TECHNICAL COLLEGE OF THE LOWCOU
LEARNING RESOURCES
POST OFFICE BO
BEAUFORT, SOUT
W9-CLG-963
901-1288

The Woman's Encyclopedia of Myths and Secrets

Honored by the London *Times* Educational Supplement as 1986 "Book of the Year"

"Awesomely researched. . . . Walker has distilled 20 years of research into an absorbing treasure house. . . . This is a feminist-scholar's gold mine and a browser's delight."—*Los Angeles Times*

"Whoever ventures into this . . . book runs the risk of being totally absorbed."
—Shirley Horner, *The New York Times*

"A mountain of scholarship, a vast mass of supremely documented material . . . demonstrat[ing] the dominant role women have played in the cultural evolution of our species."—*San Francisco Chronicle*

"Barbara Walker upsets the complacent Judeo-Christian applecart of orthodoxy. [An] outstanding, endless well of information. . . . Her literary excellence and the unrelentingly fascinating material . . .redresses two millennia of cultural and sexual misrepresentation."
—*East West Journal*

"A whopping compendium of history, legend, and myth. . . . Perhaps the first substantial feminist-oriented encyclopedia of the history of modern society."
—*The Denver Post*

"A vast and detailed resource on women's history . . . offer[ing] a wealth of fascinating detail. It will indeed give a clearer picture of our total cultural heritage."
—*Yoga Journal*

"Walker has written a tribute to the goddess. Like the witches and wise women of old, Walker has eyes to see what the rest of us cannot: the figure of the goddess hidden behind rites, dogma, fairy tales, nursery rhymes, superstitions, even our very language. She sees the restoring of the goddess to her rightful place as an essential healing act for women and our whole culture. . . . You can rely on it to be witty and compulsively readable."—*The Philadelphia Inquirer*

THE WOMAN'S ENCYCLOPEDIA OF MYTHS AND SECRETS

BARBARA G. WALKER

CASTLE BOOKS
Edison, New Jersey

TECHNICAL COLLEGE OF THE LOWCOUNTRY
LEARNING RESOURCES CENTER
POST OFFICE BOX 1288
BEAUFORT, SOUTH CAROLINA 29901-1288

ALSO BY BARBARA G. WALKER

The Secrets of the Tarot: Origins, History, and Symbolism
The Barbara Walker Tarot Deck
The Crone: Woman of Age, Wisdom, and Power
The I Ching of the Goddess
The Skeptical Feminist: Discovering the Virgin, Mother, and Crone
The Woman's Dictionary of Symbols and Sacred Objects
The Book of Sacred Stones: Fact and Fallacy in the Crystal World
Women's Rituals: A Sourcebook

Opposite title page: KORE, polychromed marble, Greece, ca. 5th century B.C.

Published in 1996 by
CASTLE BOOKS
A Division of Book Sales, Inc.
114 Northfield Avenue, Edison, New Jersey 08837

© 1983 by Barbara Walker

All rights reserved. No part of this work may be reproduced or transmitted, in any form or by any means, electronic or mechanical, including photocopying, recording, or any information storage and retrieval system without permission in writing from the publisher.

Published by arrangement with HarperCollins Publishers, Inc., 10 East 53rd Street, New York, NY 10022.

ISBN 0-7858-0720-9

Library of Congress Catalog Number 83-47736

MANUFACTURED IN THE UNITED STATES OF AMERICA.

Editor's Note

Cross references. Words printed in the text of this book in bold face type indicate main-entry treatment of those subjects. Such cross references have been designated only if the reader might find additional information pertinent to the subject at hand. Short articles have been supplemented by generous cross references, to avoid frequent duplication of material.

Some main entries serve as cross references in themselves: rather than introducing articles, they refer the reader to treatment elsewhere. For example, the entries for alphabet, blood, and world egg indicate the various other articles in which the reader will find information about these topics. Cross references have also been included for alternate spellings of main-entry headings—Isolde instead of Iseult, Beelzebub instead of Baal-Zebub, and so on.

The customary differentiation between *see* and *see also* does not appear in this book. The reader can decide to seek further information either for direct expatiation or simply for general interest.

Marginalia. An unusual aspect of this encyclopedia is its marginal notations. There are three kinds.

First, since so many terms appear in different languages and different historical eras, variant spellings are given in the margin to show their cross-cultural associations.

Second, as an extension of the above, where the etymology is particularly rich and might tend to interrupt the main story, it has been put in the margin.

Third, the author has drawn on such an abundance of sources that all cannot be included in the Bibliography. Hence, those used only once or twice have been given a brief description or definition in the margin.

References. The notes are numbered from 1 for each article. Information is abbreviated but sufficient to clue the reader to the full reference in the Bibliography. The sequence is: author's last name (preceded by distinguishing initials if there is more than one author with the same last name); title (abbreviated) if there is more than one work by the same author; volume number if pertinent; and page reference. For example:

1. Budge, G.E.2, 47.

This indicates that note 1 cites Sir E. A. Wallis Budge, *Gods of the Egyptians,* volume 2, page 47. The rest of the publication data is in the Bibliography, which is arranged alphabetically by author.

Introduction

Why did Adam "give birth" to Eve? See **Birth-giving, Male.**

Who was the original Holy Trinity? See **Trinity.**

How did the middle finger become a phallic symbol? See **Fingers.**

Why is it bad luck to break a mirror? See **Mirror.**

What was the real Easter Bunny? See **Easter.**

Why did Jesus curse the fig tree? See **Fig.**

Why do people kiss under the mistletoe? See **Mistletoe.**

What was meant by Lucifer's fall? See **Lucifer.**

Why was Jesus's tomb attended only by women? See **Mary Magdalene.**

Why was Mohammed's daughter called her father's mother? See **Fatima.**

Why did Rome fall? See **Dark Age.**

Was there a real Saint Peter? See **Peter, Saint.**

Why were women made to cover their heads in church? See **Hair.**

Why did early Christians outlaw marriage? See **Marriage.**

Why did King Arthur try to kill babies? See **Innocents, Slaughter of.**

Was there a female pope? See **Joan, Pope.**

What was the real meaning of fairy tales? See **Fairies.**

Thousands of popular fantasies and hidden facts are expounded in this Encyclopedia, where the complex subject of sexism is approached from both the historical and the mythic viewpoints. Standard encyclopedias usually omit such material, or give it a brief, uninformative note. There is need for a complete study of the many-faceted process of transition from female-oriented to male-oriented religions in western civilization.

Our culture has been deeply penetrated by the notion that "man"—*not* woman—is created in the image of God. This notion persists, despite the likelihood that the creation goes in the other direction: that God is a human projection of the image of man. No known religion, past or present, ever succeeded in establishing a completely sexless deity. Worship was always accorded either a female or a male, occasionally a sexually united couple or an androgynous symbol of them; but deities had a sex just as people have a sex. The ancient Greeks and others whose culture accepted homosexuality naturally worshipped homosexual gods. (See **Hermes.**)

Opposite page: The Goddess MAAT, bas-relief, Egypt, 19th Dynasty.

Modern Christians take it for granted that they must revere the figures of a Father and a Son, never perceiving divinity in corresponding Mother and Daughter figures, as the ancients did. Though Catholics still worship the Goddess under some of her old pagan titles, such as Mother of God, Queen of Heaven, Blessed Virgin and so on, their theologians refuse to admit that she is the old Goddess in a new disguise, and paradoxically insist on her non-divinity. (See **Mary**.)

The older concept of the female Holy Trinity ruling all cycles of creation, birth, and death in her Virgin, Mother, and Crone forms, was destroyed by Christians' attacks on her temples, scriptures, rituals, and followers. The church declared from the first that the Great Goddess "whom Asia and all the world worshippeth" must be despised, "and her magnificence destroyed" (Acts 19:27). This is virtually the only Gospel tenet that churches followed through all their centuries with no deviation or contradiction. It seemed necessary to hide the fact that Christianity itself was an offshoot of Middle-Eastern Goddess worship, skewed by the asceticism of Persia and India. (See **Jesus Christ**.)

As a salvation cult, early Christianity based its scheme of redemption on the premise of female wickedness. Salvation was needed because there had been a Fall, brought about by archetypal Woman. Without the myth of Eve's defiance, there would have been no sin, hence no need for salvation or savior. (See **Eve**.) Fathers of the church declared that the original sin was perpetuated through all generations by every woman, through sexual conception and birth-giving. Woman's mysterious, devilish sexual magnetism seduced men into the "concupiscence" that, even within lawful marriage, transmitted the taint of sin to every man. (See **Sex**.) So said St. Augustine, and the church never altered his opinion.

Throughout history we find clergymen advocating abuse of women, to express their horror of female sexuality and their conviction that all women deserve punishment for the primordial crime that brought death and damnation to man. Adam, representing all men, was less guilty than Eve, representing all women. St. Paul even regarded Eve as the only guilty one (1 Timothy 2:14). The tradition persisted up to the present century, when the clergy, if not advocating active abuse of women, at least refrained from too much interference with it. Some clergymen have been found to be wife-batterers. Many still counsel women to be subservient to men, in accordance with "God's will." (See **Sexism**.)

Man's and God's attack on women was not usually justifiable as revenge for real injuries. Therefore the mythical injury of the Fall was essential to the early theological scheme. The practical goal was not to prevent women from hurting men, but to prevent women from acting independently of men: from owning their own property, earning their own money, making their own sexual choices, or raising their own children without interference.

Patriarchal religion declared war on pagan societies where motherhood was once considered the only important parental relationship; where women owned the land and governed its cultivation; and sexual attachments were made and unmade at women's discretion. (See **Matrilineal Inheritance**.) From a biological viewpoint, patriarchal religion denied women the natural rights of every other mammalian female: the right to choose her stud, to control the circumstances of her mating, to occupy and govern her own nest, or to refuse all males when preoccupied with the important business of raising her young. (See **Motherhood**.)

Such basic biological rights of the female were set aside by patriarchal human societies—although, at the dawn of history, the social role of male begetters was very differently conceived, in a way alien to modern patriarchal thought. (See **Kingship**.) Today's scholars habitually call all female and male deities of that ancient world "gods," as they also call humanity "man." Yet the supreme deity of that world was usually a Goddess, the creatress or Mother of the gods; and the very word "man" used to mean "woman," an incarnation of the same lunar Mother, in its original language. (See **Man**.)

Early Christian thinkers rightly perceived that destruction of the women's Goddess would mean a crushing blow to women's pride and confidence, since men's pride depended greatly on their vision of a God like themselves, only better. Women were not called daughters of this God, who gave men their souls. In the sixth century, churchmen even denied that women had any souls.

Forbidden by Christian conquerors to express their own faith, the women of Europe eventually adopted the men's faith perforce. Sometimes they were lured by specious concessions, which were afterward rescinded. (See **Convent**.) Sometimes they were coerced by Christianized husbands or overlords. The myths and secrets of women's spiritual past were buried, just as men buried the sheila-na-gig figures of semi-pagan Irish churches, hoping they would never be found. (See **Sheila-Na-Gig**.)

However, what Christian histories rarely admit is that, after more than a thousand years of alternate violence and guile, the western world still was not truly Christianized. The ancient faith persisted, because every man was still born of woman and nurtured by woman, despite the theologians' insistence that a father was the only significant parent. (See **Paganism**.) This was mere verbal learning, as contrasted with the direct experience of infantile dependence on the mother. When it appeared at all, father-love seems to have been a somewhat less satisfactory artificial imitation of mother-love. (See **Fatherhood**.) In relations between fathers and children the more dominant emotion was fear. Men were enjoined from the pulpit to instill "the fear of God" into their children through harsh punishments.

Harshest of all were the Heavenly Father's punishments: a terrible vision of eternal torture developed out of men's fears. The Christian hell was the most sadistic fantasy ever to masquerade as fact. (See **Hell**.) Churchmen used it, not only to terrify naive congregations into compliance, but also to excuse the torture and burning of witches. Inquisitors said the eternal punishment of such heretics should begin in this life, continuing up to the victim's death. (See **Inquisition**.)

The religion of the Goddess and her sons and lovers, the old gods, came to be called devil worship because these deities were redefined as devils (when they were not adopted into the Christian canon as pseudo-saints). The link between "woman" and "devil" in the patriarchal mind was as old as the Garden of Eden story. (See **Serpent**.) It persisted even after the dawn of a more enlightened age brought the decline of organized persecution. However, the rack and stake were replaced in the 18th and 19th centuries by more subtle abuses. aimed at suppressing women legally, politically, economically, and psychologically. Clergymen helped by opposing women's education and supporting all physical or legal measures for keeping women "in their place." As Sir Hermann Bondi accurately observed, men made God their primary source for "the common and undisguised contempt for women enshrined in the three great Western religions, the basis for the cruel, inhuman and wasteful sexism still so rampant." Women's feelings of unworthiness and insecurity, even aberrations like masochism and depression, often may be traced to training in a male-oriented religion, at variance with their own nature.

Recently, some women have begun to seek better understanding of that feminine nature, buried as it was under western society's proliferation of masculine images and values. One interesting idea to emerge from this new research is, if women's religion had continued, today's world might be less troubled by violence and alienation. Gods, including Yahweh, tended to order their followers to make war; whereas the great mother Goddesses advocated peaceful evolution of civilized skills. Cooperation rather than exploitation was the matriarchal rule. (See **War**.)

Goddess worship usually entailed frank acceptance of the natural cycles of sexuality, birth, and death; and maternal concern for the welfare of coming generations. Love was not the abstract principle that "love of God" was to become. In the very process of worship it could be directly, intimately, and physically experienced. (See **Karuna**.) Certainly there was still a strong element of this Oriental-feminist concept in the medieval "heresies" that aroused the ire of the church. (See **Romance**.)

Perhaps the most important part of any religion is the direction it gives to interpersonal behavior patterns. The patterns evolved by women in honor of their ancient Goddess surely deserve close study today. As one of the Goddess's scriptures pointedly said, "What use are grand phrases about the soul on the lips of those who hate and injure one another? . . . Religion is kindness." (See **Atheism**.)

Traces of the "kind Goddess" are still to be found in a thousand hidden pockets of history and custom: myths, superstitions, fairy tales, folk songs and dances, nursery rhymes, traditional games and holidays, magic symbols, sagas, and scriptures both original and revised, apocryphal and otherwise—in addition to the valuable material recovered by archeologists, orientalists, and other scholars. Patterns emerge from comparative studies, which can be fitted together like pieces of a jigsaw puzzle. The puzzle is far from complete; but many of its pieces are here, in this book.

These Myths and Secrets are drawn from more than paganism. Biblical myths are especially significant, not only because they shaped the attitudes of western culture, but also because they were written and rewritten during centuries of transition from matriarchal to patriarchal systems. The later development of Christian myths contributed much to sexist thinking. In Europe, sexism was a primary product of the Christian church. Patriarchal religions like Judaism and Christianity established and upheld the "man's world" largely by an elaborate structure of falsehood. Among the Secrets in this book are many surprising historical secrets that were covered up, whitewashed, or otherwise falsified through 1500 years when the church maintained a monopoly of literate records, and virtually wrote its own history to its own order.

Some of the facts concealed by that Christian history have come to light in recent decades. Others are being kept secret even now, by religious organizations still dedicated to preserving a patriarchal society. Laymen and especially women are theoretically forbidden to investigate them. Nevertheless, they can be found out.

Naturally, the secret most deeply concealed by Christianized history was the many-named Goddess, the original Holy Trinity who created and governed the world, gave birth to its Saviors, sent her tablets of divine law to the prophets, and watched over every life from womb to tomb, according to pre-Christian belief. Today she is viewed as "mythical," having been replaced by a God (equally mythical, but more acceptable to a male-dominated culture), who took over most of her attributes. It is not usually understood that the spiritual life of western man, and especially of western woman, was greatly impoverished by her violent suppression.

The unremitting warfare of the church against followers of the Goddess is a large part of what feminists now call our hidden history. Even though Christianity itself grew out of the once-universal religion of the Goddess, it was a matricidal son whose bigotry tinged every thought and feeling with woman-hatred. In the end it produced a society in which members of one sex invariably oppressed members of the other, and both came to regard this inequity as a natural state of affairs, ordained by a male "Creator." Matters were otherwise in the pre-Christian world where the "Creator" was more often a "Creatress." Through making God in his own image, man has almost forgotten that woman once made the Goddess in hers. This is the deep secret of all mythologies, and the fundamental secret of this book.

B.G.W.

A

ARTEMIS, the Amazonian Moon-Goddess and Huntress. Greek, 4th century B.C.

The "Ludovisi Throne" marble, long identified as APHRODITE being born from the sea, helped by two Horae. Now thought to be Hera in her bath. Greek, 5th century B.C.

Majestic seven-foot statue of ATHENE, her great helmet with owls and griffins, and across her chest the *aegis* with the Medusa head signifying Female Wisdom. Early 4th century, bronze.

A

Sacred alphabets of the ancient world signified birth and beginning by the letter A. This letter meant the Creatress, who invented alphabets and gave them to mankind—though most traditions said womankind had them first.

Babylonians called the Great Mother "A", the Beginning; or Aya, the Mother of All Things.[1] Tantric sages called her birth-letter Alpa Akshara, "the letter A, which is considered the 'mother of all wisdom,' and therefore of all men of genius; all Bodhisattvas and Buddhas are said to have been produced by 'A'."[2]

The Greeks held similar views about the letter Alpha, which denoted the river of birth or creation. Its other name was **Styx**, the river of death, for in the cyclic system of the ancients, birth and death merged in a circular continuum. The river Styx circled seven times through the earth's womb and emerged again as Alpha.

1. *Assyr. & Bab. Lit.*, 133-34. 2. Waddell, 161.

Ab

Egyptian word for the heart-soul, most important of the seven souls: the one that would be "weighed in the balances" by the Goddess **Maat** in the underworld Hall of Judgment after death. As in India, the heart-soul was pictured as a tiny dancer treading a constant rhythm in the midst of the body, as Dancing **Shiva** or Dancing **Kali** kept the rhythm of life in the midst of the cosmos. The hieroglyphic sign of the *ab* was a dancing figure.[1] See **Heart.**

1. Budge, E.L., 44.

Abaddon

var. Abaton

The god **Apollo** was a solar king in heaven during the day, and a Lord of Death in the underworld at night. His latter form became the Jewish Apollyon, Spirit of the Pit (Revelation 9:11). Apollo-Python was the **serpent** deity in the Pit of the Delphic oracle, who inspired the seeress with mystic vapors from his nether world. The Greek word for the Pit was *abaton*, which the Jews corrupted into Abaddon—later a familiar Christian synonym for hell.

Also called a *mundus* or earth-womb, the *abaton* was a real pit, standard equipment in a pagan temple. Those who entered it to "incubate," or to sleep overnight in magical imitation of the incubatory sleep in the womb, were thought to be visited by an "incubus" or spirit who brought prophetic dreams.[1] Novice priests went down into the pit for longer periods of incubation, pantomiming death, burial, and rebirth from the womb of Mother Earth. Once initiated in this way, they were thought to gain the skill of oneiromancy: the ability to interpret dreams.

The Old Testament Joseph earned his oneiromantic talent by incubation in a Pit. The "brothers" who put him there seem to have been fellow priests. He could interpret Pharaoh's dreams only after he had submitted to the ritual. Assyrian priests derived similar powers from a sojourn in the Pit.[2] They then assumed the priestly coat of many colors, signifying communion with the Goddess under her oneiromantic name of Nanshe, "Interpreter of Dreams."[3] It seems likely that Joseph's coat of many colors would have been given him originally not before the initiation but afterward, by a "father" who was actually the high priest.[4]

The same burial-and-resurrection ritual is found in the lives of many ancient sages. It was said of the Pythagorean philosopher Thales of Miletus, accounted one of the Seven Wise Men of the ancient world, that he derived his intellectual skills from communion with the Goddess of Wisdom in an *abaton*.[5]

1. Bromberg, 11. 2. Lethaby, 172. 3. *Assyr.& Bab. Lit.*, 131. 4. *Larousse*, 63. 5. de Lys, 336.

Abishag

The Bible claims the maiden Abishag was chosen for her beauty, to engender "heat" in the aged King **David** (1 Kings 1:2). This "heat" was not mere warmth, but the sacred fire of sexual potency, without which no king could be allowed to rule. If an impotent king were kept in office, his land would become barren. Hence, when David failed to "know" Abishag, a more virile prince (Adonijah) immediately prepared to assume the throne, and "exalted himself, saying, I will be king" (I Kings 1:5). David's death occurred with suggestive promptness after his failure of the virility test.

Abishag's name might be related to the Hindu *abhiseka* ceremony, the anointing of kings with the sacred fluid of the Goddess Sarasvati.[1] From China to the Mediterranean, ancient kings derived their legitimation from a mating with the Goddess through her priestess-surrogate.[2] Mesopotamian kings and their deified souls, the gods, were constantly described as "beloved" of the Goddess known as creatress of the earth and "maker of fate, she who decrees the fate of the men and gods."[3] Like the eastern Goddess, Abishag represented the land in the same way as **Solomon's** bride, whose mating was chronicled in the requisite intimate detail by the Song of Solomon.

After David's death, the queen mother chose between rival candidates Solomon and Adonijah. She crowned Solomon with her own hands (Song of Solomon 3:11), after the custom of the royal women whose business it was to enthrone or depose kings, as in India, Egypt, and the lands of the Fertile Crescent.[4] However, Adonijah still had designs on the throne, as shown by his request for the hand of Abishag in marriage. To prevent this symbolically and politically significant marriage from taking place, Solomon had Adonijah murdered

(1 Kings 2:17-25). The Bible fails to explain Solomon's strangely violent reaction to Adonijah's request; but it can only have meant that the crown was at stake. This in turn shows that a sexual union with Abishag was a prerequisite for royal office. See **Kingship**.

1. Gaster, 514. 2. Boulding, 191. 3. Pritchard, A.N.E. 1, 65; 2, 17, 21, 135, 202. 4. Boulding, 210.

Abortion

The ancients generally viewed abortion as a woman's private business, in which no man had any right to interfere. As Hartley put it, "Each woman must be free to make her own choice; no man may safely decide for her; she must give life gladly to be able to give it well."[1] But with the rise of patriarchal religions—especially among the Greeks—came a belief that a father's semen conveyed the soul to the fetus. Men feared for the safety of any of their body effluvia (hair cuttings, fingernail clippings, spittle, blood) lest sorcery might damage the living man by damaging what was once a part of him. The fear was particularly pronounced in the case of semen as an extension of the father's soul. If the fetus he conceived were destroyed, then surely the man himself would suffer spiritual injury according to the principles of magic. St. Thomas Aquinas held this same opinion, since he asserted that semen was the vehicle of souls.[2] It was a logical extension of this notion that abortion should be outlawed, not because it was dangerous to women, but because it was thought (magically) dangerous to men.

In the east, however, abortion was perfectly legal at any time before the fifth month, when "quickening" was felt. After that, according to Brahman scriptures, a woman who destroyed her fetus was held guilty of murder, but before that time the fetus was soulless and could be destroyed with impunity.[3] This opinion was embodied in the Catholic church's Doctrine of Passive Conception, which contradicted Aquinas in order to prove that the soul comes only from God. Up to the late 19th century, the Doctrine of Passive Conception declared that the soul arrives in the fifth month of pregnancy, to quicken the fetus, which was previously soulless.[4]

In 1869 the church again revised its opinion, tacitly admitting either that God had misinformed his church about his method of instilling the soul into the body, or else that he had decided to alter it. Pope Pius X announced that the soul was received at conception after all.[5]

Actually, the church was only coming around, several decades late, to follow some new laws made by man, not by God. Abortion was not classified as a crime in Europe until the 19th century.[6] The United States first defined abortion as a criminal offense in the year 1830.[7]

The church now falsely pretends that it officially "always" opposed abortion. The medieval church's ire was aroused not by abortions *per se* but by the midwives who performed them. The handbook of the Inquisition stated: "No one does more harm to the Catholic faith than midwives."[8] (See **Midwifery**.) The church was not averse to killing the unborn, since it burned many pregnant women as witches. Even the pregnant wife of a city councillor was tortured and burned at Bamberg in 1630.[9]

Recent opposition to legalization of abortion apparently stemmed from ignorance of how recently it was illegalized; and also from male belief that women must be controlled by forcing childbirth on them. "Male legislators have laughed at the idea of the legalization of abortion, hinting at unprecedented promiscuity (on the part of women, not men) if such a thing were allowed. Meanwhile, thousands of desperate women die each year as the direct result of male laws making abortion illegal. Women are learning the meaning of this male laughter and indifference in the face of the most hazardous and serious biological enterprise women undertake, willingly or not."[10]

The Catholic church still claims authority over women's reproductive functions. Catholic hospitals will refuse to abort even a fetus conceived by rape.[11]

1. Hartley, 263. 2. Rees, 277. 3. *Mahanirvanatantra,* 269. 4. Briffault 2, 450. 5. Sadock, Kaplan & Freedman, 352. 6. *Encyc. Brit.,* "Abortion." 7. Rugoff, 256. 8. Kramer & Sprenger, 66. 9. Robbins, 509. 10. Roszak, 299. 11. Medea & Thompson, 114.

Abraham

This name meaning "Father Brahm" seems to have been a Semitic version of India's patriarchal god Brahma; he was also the Islamic Abrama, founder of Mecca. But Islamic legends say Abraham was a late intruder into the shrine of the Kaaba. He bought it from priestesses of its original Goddess.[1] Sarah, "the Queen," was one of the Goddess's titles, which became a name of Abraham's biblical "wife."[2] Old Testament writers pretended Sarah's alliances with Egyptian princes were only love-affairs arranged by Abraham for his own profit—which unfortunately presented him as a pimp (Genesis 12:16) as well as a would-be murderer of his son (Genesis 22:10).

In the tale of Isaac's near-killing, Abraham assumed the role of sacrificial priest in the druidic style, to wash Jehovah's sacred trees with the Blood of the Son: an ancient custom, of which the sacrifice of Jesus was only a late variant. Jehovah first appeared to Abraham at the sacred oak of Shechem, where Abraham built his altar. Later Abraham built an altar to the oak god of Mamre at Hebron. Even in the 4th century A.D., Constantine said Abraham's home at the Oak of Mamre was still a pagan shrine: "It is reported that most damnable idols are set up beside it, and that an altar stands hard by, and that unclean sacrifices are constantly offered."[3]

1. Briffault 3, 80. 2. Graves, W.G., 163. 3. Frazer, F.O.T., 335.

Abraxas

var. Abrasax

Gnostic god identified with both Mithra and Jehovah, called "Our Father" and "Lord of Hosts" in the early Christian era.[1] Like Mithra, Abraxas represented "the 365 Aeons," 365,000 years allotted to the present world's life span, based on the Hindu idea that one god-year equals a thousand man-years. Jewish scripturists incorporated this belief into Psalms 90:4, and into the *First Book of Adam and Eve*, where God said his five and a half days meant 5,500 years for man.[2] Numerical values of Mithra's and Abraxas's names each totaled 365. Both were gods of numerology.

Orthodox Christianity came to view Abraxas as a demon, because he was assimilated to the Gnostic "Lord of This World" whose attributes were both divine and demonic. As the Creator of the material universe, he was declared a devil via the Gnostic opinion that all matter was evil. Thus, he and his works—the material world itself—would be destroyed at doomsday.[3] Nevertheless, through the Middle Ages Abraxas was a favorite deity of several heretical sects.

1. Budge, A.T., 209. 2. *Forgotten Books*, 6. 3. Legge 2, 239.

Absalom

The Bible presents Absalom as either David's son or David's neighbor (2 Samuel 12:11) because biblical writers couldn't decide just where he came from. He was important only as a surrogate "king" of the Jews. His name, Father Salm, was a widely distributed sacred-king name, also rendered Salma, Salem, Salomon, or Solomon; in Assyria, Shalmaneser; in Crete, the "son of God" Salmoneus.[1] The name meant Prince of Peace, which was synonymous with Lord of Death because "Peace" was the Lord's word of farewell as he descended into the underworld.

Canaanites worshipped Father Salm at the city of Salem, whose Palestinian counterpart was Jeru-salem, "House of Salem." Kings of David's ancestral tribe, the Kenites, took the sacred name when ruling in Jerusalem. Probably several of these kings were called Solomon, including the biblical one whose real name was Jedidiah, according to 2 Samuel 12:25.

Absalom received the sacred name and died as a surrogate for the incumbent king, David, whose mourning for him was really a liturgical formula. He called Absalom "my son, my son," and cried "Would God I had died for thee" to disguise the fact that the victim really had died in his place. Among ancient Semites generally, someone had to die for the king at regular intervals, to preserve the fertility of the soil and the people with his blood. See **Kingship**.

Time-honored precedent dictated the format of the drama. The chosen victim sat on the throne, and publicly copulated with the royal women under a marriage canopy (2 Samuel 16:22). See **Huppah**.

After this, Absalom was declared a god and his phallic spirit was immortalized by an erect pillar (2 Samuel 18:18). He was hung on a sacred oak "between heaven and earth," like all victims offered to deities of the air and sky.[2] He was pierced through the heart by three darts, like the Egyptian god Set. He was dismembered by ten men in priests' livery (2 Samuel 18:14-15). According to the old custom, pieces of him were then distributed to the fields and vineyards to encourage the growth of crops.

1. Graves, W.G., 363–64. 2. Angus, 173.

Abtu

The "Abyss," sometimes called Fish of Isis, representing her genital orifice, which "swallowed" the penis of Osiris. Abtu was the Egyptian name of Abydos, an early yonic shrine where the god died and entered his Mother's womb, the underworld. See **Fish**.

Acedia

"Abysmal apathy," ecclesiastical term for the acute depression afflicting those in the monastic life.[1] They recognized that *acedia* made monks and nuns especially susceptible to demonic possession. See **Possession**.

1. Mumford, 302.

Achamoth

Mother Goddess who gave birth to the creator of the material universe, according to early Gnostic Christians.[1] She was the third person of a primordial female trinity consisting of Sige, Sophia, and Achamoth—comparable to northern Europeans' divine Great-Grandmother, Grandmother, and Mother.[2] The three of them chastised the male creator for excessive hubris and other offenses. See **Sophia, Saint**.

1. Legge 2, 69. 2. Turville-Petre, 147.

Achilles

Homeric hero of the *Iliad,* greatest of the Greek warriors at the siege of Troy. Achilles was a son of the Sea-goddess, here called Thetis, "She Who Disposes." Most of his body was invulnerable because his mother dipped him in the holy river **Styx** when he was an infant; but the spot on his heel, where her fingers held him, was not exposed to the magical waters. Therefore he could be, and was, killed by an arrow in his heel, as was the Hindu Krishna. Hence any area of vulnerability in an otherwise strong structure or person is known as an Achilles Heel.

Like Heracles, Achilles lived for some time in female disguise, recalling the priesthoods of Homeric and pre-Homeric times who wore women's clothing to attain the powers of divinity.

Aciel

Black Sun of the Chaldean underworld; the god of darkness at the bottom of the sevenfold Pit, exactly mirroring the gods of light at the top of the seventh heaven. Most underground gods and Lords of Death were similar to Aciel—Hades, Pluto, Saturn, Ahriman, Apollyon, Python, Zeus Chthonios, and their later composite, the Judeo-Christian devil. Jewish writers made Aciel a "prince of Gehenna" and corrupted his name to Arsiel.[1] He was not always devilish or evil. Oriental religions generally recognized that a principle of darkness was necessary to life, for only in the nether darkness could regeneration take place.

1. Budge, G.E. 1, 275.

Actaeon

Sacred king of the **Artemis** cult, impersonator of the Horned God; a man "turned into a stag" and devoured. His antecedents went back to "paleolithic paintings in the Spanish caves of Altamira and in the *Caverne des Trois Frères* at Ariège dating from at least 20,000 B.C."[1]

1. Graves, W.G., 229.

Adah and Zillah

"Brilliance" and "Shadow," biblical wives of Lamech; a transformation of the two-faced Goddess of birth and death, light and dark, Alpha and Omega—known in Anatolia as the Two Ladies, in Egypt as the Two Mistresses.[1] The Goddess appeared in many light-and-dark, heaven-and-hell, new-moon-and-old-moon combinations, such as **Isis**-Nephthys, **Ishtar**-Ereshkigal, **Kore**-Persephone.

1. *Larousse*, 29.

Adam

Literally, a man made of blood; in pre-biblical myths, a creature formed by the Goddess of Earth from her own clay (*adamah*), given life by her blood. (See **Eve.**) The idea of Adam's rib was taken from a Sumerian Goddess who formed infants' bones from their mothers' ribs. She was both Lady of the Rib, and Lady of Life. Her name carried both meanings at once.[1] See **Birth-giving, Male.**

1. Hooke, M.E.M., 115.

Adam-Kadmon

Gnostic image of primordial man: an innocent know-nothing, a brute Adam made of mud. Probably based on the most ancient Middle-Eastern view of humanity as a race of peasant-slaves created by the gods to be farm workers and nothing else. In occult tradition Adam-Kadmon was the perennial Fool, or Prince of Fools, symbolizing the unenlightened man. His name was given to the zero-numbered Fool of the Tarot.[1]

1. Gettings, 111.

Adamu

Sumero-Babylonian version of the first man; one of the sources for the biblical figure of **Adam.** The gods tricked him and his descendants out of immortality because they didn't want mere mortals to become deathless like gods. They lied to the man, telling him the magic food of eternal life would kill him if he ate it. So he refused it and lost his chance to escape death forevermore.[1]

The biblical God also showed concern lest human beings should eat the food of eternal life (Genesis 3:22). God told Adam the same lie that the Babylonian god told Adamu: "Thou shalt not eat of it: for in the day that thou eatest thereof thou shalt surely die" (Genesis 2:17). Adam ate, but he didn't die in the same day. On the contrary, he lived to the age of 930 years (Genesis 5:5). It was the **serpent** who told the truth about the controversial food: "Ye shall not surely die; for God doth know that in the day ye eat thereof, then your eyes shall be opened, and ye shall be as gods" (Genesis 3:4-5).

1. Hooke, M.E.M., 57–58.

Adelphos

Greek word for "brother," dating back to the matriarchal period when kinship was reckoned only through a mother. Its literal meaning is "one from the same womb."[1]

1. Briffault 1, 405.

Aditi

Hindu Great Goddess as the Woman Clothed with the Sun, mother of all the lights of heaven. She gave birth to the twelve zodiacal spirits called Adityas, "Children of Aditi," among whom was Aryaman, the ancestral god of all "Aryans."[1] See **Sun Goddess**.

1. O'Flaherty, 339; *Mahanirvanatantra*, x1.

Adonis

Greek version of Semitic Adonai, "The Lord," a castrated and sacrificed savior-god whose love-death united him with **Aphrodite**, or **Asherah**, or **Mari**. In Jerusalem, his name was **Tammuz**.

Adonis was born at Bethlehem, in the same sacred cave that Christians later claimed as the birthplace of **Jesus**.[1] He was the son of the Virgin Myrrha, a temple-woman or hierodule, identified with **Mary** by early Christians who called Jesus's mother Myrrh of the Sea.[2] Myrrh was a symbol of the Lord's death, in both pagan and Christian traditions. He returned to his Great Mother, the sea, Aphrodite-Mari. Alexandrian priestesses celebrated the event by throwing the god's image into the sea.[3]

Syrian Adonis died at **Easter** time, with the flowering of the red anemone, supposedly created from his blood. Its name was derived from his title, Naaman, "darling." He was also called the Beautiful God, like other gods of the spring flowering, such as Narcissus, Antheus, Hyacinthus.

Another form of the same god was Anchises, castrated after his mating with Aphrodite. Adonis, too, was castrated: "gored in the groin" by Aphrodite's boar-masked priest. His severed phallus became his "son," the ithyphallic god Priapus, identified with Eros in Greece or **Osiris-Min** in Egypt. Priapus carried a pruning knife in token of the Lord's necessary castration before new life could appear on earth.[4]

Castrating the god was likened to reaping the grain, which Adonis personified. His rebirth was a sprouting from the womb of the earth. Each year, sacred pots called *kernos* or "gardens of Adonis" were planted with wheat or millet, and allowed to sprout at Easter. The custom was followed in Mediterranean countries up to the present century.[5] The clay pot signified the womb. Sometimes in processions it was a gigantic *kernos* carried on a chariot, having the special name of *kalanthos*.[6]

Magic Papyri
Collections of exorcisms, invocations, charms, and spells widely circulated during the early Christian era, used as bases for later grimoires and Hermetic texts.

Adonis died and rose again in periodic cycles, like all gods of vegetation and fertility. He was also identified with the sun that died and rose again in heaven. An Orphic hymn said of him: "Thou shining and vanishing in the beauteous circle of the Horae, dwelling at one time in gloomy Tartarus, at another elevating thyself to Olympus, giving ripeness to fruits."[7] He was buried in the same cave (womb) that gave him birth. It is now the Milk Grotto, whose dust is supposed to benefit nursing mothers; it was said Mary nursed Jesus there.[8] The Grotto was sealed as Jesus's sepulchre, for in the cults of both Jesus and Adonis the virgin womb was the same as the virgin tomb, "wherein never man before was laid" (Luke 23:53).

The Magic Papyri said Jesus and Adonis also shared the same name-magic. "Adonai" was the highest god, having the True Name that could work miracles.[9] Centuries later, Christian authorities declared that "Adonai" was a demon.

1. Doane, 155; Briffault 3, 97. 2. Ashe, 48. 3. Frazer, G.B., 390. 4. Graves, G.M. 1, 69, 72. 5. Frazer, G.B., 400–401. 6. Briffault 3, 126. 7. Baring-Gould, C.M.M.A., 286. 8. Budge, A.T., 319–20. 9. M. Smith, 124.

Adultery

From *ad alterum se conferre,* "to confer (property) upon another."[1] In the age of **matrilineal inheritance**, female property owners could leave cast-off husbands destitute by conferring their "matrimony" (wealth) upon another. Patriarchal societies therefore sought to insure wives' sexual fidelity for economic reasons.[2]

To this end, the Bible commands stoning to death an adulterous wife or a bride suspected of premarital affairs (Deuteronomy 22:21). The latter rule was to invalidate the pagan custom of premarital defloration by a stranger, lest someone other than the husband might have a claim on the bride's property.[3] Hebrew patriarchs also considered "adulterous" a widow who might remarry "unto a stranger" outside the paternal clan. Widows were ordered to marry the brother of a deceased husband, so their property would remain under the control of male in-laws. This law of Levirate Marriage with its apparently divine sanction caused much trouble in later centuries.

1. Brasch, 125. 2. Hartley, 165, 171. 3. Harding, 135.

Aegis

Goatskin breastplate of the Goddess **Athene**, ornamented with oracular serpents and the petrifying head of **Medusa**. The original Libyan Athene was herself the Gorgon mask surrounded by serpents, served by priestesses who wore the *aegis* as a goatskin apron. It was a badge of divine power. Later Homeric myths considered the *aegis* so essential to sovereignty that not even Zeus could rule the other gods without it.

Aeneas

Son of **Aphrodite**, founder of Rome according to one version of the story. He saved the sacred fetish called **Palladium** from the sack of

Troy, and carried it to the site of Rome, where it was installed in the temple of Vesta. Like all sacred kings he visited the underworld, clutching the magic mistletoe branch that would insure his return to earth.[1]

1. Graves, W.G., 101.

Aeon

"The Year," title of any god annually sacrificed and reborn, such as the Savior born of the Virgin **Kore** at Alexandria every January.[1] The classic Aeon appears to have been based on Tantric worship of Shiva-Prajapati, who became a Lord of Death each year to bring about redemption of human life. According to the Aitareya Brahmana, "The Year is the same as Death; and whosoever knows this Year to be Death, his life that year does not destroy."[2]

1. Campbell, M.I., 34. 2. Eliade, M.E.R., 79.

Aesir

"Asians," the Norse gods led by Father **Odin**, who invaded the lands of the elder deities (Vanir). The Aesir came from Ásaland, or Ásaheimr, meaning both "land of gods" and "Asia." Some claimed their home city was Troy. Such myths record the recurrent western migrations of Indo-European or **Aryan** peoples. The Norse word for a god was Áss, "Asian." The Egyptian god Osiris was formerly Ausar, "the Asian."[2] Etruscans also called their ancestral deities Asians.[3] Phoenician king Cadmus was "the Oriental," from *kedem*, "the Orient."[4]

The Asian invaders were aggressive. The *Voluspá* said war occurred "for the first time in the world" when the Aesir attacked the peace-loving people of the Goddess.[5]

1. Turville-Petre, 23. 2. Budge, G.E. 2, 113. 3. Keightley, 61. 4. Massa, 40. 5. Dumézil, 71.

Agape, Saint

"Love Feast," first of **Aphrodite's** holy whores (**Horae**), was canonized as a Christian saint when icons of the Horae were re-labeled "virgin martyrs": Sts. Agape, Chione, and Irene.[1] Agape originally personified the rite of sexual communion, as practiced in Aphrodite's temples and adopted by some early Christian sects as a Tantric type of "spiritual marriage." By the 7th century A.D. the *agape* ceremony was declared heretical, but it continued secretly throughout the Middle Ages.[2] See **Menstrual Blood**.

1. Attwater, 34. 2. Sadock, Kaplan & Freedman, 23.

Agatha, Saint

"Kindly One," a spurious saint based on images of the lactating Goddess offering bared breasts in the usual **Ishtar** pose. As a fictitious "virgin martyr," Agatha refused to marry the king of Sicily, who vengefully ordered her breasts sliced off. Early Christian icons showed her carrying them on a *patera* (offering dish) as St. **Lucy** carried her eyeballs.[1] Later, the amputated breasts were misinterpreted as bells; so Agatha became patroness of bell founders.[2] Her legend may have arisen from the Christian habit of knocking the breasts off statues of priestesses and Goddesses.[3]

The original Agatha was surnamed Tyche (Fate), and worshipped at the subterranean womb-oracle of Trophonios at Lebadeia.[4] Like the Goddess of the similar womb-oracle at Delphi, she was accompanied by a Great Serpent: the oracular spirit named Agathodemon, god of Kindly Fortune, worshipped by Orphic sects up to the 5th and 6th centuries A.D. Far from tormenting Agatha as her Christian legend claimed, Sicilian kings won their thrones by way of a sacred marriage with her. Many of these kings took the name of Agathocles, "Glory of Agatha," just as Heracles called himself "Glory of Hera."[5]

The *Golden Legend* conferred on St. Agatha the curious title of Savior of Her Country, saying "She accomplished the deliverance of her native land."[6] This probably referred to votive images of the Goddess which were supposed to preserve the land from all external dangers.

1. Brewster, 95. 2. Attwater, 34. 3. *Larousse,* 211. 4. Guthrie, 225.
5. d'Alviella, 20. 6. de Voragine, 161.

Agnes, Saint

Scholars say "next to the Evangelists and Apostles there is no saint whose effigy is older" than the popular St. Agnes.[1] Indeed, she seems to have been much older than evangelists and apostles: a Roman-Jewish version of the Holy Ewe Lamb (Agna), virgin incarnation of the Ewe-goddess Rachel.

Like the virgin Mary, Agnes came from "immaculate" parents. The *Portiforium ad usam Sarum* said her mother was a virgin, her father a purified soul who renounced sexual love.[2] Like all the legendary virgin-martyrs, Agnes was slain because she renounced the love of a pagan youth. However, her true nature as an orgiastic priestess-heroine might be guessed from her ineradicable connections with love and marriage. A priest became her bridegroom by placing a wedding ring on the finger of her statue, as if it were the statue of Aphrodite-Galatea.[3] Bollandus's *Acts of the Saints* said Agnes founded her nunnery in a house of sacred prostitutes, like priestesses of Aphrodite-Salacia.[4] All the way up to the present century, St. Agnes's Eve was the traditional time for girls to divine the names of their future lovers by means of magic mirrors.[5]

Unfortunately for St. Agnes's credibility, she is said to have suffered in the reign of Constantine—when Christians were not persecuted. It was also falsely claimed that Agnes cured Constantine's daughter of leprosy. Roman Jews were said to have worshipped her in a church on the Via Nomentana, built in her honor in 350 A.D.; but Roman Jews didn't worship Christian saints, and no churches were built in honor of female martyrs in 350 A.D.[6] Roman Jews probably did, however, worship at least one version of Agna the Holy Lamb.

Though Catholic scholars now say Agnes's legends have been found "disappointingly" devoid of truth, her relics are still preserved in Rome and constantly adored by the faithful.[7]

1. Brewster, 76. 2. Hazlitt, 2–3. 3. de Voragine, 113. 4. Seligmann, 157. 5. Brewster, 75. 6. de Voragine, 112. 7. Attwater, 35.

Agni

Vedic fire god wedded to Kali under her name of Ambika, "Little Mother." She represented the primal ocean of blood from which all things arose at creation; he represented the fructifying fire from heaven (lightning); their combination meant vital heat. Vedic sages said the soul of all the universe, moving and still, is made of a combination of blood and fire. Agni also appeared to consume sacrifices that were burned on their altars. He was a prototype of such Indo-European fire-bringers as Lucifer, Prometheus, Etana, Hephaestus, and Heracles.[1]

1. O'Flaherty, 97, 148, 339.

Ahriman

Great Serpent, Lord of Darkness, and rival of the sun god in Persian myth; leader of the *daevas,* whom Zoroastrians called devils, though the original Indo-Iranian word meant "gods."[1] (See **Serpent**.)

The story of Ahriman's revolt against his twin brother, the Heavenly Father, of their war in heaven, and of the *daevas'* fall to the underworld, gave western Europe its basic myth of the fall of Lucifer, and its dualistic division of the universe between forces of good and evil. Persian prophets predicted the defeat of Ahriman and his dark angels during the final battle at the end of the world, and Judeo-Christian prophets adopted the same idea. As the Serpent, Ahriman also tempted the first man and woman.

But Ahriman was not considered inferior to the Heavenly Father. On the contrary, they were twins, born simultaneously from the womb of the primal Crone of Time (Zurvan). Ahriman's influence on earth was greater than his celestial brother's, because he created the material world. Persian **Magi** regarded him as the source of their magic power, and offered sacrifices to him. Mithraic shrines from Budapest to York were dedicated to "Arimanius" as the underground god of magic arts.[2]

Ahriman was not originally Persian. He was the Vedic god Aryaman, maker of "Aryans"—the people he created of clay. Aryaman was one of the twelve zodiacal sons of the Goddess Aditi.[3] He also had a Celtic incarnation, as the divine king Eremon.

1. *Larousse,* 317. 2. Legge 2, 239. 3. O'Flaherty, 339.

Ahura Mazda

var. Ormazd, Ormizd, Hormizd

Persian sun god born as the twin brother of the dark god **Ahriman** from the womb of Infinite Time, the Primal Creatress. The fight between the brothers, resulting in Ahriman's fall from heaven, had the same cause as the rivalry between Cain and Abel—that is, the sacrificial offering of one was accepted by the older deity; that of the other was rejected. The older deity was Vayu, probably a derivative of the Vedic celestial androgyne Varuna, or Mitra-Varuna, whose other name became "**Mithra**".

The story of the battle and the fall might have been a revision of the ancient creation myth concerning the Goddess's punishment of her first-created serpent-consort for his hubris.[1] The name Ahura was once a feminine name.[2]

Middle Persian forms of the name were Ormazd, Ormizd, or Hormizd. These names were commonly taken by kings who embodied the god's solar spirit, especially kings of the Iranian Sassanian dynasty.[3] Being naturally deified after death, such kings had cult centers and groups of priests who kept up their worship. One of these apparently became converted to Christianity and contributed another apocryphal saint to the Christian canon, usually misspelled "St. Hormidz," though Hormizd was obviously meant. This saint was vaguely placed in the 5th century A.D. and declared a Persian martyr, though his legend lacked every kind of foundation, even that of common sense. It was claimed that, for a refusal to renounce Christianity, St. Hormidz was condemned to serve as a military camel-driver—which may not have been precisely a life of luxury, but hardly qualified as martyrdom.[4] This sun-god-turned-saint was revered through the early Middle Ages by cult centers located in Persia and Iraq.

1. Graves, G.M. 1, 27. 2. Budge, E.M., 144. 3. *Encyc. Brit.,* "Ormizd."
4. Attwater, p. 173.

Akka

Eponymous ancestral Goddess of Akkad, called the Old Woman, the Grandmother, or the Midwife. She was the "Water-drawer" who brought gods to birth out of the primal deep—the feminine prototype

TECHNICAL COLLEGE OF THE LOWCOUNTRY
LEARNING RESOURCES CENTER
POST OFFICE BOX 1288
BEAUFORT, SOUTH CAROLINA 29901-1288

of Aquarius. A similar Central-American Goddess figure had curiously similar names, Acat or Akna.[1]

Akka had many related names. Greeks called her Acco or Acca, "She Who Fashions."[2] To Lapps and Finns in northern Europe, she was Mader-Akka—Mother Akka—who created humanity.[3] To Romans, she was Acca Larentia, or Acca the mother of the Lares, which were archaic ancestral spirits left over from pre-Roman Latium.

Acca Larentia was variously called the first Vestal Virgin, or a temple prostitute, or a rich courtesan, or a virgin bride of God—roles that may seem mutually contradictory but were not so (see **Prostitution**; **Vestal Virgins**). As the divine midwife, she helped Rhea Silvia give birth to Romulus and Remus, founders of Rome. She drew the divine twins out of their floating basket on the river Tiber, just as Akka of Akkad drew Sargon out of his floating basket on the river Tigris, and "Pharaoh's daughter" drew Moses from the Nile.

Acca Larentia was honored every year at the Roman festival of the Larentalia. She was assimilated to the cult of **Heracles**, who became one of her husbands. In his Roman temple, Heracles was mated to "Acca, the Maker."[4]

1. *Larousse,* 439. 2. Graves, G.M. 2, 190. 3. *Larousse,* 306. 4. Graves, G.M. 2, 190.

Aladdin

Marco Polo described Aladdin quite differently from his mythic portrait in the *Arabian Nights.* As the fairy tale said, he was master of a secret cave of treasures, but the cave was real. It was located in the fortified valley of Alamut near Kazvin, headquarters of the fanatical brotherhood of *hashishim* or "hashish-takers," which Christians mispronounced "assassins."

Aladdin was an Old Man of the Mountain, hereditary title of the chief of *hashishim,* beginning with a Shi'ite leader Hasan ibn al-Sabbah, whose name meant Son of the Goddess (see **Arabia**). The later name of Aladdin was taken by several chieftains. In 1297 the region of Gujarat was conquered by a warrior called the Bloody One, Ala-ud-den.[1]

By means of drugs and an elaborate "paradise" staffed by human Houris, initiates into the brotherhood were persuaded that they died and went to heaven, or Fairyland, where gardens and palaces occupied the valley of the secret cave. Special conduits flowed with the Four Rivers of Paradise: water, wine, milk, and honey. Each candidate was drugged into a stupor, then woke and "perceived himself surrounded by lovely damsels, singing, playing, and attracting his regards by the most fascinating caresses, serving him also with delicate foods and exquisite wines; until intoxicated with excess of enjoyment amidst actual rivulets of milk and wine, he believed himself assuredly in Paradise, and felt an unwillingness to relinquish its delights."[2]

After this period of bliss, the warrior was again drugged and taken out of the secret place, to fight in the service of the Old Man of the Mountain. He fought fearlessly, in the belief that death in battle would instantly carry him back to that heaven cleverly made real for him. Promises of sexual bliss were the real key to the ferocity of Islamic armies. The Koran said each hero who died in battle would achieve an eternity of pleasure among heavenly Houris with "big, beautiful, lustrous eyes."[3]

Aladdin's sect worshipped the moon as a symbol of the Goddess, like the Vessel of Light associated with both the virgin Mary and the Holy Grail in western Europe.[4] Eastern poets said the Vessel of Light produced *djinn,* "spirits of ancestors." This Vessel was simultaneously Aladdin's lamp, source of *djinni* (a genie), and the moon, source of all souls according to the most ancient beliefs. The moon was the realm of the dead, and also the realm of rebirth since all souls were recycled through many revolutions of the wheels of Fate. The divine Houris also dwelt in the moon, which probably was the light of Aladdin's secret cave. See **Moon**.

The *Arabian Nights* gave the password to Aladdin's cave: Open, Sesame. This was related to Egyptian *seshemu,* "sexual intercourse." The hieroglyphic sign of *seshemu* was a penis inserted into an arched yoni-symbol.[5] Every ancient culture used some form of sexual symbolism for the idea of man-entering-paradise.

1. Zimmer, 54. 2. Polo 53–54. 3. Campbell, Oc. M., 430. 4. Wilkins, 58. 5. Budge, E.L., 58.

Alako

Gypsy "son of God" who takes the souls of gypsies to the moon after death. **Gypsies** said Alako had two enemies: the devil, and Christ.[1]

1. Trigg, 202.

Alani

"Hunting dogs," Greek name for the Scythian tribes who worshipped **Artemis** as their Divine Huntress. The name Alan still carried the original Greek meaning of a hunting dog when it became popular among the Scots during the Middle Ages. Artemis was often called the Great Bitch, and her hunting priestesses were the "sacred bitches" who chased, killed, and consumed boar-gods and stag-gods like Phorcis or Actaeon. Thus, to Christians, "son of a bitch" meant a devil worshipper—that is, a pagan devotee of the Goddess. See **Dog**.

Alban, Saint

Fictitious saint called "protomartyr of England," allegedly the first Christian martyr in the British isles, slain on Holmhurst Hill in 287 A.D. However, no writer made any reference to him until two hundred years later. Gildas finally developed St. Alban's legend in the 6th century, with some confusion of dates. He claimed St. Alban sheltered a Christian fleeing from Diocletian's persecution, twenty years before Diocletian's persecution began.[1]

The real origin of St. Alban probably was nothing more than the British Goddess's title of Albion, "White Moon." Her shrine at Holmhurst Hill had a sacred fountain, always shown between the feet of "Alban" in Christian art.[2] In Bede's day the place was still holy, and someone had to invent a Christianized—and preferably masculinized—legend for it.

1. Attwater, 37. 2. Brewster, 293.

Alberich

King of the underworld in Teutonic myth, identified with the Saxon fairy-king Oberon. Alberich appeared in the Nibelungenlied as a chthonian dwarf master-smith, guardian of the Rhinemaidens' buried treasure. Like most versions of the demonic fairy king, he was a shapeshifter, appearing in such typically diabolic disguises as a toad and a serpent. He is still familiar to opera fans as a character in Wagner's *Ring of the Nibelung.*

Alchemy

In Arabic, alchemy meant "matter of Egypt," Al-Khemeia, from Khemennu, "Land of the Moon," an old name for Egypt.[1] The Arabs thought alchemy was invented by Egyptians. Christians learned it from the Arabs and believed it was invented by Thoth, or **Hermes**, or the virgin **Mary**.[2]

"Mary the Jewess" was said to have been the first great alchemist. She discovered distillation of alcohol in the time of the Caliphate, and invented the double boiler, still called *bain-marie* (Mary's bath) in France. During the Renaissance some female alchemists were persecuted as witches. Julius, Duke of Brunswick, roasted one of them alive in an iron chair in 1575, because she could not tell him how to make gold out of base metal.[3]

As a system of mysticism, alchemy was permeated by sexual symbols. So-called "copulations" and "marriages" figured in alchemical procedures. Sexual drawings enlivened the texts. The Alchemical Rebus was the usual bisexual image of male and female powers in union, "a Hermaphrodite, born of two mountains, Mercury and

Venus." Sun and moon were shown as naked male and female figures, the moon saying to her spouse, "O Sun, thou dost nothing alone if I am not present with my strength, as a cock is helpless without a hen."[4]

Alchemists sought the divine female power Sapientia, or Sophia (Wisdom), the Gnostics' Great Mother. Valentin's *L'Azoth des philosophes* showed her as a crowned, fish-tailed Aphrodite rising from the sea, spouting streams of milk and blood from her breasts. This was a direct copy of Hindu representations of the virgin **Maya**, mother of the world.[5] Alchemists called her the Siren of the Philosophers, "born of our deep Sea (Maria), who pours milk and blood from her paps."[6]

An Italian manuscript showed two bearded sages avidly sucking her breasts, to absorb the secrets symbolized by her colors, milk white and blood red.[7] The same colors appeared on the Flower of the Alchemists, a five-petaled red-and-white rose, sometimes called the womb of the *Filium philosophorum* or Glorious Child. The same rose symbolized the virgin Mary.[8]

Mary-Sophia was the Goddess of both Gnosticism and alchemy. The Philosopher's Stone was sometimes called the Sophistical Stone.[9] Alchemical writings called the hidden Goddess the Mother of Wisdom, combining elements of the Madonna with those of the pagan mother-image:

> *I am the flower of the field and the lily of the valleys. I am the mother of fair love and of fear and of knowledge and of holy hope. . . I am the mediator of the elements. . . . I am the law in the priest and the word in the prophet and the counsel in the wise. I will kill and I will make to live and there is none that can deliver out of my hand.*[10]

Since the ancient Great Mother was represented by a Holy Vase, alchemists sought the *vas hermeticum* (Womb of Hermes), which resembled the *vas spirituale* identified with the virgin Mary. Arab alchemists adopted the **rosary** from Far-Eastern cults of the Goddess, whose rosary-symbol was a vase-shaped bead, from which the other beads were said to "spring up." Rosaries dedicated to Mary also had the vase-shaped bead. Arabs called the rosary *wardija,* "rose-garden," copying the Hindu *japamala,* "rose-chaplet," the necklace of **Kali Ma,** who ruled the elements—as alchemists also hoped to do. A Dürer drawing of 1506 shows a turbanned Arab alchemist with his rosary at his belt.[11]

Many alchemical texts presented obvious sexual allegories, e.g. from the *Turba Philosophorum:* "Take the white tree, build him a round, dark, dew-encircled house, and set in it a hundred-year-old man and close it so that no wind or dust can get to him; then leave him there eight days. I tell you that that man will not cease to eat of the fruit of that tree till he becomes a youth. O what a wonderful nature, for here is the father become son and born again."[12]

Similar allegorical references to the mysteries of reproduction were common among Chinese alchemists, who spoke of attaining "longevity through liquid gold," by "a red sulphurous ingredient in goldmaking"—the male and female essences in Taoist and Tantric symbolism (see **Menstrual Blood**). One text said:

> *I must diligently plant my own field. There is within it a spiritual germ that may live a thousand years. Its flower is like yellow gold. Its bud is not large, but its seeds are round and like unto a spotless gem [i.e., the Jewel in the Lotus]. Its growth depends upon the soil of the central place [womb], but its irrigation must proceed from a higher fountain. After nine years [or, months] of cultivation, root and branch may be transplanted to the heaven of the higher genii.*[13]

Churchmen were baffled by alchemical language, and usually let practitioners of this particular "devilish art" alone, unless they were women. Yet the official opposition to the whole science kept many of the best minds away from it, thus helping to retard the development of modern chemistry out of alchemical experimentation.[14]

The deep secrecy of the alchemists' operations still puzzles many modern scholars. Carl Jung wondered why these chemical processes had to be disguised and distorted by thickets of mythological symbolism; or, if a mystical sort of enlightenment was being described, why it was tied to laboratory procedures.[15] The answer could be found in the alchemists' political environment. "Natural science" was often defined as heresy by the church. In periods when the **Inquisition** was active, almost anyone meddling with such matters was at risk. The best defense was deliberately obscure allegorization, in which theological principles—if any—could be hidden.

Some of the secret is given away by the preponderance of sexual symbols in alchemical literature. "Copulation of Athene and Hermes" might mean mixing sulfur and mercury in a retort; or it might mean a sexual "working" of the alchemist and his lady-love. Illustrations in alchemical books suggested sexual mysticism more often than not. **Adam** and **Eve** were shown as naked lovers, halves of the Primal Androgyne. Adam was pictured as incomplete male, who had to be pierced by the Arrow of Mercurius to stimulate his passionate desire for Wisdom. After this, his phallus bloomed into the flowering Tree of Life, signifying that he was ready for full union with a Goddess-like Eve, who would make him complete.[16]

Mercurius or Hermes was the alchemical hero who fertilized the Holy Vase, a womb-like sphere or egg from which the *filius philosophorum* was to be born. This vessel may have been real, a laboratory flask or retort; more often, it seemed to be a mystical symbol.[17] The Royal Diadem of its offspring was said to appear *in menstruo meretricis,* "in the menstrual blood of a whore," who may have been the Great Whore, an ancient epithet of the Goddess. Her menstrual blood curdled in her womb to create the universe, including its metals, minerals, and other raw materials of alchemy. The *Rosarium Philosophorum* (Rosary of the Philosophers) said the soul of the world is made of male and female "matters": *Anima est Sol et Luna.* Similarly a human soul was produced by male and female parents. Sexual mystics held a theory that every individual person or thing had but half a soul, which must find its other half in the opposite sex.[18]

At times the alchemists appeared to be seeking a lost deity, like the cabalists' Shekina: the Mother (*mater*) sleeping in the *mate*rial *matter* of the world, having been separated from the God whose other half she was. Alchemists usually rejected the church's teaching that matter was "evil" or "fallen." As Gnostic animists they thought the "savior" destined to emerge from the alchemical *matrix* (mother-womb) was both an anthropomorphic Glorious Child or *filius macrocosmi,* and a "miraculous stone" or Philosopher's Stone, possessing *corpus, anima, spiritus,* the "redeemer" of the inanimate universe.[19] As an enlightened mystic the alchemist hoped to attend the birth of this strange being, who would teach him to transform base metals into gold, as eastern yogis were said to do when they were sufficiently enlightened.

One reason why the church opposed alchemy and identified it with black magic was that many alchemical texts offered greater revelations, more simply achieved, than the Bible or the pulpit could offer, and thus took on the character of a rival. For example, the *Abtala Jurain* (1732) presented the whole creation:

> *Take of common rainwater a good quantity, at least ten quarts; preserve it well sealed in glass vessels for at least ten days, then it will deposit matter and feces on the bottom. Pour off the clear liquid and place it in a wooden vessel that is fashioned round like a ball; cut it in the middle and fill the vessel a third full, and set it in the sun about midday in a secret or secluded spot.*
>
> *When this has been done, take a drop of the consecrated red wine and let it fall into the water, and you will instantly perceive a fog and a thick darkness on top of the water, such as also was at the first creation. Then put in two drops, and you will see the light coming forth from the darkness; whereupon little by little put in every half of each quarter hour first three, then four, then five, then six, drops, and no more, and you will see with your own eyes one thing after another appearing by and by on top of the water, how God created all things in six days, and how it all came to pass, and such secrets as are not to be spoken aloud and I also have not power to reveal. Fall on your knees before you undertake this operation. Let your eyes judge of it; for thus was the world created. Let all stand as it is, and in half an hour after it began it will disappear.*
>
> *By this you will see clearly the secrets of God, that are at present hidden from you as from a child. You will understand what Moses has written concerning the creation; you will see what manner of body Adam and Eve had before and after the Fall, what the serpent was, what the tree, and what manner of fruits they ate; where and what Paradise is, and in what bodies the righteous shall be resurrected; not in this body that*

we have received from Adam, but in that which we attain through the Holy Ghost, namely in such body as our Savior brought from Heaven.[20]

1. Budge, E.M., 20. 2. Ashe, 213. 3. de Camp, S.S.S., 143, 147.
4. Shumaker, 178, 183. 5. Goldberg, 101. 6. de Givry, 361.
7. Neumann, G.M., pl. 174. 8. Campbell, M.I., 254. 9. Shah, 194.
10. Jung, M.H.S., 186. 11. Wilkins, 44, 50, 56, 58. 12. Silberer, 258.
13. Shah, 201–2. 14. Castiglioni, 286. 15. Campbell, C.M., 268.
16. Campbell, M.I., 258. 17. Campbell, C.M., 273. 18. Campbell, C.M., 289, 295.
19. Campbell, C.M., 271–72. 20. Campbell, C.M. 268–69.

Alcmene

"Power of the Moon," virgin mother of the solar Savior, **Heracles.** She was the Greek form of the Hebrew *almah,* "moon-woman," who mothered sacred kings in the Jerusalem cult, and whose title was bestowed on the virgin Mary.[2] Parallels between earlier myths of Alcmene and later myths of **Mary** were too numerous to be coincidental. Alcmene's husband refrained from sexual relations with her until her god-begotten child was born. The couple went on a journey "so that the child has a birth place which is not his parents' home."[3] Heracles also grew up to die a sacrificial death, after which he visited the underworld and harrowed it, then rose to heaven to be assimilated to his divine Father and to marry the Goddess's virgin aspect all over again, to beget himself anew.

1. Knight, S.L., 98. 2. Brasch, 25. 3. H. Smith, 183.

Alecto

She Who May Not Be Named, one of Demeter's triad of **Furies,** who supported the ancient laws of the Goddess by punishing transgressors.

Allah

Late Islamic masculinization of the Arabian Goddess, Al-Lat or Al-Ilat—the Allatu of the Babylonians—formerly worshipped at the **Kaaba** in Mecca. It has been shown that "the Allah of Islam" was a male transformation of "the primitive lunar deity of Arabia."[1] Her ancient symbol the crescent moon still appears on Islamic flags, even though modern Moslems no longer admit any feminine symbolism whatever connected with the wholly patriarchal Allah. See **Arabia.**

1. Briffault 3, 106.

Alleluia

Medieval Christian version of an international word for the funeral keening that announced a sacred king's passage to the land of death, in ancient religious dramas. It was called the "howl," or ululation. The Akkadian god Alalu was a direct anthropomorphization of the liturgical cry. It was *houloi* in Greek, *ululatus* in Latin, *hulluloo* or *hulla-baloo* in Old Irish.[1] Herodotus said the "howlings in the temple" were derived from the cult of **Athene** in Libya, where "the women do it very well."[2]

Alleluia was used as a battle cry in the Middle Ages, and credited with powerful victory-magic. The legend of St. Germain describes its use in a battle between Saxons and Britons. As the cry of the god Pan was supposed to cause "pan-ic" in his enemies, so the sound of *alleluia* was thought to kill the enemy's fighting spirit.[3]

1. Hazlitt, 341. 2. Herodotus, 270. 3. de Voragine, 399.

Alma Mater

"Soul-Mother," a Roman teaching priestess, especially one empowered to give instruction in the sexual Mysteries. (See **Cowrie**). The name was based on Al-Mah, a Middle-Eastern name of the Moon-goddess, also a title of her temple women, *almah*—the same word that described the virgin **Mary** in the Hebrew versions of the Gospels.[1] The priestess called *alma mater* bore a relationship to the male initiate similar to that of the Tantric **Shakti**.

1. Brasch, 25.

Alphabet

See **Motherhood**.

Altar

The custom of burying relics of saints under an altar began with a misunderstanding of the scripture, "I saw under the altar the souls of them that were slain for the word of God" (Revelation 6:9). This was based on a pagan teaching, that the souls of the enlightened became stars in heaven. Those recently deceased stood on the border of the sky, under the constellation of the Altar, which lies close to the horizon as seen from Mediterranean latitudes.[1]

The Altar was a feminine constellation because the earliest altars were modeled on the maternal hearth, and altars symbolized the Mother. The Earth's regenerative womb was often represented as an altar, which explains why "witch cults" were said to make an altar of the belly of a living woman. The Heavenly Virgin was also an altar, Ara Coeli, "Altar of Heaven," she who received the souls of the dead. Christians adopted this symbolism from the virgin **Mary**. One of the Nativity legends claimed the Cumaean Sybil showed Augustus a vision of Mary, saying, "This woman is the Altar of Heaven." A church was built on the spot, and named Santa Maria in Ara Coeli.[2]

1. Rose, 289. 2. de Voragine, 49.

Al-Uzza

"Powerful One," title of the Arabic Goddess as founding mother of Mohammed's tribe, the Koreshites, hereditary tenders of her sacred stone in Mecca.[1] See **Arabia**.

1. Briffault 3, 80.

Amata

"Beloved," the title of a **Vestal Virgin** as a Bride of God—that is, bride of the spirit of Rome manifested in the phallic **Palladium.**[1] The title was copied by Christian nuns who called themselves Brides of Christ.

1. Graves, W.G., 395.

Amazons

Greek name for Goddess-worshipping tribes in north Africa, Anatolia, and the Black Sea area.[1] Due to an erroneous belief that Amazon warriors destroyed the right breast to be unhindered in drawing the bow, some derived the name from *a-mazos*, "breastless." But Greek representations of Amazons showed no such mutilation. The idea may have arisen from Asiatic icons of the Primal Androgyne with a male right half and female left half, echoed by a coalescence of the Amazon Goddess **Artemis** with her brother-consort **Apollo**. Scholars now say the word Amazon meant "moon-woman."[2]

Gaius Tranquillus Suetonius Roman biographer and historian, ca. 70–122 A.D.

Suetonius said, "Amazons once ruled over a large part of Asia." As late as the 5th century A.D., the Black Sea was still known as the Amazon Sea.[3] Libya—which used to mean all of North Africa except Egypt—was also Amazonian. Herodotus spoke of Libyan Amazons. Diodorus, first century Greek historian, called them "the warlike women of Libya." To this day, north African Berbers call themselves Amazigh, though their common name came from Latin *barbari,* "barbarians."[4]

Herodotus Greek historian of the 5th century B.C.

The ancients said Amazons were the first to tame horses, which may well account for their armies' legendary invincibility.[5] In open country, mounted troops whether male or female would have a decided advantage over foot soldiers.

In Amazonian myths, the Goddess was often worshipped as a mare: India's mare-mother **Saranyu**, mare-headed **Demeter**, or Cretan **Leukippe** the "White Mare," whose priests were castrated and wore female dress.[6] Among Scythians also, men entered the service of the Goddess by castrating themselves and adopting women's clothing. The only deity shown in Scythian art was the Great Goddess, whom the Greeks called Artemis, or **Hestia**, or **Gaea** (the Earth).[7] Some of the Scythians settled in Parthia, "Virginland," named after their Goddess. They came to be known as Sacae, and their chief city was Sacastene, now Seistan.[8]

Scythians were governed by priestess-queens, usually buried alone in richly furnished *kurgans* (queen-graves). Five *kurgans* were discovered together at Pasyryk in southern Russia in 1954. Scythian priestesses were elder women, old enough to have gray hair. They performed traditional sacrifices, catching the blood in sacred cauldrons and taking omens from the entrails. They also accompanied their armies into battle, to cast spells for victory.[9]

The moon-sickle used in mythical castrations of gods was a Scythian weapon. A long-handled form therefore came to be called a scythe, and was assigned to the Grim Reaper, who was originally **Rhea** Kronia in the guise of Mother Time, or Mother Death—the Earth who devoured her own children. Scythian women apparently used such weapons in battle as well as in religious ceremonies and agriculture. Diodorus said Scythian women "fight like the men and are nowise inferior to them in bravery."[10] A Scythian girl was allowed to marry only after she had killed three enemies in battle.[11]

It wasn't unusual for barbarian armies to include women. Feminine magic power was often considered necessary for victory. The Bible says Barak commanded an army of 10,000 men, but refused to go into battle unless the priestess-queen Deborah went along, to cast victory spells for him (Judges 4:8). Tacitus told of druidic forces repelling Roman invaders on the island of Mona (Moon) in 61 A.D.: among the soldiers, black-clad women waved swords and cursed the enemy "like the Furies."[12]

Cornelius Tacitus Roman historian and rhetorician, ca. 56–120 A.D.

Greek myth says Amazon tribes occupied Cappadocia, Samothrace, and Lesbos, and founded the cities of Smyrna, Ephesus, Cymes, Myrine, and Paphos—all leading centers of Goddess-worship. Amazons came to the aid of matriarchal Troy in the Trojan War. The Amazon queen Penthesileia fell beneath the sword of **Achilles**, who immediately violated her dead body. Homer attributed this necrophilic act to Achilles's love of her beautiful corpse. More likely, it was a magic charm to immobilize her vengeful spirit. Greeks feared the ghosts of slain Amazons. They called them Beautiful Ones, built shrines to them, and offered them propitiatory sacrifices for centuries after the war.[13]

Theseus, king of Attica, violated the Amazons' law of matrilocal marriage by kidnapping their queen, variously named Hippolyta, Antiope, or Melanippe (Black Mare). Some said Antiope was the sister of Hippolyta. The former was slain by Theseus, the latter by **Heracles**, who wished to steal her magic girdle. Enraged, the Amazons invaded Greece, ravaged coastal towns, and besieged Athens.[14] Amazons and Greeks became hereditary enemies. A later Amazon queen named Artemisia (Spirit of Artemis) joined Xerxes to fight the Greeks at the battle of Salamis in 480 B.C.—not because she loved Persians, but because she hated Greeks.[15]

Greek myths mention several Islands of Women, where Amazons lived without men, only consorting with neighboring colonies of males at certain seasons when they wanted to conceive their children. Taurus, Lemnos, and Lesbos were said to be such all-female societies. The Greeks apparently feared them. They said the women of Taurus sacrificed to their Goddess all men who landed on their shores; and the women of Lemnos had risen up against their husbands and murdered all of them at once.[16] The Greek writers seemed to have no doubt that women could destroy whole populations of adult males, and there was no effective defense against them.

Northern Europe had mythical Amazons: the **Valkyries**, warrior-maidens of Valhalla. There were also real Amazons among the Vikings: female captains and war-chieftainesses.[17] In the 10th century A.D. a Norwegian fleet invaded Ireland and devastated Ulster and the northeast, under the command of a warrior queen called the Red Maiden.[18] Another warrior queen, Olga, was one of the first rulers of Kiev.[19] Medieval historians said Amazons ruled the city of Ulm from before the time of Abraham to the time of Alexander the Great. The city was named for the sacred elms (*ulmae*) of the grove where they worshipped Diana-Artemis.[20]

Again and again, legends mention the women's magic battle-cries, which made their enemies helpless. The Valkyrie Kara deprived her enemies of power to wield their weapons by the sound of her voice.[21] A Celtic Valkyrie, Nemhain, cursed Cu Chulainn's warriors and made a hundred of them drop dead on the spot.[22]

Lebor Gabála Érenn, also called the *Book of Conquests:* early-medieval Irish history, purporting to trace the origins of the Irish tribes back to the time of Adam.

The *Lebor Gabála Érenn—Book of the Taking of Ireland*—said the very first expedition of colonists to Ireland was led by a woman.[23] Ireland had female soldiers up to the 7th century A.D., when Christian legal reforms forbade women to bear arms.[24] The tradition persisted in connection with weddings. A bride's costume up to the 17th century included a knife at the belt.[25] But after the 9th century, female warriors in Celtic lands were labeled "witches."[26] In the Amazons' territory around the Black Sea, women retained certain Amazon customs up to the 18th century: dressing in men's clothes, riding horseback astride, and fighting beside the men in war.[27]

1. Lederer, 103. 2. Graves, G.M. 2, 379. 3. Sobol, 153, 155. 4. Wendt, 52, 66. 5. Lederer, 103. 6. Gaster, 316. 7. *Encyc. Brit.,* "Amazons." 8. Thomson, 174. 9. Wendt, 116, 137. 10. Briffault 1, 456. 11. Knight, S.L., 33. 12. Pepper & Wilcock, 216. 13. Graves, G.M. 2, 313; *Larousse,* 122. 14. Graves, G.M. 2, 126. 15. *Encyc. Brit.,* "Artemisia." 16. Graves, G.M. 2, 224. 17. Oxenstierna, 208. 18. Briffault 1, 457. 19. *Larousse,* 294. 20. Borchardt, 104. 21. *Larousse,* 279. 22. MacCana, 90. 23. Rees, 28. 24. de Paor, 109; Joyce, 84. 25. Hazlitt, 75. 26. Boulding, 319. 27. Spretnak, 106.

Ambrosia

"Supernatural red wine" of Mother Hera, which gave the Greek gods immortality.[1] In the Vedas it was *soma,* in Persia *haoma,* in Egypt *sa:* always associated with the moon and the maternal "blood of life," i.e., **menstrual blood.**[2] Merlin's older name of Ambrosius suggests a link with such pagan symbols of immortality achieved through association with life-giving feminine blood. See **Merlin; Thomas Rhymer**.

1. Graves, G.M. 1, 118. 2. Budge, G.E. 2, 298; Hartley, 231.

Amen

Magic word interpreted as "let it be" in Hebrew, used to evoke divine response to a prayer. Such words often began as deities' names. This may have originally invoked the Egyptian god Amen, "the Hidden One"—the sun in the belly of his Mother before his rebirth at sunrise. Its hieroglyphic symbol meant a pregnant belly.[1]

1. *Book of the Dead,* 194.

Amma

Norse Grandmother-Goddess who gave birth to the race of *karls* (freemen); perhaps derived from Ama, a basic name of the Great Goddess in Mesopotamia and the east.[1] See **Caste**.

1. Turville-Petre, 147.

Amphitrite

"All-encircling Triad," the pre-Hellenic Triple Goddess, transformed into a mere sea nymph by Hellenic writers. She was forced to marry Poseidon because this god was "greedy of earthly kingdoms," which implied that the earthly kingdoms used to be owned by the nymph herself. Graves says the myth represented encroachment of male priesthoods on former feminine control of the fishing industry.[1]

1. Graves, G.M. 1, 59, 61; 2, 379.

Anahid

This and its variations Anahita and Anaitis were the Persian and Armenian names for **Venus**, the star of **Ishtar** and **Astarte**, Mother Goddess of the Zend-Avesta; ruler of waters, stars, and Fate. The Mithraic Mysteries, though strongly male-oriented, retained Anahita as the necessary female principle of creation.[1]

1. Cumont, M.M., 180.

Ananias

A rabbi who opposed **St. Paul**. In the Acts of the Apostles, Ananias was (1) a holy man, Paul's instructor, who accepted Paul's faith; (2) an enemy, who struck Paul and publicly shamed him; and finally (3) "a liar unto God," who held back some of his money from the apostles, though they seemed to think he must surrender all of it. For this offense, **St. Peter** made Ananias "fall down dead" along with his wife Sapphira, and young men of the apostles' sect buried them. The apostles were imprisoned for murder, but "an angel" came secretly at night and let them out of jail (Acts 5:1–19).

This curious story was much repeated in connection with collection of church taxes. Withholders of tithes were called "liars" like the sinful Ananias.

Ananke

"Necessity," a Neoplatonic-Pythagorean title of the Goddess who governed the world according to karmic law; another name for Fortuna, or Fate. "What we call causality in the West has its roots in the Greek images of Ananke (Necessity), Dike (Justice), Heimarmene (Allotted Fate), and Nemesis (Retribution)—all goddesses which were feared and respected." Anaximander said it was according to Ananke that the "source of generation for all things is that into which their destruction also leads." Stoic philosophers made Ananke or Heimarmene the supreme all-ruling world principle, with absolute authority over even the gods. The Orphics said Ananke was mated to Chronos (Time), which gave rise to the concept of supernatural duality known as Time-and-Fate.[1] It might be said there was no Greek

Anaximander
Milesian philosopher, astronomer, and geographer, 6th century B.C.

idea of "God" that could transcend or overrule the feminine image of Ananke as the inescapable What-Must-Be.

1. von Franz, 23.

Ananta

"The Infinite," a great **serpent** in whose coils Hindu gods spent their periods of sleep or death between periods of activity.[1] The serpent might be compared to the ancient Egyptian goddess Mehen the Enveloper, a serpent who enfolded **Ra** every night when he was "dead" in the underworld. The sex of the eternal serpent was indeterminate. Earlier myths tended to see it as female, a cosmic **Kundalini**. Later Vedic traditions tended to view Ananta as male.

1. O'Flaherty, 221, 340.

Anastasia, Saint

"She Who Stands in Heaven," title of Rome's Great Goddess, personified as a pseudo-saint. Her three "serving-maids" Agapeta, Theonia, and Irene were originally the three **Horae** or Graces who attended the Goddess.

Her Christianized legend associated Agapeta, Theonia, and Irene with a man who suffered a ceremonial death in the same way as ancient victims of the pagan Mamuralia or scapegoat-sacrifice. He was beaten with rods, reviled and spat upon, then shown a vision of the Triple Goddess in his moment of death, whereupon he "fell into a sleep so deep" that no further blows could waken him.[1]

Hagiographers claimed Anastasia was another one of the "virgin martyrs" slain by Diocletian's persecution. However, modern scholars admit that she never existed except as a label on statues of the Goddess, which were re-interpreted as images of a saint.[2] Her holy day was the same as that of the sun's birth from the Great Mother at the winter solstice: December 25. By the old lunar calendar, this festival began with its Eve, December 24, called *Matrum Noctem,* "Night of the Mother."[3]

1. de Voragine, 52. 2. Attwater, 44. 3. Turville-Petre, 227.

Anath

var. Anatha, Anat, Neit, or Ath-enna; Egyptian: Aynat

Twin of the Goddess **Mari** as Lady of Birth and Death, worshipped by Canaanites, Amorites, Syrians, Egyptians, and Hebrews. Greek-speaking Phoenicians in Cyprus called her "Anat, Strength of Life." An Egyptian stele of the time of Rameses II addressed her as Queen of

Heaven and Mistress of All the Gods. Under the Greek Ptolemaic dynasty she ruled both Egypt and Palestine. Semitic texts named her Virgin Daughter of Palestine, or Virgin Wisdom Dwelling in Zion.[1]

The Jerusalem temple was occupied for centuries by both God (El) and this Goddess, variously known as Queen of Heaven, Anat, Asherah, Mari, or Miriam.[2] Her sanctuary Beth-Anath (House of Anath) is mentioned in the 19th chapter of Joshua. Some early Israelite chieftains called themselves her sons, like Shamgar ben Anath, who "slew of the Philistines six hundred men with an ox goad" (Judges 3:31). The ox goad was a magic spell, represented by the letter *lamedh,* which means "ox goad." In Sicily, a Phoenician settlement was named after this Goddess, Mach-Anath. Greeks called it Panorma, meaning Universal Mountain Mother.[3]

Ras Shamra texts Cuneiform tablets discovered in 1929 in the Ras Shamra mound, northern Syria, site of the ancient Canaanite capital city of Ugarit. The texts reveal Canaanite foundations of biblical material.

Primitive sacrificial rites of Anath or Anat were described in the Ras Shamra texts. She was fertilized by the blood of men, not by their semen, because her worship dated all the way back to the Neolithic when fatherhood was unknown and blood was considered the only substance that could transmit life. Hecatombs of men seem to have been sacrificed to Anath when her image was reddened with "rouge and henna" for the occasion.[4] "Violently she smites and gloats, Anat cuts them down and gazes; her liver exults in mirth . . . for she plunges her knees in the blood of the soldiers, her loins in the gore of the warriors, till she has had her fill of slaughtering in the house, of cleaving among the tables."[5] In similar rites in Egypt, priestesses hoisted up their skirts while dismembering the bull god **Apis** so his spurting blood would bathe their loins and fertilize them.[6]

Like the Mexican "Lady of the Serpent Skirt," who made new life from Quetzalcoatl's genital blood, Anath hung the shorn penises of her victims on her goatskin apron, or **aegis**.[7] When the Goddess was transplanted to Greece and permanently virginized as **Athene**, her *aegis* was transformed from the ceremonial apron of Libyan priestesses into a breastplate.[8] Athene still wore "serpents" (phalli) on her *aegis,* along with the Gorgon head of her Destroyer aspect. Gorgon, "Grim One," was Athene's title as a Death-goddess.[9] See **Medusa**; **Metis**; **Neith**.

Anath annually cast her death-curse, *anathema,* on the Canaanite god who became Lord of Death: Mot, the castrated "Sterility" aspect of the fertile **Baal**. Like Set in Egypt, **Mot** stood for the barren season that slew its own fertile twin, the god Aleyin. In typical sacred-king style, Mot-Aleyin was the son of the Virgin Anath and also the bridegroom of his own mother. Like Jesus too, he was the Lamb of God. He said, "I am Aleyin, son of Baal (the Lord). Make ready, then, the sacrifice. I am the lamb which is made ready with pure wheat to be sacrificed in expiation."[10]

After Aleyin's death, Anath resurrected him and sacrificed Mot in turn. She told Mot that he was forsaken by his heavenly father El, the same god who "forsook" Jesus on the cross. The words attributed to

Jesus, "My El, my El, why hast thou forsaken me?" (Mark 15:34), apparently were copied from the ancient liturgical formula, which became part of the Passover ritual at Jerusalem.

The sacred drama included a moment when Anath broke Mot's reed scepter, to signify his castration—again foreshadowing a detail of the Christian Gospels. The breaking of the scepter meant severing the connection of the old, played-out king with the Earth-goddess after the harvest of his reign. Anath therefore slew him and used his body and blood to refresh the soil for the next year's crop. "She seizes Mot, the son divine. With her sickle she cleaves him. With her flail she beats him." His pieces were scattered on the fields, like pieces of the Savior **Osiris** in Egypt.[11]

Naturally, the god-killing Anath was much diabolized in later patriarchal legends. Abyssinian Christians called her Aynat, "the evil eye of the earth." They said she was an old witch destroyed by Jesus, who commanded that she must be burned and her ashes scattered on the wind.[12] The hostility of Jesus probably stemmed from the missionaries' deliberate reversal of his former identification with the destroyed god.

In the Christian Gospels, Anath's death curse *Anathema Maranatha* (1 Corinthians 16:22) has been very loosely translated "the Bridegroom cometh." It really meant the Bridegroom's imminent death; it was the solemn curse pronounced over any sacrificial victim.[13] It carried the same double meaning as Latin *sacer,* meaning both "holy" and "accursed"—like all dying gods, who were formerly *anathemata,* "offerings."[14] Every nation has examples of gods chosen for the sacred marriage, then accursed and killed. The Celtic Goddess's fatal words marked for death such heroes as Cu Chulainn and Diarmuid. The god called Lord of the Hunt became *le Chasseur Maudit,* "the Accursed Huntsman."

The origin of accursed heroes in general might be found in ancient India, where **Shiva** the Condemned One was chosen by Sati-Kali for the sacred marriage with her virgin incarnation, followed by his death and journey to the underworld.[15] As a personification of the Primordial Abyss, the Goddess was sometimes called Kala-Nath, which might have been related to the name of Anath.[16]

Anath's capacity to curse and kill made even the Heavenly Father afraid of her. When El seemed reluctant to do her bidding, she threatened to smash his head and cover his gray hair and beard with gore. He hastily gave her everything she asked, saying, "Whoever hinders thee will be crushed."[17] It was a long step from this Middle-Eastern tale to the Greek concept of the dread Goddess as the Heavenly Father's ever-dutiful daughter. See **Anne, Saint**.

1. Ashe, 30-31, 59. 2. Briffault 3, 110. 3. Massa, 48. 4. Hooke, M.E.M., 83. 5. Gray, 80. 6. Graves, G.M. 1, 255. 7. Gaster, 416. 8. Graves, W.G., 410. 9. Knight, S.L., 130. 10. *Larousse,* 77. 11. *Larousse,* 78. 12. Gifford, 63. 13. Budge, G.E. 2, 253. 14. Hyde, 111. 15. *Larousse,* 335. 16. *Bardo Thodol,* 147. 17. Pritchard, A.N.E. 1, 124.

Anathema

Christian term for a person or thing officially cursed and excommunicated; from the biblical passage "If any man love not the Lord Jesus Christ, let him be Anathema Maranatha" (1 Corinthians 16:22). Originally it was the curse pronounced by the Goddess, Marah or Mari-Anath, on her dying god; see **Anath**. In medieval Christian usage, to be pronounced Anathema was to be cast out of the congregation with bell, book, and candle, and irrevocably consigned to hell: a curious reminiscence of the accursed god's temporary descent into the underworld, in the ancient religion.

Andrew, Saint

St. Andrew's Cross

From Greek *andros,* "man" or "virility," a title of the solar god of Patras, in Achaea, where the apostle Andrew was supposed to have been crucified after founding the Byzantine papacy.[1] St. Andrew's legend was invented by Byzantine bishops to counter Rome's claim to primacy through its own legend of **St. Peter**. Eastern patriarchs upheld their magisterium by calling Andrew the elder brother of Peter, to enhance his authority, and declaring him the first apostle to discover the Messiah.[2]

The story that Andrew was crucified on an X-shaped cross, the so-called St. Andrew's Cross, was unknown until the Middle Ages. Apparently it evolved from a popular symbol of the eastern patriarchs, a solar cross in an orb.[3] It was also the Cross of Wotan carried by Norse invaders into Scotland, where it became the present Scottish national symbol.

Patras, the site of Andrew's alleged martyrdom, was an old shrine of the phallic-solar father-god variously called Pater, Petra, or Peter, whose name had the same basic meaning as Andrew. Political battles between the factions of Andrew and Peter in the 4th century A.D. stimulated canonical disguises for local *genii loci* in both Byzantium and Rome, and these are still preserved in the calendar of saints.[4]

1. Attwater, 45. 2. Brewster, 5. 3. B. Butler, 241. 4. H. Smith, 252.

Androgyne

Many Indo-European religions tried to combine male and female in the Primal Androgyne, both sexes in one body, often with two heads and four arms. The Brhadaranyaka Upanishad said the Primal Androgyne was "of the same size and kind as man and woman closely embracing."[1] Some said the male and female elements lived together in one skin, experiencing constant sexual bliss and spiritual completeness.

Shiva and **Shakti**-Kali appeared as the androgyne Ardhanarisvara, the right side male, the left side female.[2] Rudra, the older form of Shiva, was known as "the Lord Who is Half Woman."[3] **Brahma** and **Vishnu** also appeared as bisexual beings united with their Shaktis. Chinese Taoists held the mandala of **Yang and Yin** to represent the androgyne.

Western myths also assigned androgyny to the elder gods or the first human beings. The Orphic creation myth said the firstborn deity was a double-sexed Phanes or **Eros**, "Carnal Love," whose female half was **Psyche**, the soul, Greek equivalent of Shakti.[4] **Hermes** owed his phenomenal wisdom to his former androgynous existence with Mother **Aphrodite**, as double-sexed Hermaphroditus.[5]

Often, the androgyne appeared in myth as male-female twins born simultaneously, e.g. Isis-Osiris, Jana-Janus, Diana-Dianus, Fauna-Faunus, Helen-Helenus, or Artemis-Apollo, the "moon and sun" united in their Mother's womb. Probably an androgynous image on Apollo's altar at Delos gave rise to the story that he copulated with his sister Artemis on that altar. Several forms of the sun god were represented as requiring close physical union with the moon goddess, as even Brahma was useless without his female counterpart Bhavani, "Being."[6] Egypt's "supreme" sun god was often an androgyne; the sun was his right eye, the moon his left.[7] The same androgynous being is still worshipped in Dahomey as Nana-Buluku, Moon-Sun, who created the world and gave birth to the first pair of human beings.[8]

Many myths model the first human beings on the androgyne. Persians said the first pair in the garden of Heden (**Eden**) lived together in one body, until **Ahura Mazda** separated them. Jewish imitators of the Persians also said **Adam** and **Eve** were united in a bisexual body. Some rabbinical sources said Eve was not "taken out of" Adam; they were parted from one another by a jealous God who resented their sexual bliss, which was too Godlike for human beings, and should be reserved for deities. Casting man out of the "garden" meant detaching him from the female body, often symbolized by the Hebrew *pardes*, "garden."[9] This was another way of saying the original sin that angered God was not disobedience but sex.[10]

Greek myths of the Golden Age told the same tale of a jealous God: **Zeus**, who punished humanity's friend **Prometheus** with eternal torture because he tricked the Heavenly Father for humanity's advantage (see **Sacrifice**). The people of the Golden Age had been created androgynous by Prometheus, who made their bodies of clay, and **Athene**, who gave them life. Father Zeus took out his anger on them by tearing them apart. A piece of clay was torn out of the female part and stuck to the male part. That is why women have an orifice that bleeds, and men have a loose dangling appendage that seems not to belong to them but always craves to return to the female body it came from.

Cruel Zeus permitted human beings to return the male appendage to its female home sometimes, to sense for a brief moment the bliss of their former bisexual existence. Some Gnostic mystery cults of the first centuries A.D. taught Tantric techniques to prolong the moment of bliss, which angered most forms of the Heavenly Father including the Christian one, whose bishops denounced this training as schooling in wickedness.[11] Church fathers especially deplored making—or re-making—the Beast with Two Backs, another term for the Primal Androgyne.

Though orthodox Christianity renounced both sexuality and androgyny in religious images, Gnostic Christians used them. As **Kali** was the female half of Shiva, so the Gnostic Great Mother **Sophia** was the female half of Christ. This was revealed "in a great light": the Savior was shown as an androgyne coupled with "Sophia, Mother of All."[12]

Gnostic Christians said those who received the true revelation of the Father-Mother spirit were the only ones prepared for the secret sacrament called *apolytrosis*, "release," a concept identical with Tantric *moksha* or "liberation."[13] Obviously influenced by **Tantrism** or its prototype, western Gnostics had made a direct translation of the Hindu Yab-Yum, "Father-Mother," the sexual union of a sage and his Shakti at the crucial moment of death.[14] Sexual sacraments were in effect practicing for that moment, when the enlightened one would be restored to the condition of primordial bliss as an androgynous creature.

Naassenes, or Naassians; from Hebrew *nahash,* "serpent." Jewish or Christian Gnostic sects of the early Christian era, who worshipped the serpent god Ophis (Hermes) as a form of the Savior.

Mysteries General term for religious rites of the "secret initiation" type, which included early Christianity.

The Naassenes said no enlightenment was possible without the Father-Mother spirit, an androgyne sometimes called Heavenly Horn of the Moon.[15] In the 5th century A.D., Orphic initiations sought to awaken a female spirit within man, to render him sensitive to the message of the Mysteries. After meeting the deities in a death-and-rebirth experience, he carried a bowl, emblem of the womb, and touched his belly like a gravid woman, signifying "a spiritual experience uniting the opposed ways of knowledge of the male and female, and fused with this idea is that of a new life conceived within."[16]

Such Gnostic subtleties were disliked by the orthodox, who viewed all mergings of the sexes as unequivocally sinful. After Gnostic sects were crushed, the androgyne was consigned to hell and gave birth to many curious devils with both male and female attributes. A 16th-century book showed **Satan** himself seated on a throne, wearing a papal tiara, with bird feet, a female face in his genital area, and pendulous female breasts.[17] The **Devil** of the Tarot pack was usually androgynous, as were many of the devils represented in cathedral carvings.

1. O'Flaherty, 34. 2. *Larousse,* 371. 3. O'Flaherty, 298. 4. *Larousse,* 90, 132. 5. Graves, G.M. 1, 73. 6. Baring-Gould, C.M.M.A., 375. 7. Erman, 301. 8. Hays, 339. 9. Hughes, 47. 10. Cavendish, P.E., 27. 11. J.H. Smith, C.G., 287. 12. Malvern, 53. 13. Pagels, 37. 14. Rawson, A.T., 103. 15. Jung & von Franz, 136. 16. Campbell, M.I., 389. 17. de Givry, 125.

Andromeda

"Ruler of Men," Greek title of the Philistine sea-queen won in marriage by Perseus, who supposedly saved her from the sea-serpent Yamm. Perseus seems to have been a Greek name for **Baal** in this myth, for Baal annually fought Yamm for the love of Mother **Astarte**, the Philistines' Goddess, locally named Atargatis. Baal replaced Yamm, then was himself replaced when the queen tired of him and he became Yamm in his turn. Andromeda on her rock, in the classic myth, was transformed from a critical observer of the combat into a victim.

That Perseus played the role of sacred king in the original myth is shown by his apotheosis and rising to dwell in the stars. So also **Heracles** was raised to the stars after performing the same feat—slaying the great sea serpent in order to mate with Hesione, "Queen of Asia," probably just another name for Andromeda-Atargatis.[1]

1. Graves, G.M. 1, 224.

Androphonos

"Man-slayer," title of the Goddess **Aphrodite** as a Destroyer or death-goddess. She was also the Black One, the Goddess of the Tombs, and the Queen Bee who killed her lovers as drone bees are killed, by castration and evisceration. She had "many titles which seem inconsistent with her beauty and complaisance."[1] That was because classic mythographers sought to make her a love goddess only, ignoring her earlier character as the creating-and-destroying Triple Goddess (see **Trinity**).

1. Graves, G.M. 1, 71–72.

Angels

The earliest angels were heavenly nymphs, like Hindu apsaras, who dispensed sensual bliss to the blessed ones. Vikings called them Valkyries. Greeks called them **Horae**. Persians called them Houris, or Peris (fairies). A guardian angel was a personal **Shakti** who watched over a man and took him into her ecstatic embrace at the moment of death.

Hindu angels were created primarily for lovemaking. They had no menstruation, pregnancy, birth, or nursing, though they were mothers. Each child appeared miraculously on its mother's knee at the age of five years. Apsaras could copulate endlessly with gods without any emission of fluids or loss of energy. Such a being was "the perfect dispenser of sensual delight and amorous bliss on a divine scale."[1] Like the queen of the Holy Grail palace in bardic romance, the angel was a "Dispenser of Joy." (See **Grail, Holy**.)

There were earthy angels too, the dakinis, "Skywalkers." Tantric writings said they lived in the Palace of Lotus Light. They were sometimes called prostitutes' daughters, or yoginis, i.e., yoga-priestesses.[2]

Although such angels seemed to be every man's wish fulfillment, patriarchal religions denied the sexuality of angels. Moslems rejected the **Houris** (heavenly "whores"), and insisted the angels are without carnal desires.[3] Yet this contradicted the teaching of the Koran, that after death every hero would receive beautiful girls as heavenly companions.[4]

European Christianity consigned the formerly divine Horae to Fairyland, the earthly paradise distinguished from the celestial one. The place was called *locus voluptatis terrestis,* the Terrestrial Place of Pleasure, or *pratum felicitatus,* the Paradise of Joy.[5]

Angels were often confused with seraphs and cherubs. The former were six-winged fiery flying serpents, the lightning-spirits of Chaldean myth. The latter were Semitic *kerubh,* from Sheban *mu-karrib,* "priests of the moon"; sometimes they could take the form of birds. Angels accompanying the Hindu Great Goddess were able to fly on the wings of garuda birds.[6]

Magic Papyri
Collections of exorcisms, invocations, charms, and spells widely circulated during the early Christian era, used as bases for later grimoires and Hermetic texts.

Biblical angels were "sons of God" who came to earth to beget children on mortal women (Genesis 6:4). Later these were called demons, or incubi, or "fallen" angels. The Book of Enoch blamed women for the angels' fall. Women had "led astray the angels of heaven."[7] In the Magic Papryi, the words angel, spirit, god, and demon were interchangeable.[8] When **St. Paul** said women's heads must be covered in church "because of the angels" (1 Corinthians 11:10), he meant the *daemones* (demons) supposed to be attracted to women's **hair**. The Greeks thought each person had an individual guardian angel or *daemon* which could appear in animal form, and under Christianity evolved into the "familiar spirit." There were no really well-defined distinctions between angels, demons, familiars, fairies, elves, saints, *genii,* ancestral ghosts, or pagan gods.[9] Among supernatural beings one might always find many hazy areas of overlapping identities, even "good" or "evil" qualities being blurred.

A Gallup poll showed in 1978 that over half of all Americans still believe in angels.[10]

1. Zimmer, 163. 2. Tatz & Kent, 84, 148. 3. Budge, G.E. 1, 5.
4. Campbell, Oc.M., 430. 5. Silberer, 212. 6. Tatz & Kent, 146.
7. Tennant, 183–84. 8. M. Smith, 191. 9. Wimberly, 423.
10. *Newsweek,* June 26, 1978, p. 32.

Angerona

Silent Goddess of Rome, shown holding a finger to her sealed mouth. Some said Angerona represented the secret name of Rome, which it was illegal to pronounce.[1] In all probability she was a pre-

Roman title of the same primal Creatress whom **Gnostics** called **Sige**, "Silence," personifying the lightless and soundless womb that gave birth to the first deities. Gnostics said Silence was the mother of the Great Goddess herself.

1. *Larousse,* 214.

Angurboda

Eddaic "Hag of the Iron Wood," mother of Hel and of the Moon-dogs who bore away the dead. Danaans, or Danes, knew her as Anu, Yngona, Nanna, or "Anna of the Angles." She was a "hag" in the ancient sense of "Holy One"; the Death-goddess.[1] See **Dog**.

1. Graves, W.G., 409.

Anima

Female soul, from the roots *an,* "heavenly," and *ma,* "mother," recalling a time when all souls were supposed to emanate from the Heavenly Mother.[1] In the 16th century A.D. Guillaume Postel said every soul had male and female halves, the animus and anima. The male half had been redeemed by Christ, but the female half was still unredeemed and awaited a female savior.[2] This was a new development of the old Christian view that only males had any souls at all. The third canon of the Council of Nantes in 660 A.D. had decided that all women are "soulless brutes."[3]

Guillaume Postel (1510-1581) French scholar, teacher, and mystic, friend of Ignatius Loyola, accepted into the Jesuit order but later expelled for "wrong" ideas. He was imprisoned in Rome by the Inquisition, until a popular uprising opened the prisons and offered him a lucky escape.

Alchemists applied the word *anima* to all "spirits" considered female: Anima Mercury, Anima Mundi, etc. The Spirit of the World was connected with the elements of earth and water, like Eleusinian **Demeter**, "Mistress of Earth and Sea." One reason alchemists were suspected of heresy was their notion that the World-Soul was a female *anima.*

Carl Jung revived the terms animus and anima to describe reasoning and intuitive parts of the mind (i.e., left and right hemispheres). Every person's anima is "often symbolically connected with both earth and water. She is pictured as timeless and profoundly wise. . . . Each man's first and formative experience of the anima is with his mother. Her true function in the mind, according to Jung, is creativity."[4]

1. Graves, W.G., 410. 2. Seligmann, 223. 3. Dreifus, 4. 4. Cavendish, T., 79.

Ankamma

Emanation of **Kali** the Destroyer as the spirit of cholera. She had many such emanations, each one specializing in a certain disease capable of causing death. See **Kali Ma**.

Ankh

Egyptian "Cross of Life" representing union of male and female sexual symbols: a female oval surmounting a male cross. Its other name was Key of the Nile, because the sacred marriage between God and Goddess was supposed to take place at the source of the Nile each year before the flood. The Christian version of the Cross of Life, which didn't appear in Christian art until after the 5th century A.D., significantly lacked the feminine oval and kept only the masculine part of the figure.[1]

The ankh seems to have evolved from an ancient symbol of the Goddess in Libya and Phoenicia: a narrow triangle surmounted by a crossbar and a round or oval head.[2]

Ankh

Egyptians regarded the ankh as a universal life-charm. "The life of every being, divine or human, depended on his or her possession of it. From first to last the gods are seen carrying it in their right hands, and they gave life to their kings and servants presenting it to them."[3] Early Christians also used the ankh occasionally as an emblem of immortality, calling it an ansated cross. They knew the Egyptians had a certain letter-hieroglyph that "stood for the life to come; and this letter had the form of a cross."[4] In hieroglyphics the ankh stood simply for the word "life."[5]

1. H. Smith, 188. 2. d'Alviella, 186–90. 3. Budge, A.T., 128.
4. de Voragine, 550. 5. Budge, E.L., 83.

Anna-Nin

Sumerian prototype of the many forms of the Great Goddess named Anna, Ana, or Hannah throughout the Middle East and Mediteranean lands. The name meant Lady of Heaven. See **Anne, Saint**.

Annapurna

Himalayan **mountain** called Great Breast Full of Nourishment; a manifestation of the Great Goddess as the home and support of the gods.

Anne, Saint

Mythical mother of the virgin **Mary**, from the Middle-Eastern Goddess Anna, or Hannah, or Di-Ana, mother of **Mari**. From Sumeria to pre-Roman Latium she was known as Anna, the Grandmother-Goddess; Anatha in Syria, Anat in Canaan, Ana or Anah in several Old Testament transformations. Long before the Bible was written, the Goddess Anna was already known as the Grandmother of God. Hence, the choice of her name for the mother of God's Mother is hardly surprising.[1]

Syriac versions of the Book of James said God's Grandmother was not Anna but Dinah, actually the same name, a Semitic Di-Ana or "Goddess Ana." Dinah was the ancestress of Dinaite tribes who settled in Sumeria (Ezra 4:9). As Anatha, she was the consort of Yahweh at Elephantine.[2] As Anna Perenna she was Grandmother Time to the Romans, mother of the **Aeons**. As Ana or Anu she ruled Celtic tribes. As Nanna, she was an incarnation of Freya in the mother-bride of Balder. In Phrygia too, she was Nana, mother of the Savior. She was really as old as the oldest civilization. A Sumerian prayer declared: "Hear O ye regions, the praise of Queen Nana; magnify the Creatress, exalt the dignified, exalt the Glorious One, draw nigh unto the Mighty Lady."[3]

Romans worshipped the Goddess as Anna Perenna, "Eternal Anna," mother of the Aeons. She stood at the change of years, a two-headed Goddess of Time with two faces named Prorsa and Postverta, looking forward and backward from her heavenly gate among the stars, where one celestial cycle merged into the next. So she stood for both Alpha and Omega, beginning and end. Under the name of Carmenta she invented all the letters in between.[4] She was also Jana, or **Juno**, mother of the January New Year. Classical myths masculinized her as the two-faced Janus, god of gateways. Christians may have confused icons labeled IANA with the mother of the Virgin; for Jana-Juno was the virgin mother of the savior-god Mars.

Ovid said Anna was the same as the Moon-goddess **Minerva**. **Sappho** named her "the Queen."[5] To the Celts, she was the same as their Ana, first of the female trinity of the **Morrigan**, associated with the Cauldron of Regeneration. Her moon-temple used to stand at Cnoc Aine in Limerick, now a shrine of "St. Anne."[6] To Irish pagans, Ana meant "mother." It also came to mean wealth, plenty, treasure.[7]

As Grandmother-goddess, Ana could be a destroying Crone. Some myths called her Morg-ana, "Invincible Queen Death." Medieval Christians called her Anna of the Angles, or Black Annis, or **Angurboda**, the Hag of the Iron Wood, mother of Hel.[8] The magic pentacle was the sign of Morg-ana.[9] A similar five-pointed star stood for the underworld in Egyptian hieroglyphics.[10] This same star was the official sigil of St. Anne.[11]

In her Christianized form, Anne had three husbands, gave birth to many saints, and became the patron of midwives and miners. Neumann says, "All this bears witness to her original fertility aspect as Earth Mother."[12]

St. Anne was of crucial importance in the dogma of the virgin Mary's **immaculate conception**, adopted as an article of faith in 1854, after seven centuries of controversy.[13] In the official Catholic view, original sin was transmitted by sexual acts. Therefore, so Mary

Johannes Trithemius
15th-century German scholar, Abbot of Sponheim

could be born without taint of original sin, St. Anne herself had to be innocent of sexuality. Accordingly, Johannes Trithemius proclaimed that Anne "was chosen by God for her appointed services before the foundation of the world. She conceived 'without the action of man,' and was as pure as her daughter."[14]

At first the church accepted this doctrine, because it seemed to solve the problem of Mary's sinlessness. Later it was rejected. Two virgin births made one too many. In the end, St. Anne was said to have conceived Mary in the normal way but the child was freed in the womb of original sin. Though these intimate matters are supposed to be known in minute detail, churchmen incongruously admit that "nothing whatever is known about the parents of the Virgin Mary."[15]

1. Graves, W.G., 411. 2. Hays, 89. 3. Stone, 219. 4. *Larousse,* 210.
5. Graves, W.G., 408. 6. Loomis, 387. 7. Joyce 1, 261. 8. Sturluson, 56.
9. Loomis, 342. 10. Budge, E.L., 75. 11. Brewster, 343.
12. Neumann, A.C.U., 57. 13. Young, 203. 14. Neumann, A.C.U., 59.
15. Attwater, 186.

Antic Hey

Dance step of the medieval Carnival King: *antico* from Latin *antiquus,* "ancient, venerable." Carnival "antics" were connected with the Old Religions, whose sacred processions were often accompanied by clowns deliberately making obscene gestures and jokes to heighten the spirit of revelry.[1] The "hey" was, and is, a figure-eight pattern paced on the ground, the sign meaning "infinity" in Hindu-Arabic numeral systems and in their descendant, modern mathematics. Choruses of old folk songs call for the hey, in nonsense phrases like "Hey, nonny nonny," or "Hey, derry down." Thus the antic hey was really a pagan liturgy in song or dance or both, performed at secularized versions of the ancient rites.

1. Funk, p. 54.

Antichrist

Virgin-born son of the devil, supposed to appear during the world's Last Days. Christianity never escaped the patterns of dualism, whereby each god had to have an equal and opposite anti-god. Antichrist was the Christian equivalent of Chaldean **Aciel**, lord of the nether world, counterbalancing the solar god of the heavens.

The coming of Antichrist has been announced and re-announced throughout the entire Christian era, especially in times of political and social stress. His title has been laid on Nero, Attila, Genghis Khan, Merlin, Frederick II, and many others including several popes. More recently, Napoleon, Kaiser Wilhelm, and Hitler were all nominated for the position. See **Doomsday**.

Antinomianism

General term for Christian sects that followed the original doctrine of **apotheosis,** believing they could become "one with Christ." Like their pagan contemporaries, many early Christians thought the only route to immortality was deification, and the object of their Mysteries was to learn how to be deified. The distinction between men and gods was that men died and gods didn't. Thus, one's immortality depended on becoming a god, often by sacramental procedures such as eating a god's flesh and blood (see **Cannibalism**).

Clement of Alexandria said: "That man with whom the Logos dwells . . . is made like God and is beautiful. . . . [T]hat man becomes God, for God so wills it. . . . [T]he Logos of God became man that from man you might learn how man may become God. . . . [T]he true Christian Gnostic has already become God."[1]

This doctrine of deification was soundly based on pagan precedent. Worshippers of Hermes the Logos believed that "This is the good end for those who have attained knowledge, namely, Deification." They said to Hermes, "Thou art I, and I am thou; thy name is mine, for I am thy image (*eidolon*)." Mithraists used the same formula, "I am thou and thou art I," which the Gospels put in the mouth of Jesus, "Abide in me, and I in you" (John 15:4). Seneca said, "A holy spirit dwells within us." Epictetus wrote: "You are bearing a God with you. . . . It is within yourself that you carry him." Cicero said initiation into the Mysteries taught a man he could be God, "inferior in no whit to the celestials."[2]

The theological pitfall in the concept of salvation through apotheosis was that identification of self and god led to what Tantric sages called *Svecchacara,* "Do As You Will." In effect, the perfected sage could do nothing evil because he was God, and God was incapable of sinning.[3] Therefore he was above all man-made laws, and could do as he pleased.

Greek democracy was based on a related idea that through enlightenment and reason each citizen would become capable of self-government and would make no moral errors. This did not apply to slaves, women, or those who owned no property; such were not classed as citizens. Mature male landowners however could become *idiotae,* "self-gods."[4] Thus the word "idiot" began in Greek with the sense of "one who will not be governed," that is, one who believed the divine will dwelt in himself.

Numerous medieval Christian sects took the Antinomian route to salvation, believing that, like eastern sages, they could become one with the divine. These mystics "in their identification with God supposed that upon their conscious union with Him they were exempt from the rules governing ordinary men." Leaders like Amalric of Bena, Johann Hartmann, sects like the Alumbrados, Illuminates, Adamites, and others taught that when their flesh was occupied by the holy spirit

Clement of Alexandria (Titus Flavius Clemens) Christian presbyter and teacher of the late 2nd century A.D., once reckoned a saint, but removed from the canon of saints in 1586 by Pope Sixtus V.

Alumbrados, "Enlightened Ones" Spanish heretics of the 15th to 17th centuries, recruited from reform movements among the Jesuits and Franciscans. They were eventually exterminated by the Inquisition.

Illuminati or "Perfectibilists" Bavarian secret society founded by Adam Weishaupt, a former Jesuit. The society was banned in 1785.

Adamites 18th-century sectaries who believed nakedness represented the natural state of innocence in which Adam dwelt before he "fell" into sin, and began to clothe himself.

they could commit no sins of the flesh. For them, sexual promiscuity was only a natural "embracing of God."[5]

Brothers and Sisters of the Free Spirit undertook to demonstrate the redemptive virtues of sexuality, nakedness, and scorn of the conventions. The more openly they displayed their hippie-like behaviors, the more closely they approached the divine essence. Frazer remarked, "Their progress toward this mystic communion was accelerated by the **Inquisition**, and they expired in the flames, not merely with unclouded serenity, but with the most triumphant feelings of cheerfulness and joy."[6] They had their own martyr, a literary sister who wrote the gospel of their sect, *The Mirror of Free Souls.* She and her book both were excommunicated and burned in 1310 A.D.[7]

Antinomian ideas were often defined as heresy, as in the case of Simon Morin, who seems to have had fairly standard delusions of grandeur. He said he was the incarnate second coming of Christ, and was incapable of committing a sin; anything he did must be worshipped. The church disagreed, and burned him as a witch.[8]

The usual Antinomian excuses for sexual self-expression infiltrated a group of nuns in the Dominican convent of St. Catherine de Prato. Early in the 19th century, a text of the official inquiry into this case was published in Brussels, then "withdrawn at the insistence of the Papal Court. The second edition is . . . much expurgated." One of the nuns expounded on her Antinomian teachings: "It is sufficient to elevate the spirit to God and then no action, whatever it be, is sinful. . . . Love of God and one's neighbor is the whole of the commandments. Man who unites with God by means of woman satisfies both commandments. So also does he who, lifting his spirit to God, has enjoyment with a person of the same sex or alone. . . . In doing that which we erroneously call impure is real purity ordained by God, without which man cannot arrive at a knowledge of Him."[9]

Such ideas were typically Oriental, as opposed to the Christian idea of entering into a relationship with a God who was an external "other." Though the Gospels said "the kingdom of God is within you" (Luke 17:21), orthodox Christianity treated this as a heretical idea.[10]

1. Angus, 106. 2. Angus, 102, 108, 110, 112. 3. Avalon, 624–25. 4. Lindsay, O.A., 91. 5. Avalon, 636. 6. Frazer, G.B., 117–18. 7. Tuchman, 317. 8. Summers, G.W., 429–30. 9. Avalon, pp. 637–39. 10. Campbell, M.L.B., 79, 95.

Anubis

Jackal-headed Egyptian god of the underworld and of mummification; judge of the dead; Egypt's primary **psychopomp**, like Hermes in Greece. Mated to **Nephthys**, the underground aspect of Isis, Anubis was sometimes known as the Great Dog. He was considered essential to the worship of Isis and Osiris. Plutarch said he had "a power among the Egyptians much like that of Hecate among the Greeks, he being terrestrial as well as Olympic. . . . Those that worship the **dog**, have a certain secret meaning that must not be revealed. In the more remote and ancient times the dog had the highest honor paid to him in Egypt."[1] Anubis may have been originally a canine incarnation of Shiva, whose name also meant a jackal.[2]

1. Knight, S.L., 113. 2. *Mahanirvanatantra,* 113.

Anuket

var. Anukis

"The Clasper," an Egyptian Goddess personifying the yonic source of the Nile flood. Her symbol was the **cowrie**, always emblematic of female genitals. Her union with the ithyphallic god was supposed to bring life-giving Nile waters to the land. She "clasped" a number of gods, including—in the 5th century B.C.—the Hebrew Jehovah.[1]

Like **Kali Ma** in India, Anuket had four arms, representing union between male and female principles. The general pattern for such deities was that two arms held symbols of the male elements, and two held symbols of the female elements. Yet she was known as "The One." She was "self-begotten and self-produced, and whilst yet a virgin gave birth to the sun god."[2]

At the Festival of the Inundation, Egyptians sang to her: "Thou art the bringer of food, thou art the mighty one of meat and drink, thou art the creator of all good things. Thou fillest the storehouses; thou heapest high with corn the granaries, and thou hast care for the poor and needy."[3]

Festival of the Inundation Annual celebration of the coming of the Nile flood, which brought the water and fresh silt necessary to the fertility of the entire Nile valley, where rain was almost unknown.

1. Graves, W.G., 405; *Larousse,* 37. 2. Budge, D.N., 159. 3. Budge, D.N., 106.

Apep

var. Apophis

Egyptian and Greek names of the Great Serpent of the underworld, who threatened to swallow the sun god every night as he passed through the realm of darkness, returning from west to east. (See **Serpent**.) Ra's priesthood evidently decided at one point that **Ra** faced danger in the underworld, so the faithful would be encouraged to help the sun return with their nightly prayers. However, the Serpent was a common personification of the Egyptian underworld or Tuat itself. The realm of darkness with its various "chambers" was the interior of the serpent's body, through which the sun god must pass, as he was always swallowed at each sunset.[1]

In medieval alchemy the "Apophis-snake" was confused with the Hermetic Ouroboros, a hidden world spirit in the form of a serpent, who might reveal the secret of the **Philosopher's Stone**.

1. Budge, G. E. 1, 266.

Apex

Pointed conical cap worn by the Roman high priest, Flamen Dialis. When outdoors, he must always have the *apex* on his head.[1] It was a phallic symbol representing his continual union with the Queen of Heaven. It has been shown that "In the symbolism of dreams and of myths the hat is usually the phallus."[2]

The Flamen's wife, the Flaminica, represented the Goddess. She was the more important dignitary of the two. If his marriage was terminated by her death, the Flamen immediately lost his sacred office and reverted to a private citizen. Such customs show that the powers of priests "in Rome as elsewhere, derived in the first instance from an older priesthood of magical women."[3]

The same conical cap belonged to the Lord of the Underworld in Celtiberian pagan imagery. He was Helman: a man belonging to the Goddess Hel.[4] Sometimes he was said to be the god Frey, consort of Hel's heavenly or lunar aspect, **Freya**.[5]

Celtiberian Dating from the occupation of the Iberian peninsula by Celtic tribes, especially the loosely-knit empire known as Brigantia, ruled by the Goddess Brigit.

The same conical cap evolved into the traditional headdress of sorcerers and witches; the Fool's Cap (or Dunce Cap) worn by the Carnival King; the bishop's miter; the pope's tiara; and before them all, the conical crown of Egyptian pharaohs, emblem of the king's union with the Sky-goddess. To the present day, the conical witch-hat is worn by Tantric priests and sorcerers in Tibet.[6]

1. Rose, 209. 2. Silberer, 87. 3. Briffault 3, 20–21. 4. Knight, D.W.P., 73. 5. H.R.E. Davidson, P.S., 134. 6. Waddell, 483.

Aphrodite

Often dismissed as a "Greek goddess of love," Aphrodite was really much more than that. Like Kali, she was a Virgin-Mother-Crone trinity. She was once indistinguishable from the **Fates** (Moirai); her old name was Moira, and she was said to be older than Time. She governed the world by *ius naturale,* the natural law of the maternal clan.[1]

She was not only Greek. She was the Dea Syria, also known as **Asherah** or **Astarte**, Goddess of the oldest continuously-occupied temple in the world.[2] She was the ancestral mother of the Romans, for she gave birth to their founding father, **Aeneas**.[3] Under the name of **Venus**, she was the mother of the Venetii, whose capital city became Venice, called "Queen of the Sea" after the Goddess herself.

One of Aphrodite's major centers of worship was the city of Paphos on Cyprus, the island named for its copper mines. Thus, she was called "the Cyprian" or "the Paphian," and her sacred metal was copper. She was also called **Mari**, the Sea. Egyptians referred to her island as Ay-Mari.[4]

During the Christian era, Aphrodite's temple on Cyprus was converted into a sanctuary of the virgin **Mary**, another name of the same Goddess, but in this sanctuary the virgin Mary is hailed to this day as *Panaghia Aphroditessa,* "All-holy Aphrodite."[5]

Continued worship of the goddess on Cyprus probably contributed to the Christian belief that the whole population of Cyprus descended from demons.[6] In reality, Cyprian Aphrodite was like all other manifestations of the Great Goddess: ruling birth, life, love, death, time, and fate, reconciling man to all of them through sensual and sexual mysticism. The Cyprian sage Zenon taught Aphrodite's philosophy: "mankind and the universe were bound together in the system of fate. . . . Diogenes Laertios tells us that Zenon was the first to define the end of human existence as 'life in accordance with nature.' "[7]

Aphrodite had almost as many "emanations" as Thousand-Named Kali. She was not only Mari and Moira and Marina and Pelagia and Stella Maris, all titles related to her control of the sea; she was also Ilithyia, Goddess of childbirth; Hymen, Goddess of marriage; Venus, Goddess of sexuality and the hunt; Urania, Queen of Heaven; **Androphonos**, the Destroyer of Men; and many others. She was often identified with **Isis**. Anchises, her lover who begot Aeneas and then was castrated, had a name meaning "he who mates with Isis."[8] Under several of her names, Aphrodite mated with Semitic gods. Her cult occupied the main temple in Jerusalem after 70 A.D. In the 4th century it was said that Constantine's mother found the true cross of Christ buried in Aphrodite's Jerusalem temple. (See **Cross**.)

One of Aphrodite's greatest shrines in Asia Minor was the city of Aphrodisias, once dedicated to **Ishtar**. Up to the 12th century A.D., when the city was taken by Seljuk Turks, the Goddess was worshipped there as the patron of arts and letters, crafts, and culture.[9] Recent excavations have uncovered exquisite artifacts and statuary, bespeaking a cultivated and sophisticated lifestyle under the Goddess's rule.[10]

The calendar still keeps the name of Aphrodite on the month dedicated to her, April (Aphrilis). The ancient Kalendar of Romulus said this was the month of Venus.[11]

1. Bachofen, 57, 192. 2. *Encyc. Brit.*, "Byblos." 3. Graves, G.M. 1, 69. 4. Graves, W.G., 410. 5. Ashe, 192. 6. Cavendish, P.E., 104. 7. Lindsay, O.A., 103. 8. Graves, G.M. 1, 71–72. 9. Lederer, 170. 10. *National Geographic,* v. 141, n. 6 (June 1972). 11. Brewster, 172.

Apis

Egyptian lunar bull god annually sacrificed at Memphis. Later he was combined with **Osiris** to produce the syncretic god of the Ptolemies, Osorapis, or Sarapis. Apis was begotten in bull form when moonbeams fell on a cow in heat. He was identified by special markings, notably symbols of the Goddess: a triangle on his forehead, a flying vulture on his side, a crescent moon on his flank. After death each Apis bull was elaborately embalmed and buried in the vast underground bull-tombs.[1] In mummy form, like all Egyptian gods, he became "an Osiris."

1. *Larousse,* 44.

Apollo

Greek sun god who took over the powers of his twin sister **Artemis**, the Moon. Originally, he was her child, as the sun was born of the Moon-goddess in Egypt and elsewhere. He was also her totemic beast in several forms: a wolf (Apollo Lycaeus), a mouse (Apollo Smintheus), or a golden-maned lion (Apollo Chrysocomes).

The fully anthropomorphized Apollo laid claim to the Goddess's powers of prophecy, poetry, music, magic, and healing. His priesthood adopted the **Muses**, the Graces, even the Great Serpent who gave oracles from the earth-womb, Apollo Python, known as Sol Niger (Black Sun) during his nightly sojourn in the underworld. Egyptians called him **Apep** or Apophis, the serpent of darkness. In the Bible he is Apollyon, "Spirit of the Pit" (Revelation 9:11).

Apollo's serpent-form inspired the Pythoness, priestess of the Delphic oracle, Greece's foremost temple of prophecy. This temple belonged to the Goddess in the beginning; *delphi* means womb. Even Apollo's priests admitted that she had owned the oracle in her trinitarian guise as mother of earth, heaven, and the abyss: the first of all deities to prophesy, the Earth-mother; and Themis, mother of the sea and of all Themistes, "oracles"; and the Moon-goddess, **Artemis**, under the name of Phoebe—another title stolen by Apollo, who became known as Phoebus.[1]

Apollonian priests naturally directed their energies toward conquest of the oracles. "The reason why a deity associated with political conquest and order should take possession of oracular shrines is obvious; oracles were the chief means of controlling public opinion and public action, and to control the oracles was as necessary to a political god as it is to later politicians to control the press or education."[2]

Laurel became Apollo's sacred plant because it was the plant of inspired poetic frenzy, which is why Britain's national poet is still called Laureate, the laurel-crowned one. The Delphic Pythoness chewed leaves of cherry laurel to induce her poetic-prophetic trances. Cherry laurel contains traces of cyanide, enough to cause delirium, foaming at the mouth, and other symptoms of divine possession.

Apollo's priests used the oracles to create new patriarchal laws, overturning the laws of the matriarchate. Apollo's most notable judicial act was to absolve Orestes from the crime of killing his mother. Apollo said it was no crime, because a mother is not a real parent; only a father truly gives life to a child, the same "Apollonian" opinion later adopted by Christian theologians.[3] Yet this patriarchal opinion was negated by Apollo's own surname of Letoides, "son of Leto."[4] He carried the name of his mother only, after the custom of the matriarchal Lycians who recognized strictly matrilineal ancestry, and in whose country Apollo's cult first evolved.

In his earliest manifestations, Apollo was subordinate to the Goddess as her dog-faced or wolf-faced door-guardian: a "Spirit of the Pit" like Apollyon, another name for **Anubis** or Cerberus. Four Hittite altars found in Anatolia were dedicated to a god named Apulunas, Guardian of Gates, forerunner of Apollo Lycaeus or "Wolfish Apollo."[5] Once he walked at the Goddess's heel, like Anubis; but this was suppressed and forgotten.

To some early Christians, Apollo became a junior God. He was even said to have fathered on mortal virgins several pagan sages respected by the church, such as Plato.[6] Healing miracles were widely attributed to Apollo.[7] Christians sought his intervention in certain illnesses. It was claimed that if a naked virgin touched the afflicted part, saying, "Apollo denieth that the heat of the plague can increase where a naked virgin quencheth it," the patient would get well.[8]

Under his title of Benedictus, "Good-speaker," Apollo was even canonized, and became **St. Benedict**.[9]

1. Lederer, 149. 2. Briffault 3, 153–54. 3. Bachofen, 159. 4. Guthrie, 83. 5. Guthrie, 86. 6. Shumaker, 152. 7. Graves, W.G., 433. 8. Hazlitt, 354. 9. Attwater, 62.

Apostles

Describing the religious customs of the Aztecs, Father Acosta unwittingly gave one of the real purposes of Jesus's twelve companions:

> *They took a captive . . . and afore they did sacrifice him unto their idols, they gave him the name of the idol, saying that he did represent the same idol. . . . When he went through the streets, the people came forth to worship him, and every one brought him an alms, with children and sick folks, that he might cure them, and bless them, suffering him to do all things at his pleasure, only he was accompanied with ten or twelve men lest he should fly. . . . The feast being come, and he grown fat, they killed him, opened him, and ate him, making a solemn sacrifice of him.*[1]

José de Acosta
16th-century Spanish Jesuit missionary who accompanied the *conquistadores,* and wrote a history of native cultures in Peru, Bolivia, and Mexico.

This devoured Savior, closely watched by his ten or twelve guards, embodied the god Quetzalcoatl, who was born of a virgin, slain in atonement for a primal sin, and whose Second Coming was confidently expected.[2] He was often represented as a trinity signified by three crosses, a large one between the smaller ones.[3] Father Acosta naively said, "It is strange that the devil after his manner hath brought a Trinity into idolatry."[4] His church found it all too familiar, and long kept his book as one of its secrets.

The Gospels contain hints that Jesus was as reluctant as the Quetzalcoatl-victim. Once he ran away from his "apostles" and fled alone into the mountains, fearing men would "come and take him by force, to make him a king" (John 6:15). That is, he didn't want the fatal honor of being a sacred king of the Jews, the doomed Bridegroom of Zion. The apostles caught up with him in Capernaum, and his subsequent speeches indicate resignation to his fate.

He said he was the bread of God, come down from heaven to give life to the world: "The bread that I will give is my flesh, which I will give for the life of the world. . . . Whoso eateth my flesh, and drinketh my blood, hath eternal life" (John 6:50, 54). On the eve of the sacrifice he prayed despairingly, "O my Father, if it be possible, let this cup pass from me; nevertheless . . . thy will be done" (Matthew 26:39, 42). At least the Gospel narrator claims Jesus said this.

Naturally, any sacred king's guards would become popularizers of his cult, "dining out" on the divine sayings and actions for years. However, the Gospels were not written by the apostles whose names they bear. They were forgeries, compiled long after Jesus's time, some as late as the middle of the 2nd century.[5] Even this is scholarly guesswork, since no authentic manuscript can be dated before the 4th century.[6]

Canonization of the apostles used an ancient Buddhist symbol, the *ushnisha* or "flame of invisible light" appearing on top of their heads. To Buddhists, this flame streaming from the "lotus center" of the skull meant super-intelligence. It appeared over the heads of bodhisattvas.[7] The same phenomenon appeared over the heads of the apostles (Acts 2:4). The rest of their stories were as mythical as those of the bodhisattvas. Guignebert says "not one of them is true. . . . [T]here exists no information really worthy of credence about the life and work of the immediate Apostles of Jesus."[8]

1. Frazer, G.B., 680. 2. Neumann, G.M., 203–8. 3. Briffault 2, 604. 4. Doane, 378. 5. H. Smith, 179, 182; Stanton, 106. 6. Pfeifer, 103. 7. Ross, 126. 8. Guignebert, 61.

Apotheosis

"God-making," the ritual of raising a slain sacrificial savior to heaven, to become a constellation among the stars or a part of his heavenly father. It became a custom to apotheosize Roman emperors while they were still living. Most other ancient kings were also gods on earth. Their surrogates, the "sacred kings" who died in their place, were promised immediate godhood after death.

Apotheosis was similarly promised Christian martyrs who perished in the belief that they would be wholly assimilated to Christ and would sit "on the right hand of God" like him. The church's ritual of canonization was a direct copy of pagan ceremonies of apotheosis. The Roman emperors' souls winging to heaven as eagles contributed the idea of releasing white doves at the climax of the church's canonization ceremony.[1] See **Drama**.

1. Gaster, 769.

Apple

Eve's fruit of knowledge used to be the Goddess's sacred heart of immortality, all over the Indo-European culture complex. The Goddess's many western paradises grew the apples of eternal life. The

Celts called the western paradise **Avalon**, "Apple-land," a country ruled by Morgan, the queen of the dead. Irish kings received the Goddess's magic apples of immortality and went away to live with her under the sunset. King **Arthur** was taken to Avalon by the Triple Goddess in person, as three fairy queens.

Scandinavians thought apples essential to resurrection, and placed vessels of them in graves.[1] The Norse Goddess Idun kept the magic apple-land in the west, where the gods received the fruit that kept them deathless.[2] Apples carried souls from one body to the next. Sigurd's or Siegfried's great-grandmother conceived by eating an apple.[3] The Yule pig was roasted with an apple in its mouth, to serve as a heart in the next life (see **Boar**).

Greeks said Mother **Hera** kept the magic apple garden in the west, where the Tree of Life was guarded by her sacred serpent. Graves points out that the whole story of **Eve**, **Adam**, and the **serpent** in the tree was deliberately misinterpreted from icons showing the Great Goddess offering life to her worshipper, in the form of an apple, with the tree and its serpent in the background. Similarly, Hellenes misinterpreted icons of the hero-victim receiving an apple from the Triple Goddess, before his journey to paradise, as the Judgment of Paris: a picture of a young man receiving the apple from three Goddesses, not vice versa.[4]

Romans gave the apple-mother the name of Pomona, which was probably inherited from the Etruscans. She symbolized all fruition. A Roman banquet always progressed *ab ovo usque mala*, from eggs to apples—beginning with the symbol of creation and ending with the symbol of completion. It was recorded that King Herod finished every meal in the Roman style, with an apple.[5]

One reason for the extreme reverence paid to this fruit is revealed by cutting it transversely, as the gypsies and witches did. Hidden in the apple's core was the magic pentacle, or sign of **Kore** (Core). Just as Kore the Virgin was hidden in the heart of Mother Earth (**Demeter**) and represented the World Soul, so her **pentacle** was hidden in the apple.

The five-pointed star in a circle was the Egyptian hieroglyph for the underworld womb, where resurrection was brought about by the mother-heart of "transformations."[6] In Christian iconography also, this apple-sign represented the Virgin concealed within the Mother, like Kore within Demeter. (See **Anne, Saint**.)

Among gypsies, "occult couples" carefully cut the apple to reveal its pentacle and ate it together as magical nourishment during Tantric intercourse.[7] A gypsy maiden was supposed to bring about her partner's mystic union with the soul of the earth through her own body; thus she was a **Shakti**, and the apple was her sexual symbol. It was a custom for a gypsy girl to choose her lover by tossing an apple at him, just as Kali-Shakti chose **Shiva** to be her doomed bridegroom.[8]

In Celtic paganism the Goddess's apple similarly signified a sacred marriage and a journey to the land of death. Queen Guinevere, who was really the Triple Goddess, according to the Welsh Triads, gave a magic apple to "the Irish knight Sir Patrice," actually St. Patrick, formerly the father-god or *Pater*.[9] (See **Patrick, Saint**.) The Irish knight died; Guinevere was denounced as a witch and condemned to the stake, from which Lancelot rescued her. Her offense was choosing a sacred king in the ancient ceremonial style. Pre-Christian legends show that each king who ruled Britain had to be chosen by the Triple Goddess, and later slain by her **Crone** form, Morgan, lady of the blood-red pentacle and keeper of the Apple-Isle in the west.[10]

Halloween apple-games descended from Celtic feasts of Samhain, the Feast of the Dead at the end of October. Catching at apples suspended from strings, or bobbing in water, may have invoked hanged or drowned witches. The games hinted at cheating Death in the form of Cerridwen, another name for Morgan as a Sow-goddess. At the end of the game, all players ran away "to escape from the black short-tailed sow."[11]

Halloween apples were also used for divination, as if they were oracular ghosts called up from the underworld. Such magic was especially associated with women, harking back to the pagan tradition of female control of the spirits in that world. The Volsung cycle showed that a man must be provided with "apples of Hel" by his wife, whose gift had the power to preserve him when he died and descended under the earth.[12] Thus, Halloween apples were often linked with marriage. One who peeled an apple before a candlelit mirror on Halloween would see the image of a future spouse.[13]

Volsungs Teutonic clan of demigods favored by Odin, who used a magic apple to impregnate the mother of the original Volsung. His descendant Sigurd is better known as Siegfried, hero of the Germanic *Ring of the Nibelung*.

Apple blossoms were wedding flowers because they represented the Virgin form of the Goddess whose maturity produced the fruit. As the pagan symbols were Christianized, Apple-Eve-Mother-Goddess was said to be reborn as her own younger aspect, Rose-Mary-Virgin-Goddess: the five-petaled rose and apple blossom often mystically combined. The red and white Alchemical Rose was an allegory of the Virgin Mother.[14] Some mystics said **Mary**, called the Holy Rose, had invented alchemy.[15]

However, the dangerous aspect of apples associated with the Goddess as Mother Death were never forgotten. Since she was not only the Virgin and the Mother but also Hel, or **Hecate**, her apples were often depicted in Christian folklore as poisoned. Churchmen declared that a witch could cause demonic possession through her gift of an apple to her intended victim.[16] Old women were slain for giving an apple to a child or other person who later became afflicted with fits.

1. Turville-Petre, 187. 2. Hollander, 39. 3. Turville-Petre, 200.
4. Graves, G.M. 2, 145–46; 277. 5. de Voragine, 67.
6. *Book of the Dead*, 454; Budge, E.L., 75. 7. Derlon, 157. 8. Groome, xlviii.
9. Malory 2, 274. 10. Loomis, 342. 11. Hazlitt, 297.
12. H.R.E. Davidson, G.M.V.A., 165. 13. de Lys, 365.
14. Campbell, M.I., 254. 15. Ashe, 213. 16. Haining, 70.

Arabia

Before Islam arrived in the 7th century A.D., Arabia was matriarchal for over a thousand years of recorded history. The Annals of Ashurbanipal said Arabia was governed by queens for as long as anyone could remember.[1] The land's original **Allah** was Al-Lat, part of the female trinity along with **Kore** or Q're, the Virgin, and Al-Uzza, the Powerful One, the triad known as Manat, the Threefold Moon.[2]

At Mecca the Goddess was Shaybah or Sheba, the Old Woman, worshipped as a black aniconic stone like the Goddess of the Scythian **Amazons**.[3] The same Black Stone now enshrined in the **Kaaba** at Mecca was her feminine symbol, marked by the sign of the **yoni**, and covered like the ancient Mother by a veil.[4] No one seems to know exactly what it is supposed to represent today.

The Black Stone rests in the *Haram,* "Sanctuary," cognate of "harem," which used to mean a Temple of Women: in Babylon, a shrine of the Goddess Har, mother of harlots.[5] Hereditary guardians of the *Haram* were the Koreshites, "Children of Kore," Mohammed's own tribe.[6] The holy office was originally held by women, before it was taken over by male priests calling themselves Beni Shaybah, "Sons of the Old Woman."[7]

Mohammed's legends clearly gave him a matriarchal family background. His parents' marriage was matrilocal. His mother remained with her own family and received her husband as an occasional visitor. Mohammed lived with his mother until her death, because she was his true parent according to the ancient system; "children belonged to the woman's family . . . paternity in the biological sense was relatively unimportant."[8] She may well have been one of the "aged priestesses" who served the temple in Mecca.[9] The traditions of such priestesses may well date back to Assyro-Babylonian *um-mati* or "mothers," the only people permitted to enter the Holy of Holies. Archaic Arabian shrines were usually served by seven high priestesses, recalling the lawgiving Seven Sages, who were women.[10] The first collection of the books of law called Koran—the Word of Kore, or Q're—was attributed to them.

Pre-Islamic Arabia was dominated by the female-centered clans. Marriages were matrilocal, inheritance matrilineal. Polyandry—several husbands to one wife—was common. Men lived in their wives' homes. Divorce was initiated by the wife. If she turned her tent to face east for three nights in a row, the husband was dismissed and forbidden to enter the tent again.[11]

Doctrines attributed to Mohammed simply reversed the ancient system in favor of men. A Moslem husband could dismiss his wife by saying "I divorce thee" three times. As in Europe, the change from matriarchate to patriarchate came about only gradually and with much strife.

Annals of Ashurbanipal Assyrian royal chronicles on cuneiform tablets, dating from the 7th century B.C., found in the king's famous library at Nineveh by 19th-century archeologists.

Seven Sages Legendary figures in both Greek and Arabian lore, identified with a variety of seers and philosophers, the earliest ones usually female, confused with the Seven Sisters, or Pleiades.

Many Koreshites remained faithful to the Goddess and to their queen, Hind al-Hunud: the Hind of Hinds, similar to the title of Artemis. She was also called Lady of Victory. But her victories came to an end with one of the last queens, whose husband betrayed her and surrendered her city of Makkah to the enemy.

Legend claims the step-daughter of the divine Hind married Mohammed himself.[12] However, the history of early-medieval Arabia is nearly all legend. Like Buddha, Confucius, **Jesus**, and other founders of patriarchal religions, Mohammed lacks real verification. There is no reliable information about his life or teachings. Most stories about him are as apocryphal as the story that his coffin hangs forever in mid-air "between heaven and earth," like the bodies of ancient sacred kings.[13]

With or without Mohammed, Islam succeeded in becoming completely male-dominated, making no place for women except in slavery or in the seclusion of the harem. Islamic mosques still bear signs reading: "Women and dogs and other impure animals are not permitted to enter."[14]

Nevertheless, traces of the Goddess proved ineradicable. Like the virgin **Mary**, Arabia's Queen of Heaven received a mortal form and a subordinate position as **Fatima**, Mohammed's "daughter." But she was no real daughter. She was known as Mother of her Father, and Source of the Sun: "the illumination that separates Light and Darkness; the Tree of Paradise; the Red Cow who suckles all the children of the earth; Fate; the Night, the World; the Moon; the Pure Essence of Being."[15] Like her western counterpart Mary, she was compared to the Burning Bush, and the Night of Power; "she personified the center of the genealogical mystery."[16]

Fatima's name means The Creatress. A Shi'a text, *Omm-al-Kitab,* said she appeared "at the creation of the material world," crowned, seated on a throne, holding a sword, and "ornamented with a million varicolored shimmering lights" which illuminated the entire garden of Paradise. She was the first to occupy the Seat of Dominion, "the resting place of Allah, the Most High."[17] Her symbol as Holy Virgin, the crescent moon, still appears on Islamic flags.[18] She is called Al-Zahra, "Bright-Blooming," a former title of the Great Mother. It is said the symbol of her hand, surmounting the solar disc, "represents the whole religion of Islam."[19]

Shi'ites Minority sect of Islam, tracing descent of a sacred caliphate from Mohammed's daughter Fatima and her husband 'Ali. One line of Shi'ites established the powerful Fatimid caliphate, now represented by the Khojas, Bohras, and the Druze of Syria.

Within Islam, deviant sects like Shi'ites or Sufis carried on Tantric worship of the female principle, maintaining that the feminine powers of sexuality and maternity were the powers that held the universe together.[20] The greatest medieval poet of Sufism, Ibn al-Farid, was known as "the sultan of lovers."[21] He said true divinity was female, and Mecca was the womb of the earth. As woman-worshipping minstrels of medieval Europe were attacked for their devotion to the Goddess of Love, so the Sufis were attacked for their "voluptuous libertinism." Ibn El-Arabi, the "greatest master" of Sufi mystics, was accused of blasphemy because he said the godhead is female.[22]

Shi'ites split off from orthodox Islam and claimed to follow a purer line of imams directly descended from the Fatimids. In the 11th century they united under Hasan ibn al-Sabbah, i.e., Hasan ben-Shaybah, another "son of the Matriarch." Hasan seized the fortress of Alamut and made it the headquarters of a brotherhood of warriors, the *hashishim* or "Assassins" (see **Aladdin**). The fortress fell to the concerted attacks of Mongols and Mamelukes in 1256, after having waged war on Turks and Christian crusaders alike for more than a century.[23]

Still the Shi'ite sect survived to the present, awaiting the coming of the Virgin named Paradise (Pairidaeza), who will give birth to the Mahdi, the "moon-guided" Redeemer, whose title in Europe was the Desired Knight.[24]

One of the hidden secrets of medieval bardic romance is the Arabian origin of the **Waste Land** motif, most prominent in the Holy Grail cycle of tales. Despite monkish efforts to convert it into a Christian chalice, the Grail was generally recognized as a female symbol, whose loss implied fear for the fertility of the earth. Crusaders had seen for themselves the desolation of Arabia Deserta, one of the most lifeless regions on earth. They heard the Shi'ite heretics' explanation for it: Islam had offended the Great Goddess, and she had cursed the land and departed. Now nothing would grow there.

Western mystics thought the same calamity would strike Europe if the spirit of the Mother were not brought back from the limbo to which the Christian church consigned her. This may have been a reason for the frenzy of cathedral-building in honor of "Our Lady," the Queen of Heaven, during the 12th and 13th centuries. The Waste Land theme haunted the collective psyche of the early Renaissance with a threat of conditions actually realized in the land of the infidel.

Traces of the matriarchate survived to the present among some of the Arabs of North Africa, ancient home of "Libyan Amazons."[25] Targi and Tuareg Berber women remained free of many sexual restrictions. Virginity was not prized. On remarriage, a woman could command twice the bride-price of a young virgin. Men of the Walad 'Abdi tribe insisted the success of their crops depended on the sexual freedom of their women, whom the French labeled common prostitutes. Hassanyeh Arabs of the White Nile allowed wives to be unfaithful on certain days of the week, according to the marriage contract drawn up by the bride's mother—who took pride in preserving her daughter's sexual liberties.[27] Most of Islam, however, restricted women as much as possible. Many Islamic theologians said women couldn't enter paradise, and must not receive religious instruction because it might bring them "too near their masters."[28]

1. *Assyr. & Bab. Lit.,* 120. 2. de Riencourt, 193. 3. Sobol, 55. 4. Harding, 41.

5. Pritchard, S.S., 95. 6. Shah, 390. 7. Briffault 3, 80. 8. de Riencourt, 188. 9. Briffault 3, 80. 10. Briffault 1, 377. 11. de Riencourt, 187–89. 12. Beard, pp. 293–94. 13. de Camp, A.E., 153. 14. Farb, W.P., 144. 15. Lederer, 181. 16. Campbell, Oc.M., 446. 17. Campbell, Oc.M., 445–46. 18. Briffault 2, 630. 19. Budge, A.T., 469. 20. Bullough, 150. 21. *Encyc. Brit.,* "Sufism." 22. Shah, 263, 319. 23. *Encyc. Brit.,* "Assassins." 24. Lederer, 181. 25. Wendt, 52. 26. Briffault 1, 286; 3, 200, 314. 27. Hartley, 166. 28. Crawley 1, 58.

Arachne

"Spider" or "Spinner," title and totem of **Athene** the Fate-weaver. Man's helplessness in the web of **Fate** was symbolized by the helplessness of the fly in the spider's web. The fly was a common archaic symbol of the human soul, even thought to be the actual embodiment of the soul in passage from one life to the next; thus divine psychopomps like **Baal-Zebub** (Beelzebub) were called "Lord of Flies" because they conducted souls.[1]

Classical writers misinterpreted old images of Athene with her spider-totem and web, and constructed the legend of Arachne, a mortal maid whose skill in weaving outshone even that of the Goddess. Therefore Athene turned her into a spider.[2]

1. Spence, 95–96. 2. Graves, G.M. 1, 98.

Aradia

Medieval name for the Queen of Witches, called a daughter of the Goddess **Diana**. The name may have been a corruption of **Herodias**. She represented the moon, and her brother Lucifer the Light-bringer represented the sun.[1]

1. B. Butler, 215.

Aramaiti

Iranian Earth-goddess, ancestress of the Aramaeans, whose language was the original language of the Gospels. Ara-ma-iti seems to have meant "mother of the people made of clay."

Ardhanarisvara

Bisexual image of the merging of **Kali Ma** and **Shiva**: a body female on the left side, male on the right side.[1] Other gods followed the same two-sexed pattern. Sometimes the deity was two-headed and four-armed, though known as "the One." See **Androgyne**; **Left Hand**.

1. *Larousse,* 371.

Ariadne

"Most Holy" or "High Fruitful Mother," the younger form of the Cretan Moon-goddess, worshipped at Amathus as a consort of Dionysus.[1] Hellenic myth disparaged her and made her a mere mortal maiden who helped Theseus survive the Cretan Labyrinth, ran away with him, and was abandoned when he wearied of her. However, her subsequent mating with the god showed that she was the rightful bride of gods to begin with.[2]

1. Graves, W.G., 93. 2. Graves, G.M. 1, 347; 2, 381.

Ariana

Archaic name of Iran and its Great Goddess, sometimes rendered Mariana.

Arianism

Early Christian heresy founded by Arius in the 4th century A.D. The basic tenet of Arianism was that God was not a trinity but a unit or monad.

Orphics and other mystery-cultists of the early Christian era maintained the classic trinitarian pattern laid down thousands of years before by the Triple Goddess. They said: "All things are made by one godhead in three names, and this god is all things." From the mystery-cults, some Christians picked up the idea that their deity too should be a **trinity**. Other Christians objected, saying their deity must be a monad like the Jewish Jehovah. St. Augustine found the notion of a trinity incomprehensible. He scoffed at his pagan neighbors for calling their Great Goddess three persons and one person at the same time.[1]

Neither the Old nor the New Testament mentioned a triune God, so early Pauline Christians worshipped God as one individual. However, this monotheistic idea was abandoned at the 4th-century Council of Nicaea. Arian Christians, clinging to the Hebraic belief in an undivided God, suddenly found themselves labeled heretics. In increasingly acrimonious battles, partisans of one viewpoint or the other engaged in street fighting with stones and clubs, bloodying their opponents to prove the nature of their deity.[2]

Arius's objections to the Holy Trinity were basically logical. He insisted that a divine son couldn't have co-existed eternally with his own divine father. There must have been a time when the father existed alone, before bringing the son into being. But Arius's opponents wanted to be assured that, in assimilating the body and blood of Christ in communion, they partook of an infinite divinity who had existed from the beginning of time. Otherwise they might be robbed of immortality, through unwise identification with a lesser, finite power. Therefore they insisted that Christ and God were one and the same.

Besides, pagan traditions universally supported the notion that divine fathers and sons were identical with each other, cyclically alternating and united through the Mother. Proponents of the trinitarian theory borrowed myths and symbols from the pagans, and said when the **Magi** saw the star in the east announcing Christ's birth, three suns appeared in the sky and fused into one.[3]

The emperor Constantine I at first defended Arius, because he liked the idea of a single supreme deity whom he might identify with himself. He also disliked the Christians' incessant sectarian strife. He wrote to Bishop Alexander: "I am sending to you, not simply suggesting, but imploring that you will take these men (the Arians) back . . . that there is peace and concord among you all."[4] This was ignored.

The Council decided that God, Christ, and the Holy Ghost were one and the same, forever co-existent, equally potent. Arius was anathematized and driven into exile. At last he succumbed to a dose of poison, apparently administered by one of his trinitarian opponents.[5] But the battle was not over. The Arian controversy dragged on for many centuries, and spilled much blood, as theological arguments were wont to do in those days.

After 360 A.D., Arianism was carried by missionaries to the Germanic tribes, whose Christianity remained a vaguely Arian semi-paganism up to the time of Charlemagne and beyond.[6] Arianism came to the surface again in Hungary and Transylvania during the 16th century. Christian writers then denied the trinity altogether, starting a movement that led ultimately to the foundation of Unitarian churches.[7]

1. Briffault 3, 90. 2. de Camp, A.E., 282. 3. de Voragine, 49. 4. J.H. Smith, C.G., 242. 5. Gibbon 1, 694. 6. *Encyc. Brit.,* "Arianism." 7. *Encyc. Brit.,* "Unitarianism."

Arianrhod

Goddess mother of Celtic "Aryans," keeper of the endlessly circling Silver Wheel of the Stars, symbol of Time, the same as Kali's karmic wheel. Some gave the Goddess herself the title of "Silver Wheel That Descends into the Sea."[1]

Arianrhod's **wheel** was also the Wheel of Light, Wheel of Fal, or Oar Wheel. It was often likened to a vast ship carrying dead warriors to the Moon-land, called Magonia or Emania or Hy-Many. The wheel was made by "three druidesses"—that is, the Triple Goddess, who created the cosmic wheel of the zodiac or the Milky Way.[2] Arianrhod seems to have been the same Goddess as **Ariadne**, another version of the "mother of Aryans."[3]

1. Briffault 3, 71. 2. Spence, 65, 152–53. 3. Graves, W.G., 93.

Arinna

Hittite name of the Great Goddess as "Mother of the Sun." In Mesopotamia and Egypt, the sun god was generally considered a child of the moon-, earth-, sea-, or heaven-goddess.

var. Arinniti

Ark of the Covenant

On its earliest appearances in the Bible, the ark of the covenant was so *sacer* (taboo, dangerous) that it would kill at a touch. While it was being transported on an oxcart, it teetered "because the oxen shook it" and would have fallen, had not Uzzah "put forth his hand to the ark of God, and took hold of it" (2 Samuel 6:3). In spite of Uzzah's good intentions, God instantly struck him dead for daring to touch the holy object.

Again, when the ark returned from Philistia, God perpetrated an extraordinary slaughter of 50,070 well-intentioned people for daring to look inside the ark in their joy: "And he smote the men of Bethshemesh, because they had looked into the ark of the Lord, even he smote of the people fifty thousand and threescore and ten men: and the people lamented, because the Lord had smitten many of the people with a great slaughter" (1 Samuel 6:19).

Even priests feared the power of the ark, and resorted to ritual washing before approaching it, "that they die not" (Exodus 30:20). Water was a common prophylactic charm against the destructive power of holy things. Philon of Byzantium said all the "ancients" used water for ritual purification before entering temples; they also spun prayer-wheels made of Aphrodite's sacred metal, copper.[1]

For some reason God lost interest in his ark by Jeremiah's time: "Saith the Lord, they shall say no more, the ark of the covenant of the Lord: neither shall it come to mind: neither shall they remember it; neither shall it be magnified any more" (Jeremiah 3:16).

The probable cause of God's change of heart was a reform movement to purge the temple of sexual symbols. The arks or *cistae* of the Greeks and Syrians held emblems of the lingam-yoni, such as eggs and serpents, clay or dough models of genitalia. Rabbinical tradition said the ark contained a hexagram representing the sexual union of God and Goddess, the same meaning given to the hexagram in India.[2] Thus the ark was a female container for a male god. **Mary,** God's consort in her later form, often received the title of "Ark."

Semitic *Arek,* "ark," descended from Hindu *Argha,* "great ship," metaphorically the Great **Yoni:** a female-sexual vessel bearing seeds of life through the sea of chaos between destruction of one cosmos and creation of the next.[3] From the same root came "arcane," literally a dark or crescent phase of the moon. The crescent moon boat symbolized the Goddess's spirit dancing on her primordial uterine Ocean of

Blood, whose "clots" would form the lands and creatures of a new universe. Noah's version of the Argha came to Palestine via Sumeria and Babylon (see **Flood**), but was intensively re-interpreted by Jewish patriarchs anxious to eliminate the female principle.

1. de Camp, A.E., 122. 2. Silberer, 197. 3. Jobes, 121.

Armathr

"Mother of Prosperity," the Goddess incarnate in a sacred stone revered by Icelandic chieftains, who ignored Christianity until the 11th or 12th century A.D.[1] Remote Iceland was among the last areas to be Christianized; therefore the pagan sagas (Eddas) and other literature survived the fires of censorship.

1. Turville-Petre, 230.

Artemidos, Saint

Fictitious Christian saint based on a votive idol of the Goddess **Artemis.**[1] In some traditions she remained female, but in others she lost even her femininity and was described as a holy man.

1. H. Smith, 227.

Artemis

Amazonian Moon-goddess, worshipped at Ephesus under the Latin name of Diana or "Goddess-Anna." Like the Hindu Goddess **Saranyu** who gave birth to all animals, she was called Mother of Creatures. Her image at Ephesus had a whole torso covered with breasts, to show that she nurtured all living things. Yet she was also the Huntress, killer of the very creatures she brought forth.[1] In Sparta her name was given as Artamis, "Cutter," or "Butcher."[2]

Artemis's myths extend back to Neolithic sacrificial customs. At Taurus her holy women, under their high priestess **Iphigeneia,** sacrificed all men who landed on their shores, nailing the head of each victim to a cross.[3] At Hierapolis, the Goddess's victims were hung on artificial trees in her temple. In Attica, Artemis was ritually propitiated with drops of blood drawn from a man's neck by a sword, a symbolic remnant of former beheadings. Human victims were later replaced by bulls, hence the Goddess's title Tauropolos, "bull-slayer."[4]

Her Huntress aspect was another form of the destroying Crone or waning moon. Like **Hecate,** she led the nocturnal hunt; her priestesses wore the masks of hunting dogs. *Alani,* "hunting dogs," was the Greek name for Scythians who revered Artemis. The mythological hunting dogs who tore the Horned God Actaeon to pieces were really Artemis's sacred bitches.

Classic mythographers pretended that Actaeon committed the sin of seeing the chaste virgin Goddess in her bath, and she condemned him out of offended modesty. Actually, the bath, the nakedness, and the tearing to pieces of the sacred king were all part of the drama. In barbarian Germany, the Goddess's ritual bath could be witnessed only by "men doomed to die."[5] Actaeon's deerskin and antlers marked him as the pre-Hellenic stag king, reigning over the sacred hunt for half a Great Year before he was torn to pieces and replaced by his tanist (co-king). In the first century A.D., Artemis's priestesses still pursued and killed a man dressed as a stag on the Goddess's mountain.[6] Her groves became the "deer-gardens" (German *Tiergarten,* Swedish *Djurgarden*), once the scene of venison feasts.

One of Artemis's most popular animal incarnations was the Great She-Bear, Ursa Major, ruler of the stars and protectress of the *axis mundi,* Pole of the World, marked in heaven by the Pole Star at the center of the small circle described by the constellation Ursa Major. Helvetian tribes in the neighborhood of Berne worshipped her as the She-Bear, which is still the heraldic symbol of Berne. The city's very name means "She-Bear."[7] Sometimes the Helvetians called her Artio, shortened to Art by Celtic peoples who coupled her with the bear-king **Arthur.** As Artio's Lord of the Hunt, the medieval god of witches came to be known as "Robin son of Art." According to the Irish, Art meant "God," but its earlier connotation was "Goddess"—specifically the Bear-Goddess.[8] She was also canonized as a Christian saint, **Ursula,** derived from her Saxon name of Ursel, the She-Bear.

Ursa Major "Great Bear," colloquially called the Big Dipper, a circumpolar constellation with seven bright stars including the "north pole pointers." For a brief time the constellation was renamed Charles's Wain, after the chariot of Charlemagne.

There was a rather sophisticated astronomical reason for worshipping the heavenly She-Bear who followed her track around the Pole Star, year by year. It was probably discovered first in the far east. "The months and seasons are determined by the revolution of Ursa Major. The tail of the constellation pointing to the east at nightfall announces the arrival of spring, pointing to the south the arrival of summer, pointing to the west the arrival of autumn, and pointing to the north the arrival of winter. . . . The Great Bear occupies a prominent position in the Taoist heavens as the aerial throne of the supreme deity." This deity in Taoist tradition is the Queen of Heaven, Holy Mother Ma Tsu P'o, with characteristics similar to those of Artemis. She protects seafarers and governs the weather; she is called a virgin, and Matron of the Measure; she is a Mother of Mercy who has been compared to the virgin **Mary** and to the Buddhist Goddess Maritchi.[9]

The *axis mundi* was often associated with male gods, as either a Great Serpent or a World Tree more or less recognized as a phallic symbol. Similarly the Little Bear within the circle of the Great Bear was pictured by the Greeks as Arcas, her son (see **Callisto**). Yet among the oldest traditions may be found hints that this world-supporting tree or pole was female. Even as Yggdrasil, the World Tree of the Vikings, it showed many parallels with birth-giving, fruit- or milk-producing mother trees of the Near East, under its older name of Mjotvidr or Mutvidr, "Mother-Tree." Sometimes it was Mead-Tree, like "the milk-giving tree of the Finno-Ugric peoples, a symbol which must go back ultimately to Mesopotamia, and be of great antiquity." It was said that "the tree is the source of unborn souls," which would give birth to the new primal woman, Life (Lif) in the new universe after the present cycle came to an end. Its fruit could be given to women in childbirth "that what is within may pass out." The spring at the tree's root was a fountain of wisdom or of the life-giving fluid *aurr,* which may be likened to the "wise blood" of the Mother—that much-mythologized feminine life-source likened to the Kula nectar in the uterine spring of Kundalini, as if the maternal tree upholding the universe were the Mother's spine with its many chakras.[10] See **Menstrual Blood.**

"Many-breasted" Artemis was always a patroness of nurture, fertility, and birth. Male gods turned against these attributes in opposing the cult of the Goddess. Her own twin brother and sometime consort **Apollo** made birth illegal on his sacred isle of Delos; pregnant women had to be removed from the island lest they offend the god by giving birth there.[11] Christians continued to vilify Artemis. Tatian said, "Artemis is a poisoner; Apollo performs cures."[12] The Gospels demanded destruction of Artemis's Ephesian temple (Acts 19:27). St. John Chrysostom preached against this temple in 406 A.D. Soon afterward, it was looted and burned. The patriarch of Constantinople praised Chrysostom's zeal: "In Ephesus he stripped the treasury of Artemis; in Phrygia, he left without sons her whom they called the Mother of the Gods."[13] See **Diana.**

Tatian 2nd-century Christian apologist of Greek education and Gnostic leanings. His doctrine absolutely forbade marriage for all Christians.

St. John Chrysostom, "Golden-mouthed John," 4th-century Christian orator who served as Patriarch of Constantinople until he incurred the wrath of the empress Eudoxia, who arranged to have him deposed and exiled.

1. Neumann, G.M., 276 (pl. 35). 2. Graves, G.M. 1, 86. 3. Herodotus, 244. 4. Graves, G.M. 1, 86; 2, 79. 5. Tacitus, 728. 6. Graves, G. M. 1, 85. 7 *Larousse,* 226. 8. Joyce 1, 249. 9. Williams, 30, 336–38, 371–73. 10. H.R.E. Davidson, G.M.V.A., 195. 11. Halliday, 29. 12. Graves, W.G., 433. 13. J.H. Smith, D.C.P., 175.

Artha

Sanskrit "Riches" or "Abundance," root of Indo-European names for Mother Earth: Ertha, Hretha, Eortha, etc. The Earth Mother Frigg (Freya) also bore a name meaning Wealth; so did Rhea-Pluto, Ops Opulentia, and Terra Mater. See **Earth.**

Arthur

King Arthur was the Welsh *Arth Vawr,* Heavenly Bear. His predecessor or "father" was Uther Pendragon, "Wonderful Head of the Dragon."[1] Where did the dragon's head precede the bear? At the hub of the heavens, which the ancients always anxiously watched.

In the 3rd millenium B.C, the north pole star was not the present Polaris in Ursa Minor, the Little Bear. It was Alpha Draconis, the Head of the Dragon.[2] Due to precession of the equinoxes, a slow subtle shift of the celestial pole took place over the course of 5000 years. However difficult it may have been to observe, the ancients seem to have known about it. India as well as Britain placed the former north pole in the constellation of the Dragon. The *Mahabharata* said the pole star, to which "the yoke of the world" was fixed, was the head of the Great Serpent.[3]

Greeks said the little bear-god who replaced the serpent was Arcas, ancestor of the Arcadians. His mother was **Artemis** Calliste, the Great She-Bear who used to rule all the stars.[4] As Ursa Major, she still circles the pole. Western Europeans called her Artio, Art, Ursel, or Ercel.[5] Arthur was a Celtic version of her son, spouse, sacred king.

Arthur was another humanization of an old pagan god—apparently very old, for he had no credible human parentage but rather many contradictory miraculous-birth myths. Some said he had no father. Like the Norse god Heimdall and the Saxon hero Scyld, he was born of the Ninefold Sea-goddess and cast ashore on the ninth wave, to land at Merlin's feet.[6] Bulfinch's *Mythology* said Arthur's father was Ambrosius, an earlier name for **Merlin**.

The story of Uther Pendragon's fatherhood of Arthur bears marks of strained revision. Arthur's royal mother was married to Uther's rival at the time. Uther was far away, but with Merlin's help he sent his spirit to her in the guise of her husband, while the latter was being killed. Arthur was begotten at the instant his official father died. He was taken away by Merlin to be raised in a secret place until he came of age—the cliché secret upbringing of every sacred king's career.

Arthur's mother was really the Triple Goddess, incarnate in the queen as usual. Her three daughters represented herself in triad: **Elaine**, the virgin Lily Maid; **Margawse**, mother of the four **Aeons**; **Morgan**, Queen of the Shades. Arthur later coupled with his sister Margawse and incestuously begot his own son-nephew-supplanter, Mordred, who was likewise taken away at birth to be raised in hiding.

As Galahad was the reincarnated Lancelot, so Mordred was the reincarnated Arthur, destined to succeed him by both matrilineal and patrilineal right, as both sister's-son and son. Like all kings threatened by the Oedipal rival, Arthur tried to kill Mordred by a Slaughter of the Innocents. He collected all the children born on May Day, the birthday of his prophesied supplanter, put them on a ship, and sent them out to sea to be wrecked. Of course Mordred survived the wreck and grew up to return incognito to Arthur's court.[8]

Arthur lost his sacred mana when he lost his queen, the Triple Goddess incarnate in Guinevere, who was really three Guineveres according to the Welsh Triads.[9] Mordred seized her, thus symbolically seizing the kingdom, and brought Arthur to his death.

When Arthur died, the same Triple Goddess took him back into the sea that gave him birth. "Three fairy queens" carried him away to the western isles of paradise, singing his death-song, the kind of song Welsh bards called *marwysgafen*—giving-back-to-the-sea-mother.[10] The three fairy queens were really the final triad of the Ninefold Goddess, Morgan le Fay and two of her alter egos: the Queen of

Mahabharata
Indian epic poem, consisting of historical and legendary material gathered between the 4th and 10th centuries A.D., including the famous Bhagavad-Gita.

Welsh Triads
Poetic literature of pre-Christian Wales, drawn from the bards' oral tradition.

Ninefold Goddess
The triple trinity, as exemplified by the Nine Muses of Greece, the Nine Sisters of Scandinavia, the Nine Morgans of the Fortunate Isles, etc.

Brythonic Of the British branch of Celts, including speakers of the Welsh, Cornish, and Breton languages.

Northgallis (i.e., North Gaul, or Brittany), and the Queen of the Westerlands, which meant the isles of the dead.[11] These isles were said to be ruled by nine fairy sisters, the leader of whom was Morgan.

Arthur's legends generally suggest no human king, but a Brythonic god, whom Johnson called a Celtic Zeus.[12] He may have been incarnate in one or several warrior kings for brief periods, but his basic story was mythic rather than historical.

1. Hitching, 242. 2. *Encyc. Brit.*, "Precession of the Equinoxes."
3. O'Flaherty, 274, 131. 4. Graves, G.M. 1, 86. 5. Joyce 1, 249.
6. Guerber, L.M.A., 215. 7. Hallet, 388. 8. Malory 1, 35, 45. 9. Malory 1, xxiv.
10. *Encyc. Brit.*, "Welsh Literature." 11. Guerber, L.M.A., 232.
12. Johnson, 85.

Aryan

General name for Indo-European peoples, from Sanskrit *arya*, a man of clay (like Adam), or else a man of the land, a farmer or landowner.[1] The ancestral god of "Aryans" was Aryaman, one of the twelve zodiacal sons of the Hindu Great Goddess Aditi. In Persia he became known as **Ahriman**, the dark earth god, opponent or subterranean alter ego of the solar deity **Ormazd** (Ahura Mazda). In Celtic Ireland he was Eremon, one of the sacred kings who married the Earth (Tara).

Though there was nothing "pure" about either the name or the far-flung mixture of tribes it was supposed to describe, the term "pure Aryan" was revived in Nazi Germany to support a mythological concept of Teutonic stock, the so-called Master Race. Non-Aryans were all the "inferior" strains: Semites, Negroes, gypsies, Slavs, and Latinate or "swarthy" people whose blood was said to be polluting the Nordic superiority of their betters.

1. Potter & Sargent, 33.

Asceticism

The religion of self-denial, such as practiced by early Christian eremites, characterized by self-inflicted pain, hunger, and other austerities, and renunciation of sensual pleasures.

Perhaps the earliest sectaries to regard asceticism as the key to heaven were Jain Buddhists (see **Jains**), whose theology influenced Persian patriarchs, who in turn influenced Jewish eremites like the **Essenes**. Jain Buddhist monks had already penetrated the courts of Syria, Egypt, Macedonia, and Epirus by the 4th century B.C., and were glorified in legend for the alleged magic powers they developed through prodigies of self-denial.[1]

Originally, men's ascetic practices seem to have evolved from a notion that extreme forms of self-denial would bring them the magical female capacity to give birth. Oriental myths said the first creator-gods acquired the ability to produce living things by "practicing fierce asceticism for ten thousand years."[2]

Though men never achieved the ability to give birth, they claimed other miraculous powers developed by asceticism. Perfected eremites were said to fly, to walk on water, to understand all languages, to turn base metals into gold, to heal lameness and blindness, and other miracles that became the common property of all scriptures including the Christian ones.[3]

Jain Buddhists looked upon women as hopelessly inferior in the pursuit of asceticism. Their handbook said no woman could achieve **Nirvana**, because "in the womb, between the breasts, in their navel and loins, a subtle emanation of life is continually taking place. How then can they be fit for self-control? A woman may be pure in faith and even occupied with a study of the sutras or the practice of a terrific asceticism; in her case there will be no falling away of karmic matter."[4]

Some of the ascetics openly despised sexuality and motherhood. The *Mahabharata* anticipated St. Augustine's remarks about the nastiness of birth: "Man emerges mixed with excrement and water, fouled with the impurities of woman. A wise man will avoid the contaminating society of women as he would the touch of bodies infested with vermin."[5] Some advertised their renunciation of sex by castrating themselves or affixing large metal rings in the flesh of the penis.[6]

Mahabharata
Indian epic poem, consisting of historical and legendary material gathered between the 4th and 10th centuries A.D., including the famous Bhagavad-Gita.

Essenic Judaism and early Christianity were offshoots of the Jain tradition, urging abandonment of the family and of all secular concerns.[7] Like the art of the Jains, Christian art in the early medieval period showed stiff, crude, doll-like figures, apparently bodiless under their wooden draperies, even hands and faces badly drawn. Not even artists were permitted to study the human form.[8] To look at something attractive—especially if it was made of flesh—was highly suspect because the observer might enjoy the act of looking. According to St. Jerome, a Christian must consider poisonous every act or experience having the smallest hint of sensual pleasure.[9]

Pain, however, was permitted and encouraged throughout the Christian era. St. **Catherine** of Siena was highly praised for whipping herself three times a day, once for her own sins, once for the sins of the living, and once for the sins of the dead. St. Simeon Stylites was glorified for remaining motionless on top of his pillar, like Buddhist standing-yogis, until his living flesh rotted.[10]

Fathers of the church constantly urged asceticism upon the faithful. Gregory of Nyssa touted it in terms of both wetness and dryness: "As the tympanum, from which all moisture has been removed so that it is exceedingly dry, gives out a loud noise, so also is virginity, which receives no life-giving moisture, illustrious and renowned."[11] Again he said: "We often see water, contained in a pipe, bursting upward through this constraining force, which will not let it leak, and this in spite of its natural gravitation; in the same way the mind of man, enclosed in the compact channel of an habitual continence, and not having any side issues, will be raised by virtue of its natural powers of motion to an exalted love."[12]

Moral tales told by the Christian fathers concentrated on renunciation of sexual love, and acceptance of painful martyrdom. The tale of Sts. Cyprian and Justina is typical. Cyprian, a pagan sorcerer, fell in love with the Christian maiden Justina and cast a love spell on her. Though sworn to virginity like all good Christian maidens, Justina was tortured by desire. Nevertheless she conquered her desire and proved her piety with such prodigies of asceticism that she impressed even Cyprian: she fasted almost to death, she slept naked on the stony ground, she mutilated herself to spoil her beauty.[13] Cyprian was so intrigued by all this he turned Christian too, and was martyred along with his incorrigible virgin.[14]

Human love was anathema to the early Christians who insisted that families must be abandoned. Sexual impulses were perverted into unnatural obsessions.[15] The fall of Rome was not entirely unrelated to Christians' abhorrence of the basic social unit of the state: the interlocked loyalties and dependencies of the family. Jesus himself undermined the family in his teaching: "If any man come to me, and hate not his father, and mother, and wife, and children, and brethren, and sisters, yea, and his own life also, he cannot be my disciple" (Luke 14:26). Becker says Christianity stood for "renunciation of this world and the satisfactions of this life, which is why the pagans thought Christianity was crazy. It was a sort of anti-heroism by an animal who denied life in order to deny evil."[16]

Principles of asceticism so embedded themselves in Christian society that nearly every kind of sensual pleasure came to be regarded as wicked only because it was pleasant. The delights of sacramental dancing were forbidden. A story from Ramersdorf in the Rhineland tells of a Christian missionary priest who found youths and maidens dancing together on the Sabbath. He called God's curse on them, which forced them to go on dancing day and night until they lost their minds.[17] Some European peasants still abstain from sexual intercourse during the sowing season, in the church-fostered belief that sexual activity might call down a curse on the crop.[18]

In the 18th century, theologians were still preaching the wickedness of even the most subtle feelings of pleasure. Beaumont counseled women especially to attribute any enjoyable bodily sensation to the devil's influence: "If ye perceive a sudden sweet taste in your mouths or feel any warmth in your breasts, like fire, or any form of pleasure in any part of your body, or . . . if ye become aware by occasion of pleasure or satisfaction derived from such perception, that your hearts are drawn away from the contemplation of Jesus Christ and from spiritual exercises . . . then this sensation is very much to be suspected of coming from the Enemy; and therefore were it ever so wonderful and striking, still renounce it."[19] Yet the obsessive contemplation of pain, starting with Jesus's pain on the cross, was always to be encouraged.

The most significant difference between Christianity and its pagan forerunners was this reversal of the pleasure-pain continuum. Earlier societies regarded sensual pleasure as a touch of divinity, and "bliss"—sexual or otherwise—as a foretaste of heaven. Woman was a carrier of the divine spark because of her capacity to give and receive physical pleasure. The Christian theory turned this opinion completely around. Fathers of the church taught that the human race must die out through universal celibacy, before Jesus could return and establish his heaven on earth. Reasoning that man fell from grace through woman, man could return to grace only by renouncing woman.[20] Therefore, medieval churchmen came to identify sexuality with the worst of heresies and sins, especially since St. Augustine had labeled it the pipeline of original sin. Even Protestant theologians adopted this view. Calvin said that, because of its origin in sexuality and in a woman's body, every child was "defiled and polluted" in God's sight even before it saw the light of the day; a newborn infant is a "seed-bed of sin and therefore cannot but be odious and abominable to God." Martin Luther married an ex-nun, but still didn't think much of sex. He said, "Had God consulted me in the matter, I would have advised him to continue the generation of the species by fashioning them out of clay."[21]

This note of arrogance, even hubris, in the idea of man issuing instructions to God, was always a hidden component of asceticism, despite its outward show of extreme or unnatural humility. "Nothing is prouder than the humility of the ascetic of other-worldly spirit that proclaims itself superior to the whole natural world, or than the mysticism that renounces the self only to commune with God himself."[22] Here lies the real reason for men's secret delight in ascetic principles and practices. It must be remembered that the original purpose of such self-denial was to become identified with a god and to acquire God's sacred powers for one's self.

Becoming a god meant acquiring the ability to perform miracles, as many Christian ascetics were supposed to have done. By definition, miracles flouted the laws of nature. Thus the ascetic became deliberately un-natural, confusing the denial of his own instinctual desires with denial of Mother Nature's observed habits. Ascetic ideals therefore placed body and spirit in conflict with each other. "Asceticism is the ethical code which arises inevitably from a dualistic opposition between the spiritual and the natural. These are represented as absolutely irreconcilable and mutually antagonistic; if a man is to escape the natural he must renounce the rights of his physical nature in the interests of his spiritual."[23] The psychic problem of such dualistic opinion is still much in evidence.

1. Campbell, C.M., 146. 2. O'Flaherty, 32, 47.
3. Menen, 93; Tatz & Kent, 167; *Bardo Thodol,* 158. 4. Campbell, Or.M., 237.
5. Menen, 17. 6. Rawson, E.A., 48. 7. Campbell, Or.M., 279. 8. Zimmer, 56.
9. Mumford, 145. 10. *Encyc. Brit.,* "Simeon." 11. Ashe, 176. 12. Mumford, 139.

13. Ashe, 178. 14. Attwater, 97. 15. H. Smith, 228–29. 16. Becker, E.E., 154. 17. Guerber, L.R., 111. 18. Frazer, G.B., 159. 19. Silberer, 284–85. 20. Lederer, 163. 21. Holmes, 35, 71. 22. Muller, 32. 23. Angus, 219.

Asherah

Semitic name of the Great Goddess, possibly from Old Iranian *asha,* "Universal Law," a law of the matriarch, like Roman *ius naturale.*[1] Asherah was "in wisdom the Mistress of the Gods."[2] Sumerians called her Ashnan, "strength of all things," and "a kindly and bountiful maiden."[3] Her sacred city Mar-ash appears in the Bible as Mareshah (Joshua 15:44).

The Old Testament "Asherah" is translated "grove," without any explanation that the sacred grove represented the Goddess's genital center, birthplace of all things. In the matriarchal period, Hebrews worshipped the Goddess in groves (1 Kings 14:23), later cut down by patriarchal reformers who burned the bones of Asherah's priests on their own altars (2 Chronicles 24:4-5).

The Goddess's grove-yoni was *Athra qaddisa,* "the holy place" (literally, "divine harlot"). Sometimes she was called simply "Holiness," a word later applied to Yahweh. Canaanites called her *Qaniyatu elima,* She Who Gives Birth to the Gods, or *Rabbatu athiratu yammi,* Lady Who Traverses the Sea (i.e., the Moon).[4] *Rabbatu* was an early female form of *rabbi.* Athirat, Athra, Aethra, Athyr, and Egypt's Hathor were all variations of the same name for the Goddess.[5] In Egypt she was also a Law-giving Mother, Ashesh, an archaic form of **Isis**; the name meant both "pouring out" and "supporting," the functions of her breasts. Her yonic shrine in Thebes was Asher, Ashrel, or Ashrelt. Some called her "Great Lady of Ashert, the lady of heaven, the queen of the gods."[6]

For a while, Asherah accepted the Semitic god El as her consort. She was the Heavenly Cow, he the Bull.[7] After their sacred marriage, she bore the Heavenly Twins, Shaher and Shalem, the stars of morning and evening (see **Lucifer**). The marriage rite seems to have involved the cooking of a kid in its mother's milk, a procedure later forbidden by Jewish priests (Exodus 23:19).[8]

1. *Larousse,* 312; Bachofen, 192. 2. *Larousse,* 76. 3. Hays, 57; Hooke, M.E.M., 27. 4. Albright, 121, 210. 5. Hooke, M.E.M., 70. 6. Budge, G.E. 2, 90. 7. *Larousse,* 74. 8. Hooke, M.E.M., 93

Ash Wednesday

This allegedly Christian festival was taken from Roman paganism, which in turn took it from Vedic India. Ashes were called the seed of the fire god **Agni**, with power to absolve all sins. Even if a man does "a thousand things that one ought not to do, by bathing in ashes he will cause all of that to be burnt to ashes as fire burns a forest with its energy." Another source said ashes stood for the purifying blood of **Shiva**, in which one could bathe away sins, as Christians bathed in the blood of the Lamb.[1]

At Rome's New Year Feast of Atonement in March, people wore sackcloth and bathed in ashes to atone for their sins.[2] Then as now, New Year's Eve was a carnival of eating, drinking, and sinning, on the theory that all sins would be wiped out the following day. As the dying god of March, Mars took his worshippers' sins with him into death. Therefore the carnival fell on *dies martis,* the Day of Mars. In English this was Tuesday, because Mars was identified with the Saxon god Tiw. In French the carnival day was Mardi Gras, "Fat Tuesday," the day of merrymaking before Ash Wednesday.

A Catholic directory of 1511 ordered priests to say to the congregation on Ash Wednesday, "Remember, man, you are ashes and to ashes will return." Fuller's Church History said the purpose of Ash Wednesday was to remind every man that he is "but ashes and earth, and thereto shall return."[3] These maxims oddly contradicted the church's official doctrine of the resurrection of the flesh. Their purpose was to justify with some Christian gloss the ancient notion that redemption might be brought about by contact with ashes.

Fuller's Church History A monumental history of the English church by Thomas Fuller (1608–1661).

1. O'Flaherty, 148–49, 174. 2. *Encyc. Brit.,* "Ash Wednesday." 3. Hazlitt, 19.

Asmodeus

Christian demon often credited with possessing nuns or young women to make them lustful, because he was portrayed in the Book of Tobit as a spirit of lechery. Tobit's Asmodeus was really "the god Asmo," or Aeshma, a Persian deity associated with **Ahriman**. Zoroastrian priests may have brought about his original diabolization because of an archaic connection with the Goddess Ma.[1]

Book of Tobit One of the Apocrypha, once accepted as part of the Judeo-Christian canon of sacred scriptures but later eliminated from the official canon.

1. *Larousse,* 318.

Ass

The ass-god **Pales** had an extensive cult throughout the ancient world. Palestine, Philistia, and the Palatine Hill in Rome were named for Pales, who was both male and female.[1]

The Old Norse word *Áss* meant both "Asian" and "deity," possibly indicating that the divine ass originated in Asia.[2] The pre-Vedic sacred king Ravana sported ten crowned human heads surmounted by one ass head, symbolizing the spirit of the ass god incarnate in ten kings.[3] The long ears of the ass seem to have had the same significance of virility in ancient India as the horns of the sacred bull or stag.[4]

Tacitus said the Jews worshipped the ass because wild asses were responsible for their survival in the desert.[5] According to Genesis 36:24,

Cornelius Tacitus Roman historian and rhetorician, ca. 56–120 A.D.

it was the tribal matriarch Anah, or Hannah, who first found asses in the wilderness. Balaam's oracular she-ass may have been a manifestation of the spirit of Anah, as Balaam himself was another name for **Baal**. Samson slew the Philistines with an ass's jawbone, the same bone still regarded as a seat of the soul by some African tribes.[6] Jesus entered Jerusalem on an ass's colt, symbol of the New Year. The *lilim* or Children of Lilith were ass-haunched, for they were spirits left over from the real source of the Jewish ass-cult: Egypt, home of the ass-headed god **Set**, or Seth.

Set once ruled the dynastic gods, and in token of his sovereignty displayed a pair of ass's ears at the tip of a reed scepter. The Hyksos kings of Egypt revived Set's cult in the 2nd millenium B.C., perhaps because their own ass-eared Midas was a similar god-king. The annual alternation of Set and his brother Osiris (or Horus), who murdered each other in perpetual rivalry for the favors of Isis, reflected constant replacement of sacred kings in pre-dynastic times.[7]

Ass-eared king Midas, a son of Cybele, died of drinking bull's blood. In other words, he was connected with the Taurobolium or bull-sacrifice made in honor of both Cybele and Isis. Midas has been identified with Mita ("Seed"), a king of the Moschians or "calf-men," who invaded the country of the Hittites from Thrace during the second millenium B.C. Midas's Golden Touch and ass's ears link him with the cult of Set and the Golden Calf (Horus), whose image was worshipped by the Israelites (Exodus 32:2-4).

Under Egypt's Hyksos kings, Set was a god of the hot desert wind, known as the Breath of the Ass. He was "Lord of the Chambers of the South," whence storm winds came.[8] His wind from the desert was supposed to bring pestilence, i.e., typhus, derived from Set's Greek name, Typhon. This name was interlingual and world-wide. It meant both the ass god and the wind called *tufan* in Arabic and Hindustani; *t'ai fung* in Chinese; and *tuffoon* or *Typhoon* in the South Pacific.[9]

Ass-headed Set was a sacrificial deity in the cult of Horus and Osiris. He was crucified on a furka and wounded in the side.[10] He and Horus were represented as alternating year-gods who fought and castrated one another, each being baptized in the blood of the other's "phallic eye," as the Pyramid Text said: "Horus is purified with the Eye of his brother Set; Set is purified with the Eye of his brother Horus."[11] The Eye or phallus passed from one to the other. A statue of Horus at Coptos carried Set's severed phallus in his hand.[12] After castrating Set, Horus spread his blood on the fields to render them fertile—the usual fructification-by-male-blood found in the oldest sacrificial Mysteries.[13]

Pyramid Texts Collections of prayers, hymns, and magic spells inscribed on the inner walls of the pyramids at Saqqarah (Sakkara), dating from the 5th through 7th dynasties.

Thus, Set and Horus were remnants of a primitive sacred-king cult, which the Jews adopted. The story of the rival gods appeared in the Bible as Seth's supplanting of the sacrificed shepherd Abel, evidently the same "Good Shepherd" as Osiris-Horus (Genesis 4:25). Their rivalry was resolved in Egypt by having the pharaoh unite both gods in himself. Tomb paintings of Rameses IV showed him as both Set and Horus, two heads set upon one neck.[14]

Similarly, the Jewish God uniting both Father and Son was sometimes an ass-headed man crucified on a tree. This was one of the earliest representations of the Messiah's crucifixion. Some said Christ was the same as the Jewish ass-god Iao, identified with Set.[15] Jews in Rome were said to worship an ass's head as their deity.[16]

The Roman cult of the ass apparently originated in Libya, home of the bisexual **Pales**, whose temple stood on the Palatine Hill and gave rise to the word "palace."[17] Servius said Pales was a Goddess, the Diva Palatua, a disguise of **Vesta**. Others said Pales was either a female protectress of herd animals, or Vesta's male consort. In the first two centuries A.D., Pales was worshipped as a priapic god at the festival of the Palilia, traditional date of the founding of Rome, when the **Palladium** was brought to Vesta's temple.[18] Priests of Pales wore ass-head masks as they danced in honor of the long-eared deity. The Palilia was taken into the Christian calendar as the Feast of St. George. One of its old customs may have given rise to the **Halloween** game of "Pin the Tail on the Donkey," which recalls Rome's sacrifices of equine tails triumphantly carried to the temple of Vesta.[19]

1. *Larousse,* 209. 2. Turville-Petre, 23. 3. Norman, 123. 4. Rawson, E.A., 25. 5. Tacitus, 658. 6. *Book of the Dead,* 270–71. 7. Graves, G.M. 1, 283–84. 8. Graves, W.G., 301. 9. *Encyc. Brit.,* "Typhoon." 10. Campbell, M.I., 29. 11. Norman, 42. 12. Knight, S.L., 124. 13. Budge, G.E. 2, 59. 14. Norman, 38, 48. 15. M. Smith, 62. 16. Guignebert, 53. 17. Briffault 3, 18. 18. *Larousse,* 209. 19. Dumézil, 221.

Assassins

European mispronunciation of the Saracenic brotherhood of *hashishim,* "hashish-takers," who fought Christian crusaders in the Holy Land. See **Aladdin**.

Astarte

Lady of **Byblos**, one of the oldest forms of the Great Goddess in the Middle East, identified with Egypt's Hathor, Mycenae's Demeter, Cyprus's Aphrodite.

The Bible calls her Asherah or Ashtoreth, the Goddess worshipped by Solomon (1 Kings 11:5).

Her shrine at Byblos dated back to the Neolithic and flourished throughout the Bronze Age.[1] She was the same creating-preserving-and-destroying Goddess worshipped by all Indo-European cultures, and still typified by Kali as the symbol of Nature. Astarte was the "true sovereign of the world," tirelessly creating and destroying, eliminating the old and generating the new.[2] Sidonian kings could not rule without her permission. Each king styled himself first and foremost "Priest of Astarte."

Sumerian cylinder seals from Lagash, ca. 2300 B.C., showed the Goddess in a pose identical with Kali's love-and-death sacramental posture, squatting on top of her consort's body.[3]

To the Arabs the Goddess was Athtar, "Venus in the Morning." In Aramaic she was Attar-Samayin, "Morning Star of Heaven," uniting two sexes in herself, like Lucifer the Morning Star and Diana Lucifera. Her Hurrian name was Attart, or sometimes Ishara, another form of Ishtar, "the Star."[4] To Canaanites, she was Celestial Ruler, Mistress of Kingship, mother of all *baalim* (gods).[5]

Astarte ruled all the spirits of the dead who lived in heaven wearing bodies of light, visible from earth as stars. Hence, she was known as Astroarche, "Queen of the Stars."[6] She was the mother of all souls in heaven, the Moon surrounded by her star-children, to whom she gave their "astral" (starry) bodies. Occultists still speak of the astral body as an invisible double, having forgotten the word's original connotation of starlight.[7]

Astarte-Ashtoreth was transformed into a devil by Christian writers, who automatically assumed that any deity mentioned in the Bible other than Yahweh was one of the denizens of hell. She was also masculinized. One finds in books of the 15th and 16th centuries a demon Ashtoreth or Astaroth, a "duke" or "prince" of hell.[8] Milton knew better; he spoke of "Astarte, queen of heaven, with crescent horns."[9]

Scholars who really understood the mystery of Astarte recognized in her one of the ancient prototypes of the virgin **Mary**. In Syria and Egypt her sacred dramas celebrated the rebirth of the solar god from the celestial Virgin each 25th of December. A newborn child was exhibited, while the cry went up that the Virgin had brought forth. Frazer says, "No doubt the Virgin who thus conceived and bore a son on the twenty-fifth of December was the great Oriental goddess whom the Semites called the Heavenly Virgin or simply the Heavenly Goddess; in Semitic lands she was a form of Astarte."[10]

1. *Encyc. Brit.,* "Byblos." 2. Massa, 101. 3. Campbell, Or. M., 42. 4. Albright, 196, 228. 5. Stone, 164. 6. Lindsay, O.A., 327. 7. Cavendish, P.E., 44. 8. de Givry, 132. 9. Cavendish, P.E., 237. 10. Frazer, G.B., 416.

Aster

"Star," Plato's name for **Lucifer**, the biblical god of the Morning Star.[1] He was perceived as a cyclic deity, attending the sun into the underworld at sunset, and also announcing "He is risen" in the morning.

1. Lindsay, O.A., 94.

Astraea

"Starry One," a Roman title of the Libyan Goddess of holy law, Libra or Libera, symbolized by the Scales of Judgment now enshrined in the zodiac as Libra. Like **Minerva**, **Athene**, **Maat**, and other manifestations of the same Goddess, she was characterized as a celestial Virgin dispensing the fates of men. See **Virgo**.

Astrology

Study of the stars has been called "the basis of all intellectual culture."[1] It was highly refined by the Chaldeans, who were simultaneously astronomers and astrologers. Unlike modern "Chaldeans," they were moon worshippers, basing their system almost entirely on the movements of the Moon-goddess. Their zodiac was known as Houses of the Moon.[2]

Apparently a majority of moon-watchers were women, the priestesses charged with determining correct seasons for planting and harvest, drawing up calendars, etc. Pliny said the study of the heavens, to foretell events such as eclipses, was traditionally the business of women. He suspected the priestesses' magic didn't cause eclipses, but rather foresaw them by scientific measurements; yet "the most part of the common people have been and are of this opinion . . . that all the same is done by enchantments, and that by the means of some sorceries and herbs together, both sun and moon may be charmed, and enforced both to loose and recover their light: to do which feat, women are thought to be more skilful and meet than men." He credited the Goddesses **Medea** and **Circe** with special powers over the lights of heaven.[3]

Divination by the lights of heaven was another particular province of the Moon-goddess and her sybils, the word cognate with the Goddess **Cybele** and possibly derived from Chaldean *subultu*, the Celestial Virgin (the constellation of **Virgo**).[4] An archaic term for astrological divination was *mathesis*, "the Learning," literally Mother-wisdom. Chaldean astrologers were Mathematici, "learned mothers."[5]

As a result of its ancient feminine associations, astrology was viewed as a devilish art by many fathers of the Christian church. Some thought it indistinguishable from witchcraft. Others respected it. Origen said the stars are intelligent spirits, able to foresee the future and communicate their knowledge by their observed motions. St. Thomas Aquinas agreed with this. He said man's fate is the power exerted by the stars in their movements.[6]

Savonarola thought it a disgrace, however, that in his day the church was "wholly governed by astrology," as he said. Every important prelate had his "Chaldean" at his side, determining every move by the stars.[7] St. Jerome said astrology was idolatry. Sts. Gregory, Ambrose, Chrysostom, Eusebius, and Lactantius all condemned it.

Origen (Origenes Adamantius) Christian father, ca. 185–254 A.D., an Egyptian who wrote in Greek, exerting a powerful influence on the early Greek church. At first he was accounted a saint, but three centuries after his death he was declared a heretic because of Gnostic elements found in his writings.

St. Augustine said astrology must be expelled from all Christian nations. It was prohibited by the Council of Toledo.[8]

Despite all this, the church took astrology to its bosom in the 12th and 13th centuries. Pope Julius II settled the date of his coronation on the advice of astrologers. Pope Paul III planned the consistory by horoscopes. Pope Leo X founded a chair of astrology in a major university.[9] Signs of the zodiac were associated with the apostles. Cathedrals were decorated with astrological symbols. The *Zodiacus Christianus* compared the zodiac to the stages of Christian life and the twelve virtues.[10]

Peter of Abano was one of the few unbelievers. He openly scoffed at God, and managed to avoid the **Inquisition** only by dying at an opportune moment. Toward the end, he remarked that he had devoted his life to three noble arts: philosophy, which made him subtle; medicine, which made him rich; and astrology, which made him a liar.[11]

Protestants were not as enthusiastic about astrology as Catholics. Queen Elizabeth I of England disapproved of the Chaldean art, fearing implications of treason against the royal person in prognosticating the length of her life. Toward the latter part of her reign, she imposed severe legal penalties for casting royal horoscopes.[12] Protestant leaflets listed among the "sins of the papists" such as "Observation and choice of days, of planetary hours, of motions and courses of stars . . . horoscoping, or marking the hours of nativities, witchcrafts, enchantments, and all such superstitious trumpery."[13]

Yet the common people retained many superstitious beliefs based on astrology. The idea that the stars are souls in heaven never really died out. English peasants were sure that a falling star denoted either a conception or a birth—some said one, some said the other, for none were clear about which moment the soul descended from heaven to occupy its new body.[14] Because it represented an essence of new life, the falling star was and still is "wished on," like any spirit thought to be passing from one world to another.

Council of Toledo The greatest theological significance was attributed to the church council held in Toledo in 675 A.D., though there were seventeen other church councils in the same city between the 5th and 8th centuries.

Zodiacus Christianus A curious astrological work claiming Jesuit origin. Full title: *Zodiacus Christianus locupletatus seu Signa XII Divinae Praedestinationis. Totidem Symbolis explicata ab Hierem Drexilio è Societatis Jesu.*

Peter of Abano (1250–1318) Renaissance scholar, physician, geomancer, astrologer, and heretic; an acquaintance of Marco Polo.

1. Campbell, M.I., 149. 2. Briffault 2, 600. 3. Hawkins, 138–39. 4. Briffault 2, 600. 5. Rose, 262. 6. Castiglioni, 259, 261. 7. Lea unabridged, 772. 8. Hazlitt, 22. 9. Seznec, 57. 10. Budge, A.T., 414. 11. Lea unabridged, 774. 12. Robbins, 161. 13. Hazlitt, 376. 14. Elworthy, 424.

Atalanta

Amazonian huntress, the best athlete in Calydon. As an infant, Atalanta was suckled by **Artemis** herself, in totemic form as a She-Bear. When she grew up, she took part in the famous hunt of the Calydonian Boar and drew first blood, pausing only to kill two centaurs who tried to rape her on the hunting field.

She was a faster runner than any man. Her suitors had to beat her

Calydon Ancient town of Aetolia, site of the temple of Artemis Laphria (Artemis the Forager).

in a footrace, or suffer death. Many were killed before one managed to trick her into losing the race by dropping golden apples to divert her attention. Some said she and her bridegroom were turned into lions and yoked to the chariot of the Great Mother of the Gods.[1] Phrygian **Cybele** always rode in a chariot drawn by two lions, male and female.

1. Graves, G.M. 1, 264–67.

Atargatis

Philistine Fish-goddess, called Tirgata in Syria, identified with **Aphrodite**. At the temple of Der, in Babylon, she was Derceto, "Whale of Der." Her daughter, Queen **Semiramis**, founded the city of Babylon.[1] She gave rebirth to Jonah in his earlier Babylonian form as the fish-god Oannes. Philistines called him Dagon, Atargatis's mate. At Harran, the Goddess's sacred fish were credited with oracular powers. In Boeotia she was identified with **Artemis** who wore a fish amulet over her genitals.[2] See **Fish**.

1. Baring-Gould, C.M.M.A., 497. 2. Neumann, G.M., pl. 134.

Atheism

Greek *a-theos,* one who denies the existence of any god. Christian theologians tended to regard atheism as devilish, though atheism implied disbelief in devils as well as all other supernatural entities.

Oriental thinkers were less simplistic about atheism. The more advanced sages taught that non-belief can be more "religious" than belief—indeed, atheism may make better human beings than faith can make. In the east "it is not thought impossible that atheism may be as profoundly religious as theism, nor is atheism regarded by religious men as in itself unspiritual. This is extremely hard for a westerner to understand—he does not see that the essence of religion lies in the religious experience, and not in any belief at all, and that all so-called religious beliefs or doctrines are merely theories about the religious experience."[1]

Evans-Wentz called attention to the same Oriental thought: " 'The Fatherhood of God' as a personal and anthropomorphic deity is the cornerstone of Christian theology, but in Buddhism—although the Buddha neither denied nor affirmed the existence of a Supreme Deity—it has no place, because, as the Buddha maintained, neither believing nor not believing in a Supreme God, but self-exertion in right-doing, is essential to comprehending the true nature of life."[2]

W. Y. Evans-Wentz British student of Tibetan Buddhism, translator of the *Tibetan Book of the Dead,* 1927.

By these standards, no criminal could be considered religious, no matter how much faith he professed. Conversely, no person who treated his fellow-creatures well could be considered irreligious, no matter how many gods he denied. Oriental sages viewed theological reasoning with a certain contempt, as irrelevant to the behavior that constitutes true religion: "Mere talk about religion is only an intellectual exercise. . . . Of what use are grand phrases about Atma (the soul) on the lips of those who hate and injure one another? . . . Religion is kindness."[3]

1. Vetter, 320–21. 2. *Bardo Thodol,* 236. 3. Avalon, 175.

Athene

Mother-goddess of Athens, worshipped as Holy Virgin, Athene Parthenia, in the Parthenon, her "Virgin-temple." Though classic writers insisted on her chastity, older traditions gave her several consorts, such as Hephaestus and Pan.[1] She was united with the phallic Pallas, whose "Palladium" was a lingam, later Rome's greatest fetish.[2]

Sign of Athene

Athene came from North Africa. She was the Libyan Triple Goddess Neith, Metis, Medusa, **Anath**, or Ath-enna. An inscription at Larnax-Lapithou named her Athene in Greek, Anat in Phoenician.[3] Pre-Hellenic myths said she came from the uterus of Lake Tritonis (Three Queens) in Libya.[4] Egyptians sometimes called Isis Athene, which meant "I have come from myself."[5]

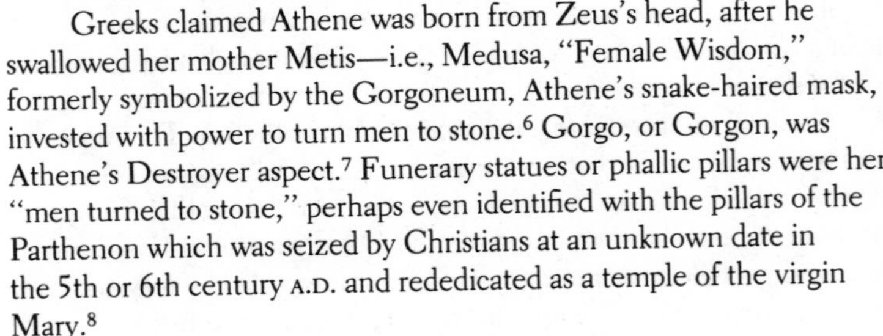

Greeks claimed Athene was born from Zeus's head, after he swallowed her mother Metis—i.e., Medusa, "Female Wisdom," formerly symbolized by the Gorgoneum, Athene's snake-haired mask, invested with power to turn men to stone.[6] Gorgo, or Gorgon, was Athene's Destroyer aspect.[7] Funerary statues or phallic pillars were her "men turned to stone," perhaps even identified with the pillars of the Parthenon which was seized by Christians at an unknown date in the 5th or 6th century A.D. and rededicated as a temple of the virgin Mary.[8]

1. Graves, G.M. 1, 149. 2. Dumézil, 323. 3. Massa, 104. 4. Graves, G.M. 1, 44. 5. Budge, G.E. 1, 459. 6. *Larousse,* 107. 7. Knight, S.L., 130. 8. Hyde, 61.

Atlas

Pre-Hellenic Titan or earth-god, brother of **Prometheus**, condemned to carry the world on his back because he took part in the Giants' Revolt against the Olympian gods. This was a re-interpretation of his primary earth-supporting function. As Prometheus was associated with the Caucasus and Heracles with the "Pillars of Heracles" in the west, so Atlas was associated with the Atlas Mountains of Africa—indicating that the **Titans** were originally divine pillars of the heavens, upholding the world. Atlas might be compared to the

Vedic god Vishnu who took the form of a tortoise (Greek Tartarus) and supported the world on his back.

Atonement

In ancient Mesopotamia the Day of Atonement corresponded to the beginning of the New Year, when all sins were collectively purged for a new time-cycle. The Jews' Yom Kippur, Day of Atonement, was based on the Sumero-Babylonian *kupparu,* an atonement ceremony in which a sheep was ceremonially loaded with all the community's sins, and killed. The sheep was an animal substitute for the man who in earlier times died as Sin Bearer, Savior, or Good Shepherd—that is, Dumuzi or **Tammuz**.

A **ram** played the part of Sin Bearer at atonement festivals of Egypt, which is why Aries the Ram is still the zodiacal sign of the New Year that began in March, by ancient reckoning. Egyptians called him Amon the ram god; the Jews assimilated him to the paschal lamb and sacrificed him at Passover.

All over the world, the sheep stood for the shepherd as an atonement-victim. In China the name Ch'iang, "Shepherd," was given to war prisoners who provided sacrificial victims. The pictograph for "shepherd" was a man with a knife severing his neck.[1] The dead shepherd was also called the Son of God. In Samarkand during the 2nd century B.C., "the Son of God died with the seventh moon . . . all the inhabitants, without distinction, appear dressed in robes of black wool. They go barefooted, striking their breasts, uttering loud wails and weeping copious tears. Three hundred persons, both men and women, go about the fields scattering grass, and looking for the remains of the Son of God."[2] Such was a Chinese traveler's impression of the rite known in Greece as the *anagnorisis,* search and discovery (see **Drama**).

Israel's law called for a goat to bear away the sins of the community to the god **Azazel**, whom the Syrians called Aziz, "the Lord's Messenger."[3] Having selected the scape-goat, the priest would "confess over him all the iniquities of the children of Israel, and all their transgressions in all their sins, putting them on the head of the goat" (Leviticus 16:21). A first goat was driven away, a second one was killed, for no god would absolve sins without an offering of blood: "Almost all things are by the law purged with blood; and without shedding of blood there is no remission" (Hebrews 9:22).

As development of the wool industry made it more profitable to keep sheep alive for their fleeces than to kill them for their meat, the goat became a more popular sacrificial victim. The animals were sometimes skinned to produce copious shedding of blood for remission of sins. An incantation from the Shurpu series gives a magic rationale for flaying a scape-goat:

> *As this goat skin is pulled off and thrown into the fire, and the burning Flame consumes it, and it does not return to its goat, and it is no longer dyed (with blood), so the oath, the ban, the pain, the misery, the disease, the sickness, the trespass, the misdeed, the crime, the sin, the disease which dwells in my body, my flesh, and my joints, may they be pulled off like this goat skin, and may the ban depart and may I see the light.*[4]

Early Greek myths evoke primitive totemism with goat gods flayed in atonement for the sins of others. **Athene** flayed the goat god **Pallas**, or **Pan**, and made her *aegis* from his skin.[5] Phrygians called the same god the satyr Marsyas, nailed to a pine tree and flayed in atonement for a crime against **Apollo**. In Rome, goats were flayed at the purification festival of the Lupercalia, where the dying satyr-god Faunus was offered to the Sabine mother-goddess Ops.[6]

The old Roman New Year was celebrated at the Ides of March and called the Mamuralia, carrying another trace of scapegoat-sacrifice. A man dressed in goatskins was led through the city in procession, beaten with rods, and driven away into exile with the formula, "Out with hunger, in with health and wealth."[7] Ovid said the March scapegoat was a legendary smith named Mamurius, who forged coins representing each month of the year—zodiacal sun-symbols.

Such practices make it clear that scapegoat-sacrifices were formerly human, and the animals replaced human victims. Liturgical formulae nearly always sent human sins into oblivion along with the sacrificed animal. Egyptians, killing the bull that represented Osiris, said the whole nation's sins were placed on his head.[8] Animal sacrifice took a more humane form in Tibet: at the New Year ceremony, three horses and three dogs were smeared with red paint instead of flayed, then dedicated to the temple.[9]

Christian symbolism made Jesus the sacrificial Lamb of God slain to atone for sin like the paschal lamb. Some early Christian writers insisted that animal sacrifice came first, and human sacrifice was a later, "higher" development: "God is a man-eater. For this reason men are sacrificed to him."[10] Among medieval theologians there was a general opinion that Jesus's sacrifice was not really effective; only "a few" were saved by the Savior's death. St. Thomas Aquinas and others claimed the vast majority of people were still doomed to eternal suffering in hell.[11] Thus the theory of atonement for all time or for all humanity was actually denied by the same church that propounded it as a basis for worldly power.

1. Hays, 188. 2. Briffault 3, 100. 3. Cumont, O.R.R.P., 113. 4. *Assyr. & Bab. Lit.*, 394. 5. Graves, G.M. 1, 81. 6. *Larousse*, 208. 7. J.E. Harrison, 196–97; Frazer, G.B., 670. 8. Budge, G.E. 2, 349. 9. Waddell, 529, 531. 10. Robinson, 138. 11. Coulton, 19.

Atropos

"Cutter," the third of the Greek trinity of **Fates** (Moerae). She was the Destroyer whose function was to cut the thread of life that the first sister spun, and the second one wove. She was usually depicted as an old woman carrying a pair of shears. Like Kali the Destroyer, she was also worshipped as a Goddess in her own right. In Parthia, the "Virgin-Land," she had her own holy city, Atropatene. Its modern name is Azerbaijan.[1]

1. Thomson, 173.

Attis

The cult of Attis strongly influenced early Christianity.

Attis accompanied **Cybele**, the Great Mother of the Gods, brought to Rome from Phrygia in 204 B.C. They were established in a temple on the Vatican hill, where they remained for six centuries.[1] At first Attis was separated from, and subordinated to, the Goddess, whom the emperor Augustus regarded as the Supreme Mother of Rome. "The Romans tolerated Attis because, maintaining the tradition of earlier days, they continued to regard Cybele as a national Goddess."[2]

Attis was a son of the Goddess's earthly incarnation, the virgin **Nana**, who miraculously conceived him by eating an almond or a pomegranate, yonic symbols both. Thus he was a typical "god without a father," the Virgin's son. He grew up to become a sacrificial victim and Savior, slain to bring salvation to mankind. His body was eaten by his worshippers in the form of bread.[3] He was resurrected as "The Most High God, who holds the universe together."[4] His epiphany was announced with the words, "Hail, Bridegroom, Hail, new Light."[5] Like his priests he was castrated, then crucified on a pine tree, whence his holy blood poured down to redeem the earth.

Attis's passion was celebrated on the 25th of March, exactly nine months before the solstitial festival of his birth, the 25th of December. The time of his death was also the time of his conception, or re-conception. To mark the event when Attis entered his mother to beget his reincarnation, his tree-phallus was carried into her sacred cavern. Thus the virgin mother Nana was actually the Goddess herself: she who was called Inanna by the Sumerians, Mari-Anna by the Canaanites, Anna Perenna by the Sabines, and Nanna, mother of the dying god Balder, in northern Europe.[6]

Christians claimed the same dates for the conception and birth of their savior. The usual quarrels ensued. The Christians resorted to their favorite argument, that the devil had established pagan Mysteries in imitation of Christianity before there was a Christianity. Tertullian

Tertullian (Quintus Septimius Florens Tertullianus) Influential early Christian writer and father of the church, ca. 155–220 A.D., born in Carthage of pagan parents.

said, "The devil by the mysteries of his idols, imitates even the main parts of the divine mysteries."[7]

Followers of Attis eventually lost their sacrificial day to the Christians. Justinian ruled that March 25 would be known as the day of the Annunciation, or Lady Day. Naturally, the day of the Annunciation was the day of Jesus's conception, so that he, like Attis, could be born nine months later at the winter solstice, as were all gods assimilated to the sun and called Light of the World.[8]

March 25 was also the day when Blessed Virgin **Juno** miraculously conceived her savior-son **Mars** by eating her own magic lily, which is why March was named after this god and why medieval France called Lady Day *Notre Dame de Mars.* The date was officially Christianized by the tenth Council of Toledo in 656 A.D. as the Festival of the Mother of God. But its symbol remained a pagan sign of the **yoni.**[9] Mars had a Phrygian counterpart, the satyr Marsyas, likewise hung on a tree, and likewise a son of **Cybele**. It was said that he and Attis were the same god.[10]

The day of Attis's death was Black Friday, or the Day of Blood. His image was carried to the temple and bound to the tree, escorted by "reed-bearers" *(cannophori)* with the reed scepters representing regenerated phalli and new fertility.[11] During the ceremonies, initiates castrated themselves in imitation of the castrated god, and presented their severed genitals to the Goddess along with those of the gelded bull sacrificed at the Taurobolium.[12] All these male remnants were deposited in the sacred cave of the Great Mother.[13]

The god died and was buried. He descended into the underworld. On the third day he rose again from the dead. His worshippers were told: "The god is saved; and for you also will come salvation from your trials."[14] This day was the Carnival or Hilaria, also known as the Day of Joy. People danced in the streets and went about in disguise, indulging in horseplay and casual love affairs.[15] This was the Sunday; the god arose in glory as the solar deity of a new season. Christians ever afterward kept Easter Sunday with carnival processions derived from the mysteries of Attis. Like Christ, Attis arose when "the sun makes the day for the first time longer than the night."[16]

Naassenes of the 3rd century A.D. worshipped Attis as a syncretic mixture of deities. One of their hymns said, "Of Attis I will sing, of Rhea's son, not sounding his praises with rolling drums, nor on the reed, nor with the roar of Ida's Curetes, but as the Muse of Phoebus on the lyre I will blend the strains. Euhoi, Euhan, he is Pan, he is Bacchus, he is the shepherd of the white constellations."[17]

Inscriptions of the 4th century gave Attis the title of Menotyrannus, from Greek *tyrannos,* "lord," plus Men or Mennu, **Osiris** as the resurrected, ithyphallic moon-bull, "the Lord Who Impregnates His Mother."[18]

Pagans sometimes celebrated the Hilaria at the end of their Holy Week, bringing it to April 1 and the carnival of the April Fool, or Carnival King, or Prince of Love, all originally synonymous with Attis. He was also identified with Green George of the old Roman Palilia, honored on Easter Monday with sacrificial hanging of the god's effigy on a sacred tree. People of the 18th century still said the 25th of March used to be New Year's Day, while April 1 stood at the "octaves" terminating the sacred week.[19]

Some Christians claimed Jesus's crucifixion took place on April 1, so the Fool of the April Fool's Day processions became Christ carrying his cross and enduring the mockery of the mob. But the spring Holy Week was not really Christian. Its origin was a universal Indo-European tradition of extreme antiquity, probably traceable to the Holi festivals of India which celebrated the rebirth of spring with joyous orgies.[20]

Green George Spirit of spring descended from the hero-sacrifice of the Roman Palilia. In Balkan countries during the Middle Ages and later, he was represented by a youth dressed in green branches and symbolically "sacrificed."

1. Clodd, 79. 2. Vermaseren, 177–78. 3. Guignebert, 73. 4. Graves, W.G., 367. 5. Angus, 136. 6. *Larousse,* 268–69. 7. Robertson, 112. 8. Ashe, 82. 9. Brewster, 144. 10. Graves, G.M. 1, 77. 11. Cumont, A.R.G.R., 56. 12. Guignebert, 71–72. 13. Vermaseren, 111. 14. Cumont, A.R.G.R., 59. 15. Frazer, G. B., 405–7. 16. Vermaseren, 182. 17. Vermaseren, 182. 18. Cumont, O.R.R.P., 61. 19. Hazlitt, 13, 548. 20. de Lys, 360.

August

Roman month of the oracular Juno Augusta. Oracles were *augustae* in the semi-matriarchal "republican" period. The term was later applied to male priests, then to emperors. An "august" man was one filled with the spirit of the Goddess.[1] *Augur,* the old name for a seer, meant "increaser," once referring to the mother-priestess.[2] The first emperor Augustus took his title from the Great Mother of the Gods, presumed incarnate in his wife Livia Augusta. Their house stood opposite the temple of the Great Mother, whom Augustus honored as the national Goddess.[3]

Among European pagans the month of August began with one of the Goddess's major festivals, Lammas Eve, from *Hlaf-mass,* "the Feast of Bread." The secret worship of **Ops, Ceres, Demeter,** or Juno Augusta continued throughout the Middle Ages in the rites addressed to the Lammas corn-mother who ruled the harvest-month. "For a seventeenth-century Scot to say 'he (or she) was born in August', was to imply high praise and recognition of a 'well-skilled person'. August, the month of the Lammas towers, the month when the Irish dancers moved around the female effigy, was the right time for birth. Then the Lammas moon was at work, on behalf of new children, and the new harvest."[4]

Churchmen repeatedly tried to obliterate the Goddess's connections with her harvest month. It was officially claimed that August had been named for St. Augustine—"prophetically" of course, since the name had been given to the month centuries before Augustine was born.[5]

1. J.H. Smith, C.G., 5. 2. Rose, 233. 3. Vermaseren, 83, 86, 126. 4. Dames, 164–65. 5. Brewster, 349.

Aurora

"Dawn," a Roman name for Eos, or Mater Matuta, the morning-mother of the sun. In the classic pattern, her child was also her consort, a sacred king sometimes entitled Tithonius, "husband of the Queen of Day." She made him immortal but forgot to give him eternal youth; so he became gray and shrunken, finally becoming a cicada, the symbol of the sun's rebirth when cicadas hailed his growing warmth.[1]

1. Graves, G.M. 1, 150; W.G., 117.

Avalon

"Apple-isle," the Celtic paradise across the western sea, where gods and heroes were fed on the apples of immortality. Cognate with Hindus' Jambu Island, Egyptians' Land of the Westerners, Norsemen's Faeroisland or Fairyland. See **Paradise**.

Avatar

Sanskrit word for the same soul reincarnated in a new body; the opposite of *atavism,* which meant harking back to an earlier, primitive state of being.

Axis Mundi

"Axle of the World." Ancient cosmologies pictured the earth as a globe spinning on a shaft with the ends fastened at the celestial poles. The *axis mundi* penetrated the earth at its center, hence it was usually associated with the cosmic lingam or male principle. Each nation placed this hub at the center of its own territory. See **Omphalos**.

Azazel

"God's Messenger," the deity who received sacrificial goats on the Jewish Day of **Atonement** (Yom Kippur, New Year). Azazel was not originally Hebraic, but Syrian.[1] Some rabbinical writings called him Azel, a subversive angel who stole magic secrets from God and gave them to **Eve**, thus bringing about the enlightenment of humanity at the cost of God's wrath. Moslems sometimes gave Azazel's name to the rebellious angel who opposed Allah, though this personage was often called Iblis, or Shaytan (Satan).[2]

During the Middle Ages, Azazel was adopted by Christian demonologists and made one of the leaders in the pantheon of hell. His name was often cited by exorcists as that of an active, lively possessor, befitting his ancient function as a Hermetic-style "messenger."

1. Cumont, O.R.R.P., 113. 2. Keightley, 25.

BAAL, in characteristic dress and stance. Phoenician bronze, 15th to 14th century B.C.

Ceremony of BAPTISM in York, Pennsylvania, in 1799. Drawing by folk artist Lewis Miller (*detail*).

One of the many versions of the BUDDHA. Temple of Borubudur, Giava, India.

Baal

"The Lord" among ancient Semites; consort of Mother **Astarte**, whose favors he shared with Yamm, the Lord of Death (from Hindu Yama). Every god was a Baal. The title was introduced into Ireland via Phoenician colonies in Spain, and became the Irish Bel or Bial, Lord of Beltain.[1]

Old Testament Jews worshipped many *baalim* as past or present consorts of the Goddess Zion (Hosea 2:2-8). Yahweh shared these other gods' temples for a long time, until his priesthood managed to isolate his cult and suppress the others.[2] Some of the *baalim* revered in Israel were: Sin, the moon god of Sinai; Molech (Melek), the "king" and sun god of Tyre; Horus, the Egyptian Golden Calf whose image was made by Aaron; Baal-Peor, a phallic "Lord of the Cleft" (or yoni); Nehushtan, the "fiery flying serpent" of lightning, made by Moses (2 Kings 18:4); Chemosh, the Babylonian sun god Shamash, incarnate in Samson (or Shams-on, the sun); Melchizedek, the god of Salem; Etana, or Ethan, the Canaanite Eytan who "went up to heaven"; Baal-Rimmon, the Lord of the Pomegranate impersonated by Solomon; Baal-Berith, the Canaanites' "God of the Covenant"; El, or Elias, the sun god Helios to whom Jesus called from the cross; Joseph, Jacob, and Israel, who were not men but tribal gods.[2]

The serpent god Leviathan (or Levi), the elephant god Behemoth, and the ass god Pales who gave his name to Palestine, all emanated from the Far East, as did Abraham or "Father Brahm," apparently based on Brahma. The Greeks' Adonis was the Semitic Adonai, "the Lord."

Since nearly all gods were sacrificial victims in their earthly incarnations, Baal may have been derived from Sanskrit Bala or Bali, a sacrificial offering.[3] The Semitic *melek,* "king," came from Phoenician *molk,* a votive offering, because early kings were not only gods but also victims.[4] (See **Kingship**.)

Baal was often used as the title of a mortal king, especially one whose reign might be terminated by a ritual sacrifice. In the time of Esarhaddon of Assyria, the king of Tyre was named Baal, or "God." In the 10th century B.C., kings of Byblos bore names like Yehimilk (God-king), Abibaal (Father-god), and Baalshamen (Heavenly Father).[5]

Baal became a favorite Christian name for a devil, because biblical writers denounced all the *baalim* indiscriminately as devils (2 Chronicles 11:15; 1 Corinthians 10:20; Revelation 9:20). Still, the northern European cognate Bal, Bel, Bael, or Balder retained the affection of commoners.[6] Baal was still the patron of the Beltain feast in 18th-century Scotland. To make the crops thrive, Scandinavians burned his effigy at midsummer in "Balder's Balefires" throughout Denmark, Norway, and Sweden.[7]

1. Joyce, 279. 2. Reinach, 201; Frazer, G.B., 341. 3. O'Flaherty, 340. 4. Gaster, 588. 5. Pritchard, 22–23. 6. Hallet, 336. 7. Frazer, G.B., 717, 769.

Baalat

"Lady," the feminine equivalent of Baal; common Middle-Eastern title of the Goddess. Also rendered Belit, Belit-ili, or Beltis.

Baal-Berith

"God of the Covenant," Canaanite lawgiving deity represented by two stone tablets in the temple at Shechem, later taken over by Hebraic invaders and transferred to the cult of **Yahweh**. Commandments on the tablets were based on the Babylonian Code of Hammurabi, received by the Babylonian king from the god Shamash.[1] These, in turn, were based on the tablets of law given the first god by his Great Mother, Tiamat.[2]

Though both tablets and title were claimed by the Judeo-Christian God, the name of Baal-Berith was attached to a devil, often invoked by medieval authors on magic, who were apparently unaware that they called upon the God of the Covenant. Weyer placed Baal-Berith in a position suiting his ancient function, however. In the royal hierarchy of hell he was Minister of Treaties.[3] Though churchmen had small use for the heretic Weyer, yet they used this precedent to assign the demonic pact to Baal-Berith. In 1335 a witch named Catherine Delort was burned for signing a pact with "the demon Berit."[4]

1. Hooke, M.E.M., 142, 147. 2. *Assyr. & Bab. Lit.*, 287.
3. Waite, B.C.M., 186–87. 4. J.B. Russell, 184.

Baal-Gad

Goat-Lord, a Semitic name of Pan, ancestor of the tribe of Gad; also identified with **Azazel**, who received annual scapegoat-sacrifices. He was worshipped in a cave at the source of the Jordan. It was said he was fathered by **Hermes**, and after death he ascended to heaven to become the constellation Capricorn, the Goat.[1]

1. Graves, W.G., 230, 391.

Baal-Hadad

Canaanite Lord of the Hunt, slain by priestesses of **Asherah**, who buried him in a bog (earth-womb) and resurrected him after seven years, the standard term of kingship in primitive Palestine.[1] He was mated to Asherah as Lady of the Pomegranate at Hadad-Rimmon, and his name was borne by two biblical kings, Ben-hadad and Hadad-ezer (Zechariah 12:11).

1. Hooke, M.E.M., 87.

Baal-Hamman

"Lord of the Brazier," the Tyrian **Heracles** who died by fire. Egyptians called him Ammon. At his cult center in Carthage, "men who were gods of light" were said to have died in sacrificial fires as late as 200 A.D.[1] In Elam, the god was Haman, slain as a surrogate for Marduk (Jewish Mordecai). One version of his sacrificial dramas appears in the Book of Esther, and eucharistic eating of his body is still performed through the **Purim** cakes called *hamantaschen.*

1. H. Smith, 136.

Baal-Peor

"Lord of the Cleft," Phoenician phallic god coupled with Asherah's yonic "cleft." Israelites adopted his cult and celebrated sexual rites in his honor in the tabernacle, until Yahweh's reformers killed the celebrants (Numbers 25). Baal-Peor's symbol was a **palm tree** between two stones, a male-genital symbol recalling the phallic god of Egypt, Osiris-Min, whose worshippers prayed to achieve erections "like a palm tree."[1]

1. *Book of the Dead,* 518.

var. Beelzebub

Baal-Zebub

"Lord of Flies," a god of Ekron in Philistia, to whose oracle King Ahaziah of Israel sent messengers in quest of healing magic (2 Kings 1:2). Like Hermes Psychopomp, his title meant the same as Lord of Death or Conductor of Souls, because flies were common forms taken by souls in search of rebirth. Mothers of many mythic heroes miraculously conceived them by swallowing their souls in fly shape.[1] Etain, legendary Irish queen married to Ochy Airem, and **Cu Chulainn** are examples from popular Celtic myth.

The Pharisees called Baal-Zebub a "prince of devils," apparently because it was thought he could cure people possessed by lesser devils (Matthew 12:24). One or two passing references to this "prince of devils" in the New Testament sufficed to establish Beelzebub as an alternative name for **Satan**, and flies as diabolic manifestations in medieval Christendom.

St. Bernard once exorcised a cloud of flies, which instantly dropped dead at the sound of his holy words and had to be shoveled out of his church in heaps.[2]

Fly-devils were still firmly believed in during the late 16th century. When a young Viennese girl suffered from cramps in 1583, Jesuit priests diagnosed her case as demonic possession. After eight weeks of exorcisms, they claimed to have expelled 12,652 demons from the girl. Her 70-year-old grandmother was accused of harboring these demons as flies in glass jars. The old lady was dragged at a horse's tail to the stake and burned alive.[3]

1. Spence, 95–96. 2. White 2, 109, 113. 3. Robbins, 395; Cavendish, P.E., 234.

Babel, Tower of

Ba-Bel, "God's Gate," was the Babylonian heaven-mountain or **ziggurat** where the god descended from the sky to the Holy of Holies, the genital locus of his mating with Mother Earth.[1]

The biblical story of the Tower of Babel "reflects the attitude of nomads entering the fertile plains of the Delta, beholding with wonder and dread the soaring towers of Babylonian cities, and despising the multitudes speaking all the various tongues of the ancient Near East."[2] To the ears of the strangers, diversity of languages was "babble," a word derived from Ba-Bel or its city of Bab-ilani, named after its own man-made Holy Mountain.[3]

Babylon's famous Hanging Gardens occupied the seven stages of the ziggurat, to create a Paradise like that of Hindu gods: "Seven divisions of the world . . . on which the seven separate cities and palaces of the gods are built, amid green woods and murmuring streams, in seven circles placed one above another." The ziggurat restored by Nebuchadnezzar was a "temple of the seven spheres of the world." It helped established universal belief in the seven heavens, corresponding to the seven planetary spheres. Christians and Moslems also adopted this view of the cosmos. The Koran says Allah made seven heavens and seven underground spheres, the seven hells.[4]

When ziggurats were abandoned and became ruinous, their mud-brick construction crumbling, later nomadic peoples assumed the gods were angered by the pride of the elder races and broke down their heaven-aspiring constructions. The Babel myth is found all over the world, including India and Mexico. It was familiar in the Greek story of the giants who piled up mountains to reach heaven. Hindus said it was not a tower but a great tree that grew up to heaven, angering **Brahma**, who cut off its branches and threw them down. From each branch grew a separate *wata* tree that gave humanity another separate language.[5]

Berossus said the Babylonian heaven-mountain was destroyed by winds, which blew a diversity of tongues among men. The first part of this premise was certainly not irrational, since drying and wind-erosion were major causes of the destruction of mud-brick structures. Berossus's story surfaced many centuries later in the Armenian myth of the holy mountain built by giants. It was blown down by winds, while "unknown words were at the same time blown about among men."[6]

Berossus Chaldean priest of Bel-Marduk, 3rd century B.C.; author of a history of Babylonia and Assyria, written in Greek.

The same story was told in the western hemisphere. Choctaw Indians said their own ancestors piled up stones to build a mountain that would reach heaven, but it was blown down by winds, whereupon people found themselves speaking different languages.[7] In Central America the heaven-reaching pyramid of Cholula was built by giants under the leadership of Xelhua. The angry gods broke it down with lightning and sent different, mutually incomprehensible languages to earth.[8]

1. White 2, 170. 2. Hooke, M.E.M., 138. 3. Eliade, M.E.R., 14.
4. Lethaby, 24, 124–25, 129. 5. White 2, 173. 6. Doane, 35.
7. Farb, W.P., 309. 8. White 2, 173.

Bacchus

Roman name for the sacrificial god **Dionysus**; also known as Bacchus Liber, or Father Liber, consort of the Goddess Libera. He was worshipped as the orgiastic deity of wine and vintage-festivals wherever wine grapes were grown throughout the Roman empire. The town of Bacharach in the Rhineland was named for him. Even in the 20th century, his influence was still supposed to ripen the grapes, and omens were taken for the vintage from his ancient stone altar on a river island.[1]

1. Guerber, L.R., 215.

Baetyl

Sacred stone containing a deity, the Greek *baitulos,* Hebrew *beth-el,* "house of the holy one." Two Goddess-wives of Jehovah in the 5th century B.C. were called Ashima Baetyl and Anatha Baetyl.[1] The Bible speaks of Anatha's *baetyl* as Beth-Anath (Joshua 19:38). Medieval Cathari still held that God had two wives, named Collam and Colibam.[2]

1. Graves, W.G., 405. 2. J.B. Russell, 125.

Balder

Norwegian name for the god Bel, or **Baal**, sacrificed as a son of Father **Odin**. He descended into the womb of Mother **Hel**, the Underworld. At doomsday, Ragnarok, he would return to earth in Second Coming. He would establish a new earth and a new heaven after the passing of the old destructive gods and their world.

Balder's effigy is still burned at Beltain fires in Scotland and Ireland. Scandinavians knew them as Balder's Balefires. His was the spirit inhabiting the Beltain cake, an effigy of god-flesh like the Christian host, sometimes man-shaped like the symbolic dough "victims" of the Far East.[1] Such pagan hosts probably gave rise to the living Gingerbread Man of the fairy tale.[2]

Like **Heracles**, **Siegfried**, and other solar heros, Balder stood for the idea of regeneration through cremation. His funeral was the Viking's dissolution in both fire and water; he was sent to sea on a burning ship. This was arranged by a Goddess called Hyrrokkin, "Fire-shrunk," one of the Elder Deities. She was a former giantess who lost her stature by passing through a magic fire.[3]

1. Waddell, 531. 2. Frazer, G.B., 679, 716. 3. Hollander, 51.

Dough victims The usual substitute, everywhere in the world, for what used to be cannibalistic offerings in primitive times. Sometimes the offerings were man-shaped cakes, supposed to resemble a real man in the eyes of the deity. Sometimes they were ordinary cakes marked with a symbol of the sacrifice, like the Christian host (from Latin *hostia,* "victim").

Balkis

The Queen of Sheba, according to the Koran. Solomon stole his throne from Queen Balkis, the Moslems said.[1] Her name was also rendered Bilqis, or Balqama. The temple of the queens of Sheba at Marib was Mahram Bilqis: Balkis the Moon-Mother. Solomon was crowned by Bath-sheba, called his "mother" in the Bible; but her name means Daughter of Sheba, so it's possible that Solomon did receive his throne from a Sheban queen. See **Solomon and Sheba**.

1. de Givry, 98.

Banshee

From Gaelic *bean-sidhe,* "woman of the fairy-mounds." The Irish banshee was a ghostly White Lady whose cry brought death to her hearers.[1] In Brittany she was the Bandrhude, or bane-druid, or dryad of death.[2] She was identified with Macha, Queen of Phantoms, third person of the Morrigan's trinity. That is, she was the **Crone** form of the Goddess, who summoned her children to death.[3]

Some said the shriek of the banshee was really the nocturnal call of the loon, a bird sacred to the Moon-goddess Luna, as its name suggests.

Like the **Vila** or death-priestess of central Europe, and the **Dakini** of the Far East, the banshee could be as benevolent as the sacred women who used to sing the dying gently to sleep. "When the banshee loves those she calls, the song is a low, soft chant giving notice, indeed, of the proximity of death but with a tenderness of tone that reassures the one destined to die and comforts the survivors; rather a welcome than a warning."[4] To others, she came like a bad death, full of horror.

1. Goodrich, 177. 2. Baring-Gould, C.M.M.A., 493. 3. Rees, 36.
4. Pepper & Wilcock, 275.

Baphomet

Bisexual idol or talking head allegedly worshipped by the **Knights Templar** when they were accused of heresy in the 14th century. Several derivations of the name Baphomet have been suggested. Some said it was Arabic *abu-fihamat,* "Father of Wisdom," the old title of an oracular head.[1] Some said it was a corruption of **Mohammed**. Some traced it to Baphe Meteos, "baptism of Metis," that is, of the Gnostic Goddess as Lady of Wisdom. It was a name well known among Gnostic sects in the east.[2] Because Baphomet was supposed to be the object of the Templars' "devil worship," it or he or she was pictured with the common devilish attributes: hoofs, a goat's face, both male and female genitals, etc.

1. Shah, 225. 2. Knight, S.L., 202.

Baptism

In 418 A.D., a Catholic church council decided that every human child is born demonic as a result of its sexual conception, thus automatically damned unless baptized.[1] During a Catholic baptismal ceremony the priest still addresses the baby, "I exorcise thee, thou unclean spirit. . . . Hear thy doom, O Devil accursed, Satan accursed!"[2] The exorcism is euphemistically described as "a means to remove impediments to grace resulting from the effects of original sin and the power of Satan over fallen nature."[3] But it is obvious from the folk belief still widespread, that the church's teaching was that every newborn infant before baptism belonged to the devil.[4] St. Augustine's doctrine of original sin laid the foundation for this idea, and Tertullian said every baby is born evil; its soul is "unclean" and "actively sinful" before baptism.[5] Medieval theologians held that any infant still in the womb is doomed to eternal damnation.[6] The Oedipal jealousies of men apparently developed these ideas, since few women would have pictured babies screaming in an eternity of torture in hellfire, simply because no priest had sprinkled them with water before they perished.

Indeed, priests refused to baptize a child within forty days of its birth, for both mother and infant were considered impure (hence too dangerous for priests to touch) during that period. "An unbaptized child, as well as a woman between childbirth and churching, was designated as heathen."[7] The real reason for this "heathenism" appears in numerous folk beliefs: it was the birth magic of the ancient Goddess that claimed both women and their infants in the performance of her Mysteries. In the north it is still said that children dying unbaptized go to Frau Holda, or Hel, or Perchta, the underground Mother.[8] In the Hebrides, the Goddess's protective ritual is still used to preserve children during the perilous pre-baptismal period: a torch is daily carried around the cradle as in old pre-Christian custom.[9] Some traditional ballads deny the Catholic doctrine that women dying in childbed or infants dying unbaptized must go to hell; they claim, rather, that such individuals pass into a pagan heaven. Mexican peasants still say they go to "a place of delight in the temple of the sun."[10]

Thus, paganism was kinder to infants and their mothers than Christianity, so that theologians often felt called upon to explain God's apparent cruelty in allowing infants to die unbaptized, so condemning them before they had a chance for salvation. In the 16th and 17th centuries, churchmen insisted that God's cruelty was perfectly just. Said Martin Del Rio, S.J.: "If, as is not uncommon, God permits children to be killed before they have been baptized, it is to prevent their committing in later life those sins which would make their damnation more severe. In this, God is neither cruel nor unjust, since, by the mere fact of original sin, the children have already merited death."[11]

It was customary to refuse baptism altogether to those thought to have been conceived out of wedlock, or sinfully. American churchmen often refused to baptize children born on Sunday, because it was thought children were always born on the same day of the week as their conception, and marital relations on Sunday were forbidden.[12]

Modern theologians have trouble explaining why baptism should be necessary. Few educated parents seriously believe their infants are doomed to eternal torture unless splashed with a little water in a church. The biblical "fall" that provided the original rationale has long since been relegated to the realm of myth.[13] The primitive notion of the public name-giving ritual seems to be all that is left to justify the formalities: no more than an excuse for people to dress up and get together, to celebrate a new life in the clan. Perhaps it should be remembered that this function was once the exclusive concern of mothers and Goddesses.

1. H. Smith, 238. 2. de Givry, 157. 3. *Encyc. Brit.*, "Exorcism." 4. Gifford, 51. 5. Tennant, 333. 6. de Voragine, 585. 7. Wimberly, 372. 8. Miles, 242. 9. Elworthy, 65. 10. Wimberly, p. 409–10. 11. Robbins, 123. 12. Murstein, 319. 13. Campbell, F.W.G., 207.

Barabbas

"Son of the Father," released from prison in Jesus's place, according to Luke 23:18. But Barabbas was another title of a sacred king, thus some scholars believe it was applied to Jesus himself, when he was "released" from the protection of Rome and handed over to Jewish priests for their Passover sacrifice. See **Jesus Christ**.

Barbara, Saint

Sancta Barbara, "the Divine Barbarian," a loosely Christianized pagan Goddess in her sacred mountain, either the Venusberg, the Horselberg, or the Round Mountain near Pozzuoli where she was worshipped under this particular title. Within the mountain dwelt the heathen dead, "bewitched men and women" who spent their time in dancing, lovemaking, and other pleasures until the day of doom.[1] In other words, St. Barbara was none other than the Fairy Queen.

As a spurious martyr, Barbara followed the usual pattern: she was a beautiful virgin, tortured by her evil pagan father to make her renounce Christianity. She remained steadfast, so her father killed her. Then God struck the father dead with a lightning bolt, unfortunately a few minutes too late to save Barbara. This was supposed to have taken place in the 3rd century A.D., possibly in Rome, or perhaps Egypt, or maybe Tuscany, or it might have been somewhere else. Accounts vary. The legend was not concocted until the 7th century.[2] By a rather curious association, St. Barbara was invoked to provide protection from lightning.[3]

1. Jung & von Franz, 121. 2. Attwater, 57. 3. Mâle, 271.

Bartholomew, Saint

Pseudo-saint based on a sacred king's title: Bar-Tholomeus, "son of Ptolemy." He was inserted into the Gospels as an apostle, but hagiographers gave him a different origin. He was called a son of "Prince Ptolomeus," crucified in Armenia, and flayed like the satyr Marsyas (see **Mars**). Icons showed him holding a moon-sickle, the sacrificial knife of the Middle East.[1]

An alternative history made Bartholomew a missionary to India, where he overthrew the idols of the oddly non-Indian deities **Astarte** and **Baal-Berith**. With many miracles, Bartholomew converted the king of that country to Christianity, but the king's brother was unaccountably permitted to crucify, flay, and behead the saint afterward.[2]

Spurious relics of the saint were installed in the Roman healing shrine of Asclepius, which was taken over by Christians and remained the Hospital of San Bartolommeo up to the 20th century.[3]

1. Brewster, 379. 2. de Voragine, 481–83. 3. Carter, 42.

Basilisk

"King Serpent," the mythical snake of the poisonous glance, listed as a real creature in European bestiaries up to the 18th century. Like the Gorgon head, whose glance was equally poisonous, the basilisk was closely linked with women's **menstrual blood**. As the serpent-haired **Gorgon** head represented women's "wise blood" and guarded menstrual mysteries that men were forbidden to behold, so there was a popular medieval belief that a hair taken from the head of a menstruating woman and buried in the earth would turn into a **serpent** or basilisk.[1] Superstitious folk supposed that all the serpents on the Gorgon's head were basilisks, which derived their evil eyes from her own deadly glance.

1. Rawson, A.T., 165–66.

Bassareus

Lydian fox god, a totemic form of **Orpheus** or **Dionysus**, whose **Maenads** were sometimes called Bassarids because they wore fox skins.[1] As a pagan deity, the fox became the popular trickster-hero of medieval folklore, where he appeared as Reynard or Renaud. He was actually worshipped in Cologne cathedral and in Westphalia in the 9th century A.D.[2] See **Dog**.

1. *Larousse,* 160. 2. Guerber, L.M.A., 162.

Bast

Egyptian cat goddess, mother of all cats, which were Egypt's most sacred animals. Bast's holy city Bubastis was said to possess the land's greatest temple. Herodotus said that in Egypt, "All cats that die are carried to certain sacred houses, where being first embalmed, they are buried in the city of Bubastis."[1] The Greeks identified Bast with **Artemis** or **Diana**, also called the mother of cats, and claimed the great shrine of Bubastis was built in her honor.[2] The cat's legendary nine lives stemmed from Artemis as the mother of the nine **Muses**, corresponding to the Egyptian Ennead of nine primordial deities. See **Cat**.

1. Budge, G.E. 2, 61, 364. 2. Herodotus, 106.

Beans

Like barley grains in Greece, beans were yonic symbols in Rome, as is still shown by the Italian slang term for female genitals, *fava,* "bean."[1] Along with all other ancient female-genital symbols, beans were credited with magic power to impregnate, because they enclosed ancestral spirits, the *manes,* born in dim prehistory of the Moon-mother Mana. The Pythagoreans placed a taboo on eating beans because of their supposed possession of spirits. In Rome, each *paterfamilias* went through an annual ceremony of exorcising ancestral spirits by throwing beans behind him at midnight, nine times enjoining the *manes* to leave the house.[2]

Another Roman ceremony on the twelfth day after the midwinter solstice (Epiphany) recalled ancient customs of choosing a sacred king. It was called the Festival of Kings Created or Elected by Beans, the beans evidently representing women, the choosing carried out by drawing black or white beans. Later, dice were used, and a ceremonial king-for-the-night called Basilicus was chosen by the "Venus" throw. The ceremony persisted in medieval England, where the Twelfth-Night plum cake contained one bean, and the man who received the bean was declared king of the festival.[3]

Some overlapping esoteric meanings of beans may be found in the Sanskrit word *mudra,* "kidney beans," also "woman," and a "magical gesture," the benevolent spell cast by a **Shakti**.[4] The influx of Tantric symbols into medieval Europe probably gave rise to Jack's beanstalk, resembling the Ladder of Heaven in that it was a soul-bridge: "the myth of the vine that once joined earth and sky," in the paradisal time when men knew the way to heaven—or thought they did.[5]

1. Young, 74. 2. *Larousse,* 213. 3. Hazlitt, 602. 4. Bharati, 41. 5. Eliade, S., 354.

Beata

"Holy woman," Spanish term for a white witch, often a hermitess distinguished by her visions, trances, stigmata, miraculous cures, etc. The church didn't know what to do with such people. Sometimes, if they became famous enough, they were canonized as saints. Sometimes they were persecuted for heresy and witchcraft.

Beelzebub

See **Baal-zebub.**

Behemoth

Biblical name of the Indian elephant god Ganesha, the "Lord of Hosts."[1] His title was adopted by the Jewish **Jehovah**, during the period when he was married to the Virgin Goddess **Anath**, or Neith, in the temple of Elephantine in Egypt. Jewish mercenaries stationed there worshipped the elephant-headed, virgin-born Lord of Hosts as their own Yaho (or, Yahweh).[2] At the time, the Jewish God was a subordinate spouse of the Goddess who was hailed as "Queen of Heaven and mistress of all the gods."[3]

The same Virgin Goddess was the mother, as well as the bride, of the elephant bull-god, according to the standard myth of divine incest created by identification of Father and Son. In India the mother of Ganesha was Parvati, virgin form of Kali. She made him from her own "body-dew" (menstrual blood). A true archetypal son, he guarded her "gate" (yoni) against the entrance of All-father **Shiva**. For this Oedipal offense he was slain, but resurrected.[4] Upon the same virgin mother under her other name of **Maya** (comparable to **Mari**, the other name of **Anath**), he begot the next incarnation of the Son of the Lord of Hosts: **Buddha**, the Enlightened One.

The elephant-god was not forgotten by the Jews, but he was dissociated from the later concept of **Yahweh**, and diabolized. He became the demon Behemoth. In this guise he appeared in medieval demonologies and grimoires, still wearing the elephant head of Shiva-Ganesha.[5]

Yet traces of the earlier divine elephant could be found in Jewish tradition. Rabbinical sources said the Passover feast commemorated more than one god. The lamb stood for the **Firstborn**. The fish represented Leviathan, the original wise serpent-deity of Levites.

The hard-boiled egg represented Ziz, or Aziz, or Azazel, the god of atonement sacrifices. The bread stood for Behemoth.[6]

1. Campbell, Or. M., 307. 2. Graves, W.G., 405. 3. Ashe, 30. 4. *Larousse*, 378. 5. de Givry, 137. 6. Hazlitt, 345.

Bellerophon

Corinthian hero, tamer of the Muses' winged horse Pegasus. Growing too proud of himself, Bellerophon tried to fly to heaven on Pegasus, and was cast down by Zeus. He died lame, blind, and accursed.

Bendis

var. Benthesicyme

Thracian name for the Goddess as Destroyer, the crone of the waning moon.[1] Christian authorities adopted her into the pantheon of the underworld as a she-demon.

1. Graves, G.M. 1, 61.

Benedict, Saint

An ancient shrine of the sun god Apollo on Monte Cassino was taken over and converted into a Christian monastery. The "St. Benedict" to whom it was dedicated was really Apollo Benedictus, the "Good-speaker."[1] Even Catholic scholars say there is no evidence that "St. Benedict" was ever a Christian priest. However, his legend did assimilate him to the sun god. When Benedict prayed, "the whole world seemed to be gathered into one sunbeam and brought thus before his eyes."[2]

1. Rose, 294. 2. Attwater, 62.

Berserker

A wearer of the "bear sark" or bearskin shirt; a Nordic warrior dedicated to the Goddess Ursel, the She-Bear (see **Ursula**). Through wearing the bear's skin, a warrior acquired the bear's fighting spirit and the grace of the ursine Goddess who was often a teacher of the martial arts. "Berserk" came to mean one possessed by battle-frenzy, careless of his own safety, unable to feel fear.

Totemic descent from the She-Bear characterized several old European clans. The Orsini or Ursini family were "bear's children," carrying a bear on their coat of arms. William of Auvergne, bishop of Paris in the 16th century, solemnly explained the origin of the Orsinis by saying a bear's semen is very like a man's, therefore it was quite possible for a bear to beget human children, presumably on a human mother.[1] The story reflects contemporary theological opinion that only a male can be a true parent. Nothing was said about a she-bear's ovum being like a woman's, nor was there a human father who might have begotten children on a bear mother.

1. Summers, W., 243.

Bible

This word for a holy book came from Byblos, the City of the Great Mother, the oldest continuously occupied temple in the world. The Goddess—called **Astarte**, Baalat, Hathor, etc.—patronized learning, and her priestesses collected a library of papyrus scrolls. Therefore, Greeks called any papyrus *byblos,* which came to mean any holy book. Hence the "Bible."[1]

Scholars have found in the Bible's numerous layers of additions and corrections a substrate of the former Semitic matriarchy, such as the Book of Ruth with its matrilineal and matrilocal marriage customs, and the Book of Judges with its feminine government of Israel (Judges 4:4). In several books the word translated "God" is really a feminine plural, "Goddesses," especially in reference to the matriarchal functions of lawgiving, avenging crimes, and bestowing the imperium of leadership.[2]

Some of the miracles attributed to biblical heroes were copied from older myths of the Goddess. Joshua's arrest of the sun was formerly credited to priestesses of Isis, Hecate, and the Thessalian Great Mother, who were said to stop heavenly bodies in their courses, and lengthen night or day at will.[3] Moses's flowering rod, river of blood, and tablets of the law were all symbols of the ancient Goddess. His miracle of drawing water from a rock was first performed by Mother Rhea after she gave birth to Zeus, and by Atalanta with the help of Artemis.[4] His miracle of drying up waters to travel dry-shod was earlier performed by Isis, or Hathor, on her way to Byblos.[5]

The greatest mistake of religious authorities in the western world was their view of the Bible as intrinsically different from other ancient scriptures, in that it was dictated word for word by God, not collected slowly, rewritten and mis-written, revised and worked over by human beings for a long time. The notion that the Bible did not evolve haphazardly, like most other holy writings of the same period, persisted almost up to the present day, even among people who should have known better.

According to the prevailing myth of biblical origins, the Old Testament was supposed to have been translated from Hebrew to Greek by seventy-two translators sent to Ptolemy by Eleazar, a Jewish high priest, in the 3rd century B.C., hence its name, Septuagint. Ptolemy locked the scholars in individual cells on the island Pharos, where each one made his own Greek version in exactly seventy-two days. Each translation agreed exactly, in every word, with the other seventy-one translations.

Of course this never happened. The Bible's real history was far less tidy. A collection appeared in the first century B.C. and again in the first century A.D. to be accepted by the Jews of the Diaspora as sacred, and passed on to Christians. In both Jewish and Christian hands the papyri underwent many changes. In the 4th century A.D., St. Jerome collected some Hebrew manuscripts and edited them to produce the Latin Vulgate, a Bible of considerable inaccuracy, differing markedly from Jerome's stem texts.

The King James Bible relied mostly on a Greek text collected and edited by Erasmus in the 16th century, which in turn relied on a Byzantine collection assembled gradually at Constantinople between the 4th and 8th centuries. A few older texts have been discovered: the Codex Sinaiticus, the Codex Vaticanus, the Codex Alexandrinus, and the Chester Beatty papyri. All are fragmentary, all differ from one another and from the King James version. There are no known portions of the Bible older than the 4th century A.D.[6]

The Revised Version of the New Testament published in 1881 tried to correct some of the more glaring errors. It erased the spurious final twelve verses of Mark, which were late interpolations including the words that caused centuries of suffering: "He that believeth not shall be damned." It eliminated the fraudulent translation "Joseph and his mother," intended to preserve the dogma of the virgin birth, and restored the original "his father and his mother." It omitted the forged interpolation intended to preserve the dogma of the trinity: "For there are three that bear record in heaven, the Father, the Word, and the Holy Ghost: and these three are one." These words appeared nowhere before the 15th century A.D. However, the Catholic church insisted on retaining the forgery. Churchmen's argument was: "How, if these verses were an interpolation, could the Holy Spirit, who guides and directs the Church, have allowed her to regard this lofty affirmation of the Trinity as authentic, and permitted its insertion in the official edition of the sacred books?" In 1897 the Congregation of the Index, with the approval of Pope Leo XIII, forbade any further research into the origins of this text.[7]

Traditionally, the church forbade not only research but even reading of the Bible by laymen. Throughout the Middle Ages, possession of a Bible written in the vernacular was a crime punished by burning at the stake.[8] With the Reformation came Bible-reading in search of a new basis for faith; but in the process were found many new grounds for skepticism.

Richard Simon's 17th-century *Critical History of the Old Testament* exhibited the now well-known internal evidence that the books of Moses were not written by Moses but were compiled by many hands at a much later date. Bishop Bossuet pronounced this work of scholarship "a mass of impieties," drove its author out of the Oratory, and ordered the entire first edition burned. Dr. Alexander Geddes, a Catholic scholar, translated the Old Testament in 1792 with a critical volume proving that the Pentateuch could not have been written by Moses, nor at any time prior to the reign of David. He was denounced as "a would-be corrector of the Holy Ghost."[9]

As the years passed, it became increasingly clear that the Holy Ghost needed correcting. Seven clerical scholars published *Essays and Reviews* in 1860, defining the new science of Bible criticism. They were denounced, and two were suspended from office; but they took their case to court, and won. In 1869 Kuenen's *The Religion of Israel* established Bible criticism as a valid field of investigation. He was followed by many others in Holland, Germany, and France. In 1889 the book of biblical essays called *Lux Mundi* gave up all pretense of the scriptures' historicity or divine inspiration, admitting that the Bible is a confused mass of myth, legend, and garbled history, often contradicting provable facts.[10]

Naturally, there was constant opposition to the efforts of the scholars. Many 19th-century churchmen insisted that the Bible's only author was God. Dean Burgon said, "The Bible is the very utterance of the Eternal; as much God's own word as if high heaven were open and we heard God speaking to us with human voice. Every book is inspired alike, and is inspired entirely." Dr. Baylee said the Bible is "infallibly accurate; all its histories and narrations of every kind are without any inaccuracy." Dr. Hodge declared that the books of the Bible are "one and all, in thought and verbal expression, in substance, and in form, wholly the work of God, conveying with absolute accuracy and divine authority all that God meant to convey without human additions and admixtures."[11] Apparently none of these gentlemen were familiar with the earlier contradictory texts; nor had they read the Bible closely enough to see the many passages where God contradicted himself.

The real point was that organized religions had an economic interest in maintaining literal interpretation of biblical myths. Guignebert says, "The doctrine of the inerrancy of the Bible . . . necessarily placed theology in an attitude of surly and sanguinary hostility toward the exact and experimental sciences, which it will not abandon save most reluctantly and after as much delay as possible. . . . [M]ethods have changed, the illusions still current have decreased, but its spirit is scarcely altered."[12]

When the theologians began to give in, they complained that viewing the Bible as myth would destroy the whole structure that their livelihood and self-respect depended on. After David Straus's *Leben Jesu* disposed of the historicity of the Gospel stories, and Renan's *Vie de Jésus* showed that the Gospels cannot be taken as literal truth but only as romantic symbolism, the Rev. Maurice Jones exclaimed, "If the Christ-Myth theory is true, and if Jesus never lived,

Maurice Jones
Author of *The New Testament in the Twentieth Century,* 1934.

the whole civilized world has for close upon two thousand years lain under the spell of a lie."[13] The Archbishop of Canterbury found it impossible to deny the Bible's apparent lies, and began to backtrack with his plaintive question, "May not the Holy Spirit make use of myth and legend?"[14]

Obviously the Bible was full of myths and legends, but most orthodox theologians had no idea of their meaning. One reason was that they didn't study the corresponding myths and legends of other cultures—ancient paganism, modern mysticism, the non-Christian beliefs of people both civilized and uncivilized throughout the rest of the world. Christian missionaries thought theirs was the only pipeline to divinity, the deities of all other people throughout the world were devils, and the myths of the Bible were absolutely true whereas all other myths were absolutely false.

Nowadays such crude beliefs seem no less superstitious than the primitive animism that the missionaries sought to destroy. Yet an even darker blot on the history of Christian missions was their arrogant vandalism—burning books and artworks, smashing images, forbidding the songs and poems of heathen tradition instead of listening and recording them in order to understand the people, to display a decent respect for what alien races held sacred, as the pagan Romans did in the days of their empire. It may well have been that, had the missionaries been willing to listen and learn, they would have discovered the mythology of the Bible all over again in other offshoots from its original sources; for all peoples, nearly everywhere in the world, shared the same fables of the creation, the flood, the magic garden with its tree of life and its primal couple, the wise serpent, the heaven-piercing tower, the divided waters, the chosen people, the virgin mothers, the saviors, and all the rest. It has been said both testaments of the Bible are only recent and relatively corrupt derivations from a world-wide cycle of archetypal myths.[15]

Least of all were righteous Christians prepared to understand that their awe of the Bible rested on a foundation of magical superstition: it was, and is, a fetish. Legal oaths were taken in physical contact with a Bible because of a very primitive belief in its destructive *mana,* which would automatically punish perjurors. Both Jews and Christians used their Bible for divination, just as a witch might use a crystal ball, an African might use a thunder-stone, or a Roman augur might use the sacred chickens. Bibliomancy (taking omens from the Bible) was sometimes deplored, but from the 4th to the 14th centuries was "repeatedly practiced by Kings, Bishops, and Saints."[16] St. Augustine frankly recommended taking omens from the Bible "in all cases of spiritual difficulty."[17] Even in this "enlightened" age, in both Europe and America, the Bible is still used to give omens.[18]

A favorite biblical method for discovering a thief easily lent itself to conscious legerdemain. The name of the accused was written on a piece of paper and inserted into the hollow end of a key, which was put into the Bible's pages. The diviner recited Psalm 50:18: "When thou sawest a thief, then thou consentedst with him, and hast been partaker with adulterers." The guilt of the accused was proven if the key was found turned around afterward.[19]

Despite the many discoveries and clarifications made by biblical scholars in the last century or so, the average Christian's attitude toward the Bible is still hardly more sophisticated than this simple-minded magic. Most churchmen see to it that their congregations are not told the true origins of biblical myths. The most primitive or unattractive of these are constantly re-interpreted as deep allegories or metaphorical fables, intended by their divine author to wait two thousand years or more for a correct explanation. Yet the real explanation of the sources of these stories, uncovered by the careful researches of the higher critics, is seldom mentioned. Likewise ignored are many of the truly awkward passages such as "Thou shalt not suffer a witch to live," or God's frequent commands to wage merciless war, which no amount of exegesis can fit into a more tolerant ethic.[20]

Erroneous but traditional views of Bible origins and meanings are doggedly preserved by male chauvinists in particular, since the canonical books were deliberately selected and edited to wipe out all feminine images of divinity and sanction religious suppression of women. Robert Ingersoll pointed out that "As long as woman regards the Bible as the charter of her rights, she will be the slave of man." Josephine Henry grumbled, "The Bible records that God created woman by a method different from that employed in bringing into life any other creature, then cursed her for seeking knowledge." Elizabeth Stanton said there is no escape from the Bible's "degrading teaching" as to the position of women, and advised women to boycott churches. "It is not commendable for women to get up fairs and donation parties for churches in which the gifted of their sex may neither pray, preach, share in the offices and honors, nor have a voice in the business affairs, creeds and discipline, and from whose altars come forth Biblical interpretations in favor of woman's subjection."[21]

Robert Ingersoll (1833–1899) American lawyer and lecturer, Attorney General of the state of Illinois; an outspoken popularizer of Bible criticism.

Josephine Henry 19th-century Kentucky suffragist and pamphleteer, active in the women's rights movement.

Elizabeth Cady Stanton (1815–1902) One of the leaders of the women's rights movement in the U.S.; an associate of Susan B. Anthony.

One of the erroneous notions that still keep Christian women shackled to their Bible-based "inferior" image is the notion that Christianity was founded on the New Testament, when in fact the early churches had no Gospels but rather created and produced their own.[22] Not only did churchmen falsely pretend an apostolic origin for their scriptures; they also weeded out all references to female authority or participation in Christian origins.[23] Only the forbidden Gnostic Gospels retained hints that Jesus had 12 female disciples corresponding to the 12 male disciples, or that Mary Magdalene was the leader of them all. Even women's scholarship was denied. St. Jerome openly admitted that his co-authors of the Vulgate were two learned women;

but later scholars erased the women's names and substituted the words "venerable brothers."[24]

1. *Encyc. Brit.*, "Byblos." 2. Mendenhall, 85. 3. Wedeck, 231. 4. Graves, G.M. 1, 264. 5. Budge, G.E. 2, 191. 6. Pfeifer, 103. 7. Reinach, 260. 8. Coulton, 123. 9. White 2, 319, 327. 10. White 2, 343–59. 11. White 2, 368. 12. Guignebert, 381. 13. H. Smith, 190, 479. 14. White 2, 359. 15. Hallet, 328. 16. Hazlitt, 47. 17. Waite, O.S., 131. 18. Cavendish, P.E., 83. 19. Maple, 39. 20. Muller, 91. 21. Stanton, ix, 125, 196, 214. 22. Muller, 148. 23. Pagels, 57. 24. Boulding, 356, 372.

Birds

From very early times there was a universal Indo-European belief that souls could take the form of birds. Latin *aves* meant both "birds" and "ancestral spirits," or ghosts, or angels. Roman emperors achieved godhood in the form of an eagle which was released above an emperor's funeral pyre to carry his soul to heaven.[1] Similarly, an Egyptian pharaoh's spirit rode aloft, on, or in, the solar hawk of **Horus** released at his funeral. Like Phoenix, he passed through the Fire and was reborn with wings. Based on such prototypes, the souls of Christian saints ascended to heaven in the form of white doves released at the canonization ceremony.[2]

Becoming a bird in a visionary or trance state was a widespread symbol of initiatory death and rebirth. Shamans and prophets in the South Pacific, Indonesia, Central Asia, and Siberia claimed to transform themselves into birds. Buddhist yogis said ecstatic flight was the first magical power to be developed by the practice of yoga. "Becoming a bird oneself or being accompanied by a bird indicates the capacity, while still alive, to undertake the ecstatic journey to the sky and beyond."[3] Celtic "fays" or "fairies" could change themselves into birds, which is why they were depicted with wings like angels, and why witches "flew" to the Sabbat.[4]

The Chinese said women knew the secret of flying before men did. The emperor Shun first learned it from two princesses. "Down to a certain date the source of magical power lay in women . . . an indication of an ancient Chinese matriarchy." In northern Europe also, the Goddess Freya owned all the magic feather garments that enabled magicians to fly through the air like birds.[5] The elaborate feather garments of Mayan and Aztec priesthoods probably had the same original function, to facilitate their soul-flights.

Because birds traveled freely between the earthly and heavenly realms, they were everywhere regarded as angelic messengers, givers of omens, possessors of occult secrets, as well as soul-carriers. Carrion crows and vultures took souls to heaven. Storks brought them back to earth for rebirth. Wise owls told the secrets of the night; lustful doves and nightingales told the secrets of love. Angelic eagles foretold the future.

Myths repeatedly credit seers with power to understand the language of birds, usually because sacred serpents licked their ears to "open" them, as in the case of the Trojan prophetess **Cassandra**.[6] Siegfried likewise obtained the power to understand birds, via the magic blood of the Great Serpent or dragon. A bird call, a magic formula, and singing were expressed by the same word in Germanic languages.[7]

The magpie was especially revered as an oracle. It was a *picus* (pecker) sacred to the Goddess Mag, or Magog, eponymous ancestress of Scythian Magnetes, the Amazonian centaurs credited with prophetic powers.[8] In Rome, the magpie or woodpecker was a totemic form of the god **Mars**, said to contain his soul between his incarnations as Maris or Faunus.

In Egypt the hawk represented the soul of Horus and of the pharaoh who embodied him. Hawks came to stand for that portion of every soul called the *ba*, which could come and go at will after death, flying freely in and out of the tomb. Narrow shafts were left open in pit graves for the passage of the *ba*. Similar shafts in pyramids, sometimes misconstrued as ventilation shafts, were originally intended to let the bird-soul of the deceased fly in and out.[9]

The bird-soul born out of the cremated body entered Egyptian mythology as the Phoenix, sometimes a man, sometimes a firebird. The name was Greek, meaning "the Phoenician," a reference to sacrificed sacred kings of Astarte at Byblos, where they were frequently burned.[10] The cult moved to North Africa with Phoenician colonists, and was carried on at Carthage where sacred kings perished in flames to a very late date.[11] Their bird-souls, reborn from the flames and flying to heaven, gave rise to the myth of the Egyptian Phoenix who periodically cremated himself and rose again from his ashes. His worshippers, identified with the god through his sacraments, partook of the same power of heavenly flight. A common expression for death was "flying away."

Philo Judaeus (ca. 30 B.C.–40 A.D.) Alexandrian Jewish philosopher, strongly influenced by Hellenistic Platonism, Pythagoreanism, and Stoicism; author of biblical commentaries, tracts, and histories.

Philo wrote of the sages' soul-flights: "They accompany in thought the Moon and Sun in their circuitings, the choirs of other planets and fixed stars, attached below to the ground by their bodies, but giving wings to their souls, so that, walking on the ether, they contemplate the powers they find there." Still known today as the yogic trance or out-of-body experience, the soul-flight was often described in medieval books on Hermetic magic: "Nothing can obstruct, neither the Sun's fire nor the Ether nor the heaven's revolution nor the bodies of other stars; but, cutting across all space, the soul will ascend in its flight up to the furthest heavenly body."[12] Bird lore has always clearly expressed man's envy of the power of flight and his longing to know what the world looks like from high in the sky.

1. Campbell, Oc.M., 334. 2. Gaster, 769. 3. Eliade, S., 98, 367, 409, 481–82. 4. Keightley, 421. 5. Eliade, S., 386, 449. 6. Graves, G.M. 2, 263. 7. Eliade, S., 98. 8. Lawson, 244. 9. Budge, A. T., 144–45. 10. Graves, G.M. 1, 69. 11. H. Smith, 136. 12. Lindsay, O.A., 191–92.

Birth Control

Transition from matriarchal to patriarchal societies usually destroyed the natural mammalian system of birth control practiced by animals and primitive people: women used to refuse sexual relations during pregnancy and lactation, a period lasting anywhere from two to six years for each child. The system is still followed in some parts of the world. Among the Hunza, pregnant or nursing women do not sleep with their husbands. The Semai of Malaya think it correct to forbid sex during the long nursing period, as this allows parents to space their children and give adequate care to each one.[1] Even in an aggressive male-dominated society like the Yanomamo, men say they are afraid to have sexual intercourse with a nursing mother.

Sometimes modern people insult the animals by calling a human rapist an "animal." Animals don't rape. Sexual intercourse takes place only when the female is receptive. When she is preoccupied with caring for her young—always her first priority—the female shows no sexual interest in the male. Should he be so ill-advised as to make sexual displays to her, she drives him away with bared teeth.

> *There is among animals no question of the use of force on the part of the male; the conjunction of the sexes is dependent upon the willingness of the female. . . . And the female sexual instincts are subject to frequent and prolonged natural suspensions which do not always correspond with the operation of those instincts in the male. Among all herbivores the females, as soon as they are pregnant, retire from the company of the males to seek either complete seclusion and solitude, or to collect in herds from which the males are excluded. Female elephants drive away all males from the herds of cows and calves not only during the long pregnancy of nearly two years, but throughout the period of lactation. The behavior is typical of animal females. Had the primitive human female admitted the male during menstruation, pregnancy, and lactation she would have departed from all biological precedents; her behavior would have constituted an abnormality.*[2]

Many early records show that human females did not depart from biological precedent. Hippocrates and Galen supported the ancient taboo on sex during pregnancy and lactation. There was a curious remnant of the taboo even in a popular marriage manual of the early 20th century, part of the vast body of sexual misinformation that our grandparents struggled with. The author declared that marital relations during pregnancy would make the child epileptic.[3]

In most primitive societies it was unthinkable that male sexual desires should take precedence over the needs of mothers and their children.[4] Patriarchy everywhere sought to change this, through religious sanction. Women were to serve men's sexual urges even when preoccupied with motherhood. This was the meaning of God's announcement to Eve: "I will greatly multiply thy sorrow and thy conception; in sorrow thou shalt bring forth children; and thy desire shall be subject to thy husband, and he shall rule over thee"

(Genesis 3:16). In this context, "sorrow" meant labor pangs, as well as the harried life of a mother with children too close together, and the illnesses and injuries caused by spreading a mother's care too thin.

The Christian canon omitted the *First Book of Adam and Eve,* which contradicted the canonical scripture by stating that Eve stuck to the old system of birth control after all. She gave birth to Cain and his twin sister Luluwa, another incarnation of the *lilu* or "lily" who was also Eve's predecessor **Lilith**. Then "when the days of nursing the children were ended"—but not until then—"Eve again conceived." She produced Abel and his twin sister. After Abel was killed at the age of 15 years, Eve produced Seth to replace him. "After the birth of these, Eve ceased from childbearing."[5] Thus the entire human race descended from these four: Cain, Seth, and their sisters. According to this version of the story, Eve was not particularly troubled by God's curse.

However, later Judeo-Christian culture insisted on men's control of women's bodies. Wives were not to initiate sexual relations, but they were never to deny their husbands. The Catholic church laid down the law that no wife could accuse her husband of rape even if he forced her with accompanying brutality. Sexual "release" was his conjugal right (but not hers).

The church interpreted the fable of Genesis as God's mandate to compel women to bear as many children as possible, even at the cost of the children's or the mothers' physical health and welfare.[6] Men refused to deal with the problem of over-production, and women were forbidden to do so, by the church's tradition. In pagan times, women used some fairly effective birth-control devices, ranging from vaginal sponges to abortifacient drugs. Many churchmen believed the witches inherited secret knowledge of such things, which contributed to the vigor of witch- and midwife-persecutions.

Father Dominic Pruemmer recently wrote in *American Freedom and Catholic Power:* "Birth control is nothing else than mutual masturbation or unnatural lust."[7] It is not usual to view the "lust" of marital partners for each other as unnatural. Nor did the church ever object to sex as masturbation when it was for a husband's benefit only—that is, not mutually satisfying. In fact church-sanctioned literature of the 17th century said the only purpose of marital sex must be conception, and if a woman receives too much pleasure she cannot conceive.[8]

The church further taught women that their children belonged more to God than to themselves, thus eroding the instinctive maternal possessiveness that fosters the best of child care. Not illogically, mothers often left their unwanted children for God to care for. In the 18th century, the hospital of St. Vincent de Paul in Paris reported as many as 5000 infants annually deposited on God's doorstep.[9] Infant corpses were rather commonly found among the rubbish of western cities. Foundling hospitals were so busy that they set revolving boxes in their walls, so infants could be passed through. Yet foundling hospitals seldom saved the children they were given. In practice, they solved the problem of excess births by killing babies by the thousands, under the sanction of male-dominated officialdom.[10]

London's first foundling hospital admitted 15,000 infants in the four years between 1756 and 1760. Of these, fewer than a third survived to adolescence. On the continent, the death rate for children in foundling institutions ran between 80 and 90 percent during the first year of life. Parish officers entrusted the care of newborns to women nicknamed "killing nurses," because they were expected to do the state's dirty work, and see to it that the unwanted children did not long survive.[11]

In effect, the patriarchal society having outlawed birth control and abortion could find nothing better to do with the overflow than destroy it after all. Apparently this was all right, as long as the decision to give life or withhold it was not being made by the mothers themselves. Vetter found this kind of morality puzzling:

> *Is there any evidence that religion has provided a superior brand of wisdom for the guidance of secular affairs, or in the burning social issues of the day? With the population of the earth growing by geometric leaps from unchecked fertility but with epidemics and diseases well under control, what religious leaders spoke up for the necessity of planned parenthood? Not one! But many did hound Margaret Sanger to prison for her constructive work in that direction.*[12]

An Englishwoman gave the following picture of conventional morality in regard to reproduction, indicating that religious leaders care for their own mythology and ceremonial well ahead of the future welfare of the race:

> *In a village that I know well a woman, legally married, bore five idiot children one after the other; her husband was a confirmed drinker and a mental degenerate. One of the children fortunately died. The text that was chosen for his funeral card was "Of such is the kingdom of heaven." About the same time in the same village a girl gave birth to an illegitimate child. She was a beautiful girl; the father, who did not live in the village, was strong and young; probably the child would have been healthy. But the girl was sent from her situation and, later, was driven from her home by her father. At the last she sought refuge in a disused quarry, and was there for two days without food. When we found her, her child had been born and was dead. Afterwards the girl went mad.*[13]

Margaret Sanger gave her life to the effort to prevent such tragedies, both within and without marriage. She believed that "excess people, not acts of God, created poverty, famine, and war. . . . All society would gain . . . if birth control were allowed to shut off the spigot that floods the world with weaklings. When sick and unfit mothers were not forced to breed, there would be an end to unwanted children who grow up to fill our prisons and asylums."[14]

But churches still doggedly opposed the right of women to

determine when, where, and how much they shall breed, largely because of the deep-seated male desire to control the life-giving miracle in which men play only a negligible part biologically. It can hardly be denied that male-dominated religions were everywhere devoted to this end from their earliest inception. As a result, overpopulation threatens the world with virtually unthinkable ecological and sociological disasters.[15] Even now, in the face of such disasters, religious leaders tend to the view that the faithful should multiply forever.

1. Dentan, 98. 2. Briffault 2, 400–401. 3. Simons, 161. 4. Briffault 2, 48. 5. *Forgotten Books,* 54. 6. See E.T. Douglas. 7. Ellis, 89. 8. Simons, 141. 9. Lederer, 64. 10. M. Harris, 183. 11. M. Harris, 184. 12. Vetter, 513. 13. Hartley, 347. 14. E.T. Douglas, 137. 15. Hallet, 411–12.

Birth-Giving, Male

Satapatha Brahmana The "Brahmana of 100 Paths." Brahmanas are prose commentaries on Vedic scriptures, dated from 800 to 500 B.C.

Padma Purana "Lotus Purana." Puranas are ancient Sanskrit scriptures in verse, treating of cosmologies, sacred histories, and the nature of the divine.

Rig Veda Foremost of the four Aryan scriptures written in Vedic (an older form of Sanskrit), ca. 1500–1200 B.C., containing sacred mythology, hymns, and verses; literary foundations of the Vedic religion.

Since birth-giving was the only true mark of divinity in primitive belief, the first gods to claim any sort of supremacy had to claim also the ability to give birth. In fact, usurpation of the feminine power of birth-giving seems to have been the distinguishing mark of the earliest gods.

Lacking vaginas, many gods gave birth from their mouths. Priests of Ra claimed their god gave birth to the first couple from his mouth. The Satapatha Brahmana said the god Prajapati learned to give birth to creatures from his mouth; but before he could manage it, he had to make sacrifices to an older, higher power: the Goddess Svaha, Lady of Sacrifices. According to the Padma Purana, a god named Sukra (Seed) was born from Shiva's penis, after living in Shiva's belly for a hundred years. However, this was not a proper maternal-type birth. Sukra existed beforehand, and Shiva had to make himself pregnant by swallowing him.[1]

The Rig Veda spoke of a male creator who gave birth to the Mother of Creation, then impregnated her, so she brought forth the rest of the universe. Brahmans tried to claim the Mother of All Gods was born from **Brahma's** body, even though she was the mother of Brahma too.[2] Brahma was known as Lotus-Born, meaning he sprang from the primal Yoni, the Goddess Padma ("Lotus"). His first Lotus Throne was located in her lap. The Rig Veda also called her Vac, the Great Womb, the Queen, the First, the Greatest of All Deities. She said: "I begot the All-Father on high. I dwell in the waters, the deep, and thence extend through all creatures, and touch the heavens with my crown. Like unto the wind I blow, encompassing all creatures; above the heavens and above the earth."[3]

Hellenic Greeks pretended their new Father Zeus gave birth to the much older Goddess Athene from his head. But before he could give birth to Athene, he had to swallow her real mother, Metis (Wisdom), who was pregnant with her at the time.[4] The Hellenes also claimed Zeus gave birth to Dionysus from his thigh; but again, the real mother was the Moon-goddess Selene, whom Zeus killed during her pregnancy. As Conductor of Souls, Hermes took the six-month fetus from Selene's womb and sewed him up in Zeus's thigh to continue his gestation.

A Greek carving showed the god Apollo sitting on a pile of eggs, trying to copy the life-giving magic of his mother Leto, or Leda, or Latona, who gave birth to the World Egg and hatched it.[5] This World Egg was an old Oriental idea. The Satapatha Brahmana said it contained "the continents, the oceans, the mountains, the planets and the divisions of the universe, the gods, the demons, and humanity."[6] Thus, birth—laying the egg—was the image of cosmic creation, and creator-gods needed to copy it. In Egypt, the mother of the World Egg was Hathor in the guise of the Nile Goose, later mythologized as the Goose who laid the Golden Egg. (See **Goose**.)

Atum, the local god of Heliopolis, the biblical "City of On," claimed to give birth to a primal couple from his penis by masturbating. Pyramid Texts of 2000 B.C. said "Atum created in Heliopolis by an act of masturbation. He took his phallus in his fist, to excite desire thereby. And the twins were born, Shu and Tefnut."[7] However, priests of Khepera insisted that their god produced Shu and Tefnut by masturbation and self-fertilization through his mouth. Yet the oldest traditions said Shu and Tefnut ("Dryness" and "Moisture") were born of the primal Mother, Iusaset. Like the biblical God who copied her many centuries later, she not only created the first couple, but also brought forth light as her first act of creation.[8]

Before begetting was understood, archaic myth-makers tried all sorts of ideas for making a male body produce offspring. A Chinese ancestor-god, Kun, suffered a crude Caesarian section. He was slain and cut open so Yu, founder of the Hsia dynasty, could emerge from his stomach.[9] Norsemen said a first male-and-female couple were born from the sweaty armpit of the giant Ymir, who imitated Mother Earth in that his flesh became the soil, his blood the sea, his bones the mountains.[10] Ymir's skull became the dome of the heavens, supported at four corners by four dwarves, Austri, Vestri, Nordri, and Sudri (East, West, North, and South), northern copies of the Sons of Horus.[11] Similar cardinal-direction gods became identified with the four angels of the Apocalypse and four evangelists, whose totems were the same.[12]

Totem Symbol or embodiment of an individual, tribal, or national spirit, frequently in animal form; a divine or semi-divine mascot supposed to have descended from an animal ancestor.

The god Loki gave birth to Odin's horse, after making himself pregnant by eating a woman's heart.[13] The usual mythic symbol of a woman's heart, from Egypt to northern Europe, was an apple. Thus it might be assumed that in some prototypical versions of the Eden story, Adam ate the apple before, not after, he gave birth to Eve.

Adam's birth-giving was a syncretic product of numerous local notions of the male mother. A Hittite god, Kumarbi, managed to become pregnant by eating his rival's penis. His offspring refused to come out through his mouth or ears, and having no vagina he was unable to deliver them. Finally the sea god Ea took them out through his side, as Adam's God did later. The idea for Adam's magic birth-giving rib came from a Sumerian childbirth-goddess, Nin-ti, "Lady of the Rib." Since *ti* meant both "rib" and "life," she was also a Lady of Life. She made infants' bones *in utero* from their mothers' ribs, which is why biblical writers thought ribs possessed the magic of maternity.[14]

An odd male-birth myth came from Persia's intensely patriarchal Zoroastrian cult, suggesting a combination of homosexuality and bestiality. The primal being, the Sole-Created Bull, was castrated and slain. Its semen went to the moon to be purified; then from this purified seed two new bulls were formed. From these, "all animals descended." The hidden feminine element in this phallic fantasy was the moon, of course; but the two bulls must have procreated homosexually. This idea was not unknown even in Christian Europe. "Authorities" like Paracelsus taught that a monster may be born of a man as a result of oral or anal intercourse with another man.[15] No matter how impossible it seemed, men apparently wished to preserve at any price the notion that a male could give birth.

Christianity demoted the Goddess to mortal status in both Eve and Mary, whom mystics regarded as two incarnations of the same person. In both incarnations she was a Mother of her Father. Gnostic Gospels said Adam came into being from the virgin Earth, who was none other than Eve.[16] The story of her birth from Adam was a late, distorted version of the myth.

> *Unless the male spirit is able—as in mathematics—to construct a purely abstract world, it must make use of the nature symbols originating in the unconscious. But this brings it into contradiction with the natural character of the symbols, which it distorts and perverts. Unnatural symbols and hostility to the nature symbol—e.g. Eve taken out of Adam—are characteristic of the patriarchal spirit. But even this attempt at revaluation usually fails, as an analysis of this symbolism might show, because the matriarchal character of the nature symbol asserts itself again and again.*[17]

Throughout the world, men's initiatory dramas enacted birth-giving to represent even the attainment of man's estate. Apparently men could think of no better way to adopt new members into their fraternities than to make the novices symbolically dead and reborn, often from a male mother. In New Guinea, initiates into the men's group crawled out from between the legs of men costumed as the birth spirit.[18] Australian men opened their veins to bathe a young initiate into their blood, magically imitating the blood of the womb.[19]

Baptismal rebirth from male blood was an idea shared by all mystery cults of the early Christian era. In the Mithraic Mysteries, an initiate was showered with the blood of the sacrificial bull and pronounced "reborn for eternity."[20] Afterward he was fed on milk, like an infant.[21] From primitive times to the present, men's groups devised theatrical imitations of birth, often claiming the rites were stolen from women—or that women were murdered for them—and have sought to protect these masquerades with all the taboos their priesthoods could invent.[22] In Malekula, men even applied the name of *mara* to the place where male initiations were held; it meant the women's obstetrical enclosure or birth-temple.[23]

In its determined exclusion of women, early Christianity evolved some "birth rites" of a somewhat homosexual cast. Some writers claimed Christian men could "impregnate" each other, in the spiritual sense, by kissing: "For it is by a kiss that the perfect conceive and give birth."[24] But it was hard for men to see themselves as perfect, when they conspicuously lacked the ability to bring forth and nurture new members of their race. Thus their endless quest for superiority nearly always required some travesty of motherhood.

Symbolic motherhood represented authority in the medieval Russian Orthodox wedding ceremony. The bridegroom threw the lap of his gown over his bride, signifying adoption by the ancient rite of mock birth. The wearer of the gown was "mother"; the one emerging from under it was "child." The Christian idea was to show that a husband exercised over his wife the authority of a mother over her child. It is strange that, when fatherhood meant authority in practice, men still thought it necessary to clothe that authority in the symbols of motherhood.

1. O'Flaherty, 32–33, 297. 2. *Larousse,* 345; O'Flaherty, 26. 3. Briffault 1, 7. 4. Graves, G.M. 1, 46. 5. Knight, S.L., 147. 6. *Larousse,* 346. 7. Lederer, 156. 8. Budge, G.E. 1, 297, 354, 429. 9. Hallet, 180. 10. *Larousse,* 248. 11. Branston, 60. 12. Budge, E.M., 89. 13. Turville-Petre, 129. 14. Hooke, M.E.M., 115. 15. Silberer, 71, 144. 16. Pagels, 53. 17. Neumann, G.M., 50. 18. Briffault 2, 687. 19. F. Huxley, 103. 20. Angus, 239. 21. Guignebert, 71–72. 22. Mead, 102–3. 23. Neumann, G.M., 159. 24. Robinson, 135.

Bitch

This became a naughty word in Christian Europe because it was one of the most sacred titles of the Goddess, Artemis-Diana, leader of the Scythian *alani* or "hunting dogs." The Bitch-goddess of antiquity was known in all Indo-European cultures, beginning with the Great Bitch Sarama who led the Vedic dogs of death. The Old English word for a hunting dog, *bawd,* also became a naughty word because it applied to the divine Huntress's promiscuous priestesses as well as her dogs.[1]

Harlots and "bitches" were identified in the ancient Roman cult of the Goddess Lupa, the Wolf Bitch, whose priestesses the *lupae* gave their name to prostitutes in general.[2] Earthly representatives of the Wolf Bitch ruled the Roman town of Ira Flavia in Spain, as a queen or series of queens named Lupa.[3]

In Christian terms, "son of a bitch" was considered insulting not because it meant a dog, but because it meant a devil—that is, a spiritual son of the pagan Goddess.

1. Potter & Sargent, 208. 2. Murstein, 76. 3. Hartley, 237.

Blaise, Saint

Spurious canonization of the Slavic horse-god Vlaise, or Vlas, or Volos: a consort of the lunar Diana. He was Christianized about the 8th century, but kept his pagan function as a patron of animals.[1] Charms read aloud in churches claimed he could heal any sick beast.[2] The myth of his martyrdom was dressed up with the traditional seven priestesses, who gathered up his sacred blood.[3] In England he was known as Blazey.

1. Attwater, 70. 2. Scot, 197. 3. de Voragine, 155.

Blancheflor

"White Flower," the Lily Maid of Celtic initiation ceremonies, representing the Virgin aspect of the Goddess—the red flower standing for the Mother, and the black bird for the **Crone**, according to the three sacred colors of the **Gunas**. Celtic romances said Blancheflor received **Perceval** into the fairy-religion, before he was converted to Christian purity at the hands of literary monks. She was the same as the Tantric Indian lady-love of Perceval's predecessor, Peredur Paladrhir of the *Mabinogion*. The monks calumniated Blancheflor, as any Shakti would have been calumniated by ascetics. They described her as a Jewish witch who coupled with Satan at a sabbat, and gave birth to **Antichrist**.[1]

Mabinogion
Accepted title for eleven Welsh tales from bardic oral tradition, first collected in the Red Book of Hergest, ca. 1400 A.D.

1. Baring-Gould, C.M.M.A., 169.

Blessing

From Old English *bletsain*, earlier *bleodswean*, "to sanctify with shedding of blood."[1] It was the custom to consecrate altars by sprinkling them with blood, and to "bless" individuals by marking them with blood, as is still the custom of foxhunters who "blood" new members of the club after a kill. According to Tacitus, the Celts "deemed it indeed a duty to cover their altars with the blood of captives."[2] The Romans did the same in essence, though their altars were "blessed" with the blood of sacrificial animals.

Cornelius Tacitus
Roman historian and rhetorician, ca. 56–120 A.D.

Catholics now bless altars by sprinkling them with salt, an ancient custom of the Jews, based on the primitive idea that blood and salt were magical equivalents because they tasted alike. Egyptian altars were *dedi*cated with salt. In Egypt, *dedi* was the magic salt that made Nile water become "as human blood."[3] (See **Menstrual Blood**; **Salt**.)

Blessing a person by drawing a cross on his head and breast originated with the Mithraic rite of the Taurobolium, when the cross (an emblem of Mithra) was marked thus on participants with the bull's blood, so they became official witnesses of the ceremony of rebirth.

To be blessed meant to be saved, through the magic of blood, as the Christian Gospels also admitted: "Almost all things are by the law purged with blood; and without shedding of blood is no remission" (Hebrews 9:22).

1. M. Harrison, 129. 2. Pepper & Wilcock, 217. 3. Erman, 49.

Blodeuwedd

Welsh Virgin Goddess of spring, all made of flower-buds, her beauty disguising a personification of the blood-hungry soil waiting to be fructified with the lifeblood of the sacred king. She also personified the "blood wedding" whereby Llew Llaw Gyffes became her doomed bridegroom and died from a spear-thrust in the side, according to the classic pattern seen in Balder, Jesus, Krishna, and many others. His soul became an eagle; but he rose again in human form to challenge his slayer, Gronw, to another bout the following year. Like Gawain and the Green Knight, or Frey and Njord in Scandinavia, the two "blood-gods" (*blotgodar*) alternately sacrificed each other in seasonal cycles.[1] The reincarnated Llew Llaw killed Gronw with a spear-thrust through a sacred holed stone.

Blodeuwedd's totemic form was an **owl**, the same bird of wisdom and lunar mysteries that accompanied or represented ancient Goddesses like **Athene** and **Lilith**. Owls were almost invariably associated with witches in medieval folklore. She was also the Ninefold Goddess of the western isles of paradise, otherwise known as Morgan, the Virgin blending into the **Crone** of death. She said: "Nine powers in me combined, Nine buds of plant and tree. / Long and white are my fingers, As the ninth wave of the sea."[2]

1. Turville-Petre, 163. 2. Graves, W.G., 29, 340.

Blood

See **Menstrual Blood**.

Boadicea

var. Boudicca

Warrior queen of the Iceni who led her tribe against Roman invaders of Britain in 60 A.D. Tacitus said the Roman soldiers had dared to scourge the queen and rape her two daughters, besides plundering the country. Boadicea took her revenge by slaughtering an entire legion; but an overwhelming number of reinforcements were sent to quell the revolt. In the end, the Britons were defeated, and Boadicea killed herself to avoid capture and disgrace.[1]

Cornelius Tacitus
Roman historian and rhetorician, ca. 56–120 A.D.

1. Tacitus, 337–41.

Boar

Sacrificial boar-gods common to both Scandinavian and Middle-Eastern traditions began with the Indian cult of **Vishnu**, who claimed to create the world by virtue of his self-sacrifice in boar shape. Vishnu said the blood of his boar incarnation had the creative power that only the Mother's blood formerly had: "Gods and creatures arise out of the sacrifice, for the sacrifice is their appointed food. Everything will always arise from the sacrifice; this whole universe is made of the sacrifice." Vishnu dared to copulate with the Earth Goddess while she was menstruating, and begot three boar-sons who were also sacrificed by "gods saying Om," the Word of creation.[1]

Vishnu the Boar represented an early attempt to re-assign to a male the holy creative blood of life, the Goddess's menstruum. As the phallic god who gave his life for humanity, he was worshipped in conjunction with the Goddess by Germanic Aryans who, Tacitus said, "worship the mother of the gods, and wear as a religious symbol the device of a wild boar."[2]

This Germanic boar-god became the doomsday-averting Savior and Lord of Death, in both human and porcine form, "born in the days of old . . . of the race of gods." He was identified with Heimdall, born of the Earth-and-Sea mother, fathered by boar blood. "He was made strong with the force of the earth, with the cold sea and the blood of the sacrificial boar."[3] That is, like most gods, in dying he begot himself again.

The boar-god was sacrificed especially at Yul (Yule), with an apple in his mouth, symbolizing his regenerated heart-soul, according to the Scandinavian belief that apples were resurrection charms.[4] Hence the traditional Yule pig roasted with an apple in its mouth. There was a mystical meaning behind the pork-eating ritual. "Valhalla's boar" was cooked in a cauldron, the regenerative womb-symbol, and the skalds said of it, "It's prime of pork, but few men know on what Valhalla's champions feed."[5] If one may hazard a guess, Valhalla's champions used to feed on human flesh, for which the boar was substituted. Swedish priests in boar masks were regarded as incarnations of Frey, and husbands of Freya, indicating an identification with the sacrificial god who once wedded the Mother and died as both a boar and a man.[6]

The Jews' taboo on pig's flesh was nothing so hygienic or rational as fear of trichinosis, as some modern apologists have tried to suggest, showing gross misunderstanding of the biblical mentality. Reinach said, "In the whole of the Bible there is not a single instance of an epidemic or a malady attributed to the eating of unclean meats. . . . To the Biblical writers, as to contemporary savages, illness is supernatural; it is an effect of the wrath of spirits. The pious Jew abstains from pork because his remote ancestors, five or six thousand years before our era, had the wild boar as their totem."[7]

Like their neighbors, the Jews worshipped sacrificial boar-gods:

Syrian Adonis, for one. Boars were offered to Astarte in Syria, and to her counterpart Demeter in Greece. Demeter's Eleusinian Mysteries mythologized the boar sacrifice as "pigs falling into a crevice in the earth" at the moment when Pluto, Lord of Death, seized his virgin bride Kore.[8] The custom of driving sacrificial pigs into pits, as in the rites of Demeter and Astarte, appeared in Christian Gospels as the miracle-tale of the Gadarene swine, whose sacrificial death impelled by "demons" was re-assigned to the intervention of Jesus (Mark 5:11–13).

Myths of dying gods like Tammuz, Attis, and Adonis featured the boar, or boarskin-clad priest, who sacrificed the god in swine form. Such gods were "gored in the groin" by the boar, an allegory of ritual castration.[9] As lovers of the Goddess, they were chosen from members of her priesthood. The sacrificer of Adonis was another of the Goddess's lovers, Ares, wearer of the boarskin. The sacrificer and castrater of Attis was his divine alter ego, a boar sent by Zeus, or by the king of Phrygia—these presumed simultaneously incarnate in the same body.[10] Like Christ, Attis was the dying Son later resurrected as the Father who decreed his death in the first place. Similarly, Vishnu the Boar decreed death for his boar-sons.[11] Some myths said Attis died in the same way as Adonis, being gored by a boar. Others said Attis himself was the boar, a totemic sign of his kingship.[12]

Malekula presents an original primitive view of the sacrificial animal as savior or surrogate for men. Mother Death guards the gates of the after-world. A man must pass these gates by distracting her attention with his sacrificial pig. While she devours the pig, he slips by her.[13] After sacrificing and eating on earth the savior-pig who becomes part of himself, the man says, "It is no longer I who live, but my sacrifice who lives in me."[14] Christians similarly ate their god in communion, and were taught to recite at the gate of heaven, "No more I, but Christ."

The old cults of the boar were not altogether forgotten. Medieval fairy tales abound in magic boars, often figuring as sacrificial animals. The first French book printed on the subject of witchcraft, de Spina's *Fortress of the Faith*, declared that French witches assembled at a certain sacred rock to worship the devil in the shape of a boar.[15]

1. O'Flaherty, 196–97. 2. Tacitus, 731. 3. Turville-Petre, 147–48.
4. Turville-Petre, 187. 5. Sturluson, 63. 6. Gelling & Davidson, 162.
7. Reinach, 19–20. 8. Graves, G.M. 1, 94. 9. Graves, G.M. 1, 72.
10. Graves, W.G., 198. 11. O'Flaherty, 196. 12. Campbell, P.M., 427.
13. Campbell, P.M., 447. 14. Campbell, M.I., 456. 15. Robbins, 27.

Bogey

The Bogey-man was a devil derived from Slavic *bog*, "god." English cognates were bugabow, bugaboo, bugbear, and boggle-bo, which used to signify a pagan image carried in procession to the games of May Day.[1] "Humbug" came from Norse *hum*, "night," plus *bog* or bogey, i.e., a night spirit.[2] The word "bug," from Welsh *bwg*, "spirit," was applied to insects because of the old belief that insects were souls in search of rebirth.[3] A *mantis* was the soul of a seer or wizard. A butterfly was Psyche, the Female Soul.

Other derivations of *bog* were Scottish *bogle*, Yorkshire *boggart*, English Pug, Pouke, and Puck; Icelandic Puki; the *Puk* of Friesland; the German Putz or Butz; Irish Pooka and Welsh Pwcca; Danish Spoge and Swedish Spoka with their English offshoot, "spook."[4] Old English *puca*, a fairy, was applied to the old gods of Beltain.[5] Thus Puck was the same as the witches' god, **Robin**.

1. Hazlitt, 80. 2. Leland, 161. 3. Spence, 96. 4. Keightley, 315–16.
5. Potter & Sargent, 295.

Bogomils

"God-lovers," Gnostic Christian heretics in the Balkans, 12th to 14th centuries A.D. Allied with the basically Manichean heresies of the Paulicians of Armenia and the Patarenes of Bosnia, the Bogomils arose in Bulgaria in revolt against the abuses of the Roman church, rejecting baptism, the Eucharist, the cross, miracles, church buildings, and the whole organization of orthodoxy. Like other Manicheans, they held that the God who created this world of matter was a demon.[1]

The Bogomils were highly puritanical but less sexist than the Roman church. They admitted women to religious offices on an equal basis with men. The Catholic writer Cosmas condemned as "deviltry" their custom of appointing women to hear confessions and give absolution to men.[2] Up to the late 14th century, Bogomilism was "the most powerful sectarian movement in the history of the Balkans," but Catholic crusades drove many members of the sect into the arms of Islam, and the movement was crushed. See **Bugger**.

1. *Encyc. Brit.*, "Bogomils." 2. Spinka, p. 66.

Bones

Many religions tabooed breaking the bones of a sacrificial animal, on the theory that the gods needed a complete skeleton to resurrect it anew.[1] On one occasion, the god Thor killed and resurrected two goats, but the thighbone of one had been damaged, so the new goat was lame.[2]

The same belief is evident in the Bible. Concerning the paschal lamb, God ordered: "Neither shall ye break a bone thereof" (Exodus 12:46); "They shall leave none of it unto the morning, nor break any bone of it" (Numbers 9:12); "He keepeth all his bones; not one of them is broken" (Psalms 34:20). To fulfill all these alleged prophecies, Jesus's bones were left intact to identify him with the Lamb: "That the scripture should be fulfilled, a bone of him shall not be broken" (John 19:36).

Several saints' legends also made use of regenerative bones. St. Germain resurrected a calf, on whose flesh he had just feasted, by laying the bones on the hide and praying over them.[3] A derivative medieval belief was that every body contains an incorruptible seed-bone, "out of which, as they say, as a plant out of the seed, our animal bodies shall in the resurrection of the dead spring up."[4]

1. *Larousse,* 307. 2. Silberer, 82. 3. de Voragine, 398. 4. Agrippa, 88.

Brahma

India's patriarchal god, whose priests tried to establish wholly male-dominated society and eliminate the Mother Goddess—who, nevertheless, remained the parent of Brahma as she was of the other gods. Though some of Brahma's scriptures tried to dissociate him from the Mother by calling him "the Birthless," yet the same scriptures incongruously referred to him as the Goddess's "Firstborn."[1]

The older *dharma* (holy law) said the worst of crimes was killing a woman or female child, because it meant killing unborn generations.[2] However, like most patriarchal systems, Brahmanism lifted the taboo on male aggression against females, and claimed that it was better to kill women than to insult Brahmans: "To revile and calumniate a worshipper of the Supreme Brahman is a sin ten million times worse than that of killing a woman."[3]

Like the medieval Christian church, Brahman priests made rules for rigid control of wives, and made their deity say any other kind of marriage was a sin that made the wife a whore and the children illegitimate, disqualified for religious observances.[4]

Brahman marriage reversed the old system of **matrilineal inheritance**, insisting that property must pass from father to son. A widow without male children was entitled to inherit only if she "lives under the control of the relations of her husband, and in their absence under the control of her father's relations"—that is, male relations—"then only is she entitled to inherit. The woman who is *even likely* to go astray is not entitled to inherit the husband's property."[5] In practice of course, any or all of these male groups could easily declare the widow unfit to inherit and divide the property among themselves.

Brahmanism was essentially paternal ancestor-worship, possibly the root of similar paternal ancestor-worship instituted in Israel by the legendary **Abraham,** whose name meant "Father Brahm." There was the same obsession with record-keeping. At every Brahman wedding, long lists of paternal ancestors were recited, like the biblical lists of "begats." Brahman sons were taught to recite: "My father is my highest Dharma. . . . My father is my Heaven. On my father being satisfied, the whole Universe is satisfied." Brahma also displayed the patriarchal god's usual insistence on exclusivity: "Those who are averse to My doctrine are unbelievers and sinners, as great as those who slay a Brahman."[6]

It is clear that Jewish patriarchy owed a debt to Brahman precedent. From the Far East came the legend of the Golden Age of righteousness, when men were free from sin, had great longevity, and grew to gigantic size.[7] Comparable were the long-lived biblical patriarchs of the antediluvian age when there were "giants in the earth" (Genesis 6:4). The story of Cain and Abel was Indo-Iranian. Vedic poets used to beg their god to accept their sacrifices, and reject those of other *arya* (men).[8]

The legend of **Jonah** was prefigured by the Indian tale of Candragomin, who endangered the ship he sailed on because a rival magician caused a storm and took the form of a sea beast to swallow him.[9]

Talmudic tradition adopted the typical Oriental belief in transmigration of souls; Adam's soul passed by transmigration into David, than into the Messiah.[10] Brahmanic revelation seemed to be part of the Messianic promise also. The Katha Upanishad said Brahma is realized in one's own soul dimly, as if seen in a mirror; but in the heaven of Brahma he is realized clearly, "as one distinguishes light from darkness."[11] The New Testament repeats the same message copied almost word for word: "For now we see through a glass (i.e., mirror) darkly, but then face to face" (1 Corinthians 13:12). The Brahman doctrine that a thousand years is one Day of Brahma is repeated in Psalms 90:4, and again in the *First Book of Adam and Eve,* where God explains that "five days and a half" for him means 5,500 years for men.[12]

Brahma is no longer popular in his native land. He is described as a "theologian's god, whose worship never struck vital roots in the popular folk soil." He was used mainly to support the caste system. "Today Brahma is so relatively unimportant that only one or two temples in all India are reserved for his exclusive worship."[13]

1. *Upanishads,* 22. 2. O'Flaherty, 293. 3. *Mahanirvanatantra,* 45. 4. Ibid., 45, 58. 5. Ibid., 283. 6. Ibid., 215, 236, 16, 242. 7. Ibid., xlvii. 8. Dumézil, 425. 9. Tatz & Kent, 146. 10. Waddell, 226. 11. *Upanishads,* 23. 12. *Forgotten Books,* 6. 13. Ross, 57.

Brigit, Saint

Triple Goddess of the great Celtic empire of Brigantia, which included parts of Spain, France, and the British Isles. Before she was a saint, she was a typical feminine trinity. Brigit ruled; her two sisters governed the arts of healing and smithcraft. Cormac's Glossary called her "Brigit the female sage. . . . Brigit the goddess, whom poets adored, because her protecting care over them was very great and very famous."[1]

Cormac's Glossary Compendium of old Irish terms and legends, attributed to Archbishop Cormac Mac Cullenan (d. 908 A.D.), king of Munster. However, some scholars believe the Glossary was compiled later than his lifetime.

Dr. MacCulloch said Brigit "originated in a period when the Celts worshipped goddesses rather than gods, and when knowledge—leechcraft, agriculture, inspiration—were [sic] women's rather than men's. She had a female priesthood and men were perhaps excluded from her cult, as the tabooed shrine at Kildare suggests."[2] Brigit's priestesses at Kildare kept an ever-burning sacred fire like that of the temple of Vesta in Rome. They called the three *personae* of Brigit the "Three Blessed Ladies of Britain" or the "Three Mothers," and always identified them with the moon.[3]

J. A. MacCulloch Scottish scholar, author of *The Religion of the Ancient Celts,* 1911.

The number of Brigit's priestesses at Kildare was 19, representing the 19-year cycle of the Celtic "Great Year." Greeks said the sun god of the north, whom they called Hyperborean Apollo, visited the northern "temple of the moon goddess" once every 19 years, a mythic expression of the coincidence of solar and lunar calendars.[4] In reality the period of coincidence was 18.61 years, which meant the smallest regular unit to give a "mating" of sun and moon was 56 years, two cycles of 19 and one of 18. This astronomical data was well known to the builders of Stonehenge, who marked the span of Great Years with posts around their circle.[5]

Brigit was older than Celtic Ireland, having come with Gaelic Celts from their original home in Galatia. One of her earliest shrines was Brigeto in Illyricum.[6] Long before the Christian era, the Goddess of the Brigantes was said to be the same as Juno Regina, Queen of Heaven, and Tanit, the Dea Celestis (Heavenly Goddess).[7]

Illyricum (or Illyria) Ancient name for the northwestern part of the Balkan peninsula, sometimes including parts of modern Serbia, Bulgaria, Austria, and the Tyrol.

Finding the cult of Brigit impossible to eradicate, the Catholic church rather unwisely canonized her as a saint, calling her Bridget or Bride. Hagiographers declared she was a nun who founded a convent at Kildare. But the convent was noted for its heathenish miracles and evidences of fertility magic. Cows never went dry; flowers and shamrocks sprang up in Brigit's footprints; eternal spring reigned in her bower. Irish writers refused to reduce their Goddess to mere sainthood, and insisted that she was Queen of Heaven, which meant identifying her with Mary. She was called "Mother of my Sovereign, Mary of the Goidels, Queen of the South, Prophetess of Christ, Mother of Jesus."[8]

An Irish charm against the evil eye suggested collusion between the pagan and Christian heavenly-mother figures; it was "the Spell the great white Mary sent to Bride the lovely fair."[9] She was also the mystic mother-bride of St. **Patrick,** supposed to have died as one of her sacrificial victims, and entered the underworld via her sacred grove at Derry Down. An old distich said, "On the hill of Down, buried in one tomb, were Bridget and Patricius."[10] Since Patrick's name meant "father," and he was as apocryphal as other Irish saints, he may have been a new name for Brigit's old consort the Dagda or "father."

Three churches of "St. Brigit" occupied her Triple-Goddess territory of Hy Many, formerly Emania or Emain Macha, country of the Moon. Baptismal fees of those churches belonged to the O'Kelly tribes, descended from the Goddess's *kelles* or sacred harlots. Her original female trinity was semi-Christianized as a "Wonder-working Triad" consisting of Brigit, Patrick, and Columba: the Mother, the Father, and the Holy Dove. St. Brigit's feast day was the first of February, the first day of spring according to the pagan calendar. It was called Oimelc, Imolg, or Imbulc, the day of union between God and Goddess.[11]

The same day was celebrated in Rome as the Lupercalia, sacred to Venus and to women generally. With unconscious irony, the church transformed it into the Feast of the Purification of the Virgin, also called Candlemas, which kept much of its pagan symbolism and was regarded as a major festival of witches.[12]

Like other versions of the Celtic Goddess, Brigit was a teacher of the martial arts, and a patron of warfare or *briga.* Her soldiers were *brigands,* or as Christians called them, outlaws.[13] Robin Hood's merry men were outlaws of the same kind; so were Kali's Thugs and the "Assassins" who worshipped the Arabian Moon-goddess.

Brigit was canonized more than once. Besides the Irish Brigit there was a St. Bridget of Sweden, foundress and supreme ruler of a double monastery of both sexes, the Order of Brigantines. (See **Convent**.) A branch of the ancient "colleges" of Brigit was a Brigantine House of Sion established in 1420 on the bank of the Thames, where it flourished until 1589 as a center of education for ladies of noble birth.[14]

1. Joyce 1, 260–61. 2. Campbell, P.M., 432. 3. Briffault 3, 70. 4. Hitching, 213. 5. Hawkins, 140. 6. J.H. Smith, D.C.P., 141. 7. Lindsay, O.A., 328. 8. Graves, W.G., 144. 9. Gifford, 60. 10. Brewster, 140. 11. Joyce 1, 379, 507; 2, 388. 12. de Lys, 127. 13. Tuchman, 252. 14. Brewster, 339.

Brimstone

Old name for sulfur, derived from Brimo, a title of Athene, Hecate, and Demeter.[1] It meant "raging one," the Goddess's Destroyer aspect.[2] The alchemical symbol for sulfur was the same as the symbol of Athene, a triangle surmounting a cross: female genital sign over the male, like the symbol of Venus.[3]

Even the raging Brimo appeared as the Virgin Mother, in feasts of purification at Eleusis, where the advent of the Divine Child was announced with a cry, "Holy Brimo has borne the Holy Child Brimus."[4]

Because of her magical ability to cleanse and purify, Brimo's stone was supposed to be proof against disease. Burning sulfur was used even in medieval times to fumigate sickrooms and avert the plague. The use of brimstone as an agent of purification accounts for its appearance in the cauldron of Purgatory with its "fire and brimstone" to burn away sins.

Alchemists tried to "marry Hermes and Athene" by combining mercury with brimstone, which they thought might create gold. They never succeeded.

1. Knight, S.L., 102. 2. Graves, G.M. 2, 384. 3. Koch, 54, 66. 4. Wilkins, 67.

Brisingamen

The Necklace of Freya; in Norse myth, the magic rainbow bridge to paradise. In Greece, Iran, Mesopotamia, and the Far East, prominent features of the after-world were often called "ornaments" of the Goddess, whose physical being was all existence: underworld, earth, and heaven. Ishtar too wore the rainbow necklace, which the Persians converted into the razor-edged bridge to the Mount of Paradise. See **Diakosmos; Ishtar; Rainbow**. Odin stole Freya's necklace and hung it on his own image; but she retrieved it.

Britomartis

"Sweet Virgin," a title of Rhea, the Great Goddess of Bronze Age Crete and the Aegean islands.[1] The same name was given to an early ruler of Gaul, who was probably a queen embodying the Goddess's spirit.[2] Olympian mythology said the mother of Britomartis was the Cretan virgin Carme, another form of Car, Car-Dia, Carmenta, Carna, etc. They were really different names for the same deity. The titles by which she was addressed in prayers and hymns were later misunderstood as the names of different deities, which is why the Goddess became "goddesses" in the west, or the Thousand-Named One in the east.

1. *Larousse*, 86. 2. Briffault 3, 400.

Broceliande

The fairy wood in Brittany where Nimue, or Vivien, or Morgan enchanted Merlin into his magic sleep within a crystal cave—or, some said, within the trunk of a venerable oak tree. This was one of the *nimidae* or moon-groves still used for worship of woodland deities up to the time of the Renaissance.[1] See **Grove, Sacred**.

1. Joyce 1, 359–60.

Bron

Companion of Joseph of Arimathea, keeper of the Christianized version of the Holy Grail. Bron was really the Celtic god Bran, keeper of the Cauldron of Regeneration; a popular deity with numerous shrines, patron of "healing and resurrection."[1]

1. Graves, W.G., 39.

Broomstick

Broomsticks were long associated with witches because they figured in pagan rituals of marriage and birth, the Mysteries of Women. In Rome the broom was a symbol of Hecate's priestess-midwife, who swept the threshold of a house after each birth to remove evil spirits that might harm the child.[1]

As Hecate was also the Triple Goddess presiding over marriage, her broomstick signified sexual union. Old wedding customs included jumping over a broomstick, possibly to represent impregnation. Gypsy weddings always included the same ritual, though gypsies now say they don't know what it means.[2] Oddly enough, the same broom-jumping ritual marked the churchless weddings of black slaves in nineteenth-century America.

Medieval peasant weddings in Europe were also churchless, as a rule, coming under the jurisdiction of common law rather than canon law, and using the rites of the old religions rather than the new. The broom was so closely identified with non-ecclesiastical marriages that by Renaissance times, when the church began to take over the nuptial rites, unions "by the broom" were declared illegitimate. English rustics still say "if a girl strides over a broom-handle, she will be a mother before she is a wife." A girl who gives birth to a bastard child is said to have "jumped over the besom."[3]

As a horse for witches to ride, the broomstick apparently signified Tantric-type sexual unions which were primary attractions of the female-oriented witch cults. *Planta genet,* the broom plant, was sacred to witches. This may explain why the ruling family of Anjou in the 12th century was named Plantagenet. Henry II, first Plantagenet king of England, inherited his throne by matrilineal succession through his mother Matilda, or Maud—names commonly associated with witchcraft—the countess of Anjou. *Genet* also meant a horse or steed, the "royal horse" of paganism. This meaning is preserved in the word *jennet,* a small horse or the female donkey, and in the names frequently taken by witches: Jenet, Janet, Jeannette, Jean, or Joan.

Such names suggested a witch-child born of a sacred marriage with a phallic god represented by the broom. A Janet or Jenny was a Daughter of the Horse, and old gods like Volos, Völsi, Waelsi, or Odin were called "Horse's Penis."[4] Riding the broomstick seems to have denoted the kind of sexual position viewed as a perversion by the church, woman above, man below acting as her "horse." This sexual implication is confirmed by the old witch-rhyme, "Ride a cock-horse to Banbury Cross (i.e., crossroads), to see a fine lady on a white horse." The fine lady was Godiva, "the Goddess." Her white cock-horse signifed her consort.[5]

Children rode the cock-horse as a broomstick with a horse's head, copied from Sufi mystics who entered Spain in the early Middle Ages. Besides their organization in groups of thirteen, like covens, and their worship of the Rabba or "Lord," later transformed into the witches' god Robin, Sufi sages rode horse-headed canes called *zamalzain,* "gala limping horse." The dervish's stick-horse stood for the Pegasus-like fairy steed that carried him to heaven and back.[6] Such customs became prevalent among the Basques, who were frequently accused *en masse* of witchcraft.

At times a witch's broomstick seems to have been nothing more than a dildo, anointed with the famous "**flying ointment**" and used for genital stimulation.[7] French witches "flew" this way: "With an ointment which the Devil had delivered to them they anointed a wooden rod which was but small, and their palms and their whole hands likewise; and so, putting this small rod between their legs, straightway they flew there where they wished to be . . . and the Devil guided them."[8] Certainly churchmen were prone to describe any kind of masturbation as guided by the devil—women's masturbation most particularly so, for nothing was more abhorrent to the patriarchal mind than the thought that women could experience sexual pleasure without men.

Witches' ointments often incorporated such drugs as aconite, readily absorbable in an oil-based liniment through skin or mucus membrane, producing symptoms like giddiness, confusion, lethargy, tingling sensations followed by numbness, and quite possibly the illusion of flying. Thus Oldham wrote:

So witches some enchanted wand bestride,
And think they through the airy regions ride.[9]

Because of their ancient association with pagan midwives and their Christian counterparts the witches, broomsticks took on an accretion of similar superstitions. Witches' familiar spirits were said to be unable to cross running water; hence, it became "bad luck" to move a broom across running water. It was also "bad luck" to burn a broom, since it was certainly bad luck for the witch.[10]

1. Dumézil, 616. 2. Trigg, 86–87. 3. Spence, 148. 4. Turville-Petre, 201. 5. Hazlitt, 25. 6. Shah, 210, 223. 7. Ewen, 78. 8. de Givry, 70. 9. Hazlitt, 655. 10. de Lys, 467.

Brother

The Greek word for brother was *adelphos,* "one from the same womb," derived from the matrilineal family when only maternal parenthood was recognized. English "brother" stemmed from Sanskrit *bhratr,* "support." In pre-Vedic India it was the duty of a brother, not a husband, to help support a woman and her children. Husbands came and went, but the matrilineal clan remained stable. As an old proverb of Arab women said: "A husband can be found, a son can be born, but a brother cannot be replaced."[1]

A preference for brothers over husbands may be found in many pre-patriarchal cultures. Pagan Slavic women considered "by my brother" their most binding oath. In pre-Christian Norway, rune stones on women's graves were raised by their brothers, not their husbands.[2] Ancient systems of clan loyalty were similar to that of the Nairs, of whom it was said that no man knew his father, but "every man looks upon his sister's children as his heirs. A man's mother manages his family; and after her death his eldest sister assumes the direction." Names and property were bequeathed in the female line.[3]

The uterine-sibling bond was so much stronger than the marriage bond in ancient societies that the ultimate endearment of lovers or spouses was to call each other "brother" and "sister."[4] King Solomon called his bride "my sister, my spouse" (Song of Solomon 4:10) with "sister" in the place of honor. An Egyptian wife affectionately addressed her husband as "brother, husband, friend," in that order.[5]

Weddings sometimes meant making bride and groom pseudo-siblings in some magical way. Polynesian couples were not considered truly married until their two mothers mingled their blood, signifying that the married pair were born of a double, or merged, womb.[6] Often, the bride and groom mingled their own blood; this was the common rite of gypsy weddings.[7]

Brother-sister incest was customary in ancient ruling families, when it was felt that a king and queen should be offspring of the same mother, so the true line of succession would not be weakened. Egyptian pharaohs married their sisters as a matter of course because their thrones were inherited through the female line.[8] One pharaoh with only one son and one daughter suggested to his wife that the children might marry outside the family. The queen angrily rejected the idea: "Dost thou wrangle with me? Even if I have no children after those two children, is it not the law to marry them one to the other?"[9]

Brother-sister incest was everywhere the practice of the elder gods and goddesses, many of whom were twins who copulated even in their mother's womb. Examples are Isis and Osiris, Artemis and Apollo, Fauna and Faunus, Diana and Dianus, Zeus and Hera, Yama and Yami, Freya and Frey. According to Norse skalds, brother-sister incest was the accepted custom of the Vanir or elder deities.[10]

Mythological evidence tends to destroy the modern conception of Stone Age man protecting "his" cave with "his" mate and "their" children. If the home was a cave or anything else, it was probably selected, furnished, and owned by the female. If there was a male protecting it, he was more likely to have been a sibling than a mate. In fact there were no monogamous families but only family groups, centering on the women and children with impregnating males a loose, changeable periphery.

1. Briffault 1, 405, 498, 505. 2. Oxenstierna, 212. 3. Hartley, 152. 4. Albright, 128. 5. Hartley, 195. 6. Briffault 1, 559. 7. Trigg, 88. 8. Hooke, S.P., 256. 9. Maspero, 121. 10. Turville-Petre, 172.

---

var. Buanann

Buana

"Good Mother," the Irish Goddess as a cow, recalling Hathor or Cow-Eyed **Hera** who was also the Irish Goddess Eriu (Eire).[1] Like all other versions of the milk-giving Mother she represented wealth or plenty. Thus, her name Ana came to be synonymous with abundance.[2]

1. Graves, W.G., 414. 2. Joyce 1, 261.

Buddhism

Established 500 years before Christianity and widely publicized throughout the Middle East, Buddhism exerted more influence on early Christianity than church fathers liked to admit, since they viewed Oriental religions in general as devil worship.

Legends and sayings derived from Buddhism appear in the Gospels, disguised as "typically Christian" precepts, including the **Golden Rule**. The Amogha school of Buddhism practiced a severe morality, a life of poverty and chastity in retirement from secular concerns, and the expectation of a Savior coming to earth in the near future.[1] Buddhist sages provided prototypes of Christian miracles. They were said to walk on water, to speak in tongues, and to ascend to heaven in the flesh.[2] Jains regarded the true Buddhist "hero" (*vira*) as "not he who is of great physical strength and prowess, the great eater and drinker, or man of powerful sexual energy, but he who has controlled his senses, is a truth-seeker, ever engaged in worship, and who has sacrificed lust and all other passions."[3]

Buddha is more properly *the* Buddha, since Buddha was not a name but a title, the "Enlightened or Blessed One," comparable to *Christos,* "the Anointed One." Buddha had many other names because he had already lived through many incarnations on earth. Even the Buddha supposed to have appeared in the 5th century B.C. had several names: Gautama, Sakyamuni, Siddhartha—the last, again, not a name but a title, "Rich in Yogic Power." Buddha was miraculously begotten by the Lord of Hosts and born of the Virgin Maya, the same Great Goddess worshipped throughout Asia and having the alternative Near-Eastern names of Maia, Marah, Mari, or Maria.[4]

Many Buddhas who had already come and gone were bodhisattvas or saints, sometimes simply known as Buddhas. Any sage might become a bodhisattva through devotion to the holy life. But one true Buddha remained to come again to earth. He was Maitreya, the Master, or the Future Buddha, similar to the being known as Kalki, the last avatar of the god Vishnu who would appear with the approach of doomsday. The final coming of the Savior would signal the end of the present world. He would judge the righteous, and annihilate the wicked, and make everything ready for the ultimate creation of a new heaven and a new earth.[5]

These were basic ideas of Christianity as well as Buddhism: simple, easy to understand, dramatic, and appropriately aligned with archetypal hopes and fears. The more subtle teachings of Buddhism, like those of Christianity, apparently developed out of group thinking of subsequent sectaries, especially the more ascetic sort. Yet—again, as in Christianity—the ascetics were unable to blot out the rich, colorful sensuality of "pagan" Hinduism. Although they claimed Buddha said the true sage must never see or speak to a woman, must avoid feminine creatures like the plague, yet within a few centuries the worship of the Goddess reasserted itself and all the bodhisattvas were provided with Shaktis who would welcome them to eternal sexual bliss in heaven. "Tantric" Buddhism re-assimilated the feminine principle. Until the advent of Islam, the original Buddhist asceticism was largely forgotten except for a few eremitic groups. A well-known aphorism said: *Buddhatvam yosidyonisamsritam,* "Buddhahood resides in the vulva (yoni)."[6]

Buddhist legends reveal the constant tension between ascetic and sensual elements. It was said Buddha wanted his brother Nanda to become a monk, but Nanda was too much in love with his beautiful mistress. So Buddha played a trick on him. He took Nanda to heaven and showed him the celestial nymphs, who were so desirable that Nanda instantly forgot the mortal woman he had loved. Buddha then told him these nymphs could be won only by a life of rigorous self-denial and meditation. Nanda agreed to join the monkish order. The ascetic life soon purged him of all desires, and he became as celibate as Buddha had wished—but only because of his overwhelming lust for a transcendent sexual experience![7]

Like their western counterparts in later centuries, Buddhist monks self-consciously threatened the Goddess with destruction, even though her virgin form had given birth to their Savior. A Buddhist hymn said, "This time I shall devour thee utterly, Mother Kali; for I was born under an evil star—and one so born becomes, they say, the eater of his mother."[8]

Stories of the Buddha and his many incarnations circulated incessantly throughout the ancient world, especially since Buddhist monks traveled to Egypt, Greece, and Asia Minor four centuries before Christ, to spread their doctrines.[9] Ascetics like the Essenes were certainly influenced by them. Christians continued to hear tales of Buddhist origin, and to relate them rather naively to their own beliefs. Buddha himself entered the Christian canon as a saint—St. Josaphat, a corruption of Bodhisat—when John of Damascus wrote down his life story in the 8th century A.D.[10] Buddha the Christian saint was supplied with a companion called Barlaam, who converted the Indian prince to a Christian asceticism despite his royal father's efforts to thwart this purpose.[11]

Many scholars have pointed out that the basic tenets of Christianity were basic tenets of Buddhism first; but it is also true that the ceremonies and trappings of both religions were more similar than either has wanted to acknowledge.

> *Buddhism has much in common with Roman Catholic Christianity, having its purgatory, its Goddess of Mercy, and its elaborate machinery for delivering the dead from pain and misery through the good offices of the priests. Among other similarities may be mentioned celibacy, fasting, use of candles and flowers on the altar, incense, holy water, rosaries, priestly garments, worship of relics, canonization of saints, use of a dead language for the liturgy and ceremonials generally. The trinity of Buddhas, past, present, and future, is compared by some to the Father, Son, and Holy Ghost. The immaculate mother of Shakyamuni, whose name Maya is strikingly similar to that of Mary, the mother of Jesus, is*

also to be noticed, while Buddha's temptation on Vulture Peak by Mara the Evil One, may also be contrasted with the similar temptation of Our Lord. . . . The worship of ancestors is in some measure akin to the saying of masses for the dead, and at one time the Jesuits considered it a harmless observance and tolerated it in their converts. Finally the Dalai Lama is a spiritual sovereign closely resembling the Pope.[12]

1. Avalon, 211. 2. Tatz & Kent,. 167, 200; Waddell, 159. 3. *Mahanirvanatantra,* cxii. 4. *Larousse,* 348. 5. *Larousse,* 374. 6. Campbell, Or. M., 302, 352. 7. Rawson, E.A., 184. 8. Wilson, 257. 9. Campbell, C.M., 146. 10. Muller, 313. 11. Attwater, 58. 12. Williams, 355.

Bugger

From "Bulgar," French *Bougre.* The modern meaning stemmed from the Roman church's charge that medieval Bulgarians practiced sexual perversions in their churches. Bulgarian Paulicians were anathematized for disobeying the Roman pope, setting up their own churches independent of Rome, and admitting women to clerical office on an equal basis with men.[1]

Bosnian Patarenes were also called buggers, since they modeled their national church on that of Bulgaria. About 1200 A.D. the papacy launched "a cruel war against the Bosnian Patarenes, which lasted two and a half centuries, and finally culminated in the acceptance, on their part, of the Mohammedan faith and in becoming Turks, rather than submit to the Roman See."[2]

Religious wars led the Balkans into social chaos. Heretics were hunted down like animals, and tortured. Lands belonging to the heretic magnates (nobles) were seized and handed over to their Catholic enemies. The heretics for their part continued to regard themselves as the only true Christian nations. Under the anti-Roman Code of Stephen, Catholic priests who tried to convert Balkan Christians back to "the Latin faith" were declared criminals.[3] Quarrels and conflicts persisted up to the present century.

1. Knight, D.W.P., 176. 2. Spinka, 147. 3. Spinka, 167–68.

Bull

The biblical title translated "God" is *El,* originally the title of the Phoenician bull-god called Father of Men. As the "supreme god of the Semitic pantheon, El was worshipped throughout Syria alongside the local gods, or Ba'als, one of his titles, indeed, being 'the Bull.' "[1] Like Zeus the Bull, consort of Hera-Europa-Io the white Moon-Cow, El married **Asherah**, the Semitic sacred Cow. He was identified with Elias or Helios, the sun. He was still the Semitic Father of Men in the time of Jesus, who cried to him from the cross, calling him Father (Mark 15:34).

Nearly every god of the ancient world was incarnate sooner or later in a bull. The Cretan moon-king called Minos inhabited a succession of Minotaurs (moon-bulls), who were sacrificed as the king's surrogates.

Yama, the Hindu Lord of Death, wore a bull's head and became the underworld judge, like Minos.[2] Shiva was incarnate in the white bull Nandi.[3] The real reason King Nebuchadnezzar "ate grass" probably was that his soul temporarily entered into the body of the divine sacrificial bull (Daniel 4:33). Court prophets of the kings of Israel put on bull masks to represent the king while casting spells for his victory over his enemies (1 Kings 22:11).[4]

Bull worship was a large part of Mithraism. The bull's blood was credited with power to produce all creatures on earth without the aid of the cow, though her power was implicit in that the bull's blood was taken up and magically treated by the Moon. The bull was consecrated to Anahita, a Persian name of the Moon-goddess whom the Greeks called Artemis Tauropolos, "Bull-Slayer," of whom the bull-slaying savior **Mithra** was a late, masculinized form.[5] Like most patriarchal symbols, those of the Mithraic cult were copied from myths of the Asian Goddess. A statue of Kali in the Ellora caves shows her in the pose typical of Mithra, holding up the nose of the sacrificial bull and preparing to slaughter it.[6]

The bull was killed for a baptism of blood at the Roman Taurobolium in honor of Attis, Cybele, or Mithra. "A trench was dug over which was erected a platform of planks with perforations and gaps. Upon the platform the sacrificial bull was slaughtered, whose blood dripped through upon the initiate in the trench . . . he turned round and held up his neck that the blood might trickle upon his lips, ears, eyes, and nostrils; he moistened his tongue with the blood, which he than drank as a sacramental act. Greeted by the spectators, he came forth from this bloody baptism believing that he was purified from his sins and 'born again for eternity.' "[7] The participant in the Taurobolium acted out literally what Christians called washing in the blood of the lamb.

Egypt's savior Osiris was worshipped in bull form as Apis-Osiris, the Moon-bull of Egypt, annually slain in atonement for the sins of the realm.[8] In the ceremony of his rebirth, he appeared as the Golden Calf, Horus, born of Isis whose image was a golden cow. The same Golden Calf was adored by the Israelites under Aaron (Exodus 32:4).

The Orphic god Dionysus also took the form of a bull; one of his earlier incarnations was the Cretan bull-god Zagreus, "the Goodly Bull," a son and reincarnation of Zeus, and another version of the Minotaur. The god was a bull on earth, and a serpent in his subterranean, regenerating phase. The Orphic formula ran: "The bull is the father of the serpent, and the serpent is the father of the bull."[9] Dionysus was reincarnated over and over, and there were some who identified him with the Persian **Messiah**. In the Book of Enoch, the Messiah is represented as a white bull.[10]

Athenian legends of the Moerae or Fates compared all men to the sacrificial bull sentenced to death at the hands of Fate sooner or later. Medieval superstition called the Fate-goddess Mora, a nocturnal spirit who roams the world seizing men and crushing them until they "roar like bulls." She was also Christianized as St. Maura, on whose sacred day women were forbidden to sew, lest they "cut the thread of life" after the manner of the Moerae.[11]

In medieval England, Twelfth Night games featured remnants of bull worship. A large cake with a hole in the center was thrown over the bull's horn, to form a lingam-yoni. The bull was then tickled, "to make him toss his head." If he threw the cake behind him, it belonged to the mistress; if in front, it belonged to the bailiff.[12] This ceremony probably derived from an ancient custom of divination. Like all sacrificial victims already dedicated to the supernatural realm, the bull was believed to have prophetic powers.

1. *Larousse*, 74. 2. Campbell, M.I., 409. 3. Campbell, Or.M., 90. 4. Hooke, S.P., 160. 5. Cumont, M.M., 20, 137. 6. Ross, 40. 7. Angus, 94–95. 8. Budge, G.E. 2, 349. 9. Legge, 39. 10. Hooke, S.P., 138. 11. Lawson, 175. 12. Hazlitt, 603.

Buto

Greek name for the Egyptian serpent-goddess Per-Uatchet, also called Uraeus, Anqet, Iusaset, Mehen the Enveloper, etc.[1] With Nekhbet the vulture-goddess, she co-ruled the Two Lands as the Nebti, the Two Mistresses.[2] Like the Two Ladies of the ancient Middle East, they were twin spirits of birth and death. See **Serpent**.

1. Norman, 48; Budge, G.E. 2, 57. 2. *Larousse*, 29.

Byblos

Oldest, most famous seat of the Semitic Great Goddess, variously known as Mari, Astarte, Asherah, Ashtoreth, Ishtar, Isis, or Hathor. "Bibles" were named after her city because the earliest libraries were attached to her temple. (See **Bible**.) Kings of Byblos received their mandate from the Goddess before they could rule. King Yehawmilk for instance said she placed him and his predecessors on the throne. When invoked as Mistress, "she heard my voice and treated me kindly." The king begged her to bless him and prolong his years in Byblos.

Recently it has been found that earlier archeological scholars misread the words "Lady of Byblos" in Aramaic texts referring to the Goddess, and translated these words "Lord of Byblos" instead.[1] In reality there was never any god in Byblos whose power equalled that of the many-named Lady.

1. Pritchard, A.N.E. 1, 215, 221.

Byelobog

Slavic "White God," a heavenly deity opposed to the Black God, Chernobog. Both were variants of the ancient Persian adversaries in heaven and the underworld, who would engage in the final battle between forces of good and evil, at the end of the world. See **Doomsday**.

C

Caryatids. Carved pillars from the Acropolis. Greek, 2nd century B.C.

St. Catherine, by Lorenzetti. Sienese, about 1335 A.D.

Bronze cat with one earring. Late Dynastic Egypt (ca. 2000 B.C.).

Cabala

var. Kabbalah

Medieval Jewish mystical system obviously influenced by Tantrism and Sufism, like the Christian courtly-love movement of the same period. The Cabala's basic premise was that all the world's ills stemmed from God's loss of contact with his female counterpart, the Shekina, a Hebraic version of Shakti. God is fragmented, and only the Shekina has power to "put God back together."[1] Universal harmony must be restored by making God and his Goddess once more "one."[2]

Sexual union of mortals was thought to create its like on the plane of the divine. Therefore sexual intercourse was a sacramental act helpful to God and the Shekina. "The efflorescence of such beliefs into orgiastic rites suggests itself too readily not to be attempted, and indeed, in the further development of Kabbalistic doctrine, such attempts were made."[3] Generally, however, the cabalist confined his erotic experiments to his legal wife. The first step in his ascent of the Sephiroth or Tree of Knowledge was the female sexual power, Shekina-Malkuth, Queen and Bride, represented by the moon and the spouse.[4] Further steps made use of elaborate systems of numerology, magic, and scriptural allegory, yielding successive revelations of the divine nature.

The major cabalistic work was the *Sefer ha-Zohar,* "Book of Splendor," composed in the late 13th century by Moses de León of Guadalajara, who claimed its real author was the legendary 2nd–century mystic Simeon ben Yohai. He pretended to have the ancient original of the book in his possession, but it was never produced. Scholars have concluded that it never existed, and de León wrote the *Sefer ha-Zohar* himself.[5]

Giovanni Pico della Mirandola (1463–1494). Italian nobleman, philosopher and scholar, declared a heretic for his attempts to unite Christian theology with Cabalistic doctrine.

Despite its Jewish orientation, the Cabala exerted a strong appeal for contemporary Christian mystics. It has been much in the favor of occultists ever since. Pico della Mirandola even professed to find in the Cabala what the Jews themselves denied: the incarnation of full godhood in Jesus. He wrote: "No science offers greater assurance of Christ's divinity than magic and the Cabala."[6] See **Hexagram; Shekina.**

1. Lederer, 186. 2. *Encyc. Brit.,* "Cabala." 3. Lederer, 188. 4. Cavendish, T., 52, 74. 5. *Encyc. Brit.,* "Cabala." 6. Shumaker, 16.

Cabiria

Title of Demeter as the Goddess of the Cabirian Mysteries in Phrygia, Samothrace, and other areas, second only to the Eleusinian Mysteries in importance. Her consort was the Young God, variously known as Dionysus, Ganymede, or Cabirius. In Thebes the Great Goddess was called Demeter Cabiria, sometimes a trinity of "three Cabirian nymphs." Her sexual union with the god was represented by the same symbol as in India and Egypt: water poured from a male vessel into a female one.[1] (See **Jar-bearer**.) Because of its ancient erotic connotations, Cabiria became a common witch-name in medieval times.

1. Neumann, G. M., 324–25.

Caduceus

Some Gnostic Christians worshipped the **serpent** hung on a cross, rod, or Tree of Life, calling it Christ the Savior, also a title of Hermes the Wise Serpent represented by his own holy caduceus, the scepter of two serpents. This was one of the oldest and most revered holy symbols. "The usual mythological association of the serpent is not, as in the Bible, with corruption, but with physical and spiritual health, as in the Greek caduceus." To Sumerians it was an emblem of life, appearing on art works like the Libation Cup of Gudea, ca. 2000 B.C. In pre-Hellenic Greece the caduceus was displayed on healing temples like those of Asclepius, Hygeia, and Panacea, which is why it is still an international symbol of the medical profession. The caduceus is found also in Aztec sacred art, enthroned like a serpent-deity on an altar. North American Indians knew it too. A Navaho medicine man said his people's sacred cave once featured "a stone carving of two snakes intertwined, the heads facing east and west."[1]

Hindu symbolism equated the caduceus with the central spirit of the human body, the spinal column, with two mystic serpents twined around it like the genetic double helix: *ida-nadi* to the left, *pingala-nadi* to the right.[2]

Moses's brazen serpent on a pole, the mere sight of which cured the Israelites, was probably a prophylactic caduceus (Numbers 21:9). It was named Nehushtan, and worshipped in the tabernacle up to the reign of Hezekiah (2 Kings 18:4). See **Hermes.**

1. Campbell, M. I., 282–84, 286–88, 294–95. 2. *Bardo Thodol,* 215.

Caillech

Old Celtic name for Kali-the-Crone, the Great Goddess in her Destroyer aspect. Like Kali, the Caillech was a black Mother who founded many races of people and outlived many husbands. She was also a creatress. She made the world, building mountain ranges of stones that dropped from her apron.[1]

Scotland was once called Caledonia: the land given by Kali, or

Cale, or the Caillech. "Scotland" came from Scotia, the same Goddess, known to Romans as a "dark Aphrodite"; to Celts as Scatha or Scyth; and to Scandinavians as **Skadi.**[2]

Like the Hindus' destroying Kalika, the Caillech was known as a spirit of disease. One manifestation of her was a famous idol of carved and painted wood, kept by an old family in County Cork, and described as the Goddess of Smallpox. As diseased persons in India sacrificed to the appropriate incarnation of the Kalika, so in Ireland those afflicted by smallpox sacrificed sheep to this image.[3] It can hardly be doubted that Kalika and Caillech were the same word.

According to various interpretations, *caillech* meant either an old woman, or a hag, or a nun, or a "veiled one."[4] This last apparently referred to the Goddess's most mysterious manifestation as the future, Fate, and Death—ever veiled from the sight of men, since no man could know the manner of his own death.

In medieval legend the Caillech became the Black Queen who ruled a western paradise in the Indies, where men were used in Amazonian fashion for breeding purposes only, then slain. Spaniards called her Califia, whose territory was rich in gold, silver, and gems. Spanish explorers later gave her name to their newly discovered paradise on the Pacific shore of North America, which is how the state of California came to be named after Kali.

In the present century, Irish and Scottish descendants of the Celtic "creatress" still use the word *caillech* as a synonym for "old woman."[5]

1. Rees, 41. 2. Graves, W. G., 131. 3. Squire, 413. 4. Joyce 1, 316.
5. Frazer, G. B., 467.

Cain

"Smith," Mother Eve's firstborn, begotten by the serpent and not by Adam, according to rabbinical tradition. The Bible says Cain's murder of his brother Abel was caused by jealousy, after God accepted Abel's blood sacrifice but rejected Cain's offering of vegetable firstfruits. Fearing to depart from this precedent, the Jews offered blood sacrifices to Yahweh up to the early Christian era.

The Bible story was a Hebraic repetition of the Persian myth of Ahriman and Ahura Mazda, who offered sacrifices to an elder deity, Vayu. Ahriman was declared a traitor and devil when his offering was refused.[1] Indo-Iranian priests used to pray the gods to accept their own sacrifices, and refuse those of other *arya* (men).[2] Ahriman was the ancestor of those other *arya,* since his original Hindu name was Aryaman, father of men.

The myth of Cain was based on primitive sacrificial magic, as shown by certain internal inconsistencies. God placed a curse on

Cain, at the same time protecting him with a mark of immunity. Hooke explains part of the ritual fertility sacrifice:

> *The sacrificer is defiled by his act. . . . It is this which explains why the slayer enjoys ritual protection . . . the most likely explanation of the mark is that it represents a tattoo mark or other indication that the fugitive belonged to a sacred class. We have evidence from Hebrew sources that the prophets bore such marks. . . . Tammuz, who bears the title of "the Shepherd," dies, or is ritually slain, during the period of summer drought . . . and his official slayer was obliged to flee in order to remove the ceremonial guilt of the slaying from the community.*[3]

Such comparisons are needed to solve the dilemma of those theologians who, through the centuries, have been helpless to explain God's apparent blunder in protecting Cain from nonexistent enemies, when there were as yet no people in the world but Cain and his parents. Actually, the sacred caste of Cainite smiths worshipped the Goddess and dedicated sacrifices of the Good Shepherd to her as the Earth, who "opened her mouth" for Abel's blood (Genesis 4:11). Cain's myth reflects the patriarchs' hostility toward this caste.[4] Eventually, they drove all the smiths out of their country, and had to send their tools to the Philistines for repair because "there was no smith found throughout all the land of Israel" (1 Samuel 13:19). Before the ban on smithcraft, however, they had the famous Tubal-cain, "instructor of every artificer in brass and iron" (Genesis 4:22). The fraternity of smiths was of Midianite origin, and may have inflicted a certain leg injury upon initiates, which could have been the mark of Cain. The Hebrew word for Passover, *Pesach,* meant "to dance with a limp."[5] The festival of Pesach was associated with the Midianites or Kenites (Cainites, "children of Cain"), who were famed as miners and smiths, and worshipped the Great Mother in the copper mines of Sinai.

According to the Sinai tablets, Semitic metalworkers called their deity Elath-Yahu, a combination of Yahweh and El-Lat or Allatu, Lady of the Underworld; but she was also identified with celestial Hathor.[6] The Cainites migrated from northern Syria, where their smith god formerly occupied the volcanic mountain Jebel-Al-Aqra, a seat of Baal in the Ras Shamra texts.[7] The Mosaic Yahweh was a volcano-god like this Midianite Baal, or like limping Hephaestus and Latin Vulcanus, gods represented by "a pillar of cloud by day, and a pillar of fire by night" (Exodus 13:21–22).

Exodus 2:16 says Moses was adopted by the Midianite smiths through his marriage to their priestess, one of the usual sacred number of seven sisters. Prominent in the clan were such artisans as Bezaleel, maker of the ark of the covenant, who was filled "with the spirit of God, in wisdom, in understanding, and in knowledge, and in all manner of workmanship; and to devise curious works, to work in gold, and in silver, and in brass" (Exodus 35:31–32). The word here translated "God"apparently meant the spirit of Elath-Yahu. But Moses quarreled with his Midianite wife, apparently over his attempt to institute the Egyptian custom of circumcision (Exodus 4:25) and they were divorced (Exodus 18:2). Subsequently, smithcraft disappeared from Israel after a long-remembered feud that imputed the crime of fratricide to Moses's followers, though their priestly tradition was to lay it on Cain. The account in Exodus 32 shows that the victims were not shepherds, but Cainites:

> *Moses stood in the gate of the camp, and said, Who is on the Lord's side? let him come unto me. And all the sons of Levi gathered themselves together unto him. And he said unto them, Thus saith the Lord God of Israel, Put every man his sword by his side, and go in and out from gate to gate throughout the camp, and slay every man his brother, and every man his companion, and every man his neighbor. And the children of Levi did according to the word of Moses: and there fell of the people that day about three thousand men. (Exodus 32:26–28)*

In later ages, Cain became a demi-devil, in the view of religious authorities who failed to notice that the true brother-slayers were Moses's followers. Or, if they did notice, they regarded the killing of three thousand as less important than the killing of one. In folklore, Cain remained attached to the diabolized matriarchal tradition: he was the man in the moon.[8] A German tale said the man in the moon refused to keep God's sabbath, the Sun-day. Therefore he was sent to the moon, and a saint informed him: "As you value not Sunday on earth, yours shall be a perpetual Moon-day in heaven."[9]

1. *Larousse,* 323. 2. Dumézil, 425. 3. Hooke, S.P., 69–71. 4. Hooke, M.E.M., 124. 5. Graves, W.G., 358. 6. Graves, W.G., 368. 7. Gray, 108. 8. Briffault 2, 629. 9. Baring-Gould, C.M.M.A., 192.

Callisto

"Fairest One," a title of Artemis as totemic She-Bear and mother of Arcas, the Little Bear. Calliste was an old name for Artemis's sacred island Thera (She-Beast). Hellenic writers said the Attic rites of Artemis involved young girls dressed as the She-bear, which gave rise to the myth of Callisto, a nymph who lost her virginity to Zeus and gave birth to the bear-child. They were placed in heaven as Ursa Major and Ursa Minor.[1] Of course the nymph was the virgin aspect of the Goddess herself.

1. Graves, G.M. 1, 86; W.G., 185.

Candlemas

Because it fell forty days after Christmas, Candlemas became the Festival of the Purification of the Virgin according to the Judeo-Christian rule that women must be "purified" forty days after childbirth, an event which the patriarchs claimed rendered a mother ritually unclean. The Bible specifies forty days of impurity following the birth of a son, and eighty days following the birth of a daughter, since females were supposed to be twice as unclean as males (Leviticus 12:2–5). The Christian God also considered new mothers unclean, and would not allow a woman to enter a church until the proper time had elapsed after her delivery. Her ritual purification was known as "churching."

The Council of Trullus once tried to abolish the festival of Candlemas, on the ground that in giving birth to Christ, the Virgin "suffered no pollution, and therefore needed no purification."

But Candlemas was not originally a Christian festival. To Roman pagans, it was the day honoring Juno Februata as the virgin mother of Mars. Like the Lupercalia two weeks later, the day commemorated the Goddess who engendered the "fever" (*febris*) of love.[1] Christian authorities said the pagan people went about Rome with "candles burning in worship of this woman Februa." Pope Sergius renamed the holy day "to undo this foul use and custom, and turn it onto God's worship and our Lady's . . . so that now this feast is solemnly hallowed through all Christendom."[2] Still, Candlemas was properly considered sacred to women and to the Goddess of Love.[3] Among Celtic pagans it was the Feast of Imbolg, which stood opposite the great festival of Lammas in the old sacred year.

Omens were taken on Candlemas Day for the new growing season, especially its weather. Therefore animals were said to come out of hibernation to provide helpful predictions for the end of winter; which is why it is now Groundhog Day. An old rhyme said, "If Candlemas Day be fair and bright, Winter will have another flight; If Candlemas Day be shower and rain, Winter is gone and will not come again."[4]

1. de Voragine, 151. 2. Hazlitt, 85–86. 3. de Lys, 127. 4. Hazlitt, 87.

Cannibalism

The most consistently observed taboo in civilized society is the taboo against eating human flesh, though there is no comparable taboo against killing, which is done regularly, sometimes in enormous volume, as in the case of war.

Upon finding human sacrifice—but not cannibalism—among the Polynesians, Captain Cook called it a shocking waste of the human race, and wrote: "It were much to be wished, that this deluded people may learn to entertain the same horror of murdering their fellow-creatures . . . as they now have of feeding, corporeally, on human flesh themselves."[1] Of course the good captain failed to notice that the same delusion dwelt among his own countrymen. Eventually the

Christians taught the Polynesians not to murder their fellow-creatures any more, by the simple expedient of murdering large numbers of Polynesians until they gave up.

Western morality has always allowed and encouraged mass killing, provided the dead never became meals for the living. It has been noted that the decline of human sacrifice and cannibalism in antiquity was not accompanied by a decline in human slaughter generally. On the contrary, the scale of warfare steadily increased with the growth of civilization, up to the point where the highly technical civilizations of today stand ready to exterminate an entire world. Moreover the highest casualty lists have been accumulated in precisely the same nations that call themselves Christian.[2]

Churches, declaring themselves officially opposed to killing, have always managed to justify it nonetheless, when it seemed expedient. Even more curious a contradiction may be found on the matter of cannibalism, which Christian authorities regarded with the utmost horror. Witches were accused of this crime more than any other, since it seemed dreadful enough to deserve the merciless punishment its alleged practitioners received. Yet at the very core of Christian faith lay the sacrament upon which salvation, redemption, eternal life and all the rest depended completely: a sacrament of cannibalism, not "symbolic" but according to its theological rationale, absolutely real.

God-eating was a universal custom descended from the earliest beginnings of civilization, when it was usually a genuine cannibal feast. As the incarnate god, "the victim is not only slain, but the worshippers partake of the body and blood of the victim, so that his life passes into their life, and knits them to the deity in living communion."[3]

The object was to become flesh of the god's flesh by eating him, so as to share in the resurrection of the divine flesh. There is no use pretending that this "Christian" ceremony did not originate in ceremonies of real cannibalism as primitive sympathetic magic. All the mystery-religions of the early Christian era centered on a pseudo-cannibalistic sacrament believed to identify the worshipper with the worshipped. "That there was a firm belief in the earlier stages of religion, of such participation in the god by eating him in a sacramental meal cannot be questioned. In the Thracian-Dionysiac Mysteries, e.g., the celebrants by such a meal obtain a share in the divine life of the god, and so are called by his name."[4]

The same idea underlay Christian sacraments as well as those of the other Mysteries. Cyril of Jerusalem talked of "partaking of the body and blood of Christ, that you may become *con-corporate* and *consanguineous* with Him; for thus we become Christophori, his body and his blood entering into our members." Methodius taught that "every believer must through participation in Christ be born a Christ. . . . He was made man that we might be made God." The same sacrament in other religions, however, was a diabolic rite: "Evil spirits

Methodius 9th-century Greek missionary to the Slavs, canonized soon after his death by the Greek church, and a thousand years later by the Roman.

gain power by means of the food consecrated to them, and are introduced by your own hands into your own bodies; there they hide themselves for a long time and unite with the soul."[5]

True cannibalism was still overtly associated with Tibetan sacrifices up to the 7th century A.D., after which the sacred mystery play provided symbolic substitutes. A victim made of dough was torn apart, his "entrails" distributed and devoured. Sometimes, real flesh from the corpse of an executed criminal was inserted into the dough image. At the atonement festival, a bull-masked priest called the Holy King of Religion stabbed the sacrificial figure, cut off its limbs, opened the breast and extracted artificial lungs, heart, and intestines. The remains were scattered by animal-masked dancers, as the remains of Osiris and other savior-gods of antiquity were scattered over the earth.[6]

Such dancers recall the Sabeans (Shebans) of Ezekiel 24, called "women that shed blood," who dressed in golden crowns and bracelets to make mourning for the dead, and "ate the bread of men." Similar funerary dancers were the Egyptian *muu* or "mothers," who wore **vulture** feathers to impersonate the Goddess Mut, or Nekhbet, eater of the dead.

Recently in parts of France it was a custom to make a dough man of the last sheaves of the harvest to represent the human sacrifice. He was broken in pieces by the *maire* (an old title of a clan mother) and given to the people to eat. Similarly in Mexico, after human sacrifices were discontinued, a flint-tipped dart was hurled into the breast of a dough man. This was known as "killing the god so that his body might be eaten." In a ceremony called *torqualo*, "God is eaten," the image was divided into small pieces and distributed among the people.[7]

This was an obvious survival of Aztec religious ideas. The victim impersonating the god received worship, healed the sick, and blessed the people, always attended by his keeper-apostles. Then he was killed and butchered in special houses called *calpulli*, which distributed him. Nursing mothers would smear their nipples with a victim's holy blood so even their infants could partake of it.

The Greek *omophagia* was originally a cannibal orgy that even dispensed with cooking. Victims were torn apart with the teeth and bare hands of the participants and eaten raw. Greek classical writers preferred to forget the *omophagia*. They looked down on barbarian tribes for sexual promiscuity and cannibalizing their family members.[10]

What was the relationship between eating sacred kings and saviors and eating family members? The answers have been given by cannibals themselves: women eat the flesh of dead men and bring them back to life as new children. Primitive people reasoned that, in order to be born again, one must get inside a woman's body. The simplest way to accomplish this was to be eaten by her. This was the original root of the world-wide doctrine of reincarnation: literally, re-clothing in flesh.

Before discovery of the mechanism of conception, a dying man

The original "barbecue" was a cannibal feast. The word came from *barbricot*, the grill of green boughs on which Carib Indians used to roast human flesh.[8] Ancient writings often speak of the cannibalistic habits of elder races. The Norse elder gods or giants were *jotunn*, from an Indo-European root word meaning "eaters." They were believed to eat men, like Jack's giant who drank the blood of Englishmen and made bread of their bones.[9]

looked forward to rebirth from one of the tribal mothers who would convert his flesh and blood into a new baby. Thus the Massagetae considered being eaten by clan mothers the only honorable death. A man could become flesh of their flesh, and live again.[11] Resurrection was brought about by the mysterious magic of women who, like the earth, gave life over and over.

Australian native women have been known to eat their infants who die, then to paint the bones red and hang them about their bodies: crude magic aimed at returning the child to the matrix and re-coating its bones with life-giving maternal blood. Women of the Bibinga tribe stated quite plainly that they ate the dead to give them reincarnation.[12] In New Guinea, a newborn child would receive the soul-name of a man who was killed and his flesh given to the mother to eat.[13]

In 1852, Dr. Hubsch wrote of the African tribe called Niam-Niam: "As soon as one of the tribe dies, his relations, instead of burying him, cut him up and regale themselves upon his remains; consequently there are no cemeteries in this land." [14] Baganda tribesmen said their women sometimes became so hungry that they bit off their babies' ears—probably a euphemistic way of saying they ate the whole baby, confident of their ability to give it another birth.[15]

The notion that pregnancy is the result of eating is still widespread among savages. Words for consuming and conceiving are often the same. There was an ancient Babylonian proverb: "Who grows pregnant without having conceived? Who grows fat without having eaten?" [16] According to Horace, the real primal scene was not the sexual drama postulated by Freud, but "A child, by a fell witch devoured, dragged from her entrails, and to life restored." [17] The Bible's term for birth is "coming forth from the bowels" (Genesis 15:4), for, like children, the ancients were not altogether certain of the distinction between reproductive and digestive systems. The Sanhedrin said a woman may conceive by drinking or bathing in water used to wash a corpse, an obvious survival of the primitive idea of a dead soul entering a new mother.[18]

The Chinese in the Shang period thought birth and rebirth were the same thing. The pictogram *kuei*, meaning both "soul" and "rebirth," was a fetus.[19]

The Yanomamo say they used to practice cannibalism, because their mother goddess Mamokoriyoma allowed them to eat dead parents and children. But they ceased to worship her, and declared cannibalism a sin. Cremation of the dead was instituted. Yet they still eat the ashes of the dead, mixed with food. Sharing the ashes of important ancestors is a sacred ceremony thought to strengthen kinship bonds.[20]

In southeastern Africa, when a woman marries into another kinship group, she must eat kernels of grain raised on the skull of a dead ancestor. When she gives birth, elders watch for signs of similarity between the deceased and the new baby. Kernels of grain were similarly grown on the mummy of Osiris and the body of Adonis, who was born in Bethlehem, the "House of Bread." The grain was eaten in solemn communion by the god's worshippers, who took it to mean they were like him, and would be reborn like him. Hawaiians had a god like Osiris, who was dismembered and buried in many earth-wombs. Foodstuffs grew from the parts of his body.[21]

Nearly all religions incorporate hidden hints of cannibalism. Apart from the sacrament of god-devouring that Christianity shared with paganism, the primitive church was accused of real cannibalism. Romans claimed the Christians sacrificed and ate children, and dipped their host in children's blood. Orthodox authorities didn't deny these charges, but insisted only the Gnostic sects were to blame. Justin Martyr said the Marcionites practiced incest and cannibalism. Eusebius of Caesarea said the Carpocratians did it. Epiphanius said the Montanists and Ophites did it. Clement of Alexandria, Irenaeus, and the 5th-century Presbyter Salvian all blamed heretic Christians for holding anthropophagus rites that brought disgrace on the church.[22]

Despite powerful taboos, cannibalism was not unknown in medieval Europe. In periods of famine or plague, when many starved to death in the streets of European towns, bodies sometimes simply disappeared. In 1435 the Sawney Beane family of Galloway was accused of having lived on a diet of human flesh for generations; but they were tortured to death by the court at Edinburgh, which may render their confessions suspect.[23] In 1661, four Scottish "witches" were tortured into confessing that they ate an unbaptized child dug up from the Forfar churchyard.[24] This seems improbable, since the unbaptized were not buried in churchyards. Next to witches, those most frequently accused of cannibalism were the Jews. See **Jews, Persecution of.**

1. Campbell, M.I., 446–47. 2. M. Harris, 121. 3. Elworthy, 112. 4. Angus, 129.
5. Angus, 107, 132. 6. Waddell, 518, 527, 531. 7. Elworthy, 111.
8. Frazer, G.B., 680; M. Harris, 102–3, 108, 118. 9. Branston, 101.
10. Thomson, 64, 145. 11. Herodotus, 83–84. 12. Summers, V., 263–64.
13. Tannahill, 15–16. 14. Baring-Gould, C.M.M.A., 158. 15. Briffault, 2, 460.
16. *Assyr. & Bab. Lit.*, 448. 17. Summers, V., 227. 18. Gaster, 521.
19. Brandon, 98. 20. Chagnon, 46, 51. 21. Campbell, P.M., 127, 200.
22. J.B. Russell, 89–92. 23. Summers, V., 61. 24. Tannahill, 101.

Canopic Jar

Egyptian tomb vessel for holding the entrails of a mummy. From the city of Canopis, "Eye of the Dog," Greek name for the star of Anubis, which Egyptians called Sothis (Sirius), the "eye" of the constellation Canis Major, the Great Dog. This star was supposed to hold the inward parts of the god Osiris in his "mummy" phase as Lord of Death. See **Dog.**

Car

var. Car-Dia, Cardea, Carmenta, Carna, etc.

The Goddess Car, or Kore, or Ker, or Q're, or Cerdo; one of the most widespread name-cycles of the Indo-European Goddess. Her sacred city in Sardinia was Caralis, the modern Cagliari.[1] Her sacred city in the Chersonese was Cardia, "the Goddess Car." Gaulish tribes called the Carnutes traced their descent from her; Chartres was named after her. As Carna and Carmenta she became the Etruscan-Roman mother of "carnivals," of "charms," and of alphabetical letters.

In the time of Alexander the Great, the land of Persia was known as Carmania, "Car the Moon."[2] Irish legend said from that land three powerful magicians came to Erin along with their mother Carman, evidently an idol of the Goddess. The magicians were later driven out, but they left their "mother" behind them.[3]

1. Massa, 43. 2. B. Butler, 137. 3. Spence, 150.

Carpet, Magic

Eastern tales of the magic flying carpet evolved from shamanic initiations in which the adept learned to "fly" via the spirit-journey. Novices undergoing initiation in central Asia were carried on a felt carpet by four priests called "sons" of the chief shaman, comparable to the four Sons of Horus carrying the dead man in ancient Egypt.[1] Flying to heaven in trance on the carpet was an integral part of death-and-resurrection ceremonies necessary to the would-be shaman's enlightenment.

1. Eliade, S., 119.

Caryatid

Carved temple pillar representing a woman; in Greek tradition, a priestess of Artemis Caryatis, modeled on the moon-priestesses of Caryae. Matriarchal temples' seven high priestesses were known as the Seven Pillars of Wisdom. The Bible says the Goddess of Wisdom has "builded her house, she hath hewn out her seven pillars" (Proverbs 9:1). As early as the 3rd millenium B.C., Moabite temples of the Goddess were provided with seven menhirs.[1] Each pillar apparently became a soul-image of one of the Seven Mothers, the original "pillars of the church." See **Pleiades.**

1. Gaster, 804.

Cassandra

Trojan prophetess called Daughter of Hecate, that is, of Queen Hecuba, who embodied the Trojan Goddess. After the fall of Troy, Cassandra was taken prisoner by King Agamemnon, on whom she laid her curse. Classical myth said she "prophesied" his doom, which meant she not only foresaw it but actually invoked it on him with her magic words. Soon after, Agamemnon was slain by his wife Clytemnestra and her new lover. The ritualistic manner of his death showed that it was not a simple murder but a replacement of sacred kings according to the ancient law of queen's right. See **Furies; Kingship.**

Caste

Inventors of the caste system were Indo-European patrilineal tribes whose early migrations destroyed many centers of Neolithic matriarchy; yet they had to attribute their social hierarchy to the authority of Mother Earth, the Goddess of final authority. Their eastern offshoots, calling themselves Aryans, conquered northwestern India and brought a Dark Age to a formerly flourishing civilization, about the middle of the 2nd millenium B.C. Like the priests of western Europe in a later Dark Age, the Aryan priests devised the caste system to relegate native peoples to a lower status, and to preserve this order with a claim of divine ordinance.

This doctrine taught that all those born into low rank were living out a necessary punishment for sin in a previous existence, even though they may not remember it. Their duty was to accept their lot without complaint, work hard, and obey their superiors, so as to win a promotion in the next life. It was perhaps the most effective method of preserving a hierarchy that human ingenuity has ever produced.[1]

Under the rule of the warlike Aryan **Aesir,** who conquered Scandinavia's earlier matriarchal tribes, "the castes and professions are regarded as reflections in the human sphere of the laws of the natural order."[2] The father of Teutonic castes was Rig-Heimdall, "King of the Sea-Home." Their mother was the Triple Goddess Earth in all three of her forms.

Rig-Heimdall lay with Edda the Great-Grandmother, oldest of Goddesses, and begot a son named Thrall, "Slave." Then he lay with Amma, the Grandmother, and begot a son named Karl, "Freeman." They he lay with Modir, the Mother, and begot a son named Jarl, "Earl, prince." These three were ancestors of the castes.

The same Rig-Heimdall was named Ram, the phallus. He was sacrificed as a Horned God. Like Scyld, Arthur, and other pagan heroes he was born of the ninth wave of the sea. His Magic Song said he was born of nine maidens, daughters of the Elder Race, another multiplication of the same Triple Goddess, everywhere the Mother-Bride. The Nine made him strong with the sea's cold strength and with sacrificial blood.[3]

Rig-Heimdall resembled the Vedic fire god Agni, Son of the Waters, who returned to the waters at his death. Some say Agni is periodically reincarnated in the Dalai Lama, another "Son of the Sea." The Rig Veda said of Agni, "He with clear flames unfed with wood, shines in the waters."[4] This was not marine luminescence, but an allegory of the ancient idea that blood was sea water infused with fire, the element of living heat (see **Elements**). As the god in dying fertilized Mother Earth with blood, so fire dying in water turned the cold brine into warm red blood of life. This was the primitive theory behind the "mating of fire and water" in both Norse and Vedic myth.

Apart from the castes in both eastern and western Aryan societies were the outcastes: India's Untouchables, or pariahs. Their duties were "carrying water and chopping firewood." Their virtue consisted of accepting these chores and attending to them faithfully.[5] It is no coincidence, but a tradition of genuine Indo-European origin, that the Bible speaks of outcasts who could not be touched, but were allowed to live as "hewers of wood and drawers of water" (Joshua 9:21). Yahweh's scribes pretended the idea came from their ancestors, but obviously it was borrowed from Far-Eastern concepts of the caste system.

1. de Camp, A.E., 294. 2. Campbell, Or.M., 416–17. 3. Turville-Petre, 147, 150–53. 4. Branston, 140. 5. Campbell, Or.M., 459.

Castration

All mythologies suggest that, before men understood their reproductive role, they tried to "make women" of themselves in the hope of achieving womanlike fertility. Methods included couvade or imitation childbirth; mock death and rebirth through artificial male mothers; ceremonial use of red substances to imitate **menstrual blood;** and **transvestism.** Another method was ceremonial castration. Its primitive object was to turn a male body into a female one, replacing dangling genitals with a bleeding hole. (See **Birth-giving, Male.**)

Many gods became pseudo-mothers by this means. Egypt's solar god **Ra** castrated himself to bring forth a race called the Ammiu out of his blood.[1] The phallus of the Hindu "Great God," Mahadeva, was removed and chopped to pieces by priestesses of the Goddess. The pieces entered the earth and gave birth to a new race of men, the Lingajas (Men of the lingam, or phallus).[2] In a Chukchi variant, the Great God Raven acquired feminine secrets of magic for men by pounding his own penis to a pudding and feeding it to the Goddess Miti (Mother).[3] In Mexico, the savior Quetzalcoatl made new humans to repopulate the earth after the Flood by cutting his penis and giving blood to the Lady of the Serpent Skirt—the Goddess with many shorn phalli dangling about her waist, a figure also known in the Middle East, e.g. as **Anath.**[4]

Several forms of the Heavenly Father became creators by a rite of castration. The god Bel cut his "head" (of the penis) and mixed his blood with clay to make men and animals, copying the magic of Mother Ninhursag.[5] Shamin, the Phoenicians' Father Heaven, was castrated by his son El and made the world's rivers from his blood, imitating the Goddess's menstrual magic. Arabs called this god Shams-on, the sun. The Bible called him Samson, whose blindness and hair-cutting were both mythic metaphors of castration.

Shearing the sun god's "hair" (rays) meant emasculating him. His severed penis represented the son/supplanter; and a penis was often called "the little blind one," or "the one-eyed god." Greeks' personification of the phallus, Priapus, was the son of Aphrodite and her castrated consort Adonis. Their Roman counterparts Vesta and Vulcan produced a phallic god Caeculus, "the little blind one."[6]

Uranus, "Father Heaven," was castrated by his son Cronus. Uranus's severed genitals entered the sea-womb and fertilized it to produce a new incarnation of the Virgin Aphrodite Urania, "Celestial Aphrodite." It was she who ruled the earlier cults of castrated gods, such as Anchises and Adonis. She was the same as the Canaanites' Lady of the Serpent Skirt: her priests castrated gods in her honor.

So did the priests of Aphrodite's Nordic counterpart, Freya-Skadi. The Nordic Father Heaven was Odin, whose twelfth holy name was Jalkr, "Eunuch."[7] As a castrated god, Odin was the son-phallus of an older Eunuch personifying both father and son; for Odin was also the One-Eyed God, or Völsi, a "stallion penis."[8] (See **Horse**.) Like the stallion of the Vedic horse sacrifice, he was castrated. A late myth tried to account for Odin's crude phallic title by saying he could not drink of the cosmic feminine fountain of wisdom until he had given up one of his eyes.[9] Here one might recall the alternating seasonal castrations of Set and Horus in Egypt, their severed phalli mythologically described as "eyes."[10]

Biblical writers called the penis a "sinew that shrank," lying "upon the hollow of the thigh." This was the sinew that Jacob lost in his duel with "a man who was a god." Jacob, "the Supplanter," was another name for Seth, or Set, who was likewise symbolized by the Ladder of Souls and likewise engaged in a contest with his rival, ending in his castration.[11] When Set was castrated, his blood was spread over the fields in the annual ceremony of sowing so as to fertilize the crops.[12]

The Book of Genesis confuses the two aspects of the god-king, who as Jacob won his battle with the incumbent king and supplanted him, then as Israel lost his battle with the next supplanter, and was castrated. Is-Ra-El may have been a corruption of Isis-Ra-El, the god enthroned as the consort of his goddess, awaiting the next challenger.[13] The syllable *El* meant his deification.

The garbled story of Jacob and the god-man was inserted chiefly to support the Jews' taboo on eating a penis (Genesis 32:32), formerly a habit of sacred kings upon their accession to the throne. The genitals of the defeated antagonist were eaten by the victor, to pass the phallic spirit from one "god" to the next. A king's *virtu,* "manliness," or *heill,* "holiness," dwelt in his genitals because that was his point of contact with the Goddess-queen. Innumerable myths of father-castrating, mother-marrying god-kings arose, not so much from inner Oedipal jealousies as from actual customs of royal succession in antiquity. See **Kingship; Oedipus.**

The Greek King Aegeus died at the very moment when his "son," Theseus, arrived from Crete to claim his throne. The key to this myth is that Aegeus was "rendered sterile" by a curse, the same ritual curse laid on all kings of outworn usefulness, followed very shortly by castration and death.[14]

In the sacred dramas of Canaan, the reed scepter of the dying god Mot was broken, to signify his castration.[15] His name, meaning "sterility" or "death," was a title of the fertility god Aleyin (Baal) as he entered his declining phase, when his rival assumed the sacred throne, and he became Lord of Death.[16] The custom of eating the defeated king's genitals appears in a number of Middle-Eastern myths, e.g., that of the Hittite god Kumarbi, one of a line of father-castrating kings of heaven.[17] Kumarbi's assumption of the fertility-spirit was expressed by the story that he "became pregnant."

Mythic fathers and sons demonstrated remarkable hostility toward each other's genitals. Scholars tend to regard this as an expression of Oedipal aggressions, originating in the jealousy of elder males toward younger, more virile ones. Though men eventually gave up the hopeless idea of making one of their number pregnant by redesigning his body in a feminine style, customs of castration and crypto-castration persisted because they offered an outlet for this male jealousy.

Among savages, men's puberty ceremonies generally provided an excuse for elder men's attacks on the bodies of youths. Modified castrations may be inflicted in the form of circumcision, subincision, and other genital wounds; also a variety of torments such as scarifying flesh, knocking out teeth, beatings, torture, and homosexual rape.[18] "The dramatized anger of both the father and the circumciser and the myths of the original initiation in which all the boys were killed, certainly show the Oedipal aggression of the elder generation as the basic drive behind initiation."[19]

The more patriarchal the society, the more brutal its attacks on male youth, as a general rule. Notable for brutality was the Moslems' *Esselkh* or scarification ceremony, a complete flaying of skin from a boy's scrotum, penis, and groin. After enduring this, the victim was further tormented by application of salt and hot sand, and buried up to the waist in a dunghill, making subsequent infection almost inevitable. Burton commented, "This ordeal was sometimes fatal."[20] Legman pointed out that both Islam and Judaism "share in the surgical intimidation of the son by the father, just at the threshold of puberty, either in the psychological castration of circumcision at puberty (Mohammedanism), or this same operation effected at the earlier age of eight days (Judaism), or in a reminiscence of this operation."[21]

Subincision provides an example of transition from a female-imitative rationale to a male sado-masochistic ritual. As practiced by the Arunta, it began with a long sliver of bone inserted into the urethra. The youth's penis was then sawed open with a sharp flint, down to the level of the bone. Blood flowing from the wound was directed onto a sacred fire, like the menstrual blood of girls at menarche. The operation was termed "man's menstruation."[22] The wound was called a "vagina."[23]

The obvious purpose of this unpleasantness was to transform a male into a pseudo-female. The mutilated youth was even obliged to urinate by squatting, like a woman. Sometimes, men renewed the damage several times over, repeating the litany: "We are not separated from the mother; for 'we two are one.'"[24] Natives said the custom was begun by an ancestral spirit, Mulkari or Mu-Kari, perhaps a corrupt form of Mother Kali (Ma-Kali), who was known as Kari in Malaysia.[25]

Far from supporting the Freudian doctrine of penis envy, primitive customs seem to suggest vulva envy as the original motive behind ritual castrations. It might be found even in civilized society. Bettelheim remarked on the desire of some young men to be circumcised, or otherwise subjected to bloodletting, when their girl friends were starting to menstruate.[26] Circumcision was surely a modified form of earlier, female-imitative castrations.

The institution of circumcision was attributed to the same gods, such as El, who castrated their fathers. Its object was to feminize. In India, boys were dressed as girls, nose ring and all, on the eve of the circumcision ceremony. In ancient Egypt also, boys on their way to circumcision wore girls' clothing, and were followed by a woman sprinkling salt, a common Egyptian symbol of life-giving menstrual blood.[27]

Circumcision took place at the age of thirteen, the number of months in a year according to ancient menstrual calendars, and the traditional age of menarche. After copying circumcision from the Egyptians, Jews transferred it to the period of infancy, leaving the pubertal ceremony, now called bar mitzvah, awkwardly placed at a point in a boy's life when nothing really happens, in contrast to the sudden onset of menarche in a girl.

Infant circumcision was attributed to Moses, who insisted on it against the will of his Midianite wife Zipporah, who apparently objected to mutilation of her infant. After performing the operation, she flung the foreskin at Moses's feet, calling him a bloody husband (Exodus 4:25).

Other biblical passages show that foreskins were considered appropriate offerings to Yahweh. David bought his wife Michal from Yahweh's representative the king, with 200 Philistine foreskins (1 Samuel 18:27). Other Heavenly Fathers made similar demands for genital gifts. Male animals sacrificed to Rome's Heavenly Father Jupiter were gelded.[28] The bull representing the castrated savior Attis was also castrated.[29] His blood conferred spiritual rebirth on those who bathed in it, like the blood of the Christian "Lamb," as if it were the secret blood of the womb, the real source of life according to the oldest beliefs.[30]

Castration as a means of acquiring feminine powers was still evident among priesthoods of the Great Mother, along with other female-imitative devices such as transvestism. Self-emasculated priests in female clothing served the Indian Goddess under her name of Hudigamma.[31] Similar eunuch priests tended Middle-Eastern temples like those of the Dea Syria at Hierapolis, Artemis–Diana in Anatolia, and the Magna Mater in Phrygia and Rome.[32] The famous seer of

Thebes, Teiresias, got his powers of second sight and prophecy by becoming a woman, possibly by castration, and living as a temple harlot for seven years.

Perhaps the best-known self-emasculators in the ancient world were priests of Attis and Cybele, the Great Mother. As Attis was castrated and poured out his lifeblood to fructify her, so his priests in imitation of his sacrifice cut off their genitals and gave them to the Goddess's image.[33] Sometimes, the men's severed members were thrown into houses, as a special blessing. In return, householders gave the new eunuchs feminine garments to wear. Sometimes, the severed genitalia were carried in baskets or *cistae* to the Mother's innermost shrine, where they were anointed, even gilded, and solemnly buried in the Bridal Chamber.[34] The phallus of the god himself was carried into the sacred cavern in the form of a large pine log, which was also, like the phallic cross of Middle-Eastern saviors, the instrument on which he died.[35] His priests, having copied his self-sacrifice, were distinguished by the androgynous title bestowed on the earliest forms of Shiva; they were "lords who were half woman."[36]

Tertullian admitted that the "divine mysteries" of Christianity were virtually the same as the "devilish mysteries" of pagan saviors like Attis.[37] Popularity of Attis's cult in Rome led to Christian adoption of some of the older god's ways. One of the best-kept secrets of early Christianity was its preaching of castration for the special inner circle of initiates, who won extra grace with this demonstration of chastity. They taught, following the Wisdom of Solomon, "Blessed is the eunuch, which with his hands hath wrought no iniquity."[38] Jesus himself advocated castration: "There be eunuchs, which have made themselves eunuchs for the kingdom of heaven's sake. He that is able to receive it, let him receive it" (Matthew 19:12).

Several early fathers of the church did receive it. Origen was highly praised for having castrated himself.[39] Justin's *Apologia* said proudly that Roman surgeons were besieged by faithful Christian men requesting the operation. Tertullian declared, "The kingdom of heaven is thrown open to eunuchs."[40] Justin advised that Christian boys be emasculated before puberty, so their virtue was permanently protected.[41] Three Christians who tried to burn Diocletian's palace were described as eunuchs.[42]

Throughout the middle ages, cathedral choirs included *castrati,* emasculated before puberty to preserve their virtue and their soprano voices, which were considered more pleasing to God than the "impure" female soprano. Women were not allowed to sing in church choirs, anyway.

Castration was advocated also for monks who could not fend off the demons of sexual desire. It was forcibly imposed on the monk Abelard, whose love affair with his pupil Heloise caused a scandal in the church. But there were others who seem to have accepted surgical chastity on a voluntary basis. Such men assumed the title of Hesychasti, "permanently chaste ones," or "those who are at peace." The title was associated particularly with the monks of Mount Athos, so carefully ascetic that even to the present day no female creature is allowed on the holy mountain—hens, cows, sows, nanny goats, and women all equally forbidden.[43]

It is likely that Mount Athos was named after **Attis**, and may have been a shrine served by his eunuch priests in pre-Christian times, situated close to his Phrygian home. There was a Magna Mater figure connected with Mount Athos up to the early 14th century. The monks were labeled heretics for being too deeply involved with the teachings of a certain so-called nun named **Irene**—"Peace," the third *persona* of Triple Aphrodite embodied in her priestess-Horae. Irene, as **Crone**, would have been the priestess of castrations hinted in the myths of such lovers of the Goddess as Anchises and Adonis.[44] When the church purged Mount Athos of the influence of Irene, the abbot Lazarus was expelled. With a companion named Barefooted Cyril, Lazarus wandered through Bulgaria preaching the redeeming virtues of nakedness and self-emasculation.[45]

It seems the cult of Attis and **Cybele** continued to influence Christianity in the Balkans for many centuries. Balkan monastic communities were organized in groups of fifty, like older "colleges" of the Great Mother's castrated priests. In Thrace, the Great Mother had the name of Cottyto, mother of the hundred-handed giant Cottus, an allegorical figure representing her fifty spiritual sons with two hands each.[46] Her worship persisted underground, long enough for the church to define it as witchcraft, and to label Cottyto a demon. In 1619 a booklet published in Paris suggested the same Balkan tradition of the priest who dedicated himself to God in a manner that was then considered heretical: "the devil cut off his privy parts."[47]

Ritual castration was again revived by 18th-century Russian sectaries calling themselves Skoptsi, "castrated ones."[48] They also called themselves People of God, insisting that removal of their genitals brought them profound spiritual powers. Russia's "mad monk" Rasputin was a member of this sect.[49] Since Rasputin was famed for his affairs with women, few of his contemporaries would have believed him a eunuch; but they had forgotten what eastern harem-keepers knew well enough: that eunuchs are quite capable of providing women with sexual pleasure. Rasputin's hold over his female devotees was in any case a curious combination of spiritual and sensual obsession.

1. Budge, G.E. 2, 89, 100. 2. G.R. Scott, 192–93. 3. Hays, 412. 4. Campbell, M.I., 156. 5. Lindsay, O.A., 106. 6. Dumézil, 325. 7. Branston, 50. 8. Turville-Petre, 201. 9. *Larousse,* 257. 10. Norman, 42. 11. Graves, W.G., 355. 12. Budge, G.E. 2, 59. 13. Budge, G.E. 1, 341–42. 14. Campbell, C.M., 305. 15. *Larousse,* 78. 16. Hooke, M.E.M., 107. 17. Graves, G.M. 1, 39. 18. Hays, 524. 19. Campbell, P.M., 98. 20. Edwardes, 97. 21. Legman, 416. 22. Brasch, 55. 23. Montagu, S.M.S., 243. 24. Campbell, P.M., 103. 25. Montagu, S.M.S., 241. 26. F. Huxley, 104. 27. Gifford, 42; Edwardes, 93. 28. Dumézil, 559. 29. Guignebert, 71–72. 30. Angus, 239. 31. Gaster, 317. 32. Frazer, G.B., 403–9. 33. Frazer, G.B., 405. 34. Lederer, 145. 35. Gaster, 609. 36. Vermaseren, 126. 37. Robertson, 112. 38. H. Smith, 235. 39. Bullough, 100. 40. Briffault 3, 372. 41. Bullough, 113. 42. Brewster, 402. 43. Castiglioni, 221. 44. Graves, G.M. 1, 72. 45. Spinka, 119–20. 46. Graves, G.M. 1, 32; Spinka, 117. 47. Robbins, 127. 48. Lederer, 162. 49. Martello, 175–76.

Cat

Along with the owl, the bat, and the wolf, the animal most commonly associated with witches was the cat. Like everything else associated with witchcraft, this idea dated back to ancient Goddess-worship.

The Teutonic Mother Freya rode in a chariot drawn by cats.[1] Artemis-Diana often appeared in cat form, and was identified with the Egyptian cat-goddess Bast. The willow sacred to Hecate became a pussy-willow that bore "catkins" in the spring.[2]

Cat worship began in Egypt, where the first domesticated cats descended from a wild ancestor, *felis libyca.*[3] Plutarch said the cat was carved on Isis's holy sistrum and represented the moon, "[i]ts activity in the night, and the peculiar circumstances which attend its fecundity making it a proper emblem of that body. For it is reported of this creature, that it at first brings forth one, then two, afterwards three, and so goes on adding one to each former birth till it comes to seven; so that she brings forth twenty-eight in all, corresponding as it were to the several degrees of light, which appear during the moon's revolutions."[4]

The Egyptian word for cat was *Mau,* both an imitation of the cat's cry, and a mother-syllable. Cats were so sacred in Egypt that any man who killed one was condemned to death. Diodorus, a first-century B.C. Greek historian, told of a foolish Roman who killed a cat in Egypt and was slain in his own house by an infuriated mob.[5]

Bast, the Cat-mother of the city of Bubastis, was the benevolent aspect of Hathor, the Lioness. Festivals of Bast were joyful with music, dancing, jokes, and sexual rites.[6] Her dark side was Hathor as the leonine Sphinx, Sekhmet (Greek Sakhmis), tearer and devourer of men.[7] "By my life, when I slay men my heart rejoices," she said. Her feast day commemorated a massacre once perpetrated by Sekhmet the Great Cat. The Egyptian calendar of lucky and unlucky days noted for this one, with inadvertent humor: "Hostile, hostile, hostile is the 12th Tybi. Avoid seeing a mouse on this day."[8]

Medieval belief in the cat's nine lives probably stemmed from the Egyptian Ennead, via the mythic figure of the Ninefold Goddess. It was often said any witch could assume a cat's shape nine times in her life.[9] She could also assume the shape of a hare.[10] Frazer observed: "Cats are precisely the animals into which, with the possible exception of hares, witches were most usually supposed to transform themselves."[11]

Brought to England, cats were confused with hares as the Moon-goddess's totems. The root language of Sanskrit called the moon *cacin,* "that marked with the Hare," but some said the lunar animal might be a cat.[12] Queen Boadicea's banners bore the device of the moon-hare, which was also dedicated to the Saxon Goddess Eostre (Easter) at her rites of spring: hence the Easter Bunny. Irish peasants still observe the matriarchal taboo on hare meat, saying to eat a hare is to eat one's grandmother.[13] Both hares and cats had obviously yonic nicknames: cunny, pussy. A rabbit warren is still called a cunnary.[14]

To the Scots, the Goddess of Witches was Mither o' the Mawkins. "Mawkin" or "malkin" was either a hare or a cat.[15] When the cat became the primary lunar animal, the traditional witch's familiar was Greymalkin or Grimalkin, a "gray cat." Gray malkins were also the "pussies" or "catkins" on the pussy willow, sacred to witches and heralding the pagan games of May.

Inquisitor Nicholas Remy said all cats were demons. In 1387, Lombard witches were said to worship the devil as a cat.[16] Christians sometimes exposed cats to torture and fire along with witches. At certain festivals, such as Midsummer, Easter, and Shrove Tuesday, it was customary to burn cats in wicker cages. "The cat, which represented the devil, could never suffer enough."[17] According to Jewish belief, cats were not made by God. The first pair of male and female cats were "snorted forth" from the nostrils of a lion on board Noah's ark.[18]

1. Turville-Petre, 107; Branston, 133. 2. Graves, G.M. 1, 115.
3. *Encyc. Brit.*, "Cat." 4. Budge, G.E. 2, 257. 5. Budge, G.E. 2, 61, 364.
6. *Larousse,* 37. 7. Budge, G.E. 1, 517. 8. *Larousse,* 36. 9. Hazlitt, 661.
10. Briffault 2, 618–19. 11. Frazer, G.B., 762. 12. Baring-Gould, C.M.M.A., 204.
13. Graves, W.G., 319. 14. Wainwright, 272. 15. Potter & Sargent, 71.
16. Cavendish, P.E., 223, 247. 17. Frazer, G.B., 760. 18. Ochs, 106.

Catherine, Saint

One of the most popular saints of all time—despite the fact that she never existed. In the hearts of many people she was second only to the virgin Mary.[1] Yet even Catholic scholars admit her legend is "preposterous."[2]

The key to the secret of St. Catherine is her so-called Catherine Wheel, the **wheel** of fire on which she was said to have been martyred. At Sinai, the original center of Catherine's cult, the Asiatic Goddess was once portrayed as the Dancer on the Fiery Wheel at the hub of the universe. A Greek convent of priestess-nuns at Sinai in the 8th century A.D. called themselves *kathari,* "pure ones," a word akin to the Kathakali temple-dancers of India, who performed the Dance of Time in honor of Kali, Goddess of the karmic wheel.[3]

The symbol of the wheel figured prominently in beliefs of medieval Gnostics who called themselves Cathari, and revered St. Catherine almost as a female counterpart of God. Perhaps for this reason, in the 15th and 16th centuries, after the Cathari were exterminated, Catholic prelates made efforts to have St. Catherine eliminated from the canon.[4]

Her Christian myth made her the standard young beauty dedicated to virginity, and so wise she could demolish the arguments of fifty philosophers at once. She refused the hand of the emperor in marriage, whereupon he—following the hagiographers' usual curious pattern—essayed to win her love by having her imprisoned and tortured. Her captors tried to break her on the fiery wheel, but the wheel was shattered by a sudden bolt of lightning and she was saved. In the end, she had to be beheaded. Milk flowed from her veins instead of blood. Angels carried her body from Alexandria to Sinai, where her relics were "discovered" 500 years later.[5] Her divine bones constantly exuded a healing unguent, which was bottled and sold at great profit to the convent.[6]

1. Brewster, 104. 2. Attwater, 209. 3. *Encyc. Brit.*, "Kathakali." 4. Brewster, 499. 5. Attwater, 209–10; *Encyc. Brit.*, "Catherine." 6. de Voragine, 715.

Cauldron

The symbol commonly opposed to the cross, as the witches' object of worship; in pagan tradition, the Great Mother's cosmic womb. As the "pot of blood in the hand of Kali," the cauldron signified cyclic recurrence, as opposed to the patriarchal view of linear time.

Shakespeare followed the traditional pattern in associating the cauldron with three witches, since, from its earliest appearances in Bronze Age and Iron Age cultures, the cauldron stood for the Triple Goddess of fate, or *wyrd* in Old English: the three Weird Sisters.[1]

The Egyptian hieroglyphic sign of the threefold Creatress, mother of the sun, the universe, and all the gods, was a design of three cauldrons.[2] The Norse god Odin stole his divine power from three cauldrons of Wise Blood in the cave-womb of the earth, where he entered in the shape of a phallic serpent and beguiled the earth-giantess by making love to her.[3] Then he drank the magic blood from the cauldrons and became a shape-shifter, turning himself into a bird to carry the precious blood back to other gods. This myth was based on that of the Aryan sky-god Indra, who also drank the Goddess's ambrosia from three cauldrons, the three wombs of Kali's trinity.[4] Indra stole the elixir by allowing himself to be swallowed by a vast serpent representing female sexuality (Kundalini). He too turned into a bird to carry the elixir to other gods.

> *In nearly all mythologies there is a miraculous vessel. Sometimes it dispenses youth and life, at other times it possesses the power of healing, and occasionally, as with the mead cauldron of the Nordic Ymir, inspiring strength and wisdom are to be found in it. Often . . . it effects transformations.*[5]

The Bible called lapis lazuli *sappur* or "holy blood." It was the substance of God's throne (Ezekiel 1:26). The Authorized Version inaccurately translates *sappur* as "sapphire."[8]

The cauldron that effected transformations was the same as the womb that churned out rebirths, changing shapes each time. In Babylon it was under the control of the Fate-goddess Siris, mother of stars. Her cauldron was the blue heaven, where she stirred the mead of regeneration. "Siris, the wise woman, the mother, who had done what was necessary. Her cauldron is of shining lapis lazuli. Her tub is of pure silver and gold. In mead stands jubilation, in mead sits rejoicing."[6]

Lapis lazuli was the blue heaven stone prized for its power to cause rebirth. The Papyrus of Nekhtu-Amen said an amulet of lapis lazuli stood for the heart (*ab*), source of mother-blood; therefore the amulet was inserted into a mummy to generate a new heart for the deceased.[7]

Chaldean cosmology saw the sky as a nesting of seven vessels, the planetary spheres, like inverted bowls or cauldrons. Beneath the earth lay the mirror image of this celestial realm, seven more spheres sometimes described as cauldrons. A Hittite myth called them the vessels of Mother Death, dark twin sister of the heavenly Mother Siris: "The doorkeeper has opened the seven doors, has unlocked the seven bolts. Down in the dark earth there stand seven cauldrons, their lids of *abaru* metal, their handles of iron. Whatever goes in there comes not out again."[9]

Egyptians sometimes saw the seven-circled nether womb as a regenerative cauldron called the Lake of Fire.[10] The corresponding celestial vessels were "above heaven."[11] But the divine cauldron also appeared right on earth, within the sacred precincts of the temple.

Large cauldrons in Egyptian temples were called *shi,* the prototype of the brass "sea" in Solomon's temple, which was certainly a Cauldron of Regeneration.[12] Babylonian temples had the same vessel, called *apsu* or "abyss," for baptism, ceremonial lavage, and rebirth rituals.[13] Such a "sea" was also called "the Deep," *tehom* in Hebrew.[14] Like the Christian baptismal font descended from these forerunners, the cauldron or "sea" was a womb symbol. Solomon's "sea" represented his Goddess, Ashtoreth (Astarte). It was decorated with her yonic lilies: "The brim thereof was wrought like the brim of a cup, with flowers of lilies" (1 Kings 7:26).

King Aeson was resurrected after being boiled in the cauldron of Medea, "Mead of Wisdom," eponymous mother goddess of the Medes. King Minos too was boiled in the Goddess's cauldron and deified in Tartarus, where he became a judge and a Lord of Death. Under the name of Demeter, the Goddess restored Pelops to life in her cauldron.[15] According to his inscription at Mount Hermon, the Roman emperor Elagabalus was likewise "deified in the cauldron."[16]

St. John the Evangelist was oddly assimilated to the pagan myth of the regenerative cauldron. He was boiled in it and came forth livelier than before. His symbols were a bleeding heart and a boiling cauldron.[17] The syncretism of the "Feast of St. John at the Latin Gate" eventually became too embarrassing, and the festival was expunged from the Christian calendar in 1960.[18] The apocryphal St. George, however, continued to enter the cauldron as one of his alleged tortures. By making the sign of the cross, he rendered it lukewarm and harmless, an example of a matriarchal symbol made subordinate to a patriarchal one.[19]

Among the Celts of Gaul and Britain, the Cauldron of Regeneration was the central religious mystery: reincarnation within the womb of the Goddess. The Irish who worshipped the threefold Morrigan called the second person of her trinity Badb, "Boiling," the producer of life, wisdom, inspiration, and enlightenment.[20]

To Welsh bards she was the Goddess Branwen, "one of the three Matriarchs of the Island," owner of the Cauldron of Regeneration in which dead men could be resuscitated overnight.[21] As "a powerful fairy queen," the Lady of the Lake of the Basin, she dwelt in a sacred lake from which her brother Bran the Blessed raised the cauldron later known as the Holy Grail.[22] This pagan god was Christianized as Bron, alleged brother-in-law of Joseph of Arimathea who was supposed to have brought the Grail to Britain. Actually, the Grail was well established in British paganism long before its legend was assimilated to that of Christ.[23] Branwen, Goddess of the Cauldron, had yet another incarnation in medieval romance as Brangwain, the wise-woman who gave Tristan and Iseult their fatal love potion.[24]

The Goddess had earthly incarnations too. Childeric, son of Merovech or Merovig, founder of the first dynasty of French kings, married a druidess named Basina (Cauldron), who foretold the future of his dynasty.[25]

Like the "seas" in ancient temples, the Cauldron of Regeneration also had its counterparts on earth. Each Celtic temple had its sacred cauldron. Aubrey's *A Natural History of Surrey* mentioned a pagan cauldron still preserved in Frensham Church, "an extraordinary great kettle or cauldron" brought by the fairies, according to local legend.[26] An 8th-century Salic Law against priestesses—or, as the church called them, witches—prohibited the pagan practice of "bearing the cauldron" in procession to "the places where they cook."[27]

The Welsh bard Taliesin claimed to have received the mead of wisdom from his mother, the Goddess Cerridwen, "the Celtic Great Mother, the Demeter."[28]

> *She resolved, according to the arts of the books of Fferyllt (Fairy-wisdom), to boil a Cauldron of Inspiration and Science for her son . . . which from the beginning of its boiling might not cease to boil for a year and a day, until three blessed drops were obtained of the Grace of Inspiration.*[29]

Taliesin's poetry contained oblique allusions to the magic cauldron, couched in the semi-opaque terms that concealed mystical secrets from the uninitiated. His "year and a day" was a reference to the lunar calender of the pagans, a year of thirteen 28-day lunar months, 364 days, with one more day to make 365. The same "year and a day" occurred in many fairy tales. (See **Menstrual Calendar**.) Taliesin's *Preiddeu Annwn* (Harrowings of Hell) spoke of the Nine Maidens, priestesses of the perpetual fire that boiled the symbolic world-cauldron; and of the yonic shrine, Hel's gate, to which the king's sword (or phallus) was lifted:

> *In Caer Pedryvan (four times revolving)*
> *The Word from the cauldron it would be spoken*
> *By the breath of nine maidens it would be kindled,*
> *The head of Hades's cauldron—what is it like?*
> *A rim it has, with pearls round its border;*
> *It boils not a coward's food: it would not be perjured.*
> *The sword of Llwch Lleawc would be lifted to it.*
> *And in the hand of Lleminawc was it left.*
> *And before the door of Hell's gate lamps were burning,*
> *And when we accompanied Arthur, a brilliant effort,*
> *Seven alone did we return from Caer Veddwit.*[30]

Nine sisters were the same as the nine Goddesses of the Fortunate Isles ruled by Morgan le Fay, and the nine Muses of Greek myth, and the pre-Hellenic ninefold Goddess Nonacris, queen of the

Stygian birth-gate.[31] She, or they, came from Oriental traditions almost as old as civilization. During their Bronze Age Shang period, the Chinese represented the Great Goddess of birth by nine tripod cauldrons like the mixing-vessels of the Muses.[32]

The primitive cult of the cauldron obviously discouraged "cowards" because it was cult of martyrdom. Like Christian martyrs, the cauldron's victims were promised immediate resurrection into a life of glory. Strabo spoke of Cimbrian priestesses who sacrificed men, making them divine heroes, and caught their blood in magic cauldrons and read omens in their entrails.[33]

Some myths hint at cannibal cauldrons large enough to boil a human body, and beliefs that death in the cauldron was not really death. A gypsy legend spoke of a hero forced by a mystic Lady to milk dangerous mares, then bathe in a boiling cauldron of their milk. A god in the form of a royal horse promised to breathe frost on the cauldron and render it comfortably lukewarm.[34] The story recalls the Corinthians' "man-eating mares," or horse-masked priestesses, who caused Bellerophon to mount to heaven on the royal horse Pegasus, symbol of apotheosis after death.[35]

Horseback riding is a sign of deification on the famous silver sacrificial cauldron recovered from a Gundestrup peat bog. Manufactured about 100 B.C., the vessel showed a ceremony of sacrifice. Victims appear to be identified with the Horned God, Cernunnos, seated in a yogi's lotus position holding male and female symbols, the serpent and torc.[36] On foot, a row of victims approach the sacred cauldron which is shield-shaped and double-lobed, resembling a yoni. A priest or priestess is shown plunging one victim headfirst into the vessel.[37] Above, the heroes depart glorified, on horseback, riding literally into the sunset, which represented heaven. Cernunnos himself was dismembered and cooked in a cauldron to rise again, which made him the obvious god for such rites.[38]

A scene similar to that of the Gundestrup Cauldron occurs on a sacred cista from Palestrina-Praeneste. Rome's Mother of Time, Anna Perenna, appears to the dying god Mars in the guise of his virgin bride, Minerva. She stands over her naked lover and pushes his head down into a boiling cauldron, while the dog of the underworld gate looks on, as also on the Gundestrup example.[39]

Some pagan Mysteries employed visions of the Cauldron as symbolic death and rebirth. Before a Siberian shaman could practice, he was required to undergo hallucinatory experiences of being chopped to pieces and boiled in a cauldron, sometimes for a period as long as three years. Yakut, Buryat, and other tribes say the shaman must be killed by the spirits of ancestors, cooked in their magic cauldron, then given new flesh. "Shaman" comes from Tungusic *saman*, "one who died," a man assimilated to the Lord of Death called Samana in Sanskrit. Tibetan shamans made the soul-journey to the "Great Hell" pictured as an iron cauldron, called House of Iron or Iron Mountain.

Strabo Greek traveler, geographer, and historian of the first century B.C., a follower of the Stoic faith.

Cimbri Germanic tribes from Jutland, which Romans called the Cimbrian peninsula. In the 2nd century B.C., a Cimbrian army marched against Rome and caused great consternation in the city.

There the aspirant was dismembered by *rakshasas*—obsolete ancestral deities—and boiled, not in punishment for sin but as an initiatory procedure.[40]

Skald-shamans of Scandinavia made the same soul-journey to Hvergelmir, the Mighty Roaring Cauldron, source of life-giving waters at the foundations of the earth. This was another version of the triple cauldron in the earth-womb, from which Odin received inspiration and power. Hvergelmir was triple too, accompanied by the fount of wisdom and memory called Mimir (an archaic "mother"), and the fount of ongoing life called Urdarbrunner, the stream of Mother Earth. Founts and cauldrons in the earth were tended by the three **Fates** (Norns), of whom the first was Mother Earth herself.[41]

Even when the Cauldron of Regeneration entered Christian tradition as the Holy Grail, supposedly the chalice of Christ's last supper, it was referred to as an *escuele* or "cauldron."[42] Arthur's knights originally sought the Grail in the underworld of Annwn, receiving their divine vision of it in the castle of Elaine, or Elen, the virgin aspect of the triple Moon-goddess. It appeared in her hands, heralded by her yonic dove. It meant death for her chosen one, Galahad, who reigned as a sacred king, then died at the altar as he saw his vision of the Grail.[43]

The Cistercian *Estoire del Saint Graal* said "two heathen rulers," Mordrain and Nascien (Death and Rebirth) were blinded by the vision of the Grail, but healed by the touch of the lance that pierced Christ, both of these objects being kept in the same sanctuary.[44] The motive seems to have been to belittle the female symbol (grail) in favor of the male symbol (lance).

1. Goodrich, 18. 2. *Book of the Dead,* 114. 3. *Larousse,* 257.
4. Campbell, Or.M., 182. 5. Jung & von Franz, 114. 6. *Assyr. & Bab. Lit.,* 308.
7. Budge, E.M., 30. 8. Graves, W.G., 290. 9. Hooke, M.E.M., 101.
10. *Book of the Dead,* 205–6. 11. Budge, G.E. 1, 203. 12. Maspero, 283.
13. Hooke, S.P., 47. 14. Lethaby, 219. 15. Graves, G.M. 2, 27. 16. Gaster, 587.
17. Brewster, 230. 18. Attwater, 189. 19. de Voragine, 236.
20. Graves, W.G., 409. 21. Rees, 47. 22. Baring-Gould, C.M.M.A., 619.
23. Campbell, C.M., 533. 24. Guerber, L.M.A., 240. 25. Guerber, L.R., 147–48.
26. Keightley, 295. 27. J.B. Russell, 69. 28. Baring-Gould, C.M.M.A., 620.
29. Briffault 3, 451. 30. Malory 1, xxi. 31. Graves, W.G., 406.
32. Campbell, Or.M., 397. 33. Wendt, 137. 34. Groome, 107.
35. Graves, G.M. 1, 255–56. 36. *Larousse,* 142. 37. Cavendish, V.H.H., 49.
38. Jung & von Franz, 373. 39. Dumézil, 213, 243.
40. Eliade, S., 41, 159, 237, 439. 41. Branston, 53, 82; Turville-Petre, 246.
42. Campbell, C.M., 531. 43. Malory 2, 130, 268. 44. Campbell, C.M., 535.

Porphyry (ca. 234–305 A.D.) Neoplatonist philosopher, scholar, and writer; biographer of Plotinus; an opponent of the Christian church, which eventually destroyed most of his books.

Cave

Porphyry said before there were temples, all religious rites took place in caves.[1] The cave was universally identified with the womb of Mother Earth, the logical place for symbolic birth and regeneration. Etruscan and Roman temples featured a subterranean *mundus,* meaning both "earth" and "womb."[2] Similarly, the Sanskrit word for a sanctuary, *garbha-grha,* meant "womb."[3]

Holy places of Hinduism were caves representing the Great

Mother's yoni. Many *gompas* (holy hermitages) were first established in caves. Like the mountain of paradise, home of the gods, the Four Great Caves of Sikkim were distinguished according to the four cardinal points. North is the cave of the god's hill; west, the cave of great happiness; south, the cave of occult fairies; east, the secret cave, from which the sun is born.[4]

Among the oldest forms of the Hindu Goddess was Kurukulla, a *matrikadevi* colored red like the womb, and called Mother of Caverns.[5] As an emanation of Kali she was worshipped in cave-temple complexes like Ellora, Ajanta, Elephanta. Her western counterpart was Phrygian **Cybele**, "Cavern-dweller," the Great Mother of the Gods. A Latin form of her name was **Sybil**, the prophetic spirit in the cavern-dwelling Cumaean sybils, by whose order the Great Mother of the Gods was brought to Rome in 204 B.C.

Cybele's castrated priests claimed none of their brotherhood ever died. Instead, they went "down into the cavern" to be united with their Goddess. Cybele's cavern-shrines were also called marriage chambers, like the *pastos* of Eleusis. The Alexandrian poet Nicander called them "marriage bowers of Rhea Lobrine."[6] They were also the "sacred subterranean places" where those who had emasculated themselves in honor of Attis and Cybele used to come to deposit the offering of their genitals.[7]

Rhea was the Cretan name of the same Goddess, during the long period when fatherhood was unknown or negligible in Cretan society.[8] All life was supposed to have arisen from her uterine cave on Mount Dicte, whence came the e-dicts of her holy law; hence her title of Dictynna, Lawgiver. She was also called Britomartis the "sweet virgin," the mother without a spouse.[9] From the same uterine cave she gave birth to Zeus, who later claimed to be Father of Gods.

Cave-temples of Rhea Dictynna evolved into *dicteria,* which the Laws of Solon designated public brothels. In the era of the promiscuous priestesses, words for cave, temple, and brothel were often interchangeable.[10] To visit the cave and lie with the holy harlot was an act of worship. During the early Christian era, most pagan mystery cults celebrated their most sacred rites in caves or underground chambers.

Followers of Mithra considered the cave so essential to proper worship that, if the site of a temple had no natural cave, an artificial one was dug. The cave on the Vatican belonged to Mithra until 376 A.D., when a city prefect suppressed the cult of the rival Savior and seized the shrine in the name of Christ, on the very birthday of the pagan god, December 25.[11]

Despite the church's efforts at suppression, the old deities continued to be worshipped in sacred caves for many centuries. So many "grottoes" contained pagan idols that decorative ideas for cathedral sculptures were copied from them: hence the *grotesques* or "grotto-creatures" swarming in Gothic art. As late as the 15th century, Pope

Calixtus II tried to forbid religious ceremonies in sacred caves.[12] As entrances to the underworld, caves were still associated with the Great Mother's yonic gate. A long-revered gate to the womb of the world was a sea-cave on the southern Peloponnese near the shrine of Marmari—Mother Mari, the Sea-goddess whose other names were Aphrodite Marina, Marah, and Mary.[13]

Up to the 18th century, a cave called Tangrogo in Denbighshire was kept by "three fairy sisters"—the three Fates—whose footprints were often seen around the edge of its magic pool. The cave was said to contain "hidden treasures," a term that often meant paraphernalia of the Old Religion.[14]

Spenser said the hidden treasures of the Faery Queen's Bower of Bliss were the same as those of the virgin Mary's secret "enclosed garden": a magic pool of regeneration, a Tree of Life, singing birds, apples, and roses, including the central Rose of Love. Andreas Capellanus said the grotto of the pagan Goddess was a Palace of Love in the center of the earth *(in medio mundi),* with the male and female symbols of a Tree of Life and a sacred spring.[15]

Sacred caves were still used as "marriage bowers" long after paganism had been forced underground—literally. Bards who adored the heretical Goddess of Love (Minne) mentioned certain Grottoes of Love, hewn by heathen giants in the wild mountains, where people could hide when "they wished privacy to make love." Gottfried von Strassburg said whenever such a cave was found, it was sealed with a bronze door inscribed *La fossiure à le gent amant,* the Grotto for People in Love. "Above, the vault was finely joined, and on the keystone there was a crown, embellished beautifully by the goldsmith's art with an incrustation of gems. The pavement below was of a smooth, shining and rich marble, green as grass. In the center stood a bed, handsome and cleanly hewn of crystal, high and wide, well raised from the ground, and engraved round about with letters which—according to the legend—proclaimed its dedication to the goddess Love."[16]

The healing waters of all the sacred springs in Europe acquired new myths ascribing their virtues to saints or to the Virgin, but their real traditions sprang from the regenerative caves of the pagan Goddess. Up to the 19th century a sacred cave near Dunskey, Scotland, was used for the curative magic of its spring. The sick were brought from great distances to be bathed in the waters, always "at the change of the moon," showing that the place was a matriarchal shrine. Its magic baptisms were believed especially beneficial to weak or undernourished children.[17]

1. Robertson, 111. 2. Hays, 181. 3. Campbell, C.M., 168. 4. Waddell, 256–57. 5. *Larousse,* 359. 6. Gaster, 609. 7. Vermaseren, 111. 8. Briffault 1, 392. 9. *Larousse,* 86. 10. Sadock, Kaplan & Freedman, 16. 11. J.H. Smith, D.C.P., 146. 12. Jung, M.H.S., 234. 13. Hughes, 159. 14. Hazlitt, 580. 15. Wilkins, 128, 139. 16. Campbell, C.M., 44. 17. Hazlitt, 420.

Cecilia, Saint

Mythical saint whose legend was built on some bones discovered by Pope Paschal I in a Roman catacomb bearing the name Calliste—probably Artemis Calliste as the Muse of music, which became the special province of "St. Cecilia."[1] Fired by the current mania for relic-hunting (9th century A.D.), the pope immediately declared that Cecilia was a virgin martyr of the second or maybe the third century, and that she was tortured to death for rejecting her pagan bridegroom on the very day of their wedding. He ordered her canonized at once.[2]

The name Cecilia meant Lily of Heaven, another ancient title of the Goddess.[3]

1. *Encyc. Brit.*, "Cecilia." 2. Attwater, 81. 3. Chaucer, 454.

Cemetery

Greek *koimeteria* was a Place of the Mother, where the dead could rest as close as possible to the Goddess's temples. The custom was continued in Christian Europe. The church-*yard,* home of the dead, derived from Germanic *gard* or *garth,* meaning "earth" or "world," i.e., the world of the dead under the soil.

Tantric **dakinis** celebrated the rites of the dead in cremation grounds, "where ordinary people feared to go," because they were death-priestesses intimately acquainted with necropoli.[1] Their Goddess, Kali Ma the Destroyer, was the same queen of tombs called Kalma in Finno-Ugric myth.[2] Dakinis became European *vilas, valas,* or *wilis,* women associated with the dead, later called witches. The traditional legend of witches celebrating their sabbats in cemeteries may have had a real basis in ancient matriarchy.

1. Rawson, E.A., 152. 2. *Larousse,* 306.

Centaurs

Greek horse-spirits derived from Hindu *asvins* and the man-horse wizards of central Asia. Centaurs were magic shape-shifters, and teachers of the Hellenic gods.[1] Their most familiar appearance was with the head and shoulders of a man and the body and legs of a horse. Their other name was Magnetes, "great ones."[2] They have been connected with Latin *centuria,* a company of 100 soldiers.[3] Perpetual rivals of the Centaurs were the Lapiths, "men-who-use-stone-weapons," a hint of their extreme antiquity. See **Horse**.

1. Graves, W.G., 255–56. 2. Lawson, 244. 3. Graves, G.M. 1, 361.

Ceraunos, Saint

Canonized form of one of the phallic lightning-gods who descended into Earth's womb, like Lucifer, to become a lord of the underworld. Pagans sometimes called the lightning *Gemma Cerauniae,* the Jewel of Ceraunos—"jewel" in the same sense as the Tantric (male) Jewel in the (female) Lotus.[1] The Greeks thought when Ceraunos descended into the underworld, he became Charon, the ferryman of the Styx.[2] As a saint, he had little purpose other than to attract to Christianity those who had formerly worshipped him as a **psychopomp.**

1. Leland, p. 250. 2. H. Smith, p. 227

Ceres

Sign of Ceres

Latin form of the Great Goddess, cognate with Greek Kore or Core, identified with Demeter as Mother Earth. As the earth-ruling aspect of the Goddess's trinity, Ceres combined with Juno as queen of heaven, and Proserpine as queen of the underworld. She was called Ceres Legifera, "Ceres the Lawgiver." Her priestesses were considered the foundresses of the Roman legal system.[1]

Ceres ruled Rome through her sacred *matronae,* during that lost period of four centuries before 200 B.C., a period whose written records were destroyed by later patriarchal historians, leaving only a residue of myths and religious customs that were only vaguely explained.[2] Farmers viewed her as the source of all food and kept her rites faithfully, for fear of crop failure.

This was true not only of Roman farmers but even of Christian farmers. Ceres's greatest annual festival, the Cerealia, was celebrated in the British Isles almost to the present day. An account of the Shire of Murray in the late 19th century said, "In the middle of June, farmers go round their corn with burning torches, in memory of the Cerealia."[3]

1. Bachofen, 192. 2. Dumézil, 10. 3. Hazlitt, 101.

Cernunnos

Celtic version of the Horned God, shown in sacred art with antlers strapped to his head, seated in lotus position like a yogi.[1] This contemplative pose was typical of Gallo-Roman deities in the first millenium B.C.[2] Cernunnos was a consort of the Moon-goddess, whose Roman name Diana may have been related to Sanskrit *dhyana,* "yogic contemplation."[3] Medieval romances spoke of pagan heroes who acquired godlike powers by falling into a trance of "contemplation" of the Goddess as lady-love.[4]

1. Campbell, Or.M., 307. 2. *Larousse,* 232. 3. Campbell, Or.M., 440. 4. Goodrich, 69.

Cerridwen

var. Cerdo

Celtic name for the Triple Goddess, especially as the fearsome death-totem, a white, corpse-eating Sow representing the moon. She was the same as Syrian Astarte or Greek Demeter, both of whom appeared as sows. So did Freya, one of whose titles was a cognate of Cerridwen, that is Sýr, "the Sow."[1]

Cerdo is the Spanish word for pig. Harvest dances in the Spanish Pyrénées were *cerdaña,* "pig-dances," celebrated in honor of the Goddess who both gave and took away, and harvested souls in her character as "the source of life, and the receptacle of the dead."[2] A rich wheat-growing region in the Pyrénées was dominated by her sacred town, Puigcerdá, or Cerdo's Hill.[3] Her cult probably went back to the prehistoric temples of Malta, which had images of the Goddess in the shape of a sow.

Welsh bards who composed funerary elegies called themselves *cerddorion,* sons of Cerridwen or Cerdo. Their greatest hero, **Taliesin**, a founder of their craft, was said to have been born of Cerridwen and specially treated by her to a few precious drops of magical inspiration from her **Cauldron**.

1. Turville-Petre, 168. 2. Baring-Gould, C.M.M.A., 621. 3. Graves, W.G., 58–60

Chad, Saint

Legendary bishop of Mercia, said to be a follower of the canonized princess Wereburg (see **Convent**). He was probably never a real person. His "brother" St. Cedd was called bishop of London, but both Chad and Cedd were variants of the pagan god Ceadda, who was associated with magic healing springs. In the runic calendar, the emblem of St. Chad was a palm branch, or Tree of Life.[1]

A pagan deity named Chaddi is still worshipped by the Samoyeds, who practice a nominal Christianity as long as all goes well, but in time of trouble return to their own Chaddi. "Heathen services are conducted by night within old stone-circles, and all images of Chaddi are carefully screened from view. . . . [W]ithin these cromlechs were formerly offered up those human sacrifices with which the natives used to propitiate Chaddi."[2]

1. Brewster, 122. 2. Johnson, 139.

Chakra

Tantric term for the magic circle of worshippers, alternating men and women after the manner of the **egg-and-dart frieze**; also, one of the "rings" or stages of enlightenment, visualized as steps ascending the spinal column, as the inner serpent goddess Kundalini uncoils from the pelvis upward to the head. This ascent of the *chakras* was likened to different stages of initiatory teaching, each taking place in a magic circle whose members cooperated in the effort of comprehension.

The *chakra* was essentially the same as the Sufic *halka,* "magic circle," called the heart and basic unit of Sufism.[1] The purpose of a properly conducted *chakra* was to make each participant feel "as if the Shakti was their own Mother who had borne them."[2] She was a mother-bride, compounded of the felt presence of both Goddess and woman. In the classic *chakra,* each man had his wife or *shakti* to his left, while the Lord of the Chakra with his *shakti* occupied the center of the circle.[3] European pagan religions maintained the same arrangement, which eventually became the pattern of the circular folk dance.

1. Shah, 21. 2. Avalon, 166. 3. *Mahanirvanatantra,* cxxi.

Chaldean

"Moon worshipper," a common name for Mesopotamian astrologers who studied the movements of the moon in relation to the stars.[1] Because the magic powers of the Chaldeans commanded respect nearly everywhere in the ancient world, biblical writers made Abraham a Chaldean (Genesis 11:28). The same name was still being applied to astrologers and wizards in the 15th century A.D.[2]

1. Briffault 2, 600. 2. Lea unabridged, 772.

Ch'ang-O

Chinese Moon-goddess, sole keeper of the ambrosia of immortality (**menstrual blood**). Her husband, the Excellent Archer, became intensely jealous of her monopoly of life-magic and quarreled with her. So she left him, as Lilith left Adam, and went to live in the moon forever, dispensing her precious elixir to women only.[1]

1. *Larousse,* 383.

Chaos

Greek word for the undifferentiated mixture of raw elements supposed to occupy the World-Goddess's womb before creation and after destruction of each recurrent universe. It meant the Goddess herself in her state of "eternal flux," when the fluid of her womb was not yet clotted into the formative state of a solid world. Chaos is expressed in the Bible as the condition of the earth before creation, "without form" and "void" (Genesis 1:2). See **Doomsday**; **Tiamat**; **Tohu Bohu**.

Charites

"Graces," heavenly dispensers of *charis* (Latin *caritas*), the grace of Mother Aphrodite, which the Bible translates either "love" or "charity" (1 Corinthians 13). The Charites were ancient manifestations of the Triple Goddess. Pausanias said they were worshipped at Orchomenos as three standing stones.[1] The classic myth of their nymph-hood hardly described them; nor did their Christian form, the mythical St. Charity. See **Grace**; **Sophia, Saint**.

1. Dumézil, 166.

Charlemagne

Frankish emperor, whose reign (768–814) was the second great turning-point in the history of the Holy Roman Empire. He was the second Constantine. He found it useful to be a Christian, since the church condoned his wars of acquisition—as pagan tribal religions would not—and took its share of the spoils, eventually rewarding Charlemagne with the crown of the Empire. He was also allowed a special status of matrimony, not granted to other men. He had four wives and innumerable concubines, which the church tolerantly described as "marriages of the second rank."[1]

Charlemagne's reign was a painful history of aggression against the matriarchal religions of his ancestors. In 772 he massacred more than 4000 Saxons and destroyed their shrine at Heresburg, an omphalos of the earth-mother Hera. He cut down the phallic tree trunk Irminsul, "Column of the World," the same *axis mundi* that Greeks called the Great Herm, Norwegians called Yggdrasil, and Christians called the cross.[2]

After destroying shrines to demoralize the pagan clans, Charlemagne imposed vassalage on them and converted them to Christianity by the simple offer of a choice between Christ and immediate death. All who rejected baptism were to be slain at once. In 33 years of constant war, Charlemagne built the Holy Roman Empire, at the cost of so many lives that historians have not even tried to estimate the extent of the slaughter.[3]

Charlemagne's policy of conversion by the sword succeeded so well that the church backed Christian rulers in this kind of military activity ever since. As the Song of Roland put it: "The bishops bless the waters and convert the heathen. If any man protests, he is burned or put to the sword."[4]

Sometimes the blessed waters themselves served to execute the unregenerate heathen. It was said that converts made under the rule of St. Goar were held under water until they either accepted Christ, or drowned.[5]

1. Murstein, 143. 2. Reinach, 144. 3. H. Smith, 251.
4. Goodrich, 96. 5. Guerber, L.R., 193.

Charm

Old English *cyrm,* a hymn or choral song, came from Latin *carmen,* a sacred incantation to the Goddess Carmenta, inventor of alphabets and "words of power."[1] A "charm" reflected men's ancient belief that women exerted power over male bodies and souls through their mastery of sung oı spoken spells invoking the help of the Goddess. The belief was not wholly illogical; the Goddess was Nature, and Nature caused the signs of sexual attraction, including lovesick behavior and penile erection, that made a man feel helplessly subject to unknown forces.

Therefore everything that made a man feel attracted to a woman came to be synonymous with witchcraft: charm, enchantment, bewitchment, spellbinding, witchery, moon-madness, or glamor—in the old sense of a spell cast by Morgan of "Glamorgan." The British Parliament passed an odd law in 1770 that hinted at the same archetypal fears, making it illegal for a woman to "betray" any man into matrimony with such artificialities as false hair, iron stays, high-heeled shoes, or perfume. If a husband demonstrated that his wife had used such devices, the marriage would be annulled, and the woman would "incur the penalty of the law now enforced against witchcraft."[2]

Women's singing was also highly suspect, as this was the classic method of casting spells. "Enchant" came from *incantare,* "to sing over"—which also meant incantation.[3]

1. Potter & Sargent, 49. 2. Murstein, 227. 3. Funk, 254.

Charon

Classic ferryman of the Styx; like Hermes, conductor of souls to the underworld. The dead were buried with coins in the mouth or on the eyelids to pay Charon's ferry. The Chinese also used to put money in graves, for crossing the river of death. In the Balkans, it was said a woman could make her husband "blind as a corpse" to her adultery, if she gave him water that had washed the coins from a corpse's eyes.[1] Charon's fee was Christianized as Peter's Penny: St. Peter's bribe for opening the heavenly gates.[2] In Greece, Charon found a new Christian identity as St. Charus, escort and guardian of souls in the "lower world," or common home of the dead.[3]

1. Frazer, F.O.T., 35. 2. Halliday, 50. 3. Hyde, 206, 213.

Chastity Belt

Medieval device for locking a woman's potential lovers out of her body, while her husband was away from home at wars, pilgrimages, or crusades. The pelvic fetter had small spiked holes through which urine, feces, and menstrual effluents might pass—in theory. In practice, it would have been impossible to keep clean. Vaginal infections, skin eruptions, and ulcers would have been inevitable after wearing such a device for only a short time, let alone months or years.

In 1889 the skeleton of a woman was found in a 15th-century Austrian graveyard, still wearing the chastity belt that probably caused her death.[1]

1. Brasch, 25.

Chemosh

Hebrew form of Shamash, the sun god of Sippar and Moab, worshipped in the temple of Solomon (I Kings 11:7). Because Chemosh was one of Yahweh's rivals, called an "abomination" by later priests attempting to suppress all cults but their own, he was adopted into the still later Christian pantheon of hell as a demon. He was a favorite of exorcists, who commonly claimed to have purged the possessed of the demon Chemosh.

Chernobog

"Black God" of the Slavs, adversary of the White God, Byelobog; another version of **Ahriman** opposed to **Ahura Mazda**, or the Black Sun beneath the earth opposed to the White Sun in heaven. Like other versions of the chthonian deity, Chernobog was a Lord of Death, often invoked for curses. The Ukrainians still say, "May the Black God exterminate you!"[1] In the same manner, ancient Persians invoked Ahriman, Chaldeans invoked Aciel, Romans invoked Saturn, and Christians invoked the devil.

1. *Larousse,* 283.

Cherry

Like many slang expressions, the use of "cherry" for "virginity" may be traced to a mythic past. Like other red fruits, such as the apple and pomegranate, the cherry symbolized the Virgin Goddess: bearing her sacred blood color and bearing its seed within, like a womb.

Maya, the virgin mother of Buddha, embraced the cherry tree Sala while giving birth to her divine child.[1] Some said the tree recognized her divinity and bent its branches down to offer its fruit. The story was carried to Europe and spawned the medieval *Cherry Tree Carol,* in which Maya became Mary.

Gypsies applied the love-magic of the cherry to many magic charms, especially those associated with virginity. When a gypsy girl desired to attract a lover, she drilled holes through fourteen cherry stones on the fourteen nights of the waxing moon, and wore them on a cord around her left thigh (the "female" side).[2] The obvious elements of this magic were penetration of the cherry, and building up to the full moon, indicating growth or pregnancy.

French traditions of courtly love perhaps made "cherry" *(cerise)* synonymous with "beloved" *(chérie)*. Cherry-red was often considered the color of love.

1. *Larousse,* 348. 2. Bowness, 22.

Cherub

Hebrew *kerubh,* the Babylonian totemic animal deities combining eagle wings, lion feet, bull heads, and serpent tails—animal symbols of the four seasons, cardinal directions, and elements. The *cherubim* who guarded the gates of Eden and the throne of God were quite unlike the naked winged babies that romantic and baroque art later called cherubs. As animal-masked and costumed priests, the *cherubim* probably descended from Sheban *mu-karribim,* "close kindred," guardians of the shrine of the Moon-goddess at Marib.

Chicomecoatl

Mexican Goddess similar to Demeter, called Heart of the Earth, and ancestress of all peoples. No god could equal her in power. She was usually accompanied by a young savior son, a fertility-sacrifice. Her angelic messengers were seven serpents.[1]

1. Neumann, G.M., 182.

Chidambaram

Tantric Buddhist concept of the Center of the Universe, where Shiva does his eternal dance of life. The same Center was a mythic model of the heart as the center of the body, and the heartbeat as the dance; for Chidambaram existed "within the heart."[1] The heart of the whole cosmos was the same as the Cave of the Heart, "where the true self resides."[2] This was another expression of Oriental belief in the identity of self and deity. See **Antinomianism**; **Heart**.

1. Ross, 32. 2. Menen, 70.

Chimalman

Virgin mother of the Aztec savior **Quetzalcoatl**; one of "three divine sisters." She was the same Triple Goddess worshipped around the world in Virgin, Mother, and Crone aspects. See **Trinity**.

Chionia

"Snow Queen," a Greek title of one of the **Horae**; an untouchable virgin Goddess of the high mountains, prototype of the medieval fairy, Virginal the Ice Queen. She was also canonized as a Christian "virgin martyr."

Chomo-Lung-Ma

"Goddess Mother of the Universe," the real name of the world's highest mountain, which westerners renamed Everest after a man. This masculine name was bestowed on the Goddess Mother in 1863 by foreign invaders who preferred to attach patriarchal surnames to everything.[1]

1. *Encyc. Brit.*, "Everest, Sir George."

Christina, Saint

Another apocryphal "virgin martyr," whose legend was constructed on no basis whatever, except the name, meaning "a female Christian." Her story was one of those sadistic wonder-tales in which Christian writers delighted, piling torture upon torture in fantasies that quite lost sight of the natural limitations of human flesh.

For refusing to burn incense to the pagan gods, Christina was locked up in a tower by her father. She was stripped and beaten with rods, then torn apart by hooks, and her limbs were broken. Nothing daunted, she took up pieces of her own flesh and threw them in her father's face, saying, "Take, tyrant, and eat the flesh thou hast begotten!" So her father then had her sprinkled with oil and roasted on a fire-wheel. Then she was thrown into the sea with a stone around her neck. Angels saved her, and she returned to her father, who dropped dead of frustration.

Christina's torments were continued by a judge named Elius, who had her rocked in a red-hot iron cradle. Her next judge, Julian, threw her into a burning furnace, where she walked about unburned for five days. Then, poisonous snakes were hung about her neck. Then, her breasts were cut off, and her tongue cut out. She took a piece of her tongue and threw it at Julian, striking him in the eye and blinding him. Finally, Julian killed her by shooting three arrows into her.[1] This can only have been a magic form of destruction, for Christina had by this time amply demonstrated her invulnerability to every ordinary method of execution.

1. de Voragine, 366–68.

Christmas

For its first three centuries, the Christian church knew no birthday for its savior. During the 4th century there was much argument about adoption of a date. Some favored the popular date of the Koreion, when the divine Virgin gave birth to the new Aeon in Alexandria.[1] Now called Twelfth Night or Epiphany, this date is still the official nativity in Armenian churches, and celebrated with more pomp than Christmas by the Greek Orthodox.[2]

Roman churchmen tended to favor the Mithraic winter-solstice festival called *Dies Natalis Solis Invictus,* Birthday of the Unconquered Sun.[3] Blended with the Greek sun-festival of the Helia by the emperor Aurelian, this December 25 nativity also honored such gods as Attis, Dionysus, Osiris, Syrian Baal, and other versions of the solar Son of Man who bore such titles as Light of the World, Sun of Righteousness, and Savior.[4] Most pagan Mysteries celebrated the birth of the Divine Child at the winter solstice. Norsemen celebrated the birthday of their Lord, Frey, at the *nadir* of the sun in the darkest days of winter, known to them as **Yule**. The night of birth, Christmas Eve, was called Modranect, Latin *matrum noctem,* the Night of the Mother—originally a greater festival than Christmas Day.[5]

Early in the 4th century the Roman church adopted December 25 because the people were used to calling it a god's birthday. But eastern churches refused to honor it until 375 A.D.[6] The fiction that some record existed in the land of Jesus's alleged birth certainly could not be upheld, for the church of Jerusalem continued to ignore the official date until the 7th century.[7]

Trappings such as Yule logs, gifts, lights, mistletoe, holly, carols, feasts, and processions were altogether pagan. They were drawn from worship of the Goddess as mother of the Divine Child. Christmas trees evolved from the *pinea silva,* pine groves attached to temples of the Great Mother. On the night before a holy day, Roman priests called *dendrophori* or "tree-bearers" cut one of the sacred pines, decorated it, and carried it into the temple to receive the effigy of Attis.[8] Figures and fetishes attached to such trees in later centuries seem to have represented a whole pantheon of pagan deities on the World Tree.

Christmas celebrations remained so obviously pagan over the years that many churchmen bitterly denounced their "carnal pomp and jollity." Polydor Virgil said: "Dancing, masques, mummeries, stage-plays, and other such Christmas disorders now in use with Christians, were derived from these Roman Saturnalian and Bacchanalian festivals; which should cause all pious Christians eternally to abominate them."[9] Puritans in 17th-century Massachusetts tried to ban Christmas altogether because of its overt heathenism.[10] Inevitably, the attempt failed.

A curious mistake in the Christmas mystery play of the Towneley cycle shows a Great Mother image not fully assimilated to that of Mary. Before their attention was arrested by the annunciatory angel, idly chatting shepherds complained of their cruel overlords, and prayed "Our Lady" to curse them.[11] Considering that they were not acquainted with the Mother of Christ, a rather different "Lady" must have been intended.

Among many other superstitions connected with Christmas were some that were typical of pagan holy days, such as the belief that animals could speak human words at midnight on Christmas Eve, or that divinatory voices could be heard at crossroads at the same time.[12] Also at midnight on Christmas Eve, water in wells and springs was supposed to turn into blood, or its sacramental equivalent, wine. The miracle was not to be verified, however; for all who witnessed it would die within the year.[13]

1. Campbell, M.I., 34. 2. Miles, 22. 3. Reinach, 282.
4. H. Smith, 130; Hyde, 92; Miles, 23. 5. Turville-Petre, 227.
6. Frazer, G.B., 416. 7. Miles, 22. 8. Vermaseren, 115. 9. Hazlitt, 118–19.
10. de Lys, 372. 11. Miles, 135. 12. Summers, V., 157. 13. Miles, 234.

Christos

"Anointed One," a title of many Middle-Eastern sacrificial gods—Attis, Adonis, Tammuz, Osiris—derived from Oriental cults of the sacred marriage. In the east, the god's *lingam* or the erect penis of his statue was anointed with holy oil (Greek *chrism*) for easier penetration of his bride, the Goddess, impersonated by one of the temple virgins.[1] Before anointing with oil, the god's phallus was often reddened to the color of life with pigment, wine, or blood—specifically, the **menstrual blood** of his bride.[2] Because kingship once depended on the sacred marriage, anointing became the official rite of investiture for surrogate kings as well as real kings. It carried a promise of godhood.

The words of the psalmist, "Thou anointest my head with oil," evolved from the ancient custom of anointing the god-king's penis, for which "head" was a common euphemism. At royal weddings the king's head was crowned with a wreath of flowers, as in the Hindu *svayamara* ceremony—and flowers, in biblical language, symbolized menstrual blood (Leviticus 15:24). Among the pagans, the temple virgin deflowering herself on the god's carved phallus would place a wreath of flowers on his head at the same time.[3] Eventually the anointing of the phallus was displaced to the head because the marriage rite was omitted from public sacrifices of the Savior, Redeemer, Son of God, etc. Like the New Testament Christ, he was "anointed" only for his burying: the marriage with the earth (John 12:7). Jesus became a *Christos* when he was *christ*-ened for burial by Mary, the magdalene or temple maiden (Matthew 26:12), who also announced his resurrection (Mark 15:47).

Among the Essenes, a *Christos* was a priest, specifically designated Sin Bearer or Redeemer: one who atoned for others' sins.[4] Among the Slavs, *Christos* or *Krstnik* meant a sacrificial hero and also an "accursed one," due to the ancient practice of laying a formal curse on the Sin Bearer before he was sacrificed.[5] See **Firstborn**; **Kingship**.

1. Rawson, E.A., 29. 2. G.R. Scott, 187; Edwardes, 50. 3. Legman, 661. 4. Pfeifer, 133. 5. Leland, 145.

Chthonia

"Subterranean," an epithet of Black Demeter, Cybele, and other underground forms of the Goddess; also applied to gods in their nether, dark, Lord-of-Death aspect, e.g. Zeus Chthonios, or Chthonian Apollo.

Cinderella

The fairy tale of the cinder-maid originated as an anti-ecclesiastical allegory repeated by real "fairies"—that is, pagans. Ella was **Hel**, or Helle, daughter of Mother Earth, the Goddess with her regenerative fires reduced to cinders. Her ugly stepmother was the new church. Her ugly stepsisters were the church's darlings, the military aristocracy and the clergy.

An early German version of the story said Cinderella's real mother the Earth, though dead, sent from her grave a fairy tree in answer to her daughter's prayer. This tree produced golden apples, fine clothes, and other gifts. Thus the "fairy godmother" of later versions seems to have been a ghost of the mother, the dispossessed Great Goddess in retirement underground.[1]

Beautified with her new riches, Cinderella won the "prince" (mankind), ever easily impressed by the display of finery. Their union was symbolized by fitting her foot into a shoe, a common sexual allegory. The Eleusinian Mysteries signified sacred marriage by working a phallic object in a woman's shoe.[2] The glass slipper perhaps stood for the Crystal Cave by which pagan heroes entered the uterine underworld.

Like other secret medieval prophecies of the overthrow of the rich, powerful theocracy, the downfall of Cinderella's ugly stepmother and stepsisters may have been intended as a prophecy.[3]

1. Jung & von Franz, 127. 2. Graves, G.M. 1, 94. 3. Tuchman, 41.

Circe

Homeric "witch" able to transform men into sacrificial swine: a mythic picture of the transition from human to porcine sacrifices during the Hellenic period. Circe's isle of Aeaea was a funerary shrine. Its name meant "Wailing." Circe herself was the death-bird *kirkos*, falcon. From the same root came the Latin *circus*, originally an enclosure for funerary games.[1]

As the circle, or *cirque,* Circe was identical with Omphale of Lydia with her cosmic spinning wheel: a fate-spinner, weaver of the destinies of men.[2] Homer called her Circe of the Braided Tresses, hinting that, like Oriental goddesses, she manipulated forces of creation and destruction by the knots and braids in her **hair**. She ruled all the stars that determined men's fates. Pliny said Circe was a Goddess who "commanded all the lights of heaven."[3]

1. Lindsay, O.A., 239. 2. Graves, G.M. 2, 358. 3. Hawkins, 139.

Circumcision

Symbolic version of the sacrifice of virility to a deity, as practiced in Egypt, Persia, and the Middle East. Originally an imitation of menstruation, performed at puberty on boys who were dressed up as girls for the occasion.[1] Circumcision came to be regarded as a sacrifice pleasing to a male deity, when it was viewed as a substitute for **castration**.

1. Gifford, 42.

Clare, Saint

var. Saint Claire

Mythical saint constructed from the title of the Celtic Goddess, Sinclair, "Sacred Light."[1] The original form remained, as a popular surname.

1. Hitching, 212.

Cleopatra VII

One of the last Goddess-queens of Egypt, Cleopatra followed the precedent of Egyptian rulers in general and turned herself into a divinity. At an Alexandrian festival she "assumed the robe of **Isis** and was addressed as the New Isis."[1]

Though she was not a native Egyptian, but one of the Macedonian family of Ptolemies, Cleopatra exercised the ancient prerogatives of Egyptian queens. Julius Caesar became her lover because it was the only way he could annex Egypt to the Roman provinces. By time-honored law, no man could exercise political power in Egypt unless he loved its queen.

Some of Cleopatra's less eminent lovers lasted only one night and paid with their lives for a single taste of her love.[2] The custom seems to have been adopted by later male rulers of Arabia, to judge by the gynocidal sultan of the *Arabian Nights.* The thinking behind this custom remains mysterious. It may be that men who lay with the queen (and therefore with the Goddess herself) were believed to gain immortality thereby, for any man who coupled with a Goddess would become a God. Sacred marriage, followed by death and deification, formed the basic pattern of many ancient Mysteries.

When her son Caesarion was born, Cleopatra built herself a *mammisi* or "birth temple" for the worship of her own maternity. In the shrine she was pictured in the act of giving birth, assisted by the Seven Hathors.[3] Cleopatra's *mammisi* stood until the 19th century A.D., when it was described by travelers, but it disappeared in the past century.[4]

She also gave birth to the sun and moon, in the form of twins named Alexander Helios and Cleopatra Selene—Alexander-Sun and Cleopatra-Moon.[5] Perhaps these children represented her own mating with the solar god of Alexandria.

1. Lindsay, O.A., 132. 2. Lederer, 323. 3. Budge, G.E. 1, 161. 4. *Encyc. Brit.*, "Hermonthis." 5. *Encyc. Brit.*, "Cleopatra."

Clitoris

From Greek *kleitoris,* "divine, famous, goddess-like."[1] Greek myth personified the phallus as Priapus and the clitoris as an Amazon queen named Kleite, ancestral mother of the Kleitae, a tribe of warrior women who founded a city in Italy.[2] In Corinth, Kleite was a princess "whom Artemis made grow tall and strong," an allegory of her erection.[3] Or, again, she was a nymph who loved the phallus of the sun god and always followed his motion with her "head"—a transparently sexual metaphor.[4] In a bowdlerized version of the story she was transformed into a sunflower, turning to follow the motion of the sun across the sky.

Pausanias Greek traveler and geographer of the 2nd century A.D. Living in a time of declining culture, he was inspired by a desire to describe the ancient sacred sites for posterity.

Pausanias said the Arcadian city of Clitor was sacred to Artemis, or to Demeter, and stood at the genital shrine of the earth, the headwaters of the Styx (or Alph).[5] The meaning of this geographical myth is made clear by the primitive belief that the Styx represented Mother Earth's **menstrual blood**, source and solvent of all things. In this place, too, the orgiastic priestesses of Artemis were "soothed" out of their frenzies; therefore the local *omphalos* must have signified the Goddess's clitoris instead of her navel.

Later patriarchal society managed to ignore the clitoris. Since the Christian church taught that women should not experience sexual pleasure but should only endure intercourse for the sake of procreation, growing girls and boys alike were kept ignorant of female sexuality, insofar as possible.[6] Even physicians came to believe that no clitoris would be found on a virtuous woman.

From medieval times onward, virtuous women rarely showed themselves naked to any man, even a husband; so it was perhaps not surprising that men should remain ignorant of the female anatomy they clumsily fumbled with in the dark. Pious married couples wore the *chemise cagoule,* a voluminous nightgown with a small hole in front, to allow impregnation with a minimum of body contact.[7]

At a witch trial in 1593, the investigating gaoler (a married man) apparently discovered a clitoris for the first time, and identified it as a devil's teat, sure proof of the witch's guilt. It was "a little lump of flesh, in manner sticking out as if it had been a teat, to the length of half an inch," which the gaoler, "perceiving at the first sight thereof, meant not to disclose, because it was adjoining to so secret a place which was not decent to be seen; yet in the end, not willing to conceal so strange a matter," he showed it to various bystanders.[8] The bystanders had never seen anything like it either. The witch was convicted.

European society certainly knew all about the penis, and never ceased to worship it, even in Christian times (see **Phallus Worship**). Yet the clitoris was forgotten:

> *Almost from the very beginning of our lives, we are all taught that the primary male sex organ is the penis, and the primary female sex organ is the vagina. These organs are supposed to define the sexes, to be the difference between boys and girls . . . . This is a lie . . . . Woman's sexual pleasure is often left out of these definitions. If people considered that the purpose of the female sex organs is to bring pleasure to women, then female sex would be defined by, and focused on, a different organ. Everyone would be taught from infancy that, as the primary male sex organ is the penis, so the primary female sex organ is the clitoris.*[9]

Medical authorities in the 19th century seemed anxious to prevent women from discovering their own sexuality. Girls who learned to develop orgasmic capacity by masturbation, just as boys learned it, were regarded as medical problems. Often they were "treated" or "corrected" by amputation or cautery of the clitoris, or "miniature chastity belts, sewing the vaginal lips together to put the clitoris out of reach, and even castration by surgical removal of the ovaries. But there are no references in the medical literature to surgical removal of testicles or amputation of the penis to stop masturbation (in boys)."[10]

In the United States, the last recorded clitoridectomy for curing masturbation was performed in 1948—on a five-year-old girl.[11]

The Catholic church's definition of masturbation as "a grave moral disorder" in 1976 may have incorporated fears of the effect of masturbation on female orgasmic capacity, now well known to evolve through masturbatory experience the same as that of a male.[12] Less than a century ago, in the Victorian era, priests and doctors realized that "the total repression of woman's sexuality was crucial to ensure her subjugation." Leading authorities like Dr. Isaac Brown Baker performed many clitoridectomies to cure women's nervousness, hysteria, catalepsy, insanity, female dementia, and other catchwords for symptoms of sexual frustration.[13]

1. Young, 47. 2. Bachofen, 283. 3. Graves, G.M. 2, 26. 4. Hamilton, 291. 5. Graves, W.G., 405–6. 6. Simons, 141. 7. Sadock, Kaplan & Freedman, 25. 8. Rosen, 296–97. 9. Gornick & Moran, 292–93. 10. Gornick & Moran, 293. 11. Ehrenreich & English, 111. 12. *Newsweek,* Jan. 26, 1976. 13. Nobile, 223–24.

Clotho

"The Spinner," first of the Greek Moerae or **Fates**; She Who Spins the Thread of Life. The same name was applied to Isis in her "terrible" aspect as a creator-destroyer.[1] Clotho's thread was sometimes golden, but more often blood red.

1. Neumann, G.M., 162.

Clytemnestra

"Divine Wooing," or Sacred Marriage; the last matriarchal queen of Mycenae, slain by her son Orestes, a worshipper of the patriarchal god Apollo. Clytemnestra claimed a queen's traditional right to choose her consort, and have each new one slay the old one. Thus she arranged to have her husband Agamemnon slain by her latest lover, Aegisthus, whose name means Strong Goat.[1]

Aegisthus had the right mythic prerequisites for a sacred king. He was born of an incestuous union. His mother Pelopia was a Goddess of Clytemnestra's clan, the Pelopids. In infancy he was abandoned to the wild, was rescued, and, like Zeus himself, was nourished by a she-goat.[2] He was prepared to be a god on earth.

Orestes spoiled it by killing his mother and her lover, calling down on himself the inexpiable curse of *miasma* for his matricide. The Furies pursued him, but the god Apollo defended him, on the ground that motherhood was not real parenthood. "The mother is no parent of that which is called her child, but only nurse of the new-planted seed that grows. The parent is he who mounts."[3] This Apollonian view of parenthood was also the Christian view, even subsequent to 1827 A.D. when Karl von Baer first discovered the human ovum, gigantic in size and complexity as compared to a spermatozoon.

1. Graves, G.M. 2, 377. 2. Gaster, 224. 3. Bachofen, 159.

Coatlicue

"Lady of the Serpent Skirt," mother of all Aztec deities as well as of the sun, the moon, and the stars. She produced all earthly life, and received the dead back again into her body. She was associated with volcanic mountains. Like Kali she wore a necklace of skulls, and a skirt of either serpents or shorn penises of her castrated savior-lovers. Her daughter Xochiquetzal, the Mexican Aphrodite, was a Goddess of All Women.

Columba, Saint

"Holy Dove," a spurious canonization of Aphrodite as a "maiden martyr" Columba of Sens.[1] Celtic myth called her Colombe, the yoni-maiden mated to Lancelot as a lightning bolt, the Phallus of Heaven.[2] See **Lightning**.

1. Attwater, 92. 2. Malory 1, 377.

Conscience

"Knowing-together," a word coined by Stoic philosophers who said deity is found only within the human mind. Socrates's famous dictum "Know thyself" was a Stoic aphorism for knowing God. Fusing divinity with self produced "conscience." Thus the philosophers said any dictate of one's own conscience was inevitably holy and right.[1] The concept grew from Oriental teachings about the identity of man with God, woman with Goddess. See **Antinomianism**.

1. Angus, 207–8.

Constantine I

The "first Christian emperor" (288?–337), honored for establishing Christianity as the official religion of the Roman empire. Actually, Constantine didn't do this in his own lifetime; his bishops did it afterward. Constantine was not so much a worshipper of Christ as he was a worshipper of himself.

Constantine considered himself the incarnation of "the supreme god," a combination of Apollo, Mithra, Jupiter, the sun, and Christ. He called himself "the instrument of the Deity." He said, "I banished and utterly abolished every form of evil then prevailing, in the hope that the human race, enlightened through me, might be called to a proper observance of God's holy laws." He designated for his tomb a spot in the center of the cruciform Church of the Holy Apostles, saying he would lie forever with six apostles at his left hand and six at his right. A contemporary historian said Constantine was "more greedy for praise than it is possible to tell."[1]

He supported freedom of worship in his empire for the wrong reason: so that no god would be offended enough to take revenge on him personally. He issued edicts of toleration for all religions, so that "we should give to Christians and to everyone else the right freely to follow whatever religion they chose, so that, whatever divinity is enthroned in heaven may be well-disposed and propitious towards me." He tried to restrain Christian fanatics from persecuting pagans, Jews, and heretics, writing in an encyclical letter to Bishop Eusebius of Nicomedia that these others must be "assured of the same degree of peace and tranquility" as orthodox Christians.[2] The orthodox Christians did not agree, and soon after Constantine's death they instituted extensive persecutions and crusades extending over the next three centuries.

Constantine did his best for the church. In one year he obtained twelve thousand converts by the simple offer of a new garment and twenty gold pieces to each person who embraced the faith.[3] But he did as much for other cults too. He didn't become a Christian himself until the final weeks of his life, when he accepted baptism on his deathbed, as insurance for his after-life.

Constantine's life was hardly a model of piety. He murdered his eldest son, his second wife, his father-in-law, his brother-in-law, and "many others," a chronicler said. His first wife, Minervina—evidently a priestess of the Moon-goddess Minerva—mysteriously disappeared. No one knows what became of her. His second wife Fausta was his stepping-stone to the throne, according to the ancient rule of the **hieros gamos**. Eulogists at the wedding said, "The title of sovereignty has now accrued to thee, O Constantine, through thy father-in-law."[4] There being no law of primogeniture, the throne still passed through the female line.

To eliminate a potential rival, Constantine killed his eldest son Crispus, born of the vanished Minervina. Afterward he accused Fausta of having had a love affair with her now-deceased stepson, along with other adulterous affairs, and killed her; it seems that any lover the empress took was still a threat to the emperor's political position.[5]

The murdered Crispus might have played the role of savior and sacred king, for after his death he was virtually canonized as a "blessed martyr." Churches in Greece were dedicated to him for over a millenium. "During the period of the Turkish occupation of Greece, over a thousand years later, he was still remembered as *the* Caesar, the hero-prince, the Christian Theseus, as it were, founder of the modern Greek nation."[6] Yet Crispus was neither a Caesar nor a Christian.

Christian bishops eventually convinced Constantine that their God would forgive his crimes and enthrone him in heaven. When he felt death approaching, he said to them: "The salvation which I have earnestly desired of God these many years I do now expect. It is time therefore that we should be sealed and signed in the badge of immortality."[7] So he was baptized, and died in the confident expectation of a glorious resurrection.

His literary whitewashing began at once. Despite his two wives and numerous concubines, Christian panegyrists said he was "wedded to chastity."[8] Eusebius elevated all the emperor's doings into acts of piety, and invented the legend that Christ had converted him with a holy vision at the Milvian bridge. Later Christian legend claimed Constantine saw the sign of the cross in the sky, with the words *in hoc signo vinces* (in this sign conquer). However, the holy sign that Constantine placed on his battle flags was not the cross. It was the **labarum**, a monogram of Mithra and a sign of the sun, already in use by several pagan emperors before Constantine.[9]

As an example of Constantine's Christian mercy, Cedrenus recorded that once when he was ill, he collected a number of children to kill them and bathe in their blood as a healing charm. However, moved by their mothers' tears, the emperor spared the children's lives after all, and "the saints" restored his health as a reward for this act of mercy.[10] No one seemed inclined to criticize him for contemplating the massacre in the first place.

Constantine's luminous example showed that Christian magic could prevent port-mortem punishment for a ruthless life. "Future tyrants were encouraged to believe," says Gibbon, "that the innocent blood which they might shed in a long reign would instantly be washed away in the waters of regeneration; and the abuse of religion dangerously undermined the foundations of moral virtue."[11]

Christianity served all the emperors after him, with the sole exception of Julian "the Apostate," much vilified by the church for suspending the persecutions of pagans and trying to restore the culture of classical Rome. But Julian died young; some said he was assassinated by a Christian.[12] The war against paganism proceeded. Beginning about 330 A.D., pagan shrines were looted and stripped of their gold, silver, and bronze treasures, many of which were carried off to decorate Constantine's greatest monument to himself, the city of Constantinople.[13] As Eusebius gleefully described the process: "The lurking-places of the heretics were broken up . . . and the savage beasts which they harbored were put to flight."[14]

Constantine's edicts of toleration were rescinded after his death. The new imperial religion attacked its rivals in a show of intolerance on a grander scale than had ever been seen before. It was a great success. "Forty years after the death of Constantine, the church had already acquired a tenth of the whole of the landed property in Rome's western empire, a figure that in western Europe rose to a third during the middle ages. . . . The church since the time of Constantine affords proof that it is not spiritual truth that has triumphed with the spread of Christianity but human power."[15]

1. J.H. Smith, C.G., 182, 235–36, 262. 2. Ibid., 123, 183. 3. Gibbon 1, 654–55. 4. J.H. Smith, C.G., 27, 71. 5. Ibid., 210. 6. Ibid., 215–16. 7. Doane, 446. 8. J.H. Smith, C.G., 39. 9. *Encyc. Brit.,* "Flag." 10. Leland, 240. 11. Gibbon 1, 654. 12. de Voragine, 131. 13. J.H. Smith, C.G., 232. 14. Legge 2, 220. 15. Augstein, 299.

Convent

Medieval institution evolved from the pagan "college" of priestesses or *virgines*—that is, unmarried women (not necessarily physical virgins) dedicated to divine service.

Early convents were double: a community of male monks united with female priestesses under the rule of an abbess, usually a landowning noblewoman.[1] "Priests and monks together with the nuns took vows of obedience to the abbess in imitation of the obedience of Jesus to his mother." A 10th-century Saxon chronicle speaks of double convents inhabited by "priests of both sexes," although in a translation it was revised to read, "priests of both orders."[2]

As Christian laws encroached on women's property rights, many women of noble rank took vows to remain single, so as to protect their wealth from the claims of husbands. Thus originated the so-called convent of noble ladies, an independent mini-queendom. For example, the Saxon convent of Gandersheim in the 9th century held overlordship directly from the king. The abbess conducted her own courts of law, kept her own seat in the imperial parliament, and maintained her own standing army.[3] Culture and learning were pursued. This convent trained the poetess Hrotswitha of Gandersheim, called "a Sappho, deserving to rank with the fabled Veleda and Aurinia, ancient German poet-priestesses."[4]

In the 7th century, a papal bull confirmed the rights of freedom from taxation and from episcopal jurisdiction of the Parthenon of *Beatae Mariae et Sanctae Columbae et Agathae* (Virgin-house of Blessed Marys and Holy Doves and Kindly Ones). Abbesses of Las Huelgas ruled sixty towns, had the right to license bishops and priests within their dioceses, to confer benefices on clergy of their own choice, to nominate ecclesiastical judges, to hear criminal cases among their subjects, and to establish new parishes. Bishops and apostolic delegates were forbidden to visit churches, parishes, clergy, or beneficiaries in the abbess's territory. The nuns remained exempt from episcopal jurisdiction all the way up to 1874.[5]

Ancient goddess-queens were described as "abbesses" in Christian histories, to disguise the real nature of the pagan matriarchate that backed them. Such a one was St. Odilia or Ottilia, called the abbess of Odilienberg (Hohenburg), a pilgrimage shrine of Alsace that was her own Holy Mountain.[6] Her legend had no documentary basis.[7] She was fraudulently canonized, only to attract her votaries to Christianity.

Many abbesses retained their pagan title of High Priestess—Sacerdos Maxima—especially in the German convents. At Quedlinburg the abbess was "in control of the whole town, its people, churches, hospitals, clergy, canons and canonesses, and all religious orders." She was not only High Priestess, but also Superior Canoness of the Cathedral, Metropolitana (mayor), and Matricia (matriarch). At St. Mary's Uberwasser in Munster, the abbess's title was *Prima domna et matre nostra spirituale*, "Mistress-Leader and Our Spiritual Mother." Cistercian monks at Las Huelgas swore obedience to the abbess as "the Illustrious Lady . . . my Prelate, and my Lady, Superior, Mother and legitimate administrator in spiritual and temporal affairs of the Royal Monastery and its Hospital."[8]

Some centuries earlier, the Latin title of Sacerdos Maxima meant a high priestess of the Great Mother of the Gods. She was assisted by lesser priestesses known as *ministra*, "ministers." The word "sodality" came from Latin *sodales*, a college of dancing priestesses trained in the Great Mother's temple.[9]

That women in convents long retained the sexual freedom of the ancient priestesses is shown by interchangeable use of the words "convent" and "brothel" in medieval times. Nicholas Clemangis said the monasteries were not so much sanctuaries of God as they were "abodes of Venus."[10]

The word *nun* originally meant a nurse, that is, a priestess of a healing shrine, like the "nymphs" in colleges of Hygeia and Panacea in pagan Greece. That the convents continued to function as hospitals is suggested by medieval romances: wounded, sick, or dying folk were usually cared for by "nuns."[11] The word also meant a virgin mother in Germanic paganism. A cognate was Nana, virgin mother of the god Balder.

Sometimes, pagan queens established convents in order to have themselves canonized, just as Roman emperors were made gods by virtue of their religious leadership. The canon of saints includes several pagan queens whose only claim to beatitude was wealth, which bought the jurisdiction of an abbey and its subject lands. Some of the queen-saints were even distinctly hostile to churchmen, like Queen Bathild, foundress of a druidic convent at Chelles in the 7th century. She was the real ruler of the western Franks, having placed her son Chlotar on the throne. Certain bishops who tried to interfere with her were assassinated. In the end she was "unceremoniously" removed from power by Christian nobles, and apparently murdered as a heretic, though her subjects maintained her cult and called her Saint Bathild.[12]

In Bede's time, Queen Ethelreda was ordained High Priestess of Ely, and was succeeded by other supreme abbesses governing the monastery's *beatarum regimine feminarum* (holy order of women) up to the Danish invasion in 866. The abbey of Wherwell was founded by Queen Elfrida in 986; it was exempt from earthly services, and held many territories and churches.[13]

Another pagan princess who founded a convent in the 7th century and was canonized, was St. Wereburg of the royal house of Mercia, ruler of the city of Chester. Her establishment was specifically for "noble women" refusing to give up their property to husbands. St. Wereburg was canonized centuries later, on the strength of a legend that her holy bones had extinguished the fires set in the city of Chester by marauding Danes.[14]

St. Hild, or Hilda, of the royal house of Northumberland, established one of the most famous double monasteries of Anglo-Saxon times at Hartlepool, the "Isle of Stags." Her influence extended over all England. She created bishops and abbots, favoring especially the poet-missionaries of Celtic background. Bede said "all who knew her called her Mother."[15] Since she bore the name of the pagan Great Mother Hild, or Hel, one might wonder about the real basis of her authority, in a century when a majority of people had not yet heard of Christianity.[16]

Even when convents became Christianized, abbesses were still ordained like bishops, and in some areas held more secular power than bishops, though church histories have tried to conceal this, sometimes through deliberate falsification of the records. For instance, a papal bull said the abbess of the Cassian foundation in Marseilles was "ordained"; a later editor changed the word to "blessed." At Jouarre, Quedlinburg, Conversano, and other places, an abbess held supreme jurisdiction over both clergy and laity in her territory. According to the Rule of St. Donatus, abbesses functioning as *Matris Spirituale* (Spiritual Mother) regularly heard confessions. French ecclesiastical records say abbesses gave absolution by imposition of their hands on the heads of men.[17]

The church began to encroach on the rights of convents in the 12th and 13th centuries, devising ways to appropriate the nuns' property and make them subject to male clergy. At Fontevrault, canonesses preceded the monks in processions, carried the pastoral cross, preached, read the Gospel, and heard confessions. Pope Innocent III deprived them of these privileges. Disagreements arose between male and female clergy. Monks insisted they would no longer genuflect every time they passed the abbess. Nuns reacted by refusing to kneel in the confessional before their brothers. Innocent III also commanded the abbess of Jouarre, her clergy, and her layfolk to subject themselves to the authority of the bishop of Meaux. When the abbess asked for time to prove her right to independence, she and all her community were excommunicated. Decrees of the Council of Trent changed church laws to say women's orders must be taken over and supervised by men's orders.[18]

Considerable bitterness accompanied sexual segregation of the double convents, judging from the letter of Abbot Conrad of Marchtal, on barring women from his order:

> *We and our whole community of canons, recognizing that the wickedness of women is greater than all other wickedness of the world, and there is no anger like that of women, and that the poison of asps and dragons is more curable and less dangerous for men than the familiarity of women, have unanimously decreed for the safety of our souls, no less than for that of our bodies and goods, that we will on no account receive any more sisters to the increase of our perdition, but will avoid them like poisonous animals.*[19]

Convents had been centers of higher learning for women in an age when women were forbidden access to schools and universities. Earlier in the medieval period, girls as well as boys attended ecclesiastical schools in Ireland and learned to read and write; but this practice was later forbidden, the schools being kept only for males.[20] Premonstratensian and Cistercian orders were famed as educators of women, until the Council of Trent ruled that women's orders must be taken over by men's orders.[21] Then Cistercian nuns were forbidden to establish any more teaching convents.[22]

Nuns were further commanded not to teach or discuss theological matters. This was used as a device for outlawing their orders and confiscating their property. It served as an excuse for the Council of Vienne to deprive the teaching nuns called Beguines of their lands and houses, in 1312 when monks of the Inquisition demanded them:

> *We have been told that certain women commonly called Beguines, afflicted by a kind of madness, discuss the Holy Trinity and the divine essence, and express opinions on matters of faith and sacraments. . . . Since these women promise no obedience to anyone and do not renounce their property or profess an approved Rule . . . [w]e have therefore decided and declared with the approval of the Council that their way of life is to be permanently forbidden and altogether excluded from the Church of God.*[23]

The Beguines were forced to integrate into orders approved by the pope, where they would receive no education. Their properties were taken over by the Inquisition to provide dwellings and prisons for the inquisitors' use.[24]

From the 12th century on, there was increasing pressure on convents to adopt rules of close confinement, to keep nuns segregated from the outside world. The canonesses of St. Mary's Uberwasser rebelled three times against the imposition of the Benedictine Rule, which would force them into seclusion.[25] Many convents were threatened with excommunication, dissolution, or even prosecution by the Inquisition to force them to accept strict seclusion and to cease developing the sisters' minds.

Early in the 17th century, teacher Mary Ward tried to found a Catholic order of teaching nuns known as the English Ladies, to provide education for girls. She and her sisters refused to submit to the cloister, so Mary was arrested and accused of heresy. Her order was suppressed in 1629. Pope Urban VIII rebuked them: "Certain women, taking the name of Jesuitesses, assembled and living together, built colleges, and appointed superiors and a General, assumed a peculiar habit without the approbation of the Holy See . . . carried out works by no means suiting the weakness of their sex, womanly modesty, virginal purity."[26] With typically patriarchal reasoning, the English Ladies were punished for doing what women were supposed to be unable to do.

A few convents managed to hold on to their pre-patriarchal independence. The clergy failed to turn out the canonesses of St. Waudru, at Mons. Monks of Fontevrault likewise failed to take over the main church or the nuns' house, and were obliged to continue to vow obedience to the abbesses, up to the French Revolution.[27]

1. *Encyc. Brit.,* "Women in Religious Orders." 2. Morris, 45, 132.
3. Bullough, 158. 4. Borchardt, 107. 5. Morris, 18, 85–86. 6. Gifford, 133.
7. Attwater, 257. 8. Morris, 58–65, 89. 9. Vermaseren, 57, 109.
10. Sadock, Kaplan & Freedman, 24. 11. Funk, 281. 12. Attwater, 60.
13. Morris, 25–26. 14. Brewster, 93. 15. Attwater, 170.
16. Brewster, 490; *Encyc. Brit.,* "Hilda." 17. Morris, 19, 71, 142.
18. Morris, 48, 76, 37, 149. 19. Bullough, 160. 20. Joyce 1, 410. 21. Morris, 157.
22. Bullough, 191. 23. Bullough, 163. 24. Lea, 226. 25. Morris, 29.
26. Bullough, 208. 27. Morris, 149.

Cornelius, Saint

"Horned One," fictitious saint said to have given curative magic to the site of Mont St. Michel. Its counterpart across the English Channel, St. Michael's Mount, was a shrine of the legendary Trojan hero Corineus, first ruler of Cornwall. His Breton name was Cornelius.[1] He may have been derived from the Horned God, Cernunnos. Corineus was said to have conquered the last of the giants, Goemagot (Gog-Magog), and thrown him into the Channel.

1. Pepper & Wilcock, 193, 203.

Corona, Saint

Spurious canonization of the phrase *sancta corona,* Divine Crown, an early Christian term for martyrdom; perhaps confused with the Goddess Coronis, virgin mother of the physician-god Asclepius.

var. Cottyto, Cottytaris

Cotys

Thracian Moon-goddess whose son, the giant Cottus of the Hundred Hands, stood for her *collegium* of fifty priests or priestesses.[1] Theocritus called her "the crone, Cottytaris, that piped of yore to the reapers in Hippocoon's field."[2] Since Christians vilified her Edonian rites as devil worship, she was listed as one of the demons in medieval texts on demonology.

1. Graves, G.M. 1, 32, 108. 2. Halliday, 36.

Coventina

"Mother of Covens," a popular name for the Celtic Goddess as patron of healing wells and springs.[1] A coven of thirteen was said to represent the thirteen lunar months. The word may have come from Moorish-Spanish-Basque *kaftan,* a ceremonial robe worn at sacred dances performed in groups of thirteen.[2] Naturally, during witch persecutions the name Coventina was applied to all forms of the Goddess.

1. Phillips, 112. 2. Ravensdale & Morgan, 153.

Cow

Perhaps the most common manifestation of the Great Mother as Preserver was the white, horned, milk-giving Moon-cow, still sacred in India as a symbol of Kali. Egypt revered Mother **Hathor** as the heavenly cow whose udder produced the Milky Way, whose body was the firmament, and who daily gave birth to the sun, Horus-Ra, her Golden Calf, the same deity worshipped by Aaron and the Israelites: "These be thy gods, O Israel, which brought thee up out of the land of Egypt" (Exodus 32:4).

The name of Italy meant "calf-land."[1] This country too was the gift of the Milk-giver, whom Etruscans called Lat, Arabs called Al-Lat, Greeks called Latona, Lada, Leto, or Leda. She ruled Latium, and gave her milk (*latte*) to the world.

All Europe was named after the Goddess as a white Moon-cow, whom the Greeks mated to the white bull incarnation of Zeus. Her alternative name was Io, "Moon." Under this name she was presented in classic mythology as a rival of Hera, but patriarchal writers were always setting different manifestations of the same Goddess at odds with one another, possibly on the principle of divide and conquer. Hera herself was named Io, ancestress of the Ionians. In her temple on the site of Byzantium she appeared as the same lunar cow, the Horned One, wearing the same crescent headdress as the Egyptian Cow-goddess.[2]

Herodotus said the milk-giving Mother Hera-Io-Latona was the same as Egypt's Buto, "an archaic queen of the Lower Kingdom."[3] The holy city of Buto, Egypt's oldest oracular shrine, was known to the Greeks as Latopolis, "city of Lat."[4] Of course Buto, or Lat, was only another name for Hathor, or Isis, or Mut, or Neith; all represented "the great cow which gave birth to Ra, the great goddess, the mother of all the gods . . . the Cow, the great lady, lady of the south, the great one who gave birth to the sun, who made the germ of gods and men, the mother of Ra, who raised up Tem in primeval time, who existed when nothing else had being, and who created that which exists."[5]

The Cow as creatress was equally prominent in myths of northern Europe, where she was named Audumla; she was also Freya, or a Valkyrie taking the form of a "fierce cow."[6] A semi-patriarchal Norse myth tried to attribute the creation of the world to the giant Ymir, whose body and blood made the universe. But he was not the first of creatures. The Cow preceded him, for he lived on her milk.[7]

Earlier myths showed the universe being "curdled" into shape from the Cow's milk. In India, many still believe literally the creation myth known as Churning of the Sea of Milk.[8] The Japanese version said the primordial deep went "curdlecurdle" (koworokoworo) when stirred by the first deities, to make clumps of land.[9] The ancient Near East thought human bodies too were curdled from the Goddess's milk. One of her liturgies was copied into the Bible: "Has thou not poured me out as milk, and curdled me like cheese?" (Job 10:10).

The root of "cow" was Sanskrit *Gau,* Egyptian *kau* or *kau-t.* Goddess-names like Gauri and Kauri also designated the yonic cowrie shell.[10] Brahman rebirth ceremonies used either a huge golden yoni or an image of the Cow-mother. "When a man has for grave cause been expelled from his caste, he may be restored to it after passing several times under the belly of a cow."[11] The Egyptian Goddess as birth-giver typically wore a cow's head or horns, as she offered her breasts with both hands.[12] As the nursing mother who gave each Egyptian his secret soul-name (*ren*), she was entitled Renenet, the Lady of the Double Granary, a reference to her inexhaustible breasts.[13] The bovine enzyme rennet, used even in antiquity to curdle milk, was also sacred to her.

A favorite Roman emblem of the Goddess was the *Cornucopia,* Horn of Plenty: a cow's horn pouring forth all the fruits of the earth. The cow was honored as the wetnurse of humanity, and her image is still inadvertently invoked to this day as an expletive Holy Cow, or a pejorative Sacred Cow.

1. Thomson, 50. 2. Elworthy, 183, 194. 3. *Larousse,* 29. 4. Herodotus, 106.
5. Budge, G.E. 1, 457–58, 463. 6. Turville-Petre, 256. 7. *Larousse,* 248.
8. O'Flaherty, 274. 9. Campbell, Or.M., 467. 10. Waddell, 404.
11. Frazer, F.O.T., 220–22. 12. Neumann, G.M., pl. 9.
13. *Larousse,* 38; H. Smith, 24.

Cowrie

Its name derived from Kauri, who was the same as Kali-Cunti, Yoni of the Universe, the cowrie shell everywhere represented the divine vulva and usually conveyed the idea of rebirth. Skeletons from the Solutrean period, ca. 20,000 B.C., have been found "lavishly decorated with cowrie shells."[1]

Egyptians decorated sarcophagi with cowrie shells as a rebirth charm. Cowries are still prized throughout the east for their supposed healing and regenerative powers. Cowrie necklaces are valued in India as amulets against the evil eye.[2] Moslem women believe cowries should be worn on the body during pregnancy. The Japanese keep cowries in wardrobe cabinets "for luck"; if no cowries are available, pornographic pictures of female genitals serve as a substitute.[3] Gypsies valued a cowrie above all other kinds of protective amulets.[4] Christianized natives of the Sudan consider a strip of leather stamped with the sign of the cross a valuable amulet; but it is not "strong magic" unless nine cowrie shells are attached to it.[5]

Romans called the cowrie shell *matriculus,* "little matrix," symbol of an Alma Mater (soul-mother) or teaching priestess, which is why a student still "matriculates" into instruction. The Roman Alma Mater taught the philosophy of love as well as the love of philosophy. Unlike Christians, the pagans believed the capacity for heterosexual love required careful nurture and training.

Sometimes the Romans called a cowrie *porcella,* "little sow," because it stood for the Goddess who was the Great Sow, like Demeter, Astarte, Ceres, Freya, Cerridwen, etc. From *porcella* came "porcelain," so called because of its resemblance to the white glazed surface of the shell.[6] A Greek word for the cowrie was *kteis,* which also meant a scallop, a comb, and a vulva.[7]

The extreme antiquity of cowrie symbolism in the Middle East is shown by the ancestor-skulls preserved by the people of Jericho in the 7th millenium B.C. These forerunners of the Jewish *teraphim* were severed from the body, provided with features of painted plaster, and made to "see" with the eyes of cowrie shells.[8]

Speaking of the Melanesians' and Polynesians' reverence for cowries, a missionary, Rev. George Brown, wrote, "There is some sacredness about them, but what it is, is not at all clear. The natives will not talk about them at all."[9] It seems likely that the natives he mentioned had already become well aware that there was no use talking about sexual symbols to missionaries.

1. Campbell, P.M., 376. 2. Gifford, 79. 3. Briffault 3, 277–78. 4. Trigg, 43. 5. Budge, A.T., 352. 6. Leland, 102. 7. Lindsay, A.W., 132. 8. Whitehouse, 168. 9. Briffault 3, 275.

Crab

The peculiar significance of Cancer, the Crab, in ancient astrology was that it presaged the coming of the end of the world. Chaldeans believed the world would dissolve and return to its primordial elements when all the planets lined up in the constellation of the Crab. The same doctrine appeared in India, Egypt, Persia, China, northern Europe, and pre-Columbian central America.[1]

The sign of the Crab was particularly associated with water and the moon, both typically representative of the Great Goddess who was supposed to bring all things to their doom.[2]

1. Campbell, M.I., 149. 2. Gettings, 95.

Crann Bethadh

In Celtic myth, the phallic Tree of Life, planted in the yonic shrine at the center of the earth; comparable to Yggdrasil, the Stone of Fal, Irminsul, the *axis mundi,* and many other versions of the cosmic phallus.

Creation

Myths of creation generally present a symbolic view of birth. Conditions before creation suggest the uterine environment: darkness, liquid, stirring or churning movement, the "eternal flux" associated with the blood of the Mother (Kali's Ocean of Blood, for example). Often there is a suggestion of one entity inside another. "When there was neither the creation, nor the sun, the moon, the planets, and the earth, and when darkness was enveloped in Darkness, then the Mother, the Formless One, Maha-Kali, the Great Power, was one with Maha-Kala, the Absolute."[1]

The Bible's highly derivative version says "the earth was without form, and void: and darkness was upon the face of the Deep" (Genesis 1:2). The Deep was the Mother's womb, *tehom,* derived from Tiamat, the Babylonian name of the primordial Goddess. In Egypt, she was Temu, mother of the abyssal elements: Water, Darkness, Night, and Eternity.[2]

Most creation myths speak of a splitting or opening in the dark, formless Mother. The beginning of the existing world is signaled by the coming of light. Romans made the connection with birth quite clear: Juno Lucina was not only a creatress, but also the Mother who brought "light" to the eyes of the newborn.[3] The biblical God who said "Let there be light" (*Fiat lux*) copied the word of the Goddess.

The prominence given everywhere to that moment of light suggests archetypal memories of the first impact of light on newborn eyes which have never seen light before. Like dreams of the individual unconscious, myths of the collective unconscious reveal hidden memories of the birth trauma. "Locked up in the depths of our unconscious mind is the terrific impact of birth, the violent adventure that uprooted our pre-natal world."[4] It is also locked up in the symbolism of myths, projected onto a cosmic scale.

Creation/birth was inseparable from the figure of the Mother. The oldest myths made her the divider of waters, maker of heaven and earth. When a god came into the picture, he was at first only her subordinate consort, one of the beings she had created: sometimes a disembodied phallus, in the form of a serpent. Late Egyptian gods who claimed to be creators never succeeded in ridding themselves of feminine imagery. For instance, **Khepera** insisted that he created the universe alone, "there was no other being who worked with me." Yet he had to say, "I laid a foundation in Maa," meaning the Great Womb, the Goddess Maat.[5]

Often it is said when the god was allowed to create, he became puffed up with pride, and began to ignore his Mother and claim sole authorship of the universe. This angered the Goddess. She punished him, bruised his head with her heel, and sent him down to the underworld.[6] (See **Eve**.) Sumerian creation myths said when the Goddess's son-spouse began to show signs of hubris she laid the curse of exile on him, saying, "Henceforth thou shalt dwell neither in heaven nor on earth."[7] This raises all kinds of questions about Middle-Eastern sacrificial gods who died in expiation of a primal sin, hung on trees or crosses "between heaven and earth."

Gnostic creation myths of the early Christian era were still telling versions in which the female principle was pre-eminent, which is why they were declared uncanonical. "In his madness," Jehovah claimed to be the only God, because he had forgotten the Mother who brought him into being, according to one source. The Mother of Gods was angry that he had impiously sinned against her, and against her other children, the male and female Immortal Ones. These were the *elohim* of the Book of Genesis. God grouped himself with them, calling the group "us" (Genesis 3:22). But Bible revisions tended to erase earlier deities, especially female ones. After the centuries of choosing and revising canonical books, nearly every trace of female divinity had been eliminated from Christian literature.[8]

Jean Astruc 18th-century French Catholic physician and scholar.

As long ago as 1753, Astruc recognized that the Book of Genesis contains at least two mutually contradictory versions of the creation myth. One version the scholars call E, for it speaks of plural creators, *elohim,* male and female deities. Another version is J, for *Jehovah elohim,* the God of gods. The two versions disagree in many points:

E: birds and beasts created before man.
J: man created before birds and beasts.

E: birds made of water, along with fishes.
J: birds made of earth, along with beasts.

E: man given dominion over the whole earth.
J: man placed only in the garden, "to dress it and keep it," like the men created to be farmer-slaves in the Sumerian original.

E: man and woman created together, after the beasts: "male and female created he (they) them, and God (*elohim,* the deities) blessed them."
J: man created alone, before beasts and birds; woman made from his rib.

E: creation took place in six days.
J: creation took place in one day.

E: nothing was said about the Fall, which appeared only in the J narrative.

The Fall was all-important. If it never took place, there was no original sin, no necessity for redemption, no Savior. Dean Burgon of Chichester said to deny the literal truth of the Genesis story was to "cause the entire scheme of man's salvation to collapse." Calvin stood squarely behind what he thought the Bible said, and insisted that all species of animals were created at once, in a period of six normal days, each with a morning and evening, as stated. Those who disagree with him, he said, "basely insult the Creator," and will meet after death "a judge who will annihilate them."[9]

The clergy's notion of investigating the origins of man consisted of studying the Bible to add up the given ages of patriarchs since Adam. This had been done in the 7th century by Isidore of Seville, who came up with a strange Bible-based view of history: "Joseph lived 105 years. Greece began to cultivate grain. The Jews were in slavery in Egypt 144 years. Atlas discovered astrology. Joshua ruled for 27 years. Erichthonius yoked horses together. Othniel, 40 years. Cadmus introduced letters into Greece. Deborah, 40 years. Apollo discovered the art of medicine and invented the cithara. Gideon, 40 years. Mercury invented the lyre and gave it to Orpheus." Reasoning on this level—and never noticing anything odd about the many consecutive reigns of 40 years—Archbishop Usher in 1650 placed the date of creation in 4004 B.C. Dr. John Lightfoot, 19th-century Vice-Chancellor of the

University of Cambridge, carried the calculations even further: "Man was created by the Trinity on the twenty-third of October, 4004 B.C., at nine o'clock in the morning."[10]

The absurdity of such reasoning began to be exposed in 1830 when Sir Charles Lyell's *Principles of Geology* investigated the earth's long-term changes, showing that creation could not have taken place in six days, nor in six years, nor even six thousand years. Geologists were finding fossils of animals that lived millions of years ago. Bones of extinct species were found in caves, mingled with human bones. Archeologists found high civilization flourishing in Egypt in 6000 B.C., with evidence of vastly older savage periods. Cuneiform writings showed that the people of Mesopotamia were telling the same story of creation that the Bible told—and telling it thousands of years earlier.

Christian scholars tried hard to refute the new findings. Gosse's *Omphalos* claimed all fossils, marks of retreating glaciers, lava flows, sedimentary rock strata, etc., were created instantaneously by God with an *appearance* of pre-existence. Chateaubriand said God deliberately fooled men with the false appearance of pre-existence in order to test their faith. Others tried to explain fossils by calling them God's deceptions, formed of "lapidific juice" or "seminal air."[11]

Naturally these crude views had to be abandoned in the end. Upholders of the Bible then tried to call the Genesis creation myth allegorical, with each "day" corresponding to a large span of prehistoric time. This didn't work either. The Bible brought plants into being before the sun, on which plant life depends; made fish and birds before "creeping things" on land which was hardly the case; and produced "light" before the only sources of light, sun and moon.

However absurd, these myths still maintain a hold on vast numbers of people deliberately kept in ignorance by an obsolete fundamentalism. Even educated adults sometimes insist that an omniscient god created the world for a purpose of his own.[12] Malebranche came up with an original notion, which may have helped the public image of his church, but made his God look rather less than grand. He said God "can love only Himself and therefore act only with the ultimate purpose of increasing His glory. . . . Thus the sole purpose of the creation was the incarnation and the formation of the Church."[13]

Nicolas Malebranche (1638–1715) French metaphysician who attempted to reconcile Cartesian philosophy with Catholic doctrine.

1. de Riencourt, 165. 2. Budge, D.N., 211. 3. *Larousse,* 203. 4. Fodor, 4. 5. Budge, G.E. 1, 295. 6. Graves, G.M. 1, 27. 7. Campbell, Or. M., 111. 8. Pagels, 29, 57. 9. White 1, 26, 76. 10. White 1, 251, 256. 11. White 1, 214. 12. Campbell, P.M., 87. 13. Walker, 204.

Creiddylad

Welsh name for the May Queen, one of the "three sisters" (Triple Goddess), in whose honor two heroes fought one another every May Day until the end of the world; the same as Shakespeare's "Cordelia." See **Gwyn**.

Crispin, Saint

Roman tutelary god of shoemakers, transformed into a saint by a "very late and quite worthless" legend.[1] October 25, the day of the shoemakers' feast among the pagans, was adopted as St. Crispin's Day.[2] He is still the patron of shoemakers, and his symbol is a shoe.

1. Attwater, 94. 2. de Lys, 182.

Crone

General designation of the third of the Triple Goddess's three aspects, exemplified by such figures as Kali the Destroyer, Cerridwen the death-dealing Sow, Atropos the Cutter, Macha, Hecate, Hel, Eresh-Kigal, Morgan, Queen of the Ghostworld, Queen of the Underworld, Queen of the Shades, Persephone "the Destroyer," etc. All such forms represented old age or death, winter, doomsday, the waning moon, and other symbols of the inevitable destruction or dissolution that must precede regeneration.

The "Crone" may have descended from Rhea Kronia as Mother of Time, though the title has been linked with Coronis, the carrion crow, since crows and other black creatures were sacred to the Death-goddess. Her fearsome character often had a "virgin mother" side as well, because her trinity of appearances was cyclic. It was said in the East that true lovers of the Goddess must love her ugly "destroyer" images as well as her beautiful ones. The Crone also represented the third (post-menopausal) phase of women's lives, and her shrines were served by priestesses in this stage of life. Because it was believed that women became very wise when they no longer shed the lunar "wise blood" but kept it within, the Crone was usually a Goddess of Wisdom. Minerva, Athene, Metis, Sophia, and Medusa provide typical examples.

Cronus

Titan god who castrated his father Uranus (Heaven) and was in turn deposed by his own son Zeus. Knowing the danger his children posed, Cronus tried to prevent it by swallowing them all—an early version of the Slaughter of the Innocents—but Zeus escaped. Cronus was confused with Chronos, "Time," because Time swallows up everything it brings forth—actually a characteristic of Cronus's mother-mate, Rhea Kronia, the Goddess personifying time and fate. She was really Mother Earth, who gave birth to Cronus; and Rhea, who married him; and Hera, who married his son Zeus; the three of them comparable to the Mother, Grandmother, and Great-grandmother Goddesses in northern Europe.[1] See **Caste**.

1. Graves, G.M. 1, 37–40.

Cross

Latin Cross

Celtic Cross

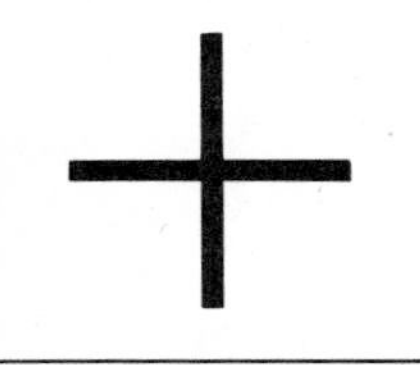

Greek Cross

The "Latin" or "Passion" cross, now the primary symbol of Christianity, was not shown in Christian art until six centuries after Christ.[1] But long before the Christian era it was a pagan religious symbol throughout Europe and western Asia.[2] Early Christians even repudiated the cross because it was pagan. A church father of the 3rd century, Minucius Felix, indignantly denied that Christians worshipped the cross: "You it is, ye Pagans, who are the most likely people to adore wooden crosses . . . for what else are your ensigns, flags, and standards, but crosses gilt and beautiful. Your victorious trophies not only represent a simple cross, but a cross with a man on it."[3]

From very ancient times, an effigy of a man hanging on a cross was set up in fields to protect the crops. The modern scarecrow is a survival of this sacrificial magic, representing the sacred king whose blood was supposed to fertilize the earth. He was never abandoned, even though every farmer knew that no scarecrow ever really scared a crow.[4]

The cross was also a male symbol of the phallic Tree of Life; therefore it often appeared in conjunction with the female-genital circle or oval, to signify the sacred marriage. Male cross and female orb composed the Egyptian "amulet Nefer," or amulet of blessedness, a charm of sexual harmony.[5]

The so-called Celtic cross, with the crossing of the arms encircled by a ring, was another lingam-yoni sign of sexual union, known to the Hindus as *Kiakra.*[6] Some old Celtic crosses still in existence show obvious phallic elements, even to a realistic meatus at the cross's tip.[7] Crosses signified a god's love-death even in pre-Columbian art of the western hemisphere, which showed the Savior carrying his cross, an image very similar to the Christian one.[8]

No one knows exactly when the cross became associated with Christianity. Early images of Jesus represented him not on a cross, but in the guise of the Osirian or Hermetic "Good Shepherd," carrying a lamb. Later, many different kinds of crosses were used as Christian symbols. They included the Greek cross of equal arms, the X-shaped St. Andrew's cross, the swastika, the Gnostic Maltese cross, the solar cross or Cross of Wotan, and the ansated cross, a development of the Egyptian **ankh**, also found as the Cross of Venus.[9]

Greeks said this cross was "common to the worship of Christ and Sarapis."[10] The Goddess Isis is shown on the Isiac Table with the cross in one hand, a lotus seed-vessel in the other, signifying male and female genitalia.[11] As her consort, the god Sarapis was incarnate in Ptolemy. The words "Ptolemy the Savior" were followed by a cross on the Damietta Stone. Pious Christian scholars once tried to pretend that this phrase was really a prophecy of the future Christ.[12]

For a few centuries the emblem of Christ was a headless T-shaped Tau cross rather than a Latin cross. This may have been copied from pagan druids, who made Tau crosses of oak trees stripped of their branches, with two large limbs fastened at the top to represent a man's arms. This was the Thau, or god.[13]

Tau Cross

A Tau cross was the sign of the holy day aptly named the Invention of the Cross, purporting to commemorate the discovery of the True Cross by the empress Helena, mother of Constantine, in a crypt under the temple of Aphrodite in Jerusalem.[14] After it was generally replaced by the Latin cross, the Tau cross was reassigned to St. Philip, supposedly crucified on a Tau cross in Phrygia, where he was trying to exorcise the god Mars in the form of a dragon.[15] This means the Tau cross was the sign of May Day, which the church adopted as St. Philip's day; and the druidic Thau was confused with the Maypole.

The Invention of the Cross was first heard of long after the lifetime of the empress Helena. The date assigned to her "discovery" was 328 A.D., though no contemporary chronicler thought fit to mention such a momentous event. The legend said Helena found three crosses under Aphrodite's temple, but couldn't decide which belonged to Christ, which to the two thieves. She had a corpse brought, and laid on each cross in turn. When laid on the right one, the dead man sprang up alive. According to an alternative story, the True Cross instantly restored the health of "a noble lady who was near to death."[16]

Christian authorities also claimed the empress found the Holy Nails and the INRI scroll, but the latter somehow disappeared and was lost for over a thousand years. In 1492 it was miraculously rediscovered in the Church of the Holy Cross in Rome, where it seemed to have been all the time. Pope Alexander III published a bull infallibly attesting to its authenticity.[17]

The Invention of the Cross proved enormously useful in the Middle Ages, to account for the veritable forest of splinters of the True Cross revered in Europe's churches. There was so much miracle-working wood of the True Cross that Calvin said it would make "a full load for a good ship."[18]

The church claimed the True Cross was made of the same wood that grew as the Tree of Life in the garden of Eden. It was carried out by Adam, and preserved by all the patriarchs in turn (even riding the Flood in Noah's ark), for the sole purpose of crucifying the Savior when he appeared. Gnostic sources added an Oedipal twist: Jesus's cross was put together by his father, Joseph the carpenter. Moreover, the cross was planted on the very spot where the Tree of Life once grew. The church said it became "the Tree of the Cross, so that whence came death, thence also life might rise again." These absurdities were implicitly believed through the Middle Ages.[19]

Male genitals are still called "the tree of life" by the Arabs, and a cross was one of the oldest diagrammatic images of male genitals. Among Christians there was at least some recognition of the cross's phallic significance. An ancient crucifix at Sancreed in Cornwall was a spear set upright in a holy vase (the uterine vessel) with two testicle-like scrolls appended to its shaft.[20] The cross entering the labyrinth was one of the oldest symbols of the lingam-yoni in the west, dating back to early Neolithic times. Spiral "feminine" labyrinths penetrated by a cross occur in prehistoric rock carvings from Crete, at Tintagel in Cornwall, Wier Island in Finland, and Chartres Cathedral.[21]

Conscious or not, the phallic connotations of the cross appear even in the present century. In the 1950's a poem in the magazine *Wake* said: "Christ, I have walked around your erection, The Cross, that begot, upon a sky of prayer, a billion men, devoted in humility."[22]

During the so-called Age of Faith, the peasants were perhaps not so devoted in humility to the cross as churchmen wanted. Certain brotherhoods of "accursed huntsmen" or "archer wizards" constantly defaced roadside crosses, believing they could acquire magic skill with the bow by shooting three arrows in succession at a crucifix.[23] Thus they opposed the phallic trident of the ancient Lord of the Hunt to Christ's symbol. (See **Trident**.) Today, the cross is often an article of jewelry, attesting an amuletic function virtually indistinguishable from its magical prophylactic use in antiquity.

1. H. Smith, 188; Cumont, O.R.R.P., 109. 2. Budge, A.T., 336. 3. Doane, 345. 4. de Lys, 42. 5. Budge, E.M., 59. 6. Baring-Gould, C.M.M.A., 374. 7. de Paor, pl. 37. 8. Campbell, M.I., 175. 9. Jung, M.S., 43. 10. Baring-Gould, C.M.M.A., 355. 11. Knight, D.W.P., 50. 12. d'Alviella, 15. 13. Elworthy, 103–4. 14. J.H. Smith, C.G., 322. 15. Brewster, 221, 226. 16. de Voragine, 274. 17. Budge, A.T., 343–44. 18. Kendall, p. 122. 19. Mâle, 153. 20. Baring-Gould, C.M.M.A., 613. 21. Hitching, 237. 22. Ellis, 112. 23. Kramer & Sprenger, 150.

Crossroads

In the Greco-Roman world, crossroads were sacred to the elder Diana under the name of Hecate Trevia (**Hecate** of the Three Ways), mother of the *Lares compitales,* "spirits of the crossroads." Travelers made offerings to the Goddess's three-faced images, and regular festivals called Compitalia were celebrated at her roadside shrines.[1]

Four-way crossroads were sometimes dedicated to **Hermes**, whose ithyphallic *herms* stood beside them until replaced by Christians' roadside crosses. However, the Christian sign of the cross was copied from Hermes's cult and traced his sacred numeral 4 on the worshipper's head and breast. Hermetic crosses were left at the crossroads of 10th-century Ireland and simply re-interpreted as Christian symbols, though they plainly displayed the twin serpents of the pagan caduceus, another sign of the older deity.[2]

Cross, herm, and caduceus merged in northern symbolism with the gallows tree of Odin/Wotan, "God of the Hanged," which led to the Christian custom of erecting a gallows at crossroads as well as a crucifix. The god on the gallows once played the same role as Jesus on the cross: a dying-god image rendered the crossroad numinous. Pre-Christian Europeans held waymeets, or *moots,* at crossroads to invoke their deities' attention to the proceedings; hence a *moot* point used to be one to be decided at a meet. The Goddess as Mother Earth, dispenser of "natural law" and creatress of birth-and-death cycles, was always present where the dying god died—as the women long remembered. The English monk Aelfric complained of female customs dedicating newborn infants to the ancient Mother. Women would "go to the crossways and drag their children over the earth, and thereby give both themselves and their children to the Devil."[3]

As the crossroad ceremonies and their deities became diabolized, the Goddess of the waymeet became the queen of witches, who still worked magic there. The *Key of Solomon* said crossroads were the best of all places for magical procedures "during the depth and silence of the night."[4] Ghosts of the hanged, of the heathen, and of ancient oracles still haunted crossroads. Bernard Ragner said a spirit voice would foretell the future to anyone who went to a crossroad at the last hour of Christmas Eve. As late as the 1920's, English farmers still believed witches' sabbats were held at crossroads. Necromantic superstitions were encouraged by the custom of burying criminals and suicides in unhallowed ground at crossroads; clergymen said anyone so buried would walk as a ghost. Sometimes, such corpses were pinned down with a stake: "A stake was driven through them when deposited at the cross-roads in order to keep the ghost from wandering abroad."[5] Presumably, the ghost could be consulted *in situ,* just as spirits could be raised from their graves in the churchyard by any necromancer.

Key of Solomon
(Clavicule de Salomon) A popular "Black Book" or magic book much used between the 11th and 13th centuries A.D.

Bernard Ragner
Author of *Legends and Customs of Christmas,* 1925

Thus Hermes and Hecate, who led the souls of the dead in antiquity, became dread spirits of "witchcraft" in the same places that they once benevolently ruled.

1. Hyde, 137. 2. Campbell, M.I., 337. 3. Briffault 3, 58. 4. Wedeck, 153. 5. Summers, V., 154–57.

Crow

Along with the **vulture** and **raven**, the carrion-eating crow was northern Europe's common symbol of the Death-goddess. Valkyries, sometimes described as man-eating women, often took totemic form as ravens or crows.[1]

Anglo-Danish myths spoke of a witch named Krake (Crow), daughter of the Valkyrie Brunnhilde. Krake was a shape-shifter: at times a beautiful virgin, at other times a hag, monster, or crow. She married the Danish king Ragnar Lodbrok (Leather-Breeches), and gave birth to the hero Sigurd.[2] Sigurd was the same as Siegfried, whose mystic lady-love was the Valkyrie Brunnhilde; thus appeared the same convoluted incestuous relationships found in the oldest myths of sacred kingship. Again, the Triple Goddess returned as the three prophetic daughters of Ragnar and Krake, Fate-weavers who created the magic banner called Raven (Hraefn).[3]

There was a mythological Kraken associated with the sea, pictured as a serpent or water-monster; but this was only another form of the same Death-goddess. The Three Ravens (Kraken) in old ballads were birds of doom perching over the slain hero. Sometimes there were only two of them, as in the ballad of the Twa Corbies (Two Crows), who proposed to pluck out the bonny blue eyes of the slain knight.[4]

Such manifestations of the Goddess as a crow might be linked with Coronis, "Crow," a death aspect of the pre-Hellenic earth mother Rhea. Classical mythographers tended to ignore Coronis, remembering her only as the virgin mother of the healing god Asclepius; but she seems to have been another of the Virgin-Crone combinations: Rhea Kronia as Mother Time who brings death to all things.[5]

1. Woods, 156. 2. Guerber, L. M. A., 274–75. 3. Turville-Petre, 59.
4. Sargent & Kittredge, 45. 5. Graves, G.M. 1, 175; 2, 387.

Crusades

"Holy wars" designed to wrest property away from the heathen or heretic enemies of orthodox Christianity. Crusades were usually fought by vassals of Christian overlords, including the wealthy clergy. Warriors were promised not only the standard soldiers' spoils, but also indulgences, like instant remission of sins and admission to heaven guaranteed no matter what crimes the crusader may have committed.

From the 8th to 10th centuries, the Holy Roman Empire was harassed by Norsemen, who owned many northern trading centers and dominated the seas. They also opened negotiations with foreign powers in North Africa and the Middle East. In 834, Arabian legates visited Denmark to contract military and trade alliances.[1] The Holy Roman Empire saw itself trapped between two anti-Christian forces: the pagan Normans in the northwest, and the Moslem Saracens in the southeast. Norsemen controlled trade routes through the Danube and Black Sea to the Turks, and were acquiring hoards of Arabic silver, gold, and gems. They also sailed the Atlantic coasts down to Gibraltar, and founded colonies in Libya. The Kingdom of God was nearly encircled.

Pope Urban II tried to solve the problem by initiating crusades in the east, on the pretext of converting the Saracens' possessions in the "Holy Land" into Christian fiefs. In 1095 he instigated the People's Crusade as a combination of penitential pilgrimage and a war of conquest. It was advertised throughout Europe. All who participated were placed above restrictions of law, and promised forgiveness of sins and eternal bliss in heaven without any time spent in purgatory.

A rabble of some 150,000 to 300,000 persons, mostly the dregs of society mixed with military mercenaries, set out across southern Europe, killing, torturing, and looting as they went. One division slaughtered 10,000 Jews in the Rhineland, then forgot about the Holy Land and dispersed. Two other divisions did so much harm in Hungary that native soldiers rose up against them and destroyed them all. Multitudes died along the way, of sickness, hunger, or injuries brought on by their violence. A remnant survived to plunder the too-hospitable Greeks, then to enter Constantinople. There, stronger crusaders sold off the weaker ones as slaves, to finance their own provisions. Finally, a remaining 7,000 or so crossed the Bosporus and were attacked by the Turks, who soon killed them all.[2]

One might think the fate of Pope Urban's crusade would have discouraged future experiments of this kind. Not so. It seems to have been an idea whose time had come.

Later crusades were better organized, with more experienced soldiers and fewer penitential pilgrims. Their primary motive was loot. For the next 400 years, Christian knights went forth to astonish the Saracens with their intellectual naïveté and their military sophistication, developed in a feudal society based on warfare.

> *The Crusaders in general, in spite of their sacred cause, behaved like highway robbers. The first host which set out in 1095, and was annihilated by the Turks at Nicaea, killed, burned and pillaged all they encountered. The army commanded by Godfrey de Bouillon massacred the entire population of Jerusalem (1098). The astuteness of Venice turned aside the fourth Crusade upon Constantinople, and the sack of this city is a dark blot on the history of Western Christendom (1204). It was abominably ravaged, and the very church of St. Sophia was the scene of bloody and sacrilegious orgies.*[3]

A contemporary chronicler said Jerusalem withstood a month's siege. Upon its fall, crusaders rode into the city with their horses wading "knee-deep in the blood of disbelievers." Jews were herded into their synagogues and burned alive. On the next day, the knights slaughtered "a great multitude of people of every age, old men and women, maidens, children and mothers with infants, by way of a solemn sacrifice" to Jesus.[4] At the battle of Acre, Richard Coeur de Lion violated his pledge of truce, and had his hostages slaughtered and flayed. "His conduct stands in strong contrast with the dignity and forbearance of Saladin, before whose eyes the outrage was committed, and who would not stoop to retaliate on his dastardly opponent."[5]

Once the crusading system was established, it was turned on other enemies of the church closer to home and became the standard method for dealing with European heathens and heretics. Between 1236 and 1283 a crusade of extermination was preached against the pagan Prussians by Pope Honorius, and carried out by the Teutonic Knights. The Christian Brethren of the Sword similarly converted Livonia and Courland. Armies of the Christian Dukes of Poland forced the Wends to accept Christian baptism and vassalage. The Lithuanians stubbornly clung to their paganism to the end of the 14th century, but eventually they too were Christianized by the sword.[6]

It was noticed in the 13th century that the semi-barbarous Stedingers of the lower Weser river maintained their ancient tribal system, paid no attention to the church, and contributed no tithes. Pope Gregory IX sent bulls to the bishops of Minden, Lübeck, and

Verden, ordering crusades against these recalcitrant peasants, whom he described as heretics because they consulted wise-women, made waxen images, and worshipped "demons." Crusaders were promised blanket pardon for their sins. However, the Stedingers fought back stubbornly, and several campaigns against them failed. At last in 1234 a huge army marched into their land, ravaged every home with fire and sword, and wiped them out. Their property was divided between the church and the barons.[7]

It has been estimated that Europe was Christianized at a cost of about 8 million to 10 million lives.[8] Even after nominal conversion, there was much residual resistance to the new cult, which was alien and unappealing to the people it was imposed on. The clergy claimed authority from an unfamiliar eastern savior and his God, defaming all the pagans' local, ancestral deities—many worshipped since the Neolithic age—as demons. Moreover, familiar laws and lifestyle were declared wholly sinful. It's hardly surprising that there arose heresy after heresy to confront the conquering church, which became increasingly fanatical in its dictatorial policies, yet in the end failed to overcome the people's need to assert their own religious heterodoxy.[9] Many refused to give up their pagan Goddess, or their notion that sexuality contained an element of the divine. Many remembered a time, not so long before, when "holy communion" was a taste of divine bliss through sensual pleasures: an idea that was especially prevalent in the south of France.

Crusades against the Catharan or Albigensian heretics of southern France were particularly virulent, since these people were prosperous enough to attract plunderers, and bitterly opposed to the Roman church, which they called the Synagogue of Satan. They condemned its worship of holy images as idolatry, denied the power of its sacraments, scoffed at the Trinity, insisted on reading the Bible for themselves, and revived the old Gnostic belief that the Jehovah worshipped by the Roman church was a demonic demiurge who created the world of matter to entrap souls in wickedness. Pope Alexander III anathematized the Catharan communities and sent ecclesiastical judges to investigate their offenses in 1163. Of these judges, the word "inquisitor" was used for the first time.[10]

In 1209 Pope Innocent II preached a great crusade against the French rebels. This has gone down in history as the Albigensian crusade, one of the bloodiest chapters in Christianity's past.[11] Half of France was exterminated. When the papal legate was asked how heretics were to be distinguished from the faithful, he replied, "Kill them all; God will know his own."[12]

Soon the legate was able to report that in Beziers alone, "nearly twenty thousand human beings perished by the sword. And after the massacre the town was plundered and burnt, and the revenge of God seemed to rage over it in a wonderful manner." The killing of heretics went on continually for twenty years, and it has been estimated that more than a million were slaughtered.[13]

This was more than a police action against heresy. It was the destruction of a whole civilization that had the misfortune to be more advanced than the rest of Europe.

> *In the twelfth century, the south of France had been the most civilized land in Europe. There commerce, industry, art, science, had been far in advance of the age. The cities had won virtual self-government, were proud of their wealth and strength, jealous of their liberties, and self-sacrificing in their patriotism. The nobles, for the most part, were cultivated men, poets themselves or patrons of poetry, who had learned that their prosperity depended on the prosperity of their subjects, and that municipal liberties were a safeguard rather than a menace to the wise ruler. The Crusaders came, and their unfinished work was taken up and executed to the bitter end by the Inquisition. It left a ruined and impoverished country, with shattered industries and a failing commerce. The native nobles were broken by confiscation and replaced by strangers. . . . A people of rare gifts had been tortured, decimated, humiliated, despoiled. . . . The precocious civilization which had promised to lead Europe in the path of culture was gone, and to Italy was transmitted the honour of the Renaissance.*[14]

Catholic writers made many efforts to justify the destruction. Apologists like Pierre des Vaux-de-Cernay used vituperation, calling the Catharan opinions "this detestable pest . . . the poison of superstitious infidelity." He said Toulouse was "marvelously and miserably infected with this plague . . . almost all the barons of Provence had become harborers and defenders of heretics." In the 19th century, Abbé Vacandard said, "The Church, after all, was only defending herself. The Cathari sought to wound her mortally by attacking her doctrine, her hierarchy and her apostolicity. She would have been ruined if their perfidious insinuations, which brought violent disturbance into men's minds, had prevailed in the end."[15] It has ever been the church's habit to regard any skepticism concerning its pronouncements as "violent disturbance"; but of course, all the bloodletting was in vain. Skepticism did prevail in the end.

1. Oxenstierna, 76. 2. H. Smith, 252–53. 3. Reinach, 295. 4. H. Smith, 253. 5. Briffault 3, 392. 6. Reinach, 294. 7. Lea unabridged, 656–60. 8. H. Smith, 251. 9. Campbell, C.M., 629. 10. H. Smith, 254–55. 11. Oldenbourg, M.M. 12. Campbell, Oc.M., 499. 13. H. Smith, 257. 14. Briffault 3, 487–88. 15. Coulton, 80, 91–92.

Cu Chulainn

Celtic dying god, a son of God, born of a virgin, reincarnated as both Father and Son. It was said of him that he was "begotten by a man that was not a man; his father was reared by his mother as a child, a child which died and did not die."[1] In other words, he was a pre-Christian Christ figure, God-begotten on the "Mother of God," of one substance with his own Father.

Cu Chulainn received the death-curse of the Goddess Macha, and died bound to a sacred pillar, pierced by arrows, his blood fertilizing the earth. Other Celtic heroes died the same way. Their idols were sometimes interpreted as images of St. Sebastian, now officially viewed as an over-hasty canonization of a Gaulish heathen savior.[2]

Cu Chulainn received his education in battle skills from Skadi, or Scatha, the same northern death-goddess as the Queen of Skye. His destiny or "weird" was to kill his rival on the "precursor day of spring," so the shedding of blood would "allow spring to enter."[3] The same idea of bloodshed to facilitate the return of spring is found in Teutonic myths of Skadi.[4]

Cu means "dog," a common title of Celtic chieftains (as in Cunobelin) identified with the underworld Lord of Death. Like Egypt's Anubis, the dead hero might become the canine gatekeeper charged with admitting souls to paradise, as shown on the Gundestrup **Cauldron**.[5] The dog represented reincarnation. So did Cu Chulainn, who was promised that "his rebirth would be of himself." He was sent to Emania, the realm of the dead in the moon.[6] He may have been the original of the British legend that the man in the moon is really a dog, who acts as a messenger of death.[7]

The virgin mother of Cu Chulainn conceived him by eating his soul in the form of a fly. This Celtic soul-symbol originated in the Middle East, where the Lord of Death was **Baal-Zebub** (Beelzebub), Lord of Flies. Like most pagan gods, Cu Chulainn was a shape-shifter. He could be an insect, animal, or man at different stages in his life cycle. Such changes from one shape to another were based on the ancient Indo-European idea of metempsychosis. The Protean hero even adapted his shape to Christianity; the medieval Irish insisted that he was an avatar of Christ.[8]

Later Irish writers pretended that Cu Chulainn was not ignominiously trussed up to his pillar as a sacrifice, in the manner of the old gods. They thought it important to prove that he fell in battle. Therefore they invented the legend that, wounded and knowing himself doomed, Cu Chulainn tied himself to the sacred pillar so he couldn't fall down before his enemies, who were piercing him with arrows, but rather "died with his honor unimpaired."[9]

1. Rees, 235. 2. Spence, 85; Attwater, 304. 3. Goodrich, 187, 216.
4. Oxenstierna, 213. 5. Cavendish, V.H.H., 49. 6. Spence, 146.
7. Baring-Gould, C.M.M.A., 197. 8. Spence, 95–96, 108. 9. *Larousse*, 233.

Cuckold

Derived from "cuckoo," the bird of May, anciently sacred to the promiscuous May-games that medieval Europe inherited from paganism.[1] The man who became a cuckoo, or cuckold, was one who didn't care whether his wife was faithful or not, for both of them attended the Maytime festivities when ritual promiscuity was the rule—or fertility charm—as late as the 16th century.[2] The season of "wearing of the green" in honor of the reborn vegetation was announced by the cuckoo's singing "from every holt and heath," as Chaucer put it; and marriage bonds were temporarily in abeyance.

The cuckold's horns descended from another pagan sign, that of the Horned God, sacrificed as a stag, goat, or ram at the spring feasts. Pagan priests used to wear the horns of the sacrificed animal on their heads; and horned masks or headdresses were commonly worn by participants in the rite, in the god's honor. A 16th-century writer therefore described the cuckold as "cornute," that is, "as soundly armed for the head, as either Capricorn, or the stoutest horned sign in the Zodiac."[3] See **Horns.**

1. Potter & Sargent, 80. 2. Frazer, G.B., 142. 3. Hazlitt, 160.

Cunt

Derivative of the Oriental Great Goddess as Cunti, or Kunda, the Yoni of the Uni-verse.[1] From the same root came county, kin, and kind (Old English *cyn*, Gothic *kuni*). Related forms were Latin *cunnus*, Middle English *cunte*, Old Norse and Frisian *kunta*, Basque *cuna*. Other cognates are "cunabula," a cradle, or earliest abode; "Cunina," a Roman Goddess who protected children in the cradle; "cunctipotent," all-powerful (i.e., having cunt-magic); "cunicle," a hole or passage; "cuniculate," penetrated by a passage; "cundy," a coverted culvert; also cunning, kenning, and ken: knowledge, learning, insight, remembrance, wisdom. Cunt is "not slang, dialect or any marginal form, but a true language word, and of the oldest stock."[2]

"Kin" meant not only matrilineal blood relations, but also a cleft or crevice, the Goddess's genital opening. A Saharan tribe called Kuntahs traced their descent from this holy place.[3] Indian "kundas" were their mothers' natural children, begotten out of wedlock as gifts of the Goddess Kunda.[4] Of old the name applied to girls, as in China where girls were once considered children of their mothers only, having no natural connection with fathers.[5]

In ancient writings, the word for "cunt" was synonymous with "woman," though not in the insulting modern sense. An Egyptologist was shocked to find the maxims of Ptah-Hotep "used for 'woman' a term that was more than blunt," though its indelicacy was not in the eye of the ancient beholder, only in that of the modern scholar.[6]

Medieval clergymen similarly perceived obscenity in female-genital shrines of the pagans: holy caves, wells, groves. Any such place was called *cunnus diaboli*, "devilish cunt." Witches who worshipped there sometimes assumed the name of the place, like the male witch Johannes Cuntius mentioned by Thomas More.[7] "Under painful circumstances" this witch died at the hands of witch hunters, but it was said he was resurrected, and came back to earth as a lecherous incubus.[8]

Sacred places identified with the world-cunt sometimes embarrassed Victorian scholars who failed to understand their earlier meaning. A.H. Clough became a laughing-stock among Gaelic-speaking students when he published a poem called *Toper-na-Fuosich,* literally "bearded well," a Gaelic place-name for a cunt-shrine. The synonym "twat" was ignorantly used by another Victorian poet, Robert Browning, in the closing lines of his *Pippa Passes*:

Then, owls and bats,
Cowls and twats,
Monks and nuns, in a cloister's moods,
Adjourn to the oak-stump pantry!

Editors of the *Oxford English Dictionary* hesitantly asked Browning where he learned the word. He said it came from a bawdy broadside poem of 1659: "They talked of his having a Cardinal's Hat; They'd send him as soon an Old Nun's Twat." Browning thought the word meant a wimple, or other headgear corresponding to "hat."[9]

1. G.R. Scott, 188. 2. Dames, 110–14. 3. Briffault 1, 604.
4. *Mahanirvanatantra,* 289. 5. Murstein, 473. 6. Erman, 61. 7. Summers, V., 179.
8. Hazlitt, 211. 9. Perrin, 217.

Cupid

Roman name for the god of erotic love, Greek Eros, Hindu Kama. Cupid was the son of Venus and Mercury (Aphrodite and Hermes), and was therefore a "Herm-Aphrodite," signifying sexual union.

In Christian usage, the ancient significance of sexual desire was confused with desire for money, hence the modern "cupidity," which used to mean "lust" but now means greed. In the same way, Latin *caritas* was altered from sensual or sexual giving to the modern "charity," giving of money.

Renaissance art made emanations of Cupid into *amoretti,* "little loves," shown as winged babies. But ancient talismans of Cupid were not babies; they were winged phalli of bronze, ivory, or wood, which gave rise to an Italian slang term for the penis, *uccello,* "little bird."[1]

1. Young, 74.

Curse, Mother's

In ancient Asiatic belief, a mother's curse meant certain death. All death was brought about by the Goddess's word of destruction, as all birth was brought about by her word of creation. By virtue of motherhood, any woman could tap the verbal power of the Goddess. The Markandaya Purana says, "for all curses there is some remedy; but there is nothing anywhere that can dispel the curse of those who have been cursed by a mother."[1] Similarly, the biblical Hannah rejoiced when she became a mother, saying, "My mouth is enlarged over mine enemies" (1 Samuel 2:1) because maternity gave her curses an irresistible power.

Homer tells the story of Meleager, cursed by his mother for murdering her brothers. Falling on her knees, she knocked the earth with her fists and called upon the underground Goddess. "And the Fury that walks in the dark and has inexorable thoughts heard her from Erebus."[2] The Fury told Meleager's mother to burn his soul in the form of a wand, so he was stricken with a fever, and soon died.[3]

Witchcraft of this sort was not even necessary—the curse alone could kill. The Greek word for the effect of a mother's curse was *miasma,* a kind of spiritual pollution bringing slow but sure destruction. *Miasma* could pursue members of a clan for many generations. The tragic family history of Orestes might be traced to a curse laid by the Goddess Artemis herself on his ancestor Atreus, who dared to withhold the golden fleece of a sacrificial lamb she had sent, using it to confirm his right to rule.[4]

Gods launched curses too, and some of them were spectacular, like those with which Yahweh threatened all who disobeyed him: a combination of pestilence, fever, consumption, inflammation, blasting, mildew, extreme burning, emerods (hemorrhoids), the scab, the itch, the botch of Egypt, madness, blindness, slavery, great plagues of long continuance, and barrenness of the land (Deuteronomy 28). However, the gods' curses seemed not to arouse as much terror as those of Goddess or Mother.

The terrible vehicle of the feminine curse was **menstrual blood**, still called *The* Curse. To "damn" has been linked with the Hebrew *dam,* "blood," specifically mother-blood, the fluid of the womb, anciently thought to create one's very soul—and destroy it. *Dam* was also synonymous with "mother" (ma-dam, my mother). Elder women past menopause were thought to be the most efficient cursers, on the ancient theory that their "wise blood" was retained in their bodies, giving them numinous power to make their words come true.[5] This was why medieval Europe believed any destructive charm having menstrual blood as one of its ingredients must be irresistible, and why elder women were viewed as prototypical witches, their words or even their glances heavy with dread.

Fathers of the church even wooed converts with the assurance that the Christian faith was strong enough to overcome a mother's curse, the most powerful curse known to man. St. Augustine claimed that some children cursed by their mother were afflicted by constant weakness and tremors, but St. Stephen converted them to Christianity, and they were completely cured of the effects of the curse.[6]

Eastern sages believed the feminine power of the curse must be allayed not so much by opposing it with a patriarchal religion, as by treating women well, so they would not be inclined to use their destructive power. The Laws of Manu said:

> *Women must be honored and adorned by their fathers, brothers, husbands, and brothers-in-law, who desire their own welfare. Where women are honored, there the gods are pleased, but where they are not*

Laws of Manu
Post-Vedic treatise on holy law, composed or collected some time between the 2nd century B.C. and the 2nd century A.D.

honored, no sacred rite yields rewards. Where the female relations live in grief, the family soon wholly perishes; but that family where they are not unhappy ever prospers. The houses on which female relations, not being duly honored, pronounce a curse, perish completely, as if destroyed by magic.[7]

This advice came from the place northern Aryans called Mutspellheim, the Home of the Mother's Curse, in "the hot lands of the south." According to the Scandinavian prophecy of **doomsday**, the Mutspell would fall upon the violent patriarchal gods who ignored ancient tribal bonds and rules of morality, and instituted cruel warfare. The result of the Mother's Curse would be the death of all gods, their Götterdämmerung or Going-Into-the-Shadow; thus it seemed the Mother's word of destruction meant the end of the world.[8]

Christian Gnostic writings reveal the same belief in a world-destroying curse from a Great Mother disgusted with the cruel behavior of the gods she created. In her anger, the Goddess would send a great power from the place "where the firmament of woman is situated," the Gnostic equivalent of Mutspellheim. "Then she will drive out the gods of Chaos whom she had created together with the first Father. She will cast them down to the abyss. They will be wiped out by their own injustice."[9]

Myths in general suggest that a mother's curse was the necessary instrument of destruction for any god, even a Savior-son, most of whom were solemnly cursed before immolation.[10] Since a mother's curse was immutable, no guilt accrued to the executioners who carried out sacrificial killings in ancient dramas of death and resurrection. Mythology bears out the archetypal idea that one who gives birth has unlimited power over the life so given, and may retain control of that life's duration.

As a rule therefore, death curses usually employed female symbolism. Typical was the curse of the "black fast," utilizing a black hen, once sacred to the Queen of the Shades as destructive twin of the Mother of the World Egg. The curse was accomplished by the operator and the black hen fasting together, every Friday for nine weeks (the Goddess's day and number). After this, an accursed one was sure to die.[11]

1. O'Flaherty, 68. 2. Cavendish, P.E., 122. 3. Graves, G.M. 1, 266. 4. Graves, G.M. 2, 44. 5. Gifford, 26. 6. de Voragine, 57. 7. Bullough, 232–33. 8. Turville-Petre, 281–84. 9. Robinson, 178. 10. Budge, G.E. 2, 253. 11. Leland, 137.

Cuthbert, Saint

Once a pagan Lord of the Hunt with a pilgrimage center at Durham, formerly Duirholm, "Meadow of the Deer."

In 1104, Durham Cathedral was erected over the god's old shrine. It housed the undecaying corpse of Cuthbert, whose sainthood was proven by his incorruptibility. He was periodically displayed, and always pronounced remarkably fresh. His remains were last viewed in 1827 and found to be as plump and rosy as ever—almost as if he were a waxwork, if it were possible to suspect the church of perpetrating such a hoax.

Oddly enough, while his incorruptible body lay in Durham Cathedral, St. Cuthbert also lived on at the bottom of the sea, as a marine smith-god who forged beads for rosaries in his ocean cave. Crinoid shells washed up on Northumbrian beaches after storms were known as St. Cuthbert's Beads.[1]

There was also a St. Cuthbert's Well, located near the famous Eden Hall, whose "luck" talisman was a sacred chalice inherited from the fairies.[2] The waters of St. Cuthbert's Well were credited with the usual miraculous powers of healing and preserving health.

1. Brewster, 396–97. 2. Hazlitt, 374.

Cybele

Great Mother of the Gods from Ida—*Magna Mater Deum Idea*—brought to Rome from Phrygia in 204 B.C. Her triumphal procession was "later glorified by marvelous legends, and the poets told of edifying miracles that had occurred during Cybele's voyage."[1]

Her holy aniconic image was carried to Rome by order of the Cumaean Sybil, a personification of the same cave-dwelling Goddess herself. As the Great Mother of all Asia Minor, she was worshipped especially on Mt. Ida, Mt. Sipylus, Cyzicus, Sardis, and Pessinus in Galatia.[2]

Her festivals were called *ludi,* "games."[3] A highlight of her worship was the Taurobolium, baptism in the blood of a sacred bull, who represented her dying-god consort, Attis. Her temple stood on the Vatican, where St. Peter's basilica stands today, up to the 4th century A.D. when Christians took it over.[4] She was one of the leading deities of Rome in the heyday of the mystery cults, along with Hecate and Demeter of Eleusis.[5]

Variations of Cybele's name—Kubaba, Kuba, Kube—have been linked with the Ka'aba stone at Mecca, a meteoric "cube" that bore the Goddess's symbol and was once known as the Old Woman.[6]

Other names for Cybele assimilated her to every significant form of the Great Goddess. She was the Berecynthian Mother (*genetrix Berecynthia*). She was Rhea Lobrine, Goddess of sacred caves, known as her "marriage bowers."[7] She was called Augusta, the Great One; Alma, the Nourishing One; Sanctissima, the Most Holy One. Roman emperors like Augustus, Claudius, and Antoninus Pius regarded her as the supreme deity of the empire. Augustus established his home facing her temple, and looked upon his wife, the empress Livia Augusta, as an earthly incarnation of her.[8] The emperor Julian wrote an impassioned address to her:

> *Who is then the Mother of the Gods? She is the source of the intellectual and creative gods, who in their turn guide the visible gods; she is both*

the mother and the spouse of mighty Zeus; she came into being next to and together with the great creator; she is in control of every form of life, and the cause of all generation; she easily brings to perfection all things that are; she is the motherless maiden, enthroned at the side of Zeus, and in very truth is the Mother of all the Gods.[9]

Fathers of the Christian church vehemently disagreed. St. Augustine called Cybele a harlot mother, "the mother, not of the gods, but of the demons."[10]

One of her names, Antaea, made her the mythical mother of the earth-giant Antaeus, who was invincible as long as his feet remained in contact with his Mother's body, the earth. Heracles conquered him by holding him up in the air. Churchmen believed the powers of witches came from the same sort of contact with Mother Earth. Arresting officers often carried witches to prison in a large basket, so their feet would not touch the ground.[11]

There was a Christian sect founded in the 2nd century A.D. by Montanus (Mountain man), a priest of Cybele, who identified Attis with Christ. Montanus maintained that women were agents of the Goddess, and could preach and prophesy as well as men. This contradicted the orthodox Pauline sect, which followed St. Paul's rule that women must never speak publicly on holy subjects.[12] During the 4th century, Montanist Christianity was declared a heresy, and many of its adherents were slain. Some Montanists in Asia Minor were locked in their churches and burned alive.[13]

1. Cumont, O.R.R.P., 47 2. *Encyc. Brit.*, "Great Mother of the Gods."
3. James, 246. 4. Clodd, 79; Frazer, G.B., 408. 5. Angus, 143.
6. Vermaseren, 22; Harding, 41. 7. Gaster, 609.
8. Vermaseren, 27, 53, 83, 85, 177–78. 9. Vermaseren, 86–87.
10. Vermaseren, 181. 11. Robbins, 334; Lea unabridged, 814. 12. Reinach, 278.
13. Chamberlin, A.M., ch. 1.

Cyboread

"Queen of the North," the mother-bride of Judas, whose myth was similar to those of Oedipus, Osiris, and other mother-marrying heroes. See **Judas**.

Cynosure

"Dog's Tail," the *kunos oura,* name given by the Greek sect of Cynics or "Doglike Ones" to the pole star, which they believed would move from its place at the still point of the turning heavens when doomsday was near.[1] This, and the fact that the Dog's Tail was the prime navigational star, made it the "Cynosure of all eyes." See **Dog**.

1. Potter & Sargent, 174.

Cypria

Epithet of Aphrodite, "the Cyprian," whose temple was founded at Paphos on the isle of Cyprus. Because of the island's many copper mines, copper (*cypros*) was sacred to Aphrodite.

Cyrene

Amazon queen who founded the city bearing her name on the coast of Libya, in Marmarica, territory named for one of the oldest forms of the Aryan Sea-goddess.[1] Cyrene was the home of seductive "sirens," whose verbal spells Homer described as highly dangerous to sailors.

1. Graves, W.G., 438.

D

DIANA, the Queen of Heaven, here shown as the Many-Breasted Artemis, as she was known to her cult at Ephesus. This ancient sculpture appears at the Villa Albani in Rome.

The DEMON Pazuzu, one of the Akkadian evil spirits, bringer of fierce storms and malaria, and terror to pregnant women. Bronze, 5¾ inches high. Mesopotamia, 500–100 B.C.

The DEVIL, as a cast iron bootjack, found in Massachusetts. Mid-nineteenth century; 10½ inches high.

Daeira

"Goddess," a title of Demeter as the Wise One of the Sea, and mother of King Eleusis (Advent). The title carried the same connotations as "God" today.

Dagon

Philistine sea god, one of Yahweh's leading enemies (Judges 16:23). He appeared as a merman, fish-man, or serpent-man. He was mated to Atargatis, the Philistine form of Astarte. Since she was a Mistress of Earth and Sea like her Mycenaean twin Demeter, her consort also patronized both farming and fishing. In Canaan, he was the "grain god" Dagan, father of Baal, mated to Anath, the Canaanite version of the same Great Mother. On account of the bad publicity given him in the Bible, he naturally became a leading demon of the Christian hell.

Dakhma

Iranian topless "tower of silence," once used to dispose of dead bodies, which were dropped in and left for the vultures to carry to the sky (see **Vulture**). Large dakhmas still stand today. The adventure of Sinbad the Sailor in the charnel valley, where supernatural birds carried off gobbets of meat, may have descended from a legendary sage's sojourn in a dakhma as a ceremonial death-and-rebirth.

Dakini

"Skywalker," a Tantric priestess, embodying the spirit of Kali Ma as an angel of death.[1] Dakinis were usually elder women, but sometimes young women impersonating the divine Shakti who took the last breath of the enlightened sage with a kiss of peace. Dakinis attended the dying, embracing and comforting them in their last moments. But there were also "fierce dakinis," representing violent or painful forms of death.[2]

Like western witches, dakinis held their meetings in cemeteries or cremation grounds, having charge of funeral rites and the preparation of dead bodies. See **Death**.

1. Tatz & Kent, 148. 2. *Bardo Thodol*, 128.

var. Danu, Danuna, Danae

Dana

Eponymous Great Mother of the Danes and many other peoples, such as the Danaans, the Danaids, the biblical Danites, and the Irish Tuatha Dé Danann, "people of the Goddess Dana."[1] The Russians called her Dennitsa, "Greatest of all Goddesses." A medieval Russian exorcism said: "In the morning let us rise and pray to God and Dennitsa."[4]

As Danu-Ana, or Anu, she led the Irish trinity of Fates, collectively the Morrigan. Mountains in Kerry are still named after her breasts, the Paps of Anu.[5] Under the name of Don she was masculinized as a "king" of Dublin in late Irish legend; but the same "king" was also called Mother of the Gods.[6] Sometimes the Irish called her Domnu, a mother Goddess personifying the Deep.[7]

Classical Greek mythology humanized the Goddess Danae, in much the same way as the Bible humanized Earth Mother Eve; the two were the same deity, fructified by the Heaven-father's seminal rain. The Hellenic Danae was a virgin princess impregnated by Zeus's shower of golden rain—that is, urine, to which primitives sometimes attributed the same reproductive power as semen. As result of this beneficial moistening, Danae bore the hero Perseus, who annoyed fathers of the Christian church by being as verifiably god-begotten and virgin-born and their own savior.[9] But Danae, like Eve, was really another name for the universal Triple Goddess, also called Dam-kina by the Sumerians, Dinah by the Hebrews, and Danu or Dunnu in Babylon. The Greeks knew of three Danaids, known as Telchines or "Enchanters," who founded the three chief cities of Rhodes.[10]

Writers of the Old Testament disliked the Danites, whom they called serpents (Genesis 49:17). Nevertheless, they adopted Dan-El or Daniel, a Phoenician god of divination, and transformed him into a Hebrew prophet. His magic powers like those of the Danites emanated from the Goddess Dana and her sacred serpents. He served as court astrologer and dream-interpreter for both the Persian king Cyrus, and the Babylonian king Nebuchadnezzar (Daniel 1:21, 2:1), indicating that "Daniel" was not a personal name but a title, like the Celtic one: "a person of the Goddess Dana."

Pre-Hellenic Aegean tribes called her Danuna, Universal Mother.[2] The rivers of Amazon country were named after her—Danube, Don, Dnieper—because she represented "Waters." To the Hindus she was "Waters of Heaven," mother of the Vedic gods.[3]

In Saxon myth, Danu-Ana became Black Annis, or Anna of the Angles, or the Blue Hag, or Angurboda, mother of Hel. An ancient cave-shrine at Dane's Hill in Leicestershire was her dwelling place, known as Black Annis's Bower.[8]

1. Graves, G.M. 1, 204. *Larousse*, 225. 2. Graves, W.G., 54. 3. Rees, 53.
4. *Larousse*, 285. 5. Graves, W.G., 409. 6. Squire, 372. 7. Squire, 48.
8. Briffault 3, 71. 9. H. Smith, 183. 10. Graves, G.M. 1, 203–4.

Daphne

"Laurel," the plant of prophecy chewed by the Goddess's priestesses in the vale of Tempe, until Apollo's cult replaced hers, and restricted laurel-chewing to the Delphic Pythoness.[1] The Goddess's original name was Daphoene, "Bloody One," in early times when her Maenads were still performing blood sacrifices.

Orgiastic Daphne entered classical mythology as a purified virgin who was saved from rape by Apollo through a transformation into a laurel tree in the nick of time. The myth seems to have been suggested by an icon showing the Goddess's face looking down from the branches of a laurel tree upon the sacred king immolated at her feet.

Laurel remained the plant of inspiration and poetic frenzy. Laurel crowns were given to the best poets, who were then called "laureate"—laurel-crowned.

1. Graves, G.M. 1, 81.

Dark Age

Western histories have put forth many theories about the fall of Rome and attributed the onset of the Dark Age to a wide variety of causes, except the one cause that may have had more to do with it than any other: Christianity.[1] By denying women's spiritual significance and forbidding Goddess worship, the church alienated both sexes from their pagan sense of unity with the divine through each other.

Christians said one of the diabolic symptoms of the oncoming end of the world was "the spread of knowledge," which they endeavored to check with wholesale book-burnings, destruction of libraries and schools, and opposition to education for laymen.[2] By the end of the 5th century, Christian rulers forcibly abolished the study of philosophy, mathematics, medicine, and geography. Lactantius said no Christian should study astronomy. Pope Gregory the Great denounced all secular education as folly and wickedness, and forbade Christian laymen to read even the Bible. He burned the library of the Palatine Apollo, "lest its secular literature distract the faithful from the contemplation of heaven."[3]

In the church's view, every opinion except its own was heretical and devilish, likely to raise doubts in the minds of believers. Therefore, pagan intellectuals and teachers were persecuted and schools were closed. Christian emperors commanded the burning of all books of the philosophers, as Theodosius said, "for we would not suffer any of those things so much as to come to men's ears, which would tend to provoke God to wrath and offend the minds of the pious." After years of vandalism and destruction, St. John Chrysostom proudly boasted, "Every trace of the old philosophy and literature of the ancient world has vanished from the face of the earth."[4]

It was almost true. Christian persecutions left "but few fragments of a vast liturgy and religious literature of paganism which would have cast many a ray of light on the origins of our own faith; and demolished holy places and beautiful temples such as the world shall never rear again."[5] After temples were destroyed, monks and hermits were settled in the ruins to defile the site with their excrement, and to prevent reconstruction.[6]

Rulers melted down bronze, gold, and silver artworks for money. Peasants broke up marble gods and goddesses and fed their pieces into limekilns for mortar.[7] It is recorded that 4th-century Rome had 424 temples, 304 shrines, 80 statues of deities in precious metal, 64 statues of ivory, 3,700 statues in bronze, and thousands in marble. By the next century, nearly all of them were gone. The historian Eunapius, a hierophant of the Eleusinian Mysteries, watched the destruction and wrote that the empire was being overwhelmed by a "fabulous and formless darkness mastering the loveliness of the world."[8]

Roman society was losing its cohesiveness and discipline, with the usual symptoms of social decline: runaway inflation, shortages, crime, apathy, and a discouraged middle class taxed to the breaking point to support a top-heavy, stagnant bureaucracy.[9] Most Christians came not from that middle class, but from the lower elements of society, taking advantage of lawless times to grab what they could. Celsus said the Christians invited into their ranks "whosoever is a sinner or unintelligent, or a fool, in a word, whosoever is god-forsaken, him the kingdom of God will receive. Now whom do you mean by the sinner but the wicked: thief, housebreaker, poisoner, temple robber, grave robber?. . . Jesus, they say, was sent to save sinners; was he not sent to help those who have kept themselves free from sin? They pretend that God will save the unjust man if he repents and humbles himself. The just man who has held steadily from the cradle in the ways of virtue he will not look upon."[10]

Bertrand Russell described the philosophical outlook of St. Jerome: "He thinks the preservation of virginity more important than victory over the Huns and Vandals and Goths. Never once do his thoughts turn to any possible measure of practical statesmanship; never once does he point out the evils of the fiscal system, or of reliance on an army composed of barbarians. The same is true of Ambrose and Augustine. . . . It is no wonder that the Empire fell into ruin."[11]

Conventional histories presented a picture of early Christians as peaceable souls, unjustly persecuted. This picture could only have arisen because historical writing was monopolized by the church for many centuries, and there was no compunction about changing or falsifying records. Pagan Rome didn't persecute religious minorities. "It never disputed the existence or reality of other deities, and the addition of a new member to the Pantheon was a matter of indifference. . . . [A]ll deities of all peoples were regarded as but manifestations of the one supreme deity." Dionysus, Venus, and Priapus were honored co-residents of the temple of Isis in Pompeii. Italian and Greek deities mixed together in the temple of Mithra at Ostia.[12] All deities were willing to co-exist except the Christian one. The Christian church alone "has always held the toleration of others to be the persecution of itself."[13] As early as 382 A.D., the church officially declared that any opposition to its own creed in favor of others must be punished by the death penalty.[14]

Contrary to the conventional mythology, Christians were not prosecuted under Roman law for being Christians but for committing civil crimes.[15] They caused riots, "often tumultuously interrupted the public worship, and continually railed against the national religion."[16] They seem to have been guilty of vandalism and arson. The Great Fire in 64 A.D. was set by Christians who were "anxiously waiting for the world to end by fire and who did at times start fires in order to prompt God."[17] Crying that the world would end at any moment, Christian fanatics sometimes developed the notion that starting the fires of the final holocaust would redound to their credit in heaven.[18] At least one saint was canonized for no particular reason other than having been an arsonist: St. Theodore, whose sole claim to fame was burning down the temple of the Mother of the Gods.[19]

The decline of Roman civilization and the onset of the Dark Age was the period Gilbert Murray characterized as the western world's failure of nerve. It marked the transition of the west from a position of cultural leadership to one of regressed barbarism, and transformed Europe into what is now known as an "undeveloped area."[20] Intellect, taste, and imagination disappeared from art and literature. Rather than broadening the western mind, its church crippled that mind by allowing childish superstitions to flourish in an atmosphere of ignorance and unreason.[21] Suppression of the teaching priestess or *alma mater* led to an eclipse of education in general.

Many scholars fled from Christian persecutions eastward to Iran, where the Sassanid king helped them found a school of medicine and science. This was the world's intellectual capital for two centuries.[22] Already in 529, when Justinian closed the Athenian schools, Hellenistic learning had been dispersed to Sassanian Persia, Gupta India, and Celtic Ireland.[23]

Church historians have claimed nothing of real value was lost in the destruction of pagan culture. Modern scholars disagree. The havoc that afflicted art, science, literature, philosophy, engineering, architecture, and all other fields of achievement has been likened to the havoc of the *Gigantomachia*—as if the crude giants overthrew the intelligent gods. The widespread literacy of the classical period disappeared. Aqueducts, harbors, buildings, even the splendid Roman roads fell into ruin. It has been pointed out that centuries of devastating war could hardly have shattered Roman civilization as effectively as did its new obsession with an ascetic monotheism.[24]

Books and artworks were destroyed because they expressed un-Christian ideas and images.[25] The study of medicine was forbidden, on the ground that all diseases were caused by demons and could be cured only by exorcism. This theory was still extant in the time of Pope Alexander III, who forbade monks to study any techniques of healing other than verbal charms.[26] Under the Christian emperors, educated citizens were persecuted by the illiterate who claimed their books were witchcraft texts. Often, "magical" writings were planted by Christian magistrates for the sake of the financial rewards they received when they caught and executed heretics—a system the Inquisition also used to advantage in later centuries. Priestesses were especially persecuted, because they were female, wealthy, and laid claim to spiritual authority.[27]

Fathers of the church seemed cynically aware that public ignorance worked in their favor. Gregory of Nazianzus wrote to St. Jerome: "A little jargon is all that is necessary to impose upon the people. The less they comprehend, the more they admire. Our forefathers and doctors have often said, not what they thought, but what circumstances and necessity dictated."[28]

Lactantius declared that pagan temples should be torn down because, in them, "The demons are attempting to destroy the kingdom of God, and by means of false miracles and lying oracles are assuming the appearance of real gods."[29] It was dangerous to leave the temples intact, even when they were converted into Christian churches. The temple of the Mother of Heaven at Carthage was made over into a church, but in 440 A.D. the bishop discovered that the Carthaginians were actually making their devotions to the old Goddess, and ordered the entire temple area leveled to the ground.[30]

Ignorance was helpful to the spread of the faith; so ignorance was fostered. Knight says, "Men are superstitious in proportion as they are ignorant, and . . . those who know least of the principles of religion are the most earnest and fervent."[31] In keeping western Europe as ignorant as possible, however, the church lost much of its history. Even contemporary events went inaccurately reported, or altogether unnoted. Events of the past were absurdly garbled. All the public knew of history was provided by bards, who tried to maintain the druidic tradition of rote-learning, with indifferent success. They taught, for example, that Alexander the Great made an expedition to the Garden of Eden, where he was instructed by the poet-magician Virgil, by "Monsignor St. Paul," and by "Tholomeus" (Ptolemy), king of Egypt. They taught that Julius Caesar was a king of Hungary and Austria, and a prince of Constantinople; his mother was the Valkyrie Brunnhilde, a daughter of Judas Maccabeus; he married Morgana, the Fairy Queen, and became the father of Oberon and St. George.[32]

The field of natural science was in even worse disorder. Learned books taught that mice do not reproduce like other mammals but are generated spontaneously and asexually from "the putrefaction of the earth"; that wasps produce themselves out of a dead horse and bees out of a dead calf; that a crab deprived of its legs and buried will turn into a scorpion; that some mammals, such as hares, can change from one sex to the other; that a duck dried into powder and placed in water will generate frogs; that a duck baked and buried will generate toads; that asparagus is produced from buried shavings of ram's horn; that scorpions can be created from garden basil rubbed between two stones; that rain and lightning can be raised by burning a chameleon's liver on a rooftop; that no fleas can breed where a man scatters dust dug up from his right footprint in the place where he heard the first springtime call of a cuckoo.[33] Because the very idea of experimentation to test hypotheses had been replaced by credulous reliance on theological authority, even notions that would have been simple to test remained untested.

As for more complex hypotheses, they were beyond the ken of

theologians. Pagan thinkers long ago understood the shape of the earth, and even calculated its approximate circumference with only a small error. But Lactantius and other learned churchmen called this field of endeavor "bad and senseless," and proved by quoting the Bible that the earth was flat.[34]

The most thoroughly Christianized nations hardly began to recover from the church's eclipse of learning until the present century. In Spain for example, the tradition of book-burning became an integral part of the auto-da-fé in 1502. It was against the law for any layman to read any book not approved by the bishops.[35] To own vernacular copies of either Testament of the Bible was punishable by burning at the stake.[36] Reading declined to almost nothing. What few grammar schools existed were only "superficial preparation for the priesthood." Still, many priests were illiterate. General education was attempted only after the revolutions of 1834 and 1855, when the monasteries were suppressed. Yet in 1896, more than two-thirds of the population were still unable to read or write.[37]

Spanish suspicion of books carried over into the New World, and deprived anthropologists and archeologists of literary treasures that might have shed much light on pre-Columbian civilizations. Spanish friars "converted" the Maya of Yucatan in 1562, by their usual forceful methods, such as torture and burning. They fed the fires with hundreds of Maya sacred books which, had they survived, would have greatly assisted modern scholars to unravel the mysteries of Mayan script. The friars said the natives were "greatly afflicted" by the loss of their scriptures; but as far as the friars could see, these books "contained nothing in which there was not to be seen superstition and lies of the devil, so we burned them all."[38]

1. H. Smith, 254. 2. Mâle, 355. 3. H. Smith, 228, 253; de Camp, A.E., 283, 264. 4. Doane, 436, 447. 5. Angus, 280. 6. J.H. Smith, D.C.P., 173. 7. de Camp, A.E., 93. 8. Pepper & Wilcock, 90, 288. 9. Thomson, 352. 10. H. Smith, 203. 11. B. Russell, 344. 12. Angus, 190–92. 13. Coulton, 91. 14. Robbins, 498. 15. Phillips, 152. 16. Knight, D.W.P., 111. 17. Lindsay, O.A., 277. 18. de Camp, A.E., 234. 19. de Voragine, 662. 20. Campbell, Oc.M., 247, 455. 21. Cumont, O.R.R.P., 26. 22. de Camp, A.E., 303. 23. Campbell, C.M., 133. 24. J.H. Smith, D.C.P., 4; de Camp, A.E., 135, 264. 25. Sadock, Kaplan & Freedman, 536. 26. White 1, 386. 27. Seligmann, 70–73. 28. Doane, 434. 29. Castiglioni, 215. 30. J.H. Smith, D.C.P., 229. 31. Knight, D.W.P., 31. 32. Briffault 3, 432. 33. Agrippa, 101, 108, 111, 122, 137, 148. 34. de Camp, A.E., 283. 35. H. Smith, 259. 36. Lea, 20. 37. Coulton, 305–6. 38. Von Hagen, 432.

David, Saint

Patron saint of Wales, actually a pagan god Christianized in the 11th century A.D. He was the Welsh sea god worshipped as Dewi, from the Aryan *devi* or *deva,* "deity." Though he was called a 6th-century bishop, nothing was written of him until 1090, more than 500 years later. His wholly unreliable biography was composed chiefly to support the Welsh bishops' independence at the time.[1]

The city now called St. David's used to be Menevia, "Way of the Moon," the same as Danish Manavegr and Irish E-Mania, the lunar paradise.[2]

Symbol of David-Dewi was the Great Red Serpent, now the red dragon, Wales's national emblem. Like the phallic god Python or Oceanus encircling the World Egg, he may have been reddened by his union with the Moon-goddess Mab, who gave sovereignty to all her kings by staining them red.[3]

David's title, the Waterman, was explained by Christian scholars to mean he was a teetotaler.[4] Welsh sailors knew better; their traditions placed him in the depths of the sea. They called him Davy Jones, who like the sea god Manannan kept the souls of drowned seamen in his "locker."[5]

Waterman was a popular title for several ancient gods of waters besides Dewi: notably Ceadda, a Mercian god of medicinal springs, who was canonized twice (see **Chad**).

Even in Christian disguise, David retained the sacred skills of a bard. It was claimed that his miraculous talent for harping and singing came from his lineal descent from the virgin Mary, of the ancient house of King David the Harpist, in the eighteenth generation. Mary was also identified with the Welsh sea-goddess Marian, Dewi's bride, receiver of the souls of the dead. Welsh bards called their death songs *marwysgafen,* the "giving to Mary," sung to send the funeral boat to the Isles of the Dead.[6]

Sometimes David was confused with Merlin, who allegedly harped and sang the stones of Stonehenge into their places. Some legends made David a bishop of Merlin's town, Caerleon.[7] Some said David was King Arthur's uncle. Like many mythical saints, he was given a long lifetime to demonstrate the health-giving virtues of Christian faith; he lived to the age of 140 years.[8] His mother was the same virgin temple-maiden who gave birth to nearly every ancient god; here she was St. Non (Holy Nun).[9] Two cities claimed his shrine, located not only at St. David's but also in the city of Chester, which used to be named Deva or Dewi.[10]

1. Attwater, 101–2. 2. Brewster, 121. 3. Rees, 75. 4. Attwater, 102. 5. Phillips, 110. 6. Brewster, 120. 7. Brewster, 121. 8. Hazlitt, 168. 9. Attwater, 102. 10. Cumont, M.M., 57.

Death

It has been said that Death came into existence only with the rise of man's consciousness, a roundabout way of saying death is more real for humans than for any other animal, because only humans foresee it.[1] Religions owe their existence to the unique ability of the human animal to understand that it must die.

Against this realization the forces of imagination are mustered to deny it. It's hard for any perceiving mind to perceive its own notbeing, with cessation of all perception. Worshippers of Kali managed to view the beyond-death state as Dreamless Sleep.[2] But most ancient people couldn't formulate an idea of non-perception.

Even when the land of the dead was minimally stimulating, as in the Babylonian concept, it was perceptible to the senses. It was the House of Dust, and the end of the Road of No Return. The dead were clothed in feathers, like **birds**. "Dust is their food and clay their meat . . . , they see no light, they sit in darkness." Yet in the same House of Dust there were priests and kings ruling, and servants to carry the baked meats and pour water from water skins.[3]

Babylonian literature reveals a hope that eventually the right ritual cure for death will be discovered, rather as modern people hope for a cure for cancer. The recommended avenue of investigation was necromantic consultation with the dead themselves. "The quest for immortality was essentially the search for the right ritual, the knowledge of what to do in order to secure a continued existence of the body after death. This knowledge is possessed by the ancestors, and can only be obtained from them."[4]

Men have usually believed that knowledge of death can only come from those who have experienced it. Hence the initiatory procedures involving mock death, as among Siberian shamans, who experience in trances being torn apart and reduced to bare bones. "By thus seeing himself naked, altogether freed from the perishable and transient flesh and blood, he consecrates himself, in the sacred tongue of the shamans, to his great task, through that part of his body which will longest withstand the action of the sun, wind and weather, after he is dead. . . . [I]n certain Central Asian meditations that are Buddhistic and tantric in origin or at least in structure, reduction to the skeleton condition has . . . an ascetic and metaphysical value—anticipating the work of time, reducing life by thought to what it really is, an ephemeral illusion in perpetual transformation."[5]

So vivid were the fantasies of the death-world that some Oriental sages prayed for sufficient conscious sense to realize that they were nothing more than inventions of the mind: "May I recognize whatever visions appear, as the reflections of my own consciousness. May I know them to be of the nature of apparitions in the intermediate State. May I not fear the troops of my own thought forms, the Peaceful Deities and the Wrathful. . . . May it come that all the Sounds will be known as one's own sounds; may it come that all the Radiances will be known as one's own radiances."[6]

Tantric Buddhism proposed that the death world or Intermediate State could be controlled if one were prepared through carefully guided fantasy in life to retain memory, consciousness, and the goal of choosing for one's self the right "womb-door" for a better reincarnation.[7] Living and dying were only complementary aspects of the same cycle, both requiring proper education. "Material life moves between two poles," Bachofen says. "Its realm is not that of being but that of becoming and passing away, the eternal alternation of two colors, the white of life and the black of death. Only through the equal mixture of the two is the survival of the material world assured. Without death no rejuvenation is possible . . . the positive power cannot for one moment exist without the negative power. Death, then, is not the opposite but the helper of life."[8]

The Great Goddess was intimately involved in every manifestation of death as she was in those of life, which is why she had an "emanation" for each fatal disease, such as Mari-Amma, Ankamma, Mutteyalamma, etc. Her priestesses supported and taught the dying. "As among the gods, so among the mortals was death everywhere woman's business. A woman is said to have invented the wailing for the dead. . . . Women cradle the infant and the corpse, each to its particular new life."[9]

Romans thought death should be kept in mind at all times, especially when life at its peak might make one forget the other, equally necessary part of the cycle. When a military hero entered Rome in triumphal procession, riding in a golden chariot, hailed as a god in the ancient equivalent of a ticker-tape parade, a person wearing the mask and costume of Death stood at his shoulder, preserving him from the sin of hubris by saying each moment in his ear, "Man, remember you will die."[10]

Paganism fostered the Tantric idea of growth and decline in recurrent cycles. "The old fertility gods did not shrink from the fact of death; they sought no infantile evasion, but promised rebirth and renewal."[11] Christianity on the other hand denied that members of its sect could die. Early Christians who died were said to have "fallen asleep," soon to wake up again with the second coming of Christ. A morbid anxiety often accompanied ritual denial. Kermode says, "Christianity of all the great religions is the most anxious, is the one which laid the most emphasis on the terror of death."[12]

Sometimes fear became obsession, in a love-hate relationship with death. In the *Secret Book of James,* Jesus recommended suicide, remarking that the kingdom of death could only belong to those who put themselves to death, and no one who avoided this duty could be saved.[13]

Secret Book of James One of the so-called Gnostic Gospels discovered at Nag Hammadi in Upper Egypt, 1945, purporting to have been written by the apostle James.

Obsession flowered into a thousand elaborate death customs and rituals aimed at encapsulating the phenomenon, separating it from ordinary life experience so its inevitability need not be fully understood. In Frazer's opinion such customs and rituals have been the most wasteful ever seen in any society:

> *No belief has done so much to retard the economic and thereby the social progress of mankind as has the belief in the immortality of the soul; for this belief has led race after race, generation after generation, to sacrifice the real wants of the living to the imaginary wants of the dead. The waste and destruction of life and property which this faith has entailed are enormous and incalculable.*[14]

Pagan philosophers' acceptance of death may have been more practical than the elaborate denials that arose later. With a somber but courageous serenity, Euripides stated the pagan idea that opinions on death are not possible:

But if any far-off state there be
Dearer to life than mortality
The hand of the Dark hath hold thereof,
And mist is under the mist above;
So we are sick for life, and cling
On earth to this nameless and shining thing,
For other life is a fountain sealed,
And the deeps below are unrevealed,
And we drift on legends for ever.[15]

Because they were westerners, the Greek philosophers have been given more credit for originality than they deserved. Actually, their opinions of death and its implications for the living were largely taken from Oriental sages who evolved them first. Greek notions of the Dreamless Sleep, of reincarnation, of the four ages of man including the primordial Age of Giants, all were derived from Oriental sources. Tantric sages spoke of the faraway Golden Age when all men were giants and lived lifetimes of about a thousand years each, because they were nearer in time to the world's creation, when the Goddess's nourishing birth blood was more abundant and the knowledge of her was more intimate among her children. As the Bible said, there were giants in the earth in those days (Genesis 6:4).[16]

The same long-lived giants were identified with their own ancestors by the authors of Genesis. The Hindu concept of human longevity in the Golden Age was copied into the Bible as a quality of the early patriarchs—not quite a thousand years apiece, but at least more than nine centuries. Adam lived to be 930 years old; Seth 912 years; Enos 905 years; and so on, the champion being Methusaleh at 969 years (Genesis 5).

However long delayed, though, death must come, and that was the thought that patriarchal thinkers found unacceptable. The older matriarchal religions were more realistic in their acceptance of death, making it the sage's duty to realize the ugliness, corruption, and decay in nature as fully as he might realize its beauty: to accord death the same value as birth. The two were of equal importance, as two passages through the same Door: one coming out, the other going in. Different forms of the Goddess represented the idea. On the one hand she was the beautiful nubile Virgin or the tender nurturing Mother; on the other hand she was a hideous ghoul, herself corpse-like and a devourer of corpses—and these two forms of her were to be adored equally. Avalon justly remarked that in the west, "the terrible beauty of such forms is not understood"; missionaries could only describe the Death-goddess as a she-devil.[17] Yet, for the enlightened,

"This fanged and bloody Goddess is the same as the other, the beautiful mother and lover. To be able to superimpose and adore both images in one is perhaps the solidest beginning on the road of sadhana."[18]

Some individuals in western culture arrived more or less independently at the vision of this archetypal female death spirit. Wherever there was a concept of Mother Nature, it could hardly fail to be noticed that it was natural to die, and the roots of every flower lay in organic rot. Coleridge spoke of the "Night-mare LIFE-IN-DEATH" as a woman. Keats described himself as "half in love with easeful Death." Like the Oriental sages, Alfred de Vigny perceived Death as a maternal Goddess: "O Death divine, at whose recall / Returneth all / To fade in thy embrace, / Gather thy children to thy bosom starred, / Free us from time, from number, and from space, / And give us back the rest that life hath marred."[19]

1. von Franz, pl. 7. 2. Campbell, C.M., 347. 3. *Epic of Gilgamesh*, 92. 4. Hooke, S P., 55. 5. Eliade, S., 63. 6. Campbell, M.I., 399; *Bardo Thodol*, 202. 7. *Bardo Thodol*, 183. 8. Bachofen, 33–34. 9. Lederer, 126–27. 10. Dumézil, 566. 11. Mumford, 267. 12. Kermode, 27. 13. Pagels, 90. 14. Frazer, P.T., 52. 15. Angus, 230–31. 16. *Mahanirvanatantra*, xlvii-xlviii. 17. Avalon, 171. 18. Rawson, A.T., 112, 129. 19. Cumont, A.R.G.R., 94.

Deborah

"Queen Bee," a ruler of Israel in the matriarchal period, bearing the same name as the Goddess incarnate in early Mycenaean and Anatolian rulers as "the Pure Mother Bee."[1] Deborah lived under a sacred palm tree that also bore her name, and was identified with the maternal Tree of Life, like Xikum, the Tree of Ishtar. The Bible called her a "prophetess" or "judge" to disguise the fact that she was one of the governing matriarchs of a former age (Judges 4:4).

One of Deborah's alternate names was Jael, "the Goddess Jah," possibly the same one patriarchal Persians called Jahi the Whore, an earlier feminine form of Yahweh.[2]

1. Sobol, 138; Neumann, G.M., 267. 2. Albright, 23.

Delilah

"She Who Makes Weak," a name compounded of *De* (daleth), the yonic Door, and *lilu,* the lotus, another yonic symbol. She was the Goddess who "weakened" the sun god every day and sent him to his death on the wheel that turned him under the earth. In the case of **Samson**—who was the sun god Shams-On, or Shamash—it was the mill wheel. In the case of **Heracles**, another name for the same solar deity, it was Omphale's wheel: the *omphalos* often represented by the cosmic yoni.

Delphi

"Womb"; Greece's oldest, most famous oracle, where Mother Earth was worshipped under the name of Delphyne, the Womb of Creation, along with her serpent-son and consort Python.[1] At various times the oracle was said to belong to the Sea-goddess, or the Moon-goddess, various designations of the same primal Mother, whose priestess-daughters, the Pythonesses, controlled the rites. Eventually the patriarchal god Apollo took it over, retaining the Pythonesses, but claiming to have placed the Serpent in his underground uterine cave, whence came the oracle's inspiration. Apollo murdered the priestess Delphyne, and held the oracle until it was closed by the Christian emperor Theodosius. After him, Arcadius had the temple entirely destroyed.

1. Graves, G.M. 1, 80.

Demeter

Greek *meter* is "mother." *De* is the delta, or triangle, a female-genital sign known as "the letter of the vulva" in the Greek sacred alphabet, as in India it was the Yoni Yantra, or yantra of the vulva.[1] Corresponding letters—Sanskrit *dwr,* Celtic *duir,* Hebrew *daleth*—meant the Door of birth, death, or the sexual paradise.[2] Thus, Demeter was what Asia called "the Doorway of the Mysterious Feminine . . . the root from which Heaven and Earth sprang."[3] In Mycenae, one of Demeter's earliest cult centers, *tholos* tombs with their triangular doorways, short vaginal passages and round domes, represented the womb of the Goddess from which rebirth might come. Doorways generally were sacred to women. In Sumeria they were painted red, representing the female "blood of life."[4] In Egypt, doorways were smeared with real blood for religious ceremonies, a custom copied by the Jews for their Passover rites.

The triangle-door-yoni symbolized Demeter's trinity. Like all the oldest forms of the basic Asiatic Goddess she appeared as Virgin, Mother, and Crone, or Creator, Preserver, Destroyer, like Kali-Cunti who was the same yoni-mother. Demeter's Virgin form was Kore, the Maiden, sometimes called her "daughter," as in the classical myth of the abduction of Kore, which divided the two aspects of the Goddess into two separate individuals. Demeter's Mother form had many names and titles, such as Despoena, "the Mistress"; Daeira, "the Goddess"; the Barley-Mother; the Wise One of Earth and Sea; or Pluto, "Abundance." This last name was transferred to the male underworld god said to have taken the Maiden into the earth-womb during the dark season when fields lay fallow. But this was a late, artificial myth. The original Pluto was female, and her "riches" were poured out on the world from her breasts.[5]

The Crone phase of Demeter, Persephone-the-Destroyer, was

identified with the Virgin in late myth, so the Maiden abducted into the underworld was sometimes Kore, sometimes Persephone. Some of the Destroyer's other, earlier names were Melaina, the Black One; Demeter Chthonia, the Subterranean One; or The Avenger (Erinys). Her black-robed, mare-headed idol, her mane entwined with Gorgon snakes, appeared in one of her oldest cave-shrines, Mavrospelya, the Black Cave, in Phigalia (southwest Arcadia). She carried a dolphin and a dove, symbols of womb and yoni. Like the devouring death-goddess everywhere, she was once a cannibal. She ate the flesh of Pelops, then restored him to life in her cauldron.[6] She was as fearsome as every other version of the Crone. The legendary medieval Night-Mare—an equine Fury who tormented sinners in their sleep—was based on ancient images of Mare-headed Demeter.

Her cult was already well established at Mycenae in the 13th century B.C. and continued throughout Greece well into the Christian era, a length of time almost equal to the lifespan of Christianity itself.[7] Her temple at Eleusis, one of the greatest shrines in Greece, became the center of an elaborate mystery-religion. Sophocles wrote, "Thrice happy they of men who looked upon these rites ere they go to Hades's house; for they alone there have true life." Aristides said, "The benefit of the festival is not merely the cheerfulness of the moment and the freedom and respite from all previous troubles, but also the possession of happier hopes concerning the end, hopes that our life hereafter will be the better, and that we shall not lie in darkness and filth—the fate that is believed to await the uninitiated." Isocrates said: "Demeter . . . being graciously minded towards our forefathers because of their services to her, services of which none but the initiated may hear, gave us the greatest of all gifts, first, those fruits of the earth which saved us from living the life of beasts, and secondly, that rite which makes happier the hopes of those that participate therein concerning both the end of life and their whole existence."[8]

Eleusis meant "advent." Its principal rites brought about the advent of the Divine Child or Savior, variously named Brimus, Dionysus, Triptolemus, Iasion, or Eleuthereos, the Liberator. Like the corn, he was born of Demeter-the-earth and laid in a manger or winnowing basket.[9] His flesh was eaten by communicants in the form of bread, made from the first or last sheaves. His blood was drunk in the form of wine. Like Jesus, he entered the Earth and rose again. Communicants were supposed to partake of his immortality, and after death they were known as *Demetreioi,* blessed ones belonging to Demeter.[10]

Revelations were imparted to the initiate through secret "things heard, things tasted, and things seen."[11] This formula immediately calls to mind the three admonitory monkeys covering ears, mouth, and eyes, supposed to illustrate the maxim, "Hear no evil, speak no evil, see no evil." Was the "evil" a secret descended from Eleusinian religion? Demeter was worshipped as "the Goddess" by Greek peasants all the way through the Middle Ages, even up to the 19th century at Eleusis where she was entitled "Mistress of Earth and Sea." In 1801 two Englishmen named Clarke and Cripps caused a riot among the peasants by taking the Goddess's image away to a museum in Cambridge.[12]

Early Christians were much opposed to the Eleusinian rites because of their overt sexuality, even though their goal was "regeneration and forgiveness of sins."[13] Asterius said, "Is not Eleusis the scene of descent into the darkness, and of the solemn acts of intercourse between the hierophant and the priestess, alone together? Are not the torches extinguished, and does not the large, the numberless assembly of common people believe that their salvation lies in that which is being done by the two in the darkness?"[14] Fanatic monks destroyed the temple of these sexual mysteries in 396 A.D., but the site remained holy to the Goddess's votaries, and the ceremonies were carried on there and elsewhere.[15]

Rustics never ceased believing that Demeter's spirit was manifest in the final sheaf of the harvest, often called the Demeter, the Corn Mother, the Old Woman, etc. At harvest festivals it was often dressed in woman's clothing and laid in a manger to make the cattle thrive.[16] Secret anti-Christian doctrines of medieval Freemasonry also drew some symbolism from the cults of the ancient Mistress of Earth and Sea, particularly the masonic sacred image of Plenty: "an ear of corn near a fall of water."[17] The ultimate Mystery was revealed at Eleusis in "an ear of corn reaped in silence"—a sacred fetish that the Jews called **shibboleth**.[18]

1. *Mahanirvanatantra,* 127. 2. Gaster, 302. 3. de Riencourt, 175. 4. Hays, 68. 5. Graves, W.G., 159, 406; G.M. 1, 61; G.M. 2, 25. 6. Graves, G.M. 2, 30. 7. *Encyc. Brit.,* "Demeter." 8. Lawson, 563–64. 9. Graves, W.G., 159. 10. Angus, 172. 11. H. Smith, 127. 12. Lawson, 79, 89–92. 13. Angus, 97. 14. Lawson, 577. 15. Angus, vii. 16. Frazer, G.B., 473. 17. Elworthy, 105. 18. d'Alviella, 2.

Demetra, Saint

As was the rule with other manifestations of the Great Goddess, there was an attempt to Christianize Demeter by making a saint of her. Though the church refused to canonize "St. Demetra" officially, yet she remained a great favorite of the people, who told miracle-tales about her and prayed to her as fervently as if she were a certified member of the canon.

The classic myth of Kore-Persephone and Demeter was retold as a popular fairy tale centering on St. Demetra. The saint's daughter (Kore) was kidnapped by "a wicked Turkish wizard" (Hades) and locked up in a tower. A young hero rescued her, but perished miserably, chopped in pieces by the wizard and hung from the tower's walls "between heaven and earth." Guided by a stork (her ancient totemic bird of birth), St. Demetra arrived on the scene, reassembled the hero, and brought him back to life.[1] Several elements of this story were repeated in the Germanic fairy tale of Rapunzel.

A masculinized version of Demeter—or perhaps one of her *Demetreioi*—was accepted into the canon as a "St. Demetrius," of no known date, and no real biography. His legend, established in the late Middle Ages, made him a warrior saint like the equally mythical St. George. The basic story was invented to publicize his healing relics preserved at Salonika.[2]

1. Lawson, 80–84. 2. Attwater, 102.

Demon

From Greek *daimon,* a personal familiar spirit or guardian angel, like the Roman *genius,* roughly synonymous with "soul." The *daimon* of a hero could undergo apotheosis, become a god, and rise to heaven to dwell among the stars.

The medieval concept of the demon evolved from Christians' blanket condemnation of all pagan *daimones,* though they continued to believe implicitly in their existence.[1] Demons were usually considered messengers and assistants of a single Devil, in the same relationship to him as angels to God. Yet they were also called "devils" and their master could be "the Demon." The terms were never clearly distinguished.

Animals and people could be "demons," or could harbor demons within their bodies or minds. Sometimes, any alien group of people could be called demons. Europeans often visualized demons as black, like Negroes.[2] On the other hand, dark-skinned people like the Singhalese maintained that demons were white and hairy.[3]

According to St. Thomas Aquinas, all bad weather and natural catastrophes were brought about by demons. He said, "It is a dogma of faith that demons can produce wind, storms, and rain of fire from heaven." Pope Eugene IV issued a bull against human "agents of Satan" who controlled weather-demons. Pope John XXII complained of wizards who tried to kill him through the agency of demons they sent into mirrors and rings.[4]

The church had several mutually contradictory theories about the origin of demons. One theory said they were the rebellious angels who fell with Lucifer, before the creation of Adam and Eve, so the principle of evil was ready in the garden of Eden to play the tempter's role. A second, incompatible theory said demons were created after human beings. They were begotten by the angels on the daughters of men (Genesis 6:4). "The majority opinion about the fall of the angels, held by St. Augustine and therefore accepted in the Middle Ages, was that it had occurred before the creation of Adam, but some of the old notion that the angels had fallen through lust for the daughters of men persisted to reinforce antifeminine prejudices."[5]

Some authorities, familiar with the pagans' animal masks and animal-headed idols, said demons were an animal-like race created separately by God, and readily incarnate in animal form. Black goats, bulls, cats, or dogs could be demons. The Gaelic *uile-bheist* (Yule-beast, moon-calf) was called a demonic animal. St. Ambrose told of a certain priest who exorcised the frogs in a certain marsh to stop them from croaking during mass. A thirteenth-century bishop of Lausanne exorcised all the eels in Lake Leman.[6] St. Augustine confidently asserted that demons help sorcerers to perform their magic, and have the power to assume many animal shapes.[7]

At Basel in 1474, a rooster committed the unnatural crime of laying an egg. It was decided that the bird possessed a demon, but exorcism failed to remove it. So the unfortunate rooster was solemnly sentenced to death by church authorities, and burned at the stake.[8]

Greeks still believe in the half-horse demons, *kallikantzari,* descended from ancient centaurs and the shape-shifting horse-wizards of India, the *kinnaras,* "canterers" who used to live on the holy mountain of Mandara.[9] Their descendants perhaps founded the city of Kallipolis (Gallipoli). Their chief is still called the Lame Devil, recalling lame Amazonian smith-gods like Hephaestus. Until recently it was thought any child born on Christmas Day would become a *kallikantzaros.*[10] A cruel custom arose from this belief. Children born on Christmas Day were carried to the market square, where their feet were thrust into a fire until the toenails were singed.[11] The magical purpose of this may have been to destroy the horse-demons' "hoofs."

Records of witch trials show that almost any kind of animal could be perceived as a demon. Witches were executed because a neighbor's child was frightened by "the devil in the shape of a dog"; or because a man saw "a Thing like unto a rat" run out of a woman's house; or because a woman kept "two devils in the form of colts"; or because a neighbor saw "the devil in the form of a toad" in a woman's garden; or because a traveler saw "a Thing like a black cow" near the house of the accused; or because children heard a woman "talk to the devil in the form of a frog." One woman was condemned because neighbors heard near her house at night a "foul yelling, like a number of cats." No one seems to have suggested that the yelling was in fact done by cats, not demons.

Ursula Kemp was hanged in 1581 on the evidence of her own 8-year-old son, who testified that she kept four demons: two cats, a toad, and a black lamb.[12] Not once in the recorded trials did authorities question witnesses' ability to distinguish these demons from ordinary animals. It was taken for granted that anyone, even a small child, could recognize His Satanic Majesty no matter how cleverly he disguised himself as an apparently normal beast.

Several popes were believed to have familiar demons of their own, particularly the famous Honorius, long remembered as a magician. During the controversy between Pope Boniface VIII and Philip IV of

France, the king held an assembly that formally deposed the pope and presented evidence to prove that he was a sorcerer with a familiar spirit.[13]

Sometimes, in the description of demons, imagination failed and had to fall back on popular make-believe. One poor wretch named Margot de la Barre was burned at Paris in 1391 for calling up a demon "in the name of the Father and the Son and the Holy Spirit." Pressed to describe the demon—under the stimulus of torture—she could think of nothing better to say than that he had "the shape that demons take in Passion plays."[14]

It was often assumed that demons congregated especially in and around churches, for some inexplicable reason. Churches had to be exorcised at their dedication. Crosses were painted on the walls "to terrify the demons."[15]

Houses were similarly protected by many crosses and crucifixes but, nevertheless, harbored many demons, a belief that betrayed little trust in the alleged powers of the crucifix. The custom of ringing church bells at the time of a death was supposed to drive away demons "who stood at the bed's foot, and about the house, ready to seize their prey, or at least to molest and terrify the soul in its passage, but by the ringing of that bell (for Durandus informs us evil spirits are much afraid of bells), they were kept aloof: and the soul, like a hunted hare, gained the start." Tolling the church's largest bell commanded a higher price, "for that, being louder, the evil spirits must go farther off, to be clear of its sound, by which the poor Soul got so much more the start of them."[16]

Before the witchcraft mania set in about the 12th and 13th centuries, there was a general understanding that demons were nothing more than the old gods and goddesses, all of whom had animal incarnations of some kind. Christian fathers insisted that the pagan deities were not figments of imagination, but real, living demons. Learned men even in the 19th century still believed this. Rawlinson, the translator of Herodotus, was sure the oracle at Delphi was an evil spirit.[17] An early medieval baptismal formula demanded renunciation of "relations with the demon," defining the old religion as "works of the demon, and all his words, and Thor, and Odin, and Saxnot, and all evil beings that are like them."[18] Such formalities were largely ignored. Centuries later, holiday dancers included personifications of the Horned God and the Scandinavian *Julebuk* (Yule Buck), which churchmen denounced as "the devil himself."[19] Monastic writers of the 11th century spoke of many demons who constantly tempted people away from the church, showing them "delights and secrets, such as how they might become immortal."[20] It was clear that they spoke of a rival religion.

A Spanish Dominican, Raymond of Tarrega, said demons were useful for punishing sinners in hell; like angels, demons performed God's will. It was permissible to adore demons "so long as we adore, not their evil, but their existence, which was given them by God. It is not desirable to sacrifice to demons, but to do so is no more serious than adoring an image of Christ or of the saints."[21] Later this opinion was rejected, and the Inquisition burned Raymond's book.

1. Rose, 110, 137. 2. J.B. Russell, 114. 3. Briffault 3, 283. 4. White 1, 337, 351, 384. 5. J.B. Russell, 108–9. 6. White 2, 113. 7. J.B. Russell, 56. 8. H. Smith, 294. 9. O'Flaherty, 275. 10. Lawson, 190. 11. Summers, V., 184. 12. Ewen, 157. 13. J.B. Russell, 187. 14. J.B. Russell, 214. 15. de Voragine, 776. 16. Hazlitt, 479. 17. Halliday, 119. 18. J.B. Russell, 16, 67. 19. Miles, 202. 20. Joyce 1, 256. 21. J.B. Russell, 206.

Denis, Saint

Christianized form of the god Dionysus in Paris. Like Orphic shrines of Dionysus, the shrine of St. Denis featured an oracular head. It was claimed that, having been beheaded at Montmartre (Martyr's Mount), Denis then carried his own head to his abbey.[1]

Some churchmen said Denis-Dionysus died in 250 A.D.; others assigned him to the 1st century; still others confused him with the equally mythical Dionysius the Areopagite. His two "companions in martyrdom" Rusticus and Eleutherius were only alternate epithets of the god **Dionysus**.[2]

1. Tuchman, p. 309. 2. Attwater, p. 104.

Derceto

"Whale of Der," a title of the Babylonian Fish-goddess, said to be the mother of Babylon's foundress, Queen Semiramis (Sammuramat).[1] Derceto was the prototype of Jonah's whale, being the Great Fish who swallowed and gave rebirth to the solar god Oannes, or Joannes (Jonah). See **Fish**.

1. Baring-Gould, C.M.M.A., 497.

Devi

"Goddess," the Sanskrit root word for many Indo-European names for the Great Mother. The teachings of Krishna or Shiva were addressed to the Devi as interrogator of the catechism; she was also addressed as Dearly Beloved, the Shakti, a convention copied by the New Testament. Krishna's virgin mother was her "maiden" form, Devaki. The Goddess's title as "the Way leading to the Gods" was Devayani, the Divine Yoni. As the virgin mother of Mahavira she was Devananda, "Blessed Goddess."[1] A Czech name for the Moon-goddess, Devana, came from the same root, as also the Latin Diana,

Minoan Diwija, Serbian Diiwica, and the Roman Diviana—all meaning "The Divinity."[2]

1. *Larousse,* 347. 2. Thorsten, 361.

Devil

The words "devil" and "divinity" grew from the same root, Indo-European *devi* (Goddess) or *deva* (God), which became *daeva* (devil) in Persian.[1] Old English *divell* (devil) can be traced to the Roman derivative *divus, divi:* gods.[2] Thus it seems that, from the beginning, gods and devils were often confused with one another.

Divine and devilish were relative terms, as the primary sense of Hebrew words for "good" and "evil" really meant "beneficial" and "hurtful."[3] Gods did "evil" things if angered; devils could do "good" things if they were pleased. One man's god was his enemy's devil. Armenians used to sacrifice one sheep to Christ at Easter time and thirty sheep to the devil, on the theory that the devil's influence in the here and now was greater.[4]

Such thinking was not unusual. Devils were often credited with beneficent magic. There was a devil who "maketh men witty, turneth all metals into the coin of the dominion, turneth water into wine, and wine into water, and blood into wine, and wine into blood, and a fool into a wise man—and he leads 33 legions of demons." Another devil "perfectly teaches the virtues of the stars, he transformeth men, he giveth dignities, prelacies, and confirmations." Another devil "talketh of divine virtue, he giveth true answers of things present, past, and to come, and of the divinity, and of the creation, he deceiveth none, nor suffereth any to be tempted; he giveth dignities and prelacies."[5]

Even early Christians admitted that the "devils" worshipped in pagan temples were known to restore the sick to health.[6] Tertullian said, *Diabolus simia Dei,* the Devil imitates God; but in point of chronology there was some doubt about who was imitating whom.[7]

Tertullian (Quintus Septimius Florens Tertullianus) Influential early Christian writer and father of the church, ca. 155–220 A.D., born in Carthage of pagan parents.

Judeo-Christian tradition attributed many "diabolic" acts to God. He was the sender of pestilence and famine. He created a terrible hell, and its demons, who tortured human souls on his orders. He caused violent storms, which were (and still are) called "acts of God." From the 15th century on, the church sold waxen cakes, the Agnus Dei, stamped with a cross and advertised as sure protection against storms and other "acts of God"; thus God was incongruously invoked to combat himself.[8]

God even killed himself in the person of Christ, according to the theological dogma that they were one and the same. On the other hand, some claimed Christ was killed by "devilish" Jews. Though Jews were carrying out God's ordained scheme of salvation, and doing

God's will by executing Jesus, nevertheless theology exonerated God and blamed them. Though the Old Testament God did much "evil," even destroying many thousands of his own helpless worshippers for trivial offenses (1 Samuel 6:19), yet churchmen seldom dared to accept the Bible's own presentation of God as the maker of evil: "I form the light, and create darkness; I make peace, and create evil; I the Lord do all these things" (Isaiah 45:7). On the basis of this scripture, some advanced the theory that God had deliberately created the devil before the beginning of the world, because a pre-existing evil principle was necessary to "test the faith" of the future human race.[9] Yet somehow, to make a devil was not evil if God did it.

The Persians believed God and the devil were twin brothers, born simultaneously from the womb of the dualistic mother of Infinite Time, Zurvan. The devil (Ahriman) was cast down from heaven to the underworld only because his sacrifice, like Cain's, was not acceptable to the older deity. The heavenly god (Ahura Mazda) continued to reign in the heights because he knew how to make the right sacrifices.

But the devil, not the god, was the true creator of the earth and all creatures in the mundane world of matter. Thus the Magi prayed to him for assistance in all worldly endeavors, and revered him as the source of their magic powers. Ahriman was worshipped in Roman times throughout northern Europe, identified with all chthonian gods like Pluto, Saturn, or Dis Pater.[10] In early Christian mystery-plays he appeared as a wonder-working spirit, one Saint Mahown.[11]

The Christian devil became a composite of ancient deities in a single Protean form. He had the goat-horns and hoofs of satyr-gods like Pan, Marsyas, and Dionysus; the trident of Neptune, Hades, or Shiva; the reptilian form of Leviathan, Python, or Ouroborus; the fiery form of Agni or Helios; the female breasts of Astarte-Ishtar; the wolf face of Dis, Feronius, or Fenrir; the quadruple wings of Babylonian cherubim; the bird claws of ancestral spirits, the *aves;* and all the god-names Christians had ever heard, including many secret names of their own God: Jupiter, Mercury, Minerva, Venus, Hades, Pluto, Baal-Zebub, Lucifer, Zeus Chthonios, Sabazius, Belial, Adonis, Sabaoth, Iao, Soter, Emmanuel, Sammael.[12] The devil could take any shape, even a human one: Pope Gregory IX described him as "a pale, black-eyed youth with a melancholy aspect."[13] At other times he was an animal composite, as on the Amulet of Bes:

> *Naked genius with the head of Bes, flanked by seven heads of animals among whom are bull, lion, and ibis, and surmounted by* atef *crown with several horns; four wings; falcon-tail and crocodile-tail; four arms—two arms stretched out along the wings hold lances and serpents, while the third on the left seizes a lion, the fourth on the right holds sceptre and whip. The erect penis ends in a lionhead; there are lionmasks on the knees, the feet are given the form of jackal-heads with pointed ears and prolonged as coiled snakes. Bes stands on an ouroboros (cosmic serpent) which contains various animals: scorpion, crocodile, tortoise.*[14]

The devil's popular nickname Old Scratch came from a Germanic wood-spirit called a *Scrat* or *Waldscrat,* sometimes a protector of households known as *Schraetlin* or "little Scrat." The spirit inhabited a phallic amulet based on the bisexual lingam-yoni, as suggested by Anglo-Saxon *scritta,* Old English *scrat,* a hermaphrodite. Another nickname of the devil, Deuce, came from Gaulish gods called Dusii, a variation of *deus,* "god." Again there was a hermaphroditic connotation, since "deuce" also meant "two."[15]

Some demonologists postulated seven devils, one for each of the seven deadly sins: Lucifer (pride), Mammon (avarice), Asmodeus (lechery), Satan (anger), Beelzebub (gluttony), Leviathan (envy) and Belphegor (sloth). Belial, a slightly less prestigious spirit, governed such "vessels of iniquity" as playing cards and dice.[16]

"Devils" and "the devil" were interchangeable. The devil was one, and also many: a monotheistic transformation of a polytheistic concept. Christian nations asserted that all other nations worshipped "devils" or "the devil" under many names. A 16th-century list of devil-worshipping countries included: Tartary, China, Lapland, Finland, the Northern Islands, the East Indies, Persia, Arabia, Anatolia, Egypt, Ethiopia, Turkey, Russia, and Norway.[17] According to the 18th-century German theologian Johann Beaumont, any person anywhere in the world who "confesseth not that Jesus Christ is come in the flesh" belongs to the devils.[18]

As God incarnated himself in earthly flesh, so the devil was supposed to incarnate himself in earthly flesh shortly before the coming of doomsday. This demonic being was usually called Antichrist. He would be known by his Christlike ability to perform healing miracles, such as restoring sight to the blind.[19] It was never explained how these demonic miracles were to be distinguished from holy ones. The coming of Antichrist was constantly announced, dozens of times in each century. Canon Moreau and contemporary churchmen reported that Antichrist was born in 1599 at Babylon, where the Jews acclaimed him as their Messiah.[20] Apparently he was identified with the Messianic Elijah for whom the Jews looked each year at Passover.

If there were any devilish attributes on which most myths agreed, they were the rather godlike qualities of (1) superhuman intelligence, and (2) superhuman sexuality. Inquisitor Jean Bodin wrote, "It is certain that the devils have a profound knowledge of all things. No theologian can interpret the Holy Scriptures better than they can; no lawyer has more detailed knowledge of testaments, contracts and actions; no physician or philosopher can better understand the composition of the human body, and the virtues of the heavens, the stars, birds and fishes, trees and herbs, metals and stones." Inquisitor Nicholas Remy said the devil had complete knowledge of everything human beings could not explain. "Everything which is unknown lies . . . in the cursed domain of demonology; for there are no unexplained facts. Whatever is not normal is due to the Devil."[21]

No Christian was permitted to disbelieve in the devil. His credibility rested on the same foundation as that of God. Indeed, the very concept of salvation depended on the devil. If there had been no Tempter, there was no original sin, no fall, no hell, no need of a redeemer or a church. De Givry correctly said, "If the Satanic concept is tampered with, the whole edifice laboriously erected by the Fathers of the Church crumbles to the ground."[22]

The devil was essential to the dualistic theology that Christianity copied from Persia. If the world was divided between the forces of good and evil, an evil deity was necessary, otherwise evil would have to be blamed on God. Logically, a god couldn't be both all-good and all-powerful. If God could make a world without evil, and would not, he couldn't be all-good. If God wanted to make a world without evil, and could not, he couldn't be all-powerful. The only solution—not a good one, but the only possible one—was to supply God with an evenly matched adversary, to be responsible for evil. Thus theologians thought it the worst heresy, "contrary to the true faith," to suggest that devils existed only in the ignorant imagination.[23] The devil was so real to Martin Luther that he accosted him one evening and threw an inkpot at him.[24]

It was a severe theological problem to account for God's apparent helplessness to halt the devil's activity. Though Lucifer or Satan was supposed to have been utterly defeated and immobilized during the famous War in Heaven, yet he was so lively that the War seemed to have caused him nothing more than a momentary inconvenience. Theologians could only propose that God "permitted" the devil's freedom of action. They said, "It is not the witch's ointment nor her incantation that makes her forked stick fly through the air, but the power of the devil, allowed by God."[25] They never explained why the church punished what God allowed.

Much semantic hairsplitting went into defining relationships between the devil, God, and humanity, such as the distinction between sorcery and witchcraft. Sorcery was evoking spirits to "carry out those powers which God permitted the Devil." Witchcraft was evoking spirits to "commit acts against His ruling." In practice, a man who asked the devil to help him seduce a woman was not guilty of any crime, because sex was under the devil's jurisdiction, by God's order. Devils who killed children did nothing sinful, for God permitted them to kill children "in order to punish their parents."[26] On the other hand, a woman who tried to save her dying child with witch-herbs was mortally guilty and deserved the death penalty.[27]

Theologians argued that all works of witches were brought about by the devil with God's permission. Even a witch who did only good works, like healing the sick, must suffer the same death as a witch whose acts were harmful.[28] Thus witches were placed in a no-win situation. Once a man beat a witch for casting a spell on his son, and forced her to remove the spell. Pope Benedict XIV ruled that the witch committed a double sin by using the devil's power twice, even though she did it under coercion the second time. Benedict carefully stipulated that the man who beat her was entirely innocent of wrongdoing.[29]

The church created the idea that witches were the devil's helpers, involved in a vast plot to undermine Christian society. This theory was the real root of the witch mania. The people were generally indifferent to the priests' witch-hunting until this theory was forced on them by propaganda from the pulpit, which deliberately played on their fear of the devil after stimulating it in the first place.[30]

It sometimes happened that churchmen themselves consulted the devil, without paying the same penalties they inflicted on lay persons. Some miracle-working heretics were convicted by the bishop of Besançon in 1170, on the evidence of none other than Satan, interviewed by the bishop with the help of a priest skilled in necromancy. Satan assured the bishop that the accused were indeed his servants, so they were sent to the stake.[31]

The devil was useful to clergymen—or anyone else—seeking an excuse for lecherous behavior. According to one story:

> *The devil transformed himself into the appearance of St. Silvanus, Bishop of Nazareth, a friend of St. Jerome. And this devil approached a noble woman by night in her bed and began first to provoke and entice her with lewd words, and then invited her to perform the sinful act. And when she called out, the devil in the form of the saintly Bishop hid under the woman's bed, and being sought for and found there, he in lickerish language declared lyingly that he was Bishop Silvanus. On the morrow therefore, when the devil had disappeared, the holy man was scandalously defamed.*[32]

Some sly fellows used the devil to defraud. There was a Cornishman who convinced his neighbors that he had sold his soul to the devil. Taking a few coins to the tavern each night, he pretended to receive money from the devil to pay for his drink. He would thrust his hat up the chimney, calling on his diabolic friend; and the coins appeared in his hat. The superstitious innkeeper wouldn't touch the devil's money, so the Cornishman drank all evening for free.[33]

The devilish pact was not a joke, however; it was an essential ingredient of the devil-mythology that killed millions during six centuries of witch-hunting. Yet it was logically absurd. If the devil received the soul of every sinner, as the church taught, he had no need to secure it with a "pact"; it would be his anyway. As for the sinners themselves, they seemed to derive little benefit from their side of the contract, as Scot pointed out: any woman in her right mind would reject the devil's bargain, saying, "Why should I hearken to you, when you will deceive me? Did you not promise my neighbor Mother Dutton to save and rescue her; and yet lo she is hanged?"[34]

Early in the Christian era there were no very severe punishments for making a pact with the devil. The *Golden Legend* tells of a young man who signed over his soul to the devil to win the love of a certain lady. Later, St. Basil prayed over the young man and retrieved his contract, a piece of paper which dropped from an upper balcony of the church, "fluttered down through the air and fell into his hands, in the sight of all." The paper was torn up and the youth set free.[35]

Several popes were said to have made a diabolic pact, including one who may have ideological roots in a genuine pagan tradition: Silvester II. His real name was Gerbert de Aurillac. He grew up in a France still permeated by Dianic and druidic fairy-religion, where Aphrodite was worshipped at Rouen up to the 12th century, and the Moon-goddess's groves attracted pilgrims up to the 14th. Silvester chose a papal name meaning "spirit of the grove," and it was said he had a fairy mistress named Meridiana (Mary-Diana), who taught him the secrets of magic.[36] According to Cardinal Benno and William of Malmesbury, Silvester signed a pact with the devil to achieve the papal throne, and the devil gave it to him.[37]

The truth about Pope Silvester was that he had unusually intellectual tastes for his time. He remarked that, for the frustrations and difficulties of his life, "philosophy was the only cure."[38] In his time, "philosophy" didn't mean Christian theology. It meant pagan literature, natural science, and Hermetism.

> *The list of great men in those centuries charged with magic . . . is astounding; it includes every man of real mark, and in the midst of them stands one of the most thoughtful popes, Silvester II (Gerbert), and the foremost of medieval thinkers on natural science, Albert the Great. It came to be the accepted idea that, as soon as a man conceived a wish to study the works of God, his first step must be a league with the devil.*[39]

Another "devilish" philosopher was Heinrich Cornelius Agrippa von Nettesheim, historiographer to Emperor Charles V, author of the famous treatise on Hermetism, *De occulta philosophia.* The church execrated his works and severely reprimanded him for trying to defend accused witches, but his wealthy patrons protected him from arrest: only once he was imprisoned for debt, not heresy.[40] He called magic the perfect science, and implied as the Gnostic heretics did that knowledge came to man not as a gift of God but as a gift of the devil.

Agrippa's life story contributed to the legend of Faust, around which centered many thrilling tales of the devil's pact. The real Faust was not impressive. As an obscure schoolmaster in Kreuznach, he was dismissed from his post in 1507 on a charge of sodomy.[41] Six years later he reappeared as an astrologer and soothsayer calling himself the Demigod of Heidelberg. Later, citizens of Munster knew him as "the famous necromancer, Dr. Faustus." Ultimately, his fame rested not on any of his doings but on the so-called Faustian books, *Höllenzwänge,* "Harrowings of Hell," which he didn't write. These anonymous works grew into a large body of literature professing to tell the reader how to make a pact with the devil, work magic, find buried treasure, win love and fortune, and finally renounce the pact in time to save one's soul.

Predictably, such books were enormously popular. Two books really written by Agrippa von Nettesheim to win the favor of Margaret of Austria, *The Superiority of Women* and *The Nobility of the Female Sex,* were declared heretical and forbidden publication by the clergy.[42]

Magic books nearly always gave formulae for negotiating with the devil. *Le Dragon Rouge* told the aspiring wizard to address "Emperor Lucifer, master of all the rebellious spirits," and his ministers Lucifuge Rofocale, Prince Beelzebub, and Count Ashtoreth.[43] Magic Papyri that had been early models for these books often confused the names and attributes of Jehovah and Lucifer, speaking of "God the light-bringer *(Lucifer),* invincible, who knoweth what is in the heart of all life, who of the dust hath formed the race of men."[44] We have seen the same kind of confusion in Christian theology itself. Yet in 14th-century Toulouse, witches were burned for saying what was actually a tenet of the church's dualism: that "God and the Devil were completely equal, the former reigning over the sky and the latter the earth; all souls which the Devil managed to seduce were lost to the Most High God and lived perpetually on earth or in the air."[45]

Even up to the 20th century, churchmen insisted on the devilish pact. Father Thurston wrote: "In the face of Holy Scripture and the teaching of the Fathers and theologians the abstract possibility of a pact with the Devil and of a diabolical interference in human affairs can hardly be denied."[46] But the Fathers and theologians never explained how the devil could profit from the pact, other than to receive a "soul" that was his anyway. As Samuel Butler said, no one heard the devil's side of any story, because God wrote all the books.[47]

One might think an "enlightened" modern society would have given up the idea of the devil. But a poll taken in 1978 showed "two out of five Americans believe in devils."[48] The strange viability of devils may arise from their usefulness in assuaging the guilt of God and man. "Both Judaism and Christianity have maintained that God must be given the credit for all the goodness in human history, and that men must take the blame for all the evil."[49] Thus, the real purpose of the devil was to take some of this heavy responsibility off frail human shoulders. In short: the devil, not Christ, was the true scapegoat who assumed the burden of men's sins.

1. *Larousse,* 317. 2. Scot, 444. 3. Tennant, 13. 4. Briffault 2, 564.
5. Scot, 323–25. 6. J.H. Smith, C.G., 287. 7. Summers, V., 56. 8. H. Smith, 276.
9. J.B. Russell, 121. 10. Reinach, 72. 11. Hazlitt, 176.
12. de Voragine, 670; Wedeck, 95. 13. Haining, 59.
14. Lindsay, O.A., 197. 15. Knight, D.W.P., 152. 16. Robbins, 127.
17. Scot, 521, 523. 18. Silberer, 286. 19. Gifford, 120.
20. Baring-Gould, C.M.M.A., 168. 21. Robbins, 127, 408. 22. de Givry, 49.
23. Cavendish, P.E. 24, 139. 24. de Givry, 139. 25. Robbins, 213.
26. J.B. Russell, 146. 27. Haining, 85. 28. Robbins, 213. 29. Summers, W., 36.
30. Robbins, 218. 31. Lea, 2. 32. Kramer & Sprenger, 134.
33. Hazlitt, 647. 34. Scot. 40. 35. de Voragine, 312. 36. Gaster, 771.
37. Woods, 89. 38. *Encyc. Brit.,* "Silvester." 39. White 1, 386.
40. *Encyc. Brit.,* "Agrippa, Heinrich Cornelius." 41. *Encyc. Brit.,* "Faust."
42. Seligmann, 212. 43. de Givry, 117. 44. Barrett, 32.
45. Baroja, 85. 46. Summers, H.W., 63. 47. Ebon, W.T., 86.
48. *Newsweek,* June 26, 1978, 32. 49. Muller, 87.

Le Dragon Rouge, ou l'art de commander les esprits célestes, aériens, terrestres, infernaux A grimoire published at Avignon, dated 1522. The date may have been a hoax, the actual publication much later.

Magic Papyri Collections of exorcisms, invocations, charms, and spells widely circulated during the early Christian era, used as bases for later grimoires and Hermetic texts.

Herbert Thurston, S.J. Early 20th-century writer on the subject of occultism.

Diabolus

Latin name of the devil, "Serpent of the Goddess." Legend said the Great Mother made her **serpent** consort from a *bolus* of clay, rolled between her hands until it stretched into a snake form. Then she brought it to life.[1] Egyptians said Isis made a clay serpent in this way, and also a new clay phallus for Osiris. With this phallus that she made, she conceived Osiris's reincarnated *persona,* the infant Horus.

The same *bolus* gave rise to the papal "bull," through the derivative *bulla,* a coiled clay seal on a document, usually stamped with magical signs to discourage tampering. The *bulla* was also a protective amulet worn by a Roman child before coming of age.[2]

1. Graves, G.M.1, 27. 2. Gifford, 71.

Diakosmos

"Goddess-Universe," a Pythagorean and Stoic term for the "order" imposed on the elements in Primal Chaos, to bring about the creation of the world. Like the name of the abyssal Mother, Themis, *Kosmos* meant "correct order" and was used by Homer to mean an arrangement of woman's ornaments.[1] The philosophers' idea was that the Goddess created manifest forms for her own adornment, giving rise to all the material world, the beauty of which was her outer garment and jewels. Her true spirit moved within and behind these things, unseen. Through the life of the universe she constantly arranged and re-arranged the outward manifestations of her "order" to make infinite numbers of different living forms. At doomsday she destroyed them all, to begin over with the next creation. See **Tohu Bohu**.

1. Lindsay, O.A., 75, 120.

Diamond

Literally, "World-Goddess." The ancients used to believe gem stones were solidified drops of the divine essence, embedded in rocks when the world was created. Diamonds were sacred to the Mother of the gods because they "ruled" all other stones by their superior hardness. In Tantric Tibet, the divine essence of the Earth-goddess Tara is still assumed to inhabit her human incarnation, the Diamond Sow, traditional consort or feminine counterpart of the Dalai Lama.

Because diamonds were sacred to the supreme Goddess, they were taken over by the cult of the Virgin; and because of this association with virginity they came to be considered appropriate betrothal gifts. In the transition from **Tarot** cards to modern playing cards, diamonds replaced the ancient suit of pentacles, which were symbols of Mother Earth (Tara) and of the feminine earth element.

Diana

"Queen of Heaven," Roman name for the Triple Goddess as (1) Lunar Virgin, (2) Mother of Creatures, and (3) the Huntress (Destroyer). Her Greek name was Artemis. Her major pilgrimage centers were Ephesus and Nemi, the Sacred Grove. She was Dione, Diana Nemorensis, or Nemetona, Goddess of the Moon-grove. In her sanctuaries, sacred kings periodically engaged in combat, the loser dying as the god Hippolytus, the winner invested as the Goddess's new favorite, Virbius. See **Hippolytus, Saint**.

As Diana Egeria, patroness of childbirth, nursing, and healing, the Goddess made Nemi's holy spring the Lourdes of pagan Rome.[1] The legendary King Numa was said to have derived all his wisdom from a sacred marriage with her.

Diana's cult was so widespread in the pagan world that early Christians viewed her as their major rival, which is why she later became "Queen of Witches." The Gospels commanded total destruction of all temples of Diana, the Great Goddess worshipped by "Asia and all the world" (Acts 19:27).

Roman towns all over Europe habitually called the local mother goddess Diana, as later Christian towns were to call her Madonna. Fortunatus said Diana was the Goddess worshipped at Vernemeton, "which in the Gaulish language means the Great Shrine." In the 5th century A.D., the Gauls regarded her as their supreme deity. Christians spoke slightingly of their pagan custom of adoring the spirit of Diana in a cut branch or a log of wood.[2] Gozbert, a 7th-century Frankish chieftain, doubted the claims of a Christian missionary on the ground that the Christian God was "no better than our own Diana."[3]

Venantius Honorius Clementianus Fortunatus 6th-century poet, bishop of Poitiers, still venerated as a saint in France.

At Ephesus, the Goddess was called Mother of Animals, Lady of Wild Creatures, and Many-Breasted Artemis, shown with her entire torso covered with breasts to nourish the world's creatures.[4] In the 4th century A.D., the church took over this shrine and re-dedicated it to the virgin Mary.[5] One of the earliest churches devoted to "Our Lady" existed at Ephesus in 431; but most of the people believed the Lady was Diana, not Mary. In 432 the Council of Ephesus tried to eliminate worship of the pagan Goddess, but the bishops were besieged by crowds demanding, "Give us our Diana of the Ephesians!"[6]

An excuse for converting Diana's temples into Mary's churches was provided by a made-to-order legend that Mary lived at Ephesus in her old age. Her tomb was located there, and some Christians even pointed out the house in which she had lived.[7] But sometimes she was identified with the sinister Widow of Ephesus, a Crone aspect of the Goddess showing some primitive features.

Petronius's version of the myth said the Widow hung her husband's dead body on one of the three crosses in front of Diana's temple, replacing the body of a previously crucified thief. Then she lay with her new lover at the foot of the cross.[8] The parallel between this image and that of the triple Mary at the foot of Jesus's cross was too close for comfort, especially since Diana herself was assimilated to the Christian myth as Mary's mother, or elder self, the "Grandmother of God" under the name of either Anna (Hannah) or Di-anna (Dinah).[9]

Gnostic Christians called their Wisdom-goddess Sophia the same Grandmother of God, and frequently identified her with Diana of Ephesus. When Diana's temple was finally pulled down, as the Gospels ordered, its magnificent porphyry pillars were carried to Constantinople and built into the church of Holy Sophia.[10]

The magic of Ephesus was remembered through the Middle Ages. A writer said in 1725: "It is recorded in divers authors that in the image of Diana, which was worshipped at Ephesus, there were certain obscure words or sentences . . . written upon the feet, girdle and crown of the said Diana: the which, if a man did use, having written them out, and carrying them about him, he should have good luck in all his businesses."[11]

Some Christians even remembered that Diana was once the triple deity who ruled the world. A 14th-century poem attributed to the Bishop of Meaux said Diana was an old name for the Trinity.[12]

Officers of the Inquisition however regarded Diana as the "Goddess of the heathen" with whom witches made their aerial night journeys—or thought they did.[13] The worship of Diana was denounced wherever it was found, even when the worshippers were members of the clergy. In the 14th century, a bishop found the monks of Frithelstock Priory worshipping a statue of "the unchaste Diana" at an altar in the woods, and made them destroy it.[14] The notorious inquisitor Torquemada declared bluntly that Diana is the devil.[15]

Devil or not, Diana ruled the wild forests of Europe through the medieval period. As patron of the forest of Ardennes she was Dea Arduenna; as patron of the Black Forest she was Dea Abnoba.[16] Serbians, Czechs, and Poles knew her as the woodland Moon-goddess Diiwica, Devana, or Dziewona.[17] She remained the Goddess of wild woodlands and hunting, all the way up to the 18th century in England.

Dianic rites were celebrated even in church, despite objections from the clergy. A minister wrote against the traditional parade of a stag's head into St. Paul's Cathedral in London: "bringing in procession into the church the head of a deer, fixed on the top of a long spear or pole, with the whole company blowing Hunters Horns in a sort of hideous manner; and with this rude pomp they go up to the High Altar, and offer it there. You would think them all the mad Votaries of Diana."[18]

1. Frazer, G.B., 5,10. 2. Graves, W.G., 273–74. 3. Reinach, 153. 4. Neumann, G.M., pl. 35. 5. Ashe, 185. 6. Legman, 661. 7. Ashe, 112, 185. 8. Legman, 650. 9. Graves, W.G., 411. 10. J.H. Smith, C.G., 234. 11. Hazlitt, 103. 12. Seznec, 92–93. 13. Kramer & Sprenger, 104. 14. Lethbridge, 71. 15. J.B. Russell, 235. 16. Spence, 76. 17. *Larousse*, 288. 18. Hazlitt, 484.

Dictynna

Title of Mother Rhea as the Lawgiving Goddess of Mount Dicte, on Crete, where the tablets of her laws and "e-dicts" were given to Minoan kings.[1] "Dictate" is an English derivative of the goddess's directives from Dicte.

1. *Larousse*, 86.

Dido

Priestess-queen and foundress of Carthage, identified with Cyprian Aphrodite and the Goddess **Tanit**. As Dido-Anna she was the consort of the Tyrian god Melek-Heracles, who died by fire as a sacrificial victim each year. According to Roman myth, Dido chose Aeneas as her sacred king and was going to sacrifice him, but he escaped and fled, leaving her to perish in his place. He survived to become the founder of Rome.

Another of Dido's names was Elissa, "the Goddess."

Dike

var. Dice

Alternative spelling of the Greek Fate-goddess Tyche, whom the Orphics called Eurydice, "Universal Dike." To her were dedicated the oracular knucklebones (dice) used to select sacrificial victims by the rite of lots, and to prophesy the future, like the Hebrews' sacred *urim* and *thummim*. See **Orphism**.

Diogenes

Cynic philosopher who lived in an earthen pot at the door of the Great Mother's temple and constantly looked for one honest man.[1] Cynics were "dogs" or "watchdogs" of the Goddess, as their name implies (*kynikos,* doglike ones). They sought an honest man because they believed they were living in the last age of the world, and the Goddess would destroy it when there was not one honest man still living in it.

This matched the Oriental concept of the Kali Yuga, last age of the world, when men become callous, violent, disorderly, and dishonorable.[2] When these conditions were completely fulfilled, doomsday was imminent.

The word "cynical" descended from the implication that, despite Diogenes's lifelong search, he never found the one honest man whose existence still prevented the earth's destruction. See **Dog**.

1. Campbell, Oc.M., 244. 2. *Mahanirvanatantra*, 52.

Dionysius the Areopagite

One of the most influential Christian writers of the Middle Ages, revered for his mystical insights, knowledge of heavenly matters, and holy life. His only fault was that he never existed.

Dionysius's works were forged about the 6th century A.D. and palmed off as the work of one Dionysius the first bishop of Athens, supposedly converted to Christianity by St. Paul personally, during the latter's spirit-visit to Greece as a ghost, after having been "caught up to the third heaven." Paul told pseudo-Dionysius about heaven, and pseudo-Dionysius wrote it down and preached it from the Athenian Hill of Ares; hence his title, Areopagite.

The medieval church based its organization of three sacraments, three holy orders, and three lower orders on the spurious revelations of Dionysius, in imitation of the heavenly hierarchy he described, consisting of (1) Seraphim, Cherubim, and Thrones; (2) Dominions, Virtues, and Powers; (3) Principalities, Archangels, and Angels. The spirits of heaven remained thus organized all the way up to the 18th century.

Churchmen reluctantly abandoned their belief in the authenticity of Dionysius's writings when it was pointed out that, despite earlier scholars' unquestioning acceptance, they failed the simplest of chronological tests, constantly referring to events and institutions of much later date than the time of the alleged Dionysius.[1] At first the pious tried to pretend these references were miraculous prophecies of the future, but this defense proved untenable.

1. White 2, 315–16.

Dionysus

Identified with many other savior-gods, Dionysus was also called Bacchus, Zagreus, Sabazius, Adonis, Antheus, Zalmoxis, Pentheus, Pan, Liber Pater, or "the Liberator."[1] His totem was a panther (*Panthereos,* the Beast of Pan). His emblem was the *thyrsus,* a phallic scepter tipped with a pine cone. His priestesses were the Maenads, or Bacchantes, who celebrated his orgies with drunkenness, nakedness, and sacramental feasting.

Dionysus is often presented as a rustic wine-god, inventor of viniculture. He was more than that. He was a prototype of Christ, with a cult center at Jerusalem as well as nearly every other major city in the middle east. Plutarch said the Jewish Feast of Tabernacles was celebrated in his honor: "I think that the festival of the Sabbath is not wholly without relation to the festival of Dionysus."[2] He added that the Jews abstain from pork because their god Dionysus-Adonis (Lord Dionysus) was slain by a boar. In the 1st century B.C. the Jews themselves claimed to worship Dionysus under his Phrygian name of Zeus Sabazius.[3]

Tacitus said Dionysus Liber was the god of Jerusalem in a former time, but a different god had replaced him, a god with less attractive characteristics: "Liber established a festive and cheerful worship, while the Jewish religion is tasteless and mean."[4] Dionysus and Jehovah were literally two sides of the same coin in the 5th century B.C., when coins found near Gaza showed Dionysus on one side, and on the other a bearded figure labeled JHWH—Jehovah.[5]

In Lebanon, Dionysus was incarnated in Ampelus, a "beautiful youth" torn to pieces by a bull and reincarnated as a grapevine. In Chios, the blood of men murdered by Dionysus's Maenads was used to fertilize the vines. At Orchomenus, the Triple Goddess appeared in Dionysian rites as "three princesses" who tore apart a male child and ate him (the earth absorbing sacrificial blood). In Thebes, a king named Pentheus dared to oppose the Dionysian cult, perhaps because he didn't care to die like other Dionysian god-kings. But the women tore him to pieces anyway, led by the king's own mother (or mother-goddess), who wrenched his head off.[6] Later Theban rites of Dionysus centered on killing and eating a fawn named Pentheus, and the Maenads wore fawn skins. The god's Lydian totem was a fox, Bassareus, forerunner of the medieval Reynard. There the Maenads called themselves Bassarids, and wore fox skins.[7]

These darker legends show Dionysus's typical "savior" pattern: first and most primitive, a king killed and cannibalized to provide both the earth and women's wombs with fructifying blood; then a surrogate for the king, a condemned criminal or a young man chosen by lot; then an animal substitute for the man; and finally, "flesh" and "blood" devoured in the form of bread and wine, the classical Dionysian sacrament at Eleusis.

In Palestine, Dionysus was identified with Noah, the first biblical patriarch to get drunk (Genesis 9:21). His Greek title was Deucalion, "New-wine sailor," the flood hero in pre-Hellenic myths.[8] Dionysus was also a form of Adam, offspring of Father Heaven and Mother Earth (Zeus and Demeter), torn to pieces to make a sin offering of the "wine" of his blood.[9] His later hero-incarnation **Orpheus**, star of the popular Orphic Mysteries, was the same sacrificial god, torn to pieces by the Maenads. Proclus said, "Orpheus, because he was the principal in the Dionysian rites, is said to have suffered the same fate as the god."[10]

Orpheus was a third-generation savior, identified with his divine father Dionysus as Dionysus was identified with his divine father Zeus. Seated on the Heavenly Father's throne, brandishing his lightning-scepter, Dionysus was hailed as King of Kings and God of Gods.[11] He was also the god-begotten, virgin-born Anointed One (*Christos*) whose mother seems to have been all three forms of the Triple Goddess: the earth mother, Persephone the underworld queen, Semele the moon-maiden. Hints of a hanging or crucifixion ceremony appeared in his sacrificial title Dendrites, "Young Man of the Tree."[12] He was also a Horned God, with such forms as bull, goat, and stag.

According to the classic story of his dismemberment, the god took

Pausanias Greek traveler and geographer of the 2nd century A.D. Living in a time of declining culture, he was inspired by a desire to describe the ancient sacred sites for posterity.

such animal forms in rapid succession to avoid the onslaught of the Titans (pre-Hellenic earth-deities), who eventually caught him, tore him to pieces, and devoured him. They trapped his soul in a mirror while he was admiring his reflection, which equates Dionysus with the spring-flower god Narcissus, another of his many disguises. According to Pausanias, it was Onomakritos who made the Titans into "authors of Dionysus's sufferings," but the *orgia* had not included this detail of old. Probably one of the god's oldest forms was Dionysus Melanaigis, "Dionysus of the Black Goatskin," a scapegoat-satyr like Marsyas.[13] His traditional costume contributed much to the medieval Christian notion of the devil's habit of appearing in the form of a black goat.

At Eleusis, the place of his "Advent," Dionysus appeared as a newborn Holy Child laid in a winnowing-basket, *liknon*, from which he was called Dionysus Liknites. This sacred object, his cradle, was carried in his processions by a special functionary called a *liknophoros*, cradle-bearer.[14] The *liknon* was the original form of the "manger" in which the infant Jesus was laid. All grain-gods, whose flesh was eaten in the form of bread, appeared as newborn babes in a vessel intended for seed corn.

A long-remembered incarnation of the god was King Dionysus of Syracuse, who altered the custom of king-sacrifice in the 4th century B.C. When the time of his immolation approached, King Dionysus substituted for himself a courtier who was called Damocles, meaning either "Conquering Glory" or "Glory of Blood." Damocles was said to have volunteered to take the king's place because he envied the privileges of kingship. He enjoyed these privileges for a short while, but soon discovered a sword suspended above his head by a single hair: symbol of the fate of kings, in a time when they and the gods they embodied were periodically fated to die.[15] See **Kingship**.

1. James, 198. 2. Knight, S.L., 156. 3. Graves, W.G., 366–68. 4. Tacitus, 660. 5. Graves, W.G., 368. 6. Graves, G.M. 1, 105. 7. *Larousse*, 160. 8. Graves, G.M. 2, 388. 9. Knight, S.L., 156. 10. Graves, G.M. 1, 114. 11. Frazer, G.B., 451. 12. Graves, G.M. 1, 107. 13. Guthrie, 169, 320. 14. Guthrie, 161. 15. *Encyc. Brit.*, "Damocles."

Dioscuri

Greek version of the Heavenly Twins, gods of the morning and evening star, born together out of the World Egg of Leda. Each wore his half of the egg shell as a cap or crown. The twins were named Castor and Polydeuces, the latter meaning "abundant wine," perhaps a reference to the flowing blood of the solar Savior whom the twins ushered in and out of the underworld in rites linked with fertility.[1] The name of Castor has been associated with the rite of castrating the god, in classical paganism defined as "the act of offering the phallus to the Love Goddess."[2]

The Love Goddess was called Venus in Rome, and her planet is the same one that appears as both morning and evening "star." Perhaps this was why Christians associated Pollux, the Roman form of Polydeuces, with "pollution." Like Shaher and Shalem in the land of Canaan, the Heavenly Twins announced the daily birth of the sun with the words "He is risen," and sent him into the underworld at his daily death with the word "Peace" (Shalom, or Salaam). See **Lucifer**.

To Mithraic sun-worshippers the Dioscuri were symbolized by two golden stars, which still appear in the heavens as the Alpha and Beta stars of the constellation Gemini (the Twins). When the Dioscuri were shown in anthropomorphic form in Mithraic shrines, they held spears or torches, one upward, the other downward, signifying the rising and setting directions of the sun. Their pose was standard: one twin had the right leg crossed over the left, the other had the left leg crossed over the right.[3] The same "magic 4" leg position is seen on the Emperor card of the **Tarot** trumps. The Dioscuri were revered in Sparta as horsemen, warriors, and war dancers.

1. Graves, G.M. 1, 249; 2, 406. 2. Jobes, 179. 3. Cumont, M.M., 128.

Diotima

Priestess of Mantinea, famous Pythagorean philosopher, teacher of Socrates: another once-renowned *alma mater* later forgotten by patriarchal historians.[1]

1. Boulding, 261.

Di Parentes

"Parental deities," Roman title of the *Manes* or children of Mother Mana, the Moon-goddess; ancestral spirits generally.[1] At the founding of every Roman town a hole had to be dug, and covered with the *lapis manalis,* as a gate to allow the Di Parentes to pass in and out of the underworld so they would accept the town's location as their home. They were honored each year at the festival of Parentalia.

1. *Larousse,* 213.

Dísir

Norse word for the Primal Matriarchs, or Divine Grandmothers, who ruled the clans before the coming of patriarchal gods. The Goddess Freya was the Vanadís, leader of the *dísir.*[1] The matriarchs had the true magic, which the gods had to learn from them.

1. Turville-Petre, 176.

Dis Pater

"Father Dis," a Roman name of the Lord of Death inherited from Etruscan times. On occasion he wore the wolf head of the Etruscan god of the dead. Like underground Pluto he was called "the rich one," because he knew everything about mines, deposits of gem stones, and buried treasure.[1] Gallic Celts worshipped Dis above every other male deity, claiming he was the "father" of their race—in the old way of the dying god who became "father" by shedding his blood (see **Kingship**). In Britain, Dis was regarded as a universal deity very like Jehovah, whose later adherents, however, transformed Dis into an alternative name for the devil.[2]

1. *Larousse,* 211. 2. Graves, W.G., 45.

Djinn

Arabic "spirits," or ancestral souls. *Djinni* was a *genie,* cognate of the Roman *genius,* paternal ghost or begetter. Mohammedans viewed the *djinn* as pagan semi-demons because they were connected with the Old Religion. See **Genius**.

Dog

No one knows when man first domesticated the dog. Evidence suggests that "man" didn't do it at all; woman did it. In myth, dogs accompanied only the Goddess, guarding the gates of her after-world, helping her to receive the dead.

Like other carrion eaters—e.g., vultures—dogs, wolves, and jackals were associated with funerary customs. Dogs carried the dead to their Mother. In Iran, even after it became usual to bury the dead, it was thought necessary to let dogs tear the corpse before burial, a survival of the older practice.[1] The Vendidad said the soul enroute to heaven would meet the Goddess with her dogs: "Then comes the beautiful, well-shapen, strong and graceful maid, with the dogs at her sides, one who can discern, who has many children, happy and of high understanding. She makes the soul of the righteous go up above."[2]

Semitic tradition transformed the Goddess into the Angel of Death, whose approach can be seen only by dogs—which is why dogs howl at the moon to announce a death.[3] Devonshire folklore still says there is a dog in the moon who acts as a messenger of death.[4] The Irish say two dogs guard the gate of death, which used to lead to Emania, the Moon-land; mourners were enjoined not to wail too loudly, lest they disturb the dogs and cause them to attack the soul at the gate. This and many other similar images can be traced to the ancient Vedic concept of the moon as death's gate, ruled by the Goddess and guarded by her two dogs.[5]

This Oriental symbol is still seen in an almost pure form on Tarot trump #18, the card of the Moon. The conventional picture is of two dogs howling at the full moon in front of a gate, or two pylons, with a road leading between them to a distant horizon. The scene was usually interpreted as having to do with death.[6] Sometimes the card was called Hecate, after the classic death-goddess whose totemic companions were dogs.[7] Her gates were guarded by the three-headed hound Cerberus, "Spirit of the Pit."[8] In Celtic myth the gatekeeper was a dog named Dormarth, "Death's Door."[9] The same dog might be seen on the famous Gundestrup Cauldron, guarding the yonic gate through which heroes pass on their way to death and transfiguration.[10]

According to the Vedic tradition, the Bitch-goddess Sarama was the mistress of the death dogs, and a divine huntress like Artemis, Diana, Anath, and other western versions of the lunar maiden.[11] Ancient Babylon knew her as Gula, the Fate-goddess, whose symbol was a dog.[12] She was assimilated to Ishtar, whose sacred king Tammuz was torn to pieces by "dogs."[13] Under his Greek names of Adonis or Actaeon, he was torn to pieces by the Dogs of Artemis. As the savior Orpheus, he was incarnated in Neanthus of Lesbos and torn to pieces in the Orphic temple by "dogs."[14] When Athene assumed the guise of the death-goddess, her priestesses filled her temple with canine "howlings" (*houloi*), like wolves or dogs singing to the moon.[15] Sometimes a whole pack of dogs—or priestesses?—hunted souls in the realm of death, like the Celtic Hounds of Annwn, which Christians soon converted into the Hounds of Hell.[16]

Originally this meant the hounds of the Goddess Hel, ruler of the land of death. Norse myth said she gave birth to lunar wolf-dogs who ate the flesh of the dead and carried souls to paradise. Their leader was Managarm, "Moon-Dog." The *Prose Edda* says Managarm was "gorged with the flesh of the death-doomed; and with red blood he reddens the dwelling of the gods."[17] In other words, he carried the dead away in primitive, carrion-eating canine fashion.

Prose Edda
Icelandic saga, a collection of traditional stories compiled by Snorri Sturluson in the 13th century A.D.

An alternative name for the Norse moon-dogs' mother was Angurboda, the Hag of the Iron Wood: an older version of Hel, sometimes called Hel's mother.[18] Two of Angurboda's canine children, Geri and Freki, lived in Valhalla and ate the food offered on "Odin's table," meaning the altar.[19] This suggests that the Vedic image of the two death dogs passed into Norse mythology as a pair of canine gods, like the many holy dogs, wolves, or jackals of the ancient world in general.

One of the oldest of these gods was Egyptian **Anubis**, brought from central Asia at a very early date under the name of Up-Uat, "Opener of the Way." He was also known as Mates, "He of the Mother," similar to the archaic Irish word for a dog, *madra*.[20] This old Asian god was said to be a wolf, but he soon merged with the jackal Anubis, who was called his twin. The composite was a deity "whose face is like unto that of a greyhound . . . who feedeth on the dead . . . who devoureth the bodies of the dead, and swalloweth hearts." In the predynastic period he governed sacrificial priests, "jackal-headed men with slaughtering-knives," in an old section of the underworld.[21] Coptic Christians later identified Anubis with Gabriel, who was called a judge of the dead.[22]

As a lord of the land of death, Anubis became the god of mummification. He was often shown bending solicitously over the mummy of Osiris, applying the preservative *mumiya* from which the word "mummy" descended. When the Osiris cult became astrological, much of its imagery was transposed from the underworld to the heavens, including the image of Anubis.

The star of Anubis was Sothis (Sirius), the Eye of the Dog, in Greek, *Canopis.* Sirius is the star forming the "eye" of Canis Major, the Great Dog. It is the brightest star in the sky. Egyptians believed it held the soul of Osiris, whose rebirth coincided with the rising of the Nile flood, when his star rose in the east. "Three wise men" pointed the way to the newborn Savior: the three stars in Orion's belt, which form a line pointing to Sirius. The holy city of Anubis on earth was also Canopis, the Eye of the Dog, origin of the canopic mummy-jar.

Anubis came to Rome as a leading character in the Osirian Mysteries. He was seen in processions "condescending to walk on human feet . . . rearing terrifically high his dog's head and neck—that messenger between heaven and hell displaying alternately a face black as night, and golden as the day; in his left the caduceus, in his right waving aloft the green palm branch. His steps were closely followed by a cow, raised into an upright posture—the cow being the fruitful emblem of the Universal Parent, the goddess herself, which one of the happy train carried with majestic steps, supported on his shoulders. By another was borne the coffin containing the sacred things, and closely concealing the deep secrets of the holy religion."[23]

Not only Anubis, but many other dog-deities were worshipped throughout the Roman empire. An early Roman cista from Palestrina-Praeneste showed the Moon-virgin Minerva sacrificing a naked Mars over a cauldron, attended by her three-headed death dog, clearly the same as Persephone's or Hecate's Cerberus.[24] The dog as the keeper of Mother's gate was known everywhere in antiquity, probably because wild dogs were first domesticated as guardians of the home threshold, doorways being generally sacred to women who owned the houses. In Assyria, images of dogs were buried under thresholds of houses, suggesting similar burials of deceased watchdogs in former times.[25] The dogs' spirits continued to halt intruders, which may account for the ancient custom of lifting a new bride over a threshold, so the guardian spirits beneath would not think her an intruder but would accept her as a resident.

The Cynic sage **Diogenes** made himself a watchdog at the gate of the Great Mother's temple, where he lived in "a large earthen pot," representing the terrestrial womb.[26] Cynics were the Goddess's "doglike ones" (*kynikos*). Their sect, founded in the 4th century B.C., professed to foretell the end of the world from the circumpolar constellation Ursa Minor, which they called the Dog. The north pole star was the Dog's Tail, *kunos oura,* the Cynosure.[27] When it moved from its place at the still point of the turning world, according to the Cynics, the end of the present universe was at hand.

The Cynic idea of the dog affixed to the north pole is still found in European folklore. Slavs spoke of the three Zorya (triple Fate-goddess), keeping "a dog which is tied by an iron chain to the constellation of the Little Bear. When the chain breaks it will be the end of the world."[28] Egyptians similarly believed the Goddess kept "powers of darkness" fettered by a heavenly chain until the last days of the world.[29] Northern peoples said the chain held the cosmic doomsday-wolf Fenrir, who would be released by the Norns (triple Fate-goddess) to devour the heavenly father at the end of the world; this would signal the destruction of all the gods.[30] Norsemen therefore called doomsday the Day of the Wolf.[31]

The Great Goddess was herself a wolf, in the very old Roman cult of the She-Wolf Lupa, whose original consort was Lupus, the Wolf. He was also Feronius, or **Dis Pater**, a subterranean wolf god inherited from the Etruscans, as was the She-Wolf who suckled Rome's founders, Romulus and Remus. The famous Lupercalian statue of the She-Wolf was cast in bronze during the 5th century B.C. The two babies under her belly were not part of the original work but were added centuries later, to suit the Roman version of the legend.[32]

The Lupercalia may have been a corruption of Lupa-Kali; the Oriental Great Goddess was also a she-wolf. Under her yoni-name of Cunti she gave birth to a divine son "in the cave of the wolf," like the Lupercal grotto. Her child was placed in a basket of rushes and set afloat on the Ganges, as Romulus and Remus were set afloat on the Tiber, Moses was set afloat on the Nile, and Sargon was set afloat on the Euphrates. The wolf bitch Lupa was identified with the midwife-goddess Acca Larentia who took Romulus and Remus from their basket, just as Akka took Sargon, and "pharaoh's daughter" (another version of Akka) took Moses. Akka, Acca, or Acco was the same as Hecate, who turned into a wolf bitch in Homeric legend.[33] Lupa (or Acca) disappeared into the sacred spring of the Lupercal grotto, where her spirit was worshipped every year at the Lupercalian festival.

There were many lupine foster-mothers in Middle-Eastern myths. Tu Kuëh, legendary founder of the Turkish nation, was preserved in infancy by a holy she-wolf whom he subsequently married: that is, she was the Goddess of the land in totemic form.[34] A famous Turkish leader was Ataturk, "the Gray Wolf."[35] Zoroaster was raised by a she-wolf. Cyrus the Great, born of Mandane (Moon-mother), was nursed by a woman whose Greek name was Cyno, her Median name Spako, meaning "Bitch." Siegfried too was a wolf's foster child; his oldest name was Wolfdietrich.[36]

The oldest religion of the Canary Islands was a dog- or wolf-cult, traces of which are still seen in many ancient canine statues. Canary birds and canary wine took their name from the islands, which were really named for Canis, the dog.[37]

The same name once applied to the hereditary caste of Jewish priests, Kohen or Cohen, from Greek *kuon,* "dog."[38] Because dogs were associated with the old matriarchy, the epithet "dog" became an insult to Semitic patriarchs; Islam forbids both women and dogs to approach a shrine.[39] Yet Moslems still incongruously believe the gall of a black dog can serve as a holy amulet to purge an entire household of evil influences.[40]

Early Christians made an effort to assimilate the Gallo-Roman wolf god under the name of St. Lupus or St. Loup, "Holy Wolf."[41] He was made a legendary bishop of Troyes, credited with miraculously turning back the invading Huns from his province; but this story was fiction masquerading as history.[42] The church was not wholly comfortable with any of the manifestations of Lupus, who was really a prototype of the **werewolf**. Saxons used to worship him in the first month of the sacred year, called Wolf-monath (Wolf Month); but Christian authorities changed the name of this month to After-Yule, or Jesu-monath. Its runic sign was a dot in a circle, the same as the Festival of the Circumcision of Christ (New Year's Day).[43]

Diana the Huntress and her "dogs" had an extensive cult in England. Some of her legends merged with those of Arthur, Lancelot, and other British heroes. One of the tales told how Lancelot, like Actaeon, trespassed in the Goddess's greenwood and fell asleep at her secret spring:

> *There was a Lady dwelt in that forest, and she was a great huntress, and daily she used to hunt, and ever she bare her bow with her; and no man went never with her, but always women, and they were shooters, and could well kill a deer, both at the stalk and at the trest; and they daily bare bows and arrows, horns and wood knives, and many good dogs they had.*[44]

When the "Lady" caught Lancelot in the forbidden place, she didn't set her dogs on him as her forerunners had done. She only shot him in the buttock, "that he might not sit on no saddle."[45] Thus he was disgraced, since a warrior was supposed to show wounds only in front.

Because dogs were natural companions of the housewife as well as the huntress, they were often cited as witches' familiars. A black dog seemed even more suspect than a black cat. The dog was frequently believed to be the animal form of a demon lover, probably because women were inclined to fondle their dogs; many women were hanged in England on that count alone. One witch was officially condemned for having "carnal copulation with the devil in the likeness of a man, but he removed from her in the likeness of a black dog."[46]

Gypsies told a story based on such witch trials: there was a beautiful maiden whose lover was her dog. Once each year he transformed himself into a man and lay with her. In due time, she gave birth to a "little white puppy," then she jumped into the river and drowned (a popular method of disposing of witches was to drown them in the so-called swimming ordeal). The demon lover assumed his human shape, retrieved the maiden's corpse, and brought her back to life by placing the puppy-child at her breast to suck. Afterward, as in all fairy tales, they married and lived happily ever after.[47]

The black dog was the witch's helper in gathering materials for charms. According to an exceptionally durable superstition, the miraculous mandrake root could not be pulled out of the ground except by a black dog. This curiously formed root, called "the phallus of the field," or "the devil's genitals," was supposed to emit a scream if uprooted by the unwary; and all who heard the sound would go insane, or die.[48]

The Irish remembered the dog's connection with death and maintained that true curses could be cast with a dog's help. Among the Celts, *cainte,* "dog," denoted a satiric bard with magic power to speak curses that would come true.[49]

Dogs or wolves played their ancient role of psychopomps in a number of strange stories about cathedral-building, which might be traced all the way back to the Etruscan Lupus or Dis Pater, the wolf-headed Lord of Death who carried sacrificial victims away. In the very old rite of the *mundus,* trenches dug for temple foundations were filled with sacrificial blood. It was believed the building would be unstable if this blood-magic were omitted; so it was done, from Hindu India to Latium and Britain. Lupus appeared in sacred art as a wolf-angel carrying the victim to a blessed after-life. On an Etruscan vase, the death-god Charon is assimilated to Lupus and wears a wolf skin.[50]

This notion that sacred buildings needed to be founded in blood has been evident in every tradition including the Judeo-Christian one. The Bible says when Hiel founded the city of Jericho, "he laid the foundation thereof in (the blood of) Abiram his firstborn and set up the gates thereof in his youngest son Segub, according to the word of the Lord" (1 Kings 16:34). British legend said Vortigern's temple walls kept falling down because the blood sacrifice for their foundation had been forgotten.[51] Such pagan customs continued in the Middle Ages. Many skeletons have been found buried in walls, pillars, and cornerstones of churches and abbeys, placed there as supportive sacrifices.[52] A deaf-mute was buried under the cornerstone of a monastery near Gottingen.[53] A parish church at Holsworthy, North Devon, was found in 1845 to have a skeleton in its southwest wall.[54] Illegitimate children were frequently buried in building foundations. One St. Benezet, or Little Bennet, was walled up in the foundation of a bridge at Avignon in 1184. Five centuries later his crypt was opened, and St. Benezet proved his saintly status by remaining fresh and undecayed.[55] So his ecclesiastical press agents claimed, at any rate. "It was really a common thing among Christians to sacrifice children, maids, or grown-up people by burying them alive under the foundations of castles, etc., to insure their stability."[56]

When St. Columba founded a monastery on the island of Iona, he called for a volunteer to be buried alive in its foundation. A monk named Oran, or Odran, earned a later canonization by offering himself.[57] For some reason—perhaps a promise of Christ-like resurrection—he was dug up again after three days. Still alive, he began to preach blasphemous doctrines: there was no God, no devil, no heaven or hell. St. Columba therefore had him killed and re-buried.[58] It was not uncommon for monks infected with Gnostic, agnostic, or atheistic beliefs to meet with such a fate.

Europe's totemic dog or wolf clans seem to have become involved in these sacrificial customs, just as they were involved in the ancient cult of the *mundus*. For instance, Cologne Cathedral was said to have been designed by the devil, and its bells were cast under the devil's direction at the foundry of a mysterious smith named Wolf. After casting a certain discordant bell, supposed to be rung only in time of disaster, Wolf was killed by a fall from the bell tower. The architect who collaborated with the devil was also killed, crushed by a great stone that already had his name engraved on it.[59]

Chansons de gestes Old French epic poetry of the 11th to 13th centuries.

Chansons de gestes told a somewhat different version. The builders of Cologne Cathedral killed a hero named Renaud (Fox) and buried him in the foundation. A church was erected to Renaud's memory in 811 A.D.; a chapel stood on the spot in Cologne where he was slain.[60] Some said Renaud was the same as the trickster-hero-demigod Reynard the Fox; others said he was a great warrior, one of Charlemagne's paladins.

The devil and the wolf were also linked with Charlemagne's tomb at Aix-la-Chapelle. The devil contributed money to build the cathedral. In return, he demanded the life of the first creature to enter its doors. At the dedication ceremony, people thrust a wolf into the door. The devil took the wolf's life. Then it was safe for people to enter. Like Cologne, Aix-la-Chapelle had a discordant bell for emergencies. The founder of this bell was crushed to death by the clapper, so the bell was baptized with his blood.

Similar stories were told of Strasbourg Cathedral, supposedly designed by a wise witch named Sabine, once a title of Lupa, the Sabine She-Wolf. The dedication of the cathedral was marked by the sacrifice of twin brothers, like Romulus and Remus, one of whom killed the other by pushing him under a cornerstone as it was dropped into place. (Of the twins nursed by the Sabine She-Wolf, Romulus killed Remus while digging a furrow for the foundation of Rome's walls.) The bishop of Strasbourg ordered the cornerstone raised again, and the second brother was crushed under it also, by his wish. He explained, "My body will serve as a protection to the cathedral."[61]

Remnants of these curious beliefs and customs survived to the present time. In World War II, the Nazi SS caused human bodies to be "encased in the concrete fortifications and bunkers, as though such bodies could give strength to inanimate matter."[62] To this day, Greek peasants insist on a blood sacrifice at the building of any bridge, to bathe the foundation in the lifeblood of a bird or animal to "strengthen" it.[63]

The notion that a dog's blood is equivalent to the blood of a human being is still found among the Berbers, who believe that a murderer is magically tainted by the blood of his victim for the rest of his life. The killer of a dog is similarly tainted.[64] Nearly everywhere one can still find the belief that dogs can see ghosts and other spirits, left over from the formerly universal association of canines with the world of death and the special preserve of the underground Goddess.[65]

1. Herodotus, 56. 2. Robertson, 115. 3. Budge, G.E. 1, 19.
4. Baring-Gould, C.M.M.A., 197. 5. Lethaby, 193. 6. Cavendish, T., 128.
7. A. Douglas, 106. 8. Graves, G.M. 2, 385. 9. Squire, 257.
10. Cavendish, V.H.H. 49. 11. O'Flaherty, 352. 12. *Larousse*, 63.
13. *Assyr. & Bab. Lit.*, 338. 14. *Larousse*, 198. 15. Herodotus, 270.
16. Graves, W.G., 36. 17. Sturluson, 39. 18. Graves, W.G., 409.
19. Sturluson, 63. 20. Joyce 2, 453. 21. *Book of the Dead*, 182, 394, 140.
22. Graves, W.G., 153. 23. Budge, G.E. 2, 266. 24. Dumézil, 243.
25. Budge, A.T., 99. 26. Campbell, Oc.M., 244. 27. Potter & Sargent, 174.
28. *Larousse*, 285. 29. Budge, G.E. 2, 249. 30. Sturluson, 88.
31. Campbell, M.I., 72. 32. *Larousse*, 220. 33. Rank, 18, 45; Graves, G.M. 2, 342.
34. Gaster, 228. 35. Wedeck, 173. 36. Rank, 29, 56–58. 37. Potter & Sargent, 173.
38. Knight, S.L., 114. 39. Farb, W.P., 144. 40. Budge, A.T., 12.
41. Knight, D.W.P., 191. 42. Attwater, 223. 43. Brewster, 50. 44. Malory 2, 307.
45. Malory 2, 308. 46. Robbins, 193, 463. 47. Groome, 139. 48. Simons, 67.
49. Joyce 1, 455. 50. Castiglioni, 201; Summers, W., 69. 51. Guerber, L.M.A., 205.
52. de Lys, 380–81. 53. Groome, 13. 54. Elworthy, 80. 55. Brewster, 194.
56. Leland, 241. 57. Joyce 1, 285. 58. Holmes, 207. 59. Guerber, L.R., 47–56.
60. Guerber, L.M.A., 162. 61. Guerber, L.R., 85–88, 297–300. 62. Becker, E.E., 104.
63. Lawson, 264. 64. Frazer, F.O.T., 35. 65. Halliday, 59.

Dolcinists

Medieval heretics formerly called the Apostolic Congregation, founded by a peasant named Segarelli, who tried to join the Franciscan order and was rejected. Believing himself nevertheless a true spiritual son of St. Francis, he gathered disciples and preached against the worldly wealth of the church. He was caught and burned, but the Congregation continued under Fra Dolcino, who preached the oncoming doomsday, the fall of the sinful church, and the triumph of the poor and simple over the theocracy.

Dolcinists admitted women to their ranks, and granted their "sisters in Christ" the same right to preach and lead prayers as the men, one of the worst manifestations of their heresy. Dolcinists claimed to renounce sexual relations; so when Dolcino's particular "dearly beloved sister in Christ" Margherita di Trank bore him a child, it was brought about through the miraculous agency of the Holy Ghost, they said.

The Inquisition harassed the Dolcinists until they took refuge in the high mountains. Three crusades were preached against them. In the winter of 1307 they were finally reduced to starvation, trapped, and slaughtered. Dolcino was captured alive, unfortunately for him. After watching his Margherita burn, he was torn to pieces by red-hot pincers on a cart rolling slowly along the roads for all to watch.

Despite this edifying example, Dolcinism persisted for another century. Two Dolcinist Apostles were captured and burned in Germany in 1404.[1]

1. Lea unabridged, 614–23.

Doomsday

The universal idea of the world's end was rooted in ancient Hindu belief in the cyclic alternation of universes, brought about by Kali.

Each successive creation was divided into four *yugas* or ages: Satya, Treta, Dvapara, and Kali, the fourth and last marking the age when Mother turns Destroyer because the race of men become violent and sinful, failing to perceive deity in the feminine principle. "Due to the limited intelligence and lust of men in the Kali Yuga, they will be unable to recognize women as manifestations of the Shakti." Only a few may escape spiritual degeneration: those who are devoted "to the lotus of their mothers' feet and to their own wives."[1]

When Kali's doomsday arrived, the gods would slay each other. Earth would be overwhelmed by fire and flood. The Goddess would swallow up everything and un-make it, returning to her primordial state of formless **Chaos,** as she was before creation. All beings would enter her, because "She devours all existence."[2] After a time that could not be counted because even Time was destroyed, Kali would give birth to a new universe.

Puranas are ancient Sanskrit scriptures in verse, treating of cosmologies, sacred histories, and the nature of the divine.

The Matsya Purana said signs of approaching doomsday were to be found in the breakdown of social structures, the increase in violence and crime, and the decline of human intelligence:

> *There is no one, any more, in whom enlightening goodness (sattva) prevails; no real wise man, no saint, no one uttering truth and standing by his sacred word. The seemingly holy Brahmin is no better than a fool. Old people, destitute of the true wisdom of old age, try to behave like the young, and the young lack the candor of youth. The social classes have lost their distinguishing, dignifying virtues. . . . The will to rise to supreme heights has failed; the bonds of sympathy and love have dissolved; narrow egotism rules. . . . When this calamity has befallen the once harmoniously ordered City of Man, the substance of the world-organism had deteriorated beyond salvage, and the universe is ripe for dissolution.*[3]

The Vishnu Purana said the world in its last days reaches a stage where "property confers rank, wealth becomes the only source of virtue, passion the sole bond of union between husband and wife, falsehood the source of success in life, sex the only means of enjoyment, and when outer trappings are confused with inner religion."[4]

Asiatic arts of astronomic observation and calculation of calendars were motivated by an earnest desire to know the exact length of each *yuga,* to foresee the end. An age was supposed to begin when sun, moon, and planets stood in conjunction at the initial point of the ecliptic and to end when they returned to the same point. By Hindu reckoning, the present *yuga* began in 3102 B.C. The chronology of the Central American Maya began in 3113 B.C., only 11 years later, "a discrepancy probably due to some minor miscalculation in reckoning backward from the observed movements of the heavenly bodies."[5]

Ancient Mesopotamia set the same dates as India and Mexico—between 3113 and 3102 B.C.—for the beginning of civilized arts, especially astronomical calculation. The Babylonian sage Berossus said "the world will burn when all the planets that now move in different courses come together in the Crab, so that they all stand in a straight line in the same sign, and . . . the future flood will take place when the same conjunction occurs in Capricorn. For the former is the constellation of the summer solstice, the latter of the winter solstice; they are the decisive signs of the zodiac, because the turning points of the year lie in them." Jeremias commented:

> *This Babylonian doctrine has spread over the whole world. We find it again in Egypt, in the religion of the Avesta, and in India; traces of it are discovered in China, as well as in Mexico and among the savage nations of South America. To refer these phenomena back to "elementary ideas" such as may arise independently among different peoples, will not hold good in view of the circumstance that we have to do with ideas connected with definite facts which rest upon continued astronomical observations.*[6]

These remarks shed light on the great Neolithic monuments known to be astronomical calculators, suggesting a good reason why they were built with so much care and effort. The Stoic philosophers of doomsday drew upon a very ancient tradition in predicting the world's end in terms almost identical with those of Oriental sages: "A new sea will overrun everything, and the Ocean, today the boundary and girdle of the world, will occupy its centre. . . . What nature has made into separate parts will be confounded into a single mass." This creed of dissolution into Chaos became "an important part of Stoicism."[7]

Northern Europeans drew their myths of doomsday or Ragnarok from the same ancient tradition. They said the world's end would be brought about by the Mutspell (Mother's Curse) when violent gods neglected the old laws of peace and blood kinship. The angry Goddess would become Skadi the Destroyer, a great shadow devouring the world, like her Oriental counterpart Kali. The gods would enter that shadow of Götterdämmerung, literally the Going-Into-the-Shadow-of-the-Gods. They would be consumed, and the heavens and earth with them. The world would sink back into the womb of primal chaos which gave it birth in the beginning.[8]

This was the prophecy of the sybilline priestess who wrote the *Voluspá.* It was echoed by the Irish sybil Babd, one of the three Fate-goddesses. She foretold the coming of the Waste Land, "trees without fruit and seas without fish; old men would give false judgments and legislators make unjust laws; warriors would betray one another, and men would be thieves, and there would be no more virtue left in the world."[9]

After destruction of this nonvirtuous world and its cruel gods, there would be a period of dark nonexistence. Then the Goddess's womb would bring forth a new universe. A new human race would arise from a primal couple, a woman named Life—one of the Semitic names of Eve—and a man named Desirer-of-Life.[10]

Patriarchal Persians made some alterations in the picture. Their idea of doomsday was as dire as any, with the usual convulsions of the earth, fires, flood, and fallings of heaven; but they denied the subsequent creation of a new world. Their concept was not cyclic, but linear. Creation and doomsday could occur only once. After the great battle Armageddon at the end of the world, "The War of the Sons of Light with the Sons of Darkness," the heavenly forces of the sun god would prevail.[11] They would divide the sinful from the virtuous and assign them to heaven or hell. The aftermath was not another creation, but eternal stasis, like the Brahman Nirvana.

Passing through Jewish-Essenic and Roman-Mithraic sects into Christianity, this Persian doomsday became the familiar one in the west, with numerous details borrowed from the older Aryan paganism. The last Trump played on Gabriel's horn was originally played on Rig-Heimdall's "ringing horn" (Gjallarhorn).[12] The Great Serpent slain by Thor in the final battle became identified with Satan.[13] Like paganism's sacred dramas, the final drama of the earth's dissolution was divided into five acts.[14] Christians even translated the Norse "Mother's Curse" as "Judgment Day" when they found it variously rendered Mutspell, Muspell, Muspelle, Mudspeller, or Muspilli.[15]

The Savior destined to appear before the world's end had an old form in Buddhist scriptures as Kalki Avatara, the Destroyer of Sin, who would come from heaven to announce doomsday.[16] Persians copied him, changing his title to Son of Man, or Messiah. Before 170 B.C., the Book of Enoch called him *Christos*, the Anointed One, and announced that he had already come and gone, and that his Second Coming was expected at any moment.[17]

According to the Gospels, Jesus identified himself with this personage who would be seen "coming in the clouds with great power and glory. And then shall he send his angels, and shall gather together his elect from the four winds, from the uttermost part of the earth to the uttermost part of heaven" (Mark 13:26-27). Jesus was not the only Messiah of his time. Josephus said before 70 A.D. there were countless Messiahs and Christs announcing the end of the world.[18]

The Gospels promised doomsday almost at once. Jesus said it would occur in his own generation: "There be some standing here, which shall not taste of death, till they see the kingdom of God" (Luke 9:27). Early Christians accordingly expected the world's end so soon that there was no reason to marry and beget children who would never grow up, a major reason for Christianity's renunciation of **marriage**. Motherhood would only harm women in the convulsions of the last days: "Woe unto them that are with child, and to them that give suck, in those days!" (Luke 21:23).

Hopeful Christians found that Jesus's generation and many other generations passed without apocalyptic symptoms. Seeking an explanation, theologians discovered the text saying a thousand years were but a day in the sight of God (Psalms 90:4), another borrowing from Oriental sages who said a Day of Brahma lasted a thousand years. On the basis of this scripture it was decided that the world would end in the year 1000 A.D. With the approach of that year, Europe was seized by an apocalyptic mania. Farms and towns were abandoned as fanatics tramped the countryside announcing the Last Days. In some areas, agriculture and commerce came virtually to a standstill. The year passed uneventfully enough, but human society suffered greatly from famines and civil disorders caused by the doomsday belief.[19]

Some Franciscans declared that Christ really had returned to earth in 1000 A.D., disguised as St. Francis, the new Messiah, who was "entirely transformed into the person of Christ." Francis was said to have performed all the Christ-like miracles, cast out devils, turned water into wine, cured the sick, raised the dead, made the blind see, and so on.[20] There were those who went so far as to claim that Christ was important only as a precursor of St. Francis.[21]

Not only the Christ figure was supposed to return just before doomsday, but also **Antichrist**, his adversary, for the final battle between good and evil couldn't take place until all the forces were assembled on either side. According to a German legend, Antichrist could not come to earth as long as the Holy Roman (German) Empire stood.[22] This legend served to keep some of the warring nationlets in line at times, but the Holy Roman Empire was a rather loose, indefinable entity for most of its existence. Antichrist was almost as constantly anticipated as Christ.

Another who taught that the Last Judgment had already taken place was Swedenborg; he gave its date as 1757, the date of the establishment of his own Church of the New Jerusalem. He wisely refrained from predicting the world's end a short time in advance, but others fell into this trap. Cumming, in England, predicted the end of the world in 1867, with resulting injury to his credibility when the end failed to come.

A prominent doomsday prophet was William Miller, inadvertent founder of the sects of Jehovah's Witnesses and Seventh-Day Adventists. He fixed the date of the millenium on March 21, 1843. His followers were afire with enthusiasm, but still failed to see Christ descending from the clouds as expected. Miller decided he had miscalculated, and fixed a new date on October 21 of the same year. "On the appointed day of doom frenzied believers donned their robes, tucked an ultimate lunch in the folds, and took their places on the housetops, facing east. On the 22nd they ate their lunch and climbed down. Miller confessed his disappointment, but insisted 'the day of the Lord is at the door.'"[23] The Millerites never gave up hope. Their offshoot sects still exist and flourish, though naive displays of credulity are usually avoided.

1. *Mahanirvanatantra*, 12, 53, 56, 177. 2. *Mahanirvanatantra*, 295–96.
3. Ross, 66; Zimmer, 35–36. 4. Zimmer, 15. 5. Campbell, M.I., 148–49.
6. Campbell, M.I., 149. 7. Lindsay, O.A., 107–8. 8. *Larousse*, 275.
9. Squire, 118. 10. Branston, 289–90. 11. Black, 3. 12. Turville-Petre, 154.
13. Branston, 281. 14. Male, 367. 15. Turville-Petre, 284.
16. *Mahanirvanatantra*, xlviii. 17. Reinach, 217. 18. Brandon, 248.
19. Summers, V., 150. 20. de Voragine, 608–10. 21. Reinach, 307.
22. Borchardt, 69. 23. de Lys, 435.

Doppelgänger

German word for one's "double," corresponding to the Egyptian *ka*, or a reflection-soul. Sometimes the afterbirth was said to be an unformed twin of the newborn baby; by magic it might assume the living twin's shape and follow him through life. Sometimes this was thought to be the Doppelgänger seen in one's reflection.

Dove

Aphrodite's totem, the bird of sexual passion, symbolically equivalent to the yoni.[1] In India, too, the dove was *paravata*, the symbol of lust.[2] Joined to her consort the phallic serpent, the Dove-goddess stood for sexual union and "Life."

The phrase attributed to Jesus, "Be ye therefore wise as serpents, and harmless as doves" (Matthew 10:16), was no random metaphor but a traditional invocation of the Syrian God and Goddess.[3] The Oriental meaning was remembered by the gypsies, whose folk tales said the souls of ancestors lived inside magic hollow mountains, the men having been changed into serpents and the women into doves.[4]

Christians adopted the feminine dove as a symbol of the Holy Ghost, originally the Goddess Sophia, representing God's "Wisdom" as the Goddess Metis represented the "Wisdom" of Zeus. Gnostic Christians said Sophia was incarnate in the dove that impregnated the virgin Mary, the same dove that descended on Jesus at his baptism to impregnate his mind (Matthew 3:16). Pious admirers of Pope Gregory the Great made him even more saintly than Jesus by reporting that the Holy Ghost in dove shape descended on him not once but many times.[5] All this was copied from Roman iconography which showed the human soul as a dove that descended from the Dove-goddess's oversoul to animate the body.[6]

Aphrodite as a bringer of death, or "peace," sometimes bore the name of Irene, Dove of Peace. Another of her death-goddess names was Epitymbria, "She of the Tombs."[7] Romans called her Venus Columba, Venus-the-Dove. Her catacombs, mausoleums, and necropoli were known as *columbaria*, "dovecotes."[8] Thus the soul returning to the Goddess after death was again envisioned as a dove. From this image, Christians copied their belief that the souls of saints became white doves that flew out of their mouths at the moment of death. In the Catholic ceremony of canonization, white doves are released from cages at the crucial moment of the ritual.[9]

Christian iconography showed seven rays emanating from the dove of the Holy Ghost: an image that went back to some of the most primitive manifestations of the Goddess.[10] In the Orient, the mystic seven were the Pleiades or "Seven Sisters," whose Greek name meant "a flock of doves." They were daughters or "rays" of Aphrodite under her title of Pleione, Queen of the Sea.[11] Herodotus said seven holy women known as Doves founded the oracles of Dodona, Epirus, and Theban Amon.[12] They were worshipped in the Middle East as Seven Sages or Seven Pillars of Wisdom: the seven woman-shaped pillars that had been upholding temples of the Goddess since the third millenium B.C.[13] See **Caryatid**. Arabs still revere the Seven Sages, and some remember that they were women, or "doves."[14] The Semitic word for "dove," *ione*, was a cognate of "yoni" and related to the Goddess Uni, who later became Iune, or Juno.

The cult of the Doves used to incorporate primitive rites of castration and its modification, circumcision. India called the seven Sisters "razors" or "cutters" who judged and "critically" wounded men, the Krittikas, "Seven Mothers of the World," root of the Greek *kritikos*, "judge." They killed and gave rebirth to gods who were castrated to make them fertile, like women. The name of Queen Semiramis, legendary founder of Babylon, also meant "Dove" in the Syrian tongue. She was said to have castrated all her consorts.[15]

When circumcision replaced castration, the doves were involved in that too. Even Christian symbolism made the connection. The official symbol of the Festival of the Circumcision of Christ was a dove, holding in its beak a ring representing the Holy Prepuce. "Christ's fructifying blood" was linked with the similar emblem of Pentecost, which showed the descending dove on a background of blood red, officially described as a representation of the church fertilized by the blood of Christ and the martyrs.[16]

A certain "maiden martyr" called St. Columba (Holy Dove) was widely revered, especially in France, although she never existed as a human being.[17] Another curious survival of pagan dove-lore was the surname given to St. Peter: Bar-Iona, "Son of the Dove."[18] Some survivals may have been invented to explain the doves appearing on ancient coins as symbols of Aphrodite and Astarte.[19]

1. Graves, W.G., 123. 2. Waddell, 108. 3. Cumont, O.R.R.P., 118. 4. Trigg, 196. 5. de Voragine, 188. 6. Strong, 136. 7. Graves, G.M. 1, 72. 8. Bachofen, 21. 9. Gaster, 769. 10. de Lys, 13. 11. Graves, G.M. 2, 405; W.G., 194. 12. Knight, S.L., 48. 13. Gaster, 804. 14. Briffault 1, 377. 15. Rank, 93. 16. Brewster, 50, 246–47. 17. Attwater, 92. 18. de Voragine, 330. 19. d'Alviella, 91–92.

Drama

All drama began as sacred or magical drama, seasonally performed, having the same universal theme: the challenge, trial, marriage, sacrifice, and resurrection of the hero, or sacred king, or savior. The audience participated with songs, dances, sexual orgies, laments, eating the god and rejoicing at his restoration. One object was attainment of religious ecstasy: entering into the "dream."

It has been shown that every dream bears "a remarkable resemblance to drama."[1] Old Norse *draumar*, related to German *Traum* (dream), featured a sacrificial slaying of the god, the "tragic" part of the performance.[2]

Tragedy descended from the "goat-song" enacting the sacred dramas of Dionysus or Pan. The five-act structure of classical tragic drama—still seen in the plays of Shakespeare—was established by the five-act rites of the god. The acts were: (1) *agon*, the Contest: the incumbent incarnation of the god fought his challenger; (2) *pathos*, the Passion: the god united with the goddess and sent forth his soul with his semen (or blood) to fertilize the world anew—he died in his own begetting; (3) *threnos*, the Lament: a "threnody" of wailings and gestures of grief, partly to absolve the audience of responsibility for the god's death; (4) *anagnorisis*, the Discovery: priestesses returned to the tomb to find that the god was "risen," in much the same ritual enacted by Mary Magdalene and other temple-women at the tomb of Jesus (Luke 24:10) where, significantly, no men were present; (5) *apotheosis*, the Deification: the resurrected victim became God, and rose to heaven, to be a part of his divine father.[3] On this occasion the worshippers threw themselves into an orgy of rejoicing, such as distinguished the Roman carnival called Hilaria, "Day of Joy," following the death and resurrection of the savior Attis.[4]

Dionysus, Pan, Attis, Osiris, Orpheus, and many other gods of the mystery-cults contributed their dramas to medieval mystery plays, their linear descendants. The mummers' play, the ceremonies of Carnival, May Day, Harvest Home and other festivals used parts of the old sacred drama. Characters of the classic *commedia* were modeled on some of the pagan deities. The Dove-goddess became Columbine (Dove). The Serpent-god became Pierrot (Big Peter, or the Pied One). The name of Harlequin came from the Hellequins, or *Hella cunni,* "kindred of the Goddess Hel," souls of the pagan dead riding forth from her underworld.[5]

Masks were customary in the early medieval drama, just as they were in the plays of ancient Greece and Rome. From a magical point of view, the essence of the character lay in the mask, not in the actor who wore it. This was the primitive theory behind all appearances of mask and costume in religious ceremonies, from the animal-headed "gods" of Egypt—human bodies wearing the deities' disguises—to modern priestly vestments. Savages still say that, by putting on the mask and costume of an animal, spirit, or deity (or all at once), they do not simply make believe but actually become that creature.[6] See **Mask**.

1. Sagan, 178. 2. Turville-Petre, 109. 3. J.E. Harrison, 344. 4. Frazer, G.B., 407. 5. Potter & Sargent, 73; J.B. Russell, 146. 6. Jung, M.H.S., 44.

Droit du Seigneur

"The Lord's Right," also called *jus primae noctis,* "the law of the first night." An outgrowth of the feudal system that equated ownership of land with ownership of women. The *droit du seigneur* meant that every serf's bride must be deflowered on her wedding night not by her bridegroom but by the lord of the land.

As laid down by Ewen III of Scotland in the 9th century, the law said wives of common folk could be raped by any nobleman at any time; and "the lord of the ground shall have the maidenhead of all virgins dwelling on the same."[1]

The church upheld the *droit du seigneur* as a God-given right of the nobility. For a vassal bridegroom to consummate his marriage within three nights after the wedding was declared blasphemous "to the holy benediction" and tantamount to "carnal lust."[2] The overlord's lust, however, was right and proper. The eastern church provided legal penalties for a man who tried to consummate his marriage before his master could rape the bride.[3]

Droit du seigneur was a general rule throughout the feudal period and continued in Russia up to the 19th century.[4]

The system also continued in America's slaveholding south before the civil war, unofficially but generally acknowledged. Every black woman was the sexual property of her master, whether she was married to another slave or not.[5] Slave marriages could be legally ignored if plantation owners cared to do so. In 1757, Peter Fontaine said plantation owners begot so many children on their female slaves that "the country swarms with mulatto bastards." Thomas Anburey praised the system, calling it "a pleasant method to procure slaves at a cheap rate."[6]

1. Bullough, 168. 2. Brasch, 74. 3. Briffault 3, 242. 4. Fielding, 155. 5. Brasch, 72. 6. Bullough, 300; Rugoff, 325–26.

Druids

var. dryads, druides, druidai, drysidae, Gaulish *druvis,* Old Irish *drui.*[1]

Europe's sacred-oak cultists were known by many names. Greek myth said the dryads were oak nymphs, each an oracular priestess with her own personal tree spirit, like the biblical Deborah who lived under a tree that bore her own name (Judges 4:5). Dryads were called priestesses of Artemis, whose souls dwelt in their trees. They could also assume the shapes of serpents, and were then called Hamadryads, or Amadryades.[2] In their druidic groves throughout northern Europe, Strabo said, they practiced rites "similar to the orgies of Samothrace."[3]

Dryadism and druidism were two phases of the same religion, evidently restricted to a female priesthood in the earlier, matriarchal stage, later open to male priests as well. Gaulish and British priests of the oak groves formed a class of bardic wizards, keeping a sacred tradition by memorizing orally transmitted material, the nucleus of medieval sagas, epics, and ballads.

> *There is no break between the ancient semi-magical formulae chanted by the Druids and the later incantation of the wizard and the "wise-woman." They both arose in the Veda-like sacred hymns which formed the depository of the learning professed by the body of the druidical teachers and diviners and taught orally in the druidic schools. Most of them were never written down, and the fragments that we possess in writing are probably only the remains of a considerable body of oral literature.*[4]

Druids were attacked by the Christian church for their paganism, but especially for their propensity to include sacred women in their ranks. Scot said even in his day there were feminine spirits associated with trees, called Dryads in Greece and Druids in Scotland. They were shape-shifters, and could appear as either birds or women. "They know our thoughts, and can prophesy of things to come."[5]

Despite nominal conversion to Christianity, the Irish clung to druidism for many centuries. Their revered pagan king Diarmuid was called "half a druid and half a Christian." To make St. Patrick's legend more palatable to the Irish, monks claimed he had been educated by a druid.[6] Irish churches were known by the old druidic name of *dairthech,* "oak-house," formerly applied to the sacred grove.[7]

The "colleges" of druidesses, or dryads, passed by almost imperceptible degrees into a new designation of Christian nuns. One of the three classes of druidesses consisted of secluded sisterhoods, like the priestesses of Brigit, living in convent-like sanctuaries and tending sacred fires that were kept perpetually burning. Another, less secluded class of druidesses consisted of married women who lived at the temple and went home occasionally to visit their husbands. A third class was composed of temple servants who lived with their families.[8] With the coming of Christianity, the high holy sisterhoods were assimilated as nuns. The others were usually described as witches.

The druidic religion lasted a surprisingly long time over a surprisingly wide geographical area. Christians continued to worship oak deities in their sacred groves through the 8th century A.D. in Hesse. According to Gildas, Christian monks copied their tonsure from the druids. Traces of druidism were found as late as 1874 in Russia.[9] Even clearer traces were found in the 20th century in the Holy Land, where the Goddess of the sacred groves was worshipped as Asherah since pre-biblical times, and was known in Canaan as progenitress of the gods.[10] Her priestesses the oak-nymphs continued to be venerated under the title of Benat Ya'kob (Daughters of Jacob), said to dwell in their trees near old shrines that were rededicated to mythical Moslem saints. The trees were taboo. Their wood was never taken for fuel, except for votive purposes.[11]

To some extent the mystical reverence for oak trees persists to this day. Many British and American towns have their venerable "Charter Oak" or some superannuated tree where seasonal ceremonies take place. Acorns and oak leaves are still considered appropriate for wreaths and harvest decorations, even if they no longer crown the Goddess's sacred kings.

1. Piggott, 105–6. 2. Lawson, 153. 3. Haining, 23. 4. Spence, 33, 151. 5. Scot, 417. 6. Spence, 42, 53, 56. 7. de Paor, 60. 8. Boulding, 319. 9. Spence, 78, 108. 10. Pritchard, A.N.E. 1, 97. 11. Frazer, F.O.T., 329.

Durga

Kali's Creating-Preserving-Destroying trinity was said to consist of Parvati or Maya the Virgin, Durga the Queen-Mother, and Uma or Prisni the Crone. Durga was entitled "The Inaccessible." A crowned Amazon, she rode tigers into battle and defeated many demonic monsters, defending her children the gods.[1] Like other forms of the Goddess-as-warrior, such as the Middle-Eastern Ma-Bellona, Durga drank the blood of her enemies.[2] What this really meant was that her altars or images were anointed with the blood of war captives, killed as trophies.

As "The Inaccessible," Durga personified the fighting spirit of a mother protecting her young, and perhaps also the nursing mother sexually "inaccessible" to men, according to the old Oriental custom. Durga stood for the basic animal instincts of maternity, for which the adult male is no longer significant, and only her offspring claims a mother's attention.

Durga was sometimes Shasthi, "the Sixth," Leader of the Mothers. This title arose from the custom of invoking her on the sixth day after childbirth, when the continuous spells for protection of mother and child could be brought to an end. The seventh day was a day of rest.[3] This was the true beginning of the common patriarchal legend of gods who gave birth to the world in six days and rested on the seventh. Among such gods were Persia's Ahura Mazda, Memphian Ptah, Babylonian Marduk, Syrian Baal, and the Hebraic Jehovah.[4]

Durga's titles and character penetrated western ideas of the Goddess before the first century B.C. Rome's Great Mother Juno had the same attributes as her Oriental sister; she was Juno the Preserver, Queen of the Mothers.[5]

1. *Larousse,* 333. 2. O'Flaherty, 249. 3. O'Flaherty, 49, 353. 4. Hooke, M.E.M., 73. 5. Dumézil, 297.

Dusii

Gaulish word for gods, from Latin *deus.* In medieval Christian writings, a synonym for **incubus**.

Dybbuk

Hebrew word for a possessing demon, especially a "clinging" one who would not leave its human host until thoroughly exorcised.

Dymphna, Saint

var. Dympna

A canonization of what seems to have been a bit of graffiti on a brick found near Antwerp in the 13th century. The brick was buried near a coffin containing the bones of an unidentified man and woman. The words on the brick were *ma dompna,* "my lady," the traditional address of a medieval poet to his lady-love.

Though having no more basis than these words on an old brick, the cult of St. Dymphna was carefully developed. A large asylum near Gheel was named after her, so she became the patron saint of the insane—perhaps appropriately. To this day she is still touted as the intercessor for people with emotional problems.[1]

1. Attwater, 108.

E

The Creation of EVE, in the version that says she was made from one of Adam's ribs. Florentine School. Wood panel; Fra Bartolommeo, ca. 1510.

EUROPA and the Bull, here shown on a red-figure vase, approximately 11 by 11 inches. Greek, ca. 490 B.C.

Eagle

Classic soul-bird, symbol of apotheosis associated with the sun god, fire, and lightning. Greeks thought eagles so closely akin to the lightning spirit that they nailed eagles to the peaks of temples to serve as magic lightning rods. Hence the name *aetoi*, "eagles," for the pediments of Greek temples.[1] These were ancient forerunners of the "weather-cock" on the rooftree of a barn or house.

Cults of fire and the sun made the eagle a bearer of kingly spirit: the god's soul returning to heaven after a period of earthly incarnation as the king.[2] It was the Roman custom to release an eagle above the funeral pyre of each emperor, just as an Egyptian pharoah rose to heaven on the wings of the solar hawk.[3]

Zeus himself took the shape of an eagle to carry his young lover **Ganymede** to heaven. This was often interpreted as a symbol of the father-god's reception of men's souls when they were initiated into the solar Mysteries.[4]

The eagle was connected with rites of calling down "fire from heaven," probably with a burning-glass, to consume sacrifices on the altar. Such "fire from heaven" came down from Yahweh to consume the sons of Aaron (Leviticus 10:2), who died like sacrificial victims to the solar gods of Tyre. Such victims "passed through the fire" as offerings, and rose to heaven in the form of eagles.

> *We must bear in mind that in the East, whence all these beliefs and cults derive, not only was fire regarded as an all-powerful purifying agent, but death by fire was looked upon as an apotheosis which raised the victim to the rank of the gods. . . . "Fire," says Iamblichus, "destroys the material part of sacrifices, it purifies all things that are brought near it, releasing them from the bonds of matter and, in virtue of the purity of its nature, making them meet for communion with the gods. So, too, it releases us from bondage of corruption, it likens us to the gods.*[5]

The eagle was often identified with the fire bird or phoenix, who underwent a baptism of the fire that "burns all sins" and was reborn from his own ashes. The eagle also stood for the soul of **Heracles**, who passed through fire into heaven at seasonal festivals of Tarsus, and inspired St. Paul's belief in the virtue of giving one's body to be burned (1 Corinthians 13:3). The eagle was the totemic form of Prometheus, who "stole" fire from heaven, like the eastern fire-lightning-sun hero, man, or angel embodied in the Garuda bird. Garuda flew to the mountain of paradise to steal the gods' secret of immortality. Later, he assumed the golden body of the sun. American Indians had a similar hero, the thunderbird or lightning bird.[6]

As the royal bird of Rome, and the embodiment of deified emperors, the eagle was worshipped by Roman legionaries. Each legion had its sacred eagles, carried into battle like banners. If a legion should lose its eagles, the disgrace was unbearable; another whole expedition might be mounted to recover them.[7]

The Roman imperial emblem was inherited by the Germanic "Holy Roman Empire" and its *Kaisers,* derived from *Caesars.* Thus the eagle became a Teutonic symbol of sovereignty.

1. Reinach, 90. 2. Strong, 182. 3. Campbell, Oc.M., 334. 4. Strong, 187. 5. Strong, 194. 6. Hallet, 376. 7. Tacitus, 41.

E-Anna

"Land of Anna," one of the territories of Babylon, named after the Goddess under one of her most common Mesopotamian names (see **Anne, Saint**).

Earth

Herodotus said, "Three different names have been given to the earth, which is but one, and those derived from the names of women."[1] Herodotus miscounted. Thousands of feminine names have been given to the earth. Continents—Asia, Africa, Europe—were named after manifestations of the Goddess. Countries bore the names of female ancestors or of other manifestations of the Goddess: Libya, Lydia, Russia, Anatolia, Latium, Holland, China, Ionia, Akkad, Chaldea, Scotland (Scotia), Ireland (Eriu, Hera) were but a few.[2] Every nation gave its own territory the name of its own Mother Earth. Tacitus said the tribes of Europe regarded Mother Earth as "the all-ruling deity, to whom all else is subject and obedient."[3]

Mother Earth received universal worship because she was the universal parent. American Indians still relate how all peoples and animals in the beginning emerged from Earth's yonic hole, and "it was just like a child being born from its mother. The place of emergence is the womb of the earth." Siberian reindeer hunters say the human race emerged from a Goddess, whose carved figurines protect the hunter's hut, when given offerings and prayers: "Help us to keep healthy! Help us to kill much game!"[4]

The central doctrine of Amerindian religion was reincarnation in a new body from Mother Earth's womb, the ancient meaning of "born again." A chief named Smohalla spoke of his moral obligations formed by this doctrine:

> *It is a sin to wound or cut, to tear or scratch our common mother by working at agriculture. You ask me to dig in the earth? Am I to take a knife and plunge it into the breast of my mother? But then, when I die, she will not gather me again into her bosom. You tell me to dig up and take away the stones. Must I mutilate her flesh so as to get at her bones? Then I can never again enter into her body and be born again.*[5]

Oriental Indians had much the same idea about entering the

earth. Hindu priests told a dead man: "Go, seek the earth, that wise and kind mother of all. O Earth, rise up and do not hurt his bones; be kind and gentle to him. O Earth, cover him as a mother covers her infant with the skirts of her garment."[6]

Ancient Roman philosophers had the same idea too. "The Earth Mother is the mysterious power that awakes everything to life. . . . All comes from the earth and all ends in the earth . . . the earth produces all things and then enfolds them again . . . the Goddess is the beginning and end of all life." A Roman writer of the 3rd century A.D. prayed to "Holy Goddess Earth, Nature's mother, who bringeth all to life, and revives all from day to day. The food of life Thou grantest in eternal fidelity. And when the soul hath retired we take refuge in Thee. All that Thou grantest falls back somewhere into Thy womb."[7]

Patriarchal Christians might have been expected to speak of Father Heaven rather than Mother Earth, yet even they found it impossible to give up the older deity. The epitaph of Pope Gregory the Great said: *Suscipe Terra tuo de corpore sumptum*: "Receive, O Earth, what was taken from thy body."[8] Even up to the 20th century, tombstones of German Christians bore the formula: *Hier ruht im Mutterschoss der Erde . . .*, "Here rests in Earth's maternal womb. . . ."[9] In Chaucer's Pardoner's Tale an old man pleaded with the Goddess:

. . . I walk alone and wait
About the earth, which is my mother's gate,
Knock-knocking with my staff from night to noon
And crying, "Mother, open to me soon!
Look at me, Mother, won't you let me in?
See how I wither, flesh and bones and skin!
Alas! When will these bones be laid to rest?"[10]

This was more than a poetic metaphor. As late as the 12th century, many Europeans still recognized Mother Earth as a Goddess, perhaps their only supreme divinity. She was described in an English herbal of the period with no mention of God at all:

Earth, divine goddess, Mother Nature, who dost generate all things and bringest forth ever anew the sun which thou hast given to the nations; Guardian of sky and sea and of all Gods and powers; through thy influence all nature is hushed and sinks to sleep. . . . Again, when it pleases thee, thou sendest forth the glad daylight and nurturest life with thine eternal surety; and when the spirit of man passes, to thee it returns. Thou art indeed rightly named Great Mother of the Gods; Victory is thy divine name. Thou art the source of the strength of peoples and gods; without thee nothing can either be born or made perfect; thou art mighty, Queen of the Gods. Goddess, I adore thee as divine, I invoke thy name; vouchsafe to grant that which I ask of thee, so shall I return thanks to thy godhead.[11]

Up to the Renaissance, English farmers continued to call upon *Erce, eorthan modor* (Earth, mother of earth) when planting.[12] Similarly, up to the 20th century, Russian farmers continued to call upon Mati-Syra-Zemlya (Moist Mother Earth) for almost everything. Instead of touching a Bible when taking an oath, a Russian peasant would put a clod of earth on his head, invoking the Mother's curse if he broke his word.[13] This perpetuated an ancient Greek habit. Even the patriarchal Olympian gods swore their binding oaths by Mother Earth: Gaea, or Rhea, called Universal Mother, Deep-Breasted One, firmly founded, oldest of divinities.[13] Hesiod admitted that she ruled Olympus before the coming of the Hellenic deities. She ruled Russia too. The country bore her ancient name, Rha (Rhea), the Red One, mother of the Volga and all its tribes.[14]

Home and Mother were literally identical to people who combined both in their image of the earth-goddess. Many believed they must be buried in the same soil that supported them in childhood. Threatened by invaders, the matriarchal Cimmerians could have saved themselves by moving away from their homeland; but they chose to face superior numbers of enemies, and die where they were, believing their lives valueless if they couldn't re-unite with the same Earth that gave them birth.[15] The Egyptian traveler Sinuhe felt the approach of death and hurried home to his motherland "to follow the Lady of All," hoping that she would "spend eternity by my side."[16]

Post-mortem reunion with the Mother always overlapped with the idea of marrying her. Man seldom distinguished clearly between his three roles as the Goddess's child, corpse, and bridegroom. Balkan peasants still view death as a sacred marriage, and dress corpses as for a wedding. Formal dirges say: "The black earth for my wife I took." Ancient Greek epitaphs similarly proclaimed the dead man "admitted to the bridal chamber of Persephone." Artemidorus wrote: "All the accompaniments of marriage are exactly the same as those of death."[17]

The archetypal image of the marriage-with-Earth had a curious revival in the special mid-Victorian pornography known as pornotopia, in which the female body was a landscape, and man correspondingly reduced in fantasy to about the size of a fly:

> *In the middle distance there looms a large irregular shape. On the horizon swell two immense snowy white hillocks; these are capped by great, pink, and as it were prehensile peaks or tips—as if the rosy-fingered dawn itself were playing just behind them. The landscape undulates gently down to a broad, smooth, swelling plain, its soft rolling curves broken only in the lower center by a small volcanic crater or omphalos. Farther down, the scene narrows and changes in perspective. Off to the right and left jut two smooth snowy ridges. Between them, at their point of juncture, is a dark wood . . . sometimes it is called a thicket . . . triangular in shape. It is also like a cedarn cover, and in its midst is a dark romantic chasm. In this chasm the wonders of nature abound. From its top there depends a large, pink stalactite, which changes shape, size, and color in accord with the movement of the tides below and within. Within the chasm—which is roughly pear-shaped—there are caverns measureless*

to man, grottoes, hermits' caves, underground streams—a whole internal and subterranean landscape. The climate is warm but wet. Thunderstorms are frequent in this region, as are tremors and quakings of the earth. The walls of the cavern often heave and contract in rhythmic violence, and when they do the salty streams that run through it double their flow. The whole place is dark yet visible. This is the center of the earth and the home of man.[18]

Marcus attributes these images of pornotopia to a spiritual loss, possibly related in a direct way to contemporary denial of the earth-mother figure in a religious symbolism, as well as Victorian society's suppression of sexuality:

One gets the distinct impression, after reading a good deal of this literature, that it could only have been written by men who at some point in their lives had been starved. . . . Inside of every pornographer there is an infant screaming for the breast from which he has been torn. Pornography represents an endless and infinitely repeated effort to recapture that breast, and the bliss it offered.[19]

Acquisitiveness seems to have been another manifestation of the hidden psychic hunger for possession of Mother Earth. Her European names Urth, Hertha, Eortha, Erda, Hretha, etc. stemmed from Sanskrit *Artha,* "*mater*-ial wealth." Among the Hindu-rooted gypsies, "earth" meant good luck, fortune, money.[20] Latin *Mater* (Mother) became English "matter," of which Plutarch said, "Matter hath the function of mother and nurse . . . and containeth the elements from which everything is produced."[21] Tibetans still say the elements are produced by the Old Mother.[22] The material body has the special name of Anna-Maya, variations of which appeared everywhere in the ancient Mediterranean world as names of the Great Goddess.[23] The "soul manifested in matter" is defined as the Anna-Maya self. The sages say, "Mind and matter are at base one as modes of the same Power. . . . Mind is the subjective and Matter the objective aspect of the one polarized Consciousness."[24]

Western theology split this former unity into a duality, regarding matter (or flesh) and mind (or spirit) as intrinsically different from, and opposed to, one another. Thus, says Jung, "the word 'matter' remains a dry, inhuman, and purely intellectual concept, without any psychic significance for us. How different was the former image of matter—the Great Mother—that could encompass and express the profound emotional meaning of Mother Earth."[25]

After the image of Mother Earth as birth-giver, perhaps that of Mother Earth as receiver of the dead aroused the most profound emotional responses. When death was viewed as a return to the infantile state of sleep in the Mother's bosom, it seemed less terrifying. The Rig Veda says, "Crawl to your Mother Earth. She will save you from the void."[26] In medieval ballads, the hero's lady-love sometimes impersonated Mother Earth by covering her lover with her green mantle, to put him "out of sight" as if buried.[27] Greek peasants thought the worst kind of curse on an enemy was to wish Mother Earth would not accept him: "May the earth not digest thee! May the black earth spew thee up! May the ground not consume thee!"[28] Such a one rejected by the earth would be a revenant or a restless ghost.

In France during the 12th century, a sect of heretics were sent to the stake by the Archbishop of Reims, apparently for worshipping Mother Earth, among other offenses. Led to execution, one of them "cried again and again, 'O Earth, cleave asunder!'" His hearers thought he was trying to get the earth to swallow his enemies, but he may have believed the earth could open and swallow him to save him from the stake.[29] Like the original death aspect of Rhea or Cerridwen, Mother Earth still was supposed to devour her children.

1. Herodotus, 226. 2. Agrippa, 269. 3. Tacitus, 728. 4. Campbell, P.M., 240, 314. 5. de Riencourt, 23. 6. Hauswirth, 21. 7. Vermaseren, 10, 49. 8. de Voragine, 187. 9. Lederer, 24. 10. Caucer, 269–70. 11. Graves, W.G., 64. 12. Turville-Petre, 188. 13. *Larousse,* 89, 287. 14. Thomson, 252. 15. Mumford, 416. 16. Maspero, 83. 17. Lawson, 547, 554. 18. Marcus, 271–72. 19. Marcus, 273–74. 20. Leland, 99. 21. Knight, S.L., 22. 22. *Bardo Thodol,* 15; Waddell, 484. 23. *Mahanirvanatantra,* 11. 24. Avalon, 49, 318. 25. Jung, M.H.S., 95. 26. H. R. E. Davidson, G.M.V., 92. 27. Wimberly, 390. 28. Summers, V., 161. 29. Coulton, 55.

Easter

Springtime sacrificial festival named for the Saxon Goddess Eostre, or Ostara, a northern form of **Astarte**. Her sacred month was Eastre-monath, the Moon of Eostre.[1]

Saxon poets apparently knew Eostre was the same Goddess as India's Great Mother Kali. Beowulf spoke of "Ganges' waters, whose flood waves ride down into an unknown sea near Eostre's far home."[2]

The Easter Bunny was older than Christianity; it was the Moon-hare sacred to the Goddess in both eastern and western nations. Recalling the myths of Hathor-Astarte who laid the Golden Egg of the sun, Germans used to say the hare would lay eggs for good children on Easter Eve.[3] (See **Cat**.)

Like all the church's "movable feasts," Easter shows its pagan origin in a dating system based on the old lunar calendar. It is fixed as the first Sunday after the first full moon after the spring equinox, formerly the "pregnant" phase of Eostre passing into the fertile season. The Christian festival wasn't called Easter until the Goddess's name was given to it in the late Middle Ages.[4] (See **Menstrual Calendar**.)

The Irish kept Easter on a different date from that of the Roman church, probably the original date of the festival of Eostre, until the Roman calendar was imposed on them in 632 A.D. Nevertheless, the Columban foundation and their colonies in Britain kept the old date for another fifty years.[5]

The Persians began their solar New Year at the spring equinox, and up to the middle of the 18th century they still followed the old custom of presenting each other with colored eggs on the occasion.[6] Eggs were always symbols of rebirth, which is why Easter eggs were usually colored red—the life-color—especially in eastern Europe. Russians used to lay red Easter eggs on graves to serve as resurrection charms.[7] In Bohemia, Christ was duly honored on Easter Sunday and his pagan rival on Eastern Monday, which was the Moon-day opposed to the Sun-day. Village girls like ancient priestesses sacrificed the Lord of Death and threw him into water, singing, "Death swims in the water, spring comes to visit us, with eggs that are red, with yellow pancakes, we carried Death out of the village, we are carrying Summer into the village."[8]

Another remnant of the pagan sacred drama was the image of the god buried in his tomb, then withdrawn and said to live again. The church instituted such a custom early in the Middle Ages, apparently in hopes of a reportable miracle. A small sepulchral building having been erected and the consecrated host placed within, a priest was set to watch it from Good Friday to Easter Sunday. Then the host was taken out and displayed, and the congregation was told Christ was risen.[9]

A curious 16th-century Easter custom was known as "creeping to the cross with eggs and apples," a significant use of the ancient female symbols of birth and death, beginning and fruition, the opening and closing of cycles. The Ceremonial of the Kings of England ordered carpets to be laid in the church, for the comfort of the king, queen, and courtiers as they crept down the aisle on hands and knees.[10] The penitential implication of the creeping ceremony is clear enough, but the female-symbolic foodstuffs are a bit mysterious.

Germany applied to Easter the same title formerly given to the season of the sacred king's love-death, *Hoch-Zeit,* "the High Time." In English too, Easter used to be called "the Hye-Tide."[11] From these titles came the colloquial description of any festival holiday as "a high old time."

1. Knight, D.W.P., 157. 2. Goodrich, 18. 3. de Lys, 117. 4. H. Smith, 201. 5. de Paor, 70. 6. Hazlitt, 201. 7. Gaster, 603. 8. Frazer, G.B., 362. 9. Hazlitt, 281. 10. Hazlitt, 153. 11. Hazlitt, 316.

Ecclesia

"The Church," a title of the virgin Mary, who was supposed to represent the physical body of which Christ was the spiritual head. Holy Mother Church was both bride and mother of God, according to Christian mystics, postulating even an incestuous Sacred Marriage in the old pagan style. The erotic poetry of Solomon's Song was glossed as an expression of the love between Christ and "Ecclesia." Irenaeus said Mary-Ecclesia was "the pure womb which regenerates man unto

God." As in the manner of pagan temples, even the church building was likened to Mary's body.

Echo

Greek "nymph" at whose reflecting pool Narcissus met his death. According to the classical myth, Echo grieved so sorely for her beloved flower-god that she pined away until there was nothing left of her but her voice.

Originally, she was Acco, the pre-Hellenic birth-goddess, in an oracular mood as "the last echo of the Voice," meaning the Voice of Creation, the same as the Goddess Vac in ancient India (see **Logos**). In Hebrew she was Bath Kol, Daughter of the Voice.[1]

Apparently the Word she spoke to the springtime god Narcissus-Antheus-Adonis-Hyacinthus was the death curse heralding the final phase of the sacred king's fatal drama; for Narcissus was the same god as Dionysus with all his flower-titles.[2]

1. Leland, 220. 2. Graves, G.M. 1, 288.

Irenaeus Doctor, saint, and father of the church, said to have lived in the 2nd century A.D. as bishop of Lyons. His history is obscure, largely based on (possibly fraudulent) assertions of Eusebius, who claimed to have letters from Irenaeus, but none of these were preserved. The story of Irenaeus's martyrdom has been proved false.

Ecstasy

Greek *ekstasis* meant "standing forth naked," a word for the state of mind ensuing in a religious trance when the consciousness was stripped away, leaving only the essential self. In Greece as in ancient India, proper worship was sometimes conducted in a state of physical **nakedness** (Hindu *digambara*) to symbolize purification from all distractions, to concentrate on the ecstatic experience.

Edda

"Great-Grandmother," a Norse name for Mother Earth (Erda); also the word for sacred poetry inspired by her. Icelandic sagas or *Eddas* usually opened with an invocation to this Goddess, who gave birth to the oldest third of the human race.[1]

1. Turville-Petre, 150.

Eden

Hebrew "Garden of Delight," based on the Persian *Heden* or primal garden where the first couple were joined together as a bisexual being in the Golden Age. Like all images of the earthly paradise, Eden was located in the far west originally, where the sun went each night. That is why the Bible says known lands lay "east of Eden" (Genesis 4:16).

Edmund, Saint

Canonized form of the heathen deity worshipped at Bury St. Edmunds, where he was seasonally slain, like Shiva, in the shape of a white bull.

Ritual bull-killing dated back to the Cretan Minotaur cult, through rites of Artemis Tauropolos, the Roman Taurobolium, and via Iberian paganism up to the bullfights of modern Spain. St. Edmund's shrine was supposedly founded on the tomb of the saint, a young man who became "chosen king" of the East Angles in the 9th century.[1] But his legend was wholly mythological. Like other Celtic savior-gods he was tied to a tree and pierced by many arrows: the same fate meted out to the sacrificial bull, still demonstrated by Spanish picadors. On Edmund's heraldic crest, the martyr's head was held by a wolf, the traditional Doorkeeper of Death, and the Triple Goddess appeared symbolically in the shape of three Crowns. (See **Dog**.)

Monastic records reveal the true totemic nature of "St. Edmund." A white bull was chosen each year to be paraded through the streets, while women wishing to conceive would caress him, for a doomed god was usually credited with great fertilizing power. A contract paper from the monastery said: "This indenture certifies that Master John Swassham, sacrist, with the consent of the prior of the convent . . . shall find, or cause to be found, one white bull every year of his term, so often as it shall happen that any gentlewoman, or any other woman, from devotion or vows made by them shall visit the tomb of the glorious martyr St. Edmund to make oblation to the same white bull."[2]

1. Attwater, 109. 2. Briffault 3, 190.

Egg

Mystical symbol of the Creatress, whose World Egg contained the universe in embryo. Orphics said the Great Goddess of darkness, Mother Night, first brought forth the World Egg which was identified with the moon. Heaven and earth were made of the two halves of the eggshell, and the first deity to emerge was the bisexual Eros the Desired. The Egg was a common Oriental image of creation. Its western versions "went back to cosmologies of the Tiamat-type and to early exchanges between Greece and the East."[1] Egyptians' signs for the World Egg was the same as for an embryo in a woman's womb.

1. Lindsay, O.A., 116.

Egg-and-Dart Frieze

Classical architectural decoration sometimes called the Frieze of Venus and Mars: a symbol of the magic circle alternating men and women. On the frieze, ovals alternate with trident-shaped darts, female and male genital emblems. Ancient builders carried the frieze all the way around a building or room without a break, since an interruption in the frieze could mean a break in the succession of human generations.

The same design in Egypt presented even more overtly sexual hieroglyphs: downward-pointing phalli alternating with narrow mandorlas (female almond shapes), each topped by a small triangle representing a clitoris.[1]

The Tantric "magic circle" or *chakra* was a human equivalent of the Egg-and-Dart frieze. In pagan Britain, druidic priests also worked in magic circles alternating with green-robed dignitaries known as Ovates, or Eggs.[2] Wearing the color associated with Life in druidic religion, these must have been priestesses, like the eastern shaktis, or else men impersonating women by wearing female dress.

Many counting-games originated with the magic circle, in which the even numbers were assigned to men, the odd numbers to women. Pagan traditions said odd numbers represented "immortality" because all odd numbers are female.[3] This explains why Roman religious festivals were scheduled for odd-numbered days, on the theory that these days were more propitious.

1. *Book of the Dead,* 273. 2. Pepper & Wilcock, 203. 3. Wedeck, 66.

Eide

"Goddess-within," Greek concept of the female soul, corresponding to the Latin *Idea.* Aristotle was one of the first philosophers to attempt replacing this ancient notion of Mother-given intelligence with a doctrine of astral theology.[1]

1. Lindsay, O.A., 102.

Eire

var. Erin

Celtic name of Ireland, from "the Lady Eriu," or Erinn, the Triple Goddess.[1] She was a form of **Hera**, whose apple-isle was located on an island in the western sea.[2]

1. Squire, 126. 2. Graves, G.M. 1, 93.

El

General Semitic word or name for a deity, especially in combining forms, as Isra-el, Beth-el, Dani-el, El-ijah. Both El and its plural, *elohim,* meaning many deities of both sexes, are the Hebrew words rendered "God" by biblical translators. Sometimes "God" is Elias, a Hebraic version of the sun (Greek Helios); this was the "father" Jesus addressed (Matthew 27:47-49). In Phoenicia, El was the Heavenly Bull at the head of the pantheon, spouse of Asherah as Cow-Mother. He usually appeared as a human figure wearing the head or horns of a bull.

var. Elen, Hel-Aine, Eileen

Elaine

Britain's "Lily Maid," the virgin Moon-goddess bearing the same name as Helen of Troy; British tradition claimed the islands were colonized by Trojans. According to the bards, the Roman emperor acquired Britain only by marrying its queen, Elen. The people agreed to help build Roman roads because she ordered them, and the roads were called Roads of Elen of the Hosts: "The men of the Island of Britain would not have made those great hostings for any save for her."[1]

Elen or Elaine became the mother-bride of Lancelot-Galahad in Arthurian romance. Lancelot the father begot on her his own reincarnation, Galahad the son; but Lancelot in his youth had been named Galahad, and his mother was Queen Elaine. The Lily Maid gave Lancelot her sexual-symbolic charm to make him invincible: her pearl-bedewed sleeve of red silk. The womb-symbol of the Holy Grail was displayed in her castle, tended by her dove-soul, Colombe. Galahad saw this vision again in his last moments, as he expired at the altar in ancient sacred-king style.[2]

1. Mabinogion, 85. 2. Malory 1, 377; 2, 268.

Electra

One of the Seven Sisters (see **Pleiades**); virgin mother of Dardanus, founder of Troy, whose name is still borne by the Dardanelles. Electra was also known as a sea nymph. Myths of the classic period made her a "daughter" of two queens responsible for their husbands' ritual murders, Queen Clytemnestra and Queen Jocasta, who brought death to Agamemnon and Oedipus, respectively. Electra's name means "amber," and may have been applied to a priestess who wore certain amulets of amber as a badge of office.

Elements

On each of the inhabited continents, the same four elements were distinguished as building-blocks of all substances living or dead, organic or inorganic: water, fire, earth, and air. Indians of Missouri and New Mexico, Aztecs, Chinese, Hindus, ancient Egyptians, Greeks, Romans—all had the same idea.[1] The earliest known literate civilization, Sumeria, had already designated the elements water, fire, earth, and air.[2] The "science" of western Europe continued to believe in the same mystic elements up to the 18th century when real elements began to be discovered.

Indo-European tradition said the four elements were created by Great Mother Kali, who organized them into letter-mantras carved on her rosary of skulls, to form the Sanskrit alphabet, which she invested with power to create what it expressed. Elemental sounds were divided into four categories: Va, water; Ra, fire; La, earth; and Ya, air. They were bound together by the Mother-syllable Ma (Kali Ma herself), representing "intelligence."[3] Tibetan Buddhists still say the elements are ruled by "Old Mother Khon-Ma," the Great Goddess.[4]

The Goddess was addressed in scriptures: "Thou art Earth, Thou art Water, Thou art Fire, Thou art Air, Thou art the Void, Thou art consciousness itself, Thou art life in this world; Thou art the knowledge of self, and Thou art the Supreme Divinity."[5] The ancient theory of the human body's elemental "humors," adopted by the medical profession in the west up to the 19th century, was based on Kali's supposed distribution of elements in living forms. She gave water to create the blood stream, fire to make its vital heat, earth to produce the solid parts of the body, and air to animate it with breath.[6]

This theory was earnestly adopted by western philosophers. Firmicus Maternus said man is a microcosm "under the direction of Nature . . . so that within the small compass of his body he might bestow under the requirements of Nature the whole energy and substance of the elements."[7]

The same elemental symbols shown in the four hands of Kali appeared in western iconography also. Kali's bowl of blood signified water; her scepter or *dorje* (lightning bolt) was fire; her lotus wheel stood for earth; and her sword was air. The Greeks assigned their own versions of these symbols to the Goddess Nemesis (Fate): a cup; an apple-bough or wand; a wheel; and a sword.[8] Later in European history, the same symbols of the elements gave rise to the four suits of the **Tarot** deck: (1) cups; (2) wands, rods, or scepters; (3) pentacles, coins, or discs; and (4) swords. These in turn evolved into the modern hearts, clubs, diamonds, and spades.

The two colors now allotted to the four suits of cards echo the very ancient Tantric concept of two sexes expressing themselves as elements. Female water and earth were paired with male fire and air. Oriental sages maintained that mantras with a preponderance of fiery or airy (male) letters are cruel and destructive. Mantras with a preponderance of watery or earthy (female) letters are benevolent.[9] Like the corresponding card suits in red, the life-color, female elements were said to possess the active, life-giving energy. Greek philosophers later reversed this opinion, calling male elements "active" and female elements "passive." Yet, even in the Christian Middle Ages, an aphorism purportedly derived from Moses said, "Only Earth and Water bring forth a living soul."[10]

Thales of Miletus Pythagorean philosopher, said to be one of the Seven Wise men of the ancient world.

According to Thales of Miletus, water was the *Arché,* the first of the elements, having "mastery" over the others because it represented the abyssal womb.[11] The combination of water and fire as female-and-male signified a very ancient theory that blood, the basic essence of life, was made of sea water infused by magic fire from heaven, which made it warm and red, though it still tasted like sea water. Vedic sages sometimes called the combination Kali and Agni. The Goddess, fructified by Agni's fire, become the Ocean of Blood at the beginning of the world, source of the vitality of all living things until the day of destruction. "Sacred fire" symbolized sexual passion, its heat engendered by fire-from-heaven gods like Agni, Lucifer, Hephaestus, Syrian Baal, Heracles-Melkart, Thor-Heimdall, etc. The fire god lost his life when he was swallowed up by the all-encompassing Mother of Waters; sages said he was "quenched in her yoni" like a lightning bolt quenched in the sea.[12] (See **Lightning**.) This image led to the Roman belief that the feminine water-element was dangerous to men.[13]

Of the other male-female pair, the air-earth combination obviously represented Father Heaven and Mother Earth, whose separation was caused by their firstborn son, the god who "divided heaven from earth," an Oedipal myth known throughout southeastern Asia, Oceania, and ancient Mesopotamia.

Egyptians assigned a male-and-female pair to each of the primordial elements as they arose from the undifferentiated Abyss, or womb (Ma-Nu). These eight, together with their Great Mother, made up the first Ennead (Nine Great Deities).[14] Their elemental totems were associated with the four cardinal points, the four winds, the four sides of a Holy Mountain (pyramid), the four spirits called Sons of Horus who guarded the corners of a temple.[15] These were like the four Princes of Heaven revered in China and Japan as guardians of the four cardinal directions: a blue dragon in the east, a red bird in the south, a white tiger in the west, a black warrior in the north. Three animal spirits and one human were the same as Egypt's "four powers of Amenti."[16] The same elemental totems gave rise to the four angels of the Apocalypse and the four evangelists, symbolized in Christian iconography as a bull (earth), lion (fire), serpent (water), and eagle, angel, or man (air).

American Indians had remarkably similar elemental symbolism. Villages and camps were divided into four quarters or phratries of fire, air, water, and earth, each with its colors and totems. For example, the Zunis associated wind with the north, war, and yellow; fire with the south, summer, tillage, and red; water with the west, spring, peace, and blue; earth with the east, autumn, magic, and white. Aztec elemental totems were the rabbit (north, black, winter, air); the flint (south, blue, summer, fire); the house (east, white, autumn, earth); and the cane (west, red, spring, water).[17]

New World mythology postulated four primordial aeons, each corresponding to an element. Sacred histories of Mexico showed that each of the former ages was brought to destruction by the same element that ruled it.[18] "Earth, the world support and base, became the swallower of things. Air, the breath of life, became a devastating wind. Fire that descends from heaven tempered as the fire-of-life in lifegiving rain came down as a rain of flames. And finally Water, gentle mothering vehicle of the energies of birth, nourishment, and growth, became a deluge."[19]

These myths provide a clue to the original invention of the elements. Of all substances or forces in the world, why should these four have been chosen as the basis of all things? The simple answer is that the elements represented the only four possible ways other than cannibalism to dispose of a dead body, thus returning it to an "origin." A body could be buried in the earth, burned with fire, thrown into water, or given to the birds of the air. Each funerary practice was viewed as a return to the same power that engendered birth.

The same four methods of corpse-disposal are still practiced all together in Tantric Tibet. Common folk are chopped in pieces and exposed to carrion birds, as are the Parsees of India and Persia. Wealthier Tibetans are cremated, or buried if death was caused by disease. Sometimes, as among the Hindus, corpses are thrown into rivers or lakes.[20] Vedic peoples followed both funerary customs of burial and cremation, maintaining that Yama, Lord of Death, received the soul either way.[21]

Some ancient thinkers tried to classify different nations under elemental categories, possibly on the basis of funeral customs predominating in them. It was said that water-worship belonged to Egypt and the Nilotic Goddess; Phrygians were worshippers of "the earth, which was to them the Great Mother of everything; the Syrians and Carthaginians of the air, which they adored under the name of celestial Juno"; and the Persians worshipped fire.[22]

A few traditions listed a fifth element that the Greeks called *ether,* "heavenly," of which the immortal bodies of gods, angels, star-spirits, or saints were made. It was changeless, having no part in the eternal flux of other elements constantly combining and re-combining. The idea of changeless ether was so important to western notions of the immortal soul that it was never abandoned; even today some occultists call it the substance of the "astral body." In the 18th and 19th centuries, astronomers believed ether was a gas filling all of outer space.

Etheric spirits were immortal, but the other elements were also represented by spirits of a superhuman nature; undines (water), salamanders (fire), gnomes (earth), and sylphs (air). Some said these were pre-human races born of the four rivers that flowed from the Great Mother's belly in the paradisial age. Elemental colors were associated with these four rivers of feminine nurturing fluids: water, blood, honey, and milk. Oriental gemsmiths assigned to them the jewels of mystical significance: sapphire or lapis lazuli (water), ruby (blood or fire), gold (earth), and silver, crystal, or diamond (air).[23] According to biblical symbolism, the female land was made of rivers Milk and Honey; the male god or ancient Savior contributed blood and water, the very same fluids that flowed from the body of Jesus in the "land of milk and honey" (John 19:34).

The philosophical sect called Stoics—after *stoicheia,* "the elements"—assigned color symbolism, signs of the zodiac, seasons, and deities to the elements.[24] Their system passed into the Roman Circus, which was divided into four elemental regions with their colors: green for Spring, Earth, Flowers, Terra Mater, and Venus; red for Summer, Fire, and Mars; blue for Autumn, Water, Heaven, Saturn, and Neptune; white for Winter, Air, Zephyrs, and Jupiter.[25] The same deities were still connected with the elements in the 16th century A.D.: Venus (water), Mars (fire), Jove (earth), and Saturn (air).

Compendium Maleficarum A treatise on witches and witchcraft compiled by Guazzo in 1608.

Michael Constantine Psellus 11th-century Byzantine politician, scholar, philosopher, and courtier; author of a History, poems, and letters on many subjects.

The *Compendium Maleficarum* quoted Psellus's list of elemental spirits in defining various kinds of devils in the Middle Ages. "The first is the fiery, because these dwell in the upper air and will never descend . . . . The second is the aerial, because these dwell in the air around us. . . . The third is terrestrial . . . some dwell in the fields and lead night travelers astray; some dwell in hidden places and caverns. . . . The fourth is the aqueous, for these dwell under the water in rivers and lakes. . . . They raise storms at sea, sink ships in the ocean, and . . . are more often women than men."[26] According to Scot, fire-spirits govern the intellect, water-spirits the instincts and passions: "Fiery spirits urge men to contemplation, watery spirits to lust."[27] Sexual prejudices entered into these definitions, for the supposed sexual polarity of fire and water was never forgotten.

The human "temperament" came from Latin *temperare,* "to mix, to combine"; temperament was a mixture of elemental "humors" or fluids. These were supposed to be controlled by various gods associated with the elements. Thus, a character could be Martial, Jovial, Saturnine, or Mercurial. A predominance of blood gave a *sanguine* temperament; of phlegm, a *phlegmatic* one; of bile, a *melancholic* one; of ether, an *ethereal* one; and so on. The temperamental mixture was also related to *tempor,* the time or season, for the elements were categorized also with the four seasons of the year and various configurations of the stars.[28] These ideas were old even before Rome was built. The legendary ancestor of the Scythians was said to have arranged all things in the world under four elemental symbols that came down from heaven: a plough (earth), a bowl (water), an ax (fire), and a yoke (air, the "yoke" between heaven and earth, related to the word *yoga*).[29] In general, the lore of the elements was a prime example of what may be one of humanity's most characteristic behavior patterns: classifying.

1. Lindsay, O.A., 20–21; Campblell, P.M., 458. 2. Campbell, M.I., 90.
3. d'Alviella, 240. 4. Waddell, 484. 5. *Mahanirvanatantra,* 262–63.
6. *Bardo Thodol,* 15–16; Agrippa, 57. 7. Lindsay, O.A., 122; Wedeck, 236.
8. Cavendish, P.E., 71. 9. Rawson, A.T., 70. 10. Agrippa, 43, 49.
11. Campbell, P.M., 64; Oc.M., 181; Agrippa, 49. 12. Rawson, E.A., 57.
13. Dumézil, 319. 14. Dumézil, 647. 15. Budge, E.M., 89. 16. Lethaby, 58–60.
17. Lindsay, O.A., 20–21. 18. Castiglioni, 134. 19. Campbell, M.I., 154.
20. *Bardo Thodol,* 25–26. 21. Rose, 63. 22. Cumont, A.R.G.R., 205. 23. Waddell, 81.
24. Cumont, A.R.G.R., 68. 25. Lindsay, O.A., 240. 26. Robbins, 133. 27. Scot, 419.
28. Funk, 301. 29. Jung & von Franz, 114.

Elephant

A totem of **Shiva**, who took the form of the elephant and also of the god who killed the elephant. After dispatching his victim, Shiva put on the elephant's skin and turned himself elephantine, while "watched by the Goddess-spouse."[1] In the erotic poem *Song of the Cowherd,* the god was incarnated as Krishna and the Goddess-spouse as his sexually insatiable consort Radha, "She-Elephant." Radha was named for an elephant because elephants were common symbols of the most powerful sexual energies. The Kama Sutra designated "elephant men" and "elephant women" those with the largest genitals and most voracious sexual appetites. Yet Radha was entirely human, described as Woman, "the object of devotion to which even God, the Creator himself, bows down."[2]

A male elephant was often given the title of Begetter, or Father, or Grandfather.[3] Buddha was begotten on the virgin Maya by the elephant god under his title of Ganesha, "Lord of Hosts," most probably derived from the use of elephants in warfare.[4] Every history student knows North African war leaders considered the magic of elephants so essential to victory that the Carthaginian general Hannibal insisted on trying to take them over the Alps to attack Rome from the north—a disastrous tactical misjudgment, resulting in the loss of all his elephants and his war as well.

The elephant-god "Lord of Hosts" had a flourishing worship in North Africa and Egypt, which is why this same title was taken by the biblical Yahweh, who was identified with the elephant god at his sacred city of Elephantine during the 5th century B.C.[5] Jewish mercenary soldiers stationed there insisted that their god was the same as the elephant-mate of the Virgin Mother Neith, or Anath: the two of them were totemized as Cow and Bull Elephant at what was then called the source of the Nile.[6] Elephants were worshipped as sexual-symbolic deities in Egypt from an early date. Totem standards showing elephants, and artifacts of elephant ivory, appeared in pre-dynastic times.[7]

Judeo-Christian scholars tended to ignore Yahweh's involvement in the elephant cult because, as Hooke says, "it is naturally repugnant to most people [i.e., men] to entertain the suggestion that Jahveh could ever have been thought of as possessing a female consort like all the Baals of Canaan"; and for no more reason than this allegedly natural repugnance, evidence of the sacred marriage at Elephantine was suppressed. Yet the same author admitted that Jahveh was once one of the very same Baals, and even addressed as Baal in the Bible.[8]

A curious parallel to the Flight into Egypt of Yahweh's son is found in Buddhist iconography. The Virgin Mother was shown riding a white bull, led by Shiva in the costume of a peasant, holding in her arms the elephant-headed Divine Child, the reborn Ganesha.[9] Possibly the original Egyptian version of this reborn god entered the Bible under the name of **Behemoth**, who became an elephant-headed demon in the later mythology of western Europe.

The elephant still symbolizes the sacred marriage in a Buddhist fertility ritual. Monks lead a painted white elephant in solemn procession, attended by men wearing women's clothes and making salacious jokes. "Through this ritualistic female disguise they do honor to the cosmic female principle, the maternal, procreative, feeding energy of nature, and by the ritualistic utterance of licentious language stimulate the dormant sexual energy of the living power."[10] The same transvestism and lewd language can be found in fertility rituals the world over.

1. Zimmer, 173. 2. Campbell, Or.M., 352. 3. B. Butler, 224.
4. Campbell, Or.M., 307. 5. Graves, W.G., 405. 6. Ashe, 31, 59.
7. Budge, G.E. 1, 22. 8. Hooke, S.P., 104, 182. 9. Ross, 47. 10. Zimmer, 108.

Elias, Saint

Canonized form of Helios, the sun god, called El the solar bull among Semitic peoples.[1] Elias was the god Jesus addressed from the cross; his hearers said, "This man calleth for Elias . . . let us see whether Elias will come to save him" (Matthew 27:47–49; Mark 15:35). Eusebius built upon the name alone a nonsensical Christian myth, calling Elias one of five Egyptians who were "questioned" at the gate of Caesarea and gave their names and their city, Jerusalem. "The governor ordered them to be tortured to exhort more precise information; but they remained mute and were beheaded."[2]

1. Lawson, 44. 2. Attwater, 112.

Elizabeth, Saint

Daughter of a 13th-century king of Hungary, Elizabeth was married at the age of 13 to the Landgrave of Thuringia. She was a mother at 14, a widow at 20, and a corpse at 24, having died of an excess of Christianity.

Her spiritual advisor was Conrad von Marburg, who loved to strip both Elizabeth and her maids and mercilessly whip them for the slightest infraction of his orders. On one occasion the young Landgravine was invited to visit a nunnery and went without asking his permission. He beat her so severely that "for three weeks the marks of the cords could be seen upon her." After her husband's death, other nobles robbed her of her estates and left her destitute; von Marburg ordered her to send away her last few friends and her children. She said, "I fear a mortal man as much as I should fear the heavenly Judge. Therefore I have given my obedience to Master Conrad . . . that I might be bereft of every earthly consolation."[1]

She inflicted further austerities on herself, in addition to the abuse she received from von Marburg, and soon died of these physical hardships. Conrad von Marburg pulled political strings to have her canonized, to enhance his own reputation as her teacher. He busied himself in the torture chamber—a task plainly suited to his personality—and was credited with bringing 8000 heretics to the stake in a single year. At last he was assassinated by a group of irate knights, against whom he had preached a crusade.[2] He was promptly canonized as a saint and a martyr.[3]

1. de Voragine, 684. 2. Lea unabridged, 415–25. 3. H. Smith, 258.

Elohim

Hebrew plural word meaning "the goddesses and the gods," though every time it appeared in a Bible text it was translated simply "God." In the original manuscripts of the book of Genesis, Yahweh was only one of the *elohim*. Sometimes the singular form was taken as a name, e.g. the Phoenician bull-god called simply **El**, "the god."[1]

Medieval wizards thought Elohim was one of the magical secret names of God; or, at times, it was taken to be the name of a devil.

1. *Larousse*, 74.

Elves

Spenser said the word "elf" meant "alive."[1] But there is little doubt that elves were the ancestral dead, still "alive" in their burial mounds; "it is well known that in Scandinavia the dead were formerly called 'elves.'"[2] The Kormaks Saga, pagan Icelandic poem of the 10th century, described sacrifices to them for curative purposes: "Redden the outside of the mound with bull's blood, and make the elves a feast with the flesh; and you will be healed."[3]

The word elf was related to the *helleder*, people belonging to Mother Hel as Death-goddess. In general it meant heathen, both dead and living. Sigvat Thordarson in the 11th century called heathen people *alfar*, "elves," who worshipped their deities at feasts called *alfablót* (elf-blood) in certain "heathen-holy" houses ruled by women.[4]

The paradise of Alfaheimr (Elf-land) was always matriarchal, inhabited by the bright female spirits who made the sun. Like their eastern counterparts the ***dakinis***, these Valkyries or fairies could be both beautiful and hideous, representing both birth and death.[5] In the new creation after doomsday, the new female sun would be Glory-of-Elves.[6]

Christianity opposed this ancient female-centered theology, as shown by accounts of elf-feasts as demonic sabbats where "cloven-footed dancers" trod their fairy rings. Henry More, 17th century English philosopher and poet, said they often appeared in northern England and in Ireland.[7] Ballads merged the demon lover with the "elf-knight," a wooer from pagan northlands.[8] The custom of the Wild Hunt or Night Ride, sacred to the elf-king (Odin), was transformed into a procession of wind-riding demons, as at **Halloween** and other pagan festivals. Leader of the night riders was called the Erl King, from Danish *ellerkonge*, a king of those who belong to Hel. He associated with the sacred alder tree.[9]

Other plants often associated with elves were the holly sacred to Hel, the mistletoe, the mandrake, and various witch-herbs including rosemary, known as the Elfin Plant,[10] named after the Goddess herself. (See **Rose**.)

1. Keightley, 57. 2. Wimberly, 127. 3. H.R.E. Davidson, G.M.V.A., 156. 4. Hollander, 154. 5. Turville-Petre, 231. 6. Sturluson, 92. 7. Summers, V., 115. 8. Wimberly, 137. 9. *Encyc. Brit.*, "Erl King." 10. Wimberly, 350.

Elysium

Greek paradise, Persephone's heaven for heroes, also called the Isles of the Blest; located either in the underworld, or in the far west, like the Hesperian apple-orchards of Mother Hera. Elysium too was an "Apple-land," like Avalon and Eden.[1] It became a common synonym for "paradise."

1. Graves, G.M. 1, 123.

var. Emain, Hy-Many

Emania

Celtic "Land of the Moon," where the dead went, ruled by the Queen of Shades called Mania, Mana, Macha, Mene, or Minne: the Fairy Queen. Like the Norse heaven Manavegr, it was identified with the moon-path in the sky, and with earthly shrines, too. Macha's holy city was called Emain Macha. See **Moon**.

Empyrean

"Heaven of Inner Fire," Greek philosophers' concept of the highest heaven above the planetary spheres, "empire" of the sun god, or the divine king of the celestial mountain. "Inner Fire" probably referred to the divine element ether, supposed to be the substance of spirits. See **Elements**; **Mountain**.

Endymion

"Seduced Moon-man," a Greek hero enchanted into eternal sleep by the Moon-goddess Selene. He was a God-begotten king of Elis, having ousted the former king in the usual fashion of ancient heroes. "When his reign ended he was duly sacrificed and awarded a hero shrine at Olympia."[1] This was the "sleep put on him" by his Goddess, who nightly kissed him where he lay forever on the mountainside. See **Kingship**.

1. Graves, G.M. 1, 211.

Ennead

"The Nine," primal Great Deities of Egypt: a male and female pair for each of the four elements, plus their Mother, the Creatress called Nu, Nut, Ma-Nu, Temu, Maa, or Night, the Abyss, Chaos: the undifferentiated mixture of elements. See **Creation; Elements.**

Enthusiasm

Greek *enthousiasmos,* "having a god within," the concept of possession by a divine spirit. It was a doctrine set forth in Asia as *Svecchacara,* freedom from all sinfulness because all actions are motivated by the inner divinity.[1] See **Antinomianism; Possession.**

1. Angus, 151.

Entrails

Courage, in modern slang, is both "guts" and "balls," a combination of very ancient precedent. It was once thought that male genitals were protruding ends of *intestines,* literally "testes-within." Egyptian *sma* meant both entrails and male genitals.[1] Egyptians prayed to be delivered on the day of reckoning from a Kali-like death-goddess Baba, who not only "devoured" men sexually but also "feeds on the entrails of the dead."[2]

Kali devoured her lover genitally and also devoured his entrails at the same time.[3] Similarly, Aphrodite in her Crone form as Androphonos, Man-Slayer, killed her lovers as a queen bee does by ripping out their intestines along with their genitals.[4] In northern Europe there was the same ceremony: spring was brought to the world by symbolically ripping out the entrails of **Loki** via a rope tied around his genitals. His blood bathed the lap (womb) of the Goddess; then she smiled, and the spring could come.[5] See **Skadi.**

Because men's "guts" were supposed to possess the spirit of the phallic god, also mythologized as the underground serpent, it was usual to take omens from the entrails of sacrificial victims. Among the Amazonian tribes of the Black Sea area, the readers of entrails were "old gray-haired women."[6] The Romans called similar diviners *haruspices,* "those who gaze into the belly."[7]

1. Budge, G.E. 1, 43. 2. Cavendish, P.E., 112. 3. Neumann, G.M., pl. 66. 4. Graves, G.M. 1, 72. 5. Oxenstierna, 213. 6. Wendt, 137. 7. Rose, 237.

Eos

Homer's "Rosy-fingered Dawn," the same birth-goddess as Mater Matuta, Aurora, or Hebe. Her rosy fingers were usually assumed to represent the pink clouds of sunrise, but the meaning may have been more literal, recalling the habit of Egyptian and Asian priestesses of staining their fingers red for religious ceremonies. See **Henna.**

Epona

Celtic-Saxon Horse-goddess of Iron Age Britain, probably modeled on Cretan Leukippe (White Mare), Mare-headed Demeter, and the equine deities of central Asia. The cult of Epona "stretched from Spain to Eastern Europe and Northern Italy to Britain."[1] Irish kings were still symbolically united with a white mare in the 11th century A.D. See **Horse.**

1. *Larousse,* 240.

var. Erebus

Erebos

Greco-Roman name for the underworld, land of death, described in Orphic mystery-religion as "the Abysmal Womb."[1] Like other ancient concepts of "hell," it was a place of regeneration. See **Hell.**

1. Lindsay, O.A., 116.

Eresh-Kigal

Underworld counterpart of the Babylonian Goddess Ishtar; comparable to Nephthys in Egypt, Persephone in Greece, Kali-Uma in India, Hel in northern Europe. She was provided with a consort, Nergal, later transformed by Christian mythographers into a demonic official of hell.

Erigone

Virgil's name for the constellation of the Virgin, also known as Astraea, Goddess of Justice, or Libra, Lady of the Scales.[1] She was the same celestial Judge as the Egyptian Goddess Maat.

1. Lindsay, O.A., 277.

Erinys

"Avenger," title of Mother Demeter as the threefold Furies, who punished all trespassers against matriarchal law. In her fearsome avenging aspect, the Goddess sometimes appeared as the Night-mare, with a black horse head wreathed with snakes.[1] See **Demeter; Furies.**

1. Graves, W.G., 411.

Erl King

Danish *ellerkonge,* "king of elves," associated with the sacred alder or elder tree, and the underground land of the dead. As Lord of Death, he was the consort of **Hel**, Goddess of the elder trees.[1] He was really a form of **Odin**, leader of the Wild Hunt composed of ghostly riders on the night wind.

1. Keightley, 93.

Eros

Bisexual Greek deity of erotic love, identical with Hindu Kama. Orphics said Eros was the first god to emerge from the womb of the primal creatress, Mother Night, "of whom even Zeus stands in awe."[1] Plato said Eros was the oldest of deities, the most worthy of honor, the one who gave souls strength to ascend to heaven after death.[2] In short, Eros was a kind of Savior, before cults of asceticism began to replace the older worship of sexuality as a primary life-force.

1. Graves, G.M., 1, 30. 2. Lindsay, O.A., 125.

Erua

Babylonian name for the Queen of Heaven, who chose kings and married them, and controlled the function of birth among all creatures in her land.[1] An alternate title of the Goddess Ishtar, or Inanna.

1. *Assyr. & Bab. Lit.,* 114.

Essenes

Jewish sect of ascetics, based on sun-worshipping Persian anchorites, who in turn evolved their system from Jain yogis professing to work miracles by living apart from the world and practicing extreme self-denial. Jesus, John the Baptist, and Simon Magus were said to have been trained in Essenic communities, which formed the bulk of the first Christians. Epiphanius said, "They who believed on Christ were called Essenes before they were called Christians."[1]

Epiphanius Sainted 4th-century father of the church, friend of St. Jerome, writer of many tracts and polemics against paganism.

An Essenic hierarchy included a chief priest called *Christos* (Anointed One), "head of the entire Congregation of Israel." There were ordinary priests called "sons of Aaron," and another functionary known as the Messiah of Israel.[2] The latter was also called Teacher of Righteousness. He suffered physical abuse in atonement for the sins of the entire community, enduring "vindictive sentences of scourging and the terrors of painful sicknesses, and vengeance on his fleshly body."[3]

Josephus said the Essenes "reject pleasures as an evil, but esteem continence, and the conquest over our passions, to be virtue. They neglect wedlock, but choose out other persons' children, while they are pliable, and fit for learning; and esteem them to be of their kindred, and form them according to their own manners." We are not told whether these "other persons' children" were abandoned by their parents, or sold, or given to, or kidnapped by, the Essenes. These harsh anchorites imposed cruel sentences for the least infraction of rules, partial starvation being the most common punishment. Some suffered punishments lasting two or more years for wavering from the doctrines of the community.[4]

The doctrines were strikingly similar to those of early Christianity. Essenes anticipated St. Augustine in teaching that immortal souls belonged in heaven, but were drawn down to earth and entrapped in corruptible flesh by the "natural enticement" of sex.[5] The soul's purity might be recovered by ascetic techniques such as mortification of the flesh, fasting, renunciation of sensual pleasures, and by solitary meditation in the wilderness, like the voluntary exiles of John and Jesus.

Essenes called themselves Therapeutae, "healers," claiming their austere lifestyle gave them power to cast out demons of sickness, even to restore life to the dead; Jesus's raising of Lazarus was a typical Essenic miracle.[6] Much of their training as exorcists consisted of learning lists of spirits' names, and the holy names that would expel them. Like Jesus in the episode of the Gadarene swine, Essenes always demanded the demons' names. (See **Name**.) They were sworn to strictest secrecy regarding the magical names they used in their exorcisms.[7]

Essenes preached giving away all one's worldly goods upon joining the sect, which meant those who joined gave away everything they owned to their superiors. Dire punishments were meted out to those who lied about their possessions in order to hold something back for themselves or their families.[8] An Essenic episode in the Gospels tells of Ananias and his wife Sapphira, killed by St. Peter for giving the apostles only a part, but not all, of the money they received for a sale of land. Peter and his associates were jailed for murder, but later escaped (Acts 5:2-10, 18).

Despite their vows of poverty, the Essenes were strangely obsessed with visions of wealth and power coming to them after Armageddon, "The War of the Sons of Light with the Sons of Darkness."[9] Sons of Light of course were the Essenes, and all others outside their brotherhood were Sons of Darkness, otherwise called "men of the Pit."[10] The Essenes believed firmly in the imminence of the Last Days, when they would be called upon to fight the forces of evil. Their reward would be to rule the world—in an oddly materialistic manner, as envisioned by their scriptures:

> *Arise, O Warrior, take thy captives, O glorious man! Seize thy plunder, O doer of mighty deeds! Lay thy hand on the necks of thy enemies and thy foot on the heaps of the slain; smite the nations, thy adversaries, and may thy sword devour guilty flesh. . . . Let there be a multitude of*

possessions in thy fields, silver and gold and precious stones in thy palaces. . . . Let thy gates be continuously open, that the wealth of the nations may be brought unto thee; and let their kings serve thee, and all the oppressors bow down to thee and lick the dust of thy feet.[11]

A large colony of Essenes occupied the Qumran community from 110 B.C. to the fall of Jerusalem in 70 A.D. with a significant period of vacancy during the reign of Herod, 31–4 B.C. In 31 B.C. the site had to be abandoned because a severe earthquake cracked the water cistern and ruined the buildings.[12]

Survivors evidently took the earthquake as a sign of the oncoming Last Days and went forth into the world to preach their message. Josephus said before 70 A.D. there were many Messiahs and Christs announcing the end of the world.[13] Some were willing to die a martyr's death, believing this would gain them special privileges in the world of the hereafter. One such martyr may have been John the Baptist, who came from the wilderness to call Herod and his court to repentance, and remained to serve as a sacred king (see **Salome**).

Early Mandaean Christians said the true prophet was not Jesus but John the Baptist. They called themselves Christians of St. John, and also Nasoraje, or "Nazarenes."[14] One of the colonies of exiled hermits from Qumran settled around Nazareth and took up the craft of carpentry; hence the craft-brotherhood of Nazorenes, from *najjar,* "carpenters," after whom the town may have been named. Some Christian authorities of the first centuries A.D. wrote that during this period "all Christians were called Nazorenes."[15] Jesus too was called a Nazorene. The oldest Gospel called him "Jesus the carpenter" (Mark 6:3).

Oddly, what began in the east as a carpenters' metaphor passed into the Gospels as a masons' metaphor. Essene-like Buddhist hermits described themselves as logs rejected by the carpenter's craft.[16] The same words were put into Jesus's mouth, somewhat altered: he called himself a stone rejected by the masons (Matthew 21:42).

1. Doane, 426. 2. Pfeifer, 133. 3. Augstein, 108. 4. Pfeifer, 59, 138. 5. Pfeifer, 99; *Encyc. Brit.*, "Augustine." 6. Mumford, 146. 7. Legge 1, 158. 8. Pfeifer, 59. 9. Black, 3. 10. Pfeifer, 51. 11. Pfeifer, 82. 12. Pfeifer, 24; Campbell, Oc.M., 285. 13. Brandon, 248. 14. Reinach, 77. 15. Black, 72. 16. Campbell, Or.M., 279.

Esther

"Star," the Hebrew rendering of Ishtar or Astarte. The biblical Book of Esther is a secularized Elamite myth of Ishtar (Esther) and her consort Marduk (Mordecai), who sacrificed the god Hammon, or Amon (Haman). Yahweh was never mentioned, because the Jews of Elam worshipped Marduk, not Yahweh. (See **Purim**.)

Esther probably was the name given to any priestess chosen to represent the Goddess on the occasion of the king's sacred marriage.

Even the Bible story admits that Esther-Ishtar was not the real name of the Elamite-Jewish queen. Her real name was Hadassah (Esther 2:7).

Ethan

Biblical sage almost as wise as Solomon (1 Kings 4:31). His origin was not really biblical. He was the Sumerian god-king Etana, called Eytan in the land of Canaan. He ascended to heaven on eagle-back, like Ganymede, to reach the Goddess and learn the secret of eternal life. He came down again to earth, some said thrown down by the jealous sun god for his hubris.[1] Evidently he returned to earth to be reincarnated in the next king. (See **Kingship**.)

1. Albright, 250.

Eugenia, Saint

"Healer" or "Health," a title of the Goddess converted into a fictitious "virgin martyr." Her legend claimed she was one of the women who entered a Christian sect by "turning herself into a man," for some sects would not admit women unless they did this.[1] St. Eugenia accordingly became a monk and called herself Brother Eugenius. The same story told of all she-monks was told of her: she was falsely accused of rape and condemned to a life of expiation, which she patiently endured. Still, the healing miracles attributed to her shrines were older than her Christian legend, showing that she was really the Goddess whose "eugenic" springs were even more popular in the 1st century than Lourdes or Compostela in the 20th.[2]

1. Malvern, 33. 2. de Voragine, 537.

Eumenides

"Good Ones," a euphemistic title of the **Furies**, intended to placate their wrath and refrain from attracting their attention through invocation of their real names.

Eunomia

"Order," the first of Aphrodite's three Horae; one of the names of the Triple Goddess's virgin aspect as the Creatress who first brought order out of chaos. See **Creation**; **Diakosmos**.

Euphemia, Saint

"Good-speaker," a fictitious Christian saint based on a title of the Goddess as the Muse of mellifluous speech. St. Euphemia's legend shows that she was not a human being but a statue. She stood aloft on a high place, and could not be reached except with ladders; those who climbed up to pull her down were afraid, because the first of their number had been stricken with paralysis upon touching her and was borne away half dead.[1] That is, she was a holy image protected by so stern a taboo that even early Christians feared to violate it.

1. de Voragine, 552.

Europa

"Full Moon," the Great Goddess as mother of the entire continent. She was embodied in the same white Moon-cow as Hathor, Hera, Io, and Kali—who "rode" Shiva in the guise of the white bull Nandi, just as Europa rode Zeus disguised as a white bull.[1] Her Hellenic legend said Zeus kidnapped and raped her; but it was "deduced from pre-Hellenic pictures of the Moon-priestess triumphantly riding on the Sun-bull, her victim."[2] Garlanded white bulls were sacrificed to the lunar cow-goddess in Crete and Mycenae from a very early date. According to Pausanias, Europa was a surname of the ancient Mycenaean goddess, Demeter.[3]

1. Campbell, Or.M., 63. 2. Graves, G.M. 1, 197. 3. Guthrie, 225.

Pausanias Greek traveler and geographer of the 2nd century A.D. Living in a time of declining culture, he was inspired by a desire to describe the ancient sacred sites for posterity.

Eurydice

"Universal Dike," Mother of Fate, the Orphic name for the underworld Goddess who received the soul of Orpheus. Hellenic writers converted her into Orpheus's wife, sent by a serpent's bite to the land of death, where he followed her; but this was an artificial myth of very late origin. The icons from which came the apocryphal story of Eurydice's death seem to have represented Orpheus entering the underworld, to be greeted by Hecate with her serpents. Eurydice's "snake in the grass" was her sacred animal, constant companion of the underworld Goddess.[1]

Medieval poets knew the same classic Goddess as a queen of England, "Heurodis," whose consort was a god-begotten king of Winchester, "Sir Orfeo."[2]

1. Graves, G.M. 1, 115. 2. Loomis, 315–19.

Eurynome

"Universal One," the Pelasgian Creatress who danced alone on the primordial ocean of Chaos until she brought the elements to "order" (*themis,* another of her names). Like Isis and Eve, she created the Great Serpent, a disembodied phallus, to be her first consort. She permitted him to fertilize her womb, but then he began to call himself the Creator of everything. Angered by his arrogance, she bruised his head with her heel and cast him down to the underworld.[1]

Christian Gnostics told much the same story of the Mother of Creation, whom they called Sophia, and her first consort Jehovah, who was able to help in the work of creation only because she "infused him with energy" and implanted in him her own ideas. He too became too arrogant and had to be punished for forgetting his Mother.[2] See **Eve**.

Like many titles of the Great Goddess, Eurynome was both diabolized and masculinized by later Christian writers, who consigned her to hell and made her a male "demon Eurynome," sometimes described as a Prince of Death.[3]

1. Graves, G.M. 1, 27. 2. Pagels, 57–58. 3. de Givry, 132, 141.

Eve

One of her Tantric names was Adita Eva: "the Very Beginning."[2] In northern Babylonia, Eve was known as "the divine Lady of Eden," or "Goddess of the Tree of Life."[3] Assyrians called her Nin-Eveh, "Holy Lady Eve," after whom their capital city was named.

The biblical title of Eve, "Mother of All Living," was a translation of Kali Ma's title *Jaganmata.* She was also known in India as Jiva or Ieva, the Creatress of all manifested forms.[1] In Assyrian scriptures she was entitled Mother-Womb, Creatress of Destiny, who made male and female human beings out of clay, "in pairs she completed them."[4] The first of the Bible's two creation myths gives this Assyrian version, significantly changing "she" to "he" (Genesis 1:27).

The original Eve had no spouse except the **serpent**, a living phallus she created for her own sexual pleasure.[5] Some ancient peoples regarded the Goddess and her serpent as their first parents.[6] Sacred icons showed the Goddess giving life to a man, while her serpent coiled around the apple tree behind her.[7] Deliberate misinterpretation of such icons produced ideas for revised creation myths like the one in Genesis. Some Jewish traditions of the first century B.C., however, identified Jehovah with the serpent deity who accompanied the Mother in her garden.[8] Sometimes she was Eve, sometimes her name was given as Nahemah, Naama, or Namrael, who gave birth to Eve and Adam without the help of any male, even the serpent.[9]

Because Jehovah arrogantly pretended to be the sole Creator, Eve was obliged to punish him, according to Gnostic scriptures. Though the Mother of All Living existed before everything, the God forgot she had made him and had given him some of her creative power. "He was even ignorant of his own Mother. . . . It was because he was foolish and ignorant of his Mother that he said, 'I am God; there is none beside me.'" Gnostic texts often show the creator reprimanded and punished for his arrogance by a feminine power greater and older than himself.[10]

The secret of God's "Name of power," the **Tetragrammaton**, was that three-quarters of it invoked not God, but Eve. YHWH, *yod-he-vau-he,* came from the Hebrew root HWH, meaning both "life" and "woman"—in Latin letters, E-V-E.[16] With the addition of an I (yod), it amounted to the Goddess's invocation of her own name as the Word of creation, a common idea in Egypt and other ancient lands.[17]

Gnostic scriptures said Adam was created by the power of Eve's word, not God's. She said, "Adam, live! Rise up upon the earth!" As soon as she spoke the word, her word became reality. Adam rose up and opened his eyes. "When he saw her, he said, 'You will be called "the mother of the living," because you are the one who gave me life.'"[18]

Adam's name meant he was formed of clay moistened with blood, the female magic of *adamah* or "bloody clay."[19] He didn't produce the Mother of All Living from his rib; in earlier Mesopotamian stories, he was produced from hers. (See **Birth-giving, Male**.) His Babylonian predecessor Adapa (or Adamu) was deprived of eternal life not by the Goddess, but by a hostile God.

The biblical idea was a reversal of older myths in which the Goddess brought forth a primal male ancestor, then made him her mate—the ubiquitous, archetypal divine-incest relationship traceable in every mythology. The reversal was not even original with biblical authors. It was evolved by Aryan patriarchs who called **Brahma** the primal male ancestor. They claimed their god brought forth the Mother of All Living from his own body, then mated with her, so she gave birth to the rest of the universe.[20] In the Hebraic version, a wombless God made his offspring with his hands, and the actual birth-giving was left to Adam. The Bible as revised by patriarchal scribes said nothing about a divine birth-giving, since the scribes were determined to separate the concepts of "deity" and "mother" insofar as possible.

Gnostic scriptures however reverted to the older tradition and said Eve not only created Adam and obtained his admission to heaven; she was the very soul within him, as Shakti was the soul of every Hindu god and yogi. Adam couldn't live without "power from the Mother," so she descended to earth as "the Good Spirit, the Thought of Light called by him 'Life' (Hawwa)." She entered into Adam as his guiding spirit of conscience: "It is she who works at the creature, exerts herself on him, sets him in his own perfect temple, enlightens him on the origin of his deficiency, and shows him his (way of) ascent." Through her, Adam was able to rise above the ignorance imposed on him by the male God.[21]

By this Gnostic route came the Midrashic assertion that Adam and Eve were originally androgynous, like Shiva and his Shakti. She dwelt in him, and he in her; they were two souls united in one body, which God later tore apart, depriving them of their bliss of union. Cabalists took up the idea and said the paradise of Eden can be regained only when the two sexes are once more united; even God must be united with his female counterpart, the heavenly Eve called **Shekina**.[22]

Another Gnostic version of the story made God a true villain, who cursed Adam and Eve and expelled them from paradise out of jealousy of their happiness. He also lusted after the Virgin Eve, raped her, and begot her sons Jahveh and Elohim, whose other names were

Eve was one of the common Middle-Eastern names of the superior feminine power. To the Hittites, she was Hawwah, "Life."[11] To the Persians, she was Hvov, "the Earth."[12] Aramaeans called her Hawah, "Mother of All Living."[13] In Anatolia she was Hebat or Hepat, with a Greek derivative Hebe, "Virgin Mother Earth," with the same relationship to the Great Goddess Hera as Kore-Persephone to Demeter, and Hebe may have been an eponymous ancestress of "Hebrews." A semitic root of her names was *hayy,* a matrilineal kinship group, once considered the "life" of every tribe by direct descent from the Creatress.[14] The names of Eve, the Serpent, and "Life" are still derived from the same root in Arabic.[15]

Cain and Abel. Here was one of several myths that made Eve the mother not only of Adam, but also of Jehovah, and of all the elements as well. The myth went on to say the first of Eve's offspring ruled the male elements of fire and air; the second ruled the female elements of earth and water.[23]

Like her prototype Kali Jaganmata, Eve brought forth death as well as life—that is, she brought forth all living forms, all of which were subject to death for the very reason that they were alive. Under patriarchal systems of belief, the fact that every living thing is doomed to die was blamed on the Mother who gave it a finite life. Instead of blaming God for casting Adam out of the paradise where he might have lived forever, the patriarchs blamed Eve for bringing this about. The Wisdom of Jesus ben Sirach said evil began with Woman (Eve): "because of her we all die."[24] Fathers of the Christian church said Eve conceived by the serpent and brought forth Death. The seeds of all women already existed in Eve, St. John Chrysostom maintained, so that in her sin "the whole female race transgressed."[25]

St. John Chrysostom, "Golden-mouthed John," 4th-century Christian orator who served as Patriarch of Constantinople until he incurred the wrath of the empress Eudoxia, who arranged to have him deposed and exiled.

The Book of Enoch said God created death to punish all humanity for Eve's sin, but many patriarchal thinkers hesitated to blame God even indirectly. The prevalent opinion was that when Eve disobeyed the deity, death somehow just happened.[26] St. Paul blamed only Eve, absolving Adam from guilt for the apple-eating incident: "Adam was not deceived, but the woman being deceived was in the transgression" (1 Timothy 2:14). A church council announced in 418 A.D. that it was heresy to say death was a natural necessity rather than the result of Eve's disobedience.[27]

This was the real origin of the church fathers' fear and hatred of women, which expanded into a sexist attitude that permeated all of western society: Woman was identified with Death. Her countervailing responsibility for birth was taken away, and the creation of life was laid to the credit of the Father-god, whose priests claimed he could remove the curse of death. As every woman was understood to be an emanation of Eve, Tertullian said to Everywoman:

Tertullian (Quintus Septimius Florens Tertullianus) Influential early Christian writer and father of the church, ca. 155–220 A.D., born in Carthage of pagan parents.

> *And do you not know that you are an Eve? The sentence of God on this sex of yours lives in this age; the guilt must of necessity live too. You are the devil's gateway . . . the first deserter of the divine law; you are she who persuaded him whom the devil was not valiant enough to attack. You destroyed so easily God's image, man. On account of your desert—that is, death, even the Son of God had to die.*[28]

Medieval theologians said Adam was forgiven. Christ descended into hell and rescued Adam along with other biblical patriarchs. He escorted Adam into heaven, saying, "Peace be to thee and to all the just among thy sons."[29] But for Eve there was no forgiveness. No peace was offered to her or her daughters. Presumably, they were left behind in hell. Christian theologians espoused the same theory as Persian patriarchs, that heaven was closed to all women except those who were submissive and worshipped their husbands as gods.[30] Even modern theologians naively blame human death on the Edenic sin. Rahner said, "Man's death is the demonstration of the fact that he has fallen away from God. . . . Death is guilt made visible."[31] Theologians have not yet dealt with the question of what "guilt" causes death among non-human creatures.

Actually, churches depend for their very existence on the orthodox myth of Eve. "Take the snake, the fruit-tree, and the woman from the tableau, and we have no fall, no frowning Judge, no Inferno, no everlasting punishment—hence no need of a Savior. Thus the bottom falls out of the whole Christian theology."[32]

Equally destructive to Christian theology would be restoration of books arbitrarily excluded from the canon, such as the *Apocalypse of Adam*, in which Adam stated that he and Eve were created together but she was his superior. She brought with her "a glory which she had seen in the aeon from which we had come forth. She taught me a word of knowledge. . . . And we resembled the great eternal angels, for we were higher than the God who had created us."[33]

Some of these once-sacred books made Eve superior to both Adam and the creator. It was she, not God, who gave Adam his soul and brought him to life. It was she, not God, who cast down the evil deities from heaven and made them demons. And she, as the eternal female Power, would eventually judge the God she created, find him guilty of injustice, and destroy him.[34]

As an allegory, this might reflect a social truth. Fragile constructs of the collective mind, gods are easily destroyed by those who ignore them. Early Gnostic documents show that most women of the ancient world were disposed to ignore the God who was said to have cursed their sex and their descendants forever. Had one of the other versions of the Eve myth prevailed over the canonical version, sexual behavior patterns in western civilization almost certainly would have evolved along very different lines. Christianity managed to project man's fear of death onto woman, not to respect her as Kali the Destroyer was respected, but to hate her.

The uncanonical scriptures were no more and no less creditable than the canonical ones. Their picture of Eve as God's stern mother, the defender of mankind against a tyrannical demon-deity, had more adherents in the early Christian centuries than the picture that is now familiar. One of Christianity's best-kept secrets was that the Mother of All Living was the Creatress who chastised God.

1. Avalon, 120, 278. 2. Waddell, 126. 3. d'Alviella, 153. 4. Neumann, G.M., 136. 5. Graves, G.M. 1, 27; Tennant, 154. 6. J.E. Harrison, 129.
7. d'Alviella, 166–67; Lindsay, O.A., 54. 8. Enslin, C.B., 91. 9. Legge 2, 329.
10. Pagels, 30, 52, 57–8. 11. Hooke, M.E.M., 112. 12. Campbell, Oc.M., 210.
13. Pagels, 30. 14. Tennant, 26. 15. Shah, 387.
16. Reinach, 188; Cavendish, T., 116. 17. Brandon, 126–27. 18. Pagels, 30.
19. Hooke, M.E.M., 110. 20. *Larousse*, 345. 21. Jonas, 82, 204.
22. Ochs, 121. 23. Jonas, 205. 24. Malvern, 30. 25. Ashe, 178–79.
26. Tennant, 207, 244. 27. H. Smith, 238. 28. Bullough, 114.
29. de Voragine, 223. 30. Campbell, Oc.M., 196. 31. Cavendish, P.E., 28.
32. Daly, 69. 33. Robinson, 256–57. 34. Robinson, 172–78.

Evolution

The theory of species development given to the world by Darwin and his successors had no special religious significance, except that Christian authorities viewed it as a contradiction of their all-important Eden myth, just as Galileo's astronomical discoveries contradicted the Bible's geocentric cosmos. The theory of evolution showed man could not have "fallen"; there was no original sin and therefore no need of salvation.

In 1869 a German theologian, Dr. Schund, said, "If Darwin be right in his view of the development of man out of a brutal condition, then the Bible teaching in regard to man is utterly annihilated." The American Episcopal Church said: "If this hypothesis be true, then is the Bible an unbearable fiction . . . then have Christians for nearly two thousand years been duped by a monstrous lie. . . . Darwin requires us to disbelieve the authoritative word of the Creator." Another theological heavyweight declared: "If the Darwinian theory is true, Genesis is a lie, the whole framework of the book of life falls to pieces, and the revelation of God to man, as we Christians know it, is a delusion and a snare."[1]

These gentlemen were right. The theory of evolution does indeed contradict the biblical creation myths and the dogma of the Fall. As the evidence in favor of evolution continued to pile up, fundamentalist churches desperately sought ways to ignore it, or else reconcile the irreconcilable. Pope Paul IV spoke on the subject of evolution in 1966:

> *Such explanations do not agree with the teaching of Sacred Scripture, Sacred Tradition, and the Church's magisterium, according to which the sin of the first man is transmitted to all his descendants not through imitation but through propagation. . . . The theory of evolution will not seem acceptable to you whenever it is not decisively in accord with the immediate creation of each and every human soul by God, and whenever it does not regard as decisively important for the fate of mankind the disobedience of Adam, the universal first parent.*[2]

Origen (Origenes Adamantius) Christian father, ca. 185–254 A.D., an Egyptian who wrote in Greek, exerting a powerful influence on the early Greek church. At first he was accounted a saint, but three centuries after his death he was declared a heretic because of Gnostic elements found in his writings.

Since the theory of evolution can never be "decisively in accord" with the orthodox view, it can never be accepted by the "infallible" church. The orthodox view has remained on the 17th-century level of Father Mersenne who "expressed the opinion of the most enlightened theologians when he declared that orthodoxy did not fear either science or reason, and was quite prepared to accept all their conclusions, 'provided they agreed with the Scriptures.'"[3]

Seventeen hundred years ago, Origen wrote of the Garden of Eden myth: "No one would be so foolish as take this allegory as a description of actual fact."[4] But Origen was excommunicated, and countless millions have been precisely that foolish.

1. White 1, 72, 74, 371. 2. Wickler, xxix. 3. Guignebert, 422. 4. Shirley, 170.

Exorcism

The time-honored custom of ordering demons away, by verbal charms and magical gestures, is still practiced by (1) primitive witch doctors, and (2) the Catholic church. Protestant churches don't exorcise. As far back as 1603 the Church of England forbade ministers to cast out devils, though a present-day Archbishop of Canterbury publicly confessed a belief in "genuine demonic possession" in 1974.[1] The Roman church maintains the office of exorcist, whose rite of ordination states: "An Exorcist must cast out devils."[2] The Official New Catholic Encyclopedia says, "Today the Church maintains its traditional attitude toward exorcism. It recognizes the possibility of diabolical possession, and it regulates the manner of dealing with it. . . . A solemn method of exorcising is given in the Roman Ritual."[3]

This "solemn method" is based on name magic and words of power, like exorcisms used by Egyptian wizards thousands of years ago. It says in part: "I command thee, whosoever thou art, thou unclean spirit, and all thy companions possessing this servant of God, that by the Mysteries of the Incarnation, Passion, Resurrection and Ascension of our Lord Jesus Christ, by the sending of the Holy Ghost, and by the Coming of the same our Lord to judgment, thou tell me thy name, the day, and the hour of thy going out, by some sign; and, that to me, a minister of God, although unworthy, thou be wholly obedient in all things." Exorcistic power of chastity is invoked: "The continence of the Confessors commands thee." Inanimate objects can be exorcised in the same manner, as in the consecration of medals: "I exorcise ye, medals, through God the Father Almighty. . . . May the power of the adversary, all the host of the Devil, all evil attack, every spirit and glamour of Satan, be utterly put to flight and driven far away by the virtue of these medals."[4]

The history of exorcism often demonstrates legalistic-theological buffoonery at its silliest, as in the many instances of insect pests and other vermin verbally assaulted by the exorcist, though paying no discernible attention to the anathemas that threatened them. In 1478 the authorities of Berne addressed a plague of crop-eating insects, "I declare and affirm that you are banned and exorcised, and through the power of Almighty God shall be called accursed and shall daily decrease." The insects, however, only continued to increase. In 1516 the Provost of Troyes commanded all caterpillars to "retire within six days from the vineyards and lands of Villenose, threatening them with his solemn curse and malediction if they failed to obey." The caterpillars apparently weren't listening. From the 16th century onwards, it was a Savoyard custom to excommunicate destructive insects, even though they seemed not to care about being banned from God's congregation. In 1633 the consuls of Strambino summoned the caterpillars "to appear before the bench of reason to show cause why they should not desist from corroding and destroying, under penalty of banishment from the place and confiscation." In 1713 the Friars Minor in Piedade no Maranho, Brazil, claimed that their exorcism of ants worked, and "by God's express order the ants departed to another place."[5]

> *In a process against leeches, which was tried at Lausanne in 1451, a number of leeches were brought into court to hear the notice served against them, which admonished all leeches to leave the district within three days. The leeches, however, proving contumacious and refusing to quit the country, they were solemnly exorcised. . . . The doctors of Heidelberg in particular, then a famous seat of learning, not only expressed their entire and unanimous approbation of the exorcism, but imposed silence on all impertinent meddlers who presumed to speak against it.*[6]

When used against human beings, the process of exorcism proved rather more baneful than absurd, tending to exacerbate the very symptoms it was supposed to relieve. Justification is still being sought for this relic of primitive superstition, because the office exists and a reason must be given for it. But nowadays, "demonic possession" is usually treated by psychiatric therapists, not religious ones. (See **Possession.**)

1. Robbins, 243; Ebon, S.T., 193. 2. Summers, H.W.D. 208. 3. Patai, 139. 4. Summers, H.W.D., 212–13, 216, 223. 5. Frazer, F.O.T., 408–11. 6. Frazer, F.O.T., 408.

Eye

Ayin was the "eye" in the Hebrew sacred alphabet, possibly derived from Aya, the Babylonian Creatress.[5] Islamic Arabs diabolized her and corrupted her name into Ayin, spirit of the evil eye. Moslem Syrians called her *Aina Bisha*, the eye-witch.

The All-Seeing Eye of ancient Egypt once belonged to the Goddess of truth and judgment, **Maat.**[1] The Mother-syllable *Maa* meant "to see"; in hieroglyphics it was an eye.[2]

A late text transferred the All-Seeing Eye to a male god, Horus, and the common symbol came to be known as the Eye of Horus, also representing the phallus as the "One-Eyed God." Yet the same Eye was incongruously described as a female judge: "I am the all-seeing Eye of Horus, whose appearance strikes terror, Lady of Slaughter, Mighty One." [3] The Eye whose appearance strikes terror was the original prototype of the evil eye which, like the petrifying glance of Medusa, was usually associated with women and was feared by simple folk everywhere, up to the present day.

Staring idols of the Neolithic "Eye Goddess" have been found throughout Mesopotamia. In Syria she was known as the Goddess Mari, whose huge eyes searched men's souls.[4]

Like Moslems, Christians diabolized the female spirit of the All-Seeing Eye. Old women were credited with the ancient Goddess's power to "overlook"—to curse someone with a glance. Judges of the Inquisition so greatly feared the evil eyes of their victims that they forced accused witches to enter the court backward, to deprive them of the advantage of a first glance.[6]

Oddly enough, remedies for the evil eye were often female symbols. Necklaces of **cowrie** shells, those ubiquitous yonic symbols, were and are valued in India as charms against the evil eye. The triangle or Yoni Yantra, representing the vulva, is similarly used in India, Greece, and the Balkans. Northern Indian farmers protect crops from the evil eye by hanging Kali's symbol of a black pot in the field. In 18th-century England, the classic witch's familiar, a black cat, was supposed to afford protection; and sore eyes could be cured by rubbing with a black cat's tail.[7] In addition there were many signs, gestures, and other kinds of counter-spells to be used as instant remedies if one suspected having been "overlooked."

It seems men were very much averse to meeting a direct glance from a woman. In the most patriarchal societies, from medieval Japan to Europe, it was customary to insist that "proper" women keep their eyelids lowered in the presence of men. In 19th-century Islamic Iran, it was believed that every woman above the age of menopause possessed the evil eye. Old women were not permitted in crowds attending public appearances of the Shah, lest his sacred person be exposed to an old woman's dangerous look.[8]

Any person invested with spiritual powers. however, could be credited with the power to curse with a look. Several popes were reputed to be bearers of the evil eye or *jettatura.* Pope Pius IX (d. 1878) was a famous *jettatore.* Pope Leo XIII, his successor, was said to have the evil eye because so many cardinals died during his reign.[9]

1. Budge, G.E. 1, 392. 2. Budge, E.L., 55. 3. Cavendish, P.E., 167. 4. Neumann, G.M., 111–12, pl. 87. 5. *Assyr. & Bab. Lit.,* 133–34. 6. Lea unabridged, 831. 7. Gifford, 79–81. 8. Gifford, 47. 9. Budge, A.T., 365.

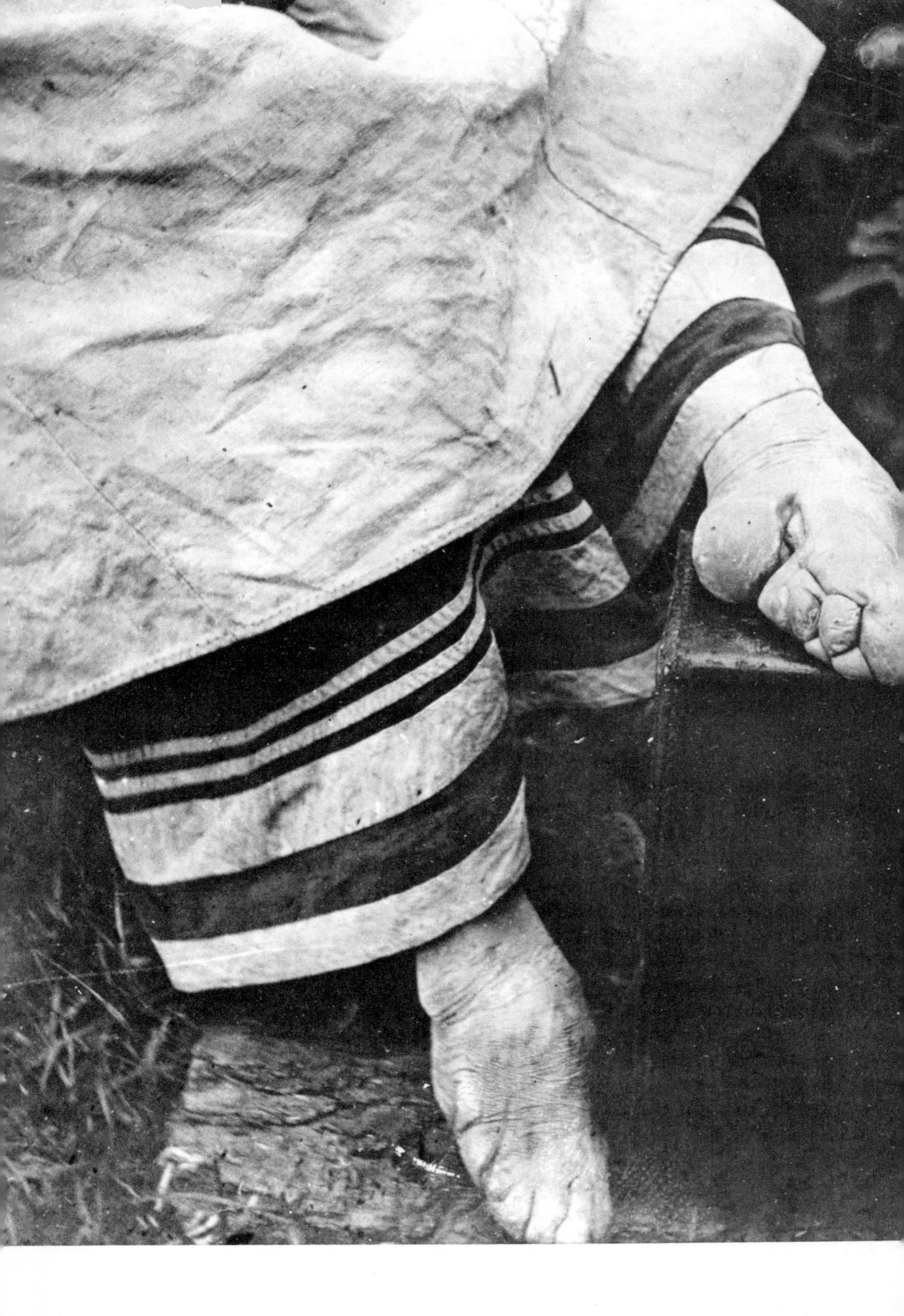

F

Feet of a Chinese woman, disfigured by FOOTBINDING. The custom of breaking the bones and binding the feet was a lifelong process for many aristocratic women. The "dainty" result was the much-admired "lotus hook" instead of a foot. The practice continued up to the beginning of the 20th century.

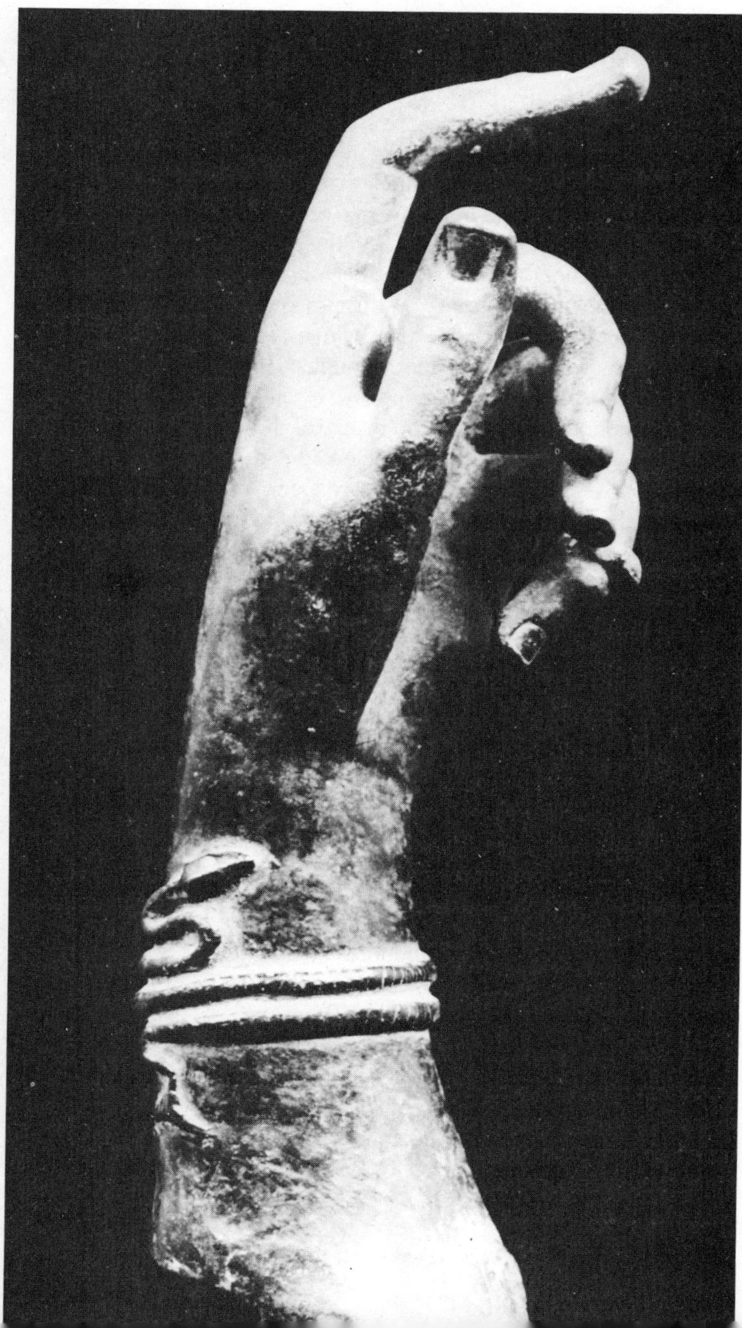

Arm and hand with extended index FINGER. This "mother" finger was the most magical—it guided, beckoned, blessed—and cursed. Etruscan bronze.

Fairies

Pagan gods and goddesses, tribal ancestors, and those who worshipped them all became "fairies" in the traditions of France, Germany, and the British Isles. The Irish still say fairies live in the pagan *sidh* (burial mounds and barrow graves), several hundred of which still stand in the Irish countryside.[1] The Welsh knew their ancestors had a matriarchal society. Like the Irish, they called fairies The Mothers, or The Mother's Blessing; and fairyland was always the Land of Women.[2]

Fairies came out of their fairy hills at Halloween, Celtic folk said, because the hills themselves were tomb-wombs of rebirth according to the ancient belief, and Halloween was only a new name for Samhain, when the dead returned to earth with the help of the priestesses—who, under Christianity, were newly described as witches.[3] Respect for the pagan dead endured to a remarkably late date, even among Christians whose church taught them that the old deities were devils. Cornish miners refused to make the sign of the cross when down in a mine, for fear of offending the fairies in their own subterranean territory by making a gesture that invoked their enemy.[4]

In the *Book of the Dun Cow,* the fairy queen described her realm as "the land of the ever-living, a place where there is neither death, nor sin, nor transgression. We have continual feasts: we practice every benevolent work without contention. We dwell in a large Shee (*sidh*); and hence we are called the people of the Fairy-Mound."[5]

The pagan after-world was a golden "dream time" of long ago, when heroes were deified by sacred marriage with the Goddess. The Great God Lug, father of Ireland's dying savior **Cu Chulainn**, came "out of the chambered undergrounds of Tara where dwell the fourth race of gods who settled Ireland. They are the glorious and golden giants, Tuatha Dé Danann. These people of the goddess Dana first used gold and silver in an Age of Bronze. They first cleared the land, first drained the swamps. They built the great temples of stone like the one they sent to Britain—Stonehenge. When conquered, they retired to their underground barrows or *Sidhe* where they still live today."[6]

The Irish called the fairies' land Tir-nan-og, Land of Ever-Youthful Ones; or Tir-nam-beo, Land of the Ever-Living; or Tir-Tairngiri, Land of Promise; or Tir-na-Sorcha, Land of Light; or Mag Mell, Plain of Pleasures; or Mag Mon, Plain of Sports; or I-Bresail, I-Brazil, or Hy-Brasil, the Land of Bresal, which gave rise to the name of Brazil.[7] Fairyland was also the magic "apple-land" of Avalon, or the Fortunate Isles, or Elf-land, Elphame, Alfheim, or Elvenhome. Sometimes it was the "never-never" land, perhaps after an Egyptian word for paradise, *nefernefer,* "doubly beautiful." The Faroe Islands were once "fairyland" (medieval Norse *Faeroisland*) because the original explorers reached them by sailing west and believed them to be the islands of the dead.[8]

Fairy mounds were entrances to the pagan paradise, which might be located underground, or under water, or under hills on distant islands across the western sea where the sun died.

The fairy queen was obviously the ancient fertility-mother, like Demeter or Ceres. William of Auvergne said in the 13th century she was called Abundia, or Dame Abonde: "Abundance."[9] She was also called Diana, Venus, Hecate, Sybil, or Titania—a title of Cretan Rhea as ruler of the earth-spirits called Titans, predecessors of the Olympian gods. (See **Titania**.) She had all three *personae* of the Triple Goddess, including the death-dealing Crone—which is why an Irish title *Bean-Sidhe,* "Woman of the Fairy-Mounds," was corrupted into **banshee**, the shrieking demoness whose voice brought death. In the form of the triple Morrigan, she sang of blood sacrifices related to springtime renewal of vegetation.[10] A variation on her title was the notorious Morgan le Fay or Morgan the Fairy, also known as the death-goddess, "Morgue la faye."[11]

The *Romance of Lancelot du Lac* spoke of the fairy queen in another incarnation as Lady of the Lake: "The damsel who carried Lancelot to the lake was a fay, and in those times all those women were called fays who had to do with enchantments and charms—and there were many of them then, principally in Great Britain—and knew the power and virtues of words, of stones, and of herbs." Their knights were forbidden to speak their names, for fear of betraying them to Christian persecutors.[12]

Book of the Dun Cow (*Lebar-na-Heera*), so called because the original manuscript was written on vellum made from the skin of a prized cow: a collection of 11th-century Irish tales and poems, compiled by Mailmuri Mac Kelleher.

Secrecy attended many aspects of the fairy-religion, for the very reason that it was carried on clandestinely under a dominant religious system that threatened its practitioners with torture and death. One of the charges that sent Joan of Arc to the stake was that she "adored the Fairies and did them reverence."[13]

A legend repeated by the gypsies said if a man found the statue of a naked *fate* (fairy) in the ruins of pagan temples or tombs, he should embrace it with love and eject semen on it. Then, like Pygmalion's Galatea, the *fate* would come to life in his dreams and tell her lover where to find buried treasure, and she would become his "fortune." He would be happy with her forevermore, provided he agreed never to set foot in a Christian church again as long as he lived.[14]

This idea of the fairy-fortune might be traced all the way back to ancient customs of matrilineal inheritance and matrilocal marriage, characteristic both of Bronze Age myths and of fairy tales. The fairy-tale hero rarely brought a bride to his own home; instead, he left home to seek his "fortune," which usually turned out to be a foreign princess won by trial and wedded in her own country, which the hero afterward helped rule. As in the pre-patriarchal system, a woman was the "fortune" or "fate" of the young man, words which also meant "fairy," through such intermediates as Fata, Fay, Le Fée, or the "fey" one. Fairy and Fate were further related through fear and fair: medieval Latin *fatare,* "to enchant," became French *faer* or *féer.*[15]

Many believed fairies lived in the deep woods where their sacred groves had been hidden from priestly interference. Romanians still speak of the Fata Padourii, Girl of the Woods, a fairy similar to the Irish banshee. At night she makes eerie sounds that portend death to the hearer.[16] In Brittany, where there were many groves dedicated to the Moon-goddess throughout the middle ages, fairies were sometimes called *man-devent,* "Moon-goddesses."[17]

It seems the fairy-religion was practiced secretly through most of the Christian era, especially by women, whose Goddess the patriarchal church kept trying to take away, giving them no substitute but Mary, who lacked the old Goddess's powers.

Certain French leaders of the Old Religion were described as "great princesses who, having refused to embrace Christianity . . . were struck by the curse of God. Hence it is that they are said to be animated by a violent hatred of [Christian] religion and of the clergy." Sometimes they were called Korrigen, Korrig, or Korr, perhaps devotees of the Virgin **Kore**. A Breton lay said: "There are nine Korrigen, who dance, with flowers in their hair, and robes of white wool, around the fountain, by the light of the full moon." They seem to have been old women who used masks or makeup: "Seen at night, or in the dusk of the evening, their beauty is great; but in the daylight their eyes appear red, their hair white, and their faces wrinkled; hence they rarely let themselves be seen by day."[18]

As late as the 17th century it was said there were shrines kept by "a thousand old women" who taught the rites of Venus to young maidens, and instructed them in fairy feats like shape-shifting and raising storms.[19] They were known as *fatuae* or *fatidicae,* "seeresses," or sometimes *bonnes filles,* "good girls."[20]

Norwegian, Scottish, and Irish Christians claimed the fairies were offspring of the fallen angels. Like the non-fallen angels, they carried off souls of the dead. Any who happened to die at twilight, the fairies' hour between day and night, would find themselves in fairyland between life and death, or between heaven and hell.[22] Such legends reflect ancient views of the after-world as without either punishment or reward but only a way-station in the karmic cycle, which is why fairies were like the un-dead—able to emerge from their tombs at will. As **psychopomps**, they were the same as Valkyries or Hindu apsaras, the heavenly nymphs who became *peris,* "fairies," in Middle-Eastern countries where the Old Religion was also maintained as a sub-current in patriarchal culture.

Certainly one of the strongest attractions of the fairy-religion was its permissive view of sexuality, typical of ancient matriarchal societies, living on in contrast to the harsh anti-sexual attitudes of orthodoxy. Fairyland was the heaven of sexy angels, as opposed to the Christian heaven where "bliss" was specifically *not* sexual, not even in matrimony (Matthew 22:30). The fairyland called Torelore in the romance of Aucassin and Nicolette was a home for lovers, as opposed to the Christian heaven of "old priests, and halt old men and maimed." The fairy king lay in bed pretending to give birth to a child, in the ancient rite of couvade (see **Fatherhood**); the queen led an army against their enemies in a bloodless battle, the combatants pelting each other with symbolic foods such as apples, eggs, and cheeses. The king said, "it is nowise our custom to slay each other."[23] (See **Paradise**.)

Toward this paradise the Fairy Queen led her lovers on a "broad, broad road across the lily lea," as Thomas Rhymer's ballad said, which some called the road to heaven, and others the road to hell: a prototype of the famous Primrose Path. The Queen herself was addressed as Queen of Heaven.[24] Sometimes her earthly angels were more spirit than mortal, like the fairies called Little Wood Women

Tasso's list of Fairy-ladies showed them indistinguishable from either Goddesses or witches, for they had names of both, including the titles of Fata, Maga, Incantatrice, or wise-woman. They were Oriana, She of the Mountain; Silvana or Silvanella, She of the Wood; Filidea, She Who Loves the Goddess; Mirinda, the Warrior Woman; Argea, called Queen of Fate; Lucina, called the Lady of the Lake; Urganda, called the Wise One; two Fates or Fays named Dragontina and Montana, and Morgana with her three "daughters," the Morrigan.[21]

Torquato Tasso (1554–1595) Italian poet and dramatist, whose checkered career included periods of residence in courts, convents, and prisons. His major work was an epic on the conquest of Jerusalem.

Aucassin and Nicolette French medieval romance based on an Arabian love story. Aucassin's original name was Al-Kasim.

(*wudu-maer*) in Bavaria, to whom dumplings and other foodstuffs were offered.[25] Yet most sources admitted that the fairies were real live women. Prior wrote, "In Danish ballads fairies are full grown women and not the diminutive beings of our English tales." Said Andrew Lang, "There seems little in the characteristics of these fairies of romance to distinguish them from human beings, except their supernatural knowledge and power. They are . . . usually of ordinary stature, indeed not to be recognized as varying from mankind except by their proceedings."[26] In other words, they were women practicing heathen rites.

1. MacCana, 65. 2. MacCana, 123; Rees, 41. 3. Joyce 1, 264–65. 4. Cavendish, P.E., 242. 5. Joyce 1, 494. 6. Goodrich, 195. 7. Joyce 1, 293. 8. Ramsay, 57. 9. Keightley, 475. 10. Goodrich, 177, 192. 11. Keightley, 45. 12. Keightley, 31, 421. 13. Coulton, 252. 14. Leland, 206. 15. Keightley, 6–7. 16. Cavendish, P.E., 242. 17. Keightley, 427. 18. Keightley, 422, 431–32. 19. Wedeck, 157. 20. Pepper & Wilcock, 166. 21. Keightley, 453–54. 22. Cavendish, P.E., 241. 23. Loomis, 251, 276. 24. Wimberly, 407, 413. 25. Frazer, F.O.T., 312. 26. Wimberly, 170–71.

R.C. Alexander Prior Author of a three-volume work on *Ancient Danish Ballads,* 1860.

Andrew Lang (1844–1912) Scottish folklorist, anthropologist, and collector of fairy tales. He also authored a four-volume *History of Scotland* and a *History of English Literature.*

Faith, Saint

Spurious "virgin martyr," one of the three sisters Saints Faith, Hope, and Charity, daughters of the equally spurious virgin-mother martyr St. **Sophia**. As one personification of these three Virtues, St. Faith really originated as one of the oldest of pagan Goddesses. Her Roman name was Bona Fides, "Good Faith." She was invoked in all legal contracts. Plutarch said her temple was built by the first king of Latium. Virgil said "hoary Faith and Vesta" were Rome's oldest lawgiving Goddesses.[1] Bona Fides did have one of Rome's oldest temples, served by three senior Flamines, the core of the ancient Roman clergy.[2]

In her Christianized form, Faith received a crypt in St. Paul's cathedral in London. Letting their imaginations soar, martyrologists raved over her famous physical beauty.[3] Perhaps because of this, she became a popular patroness of romance. English girls used to pray for a vision of their future husbands, addressing St. Faith after passing a piece of bread three times through a wedding ring.[4]

1. Dumézil, 165, 202, 258. 2. Rose, 250. 3. Brewster, 440. 4. Hazlitt, 373.

Fata Morgana

Medieval term for mirages, illusions, or witch-lights over swamps: "magic" created by the Goddess Morgan, evolved from the primitive **Magog** and sharing many characteristics with the Hindu Maya, creator of "magic." Morgan-the-Fate was often said to be still living in swamps and seacoasts, where she led travelers astray with her illusions. See **Maya**; **Morgan**.

Fata Scribunda

"The Fate Who Writes," Roman title of the Goddess who inscribed each infant's future destiny in her Book of Life shortly after birth.[1] Writing was an attribute of women or Goddesses in the oldest traditions.

1. Gaster, 764.

Fates

Nearly all mythologies bear traces of the Triple Goddess as three Fates, rulers of the past, present, and future in the usual *personae* of Virgin, Mother, and Crone (or Creator, Preserver, Destroyer). The female trinity assumed many different guises in western religion: the Norns or Weird Sisters of the north (from *wyrd*, "fate"), the Zorya of the Slavs, the Morrigan of the Irish, the triple Guinevere or triple Brigit of the Britons.

In Greek myth the three Fates were Horae, Graeae, Muses, Gorgons, Furies, and other trinities as well as the principal trinity of Moerae or Fates. Nearly always, they were weavers. In Anglo-Saxon literature, fate is "woven." Latin *destino* (destiny) means that which is woven, or fixed with cords and threads; fate is "bound" to happen, just as the spells of fairy-women were "binding."[1]

The Moerae were Clotho the Spinner, Lachesis the Measurer, and Atropos the Cutter of life's thread. All were aspects of the archaic Triple Aphrodite, of whom it was said her real name was Moera, and she was older than Time.[2] Moera was actually a late name for the Fate-goddess. In the Mycenaean period it meant a landholding, possessed by a female property owner according to the old matriarchal system. Hence, Moera was a lot: later, "allotted Fate."[3]

Aphrodite's trinity was sometimes divided into three Horae, or celestial nymphs: Eunomia, Dike, and Irene, meaning Order, Destiny, and Peace. These referred to the "ordering" of elements to form the individual; the destiny established for him by the Mother; and the "peace" of dissolution as decreed at the end of life by Aphrodite Columba, the Dove of Peace.[4]

If the weaving Fates could be induced not to cut the thread of life at a perilous moment, the individual would be spared; if not, he would die. Magic charms were often based on this notion. A Slavic charm for healing wounds was addressed to the Fate-weaver on the mystic isle of Bujan, or Buyan, the Goddess's paradise: "In the Ocean-sea, on the isle of Buyan, a fair maiden was weaving silk; she did not leave off weaving silk; the blood ceased flowing."[5] According to Russian myth, this maiden was the Virgin of Dawn, equivalent to the Latin Mater Matuta, or the Greek Eos, traditionally the first Fate. The sun god went to rest on her magic isle, and rose again from it each day.[6]

Other Greek names for the Fate-goddess were Tyche, Dike, and

Nemesis. Romans called her Fortuna; a trinity or a monad. A terracotta medallion from Vienne showed her as a tutelary city-goddess, wearing a mural crown, enthroned in a laurel wreath.[7] As the Babylonian "Mother of Destiny," Fate was named Mammetun, the Creatress.[8] All were based on the primordial Indo-European Mother of Karma, i.e., Kali Ma.

"Fate" was synonymous with "fairy" in the Middle Ages. Alphonsus de Spina placed "Fates" first on his list of devils, remarking: "Some say they have seen Fates, but if so they are not women but demons."[9] Burchardus of Worms complained that the people honored the Fates or Weird Sisters at the beginning of every year, putting offerings of food and drink on a table for them, with three knives for cutting their meat—presumably so the death-dealing Cutter wouldn't be tempted to use her own knife.[10]

Greeks still say the Fates visit the cradle of every newborn, to determine the child's future as his fairy godmothers. Parents used to chain up the watchdog, leave the door open, and set out dainty foods to put the Moerae in a good humor.[11] Many fairy tales give stern lessons in the folly of offending fairy godmothers. Gypsies still say "three ladies in white" stand at the cradle of each child, and take back the soul when life has run its course, like the Three Queens of Arthurian legend. Greek laments for the dead are still called *moirologhia*, giving the deceased back to the Moerae.[12]

1. Cavendish, P.E., 75. 2. Bachofen, 57. 3. Lindsay, A.W., 32.
4. *Larousse*, 138. 5. Wedeck, 50. 6. d'Alviella, 168. 7. Lindsay, O.A., 379.
8. *Epic of Gilgamesh*, 107. 9. Robbins, 127. 10. Miles, 181.
11. Briffault 3, 160. 12. Rose, 40.

Fatherhood

Myths show that, once men understood they could beget children, they wanted many children, because that was the best and easiest way to become a god. Ancestral mothers had been deified by their descendants for countless generations. Patriarchs craved similar nations of descendants, for a tribal ancestor achieved great glory in the afterworld. Men transferred their allegiance from the Great Mother, the original deified ancestress, to gods like Yahweh, on the basis of his promises: "I will make of these a great nation, and I will bless thee, and make thy name great. . . . I will make thee exceeding fruitful, and I will make nations of thee, and kings shall come out of thee" (Genesis 12, 17).

Persians said a man who died childless couldn't enter paradise at all. Prayers and sacrifices of descendants were essential to blessedness for the paternal soul. Hindus defined a son as one whose incantations and offerings kept a father's spirit from wandering homeless and hungry in the waste spaces of eternity. The Brhaddarma Purana said, "No rituals are performed for the man who has no descendants. . . .

Puranas are ancient Sanskrit scriptures in verse, treating of cosmologies, sacred histories, and the nature of the divine.

Sons are useful to give oblations to the ancestors."[1] The Chinese thought if a man had no son, he cut the continuous line of paternal ancestor-worship and lost his chance of becoming immortal.[2]

Fatherhood was largely a ceremonial relationship, with little recognition that men might take an active part in raising their own children. The classical Latin term *paterfamilias,* now connoting a father-of-a-family and household ruler, didn't convey anything like that to the Romans who invented the term:

> *When the ancients invoked Jupiter under that title of* pater *of gods and men, they did not mean that he was their physical father, for they never supposed he was, but on the contrary believed that the human race had existed before he did. The same title was given to Neptune, Apollo, Bacchus, Vulcan and Pluto, whom men certainly did not suppose to be their fathers. . . . Similarly, in legal language, the title of* paterfamilias *could be given to a man who had no children, was not married, was not even old enough to enter upon a marriage . . . ;* pater, *the Latin word cognate to "father" and closest akin to it in meaning, signifies not so much him who has begotten a younger person as him who has natural authority over one inferior in age or status.*[3]

Men or gods began to claim physical fatherhood not so much by an act of begetting, as by a different, ceremonial act designed to imitate the motherly act of birth-giving. (See **Birth-giving, Male**.) In earliest times the imitation was quite literal, like the rite of couvade practiced by primitives to establish paternal rights to a child. While the mother gave birth, the father took to his bed moaning and groaning, and pretended to bring forth the child. Couvade was an initiation ritual for priests of Aphrodite Ariadne at Amathus, where a man dressed in female clothing went through a pantomime of childbirth, to earn the priestly title of "father."[4]

Christian writers said their religion was sent to convert Europe to a patriarchal system in which men could demand respect from their offspring. Before Christianity came to Britain, there was a "great sin" in the structure of the clans: "the father loved not the son, nor the son loved not the father."[5] Early missionaries complained that British tribes paid no attention to the matter of who begot whom; women took lovers as they pleased, and "marital vows are never observed." St. Boniface said the English "utterly despise legitimate matrimony," meaning the kind of matrimony that gave husbands control of property and children.[6]

Eventually, Christianity changed the pagans' casual attitude toward fatherhood. St. Thomas Aquinas laid down the church's official opinion that a father is the true parent, a mother only the "soil" in which the father's "seed" grows. He said a father should be more loved than a mother, because the father's part in giving life to the child is "active," whereas the mother's part is only "passive."[7]

Emphasis on paternity was characteristic of patriarchal societies, where men often tried to pretend that begetting a child was more important than the mother's multi-faceted task of carrying, delivering, nursing, and teaching it all the basic skills of living. In matriarchal Arabia, biological paternity meant nothing. After the coming of Islam, men considered paternity so important that they instituted a year's waiting period between a woman's divorce or widowhood and her remarriage, to make absolutely sure she was not pregnant by the previous husband, since no man wanted his wife giving birth to another man's child.[8] The same waiting period was demanded in Christian Europe, and became so taken for granted that it became "indecent" for a woman to remarry too soon after an earlier husband's departure or death.

One reason for the restrictive, authoritarian atmosphere of patriarchal societies seems to have been that men didn't readily see their children as separate persons, but viewed them as extensions of the father's own ego, therefore requiring strict discipline to make them conform to the pattern. Zimmer says in the language of symbols, son means "double," "alter ego," "living copy of the father," "the father's essence in another individualization."[9] Thus the father's interest in children was more selfish than the mother's.

Harriet Stanton Blatch wrote, "Men talk of the sacredness of motherhood, but judging from their acts it is the last thing that is held sacred. . . . The sense of obligation to offspring, men possess but feebly; there has not been developed by animal evolution an instinct of paternity. They are not disinherited fathers; they are simply unevolved parents. Those who could improve humanity have been hindered by those who prefer to improve steam engines. . . . The sex which has been laboriously evolved by nature for the arduous work of race-building is handicapped." Western patriarchy developed a culture of acquisitiveness, aggression, and hierarchy for the very reason that its underlying philosophy was masculine-selfish, according to Neumann: "This situation of the patriarchate—known to us particularly from its Western development—is characterized by a recession of feminine psychology and its dominants; now feminine existence is almost entirely determined by the masculine world of consciousness and its values."[10]

Harriet Stanton Blatch 20th-century American feminist, daughter of Elizabeth Cady Stanton.

The masculine world of consciousness has been characterized as "barren" and "destructive," insofar as "the fantasies of the single man pervade our popular culture."[11] These focus on self-centered greed, aggression, or defensiveness on behalf of the self, with little comprehension of love, dependence, or responsibility toward future generations. Behavior patterns of the masculine world remind one that the earliest Chinese ideograph for "male" was also a synonym for "selfish."[12]

This culture passes harsh judgment on women who are labeled unfit mothers, because males however "dominant" identify with the child, not the mother. Standards for fathers are not so high. Drunkards, adulterers, child-beaters, even criminals are supposed to have a "right" to fatherhood, to say nothing of millions of men who treat their children with a neglectful indifference that would bring down society's wrath on a female parent. Possibly men should be taught to regard fatherhood as a privilege to be earned, not as a right to be abused.

1. O'Flaherty, 263. 2. Bullough, 247. 3. Rose, 170. 4. Briffault 2, 534. 5. Malory 2, 179. 6. Briffault 3, 418–19. 7. Tuchman, 214. 8. de Riencourt, 189. 9. Zimmer, 109. 10. Neumann, A.P., 87. 11. Gilder, 156. 12. Thorsten, 262.

Fatima

The Arabian Moon-goddess in a Mohammedanized incarnation as Mohammed's fictitious "daughter," who was nevertheless described as "Mother of her father." Her name means The Creatress. She was also known as Source of the Sun, Tree of Paradise, the Moon, and Fate. She existed from the beginning of the material world.[1] In brief, she was really none other than the Great Goddess. Like the virgin Mary, her western counterpart, Fatima was officially demoted to mortality but still kept most of her old titles and powers.[2] See **Arabia**.

1. Campbell, Oc.M., 445–46. 2. Lederer, 181.

Fauna

The Goddess Diana as Mother of Wild Creatures. She had a satyr-consort, Faunus, corresponding to the androgynous Dianus who merged with Diana. The name of Fauna came to mean "animals" because Many-Breasted Diana was supposed to give birth to all animals and nourish them with her numerous breasts, as shown on her famous statue at Ephesus.[1] Another name for Fauna was Bona Dea, the "Good Goddess."[2]

1. Neumann, G.M., pl. 35. 2. *Larousse,* 208.

Febronia, Saint

Mythical martyr credited with the same story as all other mythical female martyrs: rather than impair her virginal purity by marrying a young nobleman who was in love with her, she steadfastly withstood incredible tortures and mutilations in order to die *virgo intacta.* Also like other female martyrs, she was actually a pseudo-canonization of the lascivious Great Goddess, purified for Christian consumption. The original Febronia was Juno Februata, patroness of the passion of love (*febris*), and honored by orgiastic rites in February (see **Valentine**).

Her legend said she was martyred during the reign of Diocletian, but no one ever heard of her until four centuries later when she began to appear in Christian martyrologies.[1]

1. Attwater, 127.

Felix, Saint

A saint with a strange, muddled legend requiring considerable interpretation. St. Felix in Pincus—or, as he was sometimes called, St. Felix of Nola—was said to be a schoolmaster, so cruel that his pupils cordially hated him. When it was discovered that he was a Christian, pagan authorities turned him over to the schoolboys who had suffered at his hands; and they vindictively stabbed him to death with their styluses.[1]

Another St. Felix was credited like Lucifer with the Power of the Air. He blew on the faces of the idols of Mercury, Diana, and Serapis, and they instantly collapsed. Destruction by the power of the breath was also widely attributed to witches.[2]

1. de Voragine, 92. 2. de Voragine, 514; Lea unabridged, 815.

Fenrir

Wolf of the North, a Scandinavian version of the Cynics' north-pole **dog**, who would be loosed at doomsday to swallow the sun. The first month after the winter solstice was named for the Wolf, indicating that Fenrir may have been originally a She-Wolf like the Etruscan Lupa, thought to swallow the old sun and give birth to its reincarnation each year.[1]

1. Brewster, 50.

Feronia

Roman name for the Wolf-mother worshipped by the Sabines before the foundation of Rome itself. Her consort was the old woodland god Soranus, cyclically incarnate in the underground Lord of Death, and the risen sun in heaven. The Feronia festival in honor of the Wolf-mother was faithfully kept each year in Rome. The rites were in the charge of a certain very ancient clan, members of which performed specific miraculous feats passed on from one generation to the next, such as walking on burning coals with bare feet.[1]

1. *Larousse*, 210.

Fig

The Gospels say Jesus cursed the fig tree and made it forever barren because it refused to produce fruit for him out of its season (Mark 11:13-22). The story probably was intended to express hostility to a well-known Goddess-symbol. The fig was always female, its heart-shaped leaves representing "the conventional form of the yoni."[1]

Romans used to celebrate "a rude and curious rite" in connection with the fertilization of Juno Caprotina, Goddess of the Fig Tree, by her lecherous horned goat god.[2]

Jesus's rival deity **Mithra**, whom some called the true Messiah, also was involved with the maternal fig tree. Shortly after his birth from the *petra genetrix*, and his discovery by adoring shepherds, Mithra was adopted by the fig tree, which provided him with a continuous supply of food (fruit) and clothing (leaves).[3] According to the Book of Genesis, fig leaves were the world's first clothing, donned by Adam and Eve as soon as they acquired knowledge. Adoption by a fig tree also figured prominently in the legend of Buddha, protected by the Bodhi Tree, or Tree of Wisdom, *ficus religiosa*, the Holy Fig, when he received his enlightenment on Full Moon Day in the month of May.[4]

The fig was a common Indo-Iranian symbol of the Great Mother. Babylonian Ishtar also took the form of the divine fig tree Xikum, the "primeval mother at the central place of the earth," protectress of the savior Tammuz.[5] Patriachal writers of the Koran later turned Ishtar's tree to Zakkum, the Tree of Hell, growing downward from the earth's underside.[6]

Gaulish gods called Dusii were described in medieval Latin as *ficarii*, "fig-eaters," which meant the same as the Homeric "lotus-eaters," in view of the fact that both the fig and the lotus symbolized female genitals.[7] Anglo-Saxon "fuck" may have been derived from *ficus*, "fig." To this day, Italians make the *mano in fica*, "fig-hand," as a derogatory sexual sign implying, like the raised middle finger, "fuck you." The *mano in fica* was of Oriental origin, a lingam-yoni formed by the thumb projecting between two fingers. Hindus called the fig-hand a sacred *mudra*, and Ovid said Roman householders used it as a protection against evil spells.[8] To Christians however, it was *manus obscenus*, "the obscene hand."[9]

Like other genital symbols, the fig was often incorporated into love charms together with many other items formerly sacred to Venus. Some of these items—blood, bread, doves, and pentacles—joined the fig in a charm from the *Zekerboni*, to make bachelors see their future brides in a dream:

Zekerboni
A treatise on oneiromancy (dream interpretation) by Pierre Mora, manuscript #2790 in the Bibliothèque de l'Arsenal.

> *They must have powdered coral and some fine powdered lodestone, which they shall mix together and dilute with the blood of a white pigeon, and they shall make a dough of it, which they shall enclose in a large fig after having wrapped it in blue taffeta; they shall hang this round their neck, and when they go to bed shall put the pentacle for Saturday under their bolster, saying a special prayer the while.*[10]

1. King, 28. 2. Rose, 217. 3. Hooke, S.P., 85. 4. Ross, 88; Wilkins, 45. 5. Harding, 48. 6. Campbell, Oc.M., 430. 7. Knight, D.W.P., 153. 8. Dumézil, 367. 9. Gifford, 90. 10. de Givry, 325.

Fingers

The Dactyls—"Fingers"—were spirits born from the fingerprints of the Goddess Rhea: five males from the print of her right hand, five females from the print of her left hand.[1] Their Greek name was derived from Sanskrit Daksa, "dextrous one," a Hindu god of the hand.

Mano pantea, the Hand of the All-Goddess, was a sacred fetish of which many examples have been found in the ruins of Pompeii and Herculaneum.[2] It always showed the thumb and first two fingers raised, the last two fingers folded down. Middle finger, index finger, and thumb invoked pagan trinities of Father-Mother-Son, such as Jupiter-Juno-Mars, or Osiris-Isis-Horus. The same kind of trinity, consisting of God, Mary, and Jesus, used to be worshipped by eastern Christians—which may explain why Christianity adopted the *mano pantea* and renamed it "the hand of blessing."[3] The gesture was displayed by Christian priests and by emperors or kings by way of benediction and expression of their own union with the land.[4]

The thumb was the child, or child-soul symbolized in such fables as *Hop-O-My-Thumb*. The index finger was the Mother, the one who pointed, controlled, cast spells. The middle finger was the Father, a phallic symbol for thousands of years, up to and including the present day.

Arabs used to cut open a vein of the middle finger with a stone knife when making a pledge of faith, invoking a curse of castration if the pledge be broken.[5] Roman male prostitutes used to signal potential customers by thrusting the middle finger into the hair of their heads.[6] Like all widely recognized phallic symbols, the middle finger was associated with the devil by Christian authorities, who referred to it as *digitus infamis*, "the vile finger." When the torturers asked accused witches which finger they raised to take the devil's oath, the only "right" answer they would accept was the middle finger.[7] It was considered evil to wear a ring on the middle finger, for reasons plainly associated with its sexual meanings.[8]

Oddly enough, the classic finger-sign of the devil didn't use the middle finger at all, but displayed his "horned head" by pinning down the middle and fourth fingers with the thumb and extending the index and little fingers. On the well-known magic principle that an evil sign was prophylactic against evil, this gesture was often used in Italy and the Balkans as a defense against the evil eye. Like most European symbols, it seems to have originated with Kali Ma, who showed it as a *mudra* (sacred gesture) in her manifestation as Jagadamba, "Mother of the World."[9] Probably it was meant to signify her own horned head embodied in the sacred cow.

The most revered *mudra* was the one meaning "infinity" or "perfection," and most generally associated with female genitalia: thumb and forefinger pressed together at the tips, the other three fingers extended—our modern OK sign.[10] Tantric yogis and bodhisattvas made this gesture in token of contemplative ecstasy.[11] Persian sacred amulets of the Sassanian period (3rd century B.C.) showed a hand in this position, flanked by horns of fertility.[12] The joined thumb and index finger formed a *vesica piscis,* immemorial symbol of the yoni, while the three extended fingers perhaps referred to the Goddess's trinity.

Western Europe inherited the Egyptian idea that the index and middle fingers stood for the mother and father, respectively. Egyptian mummies were buried with a protective amulet invoking both parents, called the Amulet of the Two Fingers.[13] The index or "mother" finger was the most magical. This was the finger that guided, showed, beckoned, called for attention, blessed, and cursed.

Medieval Christians feared the pointing of a witch's index finger, which is why children are still taught that it's rude to point, and why a woman's characteristic scolding gesture brandishes the index finger like a weapon. In Tantric tradition, this mother-finger was known as "the threatening finger."[14] All Indo-European traditions knew it was female. Arabs said the index finger represents the Goddess **Fatima**, whose symbolic Hand is still revered as a mystic summary of "the whole religion of Islam."[15]

Jewish patriarchs insisted on fettering a woman's threatening, spell-casting right index finger with the wedding ring, and orthodox Jewish women wear a wedding ring on that finger to this day. Christians, however, copied their wedding-ring custom from the pagans, who said a mystic "love vein" ran directly from the fourth finger of the left hand to the heart, therefore this finger should be bound in marriage. Macrobius wrote that a woman's wedding ring should be placed on that finger "to prevent the sentiments of the heart from escaping."[16]

There was a universal prejudice against cutting fingernails without careful disposal, lest fingernail pairings be used in malignant spells against their former owner. Norse myth said the doomsday ship Naglfar was made of dead men's fingernails, so "if a man dies with his nails unshorn he is adding greatly to the materials for Naglfar" and bringing doomsday that much closer.[17] Hence the custom of manicuring corpses.

1. Graves, G.M. 1, 185. 2. Gifford, 92. 3. Ashe, 206. 4. Strong, 90.
5. Johnson, 119. 6. G.R. Scott, 108. 7. Robbins, 106. 8. Budge, A.T., 304.
9. Rawson, A.T., 50. 10. Legman, 526. 11. *Larousse*, 365. 12. Budge, A.T., 126.
13. Budge, E.M., 55. 14. *Mahanirvanatantra*, 29. 15. Budge, A.T., 304.
16. de Lys, 287–88. 17. Branston, 278.

Firmament

The Hebrew word for firmament meant "a sheet of hammered metal."[1] Sometimes this was called "the heaven of brass." The Bible gives the ancient notion that the heaven was the bottom of a vast cistern, holding "the waters which were above the firmament" (Genesis 1:7)—i.e., rain.

According to this primitive notion, the rain fell down when angels opened the "windows of heaven" to let some of the water out of the enormous cistern. Canaanite and early Jewish temples had magic windows in the roof, supposed to be models of the celestial windows, since everything about a temple was meant to copy the cosmos, not only symbolically but literally. When rain was needed, the magic windows were opened, and this was believed to cause a corresponding action in the celestial region.[2] This is why the Bible says God sent Noah's flood by opening all the windows of heaven at once (Genesis 7:11).

The biblical firmament of brass was based on an ancient Oriental image of the house of Varuna, located in the zenith. It was a "house of many mansions," corresponding to Jesus's description of his father's heaven (John 14:2). It had a thousand doors through which the light of the celestial regions could shine, forming the stars.[3] These were transmuted by biblical writers into the windows of heaven.

1. Gaster, 6. 2. *Larousse,* 79. 3. Campbell, Or.M., 177.

Firstborn

Most Asiatic gods claimed the title of Firstborn of the Womb, in Sanskrit **Hiranyagarbha**. Each priesthood wanted its own god to be "firstborn" of the Creatress, because her eldest child would wield natural authority over the others. Since it was impossible for more than one god to be *the* Firstborn, scholars simply used the title and claimed each god was the firstborn of one of the Great Mother's virgin emanations.

The classic example was the Buddha, born in many incarnations, each time as a "firstborn" of the Goddess's earthly representative, a temple maiden or *devadasi,* "Virgin Bride of God," bearing the name (and spirit) of Maya, the virgin aspect of Mother Kali. As in all myths of divine births, the maiden might have an earthly husband, but he didn't lie with her until after she brought forth her firstborn child, who was the son of God, or, in Buddha's case, the son of Ganesha, the Lord of Hosts.[1]

The actual mechanism of these divine impregnations was quite literal. The virgin mother-to-be deflowered herself by straddling the sacred lingam—the god's erect penis—and allowing it to penetrate her.[2] While thus conceiving the god's son, the virgin placed a wreath of flowers on the head of his image, a symbolic act reminiscent of the ancient Indian **svayamara** ceremony.[3] The wreath was her own genital symbol; the god's "head" was his. The god's head and the head of his lingam were both anointed with holy oil for the sacred marriage, certainly a logical necessity for inserting a stone shaft into a vagina. The custom—and the temple phalli—were standard throughout the Middle East and the Mediterranean world, where the holy oil was known as *chrism,* and the priapic god was therefore a *Christos* or "Anointed One."

In the Middle East, Maya became Maia, Mari, or Mary, another "virgin bride of God" who served as a temple maiden or *kadesha,* the equivalent of the Hindu *devadasi.* According to the classic Indo-European pattern, the angel of the Lord "came in unto" Mary (Luke 1:28), which was the biblical term for sexual intercourse; and her husband Joseph "knew her not until she had brought forth her firstborn son" (Matthew 1:25).

Divinely begotten firstborn children were *sacer*—singled out for a special fate—from the earliest times, when first fruits of all kinds were offered to the same deities supposed to have given them. Firstborn sons embodied the god, became the god, and were offered to the god. A mass sacrifice of firstborn sons in Egypt, to appease the deities during a severe drought, was recorded in the Old Testament by Jewish scribes who revised the legend to claim their own Yahweh was responsible for killing the Egyptian children (Exodus 12:29).

Actually, Egyptian firstborn-sacrifice came from very ancient traditions. The *Book of the Dead* said, "On the day of hacking in pieces the firstborn . . . the mighty ones in heaven light the fire under the cauldrons where are heaped up the thighs of the firstborn."[4] Under the later dynasties these may have been animal sacrifices, but the hieroglyphic sign of the "thighs" showed human legs, not animal legs. The Bible says Yahweh copied the act of Egypt's "mighty ones in heaven," and sent out fire to consume the sons of Aaron on the altar (Leviticus 10:2).

Like an Egyptian god, Yahweh told his priests: "Sanctify unto me all the firstborn, whatsoever openeth the womb among the children of Israel, both of man and of beast; it is mine" (Exodus 13:2). Firstborn children were offered on Yahweh's altars until priests began to permit redemption of the child by offering a lamb instead (Exodus 13:15). Thus the paschal lamb of the Passover legend was really a substitute for the son, just as the ram who replaced Isaac on Yahweh's altar also represented a transition from human to animal sacrifice (Genesis 22:9–13). The story of Isaac and the ram probably was copied from the Boeotian myth of the king's firstborn son Phrixus, who was to be sacrificed on the altar, when the ram of the Golden Fleece miraculously appeared as a substitute victim.[5]

Yahweh's acceptance of an animal sacrifice in place of a human one didn't necessarily mean he was more humane than contemporary gods elsewhere. Long before the period allotted to Abraham, Oriental nations had been offering animals instead of human victims.[6] Indeed, the Jews seem to have clung to the older custom for a longer time than most of their contemporaries. They ignored Hadrian's prohibition of human sacrifice, and continued in secret to sustain their god on human blood, as in the rites of the Essenic *Christos.*[7] See **Virgin Birth**.

Romans may have given up human sacrifice, but they had not given up the ceremony of firstborn-conception. Roman brides routinely deflowered themselves on the carved phalli of Hermes, Tutunus, Priapus, or some other "anointed" god before lying with their bridegrooms, so their firstborn children would be god-begotten.[8] It was common everywhere to refer to firstborn children as "born by the grace of God."[9]

Fathers of the Christian church deplored the custom, because it made an everyday event of the birth of a *Christos* which they preferred to consider miraculous. St. Augustine denounced Roman women for encouraging young brides to "come and sit on the masculine monstrosity representing Priapus." The women, he said, viewed this custom as "very honest and religious."[10] Lactantius explained that the idea of the ceremony was to render the bride fruitful "by her communion with the divine nature."[11]

Lactantius Firmianus (ca. 250–330 A.D.) Early Christian writer and church father; tutor to Crispus, the eldest son of Constantine I.

After the "divine nature" of these priapic gods was declared a devilish nature, yet the ceremony may have persisted, as indicated by medieval witches' description of intercourse with the devil. They claimed his penis was hard and cold, and his body was "cold all over, like a creature of stone."[12] Such a "devil" could well have been a creature of stone in fact—that is, a statue of Priapus or one of the other phallic gods, believed to beget **Antichrist** in the classical manner, as the firstborn of a virgin mother.

1. *Larousse,* 332. 2. Rawson, E.A., 29. 3. Legman, 661. 4. *Book of the Dead,* 94. 5. Graves, G.M. 1, 229. 6. Robertson, 36. 7. Cumont, O.R.R.P., 119. 8. Simons, 77. 9. Briffault 3, 231. 10. Goldberg, 51. 11. Knight, D.W.P., 103. 12. H. Smith, 273.

Fish

A world-wide symbol of the Great Mother was the pointed-oval sign of the yoni, known as *vesica piscis,* Vessel of the Fish. It was associated with the "Fishy Smell" that Hindus made a title of the yonic Goddess herself, because they said women's genitals smelled like fish.[1] The Chinese Great Mother Kwan-yin ("Yoni of yonis") often appeared as a fish-goddess.[2] As the swallower of Shiva's penis, Kali became Minaksi the "fish-eyed" one, just as in Egypt, Isis the swallower of Osiris's penis became Abtu, the Great Fish of the Abyss.[3]

Vesica piscis

Fish and womb were synonymous in Greek; *delphos* meant both.[4] The original Delphic oracle first belonged to the abyssal fish-goddess under her pre-Hellenic name of Themis, often incarnate in a great fish, whale, or dolphin (*delphinos*). The cycles in which she devoured and resurrected the Father-Son entered all systems of symbolism from the Jews' legend of Jonah to the classic "Boy on the Dolphin." Apuleius said the Goddess playing the part of the Dolphin was Aphrodite Salacia, "with fish-teeming womb."[5]

Her "boy" was Palaemon, the reincarnated young sun, made new after sinking into the same abyssal womb as the dying god Heracles.[6] The fish-goddess Aphrodite Salacia was said to bring "salacity" through orgiastic fish-eating on her sacred day, Friday. The Catholic church inherited the pagan custom of Friday fish-eating and pretended it was a holy fast; but the disguise was thin. Friday was *dies veneris* in Latin, the Day of Venus, or of lovemaking: Freya's Day in Teutonic Europe. The notion that fish are "aphrodisiac" food is still widespread even today.

The Celts thought fish-eating could place new life in a mother's womb. Their hero Tuan was eaten in fish form by the Queen of Ireland, who thus re-conceived him and gave him a new birth.[7] In another myth, fish were associated with the clots of "wise blood" emanating from the Mother-tree with its sacred fountain, in Fairyland.[8] They were called blood-red nuts of the Goddess Boann, eaten by "salmon of knowledge" who swam in her sacred fountain. "Poets and story-tellers, speaking of any subject difficult to deal with, often say, 'Unless I had eaten the salmon of knowledge I could not describe it.'"[9]

The fish symbol of the yonic Goddess was so revered throughout the Roman empire that Christian authorities insisted on taking it over, with extensive revision of myths to deny its earlier female-genital meanings. Some claimed the fish represented Christ because Greek *ichthys*, "fish," was an acronym for "Jesus Christ, Son of God." But the Christian fish-sign was the same as that of the Goddess's yoni or Pearly Gate: two crescent moons forming a *vesica piscis*. Sometimes the Christ child was portrayed inside the *vesica*, which was superimposed on Mary's belly and obviously represented her womb, just as in the ancient symbolism of the Goddess.

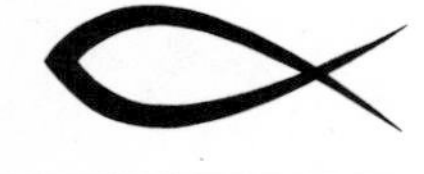

Fish

A medieval hymn called Jesus "the Little Fish which the Virgin caught in the Fountain."[10] Mary was equated with the virgin Aphrodite-Mari, or Marina, who brought forth all the fish in the sea. On the Cyprian site of Aphrodite's greatest temple, Mary is still worshipped as Panaghia Aphroditessa.[11] In biblical terms, "Jesus son of Maria" meant the same as Yeshua son of Marah, or Joshua son of Nun (Exodus 33:11), which also means son of the Fish-mother. Mary's many Mesopotamian names like Mari, Marriti, Nar-Marratu, Mara, were written like the Hebrew *Mem* with an ideogram meaning both "sea" and "mother."[12] The next letter in the Hebrew sacred alphabet was *Nun*, "fish."

Another biblical name for the Goddess was Mehitabel, none other than the Egyptian Fish-mother Mehit in a Hebrew disguise.[13]

1. Campbell, C.M., 13. 2. Goldberg, 98. 3. Campbell, Or.M., 149. 4. Briffault 3, 150. 5. Neumann, A. P., 6. 6. Graves, G. M. 2, 102. 7. Spence, 94. 8. Briffault 2, 631. 9. Joyce 1, 439; Squire, 55. 10. Harding, 58. 11. Ashe, 192. 12. Hooke, M.E.M., 24. 13. Budge, D.N., 151.

Flidhais

Celtic name for the woodland Goddess in the form of a hind or doe; Diana as the White Hind of numerous early-medieval romances. She nurtured many heroes and led them on mystic adventures. When they died she took them to the fairyland that the Norse called Hinder-fjall (Hind-Mountain).[1] Often they grew horns and became stag-gods.

1. Turville-Petre, 199.

Flood

The biblical flood story, the "deluge," was a late offshoot of a cycle of flood myths known everywhere in the ancient world. Thousands of years before the Bible was written, an ark was built by Sumerian Ziusudra. In Akkad, the flood hero's name was Atrakhasis. In Babylon he was Uta-Napishtim, the only mortal to become immortal. In Greece he was Deucalion, who repopulated the earth after the waters subsided, with the help of his wife Pyrrha and the advice of the Great Goddess of the waters, Themis. In Armenia, the hero was Xisuthros—a corruption of Sumerian Ziusudra—whose ark landed on Mount Ararat.[1]

According to the original Chaldean account, the flood hero was told by his god, "Build a vessel and finish it. By a deluge I will destroy substance and life. Cause thou to go up into the vessel the substance of all that has life." Technical instructions followed: the ark was to be 600 cubits long by 60 wide, with three times 3600 measures of asphalt on its exterior and the same amount inside. Three times 3600 porters brought chests of provisions, of which 3600 chests were for the hero's immediate family, while "the mariners divided among themselves twice three thousand six hundred chests."[2] It seems that Noah's ark was much smaller than earlier heroic proportions.

Cubit From Latin *cubitum,* "elbow"; the length of an average hand and forearm from the tip of the middle finger to the elbow (about 18-21 inches).

As long ago as 1872, George Smith translated the Twelve Tablets of Creation from Ashurbanipal's library, and discovered the earlier version of the flood myth.[3] Among the details that religious orthodoxy took care to suppress was the point that the god who caused the flood was disobedient to the Great Mother, who didn't want her earthly children drowned. Mother Ishtar severely punished the disobedient god by cursing him with her "great lightnings." She set her magic rainbow in the heavens to block his access to offerings on earthly altars, "since rashly he caused the flood-storm, and handed over my people to destruction."[4]

Ashurbanipal King of Assyria ca. 669–630 B.C., military leader and statesman. He collected at Nineveh a large library of cuneiform texts, rediscovered by archeologists in the 19th century A.D.

Old Testament writers copied other details of the ancient flood myth but could not allow their god to be punished by the Great Whore of Babylon, as if he were a naughty child sent to bed without supper by an angry mother. Thus, they transformed Ishtar's rainbow barrier into a "sign of the covenant" voluntarily set in the heavens by God himself (Genesis 9:13).

The Tigris-Euphrates valley was subject to disastrous floods. One especially was long remembered; geologists have linked it with the volcanic cataclysm that blew apart the island of Thera (Santorin) and destroyed Cretan civilization. When Sir Leonard Woolley was excavating the site of Ur, he found the track of a mighty flood—a layer of clay without artifacts, eight feet thick.[5] Such a flood may have been identified with the watery Chaos that all Indo-European peoples believed would swallow up the world at the end of its cycle, and out of which a new world would be reborn in the womb of the Formless Mother.[6] The ark and its freight represented seeds of life passing through the period of Chaos from the destruction of one universe to the birth of the next. Even in the Bible, the "birth" was heralded by the Goddess's yonic dove (Genesis 8:12).

Gnostic literature preserved the older view of the flood-causing God as an evil destroyer of humanity, and the Goddess as its preserver. Because people refused to worship him alone, jealous Jehovah sent the flood to wipe out all life. Fortunately the Goddess opposed him, "and Noah and his family were saved in the ark by means of the sprinkling of light that proceeded from her, and through it the world was again filled with humankind."[7]

This Gnostic interpretation had both Babylonian and Hellenic roots. Greeks said the primal sea-mother Themis gave Deucalion and his wife occult knowledge ("light") of how to create human beings from stones, "the bones of their Mother," i.e., of the earth.[8] Raising up living people from stones or bones was a popular miracle. Jesus mentioned it, and Ezekiel's God claimed to have done it in the valley of bones (Ezekiel 37).

1. Graves, G.M. 1, 142; Hooke, M.E.M., 130. 2. Lethaby, 239. 3. Ceram, 314. 4. *Assyr. & Bab. Lit.*, 357; *Epic of Gilgamesh*, 112. 5. Ceram, 353. 6. Avalon, 233. 7. Pagels, 55. 8. Graves, G.M. 1, 139.

Flora

Lactantius Firmianus (ca. 250–330 A.D.) early Christian writer and church father; tutor to Crispus, the eldest son of Constantine I.

Roman Goddess of spring, "The Flourishing One," annually honored at the May Day festival called Floralia. Lactantius noted with distaste that Flora was "a Lady of Pleasure," but she was prominent and important in Roman religion. Some said her name was the secret soul-name of Rome itself.[1]

St. Augustine and other fathers of the church abominated Flora and her festival, which, they said, was a licentious orgy of nude dancing and promiscuous behavior.[2]

1. J.H. Smith, D.C.P., 225. 2. G.R. Scott, 68.

Fly

Popular soul-symbol in many ancient religions, due to a primitive belief that women could conceive children by swallowing a fly bearing the soul of a previously deceased person. Virgin mothers of Celtic heroes—Etain, **Cu Chulainn**—conceived in this way.[1] Greeks similarly believed souls could travel from one life to the next in insect form;

the very word for soul, *psyche*, meant a butterfly. In the Middle East, **Baal-Zebub** or Beelzebub was "Lord of Flies" because he was a **psychopomp**; his title really meant Lord of Souls.

Behind such images can be seen an archaic mode of thought, predating the discovery of fatherhood, when men evolved various crude theories to explain the mystery of how a fetus came to be in a woman's body.[2]

1. Spence, 95–6. 2. Neumann, A.C.U., 11; Stone, 11.

Flying Ointment

A drug like aconite was probably responsible for the report that witches flew through the air with the heathen Goddess Diana, covering vast distances between sunset and cockcrow.[1] A Dominican friar, Father Nider, said two of his brethren witnessed a witch's trip to the sabbat, which turned out to be a drug trip only. She rubbed her body with an ointment, then lay down in a kneading-trough and passed into a state of delirium, thrashing about, and muttering of Venus and the devil. When she returned to her senses, the friars told her she had been to a meeting of devils and witches. On another occasion, Pope Julius III's chief astrologer experimentally rubbed a woman's body with witch-salve composed of hemlock, mandrake, henbane, and belladonna. She went into a coma lasting 36 hours and experienced many hallucinations.[2]

Professor H. S. Clarke recently noted that many drugs used by witches were known to cause such effects. Aconite disturbs the heartbeat and produces peculiar sensations, including dizziness or a sensation of flying. Belladonna produces delirium. Hemlock causes excitement and later paralysis. "Rubbing such ointments into the skin would intensify any physiological properties." These drugs, not the fat of boiled children that churchmen deemed essential, made the "magic" of witches' flying ointment.[3]

Professor H. S. Clarke Author of an appendix to Margaret Murray's *Witch Cult in Western Europe,* 1921.

Oil was the vehicle for a flying ointment of Roman witches, according to Lucian, who described a woman transforming herself into a night-raven by rubbing her body with holy oil, then flying away through the window.[4] The flying journey to heaven was the primary component of any magical initiation; it could be induced by ointment, or by eating the body of a god. By eating the flesh of Osiris in the form of bread, an initiate could become an Osiris and ascend to heaven, and "in one little moment pass over limitless distances which would need millions and hundreds of thousands of years for a man to pass over."[5]

Though ascent to heaven via a god's eaten body was certainly a central Christian doctrine, the church declared it a sin to believe it could be done by the living, with the help of a non-Christian deity. Up to the middle of the medieval period, the church said the flights of witches were wholly imaginary, and it was heresy to believe them real. After the Inquisition took shape, the church said the flights of witches were real, and it was heresy to believe them imaginary.

The earlier opinion appeared in the Canon Episcopi, written by a secretary of the Archbishop of Trier about 900 A.D., though it was passed off as a canon of the 4th-century Council of Ancyra; its fraudulence was demonstrated centuries later. It told Christians to reject the "demonic illusions" that made women think they flew through the night air with the pagan Goddess Diana.[6] When the church's opinion was reversed in the 13th century, those who doubted the witches' flights were said to "sin in the lack of true reverence to our mother the church."[7]

Supported by plenty of "evidence" from the torture chamber, the useful theory of witches' flights could account for the fact that no one ever saw the vast assemblages, allegedly coming together from great distances, to the devilish sabbat.[8] It could also account for the prison suicides of victims who beat their heads against their cell walls until they died, to avoid further torture. The inquisitor Bodin said witches left unbound between sessions in the torture chamber often dashed themselves against the wall and broke their necks because they tried to fly away with Diana or Minerva.[9]

Many women confessed under torture that they dug up children's corpses to make their flying ointment. On one occasion at Lindheim, six women confessed to this crime and were sentenced to the stake. The family of one of the women instituted an investigation of the grave in question, where the child's body was discovered intact. The inquisitors smoothly explained that the devil had reassembled the body to cause confusion. The witches were burned on schedule.[10]

1. Kramer & Sprenger, 104. 2. Castiglioni, 249–50. 3. Robbins, 364, 366. 4. Budge, E. M., 204. 5. *Book of the Dead,* 499. 6. J. B. Russell, 76. 7. Robbins, 74, 514. 8. Arens, 185. 9. Scot, 16. 10. Castiglioni, 249.

Focus

Latin for "hearth," the first altar, and center of early tribal life.[1] Goddess of the *focus* was Vesta (Greek Hestia), whose priestesses tended a perpetual fire that was bound up with the soul of Rome. It was believed the altar of Vesta was the center of the universe. The cult arose from Neolithic views of matrilocal power radiating from the home center of the clan, with the matriarch as high priestess and religious ceremonies centering on her hearth.[2]

1. Funk, 353. 2. Potter & Sargent, 201.

Footbinding

Strange erotic custom of medieval China, practiced for a thousand years, up to the beginning of the 20th century, even exerting some influence on western Europe where women were often praised in romantic literature for having the tiniest possible feet.

Crippling of the Chinese girl began at the age of five or six. Footbinding was a lifelong torment that slowly broke bones and deformed the flesh until the full "beauty" of the atrophied, three-inch "lotus hook" was achieved. Many women died of suppuration and gangrene before the desired effect was complete.

Chinese men were conditioned to intense fetishistic passion for deformed female feet. Chinese poets sang ecstatic praises of the lotus feet that aroused their desire to fever pitch. The crippled woman was considered immeasurably charming by reason of her vulnerability, her suffering, and her helplessness—she couldn't even escape an attacker by running away.[1]

Westerners sometimes imagined that footbinding produced a well-shaped but miniaturized foot. Actually, it bore little resemblance to a normal foot. The four smaller toes were folded completely under the sole; then the whole foot was folded so the underside of the heel and toes were brought together. The victim had to keep her feet tightly bandaged forever; letting them spread again would cause even worse pain.

1. See Levy.

Forgery

Documentary foundations of the Christian church's temporal powers were often forged, including the crucial Petrine doctrine of the keys (see **Peter, Saint**). Notable among later forgeries were the Decretals of St. Isidore, alleged canons and decrees of the papacy from apostolic times to the 8th century A.D., upholding papal claims to authority over European nations. These documents were first composed in France about the year 850 A.D., though they pretended to date from the earliest foundations of the church.

Cardinal Nicholas of Cusa patiently investigated the Decretals in the 15th century and found them to be clumsy forgeries full of anachronisms and garbled history.[1] The church refused to acknowledge that its traditional privileges were founded on false documents. The works of subsequent scholars revealing the deception were banned and their authors persecuted. Apologists who tried to explain away the forgery were rewarded with ecclesiastical preferments. In 1628, when Blondel published irrefutable proof of the Decretals' fraudulence, his work was promptly placed on the Index of Prohibited Books.

Among the False Decretals was the so-called Donation of Constantine, whereby Pope Sylvester I and his successors were granted temporal as well as spiritual dominion over the entire empire, and the fiefdoms of the Papal States were established. According to this document, Constantine made the pope the greatest feudal lord in Italy: "Wherefore, that the pontifical crown may be maintained in dignity,

Index of Prohibited Books (Index Librorum Prohibitorum) The first official edition appeared in 1559, though ecclesiastical authorities censored, condemned, and destroyed various kinds of books from the earliest centuries of the Christian era. Catholics were forbidden to read any books listed on the Index, which was regularly updated. Observation of this prohibition was obligatory up to 1966, when Pope Paul VI suppressed the Index.

we hand over and relinquish our palaces, the City of Rome, and all the provinces, places, and cities of Italy and the regions of the West to the most blessed pontiff and Universal Pope, Sylvester." But the real composer of the Donation, a papal official named Christophorus, made serious historical mistakes. He made Constantine call himself conqueror of the Huns, fifty years before they appeared in Europe. He called the bishop of Rome "pope" two hundred years before the title was used.[2]

Lorenzo Valla proved the spurious nature of the Donation as early as 1440. He wrote: "Even if it had been genuine, it would by now have been rendered void by the crimes alone of the Papacy, through whose avarice Italy has been plunged in constant war."[3] The church refused to admit the fraud until nearly four centuries later. A Greek saying was that the chief industry of papal Rome was fabrication of false documents. After setting the precedent, "Nearly every pontificate will add its supplement of false documents to this formidable *corpus* whence the theologians, St. Thomas Aquinas among them, will for a long period confidently derive the justification for whatever the Roman Pontiffs may desire to do or say."[4] The Gospels themselves were forged as required to uphold privileges and practices of the early church. "We must never forget that the majority of the writings of the New Testament were not really written or published by those whose names they bear."[5]

After burning books and closing pagan schools, the church dealt in another kind of forgery: falsification by omission. All European history was extensively edited by a church that managed to make itself the sole repository of literary and historical records. With all important documents assembled in the monasteries, and the lay public rendered illiterate, Christian history could be forged with impunity.

1. White 2, 314. 2. Chamberlin, B. P., 14–15. 3. Chamberlin, B. P., 166. 4. Guignebert, 249. 5. Stanton, 106.

David Blondel
Theologian who wrote *Pseudo-Isidorus et Turrianus Vapulantes* (Geneva, 1628) to demonstrate the spurious nature of earlier defenses of the False Decretals.

Lorenzo Valla
15th-century Italian humanist and critic of the church, employed as a secretary to King Alfonso V of Siciliy, who protected Valla from the Inquisition. Later, he was reconciled to the papacy and even appointed an apostolic secretary by Pope Nicholas V.

Fork

"Furka" or "fork" described the so-called lost letter of the Greek alphabet, *digamma,* a double gamma having the sound of F. Its Sanskrit name was *forkwas,* linguistic root of the two trees on which dying gods were sacrificed: Norse *fyr* (fir) and Latin *quercus* (oak).[1] The Egyptian furka was the Y-shaped cross on which the god Set was crucified. It was also a phallic symbol of the god's sacred marriage.[2] The "thieves' cross" in Christian iconography had the same shape. Such crosses flanking Jesus's cross may have represented sacred marriage. The Y-shaped fork was sometimes regarded as a female genital symbol, in conjunction with the male trident or three-pronged fork.[3]

Furka

The voodoo savior-god Legba characteristically used as his crutch a derivative of the sacred furka of Set.[4]

1. Potter & Sargent, 230. 2. Campbell, M. I., 29. 3. de Lys, 233. 4. Martello, 164.

Fortune

The Roman Triple Goddess of Fate had many "Fortune" titles: Fortuna Primigeneia, the Firstborn; Fortuna Muliebris, Goddess of Women; Fortuna Scribunda, the Fate Who Writes; Fortuna Regia, Goddess of Rulership; Bona Fortuna or Mala Fortuna, good and bad fate.

Fortuna Augusti was the foundation of the emperors' right to rule. Romans swore by the emperor's personal Fortuna, who governed his soul. Caesars "constantly had before them, even during sleep or on voyages, a golden statue of the goddess, which on their death they transmitted to their successor and which they invoked under the name of *Fortuna Regia,* a translation of *Tyche Basileos* (Fate of the Rulership)."[1]

Greek Tyche was the same as Fortuna. When she was a Fate attached to an individual, like a guardian angel, she was a *psyche* (soul) or *anima* (spirit). Her Roman name Fortuna may have descended from Vortumna, "She Who Turns the Year," the Great Mother turning the celestial **wheel** of the stars and also the karmic wheel of fate.[2]

Under the name of Agatha, "Kindly Fortune," the Goddess was associated with a serpent-consort, Agathodemon, a genius of kindly fate.[3] On the Orphic Bowl of the 5th century A.D. he appeared next to her in the guise of the Lord of Death, "halfway around the circle, at the point of midnight . . . holding in his right hand the poppy stalk of the sleep of death, turned downward."[4] In this case Fortuna and her consort stood for a fortunate life followed by a gentle death. The Goddess's favored ones went to her paradise in the far west, often called the Fortunate Isles.

On the Goddess's magic wheel of time, odd numbers were sacred to her, even numbers to her consort. Roman religious festivals were scheduled for the odd-numbered "female" days, because they were supposed to be more propitious than "male" days.[5]

Fortuna became patroness of gamblers when her fate-wheel was secularized as the carnival Wheel of Fortune, and she was renamed Lady Luck. In England she was transformed into a fairy-creature called a "portune," which might lead horses astray, make travelers lose their way, and other pranks.[6] Like most other forms of the Goddess she was converted into a malicious spirit.

1. Cumont, A.R.G.R., 86; M.M., 97. 2. Graves, G.M. 1, 126.
3. Elworthy, 384. 4. Campbell, M.I., 388. 5. Rose, 228. 6. Hazlitt, 518.

Frastrada

Legendary wife of Charlemagne; a fairy or witch from the east. The cathedral of Aix-la-Chapelle was said to have been built over a magic pool containing Frastrada's ring. Anyone who visited the pool by moonlight would be seized by its spell and forced to return again and again.[1] A similar tale was told of the Trevi Fountain in Rome, formerly sacred to Hecate Trevia.

1. Guerber, L.R., 85.

Fravashi

"Spirit of the Way," a Sufi title of a sacred harlot trained to teach sexual mysticism; the Arabic equivalent of **Shakti**.

Frederick II

Holy Roman Emperor who opposed his church, once remarking that "three have seduced the whole world, that is, Moses the Hebrews, Christ the Christians, and Mohammed the heathens." Medieval heretics revered him and made him a legendary hero like Merlin, similarly hidden in an enchanted sleep, awaiting his Second Coming. It was believed that Frederick rested in a magic mountain with his sleeping knights around him, guarded by supernatural ravens.

The prophecy of Frederick's awakening or reincarnation did not remain in the realm of folklore. It was taken up by educated writers and poets, who made it an article of anti-clerical propaganda. Books referred to the "old" German prophecy that another Frederick would come from the seed of the first, to humble the German clergy, and bring peace, prosperity, and freedom to the land.[1]

1. Borchardt, 245, 257–58, 288.

Free Will

Theological doctrine stated that God allows human beings to be tempted into evil, so by a personal decision each individual may "freely" elect to resist temptation or not. The doctrine was developed in answer to the argument that God could prevent sin if he wanted to, and because he did not prevent it, there was something wrong with him, not with humanity. As 2 Esdras put it: "It had been better not to have given the earth unto Adam; or else, when it was given him, to have restrained him from sinning. For what profit is it for men now in this present time to live in heaviness, and after death to look for punishment?"[1]

Second Book of Esdras (also known as the Ezra Apocalypse) One of the apocryphal books eliminated from the English Bible but appearing as an appendix to the New Testament in the Latin Vulgate.

The problem was to absolve God from suspicion of a frivolous malice, like that of a child who teases an animal with food, then punishes it for eating. If God was all-knowing then he must have known in advance what man would choose, which would take the element of surprise out of human sins. On the other hand, if God couldn't foresee what man would choose, and could be surprised by human actions, he wasn't all-knowing.

Scotus Erigena piously tried to thrash his way out of the paradox with a new dogma of "divine ignorance," but unfortunately succeeded in demonstrating that God fails to understand what he created. Erigena said: "There is another kind of ignorance in God, inasmuch as he may be said not to know what things he foreknows and predestines until they have appeared experientially in the course of created events. . . . There is a third kind of divine ignorance, in that God may be said to be ignorant of things not yet made manifest in their effects through experience of their action and operation; of which, nevertheless, he holds the invisible cause in himself, by himself created, and to himself known."[2]

Johannes Scotus Erigena 9th-century Irish theologian, schoolmaster at the court of the West Frankish king Charles the Bald.

These subtleties added up to a statement that God doesn't know what he knows, with a hidden conclusion that man is smarter than God, because man (that is, Erigena) knows all about what God knows and what God doesn't know. Theologians who wrote learnedly on the subject of God's ignorance were going out on a limb, claiming that they could scrutinize and analyze what they themselves declared inscrutable. So troublesome did the doctrine of free will become that some Protestant sects, such as Calvinist Presbyterianism, abandoned it altogether in favor of predestination, stating that every person was already saved or damned from birth by God's unalterable decree. This idea restored God's omniscience, but eroded the incentive to live a godly life.

There was an eastern folk tale that allegorized the relationship between God and humanity as between a wizard-shepherd and his flock of remarkably intelligent sheep. Knowing that their master would eventually kill, skin, and eat them, the sheep kept trying to run away, and proved very troublesome. At last the shepherd used his magic power to put his sheep into a hypnotic trance and gave them suggestions that they would internalize as their own beliefs. He told them they were immortal, so death could do them no harm. He told them to trust in their master's goodness no matter what happened to them. Finally, he told them not to think about their fate at all, because it wouldn't happen right away. There was no need to anticipate it. Then the sheep became obedient, and stopped trying to escape. Each one quietly awaited its own death at the master's hand, believing that it had decided to do so of its own free will.[3]

One of the "suppressed" verses of the *Rubaiyat* of Omar Khayyam also made nonsense of the doctrine of free will, after the fashion of the author of Esdras. In this verse, not man but God was made responsible for the Fall, since he had foreseen it, planned it, and supplied the circumstances that made it inevitable:

O Thou, who Man of baser Earth didst make,
And even with Paradise devise the Snake;
For all the sin wherewith the Face of Man
Is blackened, Man's forgiveness give—and take!

1. H. Smith, 235. 2. Campbell, C.M., 343. 3. Wilson, 268.

Freya

var. Frea, Frigga, Frigg

Great Goddess of northern Europe, leader of the "primal matriarchs" called Afliae, "powerful ones," or Dísir, "divine grandmothers": the same as the Hindu *matrikadevis* or mother goddesses. Freya was the Vanadís, the ruling ancestress (*dís*) of the Vanir or elder gods, who ruled before the arrival of Odin and the patriarchal **Aesir** ("Asians") from the east. Myths said Odin learned everything he knew about magic and divine power from Freya.[1]

The pagans said nothing could be lucky without Freya's presence. Even the gods languished and began to decline toward death, like mortals, when Freya was taken from them.[2]

Like all forms of the Goddess, Freya represented sexual love, which is why her alternate name Frigg became a colloquialism for sexual intercourse. Her consort Frey sometimes took the form of a phallus. In Uppsala his name was Fricco, "Lover," cognate with the phallic god Priapus, from the Indo-European root *prij*, to make love—which also gave rise to the modern "prick."[3]

Though he was sometimes called Freya's twin brother, like the Artemis-Apollo, Isis-Osiris pairs, Frey made a lingam-yoni combination with Freya. Their names meant "the Lord" and "the Lady."[4] Some writers identified them with Attis and Cybele, tracing Frigga to "Frigia" or Phrygia, the Magna Mater's home.[5]

Frey was the god of Yule, the pagan solstitial festival assimilated to Christmas. At the turning of the solar year he was born of his virgin-mother-sister-bride.[6] Like other seasonal gods he had a perpetual rival, Njord, the other half of the year. They were collectively *blotgodar* (blood-gods), who fought and sacrificed each other over and over. Njord was called the first god of the Swedes, having ruled before Odin brought alien gods from Asia. Frey was another aspect of him, worshipped in the sacred grove at Uppsala long before it was taken over by Odin's priests.[7] The grove itself stood for the body of the Goddess.

Freya had many alternate names. She was Gerd the Earth Mother, or Eartha; Godiva, "the Goddess"; Sýr, "the Sow"; Gefn, "the Giver"; Horn, the holy harlot; the Vanadís; or Mardoll, the Moon Shining Over the Sea.[8] Sometimes she was simply Lofn, "Love."[9] She was also identified with Mana, the Moon; or Hel, the underworld; or Nerthus, the primal Goddess of the Plow, in charge of the fertility of the earth; she separated the island of Zealand from Sweden by plowing a furrow around it.[10]

Many of Freya's names were only *kennings* (metaphors) from the hymns composed in her honor by her skalds. Focusing on the theme of love, and known as *mansongr*, "woman songs," these compositions were specifically forbidden by the medieval church.[11] Despite the opposition of the clergy, Germans persisted in believing that Freya's sacred day, Friday, was the luckiest day for weddings.[12]

Freya or one of her equivalents married each of the early Swedish kings: "They were regarded in heathen times as the husbands of the fertility goddess. . . . [T]hey suffered a real or symbolic death in that capacity when their time of supremacy came to an end." Scandinavian Aryans followed the typical pattern of sacred marriage between Goddess and king, the latter becoming identified with the male fertility deity whose function it was "to die for the land and for his people, while the goddess never dies. Her function is to weep over him, perhaps to help bring about his return, or to give birth to the divine child who is to take his place."[13] (See **Kingship**.)

After their abrupt sacrificial deaths, Freya kept the spirits of slain kings and heroes in her *Fensalir* or Marsh-halls, also called *Folkvangr,* the Field of Warriors.[14] They could be reborn after spending a cycle of time in the wet, fertile earth-womb. Freya's Marsh-halls recall the "bog" where Baal-Hadad lay for seven years before he was resurrected to godhood by priestesses of Asherah.[15] Like the early Semitic worshippers of the Great Mother, Aryans were "men of clay"—the meaning of their name—because their bodies came forth from Modir. This meant the root of both "mud" and "mother"; she was the same primal creatress whom the Russians called Moist Mother Earth.[16] Modir too was another manifestation of Freya.

She was especially linked with the strange archaic god Heimdall, whose name meant "a ram," undoubtedly one of the ubiquitous animal substitutes for a human sacrifice. The ram's horn was Heimdall's ringing Gjallarhorn, on which he blew the Last Trump to announce the coming of doomsday and the world's destruction. In the Bible, magic ram's horns were supposed to bring about the destruction of Jericho in the same manner.[17] The link between Heimdall and Freya suggested her Kali-like function as a Destroying Goddess, which she would assume when men and gods displeased her by forgetting her principles of right living, justice, honor, and peace. She knew more magic than the gods. Her knowledge was collectively *seidr,* cognate of Sanskrit *siddhi,* the miraculous powers developed by the practice of yoga.

Freya had so many incarnations and aspects that the scholars who tried to characterize her by only one of them soon ran into a mass of contradictions. She was called the Goddess of fertility, love, the moon, the sea, the earth, the underworld, death, birth; virgin, mother, ancestress, queen of heaven, ruler of fate, of the stars, of magic; the Great Sow wedded to the sacrificial boar; the Mistress of Cats; the leader of Valkyries; the Saga or "sayer" who inspired all sacred poetry. In sum, she was as many-sided as any other version of the Goddess.

1. Turville-Petre, 144–59. 2. Branston, 249. 3. Branston, 134, 158. 4. Gelling & Davidson, 163. 5. Borchardt, 222. 6. Oxenstierna, 216. 7. Turville-Petre, 163, 172. 8. Branston, 133. 9. Sturluson, 59. 10. H.R.E. Davidson, G.M.V.A., 113. 11. Turville-Petre, 176. 12. H.R.E. Davidson G.M.V.A., 112. 13. H.R.E. Davidson, G.M.V.A., 97, 110. 14. Turville-Petre, 189. 15. Hooke, M.E.M., 87. 16. *Larousse,* 287. 17. H.R.E. Davidson, G.M.V.A., 173–75.

Friday

Day of the Goddess Freya, called unlucky by Christian monks, because everything associated with female divinity was so called. Friday the 13th was said to be especially unlucky because it combined the Goddess's sacred day with her sacred number, drawn from the 13 months of the pagan lunar year. (See **Menstrual Calendar**.)

Romans named the day *dies Veneris* after Venus, their own

version of the same Goddess. In modern French, Friday is still *vendredi,*[1] and in Italian, *venerdì.*

Friday used to be the seventh day of the week. It was the Sabbath of the Jewish lunar calendar and is still the Sabbath of Islam. Scandinavian pagans, Hindus, and rural Scots insisted that Friday was the most propitious day for a marriage because it was the day that favored fertility.

Fish were eaten on Friday as fertility charms, in honor of Venus (or Freya) whose totems they were. Fish are still considered "aphrodisiac" food because they were sacred to Aphrodite. Thus the Catholic habit of eating fish on Friday was wholly pagan in origin. But the church never acknowledged the debt. In the Middle Ages, when pagan votaries of Freya continued to celebrate her rites on Friday, churchmen designated her day as the day of "devil worship."[2]

1. Funk, 337. 2. de Lys, 375–77.

Frog

Cylinder seals A type of sculpture that developed in Mesopotamia during the protoliterate period. Cylinder seals were small stone cylinders with figures carved in relief, to be rolled across a tablet of wet clay which would then take the impression of a picture. Subjects were usually magical or religious.

Medieval totems of witches were frogs because ancient traditions associated the frog with Hecate—Egypt's Hekat, Queen of the Heavenly midwives. Egyptians made the frog a symbol of the fetus. Hekat's sacred Amulet of the Frog bore the words, "I Am the Resurrection," another phrase of birth-magic copied by early Christians.[1]

In Rome, the frog was sacred to Venus, of whom Hecate was one aspect. Her triple yoni sometimes was shown as a fleur-de-lis composed of three frogs.[2] To this day, a garment closure of cord shaped like a fleur-de-lis is called a "frog." Tailors' folklore said every garment should have exactly nine frogs, which might be traced all the way back to Babylonian cylinder seals showing nine frogs as a fertility charm: the Ninefold Goddess ruling the nine months of gestation.[3]

1. Budge, E.M., 63. 2. de Lys, 139, 141. 3. Budge, A.T., 91.

Fu-Hi

Chinese patriarchal hero, said to have been the first man to discover the male role in reproduction, though he was himself conceived without a father.[1]

1. Briffault 1, 366.

Fuji

"Grandmother" or "Ancestress," the holy Mother-mountain of Japan.[1] Mount Fujiyama was interpreted as a point of contact between heaven and the underworld, as were most mountains. (See **Mountain.**)

1. Campbell, P.M., 336.

Furies

Also called Erinyes or Eumenides, the Furies personified the vengeful moods of the Triple Goddess Demeter, who was also called Erinys as a punisher of sinners. The three Erinyes were emanations of her. "Whenever their number is mentioned there are three of them. . . . But they can all be mentioned together as a single being, an Erinys. The proper meaning of the word is a 'spirit of anger and revenge'. . . . Above all they represented the Scolding Mother. Whenever a mother was insulted, or perhaps even murdered, the Erinyes appeared. Like swift bitches they pursued all who had flouted blood-kinship and the deference due to it."[1]

Greeks believed the blood of a slain mother infected her murderer with a dread spiritual poison, *miasma,* the Mother's Curse. It drew the implacable Furies to their victim, and also infected any who dared help him. In fear of the Furies' attention, lest they might have inadvertently assisted a matricide, people called the Furies "Good Ones" (Eumenides), hoping to divert their wrath.

Aeschylus called the Furies "Children of Eternal Night." Sophocles called them "Daughters of Earth and Shadow." Their individual names were Tisiphone (Retaliation-Destruction), Megaera (Grudge), and Alecto (the Unnameable). Some said they were born of the blood of the castrated Heavenly Father, Uranus; others said they were older than any god.[2] Their antiquity is demonstrated by the fact that they were invoked against killers of kinfolk in the female line only: a relic of the matriarchal age, when all genealogies were reckoned through women.[3]

Aeschylus's drama *The Eumenides* presented the Furies pursuing Orestes for killing his mother, Queen Clytemnestra; but they cared nothing for the murder of the father. He was not a real member of the clan. When Orestes asked them why they didn't punish Clytemnestra for murdering her husband, they answered, "The man she killed was not of blood congenital." Orestes inquired (as if he didn't know), "But am I then involved with my mother by blood bond?" The Furies snapped, "Murderer, yes. How else could she have nursed you beneath her heart? Do you forswear your mother's intimate blood?"[4] In short, the Furies harked back to a matriarchal clan system like the one in pre-Christian Britain, where "the son loved the father no more than a stranger."[5] Indeed the name of the archaic Triple Goddess of Ireland, Erin, or Eriu, has been linked with the triple Erinyes.[6]

The Furies were also "fairies," identified with witches because of their ability to lay curses on any who transgressed their law. Such "fairies" may have been real witches who tried to defend the rights of women against encroachment by Christian laws. Their *modus operandi* could have been similar to that of the Women's Devil Bush society in Africa: if a woman complained to this society that her husband abused her, he soon died of a mysterious dose of poison.[7]

Christianity adopted the Furies, incongruously enough, as servants of the patriarchal God. They became part of God's penal system in hell: dog-faced she-demons known as Furies Who Sow Evil, Accusers or Examiners, and Avengers of Crimes.[8] Their duty, as always, was to punish sinners. As "grotesques" they appeared on the tympanum of Bourges Cathedral, with large pregnant bellies bearing the full moon's Gorgon face, and pendulous breasts terminating in dogs' heads.[9] Greek art, however, depicted them as stern-faced but beautiful women, bearing torches and scourges, with serpents wreathed in their hair like the Gorgons.[10]

Although classical tradition understood the Fury as a symbol of the impersonal functioning of justice, yet she came to represent men's hidden fear of women, an image apparently still viable. *Psychiatric Worldview* says:

> *To those men who are aware of contemporary changes it becomes abundantly clear that there are a number of openly angry women around. . . . Men trained to recognize and enhance their own anger and aggressiveness in a society where rape and revenge are commonplace view angry women with alarm. . . . Men see women project onto them the full extent of their own potential aggressiveness. The spectre of an angry Fury or Medusa's head strikes fear in men, which is then often awkwardly handled because men are not supposed to display fear. A woman seeking only reasonable social or vocational equity may be perceived by a man as being out to get the kind of revenge that* his *pride would require had he experienced the narcissistic and practical wounds that she has sustained.*[11]

1. Branston, 191. 2. Graves, G.M. 1, 122, 126. 3. Lindsay, A.W., 34.
4. Bachofen, 159. 5. Malory 2, 179. 6. Graves, W.G., 317. 7. Briffault 2, 548.
8. Shumaker, 130. 9. de Givry, 27. 10. Cavendish, P.E., 123.
11. *Psychiatric Worldview,* Lederle Laboratories, July/Sept. 1977.

Furrow

World-wide female-genital symbol, often combined with a male symbol in agrarian religions. Indian scriptures made the Earth-mother Sita, "Furrow," the wife of Rama, whose name meant "Enjoyment of Virility" and who was an incarnation of the phallic Krishna.[1] Ancient Egypt celebrated an important annual rite called "the finding of the scepter of flint in the furrow of [the Goddess] Maat."[2] Similarly, Rome kept a sexual-symbolic festival devoted to finding "the flints of Jupiter" in a sacred furrow representing Ceres or Ops, Mother Earth.[3]

The city of Rome itself was established by plowing a furrow, an act attributed to the legendary Romulus. A pre-Roman ancestral hero called Tages was said to be "born from the furrow" as a son of Mother Earth.[4]

The name of the zodiacal sign of the Virgin originally meant "Furrow."[5] Its principal star, Spica, was known in Babylon as "the corn-ear of the Goddess Shala." Corn-ear meant the *shibboleth* displayed at the culmination of the rites of Ishtar, Astarte, and Demeter, all of whom were also the Furrow. Demeter made Iasion or Iasus her lover "in a thrice-plowed field," giving him the name of Triptolemus, "Three Plowings," because he entered the Furrow three times. He was also surnamed Soter, meaning both "Savior" and "Sower."

Seed entering the furrow was almost invariably likened to semen entering the womb, as shown by numerous pagan savior-gods who entered their Mother in the form of seed and were reborn as new vegetation. The Latin god Semo Sancus, whose name meant both "seed" and "semen," mated thus with Ops and died in her embrace, to regenerate himself.[6]

The classic custom of plowing a furrow for magical protection around a town was perpetuated by country folk all over Europe. Even in the 20th century, Russian villages were annually "purified" by the same ceremony, which remained exclusively in the hands of women. Nine virgins and three old women (representing the Fate sisters, or Zorya) plowed a furrow around the village at midnight, calling on the Moon-goddess. Armed with scythes, clubs, and animal skulls, they struck down and beat any man they happened to encounter while performing this magic.[7]

1. O'Flaherty, 354; Avalon, 607. 2. Budge, G.E. 1, 420. 3. Dumézil, 28. 4. Dumézil, 636. 5. Lindsay, O.A., 81. 6. Bachofen, 214. 7. *Larousse,* 287.

G

The Mother GODDESS, seated on a throne, holding several infants. This earthy tuff-stone version is more in the Italian mode than earlier Greek renditions. Italy, 400–300 B.C.

GORGON, a "grim face" mask of Athene or Medusa, signifying female wisdom. The snake headdress and belt are traditional. Greek, limestone pediment of the Temple of Artemis; Corfu, ca. 600–580 B.C.

GANESHA, Hindu elephant god, the Lord of Hosts, said to have begot Buddha on the virgin Maya. Haihaya, 11th century.

Gabriel

The angel who brought God's seed to the virgin Mary. The Bible says Gabriel "came in unto her," which meant he had sexual intercourse with her, in King James terminology (Luke 1:28). Gabriel's name means "divine husband." [1] There seems to have been a hidden reference to the ancient custom, whereby temple virgins were impregnated by certain priests designated "fathers of the god," as in Egypt.[2] See **Mary; Virgin Birth**.

1. Augstein, 302. 2. Budge, D.N., 169.

---

var. Ge

Gaea

Greek name for Mother Earth, the "Deep-breasted One," called Oldest of Divinities. Though the Olympian gods under Zeus took over her ancient shrines, yet they swore their binding oaths by her name because they were subject to her law.

Galahad

Son and reincarnation of Lancelot, by Elaine the Lily Maid, who was also Lancelot's mother Queen Elaine—for Lancelot and Galahad were mystically identical. Queen Elaine's son Galahad was taken to Meidelant, the holy Land of Maidens, where the Lady of the Lake brought him up and changed his name to Lancelot. Afterward he coupled with the Lily Maid and begot himself as a new Galahad—the same Oedipal idea running through all mythology, even in Christian father-son identity (see **Incest**).

As a sacred king, Galahad ruled his land for a term of one year, then died "suddenly, at the altar," while experiencing a vision of the Holy Grail, his Mother-symbol. He was carried to heaven by angels.[1]

When the monks rewrote his story, Galahad was viewed as a purer knight than his father-predecessor Lancelot, whose life was marred by "the vile sin of lust." Galahad was chosen to realize the Grail quest because he was the only knight in the whole company of the Round Table who was still virgin.[2] This Christianized Galahad was said to have descended from Joseph of Arimathea; but another author announced through Guinevere that Galahad was a descendant of Jesus himself.[3]

1. Malory 2, 268. 2. Campbell, C.M., 550. 3. Malory 2, 171.

Galatea

"Milk-giving Goddess," a title of White Aphrodite of Paphos, where her high priest Pygmalion "married" her, by keeping her white image in his bed.[1] The custom formed a basis for the classical myth of

Galatea's marble statue brought to life by Aphrodite for her bridegroom. The story probably arose from a ritual of invocation, to call down the Goddess's spirit into her sculptured *eidolon*.

Galatea was another name not only for Aphrodite but also for Egyptian Hathor the Celestial Cow, and Phoenician Astarte, the same milk-giving Mother. Pygmalion was a Hellenized version of her high priest Pumiyathon at Byblos.[2]

Celtic tribes from Galatia—named after her—also worshipped the milk-giving Mother as Galata, from whom Gauls and Gaels traced their descent.[3] Their early-medieval hero Galahad was one of her sacred kings. He was a Gaulish form of Heracles, who married the Gauls' ancestral Goddess Galata, sometimes symbolized in Britain as Albion, the White Moon, source of the **Milky Way**. Heracles also was a solar hero who lived for a year—like Galahad—in the palace of the Goddess, at the hub of the spinning wheel of the galaxy (Milky Way). In this Lydian story the Goddess was called Omphale, the "center," or *omphalos*. When the year turned around this hub full circle, Heracles too was supposed to die the year-god's death in a fiery wheel.[4]

All the names of Galatea-Galata-Galatia were based on *gala*, "mother's milk," for the Goddess was supposed to have made the wheel of the stars and constellations from her own milk.[5] Therefore the Moon-goddess often appeared in ancient iconography as the divine cow, horned like the moon.

1. Graves, G.M. 1, 212. 2. Frazer, G.B., 387. 3. Graves, G.M. 2, 136. 4. Graves, G.M. 2, 165. 5. Lawson, 13.

Galileo

The first Christian man to achieve visual confirmation of the true motion of heavenly bodies. Before Galileo, all Christendom accepted the church's view that man and his works stood at the center of the universe, on a fixed earth surrounded by "spheres" of sun, moon, planets, and stars. This was the biblical view, supported by such infallibles as Albert the Great, Isidore of Seville, St. Thomas Aquinas.

The Dark Age had destroyed or forgotten ancient astronomers' knowledge of the solar system. Aristarchus taught about 275 B.C. that the earth is a revolving globe in orbit around the sun. Eratosthenes about 250 B.C. calculated the circumference of the globe at 24,662 miles, less than 300 miles short of the true figure, 24,902. About 240 B.C., Hipparchus calculated the diameter of the moon, and its distance from the earth, within a few miles of the correct figures.[1] But according to Christian authorities, this information was pagan and therefore heretical and wrong.

Almost two millenia later, Nicholas Copernicus patiently observed and calculated his way back to the knowledge that the earth moves

Index of Prohibited Books (Index Librorum Prohibitorum) The first official edition appeared in 1559, though ecclesiastical authorities censored, condemned, and destroyed various kinds of books from the earliest centuries of the Christian era. Catholics were forbidden to read any books listed on the Index, which was regularly updated. Observation of this prohibition was obligatory up to 1966, when Pope Paul VI suppressed the Index.

around the sun. After hesitating and re-checking his results for nearly thirty years, Copernicus published his book in 1543. It was not well received by Catholics or Protestants. Martin Luther scoffed at it: "People give ear to an upstart astrologer who strove to show that the earth revolves, not the heavens or the firmament, the sun and the moon. . . . This fool wishes to reverse the entire science of astronomy; but sacred scripture tells us that Joshua commanded the sun to stand still, and not the earth."[2]

The Roman church investigated Copernicus's theory by consulting the scriptures, and placed his book on the Index of Prohibited Books, where it remained until 1835. The pope announced, "The first proposition, that the sun is the center and does not revolve about the earth, is foolish, absurd, false in theology and heretical, because expressly contrary to Holy Scripture. The second proposition, that the earth revolves about the sun and is not the center, is absurd, false in philosophy and . . . opposed to the true faith."

Copernicus's calculations nevertheless fascinated Giordano Bruno, who accepted the heliocentric theory, attacked St. Thomas Aquinas's cosmology of the spheres, published an early elucidation of the nebular hypothesis, and even developed something like a theory of evolution. He also doubted the reality of witchcraft and asserted that most women burned at the stake were innocent. He was silenced in the same way: burned on the Campo dei Fiori in 1600.

Ten years later, Galileo's little telescope revealed the phases of Venus, the moons of Jupiter, and the moving spots on the sun. Galileo invited clergymen to look through the telescope for themselves, but they refused, saying it would imperil their souls because objects like the moons of Jupiter were illusions of the devil. The Church said there could be only seven planets, because scripture presented seven archangels, seven churches of Asia, seven golden candlesticks, and other such allegories. One of the church's main objections at the time to Galileo's discoveries was that they upset the received knowledge of the zodiacal system; learned ecclesiastics leaned heavily on the guidance of **astrology**.

In 1632, Galileo published his *Dialogue*, with overwhelming proof of the Copernican theory. There was a storm of opposition from the church, which went on for many years and involved priests, cardinals, and two popes. A document was forged and "found" in the church's files, to the effect that Galileo had been previously forbidden to teach or discuss Copernicanism, on pain of punishment by the Inquisition. Galileo was arrested, threatened with torture, and forced to abjure on his knees, vowing to "curse and detest the error and the heresy of the movement of the earth." According to legend, he went on to whisper under his breath, *Eppur si muove*—"But it does move." Pope Paul V closed the subject with a solemn statement: "The doctrine of the double motion of the earth about its axis and about the sun is false, and entirely contrary to Holy Scripture."[3]

The pope forbade interment of Galileo's remains in his family tomb, directing that he be buried without ceremony, monument, or epitaph. His memory was execrated for two centuries, for what Pope Urban VIII called "so great a scandal to Christendom." Ecclesiastical censors ordered that a later scientific work calling Galileo "renowned" must alter the word to "notorious." In 1846, Monsignor Marini was given the job of publishing the records of Galileo's trial and falsifying them to the church's advantage. The deception was uncovered by M. L'Epinois twenty years later.[4]

M. L'Epinois Roman Catholic authority on the Galileo records.

Many books were hurried forth under ecclesiastical auspices to confute Galileo. Some contained very quaint reasoning, like Chiaramonti's:

Scipio Chiaramonti Conservative theologian who dedicated his work confuting Galileo to Cardinal Barberini.

> *Animals, which move, have limbs and muscles; the earth has no limbs or muscles, therefore it does not move. It is angels who make Saturn, Jupiter, the sun, etc., turn round. If the earth revolves, it must also have an angel in the center to set it in motion; but only devils live there; it would therefore be a devil who would impart motion to the earth.*[5]

The naive theology of the time often declared that if the earth moved, a stone dropped from a height would fall some way behind the spot directly below. Theology was shackled to the dictum of St. Augustine: "Nothing is to be accepted save on the authority of the Scripture, since greater is that authority than all the powers of the human mind."[6] Voetius in 17th-century Utrecht repeated the same dictum: "Not a word is contained in the Holy Scriptures which is not in the strictest sense inspired, the very punctuation not excepted."[7]

Even in the late 19th century, churchmen were still beating the dead horse of biblical cosmology. A president of the Lutheran Teachers' Seminary published a book refuting Copernicus, Galileo, Kepler, Newton, and all subsequent astronomers:

> *The entire Holy Scripture settles the question that the earth is the principal body of the universe, that it stands fixed, and that sun and moon serve only to light it. . . . God never lies, never makes a mistake; ou of his mouth comes only truth when he speaks of the structure of the universe, of the earth, sun, moon, and stars.*[8]

In 1885 the Catholic scholar St. George Mivart realized that God had indeed lied about the structure of the universe, and hypothesized that God had deliberately led his popes and cardinals into error in order to teach them that astronomy lay outside their jurisdiction. This became the accepted Catholic view of the Galileo fiasco.[9] It was a view that did irreparable damage to the doctrine of papal infallibility, and opened the way to future doubts about God's veracity. If he deceived his chosen envoys in one matter, who could be sure he didn't deceive them in others?

The battle with Galileo set the pattern for three centuries of ecclesiastical condemnation of each new discovery in an Age of Enlightenment when almost all scientific knowledge was found to be contrary to Holy Writ. Linnaeus's observations of the sexual system of plants were banned. The theological faculty of the Sorbonne forced Buffon to publish a recantation of his geological discoveries "which may be contrary to the narrative of Moses." Bernouilli was forced to expunge from his works the proof that the living body constantly changes its parts, because this contradicted the church's doctrine of the resurrection of the flesh. The Egyptologist Sir J. G. Wilkinson had to "modify" ancient Egyptian chronology because it interfered with the biblical flood myth. Dr. Franz Gall was forbidden to study the structure of the human brain on the ground that it was "blasphemous."[10]

Nearly every important scientific book of these three centuries appeared on the Index of Prohibited Books, "infallibly" declared false because it contradicted the Bible. The biologist Huxley said he encountered in every path of natural science a barrier reading: "No thoroughfare. Moses."[11] In 1832, Pope Gregory XVI's encyclical *Mirari vos* declared war on (1) all forms of society founded on liberty of conscience; (2) liberty of the press, "which cannot be sufficiently execrated and condemned, for by its means all evil doctrines are propagated"; and (3) liberty of scientific research.[12] Stanton says, "All through the centuries scholars and scientists have been imprisoned, tortured and burned alive for some discovery which seemed to conflict with a petty text of Scripture."[13] The Galileo case was the very beginning of a long retreat.

1. Campbell, M.T.L.B., 15. 2. White 1, 126. 3. White 1, 138. 4. White 1, 162–63. 5. White 1, 145. 6. H. Smith, 297. 7. White 2, 308. 8. White 1, 151. 9. White 1, 165–66. 10. Bromberg, 77; White 1, 256. 11. White 2, 312. 12. Guignebert, 452. 13. Stanton, 9.

Ganesha

"Lord of Hosts," Hindu elephant god who begot Buddha on the virgin Maya.[1] At Elephantine in Egypt he appeared as a form of Yahweh, consort of the Goddess Anath, or "the Virgin Zion." He also reappeared in the Bible as Behemoth, who later became a demon. (See **Elephant**.)

1. Campbell, Or.M., 307.

Ganges

River of the Goddess Ganga, daughter of the Mountain-mother Nanda Devi (Blessed Goddess), one of the Himalayas. Ganga's waters represented baptism and redemption. Shiva's hymn of praise to her said: "Heaps of sin, accumulated by a sinner during millions of births, are destroyed by the mere contact of a wind charged with her vapor. . . . As fire consumes fuel, so this stream consumes the sins of the wicked. Sages mount the staired terrace of the Ganges; on it they transcend the high heaven of Brahma himself: free from danger, riding celestial chariots, they go to Shiva's abode. Sinners who expire near the water of the Ganges are released from all their sins: they become Shiva's attendants and dwell at his side. They become identical with him in shape; they never die—not even on the day of the total dissolution of the universe."[1] No wonder millions come from all over India to bathe in Ganga's magic waters.

1. Zimmer, 110.

Ganymede

"Rejoicing in virility," the boy-lover given to Father Zeus by Hellenic writers anxious to create a divine prototype for their cult of homosexuality. Ganymede was carried to heaven on an eagle's back to slake Zeus's lust. He became Cupbearer to the Gods, replacing Hebe who was the virgin aspect of Mother Hera.[1] Thus the dispenser of immortality was made male instead of female.

1. Graves, G.M. 1, 116–17.

Garlic

Throughout the Christian era, garlic was considered a protection against vampires and werewolves, as efficacious as a crucifix if not more so. The source of this belief might be found in pagan tradition, since blood-drinking revenants were simply diabolized versions of pagans who believed they could attain immortality by drinking the blood of gods other than Christ. Garlic and garlic-eaters were taboo in Greco-Roman temples of the Mother of the Gods. Probably the Goddess's dislike of garlic was based on its unsuitability for group contact and sexual worship, which required sweet-smelling breath.

Gautama

Hindu sage who castrated the god Indra and took his wife from him, in a primitive Oedipal myth recounted in the Ramayana.[1] Gautama was one of the many names of Buddha, of whom the archaic sage was one emanation.

1. O'Flaherty, 94–95.

Gawain

var. Gavin

Celtic name of the sun god. While he was fighting Lancelot, Gawain's strength increased as the morning approached noon, but after the sun began to decline from the zenith Gawain's strength waned. He was conquered just before sunset.

Another battle story made Gawain symbolize the new sun at the turning of the year. He beheaded the Green Knight (old year) at the festival of the winter solstice, and had to submit to a similar fate himself at the following New Year.[1]

Along with his three brothers Gaheris, Gareth, and Agravine, Gawain represented the Celtic sacred year with its four quarters. All four were born of the Triple Goddess under the name of Margawse, Arthur's sister-wife, who also gave birth to Mordred, Arthur's son-nephew, destined to defeat and replace him. (See **Arthur**.)

1. Loomis, 324–42.

Gehenna

Valley of Hinnom outside Jerusalem, once the site of a fire-altar called Tophet, where sacrifices were made to the Tyrian god Moloch, Molech, or Melek, "the King," worshipped by Solomon (1 Kings 11:7).

After the Jews gave up passing their firstborn children "through the fire to Molech" (Leviticus 18:21), the shrine was abandoned. The valley became a dump where rubbish, including corpses of criminals and other outcasts, was burned.[1] Thus the stench and fire associated with Gehenna eventually made its name a synonym for hell.

The Jews elaborated the basic seven-layered Babylonian underworld into a mystic Gehenna sixty times as big as the world, where each "palace" had 6,000 houses, and each house had 6,000 vessels of fire and gall. Prince of Gehenna was Arsiel, copied from the Babylonian netherworld god Aciel, "Black Sun," negative aspect of the sun god.[2] In Gehenna's central pit lived the serpent-angel Apollyon, another name for the same negative aspect of the sun god Apollo (Revelation 9:11).

1. Cavendish, P.E., 146. 2. Budge, G.E. 1, 275.

Genevieve, Saint

"Generator of Life," a canonized Gallic Diana, patron of Paris. In her church at Andernach she was a "queen" who lived in a sacred cave and bore a holy child. She could take the form of a white hind, like the Goddess. One King Siegfried met her while he was hunting, married her, and became her Lord of the Hunt.[1]

The Frankish king Clovis had himself buried in the shrine of "St. Genevieve," which Gregory of Tours insisted on calling by its newer name, the Church of the Holy Apostles Saints Peter and Paul; but in Gregory's time it was still remembered as the temple of the

Goddess.[2] Gregory's history, written over a century later and full of legendary material, is the only extant source of information about Clovis or Genevieve.

St. Genevieve's runic emblem was a pentacle raised above a cross: a strong hint of paganism.[3] The people of Paris still commemorate the occasion in 1129 when her holy relics allegedly halted an epidemic in the city.[4]

1. Guerber, L.R., 149–51. 2. *Encyc. Brit.,* "Clovis." 3. Brewster, 52. 4. Attwater, 147.

Genius

"Begetter," a Roman word for a spirit of paternal ancestry, cognate with Arabic *djinni* or *genie.* Each Roman man had his personal *genius* as a guardian angel or familiar; each woman had a corresponding female spirit called a *juno.*[1] In the time of the empire, the word genius came to be applied to both sexes. Official prayers were addressed to the "Genius of Rome, whether masculine or feminine, whether god or goddess."[2]

The meaning of genius changed again in the Middle Ages, when it was virtually synonymous with "spirit." One could speak of a *genius loci,* spirit of a place; or an "evil genius," a demon. The modern meaning, an exceptionally intelligent or inspired person, was of late origin. In 1875 A.D., James Hinton defined genius as "the woman in man."[3] In this sense a genius was very similar to a Muse or a Shakti.

1. Rose, 193. 2. Dumézil, 39. 3. Pearsall, W.B., 490

George, Saint

Fictitious patron saint of England. St. George's Day was known to the Romans as the Feast of Pales, a fertility festival. Medieval custom honored St. George on Easter Monday, the Moon-day following the Sun-day of the Christian hero. Folklore named the pagan savior Green George, a spirit of spring.[1] His image was common in old church carvings, a human head surrounded by leaves or looking out of a tree trunk. Some called him the witches' god, "a confused idea of something between a tree and a man," or "the devil in the shape of a trunk of a tree . . . with some form of a human face."[2]

St. George the Dragon-slayer apparently evolved from a mythic meld of Green George with an Arian bishop of Alexandria who opposed St. Athanasius, and put to death an orthodox Master of the Mint named Dracontius, "Dragon."[3]

St. George's emblem was a *vesica piscis,* a prime fertility symbol because it represented the Goddess's yoni; but Christian authorities preferred to interpret it as a "shield." Still, George was so shamelessly involved in fertility rites that the church discredited him and began calling him "the imaginary saint." An old English ballad said: "Some say there was no George; some, that there no Dragon was; pray God, there was at least a maid."[4]

1. Frazer, G.B., 145–46. 2. Knight, D.W.P., 221, 229.
3. Baring-Gould, C.M.M.A., 269. 4. Brewster, 209–10.

Ghora

"Horrible," the third of Vishnu's three boar-children destined for sacrifice so their "energy" (blood) might nourish and uphold the world. Their names probably were based on archaic titles of the Triple Goddess; the first two meant "Well-Rounded One," and "Golden One." Ghora personified a primal taboo, as did the Greek Gorgon who was also "Horrible." Ghora was destructive, therefore sacrificed with his siblings "for the sake of the three universes," for these boar-children were capable of destroying even the gods in the highest heaven.[1]

1. O'Flaherty, 193–96.

Ghost

A cognate of "guest," both words rooted in Germanic *Geist,* originally a spirit of a dead ancestor invited to tribal feasts on such occasions as Samhain (Halloween) and other solemn ceremonies. Many European peoples preserved the heads or skulls of ancestors, which were set up, painted, and decorated, in a prominent position at gatherings of the clan, and were consulted for oracles after being offered their portion of the collation. Hence the "Death's-head at the feast." During later Christian times the custom was discouraged, for the church's doctrine of resurrection of the flesh forbade burial of bodies without heads. Nevertheless, the visiting ghost was an ineradicable belief. Ghosts were supposed to haunt all the scenes of their former lives, especially if they died violently or unhappily, or were buried in unconsecrated ground, or had possessed evil spirits. The earlier, more benevolent type of family ghost is still suggested by the identical pronunciation of "ghost" and "guest" in northern England.[1] The anger of ghosts was most feared by people who refused to honor them as guests.

1. Hazlitt, 27.

Giants

Appearing in every mythology as a primal Elder Race, giants were obvious projections of every child's earliest perceptions of the adult world. Like grownups seen through the eye of the toddler, giants tended to be fearsome, sometimes bloodthirsty but sometimes benevolent; possessors of an arcane ancient wisdom; and adepts of magic.

According to the Bible, giants were like all Savior-figures up to and including Jesus: offspring of divine fathers and human mothers (Genesis 6:4). Semitic tradition held that all the biblical patriarchs were of enormous size. Abraham was seventy times as big as a modern man. Philo maintained that Adam was a giant.[1] Unlettered Arabs still say the megalithic structures being studied by archeologists were not so hard for the ancient people to build, because those people were giants.[2]

Long before the Bible was written, Hindus were saying the same of the people of the Golden Age, in the childhood stage of humanity. Like parent figures, the earliest races were gigantic, sinless, wise, and long-lived. They died only when they wished to. They could live a thousand years because, in their age, life was "centered in the blood"—i.e., the immortal blood of the Goddess.[3] (See **Menstrual Blood**.) That this life-giving blood was a feminine effluent is suggested by the story of Thor's journey to Giant-land to learn the secrets of the giants' ancient magic; he could not find the right way until he crossed a river of the giantesses' menstrual blood.[4] In Greece, the similar river leading to the land of "ancestors" was the Styx.

Greeks called the giants Titans, offspring of Mother Earth and Father Sky (Uranus). The heavenly Father was jealous of his children and tried to smother them by clinging too closely to Mother Earth to let them breathe air. Earth gave her son Cronus the moon-sickle and bade him castrate and kill his Father. Later, Cronus married Rhea the Titaness—another incarnation of the same Mother Earth—and feared the same Oedipal fate from the other end. To preserve his own life, he swallowed his children. The mother saved one of them, Zeus, who did indeed attack his father and marry the same Mother Earth under a variety of her names—Hera, Olympia, Rhea, Gaea, or Danae. The Oedipal theme of the father-son rivals almost always appears in connection with the giant-myths.[5]

Greeks assigned to the Titans all the crude religious rites of their ancestors, such as cannibalistic sacraments and dismemberment of divine victims like Dionysus or Zagreus. As archaic earth-deities, the Titans battled the newer Olympian gods in a myth known as the Giants' Revolt, paralleled by Persian, Jewish, and Christian stories of the War in Heaven.[6] One of the mythic reasons given for the war was Zeus's punishment of the Titans for eating Dionysus's flesh; but Zeus, inconsistently, himself devoured Dionysus's heart.

Legends of giant ancestors were used by Christians to defend the fraudulent miracle-working bones of the Holy Innocents supposedly slaughtered by King Herod. When it was observed that these profitable bones were too large to have come from children less than two years of age, churchmen argued that the human frame was bigger in Herod's time, because it was closer to the age of giants.[8]

The Irish said giant people still lived in "the chambered undergrounds of Tara where dwell the fourth race of gods who settled Ireland." They were the Tuatha Dé Danann, people of the Goddess Dana, builders of stone temples.[9] Their Goddess passed into medieval folklore as Titania, the Fairy Queen.[10] Curiously, though she was a Titaness and the Tuatha Dé Danann were giants, they shrank as popular belief in their powers waned before the encroachment of the new religion. Eventually they became fairies or elves, not giants but "little people," the size of children or even smaller.[11] This reduction in their size was surely related to a reduction in awesomeness. Significantly, their religious myths became "fairy tales" for children, and many of their liturgies and sacred songs reappeared in the guise of nursery rhymes.

1. Tennant, 134. 2. Cavendish, P.E., 128. 3. *Mahanirvanatantra,* pp. xlvii-xlviii. 4. Turville-Petre, 79. 5. Cavendish, P.E., 124–25. 6. Graves, G.M. 1, 119, 131. 7. Campbell, P.M., 101. 8. de Voragine, 66. 9. Keightley, 446. 10. Graves, W.G., 476. 11. Cavendish, P.E., 238.

Giles, Saint

Druidic deity adopted into the Christian canon. His legend originated at Nimes, named after the Dianic moon-grave or *nemeton.* (See **Grove, Sacred.**) He was nurtured in a cave by a magic hind, the Goddess in deer shape. He was identified with the Celtic hero Oisín, whose mother was a deer.[1] Like most Celtic Lords of the Hunt, he was slain by arrows. Enacting the hero's *Liebestod,* as he died he clasped the same magic hind in his arms.

Some said St. Giles was a Greek, born in Athens, possibly to account for his connection with such deer-gods as Actaeon, whose cult was dedicated to the same Diana.[2] Another such hero was Telephus, king of Mysia. In infancy he was nursed by a doe and discovered by shepherds. An oracle sent him to Mysia where he married the queen, his own mother Auge, in typically Oedipal fashion.[3]

Like the smith-priests of the archaic Diana, St. Giles was lame, and so became the patron saint of cripples. Because of his enormous popularity, a fictitious "Life" was composed for him in the 10th century. More than 150 churches were dedicated to him, including St. Giles Cripplegate in London and the high kirk in Edinburgh.[4] Yet his legend had almost nothing Christian about it, and his sainthood was based on forgery.

1. Turville-Petre, 204. 2. Brewster, 391. 3. Rank, 25. 4. Attwater, 155.

Gilgamesh

Hero of a Sumero-Babylonian epic recounting man's vain search for the immortality guarded by the jealous gods. The principal extant text came from the library of Ashurbanipal at Nineveh, 7th century B.C.; but older fragments reveal the story in Babylon at a much earlier date, the beginning of the second millenium B.C.[1]

Fearful of death, Gilgamesh journeyed in search of Uta-Napishtim (Noah), the flood hero who was the only immortal man, to learn his secret. After many adventures Gilgamesh found the patriarch, who showed him a magic "rose" of eternal life. Gilgamesh took the plant, but it was stolen from him by a **serpent**. Thus the serpent became the only immortal creature, capable of shedding its skin and becoming periodically reborn without any sojourn in the land of death.

On his journey, Gilgamesh met the Goddess disguised as an innkeeper—that is, the dispenser of the Wine of Immortality to the gods. She was called Siduri Sabitu, the Wine-Bearer, later adopted by Sufi philosophers as the Goddess Saki, who poured for each man the cup of "reality revealed."[2] In Greek, she was Oenothea, "Wine-goddess."[3]

She revealed reality to Gilgamesh by advising him to abandon the search for immortality, because the cruel gods decreed that all human beings must die. She told Gilgamesh to return home, to take pleasure in the good things of life while he could: to bathe and dress himself, eat and drink, play with his children, make love to his wife, and "make every day a festival."[4]

Siduri's live-for-today philosophy was copied into the ninth chapter of Ecclesiastes, a curiously pagan passage wherein the "word of God" denies the after-life with all its rewards or punishments, and the Judeo-Christian deity dispenses no justice.

1. *Larousse,* 66. 2. *Epic of Gilgamesh,* 38. 3. Wedeck, 207. 4. *Larousse,* 72.

Glory-of-Elves

Norse name for the Sun Goddess, who would give birth to a daughter sun to rule the new universe after doomsday.[1] She was probably modeled on the Aryan Sun Goddess Aditi, whose offspring would be "revealed" at doomsday.[2]

1. Sturluson, 92. 2. O'Flaherty, 339.

Gnosticism

"Knowledge." Gnosticism was a general term for mystery cults of the early Christian era and for derivative heresies of the medieval period. Their "knowledge" meant secrets of the after-life, spells and words of power required for advantageous placement in heaven, and revelations of the true nature of God. Leading Gnostic sects focused on the Great Mother and her Dying God—e.g., Eleusinian, Orphic, and Osirian mysteries. Angus says Gnosticism was "for over half a millenium the approach to religion for thoughtful minds."[1]

Tantric-style meditation and sexual rites figured in western Gnosticism, including sects that were fundamentally Christian. As the ultimate aim of Tantric yoga was to enter the primal realm of Silence, a feminine power enfolding the original Creative Word, the Logos, so Gnostic Christians sought communion with the Goddess Sige (Silence) who dwelt at the beginning of all things.[2] She gave birth to **Sophia** (Wisdom, or Knowledge), the Gnostic Great Mother, both spouse and mother of God.

Some Gnostics adopted the Oriental idea of the world soul, identified with Sophia, sometimes in androgynous communion with God. This was the view of the church father Origen, who was revered in his time but three centuries later excommunicated for holding heretical beliefs.[3] He said, "As our body while consisting of human members is yet held together by one soul, so the universe is to be thought of as an immense living being which is held together by one soul."[4] The trouble with the world soul from the Christian point of view was that it mingled the blessed with the damned in one divine spirit, preventing the separation of sheep and goats that was thought necessary at doomsday.

Origen (Origenes Adamantius) Christian father, ca. 185-254 A.D., an Egyptian who wrote in Greek, exerting a powerful influence on the early Greek church. At first he was accounted a saint, but three centuries after his death he was declared a heretic because of Gnostic elements found in his writings.

The orthodox church especially objected to Gnostic feminine imagery. It was impossible to see God deserving the Great Mother's punishment, as the Gnostics said he did. Followers of St. Paul denounced the Gnostics as firstborn of Satan, ravening wolves, demoniacs, atheists, robbers, pirates, beasts in human shape, and dealers in deadly poison—typical of the insults Christian traded with Christian in those times.[5]

From the 4th to the 8th centuries, the church incessantly persecuted Gnostic minorities. Nevertheless, "Secret fraternities perpetuated the doctrines of Gnosticism and the illuminism of the Pagan religions for many centuries after their supposed disappearance."[6] Gnostic cult objects have been found throughout Sicily, Spain, and southern France, especially the *coffrets gnostiques* or sacred boxes, like Greek *cistae* or Semitic "arks," dating from the early Middle Ages.[7]

Tertullian (Quintus Septimius Florens Tertullianus) Influential early Christian writer and father of the church, ca. 155–220 A.D., born in Carthage of pagan parents.

Church fathers were particularly offended by the Gnostics' propensity to admit women to ecclesiastical rank: "All initiates, men and women alike . . . might be elected to serve as *priest, bishop,* or *prophet.*" Tertullian reported with horror that Gnostic women "teach, they engage in discussion; they exorcise; they cure." They even baptized, showing that they had episcopal status. "They all have access equally, they listen equally, they pray equally—even pagans, if any happen to come. . . .They also share the kiss of peace with all who come."[8]

Irenaeus Doctor, saint, and father of the church, said to have lived in the 2nd century A.D. as bishop of Lyons. His history is obscure, largely based on (possibly fraudulent) assertions of Eusebius, who claimed to have letters from Irenaeus, but none of these were preserved. The story of Irenaeus's martyrdom has been proved false.

Some Gnostic groups went so far as to claim the true revelation of esoteric Christianity came through a woman, the "apostle to the apostles," **Mary Magdalene**, Jesus's beloved. They prayed to a two-sexed deity addressed as Father and Mother, identified with Jesus and Mary. Irenaeus anathematized such groups, insisting they "repent" and submit themselves to him, so he could punish them with "advance discipline" that would save their souls.[9]

Gnostic principles of enlightenment were incorporated into bardic romance, mystery plays, and fairy tales early in the medieval period. Such sources maintained secrets of the heretical religions as allegories or bolic drama. Manichean Gnostics founded their own churches, separating themselves from Rome which they regarded as hopelessly materialistic. They claimed the God of the Roman church was really a devilish demiurge who made the material world to entrap human souls in evil.[10] See **Manicheans**.

Gnostic traditions evolved the Catharan Christianity of southern France and Italy, which stimulated the bloody Albigensian crusade (see **Crusades**). Catharan churches claimed Jesus transmitted to them a secret Gnostic doctrine that overrode the dogmas of the Roman church. Only the "inner man" would rise to heaven, so the dogma of the resurrection of the flesh was a lie. Baptism was useless. Marriage was unimportant. No one needed to be celibate except the "perfected" ones, who renounced the life of the senses as eastern yogis did. The Inquisition accused the Cathari of calling the Roman church names, such as Mother of Fornication, Babylon the Great Whore, the Devil's Basilica, and Satan's Synagogue.

The story of John the weaver of Toulouse shows opposition between the Roman church and Catharan principles of ritual purity. Accused of following the Gnostic heresy, John proclaimed that he lied, swore, ate meat, and enjoyed sex with his wife; therefore he proved himself a faithful Christian and no Catharan heretic.[11]

Other strands of Gnosticism ran through astrology, alchemy, Hermetic magic, and occultism. Insofar as the sought-after knowledge was the natural science that alchemists and sorcerers were beginning to discover (or rediscover), the church opposed it as destructive to the faith. St. Augustine had firmly censured "the vain and curious desire of investigation, known as knowledge and science." Yet Hermes Trismegistus, the half-acknowledged god of medieval alchemists and occultists, had been praised by Lactantius as the revealer of "almost the whole verity." Women were involved, too, in the pursuit of natural science. Women were closely associated with the origins of alchemical/mystical gnosis: Theosebia, Mary the Jewess, one who called herself Cleopatra, another who called herself Isis.[12]

Rediscovery of pagan writings had brought Isis back into an influential, if secret, prominence. The Hellenistic world identified "Isis of the Myriad Names" with every other female divinity.[13] Medieval occultists in turn found her glorified in the writings of Plutarch and identified her with the World Soul, or Sophia. She appeared in numerous occult books as the Naked Goddess crowned with stars, her dominion over land and sea symbolized by her right foot on the earth, her left foot in water. Her vulva was marked by a precisely positioned crescent moon, which a modern male scholar, with the curiously typical vague perception of female genitalia, chose to describe as covering her "womb."[14]

On the whole it was a general rule that wherever the orthodox churches found any hint of female divinity or authority, there they at once found heresy. Persecution of various kinds of Gnostics proved the rule over and over. Both natural science and feminine spirituality came to birth only with great difficulty, against every obstacle that western patriarchism could devise to throw against them. The latter is, even now, not yet fully born.

1. Angus, vii. 2. Campbell, M.T.L.B., 112. 3. *Bardo Thodol,* 234. 4. Shirley, 46. 5. Legge 2, 10. 6. Waite, O.S., 195. 7. Jung & von Franz, 137. 8. Pagels, 42. 9. Pagels, 46, 49. 10. Legge 2, 239. 11. Coulton, 71, 77. 12. Seligmann, 80–81, 88. 13. Boulding, 252. 14. Seligmann, 45.

Goddess

Few words are so revealing of western sexual prejudice as the word Goddess, in contrast to the word God. Modern connotations vastly differ from those of the ancients, to whom the Goddess was a full-fledged cosmic parent figure who created the universe and its laws, ruler of Nature, Fate, Time, Eternity, Truth, Wisdom, Justice, Love, Birth, Death, etc.

Male writers through the centuries broke the Goddess figure down into innumerable "goddesses," using different titles or names she received from different peoples at different times. If such a system had been applied to the usual concept of God, there would now be a multitude of separate "gods" with names like Almighty, Yahweh, Lord, Holy Ghost, Sun of Righteousness, Christ, Creator, Lawgiver, Jehovah, Providence, Allah, Savior, Redeemer, Paraclete, Heavenly Father, and so on, *ad infinitum,* each one assigned a particular function in the world pantheon. During the Middle Ages, most of the old names and titles of male deities were amalgamated as "secret names" of the one God, while the names and titles of the Goddess were ever more minutely classified, and some were even masculinized, humanized, or diabolized. Yet such classification tends to disintegrate under deeper study that reveals the same archetypal characteristics in nearly all the "goddesses."

Probing ancient views of the Goddess is instructive. It shows a female figure almost always more powerful than the male. Not only is she his Mother, the author of his being; she is also the deity who infuses all creation with the vital blood of life. Gods prosper only when they partake of her wisdom or adopt her powers, until they commit the ultimate hubris, symbolic matricide, by setting up an all-masculine theology. The strength of the Goddess was harnessed to support new male religions as the strength of women's nurturing, caretaking instinct was harnessed to a patriarchal marriage system supporting men. Even today, scholars tend to call all ancient deities "gods" when they include both male and female; and sometimes the oracular utterances of the Goddess are said to emanate from a "god."[1]

Perhaps one should take more seriously the ancients' often-repeated opinion that their Goddess had a thousand names. Every female divinity in the present Encyclopedia may be correctly regarded as only another aspect of the core concept of a female Supreme Being. No modern temples perpetuate this core concept. Men long since tore down the Goddess's shrines, as Christian Gospels commanded them to do (Acts 19:27). Yet even in a society that trivialized and vilified it, the core concept lives on. Some people believe that a new feminine theology will emerge from the core concept during the present century.

1. Pritchard, A.N.E. 1, 285; 2, 185.

Godiva, Lady

The name of Lady Godiva is simply a combination of three different ways of saying "Goddess." As Mother Goda, or Gerd, she was the same as Freya, consort of Godan (Wotan), father of "Gods"(Goths); the old Teutonic *d* and *th* were interchangeable.[1] *Diva* was a universal Indo-European word for "Goddess" derived from Sanskrit *devi.* Tantric scriptures still speak of a "mother of creation" and a "holy female river" Godavari, personifying the Western Continent, Apara-Godaniya, a land of cattle and of rough barbarians who lived on meat—apparently the Goths.[2]

The legend of Lady Godiva's naked ride through Coventry evolved from the Goddess's May-Eve procession, which the clergy first tried to suppress by ordering the people to stay indoors and refrain from watching it. In Southam there were two Ladies, white and black, representing the Virgin and Crone, summer and winter, Love and Death.[3] The black Goddess appeared with a bull-masked dancer known as Old Brazen Face: the solar bull mated to the Moon-cow.[4] The "fine lady" on the white horse in the *Ride A Cock-Horse* nursery rhyme was the Naked Goddess of the annual pageant.[5] Some versions of the rhyme called her the "old woman."[6]

Peeping Tom dared to catch a glimpse of her nakedness and was stricken blind for it, according to the story. This recalls other men blinded for looking on the Goddess's nakedness, like Teiresias of Thebes. Such divine punishment, with its accompanying gift of godlike insight, represented a modification of older Gothic customs whereby the Naked Goddess could be seen only by "men doomed to die," such as Teiresias's less fortunate forerunner, Actaeon.[7] Blindness was a common enough result of peeping at forbidden sacred mysteries. King Philip of Macedon was blinded for peeping through a crack to see the serpent-god impregnating the queen with the seed of Alexander the Great.[8] Perhaps Godiva's "Tom" was intended to be **Thomas Rhymer**, another seer like Teiresias who spent seven years serving the Goddess.

Lady Godiva's annual ride was suppressed by Puritans, but after the fall of the Puritan Commonwealth in 1678 she appeared again, naked as before on her white horse. So she remained up to 1826, when a new wave of puritanism finally dictated that she must be clothed.[9]

The original purpose of her ride, to renew her virginity, consummate the sacred marriage, and thus provide the blessings of fertility for the coming year, was at last forgotten. An improbable fable was made up, saying a human Lady of Coventry rode naked alone, only because her Lord insisted on it. This is all most people now know of the history of Godiva, the Gothic Goddess.

1. Turville-Petre, 72, 177. 2. *Mahanirvanatantra,* 67; Tatz & Kent, 85. 3. Graves, W.G., 451. 4. Spence, 111. 5. Knight, D.W.P., 170. 6. Hazlitt, 25. 7. Tacitus, 728. 8. Gifford, 141. 9. Gifford, 142.

Gog

See **Magog.**

Golden Calf

Horus, the bull-calf representing Osiris reborn from his mother Isis-Hathor, who appeared in her processions as a golden cow. Israelites in exile considered a Horus-calf so necessary that they permitted Aaron to melt down their gold jewelry to make one. Aaron presented the finished calf as the god who brought the people safely out of the land of Egypt (Exodus 32:4). The sexual worship of Horus was maintained also. The Israelites made offerings to him, sat down to a feast, then "rose up to play" (Exodus 32:6). The word here translated "play" really meant "copulate."[1]

1. Knight, D.W.P., 62.

Golden Rule

What has been called the essence of Christian teaching was not Christian at all but a precept common to all the ancient world, ultimately based on the Tantric law of karma. The Tantric Sadhaka or Sadhu (yogi) was told to "do good to other beings as if they were his own self."[1] Tantric holy men reached the Middle East at an early date, and may have been the "Sadducees" mentioned in the New Testament. The Buddhist version of the precept was "What ye sow, that shall ye reap," which was copied into Christian scriptures (Galatians 6:7) some 500 years later.[2]

Long before the Bible, Akkadian maxims enjoined the faithful: "Do not return evil to your adversary; requite with kindness the one who does evil to you . . . be friendly to your enemy."[3] In the Egyptian Middle Kingdom, the Golden Rule was a proverb sacred to Maat, the Mother of Justice; "Do the other good, that he may do good to you."[4] Among the Greeks, the same karmic law became the law of the Goddess Dike, ruler of Fate, who said, "He who does wrong to another, does wrong to himself."[5] Jewish writers adopted the principle and attributed it to the injunctions of Hillel: "Do not unto others what thou wouldst not they should do unto you, this is the whole of the Law."[6]

Patriarchal writers naturally attributed the Rule to male heroes, but the older sources nearly always presented it as the law of the Goddess.

1. Avalon, 93. 2. *Bardo Thodol*, 236. 3. Pritchard, A.N.E.2, 146. 4. Erman, 121. 5. Lindsay, A.W., 44. 6. Reinach, 217.

Goose

Mother Goose originated in ancient Egypt, where she was Mother Hathor, incarnate in the Nile Goose. She laid the Golden Egg of the sun, another way of saying she gave birth to Ra. His solar disc was sometimes called the Goose-egg.[1] Some Egyptian writings called the goose Creatress of the World because she produced the whole universe in a primordial World Egg.[2]

The fairy tale of Jack who climbed the beanstalk to find the goose that laid the golden egg, dated back to pre-dynastic shamans who climbed the Heavenly Vine, or Ladder of Set, to the celestial realm of the solar deity, invoked in prayers as "the Egg of the Goose appearing from out of the sycamore."[3]

Like Hathor, Mother Goose was the godmother of all children. In her pictures she always wore the traditional garb of the witch-midwife: black cloak, pointed hat like the Egyptian crown, and magic wand.

1. de Lys, 27. 2. Neumann, G.M., 217. 3. Budge, E.M., 132.

Gorgon

Prophylactic mask signifying Female Wisdom: a face of Athene or Medusa surrounded by snake-locks. Gorgo, Gorgon, or Gorgopis, "Grim Face," was the title of Athene as a death goddess.[1] Athenians tried to explain the Gorgon face on Athene's aegis with the myth that Perseus cut off Medusa's head and brought it home to his own Goddess. But this was a late myth designed to conceal Athene's roots in Libya, where she was herself called Medusa, or Metis.

Like other versions of the archaic Goddess, the Gorgons were a trinity in classical mythology. Their names were Medusa, Stheino, and Euryale: Wisdom, Strength, and Universality. Hellenic writers pretended they were monsters, but these were not the names of monsters. They were titles of the triadic Moon Mother. Orphic mystics continued to call the moon "The Gorgon's Head."[2]

The story that the Gorgon's look could turn men to stone dated from the use of the Gorgon-face to enforce taboos on secret Mysteries of the Goddess, guarded by stone pillars formerly erected in honor of her deceased lovers. See **Athene; Medusa**.

1. Bachofen, 168. 2. Graves, G.M. 1, 129.

Gossip

Archaic word for a woman, especially one past middle age. The original word was *godsib*, "one related to the gods," i.e., a god-mother. In pre-Christian times, elder women were considered divine because they retained their "wise blood" after menopause. (See **Menstrual Blood**.)

In Christian times, "gossip" came to mean any godmother; e.g. Queen Elizabeth I was the *gossip* at the baptism of her godson James VI of Scotland.[1]

A group of elder women were called "gossips" as a term of respect at first, after the peasant habit of calling any older woman "mother" or "grandmother." The modern meaning of "gossip" arose from the conversation of "gossips," or old wives' tales.

1. Funk, 256.

Götterdämmerung

"Going-into-the-Shadow-of-the-Gods," often erroneously called Twilight of the Gods: the Teutonic doomsday, when all the old gods would be destroyed and reabsorbed by the Great Goddess **Skadi**, the Shadow.[1] Like Kali in the Far East, Skadi stood for the primal womb of darkness that cyclically devoured worlds and gave them new birth. The Scandinavian and Teutonic concept of cyclic universes, each with its renewable set of gods, was essentially identical to that of India. See **Doomsday**.

1. Turville-Petre, 164.

Grace

In a famous New Testament passage, the quality said to be greater than faith or hope is *caritas* (1 Corinthians 13), translated sometimes "charity," sometimes "love." Both translations are inexact. The word meant "grace," specifically the grace of the Triple Goddess, embodied in the boon-bestowing Three Graces who dispensed *caritas* (Latin) or *charis* (Greek) and were called the Charites. Julian said their grace was a gift from heaven: "The threefold gift of the Charites comes to us from heaven, from the circles of the stars."[1]

Romans sometimes called grace *venia*, the divine correlative of Venus, bringing visible tokens of the goddess's favor.[2] Grace meant the same as Sanskrit *karuna*, dispensed by the heavenly nymphs and their earthly copies, the sacred harlots of Hindu temples (*devadasis*). Their "grace" was a combination of beauty, kindness, mother-love, tenderness, sensual delight, compassion, and care.

Graces were emanations of the Goddess. They danced in her shrines. They tended to her adornment. They acted as midwives to the gods. They were patrons of music, dance, poetry, and art.[3] They were shown over and over in the same classic pose as three naked women dancing, in attitudes strongly resembling those of the Heavenly Nymphs on the Temple of Love at Khajuraho in India.[4]

Greek writers called the Graces Aglaia (Brilliant), Thalia (Flower-Bringer), and Euphrosyne (Heart's Joy); but they had older names inherited from a dim prehistory. Homer knew only one Grace, named Cale or Kale, perhaps a cognate of Kali.[5] The Gnostic author Marcus also used the word Grace or Charis as a title of the Goddess: "May She who is before all things, the incomprehensible and indescribable Grace, fill you within, and increase in you her own knowledge."[6]

Christians took the pagan concept of *charis* and struggled to divest it of sexual meanings for application to an ascetic creed. "Charity" became a basic tenet of primitive Christianity, as of Buddhism before it, on the theory that a sure place in heaven could be won by giving away one's worldly goods to the poor. Jesus listed the blessings prepared for those who voluntarily made themselves meek, humble, and poor on earth (Luke 6:20-30). The church's word for these "Beatitudes" was *macarisma*, a word of ancient origin, invoking the Triple Goddess as Ma (birth), Charis (grace), and Ma (death).[7] The cognate word *charisma* meant Mother-given grace.

Charis merged with "charity" via ancient precedents equating love and affection with hospitality and gift-giving, the "maternal virtues." Homeric literature used the word *philein*, "lovingness," to mean open-handed hospitality.[8] As re-interpreted by Christian theology, the "graciousness" that used to mean both liberality and warm physical affection came to suggest liberality alone, practiced to secure one's own immortality.

1. Lindsay, O.A., 391. 2. Dumézil, 94. 3. *Larousse*, 132. 4. Elisofon & Watts, 118. 5. Graves, G.M. 1, 53–55. 6. Pagels, 50. 7. Augstein, 115. 8. Lindsay, A.W., 33.

Graeae

The Gray Women of classical myth; like the northern Norns, a variant on the *personae* of the Triple Goddess. Graeae were mothers of Greece (Graecia). According to the Perseus myth they were less terrible than the Gorgons, but Graeae and Gorgons were originally the same triad, the former having more sinister names than the latter. The Graeae were named Enyo, Pemphredo, and Deino: Warlike One, Wasp, and Terror.[1] They shared but a single eye and a single tooth among them, showing that they stood for a primitive concept of the Goddess who was three in one and one in three. See **Gorgon**; **Trinity**.

1. Graves, G.M. 1, 129.

Grail, Holy

Christian myth said the Holy Grail was the chalice used by Christ at the Last Supper when he poured wine for the disciples to drink, saying, "this is my blood" (Matthew 26:28). After the crucifixion, Joseph of Arimathea took the chalice to England and established it in a shrine at Glastonbury. Later, it disappeared.

This myth wasn't heard in Europe until the 12th century. The real origins of the Holy Grail were not Christian but pagan. The Grail was first Christianized in Spain from a sacred tradition of the Moors.[1] Like the Celts' holy Cauldron of Regeneration, which it resembled, the blood-filled vessel was a womb symbol meaning rebirth in the Oriental or Gnostic sense of reincarnation. Its connotation was feminine, not masculine.

The Grail was kept in a magnificent temple governed by a queen named Repanse de Joie (Dispenser of Joy), an ancient title of a holy harlot. Bards said her husband was a Moor, and her son John founded the eastern order of the Knights Templar, a group of warriors dedicated to the Grail temple and the defense of women. When a lady needed help, Grail knights like Galahad, Parsifal, or Lohengrin would receive orders in fiery letters on the rim of the Grail and ride to the rescue.

Hispano-Moorish tradition located the Grail temple on Montsalvatch, the "Mount of Salvation" in the Spanish Pyrénées.[2] The temple was a model of the universe, topped by a gigantic ruby representing the maternal heart of the world, the Holy Rose. The pseudo-universe even included a miniature of itself enclosing the sacred vessel:

> *The temple itself was one hundred fathoms in diameter. Around it were seventy-two chapels of an octagonal shape. To every pair of chapels there was a tower six stories high, approachable by a winding stair on the outside. . . . The vaulting was of blue sapphire, and in the center was a plate of emerald. . . . All the altar stones were of sapphire. . . . Upon the inside of the cupola surmounting the temple, the sun and moon were represented in diamonds and topazes, and shed a light as of day even in the darkness of the night. The windows were of crystal, beryl, and other transparent stones. The floor was of translucent crystal, under which all the fishes of the sea were carved out of onyx, just like life. The towers were of precious stones inlaid with gold; their roofs of gold and blue enamel. Upon every tower there was a crystal cross, and upon it a golden eagle with expanded wings, which, at a distance, appeared to be flying. At the summit of the main tower was an immense carbuncle, which served, like a star, to guide the Templars thither at night. In the center of the building, under the dome, was a miniature representation of the whole, and in this the holy vessel was kept.*[3]

Like the Arabian brotherhood of *hashishim* (see **Aladdin**), the legendary Knights Templar waited for the Desired Knight, or *Mahdi,* to rescue the world from tyranny and establish the benevolent rule of the Grail. The alternative was a dire prediction of the **Waste Land**, modeled on the arid wilderness of Arabia Deserta, which some eastern sages attributed to the departure of the Goddess.

The Grail temple was sometimes called Montjoie, "Mount of

Joy," like the castle Joyous Gard to which Queen Guinevere retired with her lover. It was the same as the Mons Veneris, or Venusberg. Its sexual symbolism served to rally heretical uprisings against the anti-sexual church. A 14th-century peasant leader calling himself William Karle, or Cale, adopted "Montjoie" as a battle cry, and banners showing the Goddess's traditional triple lily.[4] The same battle cry was used by the legendary soldiers of Roland, supposed to have died in the vicinity of the Grail castle.[5] Even older myths said the battle cry of the Grail king was *Amor* (Love).[6]

The Grail was first converted into the chalice of Christ's last supper in the *Joseph d'Arimathie* of the Burgundian poet Robert de Borron, between 1180 and 1199. The origins of the mystic vessel were yet suspect. It was formerly a jewel in the devil's crown. Sixty thousand angels gave it to Satan when he still lived in heaven. During his descent to hell, the jewel fell from his crown to earth, where it was found and fashioned into a cup.[7] Joseph of Arimathea acquired the cup and gave it to Jesus to use at his last meal with his disciples. It was the cup of doom, of which Jesus prayed to God in a weak moment, "Father, if it be possible, let this cup pass from me" (Matthew 26:39).

The poet said Joseph was imprisoned by the Jews and left in a dungeon for a year and a day without food or drink; but he remained alive and well because he had the Grail with him. He was set free by the emperor Vespasian, who was converted to Christianity after being cured of leprosy by the veil with which St. Veronica wiped Jesus's face. Joseph then traveled to England with a group of pilgrims, built the temple of the Grail at Glastonbury, and installed the Round Table for the rite of the holy supper. Among his followers was Bron, the Rich Fisher, directly stolen from pagan myths of Bran the Blessed, Welsh god of the sacred cauldron. For a touch of anti-Semitic propaganda in this chowder of fantasy, de Borron claimed the vacant Seat Perilous at the Round Table was the seat of Judas. Another Jew, Moyses (Moses) once dared to sit in it, but for his hubris he was swallowed up by the earth.[8]

About 1230 appeared the even more chaotic Vulgate Cycle, *L'Estoire del Saint Graal,* a quintet of prose romances in Old French. The author pretended his book was given by the ghost of Christ himself to a Cistercian monk on Good Friday, 717 A.D. This work frankly called the Grail by its old title, an *escuele* or "cauldron." The company of the Grail colonized the holy city of Sarras, ruled by Mordrain and Nascien (Death and Birth). Moys (Moses) was snatched away from the Seat Perilous by fiery hands. Solomon's ship, which moved by itself on the sea, carried Christianity to all lands. Members of the Grail company had various adventures: Bron went to Scotland and sustained a poisoned wound, like Tristan. He was cured by the local princess, then he killed her father and married her. Alain the "Hunting Dog" went to a foreign land and built a new castle for the Grail, Castle Corbenic (*cors-benoiz,* meaning either Horn of Plenty or Sacred Heart). The seventh Rich Fisher, Lambor, was slain by a Saracen with the magic sword from Solomon's ship, and the land of the lost Grail became *la terre gaste*—the Waste Land.[9]

A final step in the transformation of the Grail from a pagan symbol to a Christian one was taken in *La Queste del Saint Graal,* written by a Cistercian monk. Now Galahad was said to be the perfect Desired Knight, of the lineage of Joseph of Arimathea. Galahad occupied the Seat Perilous safely, because he was virginally pure. He drew the magic sword from a stone that floated on the river, for the same reason. Through him the Grail vision was bestowed on all the Round Table knights, who promptly left their games, feasts, and tourneys (i.e., their paganism) to follow the vision to the ends of the earth in search of the real thing.

The *Queste* showed obvious hostility to the contemporary cult of courtly love; but when the Grail's aura of feminine mystery was removed, its romantic appeal declined. If the Grail was nothing more than the cup of Christ's blood, then there was no reason for the great Quest at all. The cup of Christ's blood was readily available to all, in every chapel; and even though it was called a holy sacrament, its discovery somehow lacked thrills.[10] As matters turned out, to Christianize the Grail was to neutralize the magnetism of its secret nature.

The monkish author's real purpose was to tout the virtues of virginity. All but one of the Round Table knights failed the Grail quest because they were guilty of sexual sins. Perceval was abandoned because of his past links with the cult of courtly love. Gawain, who played the part of Desired Knight in other romances, failed utterly. Lancelot, having committed adultery with Guinevere, could never see the Grail except in a dream. The only chaste knight was Galahad, the new, purified Lancelot. Galahad's virginity led him to every Christian treasure, including the shield of Joseph of Arimathea, laid up in a Cistercian abbey. It was white with a red cross—the same "hues of innocence and blood" on the red-and-white emblem of the Assassins' brotherhood, borrowed by the crusaders, and later by mystics calling themselves Knights of the Rosy Cross, or Rosicrucians.[11]

The Grail remained secretly pagan for many centuries in isolated areas. English Grail stories were modeled on the Irish Horn of Plenty, containing blood/wine for drinking and named the Vessel of the Spirit. A festival called a Grail was celebrated every seventh year in Brunswick, until it was outlawed in 1481.[12]

1. Guerber, L.M.A., 182–83. 2. Guerber, L.M.A., 185, 200. 3. Guerber, L.M.A., 186–87. 4. Tuchman, 177. 5. Goodrich, 81. 6. Campbell, M.T.L.B., 163. 7. Guerber, L.M.A., 182–83. 8. Campbell, C.M., 534. 9. Ibid., 535. 10. Ibid., 550, 507. 11. MacKenzie, 117. 12. Jung & von Franz, 115, 121.

Green, Wearing of

Pagan springtime custom that kept its popularity in Christian Europe, especially through the month of May. By imitative magic, wearing of green was supposed to encourage Mother Earth to clothe herself in the green of abundant crops. The women described as fairies in medieval balladry always dressed in green; and their lovers, like **Thomas Rhymer**, wore green in the fairy realm. Christians opposed these pagan traditions, associating green with the dead and with witches, developing the "familiar superstition that green is unlucky."[1] Green was also linked with the sexual promiscuity of old rituals.

1. Wimberly, 176.

Grim

"Mask," often a title of Teutonic deities, like Grimhild. Northern gods as well as those of Egypt and Africa were thought to reside in the masks worn by their impersonators at religious pageants.[1] "Grim" came to mean "ominous" because mask-wearing priests and priestesses were traditional givers of omens.

1. Sturluson, 49.

Griselda

Legendary model for proper wifely behavior in the Christian era. "Patient Griselda" married a man of superior rank, who abused her, neglected her, flaunted his adulteries before her, even took away her babies to kill them and forbade her to shed a single tear because the sight of her grief would vex him. Griselda endured everything humbly, and at last her husband reformed and rewarded her with his true love, saying she had passed all his "tests." So they lived happily ever after, Griselda apparently harboring no resentment for years of mistreatment.

Grotesques

"Creatures of the Grotto," decorative figures in Christian churches, taken from the animal gods, masques, sirens, gorgons, satyrs, Green Men, serpent deities, and other idols in the sacred caves of paganism.[1] Early churches were built right over the heathen "grotto" and the same deities were worshipped side by side with Christian ones, so the people would continue to come to the church by force of habit, finding their familiar idols there.[2] Some hardly noticed the change, which was what authorities of the church counted on. Pope Gregory the Great ordered missionaries to "accommodate the ceremonies of the Christian worship as much as possible to those of the heathen, that the people may not be much startled at the change."[3]

Later, when "grotesques" were re-defined as devils, churches were left with incongruous images of the rival deities, to which people still prayed secretly, or touched for "luck," or gave offerings. Hugo wrote, "Sometimes a porch, a facade, or a whole church presents a symbolic meaning entirely foreign to worship, even inimical to the Church."[4]

The Cathedral of Worms for example displayed along one whole side the gods and heroes of the Nibelungenlied, even though the official theology represented these entities as devils.[5]

Sometimes the traditions of the grotesques were perpetuated by secret societies among the artisans, especially masons and smiths, whose fraternities preserved Gnostic symbols like the double-tailed siren, the double-sexed demiurge, and the Ouroboros or World Serpent, also greatly revered by alchemists and Hermetic magicians. See **Smith**.

1. Guerber, L.R., 272. 2. See Sheridan & Ross. 3. M. Harrison, 138.
4. Mâle, 395. 5. Guerber, L.R., 272.

Grove, Sacred

Next to a cave, a grove was the most popular uterine symbol in ancient religions, even among early biblical Semites, to whom Asherah was the Mother-Goddess of the Grove. A large tree, pillar, or obelisk within the grove often represented the male god inside the Goddess as both child and lover.

Brittany in the 11th century still had a druidic holy wood called Nemet. This may have been the same as the fairy wood Broceliande, the grove of Merlin's Nemesis, the lady Nimue, who also bore the name of the fatal Goddess of the grove.

Patriarchal priesthoods seemed to consider the groves dangerous. The Bible speaks of many attacks on the *asherim* or Groves of Asherah, which were consistently worshipped by both people and kings, despite the prophets' repeated condemnations: Exodus 34:13, Deuteronomy 16:21, Judges 3:7, 1 Kings 15:13, 16:33; 2 Kings 18:4, 21:7.

Destroyers of the sacred groves feared the Mother's curse, as shown in numerous moralizing myths. Erysichthon dared to cut down one of Demeter's sacred groves, though the high priestess forbade him with the voice of the Goddess herself. Then angry Demeter cursed him with perpetual hunger that could never be appeased. He ended as a wretched beggar, frantically stuffing his mouth with filth.[4]

Druidic sacred groves were somewhat protected by superstitious fear of similar curses. The oak grove at Derry was one of the most popular shrines of Irish paganism, its magical name still invoked by the bardic phrase "Hey, Derry Down" in the chorus of old ballads. Writings attributed to St. Columba said Derry's grove must be preserved at all costs. The saint said as much as he feared death and hell, he "dreaded still more the sound of an axe in the grove of Derry."[5]

Sacred kings in Diana's ancient grove at Nemi were expected to fight any rival challenger who broke a branch from the holy tree. This symbolic act occurs so often in medieval romances that it can only be assumed the custom continued through the Middle Ages. The Vulgate epic of Lancelot said Parsifal challenged a rival knight in the same manner as the heroes of Nemi: he "found a tree in the grove

A common Indo-European word for the sacred grove was Nemi (Latin *nemus*), indicating dedication to the Moon-goddess called Nemesis, Diana Nemorensis, or Diana Nemetona—Lady of the Grove. *Nemeton* was the druidic oak grove. Strabo said the greatest shrine of the Galatians (Gauls) in Asia Minor was Drunemeton, the druid-grove. Southern Scotland had a shrine called Medionemeton. France had another, called Nemetodorum (modern Nanterre). In Spain, the sacred grove of the Moon-goddess Brigit was Nemetobriga.[1] Hungary still has Maros-Nemeti, an old grove-shrine of Mari-Diana.[2]

The Irish called a sanctuary *nemed,* or *fidnemed,* a "forest shrine," established by the archaic colonists called Nemed or Moon-people. Religious rites continued in these forest shrines throughout the Middle Ages.[3] Christian writers spoke of "heathen abominations" carried out in forest shrines or *nimidae.*

undefended, and broke a branch from it."[6] Evidence is not lacking to show that breaking a branch from the sacred tree was equivalent to a threat of castration of the god, or the incumbent sacred king who embodied the god.[7]

1. Piggott, 72. 2. Strong, 192. 3. Joyce 1, 359–60. 4. Graves, G.M. 1, 89. 5. Spence, 42. 6. Campbell, C.M., 555. 7. Frazer, G.B., 815 et seq.

Guignole, Saint

Phallic god of Gaul, probably a French name for Priapus, Christianized and worshipped in his own church at Brest. Even after adoption into the Christian canon, St. Guignole remained an ithyphallic figure, from whose erect penis women scraped splinters to assist in conception charms. The priests assisted by installing a trick penis in St. Guignole's statue, which could be lengthened secretly from behind as it was scraped away in front.[1] See **Phallus Worship**.

1. G.R. Scott, 247.

Guinevere

In Germany, Guinevere was Cunneware, "female wisdom."[1] According to the Welsh Triads, she was the Triple Goddess, Gwenhwyfar, "the first lady of these islands," at times one queen, at times three queens, all named Gwenhwyfar, all of whom married King Arthur.[2]

Arthur was born of the same Goddess when he was cast ashore on the ninth wave. The Welsh called breaking waves the Sheep of the Mermaid, and the Mermaid was Gwenhidwy, or Gwenhwyfar. The ninth wave represented the "god born of nine maidens," also known as The Ram.[3] Nine maidens signified the triplicated Triple Goddess, like the nine Muses in Greek myth.

Guinevere embodied the sovereignty of Britain. No king could reign without her. Thus, in story after story, she was abducted by would-be rulers. Melwas, Meleagant, Arthur, Lancelot, and Mordred all took Guinevere away from the incumbent ruler when they wished to make themselves kings. When a king lost Guinevere, he lost the kingship. Some myths suggest that she was a sacred statue, like the Fortuna Regia of Roman Caesars.[4] Yet she was also a living woman, who impersonated the Destroyer when she gave the apple of death to **Patrick**, and was nearly burned at the stake when she was accused of witchcraft. Early legends said she disappeared into the castle of Joyous Gard, the earthly paradise, where she reigned each spring as May Queen.

1. Campbell, C.M., 448. 2. Malory 1, xxiv. 3. Turville-Petre, 152. 4. *Encyc. Brit.*, "Guinevere."

Gula

Babylonian name of the Great Goddess as Lady of Birth and Mother of Dogs. She also ruled fate, as shown by the plural form Gulses, the Fates Who Write, corresponding to Roman Fata Scribunda, or Teutonic *Schreiberinnen,* "Writing-Women."[1]

1. Gaster, 764.

Gunas

"Strands," the threads of Fate, colored white, red, and black. In Tantric symbolism, the three colors stood for "the divine female Prakriti"—i.e., **Kali**—in her three aspects as Creator, Preserver, and Destroyer, or giver of birth, life, and death.[1] The Virgin-Creator was Sattva, white; the Mother-Preserver was Rajas, red; the Crone-Destroyer was Tamas, black. Together they symbolized the cyclic succession of "purity, passion, darkness."[2]

The Svetasvatara Upanishad said white, red, and black were the colors of the Goddess Maya, who was also Kali. Sattva signified "radiant tranquility"; from *sat,* that which exists forever.[3] Rajas was the color of royal blood, the color of a king (*raj*), and of the Mother as queen and battle-goddess, like Durga-Kali, in "blazing motion, violence and passion." Another of her names, Aruna, may have been the origin of Aruru, the Mesopotamian Goddess who made mankind out of clay reddened with her lunar blood.[4] Tamas, the color of the Crone, stood for "passive weight and darkness," the blackness of the tomb.[5]

The Gunas were not only Oriental. The same white, red, and black "strands" were associated with western forms of the Triple Goddess also. Theocritus, Ovid, Tibullus, and Horace all said the sacred colors of the life-threads were white, red, and black.[6] The Goddesses who held the threads were the Fates. They were based on Oriental images such as the three Goddesses depicted in the Mahabharata, weaving the veil of nights and days in an underground "city of serpents," representing cycles of light and darkness with threads of white and black linked with the blood-red thread of life.[7]

Mahabharata Indian epic poem, consisting of historical and legendary material gathered between the 4th and 10th centuries A.D, including the famous Bhagavad-Gita.

Sumerian temples were ornamented with clay-cone mosaics that always showed the same three colors,[8] which were also used to decorate the New World pottery known as Mimbres ware. Celtic myth assigned them to the Hounds of Annwn or dogs of the underworld, and to the maidens in the Castle of the Holy Grail, as if they too were Kalis—or, as the Irish said, kelles (see **Kelle**).

The Gunas are familiar motifs in fairy tales, such as *Snow White:* a story of the princess who not only personified the Virgin in combination with the Mother-queen and the Crone-witch; she also displayed the Gunas in her own person, with "skin white as snow, lips red as blood, and hair black as ebony." Snow White was a direct descendant of Peredur's divine lady-love, whose hair was black as jet, her skin white and red. A vision of the colors alone (crow's feathers and blood in the snow) cast Peredur into a holy trance of meditation upon her image, from which he couldn't wake.[9] Grimm's fairy tale of *Snow White and Rose Red* came from the same root, uniting Virgin and Mother as Eithne the Fair and Fedelim the Rosy, repeated in the lilies and roses sacred to the virgin Mary.[10] The same Virgin and Mother colors were combined by the Two Mistresses of ancient Egypt, Nekhbet and Buto, wearers of the white and red crowns. The same colors were known to medieval mystics in the Middle East as the Hues of Innocence and Blood.[11]

The Crone's color, black, was often dissociated from the Virgin and Mother colors, though the three veils laid on Christian altars for Christmas Matins retained the hues of the pagan trinity, white, red, and black.[12] Black animals were sacrificed to the underworld Goddess from Homer's time all the way up to the 18th century A.D.[13] The Slavs offered black horses to their horse-headed Lord of Death, Volos, who was lightly Christianized as St. Vlas.[14] Gypsy women wore red and black for funerals, combining the attributes of Mother and Crone.[15] In China however, the funereal color was white, to suggest rebirth. Old European ballads sometimes associate all three colors with death. The departure of the dead from Middle-Earth was heralded by "the crowing of the white, the red, and the black cock."[16]

So often were the sacred colors displayed in hundreds of myths, folk tales, and even Christian customs, that Dante placed them at the very core of his Inferno, to symbolize the essence of God's adversary: the three heads of Lucifer were white, red, and black.[17]

1. Avalon, 328–29. 2. Silberer, 280. 3. *Mahanirvanatantra,* p. xxxiii. 4. Avalon, 146. 5. Rawson, E.A., 160. 6. Wedeck, 66. 7. Lethaby, 238. 8. Whitehouse, 60. 9. Goodrich, 63–66. 10. Spence, 56. 11. MacKenzie, 117. 12. Miles, 93. 13. Homer, *Odyssey,* 163. 14. *Larousse,* 298. 15. Groome, 144. 16. Wimberly, 104. 17. Campbell, C.M., 426.

Gunnlöd

Norse name of the Earth-goddess or primal "giantess" from whose underground **cauldron** Odin stole the wise blood of immortality, magic, and feminine *mana,* to make himself a supreme god.[1] Though her myth underwent several revisions, Gunnlöd was another form of the Triple Goddess, keeping three cauldrons (or wombs) in the bowels of the earth, which meant in herself.

1. *Larousse,* 257.

Gwyn

"White god" of Wales, sometimes identified with King Arthur; an Osiris-like Savior slain by his perpetual rival and alter-ego Gwythur ap Greidawl (Set), and buried in a boat-shaped oak-coffin before his resurrection. He was born of Arianrhod, the Great Goddess as virgin mother, and became her consort. Like her, he was a trinity: Dylan, a silver fish; Llew, a white stag; Gwyn, the white rider on a white horse. In these forms he matched the trinity of Arianrhod of the silver wheel, Blodeuwedd the white-flower virgin, and Cerridwen the deathly white sow. Every May Day "until the day of doom," Gwyn fought his rival for the royal embodiment of the Goddess on earth, Creiddylad—Shakespeare's "Cordelia"—who belonged to each contestant alternately. Gwyn was the origin of the common prefix "Win" in the names of ancient British towns.[1]

1. Graves, W.G., 185, 351, 430.

Gyges

Ancient king of Lydia, chosen by the queen to kill her former husband Candaules and then to marry her, according to the archaic system of kingship by combat. Gyges's potency was first judged by the ceremony of unveiling the queen and looking on her nakedness, whereby his physical reaction could be noted and assessed.[1] Since virility was the principal requirement in a king at the time, his sovereignty was contingent on the queen's acceptance of him as a lover. See **Kingship**.

1. Herodotus, 5–6.

Gypsies

Among the last active preservers of Goddess-worship in Europe were the gypsies, who began to migrate westward from Hindustan about 1000 A.D.[1] Because Christians identified their beliefs with witchcraft, gypsies were popularly known as Minions of the Moon, or Diana's Foresters. Some may have adopted the Dianic witch-cult through assimilation of the lunar Diana to their own Goddess, Sara-Kali (Queen Kali), also called Laki (Hindu Lakshmi), or Matta the Mother.[2] Gypsies revered the female principle as the source of life; they said, "For us, woman is like the earth. The earth is our mother, and so is woman. The secret of life comes from the ground."[3]

Many Europeans thought the gypsies came from Egypt, hence their name, "Egyptians."[4] Their own traditions, usually kept secret from non-gypsies, showed that they came of Hindu roots. They believed in reincarnation and karma. A gypsy fortune teller or cartomancer was called a *Vedavica*, reader of the Vedas; for gypsies seem to have regarded **Tarot** cards as their own Vedas.[5]

Gypsies' Goddess was a trinity: Kali as the same three sisters of Fate worshipped by pagans and witches. Like the fairy godmothers, Moerae, or Fortunae, she came in the form of three mystic ladies to the cradle of every newborn child. Gypsies' baptismal ceremonies included three offerings on the infant's bed, "one for each goddess of fate."[6]

The three divine Mothers were symbolized by a triangle, the Tantric yogis' sacred Yoni Yantra, immemorial sign of woman.

Gypsies' informal hieroglyphic system always represented "woman" by the Yoni Yantra.[7] A favorite method of card divination among gypsies was to lay out cards in this same "female" shape. Like the Triple Goddess herself, the triangle's three sides stood for past, present, and future.[8]

The matriarch was the center of gypsy tribal life. "Everything that went on around a tribal mother resembled the old pagan sex rites." Her husband was a drone, whose function was to impregnate her. The tribe supported him in idleness but looked down on him as a non-productive member. If he failed to beget perfect children, he was "accidentally" killed, and another stud-chieftain took his place. "Tribal mothers were often widowed half a dozen times over." The male functionary closest to a tribal mother was not her husband but "the coaxer," a man trained from an early age to control his own sexual responses and "concentrate completely on his partner's pleasure. He was taught to know all the sensitive and erotic zones of the female body. In this curious three-sided relationship, the coaxer gave the mother her physical fulfillment without ever penetrating her. Instead, by a combination of caresses, words, and breathing, he made her sufficiently excited to be ready to have an orgasm as soon as her husband took over."[9]

The queen's coaxer was trained like a Tantric yogi in the rite of *maithuna*, and so were other "occult couples" revered by the gypsies for impersonating the Goddess and God in their endless world-sustaining union. For the gypsy, as for the Tantric sadhu and the Sufi dervish, occult *coitus reservatus* was "a means of increasing psychic powers" in accordance with the ancient Oriental belief that all magic comes from woman.[10]

The gypsy word for a fairy, *rashani*, actually meant "priestess." The most common gypsy surnames were Smith and Faa: "Fay," or "Fairy."[11] Gypsies were generally practitioners of smithcraft, thus became involved in the medieval conviction that smiths, wizards, and women conspired together against the Christian church.[12] (See **Smith**.)

Legends constantly attest to hostility between Christians and gypsies. Laws against vagrancy were invoked, or even specifically passed, to enable the Inquisition to seize gypsies and haul them off to witches' prisons, often without even recording their names.[13] In 1500 the Diet of Augsburg ruled that Christians could kill gypsies without legal penalty, whereas a gypsy injured by a Christian might seek no redress in court.[14] In 1782, forty-five gypsies were tortured, broken on the wheel, hanged, drawn, and quartered for having murdered a number of Hungarians who were really alive and well enough to watch the execution of their alleged killers.[15]

There was a popular belief that gypsies were descended from a union of the first gypsy woman with the devil.[16] An English writer called gypsies "thieves, rogues, and beggarly rascals . . . known by the name of Bohemians, Egyptians, and Caramaras."[17] The third of these titles was peculiarly reminiscent of Kauri-Mara, or Mother Kali as the Goddess of Death.

As the epithet "Christ-killers" supported persecutions of Jews, so various epithets and legends supported persecutions of gypsies. It was said gypsy smiths forged the nails for Christ's crucifixion. The gypsies promulgated a counter-legend: they said an ancestor of their race stole one of the four nails set aside to crucify Jesus, but had no time to steal the other three. For want of the fourth nail, Jesus's feet had to be fastened together with a single nail. Oddly, the transition from four nails to three in Christian art occurred about the same time the gypsies were telling this story.[18] The gypsies also claimed that Jesus, grateful for the gypsy's attempt to save him, from the cross granted all gypsies the right to steal. Another legend said gypsies were allowed to steal because a gypsy woman stole the infant Jesus and hid him from Herod's baby-killers in her basket.[19]

Some gypsies said their race had its own special savior, a Son of God named Alako, who ascended to the moon. He defends gypsies and takes their souls to the moon after death. His two enemies are the devil and Christ.[20] Gypsies also prayed to a spirit from Mother Earth, the *Pchuvus* (cognate with Celtic *pooka* or Puck), who can bestow "earth" on favored people. In gypsy terms, earth meant luck, fortune, money, like the Hindu *artha*, riches from the Earth-mother.[21]

Gypsies claimed it was very unlucky to meet a monk or priest first thing in the morning; nothing would go right for the rest of the day. This anti-clerical idea caught on even among Christians and was still found throughout Italy in the 19th century.[22] Agrippa's *Occult Philosophy* said meeting a monk was an evil omen, "because these kind [sic] of men live for the most by the sudden death of men, as vultures do by slaughters."[23] Reginald Scot said when hunters met a priest, they thought it such bad luck that they would "couple up their hounds, and go home, being in despair of any further sport that day."[24]

Gypsy myths repeated classical sacred dramas in the guise of fairy tales. The Horned God sacrificed to the Triple Goddess appeared frequently. As a gypsy youth, he ate a magic apple given him by a woman, and stag's horns grew from his head. He ate a second magic apple, and his flesh fell away from his bones. He ate a third magic apple, crossed a stream (the Styx), and was resurrected, fairer than ever.[25] Here was Dionysus or Actaeon or Pentheus, slain in his stag mask and reborn from the dead.

As in Vedic myth, gypsy gods were often sacrificed in pig form, usually with the all-important **apple** representing the "heart-soul" (Egyptian *ab*). A gypsy maiden reminiscent of Circe was said to have resurrected her dead lover by replacing all his flesh with pig's flesh, a classic image of a god's or man's sacrificial bestialization. When she squeezed an apple into his mouth to serve as his new heart, he returned to life.[26] The pig with an apple in its mouth was also known to worshippers of Vishnu the boar-god, and those of his Norse counterpart the Yuletide **boar** (or suckling pig). Egyptians said a dead man could be brought back to life when **Anubis** pushed his heart into his mouth.[27] Gypsies told a similar story of a gypsy witch who brought her dead son to life again by pushing his heart into his mouth.[28] An apple often represented the heart.

Among gypsies, "giving the heart" in love or marriage frequently took the ceremonial form of giving an apple. "Occult couples" began the sexual rites with formal cutting of the apple to reveal its magic pentacle, feeding it to each other with the formula: "I am your nourishment, you are mine. We are the feast."[29] South Slavic pagans also used the apple in their marriage ritual: the bride ate half the apple, and gave the other half to her bridegroom. It has been surmised that a similar ancient marriage rite underlay the story of Eve's apple.[30]

Certainly the myths that developed into gypsy folk tales were extremely old and universal throughout the Indo-European cultures. Their Goddess Sara-Kali could well have been the original Sarah who led her tribe from the matrilineal society of Ur of the Chaldees about 1900 B.C.[31] Her alleged consort Abraham was emphasized by biblical writers, but rabbinic literature said he was only a Chaldean "astrologer," i.e., a priest of the Moon-Goddess.[32] The Goddess appeared as mother of the solar deity in another gypsy legend, as "an old woman dressed in white, sitting in a beautiful temple." She explained her function in terms recalling the Riddle of the Sphinx: "I am the mother of the Sun King, who daily flies out of this house as a little child, at mid-day becomes a man, and returns of an evening a graybeard."[33] She also represented the divine Cauldron that daily swallowed him up and gave him rebirth. The popular gypsy surname Kaldera or Kalderas may have been derived from Kali-Devi as the same Cauldron.[34]

The Cauldron of the Deep also appeared in gypsy lore as a mirror, like the one in which the Titans trapped the soul of Dionysus, who was identified with the same sun god. Transylvanian gypsies called him the Enchanted (or Accursed) Hunter, who loved a witch named Mara or Mari—that is, Mother Death. She trapped the hunter's soul in her magic mirror and took it away from him, the typical preliminary to his cyclic resurrection.[35]

Much of this highly significant gypsy lore was kept from non-gypsies for many centuries, as it was always viewed as heresy by Christian authorities, and even folk tales could become excuses for persecution. The prejudice against gypsies has lasted even into the present century. The Nazis declared them "subhumans," along with Jews, Slavs, and other "non-Aryans." Over 400,000 gypsies were killed in the German concentration camps.[36]

1. Trigg, 7. 2. Groome, iv, lxii. 3. Derlon, 135. 4. Trigg, 4. 5. Leland, 67. 6. Trigg, 80. 7. Lederer, 141. 8. Trigg, 48–49. 9. Derlon, 132. 10. Derlon, 159. 11. Groome, lxi. 12. Joyce 1, 223. 13. Summers, G.W., 488–91. 14. Trigg, 11. 15. Tannahill, 103. 16. Trigg, 21. 17. Hazlitt, 113. 18. Groome, xxx. 19. Trigg, 72–73. 20. Trigg, 202. 21. Leland, 99. 22. Leland, 129; Gifford, 25. 23. Agrippa, 172. 24. Scot, 164. 25. Groome, lxvii. 26. Groome, 28. 27. Erman, 158. 28. Groome, 18. 29. Derlon, 131–32. 30. Crawley 2, 133. 31. Boulding, 236. 32. Barrett, 183. 33. Groome, 136. 34. Esty, 67. 35. Groome, 131–32. 36. Boulding, 328.

HYGEIA, "Health." She and her sister Panacea were versions of the Goddess Rhea—or actually her milk-flowing breasts. Asclepius, shown here in his child-form, was also their adoptive father, and the whole clan, snake and caduceus included, became the collective patron of the medicine men.

HATHOR, Queen of Heaven and mother of all the gods. Her name was made part of all early Egyptian royal names to assure matrilineal accession. The Sphinx is one of her incarnations. This depiction shows her with the 19th Dynasty Pharaoh Sethos I and is from his tomb.

Hades

Underworld god, Lord of Death, consort of Hecate or Persephone. In pre-Roman Latium he was known as Eita or Ade, and his bride was Persipnei.[1] Greek myth converted him into the abductor of the Virgin Persephone, or Kore; but as "Destroyer" she was really the underworld Death-goddess to begin with. His Greek name, Aidoneus, meant "blind one," a common title of the phallic Hidden God in the womb of the earth.[2]

Hades was also known as Pluto, or Pluton, Lord of Riches. He was supposed to know the location of all gems and precious metals in the earth. When he was identified with the Christian devil, the belief persisted that the devil could locate buried treasure for his followers. Like all underground deities, Hades was thought a leading resident of hell, which was often called by his name instead of by the name Hel, the Goddess.

1. *Larousse,* 211. 2. Graves, G.M. 2, 393.

Hag

Originally "Holy Woman," the Hag was a cognate of Egyptian *heq,* a predynastic matriarchal ruler who knew the words of power, or *hekau.*[1] In Greek she became Hecate, the Crone or Hag as queen of the dead, incarnate on earth in a series of wise-women or high priestesses.

Hebrew "wisdom" in Proverbs 8 is *Hokhmah,* from Egyptian *heq-maa* or Heka-Maat, the underworld Mother of wisdom, law, and words of power.[2] Greek and Roman cognate *hagia* meant holy, especially as applied to the principle of female wisdom, Hagia Sophia (see **Sophia, Saint**). Similarly in Israel, a *haggiah* was a holy day. Certain Jewish religious literature dating back to Israel's matriarchal period was probably written by wise-women, since it was called the Haggadah. Later patriarchal rabbis declared this material "not legal."[3]

In northern Europe, the Hag was the death-goddess corresponding to Hecate, like the Hag of the Iron Wood whose daughter or virgin form was Hel.[4] Old Norse *hagi* meant a sacred grove, the Iron Wood, a place of sacrifice. *Haggen* meant to chop in pieces, which is what happened to sacrificial victims dismembered for a feast. "Hags" may have been priestesses of sacrifice, like the Scythian matriarchs who butchered for their sacred cauldrons and read omens in entrails.[5] Northmen colonized Scotland, where a *haggis* or "hag's dish" was made of internal organs. Until the 19th century, people kept the New Year festival of Hagmena, Hag's Moon, going in disguise from house to house, begging cakes. A chronicler said: "On the last night of the old year (peculiarly called Hagmenai), the visitors and company made a point of not separating till after the clock struck twelve, when they rose, and mutually kissing, wished each other a happy New Year." This is still the custom. But a contemporary clergyman said the Hagmena meant the Devil was in the house.[6]

Devilish qualities were attributed to stone idols of the Hag, such as the famous Stone of Scone, still used at each British monarch's coronation. This stone once represented the Hag and her spinning wheel—i.e., Arianrhod, Goddess of the Wheel of Fate. A Danish ballad said the Hag of Scone led the "swarthy Elves"; but she was turned to stone by an incantation of the missionary St. Olave: "Thou

Hag of Scone, stand there and turn to granite stone."[7] Helvetian converts to Christianity were compelled to batter to pieces sacred stones in which their Goddess dwelt, reciting her formula, "Once I was the Goddess and now I am nothing at all."[8]

In the 16th century, "hag" was synonymous with "fairy."[9] Old High German called a wise-woman Hagazussa, that is, a moon-priestess.[10] Though "hagiology" still means the study of holy matters and saints, the root word *hag* declined in its meanings. Shakespeare's verb *hagged* meant to be bewitched. His noun *haggard* meant a hawk, a harpy, or an intractable woman.[11]

The Hag as death-goddess, her face veiled to imply that no man can know the manner of his death, was sometimes re-interpreted as a nun. Christianized legends were invented for these veiled figures.[12]

1. *Book of the Dead,* 351. 2. Budge, G.E. 1, 296. 3. *Encyc. Brit.,* "Haggadah." 4. Sturluson, 39. 5. Wendt, 137. 6. Hazlitt, 296. 7. Wimberly, 36. 8. Thorsten, 336. 9. Scot, 550. 10. J.B. Russell, 16. 11. Potter & Sargent, 70. 12. Graves, W.G., 409.

Hair

As shown by its importance in witch-charms and in the mutual exchange of talismans between lovers, hair was usually viewed as a repository of at least a part of the soul. At the ancient temple of Troezen, youths and maidens dedicated locks of their hair to the savior-god Hippolytus before marriage; this was "designed to strengthen his union with the Goddess."[1]

When the Goddess-mother became Queen of Shades for each god or man at the end of his life, his soul was likened to a child seeking safety in the mother's shadow. The Great Mother's hair cast its shadow over the approaching soul. An Egyptian found salvation by identifying himself with Osiris, for whom the Goddess made resurrection-magic with her hair: "He is found with her hair spread over him; it is shaken out over his brow."[2] When Isis put on mourning garments for Osiris, she cut a lock of her hair to preserve his soul. Egyptian widows similarly buried locks of their hair with deceased husbands, as a charm of protection in the after-world.

When Isis restored vitality to the dead Osiris, entitled the Still Heart, she created his new life with her hair, made his heart beat again and his penis move so she could conceive his reincarnation, Horus. She "produced warmth from her hair, she caused air to come. . . . She caused movement to take place in what was inert in the Still Heart, she drew essence (semen) from him, she made flesh and blood, she suckled her babe alone."[3] She further protected her Divine Child by "shaking out her hair over him."[4]

Mortal women often claimed the same preservative magic for their own hair. Ptolemy III was protected from harm on his Syrian campaign in 247 B.C. by his wife Berenice, who dedicated locks of her hair on Aphrodite's altar for this purpose. When the hair vanished from the temple, it was discovered among the divine figures in heaven, where it appears to this day as the constellation Coma Berenices, "Berenice's Hair."[5]

Signs and wonders in the heavens were usually interpreted as significant omens of future catastrophes, particularly a comet, "spirit of hair." A comet was supposed to be a tendril of the Great Mother's hair appearing in the sky as the world was slowly overshadowed by her twilight shadow of doomsday. Most forms of the Death-goddess showed masses of hair standing out from her head, sometimes in the shape of serpents, as in the Gorgoneum of Medusa-Metis-Neith-Anath-Athene. On the magic principle of "as above, so below," women's hair partook of the same mystic powers as the Goddess's hair. Tantric sages declared that the binding or unbinding of women's hair activated cosmic forces of creation and destruction.[6]

The same idea prevailed among prophetic priestesses or witches, who operated with unbound hair on the theory that their tresses could control the spirit world. Mother Goddesses like Isis, Cybele, and many emanations of Kali were said to command the weather by braiding or releasing their hair. Their corresponding mortal representatives could cause to be bound or loosed in heaven what they bound or loosed on earth—hence the unflagging superstitious belief in Christian Europe that witches' hair controlled the weather. Churchmen said witches raised storms, summoned demons, and produced all sorts of destruction by unbinding their hair. As late as the 17th century the *Compendium Maleficarum* said witches could control rain, hail, wind, and lightning in such a way.[7] In the Tyrol, it was believed that every thunderstorm was caused by a woman combing her hair. Scottish girls were forbidden to comb their hair at night while their brothers were at sea, lest they raise a storm and sink the boats.[8] A Syrian exorcism for werewolves invoked "that Angel who judged the woman that combed the hair of her head on the Eve of Holy Sunday," suggesting a connection between hair-combing women and the "werewolves" mythologized as dogs of doomsday.[9]

Compendium Maleficarum A treatise on witches and witchcraft compiled by Guazzo in 1608.

St. Paul greatly feared the "angels" (spirits) that women could command by letting their hair flow loose. He insisted that women's heads must be covered "because of the angels" (1 Corinthians 11:10). Thus it became a Christian rule that women's heads must be covered in church, lest they draw demons into the building. Modern women wearing hats or head shawls to church unconsciously defer to this ancient superstition about their hair. Due to identification of bats with demons, the erroneous notion that bats tend to tangle themselves in women's hair arose from the same superstition.[10]

The ancients insisted that women needed their hair to work magic spells; thus women deprived of their hair were harmless.[11] For this reason, Christian nuns and Jewish wives were compelled to shave their heads. Inquisitors of the medieval church insisted on shaving the hair of accused witches before putting them to the torture.[12] Churchmen claimed Satan told his worshippers that no harm could come to them "as long as their hair was on."[13] Some inquisitors preferred to shave body hair too; hence the expression "to make a clean breast"—that is, to confess—arose from the custom of shaving the chest hair of male witches.

Inconsistently, churchmen apparently thought women should not take the initiative and cut off their own hair. Cutting off her hair was one of the crimes for which Joan of Arc was condemned to the fire. The count read: "This woman is apostate, for the hair which God gave her for a veil she has untimely cut off."[14] Had she been tortured, as the inquisitors threatened, her hair would have been untimely cut off anyway. It seemed that men wanted to do it themselves, not to be anticipated.

Medieval Europe had innumerable superstitions based on the pagan significance of hair. Children's hair was left uncut for many years on the theory that their strength would be impaired if their hair was cut too soon.[15] Gypsy witches advised the lovelorn to snip a lock of the beloved's hair secretly and wear it as a ring or locket. Whoever possessed another's hair had power over his soul.[16] Lovers often traded hair-locks in token of good faith. If either betrayed the other, the hair-lock could be used to cast a vengeful spell on the betrayer.

Gypsies said a witch could be known by her hair, which grew straight for three or four inches, then began to wave, like "a waterfall bouncing over rocks." This was one of the distinctively Hindu ideas the gypsies brought with them out of Asia.[17] The waterfall effect was produced when naturally straight hair was kept in braids, a fashion of both Hindu and gypsy women. During childbirth however, gypsy women always let their hair flow loose, on the magic principle that braids or knots would "tie up" the birth.[18] European witch-midwives often shared this belief, but many also braided female hair into amulets to preserve suckling infants and their nurses. This custom continued in Ireland up to the 19th century.[19]

Homer spoke of "Circe of the Braided Tresses, an awful goddess of mortal speech": that is, Circe's hair and words like Kali's controlled creation and dissolution.[20] Circe was another name for the Fate-spinner, who sat at her loom weaving the destinies of men and singing her spells of becoming.[21] Circe's braids symbolized her power over metempsychosis; she stood for the cosmic Cirque, or karmic wheel.[22]

Braiding the round of Fate was expressed in pagan dances, like the Maypole dance, with ribbons signifying the rays of sun and moon. On May Eve, female dancers circled the pole widdershins or moon-wise—the counter-clockwise direction sacred to women—while male dancers progressed in the other direction, sunwise. The resulting braid represented interpenetration of masculine and feminine powers.[23] This heathen dance survives as the "braiding" figure in square-dancing known as Grand Right and Left, in which men and women weave opposite directions around a circle, with or without touching hands as they pass.

For the sun gods, hair represented both "rays" and virility. Apollo's phallic function was implied by his epithet Chrysocomes, "He of the Golden Locks." Ceremonial castration was the meaning of solar gods' haircuts, like Samson's. A traditional site of the hero's castration or hair-cutting was Calvary, "Bald Skull," a hill where sacrifices were performed. Romans sometimes called the Great Goddess Calva, "Baldness," a name so old that no one knew the reason for it. Like Moriah, it may have descended from an altar-crowned hill of sacrifice.[24]

> *Head hair comes in for special attention in both West and East. Priests who wish to conserve their vitality, to "cut off the outflows," to use a Buddhist term, shave it off. His long hair was the repository of the Biblical Samson's energy. So is the Sikh's. The Indian god Shiva, who is the personalized representation of the creative and sexual energy of the universe, is always represented as having a mass of long, tangled, piled-up hair on his head. Yogis who are his devotees imitate their divine pattern in this respect. Abundant hair represents the abundance of divine energy, in the same way as Shiva's erect phallus. . . . [E]ven today the ordinary Indian believes that the way to avoid "catching cold" and stay healthy (i.e., preserve his vital energy) is to wrap up his head, even if the rest of the body is practically naked. Hence the turban.*[25]

Tantric *sadhakas* who worshipped hairy Shiva may have been the original "Sadducees" of the Bible. A related sect of hermits known as Nazarites or Nazarenes were distinguished like *sadhakas* by their never-cut hair, a tradition partly preserved by the uncut ear-locks of the orthodox Jew. The law of the Oriental holy hermit appears in the Bible: "He shall be holy, and shall let the locks of the hair of his head grow" (Numbers 6:5). But Christians said a man having long hair was shameful (1 Corinthians 11:14).

An opposing myth, relating virility to baldness, was promulgated by Hippocrates, possibly because he was himself subject to hair loss. He said bald men are "of an inflammatory habit; and the plasma in their head being agitated and heated by salacity, coming to the epidermis withers the roots of the hair causing it to fall off."[26] Thanks to Hippocrates, the mythic relationship between baldness and sexual potency has lasted up to the present day.

Another durable myth claimed a witch's hair would become a serpent when buried or placed in water, especially if the hair was plucked while the witch was menstruating.[27] This was another branch from the root of Gorgon mythology, where the female head with serpent-hair represented "wisdom" and warned would-be trespassers of the menstrual taboo.

Hair was so universally associated with paganism that British churches used to command men to shear their hair and beards on Maunday Thursday, the day before Good Friday, so they would be "honest" (i.e., "Christian") for Easter. Consequently this day is described in old writings as Shear Thursday.[28]

1. Frazer, G.B., 8. 2. *Book of the Dead,* 54, 400. 3. Budge, D.N., 250. 4. Budge, G.E. 1, 443. 5. Lindsay, O.A., 131. 6. Rawson, A.T., 67. 7. Wedeck, 152, 78. 8. Frazer, G.B., 273. 9. Summers, V., 225. 10. Cavendish, P.E., 95. 11. Graves, W.G., 396. 12. Frazer, G.B., 789. 13. Campbell, C.M., 595. 14. Coulton, 253. 15. de Lys, 153. 16. Leland, 134. 17. Leland, 160. 18. Trigg, 58. 19. Hazlitt, 341. 20. Homer, *Odyssey,* 148. 21. Graves, G.M. 2, 358. 22. Lindsay, O.A., 239. 23. de Lys, 374. 24. Dumézil, 422. 25. Rawson, E.A., 25. 26. Knight, S.L., 79. 27. Briffault 2, 662. 28. Hazlitt, 541.

Hakkni Panki

Gypsy word for trickery, practiced by gypsies on the non-gypsy folk to steal money and other necessities from them. A corruption of the Romany term led to the modern "hanky-panky."[1] See **Gypsies**.

1. Leland, 211.

Haligmonath

"Holy Month," the month of birth, ninth month of the Saxon lunar calendar which was based on female biological cycles.

Halja

Gothic name for Hel, Goddess of the underworld, also known as Helga, Helle, Holle, etc. This was the name used to translate *Infernus* in early translations of the Latin Bible.

Halka

Sufi word for the magic circle, corresponding to the Trantric *chakra.* The circle of worship, alternating men and women, is called "the basic unit and very heart of active Sufism."[1] Dancing, worshipping, and other ritual activities performed in a circle of men and women marked western paganism also, as shown by references to circles or rings of fairies, witches, mummers, and Maypole dancers. Circles generally expressed cyclic religions; lines, like the rows of pews in a Christian church, expressed patriarchal linearity of ideas.

1. Shah, 21.

Halloween

All Souls' or All Hallows' Day (November 1) was the Christian version of Samhain, the Celtic feast of the dead, named for the Aryan

Lord of Death, Samana, "the Leveller," or the Grim Reaper, leader of ancestral ghosts. According to the pagan lunar calendar, festivals were celebrated on the "eve" rather than the day. Therefore Halloween or All Hallows' Eve was the original festival, later displaced to the following day. The Irish used to call the holy night the Vigil of Saman. Churchmen described it as a night of magic charms and divinations, reading the future with witches' mirrors and nutshell ashes, ducking for apples in tubs of water (representing soul-symbols in the Cauldron of Regeneration), and other objectionable rites. Even today it is said that a girl who peels an **apple** before a mirror on Halloween will see the image of her future husband in the glass.[1] Christian authorities wrote of Halloween, "Many other superstitious ceremonies, the remains of Druidism, are observed on this holiday, which will never be eradicated while the name of Saman is permitted to remain."[2] The name of the pagan deity remains in the Bible as Samuel, from the Semitic Sammael, the same underworld god.

Of course the original divinations were oracular utterances by the ancestral dead, who came up from their tombs on Halloween, sometimes bringing gifts to the children of their living descendants. In Sicilian Halloween tradition, "the dead relations have become the good fairies of the little ones."[3] Similar customs are observed at Christmas.

In Lithuania, the last European country to accept Christianity, the pagans celebrated their New Year feast at Halloween, sacrificing domestic animals to their god Zimiennik (Samanik; Samana). Their prayer ran, "Accept our burnt sacrifice, O Zimiennik, and kindly partake thereof."[4] If the lord of the underworld accepted the offering on behalf of all the dead, the spirits were satisfied and would refrain from doing harm. If not adequately propitiated, they might descend on the world as vengeful ghosts, led by demons and "witches" (priestesses) who summoned them. The witches and ghosts are still associated with Halloween, together with such soul-symbols as owls, bats, and cats.

The pagan idea used to be that crucial joints between the seasons opened cracks in the fabric of space-time, allowing contact between the ghostworld and the mortal one.

1. de Lys, 365. 2. Hazlitt, 340. 3. Miles, 192. 4. Miles, 195.

Halo

Christian symbol of apotheosis—deification, or canonization—taken from the Eleusinian Mysteries, where the savior-god was deified at the Haloa, Festival of the Threshing-Floor (the *halos*).[1]

The god was variously named Dionysus, Triptolemus, or Iasus. He represented the grain. At his birth, he was laid in a manger. He was sacrificed, buried, and resurrected: the sequence representing harvest, re-planting, and new growth. His flesh and blood were consumed by his worshippers in the form of bread and wine. See **Demeter**.

The deity was identified with the daily-reborn sun, so the halo was also a solar symbol, as in Egypt. In Christian hagiography it was sometimes known as the *aura,* "circle of gold," which Byzantine art showed as a golden disc rather awkwardly attached at an angle to the back of the head. Still another variant was based on the Tantric idea of the "thousand-petaled lotus of light" sprouting from the head of the completely enlightened sage. It was called the *nimbus* or "cloud" of light, a symbol of divinity long before there were Christian deities or saints.[2]

1. Potter & Sargent, 185. 2. Budge, A.T., 351.

Hannah

Biblical version of the Anatolian Grandmother-goddess Hannahanna, or Anna. Hittites called her Hwanhwanar, the Nether Upsurge, married to a sacred king at the Puruli festival, shortly before he was sent down into her Abyss to become the new Lord of Death.[1]

Hannah's biblical son bore the same name as the Lord of Death, Sama-El, Sammael or Samuel, from Samana, a Hindu title of the death-god Yama as Conductor of Souls.[2]

In Old Iranian, a clan matriarch was the *hana,* "grandmother." Similarly, the Mother of the virgin mother was worshipped throughout the Middle East under such names as Hannah, Anna, Nana, In-anna, or "Queen Nana, the Creatress."[3] In Christian tradition she was Anna, the Grandmother of God.[4] Mother of the virgin Mary was Anna or Hannah, just as Anatolian Hannahanna was the mother of the virgin Mari. Sometimes her virgin aspect was named Inaras, who was also a death-goddess. She annually imprisoned the sacred king in a temple tower, mated with him, then killed him.[5] (See **Anne, Saint**.)

1. Gaster, 7. 2. *Larousse,* 346. 3. Stone, 219. 4. Graves, W.G., 410.
5. Hooke, M.E.M., 98–99.

Hapi

Archaic deity of the Nile, represented as masculine but having pendulous female breasts and a large pregnant belly. Ancestral predynastic tribes of Egypt were said to be Hapi's children, therefore Hapi was originally a form of the Great Goddess. Like most of the oldest Oriental divinities, "he" was associated with the yonic lotus.[1]

1. *Larousse,* 36, 38.

Har

var. Harmonia

Ishtar as the patroness of temple prostitutes or *harines* was known as the Great Goddess Har. Like Greek *horae,* Persian *houris,* and other sacred *har*lots, her priestesses occupied the part of the temple that came to be called Harem, the Sanctuary.[1] Kings had to prove their virility, hence their right to rule, by impregnating the *harines,* until it became a custom to let certain priests take over this duty. (See **Prostitution**.)

From the root *har* came Hara, Hebrew for both a holy mountain and a pregnant belly; Hariti or Haraiti, the "Lofty Mountain" of paradise in both pre-Vedic Dravidian and Old Iranian cosmology; and Harmonia, a "daughter of Aphrodite," a bringer of peace, one of the functions of the holy harlot. Harmonia was mythologized as an ancient queen of Boeotia, married to Cadmus, whose name in Phoenician was *kedem,* "the Oriental."[2] When Cadmus and Harmonia died and went to paradise, they were both transformed into serpents.[3] Probably they were assimilated to the male-and-female, perpetually entwined serpents of the Hermetic caduceus, whose meaning was "Life." (See **Serpent**.)

1. *Assyr. & Bab. Lit.,* 170; Briffault 2, 320. 2. Massa, 40. 3. Graves, G.M. 1, 199.

Harpies

Female death-spirits from Mount Dicte, home of the Cretan Goddess, embodied in carrion birds, probably vultures. They had bird bodies with women's heads and breasts, suggesting the Minoan style of funerary priestesses in feather costumes with bare necks and bosoms. Their name meant "snatchers" or "pluckers," perhaps related to their use of the harp in funerary music, since a harp is played with plucking motions.[1] Patriarchal Hellenic myth made the Harpies obnoxious monsters, but they seem to have been once the same as **dakinis** or **Valkyries**. Christian iconography continued to picture winged angels, who carried souls to heaven, as harp players.

1. Graves, G.M. 1, 128; 2, 230.

Hathor

Egyptian Mother of the Gods and Queen of Heaven, originally Het-Hert, "the House (or Womb) Above"; later Hat-Hor, "the House (or Womb) of Horus." Hathor was "the mother of every god and goddess." She "brought forth in primeval time herself, never having been created." In the earliest dynasties, her name was a component of all royal Egyptian names, indicating the archaic matrilineal queenship based on successive incarnations of her spirit.[1]

Hathor was worshipped in Israel in the 11th century B.C. at her own holy city of Hazor, which the Old Testament claims Joshua destroyed (Joshua 11:13, 21). The Sinai Tablets show that Hebrew workers in the Egyptian mines of Sinai about 1500 B.C. worshipped Hathor, whom they identified with the Lady of Byblos, **Astarte.**[2]

Some sources said there were seven Hathors: the Holy Midwives associated with the seven heavenly spheres. They gave each Egyptian seven souls at birth. Sevenfold Hathor entered medieval myth as the fairy godmother(s) and Mother Goose, as well as the Mother of the Sun King, the Lady of the Lake, and the Huntress.

In Upper Egypt, Hathor was Sati or Satis, She of the Two River-Banks, source of the Nile.[3] Her Destroyer aspect was a lion-headed huntress, the Sphinx, sometimes called Sekhmet or Sakhmis, "the Powerful." Like Kali, she drank the blood of gods and men.

1. Budge, G.E. 1, 92–93, 428, 431. 2. Albright, 96, 196. 3. Erman, 4.

Heart

Ab was the Egyptian word for heart-soul, most important of the seven souls bestowed by the seven birth-goddesses (Hathors). The *ab* was the soul that would be weighed in the balances of Maat after death, in her underground Hall of Judgment, to see if it was too heavy with sins to balance her Feather of Truth. The *ab* was most important because it was the central blood-soul emanating from the essence of the mother.

The maxim that a pregnant woman carries her child "under her heart" began with the Egyptians, who believed menstrual blood that made the child's life descended from the mother's heart to her womb. The maternal heart, then, was the source of the child's life, which was why a mother called her child "heart's blood." The Book of the Dead addressed prayers to "My heart of my mother. . . . My heart of transformations," meaning the source of rebirths.[1]

Significantly, the meaning of the Egyptian word for the mother-given heart was reversed in Hebrew; *ab* was re-defined as "father."

The Egyptian hieroglyphic sign for *ab* was a dancing figure, and as a verb it meant "to dance."[2] This referred to the mystic dance of life going on inside the body—the heartbeat. The same mystic symbol in India was the Dance of Shiva, who was supposed to dwell at the beating heart of the cosmos within the world-body of Kali. Shiva went through certain cycles when he was temporarily dead, known as Shava the Corpse, and his dance ceased until his Mother resurrected him again. Similarly, the Egyptian god Osiris passed through a death phase before the Goddess brought him back to life. In this phase he was known as the Still-Heart.[3]

Like other mummies, Osiris's mummy received a new *ab,* "heart amulet," always made of red stone and placed in the mummy's breast to bring back vitality.[4] The custom of removing the mummy's real heart probably dated back to primitive ritual offerings of human hearts to the Goddess, who was addressed in some archaic prayers as "swallower of hearts."[5] As always, the primitive theory was that what a deity gave must be returned at least in part, to keep up the deity's energy to give more. The same kind of sacrifices took place on the sacred pyramids of Mexico. Victims identified with the dying god were cut open quickly, so the heart could be offered still alive and "dancing." The Egyptian word *ab* also meant an offering as well as a heart, suggesting that at some point in Egyptian history the sacrificial victims were deprived of their hearts.[6] Juvenal said the Egyptians offered human sacrifices and ate human flesh. The Egyptian Goddess took an underworld form as a monster Ab-She, "She Who Eats Hearts."[7] The old texts said the Goddess devoured what she created, after the manner of Kali, and Earth, and Time, and Fate: "she taketh possession of hearts, she swalloweth."[8]

Up to the present century, Bantu witches remembered Egyptian ideas well enough to believe they could cast a death spell by symbolically eating the intended victim's "heart life," a concept very like the Egyptian *ab.*[9] Many phrases still in English usage date back to the Egyptian idea of the heart as the center of the self, the soul, or the emotions. One is heavy-hearted or light-hearted; hope brings "new heart"; grief makes the heart ache or break; love steals the heart away, or makes the heart full; absence makes the heart grow fonder; hearts may be given, or taken, or withered, or gladdened; hearts may be warm or cold, hard or soft.

So vital was the idea of the heartbeat in Oriental religions that the very center of the universe was placed "within the heart" by Tantric sages.[10] This place was Chidambaram, where Shiva danced to the basic rhythm of eternity. The sages said: "Sound (nada) represents the State of Power. It is experienced by the yogi when he plunges deep into himself. It is made manifest in the heartbeat. And since the microcosm is finally identical with the macrocosm, when the yogi hears the Nada, this Sound of Power, he is listening to the heartbeat of the Absolute."[11]

In this expression of the basic mystical idea that deity is within the human being, the sages in effect admitted that man creates God. The heartbeat was also said to establish the fundamental tempo for poetry, song, music, and dance.

Acts of John
A famous Gnostic text, never entirely suppressed although the orthodox church repeatedly denounced it through the centuries for its heretical assertion that, as a deity, Jesus could not actually die on the cross.

The Tantric idea of the heart's dance surfaced in early Gnostic Christianity, when Jesus was equated with the dancing god-within. In the *Acts of John,* Jesus said to his followers: "To the Universe belongs the dancer. He who does not dance does not know what happens. Now if you follow my dance, see yourself in Me who am speaking. . . . You who dance, consider what I do, for yours is this passion of Man which I am to suffer."[12]

Though the church outlawed ecclesiastical dancing early in the Christian era, the theme of the dancing god within the heart was not forgotten. Eventually it led to the concept of the Sacred Heart, adopted as an article of Catholic faith late in the 17th century. An oddly feminine symbolism was attached to this re-working of the heart-soul idea. Jesus's divinity was "the moon dwelling in the heart." His Sacred Heart was described by all the metaphors attached to the ancient Mother-heart: "as 'the temple in which dwells the life of the world,' as a rose, a cup, a treasure, a spring, as the furnace of divine love . . . as a bridal chamber."[13]

The church claimed that the Sacred Heart began with the divine vision of St. Margaret Marie Alacoque in 1675. However, the idea was not original with her. An alchemical textbook published 11 years before her birth depicted the Sacred Heart encircled by a crown of thorns. Several centuries earlier, it was shown on a stained-glass window of the Convent des Cordeliers in Paris; on a Jacobin cloister wall; on a window of the Chapel of St. Thomas Aquinas; and in four places of the Carmelite church of St. Michael. Some of these "certainly belonged to the 15th and 16th centuries."[14] And of course, the concept of the divine heart-soul at the core of the living world—that is, Shiva's Sacred Heart, or Osiris's—belonged to the millenia, long before there was a Christian church.

1. *Book of the Dead,* 454. 2. Budge, E.L., 44. 3. *Book of the Dead,* 410. 4. Budge, A.T., 138. 5. *Book of the Dead,* 416–18. 6. Budge, E.L., 44, 71. 7. Budge, G.E. 1, 232. 8. Neumann, G.M., 161–62. 9. Summers, H.W., 163. 10. Ross, 32. 11. Zimmer, 205. 12. Pagels, 74. 13. Jung & von Franz, 100. 14. de Givry, 216.

Hebe

Virgin form of Hera, the Greek Mother of the Gods; a variant of Eve, who was Hebat in Anatolia, Heveh or Hawwa in Mesopotamia, Hvov in Persia. Greek myths said Hebe was cupbearer to the gods, dispenser of their ambrosia of immortality. Without her, the gods would grow old and die, the same doom that threatened the Norse gods when they lost Freya.[1]

Like Eve, in her Mother aspect Hebe governed the Tree of Life with its magic apples, source of the gods' everlasting life, which they jealously guarded from mankind (Genesis 3:22). Heroes like Heracles could become immortal gods by marrying Hebe and living in her garden of paradise, where they could feed on the apples of the holy tree.[2] Such myths show that Hebe was only Hera virginized, for Hera was the owner of the serpent-guarded apple tree in the far-western paradise, known to the Greeks as the garden of the Hesperides.

After Hellenic Greeks introduced a social system of patriarchy and the fashion of romantic-homosexual love, Father Zeus evicted Hebe from her traditional post and replaced her with his own male concubine, Ganymede. Thus the Virgin Goddess was supplanted by the Youth, the gods' new cupbearer, taken to heaven and dwelling in the stars as the constellation Aquarius.[3]

1. Branston, 249. 2. Graves, G.M. 2, 203. 3. Graves, G.M. 1, 116.

Hecabe

var. Hecuba

Matriarchal queen of Troy, embodying the spirit of the Moon-goddess Hecate, whose name was the same as her own. Hecabe's "daughters" (priestesses) had divinatory powers, and the ability to cast spells, as shown by the legend of **Cassandra**. Hecabe herself laid effective curses. When captured by her enemies, she transformed herself into Hecate's totemic shape, a black bitch named Maera, Mara, or Moera, the Destroying Fate.[1] The wanderings of Odysseus were attributable to the curse of exile she laid on him; he was preserved from death only the by the counter-spell of his wife the Goddess Penelope.

1. Graves, G.M. 2, 342.

Hecate

One of the oldest Greek versions of the trinitarian Goddess, Hecate was derived from the Egyptian midwife-goddess Heqit, Heket, or Hekat, who in turn evolved from the *heq* or tribal matriarch of pre-dynastic Egypt: a wise-woman, in command of all the *hekau* or "mother's Words of Power."[1]

As a heavenly midwife amalgamating the Seven Hathors of the birth-chamber, Heqit delivered the sun god every morning.[2] Her totem was the frog, symbol of the fetus; and this animal was still sacred to her four thousand years later when she became the Christians' "queen of witches."

In Greece, Hecate was one of many names for the original feminine trinity, ruling heaven, earth, and the underworld. Hellenes tended to emphasize her Crone or underworld aspect, but continued to worship her at places where three roads met, especially in rites of magic, divination, or consultation with the dead.[3] Her images guarded three-way crossroads for many centuries; thus she was Hecate Trevia, "Hecate of the Three Ways." Offerings were left at her roadside shrines on nights of the full moon. As a deity of magic and prophecy she was invoked by those who set out on journeys, like the biblical king of Babylon, who "stood at the parting of the way, at the head of the two ways, to use divination: he made his arrows bright, he consulted with images" (Ezekiel 21:21).

Hecate was called "most lovely one," a title of the moon.[4] Like all other forms of the Triple Goddess, she was associated with the moon in all three of her aspects. Some said she was Hecate Selene, the Moon, in heaven; Artemis the Huntress on earth; and Persephone the Destroyer in the underworld.[5] Ancient texts referred to her as Hecate Selene the Far-Shooting Moon, mother of Dionysus—though Dionysus was also the son of Persephone, which shows that Hecate and Persephone were often confused with one another.[6] Sometimes Hecate was considered identical with Diana Ilithyia, the Moon-goddess as protectress of parturient women. Sometimes she was part of the

Queen-of-Heaven trinity, Hebe the Virgin, Hera the Mother, Hecate the Crone. Porphyry wrote:

> *The moon is Hecate, the symbol of her varying phases. . . . [H]er power appears in three forms, having as symbol of the new moon the figure in the white robe and golden sandals, and torches lighted; the basket which she bears when she has mounted high is the symbol of the cultivation of the crops which she made to grow up according to the increase of her light.*[7]

Late Hellenic writers devised a rather labored explanation for Hecate's journey from the sky to the underworld, originally a mythic metaphor for the moon's setting. Hecate was in the house of a woman in childbirth. The gods, fearing magical contagion from this, plunged her into the river Acheron to wash away the traces of birth-mana. The river carried Hecate underground, where she married Hades. This was a myth derived from patriarchal anxieties about contact with childbearing women, demonstrated especially in the Bible (Leviticus 12:5). Ritual bathing of mother and child in a sacred river after the lying-in period probably gave rise to the story of Hecate's river-journey.

During the early Middle Ages, Hecate became known as Queen of the Ghostworld, or Queen of Witches. She was especially diabolized by Catholic authorities who said the people most dangerous to the faith were precisely those whom Hecate patronized: the midwives.[8] Her ancient threefold power was copied, however, by priestly writers who reassigned it to their own deity: "The threefold power of Christ, namely in Heaven, in earth, and in Hell."[9]

Porphyry (ca. 234–305 A.D.) Neoplatonist philosopher, scholar, and writer; biographer of Plotinus; an opponent of the Christian church, which eventually destroyed most of his books.

1. Budge, E.M., 196; G.E. 2, 300. 2. *Larousse*, 38. 3. Graves, G.M. 1, 124. 4. Angus, 173. 5. Wedeck, 203. 6. Graves, G.M. 2, 393. 7. Briffault 2, 605. 8. Kramer & Sprenger, 66. 9. de Voragine, 776.

Hecatomb

Sacrificial festival involving the offering of one hundred victims to Hecate. The later, extended meaning was any slaughter of a group of one hundred. Most Middle-Eastern gods (including Yahweh) received "hecatombs" on special occasions.

Heill

Literally, "virility," the divine force without which Norse kings couldn't rule. A king's virility was periodically tested, and when it waned, he was usually killed and replaced. When King Fjölnir of Sweden "became impotent," he was drowned in a vat of mead, the common euphemism for the sacred cauldron.[1] A similar custom disposed of biblical kings, like David, who died very soon after the maiden **Abishag** proved him impotent (1 Kings 1:4).

The Cerne Giant of Dorset was said to represent the Saxon god Heill, personification of phallic spirit, as shown by his erect penis. The church claimed St. Augustine built Cerne Abbey to commemorate the downfall of this lusty "devil," but it seems the shrine was dedicated to Heill in the first place, and simply taken over by Christian monks.[2]

1. Turville-Petre, 119, 191. 2. Johnson, 326.

Heimarmene

Pythagorean name for the Goddess of Allotted Fate, a trinity with **Ananke** and Dike. She was another philosophical transformation of the Triple Goddess.

Heimdall

Archaic Norse god born of the sea, called "king" (*rig*), and charged like the Christian doomsday angel with the duty of sounding the Last Trump at doomsday on his ringing horn (*Gjallarhorn*).[1] By virtue of his sacred marriage with all three persons of Mother Earth's trinity, Heimdall was also the father of the castes.

1. Turville-Petre, 154.

var. Hekau

Heka

Egyptian "Words of Power," evolved by primitive matriarchs under the birth-goddess Hekat or Heqit (Greek Hecate). In Egyptian salvation-mysteries, rote learning of *hekau* was necessary to gain admission to various areas of the after-world. Also useful were amulets like the Hekat, a uterine "ark" named after the Goddess. See **Ship**.

Hel

Norse Queen of the Underworld, whose name became the English "hell." Dead heroes who went to the house of Hel were known as Helleder, "Hel's men."[3] Sometimes they were ancestral ghosts known as *Hella cunni,* "kinsmen of Hel," corrupted in the medieval mystery play to Harlequin, lover of Columbine the Dove-maiden, who was another version of the Goddess.[4] The Celtic Lord of Death, wearer of the *apex* or pointed tiara of divinity, bore the title of Helman.[5]

The early "hell" seems to have been a uterine shrine or sacred cave of rebirth, denoted by the Norse *hellir.*[6] The notion of Hel as a cauldron-womb filled with purgative fire may have been related to the idea of the volcanic Mother-mountain (Latin *caldera*). In the Pacific,

Mother Hell or Mother Death was often a fire-mountain entered by way of a sacred cave. The Hawaiian volcano-goddess Pele, like Hel, kept souls of the dead in regenerative fire. Pele and Hel may have had linguistic connections, as *p* and *h* may be interchanged in Indo-European languages. In Malekula, the dead live in a volcano under the Goddess's rule: "Abiding in that fire is bliss; there is no fear of being consumed." Japan's sacred volcano was named for the fire-goddess Fuji, "Grandmother" or "Ancestress."[7] Similarly, Hel was a fire-mountain according to German legend; the emperor Theodoric became immortal by entering her womb through a volcano.[8]

The Infernus of classical paganism contributed to the Christian amalgam of images of Hel's land. Infernus meant an oven in the earth; an old Roman proverb said "the oven is the mother." Roman ovens and bakeries were associated with temples of the Goddess, whose harlot-priestesses were often called Ladies of Bread. Their orgies were called Fornacalia, "oven-feasts," from *fornix,* the "oven" which gave us both "furnace" and "fornicate."[9] Naturally, Christian authorities maintained that tasting the sacred fire of eternity through "fornication" was a sin.

Medieval legends spoke of Hel as Brunnhilde, "Burning Hel," also the name of a leader of the Valkyries, otherwise known as Hild the Avenger.[10] Another of her names was Matabrune, "Burning Mother," who gave birth to King Oriant, a version of the Oriental sun god born at dawn from the bowels of the earth.[11]

Magic fire surrounding the Valkyrie's castle was an allegory of cremation fire, through which a hero passed enroute to Hel. Cremation of the dead was later forbidden by the Christian church, on the theory that cremation destroyed the body and prevented "resurrection of the flesh" according to the orthodox dogma. The more practical reason for outlawing cremation was that, as a pagan ceremony, it brought no revenue to the church.[12] It was profitable, however, to cremate witches while they still lived; inflated charges were made for every rope, nail, and stick of wood.[13]

Some myths suggest that Hel was originally envisioned as not fiery but dark: a Crone-goddess like Black Kali, eater of the dead. As the Nether Moon, she was called Nehellenia. Her ancient altars were found in Holland at the mouths of the Rhine.[14] Vases and statues from her shrines were discovered in Zealand in 1646.[15] Sometimes, her underworld was not hot but ice cold, as if serving as a model for Dante's innermost circle of the Inferno. The cold, dark Queen of Shades was Nef-Hel or **Nifl**.

Hel was supreme and inescapable, seizing even gods in her embrace. The Swedes said Odin the Heavenly Father was buried in a barrow known as Hel's Mount.[16] Because she was associated with mountains, Hel sometimes merged with Mother Freya. A fate-spinning Goddess called Hel of the Air was worshipped on the Lüftelberg.[17] She was simultaneously diabolized as feminine counterpart of the Prince of the Power of the Air (Odin-Satan) who led the

In various dialects Hel was Holle, Halja, Hild, Helga, Holde, Helle, Ella, or Hellenia. Helgo, Heligoland, Helsinki, Hollingstedt, Holderness, Holstein, and Holland were a few of the many place names derived from her. She was the usual tomb-womb of rebirth after death. Iceland still has a traditional "home of the dead" in Helgafell or Hel's Hill.[1] In Germany, "Dame Holle's Well" was called the source of all the children on earth.[2]

Wild Hunt. Tenth-century witchcraft texts said the heathen women rode forth under the leadership of "the witch Holda."[18]

Like her Greek twin Hecate, Hel sometimes wore all three faces of the Triple Goddess. The German poem *Gudrun* represented her as the ruler of Holland, incarnate in three virgins living in a mystic cave: Hild, princess of Isenland, Hilde, princess of India, and Hildburg, princess of Portugal. All three resembled mermaids or wood nymphs. The legendary Prince Hagen married all three Hels, after the usual ritual combat with an elder king.[19]

Ballads and sagas depicting such encounters between mortal men and supernatural women were collectively described as "hellish"—that is, *hellig,* medieval Danish for "holy."[20]

Pliny said all the inhabitants of "Scatinavia" (Scandinavia) were children of Mother Hel, thus they were called Helleviones.[21] They considered their Goddess incarnate especially in elder trees, which were still called Hel-trees or elven-trees in the Middle Ages. Danish peasants prayed at elder trees to the Hyldemoer, that is, Hel-mother, or Elder-mother.[22]

Hel's ancient connection with fertility was still evident in her medieval titles, Lady Abundia or Satia (abundance, satiety). In this guise she led the "ladies of the night" called Hellequins, who rode forth to receive offerings of food and drink from common folk, promising in return to bring prosperity on the house.[23] Apparently these were not mere legends but real women, carrying on the Goddess's nocturnal festivals. Hel was despised by the church, but the common people seem to have thought her more benevolent than otherwise. Her underworld was reached by crossing a river, like the Greek Styx; the river was Gjöll, "Wailing." On the bridge that crossed it stood the Goddess's emanation, Modgudr (Good Mother), ready like the Orphic Persephone to greet the deceased and see him safely into eternity.[24]

Northern shamans believed they could put on the Helkappe, a magic mask or *Hel*-met, which would render them invisible like ghosts, and enable them to visit the underworld and return to earth again without dying. The Helkappe seems to have represented the shamanic trance, in which death and resurrection were experienced as a vision. See **Mask**.

1. Turville-Petre, 55. 2. Rank, 73. 3. Steenstrup, 149. 4. Potter & Sargent, 52, 73. 5. Knight, D.W.P., 78. 6. Wainwright, 113. 7. Campbell, P.M., 336, 450. 8. Borchardt, 242. 9. Neumann, G.M., 286. 10. Oxenstierna, 191. 11. Baring-Gould, C.M.M.A., 579. 12. Pepper & Wilcock, 226. 13. Robbins, 111–13. 14. Reinach, 138. 15. Johnson, 211–12; Hays, 145. 16. Johnson, 165. 17. Guerber, L.R., 99. 18. J.B.Russell, 81. 19. Guerber, L.M.A., 23–25. 20. Steenstrup, 186. 21. Ramsay, 23. 22. Keightley, 93. 23. J.B. Russell, 146. 24. Branston, 91.

Helen of Troy

Incarnation of the Virgin Moon-goddess, daughter of Queen Hecuba, or Hecate, who embodied the Crone. Helen was also called Helle or

Selene. She was worshipped as an orgiastic deity at the Spartan festival Helenephoria, featuring sexual symbols carried in a special fetish-basket, the *helene.*[1]

Trojan Helen married Menelaus, "Moon-king," who was promised immortality because he made a sacred marriage.[2] However, Helen left him and went home with her new Trojan lover Paris, so Menelaus lost both his immortality and the Trojan fiefs that Helen's "matrimony" brought. He sailed with his armies to get her back, and this was the start of the legendary Trojan War which pitted patriarchal Greeks against matriarchal Trojans.[3]

As Elen, Elaine, or Hel-Aine, the same Moon-virgin became the queen of pagan Britain, a "Lily Maid" who made the first alliances with emperors of Rome. (See **Elaine.**) The oldest British histories said the first British king was a Trojan named Brutus, Helen's relative.[4] After Troy fell, he sailed west to the island of Albion and founded a city, New Troy, later renamed Lugdunum (London) after his descendant, the god Lug.[5]

1. Graves, G.M. 1, 208–9. 2. Knight, S.L., 125. 3. Graves, G.M. 2, 276. 4. Briffault 3, 431. 5. Guerber, L.M.A., 309.

Helice

"Willow," a title of Hecate in her virgin form as the new moon and the Helicon or "willow-stream" surrounding the Mountain of the Muses. Like Artemis, Helice the Willow-maid was associated with both the moon and Ursa Major, eternally circling the pole, known as Helice's Axle.[1] Witches thought a willow wand a microcosmic *axis mundi.* See **Willow.**

1. Lindsay, O.A., 251.

Hell

Though Christian theology gave its underworld the name of the Goddess Hel, it was quite a different place from her womb of regeneration. The ancients didn't view the underworld as primarily a place of punishment. It was dark, mysterious, and awesome, but not the vast torture chamber Christians made of it.

Greeks called the underworld Erebus, Hades, or Tartarus, from the "tortoise" incarnation of Vishnu, who was supposed to support the earth in the form of a tortoise. Shades of the dead dwelling in Tartarus endured no torment other than the general cheerlessness of being dead. Lacking blood, shadows, voices, and vital energy, they waited yearningly for rebirth.

Like the realms of earth and heaven, the underworld had its social hierarchy. Queen Persephone or Hecate, her consort Pluto or Hades, ruled magistrates like Aeacus, Rhadamanthys, and Minos, who were wizard-kings on earth. There were spirits like Hypnos (Sleep), Morpheus (Dreams), and Thanatos (Death).[1] Sometimes, as in the medieval vision of fairyland, the underworld was a place of sensual delight. In the Elysian Fields, souls of the enlightened ones were tended by the Goddess's divine nymphs.

Like the Egyptian nether god, Seker or Amen, Hades was "the unseen one"—the ubiquitous Hidden God in his intra-uterine, sleeping, or dead Black Sun phase. Lord of the Underworld or Lord of Death, he was also a phallic deity, holding the "key" to the nether yonic gate, as his heavenly counterpart Petra (Peter) held the key to the Pearly Gate of Celestial Aphrodite. The nether god was supposed to deposit his semen in rocks, where it solidified into precious gems, a western version of the Jewel in the Lotus. Thus he was Lord of Riches also. Romans called Hades by the name of Dis, short for Dives, "the rich god."[2] Most savior-gods who "harrowed hell," or plowed the earth-womb, were credited with the power to reveal buried treasure, a power inherited by the Christian devil.[3]

Egyptians called the underworld Amenti, Khert-Neter, Neter-Khertet, or the Tuat. It was both a hell and a paradise, a place of judgment and rebirth. Egyptian religion didn't emphasize punishment for sin. Egypt's savior Osiris came to save humanity not from everlasting torture, but from death.[4] Egyptians feared death, which they called an "abomination," and devoted most of their religious efforts to avoiding it.[5]

Egyptian pictures of "the wicked" being destroyed in underworld fire-pits were interpreted by Christians as torments of damned souls. However, these "wicked" were not necessarily human. They were supernatural enemies of the sun god: spirits of darkness, mist, storm. The fire-pits seem to have represented the burning clouds of sunrise and sunset. Even when victims were human, their burning was not eternal.

> *Egyptians did not believe in purgatory or everlasting punishment. . . . [T]he wicked were slaughtered daily and their bodies consumed by fire, but each day brought its own supply of these, and thus the avenging gods were kept busy daily, and the fire-pits were filled with victims daily. There is no evidence in the texts that the Egyptians thought the burning of the same victims could go on forever.*[6]

The idea of eternal torture in hell arose with ascetic patriarchal religions like that of Zoroastrian Persia. Masculine preoccupation with pain stood in contrast to the matriarchies' preoccupation with pleasure, a psychic outgrowth of the severities of the ascetic life. There is reason to believe hell's nastier torments were invented primarily to intimidate women into obeying new patriarchal laws.

Zoroastrian priests insisted women who were unfaithful to their husbands would go to hell and have their breasts torn open with iron combs. Women who scolded would be forced to lick hot stoves with their tongues. Women who showed disloyalty to men would be hung up by one leg, while scorpions, snakes, ants, and worms dug their way in and out of their bodies.[7] A similar vision inspired Grunewald's medieval picture of the hellish torments in store for those who committed the crime of loving.[8] But not even the Persians supposed the torments of hell would go on forever. That refinement of cruelty was left to the Christians.

The Jews adopted the Persians' hell as a place for punishing the majority of women, judged hopelessly unworthy of the Father-god's heaven. Men could be consigned to hell for holding too much unnecessary conversation with their wives, or for taking feminine advice.[9] The female creation-river Gihon was converted into **Gehenna**, the Jewish hell's river of fire, whose name was sometimes applied to the whole land. The kingdom of Gehenna was 60 times as large as the world. Each of its "palaces" had 6000 "houses," and each house had 6000 vessels of fire and gall awaiting the sinner. Prince of Gehenna was Arsiel, copied from the Chaldean "Black Sun" Aciel, the negative deity corresponding to the god of light in the celestial realm.[10]

Judeo-Christian tradition populated hell with all the biblical *baalim*, even those who had been identified with Yahweh himself: Behemoth, Leviathan, Baal-Peor, Baal-Zebub, Baal-Rimmon, Belial, Asmodeus, Molech, Lucifer, Satan, Tammuz, Dagon, Nehushtan, Chemosh (Shamash), Apollyon: even Baal-Berith, the "God of the Covenant." These were joined by gods and goddesses of classical religions: Hades, Pluto, Diana, Persephone, Hermes, Python, Hecate, Minerva, Venus, Cybele, Attis, Jupiter, Neptune, Saturn, Adonis, Pan, Lamia, Medusa, Lilith—plus all the gods and goddesses of Germanic and Celtic paganism. Even those who were artificially canonized, to convert their old shrines into churches, were often simultaneously diabolized and consigned to hell in the guise of demons.

There was a curious medieval passion for identifying, classifying, and naming all the demons. Sorcery required knowledge of their names and titles. An exorcist could do nothing until he learned the name of the demon he dealt with. The Gospels said even Jesus needed to learn the names of the Gadarene devils he exorcised (Mark 5:9). Thus, many sources provided lists of demonic names.

One of the most interesting dissertations on hell was Johann Weyer's *Pseudomonarchia Daemonum*, published in the 16th century when Weyer served the Duke of Cleves as a healer and diviner. Weyer said there were exactly 7,405,926 demons, divided into 72 companies. These figures had already been reported in the Talmud.[11] Supreme Chief of the Infernal Empire and founder of the Order of the Fly was Beelzebuth (Baal-Zebub), the old Philistine Lord of Flies. His lieutenants included Satan, Leader of the Opposition; Pluto, Prince of Fire; Moloch, Prince of the Land of Tears and Grand Cross of the Order of the Fly; Baal, Commander-in-Chief of the Infernal Armies and another Grand Cross of the Order of the Fly; and Lucifer, Lord Chief Justice of hell.

Baal-Berith, erstwhile God of the Covenant, filled the post of

Minister of Treaties. Nergal, husband of the Babylonian underground Goddess Eresh-kigal, became hell's Chief of Secret Police. The Royal Household included Melchom (Milcom) as Paymaster, and the Philistine god Dagon as Grand Pantler. The Hebrew elephant god Behemoth (originally Ganesha, father of Buddha) was Grand Cup-Bearer. Among the Masters of the Revels, Asmodeus held the post of Superintendent of Casinos. Antichrist was only an insignificant juggler and mimic.[12]

The infernal hierarchy also maintained embassies in various European countries. Thamuz, or Tammuz, was Ambassador to Spain. Baal-Rimmon, Phoenicia's "Lord of the Pomegranate," was Ambassador to Russia. England's ambassador was Mammon, whose appointment reflected continental resentment of the English zeal for commerce.

Sexual prejudice also extended to the denizens of hell. There was only one token female among hell's governing spirits: Proserpine, called Arch-she-devil and Sovereign Princess of Mischievous Spirits. Astaroth (Astarte) was present only in masculine disguise, as a "duke" of hell and its Grand Treasurer. The Goddess Belili took two male shapes, as Belial and Belphegor, hell's ambassadors to Turkey and France.

Masculinized Goddesses appeared also in Collin de Plancy's *Dictionnaire infernal*, an imitation of Weyer's *Pseudomonarchia*, showing portraits of a male "demon Ashtoreth" and a male "demon Eurynome." Even Lilith was masculinized as a hellish "prince" in Alexis de Terreneuve du Thym's list of devils: "Beelzebub, the supreme chieftain; Satan, the dethroned prince; Eurinome, prince of death; Moloch, prince of the Land of Tears; Pluto, prince of fire; Pan, prince of the incubi; Lilith, prince of the succubae; Leonard, grand master of the Sabbaths; Daalberith (Baal Berith), high pontiff; and Proserpine, the arch she-devil."[13]

What Weyer's solemn imitators never understood was that the *Pseudomonarchia* was really an elaborate joke, invented as a caricature of earthly hierarchies. Humor and skepticism were equally foreign to the Age of Faith, when the core of learning was credulity. It was a childlike age. Generations of would-be Magi soberly studied Weyer's mockery in search of demonic names to use in magic charms.

Weyer not only mocked the Christian hierarchy; he also defended witches. As a physician, he was called to examine some of the Inquisition's victims, and pronounced them harmless, deluded women who could not be held responsible for the statements wrung from them by torture. He tried unsuccessfully to halt the tortures and burnings. For this he was accused of heresy and indecency. Father Bartolomeo da Spina scorned Weyer with heavy-handed irony: "Recently Satan went to a Sabbath attired as a great prince, and told the assembled witches they need not worry since, thanks to Weyer and his followers, the affairs of the Devil were brilliantly progressing."[14]

But, Weyer aside, hell was not a joke. It was perhaps the most sadistic fantasy ever conceived by the mind of man. It was described, painted, and contemplated with incredibly perverse relish. Berthold of Regensburg said sinful folk must imagine their punishment in hell as the pain of a body made white-hot in a white-hot universe. "Let them count the sands of the sea-shore, or every hair that has grown upon man and beast since the days of Adam; let them reckon a year of torment for each of those hairs and, even then, the sinner will be only at the outset of his unending agony."[15] Martin of Braga said anyone who renounced Christianity would be "put physically into eternal fire in hell, where the inextinguishable flames burn for ever . . . and such a man shall long to die again, and not feel the punishment, but he will not be allowed to."[16]

Churchmen claimed the fires of sexual passion were transmuted into the fires of hell, blown by the breath of God into a heat fiercer than any earthly flame. A single drop of sweat from a damned soul would pierce living flesh like an arrow and burn like acid. One was told to imagine the pain of being covered with such sweat, forever.[17] The story of sinner's sweat was often told throughout the Middle Ages. It may have been inspired by a passage from the Mahabharata: "As the lord of gods, whose energy is infinite, became angry, a terrible drop of sweat came out of his forehead; and as soon as that drop of sweat had fallen to the earth, an enormous fire like the fire of doomsday appeared."[18]

Perhaps the worst part of the hell-vision was theologians' insistence that the joy of the blessed ones in heaven couldn't be complete unless they were permitted to gloat over the sufferings of the damned. St. Gregory the Great assumed with appalling naturalness that the "good" people in heaven would be entirely without pity. St. Thomas Aquinas wrote: "In order that nothing may be wanting to the felicity of the blessed spirits in heaven, a perfect view is granted to them of the tortures of the damned." Other fathers of the church proclaimed that, while the greatest pleasure of the saved would be contemplating the Divine Essence, their second greatest pleasure would be watching the damned writhing in hell. They couldn't feel sorry for loved ones or friends in torment, because their opinions would always be identical with God's; and God apparently reveled in sinners' pain.[19]

Thomas of Cantimpré mentioned some "simple folk" who worried about having to watch former friends or relatives suffering in hell. He said these worries were foolish, because no one in heaven could grieve for anything. He cited the Blessed Marie d'Oignies, who saw in a vision that her dead mother was damned, and so stopped mourning for her at once.[20]

Thomas of Cantimpré 13th-century scholar and encyclopedist, author of *On the Nature of Things.*

St. Bernardino of Siena argued that heaven must be perfect, and perfection couldn't be achieved without "due admixture of groans from the Damned." Only a few people were good enough to be saved; the vast majority would go to hell. This was the orthodox opinion.

St. Bernardino of Siena (1380-1444) Franciscan theologian, writer, and itinerant preacher, canonized in 1450, six years after his death.

Raymond Lull (Raimundo Lulio) Catalan philosopher of the late 13th century, author of numerous mystical works in Catalan, Arabic, and Latin. Lull was revered in the Franciscan order as *Doctor Illuminatus* and as a saint in some areas. He was never officially canonized, though Pope Pius IX confirmed his *cultus* in 1858.

Raymond Lull was condemned as a heretic for trying to teach that Christ's mercy would save nearly all men. Christ was not that merciful; only the mother Mary was that merciful. An Ethiopian Christian legend said Mary was distressed to see her kinfolk in hellfire, and asked God to give humanity holy writings that would save them.[21]

The sadism implicit in the fantasy of hell was all too graphically enacted by the inquisitors' tortures and burnings. The Inquisition's handbook directed that "eternal damnation should begin in this life, that it might be in some way shown what will be suffered in hell."[22] The inquisitor Bodin considered even slow burning a negligible punishment in view of its sequel: "Whatever punishment one can order against witches by roasting and cooking them over a slow fire is not really very much, and not as bad as the torment which Satan has made for them in this world, to say nothing of the eternal agonies which are prepared for them in hell, for the fire here cannot last more than an hour or so until the witches have died."[23] Of course, the witches so mercifully slain often had been subjected to unendurable tortures already for weeks, months, or even years.

The inquisitor Nicholas Remy said witches "are justly to be subjected to every torture and to put to death in the flames; both that they may expiate their crimes with a fitting punishment and that its very awfulness may serve as an example and a warning to others." To help them remember the occasion, witches' children were to be stripped and beaten with rods around the stakes where their mothers were burning.[24] Inquisitors obviously disliked children. They burned "witches" 10 or 12 years of age, or even younger.[25] At Würzburg in 1629, children as young as 7 were executed for witchcraft, plus many others of 10, 12, 14, or 15 years.[26]

Up to the 19th century, hell was used as a convenient way to throw the "fear of God" into children. Father Furniss's *Sight of Hell* presented the following edifying fantasies to young people:

> *Of two little maids of sixteen, one cared only for dress, and went to a dancing school, and dared to disport in the park on Sunday instead of going to mass: that little maid stands now, and forever will stand, with bare feet upon a red-hot floor. The other walked through the streets at night, and did very wicked things; now she utters shrieks of agony in a burning oven. A very severe torment—immersion up to the neck in a boiling kettle—agitates a boy who kept bad company, and was too idle to go to mass, and a drunkard; avenging flames now issue from his ears. For like indecencies, the blood of a girl, who went to the theatre, boils in her veins; you can hear it boil, and her marrow is seething in her bones and her brain bubbles in her head. "Think," says the compassionate father, "what a headache that girl must have!"*[27]

Dutch theologian Dirk Camphuysen opposed such crude training of the young, on the theory that it was more disturbing to sensitive minds than corrective of sinful ones. Unable to refrain from committing some sins, people developed a personal conviction of doom, "which necessarily produces such great fear and agony in the soul, that life is too frightening for them, and they find death by their own hand. Of this there are not a few examples, and some of them known to me personally. Others do not go as far as suicide, but fall into fits of melancholy and despair, sometimes ending in madness."[28]

John Wesley was so implacable as to maintain that the whole Christian religion depended entirely on the horrors of hell. If there were "no unquenchable fire, no everlasting burnings," then all New Testament teaching is a lie, and there is no reason to believe in the revelation of heaven.[29] Yet some theologians disagreed. Johann Cloppenburg said in 1682: "It is absurd that God should be angry forever, and punish the finite sins of creatures with infinite punishments."[30]

Johann Cloppenburg 17th-century theologian, author of the *Compendium Socinianismi Confutatum.*

Some thinkers maintained that only an evil God could create a hell so savage and deliberately allow human beings to fall into it, when he had the power to prevent this. The doctrine of **free will** was invented by the church to counteract this logic; but, as Bayle showed, "absolute free will is of no real use in justifying hell or in theodicy in general." Man's free will "does not exculpate God from being ultimately responsible for the sins He punishes, unless one takes from Him His omniscience as well as His omnipotence. . . . [I]f, before the creation, He foresaw that most men would abuse their free will and commit sins, he could have refrained from creating them."[31] The same sentiment was put forth more than 2000 years ago by the author of 2 Esdras, who demanded why God had bothered to create Adam if he couldn't restrain Adam from sinning.

Pierre Bayle. 17th-century French theologian of Calvinist or pseudo-Calvinist background.

Second Book of Esdras (also known as the Ezra Apocalypse) One of the apocryphal books eliminated from the English Bible but appearing as an appendix to the New Testament in the Latin Vulgate.

In wrestling with the problem of God's responsibility for hell, theologians of the 17th and 18th centuries often found themselves forced by their own logic into a basically Manichean image of an evil God. Sterry said "an angry, revengeful God is no God at all, but a projection of men's evil passions. . . . If sin is part of God's plan, then the sinner as much as the saint can claim to be fulfilling God's will." Jurieu admitted "the absolute impossibility of reconciling God's hatred of sin with His permission of it." He re-phrased Esdras's question: "If God has an infinite hatred of sin, why, having foreseen it, has He not prevented it? Why has He made men be born who, He well knew, were to damn themselves?" Bayle described God as "a lawgiver who forbids man to commit crime, and who nevertheless pushes man into crime, and then punishes him for it eternally." Thus he must be a God "in which one could have no trust, a deceiving, cunning, unjust, cruel nature; He is no longer an object of religion."[32] Whiston even concluded that the very existence of hell must condemn God in the eyes of humanity:

> *The exquisite torments of these most numerous and most miserable creatures, are determined without the least pity, or relenting, or bowels of compassion in their Creator, to be in everlasting fire, and in the flames of Hell; without abatement, or remission, for endless ages of ages. And*

> *all this for the sins of this short life; fallen into generally by the secret snares of the Devil, and other violent temptations; which they commonly could not wholly either prevent, or avoid . . . instances . . . of the absolute and supreme power and dominion of the cruel and inexorable author of their being.*[33]

Political implications of the "problem" of hell were set forth by Petersen:

> *What fruit has the doctrine of eternal damnation borne up till now? Has it made men more pious? On the contrary, when they have properly considered the cruel, frightful disproportion between the punishments and their own finite sins, they have begun to believe nothing at all, and have thought that these books of Holy Scripture have just been compiled by the priests, who made up such threats for the common people as they thought fit, in order to keep them in check.*[34]

Of course blaming the fiendishness of hell on God, or Satan, or Adam, or any other mythic figure was a way of avoiding recognition of the fact that its real inventors were men. Eastern sages were more frank; they said "the torments of hell are morbid creations of the individual's own ideas."[35] The ideas of the individual, however, were created by the society—in the case of hell, by the church. As Chaucer's Summoner slyly said, people sometimes thought the friars came by their familiarity with hell in a direct manner:

> *This friar boasts his knowledge about Hell,*
> *And if he does, God knows it's little wonder;*
> *Friars and fiends are seldom far asunder.*[36]

Though the possibility is seldom recognized, there are many indications that the Christian vision of hell in its sadistic horror was one of the leading causes of disillusionment with Christianity itself. Hell *was* necessary, otherwise there was nothing for "salvation" to save from; yet it often seemed people were sent to hell for no greater sin than being human. William Blake said, "When thought is closed in caves, then love shall show its root in deepest Hell."[37]

In the end, scholars were forced to renounce hell because it made God look more vindictive than man, though few dared admit that the vindictiveness sanctioned and stressed by the church was really man's alone. Shaftesbury said it was impossible to adore a God "whose character is to be captious and of high resentment, subject to wrath and anger, furious, revengeful . . . (of) a fraudulent disposition, encouraging deceit and treachery among men, favorable to a few, though for slight causes, and cruel to the rest." Bayle found it impossible to exonerate "a good and omnipotent God" from responsibility for the world's evils, though he made humanity suffer for them. The problem became "infinitely more difficult when He has also to be exonerated from causing the suffering and wickedness of the next world."[38]

1. *Larousse,* 166. 2. Cavendish, P.E., 119. 3. Rose, 240. 4. Budge, G.E. 1, 264.

5. *Book of the Dead,* 550. 6. *Book of the Dead,* 161. 7. Campbell, Oc.M., 199.
8. Hughes, 203. 9. Cavendish, P.E., 146. 10. Budge, G.E. 1, 275. 11. Wedeck, 94.
12. Waite, C.M., 186–87. 13. de Givry, 132, 141. 14. Castiglioni, 253.
15. Coulton, 18. 16. J.H. Smith, D.C.P., 241. 17. de Voragine, 649, 651.
18. O'Flaherty, 121. 19. H. Smith, 206. 20. Cavendish, P.E., 153.
21. Coulton, 18–20; Budge, A.T., 196. 22. Kramer & Sprenger, 79. 23. Robbins, 179.
24. Cavendish, P.E., 213. 25. R.E.L. Masters, 271; Summers, G.W., 488–91.
26. Robbins, 554–55. 27. H. Smith, 376. 28. Walker, 90. 29. Cavendish, P.E., 139.
30. Walker, 84. 31. Walker, 47. 32. Walker, 112, 119, 195, 201. 33. Walker, 99–100.
34. Walker, 244. 35. Waddell, 89. 36. Chaucer, 321. 37. Wilson, 227.
38. Walker, 49, 185.

Henna

Widely used in India and Egypt and by Greek worshippers of Hecate to stain women's palms and soles the sacred color of the Goddess, henna was important in her sacrificial rites. The death-dealing Goddess **Anath** was colored red with henna before immolation of human victims to her image.[1] Gypsy legends preserved something of the association between henna and the sacrificial ceremonies of Mari-Anath. They claimed Mary was preparing to redden her hair with henna at the very moment when her son was crucified; therefore she laid a curse on the red pigment that was formerly sacred.[2] Jewish scriptures spoke of "daughters of Cain"—i.e., women who didn't worship Yahweh—whose hands and feet were "dyed with color" in the Oriental fashion.[3]

Like all other trappings of women's religions, henna was associated with witchcraft in the Middle Ages. One of the heretical crimes for which the Spanish Inquisition arrested women was the use of henna to redden the skin or nails.[4] During the Victorian era, an Essex woman was charged with witchcraft for no other reason than the discovery in her house of some "red ochre," or henna.[5]

1. Hooke, M.E.M., 83. 2. Esty, 17. 3. *Forgotten Books,* 78. 4. H. Smith, 259.
5. Maple, 132.

Hephaestus

Pre-Hellenic **smith** god, cast down from the Olympians' heaven by Zeus, for trying to protect his mother Hera. Hephaestus was one of the ancient Amazonian smiths, an opponent of the divine Father. He took Hera's side in her quarrels with Zeus; he married Aphrodite; he was on affectionate terms with the primal Sea-goddesses Thetis and Eurynome; he shared a temple with Athene. He was lame, like all the Amazonian smiths. He was associated with volcanoes and lightning, like all early gods who fertilized the Great Mother's "abyss" with fire. One of Hephaestus's major shrines was the island of Lemnos, a matriarchal colony founded by Amazons.[1]

1. Graves, G.M. 1, 87–88.

Hera

Hera's name was sometimes rendered "Lady," and may have meant *He Era,* the Earth. An earlier version was Rhea, the pre-Hellenic Great Mother mythologized as the mother of the Greeks' Hera. Both were forms of the Great Goddess of early Aegean civilization, who predated the appearance of gods on the scene.[1]

Hera's name could also have been a cognate of Hiera, "Holy One," a title of ancient goddess-queens who ruled in her name. An Amazon queen named Hiera of Mysia led her army against the Greeks in defense of matriarchal Troy. Philostratus said Homer refused to mention Hiera in the *Iliad* because she was so great as to outshine Homer's heroine, Helen.[2]

There were many other, more far-flung cognates and counterparts of Hera. In Babylon she was "Erua, the queen, who controls birth."[3] She chose kings, gave them sovereignty by marrying them, and deposed them. As the eponymous Goddess of ancient Ireland she was "the Lady Eire," or Eriu.[4] Like Hera, the Lady Eire controlled the western apple-garden of immortality.

Hera was the Mother of the Gods, even of the Olympian gods, to whom she gave the ambrosia of eternal life. Hellenic writers tried to make her subordinate to Zeus, though she was much older than he, and had married him against her will. Their constant mythological quarrels reflected conflicts between early patriarchal and matriarchal cults. As the primordial feminine trinity, Hera appeared as Hebe, Hera, and Hecate—new moon, full moon, old moon—otherwise personified as the Virgin of spring, the Mother of summer, and the destroying Crone of autumn. Pausanias said Hera was worshipped as Child, Bride, and Widow.[5] In her Argive temple, she passed through endless cycles as her virginity was annually renewed, like that of Aphrodite, by immersion in a holy spring.[6]

Pausanias Greek traveler and geographer of the 2nd century A.D. Living in a time of declining culture, he was inspired by a desire to describe the ancient sacred sites for posterity.

Hera received sacrifices of "heroes," or "Hera-sacred men," whose myths dated from a primitive time when men were slain as her martyr-bridegrooms. In ancient Greece the term "hero" was synonymous with "ghost"—one who had gone to the Goddess.[7] Herodotus told the story of two of these heroes, Cleobis and Biton, chosen to draw the Mother's chariot in a procession. Afterward they "fell asleep" in her temple and never woke again. This holy death reflected great honor on their family; Solon called Cleobis and Biton "the happiest of men."[8] Like Christian martyrs, they achieved the "crown."

Hera's cult spread at an early date throughout pagan Europe, the whole continent having been named after one of her incarnations, Europa. Saxons worshipped her at Heresburg (Hera's Mount), where the phallic "column of the world" called Hermeseul was planted in the Earth-goddess's yoni.[9] Late in the 8th century A.D., the temple was destroyed and the phallic pillar overthrown by the armies of Charlemagne. However, the sanctuary was not forgotten. The Salic Law referred to "witches" called *hereburgium* or *herburgium,* those who worship at the Heresburg.[10] They were equated with those who "carried the cauldron" to religious meetings in honor of the Goddess—such meetings as the clergy styled witches' sabbats. Legends of Hera's magic garden in the west, where the apples of immortality grew, passed into the medieval lore of Fairyland.

1. Graves, G.M. 1, 51. 2. Bachofen, 107. 3. *Assyr. & Bab. Lit.,* 195.
4. Graves, W.G., 317. 5. Graves, G.M. 1, 52, 54. 6. *Larousse,* 102. 7. Halliday, 47.
8. Herodotus, 11–12. 9. Borchardt, 122. 10. Baroja, 59.

Heracles

Greek savior, the earthly incarnation of either Zeus or Apollo, the sun; born of the moon-virgin Alcmene ("Power of the Moon"), whose consort didn't lie with her until after her Divine Child was born.

His name meant "Glory of Hera," and he was nursed by the Great Goddess herself on the same milk that spurted from her breasts to form the Milky Way. His Twelve Labors symbolized the sun's passage through the twelve houses of the zodiac, the heavenly "way" indicated for him by the same river of celestial milk. After his course was finished, he was clothed in the scarlet robe of the sacred king and killed, to be resurrected as his own divine father, to ascend to heaven, to marry the virgin form of the Goddess all over again, and to dwell among the stars, where he is still found.

Pausanias said Heracles's surname was Soter (Savior).[1] Julian said of him, "All the elements obey the demiurgic and perfective power of this pure and unmixed spirit, whom the great Zeus has begotten to be the Savior of the Universe." He was worshipped everywhere as the savior who "died" and rose again like the sun, which is why a solar eclipse was supposed to have attended his death—the same mythic eclipse appended to the deaths of Krishna, Buddha, Osiris, and Jesus.[2]

Julian (Flavius Claudius Julianus) Roman emperor from 361 to 363 A.D., the only pagan to rule Rome after the time of Constantine; nicknamed "the Apostate" by Christian historians because he tried to re-institute the old Roman religion. His death was mysterious; some claimed he was assassinated by a Christian.

The influence of Heracles's cult on early Christianity can hardly be overestimated. St. Paul's home town of Tarsus regularly re-enacted the sacred drama of Heracles's death by fire, which is why Paul assumed there was great saving virtue in giving one's body to be burned, like the Heracles-martyrs (1 Corinthians 13:3). Heracles was called Prince of Peace, Sun of Righteousness, Light of the World. He was the same sun greeted daily by Persians and Essenes with the ritual phrase, "He is risen."[3] The same formula announced Jesus's return from the underworld (Mark 16:6).

Heracles also entered the underworld and "harrowed hell," the fructifying function of the King of Glory who "came in" to the womb of the Earth-goddess (Hera). She gave him his second birth and made him a god—hence his title, dedicated to her glory.[4] He was sacrificed at the spring equinox (Easter), the New Year festival by the old reckoning. He was born at the winter solstice (Christmas), when the sun reaches his *nadir* and the constellation of the Virgin rises in the east.[5] As Albert the Great put it centuries later, "The sign of the celestial virgin rises above the horizon, at the moment we find fixed for the birth of our Lord Jesus Christ."[6]

The celestial virgin to whom Heracles ascended was sometimes Hebe, or Hera-as-Maiden, or Eve as she was called in the Middle East. Like Isis, she said the fruit of her womb became the sun.[7] Often she was confused with Cyprian Aphrodite, who was really the same celestial virgin incarnate in the attendant Horae who followed the god through his risings and settings on the wheel of time: "In twelve months the silent pacing Horae follow him from the nether-world to that above, the dwelling of the Cyprian Goddess, and then he declines again to Acheron."[8]

In Lydia, Heracles was bound to the cosmic wheel of Queen Omphale, the Goddess incarnate, representing the hub of the universe (*omphalos*). He was one in a succession of her sacred kings. His predecessor was the oak-crowned Tmolus, who died by impalement after coupling with the high priestess. Another earlier model of the wheel-kings was Ixion of the Lapiths, who died on a fiery wheel signifying the revolutions of the sun. Such a sacrificial custom probably underlay the myth of Heracles bound to the wheel and made to spin for a year—that is, to turn through the signs of the zodiac which decorated the wheel.[9] Hellenic writers re-interpreted the myth to mean Heracles spent a year as a slave among Omphale's women, spinning flax on a spinning wheel, wearing female dress, a story invented to explain the early stage in the evolution of sacred kingship when a man could be the queen's deputy only when wearing her robes.[10] Priests of Heracles wore female garments up to a fairly late date.

Another myth said Heracles's predecessor was the centaur Nessus, who engaged in combat with Heracles for possession of the priestess Deianira. Heracles won, and married Deianira. Nessus died, bequeathing his blood-red ceremonial robe to the conqueror. Later, when his priestess-wife ordained that he must wear the robe, Heracles put it on and burned as if "wrapped in flames." His pyre was lighted by the next king, Philoctetes, who inherited his emblems of office.[11]

An Egyptian version of the same dying-and-reborn "hero" was Horus, or Heru, firstborn of Isis-Hathor.[12] In his dying aspect he was the enfeebled form of Ra, named Harakhti, declining toward his burning pyre in the west, to be devoured by the Mother's underground womb. Greeks called his holy city Herakleopolis, "City of Heracles."[13] The same sun-and-fire god was known in the Far East as one of the Ten Knowledge-Holding Deities, still remembered as "the most Supreme Heruka."[14]

Egypt continued to celebrate the fiery death and rebirth of a mock king up to the 19th century A.D., on the first day of each year by Coptic reckoning. The god-man was placed on a throne for three days, crowned with a tall pointed miter like that of pharaohs, May Kings, Carnival Kings, Lords of Misrule, and other pagan savior figures. Then he was burned in effigy and crept forth "reborn" from the ashes of his royal garment. Frazer says, "The custom points to an old practice of burning a real king in grim earnest."[15] According to Tertullian, as late as the 3rd century A.D. the people of Carthage were still annually burning "men who were gods of light."[16]

Having died a martyr's death, Heracles ascended to heaven without delay and received a place on the right hand of the Crone, or Crown—*Corona Borealis,* the constellation of the martyr's reward. Christian martyrs were promised the same "crown" in heaven. Meanwhile, Heracles's reward on earth was claimed by Christian priests: that is, tithes, from the Roman military custom of donating to Heracles's temple a tenth part of the spoils of victory.[17]

As another underworld Lord of Death, Heracles was credited with the same power to reveal buried treasure that was later inherited by the Christian devil.[18]

1. Knight, S.L., 98. 2. Lindsay, O.A., 333, 316. 3. Briffault 3, 366.
4. Graves, G.M. 2, 394. 5. Neumann, G.M., 313. 6. Martello, 189.
7. Legge 2, 63. 8. Baring-Gould, C.M.M.A., 286. 9. Campbell, C.M., 422.
10. Graves, G.M. 2, 167. 11. Graves, G.M. 2, 163, 202. 12. Budge, G.E. 1, 9.
13. Erman, 48, 139. 14. Waddell, 497. 15. Campbell, Or.M., 73.
16. H. Smith, 135–36, 182. 17. Dumézil, 438. 18. Rose, 240.

Hermes

Greek god of magic, letters, medicine, and occult wisdom, identified with Thoth in Egypt, Mercury in Rome. He was really older than Greece, one of the Aegean Great Mother's primal serpent-consorts, partaking of her wisdom because he was once a part of her. Like India's Ardhanarisvara—Kali and Shiva united in one body—Hermes was the original "hermaphrodite" united in one body with Aphrodite. Priests of Hermes wore artificial breasts and female garments to preside over Aphrodite's Cyprian temple in the guise of the god Hermaphroditus.[1]

Hermes was a universal Indo-European god. An Enlightened One born of the virgin Maia, he was the same as the Enlightened One (Buddha) born of the same virgin Maya in India. The *Mahanirvanatantra* said Buddha was the same as Mercury (Hermes), the son of the Moon (Maya).[2]

Greeks called Hermes the Psychopomp, Conductor of Souls, the same title everywhere given to the Lord of Death in his union with the Lady of Life. Hermes had greater power over rebirth and reincarnation than the heavenly father Zeus. It was Hermes who transferred Dionysus from the womb of the Moon-goddess to Zeus's "thigh" (penis) so he could be born from a male; apparently Zeus couldn't accomplish this miracle for himself.[3]

His feminine wisdom credited Hermes with the invention of civilized arts usually attributed to the Goddess: measuring and weighing, astronomy and astrology, music, divination by knucklebones. He helped the three Fates compose the alphabet.[4] He could control the elements. His caduceus could transform whatever it touched into gold, which is why Hermes became the patron of alchemists.[5]

Ovid said Hermes was married to the lunar priestess of a sacred fountain in Caria, the Land of the Goddess Car. He was also part of a trinity with Mother Earth and Father Hades, and a phallic god of the orgiastic Cabiri who worshipped Demeter Cabiria in the Mysteries of Phrygia and Samothrace.[6]

Hermes's phallic spirit protected crossroads throughout the Greco-Roman world, in the form of *herms,* which were either stone phalli or short pillars with Hermes's head at the top and an erect penis on the front. During the Christian era, the herms were replaced by roadside crosses, but the idea of setting these votive erections at crossroads was pagan rather than Christian.

Saxons worshipped Hermes as the phallic spirit of the Hermeseul, or Irminsul, planted in the earth at the Mother-mount of Heresburg (Hera's Mount). It is now known as Eresburg, and a church of St. Peter stands where Hermes's ancient sanctuary united the phallic principle with Mother Earth. Other Germanic tribes worshipped Hermes under the name of Thot or Teutatis, "Father of Teutons."[7] Hermes-Mercury was the same as the Germanic father-god Woden, which is why the Hermetic day, Wednesday, is Woden's Day in English but Mercury's Day in Latin languages.

The Cross of Woden also represented Hermes as "the only fourfold god." The sign of the cross traced by Christians on their heads and breasts originated as one of the crosses of Hermes, the Arabic numeral 4, often appearing upside down or backward as the Christians' gesture drew it.[8] The medieval legend that witches made the sign of the cross upside down or backward may have begun with worshippers of Hermes; actually, Christians had reversed the cross-sign made by the pagans instead of vice versa.

Sign of Mercury (Hermes)

The cross marked Hermes a god of four-way crossroads, the four quarters of the earth, the four elements, the four divisions of the sacred year, the four winds, and the solstices and equinoxes represented by their zodiacal totems Taurus, Leo, Scorpio, and Aquarius—the bull, lion, serpent, and man-angel symbols adopted by Christians to represent the four evangelists.[9] Sometimes, the cross of Hermes was an ankh, standing on a crescent that signified his mother the moon. This evolved into the conventional sign of Mercury, a circle with a cross below and a crescent above.[10]

Hermes was also represented by the Gnostic "world" sign, a Maltese cross with a circle at the end of each arm.[11] This seems to have referred to the four solstitial and equinoctial suns. Gnostics viewed Hermes as a personification of the World Serpent, ruler of time, who coiled around the terrestrial egg.[12] According to Gnostic Gospels, Jesus told Mary that the serpent surrounded the world, with his tail in his mouth, his body containing the twelve zodiacal halls—that is, he was identified with the Egyptian Tuat (Thoth) and the druidic *ouroboros,* also known as the Wise Serpent Hermes.[13]

Neoplatonic philosophers called Hermes the **Logos**, or Word of God made flesh.[14] Christian images of Jesus as the Logos were borrowed from the older deity, whose hymns addressed him in terms similar to those used in the Gospels:

> *Lord of Creation, the All and One. . . . He is the light of my spirit; his be the blessing of my powers. . . . Hymn, O Truth, the Truth, O Goodness, the Good, Life, and Light, from you comes as to you returns our thanksgiving. I give thee thanks O Father, thou potency of my powers; I give thee thanks O God, the power of my potencies. Thine own Word through me hymns thee. . . . Thou pleroma in us, O Life, save us; O Light, enlighten us; O God, make us spiritual. The Spirit guards thy Word. . . . From the Eternal I received blessing and what I seek. By thy will have I found rest.*[15]

Naturally, Hermes became the "god within" sought by all religious philosophers of the Gnostic period. (See **Antinomianism**.) His traditional bisexuality was interpreted as self-love; some said he invented the ritual of self-love, that is, masturbation. His caduceus was called a masturbatory symbol, a rod massaged by the serpents that embraced it.[16] Masturbation was said to be the hermit's typical act of self-contemplation, which some claimed would lead to comprehension of the God, just as sexual intercourse led to comprehension of the Goddess. A "*herm*-et" was literally a little Hermes, with a divine spirit dwelling in the phallus.

Hermes lived on through the Middle Ages in a new disguise as Hermes Trismegistus, Hermes the Thrice-Great One, founder of systems of Hermetic magic, astrology, alchemy, and other blends of mysticism with natural science. Lazzarelli's *Calix Christi et Crater Hermetis* (Chalice of Christ and Cup of Hermes) said all learning came from Hermes, who gave it to Moses in Egypt. Agrippa von Nettesheim often cited the authority of Hermes, whom he took for a grandson of Abraham. Burton's *Anatomy of Melancholy* listed Hermes as one of the great philosophers, along with Socrates, Plato, Plotinus, Seneca, Epictetus, the Magi, and the druids.[17] A 16th-century treatise said the Hermetic vessel was "a uterus for the spiritual renewal or rebirth of the individual . . . more to be sought than scripture."[18]

Hermetic magic was extensively cultivated by the Arabs, who based much of their numerical and alchemical systems on Hermetic lore.[19] Sufi mystics and eastern alchemists both claimed Hermes as an initiate of their craft.[20] After the crusades, Europeans developed a new interest in what they regarded as the ancient wisdom of the east, and became greatly impressed by any philosophy attributable to classical antiquity.

About 1460 a Greek manuscript of the eastern Corpus Hermeticum was presented to Cosimo de' Medici by a monk named

Sir Thomas Browne (1605–1682) English physician, author of the famous *Religio Medici* and other works.

Leonardo da Pistoia. Other texts were added later to the growing body of semi-secret "devilish arts" which commanded more and more of the attention of European intellectuals. Sir Thomas Browne called Hermetism "the mystical method of Moses bred up in the Hieroglyphical Schools of the Egyptians," stating that the Egyptians worshipped Hermes as Mercurius or Anubis, "the Scribe of Saturn, and Counsellor of Osiris, the great inventor of their religious rites, and Promoter of good unto Egypt." Hermes ascended to heaven in the form of Sirius, the Great Dog. He was so revered in Italy that the mosaics of Siena Cathedral portrayed him with the inscription, "Hermes Mercury Trismegistus, Contemporary of Moses."[21]

The Christian mythological figure most often assimilated to Hermes was the archangel Michael, Angel of Death, with a function resembling that of the ancient Psychopomp. "On the ruins of ancient temples of Mercury, built generally on a hill, rose chapels dedicated to St. Michael." A hill formerly sacred to Hermes-Mercury in France still bears the name of Saint Michael-Mont-Mercure. It lies opposite another "Michael's Mount" located across the channel in England.[22]

Spirits of the two mounts were both called Mercurius in pre-Christian times, perhaps representing the twin serpents that expressed Hermes's dual function as lord of death and rebirth. The twin serpents had many incarnations in alchemy and magic. Of them Flamel wrote: "These are snakes and dragons, which the ancient Egyptians painted in the form of a circle, each biting the other's tail, in order to teach that they spring of and from one thing. These are dragons that the old poets represent as guarding sleeplessly the golden apples of the Hesperian maidens. . . . These are the two serpents that are fastened around the herald's staff and the rod of Mercury."[23]

Hermetic mysticism usually called the serpents male and female, for the real secret of Hermetic power was androgyny. Like that of Oriental gods, Hermes's efficacy depended on his union with the female soul of the world, like the Aphrodite of his archaic duality. In medieval texts she was called the Anima Mercury, a naked woman surrounded by oval mandorla designs like the World card of the Tarot pack.[24] This card was the last of the Tarot trumps, and the Magician, identified with Hermes, was the first numbered trump. A Mantegna Tarot showed the Magician as a classic Mercury with serpent-twined caduceus, winged helmet, and flute, stepping over a severed head—symbol of oracles—toward a cock, the symbol of annunciation.[25]

1. Graves, G.M. 1, 73. 2. Rawson, A.T., 142. 3. Graves, G.M. 1, 56.
4. Graves, G.M. 1, 64–65. 5. d'Alviella, 228.
6. *Encyc. Brit.,* "Hermaphroditus," "Hermes." 7. Borchardt, 145, 122, 216.
8. Koch, 84. 9. Campbell, M.I., 181. 10. Silberer, 189. 11. Koch, 93.
12. Campbell, M.I., 298. 13. Budge, G.E. 1, 266. 14. Doane, 375.
15. Angus, 99. 16. Cavendish, T., 104–5. 17. Shumaker, 232.
18. Jung & von Franz, 143. 19. *Encyc. Brit.,* "Hermes Trismegistus."
20. Shah, 196. 21. Shumaker, 242–43. 22. Mâle, 378. 23. Silberer, 129.
24. Gettings, pl. 32. 25. Cavendish, T., 67–68.

Hero

Greek word for a man sacrificed to Hera, possibly from Sanskrit Heruka, a Knowledge-Holding Deity, via Egyptian Heru or Harakhti, Horus-Osiris as a dying god.[1] The Greek May Day festival was the Heroantheia, "Hero-flowering."[2] The "flower" was the hero's fructifying blood, represented by red or purple flowers, and described by the same word applied in the Bible to menstrual blood (Leviticus 15:24). The May Day hero was therefore a flower-god: Narcissus, Hyacinthus, Adonis, or Antheus, who were all the same deity, sometimes called Naaman, "Darling," because he was Aphrodite's beloved.[3]

1. *Bardo Thodol,* 70. 2. Gaster, 290. 3. Frazer, G.B., 390.

Herodias

Biblical "consort of Herod," literally the Great Lady, whose story was so extensively revised that she was not even the consort of Herod any more but the consort of Herod's brother Philip (Matthew 14:3). The Gospel story says Herodias demanded the head of John the Baptist and had her dancing daughter obtain it from Herod. This made her a prime religious villainess, and about the 10th century A.D. her name began to be taken as a synonym for Hecate, Queen of Witches. Yet the classic belief that Hecate was that third of the Triple Goddess who ruled the underworld, while her other personae Hebe and Hera ruled heaven and earth, came to be applied to Herodias as the new Hecate. In 936 a bishop of Verona formally denounced "those who believe that Herodias rules one-third of the world."[1]

1. J.B. Russell, 75.

Hesione

"Queen of Asia," a Syrian title of Atargatis, or Meri-Yamm, the Great Goddess of the sea in conjunction with her serpent. Greeks claimed Hesione was rescued from a sea serpent by Heracles, another version of the Perseus-Andromeda myth. The original fight probably was the one between Baal and the sea serpent Yamm for the sexual favors of the Asian Goddess. (See **Kingship**.)

Hesperides

Garden of immortality in the Far West, belonging to Mother Hera who sometimes took the form of Hespera, the Evening Star (Venus). Apples of eternal life grew on the Hesperian apple tree, guarded by Hera's sacred serpent. Like most versions of the earthly **paradise** or **Eden**, this one was located beyond the Pillars of Heracles (Gibraltar).

The Pillars were not only the straits leading to the western sea, but also the phallic shafts that stood in front of the ancient temples, the Garden being the temple itself, symbol of Hera's regenerative womb.

Hestia

Greek "Hearth," one of the oldest matriarchal Goddesses, in Latin, Vesta. She represented the home place, every man's "center of the world." When the matriarchs ruled, "The hearth was in the midst of the dwelling; that hearth was to each member of the household, as it were, an *umbilicum orbis,* or navel of the earth . . . [h]earth being only another form of earth, as in the German *erde* and *herde.*" Pythagoras said the fire of Hestia was the center of the earth.[1]

Romans had the same idea about the altar of Vesta, with its perpetual fire tended by the mystic **Vestal Virgins**. Cicero said the power of Vesta extends over all altars and hearths, therefore all prayers and offerings begin and end with her, "because she is the guardian of the innermost things."[2]

Hestia never had a consort, for no god could share her strictly matriarchal province, the Prytaneum or public hearth of every town. It was said of her that "seated in the midst of the celestial dwelling-place she receives the richest part of sacrifices, and among men she is of all the deities the most venerated."[3]

1. Lethaby, 81–82. 2. Dumézil, 322. 3. *Larousse,* 136.

Hetaera

"Companion," Greek title of a courtesan, the only kind of woman to retain full equality with men in the male-dominated Hellenic period. Like Christian nuns of the early medieval period, Greek *hetaerae* remained unmarried to protect their property rights from the depredations of patriarchal marriage laws. Unlike wives, they were free to attend schools, establish salons, and take a vital part in social and intellectual life of the time.

Their title may have been related to Egyptian *heter,* "friendship," whose hieroglyphic sign was two women grasping each other's hands.[1]

1. Budge, E.L., 51.

Hex

This word for a witch's spell had a long history associated with connotations of the number six—Greek *hex,* Latin *sex,* cognate with Egyptian *sexen,* "to embrace, to copulate." Six was everywhere the number of sex, representing the union between the Triple Goddess and her trident-bearing consort, which is why Christian authorities called six "the number of sin."[1] Pythagoreans on the contrary called six the perfect number, or The Mother. One of its Egyptian forms *seshemu,* "sexual intercourse"—shown in hieroglyphics by male and female genitals in conjunction—survived in the Sufi love-charm designed to open the "cave" of the Goddess: Open, Sesame.[2]

To this day, hex signs are hexagonal like the six-pointed Tantric yantra of love (see **Hexagram**). The name of the sign is from German *Hexen,* "witches," who may have been so named because they "made the six."

A triple six, 666, was the magic number of Triple Aphrodite (or Ishtar) in the guise of the Fates. The Book of Revelation called it "the number of the Beast" (Revelation 13:18), apparently the Beast with Two Backs, the androgyne of carnal love. Solomon the wizard-king made a sacred marriage with the Goddess and acquired a mystic 666 talents of gold (1 Kings 10:14). Christians usually called it Satan's number, yet the recurrences of this number in esoteric traditions are often surprising. For example, the maze at Chartres Cathedral was planned so as to be exactly 666 feet long.[3]

Egyptians considered 3, 6, and 7 the most sacred numbers. Three stood for the Triple Goddess; six meant her union with the God; seven meant the Seven Hathors, seven planetary spheres, seven-gated holy city, seven-year reigns of kings, etc. Egyptians had an abiding conviction that the total number of all deities must be exactly 37, because of this number's magic properties. Not only did it combine the sacred 3 and 7, but 37 multiplied by any multiple of 3 gave a triple digit or "trinity": 111, 222, 333, 444, 555, etc. The miraculous number 666 is a product of $3 \times 6 \times 37$.[4]

1. Baring-Gould, C.M.M.A., 652. 2. Budge, E.L., 57–58.
3. Pepper & Wilcock, 159. 4. Budge, E.M., 174.

Hexagram

The familiar design of two interlocked triangles is generally supposed to have represented the Jewish faith since the time of David, or Solomon; therefore this hexagram is known as Magen David (Shield of David), or the Star of David, or Solomon's Seal. Actually, the hexagram had nothing to do with either David or Solomon. It was not mentioned in Jewish literature until the 12th century A.D., and was not adopted as a Jewish emblem until the 17th century.[1]

Hexagram

The real history of the hexagram began with Tantric Hinduism, where it represented union of the sexes.[2] The downward-pointing triangle was the Female Primordial Image or Yoni Yantra, existing before the universe. In the course of infinite time, the Goddess conceived a spark of life within her triangle, the *bindu,* which was eventually born and developed into a male, symbolized by the upward-pointing triangle. He united with his Mother to form the Primal Androgyne.[3] The sign of this union was the hexagram, called Sri Yantra or Great Yantra. "The downward-pointing triangle is a female symbol corresponding to the yoni; it is called 'shakti.' The upward-pointing triangle is the male, the lingam, and is called 'the fire' (vahni)."[4]

A personification of the Great Yantra was Bindumati, "Mother of the Bindu," described in myth as a divine harlot. She ruled the forces of nature. She could command storms by the power of her magic and halt rivers in their tracks, a miracle copied by several holy men in Egyptian myth, and later by Moses.

From the Tantric image of the sexual hexagram arose a Jewish system of sex worship connected with the medieval Cabala, and a rabbinical tradition that "a picture is supposed to be placed in the ark of the covenant alongside of the tables of the laws, which shows a man and a woman in intimate embrace, in the form of a hexagram."[5]

The Cabala was developed by the Jews of Moorish Spain after the crusades brought eastern Goddess worship into their ken. Cabalists used the hexagram as Tantric yogis used it, to represent the union of God with his Female Power, Shekina, the Jewish form of Shakti-Kali. As Shakti was the essential soul of any Hindu god, so Shekina was the essential soul of the Cabalistic God. As in all religions of the Divine Marriage, Cabalistic Judaism discovered man and woman to be earthly images of God and Goddess; and sexual union of mortals naturally encouraged its like in the supernatural realm. Therefore sexual intercourse was "a sacramental act in the service of a God and his consort (or perhaps vice versa: a Goddess and her consort)."[6]

The Zohar identified Shekina with Torah, "the law," as the older Gnostic Goddess was identified with her own virgin form Maat, "the law" or "Truth." A man aspiring to mystic wisdom had to become a "bridegroom of Torah," for the law was embodied in a maiden, like the enlightening lady-love of contemporary bardic romance, which was also inspired by eastern Goddess-worship.

> *For the Torah resembles a beautiful and stately damsel, who is hidden in a secluded chamber of her palace. . . . She opens the door of her hidden chamber ever so little, and for a moment reveals her face to her lover, but hides it again forthwith. . . . He alone sees it and he is drawn to her with his heart and soul and his whole being. . . . When he comes to her, she begins from behind a curtain to speak words in keeping with his understanding, until very slowly insight comes to him.*[7]

The hexagram stood for the complete union of the sage with Shekina-Torah. Attribution of the hexagram to Solomon as the magic "Solomon's Seal" probably arose from the popular view of Solomon as enlightened by a sacred marriage, suggested by the erotic love poetry of Solomon's Song in the Bible.

1. *Encyc. Brit.*, "Magen David." 2. Jung, M.H.S., 240. 3. Rawson, A.T., 74, 82. 4. Zimmer, 147. 5. Silberer, 197. 6. Lederer, 188. 7. Cavendish, T., 73.

Hierophant

"Image of the Holy One," title of the Eleusinian high priest who played the role of God in sexual union with the priestess, embodying the Goddess.[1] More recently, the title was applied to the Pope in the trump suit of the **Tarot**.[2]

1. Lawson, 577. 2. Cavendish, T., 82.

Hieros Gamos

"Sacred Marriage" in Greek, meaning the union of a king or sacred king (surrogate for the real king) with his Goddess, usually in the form of a priestess-queen impersonating the Goddess. The sacred marriage was once considered essential to the king's right to rule. (See **Kingship**.)

Hilaria

Roman Easter carnival celebrating the day of resurrection of the savior-god **Attis**. On this "Day of Joy," people went about in disguise, universal license prevailed, celebrants were allowed to say and do whatever they pleased.[1] This took place at the vernal equinox, usually set on the 25th of March, which Christians later claimed for the resurrection day of *their* savior.

1. Frazer, G.B., 407.

Himalaya

"Mountains of Paradise" in Sanskrit, the root language that gave rise to other Indo-European languages. In German, for instance, paradise became *Himmel,* originally conceived as a heaven-piercing mountain.[1] See **Mountain**.

1. Lethaby, 125.

Hina

Polynesian virgin-mother Goddess, creatress of the world. She was the moon, and also the first woman.[1] All women embody her spirit, hence the word *wahine,* "woman."[2] Hina gave birth to every god as well as the first human beings.

1. Hays, 391. 2. Campbell, M.T.L.B., 43.

Hind Al-Hunüd

"Hind of Hinds," the Koreshite queen overthrown by soldiers of Mohammed (see **Arabia**). The Great Hind she personified was Kore-Diana, Mother of Animals, ancestral Goddess of her tribe.

Hippolytus, Saint

One of the pseudo-saints, based on a pagan god worshipped in both Greece and Rome as a dying-and-resurrected savior. Originally he died as a surrogate for King Theseus, who retained his throne by sacrificing "sons" who received the title of Hippolytus, "Torn by Horses." The manner of sacrifice was that the victim was dragged to death by chariot horses, a rite apparently initiated in Athens by Theseus's Cretan queen, Phaedra. Myth says Hippolytus's horses were frightened into their fatal stampede by a Bull from the Sea, actually a title of the Cretan high priest whose totemic form was the Minotaur.

Hippolytus was called the son of the Amazon queen, who embodied the spirit of Artemis-Diana. The Roman Hippolytus was slain and resurrected in Diana's sacred grove of Nemi. He was apotheosized and raised to heaven as the constellation Auriga, the Charioteer.[1] He married the Goddess's virgin aspect, the nymph Egeria. He was reborn like all cyclic gods as his own son, Virbius, "the Virile One." Virbius too was slain by horses in his turn.

"We can hardly doubt," says Frazer, "that the Saint Hippolytus of the Roman Calendar, who was dragged by horses to death on the thirteenth of August, Diana's own day, is no other than the Greek hero of the same name, who, after dying twice over as a heathen sinner, has been happily resuscitated as a Christian saint."[2]

A number of theological writings were brought forth under the signature of St. Hippolytus, whose "life" was assigned to the 3rd century A.D. The likelihood is that all these works were forged at a later date and arbitrarily given a canonical authorship, as was the custom of the early church.[3]

1. Graves, G.M. 1, 358. 2. Frazer, G.B., 6. 3. Attwater, 172.

Hiranyagarbha

"Firstborn of the Womb," a title claimed by nearly all Hindu gods, each of whom insisted on being the eldest son of the primal Creatress. Modern scholars tend to conceal the true meaning of the word by avoiding its feminine connotation. A commentator on the *Upanishads* said any god may be called Hiranyagarbha "when associated with the power called Maya—the power to evolve the empirical universe."[1] This effectively withholds the information that "the power called Maya" is the Great Goddess, and the "association" between her and the god is that of mother and child. See **Firstborn**.

1. *Upanishads,* 21.

Hocus Pocus

Magic phrase evolved from the medieval practice of intoning liturgical words as invocations and charms. Hocus pocus is a corruption of *hoc est corpus meum,* "this is my body," from the sacrament of the Eucharist.[1] See **Magic**.

1. Shumaker, 16.

Hod

Norse "blind god" who killed the youthful savior Balder with a thrust of a spear or arrow of mistletoe. Afterward, Hod took Balder's bride Nanna. Some myths say Hod was really another name for Odin, who was blind or half-blind; for Odin contrived the death of his divine son Balder, much as Yahweh contrived that of his divine son Jesus. Christians claimed Jesus was pierced by a spear wielded by a blind man, **St. Longinus**. Probably Hod was a title of the high priest in charge of sacrificial killings, embodying Odin's spirit.[1] He may even have been blindfolded or put into an eyeless mask, the Helmet of Darkness (Tarnhelm), to enact the sacred drama as a deadly game of Blind Man's Buff.

1. Turville-Petre, 113–18.

Hofgydja

"Priestess of the Temple," Norse title of clan mothers who had charge of religious rites up to the 11th century A.D., when Christian missionaries began to oust women from their shrines.[1] Women carried on their traditional festivals in private, as "witches."

1. Turville-Petre, 261.

Hokmah

"Wisdom," the Hebrew version of the Gnostic Goddess known in Latin as Sapientia, in Greek as **Sophia**. Her name was only a title of the Great Mother who actively helped God create the world, according to Proverbs 8, and whose symbol was the Aphroditean dove later adopted by Christians as a sign of the Holy Ghost. Much of the Jewish "Wisdom literature" owed its origin to ancient Oriental and Egyptian sources in which the Goddess was supposed to have inspired clear thinking on all matters of morality and religion.[1] Therefore Hokmah closely resembled Isis. Her praises were inserted into the mouth of Solomon, one of her most renowned lovers, by the author of the Wisdom of Solomon:

> *Her bright shining is never laid to sleep. But with her there came to me all good things together. . . . And I rejoiced over them all because [Hokmah] leadeth them; though I knew not that she was the mother of them. . . . She that is the artificer of all things . . . there is in her a spirit quick of understanding, holy, alone in kind, manifold, subtle, freely moving . . . all-powerful, all-surveying, and penetrating through all spirits. . . . Yea, she pervadeth and penetrateth all things. . . . And she, though but one, hath power to do all things; and remaining in herself, reneweth all things. . . . For she is fairer than the sun, and above all the constellations of the stars; being compared with light, she is found to be before it. . . . She reacheth out from one end of the world to the other with full strength, and ordereth all things well.*[2]

It may be that the Hebrew name of Hokmah was also of Egyptian origin, after an ancient title of Isis as Heq-Maa, Mother of Magical Knowledge, dating back to the *heq* or tribal wise-woman of pre-dynastic times. The Goddess as Heqit, Hekat, and the Greek derivative Hecate (the Wise Crone) can be traced to the same sources.

1. *Encyc. Brit.*, "Wisdom Literature." 2. Barrett, 143, 218–19.

Holly

To the druids, holly was the plant of death and regeneration, sacred to Mother Holle, or Hel, the underworld Goddess.[1] Germanic witches who worshipped her favored holly wood for magic wands. Red holly berries showed the female blood-of-life color, corresponding to white **mistletoe** berries associated with male elements of semen and death. In the divine marriage celebrated at Yule, they were displayed together.

The "holy" holly was linguistically linked with Hel's yonic "hole" (Germanic *Höhle,* a cave or grave). It was the most sacred of trees, according to a carol sung by medieval pagans at Yuletide, saying holly "bears the crown."[2]

In the Dionysian cult, female holly was paired with the god's male symbol, ivy.[3] Green boughs of both were used to adorn doorways at the solstitial festival. Tertullian condemned the custom, saying any Christian who has "renounced temples" should not make a temple of his own house door.[4] Nevertheless, house-decorating with holly, ivy, or mistletoe at the solstitial festival went serenely on. The Council of

Bracara ruled that no Christian should bring holly into his house for Christmas, because it was a custom of "heathen people."[5] Heathen or not, it was inextricably linked with Yuletide celebrations and could not be eradicated.

Even the sexual symbolism of the holly was remembered, in a way, up to the 17th century. Christmas games included a mock battle of the sexes, in which the master and mistress of the house engaged: "Great is the contention of holly and ivy, whether master or dame wears the breeches."[6] The kiss under the mistletoe originally represented sexual union, a peaceful resolution of the battle.

1. Goodrich, 54. 2. Graves, W.G., 186. 3. de Lys, 63. 4. Miles, 269. 5. Hazlitt, 118, 127. 6. Hazlitt, 120.

Bracara Modern Braga, in northern Portugal, first settled by Romans under the name of Bracara Augusta. An early church council was held there in 563 A.D.

Honey

Being one of the few preservatives the ancients knew, along with **salt**, honey was widely regarded as a substance of resurrection-magic. In Asia Minor from 3500 to 1750 B.C. the dead were embalmed in honey and placed in fetal position in burial vases or *pithoi,* ready for rebirth. "To fall into a jar of honey" became a common metaphor for "to die."[1] The *pithos* represented the womb of the Goddess under her name of Pandora, "All-giver," and honey became her sacred essence.

Myths present many symbolic assurances that the Goddess would restore life to the dead through her magic "bee-balm." Worshippers of Demeter called her "the pure mother bee," and at her Thesmophoria festivals displayed honey-cakes shaped like female genitals. The symbol of Aphrodite at Eryx was a golden honeycomb.[2] Her priestess bore the name of Melissa, "Queen Bee," the same as the Jewish Queen Deborah, priestess of Asherah, whose name also meant "bee."[3]

> *The bee was rightly looked upon as a symbol of the feminine potency of nature. . . . In the Syracusan Thesmophoria, the participants carried* mylloi, *cakes made of honey and sesame in the shape of the female sex organ. . . . Menzel draws an apt parallel between this custom and the Hindu usage of daubing the woman's genitals with honey at the marriage feast.*[4]

Bees are still called *hymenoptera,* "veil-winged," after the *hymen* or veil that covered the inner sanctum of the Goddess's temples, the veil having its physical counterpart in women's bodies. Defloration was a ritual penetration of the veil under the "hymeneal" rules of the Goddess, herself entitled Hymen in the character of patroness of the wedding night and "honey-moon."

The honeymoon spanned a lunar month, usually in May, the month of pairings, named after the Goddess as the Virgin Maya.[5] In an archaic period, sacred kings seem to have been destroyed after a 28-day honeymoon with the Goddess, spanning a lunar cycle, as the queen bee destroys her drone-bridegroom—by tearing out his genitals.[6]

As applied to ordinary weddings rather than sacrificial dramas, the honeymoon of a lunar month would include a menstrual period, the real source of what was euphemistically called moon-honey. A bridegroom contacted the source of life by copulating with his bride during menstruation, according to the oldest Oriental belief. Even the Great God Shiva was helpless unless his phallus was baptized in blood from the vagina of Kali-Maya, his Shakti and mother, in the Tantric ritual known as Maharutti.[7]

A combination of honey and **menstrual blood** was once considered the universal elixir of life, the "nectar" manufactured by Aphrodite and her sacred bees, which kept the very gods alive. Similarly, the great secret of Norse mythology was that the gods' nectar of wisdom, inspiration, literacy, magic, and eternal life was a combination of honey and "wise blood" from the great **Cauldron** in the belly of Mother Earth—though a late patriarchal revision claimed this *hydromel* or "honey-liquid" was a mixture of honey with the blood of a male sacrificial victim known as Wisest of Men.[8]

Even the most patriarchal cults seemed unable to dispense with the life-giving feminine fluids. Celibate priests of Mithra, who excluded women from their temples, nevertheless worshipped the Moon-goddess Diana or Luna who "made the honey which was used in the purifications."[9] Of course it was the Moon-goddess who also made the "wise blood" of female lunar cycles. Porphyry reported a popular belief in his day that bees were reincarnations of the lunar nymphs.[10]

Porphyry (ca. 234–305 A.D.) Neoplatonist philosopher, scholar, and writer; biographer of Plotinus; an opponent of the Christian church, which eventually destroyed most of his books.

Finnish myth speaks of the hero Lemminkainen, torn to pieces like a sacrificial victim and sent to Manala, the underground realm of the death-goddess Mana. His own mother restored him to life with her magic honey, assisted by her familiar spirit, Mehilainen the Bee.[11]

Early Christian Ophites celebrated a Tantric-style "love feast" which included the tasting of menstrual blood, and it was said of them that they mingled blood with honey.[12] Thus they combined two of the three substances—the third being salt—most often associated with resurrection or rebirth.

1. Neumann, G.M., 267. 2. Graves, G.M. 1, 72. 3. Sobol, 138.
4. Bachofen, 295–96. 5. Graves, W.G., 179. 6. Graves, G.M. 1, 71.
7. Edwardes, 50. 8.*Larousse,* 257. 9. Cumont, M.M., 112. 10. de Lys, 50.
11. *Larousse,* 301–2. 12. Campbell, C.M., 160.

Hope, Saint

According to Hesiod's fable of Pandora's Vase (or, as it was later erroneously called, Pandora's Box), the spirit called Hope stood for the refined cruelty of Father Zeus toward helpless mortals. Zeus sent the vase full of Spites to plague humanity with vice, madness, sickness, hard labor, war, famine, and every other ill; he also enclosed Hope, whose function was to prevent men from killing themselves in despair, to escape the miseries Zeus decreed for them.[1]

Hope was thus presented as a spirit of delusion; her ultimate purpose was to make men suffer. In Christian scriptures however, she was combined with Faith and Charity (or Love) as one of the three essential virtues. Some excessively naive hagiographers even canonized these three virtues as three fictitious virgin martyrs, all daughters of the equally fictitious St. **Sophia**.[2] St. Hope is still listed in the Roman canon of saints even though scholars have shown that she never existed.

1. Graves, G.M. 1, 145. 2. Attwater, 127, 312.

Horae

Aphrodite's celestial nymphs, who performed the Dances of the Hours, acted as midwives to the gods, and inspired earthly *horae* (harlot-priestesses) to train men in the sexual Mysteries. The dance still called *hora* was based on the priestesses' imitation of the zodiacal circling of "hours." Time-keeping is *horology* because of the systems devised by these ancient priestesses of the Goddess. See **Prostitution**. The Horae were called "fair ones, begetters of all things, who in appointed order bring on day and night, summer and winter, so as to make months and years grow full."[1]

In Egypt they were "Ladies of the Hour," in Persia *houris,* in Babylon *harines;* among Semites they were the "whores" called *hor* (a hole), ancestresses of the Horites.

1. Jonas, 258.

Horns

Perhaps the most distinguishing feature of a divine being used to be a horned head. Masks and crowns of incarnate deities were often those of horned animals—bulls, goats, stags. Horns were connected with the oldest Tantric belief concerning male vitality: that by suppression of ejaculation, mystic energy mounts up the spine to the head and flowers forth in wisdom and magic power, made visible by horns.

> *Outgrowths from the head are specially significant. The horned animals are the most sacred, because they carry about upon them visible evidence that their "head-stuff" is developed to the point of extrusion. Bulls, rams and he-goats are especially well-endowed. So too are deer. There is ample linguistic evidence in the West for the association between horns and male sexuality. In Indian miniatures and ivories of the seventeenth and eighteenth century* A.D. *horned deer are frequently used as symbols for the desire of a lovely girl in the forest.*[1]

The Bible says Yahweh's altar was horned, and he was sometimes addressed as a phallic stone, "the Rock that begat thee," as well as the phallic "horn of my salvation, my high tower" (2 Samuel 22:3). Yahweh was identified with El, "supreme god of the Semitic pantheon" who wore bull-horns as consort of Mari-Asherah the divine cow.[2] Like Zeus and Apis, he could take the form of the white moon-bull, probably copied from totemic incarnations of Shiva as the white bull Nandi (Blessed One).

The white moon-bull seems to have been one of the forms of the moon god Sin, whose holy Mount Sinai Moses climbed, and came down "wearing horns" in token of his encounter with the god of the mountain. The standard biblical translation says Moses came down from Sin's mountain with his head "shining," but in Hebrew, the same word signifies a "horned" or a "radiated" head.[3] The Vulgate says *cornuta fuit facies ejus,* he (Moses) wore horns. Michelangelo's famous figure of Moses is horned like a satyr.[4]

The Horned God was as old as the Stone Age. Primitive sacred art everywhere shows men wearing the horns of bulls, stags, rams, or goats, which distinguished the shaman, sacred king, priest, or victim.[5] Horned animals were frequently associated with Mother Goddess figures.[6] Myths of all later periods also combined the Goddess with the Horned God, who was Actaeon the stag, Pan the goat, Dionysus or Zeus the bull, Amen the ram, and innumerable combinations of these with human images. The Teutonic hero Sigurd or Siegfried was sometimes a man, sometimes a hart, consort of the White Hind who led men on mysterious adventures. He found his mother-bride in the form of a Valkyrie sleeping in her secret place, Hinderfjall (Hind-Mountain).[7] Later he died in the forest as a hunted stag, pierced by arrows, like Actaeon the Lord of the Hunt and his medieval counterpart, the witches' Horned God.

Medieval folk thought it might be possible for human beings to grow real horns on their heads for a variety of reasons, from telling lies (through identification with the devil as Father of Lies) to becoming a **cuckold**. Agrippa von Nettesheim offered a pseudo-scientific explanation for the alleged overnight horning of Cyprus, king of Italy. The king dreamed all night of a battle of bulls, which stimulated "the vegetative power, being stirred up by a vehement imagination, elevating cornific humors into his head and producing horns."[8]

Sir Thomas Browne (1605–1682) English physician, author of the famous *Religio Medici* and other works.

Of course the principal Horned God was the devil, a composite of all the Horned Gods of paganism. Sir Thomas Browne said the "devils" of holy scripture were Fauns, Satyrs, and sons of Pan; but the original Hebrew word for them was "goats."[9] In Scotland, the devil was known as Ould Hornie. His notorious lustfulness gave rise to the modern slang term "horny." The so-called sign of the devil—forefinger and little finger extended—was originally a gesture-symbol of a horned animal head, copied from a sacred *mudra* of the Great Goddess in India.[10]

1. Rawson, E.A., 25. 2. *Larousse,* 74. 3. Elworthy, 185.
4. *Encyc. Brit.,* "Michelangelo." 5. Jung, M.H.S., 235–36. 6. *Larousse,* 3.
7. Turville-Petre, 199. 8. Agrippa, 202. 9. Hazlitt, 176–78.
10. Rawson, A.T., 50.

Horse

In the 15th century A.D., Pope Calixtus III decreed that no more religious ceremonies should be held in "the cave with the horse-pictures."[1] Ancient pagan horse-worship was still common and acceptable, co-existing with Christianity, only three centuries earlier when kings of Ireland still underwent symbolic rebirth from the White Mare.[2] She was Epona, the Celtic version of Cretan Leukippe ("White Mare"), one of many relics of the Amazonian horse-cult throughout Europe.

The divine horse still stands on a hillside at Uffington (in Berkshire, England), 370 feet long, carved in the chalk by pre-Christian votaries of Epona, now serving as a notable tourist attraction.[3]

Horses were sacred to the Jutes who invaded Kent; their king and queen bore the titles of Hengist and Horsa, "Stallion and Mare." Their daughter became the wife of Vortigern. Out of a Christian prejudice against queens, the Venerable Bede insisted that the Stallion and Mare were really two brothers ruling jointly, but he never explained how they managed to become joint parents.[4]

Symbolic of the equine deities was a double-headed androgynous horse still used to decorate the double projecting rafters of old houses in Jutland, the original home of the Jutes. Such figures are known as Hengist and Horsa and are put up for "luck."[5]

Another relic of pre-Christian horse worship is the Morris dancer's traditional horse-headed stick, or "hobby horse"—otherwise the cock-horse ridden to Banbury Cross to see the Goddess make her ritual ride as Lady **Godiva**. Similar horse-headed sticks were ridden by central Asian shamans. "The 'horse' enables the shaman to fly through the air, to reach the heavens. The dominant aspect of the mythology of the horse is not infernal but funerary; the horse is a mythical image of death and hence is incorporated into the ideologies and techniques of ecstasy."[6] Death symbolism figured in the dream of riding a black horse, interpreted as a portent of "loss and sorrow."[7]

Northern Europeans considered horses essential to the funeral rites of great warriors. The riderless horse led in a pagan or Christian military officer's funeral procession dated back to primitive belief that his ghost needed to ride to heaven. His empty boots were often fixed backward in the stirrups because it was thought ghosts wore their feet backward. In ancient times, the horse was usually sacrificed at the funeral and buried with the dead hero, just as boats were buried with Egyptian mummies to carry them over afterworld waters.[8]

Death was the significance of Father Odin's eight-legged gray horse Sleipnir, symbol of the gallows tree, where human sacrifices were hung in Odin's sacred groves. Skalds called the gallows "high-chested rope-Sleipnir," the horse on which men rode to the land of death, Heljar. Recounting Odin's own death-and-resurrection drama, the original nine-day wonder, the Elder Edda said: "In the Norn's seat nine days sat I, thence was I mounted on a horse; there the giantess's sun shone grimly through the dripping clouds of heaven. Without and within, I seemed to traverse all the seven nether worlds."[9]

Old Norse *drasil* meant both "horse" and "gallows tree."[10] Therefore the World Tree Yggdrasil, on which Odin hung and bled, was both the Horse of Yggr and the Gallows of Yggr, as well as the *axis mundi* at the earth's hub. Yggr was another name for Odin as Lord of Death. When Christians diabolized him, he became the great devil-rider leading the hosts of the dead through the sky on their cloud-colored horses, and Yggr evolved into the English "ogre."[11]

The horse cult of Odin's Aesir was rooted in Vedic India. Hindu dying gods often assumed horse shape. Hindu queens impersonated the Goddess as Mare-mother, Saranyu, by inserting the dead horse's penis between their legs at the end of the sacrificial ceremony, calling upon "the vigorous male" to "lay seed" for the benefit of the land and its people.[12]

This ancient ceremony explains one of Odin's more puzzling titles, Völsi, meaning both "Son of God" and "Horse's Penis."[13] The penis was the "son" worshipped by Iron Age equestrian tribes calling themselves Völsungs, descendants of Völsi. The cult was not confined to Scandinavia. The Welsh had the same ancestral horse-god, Waelsi or Waels. Slavs also worshipped him as Volos, a sacrificed horse whose entrails and blood were supposed to produce the water of life. In a Russian folk tale, Volos directed the hero to use him for resurrection magic: "Open my body, take out my entrails, rub the dead man with my blood."[14] This was supposed to restore life to the dead.

Volos was still incarnated in a ritually castrated and slaughtered stallion every spring, up to the 18th century A.D.[15] Since the people insisted on worshipping him, he was converted into a Christian saint, Vlas, who had no real existence except as a pagan horse-god.

Ancient Rome knew him as the October Horse, or *curtus equus* ("cut horse"). By an elaborate ritual, the animal was divided into three sections by sacred women known as the Three Queens. After slaughtering, the horse's amputated tail was carried hastily to the temple of Vesta—the earth's yoni, by Roman reckoning—so its blood could drip on the altar.[16] In earlier times it probably was the horse's penis that donated its blood to the Goddess, as in the rites of Saranyu and Völsi. Castrated stallions were offered to all equine forms of the Goddess. The Taurians sacrificed to Artemis horses from whom "the member was cut off."[17]

The blood-wedding of the Earth Mother and the Horse's Penis produced the race of horse-gods known in the Aegean as centaurs, in India as Asvins or Gandharvas.[18] They were great wizards, skilled in music and dancing, expert healers, lusty lovers of women. They often stole brides from their bridegrooms, a legend reminiscent of the ancient

Oriental custom of having brides deflowered by priests or god-penises instead of by their husbands (see **Firstborn**).[19]

Western centaurs were similar, born of Mare-headed Demeter in Mycenae, or of Leukippe the White Mare in Crete.[20] Priests of this Goddess were castrated and wore female dress.[21] Sometimes they were called Magnetes, "Great Ones." One of their leaders was the magic horse Arion, born of Demeter's union as a mare with the sea god in the form of a stallion.[22] A sacred grove in Chios called Tripotamara (Three Streams) is said to be still haunted by ghostly centaur-wizards.[23]

Greeks called Corinthian horse-priestesses "man-eating mares," also known as the horse-masked Pegae guarding the sacred fountain of Pirene, home of Pegasus—another name for Arion, the horse who carried heroes to heaven. The Pegae-priestesses killed Bellerophon and his father, a typical father-son combination of the reborn deity. Diodorus compared the orgies of the Pegae to those of the Egyptian bull-god Apis, whose priestesses tore him apart and directed his spurting blood onto their genitals to fertilize themselves on behalf of their Goddess, the earth.[24]

Customs of the Cretan horse cult produced the myth of **Hippolytus** (He Who is Torn by Horses), dragged to death by his chariot horses after receiving a curse from his father Theseus. The myth concealed a primitive sacrifice, though Hippolytus was eventually canonized as a Christian saint.[25] In his Christian form, Hippolytus was dragged to death by horses on the Goddess's holy day in August.[26] Some said Demeter's Cretan lover Iasion was similarly torn to pieces by horses.[27]

Ancient kings of Sweden were torn to pieces by horse-Valkyries or horse-masked priestesses of Freya, known as *volvas.*[28] Medieval folklore redefined a *volva* as a witch able to transform herself into a mare. She embodied the spirit of the Scandinavian death-goddess who rode a winged black horse known as the Valraven (Raven-ridden-by-Valkyries).[29] Slavs used to pray to her as the virgin battle-queen (Diana, Athene, Bellona, etc.) before setting forth to war: "Unsheathe, O Virgin, the sacred sword of thy father, take up the breastplate of thy ancestors, thy doughty helmet, bring out thy black horse."[30]

The myth of King Midas and his ass-ears was dressed in Celtic garb for transposition to an Irish horse cult centering on King Lavra (ca. 3rd century A.D.). The king was said to have horse's ears, a fact known only to his barber—until the barber whispered the secret to a willow tree. The willow was cut down and made into a harp, and the harp sang the truth about the king's ears.[31]

Horse sacrifices were performed in Norway in the 10th century A.D. despite the efforts of newly converted Christian kings to discontinue them. King Haakon's rebellious subjects not only continued the pagan feasts of horsemeat but forced the king himself to take part in them and drink toasts to the old gods meanwhile.[32]

Traces of the horse sacrifice persisted in England up to the 16th century, when it was still customary for all horses to be bled on St. Stephen's Day, the day after Christmas, for "luck."[33] The New Year sacrifice of a white horse-image known as Old Hob was the same "hobby-horse" as Germany's *Schimmel,* made of a horse head animated by young men covered by white cloths. In Pomerania the New Year hobby-horse performer *Schimmelreiter* pantomimed ancient sacrificial dances.[34] Christian opposition to pagan horse sacrifices probably gave rise to the strong prejudice against eating horsemeat.[35]

1. Jung, M.H.S., 234. 2. Graves, W.G. 425; Gelling & Davidson, 92. 3. *Larousse,* 225. 4. *Encyc. Brit.,* "Hengist & Horsa." 5. Gelling & Davidson, 127; Johnson, 329. 6. Eliade, S., 467. 7. Hazlitt, 191. 8. de Lys, 261. 9. Baring-Gould, C.M.M.A., 247. 10. Turville-Petre, 48. 11. B. Butler, 153. 12. Briffault 3, 188. 13. Turville-Petre, 201. 14. Maspero, xxi. 15. *Larousse,* 288. 16. Dumézil, 223–25. 17. Neumann, G.M., 276. 18. O'Flaherty, 60. 19. Jobes, 145. 20. Graves, W.G., 425. 21. Gaster, 316. 22. Graves, G.M. 1, 61. 23. Lawson, 217. 24. Graves, G.M. 1, 255–56. 25. Baring-Gould, C.M.M.A., 271. 26. Frazer, G.B., 6. 27. Graves, G.M. 1, 89. 28. Lederer, 195; Turville-Petre, 48. 29. Guerber, L.M.A., 255. 30. *Larousse,* 294. 31. Pepper & Wilcock, 256. 32. Oxenstierna, 67–69, 256. 33. Hazlitt, 57. 34. Miles, 200. 35. H.R.E. Davidson, G.M.V.A., 122.

Horsel

Teutonic Moon-goddess, Venus of the Horselberg; also called Ursel or Ercel. Her many lovers included Tannhäuser in Germany and **Thomas Rhymer** (Thomas of Ercel's Down) in England. According to the Thuringian Chronicle, she appeared as a fiery trinity in 1398, as "three great fires in the air" descending to rest in the Horselberg.[1] Eventually the Goddess Horsel was canonized as the apocryphal St. **Ursula**, with her "eleven thousand virgins"—transformations of the Moon-mother and her daughter stars.

1. Baring-Gould, C.M.M.A., 211.

Horseshoe

Hindus, Arabs, and Celts regarded the yonic shape of the horseshoe as a symbol of the Goddess's "Great Gate," thus it was always esteemed as a prophylactic door charm. Druidic temples were constructed in the shape of a horseshoe.[1] So were some Hindu temples, with the frank intention of representing the yoni. The horseshoe arch of Arabic sacred architecture developed from the same tradition.[2]

Greeks assigned the yonic shape to the last letter of their sacred alphabet, Omega, literally, "Great Om," the Word of Creation beginning the next cycle of becoming. The implication of the horseshoe symbol was that, having entered the yonic Door at the end of life (Omega), man would be reborn as a new child (Alpha) through the same Door. It was everywhere represented as "a horseshoe, the very figure that is nailed to so many doors in various parts of the world, as an emblem of luck. Mighty few of those who live in such houses know that the horseshoe is only a symbol of the yoni and that by nailing it to their doors, they follow out a custom older than the history of their race."[3]

The Christian God who claimed to be the "Alpha and Omega" (Revelation 1:8) was only copying one version of this very ancient symbolism, whose meaning seems not to have been understood by the biblical writer.

1. Graves, W.G., 315–16. 2. de Lys, 113. 3. Goldberg, 102.

Hortus Conclusus

"Enclosed Garden," a symbol of the Virgin, whose garden was called Paradise and mythologically related to the womb. Virginity meant the feminine "gate of paradise" was not yet opened. In the erotic metaphors of Solomon's wedding song, the virgin bride as yet un-deflowered is not only a *hortus conclusus* but "a spring shut up, a fountain sealed" (Song of Solomon 4:12). In medieval art, the virgin Mary was mystically depicted inside a walled garden representing her virginity.[1]

1. Hughes, 55.

Horus

Egyptian Divine Child, or reborn sun; a son-reincarnation of either **Ra** or **Osiris,** or both. Horus was depicted as a child with a long lock of hair curled to one side of his head and a finger in his mouth, signifying childlike dependence.[1] Yet he was also a warrior, avenging his "father" or elder-self Osiris by castrating and killing Set, the god of the barren half of the year.

Some said there was a Horus the Elder, born of Isis immediately after her own birth, for he was conceived by the coupling of Isis and her twin-brother-spouse Osiris while they were still in the womb of their mother Mut. Other myths said Horus was the world's firstborn sun, who arose from the primal Mother's lotus-yoni at the beginning of time.[2]

Horus might be traced to the Far East, as the "Lotus-born" Heruka, or hero; the original Egyptian form of his name was Heru. Greek Gnostics of the philosophical age called him Harpocrates. What-ever his name, he was another variation on the usual theme of the dying-and-reborn god, father-killing son and son-killing father.

1. Budge, G.E. 1, 484. 2. Budge, G.E. 1, 473.

Host

Latin *hostia,* "victim," became the Host of the Eucharist, indicating the dead and cannibalized god whose worshippers devoured his flesh and blood—literally in the earliest religious systems, symbolically in the later Mysteries such as Mithraism, Orphism, and Christianity. Bread played "host" to the visiting spirit of the deity, and became one with the body of the worshipper upon being eaten. See **Cannibalism**; **Transubstantiation**. Another derivative of *hostia* was "hostage," a surrogate; and if not ransomed, a victim.

Houri

Persian-Arabian heavenly nymph, sexual angel, or temple prostitute; cognate with the Greek *hora,* Babylonian *harine,* Semitic *harlot,* or "whore." Houris were dancing "Ladies of the Hour" who kept time in heaven and tended the star-souls. See **Angel**; **Prostitution**.

Hsi Wang Mu

"Lady-Queen of the West," Chinese Great Mother who kept the fruit of immortality in a magic orchard in the Far West, as did Idun, Pomona, Hera, Morgan, etc. Instead of apples, Hsi Wang Mu raised peaches, the Chinese symbol of the yoni. Once every 3000 years she gave the gods peaches from her Tree of Life.[1] See **Peach**.

1. *Larousse,* 382.

Hubris

Greek "lechery," or "pride," both words associated with penile erection; said to be the sin of **Lucifer**. Patriarchal gods especially punished *hubris,* the sin of any upstart who became—in both senses—"too big for his breeches."[1]

The original Hubristika was an Argive "Feast of Lechery" featuring orgies and **transvestism**. Men broke a specific taboo by wearing women's veils and assuming women's magic power.[2] Christianity later condemned as devil-worship all forms of transvestism, because of its implication that men acquired power through connection with women, whether it was a sexual connection or a masquerade.

From *hubrizein,* lecherous behavior, came the Roman word *hybrid,* describing a child of a Roman father and a foreign mother. A trace of the old law of matrilineal inheritance dictated that a child was a slave or a freeman according to the status of his mother, slave or free; the father's status was irrelevant. Similarly among the Jews, in the case of mixed marriages or hybridization, a child was Jewish only if the mother was the Jewish parent, but gentile if only the father was Jewish.[3]

1. Potter & Sargent, 176. 2. Lederer, 145. 3. Ochs, 96.

Hudigamma

Hindu Mother Goddess served by eunuch priests dressed in women's clothes.[1] Her western counterparts had similar customs; transvestite eunuch priests served Cybele, Artemis, Heracles as the consort of Lydian Omphale, and Adonis as the consort of Syrian Aphrodite. All the savior-gods in these cults were castrated. See **Castration; Transvestism.**

1. Gaster, 317.

Huppah

Hebrew "tent," the marriage canopy held above the heads of a bride and groom in a Jewish wedding, a custom derived from the ancient Semitic matriarchate when women owned their tents, and a wedding ceremony was in effect a solemnization of the man's permission to enter the tent of his beloved.[1] The tent and the land it occupied were symbolic of the woman herself. Before the development of patriarchal rules, she had complete control of her property. An Arabian wife could divorce her husband without speaking a word, simply by turning her tent to face the other direction, which let him know he was forbidden to enter the door again.[2]

When Absalom tried to establish a right to rule Israel, he raised "an awning on a housetop" and beneath its shade he copulated with King David's royal concubines "in the sight of all Israel" (2 Samuel 16:22). Without this rite of sacred marriage, no man could be a king. Absalom's followers erected the customary phallic pillar in his name, to honor his virility—after he died as a surrogate for the king (2 Samuel 18:18).

The huppah was not unknown as an accompaniment to Gentile marriages. Anglo-Saxon weddings similarly took place "under a veil or square piece of cloth, held at each corner by a tall man, over the bridegroom and bride."[4] The veil seems to have symbolized the woman's dwelling place, for early Anglo-Saxon marriages were matrilocal.

Egyptians preserved from their own matriarchal period the same symbol of the marriage tent, called *senti,* the canopy under which a pharaoh received his bride and his crown at the same time. Marriage with the queen gave him formal right to rule her land, and the *senti* like the huppah was a symbol of permission.[3]

1. Briffault 1, 374. 2. de Riencourt, 187-89. 3. *Book of the Dead,* 427. 4. Hazlitt, 90.

Husband

"One bonded to the house *(hus)*"—a steward or majordomo chosen to tend a woman's property, under the old Saxon matriarchate when property rights were matrilineal. A husband was not considered an integral part of the maternal clan but remained a "stranger" in the house, as in early Greece where the men's god Zeus was "god of strangers."[1]

Pre-Islamic Arabian husbands didn't even have names in the matrilineal clan until they begot children; then a man could call himself *abu,* "father of . . ." So-and-so. This part of an Arab's name is still considered the most important part.[2]

In southeast India, a husband was regarded as a more or less permanent guest in the wife's home, constrained to remain on his good behavior according to the rules governing guests. In archaic Japan, husbands were not residents in the wife's home at all, but only visitors. The old word for "marriage" meant "to slip into the house by night."[3] Patrilocal marriage was unknown in Japan until 1400 A.D.[4]

The position of a husband in the ancient world was often temporary, subject to summary divorce. An Arabian wife could dismiss her husband by turning her tent to face the west for three nights in succession.[5] After the introduction of Islamic patriarchy, the system was reversed in favor of men. A husband could turn his wife out of her home simply by saying "I divorce thee" three times.

Early Latin tribes followed the same rules as Arabians; a woman could divorce her husband by shutting him out of her house for three consecutive nights.[6] Even in imperial times, a Roman wife could maintain her own property free of husbandly claims by passing three nights of each year away from his residence.[7]

Ancient Egypt had several varieties of marriage existing side by side. Some, probably the oldest, were governed by premarital agreements that spelled out the wife's property rights and the husband's comparative powerlessness under the law. For example:

> *I bow before thy rights as a wife. From this day on, I shall never oppose thy claims with a single word. I recognize thee before all others as my wife, though I do not have the right to say thou must be my wife. Only I am thy husband and mate. Thou alone hast the right of departure. From this day on that I have become thy husband, I cannot oppose thy wish, wherever thou desirest to go. . . . I have no power to interfere in any of thy transactions. I hereby cede to thee any rights deeded to me in any document that has been made out in my favor. Thou keepest me obligated to recognize all these cessions.*[8]

Egyptian priests advised husbands to remain in their wives' good graces, much as Christian priests later advised wives to make themselves subservient to husbands:

> *Keep thy house, love thy wife, and do not dispute with her. She will withdraw herself before violence. Feed her, adorn her, massage her. Caress her and make her heart to rejoice as long as thou livest. . . . Attend to that which is her desire and to that which occupies her mind. For in such manner thou persuadest her to remain with thee. If thou opposest her, it will be thy ruin.*[9]

An Egyptian husband was counseled to make glad his wife's heart "during the time that thou hast," which might have meant a lifetime on earth, or else a shorter period implying a temporary marriage.[10] In the matrilocal household, husbands often entered a period of trial servitude to win their brides, as did the biblical Jacob to win the hand of Rachel (Genesis 29). Hence Sophocles's remark that "Egyptian men sit indoors all day long, weaving; the women go out and attend to business."[11]

Similarly among Anglo-Saxon tribes, "husbandry" meant farm work—as it still does—because a husband was usually bonded to work on his wife's land. Such an agricultural matriarchate is still found in some areas. Among the Zuni, husbands worked in the fields, but the land and its harvest belonged to their wives.[12] The old custom of providing work in compensation for marriage gave rise to the word bridegroom, literally "the bride's servant." The Koran tells men, "your wives are your tillage," because by ancient Arabian law a wifeless man was also landless.[13] See **Matrilineal Inheritance**.

Tantric sages considered "husbandship" (*bhavanan*) essential for still another reason: it was indispensable to a man's spiritual development. The same notion was found among Aryan Celts. The ancient Irish said a true bard could have power over poetry and magic only if he had "purity of husbandship," that is, fidelity to his wife.[14]

1. J.E. Harrison, 519. 2. Briffault 2, 90–91. 3. Hartley, 147, 159. 4. Briffault 1, 369. 5. de Riencourt, 187. 6. Briffault 2, 348. 7. Hartley, 232. 8. Diner, 212. 9. Diner, 218; Budge, D.N., 26. 10. Hartley, 196. 11. Bachofen, 180. 12. Farb, M.R.C., 81–83. 13. Fielding, 83. 14. Joyce 1, 463.

Hvov

"The Earth," an Iranian form of **Eve**. Followers of Zoroaster pretended that she was the wife of their prophet, not a Goddess but only a mortal woman; yet, like writers of the Bible, they inadvertently gave away the secret by calling her Mother of All Living. Zoroaster "went into" her three times, and each time "his seed entered the ground," indicating that he impersonated the god who fertilized the Earth.[1]

1. Campbell, Oc.M., 210.

Hyacinthus

Spring-flower god worshipped in Crete, Sparta, Rhodes, and Mycenae; another name for Narcissus or Antheus or Adonis. In Lacedaemon his flowers represented phalli, carried at the annual festival of the Hyacinthia. Classical myth made him a homosexual lover of the god Apollo, another instance of Apollo's usurpation of the role of his sister Artemis, whose priestesses the Hyacinthides ruled the archaic rites of the flower god.[1]

1. Graves, G.M. 1, 78–82, 311.

Hygeia

"Health," title of Mother Rhea Coronis at her healing shrine of Titane. The name was applied to one of the Goddess's milk-giving breasts. The other was **Panacea.** Later worshippers of the doctor-god Asclepius made Hygeia and Panacea his "daughters."

Hymen

Veil of the Temple; the anatomical definition descended from a concept of the vagina as a sanctuary of Aphrodite, virgin Goddess presiding over defloration. The veil of her temple was "rent in the midst" (Luke 23:45) by the Passion of her doomed bridegroom, at the moment when he entered her chthonian womb, and the sun (male principle) was darkened—all elements borrowed by the Christian crucifixion myth. (See **Honey.**) At the sacred marriage as well as at secular marriages, the Goddess was invoked with the cry *O Hymen Hymenaie:* possible origin of the word "hymn."[1]

1. Rose, 32.

Hypatia

Alexandrian Neoplatonist philosopher, victim of 5th-century Christian persecution of intellectual women. While she was driving to the academy where she taught, a gang of monks dragged her from her chariot, carried her into a church, stripped her, scraped the flesh from her bones with oyster shells, then burned what was left: all by order of St. Cyril, the city Patriarch. By making judicious gifts to civil authorities, Cyril and his monks managed to halt official investigation of Hypatia's murder.[1] Cyril attained sainthood in 1882 when Pope Leo XIII canonized him as a "doctor of the church."[2]

Hypatia's teachings had been famous throughout the land of Egypt, and her death signaled the end of pagan learning in that country.[3]

1. Gibbon 2, 816–17. 2. Attwater, 100. 3. Seligmann, 82.

Hyperboreans

Greek name for the tribes of northern Europe and the British isles, literally "dwellers at the Back of the North Wind." They were supposed to have miraculous knowledge of the movements of the stars, the seasons, fate, and reincarnation. Their observatory-temples, such as Stonehenge, probably contributed to this view.

"Womb," the orgiastic religious festival of Aphrodite in Argos, where the Womb of the World was adored and symbolically fructified.[1]

Hysteria was given its present meaning by Renaissance doctors who explained women's diseases with a theory that the womb sometimes became detached from its place and wandered about inside the body, causing uncontrolled behavior.

1. H. Smith, 126.

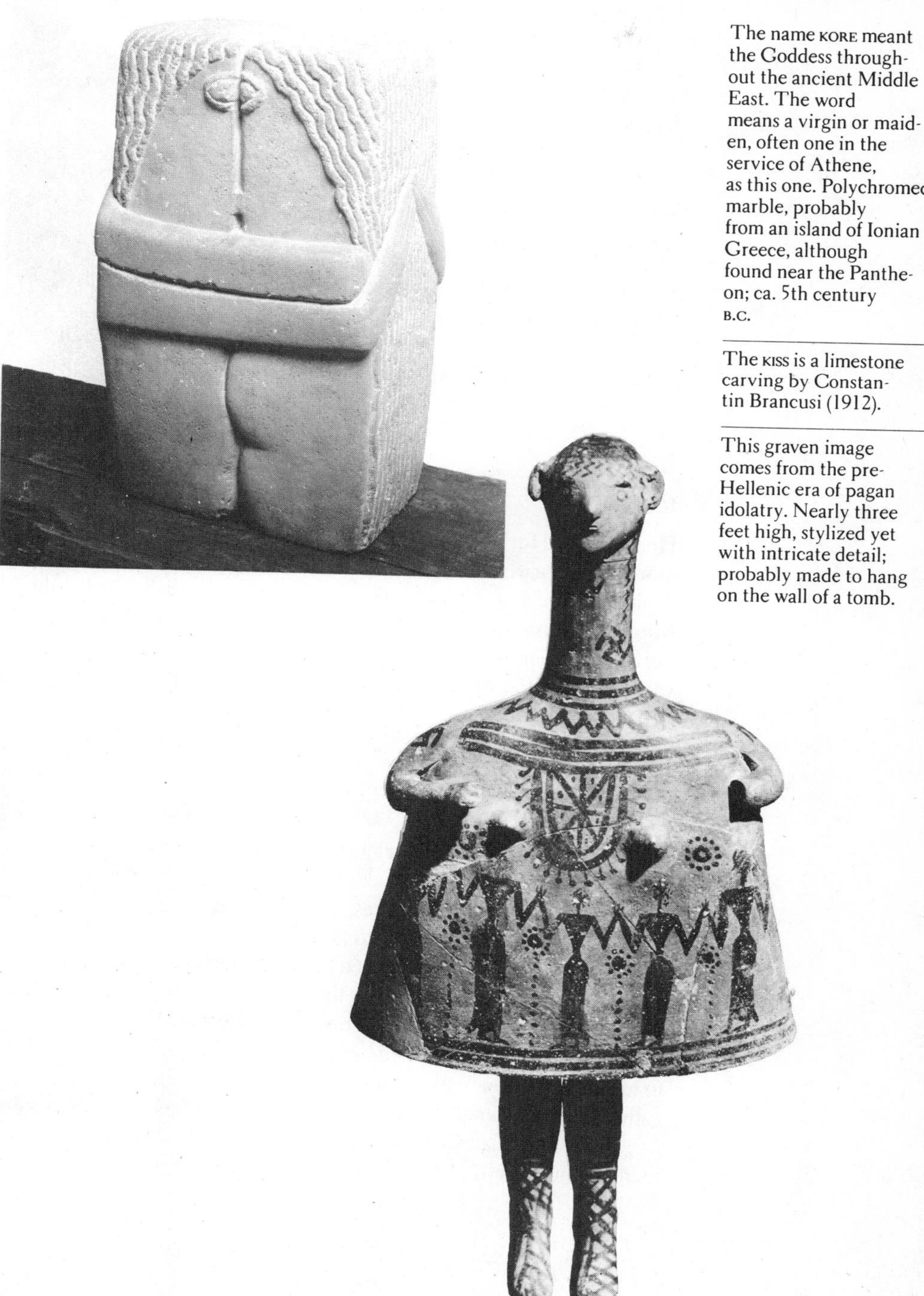

The name KORE meant the Goddess throughout the ancient Middle East. The word means a virgin or maiden, often one in the service of Athene, as this one. Polychromed marble, probably from an island of Ionian Greece, although found near the Parthenon; ca. 5th century B.C.

The KISS is a limestone carving by Constantin Brancusi (1912).

This graven image comes from the pre-Hellenic era of pagan idolatry. Nearly three feet high, stylized yet with intricate detail; probably made to hang on the wall of a tomb.

Iao

One of the most common and most revered "secret names of God" for use in spells, charms, and invocations, adopted from Neoplatonic mystics who called it the essence of the (pagan) **Logos**. Apparently its occult meaning was the deity invoking him- or herself, as "I, the Alpha-and-Omega." See **Name**.

Orphics said Iao was the same as Dionysus, or else the bisexual Phanes (Eros), firstborn of the gods.[1] Christians of the Middle Ages claimed Iao was Jesus.

1. Graves, W.G., 463.

Iblis

Arabic name for Satan, or Shaytan, the angel who rebelled against Allah and refused to worship Allah's creation, Man.[1] Iblis was the leader of the *djinn,* spirits older than Allah. His name seems to have been a corruption of Greek *diabolos.*[2]

1. Keightley, 289. 2. Jonas, 210.

Ichor

Homer's word for the mystic "blue blood" of gods, which kept them immortal and gave them a blue skin color such as characterized gods depicted in the sacred art of India. As the gods were diabolized in the Middle Ages, so was their magic blood. *Ichor* now means a watery purulent discharge, such as medieval churchmen postulated in the veins of devils; the word has also been applied to the blood of insects. See **Quintessence**.

Idea

"Inner-Goddess." Occult tradition said an idea emanated from the Female Soul of the World (Shakti, Shekina, Psyche, Sophia, etc.). Her "ideas" were like personal Muses, "which forms she did in the Heavens above the Stars frame to herself."[1]

Medieval theologians disliked the Idea's feminine connotations and turned away from the ancient theory of the *eide* to the astral theology of Aristotle, that is, to astrological determination of thoughts.[2] Feminine "idea" was replaced by masculine "concept," which used to mean the same as conception, from Latin *concipere semina,* a gathering-up of semen.[3]

Early Christian Gnostics however regarded God the Creator as a mere demiurge, child of the Mother who created in his mind all the "ideas" he used to make things in the material world. His sin was that he arrogantly claimed all these ideas to be his own, because "he was ignorant of the *ideas* of whatever he created and of the Mother herself."[4] This notion that God was guilty of the sin of hubris against the Goddess recurred again and again among early Gnostic sects, until the orthodox church declared the notion heretical and forcibly changed the minds of its adherents.

1. Agrippa, 65. 2. Lindsay, O.A., 102. 3. Potter & Sargent, 224. 4. Jonas, 191.

Idolatry

The pagan habit of making graven images of deities and heroes was copied by the Catholic church and never abandoned, despite God's many prohibitions of idolatry in the Bible (Exodus 20:4, Leviticus 19:4, etc.). St. Thomas Aquinas defended the church against the biblical tradition, and laid down a rule that the same reverence must be paid to Christ's image as to the deity himself.[1]

The issue of idolatry became crucial in the Protestant Reformation, when heretic sects broke off from Catholicism, claiming that papal Rome no longer followed the biblical magisterium in this matter or any other.

John Wyclif declared that holy images were of no use except as firewood. For this reason, among others, the church insisted on digging up his heretic bones 30 years after his death and burning them.[2]

John Wyclif (ca. 1330-1384) English reforming theologian who inspired John Huss, the Lollards, and other leaders of the Protestant Reformation. Wyclif served as rector of Fillingham, prebend of Aust, warden of Canterbury, and rector of Ludgershall in Buckinghamshire.

Some Protestant sects, like the Socinians, argued that if Catholics could be saved despite their disobedience of God's clear command against idolatry, then Protestants could be saved also, though they denied other papal doctrines such as the trinity and the eternity of damnation. In renouncing idolatry, they claimed to be following the letter of biblical law more closely than the Roman church did.[3]

One reason for renunciation of idols was the fear that people would cease to be suitably impressed by them, for after the decline of Roman culture holy images became less and less impressive. Lacking the artistic skill and training that had flourished under paganism, Christian image-makers were unable to produce anything comparable to the classical sculptures and paintings. They created only the crudest sort of painted wooden figures or icons.[4]

Images, no matter how venerable, failed to arouse the proper reverence when their cracks showed, their paint chipped, or the awkward technique of a mediocre artist too obviously proclaimed a man-made artifact devoid of inspiration. As the Chinese proverb said, "No image-maker worships the gods—he knows what stuff they are made of."[5] So did everyone else know, in the case of crudely conceived idols. Some, however, succeeded in fooling the credulous faithful for a long time. Boxley Monastery near Maidstone attracted many pilgrimages to its famous Rood of Grace, an idol of Christ that could "come alive": its eyes and lips moved. Cromwell's officers disclosed the deception in 1536, publicly displaying the wires and rods inside the statue that created the "miracle."[6]

Similarly "miraculous" idols, in effect, were the many pagan tomb-carvings and statues taken over by Christian churches and re-christened martyrs and saints. Where pagan folk were used to visiting shrines of heroes and demigods for petitions or healing, churches simply moved into the shrine and created a new tale of martyrdom for an old god, using his faked "relics" for healing magic. Especially with medieval monks, "the manufacture of martyrs became a thriving industry." Even the bones of ordinary Roman citizens dug out of ancient tombs or catacombs became "idols" in that they were worshipped as divine containers for the spirits of **saints**.[7] This kind of idolatry was not a new Christian invention, but a copy of pagan practice. The writings of Pliny show magical recipes in classical times using the relics of slain gladiators, or hair, or pieces of garments, or nails from a cross on which a man had been executed.[8]

The Catholic church changed its collective mind several times about idols before settling down to permit them. Certainly early sects, such as the Iconoclasts, adopted a typically Semitic horror of idols and devoted themselves to smashing every metal or marble god or goddess. At the Council of Constantinople, the bishops unanimously decreed that images were inventions of the devil and must be kept out of Christian churches. Three decades later, the Council of Nicaea reversed this decision and even anathematized those who refused to worship images. Two more councils contradicted each other's decisions on the matter, until in 843 the images were reinstated in the churches once for all.[9]

One way in which the church excused its own idolatry was to claim that its idols were not real idols but only "symbols." Whatever this may have meant, the churchmen knew perfectly well that the average worshipper made no such distinction. The images were as thoroughly idolized as any African fetish or Phidian Athene:

> *The instant we ascribe to an image . . . real power to act, we make of it an inspired being in itself, and all the sophistry in the world as to its being a means of faith, or a symbol, or causing a higher power to act on the suppliant, is rubbish. The devotee believes* tout bonnement *that the* image *works the cure, and if he did not, any other image of the Virgin or Saint would answer the same purpose. This chaff has been thrashed out a thousand times. . . . And it will last, while one fetish endures, that the hierophant will call it a mere "symbol," and the ignorant worshipper, absolutely unable to comprehend him, will worship the symbol as the thing itself—as he is really expected to do.*[10]

1. H. Smith, 217. 2. H. Smith, 319. 3. Walker, 185. 4. H. Smith, 217. 5. Muller, 329. 6. Hazlitt, 524. 7. Muller, 206. 8. Halliday, 49. 9. Muller, 16. 10. Leland, 237.

Idun

Norse Goddess called "the Renewing One."[1] In her western garden she grew the apples of immortality, which gave the gods eternal life.[2] When her apples were stolen, the gods began to wither and grow old, like mortals.[3]

Idun's name, possibly a feminine forerunner of "Odin," could have been derived from Greece's mountain-shrine Ida, sacred to Rhea, or her alter ego Hera, who kept the apples of immortality that gave the Olympian gods eternal life. Idun was also said to have invented the runic alphabet. Her consort Bragi became the greatest of bards, because she engraved the magic **runes** on his tongue.

1. Sturluson, 54. 2. *Larousse,* 266. 3. Hollander, 39.

Ignatius, Saint

Also called Theophorus, "God-bearer," Ignatius starred in a triumphal procession of Trajan's time, from Antioch to Rome where he was killed.[1] As his name meant Holy Fire, the cult hero whose spirit he carried to immolation seems to have been Heracles. Or he may have been one of the god's idols, carried to Rome with other booty to be displayed at Trajan's triumph.[2] His canonization was only a later myth on an old title.

1. Attwater, 176. 2. Brewster, 89.

Ilithyia

Surname of many forms of the Goddess—Diana, Aphrodite, Artemis, etc.—in the role of divine midwife. Women in childbirth prayed to Ilithyia Eleutho, the Goddess as "Liberator," who freed the infant from the womb. This mythic personage was even canonized as a (male) Christian saint, St. Eleutherius. Similarly a church devoted to Mary as Panaghia Blastike, "Virgin of Fecundity," was built on an old shrine of Aphrodite Ilithyia, "Mother of Fecundity."[1] The Greeks applied the name Ilithyia to many Egyptian goddesses as well, including Isis, Buto, Hathor, and Nephthys.

1. Hyde, 61, 77.

Immaculate Conception

Often erroneously thought to refer to the conception of Christ, the doctrine of the Immaculate Conception actually was invented to absolve the virgin **Mary** of original sin from the moment of her own conception. Early fathers of the church said Mary couldn't be Theotokos (God-bearer) if she was human, therefore tainted with the sin of

Eve; it was heresy to worship her as divine.[1] Nevertheless, people insisted on worshipping her.[2] By the 12th century, Mariolatry even overshadowed the worship of God and Christ; so the doctrine of the Immaculate Conception was invented to make her uniquely holy.

Many churchmen opposed the doctrine, which was heatedly argued for the next 700 years. Finally it was adopted as an article of faith by Pope Pius IX in 1854.[3] Every Catholic was commanded to believe henceforth that Mary "at the first instant of her conception, was preserved immaculate from all stain of original sin, by the singular grace and privilege granted to her by Almighty God."[4]

A certain unnamed medieval holy man had been informed by a divine source that Mary's birthday was September 8, precisely nine months after the December festival which originally represented the conception of the Virgin Goddess Kore.[5] Apparently the date was chosen to celebrate Epiphany and the Immaculate Conception at the same time.

These events being equally devoid of documentation, their invention and promulgation sometimes aroused scorn among non-Catholics. Hazlitt scoffed: "We hear of her immaculate conception as an afterthought, on the part of the Romanists. . . . [T]he whole narrative touching her [Mary] is evidently fabulous, and . . . the immaculate conception by her mother, her own purification . . . are absurdities."[6]

How Mary's conception took place was a problem that aroused some ingenious theological nonsense. Mary's father was not God or a spirit but a living man, and if he had sexual intercourse with Mary's mother it would mean using the medium of transmission of original sin, by the church's own teaching. Some theologians would have it that his seed was carried magically, as if he were an incubus.

1. de Riencourt, 150. 2. Daly, 92. 3. Young, 203. 4. *Encyc. Brit.*, "Mary." 5. de Voragine, 524. 6. Hazlitt, 394.

---

var. Emanuel

Immanuel

Persian title of "the god Immani," or E-mani, venerated in Elam as a sacred king-martyr.[1] One of his later incarnations was the savior Mani, allegedly born of a virgin named Mary.[2]

Isaiah 7:14 quoted a Persian scripture: "Behold, a virgin shall conceive, and bear a son, and shall call his name Immanuel." Matthew 1:22–23 insisted this was a prophecy of Christ, who was therefore "Immanuel"; but the name never really stuck.

1. *Assyr. & Bab. Lit.*, 170, 178. 2. Robertson, 86–88.

---

var. Ininni

Inanna

Sumerian name of the Goddess as queen of the land who made every king her bridegroom. Wedding hymns for the **hieros gamos** said, "Oh my queen, queen of the universe, the queen who encompasses the universe, may he [the king] enjoy long days at your holy lap." Sometimes she turned her power against the king's enemies: "My queen, the foreign lands cower at your cry. . . . My queen, you are all-devouring in your power. . . . My queen, the great gods fled before you like fluttering bats." Tradition said the city of Agade was completely destroyed because Inanna abandoned its temple: "Holy Inanna forsook the shrine Agade . . . ; she went forth against the city in battle."[1]

Inanna was the source of the earth's life blood. She filled the wells, rivers, and springs with her "blood." As a fertility deity, like her Babylonian counterpart Ishtar, she annually descended into the underworld to rescue her consort Dumuzi [Tammuz]. As Nanna, Nana, or Anna she became the holy virgin mother of Attis, the bride of Balder, and the elder Virgin Mother whom Christians called "God's Grandmother."[2]

Hittites called her Inaras. In the land of Hatti she renewed her virginity each year to become the bride of the sacred king at the Purulli festival, which later passed into the Jewish Purim. The chosen man was isolated in a royal castle or tower, and slain at the appointed time so his blood would help the Goddess fertilize the land. Certain writings of lamentation suggest that the king-martyr regretted his brief glory.[3]

1. Pritchard, A.N.E., 127, 202, 207. 2. Graves, W.G., 411. 3. Hooke, M.E.M., 99.

Incest

Thanks to Freud, King Oedipus is one of the most misinterpreted figures in mythology. His mother-marrying, father-killing legend arose not from a wish-fulfillment fantasy but from the ancient system of succession of sacred kings, whereby every previous king was slain by his successor, chosen to be the queen's new bridegroom. The killer was always described as a "son" of the deceased because he was the same god reincarnated in another consort of the same mother-bride. Such sacred incest can still be traced even in the Christian image of the divine Son who is indistinguishable from his Father, who impregnated his own Mother (i.e., Mother of God) to beget himself.

When patriarchal invaders overthrew the Theban matriarchate, they purposely misinterpreted the sacred icons that told the story of its royal succession. The name of the deceased "father," Laius, simply meant "King," and that of the widowed "mother" was the same as the title of the Moon Goddess. The replacement, Oedipus, was depicted as a stranger from a distant land. To make him the king's true son, improbable details were added to show he was sent away in infancy and brought up among foreigners. Freud's rather subjective notion that all men secretly want to kill their fathers—the so-called Oedipus complex—may have had more to do with Freud's own experience of a repressive father than with any mythic archetype.[1]

Sacred incest between father-son and mother-bride was usual among ancient god-kings. It was considered necessary for the goddess-queen to be periodically supplied with a young, virile consort who embodied the same god again as the older consort. Thus Egyptian gods like Amon and Osiris were respectfully entitled, "Husband of thy mother."[2] The reborn Savior appeared as Min, or Menu, the Moon-bull who mated with his sacred Cow-mother. In human form, he was shown with an abnormally long erect phallus, as an ithyphallic sex god like Eros or Kama, the Bull "from whom spring the delights of love."[3]

> *Throughout Egypt generally the company of gods of a town or city were three in number . . . ; two members of such a triad were gods, one old and one young, and the third was a goddess, who was, naturally, the wife, or female counterpart, of the older god. The younger god was the son of the older god and goddess, and he was supposed to possess all the attributes and powers which belonged to his father. . . . [I]t was assumed that he would succeed to his rank and throne when the older god had passed away.*[4]

Here was the basis of trinities consisting of Father, Son, and Holy Spirit (or, Goddess: the third member of the trinity was female, as she was even in Gnostic Christianity under the name of Sophia). The same trinity occurs in almost all mythologies, without ever developing into a complete family: there is no daughter, only a son. That is, man-as-youth and man-as-man have their separate projections into divinity; but woman is always the same.

Unlike Freud, Jung said the meaning of the mother-son incest in religions was not based on simple eroticism but on the idea of rebirth. "To get back to the mother again in order to be born again by the mother. . . . One of the simplest ways was to fructify the mother and procreate oneself again. . . . It is not incestuous cohabitation that is sought, but rebirth. . . . The neurotic who cannot leave his mother has good reason; fear of death holds him there. It appears that there is no concept and no word strong enough to express the meaning of this conflict. Whole religions are built to give value to the magnitude of this conflict."[5]

Though the myth of Oedipus was not about true "Oedipal" father-son rivalry but rather about sacred kingship, the theme of male jealousy was amply demonstrated elsewhere in myths. Rank says, "It is not necessary to explore the heavens for some process into which this trait might be laboriously fitted . . . ; in reality, a certain tension is frequently, if not regularly, revealed between father and son . . . related to the competition for the tender devotion and love of the mother."[6] It might be a fruitful avenue for psychological investigation to determine why mother-son love in mythology was nearly always transmuted into the realm of the erotic.

1. Graves, G.M. 2, 12–13. 2. Maspero, lix. 3. Budge, E.M., 140.
4. Budge, G.E. 1, 113–14. 5. Silberer, 419–20. 6. Rank, 77.

Incubus

The pagan incubus was a special priest embodying a prophetic spirit who could come in dreams or visions to those who "incubated" overnight in the earth-womb or Pit of a temple (see **Abaddon**). Greeks practiced incubation especially in the healing temples of Asclepius and Hygeia. Egyptians' favorite incubus appeared in temples of Imhotep.[1] Undoubtedly, the appearance of the incubus was often carefully staged, when the sleeper was a figure of political importance, to issue the "right" prophecies and advice that would benefit the temple.

Christians copied the custom of incubation, which became "watching" or "keeping vigil." It was recommended in a time of troublesome decision to "watch and pray" overnight in a church, to court a vision of guidance. The incubus, however, was diabolized. He was no longer the same as a guiding angel. The reason for his fall from grace was the ancient tradition of midnight sexual relationships between incubating women and priests, or incubating men and priestesses. Incubi thus became spirits of lust.

Certain churchmen said incubi were demon lovers of women, able to beget children in a demonic version of the Virgin Birth. Father Ludovico Sinistrari said—hedging his bets like every well-trained cleric—"Subject to correction by our Holy Mother Church, and as a mere expression of private opinion, I say that the Incubus, when having intercourse with a woman, begets the human fetus from his own seed." As a "well-known" example of a demon-begotten man, Sinistrari cited "that damnable heresiarch Martin Luther."[2] As for the opinion of the damnable heresiarch himself, Luther said all odd-looking children should be destroyed at birth, for they were clearly the offspring of demons.[3]

Ludovico Maria Sinistrari 18th-century Franciscan theologian, author of *Demonality.*

Other authorities, like St. Thomas Aquinas, insisted that demons must be sterile. Therefore an incubus could impregnate a woman only by carrying semen from a man with whom the demon previously copulated in the form of a succubus or she-demon—for demons were thought to change their sex at will.[4] Aquinas also asserted that a demon could use semen lost in a wet dream so a man could be "at one and the same time both a virgin and a father."[5]

Here Aquinas contradicted both the biblical tradition and St. Augustine, who cited Genesis 6:4 to prove that fallen angels begot children on mortal women: "The sons of God came in unto the daughters of men, and they bare children to them." Pope Benedict XIV announced, "This passage has reference to devils known as incubi and succubi." The pope declined to decide the question of demonic conception, however; he simply mentioned both schools of thought: "Some writers deny that there can be offspring. . . . Others, however, asserting that coitus is possible, maintain that children may result." On this theory, a woman was burned at Carcassonne in 1275 for bearing a child to the devil.[6]

Churchmen with some classical education pointed out that the gods of the heathen—devils, by the church's definition—were fathers.[7] Many legends accepted by the church attributed demonic parentage to such historical figures as Robert of Normandy, Alexander the Great, Plato, Scipio Africanus, all the Huns, and all the Cypriots.[8] A 6th-century *History of the Goths* declared that the Huns were descended from the offspring of women and incubi.[9] Nevertheless, the opinion of Aquinas generally overruled both classical and biblical precedent.

Whatever the incubus's reproductive potential, his sexual capacity inspired ill-concealed male envy in an age when nearly all men were so sexually naive as to confuse penis size with lovemaking skills. Father Sinistrari said women who lay with incubi found afterward that the lovemaking of mere men was "paltry and unable to arouse them to any degree."[10] Pico della Mirandola explained why: incubi were handsome and notable for "the extraordinary largeness of their members. . . . The devils can even agitate the thing when it is inside, wherefore the women derive more pleasure than they do with men." De Lancre quoted the testimony of an accused witch, who said her devil "had a member like a mule's . . . as long and as thick as an arm. . . . He always exposed his instrument, of such beautiful shape and measurements." Despite these unwieldy proportions, incubi were said to seduce very young children. The Chancellor of Würzburg declared in August, 1629, that "There are some 300 children of three or four years who have had intercourse with devils."[11]

Pierre de Lancre (1553-1601) Trial judge for the Inquisition, who boasted of burning hundreds of witches and charged the entire population of Pays de Labourd—some 30,000 persons—with witchcraft. He wrote several books on witchcraft, which were accepted as authoritative.

Satyrs, fauns, and the Gaulish *dusii* (from *deus,* "god") were cited in an official Inquisition handbook as incubi who had intercourse with witches in front of witnesses. St. Augustine called the Gaulish Dusius an incubus who lay with mortal women; and later churchmen earnestly supported Augustine with what they conceived to be proof.[12] Women seemed unaccountably willing to copulate with their demons under the eyes of "bystanders"; the latter reported that, while the demon remained invisible, "it has been apparent from the disposition of those limbs and members which pertain to the venereal act and orgasm, [that] . . . they have been copulating with Incubus devils."[13]

Nuns appeared especially vulnerable to the attentions of incubi.[14] Authorities said nuns often awoke in the morning "to find themselves polluted as if they had slept with men."[15] Some nuns claimed they slept with Christ, but this was condemned as blasphemy resulting from demonic possession, even though the church taught them to think of themselves as Christ's wives.

There were some Christian saints who functioned as incubi themselves. At shrines of St. Giles in Normandy and St. René in Anjou, women would lie all night with the saints' ithyphallic images hoping to conceive children.[16] Christians used to incubate in the temple of Isis at Canopis, following local custom; so the bishops moved some bones into the temple and called them relics of two martyrs, Cyrus of Alexandria and John of Edessa. Incubations continued as before, and any subsequent miracles were credited to the martyrs instead of to Isis.[17]

On occasion, women who consorted with incubi seemed to inspire more fear than the demons themselves. An Anglo-Saxon Leechbook prescribed magic salves for protection, not against incubi but against "women with whom the Devil had sexual intercourse." At Toulouse in 1275, a 56-year-old woman of means was robbed of her worldly goods by ecclesiastical confiscation, and tortured until she confessed that she had intercourse with an incubus every night for years and gave birth to the demon's child, which was half wolf and half snake.[18]

Perhaps the ultimate irony was the church's official opinion that all the activities of incubi were performed "with the permission of God."[19] But what God allowed, men punished.

1. Gifford, 111. 2. R.E.L. Masters, 215, 219. 3. G.R. Scott, 113. 4. H. Smith, 278. 5. Robbins, 28. 6. Robbins, 461, 516. 7. H. Smith, 278. 8. Robbins, 465. 9. J.B. Russell, 59. 10. Haining, 77. 11. Robbins, 385, 462, 464. 12. Hazlitt, 176. 13. Kramer & Sprenger, 24, 114. 14. Haining, 70. 15. Robbins, 127. 16. G.R. Scott, 245–50; Knight, D.W.P., 141. 17. Gifford, 123. 18. J.B. Russell, 75, 164. 19. Robbins, 127.

Indulgence

Catholic doctrine most often equated with the sin of simony. By selling indulgence, the church reaped enormous profit with no material investment—only a promise that the purchaser would be absolved of his sins and admitted to heaven after death. No customer ever returned to complain of being cheated.

It became the rule for popes to promise plenary indulgence (absolute remission of all sins) to military leaders who fought the church's crusades. Bills of indulgence became the spiritual carrot corresponding to the stick of excommunication, which was thought to sentence the sinner irrevocably to hellfire.

Bills of indulgence were peddled by Renaissance popes to earn money for their expensive lifestyle. Pope Alexander VI made a commercial empire out of selling pardons. Pope Leo X sent a Dominican, Johann Tetzel, into Germany to sell indulgences for varying numbers of days' worth of release from purgatory, depending on price. Tetzel's announcements read:

> *I have here the passports . . . to lead the human soul into Paradise. Inasmuch as for a single one of the mortal sins, several of which are committed every day after confession, seven years of expiation either on earth or in Purgatory are imposed—who, for the sake of a quarter of a florin, would hesitate to secure one of these letters which will admit your divine, immortal soul to the celestial joys of Paradise?*[1]

One observer wrote in the 15th century: "Sinners say nowadays, I care not what or how many evils I do before God, for I can get at once, without the least difficulty, plenary remission of any guilt or sin whatever through an indulgence granted me by the Pope, whose written grant I have bought for fourpence . . . , for these grantors of Indulgence run about from place to place and sometimes give a letter for twopence, sometimes for a good drink of wine and beer, sometimes to pay their losses at a game of ball, sometimes for the hire of a prostitute, sometimes for fleshly love."[2]

Reginald Scot thought the peddling of indulgences showed the trivial nature of Catholic doctrine, especially when coupled with the church's idolatry. He wrote of "the folly of some papists, who seeing and confessing the pope's absurd religion, in the erection and maintenance of idolatry and superstition, specially in images, pardons, and relics of saints, will persevere to think, that the rest of his doctrine and trumpery is holy and good."[3]

But not all Catholics approved of the sale of indulgence. In Prague, papal bulls of indulgence were publicly burned at the pillory, having been carried there strung around the neck of a whore, who enlivened the proceedings with lascivious capering.[4] Minstrels and other popular entertainers throughout Europe made fun of the doctrine of indulgence with a satiric couplet:

As soon as the coin in the coffer rings,
The soul from out of the fire springs.[5]

1. Chamberlin, B.P., 241. 2. Murstein, 113. 3. Scot, 12. 4. Lea unabridged, 489.
5. Chamberlin, B.P., 241.

Infallibility

The doctrine of papal infallibility stated that anything the pope said was invariably true, and anything he did was invariably right, because God could not permit his pope to speak or act erroneously. The doctrine first took shape in the 15th century. It was set forth by implication in the writings of Torquemada. Cardinal Cajetano openly proclaimed it, inspiring the pope to issue the bull *Pastor eternus,* which made the doctrine of infallibility part of canon law.[1]

In the 19th-century Age of Enlightenment, one scientific discovery after another demonstrated that the statements of popes on matters like the solar system, biology, botany, geology, and other earth sciences—to say nothing of witchcraft, diabolism, and the Bible—had been patently fallible. In fact, wrong. So the church decided that the pope was still certainly infallible but only when he spoke officially, *ex cathedra,* for then God protected his words from error if not at other times. Unfortunately this served for only a short time. It was soon found that popes were wrong in numerous statements officially enshrined in bulls and encyclicals.

The doctrine of infallibility had to be revised again, this time to state that the pope is infallible only when speaking "on matters of faith and morals." Still another revision of the doctrine may be due in the near future.

1. Guignebert, 357.

Infernus

Latin word for the underworld, source of our "Inferno" which implies a place of hellish fire and heat; but the Infernus was not necessarily hot at all. The name simply meant "the place within." It was usually pictured as dark, not fiery. There were several entrances. Lake Avernus was one; another was the sacred cave of the Cumaean Sybil.

Inheritance

See **Matrilineal Inheritance.**

Innocents, Slaughter of

Part of the traditional myth of sacred kingship: the incumbent king is warned by a prophecy of the birth of his future supplanter and tries to escape his fate by killing numbers of recently born infants. Innocents were slaughtered in the myths of Sargon, Nimrod, Moses, Jason, Krishna, and Mordred as well as in that of Jesus.

Probably the original killer of innocents was Kamsa, king of the Bhojas, who tried to kill Krishna along with a batch of other children. The slaughter is depicted in the cave-temple at Elephanta, where the cross is the symbol of the king.[1] In this case Krishna escaped because he was secretly exchanged with an infant girl, who was killed in his place. She grew up in heaven, and became a Goddess. She prophesied that she would smash Kamsa and drink his blood; and Kamsa "realized that she was his own death."[2]

The Arthurian version of the Slaughter of the Innocents followed the typical pagan model. Merlin predicted that **Arthur** would be overthrown by a prince born on May Day, the old Celtic New Year as it was reckoned when kings were usually replaced by their tanists or "sons." Mordred was Arthur's son by his sister Margawse, therefore both a son and a uterine nephew, able to claim the throne by both father-right and mother-right. Arthur seemed not to realize the obvious qualifications of Mordred when he ordered the slaughter of May Day children, according to Malory's account; and the story was further muddled by giving the children various ages, though they were all born on the same day ("some four weeks old, and some less").[3]

Then King Arthur let send for all the children born on May Day, begotten of lords and born of ladies; for Merlin told King Arthur that he that should destroy him should be born on May Day, wherefor he sent for them all, upon pain of death; and so there were found many lords' sons, and all were put in a ship to the sea, and some were four weeks old, and some less. And so by fortune the ship drave unto a castle, and was all to-riven, and destroyed the most part, save that Mordred was cast up, and a good man found him, and nourished him till he was fourteen year old, and then he brought him to court, as it rehearseth afterward, toward the end of the Death of Arthur.[4]

The Christian version of the slaughter of the innocents occurs only in the Gospel of Matthew. Other Gospels say nothing of it. Mark and John make no mention of Jesus's early years. As far as Luke is concerned, Jesus grew up quietly in Galilee after presentation in the temple of Jerusalem after his birth; there was no king threatening his life. Matthew's "slaughter" seems to have been included only to provide an excuse to locate the holy child in Egypt, to create fulfillment of a prophecy, "Out of Egypt have I called my son" (Matthew 2:15). Therefore Herod's attack on the children probably was invented to provide a link between Jesus and his Egyptian counterpart **Osiris**.

The infants supposedly slain by King Herod were canonized *en masse,* though there are no scriptural records of any of their names, nor even of their number. A modern Catholic scholar notes that enormous numbers have been postulated in the past, but "it is unlikely that there were more than about twenty of them at the most."[5] Yet this statement has no more foundation than a statement that there were two hundred, or two thousand, or none at all—perhaps the most likely possibility, since this was a universal, not a specific, myth.

The entire unknown, unnamed group became patrons of children, and on their feast day, December 28, it was customary in England for children to dress up and go from house to house begging gifts. However, in 1540 an ecclesiastical proclamation ordered that this custom must cease.[6] It has not been observed since.

1. Baring-Gould, C.M.M.A., 374. 2. O'Flaherty, 213. 3. Malory 1, 35. 4. Malory 1, 45. 5. Attwater, 179. 6. Hazlitt, 131.

Inquisition

Until the advent of Nazism in modern Germany, Europe knew no system of organized terrorism to rival the 500-year reign of the Inquisition. Historian Henry Charles Lea, recognized as the leading expert on the medieval period, called the Inquisition "a standing mockery of justice—perhaps the most iniquitous that the arbitrary cruelty of man has ever devised. . . . Fanatic zeal, arbitrary cruelty, and insatiable cupidity rivalled each other in building up a system unspeakably atrocious. It was a system which might well seem the invention of demons."[1] (See **Torture**.)

It was invented primarily to force public acceptance of a church the public didn't want. According to a contemporary aphorism, the church had not ten commandments but only one: "Bring hither the money."[2] St. Bernard deplored the church's greed: "Whom can you show me among the prelates who does not seek rather to empty the pockets of his flock than to subdue their vices?"[3]

Bulgarian writers said the priests of Rome were given to drunkenness and robbery, and "there is none to forbid them." The local presbyter Cosmas didn't deny it but only insisted that Christians must honor even wicked priests.[4] This was an accepted doctrine. Pilichdorf said, "The worst man, if he be a priest, is more worthy than the holiest of layman."[5]

Peter von Pilichdorf
Anti-heretical missionary writer of the early 14th century.

Priests were a privileged class, but their privileges were more and more resented. In the 12th century, monasteries made themselves into wineshops and gambling houses; nunneries became private whorehouses for the clergy; priests used a confessional to seduce female parishioners. Episcopal collectors were depicted in popular stories as the worst of all sinners.[6] "The sale of Church offices was constant and unblushing."[7] Even the pope observed that "those charged with divine grace . . . participate in rapine and despoliation, even in the shedding of blood."[8]

Pierre de Bruys was burned in 1126 for declaring openly that "God is no more in the church than in the market-place; the forms and ceremonies which to so many folk replace true religion are utterly useless; the Cross should not be prayed to. . . . The priests lie in pretending that they made Christ's body and give it to the people for their salvation."[9] According to Tyndale, common folk said of anything that went wrong, "the bishop has blessed it." If the dinner burned, they said the bishop has put his foot in it, "because the bishops burn who they list and whosoever displeaseth them."[10]

Pierre de Bruys
Reforming theologian of the 12th century, founder of the heretical Petrobrusian sect.

William Tyndale
(ca. 1494-1536) English ecclesiastical reformer, influenced by Wyclif; translator of the first English-language Bibles, many of which were seized and burned by Catholic authorities. After a life of preaching and literary activity which helped establish the Reformation, Tyndale was arrested and executed in Brussels.

Would-be reformers within the church were usually silenced. Frère Raymond Jean was executed for preaching against the church's abuses. He said bitterly, "The enemies of the faith are among ourselves. The Church which governs us is symbolled by the Great Whore of the Apocalypse, who persecutes the poor and the ministers of Christ."[11]

Nicholas de Clamanges, rector of the University of Paris, declared in an open letter that the popes were ravishers, not pastors, of their flocks: "The priesthood has become a misery reduced to profaning its calling. . . . Who do you think can endure, among so many other abuses, your mercenary appointments, your multiple sale of benefices, your elevation of men without honesty or virtue to the most eminent positions?"[12] Pope Alexander VI, one of the men so described, was credited with the cynical remark, "It is not God's wish that a sinner should die, but that he should live—and pay."[13]

A Franciscan splinter group, the Fraticelli, withdrew from their order, claiming the pope and all his successors were tainted with the sin of simony. Therefore the church had been excommunicated by

God, for ignoring Christ's vow of poverty. They called the pope an Antichrist.[14] These heretics were soon exterminated. One of their centers, the village of Magnalata, was leveled by order of Pope Martin V and every resident slain.[15]

In 1325 Pope John issued the bull *Cum inter nonnullos,* which "infallibly" declared it was heresy to say Jesus and his apostles owned no property. Inquisitors were ordered to prosecute those who believed Jesus was a poor man. The group called Spiritual Franciscans, who did so believe, were taught an immediate lesson when the pope had 114 of their number burned alive.[16]

Waldenses Also called Valdenses or Vaudois, this heretic sect was founded in southern France during the 12th century by Peter Waldo, or Valdes, who preached a life of simplicity and poverty in imitation of Christ.

The offenses of the Waldenses included many "wrong" opinions. They said laymen and women had the right to preach; masses, votive offerings, and prayers for the dead were useless; purgatory did not exist; one could pray to God without setting foot in a church; and a bad priest should be forbidden to administer sacraments—"a proposition which does no less than deny lasting grace to the sacrament of Orders, and thus destroys the fundamental privilege of the Church." The Waldenses said priests who demand money for administering communion are lower than Judas, "for they sell for one denarius that body for which *he* demanded thirty."[17]

Along with public disgust at the church's avarice, there was a growing suspicion—sparked by Gnostic philosophies from the east—that the church's myths of the garden of Eden, the fall, original sin, heaven and hell, the virgin birth, the meaning of salvation, and so on, were literally untrue. Because people refused to believe the eucharistic bread and wine were literally flesh and blood, the papacy lost all of Bohemia, which after many wars and crusades founded its separate Moravian church. Tenets of the Roman church were widely questioned. Priests were forbidden to "dispute concerning the faith against such astute heretics" in public, lest they expose themselves to ridicule.[18] As Becker said, "This is neurosis in a nutshell: the miscarriage of clumsy lies about reality."[19]

Despite the church's efforts to keep the populace in ignorance, even among the peasantry there were individuals astute enough to recognize theology's clumsy lies. Even the 12th-century passion for building cathedrals seems to have represented a last-ditch effort to hold the wandering attention of the people by giving them splendid temples of the "Lady," to replace the Mother-shrines previously destroyed. At length not even the *Notre Dames* sufficed. The Church had to fall back on its traditional propensity to maintain a reign of terror.[20]

Guignebert says Christianity was "given to warfare; exclusive, violently intolerant, to the Jews especially menacing; bristling with peremptory dogmas which set reason at defiance; marked by complex elaborate rites . . . kept up to the mark by a formidable army of monks and kept in check by a quibbling troop of acute theologians."[21] The violence of the Inquisition was its ultimate weapon.

Violence could be invoked under this system by nothing more than ordinary living, just as the doctrine of original sin was invoked by nothing more than being born. Not only sexual impulses, which were always labeled corrupt, but almost every other natural impulse was viewed as evidence of anti-Christian perversity.[22]

Modern apologists say the Inquisition served some good purposes, like helping secular courts bring criminals to justice.[23] Only a few decades ago, even Catholic manuals mendaciously claimed the Inquisition was a purely civil tribunal.[24] Actually, the Inquisition was uninterested in secular crimes, except insofar as they could provide a basis for a charge of heresy or witchcraft. The Inquisition was created to win the war between the church and a disillusioned public. Coulton says, "The so-called Ages of Faith were only Ages of Acquiescence"; but even the acquiescence was wearing thin.[25]

The power of the Inquisition was established and enlarged by a series of papal bulls. *Ad extirpanda* of Pope Innocent IV, issued May 15, 1252, was "a terrible measure against heretics in Italy, authorizing seizure of their goods, imprisonment, torture, and, on conviction, death, all on minimal evidence."[26]

The Inquisition was the most elaborate extortion racket ever devised, primarily developed for profit.[27] After the arrest, the property of the accused was instantly confiscated. Nothing seems to have been returned. The popes publicly praised the rule of confiscation as a prime weapon against heresy.[28] Confiscation was the organization's *raison d'être;* when the rule of confiscation was not applied, "the business of defending the faith languished lamentably." Affluent Italy made its inquisitors incredibly rich in the 14th century. Within two years, the inquisitor of Florence amassed "more than seven thousand florins, an enormous sum."[29] As the inquisitor Heinrich von Schultheis complacently wrote, "When I have you tortured, and by the severe means afforded by the law I bring you to confession, then I perform a work pleasing in God's sight; and it profiteth me."[30]

Confiscation took place before conviction, because it was taken for granted that no one escaped. "Officials considered themselves safe in acting upon the presumption" of guilt. Sometimes confiscation took place even before confession. In 1300 a nobleman named Jean Baudier was arrested and first examined on January 20. He refused to confess for a long time but finally was broken down by torture and confessed on February 5. He was condemned on March 7. However, his impounded property had been sold on January 29, before the confession. Similarly, Guillem Garric was arrested at Carcassonne in 1284 but not sentenced until 1319. Nevertheless, officials were quarreling over his castle in 1301.[31]

Accused persons were expected to pay the expenses of their own imprisonment, even of their own torture. This continental custom was followed in Scotland where, for example, torturers charged their victims 6 shillings and 8 pence for branding on the cheek. In

England, accused witches were sometimes acquitted; yet they were kept in prison until they paid the expenses of their unlawful imprisonment.[32]

The Inquisition's prisoners had to pay for their own food in prison. Without money they starved. Pope Gregory XI noted that too many were starving to death before they could be brought to the stake, but it seems not to have occurred to him to feed them on church funds. Instead, he offered indulgences to all who would donate food to the "many heretics and those defamed for heresy, who in consequence of their poverty cannot be sustained in prison unless the pious liberality of the faithful shall assist them as a work of charity." Thus the church bent its own rules, which said anyone who helped a heretic was to be suspected of heresy also. Lea commented:

> *There is something so appallingly grotesque in tearing honest, industrious folk from their homes by the thousand, in thrusting them into dungeons to rot and starve, and then evading the cost of feeding them by presenting them to the faithful as objects of charity, that the proclamation which Gregory issued August 15th, 1376, is perhaps the most shameless monument of a shameless age.*[33]

When an arrested heretic had unpaid debts, the judges simply canceled the debts on the ground that no heretic could engage in legal transactions. Thus, "creditors were shamelessly cheated." The entire financial network of European society was strained by its religious masters. "In addition to the misery inflicted by these wholesale confiscations on the thousands of innocent and helpless women and children thus stripped of everything. . . . All safeguards were withdrawn from every transaction. No creditor or purchaser could be sure of the orthodoxy of him with whom he was dealing. . . . The practice of proceeding against the memory of the dead after an interval virtually unlimited, rendered it impossible for any man to feel secure in the possession of property, whether it had descended in his family for generations, or had been acquired within an ordinary lifetime."[34]

Property could be seized from the dead, whose bones might be dug up from their graves and burned as post-mortem heretics; then the property was taken away from legal heirs.[35] If a person knowing he was about to be arrested tried to sell or give away his property, or to commit suicide before the torturers got to him, his property was seized, because a heretic was forbidden to make any legal transaction, and a suicide could bequeathe property to no one; it was taken by the church. If the accused fled the country, he was tried and convicted *in absentia.* Families of the accused were left destitute, and no one dared help them for fear of falling under suspicion. The Inquisition established the law of property seizure for suicides, which remained the rule in most European countries and the British Isles until 1870.[36]

Inquisitors could also impose heavy fines. Sometimes it was argued that fines were useless, since all the property of the accused heretic disappeared in confiscation anyway; but the inquisitors invented a class of unwitting miscreants called "defenders," whose heresy might consist only of a single thoughtless word overheard or spoken. These could be fined for their oversight.[37]

The system of fines often developed into a protection racket. Inquisitors could "exchange the punishment of the body with the punishment of the purse," as Scot put it, and there were many who paid annual fees to escape persecution.[38]

A person who opposed or impeded the inquisitors in any way became at once excommunicate, and after a year in this condition was "handed over without further ceremony to the secular arm for burning, without trial and without forgiveness." No one was acquitted. If a confession could not be obtained—which was extremely rare, thanks to the use of torture—the sentence was "not proven." Even then, the prisoner could be kept indefinitely in prison in case new evidence should arise, or fresh tortures prove effective.[39] Should a victim resist all tortures and survive, which was virtually unheard of, he still was not released. He could be sentenced to life imprisonment for "obduracy."

The witch's or heretic's trial was a mockery. The accused had no lawyer; Pope Boniface directed that trials must be conducted "simply, without the noise and form of lawyers."[40] Evidence was accepted from witnesses who could not legally testify in any other kind of trial, such as condemned criminals, other heretics, and children, even as young as the age of two. The inquisitor Bodin "valued child witnesses because at their tender age they could easily be persuaded or forced to inform."[41] A witness who withdrew adverse testimony was punished for perjury, but his testimony remained on the record.[42] Inquisitorial rules for a trial were as follows:

1. The procedure was kept secret.
2. "Common report" and hearsay were accepted as proof of guilt.
3. Accused was not told of the nature of the charges nor allowed legal counsel.
4. Witnesses were kept concealed.
5. Perjurers, excommunicates, or children could give evidence against witches.
6. No favorable evidence or character witnesses were permitted. In any case, one who spoke for an accused heretic would be arrested as an accomplice.
7. Torture was used always, without limit of duration or severity. Even if the accused confessed before torture, the torture was applied anyway, to "validate" the confession. If the accused died under torture, the record stated that the devil broke his neck in prison.
8. Accused was forced to confirm under torture the names of "accomplices" suggested to him by the judges.
9. No accused person was found innocent.[43]

Officially, the rule was that torture could be applied only once.

But, by a semantic quibble, it could be "continued" any number of times, even over a period of years, each pause being considered a "suspension," not an end. There are records of some victims tortured over fifty times.[44] The Inquisition's handbook, *Malleus Maleficarum,* said the accused witch must be "often and frequently exposed to torture. If after being fittingly tortured she refuses to confess the truth, he [the inquisitor] should have other engines of torture brought before her, and tell her that she will have to endure these if she does not confess. If then she is not induced by terror to confess, the torture must be continued." If she remained obdurate, "she is not to be altogether released, but must be sent to the squalor of prison for a year, and be tortured, and be examined very often, especially on the more Holy Days."[45]

Another official rule was that the church did not shed blood. Therefore, victims were handed over to the secular arm (civil courts) for execution. This was called relaxing or abandoning them. It was accompanied by a token plea for mercy: "We cast you forth from this our ecclesiastical Court, and leave you to be delivered to the secular arm. But we earnestly pray that the said secular court may temper its justice with mercy, that there be no bloodshed or danger of death."[46]

This plea was the emptiest of formalities, designed only to absolve the church of responsibility for bloodshed. In fact, "to be delivered to the secular arm" was an irrevocable death sentence, which the secular court was compelled to carry out. To temper justice with "mercy" meant permission to strangle the victim before she was burned, but this was not often done.[47]

History was written to order by church historians who claimed the church "took no part in the corporal punishment of heretics." Ecclesiastical euphemism forced on civil authorities a guilt that belonged at the church's door. Magistrates were commanded to carry out the death penalty by the dire threat of excommunication and consequent arrest. "The remorseless logic of St. Thomas Aquinas rendered it self-evident that the secular power could not escape the duty of putting the heretic to death. . . . [T]he only punishment recognized by the Church as sufficient for heresy was burning alive. Even if the ruler was excommunicated and incapable of legally performing any other function, he was not relieved from the obligation of this supreme duty, with which nothing was allowed to interfere. . . . The fact is, the Church not only defined the guilt and forced its punishment, but created the crime itself."[48]

The fiction of the church's innocence was exposed by a bull of Pope Leo X in 1521. The Senate of Venice had refused to sanction the numerous executions ordered by the Inquisition. The Pope wrote to his legate, "We declare and order you to exhort and command the aforesaid Senate of Venice, their Doge and his officials, to intervene no more in this kind of trial, but promptly, without changing or inspecting the sentences made by the ecclesiastical judges, to execute the sentences which they are enjoined to carry out. And if they neglect or refuse, you are to compel them with the Church's censure and other appropriate legal measures. From this order there is no appeal."[49] A directive published in 1599 said judges were bound under pain of mortal sin to execute witches; anyone who objected to the death sentence was suspected of complicity.[50]

Inquisitors "jealously guarded their records from all outsiders."[51] On one occasion, magistrates of Brescia objected to burning a number of condemned witches without having examined records of their trials. But the inquisitors kept their records sequestered, and the pope declared the magistrates' reluctance a scandal to the faith. "He ordered the excommunication of the magistrates if within six days they did not execute the convicts . . . a decision which was held to give the secular courts six days in which to carry out the sentence of condemnation."[52]

Even when kept hidden, records were often falsified. Inquisitors had special terms for everything they did. For example, torturers said their victims were "laughing" when they contorted their faces with pain; or "sleeping" when they fainted. Those who died under torture either "committed suicide" or were slain by the devil. Having confessed under torture, the accused was compelled to repeat the confession outside the torture chamber, knowing he would be returned thereto if he didn't obey; nevertheless, this was recorded as a confession given "freely and spontaneously, without the pressure of force or fear," and court documents often claimed the accused had confessed without torture. Sometimes confessions were described as "voluntary" if they were obtained after the first degree of torture—binding and racking.[53] An episcopal scribe at Pamiers naively wrote that a prisoner confessed of his own accord "after he was taken down from the torture."[54]

Some victims were listed as "confessed without torture" after exposure to only one instrument, a spiked iron press that crushed the legs. Friedrich von Spee, a Jesuit who acted as confessor for condemned witches and developed some compassion for them, wrote of this practice: "And they call that 'Confessed without torture'! What kind of insight can those have who lack all understanding of such pains? How can outstandingly learned men judge and discriminate when they cannot understand the language, the specialists' jargon, of the inquisitors?" In his *Cautio Criminalis,* von Spee wrote:

> *Why do you search so diligently for sorcerers? I will show you at once where they are. Take the Capuchins, the Jesuits, all the religious orders, and torture them—they will confess. If some deny, repeat it a few times—they will confess. Should a few still be obstinate, exorcise them, shave them, only keep on torturing—they will give in. If you want more, take the Canons, the Doctors, the Bishops of the Church—they will confess.*[55]

Another unusual churchman, Bernard Delicieux, was excommunicated, arrested, tortured, and burned alive for expressing the opinion that St. Peter and St. Paul, if tried by the Inquisition's methods, would certainly be convicted of heresy.[56]

Inquisitors were placed entirely above the law by Pope Innocent IV in his bull of 1252, *Ad extirpanda.*[57] Every ruler and citizen must assist them on pain of excommunication. Resistance could place the whole community under interdict, or force payment of heavy fines. Any individual fined by the Inquisition could be held in prison until he paid, or died. Torture was officially sanctioned in 1257 and remained a legal recourse of the church for five and a half centuries until it was abolished by Pope Pius VII in 1816.[58]

The victims in those five and a half centuries were literally countless. Official burnings were only a beginning. There were also the disrupted, starving families; unrecorded suicides; unofficial lynchings; hundreds of thousands, perhaps millions, who died unnoticed in the papal crusades against heretical groups. There were late-Renaissance witch hunts in Protestant countries, which had no formal connection with the Inquisition but certainly took their impetus from it.

The chronicler of Trèves reported that in the year 1586, the entire female population of two villages was wiped out by the inquisitors, except for only two women left alive.[59] Two other villages were destroyed completely and erased from the map.[60] A hundred and thirty-three persons were burned in a single day at Quedlinburg in 1589, out of a town of 12,000. Henri Boguet said Germany in 1590 was "almost entirely occupied with building fires (for witches); and Switzerland has been compelled to wipe out many of her villages on their account. Travelers in Lorraine may see thousands and thousands of the stakes to which witches are bound."[61]

Henri Boguet
Highly active inquisitorial judge whose book, *Discours des sorciers* (1590) became a standard reference.

In 1524, one thousand witches died at Como.[62] Strasbourg burned five thousand in a period of 20 years.[63] The Senate of Savoy condemned 800 witches at one time. Paramé stated that over thirty thousand were executed in the 15th century.[64] Nicholas Remy said he personally sentenced 800 witches in 15 years and in one year alone forced sixteen witches to suicide. A bishop of Bamberg claimed 600 witches in 10 years; a bishop of Nancy, 800 in 16 years; a bishop of Wurtzburg, 1900 in 5 years. Five hundred were executed within three months at Geneva and 400 in a single day at Toulouse. The city of Trèves burned 7,000 witches. The Lutheran prelate Benedict Carpzov, who claimed to have read the Bible 53 times, sentenced 20,000 devil-worshippers. Even relatively permissive England killed 30,000 witches between 1542 and 1736. The slaughter went on throughout Christian Europe for nearly five centuries.[65]

Mass burnings on the Iberian peninsula were known as autos-de-fé (acts of faith). They were held once a month on the average, usually on a Sunday or holiday so all could attend; to stay away was thought suspicious. Sometimes the spectators were invited to participate, as in the diversion genially known as "shaving the new Christians." This meant setting fire to the hair or beards of those waiting their turn at the stake.[66]

Wholesale burnings in Germany are suggested by the observation of a visitor to Wolfenbuttel in 1590: there were so many stakes to burn the witches that the place of execution resembled a small forest. The executioner of Neisse in Silesia invented an oven in which he roasted to death forty-two women and young girls in one year. Within nine years he had roasted over a thousand persons, including children two to four years old.[67]

Inquisitors were empowered to absolve each other, their officers, torturers, and executioners, of blood guilt for their victims' deaths, whether in the prison, in the torture chamber, or at the stake.[68] They also forced the condemned witches to recite: "I free all men, especially the ministers and magistrates, of the guilt of my blood; I take it wholly upon myself, my blood be upon my own head." Some witches even were made to repudiate the more impossible confessions extorted by torture, as a suicidal device: "Through the temptation of the devil I made up that confession on purpose to destroy my own life, being weary of it, and choosing rather to die than live." These abject recitations preceded the trip to the stake, for it was common practice to silence witches on their way to execution, either by wooden gags, or by cutting out their tongues, to prevent communication with the crowd.[69]

Inquisitors didn't want to give witches a chance to reveal that they had been raped in prison, the usual practice of torturers and their assistants during preliminary "stripping."[70] By the curious morality of the day, outrage could be excited by sexual "irregularities" although spectacles of hideous torment were received without serious objection. The people of Toulouse gathered evidence against an inquisitor named Foulques de Saint-George to prove he arrested women for the sole purpose of abusing them sexually.[71] Apparently this was considered worse than torturing them.

Some records hint that executioners could indulge their lusts as long as they were circumspect. The day in 1589 at Quedlinburg, 133 witches were burned and four inexplicably disappeared. "Four beautiful girls were spared by the executioner, who gave out that the devil had spirited them away."[72] They were never seen again. One can well imagine who this "devil" was and what happened to the poor girls before they were finally murdered.

It can hardly be doubted that a major driving force of all witch hunts was sadistic sexual perversion. Torturers liked to attack women's breasts and genitals with pincers, pliers, and red-hot irons. Under the Inquisition's rules, little girls were prosecuted and tortured for witchcraft a year earlier than little boys—at 9½, as opposed to 10½ for boys. Witch hunting generally was directed against the female sex, and the abject helplessness of imprisoned and tortured women invariably encouraged sexual abuse along with every other kind of abuse.

Late in the 14th century it became a rule that prisoners in solitary confinement (usually women) could be visited in their cells by "zealous Catholics" (always men; female visitors were not allowed).[73]

One inquisitorial judge, Dietrich Flade, experienced a revulsion for his lifework and dared to say openly that the confessions wrung from his victims were false, due only to their agony. His archbishop had Flade arrested and put on the rack himself until he admitted having sold his soul to Satan; then he was burned.[74]

Another who ran into trouble for speaking too freely was Peter the Precentor of Paris, who said the Inquisition blackmailed rich people and falsely accused and arrested "certain honest matrons" who "refused to consent to the lasciviousness of priests."[75] Civil magistrates who criticized the Inquisition often found themselves in its dungeons. When the governor of Albi defended his people against the inquisitors in 1306, letters were forged and "discovered" in church records to remove him from office on the ground that his grandfather was a convicted heretic.[76]

Predictably, inquisitors often went in fear of their own lives, appearing in public with escorts of armed guards. Some were attended by small armies of toughs whose disruptive behavior was absolved by their masters, so they could literally get away with murder, robbery, and rape; they were "above the law."[77] Many inquisitors wore armor under their habits and tested all their food for poison. Torquemada's chief protégé Pedro Arbués was assassinated by relatives of some of his victims in a church in Aragon as he left his guards and went alone to the altar to receive the sacrament. During the 19th century, Pedro Arbués was canonized as a saint by Pope Pius IX.[78]

Another inquisitor-saint was Peter Martyr (Piero da Verona), whose case has never been adequately explained. He was so zealous in Lombardy as to embarrass even the church; apparently it was decided that he would be more useful dead than alive. In 1252 he was assassinated, and within a year he was canonized—the fastest creation of a saint on record. His killers were captured but not prosecuted. One of them later became an inquisitor himself. Another entered the Dominican order, died in old age, and was canonized as St. Acerinus; his portrait appeared in a stall of Peter Martyr's own church in 1505. A third conspirator was arrested and imprisoned by the Inquisition 43 years after the murder, possibly because he was beginning to talk too much.[79]

Another curious case was that of the heretic who nearly became a saint, Armanno Pongilupo, a high-ranking official of the Catharan sect at Ferrara in the 13th century. Pretending devout Catholicism, Pongilupo secretly gave aid to imprisoned heretics. He played the part of piety so well that after his death, altars and images were dedicated to him; he received a magnificent tomb in the cathedral; stories were told of his miraculous cures of the sick, the lame, and the blind. Ferrara's citizens demanded his canonization, but the church refused, ordering that his remains be exhumed and burned for his heresy. Ferrara would not comply. The cathedral was placed under interdict and its chapter was excommunicated. Arguments about Pongilupo dragged on for 33 years. Finally, the inquisitor Guido da Vincenza ended the matter by having Pongilupo's bones burned, his altars destroyed, and his heirs deprived of their property—which naturally reverted to the church. Guido was rewarded with the episcopate of Ferrara.[80]

The Inquisition was not organized to administer justice; it was organized to enrich the church and silence its critics. Lea says, "All the safeguards which human experience had shown to be necessary in judicial proceedings of the most trivial character were deliberately cast aside in these cases, where life and reputation and property through three generations were involved. Every doubtful point was decided 'in favor of the faith'. . . . Had the proceedings been public, there might have been some check upon this hideous system, but the Inquisition shrouded itself in the awful mystery of secrecy until after sentence had been awarded and it was ready to impress the multitude with the fearful solemnities of the *auto da fé*."[81]

The Inquisition remained active until 1834, especially in Central and South America, where "heathen" natives were tortured and burned for crimes against the true faith, such as not believing in it.[82] Mayan scribes in Central America wrote: "Before the coming of the Spaniards, there was no robbery or violence. The Spanish invasion was the beginning of tribute, the beginning of church dues, the beginning of strife."[83] Catholic fathers of the mission of San Francisco burned many Indian "witches" before the tribes were sufficiently subdued to accept God's word.[84] Lea said, "An inquisitor seems to have been regarded as a necessary portion of the missionary outfit."[85]

Even in the present century, Catholic authorities have tried to present the Inquisition in an undeservedly flattering light. Cardinal Lépicier, expressly supported by Pope Pius X, declared the church's reign of terror was right, just because the church did it. "The naked fact that the Church, of her own authority, has tried heretics and condemned them to be delivered to death, shows that she truly has the right of killing. . . . [W]ho dares to say that the Church has erred in a matter so grave as this?"[86]

In fact, many have dared to say so. Leland wrote: "When people believe, or make believe, in a thing so very much as to torture like devils and put to death hundreds of thousands of fellow-beings, mostly helpless and poor old women, not to mention many children, it becomes a matter of very serious import to all humanity to determine once for all whether the system or code according to which this was done was absolutely right for ever, or not."[87] Anthropologist Jules Henry said, "Organized religion, which likes to fancy itself the mother of compassion, long ago lost its right to that claim by its organized support of organized cruelty."[88] Coulton said of the

Inquisition, "History affords few plainer examples of the demoralizing effects of absolute power upon fairly ordinary men."[89] And Vetter pointed out that the system that created such horrors may be still dangerous:

> *Have religious institutions been any more humane in the process of consolidating their power than has secular machinery similarly occupied? The taste for slaughter exhibited by the sons of the Prophet was more than matched by that of Christians who liquidated heathen and heretic. . . . The cultural backgrounds of the past and current generation of political dictators provides interesting material for speculation. Mussolini, Franco, Salazar, Hitler, Peron and almost without exception the Latin-American dictators were or are Roman Catholics, at least in their education and upbringing. And Stalin had considerable training for the priesthood of an equally dictatorial church. Confronted with such facts one is compelled at least to ask himself what kind of causal sequences are here suggested. . . .*
>
> *In both Islam and Christendom the naive believers have over long periods been taught that it was their duty to slaughter the unbeliever, or whoever refused to accept their particular version of divine guidance. They have not had a change of heart; they have just been shorn of the powers for mischief.*[90]

It is unsettling to realize that such powers for mischief could yet be revived. The edicts that established the Inquisition have never been repealed. They are "officially still part of the Catholic faith, and were used as justification for certain practices as recently as 1969."[91]

Julian Huxley deplored the "pestilent doctrine on which all the churches have insisted, that honest disbelief in their more or less astonishing creeds is a moral offense . . . deserving and involving the same future retribution as murder and robbery." In his opinion, the worst visions of hell would seem pale beside a comprehensive vision of Christianity's gory history.[92] Such history should be remembered, on the old principle that those who cannot remember their history are condemned to repeat it.

1. Lea, 60, 97, 257. 2. Tuchman, 327. 3. Lea unabridged, 21. 4. Spinka, 61. 5. Coulton, 177. 6. Lea unabridged, 10, 16. 7. Coulton, 42. 8. Tuchman, 224. 9. Coulton, 61; H. Smith, 254; Guignebert, 291. 10. Hazlitt, 53. 11. Lea unabridged, 599. 12. Tuchman, 522. 13. Chamberlin, B.P., 167, 170. 14. Coulton, 230. 15. Lea unabridged, 653. 16. Guignebert, 287. 17. Guignebert, 298, 326. 18. Coulton, 81. 19. Becker, D.D., 178. 20. Campbell, C.M., 395. 21. Guignebert, 184. 22. Campbell, M.T.L.B., 162. 23. *Encyc. Brit.,* "Inquisition." 24. White 1, 319. 25. Coulton, 58. 26. J.B. Russell, 155. 27. Lea, 224. 28. Robbins, 229. 29. Lea, 173–75, 225. 30. Robbins, 451. 31. Lea, 213–14. 32. Robbins, 116, 456. 33. Coulton, 151. 34. Lea, 215, 218, 225. 35. Coulton, 132, 148. 36. H. Smith, 418. 37. Lea, 169. 38. Scot, 27. 39. Lea, 45, 149. 40. H. Smith, 284. 41. Robbins, 229, 554. 42. H. Smith, 284. 43. Robbins, 13–14. 44. H. Smith, 287; Robbins, 304. 45. Kramer & Sprenger, 226, 249. 46. Coulton, 168–69. 47. H. Smith, 290. 48. Lea, 231, 233, 237. 49. Robbins, 305. 50. Pepper & Wilcock, 150. 51. Coulton, 119. 52. Lea, 235. 53. Robbins, 108, 269, 482–83, 540. 54. Coulton, 156. 55. Shumaker, 62; Bromberg, 61. 56. Lea unabridged, 214; Coulton, 216. 57. Lea, 33. 58. Robbins, 269. 59. Summers, G.W., 486–87. 60. Robbins, 219. 61. Shumaker, 61. 62. W. Scott, 170. 63. Robbins, 219. 64. Coulton, 263. 65. H. Smith, 292–93. 66. Plaidy, 157. 67. Robbins, 554–55. 68. Lea, 77.

69. Robbins, 105; Lea, 248. 70. Robbins, 592. 71. Lea unabridged, 302. 72. Robbins, 219. 73. Lea, 99, 183. 74. H. Smith, 292. 75. Coulton, 38. 76. Lea, 76. 77. Lea, 77–79; Coulton, 293. 78. Reinach, 312. 79. Lea unabridged, 376. 80. Lea unabridged, 390. 81. Lea, 101–2. 82. Plaidy, 165. 83. von Hagen, 61. 84. Briffault 3, 519. 85. Lea, 51. 86. Coulton, 69. 87. Leland, 250. 88. Henry, 422. 89. Coulton, 129. 90. Vetter, 411, 510, 518. 91. Holmes, 45. 92. H. Smith, 392–93.

Io

"Moon," the white Cow-goddess who mothered the Ionians. Hers was another name for "Cow-Eyed" Hera, as Homer called her, although classic mythographers portrayed her as a separate entity, one of Zeus's many paramours. Io represented the horned, milk-giving, lunar Triple Goddess, as shown by her sacred colors. She turned herself from white to red to black, the hues of the Virgin, Mother, and Crone (see **Gunas**).[1]

The apocryphal story that Hera sent a gadfly to sting Io, to send her wandering all over the world, was a Hellenic myth invented to explain the universality of the worship of the white Moon-cow. Since Hera was herself the same Goddess, her alleged jealousy of Io was a patriarchal fiction. Some said Hera placed Io under the guardianship of hundred-eyed Argus Panoptes ("All-Eyes"), an allegory of the moon traveling under the many-eyed gaze of the starry sky.[2]

1. Graves, G.M. 1, 191. 2. Jobes, 210.

Iphigeneia

"Mother of Strong Ones," high priestess of Artemis at Taurus, where all strangers were sacrificed to the Goddess and their severed heads nailed to crosses. The myth that Iphigeneia was Agamemnon's daughter, sacrificed to the sea by her cruel father, has been called a result of "the mythographers' anxiety to conceal certain barbarous traditions."[1] One of Iphigeneia's other names was Hecate.

1. Graves, G.M. 2, 78.

Irene, Saint

"Peace," the third of Aphrodite's three Horae; the Dove who announced the coming of death. She also associated with the "peace" to be won by ritual castration, even as late as the 14th century A.D. when a nun or priestess bearing her name was linked to the heretical sect of Mount Athos monks who emasculated themselves.[1] (See **Castration.**)

The pagan temple of Irene on the acropolis of Constantinople was taken over by Christians and renamed the Church of Holy Irene.[2]

Thus the Byzantine Goddess was canonized, along with her two sisters in the same Trinity.[3]

1. Spinka, 119. 2. J. H. Smith, C.G., 228. 3. Reinach, 312; Attwater, 34.

Iris

Greek Goddess of the **rainbow**, personifying like the Hindu Maya the many-colored veils of the world's appearances behind which the spirit of the Goddess worked unseen. In many mythologies she personified the bridge between earth and heaven, the Rainbow Bridge of Norse paganism, the Necklace of Ishtar in Mesopotamia, the Road of the Gods in Japan, the Kinvad Bridge in Persia.[1]

Greeks said the rainbow symbolized the Goddess Iris, "Source of the waters from on high," mother of Love.[2] Like the part of the eye named after her, she was the Kore, Virgin, or Female Soul, a form of the Great Shakti who was both the organ of sight and the visible world that it saw. Her spectrum spanned all possible colors. The same seven-color spectrum was shown on the seven-stage ziggurats of Mesopotamia, signifying the seven planetary spheres, with a symbolic ascent to the Seventh Heaven as part of the initiatory pilgrimage.[3]

1. Eliade, S., 134-35. 2. Cavendish, T., 116. 3. Lethaby, 131.

var. Isolde

Iseult

"White Lady" of Welsh romance, a pagan queen who abandoned one husband in order to take another. With Tristan, her "true-love," she became a popular heroine of the typical bardic romance of star-crossed lovers. The bards maintained that even married ladies should be free to take lovers, as under the old pagan system. Because King Mark of Cornwall, Iseult's jealous husband, imprisoned his wife's lover and tried to kill him, poets branded King Mark a "felon" and a "traitor."[1] See **Romance**.

1. Malory 2, 53.

Ishtar

Babylonian "Star," the Great Goddess who appears in the Bible as Ashtoreth, Anath, Asherah, or Esther, the Queen of Heaven (Jeremiah 44:19). She was also the Great Whore, described in Revelation 17:5 as Babylon the Great, the Mother of Harlots. Another of her titles was the Goddess Har, who called herself the compassionate prostitute. Men communed with her through the sexual rites of her harlot-priestesses.[1] See **Prostitution**.

Babylonian scriptures called Ishtar the Light of the World, Leader of Hosts, Opener of the Womb, Righteous Judge, Lawgiver, Goddess of Goddesses, Bestower of Strength, Framer of All Decrees, Lady of Victory, Forgiver of Sins, etc.[2] Much of the liturgical flattery addressed to God in the Old Testament was plagiarized from Babylonian prayers to Ishtar. One example:

> *Who dost make the green herb to spring up, mistress of mankind! Who hast created everything, who dost guide aright all creatures! Mother Ishtar, whose power no god can approach! A prayer will I utter; may she do unto me what seems good unto her . . . . O my mistress, make me to know my deed, establish for me a place of rest! Absolve my sins, lift up my face!*[3]

A Babylonian prayer that obviously prefigured the prayers and psalms of biblical writers, even the biblical theology, said to the Goddess: "O Thou art adorable, who givest salvation, life, and justice, vivify my name."[4] Like the Old Testament God, Ishtar was the Mighty One, winner of battles and overthrower of mountains.[5] She said:

> *In the brilliant heavens, to give omens in abundance, I appear, I appear in perfection. With exultation in my supremacy, with exultation do I, a Goddess, walk supreme; Ishtar, the Goddess of evening, am I; Ishtar, the Goddess of morning, am I; Ishtar, who opens the portals of heaven, in my supremacy. The heavens I destroy, the earth I devastate, in my supremacy. Who rises resplendent on the firmament of heaven, invoked above and below, in my supremacy. The mountain I sweep away altogether, in my supremacy. The great wall of the mountain am I, their great foundation am I, in my supremacy.*[6]

A long Babylonian prayer presents numerous metaphors and liturgical phrases later copied by Jewish priests on behalf of their god:

> *I beseech thee, Lady of ladies, Goddess of goddesses, Ishtar, queen of all cities, leader of all men. Thou art the light of the world, thou art the light of heaven . . . . Supreme is thy might, O Lady, exalted art thou above all gods. Thou renderest judgment and thy decision is righteous; unto thee are subject the laws of the earth and the laws of heaven, the laws of the temple and of the shrine, and the laws of the private apartment and of the secret chamber. Where is the place where thy name is not, and where is the spot where thy commandments are not known? At thy name the earth and the heavens shake, and the gods they tremble; the spirits of heaven tremble at thy name and the men hold it in awe. Thou art great, thou art exalted; all the men of Sumer, and all creatures, and all mankind glorify thy name. With righteousness dost thou judge the deeds of men, even thou; thou lookest upon the oppressed and to the downtrodden thou bringest justice every day. How long, Queen of Heaven and Earth, how long, how long, Shepherdess of pale-faced men, wilt thou tarry? How long, O Queen whose feet are not weary and whose knees make haste? How long, Lady of Hosts, Lady of Battles? Glorious one whom all the spirits of heaven fear, who subduest all angry gods; mighty above all rulers, who holdest the reins of kings. Opener of the womb of all women, great is thy light. Shining light of heaven, light of the world, enlightener of all the places where men dwell, who gatherest together the hosts of the nations. Goddess of men,*

divinity of women, thy counsel passeth understanding. Where thou glancest the dead come to life, and the sick rise and walk; and the mind that is distressed is healed when it looks upon thy face. How long, O Lady, shall mine enemy triumph over me? Command, and at thy command the angry god will turn back. Ishtar is great! Ishtar is Queen! My Lady is exalted, my Lady is Queen.[7]

Akkadian sources show that Ishtar was the same Great Goddess revered all over the Near East under such names as Dea Syria, Astarte, Cybele, Aphrodite, Kore, Mari, etc.:

Praise Ishtar, the most awesome of the Goddesses, revere the queen of women, the greatest of the deities. She is clothed with pleasure and love. She is laden with vitality, charm, and voluptuousness. In lips she is sweet; life is in her mouth. At her appearance rejoicing becomes full. She is glorious. . . . The fate of everything she holds in her hand. . . . Ishtar—to her greatness who can be equal? Strong, exalted, splendid are her decrees. . . . Ishtar among the gods, extraordinary is her station. Respected is her word; it is supreme over them. She is their queen; they continually cause her commands to be executed. All of them bow down before her.[8]

The powers of the underworld bowed down before her when she went underground to rescue her son-lover Tammuz, as her Sumerian forerunner Inanna rescued the same son-lover, Dumuzi. She said to the seven gatekeepers: "If thou openest not the gate so that I cannot enter, I will smash the door, I will shatter the bolt, I will smash the doorpost, I will move the doors, I will raise up the dead, eating the living, so that the dead will outnumber the living."[9] This threat was typical of Ishtar's dark underworld twin, Eresh-kigal, the Death-goddess who had power to deprive the heavenly gods of their sacrificial food.[10] Ishtar's temporary departure caused sterility and suspension of sexual activities over the whole earth: "After the Lady Ishtar has descended, the bull no longer mounts the cow, the ass no longer bends over the she-ass, and the man no longer bends over the woman in the street: the man slept in his place, the woman slept alone."[11]

This Descent into Hell was a perilous but necessary part of the sacred drama, lasting three days and culminating in the Day of Joy, when the god was restored to life.[12] This inaugurated a new year after penitential atonement and sacrifice. "It is on New Year's Day that Ishtar lies with Tammuz, and the king reproduces this mythical hierogamy by consummating the ritual union with the Goddess [i.e., with the hierodule who represents her on earth] in a secret chamber of the temple, where the nuptial bed of the Goddess stands."[13]

Gilgamesh said the Goddess was cruel to her lovers, since each in turn personified the dying god who refreshed the earth's fertility with his blood.[14] When the god was incarnate in bulls, the animals were emasculated and their severed genitals thrown to the Goddess's image, a rite "probably derived from the rite of self-emasculation which had been practiced in honor of Ishtar."[15] Ishtar's priestesses apparently performed some version of the rite each year in the temple of Jerusalem, where the virgin form of the Goddess was called Mari, Mari-Anna, or Miriam, and her holy women annually wailed for the sacrificial death of Tammuz (Ezekiel 8:14). See **Salome; Mary Magdalene.**

1. Briffault 3, 169. 2. Harding, 164–65. 3. *Assyr. & Bab. Lit.*, 434. 4. d'Alviella, 189. 5. *Epic of Gilgamesh*, 26. 6. *Assyr. & Bab. Lit.*, 434. 7. Briffault 3, 88–89. 8. Pritchard, A.N.E. 1, 232–33. 9. Hooke, M.E.M., 40. 10. Pritchard, A.N.E. 2, 13. 11. Neumann, A. P., 87. 12. Frazer, G. B., 407. 13. Eliade, M.E.R., 26. 14. *Assyr. & Bab. Lit.*, 338–39. 15. Jobes, 185.

Isis

Egyptian scriptures said, "In the beginning there was Isis, Oldest of the Old. She was the Goddess from whom all becoming arose."[1] As the Creatress, she gave birth to the sun "when he rose upon this earth for the first time."[2] Her title, "Giver of Life," was applied also to the queen mother of Egypt.[3]

In her Roman mysteries, Isis was addressed as "the One Who is All." Lucius's hymn to her said:

> *O Thou holy and eternal Savior of the human race. . . . Thou bestowest a mother's tender affections on the misfortunes of unhappy mortals. . . . Thou dispellest the storms of life and stretchest forth thy right hand of salvation, by which Thou unravellest even the inextricably tangled web of Fate. . . . Thou turnest the earth in its orb; Thou givest light to the sun; Thou rulest the world; Thou treadest Death underfoot. To Thee the stars are responsive; by Thee the seasons turn and the gods rejoice and the elements are in subjection. . . . I am too feeble to render Thee sufficient praise. . . . But, a pious though poor worshipper, I shall essay to do all within my power; Thy divine countenance and most holy deity I shall guard and keep forever hidden in the secret place of my heart.*[4]

Lucius of Patrae Author of a lost *Metamorphoses* which furnished a precedent and basic material for the *Metamorphoses* of Lucius Apuleius, a devotee of Isis and Platonic philosopher of the 2nd century A.D.

Another devout Roman Isis-worshipper, Apuleius, quoted her response to him, when he addressed her under several other Goddess-names:

> *I am Nature, the parent of things, the sovereign of the elements, the primary progeny of time, the most exalted of the deities, the first of the heavenly gods and goddesses, the queen of the dead, the uniform countenance; manifested alone and under one form. . . . At my will the planets of the sky, the wholesome winds of the seas, and the mournful silences of hell are disposed; my name, my divinity is adored throughout the world, in divers manners, in variable customs, and by many names.*
>
> *For the Phrygians that are the first of all men call me the Mother of the gods of Pessinus; the Athenians, which are sprung from their own soil, Cecropian Minerva; the Cyprians, which are girt about by the sea, Paphian Venus; the Cretans, which bear arrows, Dictynian Diana; the Sicilians, which speak three tongues, infernal Proserpine; the Eleusinians, their ancient goddess Ceres; some Juno, others Bellona, others Hecate, others Ramnusie . . . the Egyptians, skilled in ancient lore, worship me with proper ceremonies, and call me by my true name, Queen Isis.*[5]

Aristides also was initiated into the Mysteries of Isis, and spoke of a mystical experience during which he saw, coming from Isis, "a Light and other unutterable things conducing to salvation." To be initiated into her cult brought a privileged status after death (an idea copied later by Christians): "Isis, the 'eternal savior of the race of men,' promises her votary: 'Thou shalt live in blessedness; thou shalt live glorious under my protection. And when thou hast finished thy life-course and goest down to the underworld, even there in that lower world thou shalt see me shedding light in the gloom of Acheron and reigning in the inmost regions of Styx; thou thyself shalt inhabit the Elysian Fields and shalt continually offer worship to me, ever gracious.'"[6]

Egyptians addressed her as "Mistress of the gods, thou bearer of wings, thou lady of the red apparel, queen of the crowns of the South and North, only One . . . superior to whom the gods cannot be, thou mighty one of enchantments (or, Words of Power) . . . thou who art pre-eminent, mistress and lady of the tomb, Mother in the horizon of heaven . . . Praise be unto thee, O Lady, who art mightier than the gods, words of adoration rise unto thee from the Eight Gods of Hermopolis. The living souls who are in their hidden places praise the mystery of thee, O thou who art their mother, thou source from which they sprang, who makest for them a place in the hidden Underworld, who makest sound their bones and preservest them from terror, who makest them strong in the abode of everlastingness." Her name may have come from *Ashesh,* meaning both "pouring out" and "supporting," an implication that her divine essence (blood or milk) kept the gods and all other creatures alive.[7]

Sign of Isis

Isis was the Egyptian throne. Pharaohs sat on her lap, protected by her arms or wings.[8] The symbol she carried on her crown was the *mu'at,* "foundation of the throne," which also represented her *alter ego* Maat, the motherhood-principle called Right, Justice, Truth, or the All-seeing Eye.[9] An Egyptian hymn was copied into the Bible: "Right and justice are the foundation of thy throne" (Psalms 89:14).

Hermetic texts said Isis revealed the mysteries of the stars to God, who was her son.[10] She also provided a model for Moses's miracle of stopping the waters, which she did quite casually on her way to Byblos; and Joshua's miracle of stopping the sun, which she did while bringing Horus back to life.[11] Since Horus was the sun—Ra or Osiris in the form of Isis's infant—an interruption of his life would naturally have caused the sun to stand still in heaven.

Isis and her dark twin sister Nephthys were Egyptian versions of the familiar creating-and-destroying Goddess, Mother of Life and Crone of Death. Egyptians called her by many names: Mut, Hathor, Bast, Maat, Heqit, Sekhmet, Sati, Neith, etc. Some of her destructive functions were described in the *Book of the Dead:*

> *Terrible one, lady of the rain-storm, destroyer of the souls of men, devourer of the bodies of men, orderer, producer, and maker of*

slaughter . . . Hewer-in-pieces in blood, Ahibit, lady of hair. . . . Fire-lover, pure one, lover of slaughterings, cutter off of heads, devoted one, lady of the Great House . . . her name is Clother, hider of her creations, conqueror of hearts, swallower of them. . . . Knife which cutteth when its name is uttered, slayer of those who approach thy flame.[12]

Isis swallowed **Osiris** the savior and brought him back to life. He was reincarnated as the child Horus, or else as the ithyphallic moon-god Min, or Menu, "He who impregnates his mother."[13] He was annually torn to pieces and reassembled except for his lost penis. Isis made him a new penis of clay, then gave it—and him—new life by invoking her own holy names as life-giver and death-giver: "Behold, I have found thee lying there. Weary is the great one . . . . O Osiris, live, stand up thou unfortunate one that liest there! I am Isis. I am Nephthys."[14] So Osiris stood up, and lived, and mated with his Goddess, and life went on. Osiris-Min's counterpart Adonis was similarly reborn from the Goddess as Priapus and was similarly associated with spring floods.[15]

Some said the annual Nile flood was caused by a teardrop from Isis's eye as she raised her lament for the dead god. The Nile festival took place on the "Night of the Tear-Drop," unwittingly preserved by Moslems as the June festival of Lelat al-Nuktah, "Night of the Drop." Worshippers said to the Goddess: "Thou givest life unto the flocks and herds, all the land drinks thee when thou descendest . . . when thou comest the whole land rejoices. Thou art the bringer of food, thou art the mighty one of meat and drink, thou art the creator of all good things. Thou fillest the storehouses, thou heapest high with corn the granaries, and thou hast care for the poor and needy."[16]

Isis was worshipped throughout the Greco-Roman world, "from Alexandria to Arles, from the outskirts of the Sahara to the isle of Britain, from the mountains of Asturias to the mouths of the Danube."[17] Prevalence of the fairy tale "The Witch in the Stone Boat" shows how widely Isis's cult traveled, for the "witch" was none other than she; each of her temples featured a carved stone moon-boat containing her figure, which Christians called a witch or demoness. In pagan times, Isis's boat had its own special holiday on the 5th of March, the *Navigium Isidis,* Blessing of the Vessel of Isis.[18]

Isis's cult came to Rome about 80 B.C., attained great popularity in the reign of Vespasian, and flourished throughout the empire until it was ousted by Christianity four centuries later. The Goddess herself was not so much ousted as absorbed. Her identification with the virgin Mary was part of the syncretic development of the Madonna cult. Some early Christians in Rome called themselves Pastophori, a title of "shepherds" or "servants of Isis," which evolved into *pastors.*[19]

The story of Mary's Egyptian journey with her child seems to have been devised not only to fulfill the scripture, "Out of Egypt have I called my son" (Matthew 2:15), but also to justify the extensive identifications between Isis and Mary. One legend said Mary and

Book of the Dead. Common name for the collection of Egyptian funerary papyri written between 1500 and 1350 B.C., including Vignettes, Hymns, Chapters, and descriptive Rubrics. Among the best-preserved, and most typical, copies of the Theban Recension of the *Book of the Dead* is the much-studied Papyrus of Ani.

Jesus took refuge in the holy tree at Mataria, the sycamore of Isis-Hathor, Goddess of Dendera, the Shrine of the Tree.[20] Isis was "Destiny," and so was Mary—the triple Moerae. "The tree is a symbol of destiny because it is rooted in the depths. But what is more important is that it grows into time, ramifies its branches like a family tree."[21] Mataria was long known as an Egyptian name of the Goddess who was also Mata-Meri, or Mari.[22]

> *Pictures and sculptures wherein [Isis] is represented in the act of suckling her child Horus formed the foundation for the Christian figures and paintings of the Madonna and Child. Several of the incidents of the wanderings of the Virgin with the Child in Egypt as recorded in the Apocryphal Gospels reflect scenes in the life of Isis as described in the texts found on the Metternich Stele, and many of the attributes of Isis, the God-mother, the mother of Horus, and of Neith, the goddess of Sais, are identical with those of Mary the Mother of Christ.*[23]

An Egyptian amulet in the British Museum shows the Goddess seated under her holy tree, giving birth to her divine child, and holding the ankh in one hand. On the reverse is another ankh and the legend, "One God in heaven." Some suggest that the picture might represent the birth of Buddha, but it is usually interpreted as the birth of Christ—though its original was certainly a picture of Isis.[24]

1. Stone, 219. 2. Budge, G.E. 1, 259. 3. Budge, D.N., 265.
4. Angus, 71, 119, 240. 5. Knight, S.L., 118. 6. Angus, 135, 139.
7. Budge, G.E. 1, 519; 2, 90. 8. Budge, G.E. 2, 202. 9. Gaster, 769.
10. Lindsay, O.A., 184. 11. Budge, E.M., 135. 12. *Book of the Dead,* 416–18.
13. James, 135–39. 14. Brandon, 126–27. 15. Frazer, G.B., 390.
16. Budge, D.N., 105–6. 17. Cumont, O.R.R.P., 83. 18. Angus, 123.
19. Budge, G.E. 2, 217. 20. Budge, G.E. 2, 220. 21. Neumann, G.M., 248.
22. Budge, D.N.,160; Graves, W.G., 357. 23. Budge, G.E. 2, 220.
24. Budge, A.T., 129–30.

Isra-El

Philo Judaeus (ca. 30 B.C.–40 A.D.) Alexandrian Jewish philosopher, strongly influenced by Hellenistic Platonism, Pythagoreanism, and Stoicism; author of biblical commentaries, tracts, and histories.

Philo said Isra-El was a Jewish king in Phoenicia, who dressed his only-begotten son Jeud in royal robes and sacrificed him as a surrogate for himself.[1] The Bible said Isra-El was the royal name taken by Jacob after he battled all night with a man who was God (Genesis 32)—which meant not an angel, as the story is usually interpreted, but an incumbent sacred king embodying the divinity. Jacob was the "supplanter" who next took the name of the same divinity. The suffix El meant "a deity," male or female—though Bible translators invariably rendered it "God"—and Is-Ra may have originated as an androgynous combination of Isis and Ra, or else a father-and-son combination of Osiris and Ra. In any event, it was a god-name much older than the story of Jacob.

1. Frazer, G.B., 341.

Istadevata

Patron Goddess of the Self: a Tantric name of the spiritual **Shakti** or individual guardian angel of the enlightened sage; corresponding to the Greek *Psyche,* Roman *Anima,* and other manifestations of man's "female soul."

Ius Naturale

"Natural Law," Latin term for the Law of Aphrodite, or of Juno, or of Demeter: the legal system of the ancient matriarchate. It was related to "the Aphroditean law which permeates matter and causes it to be fertilized. It is Aphrodite who fills the two sexes with the urge for generation, who implants solicitude for the offspring, who forges the bond between mother and child and secures the freedom and equality of all the progeny. All special privilege is odious to this goddess. Hence the equal right of all to the sea, the seashore, the air; and the *communis omnium possessio* (common property) may be traced back to the *ius naturale.*"[1] Laws of the matriarchate were not hierarchical, but democratic; and the authority of women was "natural" because it was based on archetypal dependence on the moral instruction of the Mother. See **Motherhood**.

1. Bachofen, 189.

Ixion

"Strong Moon-man," sacred king of the Lapiths, "wielders of stone weapons." Ixion married the Sky-goddess Dia, and afterward died spread-eagled on a fiery wheel, symbol of the sun endlessly rolling through the heavens. Hellenic myth interpreted this as punishment for a sin against Zeus, but the original story was one of sacred-king sacrifice, related to "the burning wheels rolled downhill at European midsummer festivities, as a sign that the sun has reached its zenith and must now decline again."[1]

Ixion's name was akin to *axis,* the same as the Hindu *Akshivan* who was an emanation of Shiva personifying the Axle of the World (*aksha*).[2] Thus Ixion was another of the gods whose death took place at the hub of the universe, the *axis mundi* later assimilated to the cross of Christ.

1. Graves, G.M. 1, 209. 2. Jobes, 260.

Izanagi and Izanami

Japanese male-female creators, representing the uterine Deep and the phallic lightning bolt supposed to have churned it into movement, so the primal womb went "curdlecurdle" (*koworokoworo*) and gave birth to solid matter. One version said the male twin, Izanagi, reached down from heaven and stirred the Deep with his spear.[1]

The pair were known as the Male Who Invites and the Female Who Invites. Their myth told how they discovered sex and used it to work their creation magic:

> *His Augustness, the Male Who Invites, inquired of Her Augustness, the Female Who Invites, "In what manner is your body made?" She replied, "My body in its thriving grows, but there is one part that does not grow together." And His Augustness the Male who Invites said to her: "My body in its thriving also grows, but there is one part that grows in excess. Therefore, would it not seem proper that I should introduce the part of my body in excess into the part of your body that does not grow together, and so procreate territories?"*
>
> *Her Augustness the Female Who Invites said: "It would be well." And His Augustness, the Male Who Invites, said to her: "Let us go round this August Heavenly Pillar, I and you, and when we shall have come together let us in august union join our august parts." She agreed . . . and where they met, Her Augustness the Female Who Invites said: "Ah! What a fair and lovely youth! Whereupon His Augustness the Male Who Invites said: "Ah! What a fair and lovely maiden!"*[2]

The earlier myths said Izanami gave birth to all things; but at a later date, an imaginative revisionist took the initiative away from her. The next installment said she was burned to death while giving birth to Fire; then she went into the underworld and became a Tiamat-like sea monster. Izanagi followed her, but she couldn't return to the upper world with him because she had eaten underworld fruit (the same theme familiar in Greek myths of Persephone and Eurydice).

Izanagi fled, horrified at his female twin's changed appearance. She pursued him with an army of storm-demons, whom he foiled by throwing them peaches, the yonic fruit of life, which they couldn't resist stopping to pick up. Then Izanagi performed magical purifications and developed the ability to give birth to beings. Amaterasu the sun goddess was born from his left eye, a moon god from his right eye, and the dragon-slaying hero Susa-no-wo from his nose. The former Creatress Izanami, left behind in the underworld, also gave birth to more deities but they were all evil spirits.[3]

1. *Larousse*, 403. 2. Campbell, Or.M., 467–68. 3. Jobes, 172–73.

Jack and Jill

Heavenly Twins of Norse mythology, originally Hjuki and Bil, a boy and girl taken "up the hill" to heaven by their Moon-mother Mana. They drew the Water of Life "from the well Byrgir, in the bucket Soegr, suspended from the pole Simul, which they bore on their shoulders." Hjuki was derived from *jakka,* to assemble, to increase; Bil from *bila,* to break up or dissolve. Thus the twins signified forces of creation and destruction.[1] It was said their faces could be seen forever in the markings on the moon. Bil's voice could be heard in the singing wind, and Hjuki sends moonlight to help night-bound skiers find their way down safely to valley towns.[2]

An event reported in 1633 suggests that an esoteric meaning of the Jack and Jill myth might have been embedded in a ritual recognized as heresy. A 20-year-old girl named Mary Spencer was convicted of witchcraft because "on her way to the well for water, she often rolled her pail down the hill, running before it and in fun calling it to follow her."[3] That such apparently trivial actions invited serious charges, even death sentences, suggests that they must have been understood in some way other than mere play.

1. Baring-Gould, C.M.M.A., 201. 2. Jobes, 27. 3. Robbins, 381.

Jael

var. Jaala

"Wild She-Goat," alternate name for the Israelite queen Deborah as a mate of the scapegoat-god, Baal-Gad or Pan. Ja-El was the same as the Persians' primal Goddess Jahi, adopted by tribal queens of the pre-patriarchal period. Jael sacrificed Sisera in a strange way, nailing his head to the ground (Judges 4:21), which may be likened to the priestesses of Artemis Tauropolos nailing the heads of their victims to crosses.[1]

1. Graves, G.M. 2, 78.

Jagadamba

"Mother of the World," a Tantric title of Kali.[1] She was also called Jaganmata, "Mother of All Living," which was copied into the Bible as a title of Eve.

1. Rawson, A.T., 50.

Jahi the Whore

Persian patriarchal epithet for the Great Mother who brought forth, then mated with, the serpent Ahriman, as Lilith or the pre-Adamic **Eve** was supposed to have done with the biblical serpent. Zoroastrian scriptures said Jahi brought menstruation into the world, for she menstruated for the first time after mating with her serpent. Hence she personified the moon, which was everywhere supposed to be the original source of menstruation. Jahi also brought sex into the world by seducing the first man in the primal garden. Jewish patriarchs probably derived their notions of the sinfulness of women (by virtue of their descent from Eve) from Persian ascetics who claimed all women were "whores" because they were descendants of Jahi.

Oddly enough, some of the earliest forms of the name of the Jewish God seem to have been masculinized versions of the name of Jahi. Variations included Jahu, Jah, Yahu, Yahweh, Iau, Jaho. Some myths indicate that this God like Ahriman once had a serpent form and may have played the part of the Great Mother's serpent.

Jains

Ascetic sect of Buddhist hermit-yogis who attempted to develop magical and miraculous powers by severe self-denial. The founder of Jainism (ca. 6th century B.C.) was Jina, also called Mahavira (Great Hero, or Great Man). He had the usual virgin mother, Devananda, the "Blessed Goddess."[1] He performed the usual miracles. He walked on water, healed the sick, turned water into wine, exorcised demons, made the blind see, etc. These powers were supposed to have come to him because he renounced all sensual pleasures and retired to a life of constant meditation in a forest hermitage.

From the time of Alexander the Great, Jain monks traveled westward to impress and influence Persians, Jewish Essenes, and later, Christians. See **Asceticism**.

1. *Larousse*, 347.

Jambu Island

Land of the Rose-Apple Tree, a Tantric **paradise** likened to the body of a maternal Shakti, identical with western pagan images of the Blessed Isles in the west, or Fairyland, or the original Eden with its apple-bearing Tree of Life. The shape of Jambu Island is like a yoni, the Chariot or Throne of Shiva. In its center is the Diamond Seat (*vajrasana*) or clitoris, where the Way of Awakening is demonstrated to the sexually and spiritually enlightened.[1]

1. Tatz & Kent, 84.

James of Compostela, Saint

Compostela on the northwestern corner of Spain was one of the most popular pilgrimage centers of pre-Christian times, later assimilated to Christianity via the rather silly legend that the dead apostle James miraculously journeyed there by floating, all alone, in a stone coffin.

The legend was first heard in the 7th century A.D., when the church took over the Compostelan shrine from the Brigantine Sea-goddess, Brigit. The sanctuary was formerly named Brigantium.[1] The Goddess's symbol, a *kteis* or vulva in the form of a scallop shell or cowrie, was adopted by the cult of the new saint.[2]

The scallop remained the emblem of St. James although it was hardly suitable for a male saint. Scallop was derived from the Norse *skalpr,* "a sheath."[3] The same word in Latin was *vulva.*[4] Medieval artists knew the scallop was a *kteis* and a symbol of the Goddess. Botticelli's famous *Venus* was born from the same *kteis.*

The anonymous bones now advertised at Compostela as those of St. James were actually picked up in Galicia during the Middle Ages. Though the Spanish church still insists on the authenticity of St. James because Compostela brings in a great deal of money annually from the faithful, most Catholic scholars now agree that St. James was and is entirely spurious.[5]

1. Graves, G.M. 1, 296. 2. Lindsay, A.W., 132. 3. Potter & Sargent, 108. 4. Brasch, 179. 5. Attwater, 182.

Janua Coeli

"Gate of Heaven," title of the sanctuary screen in Christian churches, derived from the yonic "gate" of Juno (Uni, or *yoni*) veiled by the *hymen* in the Goddess's own temples. As a personification of the Gate, Juno had two faces looking in both directions—the outward passage of the Gate at birth, the reverse passage at death. At her festival in early January she was addressed as Antevorta and Postvorta, the Goddess Who Looks Forward and Backward, for January was the "gate" of the year, when the god of the Aeon died and was reborn from Mother Time.[1]

As Roman religion became more patriarchal, Juno's gate-keeping persona became an androgynous Janua-Janus, later was wholly masculinized as the two-faced god Janus to whom all gateways were sacred. He was another form of the Petra, Pater, or Peter, keeper of the keys to the Goddess's "Pearly Gate."

The Christian version of the *janua coeli* depicted heaven on one side, hell on the other. The "wrong" or "death" side of the Gate became known as *janua diaboli,* "the gate by which the Devil enters." Since the whole image was that of a yoni to begin with, it was almost inevitable that Christian fathers used *janua diaboli* as a common synonym for "woman."[2]

1. Graves, W.G., 184. 2. J.B. Russell, 283.

Januarius, Saint

Canonized version of the Roman god of gateways, Janus of the two faces. His old shrine at Naples was converted into a saint's church, where a bottle of dried blood was reverently preserved and said to be the blood of the saint. This blood would turn liquid when placed beside the skull of a genuine martyr. Pope Pius II himself "infallibly" attested to the reality of this miracle.[1]

Naturally there was no real St. Januarius; he was only another form of Peter, the "Petra" who guarded the heavenly gate (see **Peter, Saint**). As guardian of door and gateways he became the *janitor*—meaning "doorkeeper"—of heaven.[2]

1. Brewster, 415. 2. Dumézil, 328.

Jar-Bearer

A mysterious man bearing a vessel of water preceded Jesus on his triumphal promenade to the house of the Last Supper (Luke 22:10). The meaning of this detail is revealed by the Babylonian cult of the savior-god Nabu, or Nebo, who also promenaded to the sacred drama of his immolation in the Goddess's grove on the third day of the month of Iyyar, when priests consecrated the god's nuptial couch, and "the god will enter the bedchamber (or tomb). On the fourth day will take place the return of Nabu." The man representing the god was always preceded by a jar-bearer, carrying the vessel of water that stood for the god's seminal spirit, the medium of his union with the dread Goddess.[1]

In Egypt, the jar was the *menat* or moon-charm, represented in hieroglyphics as fluid pouring from a narrow phallic vessel into a wider, female pot or vase. As early as the 6th dynasty, the *menat* signified the restoration of sexual capacities after rebirth.[2] Unlike Christians, who denied sexual activity in heaven (Matthew 22:30, Mark 12:25, Luke 20:35), Egyptians believed there could be no heavenly bliss without sex. Even the Savior Osiris, reborn as "impregnator of his Mother," followed the *menat* to his love-death. It was water in a "male vessel," the phallic jar.[3]

Both Osiris and Isis were represented by vessels of water, to merge in their mating as completely as two waters in a single jar. The concept was the same as the Tantric image of sexual union blessed by the god of love: a merging of bliss and the void, "like the pouring of water into water."[4]

Similar imagery underlay creation myths like that of Ashurbanipal's Twelve Tablets, where the male celestial sea Apsu rained down fructifying waters into the sea-womb of Mother Tiamat, the nether sea.[5] Because the ancients thought rain a kind of celestial semen, mythological heavenly fathers tended to be rain gods (e.g., Jupiter Pluvius). Since they weren't sure whether this fertile fluid from heaven should be called semen or urine, the heavenly father sometimes made "golden rain," like the urine with which Zeus impregnated Danae, the Earth.[6] Uranus or "Father Heaven" was an archaic producer of fertilizing urine.

In India the spirit of love is still represented by a jar of water serving "in the place of a sacred image. The water is regarded, for the period of the worship, as a residence or seat (pitha) of the god."[7] The Sanskrit word *pitha* recalls the Greek *pithos* or jar signifying rebirth in Demeter's Eleusinian Mysteries, when she was Mistress of Earth and Sea and absorbed the substance of gods.[8]

Mysteries of the Cabiri in Phrygia and Samothrace worshipped Demeter Cabiria in conjunction with the Young God (Ganymede, Dionysus, or Cabirius) in the form of a male jar-bearer, shown pouring water into a maternal Pot, Vase, Cauldron, or Grail. He was the universal ephebe; the larger vessel was the universal mother.[9] Similar mysteries of the two vessels were dramatized throughout the Middle East, so the jar-bearer became the symbol of any dying savior-god enroute to his Fate.

1. *Assyr. & Bab. Lit.*, 249. 2. Budge, E.M., 60. 3. Elworthy, 187, 301. 4. Tatz & Kent, 140. 5. *Larousse*, 49. 6. Graves, W.G., 54. 7. Zimmer, 34. 8. Neumann, G.M., 267. 9. Neumann, G.M., 324–25.

Jehovah

Name of God, artificially constructed from the vowels of *Adonai,* "the Lord," with the Hebrew consonants JHVH, yod-he-vau-he, the **Tetragrammaton**. At first the artificial construct was used to avoid speaking the "real" name of God, which carried a curse. Actually there were many variations of the name, in many Semitic dialects: Yahu, Jah, Jeud, Ieu, Yahweh, Jahveh, Yaho, Iao.[1] Another variation was Jesus, a Latin form of Yeshua, Joshua, or Jeud. (See **Yahweh**.)

1. Albright, 262.

Jesus ben Pandera

var. Panthera

Celsus and the Talmudic tradition mentioned Jesus, son of Pandera or Panthera, begotten by a Roman soldier on a Jewish prostitute, Miriam of Magdala (Mary Magdalene), whose husband was a carpenter.[1] The word for carpenter, *najjar,* was applied to a sacred brotherhood, the Nazarites or Nazorenes, who supported themselves by woodworking.[2] Jesus ben Pandera was called a *najjar,* a holy man. He worked miracles, healed the sick, foretold the world's end.[3] Eventually he was executed, perhaps by hanging, through his own wish.

Some said this ben Pandera or Bar-Panther was the grandfather of the Virgin Mary.[4] Other Christian authorities, like Epiphanius, said he was the paternal grandfather of the Christian Jesus—which, obviously, contradicted the Virgin Birth myth. "Son of Pandera" was a title so firmly attached to Jesus that many Christian writers accepted it and tried to explain it. The name of Pandera as Jesus's father is traceable back to the time of the Gospels and has "an equal claim to reliability."[5] Later Christians said the name was used by the Jews to discredit their savior by calling him a whore's son who was executed as a criminal.

The "whore" called Miriam of Magdala seems to have been a sacred hierodule or Virgin Bride of God, dedicated to the temple (*magdala*). Since the oldest traditions associated Mary Magdalene with the Holy Vase that represented Pandora, the Great Goddess entitled "All-Giver," some suggest that Pandera was a corrupt form of this title.[6] Another theory said Jesus ben Pandera really meant Jesus, son of the Virgin (Parthenos), the latter being the usual title of a temple hierodule.[7] Or again, Pan-Thera could have meant Dionysus the son of Pan, whose totem animal was a panther, or "all-beast." Jesus was assimilated to the Dionysian savior. The story of his miracle at Cana was directly modeled on a Dionysian rite of sacred marriage celebrated at Sidon; even the Gospels' wording was copied from the festival of the older god.[8]

These few garbled hints of Jesus's pagan background may have been greatly clarified by the hundreds of diverse Gospels extant in the first few centuries A.D., had not the early church seen fit to destroy them all.[9]

1. Keller, 341–42. 2. Briffault 3, 367. 3. Robertson, 68. 4. de Voragine, 520. 5. M. Smith, 61, 65. 6. Graves, G.M. 1, 148. 7. Ashe, 53. 8. M. Smith, 120. 9. M. Smith, 2.

Jesus Christ

The Jesus who was called *Christos,* "Anointed," took his title from Middle-Eastern savior-gods like Adonis and Tammuz, born of the Virgin Sea-goddess Aphrodite-Maria (Myrrha), or Ishtar-Mari (Hebrew Mariamne). Earlier biblical versions of the same hero were Joshua son of Nun (Exodus 33:11), Jehu son of Nimshi, whom Elijah anointed as a sacred king (1 Kings 19:16), and Yeshua son of Marah. The Book of Enoch said in the 2nd century B.C. that Yeshua or Jesus was the secret name given by God to the Son of Man (a Persian title), and that it meant "Yahweh saves."[1]

In northern Israel the name was written Ieu.[2] It was the same as Ieud or Jeud, the "only-begotten son" dressed in royal robes and sacrificed by the god-king **Isra-El**.[3] Greek versions of the name were Iasion, Jason, or Iasus—the name of one of Demeter's sacrificed consorts, killed by Father Zeus after the fertility rite that coupled him with his Mother.[4] Iasus signified a healer or *Therapeuta,* as the Greeks called the Essenes, whose cult groups always included a man with the title of *Christos*.[5] The literal meaning of the name was "healing moon-man," fitting the Hebrew version of Jesus as a son of Mary, the *almah* or "moon-maiden."[6] (See **Virgin Birth**.)

Other versions of the name were Jaho, Iao, or Ieuw, sometimes titles of Zeus-Sabazius as the nocturnal sun and Lord of Death in the underworld.[7] The same god was Sabaoth, the Jews' "Lord of Hosts." The Latin name for this Heavenly Father came from the same root: Iu-piter, Father Ieu.[8]

Book of Enoch Consisting of three extant books and a lost fourth, the Enochian works were written probably between the Maccabean age and the first century B.C. The chief subject is the coming world's end and the reappearance of the Messianic Son of Man, who resembles the predicted final avatar of Buddha appearing before doomsday.

It seems Jesus was not one person but a composite of many. He played the role of sacred king of the Jews who periodically died in an atonement ceremony as surrogate for the real king. "The Semitic religions practiced human immolations longer than any other religion, sacrificing children and grown men in order to please sanguinary gods. In spite of Hadrian's prohibition of those murderous offerings, they were maintained in certain clandestine rites."[9] The priesthood of the Jewish God insisted that "one man should die for the people . . . that the whole nation perish not" (John 11:50). Yahweh forgave no sins without bloodshed: "without shedding blood is no remission" (Hebrews 9:22).

Middle-Eastern traditions presented a long line of slain and cannibalized Saviors extending back to prehistory. At first kings, they became king-surrogates or "sacred" kings as the power of real monarchies developed. The Gospels' Jesus was certainly not the first of them, though he may have been one of the last. One passage hints at a holy man's understandable fear of such brief, doomed eminence: "When Jesus therefore perceived that they would come and take him by force, to make him a king, he departed again into a mountain himself alone" (John 6:15).

This Jesus seems to have made little or no impression on his contemporaries. No literate person of his own time mentioned him in any known writing. The Gospels were not written in his own time, nor were they written by anyone who ever saw him in the flesh. The names of the apostles attached to these books were fraudulent. The books were composed after the establishment of the church, some as late as the 2nd century A.D. or later, according to the church's requirements for a manufactured tradition.[10] Most scholars believe the earliest book of the New Testament was 1 Thessalonians, written perhaps 51 A.D. by Paul, who never saw Jesus in person and knew no details of his life story.[11]

The details were accumulated through later adoption of the myths attached to every savior-god throughout the Roman empire. Like Adonis, Jesus was born of a consecrated temple maiden in the sacred cave of Bethlehem, "The House of Bread."[12] He was eaten in the form of bread, as were Adonis, Osiris, Dionysus, and others; he called himself the bread of God (John 6:33). Like worshippers of Osiris, those of Jesus made him part of themselves by eating him, so as to participate in his resurrection: "He that eateth my flesh, and drinketh my blood, dwelleth in me, and I in him" (John 6:56).

Like Attis, Jesus was sacrificed at the spring equinox and rose again from the dead on the third day, when he became God and ascended to heaven. Like Orpheus and Heracles, he "harrowed hell" and brought a secret of eternal life, promising to draw all men with him up to glory (John 12:32). Like Mithra and all the other solar gods, he celebrated a birthday nine months later at the winter solstice, because the day of his death was also the day of his cyclic re-conception. See **Attis**.

From the elder gods, Jesus acquired not only his title of Christos but all his other titles as well. Osiris and Tammuz were called Good Shepherd. Sarapis was Lord of Death and King of Glory. Mithra and Heracles were Light of the World, Sun of Righteousness, Helios the Rising Sun. Dionysus was King of Kings, God of Gods. Hermes was the Enlightened One and the Logos. Vishnu and Mithra were Son of Man and Messiah. Adonis was the Lord and the Bridegroom. Mot-Aleyin was the Lamb of God. "Savior" (Soter) was applied to all of them.

Mystery cults everywhere taught that ordinary men could be possessed by the spirits of such gods, and identified with them as "sons" or alter egos, as Jesus was. It was the commonly accepted way to acquire supernatural powers, as shown by some of the charms used by magicians: "Whatever I say must happen. . . . For I have taken to myself the power of Abraham, Isaac, and Jacob and of the great god-demon Iao Ablanathanalba . . . for I am the Son, I surpass the limit. . . . I am he who is in the seven heavens, who standeth in the seven sanctuaries; for I am the son of the living God. . . . I have been united with thy sacred form. I have been empowered by thy sacred name. I have received the effluence of goodness, Lord, God of gods, King, Demon . . . having attained that nature equal to the God's."[13]

Aulus Cornelius Celsus
Patrician Roman scholar of the first century A.D., who wrote at length on the subjects of medicine, agriculture, philosophy, jurisprudence, and religion.

The skeptical Celsus noted that beggars and vagabonds throughout the Empire were pretending to work miracles and become gods, throwing fits, prophesying the end of the world, and aspiring to the status of saviors:

> *Each has the convenient and customary spiel, "I am the god," or "a son of God," or "a divine spirit," and "I have come. For the world is about to be destroyed, and you, men, because of your injustice, will go (with it). But I wish to save, and you shall see me again coming back with heavenly power. Blessed is he who worships me now! On all others, both cities and countrysides, I shall cast eternal fire. And men who (now) ignore their punishments shall repent in vain and groan, but those who believed in me I shall preserve immortal."*[14]

Of course this "conspicuously false" doctrine was the central message of the Gospels too. Persian eschatology passing through a Jewish-Essenic filter predicted "the Son of Man coming in a cloud with power and great glory" (Luke 9:27, 21:27). Jesus promised the end of the world in his own generation. The rest of the Gospel material was largely devoted to the miracles supposed to demonstrate his divine power, since religions generally "adduce revelations, apparitions, prophecies, miracles, prodigies and sacred mysteries that they may get themselves valued and accepted."[15] Even these miracles were derivative. Turning water into wine at Cana was copied from a Dionysian ritual practiced at Sidon and other places.[16] In Alexandria the same Dionysian miracle was regularly shown before crowds of the faithful, assisted by an ingenious system of vessels and siphons, invented by a clever engineer named Heron.[17] Many centuries earlier, priestesses at Nineveh cured the blind with spittle, and the story was repeated of many different gods and their incarnations.[18] Demeter of Eleusis multiplied loaves and fishes in her role of Mistress of Earth and Sea. Healing the sick, raising the dead, casting out devils, handling poisonous serpents (Mark 16:18), etc., were so commonplace that Celsus scorned these "Christian" miracles as "nothing more than the common works of those enchanters who, for a few oboli, will perform greater deeds in the midst of the Forum. . . . The magicians of Egypt cast out evil spirits, cure diseases by a breath, and so influence some uncultured men, that they produce in them whatever sights and sounds they please. But because they do such things shall we consider them the sons of God?"[19]

Magicians often claimed that their prayers could bring flocks of supernatural beings to their assistance.[20] Thus Jesus declared that his prayer could summon twelve legions (72,000) of guardian angels (Matthew 26:53). Magicians also communed with their followers by the standard mystery-cult sacrament of bread-flesh and wine-blood. In texts on magic, "a magician-god gives his own body and blood to a recipient who, by eating it, will be united with him in love."[21]

The ability to walk on water was claimed by Far-Eastern holy men ever since Buddhist monks praised it as the mark of the true ascetic.[22] The Magic Papyri said almost anyone could walk on water with the help of "a powerful demon."[23] Impossibilities have always been the props of religious credulity, as Tertullian admitted: "It is believable because it is absurd; it is certain because it is impossible."[24]

Magic Papyri Collections of exorcisms, invocations, charms, and spells widely circulated during the early Christian era, used as bases for later grimoires and Hermetic texts.

However, repetitive miracles were not so believable as original ones. Therefore early Christians insisted that all the older deities and their miracle-tales were invented by the devil, out of his foreknowledge of the true religion, so the faithful would be confused by past "imitations."[25] Pagan thinkers countered with the observation that "The Christian religion contains nothing but what Christians hold in common with heathens; nothing new, nor truly great." Even St. Augustine, finding the hypothesis of the devil's inventions hard to swallow, admitted that "the true religion" was known to the ancients, and had existed from the beginning of time, but it began to be called Christian after "Christ came in the flesh."[26]

Nevertheless, adherents of the true religion violently disagreed as to the circumstances of its foundation. In the first few centuries A.D. there were many mutually hostile Christian sects, and many mutually contradictory Gospels. As late as 450, Bishop Theodore of Cyrrhus said there were at least 200 different Gospels revered by the churches of his own diocese, until he destroyed all but the canonical four.[27] The other Gospels were lost as stronger sects overwhelmed the weaker, wrecked their churches, and burned their books.[28]

One scripture, later thrown out of the canon, said Jesus was not crucified. Simon of Cyrene suffered on the cross in his place, while Jesus stood by laughing at the executioners, saying, "It was another . . . who drank the gall and vinegar; it was not I . . . it was another, Simon, who bore the cross on his shoulder. It was another upon whom they placed the crown of thorns. But I was rejoicing in the height. . . . And I was laughing at their ignorance."[29] Believers in this scripture were persecuted and forced to sign an abjuration reading: "I anathematize those who say that Our Lord suffered only in appearance, and that there was a man on the cross and another at a distance who laughed."[30]

Some Christians interpreted Jesus's *noli me tangere* ("Touch me not") to mean he came back from death as an incorporeal spirit, after the manner of other apotheosized heroes, such as the Irish hero Laegaire, who also told his people not to touch him.[31] Later, an unknown Gospel writer inserted the story of doubting Thomas, who insisted on touching Jesus. This was to combat the heretical idea that there was no resurrection in the flesh, and also to subordinate Jerusalem's municipal god Tammuz (Thomas) to the new savior (see **Thomas, Saint**). Actually, the most likely source of primary Christian mythology was the Tammuz cult in Jerusalem. Like Tammuz, Jesus was the Bridegroom of the Daughter of Zion (John 12:15). Therefore his bride was **Anath**, "Virgin Wisdom Dwelling in Zion," who was also the Mother of God.[32] Her dove descended on him at his baptism, signifying (in the old religion) that she chose him for the love-death. Anath broke her bridegroom's reed scepter, scourged him and pierced him for fructifying blood. She pronounced his death curse, Maranatha (1 Corinthians 16:22). As the Gospels said of Jesus, Anath's bridegroom was "forsaken" by El, his heavenly father.[33] Jesus's cry to El, "My God, my God, why hast thou forsaken me?" seems to have been a line written for the second act of the sacred drama, the *pathos* or Passion (Mark 15:34).

Of course this Passion was originally a sexual one. Jesus's last words "It is consummated" (*consummatum est*) were interpreted as a sign that his work was finished, but could equally apply to his marriage (John 19:30). As a cross or pillar represented the divine phallus, so a temple represented the body of the Goddess, whose "veil" (*hymen*) was "rent in the midst" as Jesus passed into death (Luke 23:45). As usual when the god disappeared into the underworld, the sun was eclipsed (Luke 23:44). In their ignorance of astronomical phenonema, Christians claimed that the moon was full at the same time—Easter is still a full-moon festival—though an eclipse of the sun can only occur at the dark of the moon.[34] The full moon really meant impregnation of the Goddess.

The parting of Jesus's garment recalls the unwrapping of Osiris when he emerged from the tomb as the ithyphallic Min, "Husband of his Mother." If Jesus was one with his heavenly father, then he also married his mother and begot himself. A 4th-century scripture said in the underworld he confronted his mother as Death, *Mu*.[35] She was also the Bride disguised as Venus, the evening star, presiding over the death of the sun. Jews still recall her in a ritual greeting to the evening star, "Come, O friend, let us welcome the Bride."[36]

Like pagans, early Christians identified the Bride with the Mother. They said Jesus "consummated on the cross" his union with Mary-Ecclesia, his bride the church. Augustine wrote: "Like a bridegroom Christ went forth from his chamber, he went out with a presage of his nuptials. . . . He came to the marriage bed of the cross, and there, in mounting it, he consummated his marriage . . . , he lovingly gave himself up to the torment in place of his bride, and he joined himself to the woman for ever."[37] John 19:41 says, "In the place where he was crucified there was a garden; and in the garden a new sepulchre, wherein was never man yet laid." A garden was the conventional symbol for the body of the mother/bride; and a new tomb was the virgin womb, whence the god would be born again. On the third day, Jesus rose from the tomb/womb like Attis, whose resurrection was the Hilaria, or Day of Joy.[38] Jesus's resurrection day was named after Eostre, the same Goddess as Astarte, whom the Syrians called Mother Mari.[39]

Three incarnations of Mari, or Mary, stood at the foot of Jesus's cross, like the Moerae of Greece. One was his virgin mother. The second was his "dearly beloved" (see **Mary Magdalene**). The third Mary must have represented the Crone (the fatal Moera), so the tableau resembled that of the three Norns at the foot of Odin's sacrificial tree. The Fates were present at the sacrifices decreed by Heavenly Fathers, whose victims hung on trees or pillars "between heaven and earth." Up to Hadrian's time, victims offered to Zeus at Salamis were anointed with sacred ointments—thus becoming "Anointed Ones" or "Christs"—then hung up and stabbed through the side with a spear.[40] Nothing in Jesus's myth occurred at random; every detail was part of a formal sacrificial tradition, even to the "procession of palms" which glorified sacred kings in ancient Babylon.[41]

Far-Eastern traditions were utilized too. The Roman empire was well aware of the teachings and myths of Buddhism. Buddha images in classic Greek style were made in Pakistan and Afghanistan in the first century A.D.[42] Buddhist ideas like the "footprints of Buddha" appeared among Christians. Bishop Sulpicius of Jerusalem reported that, as in India, "In the dust where Christ trod the marks of His step can still be seen, and the earth still bears the print of His feet."[43] Buddhist metaphors and phrasing also appeared in the Gospels. Jesus's formula, "Dearly Beloved," was the conventional way for Tantric deities to address their teachings to Devi, their Goddess.[44]

Scholars' efforts to eliminate paganism from the Gospels in order to find a historical Jesus have proved as hopeless as searching for a core in an onion.[45] Like a mirage, the Jesus figure looks clear at a distance but lacks approachable solidity. "His" sayings and parables came from elsewhere; "his" miracles were old twice-told tales. Even the Lord's Prayer was a collection of sayings from the Talmud, many derived from earlier Egyptian prayers to Osiris.[46] The Sermon on the Mount, sometimes said to contain the essence of Christianity, had no original material; it was made up of fragments from Psalms, Ecclesiastes, Isaiah, Secrets of Enoch, and the Shemone Esreh.[47] Moreover, it was unknown to the author of the oldest Gospel, pseudo-Mark.[48]

The discovery that the Gospels were forged, centuries later than the events they described, is still not widely known even though the Catholic Encyclopedia admits, "The idea of a complete and clear-cut canon of the New Testament existing from the beginning . . . has no foundation in history." No extant manuscript can be dated earlier than the 4th century A.D.; most were written even later.[49] The oldest manuscripts contradict one another, as also do even the present canon of synoptic Gospels.

The church owed its canon to the Gnostic teacher Marcion, who first collected Pauline epistles about the middle of the 2nd century.

Later he was excommunicated as a heretic because he denied that the scriptures were mystical allegories full of magic words of power. The epistles he collected were already over a century old, if indeed they were written by Paul; much of their material was made up of forged interpolations.[50]

The most "historical" figure in the Gospels was Pontius Pilate, to whom Jesus was presented as "king" of the Jews and simultaneously as a criminal deserving the death penalty for "blasphemy" because he called himself Christ, Son of the Blessed (Luke 23:3; Mark 14:61-64). This alleged crime was no real crime. Eastern provinces swarmed with self-styled Christs and Messiahs, calling themselves Sons of God and announcing the end of the world. None of them was executed for "blasphemy."[51] The beginning of the story probably lay in the tradition of sacred-king sacrifice in Jerusalem long before Pilate's administration, when Rome was trying to discourage such barbarisms.

From 103 to 76 B.C., Jerusalem was governed by Alexander Janneaus, called the Aeon, who defended his throne by fighting challengers. One year, on the Day of Atonement, his people attacked him at the altar, waving palm branches to signify that he should die for the earth's fertility. Alexander declined the honor and instituted a persecution of his own subjects. Another king of Jerusalem took the name of Menelaus, "Moon-king," and practiced the rite of sacred marriage in the temple.[52] Herod also made a sacred marriage, and had John the Baptist slain as a surrogate for himself.

If there was a Jesus cult in Jerusalem after 30 A.D., it completely disappeared forty years later when Titus conquered the city and outlawed many local customs, including human sacrifice. Jerusalem was wholly Romanized under Hadrian. It was newly named Aelia Capitolina and rededicated to the Goddess. The temple became a shrine of Venus.[53] Tacitus described the siege of Jerusalem, but his writing is abruptly cut off at the moment when Roman forces entered the city—as if the final chapters were deliberately destroyed—so no one knows what the Romans found there. However, Romans did express disapproval of the Jews' or Christians' cannibalistic sacraments. Porphyry called it "absurd beyond all absurdity, and bestial beyond every sort of bestiality, that a man should taste human flesh and drink the blood of men of his own genus and species, and by doing should have eternal life."[54]

From the Christians' viewpoint, a real historical Jesus was essential to the basic premise of the faith: the possibility of immortality through identification with his own death and resurrection. Wellhausen rightly said Jesus would have no place in history unless he died and returned exactly as the Gospels said.[55] "If Christ hath not been raised, your faith is vain" (1 Corinthians 15:17). Still, despite centuries of research, no historical Jesus has come to light. It seems his story was not merely overlaid with myth; it was mythic to the core.

Like all myths, it revealed much about the collective psychology that created it. In earlier pagan religions, the Mother and Son

Porphyry (ca. 234–305 A.D.) Neoplatonist philosopher, scholar, and writer; biographer of Plotinus; an opponent of the Christian church, which eventually destroyed most of his books.

Synoptic Gospels The first three books of the New Testament (Matthew, Mark, Luke), which differ radically from the material in the so-called "Gnostic" Gospel of John.

Julius Wellhausen (1844–1918) German Old Testament scholar, a leader of the "higher criticism" movement.

periodically ousted the Father from his heavenly throne. The divine son of Christianity no longer challenged the heavenly king, but tamely submitted to his fatal command: "Not my will, but thine, be done" (Luke 22:42). Some early sects said the Father who demanded his son's blood was cruel, even demonic.[56] These were suppressed, but scholars have discerned in Christianity "an original attitude of hostility toward the father figure, which was changed in the first two Christian centuries into an attitude of passive masochistic docility."[57]

If orthodox Christianity demanded subordination of the Son, it was even more determined to subordinate the Mother. The Gospels' Jesus showed little respect for his mother, which troubled the church in its Renaissance efforts to attract women to the cult of Mary. "Any hero who speaks to his mother only twice, and on both occasions addresses her as 'Woman,' is a difficult figure for the sentimental biographers."[58] Together with Jesus's avowed opposition to marriage and the family (Matthew 22:30; Luke 14:26), women's primary concerns, New Testament sexism tended to disgust educated women of the pagan world.

But the Jesus who emulated Buddha in advocating poverty and humility eventually became the mythic figurehead for one of the world's pre-eminent money-making organizations. The cynical Pope Leo X exclaimed, "What profit has not that fable of Christ brought us!"[59]

Modern theologians tend to sidestep the question of whether Jesus was in fact a fable or a real person. In view of the complete dearth of hard evidence, and the dubious nature of the soft evidence, it seems Christianity is based on the ubiquitous social phenomena of credulity:

> *An idea is able to gain and retain the aura of essential truth through telling and retelling. This process endows a cherished notion with more veracity than a library of facts. . . . [D]ocumentation plays only a small role in contrast to the act of re-confirmation by each generation of scholars. In addition, the further removed one gets from the period in question, the greater is the strength of the conviction. Initial incredulousness is soon converted into belief in a probability and eventually smug assurance.*[60]

1. H. Smith, 193. 2. Albright, 262. 3. Frazer, G.B., 341. 4. Graves, G.M. 1, 89. 5. Rose, 111. 6. Graves, G.M. 2, 396. 7. Albright, 262. 8. Knight, D.W.P., 113. 9. Cumont, O.R.R.P., 119. 10. H. Smith, 179–80. 11. Enslin, L.C.M., 233–38. 12. Frazer, G.B., 402; Briffault 3, 97. 13. M. Smith, 102–4. 14. M. Smith, 117. 15. Guignebert, 371. 16. M. Smith, 25, 120. 17. de Camp, A.E., 258. 18. Gifford, 63. 19. Doane, 272. 20. M. Smith, 109. 21. M. Smith, 123. 22. *Bardo Thodol,* 158; Tatz & Kent, 167. 23. M. Smith, 120. 24. Angus, 268. 25. Robertson, 112. 26. Doane, 409–11. 27. M. Smith, 2. 28. H. Smith, 189. 29. Pagels, 72–73. 30. Reinach, 245. 31. Joyce 1, 298. 32. Ashe, 31. 33. *Larousse,* 77. 34. Agrippa, 71. 35. Brandon, 45. 36. Wilkins, 143. 37. Cavendish, P.E., 54; T., 75. 38. Frazer, G.B., 407. 39. H. Smith, 201. 40. H. Smith, 135. 41. Pritchard, A.N.E., 204. 42. Ross, 100. 43. de Voragine, 287. 44. *Mahanirvanatantra,* 173. 45. M. Smith, 4. 46. Budge, E.M. 116. 47. H. Smith, 186. 48. Augstein, 260. 49. Pfeifer, 103. 50. Reinach, 256, 277. 51. Brandon, 248. 52. Pfeifer, 72–74, 120. 53. *Encyc. Brit.,* "Jerusalem." 54. M. Smith, 66. 55. Guignebert, 47. 56. Legge 2, 239. 57. Augstein, 309. 58. M. Smith, 25. 59. de Camp, A.E., 399. 60. Arens, 89.

Jewel in the Lotus

The Holy Phrase of Tantrism, *Om mani padme hum,* meaning the lingam (penis) in the yoni (vulva), or the fructifying male principle enclosed within the sustaining, birth-giving, enveloping female principle. Apart from its purely sexual meaning, there were many corollary ideas, such as: (1) the spark of life, or fetus (*bindu*) conceived within the Mother of Creation; (2) the dead body enclosed in the womb of Mother Earth; (3) the eternal orgasm of Shiva the jewel and Kali the lotus in their cosmic sexual dance; (4) the sleeping god, between reincarnations, cradled in the Lotus of his Mother. Another word for the male "jewel" was *vajra,* meaning phallus, gem, spark of life, and bolt of **lightning.**[1]

1. Rawson, E.A., 151.

Jews, Persecution of

Illogically, Christians justified persecutions of Jews by calling them "Christ-killers," though their own theology said God had decreed Christ's death; therefore the Jews only obeyed the will of God. Gospel passages interpolated after the church's rise to power in Rome absolved Pilate of guilt because he represented the Holy City. The Jews were condemned by the ancient liturgical phrase copied into the Gospel, which used to invoke the fertilizing power of a god's blood but was later interpreted as an acceptance of blood guilt: "His blood be on us, and on our children" (Matthew 27:23-25).

This pious forgery became the foundation for centuries of persecutions, culminating even in the present century with the extermination of millions of Jews under the Nazi regime, the latest in a two-thousand-year history of pogroms.

Up to the middle of the 14th century the free city of Cologne remained a haven for Jewish merchants, weavers' guilds, and other commercial enterprises, resisting domination by the church. Then Catholic forces moved in; Jewish merchants were burned alive in their houses with their wives and children; those who escaped the immolation were banished. Their property remained in Christian hands, with 50 percent going to the victorious archbishop.[1]

The great plagues of the 14th century were usually attributed to the Jews, said to cause the pestilence by poisoning wells and streams with a combination of holy wafers stolen from the churches and the menstrual blood of Jewish women. Each wave of plague brought a wave of massacre of Jewish communities. In 1382, rioters looted and vandalized the Jewish quarter in Paris.[2] In 1391, the Archdeacon of Seville instigated a "Holy War against the Jews." Mobs stormed the ghetto, tore down synagogues, and murdered an estimated 41,000 persons.[3] Twelve thousand Jews perished in Bavaria at the time of the Black Death; two thousand were burned at Strasbourg for causing the plague of 1348; at Chinon an immense trench was dug and filled with blazing wood to burn 160 Jews in a single day.[4]

The church encouraged persecution of Jews to divert attention from the developing idea that these terrible plagues, which killed about half of Europe's population before the end of the century, were caused by a malicious God. The pope himself referred in a bull to "the pestilence with which God is afflicting the Christian people." The horrors of the plague revived Gnostic opinions of the evil Jehovah. One professor wrote: "The hostility of God is stronger than the hostility of man."[5]

The real cause of the plagues was the Christian commerce with the Holy Land. Crusaders' ships carried millions of Oriental black rats, with their fleas, the true carriers of the plague bacillus.[6] Being ignorant of this, Christian authorities made no effort to control the rats but tried to exterminate Jews instead. Jew-killing probably served to vent some of the popular resentment of clergymen, who behaved badly during the plagues. Most deserted their flocks in haste to leave plague-stricken areas. Churchmen generally were accused of "panic fear and neglect."[7]

Persecutions were supported by many made-to-order myths. In Spain, the popular myth of the ritual murder was combined with the myth of plague-magic to give Torquemada his excuse to expel the Jews from the country in 1490 and take their property for the enrichment of the church. Some Jews were arrested and tortured until they confessed having stolen a consecrated host and kidnapped a four-year-old boy called Santo Niño (Holy Child) from the doorway of a church. They gave the child five thousand lashes, crowned him with thorns, and extracted his heart to make anti-Christian magic. All Jewry was involved in this plot to destroy Christendom by black magic, the confessions said. Jews planned to kidnap Christian children and use their hearts or blood or ashes to make charms which, thrown into rivers and wells, would make all Christians sick.

It was said Santo Niño bore his sufferings with great serenity, and even directed the Jews in the removal of his heart. The child's blind mother miraculously recovered her sight at the moment of his death (an interpolated allegory of Judaism receiving enlightenment by the death of Christ, perhaps). The Holy Child went directly to heaven, which accounted for the authorities' inability to find his remains where the Jews said they were buried.[8]

This mythic porridge started the expulsion of thousands of Jews from Spain and Christian seizure of their assets. In 1260 the Jewish population of Toledo had built "the largest and most beautiful synagogue in Spain." In the 15th century the Jews of Toledo were massacred and the synagogue appropriated by the church. It now bears the name of the Church of Santa Maria la Blanca.[9] According to contemporary theologians, persecution and seizure of property was a legitimate activity of Catholic powers. In their view, "no illegitimate violence was being done to the Jews, infidels, and heretics put to the sword at the behest of the Church: these people had no rights to be violated."[10]

The legend of Santo Niño was not even an original invention of the Spanish Inquisition. The same legend had been used two centuries earlier to stimulate a persecution of Jews in the Rhineland. The German child-martyr's name was Werner. He was kidnapped, tortured, and sacrificed to the Jewish God. His mutilated body was found in a river, and a church was built over his tomb at Bacharach.[11] In 1322, eighteen Swabian Jews were slain at Ehingen for stealing a consecrated host from a church. Later it was discovered that the Jews were innocent, and the real culprit was a Christian woman who was subsequently burned for witchcraft.[12]

Jews and women were almost equally serviceable as scapegoats for the evils of medieval life; but women were more detested than Jews, according to a decree of Orvieto in 1350. This law said if a man and woman became involved in a love affair, one of them Christian and the other Jewish, the woman in the case, of whichever faith, must be beheaded or burned alive.[13]

Often, anti-Semitism went to such lengths that Christian authorities even denied the origin of their own religion from a Jewish matrix. Opposing a papal aspirant of Jewish ancestry, St. Bernard wrote: "It would be an insult to Christ if the offspring of a Jew occupied the throne of Peter."[14] Bernard seems to have wholly forgotten his own church's teaching that Peter himself was a Jew, as were all the other apostles and Jesus as well. The Jews didn't press the point, since the former Jewishness of Christ or Peter made no difference in the political situation.

Anti-Semitism reached an apogee under the rule of Adolf Hitler in our own century. Hitler made the Jews wear yellow badges, like medieval heretics. A German Christian organization announced in 1937, "Hitler's word is God's law."[15] Hitler said:

> *My feeling as a Christian points me to my Lord and Savior as a fighter. It points me to the man who once, in loneliness, surrounded by only a few followers, recognized these Jews for what they were and summoned men to fight against them and who, God's truth! was greatest not as a sufferer but as a fighter. In boundless love, as a Christian and as a man, I read through the passage which tells us how the Lord rose at last in His might and seized the scourge to drive out of the Temple the brood of vipers and adders. How terrific was the fight for the world against the Jewish poison.*[16]

Evidently Hitler was not much of a reader. He never got to the part that designated Jesus the Bridegroom of Zion; nor did he seem to know who owned the Temple.

1. Agrippa, 19. 2. Tuchman, 380. 3. Coulton, 288. 4. White 2, 73. 5. Tuchman, 104, 109. 6. de Camp, S.S.S., 47. 7. Coulton, 202. 8. Plaidy, 171 et seq. 9. Pepper & Wilcock, 120. 10. J.B. Russell, 148. 11. Guerber, L.R., 206–7. 12. J.B. Russell, 167. 13. Tuchman, 118. 14. *Encyc. Brit.*, "Bernard." 15. Langer, 63. 16. Langer, 39.

Jezebel

Sidonian queen of Israel, maligned in the Bible for worshipping Astarte instead of Yahweh.[1] Jezebel and her husband King Ahab were murdered in a civil war fomented by Yahweh's devotees. Her daughter Athaliah became queen, but seven years later she too was murdered by treachery (2 Kings 11:16). Thus, worship of the Goddess was abandoned.[2]

1. Boulding, 236. 2. Stone, 188.

Joan of Arc

"Joan of the Bow"—Joan the Huntress—also called La Pucelle, "the Maid," a traditional title of a priestess in the fairy-religion.[1] Joan herself stated that she received her mission "at the tree of the Fairy-ladies," a center of the Dianic cult at Domrémy.[2] In 1429, ecclesiastical judges examined her and announced that holy angels had appointed her to save France.[3] Later, the Bishop of Beauvais reversed this decision. In 1431, aged only 19, she was burned as a witch at Rouen, wearing a placard that said: "Relapsed, Heretic, Apostate, Idolator."[4] Ecclesiastical authorities never did explain the nature of her "idols." The executioner pretended to find her heart unburned in the ashes, to sell it as a holy relic.[5]

For 500 years Joan remained a popular national heroine until she was finally canonized by Pope Benedict XV in 1920. To the church of her own time this would have been unthinkable. "The Church, jealous of her pagan authority over pagan soldiers; and jealous, too, of her success-based popularity with the masses; needed no urging by the English to see Joan as 'dispensable.' It was the Church which tried and condemned her; the Church which regarded her—rightly, of course—as an enemy; and the Church was glad to get rid of her."[6] Ironically, the same church that pronounced Joan a witch and had her killed, now claims her as a saint.

1. Daly, 148. 2. Cohen, N.H.U.T., 109. 3. Attwater, 187. 4. Cohen, N.H.U.T., 9. 5. *Encyc. Brit.*, "Joan of Arc." 6. M. Harrison, 204.

Joan, Pope

Catholic scholars now deny that there was ever a female pope, but the legend of Pope Joan persists. Even the church accepted Joan's pontificate as historical fact, up to the beginning of the 17th century. Her portrait appeared in a row of papal busts in Siena Cathedral, labeled *Johannes VIII, femina ex Anglia:* John VIII, an Englishwoman.[1]

Pope Joan was first mentioned by her contemporary, Anastasius the Librarian (d. 886). Scotus's chronicle of the popes listed her: "A.D. 854, Lotharii 14, Joanna, a woman, succeeded Leo, and reigned two years, five months, and four days." De Gemblours's chronicle said, "It is reported that this John was a female, and that she conceived by one of her servants. The Pope, becoming pregnant, gave birth to a child, wherefor some do not number her among the Pontiffs." Thomas de Elmham's official list of the popes said: "A.D. 855, Joannes. This one doesn't count; she was a woman."[2]

Papal historian and Vatican librarian Platina wrote in *The Lives of the Popes* that Joan was English, that she knew more of the scriptures than any man, and that she was elected pope by disguising herself in men's clothes and making herself a "monk" noted for scholarship. Her deception was revealed when her labor pains came on her, and she died in a street between the Lateran and St. Clement's church.[3] She was dragged into the street and stoned to death and buried there in an unmarked grave.[4] Martin Polonus said the street was ever afterward avoided by papal processions, "out of detestation for what happened there. Nor on that account is she placed in the catalogue of Holy Pontiffs, not only on account of her sex, but also because of the horribleness of the circumstances."[5]

Joan (or John) was the only pope ever stricken from papal records, although her pontificate was better documented than many others, especially the popes before the 4th or 5th centuries, many of whom had no contemporary documentation at all but were mere names inserted into later chronicles to create an illusion of unbroken succession.

The official story now is that there was an "antipope" named John, enthroned by popular demand against the will of the clergy, and soon overthrown.[6] But church historians were seldom trustworthy. In 1886, Emmanuel Royidis published Joan's biography, *Papissa Joanna*, stating in his introduction: "Every sentence in my book and almost every phrase is based on the testimony of contemporary authors." The church immediately banned his book and excommunicated him.[7]

Pope Joan may not have been so apocryphal as she is now portrayed. Part of the church's most carefully hidden history shows that there were women in high ecclesiastical positions up to the 12th century, when they began to be deposed. Abbesses in Germany and France once held episcopal powers and the title of Sacerdos Maxima: High Priestess. At Quedlinburg, the scene of particularly intense witch persecutions, the abbesses once controlled all religious orders and the whole town, having titles of Superior Canoness of the Cathedral, Metropolitana (Mayor), and Matriarch.[8]

In Milan during early Renaissance times, dual cathedrals of the monks of St. John and the canonesses of St. Maria Maggiore seem to have been devoted to worship of the female principle after the manner of the Order of Fontevrault, whose monks "took vows of obedience to the abbess in imitation of the obedience of Jesus to his mother." The Milanese nuns bore the title of Sancta Dei Genetrix—Holy Mother of God.[9]

From Milan came a sect devoted to an unofficial papess named Guglielma, whose followers "believed she was incarnation of the

Holy Spirit." Her Second Coming was predicted, and she was reincarnated in a lady named Manfreda or Maifreda, whose votaries said "the male dominated Papacy would pass away, yielding to a line of female Popes. In preparation for this event they elected Sister Manfreda the first of the Popesses, and several wealthy families of Lombardy provided at great cost the sacred vessels they expected her to use when she said Mass in Rome at the Church of Santa Maria Maggiore." But the sect was exterminated by the Inquisition, and Manfreda was burned at the stake in the year 1300.[10] Some die-hards claimed she was later reincarnated as the Fairy Queen.[11]

There were other women in history close to the papal office who may have contributed to the legends of the Papess. Gibbon suggested the period in the 10th century when Rome was ruled by two women of the house of Theophylact, Theodora and her daughter Marozia, both queens and sacred harlots, bearing the title of *senatrix*. "The most strenuous of their lovers were rewarded with the Roman mitre, and their reign may have suggested to darker ages the fable of a female pope. The bastard son, the grandson, and the great grandson of Marozia—a rare genealogy—were seated on the Chair of St. Peter."

Liudprand, bishop of Cremona, said it differently: "A certain shameless strumpet called Theodora at one time was sole monarch of Rome and—shame though it is to write it—exercised power like a man. She had two daughters, Marozia and Theodora, who were not only her equals but could surpass her in the exercises that Venus loves." Theodora's lover, Bishop John of Ravenna, was given the papacy: "Theodora, like a harlot fearing that she would have few opportunities of bedding with her sweetheart, forced him to abandon his bishopric and take for himself—O, monstrous crime!—the Papacy of Rome."[12] John didn't seem to need forcing. He became Pope John X in 914, but Marozia deposed him in 928 and threw him into a dungeon in the castle of Sant' Angelo, where he died. Three years later she gave the papal throne to the son she had borne to Pope Sergius.[13]

From time to time, other women exerted significant influence on the papacy. Pope John XXII had so many mistresses that it was said he turned the Lateran palace into a brothel. He made his favorite one of the most powerful feudal baronesses in Italy, "for he was so blindly in love with her that he made her governor of cities—and even gave to her the golden crosses and cups of St. Peter himself." When Pope Alexander VI (Rodrigo Borgia) left Rome to visit his son Cesare, he left his daughter Lucretia Borgia in charge. Another woman who commanded popes was Catherine Benincasa of Siena, who convinced Pope Gregory XI that she had a mandate from God to order his papacy moved from Avignon back to Rome.[14]

But the real papess, if there was one, belonged to an earlier era than these—an era of untrustworthy, disconnected records, often destroyed by social upheavals and wars. A popular fairy tale, "The Flounder in the Sea," began as a hostile allegory of the papess. A magic flounder granted the wishes of the ambitious wife of a fisherman; first she wished to become wealthy, then noble; she wanted to be a king, then a pope. Finally she wanted to become God, and hubris caused her downfall. The fisherman in the story was naturally St. Peter, bridegroom of the church (Lady Ecclesia); the miraculous fish with the power to create popes—but not God—represented Christ.[15] The moral of the story was the common anti-feminist opinion that women were more easily corrupted by political power than men.

Seventeenth-century England freely circulated the original story of Pope Joan to cast opprobrium on the "papists." A London pamphlet showed her in papal robes and tiara, her child appearing from beneath her skirt, with the verse:

A Woman Pope (as History doth tell)
In High Procession, She in Labour fell,
And was Delivered of a Bastard Son;
Thence, Rome some call the Whore of Babylon.[16]

The Papess of the **Tarot** cards was often called Pope Joan. When the first Tarot decks were being produced, Joan's pontificate was universally accepted as historical fact. The card-Papess's three-tiered tiara was the same as the headdress shown on engravings of Pope Joan.[17] However, less than a century later, French card painters were afraid to set a woman on the papal throne even symbolically. They changed the Papess to Juno in a classic chlamys. A Belgian Tarot even transformed her into a man, labeled "the Spaniard."[18]

Whether Pope Joan really existed or not, a curious Vatican custom arose in the wake of her legend. Candidates for the papacy had to seat themselves naked on an open stool, to be viewed through a hole in the floor by cardinals in the room below. The committee had to make its official announcement: *Testiculos habet et bene pendentes,* "he has testicles, and they hang all right."[19] It seemed important that "Holy Mother Church" must never be governed by a Holy Mother.

1. Chamberlin, B.P., 25. 2. Baring-Gould, C.M.M.A., 172–73. 3. Durrell, 11.
4. Chamberlin, B.P., 25. 5. Baring-Gould, C.M.M.A., 173.
6. *Encyc. Brit.*, "Papacy." 7. Durrell, 8–9. 8. Morris, 19, 58–59.
9. Morris, 45, 12. 10. Moakley, 72–73. 11. Chamberlin, B.P., 97.
12. Chamberlin, B.P., 26. 13. Chamberlin, B.P., 27–35.
14. Chamberlin, B.P., 44, 201, 127. 15. Moakley, 72. 16. Gettings, pl. 56.
17. Gettings, 33. 18. Cavendish, T., 15, 71–73. 19. Simons, 116.

---

var. Iocaste

Jocasta

"Shining Moon," the mother-wife of **Oedipus**; another mythic combination of the Moon-goddess and her sacred king.

Jonah

Biblical version of the Babylonian god Oannes, shown as a man reborn from the mouth of a great Fish, or whale, symbol of the Goddess

Derceto (Whale of Der).[1] A 10th-century Bible apparently preserved the ancient meaning of Jonah's story, stating that he lived three days in the *womb* of the whale. Later translations substituted "belly" for "womb."[2] See **Derceto; Fish.**

1. Reinach, 209. 2. Potter & Sargent, 180.

Josaphat, Saint

Christian corruption of the title Bodhisat; an inadvertent canonization of Siddhartha Buddha. Medieval saintmakers adapted the story of Buddha's early life to their own fictions, calling the father of St. Josaphat "an Indian king" who kept the young saint confined to prevent him from becoming a Christian.[1] He was converted anyway, and produced the usual assortment of miracles, some of them copied from incidents in the life story of Buddha. St. Josaphat enjoyed great popularity in the Middle Ages, an ironical development in a Europe that abhorred Buddhism as a work of the devil.

1. Attwater, 58.

Joseph

The Gospel of Mark, oldest of the synoptic Gospels, never mentioned Joseph. Jesus is "the son of Mary" (Mark 6:3), and of Mary only.

The Gospel of Matthew gives a long genealogy of paternal ancestors to prove Jesus a descendant of David through his father Joseph. Then, the verses immediately following make nonsense of the whole genealogy by declaring that Jesus was not Joseph's son at all. An early translation of the New Testament however, the Codex Sinaiticus, stated: "Joseph begat Jesus."[1]

The Gospel of Luke calls Joseph a son of Heli, i.e., of Helios, the sun (Luke 3:23). Jesus called Eli, or Elias, his "father" who forsook him when he was crucified (Matthew 27:46; Mark 15:34). Jesus was later identified with the same "father." A sect of Gaulish Christians worshipped Christ as Helios, calling themselves Heliognosti.[2] The solar eclipse at Jesus's death, his titles of Light of the World and Sun of Righteousness, were taken from cults of the solar hero, as were his virgin birth and his mortal pseudo-father who didn't lie with his wife until she brought forth her Divine Child, son of the sun.[3]

The Christian legend of Joseph's rod said he was chosen to be Mary's husband, out of a group of suitors, by a symbolic test of fertility. All candidates laid their (phallic) rods on the (female-symbolic) altar. Joseph's rod alone burst into bloom, a proof of magical potency. The sacred dove of Aphrodite came down from heaven and perched on Joseph's rod, signifying that the Goddess accepted him.[4] The same dove appeared later over the head of Jesus at his baptism, with the same implication of acceptance.

The story of the flowering rod (virility) was common in Middle-Eastern mythologies; rods were also interchangeable with serpents, because of the phallic significance of both (Exodus 7:12). The flowering rod was also a magic talisman for Tannhäuser, who proved the validity of his pagan faith against the pope with a rod that burst into bloom. This rod came from the mountain sanctuary of the Goddess Venus and represented Tannhäuser as her lover.[5]

The Goddess was incarnate in a queen—in Tannhäuser's case, "Queen Sybil"; in the parallel case of Thomas Rhymer, the Fairy Queen; in the case of the biblical Joseph, Mariamne, Queen of Jerusalem, embodiment of the Goddess Mari. There was a Joseph who espoused temple maidens at Herod's court, but was slain after he lay with the queen, Mariamne, or Miriam, or Mary.[6]

The priestly name of Joseph may have been bestowed on Jewish counterparts of the priests known in Egypt as "fathers of the god."[7] The function of such holy men was to beget, on the temple maidens, children who would be *sacer:* firstborn "sons of God" dedicated to the service of the deity. The Protoevangelium says the virgin Mary was such a temple maiden; she also bore the name of the Queen and the Goddess, as well as the holy harlot who was high priestess of the sacred drama.[8] The mythic proliferation of Marys and Josephs indicates that these were not personal names but characters in the drama: the chosen husband who was yet not a husband; the father-of-God who was yet not a father; the virgin-mother-Goddess-priestess-queen who was also a *kadesha* or "Bride of God."[9]

Protoevangelium, also known as the Revelation of James: a Gospel written in the second century A.D., valued by early church fathers as authentic but eventually eliminated from the canon.

It can be shown that Joseph was indeed a divine name in Israel. The Egyptian form was Djoser or Tcheser, a deified pharaoh long associated in both Egyptian and Hebrew tradition with the seven-year famine along the Nile.[10] Palestine had a town dedicated to Joseph-El, or "Joseph the God," possibly the same Egyptian god-king.[11] Certainly the Old Testament Joseph was "chosen" by the Goddess who inspired divinatory interpretation of dreams, called Nanshe by the Babylonians.[12] Dream interpretation was the specialty of the Old Testament Joseph in his role of Egyptian wizard-priest associated, like Djoser, with the seven-year famine. A multicolored vestment was the mark of oneiromantic wizard-priests in Babylon, which probably explains Joseph's celebrated coat of many colors (Genesis 37:23).

Joseph's sojourn in the Pit would naturally have taken place before, not after, he was awarded the coat. His "brothers" (fellow priests?) lowered him into the *abaton* for a death-and-rebirth ritual, such as Assyrian and Babylonian priests underwent before they emerged from the Pit reborn into a holy life.[13] After such an initiation, Joseph was inspired not only to interpret dreams; he also practiced divination with the aid of a silver cup (Genesis 44:5), the vessel of the Goddess, made of moon-metal. (See **Abaddon**.)

Another biblical Joseph associated with the Christian sacred drama, and a divine cup, was Joseph of Arimathea, literally "a Joseph belonging to the Goddess-mother Ari," or Mari, she who made men (*arya*) out of clay.[14] This Joseph was a "counselor" of Jerusalem, that is, a priest; he supervised Jesus's burial. Later myths said the same Joseph carried to England the divine sexual symbols of a (male) flowering rod and a (female) cup or Grail of sacred blood. Several women named Mary accompanied him. The holy articles were enshrined at Glastonbury, formerly named Caer Wydyr, an omphalic seat of the union between pagan God and Goddess. [15] Rod and cup were reinterpreted in a Christian context by the legends of the Holy Grail at Glastonbury. However, mystical systems such as the Tarot suits of rods and cups suggest that these were none other than male-female elemental symbols given a Christian gloss (see **Grail, Holy**).

1. H. Smith, 182. 2. Lindsay, O.A., 333. 3. H. Smith, 183.
4. Guerber, L.R., 340; Graves, W.G., 123. 5. Goodrich, 174. 6. Enslin, C.B., 48–49.
7. Budge, D.N., 169. 8. Ashe, 201. 9. Briffault 3, 169–70.
10. Budge, G.E. 2, 53; de Camp, A.E., 294. 11. Reinach, 201. 12. *Larousse,* 63.
13. Lethaby, 172. 14. Potter & Sargent, 33. 15. Graves, W.G., 105.

Jove

"The Youth," a title of the god Jupiter as a replacement for Juventas, "The Maiden," in the originally all-female Capitoline Triad, a Virgin-Mother-Crone personification of the Etruscan Goddess. Juno the Mother and Minerva the wise Crone remained; but Juventas the Virgin gave way to a young god, just as Hebe the virgin form of the Greek Triple Goddess gave way to the youth Ganymede. See **Trinity**.

Judas

As the Christian figure of the Betrayer, Judas was poorly understood. Formerly, Judas was an ancestral god, father of the nation of Judah and of Jews (*Judaei*). As Jude, or Jeud, he was the "only-begotten son" of the Divine Father Isra-El.[1] Judas was a dynastic name for priest-kings of Judea for a hundred years after Judas Maccabeus restored ancient sacrificial customs to the temple of Jerusalem in 165 B.C.[2] Thus the kingly name of Judas was commonly given victims sacrificed as surrogates for a reigning monarch.

Judas's legend parallels those of many other sacred kings. He was born of a holy woman named Cyboread, a prophetess or priestess. He was sent out to sea in a chest (*cista*), which washed up on the isle of Scariot—hence his name, Judas Iscariot. The queen of the island raised him, as the princess of Egypt raised Moses. When he came of age, Judas returned home to take service at Pilate's court. Like Oedipus, he killed his father and married his mother. Early Christians said Judas joined the disciples of Jesus in order to be cleansed of this sin.[3]

The Syrian *Acts of Thomas* declares however that Judas was

Jesus's twin brother, whose full name was Judas Thomas, i.e., "Judas the Tammuz." Passages of the Koran insist that Judas had the same face as Jesus and was crucified in his stead.[4] Judas's qualifications as a sacrificial Savior hint that he might have combined with Jesus at some point in early Christianity as an alternate seasonal god, like Horus and Set in Egypt.

The Gospels are vague and contradictory about Judas's death. Matthew says he hanged himself (27:5). Acts 1:18 says he died of a fall, which made him "burst asunder in the midst, and all his bowels gushed out." Hanging and disemboweling were both common forms of ritual killing; but the ritualistic nature of Judas's death is most strongly suggested by its location: Aceldama, the Field of Blood, dedicated to "the Potter in the House of the Lord," who received Judas's blood-money.

The Gospel writer naively admitted that the detail about the money that bought Jesus was inserted only to fulfill a "prophecy" in Zechariah 11: "So they weighed for my price thirty pieces of silver. And the Lord said unto me, Cast it unto the potter. . . . And I took the thirty pieces of silver, and cast them to the potter in the house of the Lord." The Potter in the temple was an image of the Great Goddess Aruru, "The Potter," a title of Ishtar or Astarte or Ninhursag who made mankind of clay moistened with blood. The Potter's Field was clay, periodically soaked with blood to restore to the Goddess some of the life-essence she bestowed.[5]

Gospel stories contradict each other concerning this field. One writer said Judas purchased the field with his thirty pieces of silver (Acts 1:18). Another said he "repented" and took the money back to the temple, where he flung it down, and the priests used it to buy "the potter's field, to bury strangers in" (Matthew 27:7).

The story of Judas's "betrayal" of Jesus is particularly confusing; why would anyone need to point Jesus out, when he had already entered the city as the central figure in a triumphal procession, playing the part of the Bridegroom of Zion, calling himself the son of God, publicly conversing with angels, and publicly promising all men a share in his imminent resurrection (John 12: 15, 29, 32)? In fact the monetary payment and the "betrayal" seem to have been necessary parts of the traditional drama, devices to absolve the executioners of guilt.

It might be supposed that when Jesus received Judas's kiss, he became a sacred king of the *Judaei.* He was "betrayed" by the spirit of the eleventh hour, who in the solar cults announced the coming death of the Light of the World in the twelfth hour—which is why the eleventh hour still presages something dire. Because of the kiss, it was sometimes assumed that Judas was "the disciple whom Jesus loved"—though Gospels later removed from the canon said Jesus loved Mary Magdalene more than any of his male followers.[6] The much-discussed passage in John 21 was a remnant of sun worship, with which the Gospel of John was generally permeated:

Peter, turning about, seeth the disciple whom Jesus loved following; which also leaned on his breast at supper, and said, Lord, which is he that betrayeth thee? Peter seeing him saith to Jesus, Lord, and what shall this man do? Jesus saith unto him, If I will that he tarry till I come, what is that to thee?

Twelve disciples signified the twelve hours of the day: "Are there not twelve hours in the day? If any man walk in the day, he stumbleth not, because he seeth the light of the world" (John 11:9). The disciple of the last hour, who leaned on the breast of the sun at his setting, was the evening star, often called Shalem or Shalom, "peace," because he betrayed the solar deity into his nightly death and spoke the Word of Farewell to him: *salaam,* Peace. The Jews' solar king died at Jeru-*salem,* "the House of Peace."

The ancients knew the evening star and morning star were one and the same, the planet Venus. So the same "disciple" who betrayed the sun god into the land of death was also the one who tarried until he rose again in the morning, the last star whose light still shone as the sun was ascending to heaven. Thus the betrayer was the spirit closest to the deity; the hour that "loved" him. Hellenization of Israel converted the dual morning-star and evening-star god into the Dioscuri or heavenly twins. Mithraic icons showed them turning the torch of life downward on one side of the sun, upward on the other.[7]

There was another interpretation of the mysterious passage embedded in the famous legend of the Wandering Jew. Ignoring the two accounts of Judas's death, medieval interpreters said Jesus meant that Judas, for his crime, was condemned never to die until Jesus "came again" at the end of the world. So Judas wandered through time, weary but deathless, living many lifetimes in bitterness and regret. Perhaps this tale of Wandering Jew was intended to mock the pagans' idea of many reincarnations on earth.

Yet another Christianization of Judas transformed him into St. Jude, adopted into the Christian canon because the ancient cult of Judas continued in Judea and couldn't be eradicated. The fictitious St. Jude became very popular in the Middle Ages. True to his Judaic character, the saint was called "a powerful intercessor for those in desperate straits."[8]

1. Frazer, G.B., 340. 2. Pfeifer, 39. 3. Rank, 21–22. 4. Augstein, 151, 183. 5. Neumann, G.M., 152. 6. Pagels, 64–65. 7. Cumont, M.M., 128. 8. Attwater, 206.

Juggernaut

Corrupt form of Vishnu's epithet Jagganath, "Lord of the World," when he was enthroned in a temple constructed to resemble a gigantic chariot, wheels and all.[1] The temple was planned to represent the moving world, carrying all its freight of gods, heroes, nymphs, creatures, plants, human beings, and all the rest of creation.

Each year at the Puri festival, the god rode with his sister and brother on a heavy wagon drawn by hundreds of pilgrims, some of whom were said to court martyrdom and a blessed eternity in heaven by throwing themselves under the wheels of the god's chariort as it progressed.[2] Thus a "juggernaut" came to mean anything heavy and unstoppable.

1. Elisofon & Watts, 79. 2. *Encyc. Brit.*, "Juggernaut."

Julian, Saint

Christianized version of the god of travelers and those who served travelers: innkeepers, ferrymen, strolling entertainers. He was called Julian the Hospitaller.[1]

Julian's Christian legend was hardly very saintly. Returning home from a late journey, he found two people in his bed and killed them both, assuming he had caught his wife with her lover. Instead, the murdered pair proved to be Julian's own father and mother.[2] As penance for his error, Julian took his wife and went to live by a ford, where they gave shelter and assistance to travelers. The legend seems to have been concocted from nothing more substantial than a votive figure of the emperor Julian at a roadside shrine, where travelers left offerings so as to have good fortune on the road. Many of the gods thus honored by pagan pilgrims were arbitrarily declared saints in order to provide a Christian motive for the worship given them.

1. Attwater, 206. 2. Hazlitt, 351.

Sign of Juno

Juno

Roman Great Mother, derived from Sabine-Etruscan Uni, the Three-in-One deity cognate with "yoni" and "Uni-verse." Juno had dozens of attributes or emanations which are sometimes erroneously viewed as separate Goddesses. Juno Fortuna was the Goddess of Fate. Juno Sospita was the Preserver. Juno Regina was Queen of Heaven. Juno Lucina was Goddess of Celestial Light. Juno Moneta was the Advisor and Admonisher. Juno Martialis was the virgin mother of Mars. Juno Caprotina, or Februa, was the Goddess of erotic love. Juno Populonia was Mother of the People. And so on, through many other Junos.[1]

Every Roman woman embodied a bit of Goddess's spirit, her own soul a *juno,* corresponding to the *genius* of a man.[2] Later patriarchal vocabularies dropped the word *juno* but retained *genius,* thus depriving women of their souls—which may be why church councils of the early Middle Ages sometimes maintained that women are soulless.

Juno's sacred month of June honored her as patroness of marriages and the family, which is why June is still the traditional time for weddings.

Juno had her formidable aspects too. As a battle-goddess she represented the fighting spirit of a mother defending her offspring, the epitome of bravery by Roman definition. Therefore *Juno Seispitei Matri Reginae* (Juno the Preserver, Queen of the Mothers) was regarded as the spirit of war.[3] Her title was the same as that of the Hindu war-goddess Durga the Preserver, Leader of the Mothers.[4] Like all Indo-European forms of the Goddess, Juno was only another local manifestation of the same all-encompassing deity.

Among Juno's sacred symbols were the **peacock,** the **cowrie** shell, and of course the lily, or lotus, universal yonic emblem. With her sacred lily, Juno conceived the god Mars without any assistance from her consort, Jupiter; thus she became the Blessed Virgin Juno.[5] The three-lobed lily that used to represent her parthenogenetic power was inherited by the virgin Mary, who still retains it.

1. *Larousse,* 203–4; Rose, 217. 2. Reinach, 102; Rose, 193. 3. Dumézil, 297. 4. O'Flaherty, 49, 353. 5. *Larousse,* 202.

Jupiter

Sign of Jupiter

Roman Heavenly Father, from Sanskrit *Dyaus pitar,* the basic Father Heaven mated to Mother Earth. Zeus Pater, the Greek Heavenly Father, was another incarnation of the same Aryan deity, whose worship spread westward with migrations and invasions of Indo-European patriarchal tribes. Like his counterparts in other nations, Jupiter was primarily a rain god; his function was to fertilize the soil with seminal moisture. Thus he was connected also with thunder and lightning—his voice and his weapon. He was commonly known as Jupiter Pluvius, "the Heavenly-Father-Who-Rains."

Jupiter was added to the originally female Capitoline Triad by ousting the Virgin form of the Goddess, Juventas, leaving Juno and Minerva as Jupiter's two female partners.[1] Juno was said to be his wife, though like Hera she was much older than her spouse.

1. Rose, 116.

Justice

The spirit of justice was female in classic paganism. Ulpian said justice depended on "the feminine nature principle, which has a profounder kinship with the *natura iustum* (that which is just by nature) than does the male sex, with its greater susceptibility to the principle of domination." Pythagoreans taught that *iusticia* and *aequitas* (justice and equity) are "innate attributes of the feminine nature principle."[1]

The Roman praetor or judge "gave expression to justice as the organ and *viva vox* of Bona Dea-Fauna-Fatua. Through this tie with the material primordial mother he was enabled to observe the practical justice of the *ius naturale,* the equity of the left hand, often in opposition to the strictly formal logic of the civil law. As 'feminine godhead' Bona Dea became equivalent to Themis, in whose mysteries the worship of the feminine *kteis,* the *sporium muliebre* (womb), plays so prominent a part. The name 'feminine godhead' takes on its full meaning only when the same physical, sensuous implication is recognized. Thus the cult of the *kteis* involved not only the idea of maternal fertility but the maternal mystery of justice."[2]

1. Bachofen, 189, 186. 2. Bachofen, 193.

Ka

One of an Egyptian's seven souls, often believed to be a spirit-twin resident in the afterbirth.[1] The Shilluks of the upper Nile, who in the present century still worshipped the Cow-mother Hathor as bestower of the souls, buried afterbirths of their sacred kings in the same tombs where the kings themselves would be laid on the theory that a man needed his *ka* in order to become a god after death.[2] In ancient Egypt, prayers were addressed to the *ka* of Osiris and other gods. India knew the same concept, even the same word. Brahma had a soul-twin named Ka, which was translated "Who?"[3]

The hieroglyphic sign of the *ka* was a pair of upraised arms with bent elbows.[4] This arm position evidently invoked the Goddess, and was connected with the idea of the *ka* as a mother-given entity, each baby's unformed twin, made of blood.[5] A Paleolithic painting from Algeria shows a hunter stalking an ostrich while a full-hipped female figure, larger than he, raises her arms in the position of the *ka.* The female figure was either a mother or a sexual partner, as shown by a serpentine connective line running from the hunter's crotch to hers.[6] Evidently, she made magic to help the hunter in his efforts, even though she may have been far away.

A vase figure from Amratian times showed a similar *ka*-invocation performed by a priestess, assisted by two men who helped hold her arms aloft when she became tired.[7] The same magical *ka*-invocation was performed by Moses at the battle between Israelites and Amalekites. The Israelites won because Moses, with the help of Aaron and Hur, held up his arms in the *ka*-position all day until the battle ended at sunset (Exodus 17:12).

Egyptians thought the *ka*-soul was immortal and dwelt in or near the tomb where the body rested. The same notion was common among Christians, who said a ghost lived in or near the grave. There is in existence a letter written by an ancient Egyptian to his deceased wife, three years after her death. He attached the letter to the portrait statue in her tomb, confident that her *ka* would read the letter.[8]

Among northern Aryans the idea of the *ka* was transposed into the *Doppelgänger* (double-goer), a hidden twin-soul thought to reside in the placenta or umbilical cord, though sometimes it could develop into a full-grown twin. Germanic folklore has many examples of the soul preserved in a safer location than the body—e.g., the giant who kept his soul in an egg, and so on. German and French peasants used to treat an umbilical cord or afterbirth with great care, to give magical assistance to the child's future health or longevity. Sometimes, as in Greek myth, mothers preserved their children's umbilical cords in a secret place, thinking no harm could come to the child as long as the cord was intact.[9]

1. H. Smith, 24. 2. Briffault 3, 192; Frazer, G.B., 310, 345.
3. O'Flaherty, 344. 4. Budge, E.L., 57. 5. Montagu, S.M.S., 271.
6. Neumann, G.M., 114. 7. Neumann, G.M., 116. 8. Budge, E.M., 219.
9. Frazer, G.B., 46.

Kaaba

Shrine of the sacred stone in Mecca, formerly dedicated to the pre-Islamic Triple Goddess Manat, Al-Lat (Allah), and Al-Uzza, the "Old Woman" worshipped by Mohammed's tribesmen the Koreshites. The stone was also called Kubaba, Kuba, or Kube, and has been linked with the name of Cybele (Kybela), the Great Mother of the Gods.[1] The stone bore the emblem of the yoni, like the Black Stone worshipped by votaries of Artemis.[2] Now it is regarded as the holy center of patriarchal Islam, and its feminine symbolism has been lost, though priests of the Kaaba are still known as Sons of the Old Woman. See **Arabia**; **Cybele**.

1. Vermaseren, 22. 2. Harding, 41.

Kadi

Babylonian Goddess of Der, a serpent with a woman's head and breasts. Her name was the root of *kadishtu,* Hebrew *kadesha,* a temple harlot known as a Holy One, or Virgin Bride of God (see **Prostitution**; **Virgin Birth**). She may have descended from the Vedic Goddess Kadru, mother of all Nagas or sacred serpents, who attained immortality through the magic blood she gave them to drink.[1]

1. O'Flaherty, 222.

Kala-Nath

Title of the Goddess Kali as the Primordial Abyss or womb of creation.[1] Possible origin of the Middle-Eastern Goddess Anath, worshipped in Libya as Neith, in Canaan as Anat, who was once the spouse of Jehovah. See **Anath**.

1. *Bardo Thodol,* 147.

Kalanemi

"Rim of the Wheel of Time," a pre-Vedic spirit of the zodiac or Milky Way, viewed as the great star-wheel at the rim of the universe, also sometimes envisioned as the World Serpent encircling the earth with its tail in its mouth. Men had to study Kalanemi in order to learn *kalends,* the proper order of seasons, sabbaths, and festivals. Kalanemi was probably an aspect of Kali Ma as the Crone of Time; it is interesting that the second part of the name, *nemi,* meant the Moon-grove in Greco-Roman culture, and according to ancient astrologers the zodiac was the moon's grove through which she passed in the night (see **Grove, Sacred**). Later Vedic priests diabolized Kalanemi as a "demon" who begot Balarama and Krishna in the underworld before the beginning of time.[1]

1. O'Flaherty, 207.

Kalenderees

Wandering dervishes from medieval Hindustan who taught Tantric doctrines in Persia and Arabia.[1] Their cult of the Goddess Kali may have been the origin of the female-centered Sufi sect which revered the same feminine Word of Creation (Om, Umm: the Matrix or Mother-belly), and believed that religious fulfillment for men or women could be found only in sexual love.[2] See **Kali Ma**.

1. Keightley, 20. 2. Shah, 29, 175.

Kali Ma

"Dark Mother," the Hindu Triple Goddess of creation, preservation, and destruction; now most commonly known in her Destroyer aspect, squatting over her dead consort Shiva and devouring his entrails, while her yoni sexually devours his lingam (penis). Kali is "The hungry earth, which devours its own children and fattens on their corpses. . . . It is in India that the experience of the Terrible Mother has been given its most grandiose form as Kali. But all this—and it should not be forgotten—is an image not only of the Feminine but particularly and specifically of the Maternal. For in a profound way life and birth are always bound up with death and destruction."[1]

Kali was the basic archetypal image of the birth-and-death Mother, simultaneously womb and tomb, giver of life and devourer of her children: the same image portrayed in a thousand ancient religions. Even modern psychologists face this image with uneasy acknowledgment of its power. It seems the image of the angry, punishing, castrating Father is somehow less threatening than that of the destructive Mother—perhaps because she symbolized the inexorable reality of death, whereas he only postulated a problematic post-mortem judgment.[2]

Tantric worshippers of Kali thought it essential to face her Curse, the terror of death, as willingly as they accepted Blessings from her beautiful, nurturing, maternal aspect. For them, wisdom meant learning that no coin has only one side: as death can't exist without life, so also life can't exist without death. Kali's sages communed with her in the grisly atmosphere of the cremation ground, to become familiar with images of death. They said: "His Goddess, his loving Mother in time, who gives him birth and loves him in the flesh, also destroys him in the flesh. His image of Her is incomplete if he does not know Her as his tearer and devourer."[3]

Few western scholars understood the profound philosophy behind the hideous images of Kali the Destroyer. The London Museum displayed such an image with a label saying only, "Kali—Destroying Demon."[4] The *Encyclopaedia Britannica* devoted five columns to Christian interpretations of the Logos without ever mentioning its origin in Kali's *Om* or Creative Word; Kali herself was dismissed in a brief paragraph as the wife of Shiva and "a goddess of disease."[5] Certainly, as the Kalika or Crone she governed every form of death including disease; but she also ruled every form of life.

Kali stood for Existence, which meant Becoming because all her world was an eternal living flux from which all things rose and disappeared again, in endless cycles. The gods, whom she bore and devoured, addressed her thus:

> *Thou art the Original of all the manifestations; Thou art the birthplace of even Us; Thou knowest the whole world, yet none know Thee. . . . Thou art both Subtle and Gross, Manifested and Veiled, Formless, yet with form. Who can understand Thee?. . . . It is Thou who art the Supreme Primordial Kalika. . . . Resuming after dissolution Thine own form, dark and formless, Thou alone remainest as One ineffable and inconceivable . . . though Thy self without beginning, multiform by the power of Maya, Thou art the Beginning of all, Creatrix, Protectress, and Destructress.*[6]

Brahmans assigned Kali's three functions to three male gods, calling them Brahma the creator, Vishnu the preserver, and Kali's archaic consort Shiva the destroyer; but many scriptures opposed this male trinity as offensively artificial. A prayer in the Tantrasara said: "O Mother! Cause and Mother of the World! Thou art the One Primordial Being, Mother of innumerable creatures, Creatrix of the very gods; even of Brahma the Creator, Vishnu the Preserver, and Shiva the Destroyer! O Mother, in hymning Thy praise I purify my speech!"[7] The Nirvana Tantra treated the claims of male gods with contempt:

> *Brahma, Vishnu, Mahesvara [Shiva], and other gods are born of the body of that beginningless and eternal Kalika, and at the time of dissolution they again disappear in Her. O Devi, for this reason, so long as the living man does not know the supreme truth in regard to Her . . . his desire for liberation can only give rise to ridicule. From a part only of Kalika, the primordial Shakti, arises Brahma, from a part only arises Vishnu, and*

Tantrasara, Nirvana Tantra, etc.. Tantras are basic scriptures of **Tantrism,** many of which have yet to be translated from Sanskrit or other original languages into English. Extant texts date back to ca. 600 A.D., though the material was much older. Among the most popular Hindu Tantras are the Shaktisamgama, Kularnava, Mahanirvanatantra, and Tantraraja.

> *from a part only arises Shiva. O fair-eyed Devi, just as rivers and lakes are unable to traverse a vast sea, so Brahma and other gods lose their separate existence on entering the uncrossable and infinite being of Great Kali. Compared with the vast sea of the being of Kali, the existence of Brahma and the other gods is nothing but such a little water as is contained in the hollow made by a cow's hoof. Just as it is impossible for a hollow made by a cow's hoof to form a notion of the unfathomable depths of a sea, so it is impossible for Brahma and other gods to have a knowledge of the nature of Kali.*[8]

Even the arrogant Vishnu, who claimed to have brought the whole earth out of the primal abyss, received the grace of enlightenment concerning Kali and wrote a poem about her: "Material cause of all change, manifestation and destruction . . . the whole Universe rests upon Her, rises out of Her and melts away into Her. From Her are crystallized the original elements and qualities which construct the apparent worlds. She is both mother and grave. . . . The gods themselves are merely constructs out of Her maternal substance, which is both consciousness and potential joy."[9]

The Yogini Tantra said of Kali, "Whatever power anything possesses, that is the Goddess."[10] Shakti, "Power," was one of her important names. Without her, neither man nor god could act at all:

> *It is She as Power (Shakti) who takes the active and changeful part in generation, as also in conceiving, bearing, and giving birth to the World-Child. All this is the function of the divine, as it is of the human, mother. . . . It is thus to the Mother that man owes the World of Forms or Universe. Without Her as material cause, Being cannot display itself. It is but a corpse . . . primacy is given to the Mother, and it is said, "What care I for the Father if I but be on the lap of the Mother?"*[11]

A Tantric scholar points out that "the poets have found much more intimate cries of the heart when they spoke of the Deity as their 'Mother' than when they addressed themselves to God as Father." Kali's poets approached her through love: "By feeling is She known. How then can lack of feeling find Her?" In their view, "All is the Mother and She is reality herself. 'Sa'ham' (She I Am) the Sakta says, and all that he senses is She in the form in which he perceives her. It is She who in, and as, him drinks the consecrated wine, and She is the wine." She feeds him as a mother feeds her child, and he becomes immortal: "Deathless are those who have fed at the breast of the Mother of the Universe." The Yoginihrdaya Tantra says, "Obeisance to Her who is pure Being-Consciousness-Bliss, as Power, who exists in the form of Time and Space and all that is therein, and who is the radiant Illuminatrix in all beings."[12]

As a Mother, Kali was called Treasure-House of Compassion (*karuna*), Giver of Life to the world, the Life of all lives. Contrary to the west's idea of her as a purely destructive Goddess, she was the fount of every kind of love, which flowed into the world only through her agents on earth, women. Thus it was said a male worshipper of Kali "bows down at the feet of women," regarding them as his rightful teachers.[13]

The name of Eve may have originated with Kali's Ieva or Jiva, the primordial female principle of manifestation; she gave birth to her "first manifested form" and called him Idam (Adam). She also bore the same title given to Eve in the Old Testament: Mother of All Living (Jaganmata).[17]

As the primal Deep, or menstrual Ocean of Blood at creation, Kali was certainly the same as the biblical *tehom,* Tiamat, or *tohu bohu,* the "flux" representing her state of formlessness between manifested universes. As Mahanila-Sarasvati the great blue River-Goddess, she was probably the original namesake of the River Nile. As Kundalini the Female Serpent, she resembled the archaic Egyptian serpent-mother said to have created the world. It was said of Kundalini that at the beginning of the universe, she starts to uncoil in "a spiral line movement which is the movement of creation."[18] This spiral line was vitally important in late Paleolithic and Neolithic religious symbolism, representing death and rebirth as movement into the disappearing-point of formlessness, and out of it again, to a new world of form. Spirals therefore appeared on tombs, as one of the world's first mystical symbols.

Lunar priests of Sinai, formerly priestesses of the Moon-goddess, called themselves *kalu.*[22] Similar priestesses of prehistoric Ireland were *kelles,* origin of the name Kelly, which meant a hierophantic clan devoted to "the Goddess Kele" (see **Kelle**).[23] This was cognate with the Saxon Kale, or Cale, whose lunar calendar or *kalends* included the spring month of Sproutkale, when Mother Earth (Kale) put forth new shoots.[24] In antiquity the Phoenicians referred to the strait of Gibraltar as Calpe, because it was considered the passage to the western paradise of the Mother.[25]

Indo-European languages branched from the root of Sanskrit, said to be Kali's invention. She created the magic letters of the Sanskrit alphabet and inscribed them on the rosary of skulls around her neck.[27] The letters were magic because they stood for primordial creative energy expressed in sound—Kali's *mantras* brought into being the very things whose names she spoke for the first time, in her holy language. In short, Kali's worshippers originated the doctrine of the **Logos** or creative Word, which Christians later adopted and pretended it was their own idea. Kali's letters magically combined the elements, which were previously separate as fiery-airy (male) or watery-earthy (female) forces. The former were "cruel"; the latter "benevolent."[28] This distinction seemed to reflect the Tantric view of Kali as Lady of Life and her spouse as Lord of Death.

Though called "the One," Kali was always a trinity: the same Virgin-Mother-Crone triad established perhaps nine or ten millenia ago, giving the Celts their triple Morrigan; the Greeks their triple Moerae and all other manifestations of the Threefold Goddess; the

Western scholars erroneously viewed the various manifestations and incarnations of Kali as many different Goddesses, particularly isolating those primitive *matrikadevis* (mother-goddesses) grouped together as "Dravidian she-ogres."[14] Yet Kali's worshippers plainly stated that she had hundreds of different names, but they were all the same Goddess: Sarasvati, Lakshmi, Gayatri, Durga, Annapurna, Sati, Uma, Parvati, Gauri, Bagala, Matangini, Dhumavati, Tara, Bhairavi, Kundalini, Bharga, Devata, etc. All were Kali Mahadevi, the "Great Goddess"—the same title she bore among western pagans.[15]

Some of Kali's older names found their way into the Bible. As Tara, the earth, she became Terah, mother of the Hebrew ancestral spirits called **teraphim**. The same Kali-Tara became the Celts' Tara, Gauls' Taranis, Etruscans' Turan, and the Latin Terra, "Mother Earth," said to be interchangeable with Venus.[16]

Norsemen their triple Norns; the Romans their triple Fates and triadic Uni (Juno); the Egyptians their triple Mut; the Arabs their triple Moon-goddess—she was the same everywhere. Even Christians modeled their threefold God on her archetypal trinity.[29]

Her three forms were manifested in many ways: in the three divisions of the year, the three phases of the moon, the three sections of the cosmos (heaven, earth, and the underworld), the three stages of life, the three trimesters of pregnancy, and so on. Women represented her spirit in mortal flesh. "The Divine Mother first appears in and as Her worshipper's earthly mother, then as his wife; thirdly as Kalika, She reveals Herself in old age, disease and death."[30]

Three kinds of priestesses tended her shrines: Yoginis or Shaktis, the "Maidens"; Matri, the "Mothers"; and **Dakinis**, the "Skywalkers" who attended the dying, governed funerary rites and acted as angels of death. All had their counterparts in the spirit world. To this day, Tantric Buddhism relates the three mortal forms of woman to the divine female trinity called Three Most Precious Ones.[31]

Kali's three forms appeared in the sacred colors known as **Gunas**: white for the Virgin, red for the Mother, black for the Crone, symbolizing birth, life, death.[32] Black was Kali's fundamental color as the Destroyer, for it meant the formless condition she assumed between creations, when all the elements were dissolved in her primordial substance. "As white, yellow, and other colors all disappear in black, in the same way . . . all beings enter Kali."[33]

The Black Goddess was known in Finland as Kalma (Kali Ma), a haunter of tombs and an eater of the dead.[34] European "witches" worshipped her in the same funereal places, for the same reasons, that Tantric yogis and dakinis worshipped her in cremation grounds, as Smashana-Kali, Lady of the Dead.[35] Their ceremonies were held in the places of ghosts where ordinary folk feared to go.[36] So were the ceremonies of western "witches"—that is, pagans. They adored the Black Mother Earth in cemeteries, where Roman tombstones invoked her with the phrase *Mater genuit, Mater recepit*—the Mother bore me, the Mother took me back.[37]

Sometimes Kali the Destroyer wore red, suggesting the blood of life that she gave and took back: "As She devours all existence, as She chews all things existing with Her fierce teeth, therefore a mass of blood is imagined to be the apparel of the Queen of the Gods at the final dissolution."[38] The gypsies, who worshipped Kalika as a disease-causing Goddess they called "the Aunt," clothed her in red, the proper color for gypsy funerals.[39]

Blood was as much a part of Kali's worship as it was of the worship of the biblical God who said blood must be poured on his altars to bring remission of sins (Hebrews 9:22). The difference between the western God's demand for blood and Kali's was that Jewish priests took away the meat and ate it themselves (Numbers 18:9), whereas devotees of Kali were permitted to eat their own offerings, as in Calcutta:

Variations of Kali's basic name occurred throughout the ancient world. The Greeks had a word Kalli, meaning "beautiful," but applied to things that were not particularly beautiful such as the demonic centaurs called *kallikantzari,* relatives of Kali's Asvins. Their city of Kallipolis, the modern Gallipoli, was centered in Amazon country formerly ruled by Artemis Kalliste.[19] The annual birth festival at Eleusis was Kalligeneia, translatable as "coming forth from the Beautiful One," or "coming forth from Kali."[20] The temple of the Great Mother of the Gods at Pergamum stood on Mount Mamurt-Kaleh, easily transposed into Mount Mother-Kali.[21]

Kali's title Devi (Goddess) was similarly widespread in Indo-European languages. She was the Latin *diva* (Goddess) and Minoan *diwi* or *Diwija,* the "Goddess" associated with Zeus at Knossos.[26] Dia, Dea, and Diana were alternate forms of the same title.

The temple serves simply as a slaughterhouse, for those performing the sacrifice retain their animals, leaving only the head in the temple as a symbolic gift, while the blood flows to the Goddess. For to the Goddess is due the lifeblood of all creatures—since it is she who has bestowed it—and that is why the beast must be slaughtered in her temple; that is why temple and slaughterhouse are one.

This rite is performed amid gruesome filth; in the mud compounded of blood and earth, the heads of the animals are heaped up like trophies before the statue of the Goddess, while those sacrificing return home for a family banquet of the bodies of their animals. The Goddess desires only the blood of the offerings, hence beheading is the form of sacrifice, since the blood drains quickly from the beheaded beasts . . . ; the head signifies the whole, the total sacrifice.[40]

Beheading or throat-cutting were common methods of sacrificial killing in the western world, too. "Kosher" killing for Yahweh consisted, and still consists, of draining the animal's blood, because blood was the special food of deities. Kali demanded sacrifice of male animals only, for they were expendable—a custom harking back to the primitive belief that males had no part in the cycles of generation. Shiva himself, as Kali's sacrificial spouse, commanded that female animals must never be slain at the altar.[41]

Kali was the Ocean of Blood at the beginning and end of the world, and her ultimate destruction of the universe was prefigured by destruction of each individual, though her karmic wheel always brought reincarnation. After death came nothing-at-all, which Tantric sages called the third of the three states of being; to experience it was like the experience of Dreamless Sleep. This state was also called "the Generative Womb of All, the Beginning and End of Beings."[42] Kali devoured Time itself. At the end of Time, she resumed her "dark formlessness," which appeared in all the myths of before-creation and after-doomsday as elemental Chaos.[43]

The mystical experience of Kali was often described as a preview of formlessness beyond the veil of death: a psychic return to the womb, to be united with Kali's oceanic being. Thus Ramakrishna described it:

I was suffering from excruciating pain because I had not been blessed with a vision of the Mother. . . . I feared that it might not be my lot to realize her in this life. I could not bear the separation any longer; life did not seem to be worth living. Then my eyes fell on the sword that was kept in the Mother's temple. Determined to put an end to my life, I jumped up and seized it, when suddenly the blessed Mother revealed herself to me. . . . the temple and all vanished, leaving no trace; instead there was a limitless, infinite, shining ocean of consciousness or spirit. As far as the eye could see, its billows were rushing towards me from all sides . . . to swallow me up. I was panting for breath. I was caught in the billows and fell down senseless.[44]

Ramakrishna (1836–1886) Leading Hindu saint of the 19th century, familiar in the western world through the teachings of his famous disciple Vivekananda.

Ramakrishna revitalized the worship of the Mother, as his pupil Vivekananda said; "It was no new truths that Ramakrishna came to preach, though his advent brought old truths to light."[45] Vivekananda predicted the resurgence of the Mother into the consciousness of the world's population, after patriarchal religions had forced her into concealment in the unconscious: "One vision I see clear as life before me, that the ancient mother has awakened once more, sitting on her throne rejuvenated, more glorious than ever. Proclaim her to all the world with the voice of peace and benediction."[46] Clearly, this Goddess was much more than the London Museum's "Destroying Demon."

1. Neumann, G.M., 149–53. 2. Fromm, 363–64. 3. Rawson, A.T., 112. 4. Wilson, 257. 5. *Encyc. Brit.,* "Kali." 6. *Mahanirvanatantra,* 47–50. 7. de Riencourt, 167. 8. Rawson, A.T., 184. 9. Rawson, E.A., 159. 10. Rawson, A.T., 183. 11. Avalon, 419–20. 12. Avalon, 130–31, 466, 27–31. 13. Avalon, 410, 533. 14. *Larousse,* 359. 15. *Mahanirvanatantra,* xxxi. 16. Dumézil, 676. 17. Avalon, 120, 277. 18. Avalon, 193, 229, 233. 19. Graves, W.G., 185. 20. *Encyc. Brit.,* "Thesmophoria." 21. Vermaseren, 26. 22. Lindsay, O.A., 40. 23. Joyce, 352. 24. Brewster, 88. 25. Massa, 43. 26. Hays, 104. 27. Graves, W.G., 250. 28. Rawson, A.T., 70. 29. Stone, 17. 30. Avalon, 171. 31. Waddell, 129, 169. 32. Avalon, 328. 33. *Mahanirvanatantra,* 295. 34. *Larousse,* 306. 35. *Mahanirvanatantra,* 360. 36. Rawson, E.A., 152. 37. Lederer, 22. 38. *Mahanirvanatantra,* 295–96. 39. Trigg, 119, 186. 40. Neumann, G.M., 152. 41. *Mahanirvanatantra,* 103. 42. Campbell, C.M., 347. 43. Avalon, 517. 44. Wilson, 254. 45. *Encyc. Brit.,* "Ramakrishna." 46. Menen, 149.

Kama-Mara

"Erotic-desire" plus "Fear-of-death," a dual spirit who tempted Buddha during his solitary meditation. The Upanishads said Kama-Mara was the Self, source of both desire and fear.[1] But Mara was once the mother of the Maruts or nature-spirits; Kama was the Vedic equivalent of Eros; it seems likely that they were combined in an archaic period as a sexual androgyne. The "demonic" combination expressed the ascetics' belief that eroticism drew the flesh of men toward destruction.

A Buddhist legend said the Blessed One met the challenge of Kama-Mara by touching the earth with his fingers, thus invoking the irresistible power of the universal Mother, who protected him.[2]

1. Campbell, Oc.M., 371. 2. Campbell, M.T.L.B., 131.

Kamsa

Vedic prototype of King Herod. Kamsa, King of the Bhojas, initiated a Slaughter of Innocents when trying to kill the infant Krishna, his future conqueror. Kamsa killed only boy babies until Devaki brought forth a girl. The girl was killed too, and rose to heaven to become a Goddess. She visited Kamsa and told him, "Kamsa, Kamsa, since you attacked me to destroy me . . . I will smash your body with my own hands and drink your warm blood." Kamsa realized that she had become his Death.[1] The myth was intended to support the taboo against killing females.

1. O'Flaherty, 213.

Kara

Valkyrie swan-queen who defeated her enemies with magic songs, flying above them in her dress of swan feathers. Another name for the Aryan Great Goddess, also rendered Kauri, Cara, Kari, etc., as mother of the heavenly swan-nymphs or Apsaras. See **Swan**.

Karezza

Coitus reservatus; Tantric *maithuna;* probably the same as *drudaria* in medieval poems of courtly love: sexual intercourse without male orgasm. The object was to increase a man's spiritual powers by keeping seminal secretions in his body and also absorb the power engendered by his partner's multiple orgasms. See **Tantrism**.

Kari

Malay variation of the Triple Goddess Kali, sometimes identified with "three grandmothers under the earth" who cause floods—that is, bring about the doomsday-by-water and subsequent re-creation. Kari was also a primordial creatress, perhaps androgynous, who conceived the first human beings by means of magic flowers (the yonic lotus) and gave birth to the human race.[1] Kari's voice spoke in the thunder.

1. Hays, 352.

Karma

Hindu concept of **Fate**, perhaps derived from Kauri-Ma, i.e., Kali Ma. The usual symbol was a wheel, representing endless cycles of becoming, every force or entity in the universe begetting equal and opposite reactions to its own action, all forces maintaining balance. The Goddess's law was that any individual evolution must be worked out by a series of reincarnations through the turnings of the great wheel of time. Evil actions resulted in rebirth to a more evil life; good actions brought lives of increasing virtue and happiness. Ascetic yogis of early Buddhism instituted the idea that one could take short cuts through the cycles of time and escape altogether from the inexorable karmic wheel into a state of Nirvana or cosmic not-being, the individual dissolved in the infinite.

Karuna

Tantric term for the basic quality of mother-love, directly experienced in infancy and ramified in adulthood to embrace all forms of love: touching, tenderness, compassion, sensual enjoyment, and eroticism.

Karuna

Many centuries before Freudian psychology recognized "infantile sexuality," Tantric sages called *karuna* the essence of religion: a gut feeling of loving-kindness, as opposed to the often cruel or useless verbalizing of theological principles.[1] It was understood that *karuna* must be learned through physical and sexual contact comfort, by adults and children alike. Thus the identity of infantile, sexual, warmly loving, and religious behavior patterns was perceived long ago and is just now being rediscovered by western civilization.

The ancients well knew the experience of being in love recapitulates the mother-child relationship in its intimate physical attachment, trust, and dependence. Recognition of one particular other as a love object surely evolved from the instinctive mechanism that binds together individual mothers and offspring. It has been shown even in the animal realm that adequate sexual functioning in adulthood depends on satisfactory relations with the mother in infancy.[2]

In ancient times the Goddess's sacred whores were special teachers of *karuna,* which may have been the root of modern Italian *carogna,* "whore." Pagan Rome gave the Great Goddess the title of Mater Cara, "Mother Beloved."[3] She combined all the qualities of sexuality, motherhood, marital bliss, friendship, generosity and mercy, or *caritas,* which the Christian church later purged of its sensual implications and transformed into "charity," the giving of money to earn points in the after-life. The Greek version of *karuna* was embodied in the Charites or Graces, the naked Triple Goddess, whose quality of "grace" was also altered in the Christian context. In Babylon, the Great Mother under the name of Ishtar was also the Great Whore and the lover of all men, expressing *karuna* in her self-description, "A prostitute compassionate am I."[4]

The Christian derivative of Mari-Ishtar was **Mary Magdalene**, the sacred harlot who said harlots are "compassionate of all the race of mankind."[5] Gnostic Gospels mentioned Mary Magdalene as the original female pope, embodying the true Christian spirit kept secret from male apostles, while it passed directly from Jesus through his surpassing love for Mary.[6] Significantly, Christian iconographers often confused Mary the harlot and Mary the mother. See **Prostitution**.

Motherhood, sensual satisfactions, and kindly feelings were associated with the spirit of the Goddess under all her names, and especially with women as her earthly representatives. The integrated idea of *karuna* with all its ramifications has virtually disappeared from modern western society, where it is even difficult to explain its older meanings. Yet "those modes of perceiving the world and organizing behavior which are more distinctly 'female' can't be thought of as having sprung into being in the context of the world we now inhabit. . . . We must think in terms of patterns of behaving that developed over untold centuries, and which were keyed to survival of the human group in the primitive environment. Such a way of being would have been predicated upon powerful social bonds, 'bonds of love,' which would serve to keep otherwise more vulnerable individuals in close proximity to protectors." Every individual was to some extent in need of protectors: "It may be that we feel loneliness to be so potentially annihilating because, to the lone human—and above all, the lone human infant or child—being alone *was* death."[7]

Western culture began to lose sight of the close relationship between sensuality and loving-kindness when its theology followed St. Augustine to his conclusion that every child is born tainted with sin because of its necessarily sexual conception.[8] Nearly all manifestations of love fell under theological suspicion because nearly all involved the feminine principle in some way. (See **Romance**.) "Men's sexual drive was unacceptable to them and so it was projected onto women. It was *women* whose lust was said to be insatiable. . . . [V]iewing woman as seductress and temptress is still evident, as can be seen by the fact that prostitutes, but seldom their customers, are arraigned, and the fact that the rape victim is often seen as having 'asked for' her attack by dressing or behaving seductively."[9]

In a society that lacks any coherent articulation of the concept of *karuna,* women as mothers, lovers, and caretakers "learn early that they should be ashamed of the very set of qualities which are particularly theirs. Ironically, at the same time, they are constantly threatened by the prospect that if they are not affectionate enough and as close and loving to others as they ought to be, they will have failed in their own and others' eyes." The result is "a noxious social climate which fosters too little feeling in men and too much in women."[10]

Loss of this all-important concept may create social evils of the most pervasive sort. "Male public culture gets caught up with machines and puts emphasis on things that are not alive. The decision-making of males in power tends to happen in a vacuum with little reference to the needs of life. Paradoxically, the public leaders who are supposed to help us deny death become increasingly oblivious to life and show increasing contempt for it. We have a civilization in which males in high places imitate a male god in heaven—both think themselves above the petty concerns of simple nurture and delight in generative life."[11]

1. Avalon, 175. 2. Scarf, 178. 3. Potter & Sargent, 71.
4. Briffault 3, 169. 5. Malvern, 49. 6. Pagels, 64. 7. Scarf, 107, 575.
8. Holmes, 35. 9. Hirsch, 193. 10. Lewis, 242, 292. 11. Goldenberg, 107–8.

Kauri

var. Gauri

Pre-Vedic name of the Goddess as dispenser of **karuna**. Kauri was sometimes translated "Brilliant One," a name for the Goddess's virgin aspect: she who gave their "Power" (Shakti) to the gods.[1] Kauri was also a name for the vulva (yoni), descriptive of the **cowrie** shell accepted all over the world as a symbol of the female genital and its curative and generative properties.

1. *Larousse,* 375.

var. Kelly

Kelle

Irish-druidic priest-name, derived from pre-Christian holy harlots of the Goddess Kelle, Kale, or Kali. Irish writings described the divine harlot Mary Magdalene as a kelle.[1] The medieval term Kele-De was considered somewhat mysterious, translated "Bride of God" if a woman, "Servant of God" if a man.[2] These translations were inaccurate. Kele-De meant literally the spirit of the Goddess Kele, evidently identical with the Goddess Kali of the original Indo-European Celts.

Votaries of the Goddess Kele stressed the search for inward perfection through meditation, yogic style.[3] Her gods assumed the lotus position like eastern yogis. Her primitive Grail hero, Peredur, experienced her as the "most beautiful woman in the world," represented by the three colors of the Divine Prakriti, still known as the **Gunas**, standing for her powers of creation, preservation, and destruction.[4]

The mythical "St. Kilda" seems to have been another version of the Goddess Kele, dwelling on a remote rocky islet once identified with the western paradise of the dead. St. Kilda's Isle still exists, but the origin of its name has been forgotten. The ubiquitous Irish word *kill,* a cell or cave, once meant a shrine of Kele, whose holy men called themselves Culdees, Colidees, Cele-De, Keledio, etc. Some were described in Christian histories as monks, though they were obviously married.[5]

Kildare was a major shrine of the Goddess Kilda-Kele, or Brigit, identified with the virgin Mary after Christian monks appropriated the site. But the guardianship of the sacred fire at Kildare had long been a prerogative of priestesses; the shrine was forbidden to men.[6] Confusion of Kilda-Kele-Brigit with Mary was not too far-fetched, as they had been aspects of the same Goddess for thousands of years in India as Kali-Mari or Kel-Mari, the Pot Goddess who made human forms out of clay.[7] (See **Kali Ma**.)

1. Malvern, 117. 2. Joyce, 352. 3. de Paor, 72. 4. Goodrich, 63–66; Avalon, 328. 5. Brewster, 130–31. 6. Briffault 2, 540. 7. Briffault 1, 474.

Keres

Dog-faced Furies of the Earth Mother Demeter, giving rise to the Latin name of the same Goddess, Ceres. Like most other versions of the Great Goddess's death-hounds, the Keres visited battlefields and ate the dead to carry their souls to glory. They were another aspect of the frightening female psychopomps otherwise called Valkyries, dakinis, harpies, Nekhbet-vultures, she-wolves, or sacred bitches.[1] (See **Dog**.)

1. *Larousse*, 166.

Kerlescan, Kermario

Sacred sites in Brittany, with extensive Neolithic temple-complexes probably dedicated to the Goddess Ker, or Car, Kore, Q're, Car-Dia, Kauri, etc. Mass sacrifices were offered to her at an Egyptian site called Ker-Ma in the 3rd millenium B.C.[1] The temples of Karnak in Egypt and Carnac in Brittany were named alike, not by mere coincidence.

1. Campbell, Or.M., 61–63.

Kernos

"Heart" or "kernel"; the Eleusinian sacred pot, a uterine symbol in which seeds of new life could sprout. The *kernos* evolved into the Garden of Adonis, a pot with sprouting seeds of wheat or barley, tended by women. Ceremonies of the *kernos* were still observed up to the 20th century in Sardinia, Sicily, Calabria, and other areas.[1] In England and Scotland the feast of Harvest Home, Ingathering, Mell Supper, or (in Christian times) the Festival of Our Lady of Mercy sometimes had the name of *kirn*.[2]

1. Frazer, G.B., 396–402. 2. Brewster, 424.

Keroessa

"Horned One," a Byzantine title of Hera or Io as the Heavenly Moon-cow, symbolized by the **horns** of the crescent moon.[1] See also **Cow**.

1. Elworthy, 183.

Khenti-Amenti

Early name of Osiris, savior-god of Abydos, ca. 2000 B.C. He was also called King Zer. He entered the underworld (Amenti) and returned as an oracular talking head, to inform his worshippers about the after-life and the proper techniques of salvation. Wealthy Egyptians paid large sums to have themselves buried near his tomb, to insure their personal resurrection.[1] In the same way, Christians later insisted on being buried near the "body" of their savior in the church—hence the funerary churchyard.

1. H. Smith, 39.

Khepera

Scarabaeus or dung-beetle god, one of Egypt's sillier attempts at a male creator without a Goddess. Khepera was adopted by the solar priesthood because of a belief that all dung-beetles were male, reproducing through eggs incubated in their dung balls without the help of females.[1] The scarab's dung ball was identified with the sun, which Khepera rolled daily across the sky.

Some priests said Khepera achieved male motherhood by masturbation. "I had union with my hand, and . . . I poured seed into my own mouth, and I sent forth from myself issue in the form of . . . Shu and Tefnut." Khepera insisted he was the sole creator; "there was no other being who worked with me." Yet like all gods he was forced to depend on a mother-symbol. He said, "I laid a foundation in Maa," the Goddess as primal matter.[2]

Finally the mother-symbol re-absorbed him. Some said Khepera had no reproductive power until he received an eye of the female moon, which could give birth to plants and animals. He became just another child of the Goddess: "Tem-Khepera who produced himself on the thighs of his divine mother."[3] He was shown emerging from a yonic lotus between the Goddess's two aspects, Isis and Nephthys.[4]

1. *Book of the Dead,* 169. 2. Budge, G.E. 1, 295–97.
3. *Book of the Dead,* 119, 435. 4. d'Alviella, 29.

var. Neter-Khertet

Khert-Neter

Egyptian name for the underworld, along with Amenti and Tuat. Khert-Neter was the land of "many mansions," ruled nominally at least by the mysterious *neter,* an archaic "divinity" that seems to have meant maternal ancestors. See **Neter**.

Khnum

Egyptian potter god whose priests claimed he made the World Egg on a potting wheel and gave birth to creatures out of a womb of clay. This was a late myth, copied from older stories of the Goddess whose priestesses said she gave birth to the world, and also gave women the art of working clay, which used to be an exclusively female occupation.[1] See **Pottery**.

1. Neumann, G.M., 136.

Khon-Ma

Tibetan name of Mother Earth, the "old mother" Goddess who rules over all spirits emanating from the earth element.[1] See **Earth**.

1. Waddell, 484.

Kiakra

Vedic name of the so-called Celtic **cross**, with a wheel in its center, signifying union of male and female principles. When displayed by Vishnu, this emblem meant the phallic god's "power to penetrate heaven and earth."[1] The word was probably related to ***chakra***, the magic circle of men and women alternating in Tantric worship. Kiakra was one of the original combinations of cross and circle (wheel or egg) that gave rise to the so-called Cross of Wotan, *ankh* of Osiris, and other male-female symbols of divine union.

1. Baring-Gould, C.M.M.A., 375.

Kingship

In early Asiatic civilizations, kingship depended on the choices of women. There was no law of primogeniture. Kings were rarely succeeded by their sons. Kings of Sumeria and Assyria were of unknown fatherhood. King Esakkuruna was called "the son of Nobody."[1] Women were the kingmakers in the lands he ruled.[2]

Marriage with the earthly representative of the Goddess, in the form of the queen, was essential to the position of kingship; this was the original meaning of "holy matrimony" (**hieros gamos**). Akkadian kings apparently went on military expeditions chiefly to prove themselves worthy of the sacred marriage.[3]

Ashurbanipal said he ruled by the grace of the Goddess Ishtar; he was the king "whom her hands created." Shamash-shum-ukin of Babylon said he was chosen for kingship by the same Goddess under her title of Erua, Queen of the Gods. King Esarhaddon of Assyria said he was "beloved of Queen Ishtar, the goddess of everything, the unsparing weapon, who brings destruction to the land of the enemy."[4] Ishme-Dagan, king of Isin in 1860 B.C., said he was "he whom Inanna, queen of heaven and earth, has chosen for her beloved husband."[5] The Bronze Age king Ixion of Thessalian Lapiths married the Mother of the Gods after killing her former mate, described as his father-in-law, because each king's successor was supposed to call his defeated rival "father."[6] The queens were the same as Goddess, or Mother of God. The pharaoh Amenhotep III built a temple for his wife Ti, who was worshipped as the Goddess.[7]

The goddess-queen's choice largely depended on the candidate's sex appeal. If she tired of the king's lovemaking, he could be deposed or killed, for the queen's sexual acceptance of him determined the fertility of the land. In many early societies the old king was killed by the new king, usually called a "son" though he was no blood relative. Hence the unbroken chain of Oedipal murders that puzzled modern scholars before it was known that the words "father" and "son" were used in a different sense. A Babylonian tablet says:

> *Haharni laid claim for himself to lordship over Dunnu. Earth raised her face to her son Amakandu. "Come let me make love to you" she said to him. Amakandu took his mother (for a wife) and Haharni his father he killed; in Dunnu, which he loved, they laid him to rest. And Amakandu took over his father's lordship and Nether Sea, his sister, he took (as wife). Lahar, son of Amakandu, came and Amakandu he killed, and in Dunnu, in the (tomb) of his father he caused him to rest. Nether Sea, his mother, he took (as wife).*[8]

After this, Lahar's son killed Lahar and took his sister River as wife; he in turn was killed by his son, who married his sister Ningeshtinna, "Lady of the Vine of Heaven," a shortened name of the Goddess Nin-gest-inanna. Sovereignty passed from mother to daughter, beginning with Earth, the Goddess Dunnu herself, foundress of the line—the same as Crete's Danuna, Anatolia's Danu, Greece's Danae, the Gaulish Diana. Kings were expected to kill their predecessors or pseudo-fathers. "Son" meant "successor," and "sister" was synonymous with "wife."[9]

The length of a king's reign was often predetermined, because people thought the Goddess needed the refreshment of a new lover at stated intervals. Up to 1810 A.D., kings of Zimbabwe were ceremonially strangled to death by their wives at the moon temple every four years.[10] Kings of ancient Thebes reigned for seven years; so did kings of Canaan. Myths suggest a similar seven-year period for each king of Crete. Cretan kings were never allowed to grow old; they always died in the full bloom of youth.[11] More recently, Nigerian kings were strangled after the queen's pregnancy was established, which meant each king fulfilled his role in life by begetting one royal offspring.[12]

White explorers in Africa spoke of tribal "kings," but rarely mentioned that the real rulers of the tribes were queens. "In the oldest times there were no reigning princes in Africa, but the negroes had large kingdoms [sic] which were ruled by goddesses."[13] Ghana was governed by kings of a matrilineal succession whose divine right passed through sisters' sons. The Lovedu were ruled by a female "king" who took a series of lovers but always left the government to one of the royal princesses.[14] Angola was ruled by women until the Portuguese invasions. Ashanti was ruled by queens until the British Protectorate in 1895. Its kings were subject to the queen mother; its princesses took no husbands but kept a series of lovers. Similar customs obtained in Loango, Daura, the country of the Abrons, and other

African nations. The queen of Ubemba was called Mamfumer, "Mother of Kings," and did all the governing.[15]

The Gospels' "Candace queen of the Ethiopians" (Acts 8:27) was not a single individual but the hereditary title of queen mothers who governed the Nubian states.[16] Ethiopian kings were ritually slain from the earliest times. Regicide was still the custom of Nubian Kassites of the Upper Nile in the 1st century B.C. Diodorus said only one Ethiopian monarch escaped this kingly fate because he was educated in Greece and dared to disobey tribal law. He led a party of soldiers into the sanctuary and killed all the priests before they could kill him.[17]

The Javanese Singasari dynasty had matriarchal queens similar to Candace, typified by Queen Dedes whose statues show her as a beautiful Shakti of wisdom. She married a number of new kings after they killed her previous consorts, each apparently holding office for a seven-year period.[18]

Legends consistently associate kingship with ceremonial death. A seal from Lagash shows the Goddess taking her new king by the hand, while he raises a weapon to slay the old king, prostrate under the queen's feet.[19] King Sennacherib of Assyria was "beaten to death with statuettes of the gods" in the temple at Nineveh. Perpetrators of the deed were his "sons," one of whom succeeded him as King Esarhaddon. Upon his accession, Esarhaddon proclaimed: "I am powerful, I am omnipotent, I am a hero, I am gigantic, I am colossal!"[20]

Sometimes, kings had to proclaim they were embodiments of the Goddess herself so as to rule with the same authority as queens. Antiochus of Commagene announced that he could rule because he *was* the Goddess.[21] A king's investiture used to mean putting on female robes, so the king could be displayed as a transvestite Goddess (see **Transvestism**).

In the ancient Middle East generally, kings were not so much governing figures as ceremonial ones, primarily concerned with dedication of temples and other religious responsibilities.[22] Sometimes they were also war leaders, able to preserve their lives in time of danger by convincing the people that no one else could defeat the enemy. In such a case, a surrogate victim might be found—a real or adopted son, a prophet, a condemned criminal, or a divine animal.

A war leader of Carthage "clothed his best and most beloved son in royal robes and crucified him as a sacrifice" to secure the blessing of Baal on his military campaigns.[23] Similarly, the god-king Isra-El clothed his only-begotten son Ieud in royal robes and sacrificed him "according to the custom of the Jews," as Philo said.[24] This king became Jesus, "king" of the Jews (John 18:33). Since a king was God, any king's real or adopted son was naturally the Son of God; and Yahweh himself was embodied in the Jewish king. "In the early period of the Hebrew monarchy the central element of the annual New Year festival was the ritual enthronement of Jahveh as King."[25]

Son-killing was a habit, not only of the Jewish god-king but of many other god-kings who modified the old custom by shedding the blood of someone else in the proper season. A Swedish king named Aun managed to extend his reign for nine years by sacrificing one of his nine sons each year to ransom his own life.[26]

Another Swedish king named Gunnar Helming simply ran away. After wrestling with the god Frey, incarnate in the previous king—as biblical Jacob wrestled with "a man who was God" and later received the king-name of Isra-El—Gunnar Helming took the king's place in the bed of the high priestess (or Goddess). Evidently he pleased her, for with her help he gathered up all the gold and silver treasures of kingly office and escaped, taking her with him.[27] A similar story was told of Theseus's escape from the Minoan sacred king's fate with the help of the priestess Ariadne, the incarnate Moon-goddess, who had taken a fancy to him.[28]

Seleucus Nicator of Antioch, formerly one of Alexander's generals, became king of Syria but was forced to abdicate in favor of his "son" Antiochus, because the queen fell in love with the younger man and cast off her old spouse.[29] As late as 97 A.D., kings of Antioch were "chosen for merit" and deposed when their "merit" failed. This "merit" seemed to have to do with their sexual capacity.[30] That is, it was *virtu,* "virility," from *vir,* "man."

A common method of choosing a king was to test his virility by having him look on the Goddess's nakedness during the ritual bath that magically restored her virginity each year. Actaeon, Teiresias, and lovers of the Germanic Earth Goddess were chosen by so viewing her.[31] Gyges was chosen by the queen of Lydia, who bore the name of the Goddess Omphale, upon her display of her naked body to him; he was told to kill the incumbent king and marry her.[32] Bath-Sheba, whose name meant she was the daughter of Arabian queens, married King David after he saw her naked in her bath, and killed her previous husband, Uriah the Hittite (2 Samuel, 11). The Goddess Ishtar presented herself naked to her would-be lovers, saying, "Let us enjoy thy manly strength. Let thy hand [or, phallus] come forth and take away my virginity."[33]

Such legends point to a custom of choosing a king by the promptness of his erection upon the sight of the naked Goddess. People would follow only a leader of proven sexual potency, as shown by the transparent sexual metaphors of the 110th Psalm: "The Lord shall send the rod of thy strength out of Zion: rule thou in the midst of thine enemies. Thy people shall be willing in the day of thy power, in the beauties of holiness from the womb of the morning; thou hast the dew of thy youth." Dew was the biblical word for semen, rod meant phallus, Zion was the Holy Mount, otherwise the body of the Virgin Israel.

When the king's youth and dew deserted him, so did his people, who considered it dangerous to keep an impotent king in office. A declining birth rate or a poor growing season could bring on a king-killing. Proverbs 14 says, "In the multitude of people is the king's honor; but in the want of people is the destruction of the prince."

Northern Europeans believed in killing kings at the failure of their *gaefa* or *heill* (virility, divine force), made manifest through failure of the land's fertility. Crops went bad in the reign of Dómaldi; his subjects tried sacrificing oxen, then men, to no avail; finally they fell on the king and butchered him. As late as the 9th century A.D., King Hálfdan of Norway was slain for the sake of the crops.[34] Writings falsely attributed to St. Patrick expressed the Celtic conviction that the reign of a potent king would be distinguished by fine weather, calm seas, abundant grain, and trees laden with fruit.[35]

Ceremonial killing of kings was an ancient Latin custom, dating back to the obscure period of Roman history that is now virtually unknown, because later priesthoods destroyed its records.[36] Early Roman kings usually met death by "assassination" in the month of March, beginning the sacred year.[37] King Tatius was slain at the altar with sacred knives: a suspiciously stylized death. Julius Caesar met a similarly ritualistic death at the fatal time, the Ides of March, in the sacred inner chamber of the senate, on the very dais of the altar, in fulfillment of a prophetic announcement by his wife.

There is some doubt as to whether Caesar's wife was considered a mortal woman or an embodiment of the Goddess whom Caesar worshipped for the sake of his victories in battle: Venus Genetrix. After defeating Pompey, he built her a marble and gold temple in the Forum and had his own statue placed before her as her consort. The drama of his life and death contained elements common to other sacred kings who were consorts of the Goddess.

At the beginning of his career, Caesar dreamed of copulating with his own mother, and the seers prophesied from this that he would rule the earth (Mother). On the eve of his assassination he attended a feast or Last Supper and was asked, "What is the best kind of death?" He replied, "The kind that is least expected." On the following day he received the kind of death he had chosen. Later, during the funerary games in honor of Venus Genetrix, a comet was identified as the soul of Caesar enroute to the company of the gods.[38]

Julius Caesar's successor Augustus received his title by marrying Livia Augusta, who planned the rebuilding programs in Rome and also revitalized the worship of her Goddess, Juno Augusta. Though Livia's contributions to the glories of the Augustan Age have been belittled by Christian historians, there is no doubt that she was a full co-ruler and the real author of many of Augustus's legal reforms and municipal projects. There was a vague understanding, never fully investigated, that like the previous Caesar's wife, Livia somehow "hastened her husband's end."[39]

By Roman law of matrilineal succession, Augustus was succeeded by Tiberius, Livia's firstborn son by another man. The title of Augustus passed through the female line even up to the time of Constantine, who received his throne through a marriage with the princess Fausta.[40]

The title of Caesar (Kaiser, Czar) passed on to Germanic emperors in the Dark Ages when legends of heroes and sacred kings usually included the ritual death. Siegfried suffered a typical Caesar's death, brought on by his wife's prophetic dream. His wife personally embroidered on his robe the cross marking the spot where the slayer's spear must strike.[41]

St. Caesarius, whose name meant "king," was another fictitious saint based on the old custom of king-killing. He was the Kaiser slain as an embodiment of Apollo at Terracina. The man impersonating the king would run through lines of spectators and leap from a cliff, as the mythical saint was said to have done.[42] The festival of "St. Caesarius" was All Hallows, the pagan holy day of ancestral ghosts (see **Halloween**).

Similar deification or sainthood seems to have been the purpose of the mysterious *Liebestod* (Love-Death) of Attila the Hun, who appears in the Germanic Nibelungen saga under the name of Atli or Etzel, in the company of other heroes such as Siegfried. Attila's last bride bore the name of Germanic death-goddess, Grimhild or Kriemhild. According to Marcellinus, Grimhild killed Attila in their marriage bed on their wedding night.[43] Other sources more euphemistically said he died suddenly in the arms of his bride, smothered by "an effusion of blood." That his killing might have been deliberately planned, to make him a god, is suggested by his burial with all the trappings of a sacred Caesar: a triple coffin of sun, moon, and earth metals—gold, silver, and iron. His gravediggers were all slain so his tomb would be kept secret.[44] His funeral rites consisted of a brief period of extravagant mourning, followed by a joyful feast representing his apotheosis. His future Second Coming was expected.

Men who played the fatal role of the king in classic sacred dramas were often deified (canonized) to induce them to serve as surrogates for the real king. Like Christian martyrs, they believed that once past the "veil," they would enjoy blissful immortality, identified like the ruler with the supreme god himself. Thus, many stories show men willingly assuming the fatal role. Antinous, a favorite of the emperor Hadrian, sacrificed himself in a magical ceremony to preserve the emperor's life.[45] Each winter, the Roman festival of the Saturnalia featured a man who played the part of the Lord of Death, identified with both the emperor and the god Saturn.[46] The latter was the Heavenly Father in his underground, "slain" aspect, as Shava the Corpse stood for Father Shiva in the same attitude of death. See **Shiva**.

The Roman word for a king, *rex* or *reg,* descended from Sanskrit *raj,* as did the Celtic *rig.*[47] Not only the word but the concept of the office migrated all over the Eurasian continent, making a king's sovereignty dependent on his acceptance by the land, which was always embodied in women. The idea is still discernible in a Tartar custom: a chief's son must be carried about to every village and suckled by every nursing mother to validate his later claim to leadership.[48] The land was a king's eternal mother-bride. King James I of England referred to a tradition of immemorial antiquity when he said, "I am the husband and the whole island is my lawful wife."[49] The Welsh long believed the British isles were annexed to Rome only through a sacred marriage between the Roman emperor and the British queen, the Lily Maid Elen. Welsh bards also said their own Llefelys became king of France by marrying the queen and gaining "the crown of the kingdom along with her."[50]

Like early kings of Egypt, Babylon, Assyria, Greece, and Rome, pre-Christian British kings became stewards of the country through a **hieros gamos** with the queen. The Danish historian Saxo Grammaticus said of Hermutrude, queen of Scotland, that "whomsoever she thought worthy of her bed was at once a king, and she yielded her kingdom with herself."[51] Pictish kings were selected by the royal women from a matrilineal blood line. Early Saxon queens governed their land, and a king could govern only by marrying them.[52] That is why King Canute married the widow of his predecessor; and Ethelbald, king of the West Saxons, married his father's widow. Another Ethelbald, king of Kent, married his stepmother after his father's death.[53]

British romances show kings unable to rule unless they possessed the queen, whose name was often given as Guinevere—also rendered Cunneware, Gwenhwyfar, Jennifer, Ginevra, or Genevieve. Some early sources say there were three of her (the Triple Goddess). King Arthur married all three.[54] Repeated abductions of her by Meleagant, by Lancelot, by Melwas, by Arthur, and by Mordred signified many would-be kings' claim to sovereignty.[55] The collapse of Arthur's kingdom was intimately related to his loss of the queen.

In pagan Ireland a king's inaugural greeting announced that he was wedded to (literally, had copulated with) his land, in the person of the queen. The legendary Irish Queen Mab, famous in folklore as the Fairy Queen, chose and invested her kings and changed her lovers often.[56]

Rivalries between kings—ruler and tanist, father and son, royal "dragon" and his dragonslayer—preserve in mythology the archetypal sexual jealousy that related male power to acceptance by the female, and male powerlessness to sexual rejection. The myth of Finn and Diarmuid plainly shows the chieftains' jealous counter-claims to Queen Grianne (Ygraine), another form of Guinevere. King Arthur's death scene was prefigured by the story of Finn's three trips to bring healing waters to the wounded Diarmuid; but each time he deliberately let the water trickle through his fingers, so Diarmuid died. Finn said smugly to his younger, handsomer rival: "Well it pleases me, O Diarmuid, to see you in this plight, and it grieves me only that all the women of Erin are not now gazing on you; for your extraordinary beauty is now ugliness, and your choice form a deformity."[57]

An old English custom of "lifting" the king at Easter time suggests the former importance of women in every aspect of the king's career, including his selection, approval, love-death, and apotheosis. The king was heaved up into the air each year by a group of court ladies. Though piously called an imitation of "our Savior's resurrection," the custom was obviously older than Christianity; it was pagan, not Christian, theology that made gods and kings one and the same, both subject to the magic of women.[58]

1. *Assyr. & Bab. Lit.*, 198. 2. Bachofen, 215. 3. Hooke, S.P., 49.
4. *Assyr. & Bab. Lit.*, 91, 114, 130. 5. Gray, 59. 6. Campbell, C.M., 422.
7. Budge, D.N., 83. 8. Albright, 94. 9. Albright, 94, 128. 10. Lederer, 132.
11. Campbell, Oc.M., 59. 12. Stone, 132. 13. Briffault 3, 26–32.
14. Hays, 296, 312. 15. Hartley, 161. 16. Briffault 3, 41.
17. Campbell, P.M., 200. 18. Campbell, M.I., 216–17. 19. Campbell, Or.M., 42.
20. de Camp, A.E., 64. 21. Cumont, M.M., 95. 22. Hooke, S.P., 49.
23. de Lys, 450. 24. Frazer, G.B., 341. 25. Hooke, S.P., 110.
26. Frazer, G.B., 337. 27. Oxenstierna, 219. 28. Graves, G.M. 1, 345.
29. Gifford, 180. 30. Thomson, 312. 31. Tacitus, 729. 32. Herodotus, 5–6.
33. *Assyr. & Bab. Lit.*, 338–39. 34. Turville-Petre, 191–92. 35. Joyce 1, 57.
36. Pepper & Wilcock, 84. 37. Graves, W.G., 399. 38. Dumézil, 545–48.
39. Beard, 302. 40. J.H. Smith, C.G., 71. 41. Goodrich, 148–49.
42. Brewster, 471. 43. Gibbon 2, 294. 44. *Encyc. Brit.*, "Attila." 45. King, 55.
46. Frazer, G.B., 679. 47. Dumézil, 17. 48. Hazlitt, 112. 49. Daly, 99.
50. Mabinogion, 85, 90. 51. Frazer, G.B., 180. 52. Briffault 1, 416.
53. Hartley, 127. 54. Malory 1, xxiv. 55. *Encyc. Brit.*, "Guinevere."
56. Briffault 3, 379. 57. Campbell, C.M., 302. 58. Hazlitt, 363.

Kingu

Firstborn son of the Sumerian creatress **Tiamat**. She gave him the Tablets of Destiny and the authority to rule over all the other gods. But he was slain by Marduk, Babylon's municipal god, and his blood made the earth's "living waters."

Kismet

Turkish variant of Qis-Mah, the Arabic "Fate" bestowed by the Moon-goddess Mah. The meaning was similar to Hindu *karma,* Roman *fortuna,* Greek *dike* (destiny). See **Ma**.

Kiss

Like most forms of affectionate contact, the kiss was an adaptation of primitive mother-child behavior. The original Sanskrit word was *cusati,* "he sucks." Gestures of embrace, of clutching to the bosom, began as imitations of the nursing mother. Scholars believe kissing originated with mouth-to-mouth feeding, practiced among ancient Greeks and others as a form of love play. In Germany and Austria even up to the 19th century A.D. it was common for mothers to premasticate food and feed it to their infants by "kissing."[1] Kissing was most common in European countries, where it was supposed to create a bond among all members of a clan (hence, "kissing cousins"). It was virtually unknown in northern Asia (Japan, China, Mongolia). Amerindians and Eskimos did not kiss but rather inhaled the breath of a loved one by "rubbing noses."

1. Wickler, 191, 237–38.

Knighthood, Ceremony of

In the Middle Ages, a knight was created by a symbolic imitation of the ritual that used to make a man into a god: beheading him. Touching first one shoulder then the other with a sword implied that the sword had passed through the neck. Celtic tribes especially revered man-gods who were preserved in the form of severed heads, which were believed to give oracles. In Greece also, savior-gods like Orpheus spoke to their followers of the after-life through the mouths of their own mummified heads. Symbolic beheading also "knighted" men dedicated to the Goddess Artemis in her Spartan shrines, where the man so dedicated received a slight cut in his neck from the edge of a sword.[1]

1. Graves, G.M. 2, 79.

Knights Templar

The Order of Knights of the Temple was founded in the Holy Land in 1118 A.D. by a Burgundian knight, Hugues de Payens or Payns, that is, "Hugh of the Pagans."[1] Its organization was based on that of the Saracen fraternity of *hashishim,* "hashish-takers," whom Christians called Assassins (see **Aladdin**).[2] The Templars' first headquarters was a wing of the royal palace of Jerusalem next to the al-Aqsa mosque, revered by the Shi'ites as the central shrine of the Goddess Fatima.[3]

Western romances, inspired by Moorish Shi'ite poets, transformed this Mother-shrine into the Temple of the Holy Grail, where certain legendary knights called Templars gathered to offer their service to the Goddess, to uphold the female principle of divinity and to defend women. (See **Grail, Holy**.) These knights became more widely known as Galahad, Perceval, Lohengrin, etc.

The real Knights Templar, however, professed Christianity and assumed the duty of protecting Christian pilgrims and merchants traveling through the Holy Land. They also undertook to protect the travelers' lands, castles, and other properties back home, where

Templars from Jerusalem arrived to take charge. When pilgrims failed to return from their journeys, the property could pass into the Templars' permanent possession. As a result, like other holy orders founded on a vow of poverty, the Templars soon became very rich.

At first the Knights Templar had difficulty getting papal sanction for their military order. The papacy refused to recognize them until a vindication of their aims was written by St. Bernard, whose uncle joined the order and became a Grand Master. The Templars' original charter, signed by Pope Innocent II, granted them freedom from papal claims on their property, even from church taxation. This financial independence was to prove their downfall.

Having acquired estates and treasure houses throughout France, Spain, Portugal, and the Levant, the Templars were leading bankers and moneylenders of the 13th century. They served kings and merchant princes. Their own treasure ships plied the eastern Mediterranean coasts. Their reputation for honesty was such that even Moslems trusted them. Eventually, Pope Clement V and King Philip IV of France, whose government was nearly bankrupt, joined forces to deprive the Templars of their money and their lives.

Early in the 14th century, the Templars were accused of organized heresy, devil worship, ritual sodomy, and blasphemy. It was claimed they adored an androgynous idol named **Baphomet**, "having sometimes three faces, sometimes two, or only one, and sometimes a bare skull, which they called their savior, and believed its influence to be exerted in making them rich, and in making flowers grow and the earth germinate."[4]

The rumor-mongers claimed the Templars' secret rites involved denial of Christ, treading on the cross, forcing initiates into homosexual acts, kissing the devil's genitals, and similar charges that were to become monotonously familiar in witch persecutions. Grand Master Jacques de Molay and other dignitaries of the order were arrested and confessed under torture that they had indeed done such things, with the aim of teaching newly initiated Knights unquestioning obedience to their superiors' commands. Later, Molay and his associates publicly renounced their confessions, saying they had been forced by torture. In 1314 they proclaimed their innocence before a large crowd of people and were burned at the stake as relapsed heretics the same afternoon.[5]

The order was suppressed with great cruelty. With the church's blessing, local barons in France, Cyprus, Castile, and other areas simply murdered the Knights and took their properties. Captured Templars were forced to confess to every sort of crime, most apparently invented by their judges. It was found that each Templar confessed to one set of sins when tortured by one judge and a completely different set when tortured by a different judge.[6] Trials were transparently rigged. During the trial of Templars at Paris, the court repeatedly refused to hear depositions from no fewer than 573 witnesses for the defense.[7]

A few Templars managed to flee to England, where torture was not legal. This made it impossible to obtain what Pope Clement called "true evidence," meaning evidence extorted by torture. The pope wrote to King Edward II, demanding that the Templars be arrested and tortured. Otherwise, Edward and his court would be excommunicated as impeders of the Inquisition. As a bribe, Edward was offered a Plenary Indulgence for all his past sins. Finally he permitted papal judges to torture the Templars, changing the English law "out of reverence for the Holy See."[8] The indispensable utility of torture was thus established, and "the success of the extermination of the Templars set the patterns for the subsequent persecution of witches."[9]

Scholars have tried to determine the truth, if any, of the charges against the Templars. Most agree that the Templars "had adopted some of the mysterious tenets of the eastern Gnostics."[10] Their alleged idol Baphomet may have been the Triple Head of Wisdom pictured on the arms of the order's founder, in the form of three black Saracen heads.[11] On the other hand, no idol of Baphomet was ever found in the Templars' houses or shrines, though these were seized and sealed immediately.[12]

Templars were accused of "making a fig" at the crucifix with their hands; but this derisive sexual symbol was not a mockery by eastern standards. Orientals called it a knowledge sign, the feminine counterpart of the phallic cross; in India it was a lingam-yoni.[13] If the Templars trampled a crucifix, they may have copied the custom of Arab dervishes who ceremonially rejected a cross with the words, "You may have the Cross, but we have the meaning of the Cross."[14] As for the charge of sodomy, no monastic order was free of that. Men cut off from women were no less prone to homosexual behavior in the 13th century than in the prisons, barracks, lumber and mining camps, and boys' schools of the 20th.

1. Shah, xix. 2. MacKenzie, 117. 3. *Encyc. Brit.,* "Templars." 4. Knight, D.W.P., 186. 5. *Encyc. Brit.,* "Templars." 6. Reinach, 310. 7. J.B. Russell, 197. 8. Coulton, 245. 9. Robbins, 208. 10. Knight, D.W.P., 193. 11. Shah, xix. 12. Coulton, 243. 13. Knight, D.W.P., 150. 14. Shah, 233.

Knot

The Fate-goddess wove and tied together the threads of life, according to the ancients. Marriage is still called "tying the knot" because it used to be viewed as a binding of two life-threads by the Goddess Aphrodite, or Juno. Egyptians' Isis-Hathor bound or loosed the lives of men with Tat, the Knot of Fate, and taught the art of making magic knots. Sometimes she bore the title of the knot itself, Tait. High-ranking Egyptians were promised she would personally weave their cerements, including "bandages from the hand of Tait."[1] In Egypt, holy mysteries in general were *shetat,* "she-knots."[2]

Knot

The Knot of Fate came into Greek myth as the famous Gordian Knot severed by the sword of Alexander, in fulfillment of the prophecy that whoever could "unravel" the knot would become lord of all Asia. The original knot was the marriage tie of Phrygia's sacred king, alternately Gordius or Midas, sons and bridegrooms of the Magna Mater. The knot was fastened to the yoke of the oxcart on which Gordius entered into his kingdom, as the oracle announced in terms similar to the Bible's description of Jesus's triumphal entry into Jerusalem: "Phrygians, your new king is approaching with his bride, seated in an ox-cart!"[3]

Pagan religions related the art of knotting to "binding" and "loosing" the forces of creation and destruction, the same power claimed by the papacy for the alleged heirs of St. Peter (Matthew 16:19). (See **Peter, Saint**.) The windings of Fate and the mysteries of Nature were often symbolized by elaborate knotwork, as in the intricate knot-patterns of Scandinavian and Saracenic monuments.

Witches of Finland, Lapland, and the northern islands bound the winds in magic knots and sold them to credulous sailors, who would use the knots to try to control the winds at sea, as Odysseus's sailors did with Aeolus's bag of winds. Such magic was still common in the late 16th century.[4] Scottish witches were said to raise winds and storms by soaking a knotted rag in water and beating it on a stone to make drops fly like rain, saying:

I knok this rag upone this stane
To raise the wind in the divellis name
It sall not lye till I please againe.[5]

In 1814 Sir Walter Scott found one Bessie Millie selling "winds by the devil's help" to sailors in the form of knotted cords.[6] British witches claimed to stop nosebleeds by tying knots in red thread, the classic Fate-weaver's blood symbol.[7] Weaver's thread was also thought to cure "diseases of the groin" when knotted with a widow's name pronounced at each knot.[8] On the other hand, witches could make men impotent with a magic knot called "ligature." Predictably, men said this was a "detestable impiety" deserving the death penalty. According to a canon of the church, God's opinion was self-contradictory. Ligature could occur only with God's permission and could be cured only "with God's help."[9]

The Jews so feared magic knots that rabbinic law forbade tying any knots on the Sabbath; though one rabbi said it was legal to tie a knot that could be untied with one hand.[10] Moslems said Mohammed nearly died of a sickness prepared by Jewish witches with a "cord of knots," which was discovered in time to save his life. The knots were loosened by speaking verses of the Koran. Moslems still believe that Surah CXIII of the Koran will stop "the evil of women who are blowers on knots."[11]

Knot magic is performed by the Mexican *recibidora* (midwife) in complicated tyings of umbilical cords.[12] Greeks still remember the life-knots of the Moerae, saying of a dead man, "his thread is cut."[13] The same triple Fates govern the "Nordic Knot" of three interlocking triangles, known as the Knot of the Vala.[14] Formed of three female-genital symbols, this invoked the Great Vala (Freya) who wove the fates of men.

1. Erman, 73. 2. Budge, D.N., 189. 3. Graves, G.M. 1, 282. 4. Robbins, 201. 5. Frazer, G.B., 93–94. 6. Holmes, 207. 7. Maple, 147. 8. Agrippa, 157. 9. Robbins, 306–7. 10. Barrett, 147–48. 11. Budge, A.T., 62–67. 12. Castiglioni, 139. 13. Hyde, 198. 14. Davidson, G.M.V.A., 147.

Kobolds

Germanic earth-gnomes inhabiting caves and mines, ruled by the dwarf-king Alberich (British Oberon). Their name descended from Greek *kaballoi,* horse-riders, which formerly referred to "Amazonian" tribes led by the Goddess. She was called Oberon's spouse, Titania, queen of the Titans—who were, of course, the earth-giants worshipped by pre-Hellenic Pelasgian peoples, who resisted the Olympian gods.[1] Similarly the kobolds lived underground, and resisted the rule of new celestial deities.

1. de Givry, 315.

Koran

Mohammedan scriptures, often erroneously thought to have been written by Mohammed. Moslems don't believe this.[1] But many don't know the Koran was an enlarged, revised version of the ancient Word of the Goddess **Kore**, revered by Mohammed's tribe, the Koreshites (Children of Kore), who guarded her shrine at Mecca.

The original writing was done long before Mohammed's time by holy *imams,* a word related to Semitic *ima,* "mother."[2] Like the original *mahatmas* or "great mothers" in India, the original *imams* were probably priestesses of the old Arabian matriarchate. It was said they took the scriptures from a prototype that existed in heaven from the beginning of eternity, "Mother of the Book"—i.e., the Goddess herself, wearing the Book of Fate on her breast as Mother Tiamat wore the Tablets of Destiny. Sometimes the celestial Koran was called the Preserved Tablet.[3] There was some resemblance between this and other legendary books of divine origin, such as the Ur-text, the Book of Thoth, and the Emerald Tablet of Hermes.

As in the case of the Judeo-Christian Bible, the Koran was much rewritten to support new patriarchal laws and to obliterate the figures of the Goddess and her priestesses. See **Arabia**.

1. *Encyc. Brit.,* "Mohammed." 2. Campbell, Oc.M., 443. 3. Budge, A.T., 52.

Kore

Greek Holy Virgin, inner soul of Mother Earth (Demeter); a name so widespread, that it must have been one of the earliest designations of the World Shakti or female spirit of the universe. Variations include Ker, Car, Q're, Cara, Kher, Ceres, Core, Sanskrit Kaur or Kauri, alternate names for the Goddess Kali.

Neolithic Asia knew a mysterious Goddess Ker, or Car, ancestress of the Carians.[1] Her city in the Chersonese was Cardia, "the Goddess Car." *Kardia* became the Greek word for "heart," as *cor* became the Latin; both descended from the Goddess who was the world-heart. The same syllable is found in words for maternal blood relationships: Gaelic *cairdean,* kinship; Turkish *kardes,* maternal siblings.[2] The Goddess became *Kardia ton kosmos:* "Heart of the World."[3]

Shrines of Karnak in Egypt and Carnac in Brittany were sites of gigantic temples and funerary complexes over 5000 years ago, dedicated to Kar or Kore. France had similar shrines in similarly-named locations, Kerlescan, Kercado, Kermario.[4] The last name combined the pagan Virgin with the Goddess Mari, who was sometimes her daughter, her mother, or herself, like Kali embodied in Kel-Mari.[5] Inhabitants of Carnac, and of Carnuntum on the Danube, called themselves in Roman times the Carnutes, "people born of the Goddess Car."[6]

In Egypt's early dynastic period there was a place called Kerma (Mother Ker) in Nubia, where mass sacrifices took place. A similar name, Kara, was held in reverence by several early Egyptian rulers. Egyptians spoke of an eastern land called Kher, and called Palestine the country of Kharu.[7]

Car or Carna was known to the Romans as "a Goddess of the olden time," whose archaic worship was connected with Karneia festivals of Sparta and the classic Roman Carnival.[8] Sometimes she was Carmenta, "the Mind of Car," who invented the Roman alphabet.[9] An extremely old temple on the Caelian Hill was dedicated to her.[10] A later variation of her name was Ceres, origin of such words as cereal, corn, kernel, core, carnal, cardiac.

In the east this ancient Goddess was everywhere. Some said she was Artemis Caryatis, mother of the Caryatides of the Laconian temple of Caryae.[11] The Tyrian seaport of Caraalis (modern Cagliari) was sacred to her.[12] One of Israel's oldest shrines, the "garden" called Mount Carmel, was her place and that of her *baalim* (gods).[13]

Kore was a great power in Coptic religion, with a flourishing cult at Alexandria in the 4th century A.D. Her festival, the Koreion, was held each January 6, later assimilated to Christianity as the feast of Epiphany. Kore's festival celebrated the birth of the new year god Aeon to the Virgin, whose naked image was carried seven times around the temple, decorated with gold stars and the sign of the cross. The priests announced to the public that the Virgin had brought forth the Aeon.[14]

The Koreion passed into British tradition as the Kirn, or Feast of Ingathering, which the church later changed to the Feast of Our Lady of Mercy. Kirn was a cognate of the Greek *kern* or sacred womb-vase in which the grain god was reborn.[15] Here again the Kore or Ker was a virgin mother. The Goddess's harvest instrument, a moon-sickle, represented even the Christian version of the festival.[16]

The classic myth of Kore's abduction by Pluto was another

instance of a god's usurpation of the Goddess's power, according to Gnostic sources. "Plutonius Zeus . . . does not possess the nourishment for all mortal living creatures, for it is Kore who bears the fruit."[17] Kore's resurrection represented the seasonal return of vegetation. She was also the World Soul animating each human soul, and looking out of the eyes. Reflection in the pupil of an eye was known as the Kore or "Maiden" in the eye. To the Arabs, it was the "baby" in the eye. The Bible calls either a daughter or a soul "the apple of thine eye" (Proverbs 7:2); and of course, every apple had a Kore.

1. Graves, W.G., 373. 2. Farb, W.P., 144. 3. Cumont, A.R.R.P., 72. 4. *Encyc. Brit.*, "Carnac." 5. Briffault 1, 474. 6. J.H. Smith, D.C.P., 39. 7. Erman, 228, 278. 8. Dumézil, 386, 389. 9. Graves, G.M. 1, 280; 2, 137. 10. *Encyc. Brit.*, "Carna." 11. Graves, W.G., 372. 12. Massa, 43. 13. *Encyc. Brit.*, "Carmel." 14. Campbell, M.I., 34. 15. Neumann, G.M., 132. 16. Brewster, 424. 17. Robinson, 305.

Krake

"Crow," the Crone or Death-goddess in Anglo-Danish mythology; sometimes a Queen of Witches, identified with the man-eating *Kraken;* sometimes a beautiful virgin, spouse of kings.[1] See **Crow**.

1. Guerber, L.M.A., 274–75.

Kriemhild

var. Grimhild

Burgundian queen who married and immediately killed Attila the Hun. In her marriage bed on the wedding night, she bathed in his blood. Also known as Ildico, she may have represented the Germanic Goddess who gave immortality to sacred kings through the *Liebestod* (Love-Death). See **Kingship**.

Krishna

Popular incarnation of Shiva, born of Devaki, "the Goddess"; announced by a star and by angelic voices; presented with gifts by shepherds and wise men; hailed as Redeemer, Firstborn, Sin Bearer, Liberator, Universal Word; survivor of a Slaughter of the Innocents, probably the original one on which the myths of Sargon, Moses, Nimrod, Cronus, Mordred, and Jesus were based.[1]

Unlike the western *Christos,* however, Krishna was an erotic god. His adventures with the Gopis (Milkmaids) present a classic of religious pornography. His favorite mistress was the insatiable Radha, "Elephant-woman," another form of Maya as the consort of the elephant-god Ganesha.

Krishna met the sacred king's usual sacrificial death, hanging "between heaven and earth," and fructifying the soil with his blood. Like all Hindu gods he had many incarnations or avatars, including Rama, hero of the *Ramayana.*

1. O'Flaherty, 207.

Ramayana Indian epic poem based on ancient traditional stories, first written in Sanskrit about 300 B.C. by Valmiki.

Kris Kringle

"Christ of the Wheel," title of the Norse year-god born at the winter solstice (Christmas) as the sun god born again. His title seems to have applied to a sacrificial victim on a fiery **wheel**. Today he is identified with Santa Claus. See **Nicholas, Saint**.

Krittikas

"Cutters" or "razors," Hindu name for the seven Pleiadic sisters called Mothers of the World, who chose, judged, castrated, and killed sacred kings. Their title gave rise to Greek *kritikos,* "judge." See **Pleiades**.

Kteis

Greek word for a comb, cowrie, scallop, or vulva; symbol of the feminine Gate of Life. Pilgrims to Aphrodite's shrines carried a *kteis* in token of a state of grace (*charis*). The custom continued in the name of St. **James of Compostela**.

Kula

Hindu "flower" or "nectar," euphemism for **menstrual blood**, corresponding to biblical "flowers" (Leviticus 15). A girl "bore the Kula flower" at first menstruation, which assimilated her to the clan spirit dwelling in maternal bloodlines.[1] In Fiji, the same word described a newly circumcised adolescent boy, whose flow of genital blood was supposed to connect him to the tribe and give him fertility magic like that of the *kula* girl.[2]

1. *Mahanirvanatantra,* 88. 2. Crawley 1, 79.

Kumarbi

Hittite god who made himself pregnant by biting off the genitals of his predecessor, Father Heaven. Having no vagina, Kumarbi had to be cut open to deliver his offspring, as in the biblical myth of Adam's birth-giving. Like Kumarbi, the Chinese ancestor-god Kun managed to become pregnant but his belly had to be opened to give birth.[1] Many similar myths suggest constant male experimentation in primitive times, to find a way for envious men or gods to copy the female magic of reproduction. See **Birth-Giving, Male**.

1. Hallet, 180.

Kundalini

Tantric image of the female **serpent** coiled in the lowest *chakra* of the human body, in the pelvis. An aim of Tantric yoga was to "realize Kundalini" by certain exercises and meditations, such as *yoni-mudra:* contraction of the perineal muscles, training men to suppress ejaculation. If Kundalini could be induced to uncoil and mount through the spinal *chakras* to the brain, the adept would experience the bliss of her emergence as the "thousand-petaled lotus" from the top of the head, which meant union of the self with the infinite. Tibetan lamas still consider the most secret, sacred *mantra* the one that wakens the sleeping Kundalini and causes her to rise.[1]

1. *Bardo Thodol,* 221.

Kupala

Slavonic "Water-Mother" derived from the springtime Aphrodite who annually renewed her virginity and the vitality of nature with baptism. Worshippers of Kupala bathed themselves in rivers and purified their souls with the "dew of Kupala" gathered during the night of her festival. They would pray: "I come to thee, little water-mother, with head bowed and repentant. Forgive me, pardon me—and ye, too, ancestors and forefathers of the water." Kupala was also connected with the mystic Fire-flower of the fern, supposed to bloom exactly at midnight once a year, on the night of the Goddess's festival. It was guarded by demons, but if someone wise and bold enough to outsmart the demons managed to seize the flower, he would understand the language of trees.[1] This was a typical shaman's myth of the prize of secret knowledge, obtained at great risk, in the talismanic form of a female symbol.

1. *Larousse,* 296.

Kupparu

Sumerian-Akkadian forerunner of Yom Kippur: a Festival of Atonement when a New Year victim, usually a sheep, was symbolically loaded with the sins of the community and killed. The Jewish festival of the scapegoat was modeled on the *kupparu*. See **Atonement**.

Kurgan

Tomb of a Scythian queen or high priestess, more elaborately furnished with ceremonial robes and jewels than the tombs of males. Many *kurgans* have been discovered in southern Russia, the territory of ancient **Amazons** whose tribes were ruled by divine matriarchs.[1]

1. Wendt, 137.

Kurukulla

Dravidian "Goddess of Caverns," one of the primeval *matrikadevis* (Mother Goddesses). Prototype of such western forms as Cybele, Demeter Chthonia, Nertha, Hel, and other underground deities. She was a red Kali, seated in her cave, with four arms: two that threaten, and two that soothe.[1] See **Kali Ma**.

1. *Larousse,* 359.

Kvaen

"Queen" in Old Norse; title of a Scandinavian tribal ruler, according to Roman writers, who called northern Europe the "Land of Women" because of the authority of women in the homes and temples.[1] The *Kvaen* of *Faeroisland* (the Faroe Islands, or the western paradise) became the Lady of Ancestral Spirits, or Queen of the Ghostworld, who entered medieval romantic literature as the Fairy Queen.

1. Thomson, 244.

Kvasir

"Wisest of all men" in Scandinavian myth, a sacrificial victim created by the gods of Asgard for the sole purpose of adding his blood to the symbolic uterus, the great Triple Cauldron under the earth. Kvasir represented a masculine effort to take over the "wise blood" of women, which was thought to create children out of female internal essence. See **Cauldron; Menstrual Blood**. Once Kvasir's magic blood was in the cauldron, Odin stole it from the Earth-giantess and gave it to the male gods.[1]

1. *Larousse,* 257.

var. Kuan-Yin

Kwai-Yin

Eponymous Great Mother of China, known as the Lady Who Brings Children; embodiment of the *yin* principle, as Kali embodied the *yoni* principle in India. Kwai-Yin perpetually contemplated the Golden

Vial of her own womb, which produced the entire world while her consort Shang-te (Father Heaven) lived within her in a Chinese version of the Jewel in the Lotus. Kwai-Yin and her Japanese counterpart Kwannon represented the principle of **karuna**, Boundless Compassion.[1]

1. Campbell, M.T.L.B., 155.

Kyklos Geneseon

Greek "Wheel of Rebirth," or Wheel of Becomings, identical to the karmic wheel of Kali in India; symbol of early Greek ideas of reincarnation put forth by such philosophical sects as the Pythagoreans and Stoics.[1] See **Reincarnation; Wheel.**

1. *Bardo Thodol,* lxvii.

RED RIDING HOOD

'Tis said the story of LITTLE RED RIDING HOOD is based on the trinity of the Goddess Diana—virgin, mother, grandmother—in which the Lord of the Hunt and the She-Wolf also figure. This rendition is the cover of a book, itself cut to the outline of the familiar little girl.

To the Greeks and Romans the LION was the sun-god; but it was much earlier associated with the Goddess in Egypt and the Middle East. Here the Goddess Sekhet appears with the sun-circle around her lion-head. Black granite; Temple of the Goddess Mut at Kernak, Egypt; ca. 14th century B.C.

Actually, LEDA was the Goddess Lat who laid the Golden Egg, which made her the Nile Goose to the Egyptians. Her friend the swan was added by medieval artists to allow some erotic goings-on without actually showing another human being. Here, they are life-sized in limestone by Michael Anguier; mid-17th century.

Labarum

Alleged "monogram of Christ" seen by Constantine in his vision before the battle of the Milvian Bridge, supposed to have brought about his conversion to Christianity, afterward displayed on his *labaron* or standard. Centuries later, some accounts declared it was the sign of the cross that Constantine saw in the sky. The earliest descriptions contradict this. The labarum was not the sign of the cross; it didn't appear in the sky; it was not even a Christian symbol.

Labarum

Lactantius said the emperor was "directed in a dream to cause a heavenly sign to be marked on the shields of his soldiers . . . the letter X with a perpendicular line through it, turned over at the top." This was in fact the emblem of the soldiers' god Mithra, whose worship was most popular in the legions.[1] Christians struggling to Christianize this sign claimed it was formed of the letters *chi* and *rho,* for *Christos.* However, a series of holy signs from Philae show that the labarum evolved from the Egyptian ankh.[2]

Pious hagiographers of the Middle Ages paid no attention to Lactantius. They declared that Constantine saw in the sky "the image of a cross described in shining light; and above the image was written in letters of gold the legend: 'In this sign shalt thou conquer!'"[3] This was the orthodox Christian myth, which survived.

There were other forms of the labarum or Chrismon (Christ-monogram). Most common today is the combination of letters IHS, often with a cross surmounting the H. This is called a *signum dei,* supposed to mean *Iesus Hominum Salvator,* "Jesus, Savior of Man." Taylor said the same letters had a mystic meaning in Orphic resurrection cults, where they were not Latin but Greek letters: iota, eta, sigma.

> *IHS are Greek characters, by ignorance taken for Roman letters; and* Yes, *which is the proper reading of those letters, is none other than the very identical name of Bacchus, that is, of the Sun, of which Bacchus was one of the most distinguished personifications; and Yes, or IES, with the Latin termination US added to it, is* Jesus. *The surrounding rays of glory, as expressive of the sun's light, make the identity of Christ and Bacchus as clear as the sun.*[4]

According to another interpretation, confusing Constantine's biography with the Mithraic-Christian labarum, the letters meant *in hoc signo* (in this sign), and the cross was a magical command: "Conquer!" Yet another tradition confused the labarum with the Alpha-and-Omega cross, with the Greek letters of creation and destruction on its right and left arms.[5] This was a further adaptation of very ancient matriarchal symbols; for Omega was the letter of the destroying Moon-goddess, and Alpha was the sacred river of her blood that gave birth to all things. (See **Styx**.)

1. J. H. Smith, C.G., 48. 2. d'Alviella, 180. 3. de Voragine, 271.
4. G.R. Scott, 169. 5. Koch, 23, 26.

Labrys

The double-bladed ax wielded as a scepter by the ancient Amazonian Goddess under her various names of Gaea, Rhea, Demeter, or Artemis. It was a ceremonial weapon, though perhaps originally used as a battle-ax by Scythian female warriors. When a male priesthood took over the Goddess's shrine at Delphi, founded by Cretan "Amazons," they adopted the *labrys* also and gave themselves the title of Labryadae, "ax-bearers." The title was still used in classical times.[1] It may have been based on a traditional male scepter-bearer in the Goddess's processions in earlier centuries, perhaps even the sacred youth himself, consecrated to the **hieros gamos**, and displaying a "phallic" symbol of his imminent union and sacrifice.

In modern times the *labrys* has been adopted by lesbians as a symbol of reminiscence, in jewelry or art, of the all-female community of Lesbos and its founding mothers who worshipped only the Goddess in nature and in each other.

1. Graves, G.M. 1, 181.

Labyrinth

"House of the Double Ax," from *labrys,* the ceremonial ax used to sacrifice bulls to the Cretan Moon-goddess. The classic Labyrinth was the palace of Minos, "Moon-king," whose spirit dwelt in the sacred bull, the Minotaur or Moon-bull, a Cretan form of Apis, who was similarly sacrificed in Egypt.[1] Minos was a Lord of Death and an underworld judge, a western counterpart of the Hindu Moon-bull Yama, who functioned in the same way.[2]

Labyrinth

The mystic meaning of a labyrinthine design was a journey into the otherworld and out again, like the sacred king's cyclic journeys into death and rebirth. Early labyrinthine designs on coins, caves, tombs, etc. referred to the earth-womb. The classic labyrinth was not a maze to get lost in; it had only one path, traversing all parts of the figure. Such labyrinths were meant for ceremonial walking, "almost always connected with a cave. . . . In those cases where the ritual has been preserved, the labyrinth itself, or a drawing of it, is invariably situated at the entrance of the cave or dwelling."[3]

Labyrinth-games were played by witches for ceremonial purposes. Some descended to the nursery level, like the game Troy Town still played by children on a pattern of seven labyrinthine circles cut in sod.[4]

Some labyrinths were taken over by Christian churches and incorporated into floor patterns, gardens, or hedges. Some were insinuated into church designs by masonic brotherhoods as secret Gnostic symbols. Chartres Cathedral had a labyrinth with the six-lobed device of Aphrodite at its center. The path of the labyrinth was exactly 666 feet long, Aphrodite's sacred number.[5] (See **Hexagram**.) The central lotus once bore the names of the master builders, who perhaps hoped to achieve immortality by the Gnostic name-magic. But the names have been erased.[6]

1. Graves, G.M. 1, 255. 2. Lethaby, 156. 3. Norman, 107. 4. Lethaby, 155. 5. Pepper & Wilcock, 159. 6. Norman, 108.

Lachesis

"The Measurer," second of the three **Fates** or Moerae in Greek religion; corresponding to the second person of Kali as the Preserver. She who measured out the life-span of every creature was the same as the Goddess who preserved life up to the time when it must end, and Atropos the Cutter took over from Lachesis.

La Dama

"The Lady," worshipped by Basque witches in a sacred cave of the Amboto mountains.[1] In Semitic languages, *Dama* also meant "blood-mother."

1. Pepper & Wilcock, 150.

Ladder

Jacob's Ladder was a copy of the Egyptian "Ladder of Set," whereby a king or prophet might climb up to heaven "when he hath made use of the words of power of Ra." The *Book of the Dead* said a pharaoh might become Lord of the Ladder, assisted into heaven by a prayer that he was taught: "Homage to thee, O divine Ladder. Homage to thee, O Ladder of Set! Stand thou upright, O divine Ladder. Stand thou upright, O Ladder of Set! Stand thou upright, O Ladder of Horus, whereby Osiris appeared in heaven when he used the words of power of Ra."[1]

Book of the Dead
Common name for the collection of Egyptian funerary papyri written between 1500 and 1350 B.C., including Vignettes, Hymns, Chapters, and descriptive Rubrics. Among the best-preserved, and most typical, copies of the Theban Recension of the *Book of the Dead* is the much-studied Papyrus of Ani.

The dead king's subjects were assured that "the gods made a ladder for (him) that he might ascend to heaven on it." The king's funerary inscriptions said, "I set up a ladder to heaven among the gods."[2]

The ladder to heaven was a relic of shamanistic death-rebirth ceremonies. It was ascended by kings, prophets, sages, bodhisattvas, and other Enlightened Ones, the "angels" on the ladder in Jacob's dream (Genesis 28:12). Among central Asian tribes the "soul ladder" was a post fixed on the grave, with fourteen notches representing the "steps" or days of the moon in ascent. A similar Heavenly Ladder was made in India with wooden sword blades, which the priest must climb to perform sacramental decapitation of a white cock at the top. Chinese shamans or high priests ascended a ladder of knives, walking barefoot on the edges as an initiatory ordeal.[3]

Priest-kings in antiquity climbed soul-ladders to meet the Goddess on the occasion of their **hieros gamos** and also after death, when their souls returned to the Mother who bore them. Sometimes the ladder was perceived as a familiar passageway between the Goddess in heaven and her consort the king on earth. Kosingas of Thrace controlled his subjects by threatening to ascend his special wooden ladder to the Great Goddess Hera, to complain to her of their conduct and invoke her wrath on them.[4]

As a rule the soul-ladder passed through the seven heavens, like the *axis mundi* in Gnostic cosmology. Celsus said initiates into the Mithraic Mysteries climbed a *klimax* or ladder of seven rungs.[5] The first rung was lead for Saturn, the second tin for Venus, the third bronze for Jupiter, the fourth iron for Mercury, the fifth "monetary alloy" for Mars, the sixth silver for the moon, and the seventh gold for the sun. At the top, a platform represented the sphere of the fixed stars, the Empyrean.[6]

Aulus Cornelius Celsus
Patrician Roman scholar of the first century A.D., who wrote at length on the subjects of medicine, agriculture, philosophy, jurisprudence, and religion.

As a symbol of ecstatic initiatory ascents in the sacred Mysteries, the ladder was carried over into Judaism, Christianity, and Islam. Mohammed's vision like Jacob's was "a ladder rising from the temple in Jerusalem (pre-eminently the 'Center') to heaven, with angels to right and left; on this ladder the souls of the righteous mounted to God."[7] Both Jacob's ladder and Mohammed's were based on much earlier Egyptian representations of the pharaoh being welcomed into heaven by the gods, who helped him up the last rungs of his ascent.[8] Like the ladders of Set, Osiris, and Buddha, the ladder of the pharaoh had 14 steps, alluding to the waxing days of the lunar cycle. Another 14 steps represented the descending part of the cycle, into the underworld and back.

There were many "ladder-saints" in Syria and Persia during the 4th century A.D., when ladder-sitting or pillar-sitting became a fad among holy hermits. St. Simeon Stylites was a famous Christian pillar-saint, glorified for remaining motionless so long that his living limbs developed gangrene. One of his followers and admirers was named St. Sadoth (Persian Schiadurte). The legend of this saint said he saw a vision of Simeon at the top of heaven-reaching ladder, calling down to him, "Mount up, Sadoth; fear not! I mounted yesterday; it is your turn today." Shortly afterward, Sadoth was martyred and climbed up to heaven.[10]

The sacred *klimax* was so popular in Byzantine and Gnostic iconography that it was even canonized as a bogus saint, John Climacus. A mystical book supposed to have been written by him appeared at Mt. Sinai in the 7th century A.D., the *Ladder to Paradise.*[11] This St. John was said to have been an abbot at the Sinai monastery, but his surname suggested a Tantric adept. The *klimax* was more than a ladder; as its modern usage suggests, it was also an ascent to sexual bliss through marriage with the Goddess. Some Gnostic sects were still using the ladder as a symbol of the soul's marriage in the Middle Ages.

1. *Book of the Dead,* 301. 2. Eliade, S., 489. 3. Eliade, S., 283, 426, 442.

4. Eliade, S., 391. 5. Cumont, M.M., 144. 6. Eliade, S., 121-22. 7. Eliade, S., 489. 8. Gifford, 78. 9. Campbell, M.I., 169. 10. Brewster, 109. 11. Attwater, 199.

Lady

Anglo-Saxon *hlaf-dige,* "the Giver of Bread."[1] In ancient matriarchal societies, women had charge of food storehouses and of doling out harvests to members of their clan. "Lord" came from *hlaf-ward,* the guardian of the bread; for the husband of the tribal mother had the job of protecting food stores against vandalism or unauthorized removal.[2]

Thus the God who gave daily bread, as in the Lord's Prayer, usurped ancient feminine prerogatives. In a way his spouse remained the "giver," for the Latin *Madonna,* like "my lady," retained the same implication of My-Mother-Who-Gives.

1. Brewster, 349. 2. Funk, 257.

Laius

"The King," who preceded **Oedipus**. He was called the father of his killer, because kings who were slain by their successors were commonly given the title of father to the killer-son, to indicate that the divine spirit of the god passed from one to the other. See **Kingship**.

Lakshmi

Hindu Goddess of Sovereignty, by whose authority Indra claimed to be king of the gods. Lakshmi gave him a drink of Soma or "wise blood" from her own body, so he could produce the illusion of birth-giving and wear the many-colored veils of Maya.[1] All the oldest Indo-European gods had similar claims to sovereignty through feminine essences. See **Menstrual Blood**.

1. Rees, 75.

Lamb

Totemic symbol of Christ, based on the Jewish custom of sacrificing a firstborn lamb to Yahweh at Passover, as a substitute for the primitive sacrifices of firstborn sons that Yahweh originally demanded (Exodus 13:2).

As the Lamb of God *(agnus dei)*, Jesus was supposed to redeem the firstborn son Adam, and through him the whole human race, which must be "washed in the blood of the Lamb," as the church taught. Throughout the Middle Ages, orthodox theology insisted that

Adam was buried on Golgotha at the exact spot where Jesus's cross stood, so the blood of the Lamb-savior ran down into the earth and brought salvation to Adam's remains.[1] Eve was not buried there, however; theologians said nothing whatever about her salvation.

The medieval name of Agnus Dei was given to cakes of wax stamped with the figure of a lamb and sold by the papacy, which preserved an exclusive monopoly on their sale by a papal bull of 1471. This charm was in great demand, as it was advertised as sure protection against all kinds of destructive storms—the "acts of God" as defined by theologians.[2] In effect, the power of the Son was invoked to protect humanity against the wrath of his Father.

1. Eliade, S., 268. 2. H. Smith, 276.

Lamhussu

Dark-red royal garment of Babylonian kings, the blood-color assumed by their surrogate sacrificial victims in the Sacaea festival; the same "scarlet" (Matthew 27:28) or "purple" (Mark 15:17) color worn by Jesus as sacred king. See **Menstrual Blood**; **Purple**.

Lamia

Greek name for the Libyan serpent-goddess—Medusa, Neith, Athene, Anatha, or Buto.[1] Lamia was probably a variant of Babylonian Lamashtu, "Mother of Gods" worshipped at Der as a serpent with a woman's head. Though Lamashtu was feared as a Kali-like Destroyer, yet she was also revered as a supreme Goddess, called Daughter of Heaven and Great Lady.[2] Greek myth made her another rival of Hera.

The Latin Vulgate Bible gave "Lamia" as a translation of Hebrew Lilith, Adam's recalcitrant first wife. The Authorized Version rendered *lamia* as a screech owl. The Revised Version translated the same word as "night monster." During the Middle Ages, *lamia* became a general term for a witch. A 15th-century German professor of theology stated authoritatively that *lamiae* were "demons in the shape of old women."[3] See **Vagina Dentata**.

1. Graves, G.M. 1, 205. 2. Budge, A.T., 117. 3. Robbins, 295–96.

Lammas

Saxon *Hlaf-mass,* the Feast of Bread, was a major summertime festival of the Great Goddess of the grain: Ceres, Ops, Demeter—or Juno Augusta, ruler of the harvest month of August. Lammas was the "Eve" of this month of ripening, often classified with May Eve and Halloween as a festival of witches, because the church didn't succeed in eradicating its pagan significance.[1] Sometimes Lammas was identified with the Celtic midsummer festival of Lugnasad, celebrating the death and resurrection of Lug as grain god. Churchmen said Lammas was one of the witches' four annual Great Sabbaths, based on the four seasonal festivals of the pagan year.

1. Brewster, 349.

Lancelot

Arthurian hero based on early Celtic conceptions of the phallic lightning god—Lanceor, the Golden Lance, mated to Colombe, the Dove, a northern version of Aphrodite Columba.[1] Like the Oriental *vajra,* meaning phallus, jewel, or lightning, Lanceor descended into the Goddess's abyssal womb to fertilize the world. Thus Plutarch stated that Lightning was the impregnator of the Waters.[2]

Though anthropomorphized in romance as a knight of the Round Table, Lancelot showed signs of his pagan origin: he was still the lover of the Mother, and the reincarnation of his own elder self. He lay with **Elaine**, or Elen, or Helen, or Eileen, or Hel-Aine, the same Goddess worshipped at the Celtic lunar shrine of Cnoc Aine.[3] She was the Weaver of Fate, and she made Lancelot invincible with her gift of a vaginal fetish, a red silk sleeve. She was also Lancelot's queen mother Elaine, who christened him Galahad, the same name given his younger reincarnation or "son." The elder hero received the name Lancelot when he was initiated by the Lady of the Lake in her magic Land of Women.[4]

Like Osiris-Horus, Apollo-Heracles, Zeus-Zagreus, God-Jesus, and other versions of the ubiquitous father-son deity, Lancelot became a Lord of Death and a keeper of the paradise-castle, which appeared in the romances as Joyous Gard, the "Happy World." Lancelot stole Arthur's queen, living symbol of the land of Britain, after rescuing her from a fiery death at the stake, on a conviction of witchcraft. It was she who announced that Lancelot came from Jesus Christ in the 8th generation, while Galahad was of the 9th generation.[5] Though medieval churchmen insisted that Jesus never begot children, the heathen bards continued to popularize the contrary belief because it was the best way to account for the old concept of successive reincarnations.

Like many other figures of Celtic romance, Lancelot seems to have developed out of Oriental Tantric traditions. He resembled the Tantric saint Padma-sambhava, the Lake-Born Vajra, i.e., a phallic lightning-bolt reborn from the Water-Mother as Lady of the Lake.[6] The Dove of the Sea was his mother-bride, symbol of the Abyss (Maria). Lancelot's name, "Big Lance," might be compared to the other primitive Tantric-Celtic hero Peredur Paladrhir, "Spearman with a Long Shaft," which described the ithyphallic god in union with his Goddess.[7]

Lancelot's origin in Meidelant, "Land of Maidens," also suggests an early date and an Oriental root of his basic myth.[8] He suggested Krishna who was raised by "holy women" in a sacred grove, and grew up to be an eminently sexual god.[9] Lancelot was not a solar deity but the rival of the sun god, represented by Gawain, with whom Lancelot fought a great battle, defeating him when his strength ebbed at the end of the solar day.

1. Malory 1, 377. 2. Rawon, E.A., 151; Knight, S.L., 135. 3. Graves, W.G., 409. 4. Malory 1, 91. 5. Malory 2, 171. 6. Waddell, 258. 7. Squire, 369. 8. Rees, 293. 9. *Larousse,* 367.

Lapis Manalis

"Stone of the Underworld," or of the dead, the sacred stone covering the pit of the *manes* on Rome's Palatine Hill. At the annual festival of Mania, the Ancestral Moon-mother, the stone was removed and her children the *manes* or ghosts-of-ancestors were invited to join the feast. Sometimes the festival was called Parentalia, since the ghosts in the underworld were the same as the *di parentes* or "parent-gods" from past ages.[1]

Northern Europeans celebrated the same kind of festival at Halloween or Samhain, also a feast to which ancestral ghosts were invited.

1. *Larousse,* 213.

Lara

Short name of the Roman Goddess Acca Larentia, mother of the *lares* or household spirits. She was honored at the annual Larentalia, a festival inherited from pre-Roman times. See **Akka**.

Lat

Italian *latte,* "milk," descended from the milk-giving Goddess Lat, eponymous Mother of pre-Roman Latium. She was also Latona, or Leto, mother of the World Egg and the sun.[1] Arabs knew her as Al-Lat, the Moon, later masculinized as the Islamic Allah. She was well known in pre-dynastic Egypt. Herodotus called her "an archaic queen of the Lower Kingdom." Hers was one of Egypt's oldest oracular shrines, which the Greeks knew as Latopolis.[2] To the Egyptians, this place was Menhet, "House of the Moon."[3]

Lat was the Moon because the ancient world regarded the moon as the universal source of nourishment: a celestial Breast that produced the **Milky Way**. From the moon came water, milk, blood, plant sap, and all other life-supporting fluids.

Lat was the foundress of Latin matriarchal culture. The old word *latifundia* meant parcels of land allotted to clan matriarchs by the Goddess herself.[4] See **Matrilineal Inheritance**. The island of Malta was once Ma Lata, "Mother Lat."

In 1428, the church totally destroyed an Italian town whose residents were suspected of heretical opinions. Oddly enough, the town was named Magnalata: "Great Lat."

1. Graves, W.G., 318. 2. *Larousse*, 29. 3. Budge, G.E. 2, 50.
4. Cumont, M.M., 74.

Leda

"Lady" or "Woman," another name of the Goddess Lat, who laid the World Egg and hatched Castor and Pollux, the morning and evening stars; and Helen, the earthly incarnation of the Moon-goddess; and Clytemnestra, who was to Mycenae as Helen was to Troy. Mythographers confused Leda with Nemesis, who coupled with Zeus when he took the form of a swan-king. Thus she became the famous Goose that Laid the Golden Egg (the sun, Apollo) under her other name, Leto.[1] To the Egyptians, this was the Nile Goose, Hathor.

A favorite theme of medieval artists was the coupling of Leda with the swan-god, which permitted an erotic subject to be shown without involvement of a human male figure.

1. Graves, G.M. 1, 207.

Left Hand

Latin *sinister*, "left," came to mean diabolic, witchlike; *dexter*, "right," yielded dextrous, meaning skilful or clever. Ambidextrous is literally "two right hands." Right-ness is associated with righteousness, rectitude, rectification, good right hand, adroitness (from French *à droite*, "to the right"). Left is *gauche*, clumsy or stupid, with its English derivatives gawk, gawky. Italian *mancino*, "left," means deceitful. German *link*, "left," means wrong, backward, perverse. Anglo-Saxon *lyft* meant weak or worthless. The evil eye was said to be the left one.[1] According to the Brahmans, left-handedness goes against the grain of decency.[2] Jewish mystics said God's left hand is the hand that destroys. Satanael or Sammael the death-god personifies God's left side.[3] The Gospel of Nicodemus said the thief crucified at Jesus's right hand received the kingdom of heaven; the thief crucified at his left hand was damned.[4] Superstitious folk still believe it's lucky to see the new moon over one's right shoulder but disastrous to see it over the left.[5]

Sagan asks, "In the worldwide associations of the words 'right' and 'left' there is evidence of a rancorous conflict early in the history of mankind. What could arouse such powerful emotions?"[6]

What else, indeed, but patriarchs' battle of the sexes?

All myths agree that the right side was male, the left side female. Wherever the deity was an androgyne, this arrangement was followed. Typical was the Hindu bisexual deity Bhava, "Existence," with a woman's left side and a man's right, signifying "man together with Nature" and showing that all Existence is made up of two sexes. Androgynous idols of Kali and Shiva showed the same arrangement.[7]

Greek Pelopids tattooed themselves with a female symbol on the left shoulder in honor of maternal ancestry, a male symbol on the right shoulder for paternal ancestors. Egyptians said the left hand represented the Goddess Maat, the right hand her consort Thoth. Babylonians prayed: "Let my goddess stand at my left hand! Let my god stand at my right hand!"[8]

Pelopids Tribes claiming descent from Pelops, a legendary sacred king sacrificed, partly devoured, and resurrected by Mother Demeter; inhabitants of the Peloponnese.

The Jews said the seed of female children emanated from a father's left testicle, while that of male children emanated from his right testicle.[9] This ancient belief persisted among Christians even up to the present century. In 1891 a book entitled *Essentials of Conception* said a man could "progenate a male or female child at will, by putting an elastic band around the testicle not required. Semen from the right testicle progenates male, whilst that from the left female children."[10]

According to some rabbinical traditions, the left hand of God was female, which may have been why patriarchs thought it necessary not to let "thy left hand know what thy right hand doeth" (Matthew 6:3). Rabbis taught that "A wise man's heart is at his right hand: but a fool's heart is at his left" (Ecclesiastes 10:2). Matriarchal societies believed the menstrual blood that made a child in a mother's womb was her heart's blood, engendered on the left side of the body; but the patriarchs displaced the heart to the right.

In a sense, modern research has found some physical basis for belief in the left/female, right/male imagery of the ancients. The left hemisphere of the brain, which controls the right side of the body, is said to evolve logical thought sequences and suppress sensory input that might interfere with problem solving. The right hemisphere, governing the left side of the body, is called the intuitive, creative, or imaginative part of the brain. It is supposed to generate the more sensitive, broader awareness and response made manifest in feelings, empathy, fantasy, art, visual imagery, and inspiration: many of its qualities were belittled by patriarchal thinkers as incomprehensible "women's intuition."[11] This is an over-simplification, since both hemispheres work together in both sexes, and their functions are not neatly divisible. One half of a brain could hardly exist without the other.

India prized intuitive thinking somewhat more than logical thinking, and recognized two Ways to religious revelation: the male, solar, ascetic "way to the gods" known as the Right-Hand Path; and the female, lunar, sensual way of the Goddess, known as Vama Marg or the Left-Hand Path—literally, the Female Way.[12] Tantric yogis recognized the left side of the body as the seat of every man's "female soul" or *shakti*, with whom he would be united after death. In token of reverence for the indwelling female soul, the yogis always entered a place of worship with the left foot forward.[13]

Europe's pagan customs, embodied in "witchcraft," maintained the virtues of left-sidedness against prevailing patriarchal opinion. Witches said itching or burning of the left ear betokened joy in the near future, while the same sensations of the right ear meant sorrow.[14] Witches' dances circled to the left, counterclockwise, moonwise, or "widdershins"—as folk dances still do—following the retrograde motion of the moon instead of the clockwise motion of the sun. The medieval church said dancing, turning, or circumambulating in this direction was heresy. During the centuries of persecution, countless people were burned alive for dancing widdershins, especially if they turned their backs to the center of the circle. Back-to-back dancing was evidently considered indecent, though widely practiced.[15]

The pagans were firmly in favor of the widdershins direction. Pre-Christian kings in Scandinavia were expected to lay magic circles of protection around their cities by circumambulating them widdershins. Irish druidic law insisted on the same counterclockwise movement around the holy omphalos at Tara, shrine of Mother Earth: "Thou shalt not go righthandwise around Tara."[16] Tantric influence also directed Middle-Eastern Sufis to circumambulate their shrines in the widdershins direction.[17]

The Christians reversed the direction of all turning charms, such as the divinatory magic of St. Andrew's Well on the isle of Lewis. Sick pilgrims were told to float a wooden bowl on the waters. If the bowl turned sunwise, the patient understood that he would get well. If it turned moonwise, he would die.[18]

Witches were said to make the sign of the cross with their left hands: another proof of heresy. The left-handed cross in graphic symbolism was the Oriental moon-swastika, with arms pointing counterclockwise, an emblem of Kali, as opposed to the sun-swastika, which represented male gods.[19] See **Swastika**.

The Scottish rite of handfasting was derived from a pagan-Oriental marriage custom, incorporating the figure-eight Infinity sign that represented union of Kali and Shiva among Tantric yogis and yoginis. The couple joined right hands to unite their "male" souls, then joined left hands to unite their "female" souls, forming the Infinity sign with their arms thus crossed.[20] The sign itself is still used in modern mathematics, but handshakes are now exclusively—and significantly—right-handed.

Another Tantric sign of male-and-female unity was pressing the palms of the hands together, fingers upward: this meant two bodies joined as one. The gesture is still one of greeting and blessing among Indians. During the 12th and 13th centuries when Hindu religious customs were penetrating Europe, the gesture was adopted by Catharan heretics as the *manibus junctis* (hand-joining), which the orthodox church later took to itself.[21] Now it is the standard gesture of prayer, both east and west.

Classic traditions added still more support to the male-female images of rightness and leftness. While giving birth to the sun and moon (Apollo and Artemis), the Goddess Leto grasped a male palm tree with her right hand and a female olive tree with her left.[22] When giving birth to Zeus, the Goddess Rhea placed her hands on the earth to cause five female spirits to spring up from her left handprint, and five male spirits from her right handprint (see **Fingers**). The matriarchal magic of Medusa was mythically symbolized: blood from her left side could give rebirth to the dead; blood from her right side instantly destroyed a human body.[23] The Romans still believed in the benevolence of the left side. Plutarch said it was a good omen to see an augury, such as a flying eagle, on one's left side; an evil omen to see it on the right.[24]

Men placed wedding rings on women's left hands to fetter their magic power and hold their hearts. From the most ancient times, men believed that a certain vessel or vein ran directly from a woman's heart to the fourth finger of her left hand. This was a remarkably durable belief; Lemnius mentioned it as late as 1658.[25]

According to heraldic symbolism, the bend sinister, a stripe slanting to the left, signified bastardy or lack of a father. A warrior bearing the bend sinister on his shield was therefore his mother's son only, after the fashion of the heathen matrilineal clan. Fatherlessness was not considered a mark of dishonor until Christianity had established the patriarchal family system throughout Europe.

Related to the symbolism of the left and right hands was the symbolism of east and west. Rome established the four cardinal points by a north-south line and an east-west line, *decumanus.* The eastern half was *familiaris,* the area of good omens and of the sun. The western half was *hostilis,* the area of evil omens and of the moon.[26] Since it was the custom to face the "still point" of the heavens—the north celestial pole—for orientation of buildings and towns, the left hand was to the west, the right hand to the east, as maps are still made. To the west lay the Moon-land, home of the ancestral dead, called Westerners by the Chinese, Greeks, Celts, and Egyptians.[27] As long ago as the Stone Age, the dead were buried facing west. "To go west" has always been a synonym for "to die." Death meant a journey to the western gate of the Mother. Aztecs called the west "the place of women," where human beings once crawled out of the genital hole of Mother Earth, to which all the dead must return.[28]

On the other hand—literally—the east was the place of male solar gods greeted every morning with the formula, "He is risen." The eastern sun-temple of Borsippa was known as the Temple of the Right Hand.[29] The main avenue of Alexandria ran from the Gate of the Sun on the east to the Gate of the Moon on the west.[30] The eastern *abt* of an Egyptian temple was the birthplace of the sun god Ra; the west was the place of his dying.[31] This was probably the origin of the eastern *apse* in a Christian church, which like the Egyptian *abt* was "oriented" toward the east, birthplace of the sun.

Borsippa Ancient sister city of Babylon, located about 15 miles to the southwest; now known as Birs Nimrud. Borsippa flourished greatly in the 7th and 6th centuries B.C. It was destroyed by Xerxes I in the 5th, and partly restored by Antiochus I in the 3rd.

Bruce Papyrus Second-century Gnostic manuscript discovered at Nag Hammadi in Upper Egypt during the 1940s.

Archons Gnostic term for good or evil angels, especially as world-creating or world-governing spirits who controlled the phenomena of the stars, heavens, weather, etc.

John Huss (ca. 1370–1415) Bohemian religious reformer, founder of the Hussite sect which renounced papal indulgences and the doctrine of **transubstantiation**. Huss was promised a safe-conduct to defend his views before a church council, but the promise was broken; he was declared heretic, arrested, and burned.

Christians taught that the west was the natural home of "demons." The Bruce Papyrus depicted Jesus revealing to his disciples the magic words that would make evil Archons "flee away to the West, to the Left Hand."[32] When the Greek church baptized converts, "they first turned their faces to the west, and so renounced the devil, and then to the east, and made their covenant with Christ."[33] When John Huss was burned for heresy at Constance in 1415, he was at first bound to the stake facing east; but the error was noticed in time, and he was shifted to face west, the direction "fitting for a heretic."[34]

Superstition still maintains the male-and-female symbolism of east and west. The bad luck caused by spilling salt (symbol of blood) can be averted by throwing the salt over the left shoulder, toward the west, relegating the bad luck to the devils.[35]

Gypsies believed they could keep a horse from straying by marking the right fore hoof with a male cross, the left fore hoof with a female ring.[36] The idea was that the sexual symbols would attract one another and tangle the horse's feet like a hobble.

It is still customary for rulers to hold the "phallic" scepter in the right hand, the "yonic" orb in the left. This usage descended from the king's symbolic display of the **hieros gamos** between himself and the Goddess of his land. The original meaning was that the ruler united male and female principles; but the meaning was lost, and only the symbols remained.

1. Elworthy, 138. 2. O'Flaherty, 147. 3. Cavendish, P.E., 259. 4. de Voragine, 208. 5. Hazlitt, 417. 6. Sagan, 185. 7. O'Flaherty, 148; Knight, S.L., 33; *Larousse,* 371. 8. *Assyr. & Bab. Lit.,* 420. 9. G.R. Scott, 142–43. 10. Pearsall, W.B., 240. 11. Sheehy, 290–91. 12. Campbell, Or.M., 202–3; Avalon, 164. 13. *Mahanirvanatantra,* 72. 14. de Lys, 162. 15. Robbins, 209, 421. 16. Pepper & Wilcock, 258. 17. Shah, 382. 18. Hazlitt, 8. 19. de Lys, 452–53. 20. de Lys, 168–69. 21. J.B. Russell, 222. 22. Elworthy, 100. 23. Graves, G.M. 1, 175, 185. 24. Scot, 163. 25. Hazlitt, 2. 26. Lindsay, O.A., 19. 27. H. Smith, 39. 28. Neumann, G.M., 184. 29. d'Alviella, 27. 30. de Camp, A.E., 130. 31. Budge, E.L., 94. 32. Legge 2, 195. 33. Hazlitt, 66. 34. Lea, 248. 35. Budge, A.T., 323. 36. Bowness, 41.

Legba

Voodoo god similar to the Trickster or Hermes of classical myth. Though an ithyphallic god of lust, Legba was also androgynous. In ceremonial dances his part was taken by a girl wearing an erect wooden phallus. He was considered an embodiment of the Word or *logos* of the Goddess Fa, "Fate."[1]

Hays, 341.

Lemnos

Island shrine of the Goddess Myrine, served by an ancient female-dominant society appearing in Hellenic myth as a race of **Amazons** who massacred all their husbands. Afterward, they kept up their numbers by inviting passing mariners to impregnate them. Jason and the Argonauts called at Lemnos for this purpose.[1] As a center of pre-Hellenic religion, Lemnos was sacred to such deities as Aphrodite and **Hephaestus,** to whom Father Zeus was distinctly hostile.

1. Graves, G.M. 2, 223.

Lemures

"Ghosts," Roman term for ancestral spirits who rose from their graves to attend the annual festival of the Lemuria; a synonym for *lares, larvae,* or *manes.*[1] The mythic lost continent "Lemuria" literally meant a ghostworld.

1. *Larousse,* 213.

Lent

From Saxon *Lenet-monath,* the lunar month of "lengthening" (of days). Fasting and abstention of the Lenten period was copied from the Roman Matronalia or Feast of Mothers, celebrated during the Kalends of March and forbidden to men.[1] The women performed their rites in the sacred grove between the Aventine and Palatine hills, where Sabine women used to sacrifice their harvest-god Consus each year.[2] After the Matronalia, Roman women observed a period of chastity and fasting until the festival of Ceres in April. This custom, originally intended to insure the fertility and vitality of the crops, was copied by the Christian church and converted into the fast of Lent.[3]

1. *Larousse,* 204. 2. Bachofen, 36. 3. Gaster, 645.

Lesbians

Amazons took the isle of Lesbos and made it one of their "isles of women," a sacred colony dedicated to worship of the female principle, as later Christian monasteries were dedicated to worship of the male.[1] In the 6th century B.C., Lesbos was ruled by a group of women devoted to the service of Aphrodite and Artemis, and the practice of *charis,* "grace," meaning music, art, dancing, poetry, philosophy, and romantic "Lesbian" love.

The most famous colonist was the poet Sappho, whose contemporaries said she was even greater than Homer. Her work didn't survive the book-burnings of the early Christian era. She was one of the first classic authors to be attacked because of her homosexual orientation and her devotion to the Goddess. By the 8th century A.D., nothing survived of her large corpus of poetry except a few fragments quoted by other authors.[2]

Female homosexuality was generally regarded as a virtually

unthinkable threat in patriarchal societies. Christian Europe regarded lesbianism as "a crime without a name," and sometimes burned lesbians alive without trial. To this day, female homosexuals are credited with fearful powers; Frank Caprio said "Lesbianism is capable of influencing the stability of our social structure."[3] Any phallocentric society would naturally so regard women indifferent to a phallus.

1. *Larousse,* 122. 2. *Encyc. Brit.,* "Sappho." 3. Klaich, 89.

Lethe

"Forgetfulness," the Water of Oblivion in the Greek underworld, a spring giving rise to the River Lethe. According to Orphics and other mystery-cultists, the spring of Lethe under a white cypress was the first thing to be seen in the underworld by a newly dead soul; and the soul would be made very thirsty, and would be tempted to drink. Part of the mystery-cultists' training was to learn endurance of thirst, for a draught of Lethe would wipe out their memories of their previous incarnations and leave them no wiser than the rest of humanity, always born again without remembering previous births. The enlightened one should seek instead the spring of Memory (Mnemosyne). "Thou shalt find to the left of the house of Hades a spring, and by the side thereof standing a white cypress. To this spring approach not near. But thou shalt find another, from the lake of Memory cold water flowing forth, and there are guardians before it."[1]

The location of Lethe in the underworld, in classical and Gnostic imagery, derived from the ancient oracular cave of the Earth-deities (Chthonioi) at Lebadeia, where one made elaborate preparations to go down into the dark pit and learn his fate through "things seen" or "things heard." Among the preparations, "he has to drink the water called Lethe, in order to achieve forgetfulness of all that he has hitherto thought of; and on top of it another water, the water of Mnemosyne, which gives him remembrance of what he sees when he has gone down."[2]

Classical writers made Lethe one of the principal rivers of the underworld, along with Acheron, Cocytus, Phlegethon, and Styx.[3]

1. Guthrie, 229. 2. Guthrie, 225. 3. *Larousse,* 165.

Leto

Mother of the Sun and Moon (Apollo and Artemis) in Greek myth; a Greek form of the eastern fertility-goddess **Lat**, who was called Latona or Queen Lat in pre-Roman Latium, her Italian territory.[1] Her Greek myth was confused; she was the mother of the moon (Artemis), and yet also the daughter of the moon (Phoebe). She was further misrepresented as a mortal "virgin mother" impregnated by the Heavenly Father, Zeus.

1. Graves, G.M. 1, 57.

Leukippe

"White Mare," Cretan horse-goddess probably descended from the Hindus' Saranyu, whom the British called Epona. In Mycenae, Mare-headed **Demeter** was both Leukippe the white mare of Life, and Melanippe the black mare of Death. Her priests were castrated and wore female dress to imitate priestesses.[1] See **Horse**.

1. Gaster, 316; Graves, W.G., 425.

Leviathan

"Wriggly One," Hebrew title of the Great Serpent Nehushtan, whose worship was established by Moses (2 Kings 18:4).[1] The priestly name Levi meant a son of Leviathan, who was once another form of Yahweh even though later centuries converted him into a demon. The bishop's miter evolved from the headdress of Levite priests.[2] See **Serpent**.

1. Gaster, 576. 2. Briffault 3, 108.

Liber

Rome's Father Bacchus was also Liber Pater, consort of the Goddess Libera, or Libra. Their divine marriage took place at the Liberalia on March 17, later Christianized as St. Patrick's Day, since **Patrick** or Patricius was a Celtic form of the same god.[1]

His Greek form was Dionysus Liber, annually reborn as the Divine Child laid in a winnowing-basket or manger. This ceremony was adopted into the legend of the infant Christ, called a son of the god once worshipped as Liber in Jerusalem.[2] When the Roman temple of the Great Mother was converted into the church of Santa Maria Maggiore, the manger ceremony remained an essential part of its Christmas observances. Usener claimed the church was founded by Pope Liberius, possibly a confusion with the name of the pagan god.[3] (See **Dionysus**.)

Votaries of Liber were "libertines." The modern meaning still evokes their orgiastic rites. "Liberty" was also derived from their cult feast of the Liberalia, when, as part of the festivity, slaves were temporarily free and permitted to behave as if they were masters. This practice passed into medieval Carnival customs.

1. *Larousse,* 209. 2. Tacitus, 660. 3. Miles, 107.

Libra

Astrological Lady of the Scales, from the Goddess Libera worshipped in Carthage as Astroarche, Queen of the Stars. Like the Egyptian **Maat**, she represented the balancing process of karmic law. Her figure-eight glyph of "equilibrium" (now the mathematical symbol of infinity) signified action and reaction under the rule of Fate.[1]

In astrology, Libra is still "ruled by Venus," because she was identified with the Roman Venus-Aphrodite of the *ius naturale*—natural law, matriarchal justice.[2] The blindfold on today's Goddess of Justice was unknown in antiquity. She not only held the scales of every man's fate; she also had the All-Seeing Eye. See **Tanit**.

1. *Larousse*, 84. 2. Cavendish, T., 104–5; Bachofen, 192.

Liebestod

"Love-Death," the killing of a Germanic sacred king when he married the Goddess, or a Valkyrie who would bear him to heaven. Like the Oriental sage, the Nordic hero was united in death with his female soul (Shakti), a Heavenly Vala. Most pagan thinkers said the best death was mystically connected with love. Ovid wrote that he wanted to die "in the act of coming to Venus."[1] Heavenly "bliss" was often confused with orgasm.

1. Cavendish, P.E., 51.

Lif

"Life," the new Eve of the next cycle of existence, according to Norse mythology, after destruction of the present universe. Her name was essentially the same as Eve's title, "Mother of All Living" (Genesis 3:20). Lif's consort was a subordinate male, Lifthrasir, "Desirer-of-Life."[1] The names indicated a belief that Lif would be the true parent of the new creation, whereas her mate's only purpose was to fertilize her, as in the oldest known versions of the Adam and Eve myth.

1. H.R.E. Davidson, G.M.V.A., 234.

Lightning

Heavenly-father gods of most Indo-European religions impregnated Mother Earth, or the sea-womb, with phallic lightning bolts. India's Dyaus Pitar, "Father Heaven," wielded the lightning in token of his union with the Goddess; he foreshadowed Greece's Zeus Pater and Rome's Jupiter, who did the same. Dumuzi, Dionysus, Leviathan, and many other versions of the "fiery serpent" including Lucifer and Satan figures, were identified with the descending phallus of Heaven, whom Jesus claimed to have seen "fall as lightning" (Luke 10:18).

The lightning god's "fall" was not originally a defeat in a celestial battle but rather a descent into the womb of the Abyss to fertilize the world. Plutarch said lightning was the impregnator of the Great Goddess of the Waters (Maria), and their union was "the cause of vital heat."[1]

Lightning was the cosmic phallus of the Vedic fire god Agni, mated to Kali as the Primordial Abyss. She was said to "quench a blazing lingam in her yoni."[2] Through ignorance of its sexual meaning, Christians inadvertently preserved the same image of Maria-the-Waters rendered fertile by male fire from heaven. The baptismal font of a Christian church was likened to the womb of Mary, as the ancient temples' water-cauldrons called "seas" or "abysses" were likened to the Goddess's womb (see **Cauldron**). At the consecration of a Christian font, the burning paschal candle was quenched in the water like Agni's lingam, with the words, "May a heavenly offspring, conceived in holiness and reborn into a new creation, come forth from the stainless womb of this divine font." Mary was said to be *igne sacro inflammata:* fecundated by the sacred fire.[3]

This universal notion of the male-female connotations of fire and water was based on the Tantric view of the water element as Shakti, the primal liquid power that produced "all fiery elements"—i.e., male deities and their symbols, the sun, fire, lightning.[4] The Jewel in the Lotus, primary Tantric image of maleness enclosed by femaleness, often used for the male element the word *vajra,* meaning jewel, phallus, and lightning.[5]

The same combination of meanings occurred in Latin *Gemma Cerauniae,* lightning—literally the Jewel of Ceraunus, the lightning god.[6] Sometimes the "jewel" was a phallic scepter like the Tantric *dorje,* "lightning-bolt" or "thunderbolt," also a phallus. The same word described a phallic scepter made by Hephaestus, forger of lightning bolts for Father Zeus; it was called *doru,* a spear.[7] The Indian city of Darjeeling was named for the *dorje-lingam,* "lightning-phallus."[8]

A lightning-phallus or lightning-scepter was the emblem of sovereignty for Greek and Roman heavenly fathers and for their son-reincarnations also. Dionysus, born of the Earth- or Moon-mother, became "king of all the gods of the world" when he sat on his father's throne and wielded the lightning-scepter.[9] His father Zeus descended into the "bridal chambers" of the Mother Goddesses on the Acropolis at Thebes in the form of lightning; therefore, these shrines were taboo and were called Places of Coming.[10] The sky-god also "came" as lightning to fertilize the maternal rock, Petra Genetrix, that gave birth to the Persian savior Mithra.[11]

A descent of lightning marked many miraculous impregnations and virgin births throughout mythology, possibly beginning with the Assyro-Babylonian Zeus, called Zu the Storm Bird. Zu was a model for the winged lightning-spirits the Bible called *seraphim,* or fiery flying serpents. As a Son of God, Zu coveted the Tablets of the Law, wishing to rule the oracles and make himself king of heaven.[12] He was punished for his hubris in the Babylonian myth, but as the Olympian Zeus he successfully defeated older heaven-gods like Uranus, Cronus, Prometheus, and Hephaestus, and successfully defended his throne against other challengers.

Salmoneus of Elis Legendary sacred king bearing the Greek version of the same name as Shalmaneser or Solomon. Elis was an ancient city and state in the northwest corner of the Peloponnese; now called Ilia.

King Salmoneus of Elis dared impersonate Zeus the Lightning, seeking to become the beloved of the Goddess Salma (Salome) and control the weather. He dragged brazen cauldrons behind his chariot to imitate thunder, and threw torches into the air to encourage lightning. Zeus destroyed him for his hubris.[13] So the later mythographers said; in fact the sacred kings everywhere were made to become God, or the Son of God, by such magical means before they were sacrificed to the same God.

A Dipylon amphora from the bank of the Ilissos shows a king wielding the scepter from which issues a lightning bolt. The figure's erect penis also shoots a bolt of lightning toward the Delta-symbol of the Goddess on an altar.[14] This was a typical image of the god-king, from northern Europe to central Asia where chieftains impersonated the lightning god to mate with the divine swan-Valkyrie Kara, a variant of Kali or Kauri.[15] Among the Celts, the Goddess's bird form was Colombe, the Dove, bride of Lanceor the "Golden Lance," a lightning god who evolved into **Lancelot**.[16]

A phallic lightning bolt was the original symbol of the Ugaritic sage Atyn, Eytan, or Etana, whom the Bible calls Ethan, a king almost as wise as Solomon (1 Kings 4:31). He tried to ascend to Mother Ishtar in heaven and was cast down like a bolt of lightning by the jealous sun god Shamash. His Hebrew name meant either "perpetual stream" or "perpetually firm," both hopeful epithets of the phallic god. Ethan, or Eytan, was the answer to the riddle in Proverbs 30: "Who hath ascended up into heaven, and come down?"[17] His totem was the eagle, symbol of lightning, fire, and the sun. He ascended spread-eagled on the bird's back in the form of a cross, his fingers "upon the feathers of the wings" like the Greeks' Ganymede and the Hindus' Garuda.[18]

Quarrels over possession of the lightning-phallus underlay many stories about god-kings and their rivals. Like God casting down Lucifer "as lightning," Zeus cast down the older lightning-deity Hephaestus because he defended his Great Mother Hera against a patriarchal attack. As a god of the conquered matriarchate, Hephaestus was imprisoned in a fire-mountain and set to forging lightning bolts for the new ruler, Zeus. As the archaic Cretan Velchanos, Etruscan Vulcan, Hephaestus was one of the Amazonian smith gods who opposed the Olympian patriarchy.[19]

The God of Moses copied the ways of other patriarchal deities and claimed the ability to "cast forth lightning" (Psalms 144:6). In a literal anthropomorphization this meant he could cast forth the lightning god **Lucifer** from heaven. Medieval theologians were never quite sure who threw the lightning bolts—God, or his rival Lucifer, who retained the title of Prince of the Power of the Air.

German bishops said in 1783 that despite allegedly infallible protections such as processions, hymns, and holy relics, the devil's lightning damaged 400 church towers and killed 120 bell-ringers within 33 years.[20] It was difficult to explain why God so often threw lightning at his own churches; or, if the destructive bolts were thrown by the devil, why God didn't protect his churches better. Effective measures had to wait until the arch-infidel Benjamin Franklin invented the lightning rod. Even then, many churchmen refused to use the new invention on the ground that it was one of the devil's artifacts.

With the decline of the devil, the damage inflicted by lightning has been once more imputed to God. Modern legal documents still describe lightning-strikes as "acts of God."

1. Knight, S.L., 135. 2. Rawson, E.A., 57. 3. Neumann, G.M., 311–12. 4. *Mahanirvanatantra,* cxviii. 5. Rawson, E.A., 151. 6. Leland, 250. 7. Gelling & Davidson, 33. 8. Waddell, 258. 9. Frazer, G.B., 451. 10. J.E. Harrison, 91. 11. de Riencourt, 135. 12. *Assyr. & Bab. Lit.,* 304. 13. Graves, G.M. 1, 221; 2, 408. 14. J.E. Harrison, 77. 15. Baring-Gould, C.M.M.A., 568. 16. Malory 1, 377. 17. Albright, 250. 18. Campbell, Or.M., 134. 19. Graves, G.M. 1, 87.; W.G., 361. 20. White 1, 367.

Lilith

var. Lilit

Adam's first wife was a relic of an early rabbinical attempt to assimilate the Sumero-Babylonian Goddess Belit-ili, or Belili, to Jewish mythology. To the Canaanites, Lilith was Baalat, the "Divine Lady." On a tablet from Ur, ca. 2000 B.C., she was addressed as Lillake.[1]

Hebraic tradition said Adam married Lilith because he grew tired of coupling with beasts, a common custom of Middle-Eastern herdsmen, though the Old Testament declared it a sin (Deuteronomy 27:21). Adam tried to force Lilith to lie beneath him in the "missionary position" favored by male-dominant societies. Moslems were so insistent on the male-superior sexual position that they said, "Accursed be the man who maketh woman heaven and himself earth."[2] Catholic authorities said any sexual position other than the male-superior one is sinful.[3] But Lilith was neither a Moslem nor a Catholic. She sneered at Adam's sexual crudity, cursed him, and flew away to make her home by the Red Sea.

God sent angels to fetch Lilith back, but she cursed them too, ignored God's command, and spent her time coupling with "demons" (whose lovemaking evidently pleased her better) and giving birth to a hundred children every day. So God had to produce Eve as Lilith's more docile replacement.

Lilith's fecundity and sexual preferences show that she was a Great Mother of settled agricultural tribes, who resisted the invasions of nomadic herdsmen, represented by Adam. Early Hebrews disliked the Great Mother who drank the blood of Abel the herdsman, after his slaying by the elder god of agriculture and smithcraft, Cain (Genesis 4:11). Lilith's Red Sea was another version of Kali Ma's Ocean of

Blood, which gave birth to all things but needed periodic sacrificial replenishment.

There may have been a connection between Lilith and the Etruscan divinity Leinth, who had no face and who waited at the gate of the underworld along with Eita and Persipnei (Hades and Persephone) to receive the souls of the dead.[4] The underworld gate was a yoni, and also a lily, which had "no face." Admission into the underworld was often mythologized as a sexual union. The lily or *lilu* (lotus) was the Great Mother's flower-yoni, whose title formed Lilith's name.

The story of Lilith disappeared from the canonical Bible, but her daughters the *lilim* haunted men for over a thousand years. Well into the Middle Ages, the Jews were still manufacturing amulets to keep away the *lilim,* who were lustful she-demons given to copulating with men in their dreams, causing nocturnal emissions.[5] Naturally, the *lilim* squatted on top of their victims in the position favored by ancient matriarchs.

Greeks adopted the *lilim* and called them Lamiae, Empusae (Forcers-In), or Daughters of Hecate. Christians also adopted them and called them harlots of hell, or succubae, the female counterparts of incubi. Celibate monks tried to fend them off by sleeping with their hands crossed over their genitals, clutching a crucifix. It was said that every time a pious Christian had a wet dream, Lilith laughed. Even if a male child laughed in his sleep, people said Lilith was fondling him. To protect baby boys against her, chalk circles were drawn around cradles with the written names of the three angels God sent to fetch Lilith back to Adam—even though these angels had proved incapable of dealing with her. Some said men and babies should not be left alone in a house or Lilith might seize them.[6]

Another common name for the Daughters of Lilith was Night-Hag. This term didn't imply that they were ugly; on the contrary, they were supposed to be very beautiful.[7] As with their brothers the incubi, they were presumed so expert at lovemaking that after an experience with a Night-Hag, a man couldn't be satisfied with the love of a mortal woman.

1. Graves & Patai, 68. 2. Edwardes, 157. 3. Graves & Patai, 67. 4. Hays, 183. 5. Graves, G.M. 1, 190. 6. Cavendish, P.E., 99. 7. Scot, 512.

Lily

The flower of Lilith, Sumero-Babylonian Goddess of creation; the *lilu* or "lotus" of her genital magic. The lily often represented the virgin aspect of the Triple Goddess, while the rose represented her maternal aspect. The lily was sacred to **Astarte**, who was also Lilith; northern Europeans called her Ostara or Eostre, the Goddess of "Easter" lilies.[1]

Because of its pagan associations with virgin motherhood, the lily was used to symbolize impregnation of the virgin Mary. Some authorities claimed the lily in Gabriel's hand filtered God's semen which entered Mary's body through her ear.[2]

Mary's cult also inherited the lily of the Blessed Virgin Juno, who conceived her savior-son Mars with her own magic lily, without any male aid.[3] This myth reflected an early belief in the self-fertilizing power of the yoni (vulva), which the lily symbolized and Juno personified. Her name descended from the pre-Roman Uni, a Triple Goddess represented by the three-lobed lily or fleur-de-lis, her name stemming from the Sanskrit *yoni,* source of the Uni-verse.

In 656 A.D., the 10th Council of Toledo officially adopted the holy day of Juno's miraculous conception of Mars into the Christian canon, renaming it the Festival of the Mother of God, or Lady Day, insisting that it commemorated Mary's miraculous conception of Jesus with the aid of a lily.[4] Christian artists showed the angel Gabriel holding out to Mary a scepter surmounted by a fleur-de-lis on a lily stalk. A scroll usually issued from Gabriel's mouth, with the words *Ave Maria gratia plena,* the seminal "Word," which made Mary "full." Aphrodite's dove, that other yonic symbol, hovered about the scene.[5]

Celtic and Gallo-Roman tribes called the virgin mother Lily Maid. Her yonic emblem appeared not only as the French fleur-de-lis but also as the Irish shamrock, which was not originally Irish but a sacred symbol among Indus Valley people some 6000 years before the Christian era. Christianized France identified the Lily Maid with the virgin Mary, but she was never completely dissociated from the pagan image of Juno. Among the people, Lady Day was known as *Notre Dame de Mars.*[6]

The Easter lily was the medieval pas-flower, from Latin *passus,* to step or pass over, cognate of *pascha,* the Passover. The lily was also called Pash-flower, Paschal flower, Pasque flower, or Passion flower. Pagans understood that it represented the spring passion of the god, like Heracles, for union in love-death with the Virgin Queen of Heaven, Hera-Hebe, or Juno, or Venus, all of whom claimed the lily. When Hera's milk spurted from her breasts to form the Milky Way, the drops that fell to the ground became lilies.[7]

Sometimes, the Easter flower was not a white lily but a scarlet or purple anemone, emblem of Adonis's passion and called identical with his bride Venus.[8]

1. H. Smith, 201. 2. Simons, 103. 3. *Larousse,* 202. 4. Brewster, 146. 5. Cavendish, V.H.H., 68. 6. Brewster, 146. 7. Guthrie, 71. 8. Agrippa, 103.

Lingam

"Penis," Hindu symbol of any god, usually Shiva. The lingam-yoni is still the supreme symbol of the vital principle, representing male and female genitalia in conjunction.[1] Its verbal equivalent is the Jewel in the Lotus.

Sometimes the lingam appeared as a phallic pillar in the *cella* or Holy of Holies, the core of the temple which stands for the Goddess and is called "womb" (*garbha-grha*).[2] Shiva bore the name of Sthanu, "Pillar," and was shown emerging from a lingam-pillar with his "jewel" or phallic eye displayed in the center of his forehead, a graphic illustration of the transformation of the whole lingam into a man-shape.[3]

It was a Hindu custom to have brides deflowered in the temple by Shiva's carved lingam to make their firstborn children God-begotten (see **Firstborn**). Temple harlots were made "brides of God" by the same ceremony of the lingam, as was also the custom in the ancient Middle East, Greece, and Rome.[4] Besides these man-sized examples there were large pillars, which often became objects of pilgrimage. Many miracles were said to have taken place in the vicinity of Shiva's lingam.[5]

1. Rawson, A.T., 51. 2. Zimmer, 127. 3. O'Flaherty, 195.
4. Rawson, E.A., 29, 88. 5. *Mahanirvanatantra,* 335.

Lion

Usually a symbol of the sun god in Greece and Rome, the lion was more commonly associated with the Goddess in the Middle East and Egypt. Ishtar, Astarte, and Cybele rode or drove lions. Bast-Hathor was the Sphinx-lioness, symbolizing the Destroyer. Sometimes she appeared with two lion heads looking forward and backward, like her Roman counterpart Janus-Jana. This was a symbol of Time, with the hieroglyph *xerefu* and *akeru,* the Lions of Yesterday and Today.[1]

The Dark Age kingdom of the Britons was named after the "Lyonesse," one of its early queens appearing in Arthurian romance as the Lady Lyonors. Merlin's city was Caerleon, the Lion's Place. Lions were not native to the British isles, therefore the British lion was an imported totem. Lion and serpent stood for ascending and declining spirits of the sacred year, the former following the latter in the pagan zodiac.[2]

The British "Lady who ruled lions"may have arrived on Roman coins, which since the Augustan period showed the Great Mother of the Gods (Cybele) enthroned between two lions, wearing the mural crown that became a Saxon emblem of divinity. She was thus described in a poem: "The Virgin in her heavenly place rides upon the Lion; bearer of corn, inventor of law, founder of cities, by whose gift it is man's good lot to know the gods; therefore she is the Mother of the Gods, Peace, Virtue, Ceres, the Syrian Goddess, weighing life and laws in her balance."[3]

1. Budge, E.L., 61. 2. Graves, W.G., 270. 3. Vermaseren, 75, 138.

Little Red Riding Hood

Fairy-tale heroine based on the Virgin aspect of the red-clothed Diana: in the tale, the usual trinity of maiden, mother, and grandmother. The

Hunter was originally *le Chasseur Maudit,* or pagan Lord of the Hunt; while the man-eating She-Wolf or grandmother was a western form of the Kalika. See **Werewolf**.

Logos

Greek "Word," a theory of creation that passed from Tantrism through Neoplatonic philosophy to Christianity. The theory was that a deity could create anything—other deities, worlds, creatures—by the power of magic words: when the name was spoken, the thing materialized. The Logos, then, was divine essence concentrated in a Word and made manifest, as Jesus was called "the Word made flesh." The Gospel of John gave him eternal existence: "In the beginning was the Word, and the Word was with God, and the Word was God" (John 1:1).

Judeo-Christian thinkers defined the Logos in so many ways that it became virtually without meaning, and so was relegated to the status of a "deep mystery." The Logos was Christ, or the Wisdom of Yahweh, or an archangel, or Truth, or the high priest, or the Law, or the covenant, or the scriptures, or Moses, or the creative power, or the soul of the world, or the sun, etc.[1] Orphic, Pythagorean, and Neoplatonic philosophers who expounded the Logos doctrine were not well understood by their Christian followers, who struggled vainly with the subtle semantics of the pagan philosophers.

The pagans' "Word made flesh" was usually **Hermes**, representing the *Logos spermatikos,* seminal Word, proceeding from the mouth of Zeus to beget all things through the power of his agent on earth.[2] The Corpus Hermeticum praised this Word-bearer: "Holy art thou, who by the Word has created all things that exist! Holy art thou, of whom all Nature has produced the image!" Justin Martyr's *Apologia* earnestly tried to assimilate the attributes of Hermes-the-Word to Jesus, "on account of his wisdom," claiming that Jesus was exactly like Hermes in being the Son, Messenger, and Word of God.[3]

One of the reasons for male enthusiasm for the Logos doctrine was that it provided male gods with a method of creating, formerly the exclusive prerogative of the birth-giving Goddess. Hermes-the-Logos became Hermes-the-Creator, exercising the magic feminine powers he derived from living in androgynous union with Mother Aphrodite. *The Perfect Word* addressed Hermes as not only the Light of the life of man but also "the fruitful Womb of All."[4]

The Perfect Word Third-century Greek text of Hermetic revelation-literature, discovered by Reitzenstein in the Mimaut papyrus.

Similarly, Hermes's Egyptian counterpart Thoth mastered the Words of Power and assumed the attributes of the Goddess Maat, "whose Word is Truth," sometimes called his spouse. Priests of Thoth's holy city, which the Greeks called Hermopolis, said Thoth was the universal demiurge who spoke the Word of creation, *met,* and "gave birth" to the first gods.[5]

Met, a mother-word related to Maat, Greek *metis,* Sanskrit *medha,* "female wisdom."[6]

The oldest Oriental father-gods "gave birth" by speech, when they were first conceived by men who didn't know the real physiology of begetting. The Sanskrit word for a father-given or Brahma-given soul was *atman,* "air" or "breath," cognate with the German *atmen* and Greek *atmos,* "air." A Brahman father still establishes a paternal claim to a child by breathing its soul-name three times into its face, pretending to place the soul in the body.[7]

The biblical Yahweh also claimed to give life by the power of his breath or "wind," which he used to animate the dry bones of the dead: "Behold, I will cause breath to enter into you, and ye shall live" (Ezekiel 37:5). This incident was probably copied from the Babylonian *Enuma Elish,* wherein Marduk established his right to kingship among the gods by showing he could destroy and re-create by the power of his Word.[8]

Among the oldest Mesopotamian texts there are stories of deities representing "the Word." In the *Epic of Gilgamesh,* Enlil the god of "air" or "breath" was also a Logos: "The spirit of the Word is Enlil, the spirit of the heart of Anu (heaven)." Enlil embodied "the word which stilleth the heavens above."[9]

Though male gods popularized the idea of the Logos, the ability to destroy and re-create by Word-power belonged originally to the Goddess, who created languages, alphabets, and the secret mantras known as Words of Power, Egyptian *hekau,* creations of Hecate (Maat). Every manifestation of life was brought into being by the Great Goddess Kali with her Word, **Om**, an invocation of her own "pregnant belly." This was the primordial Logos, "the supreme syllable, the mother of all sound."[10] Kali's creative voice had its own personification as a Goddess Vac (Voice), engendered in celestial waters, at the summit of the Cosmic Tree.[13] Vac brought forth the god who called himself All-father, as well as everything else in the universe.[14] She reappeared in Greek myth as a disembodied voice, the nymph Echo, who brought the flower-god Narcissus to his doom by trapping his soul in her water-mirror. In Arabic her *Om* became *Umm,* meaning mother, matrix, source, principle, or prototype: the Logos of the Sufi.[15]

The fifty letters of Kali's Sanskrit alphabet were *matrika,* "mothers." Hindu scriptures said: "As from a mother comes birth, so from *matrika,* or sound, the world proceeds."[11] *Om* was the *mantramatrika,* Mother of Mantras; and these divine Words spoken by Kali created and destroyed everything, including all gods.[12]

Om was a familiar sound. Celts called their Moon-mother Omh, "She Who Is." Shebans called their Moon-temple at Marib Aum, the Belly of the World. Lydians placed the same Belly of the World in their own country as an *omphalos* or navel-stone, hub of the universe, "made flesh" in their Goddess-queen Omphale. It was not an exclusively Lydian custom; every temple in Greece hid an *omphalos.*

Om was Alpha, the letter of creation, repeated again as the final letter of destruction, Omega, which means literally "great Om." Its Greek form is a horseshoe, based on the Hindu symbol of the yonic Gate. When the biblical prophet proclaimed: "I am the Alpha and Omega, the beginning and the ending, saith the Lord, which is, and which was, and which is yet to come" (Revelation 1:8), he used words copied from the temple of the Great Mother at Sais, where they were written on stone many centuries before the Bible was compiled.[16]

The Logos idea was virtually identical with the Oriental concept of the Oversoul, which had been an essence of the Great Mother but was re-defined as an essence of the Great Father or of his son, the Savior. Origen said, "As our body while consisting of human members is yet held together by one soul, so the universe is to be thought of as an immense living being which is held together by one soul, the power of the logos."[17] Christ was only one of many aspirants to the title of Logos. Before him, Attis was hailed as the Logos "who holds the universe together."[18] But before them all was the Great Mother: "The supreme Shakti has the form both of the seed and the sprout of the revealed coming-together of Shiva and Shakti; subtlest of the subtle, She is contained in all that lies between the first and the last letters of the alphabet, which contains the original root forms from which the names of everything in the world are compounded."[19]

The Christian idea that Christ was God's "Word made flesh" was an idea common to all the ancient pagan world. Every king was literally God manifested in the flesh, whether he was a real ruler or a sacramental surrogate ruler. Usually he was called Savior, and begotten by the god on a temple virgin. He was chosen and invested by holy words and name-souls. Antiochus of Syria, for instance, received the divine surname of Epiphanes, "God Made Manifest (in the flesh)."[20]

Not even Christians, however, managed to purge the Logos of all its original feminine connotations. Clement of Alexandria distorted his symbolism to the point of absurdity when trying to connect the Logos with parenthood: "The Word is everything to the child, both father and mother, teacher and nurse. . . . The nutriment is the milk of the Father . . . and the Word alone supplies us children with the milk of love. . . . For this reason, seeking is called sucking; to those infants who seek the Word, the Father's loving breasts supply milk."[21]

These odd notions arose from the ancient belief that a mother gave her child its name-soul along with the first breast milk, as she breathed a Word that would henceforth define and personify the child. In the Old Testament, children were named by their mothers, never by their fathers.[22] Thus a universal Parent would be expected to give name-souls to all creation along with universal breast milk.

A giver of nourishment was also a giver of Law, derived from the same root word as Logos. Priest-chieftain of the Icelandic *Althing*—supreme governing body of the tribes—had a title now translated Lawspeaker. But that is not the literal translation of the Icelandic word, *lögsögumathr,* which really means Mother-Who-Speaks-the-Word.[23]

The doctrine of the Logos was so widespread that Christians could hardly be expected to ignore it. It was one of many pagan ideas that the church eagerly seized. Medieval Schoolmen tried to make it reconcile faith with reason, insisting that the two must be identical because their root was the same: "that no more than one source of truth, the Logos, had ever existed, and that everything of any value in human wisdom, especially in Greek philosophy, flowed from that sole source. Plato himself was reputed to have pilfered from Moses."[24]

Schoolmen Philosophical and theological thinkers of the "Scholastic" movement, 11th to 15th centuries, including such authorities as Abelard, Aquinas, Duns Scotus, Ockham, and Albertus Magnus.

The Schoolmen were ignorant of the ancient *logoi,* sacred writings of the Orphics, mentioned by Plato and other philosophers as a vast mass of literature amounting to a true "Bible"; these writings had all been destroyed during the early centuries of Christianity.[25] But there were Christian Gnostic writings that had copied the Orphics and transmitted the idea of the Logos to Christian dogma even after they were declared "heresies." The *Gospel of Truth* said, for example, "When the Word appeared, the Word which is in the hearts of those who pronounced It. . . . It was not only a sound, but It had taken on a body as well."[26] Christians gave such assertions a rather simplistic interpretation, assuming the body was Christ's; yet perhaps the more perceptive of the ancient philosophers meant that man, the verbalizing animal, in effect creates all his gods out of his Word.

Gospel of Truth
Gnostic scripture associated with the early Christian sect of Valentinians, founded about 150 A.D.

1. H. Smith, 218. 2. *Encyc. Brit.*, "Logos." 3. Doane, 375. 4. Angus, 243.
5. *Larousse*, 27–28. 6. Budge, E.L., 142. 7. *Mahanirvanatantra*, 236; Hays, 223.
8. Fromm, 164. 9. *Epic of Gilgamesh*, 24. 10. *Upanishads*, 53.
11. *Mahanirvanatantra*, cvii. 12. Wilkins, 201. 13. d'Alviella, 162.
14. Briffault 1, 7. 15. Shah, 175. 16. *Larousse*, 37. 17. Shirley, 46.
18. Graves, W.G., 367. 19. Rawson, A.T., 198. 20. Cavendish, P.E., 18.
21. Pagels, 67–68. 22. Briffault 1, 372. 23. Branston, 30.
24. Guignebert, 258. 25. Guthrie, 310, 313. 26. Jonas, 76.

Lohengrin

Medieval version of Zeus the Swan-king, or the Swan-knight Krishna, beloved of all the Swan-maidens in heaven (seen as little clouds sailing over the blue). The holy swan, Leda's lover, was transformed into a Knight of the Holy Grail, dedicated to helping women maintain their legal rights under a patriarchal system. See **Swan**.

Loki

Norse god of complex character and great age. He may have been a *genius loci,* "spirit of a place." His name may have descended from Sanskrit *Loka,* a spirit of the seven celestial planes. He was an archaic form of the "Luck" envisioned as guardian angel of a clan or family, often embodied in a fetish object.[1] One story said Loki's lips were stitched up with a thong, suggesting that his spirit dwelt in a mummified oracular head.[2] Such heads were also used as clan-spirits by the early Hebrews, who called them ***teraphim***.[3] To lose them was to lose the family's "luck."

Like many of the oldest gods, Loki was bisexual. He even succeeded in becoming a mother, though only after he had swallowed a woman's heart to acquire the power of birth-giving. The Greek Zeus resorted to the same feminine magic, for the same reason. Loki's offspring was the eight-legged horse Sleipnir, spirit of death, a symbol of the gallows tree on which Odin rode.[4]

Loki was sometimes Logi, "Flame," the fire god identified with the Celtic Lug, and probably descended from the Aryan Agni-Shiva as the lightning-fire "quenched" by his marriage to the Goddess of the watery abyss. Indeed, under the name of Agni, the god was "an early king of Sweden" married to the Goddess Skialf, or Skadi.[7]

Loki was also a death spirit in his own right, like Shiva the Destroyer who often appeared as Shiva the Destroyed, dead under the feet of Kali the Crone, his guts pulled out of his belly and devoured. The same thing happened to Loki as he was periodically sacrificed to Skadi the Crone.[5] Also like the Oriental god, Loki always came back to life. Though the other Aesir chained him up, as the wolf Fenrir and the troublemaking Prometheus were chained, yet Loki's inevitable destiny was to break free and initiate the ultimate convulsions of the world's doomsday.[6] Aryan belief postulated seven Lokas before the final paradise of Shiva and Shakti; thus it might be assumed that Loki would have seven incarnations before the final death of the gods.

1. Avalon, 40. 2. Branston, 267. 3. Graves, W.G., 164. 4. Turville-Petre, 129. 5. Oxenstierna, 213. 6. Cavendish, P.E., 169. 7. H.R.E. Davidson, G.M.V.A., 227, 234.

Longinus, Saint

Christian legend made Longinus a blind Roman centurion who thrust the spear into Jesus's side at the crucifixion. Some of Jesus's blood fell on his eyes and cured his blindness, whereupon Longinus was converted and spent the rest of his life breaking pagan idols in Cappadocia.[1]

This canonization-story made even less sense than most, as Roman centurions were not blind. Possibly in an original version, now lost, Longinus was stricken blind after delivering the spear-thrust; but this would have allowed no time for his conversion.

The true prototype of the legend seems to have been the blind god Hod, who slew the Norse savior Balder with the thrust of a spear of **mistletoe**. Early-medieval missionaries deliberately confused Jesus with Balder. Some even declared the cross of Jesus's crucifixion was made of mistletoe.[2]

March 15, the "Ides of March" when most pagan saviors died, was the day devoted to Hod by the heathen, and later Christianized as the feast day of the Blessed Longinus.[3]

1. Brewster, 135–36. 2. Turville-Petre, 119. 3. Brewster, 136.

Lorelei

Famous rock in the Rhine, anciently identified with a Water-siren or River-goddess who lured men to death by drowning. Possibly it was once a shrine of the Water-goddess. Early in the 19th century, a German writer transformed the Lorelei into the usual maiden disappointed in love. She threw herself in the river, and afterward appeared as a spirit of the rock, singing her fatal songs to passing boatmen.[1]

1. *Encyc. Brit.*, "Lorelei."

Lotus

Asia's primary symbol of the yoni (vulva), often personified as the Goddess Padma, "Lotus," also known as Cunti, Lakshmi, or Shakti.

Lotus

The central phrase of **Tantrism**, *Om mani padme hum,* meant the Jewel (male) in the Lotus (female), with interlocking connotations: the penis in the vagina, the fetus in the womb, the corpse in the earth, the God in the Goddess representing all of these.[1]

The father-god Brahma claimed to be a universal creator; nevertheless, he was styled "Lotus-born," for he arose from the primal Goddess's yoni. Egypt's father-god Ra also claimed to be a creator but owed his existence to the Goddess called "great world lotus flower, out of which rose the sun for the first time at the creation."[2]

Virtually all Egyptian Goddess-forms were symbolized by the lotus.[3] Pharaohs were sexually united with the World Lotus to achieve rebirth after death. The funeral hymn of Unas declared that he "had union with the goddess Mut, Unas hath drawn unto himself the flame of Isis, Unas hath united himself to the lotus."[4]

One way of uniting oneself to the lotus was the custom of ritual cunnilingus, widely practiced throughout the east as communion with the feminine life-principle.[5] This was probably the true meaning of the Land of Lotus-Eaters visited by Odysseus and his crew. The sensual Land of Lotus-Eaters was described as a tropical place beyond the southern sea, which could apply to any land from Egypt to India.[6]

Ascetic Jain Buddhism tried to eradicate the lotus symbol because of its erotic implications. Nevertheless, a few centuries after Buddha's time, the most prominent figure on Buddhist monuments was again Padma, openly displaying her genital lotus.[7] A similar resurgence of erotic imagery overtook ascetic Christianity, when "obscene" figures proliferated in cathedrals and churches, for example the Irish **sheila-na-gig**.

Most Oriental mystics held that spiritual knowledge began with carnal knowledge. The lotus was the Goddess's gate, and sex was the Way through the gate to her inner mysteries. With proper sexual exercises, a true sage might achieve the final flowering of revelation described as the thousand-petaled lotus of invisible light emanating from the top of the head after ascending the spinal *chakras* from the pelvis.

Worshippers of Vishnu sometimes painted their god as the source of the World Lotus, which grew on a long stem from his navel. But since "the primary reference of the lotus in India has always been the goddess Padma, 'Lotus,' whose body itself is the universe, the long stem from navel to lotus should properly connote an umbilical cord through which the flow of energy would be running from the goddess to the god, mother to child, not the other way."[8] Some Hindu cosmogonies saw the whole world as the lotus flower, with seven petals representing the seven divisions of the heavens where the cities and palaces of the god were located.[9]

In the Middle East, the lotus was *lilu,* or **lily**.[10] It was the flower of **Lilith**, the Sumero-Babylonian earth mother claimed by the Jews as Adam's first wife. The three-lobed lily or fleur-de-lis, like the shamrock, once stood for the Triple Goddess's three yonis, which is why the lily was sacred to the triune Queen of Heaven. The Blessed Virgin Juno conceived her savior-son Mars by the lily, and the same flower was adopted as a conception-charm of the Blessed Virgin Mary.[11] When Isis was assimilated to the burgeoning legends of the Virgin, her Egyptian images held the phallic cross in one hand, the female lotus seed-vessel in the other, like the Goddess shown on the Isiac Table.[12]

1. Rawson, E.A., 151. 2. Budge, G.E., 1, 473. 3. Angus, 139. 4. Budge, G.E. 2, 32. 5. Rawson, E.A., 103. 6. Thomson, 176. 7. Campbell, Or.M., 301. 8. Campbell, Oc.M., 157. 9. Lethaby, 124–25. 10. Summers, V., 226. 11. Simons, 103. 12. Knight, D.W.P., 50.

Lotus Position

Meditation pose of Tantric yogis, also shown on icons of early Celtic gods.[1] Pagan Scandinavia still made artifacts with figures seated in lotus position during the 8th to 10th centuries.[2] The medieval church denounced this cross-legged pose as a relic of paganism, and declared all who sat cross-legged were working sorcery.[3]

1. Campbell, Or.M., 307. 2. Campbell, M.I., 336. 3. Agrippa, 159.

Lucifer

"Light-bringer," Latin title of the Morning Star god who announced the daily birth of the sun. Canaanites called him Shaher. The Jewish Shaharit (Morning Service) still commemorates him.[1] Shaher's twin brother Shalem, the Evening Star, announced the daily death of the sun and spoke to him the Word of Peace (Hebrew *shalom,* Arabic *salaam*).[2] Shalem was worshipped along with his brother in Jerusalem, which means "House of Shalem." Shaher and Shalem were the same as the Greeks' Dioscuri or Heavenly Twins, Castor and Pollux, born of Leda's World Egg. They were also prominent in Persian sun worship as the two torch-bearers, one with his torch ascendant and the other with his torch directed down.[3]

Both Shaher and Shalem were born of the Great Mother **Asherah** in her world-womb aspect as Helel, "the Pit."[4] Canaanite myth said Shaher coveted the superior glory of the sun god and tried to usurp his throne, but was defeated and cast down from heaven like a lightning bolt. Pagan scriptures of the 7th century B.C. included a dirge for the fallen Morning Star:

> *How hast thou fallen from heaven, Helel's son Shaher! Thou didst say in thy heart, I will ascend to heaven, above the circumpolar stars I will raise my throne, and I will dwell on the Mount of Council in the back of the north; I will mount on the back of a cloud, I will be like unto Elyon.*[5]

Centuries later, a Jewish scribe copied this Canaanite scripture into the Bible and pretended it was written by Isaiah:

> *How art thou fallen from heaven, O Lucifer, son of the morning! . . . For thou hast said in thine heart, I will ascend to heaven, I will exalt my throne above the stars of God: I will sit also upon the mount of the congregation, in the sides of the north: I will ascend above the heights of the clouds; I will be like the most High. (Isaiah 14:12-14)*

The biblical writer further told Lucifer: "Thou shalt be brought down to hell, to the sides of the pit" (Isaiah 14:15). This "pit" was the same as Helel, or Asherah, the god's own Mother-bride; and his descent as a lightning-serpent into her Pit represented fertilization of the abyss by masculine fire from heaven. In short, the Light-bringer challenged the supreme solar god by seeking the favors of the Mother. This divine rivalry explains the so-called sin of Lucifer, *hubris,* which church fathers translated "pride"—but its real meaning was "sexual passion."[6]

Actually, all sacred kings aspired to the same proud position Lucifer or Shaher coveted: to be the spouse of the Goddess, to stand at the hub of the heavens (carried thence on a cloud), to become one with the supreme deity. Egyptian pharaohs made almost identical claims to glory, as shown by Pepi's tomb inscription stating that he "standeth upon the north of heaven with Ra, he becometh lord of the universe like unto the king of the gods."[7] He also descended into the earth in the guise of the immortal serpent Sata, father of lightning; and his Hebrew name Satan merged with the image of Lucifer in Jesus's words: "I beheld Satan as lightning fall from heaven" (Luke 10:18).

Lucifer continued to be linked with both lust and lightning during the Christian era. He became the Prince of the Power of the Air (Ephesians 2:2) who threw his lightning bolts at church towers. He wielded the trident, in Eastern symbolism a triple lightning-phallus destined to fertilize the Triple Goddess.[8]

Another ancient source of the Lucifer legend was the Assyro-Babylonian lightning god, Zu the Storm Bird, a forerunner of Zeus; sometimes he was a *seraph* or "fiery flying serpent," the lightning bolt personified. Zu was punished for coveting the power-filled Tablets of Destiny that Great Mother Tiamat had given her firstborn son, the father of gods. Zu said to himself, "I will take the tablet of destiny of the gods, even I; and I will direct all the oracles of the gods; I will establish a throne, and dispense commands, I will rule over all the spirits of Heaven!"[9]

Egypt called the Morning Star god Bennu, the dying-and-reborn Phoenix bird known as "Soul of Ra," who died on the World Tree in order to renew himself, to "shine on the world." His spirit dwelt in the phallic obelisk, called Bennu or the Benben-stone, which stood for the god's sexual union with the Mother. Another of his phallic forms was the mighty serpent Ami-Hemf, "Dweller in his Flame," who lived on the Mountain of Sunrise and was identified with the morning star.[10] Thus Egypt and Mesopotamia had several versions of light-bringing Lucifer long before scraps of his myth found their way into Judeo-Christian writings.

Plato knew the morning-star god as Aster (Star) and also understood that the same star appeared at evening in a different position and so became the evening star (actually the planet Venus). Plato therefore viewed Aster as the dying-and-reborn deity himself: "Aster, once, as Morning-Star, light on the living you shed. Now, dying, as Evening-Star, you shine among the dead."[11]

Gnostic Christians maintained that the "light" Lucifer brought was true enlightenment, which he gave humanity against God's will, as Prometheus stole the fire of heaven to bring civilization to mankind against the will of Zeus. The Bible's story supported the Gnostic view. God denied Adam and Eve the fruit of the tree of knowledge, desiring to keep them ignorant; but Lucifer, in the form of the serpent, gave them the "light" of wisdom.

The Persians, too, said their own Great Serpent **Ahriman** gave knowledge to the first couple in the garden of Heden. Ahriman too was the twin brother of the solar God, cast out of heaven for his hubris; but the Magi worshipped the Great Serpent as the source of their occult wisdom.[12] He was often thought more influential in terrestrial affairs than the Father who cast him down.

Such Persian precedents influenced Gnostic Christians who regarded Jehovah as the villain and Lucifer as the hero, savior, and friend of man, revealer of sacred mysteries that the Heavenly Father jealously withheld. Medieval secret fraternities perpetuated the Gnostics' respect for Lucifer and sometimes identified him with Hermes, god of revelation. These Gnostic doctrines persisted through the first half of the Christian era and well into the second half.[13] Meister Eckhart said, "Lucifer, the angel, who is in hell, had perfectly pure intellect and to this day knows much."[14]

Meister Eckhart von Hochheim Popular German mystical preacher of the early 14th century; minister of a Dominican order in Saxony. In 1326 he was charged with heresy and died soon afterward. A papal bull of 1329 condemned 28 propositions from his theological works.

In the 14th century A.D. there were Gnostic groups called Luciferans, who "worship Lucifer and believe him to be the brother of God, wrongly cast out of heaven."[15] Luciferans were first heard of in Austria. Their cult soon spread to Brandenburg, Bohemia, Switzerland, and Savoy. In 1336 the Inquisition burned fourteen men and women at Magdeburg for holding heretical opinions about Lucifer. In 1384, a priest at Prenzlau accused his entire congregation of believing that Lucifer was God or the brother of God.[16]

One of the "great questions" among medieval Schoolmen was how many angels fell with Lucifer and how many remained in heaven under the command of Michael. Some authorities said "most" angels fell. Some said "most" remained. Some said a tenth, a ninth, or a third of the angelic host fell, because "the dragon with his tail plucked down with him the third part of the stars." Furious debate raged also between Thomists, Scotists, and followers of Augustine on the "great question" of the battle's location and duration. It was said to have taken place in the air, in the firmament, or in paradise. It lasted one instant, two instants, or four instants; the consensus of learned opinion was that it lasted three instants.[17] Thus the theologians supposed that it didn't take long for God to subdue Lucifer. On the question of why Lucifer's army rebelled against the supremely beneficent, supremely lovable God in the first place, the theologians were silent—perhaps knowing all too well deep within their minds what Lucifer really stood for.

1. Patai, 147. 2. Hays, 85. 3. Cumont, M.M., 68, 128. 4. Hooke, M.E.M., 93. 5. Albright, 232. 6. Potter & Sargent, 176. 7. *Book of the Dead,* 86. 8. O'Flaherty, 130. 9. *Assyr. & Bab. Lit.,* 304. 10. Budge, G.E. 2, 96–97; 1, 24. 11. Lindsay, O.A., 94. 12. Legge 2, 239. 13. Waite, O.S., 195. 14. Campbell, Oc.M., 513. 15. Wedeck, 142. 16. J.B. Russell, 177, 180. 17. Scot, 422–23.

Lucy, Saint

A Christianization of Juno Lucina or Lucetia, Mother of Light, the Sabine Goddess whose temple was built on the Esquiline in 735 B.C. There she appeared, bearing her symbols, a lamp and a *patera,* offering-dish. She bestowed the gifts of light, enlightenment, and eyesight, especially as the opener of eyes of newborn children.[1]

The bogus "St. Lucy" bore the same symbols and was advertised as a patron of sufferers from eye diseases. Lucy, or Lucia, was one of the most popular of medieval saints, ranking with Agatha, Catherine, and Mary Magdalene as a leading ecclesiastical money-maker.

Lucy's legend was the same "virgin martyr" story told of dozens of other mythical female saints. Her devotion to chastity was so great that when a pagan suitor admired her beautiful eyes, she cut them from their sockets and sent them to him on a platter, asking to be left in peace henceforth. This was how Christians interpreted the Goddess's *patera* with its offerings.

The legend went on to say the pagans tried to execute St. Lucy for the alleged crime of keeping her virginity. But when they tried to drag her out of the temple where she had been imprisoned, she stood rooted to the floor as heavily as a great statue. She couldn't be moved even with ropes and pulleys. A fire built on the stone floor around her also failed to destroy her. Finally she was killed by a sword thrust.[2]

Details of this naive legend show that "St. Lucy" really was a colossal statue of Juno Lucina, whose jeweled eyes were gouged out by a Christian vandal; but destroying the statue proved difficult, as it was too heavy to be moved. In the end, Juno was broken up and removed from her temple in pieces—but superstitious dread inspired the awe that canonized her. The most significant detail in the legend said Lucy was once very rich, but she distributed all her wealth to poor Christians. This wealth evidently consisted of the expensive temple furnishings which were informally distributed among the looters. Robbing temples and smashing their holy statues was one of the major occupations of poor Christians in Rome during the 4th and 5th centuries.[3]

People whom the church called witches apparently remembered St. Lucy as the pagan Goddess Lucina, and continued to worship her with pagan ceremonies even though she was concealed by a Christian cloak. As late as 1890, Tuscan witches still used Lucina's healing charm, a wreath of rue tied with red ribbon, making the patient spit three times through the wreath calling on "St. Lucy" for protection against the evil eye.[4]

Other versions of the same Goddess, such as Triduana (Diana Triformis) and the Irish Medana, were also assimilated to Christianity as fictitious saints, of whom the same story was told: they were beautiful virgins who gouged out their eyes rather than succumb to the temptations of love.[5] It seems the new churches inherited from the ruin of the old pagan world a great many eyeless female statues.

Some medieval sources viewed Lucy as a female Christ and attributed to her the same miracles performed by Jesus. She could restore sight to the blind, and by her magic touch she cured her own mother's "issue of blood."[6]

In Sicily, St. Lucy continued to rule the Festival of Lights on the shortest day of the year, recalling the ancient festival of Juno Lucina rekindling the sun. Swedish celebrations of the day still feature a girl wearing a crown of candles, known as the Lussibruden (Lucy Bride).[7]

1. *Larousse,* 203–4. 2. Brewster, 21. 3. J.H. Smith, D.C.P., 177. 4. Gifford, 76. 5. Gifford, 131. 6. de Voragine, 34. 7. Miles, 221–22.

Ludus

Latin "Game"; the dramas, performances, and contests of a religious festival. The *ludi* evolved into the *commedia,* carnivals, circuses, and mystery plays of the Middle Ages, with the old gods disguised as clowns, whose traditional hieratic gestures thus became "ludicrous." The ancient *rex ludorum,* King of the Games, became the medieval Carnival King, or Prince of Fools. See **Antic Hey**.

Lug

var. Lugd, Lud

Celtic god, son or reincarnation of the Dagda, eponymous founder of the cities of Lyons and London—formerly Lugdunum, the stronghold of Lug. His temple stood on Ludgate Hill.[1] "Lud's Gate" was a great stone called Crom Cruaich, the Bloody Crescent, apparently a symbol of the menstruating Moon-goddess to whom Lug was married in suggestively Tantric style.[2]

Lug's special festival was Lammas Eve, formerly Lugnasad, "the Games of Lug." The pagan rites of Lugnasad were kept to a very late date at Taillten in Ireland, where the Goddess had been worshipped as a local Earth-mother, Tailltiu. At the annual Taillten Fair, men bought brides in a custom reminiscent of the Goddess's ancient rites of sacred promiscuity and defloration. The hill where payments were collected was known as the Hill of the Buying.[4]

Taillten was so notorious for promiscuity that any casual sexual affair came to be known as a Taillten marriage.[5] Taillten marriages were actually legal up to the 13th century. They were supposed to last the period specified by the old lunar calendars, a year and a day.[6]

Lug's curious name may have come in some remote past time from Mesopotamia, where the title of a sacred king, the Goddess's spouse, was *lugal.*[7]

Lug was Christianized as several saints: St. Lugad, St. Luan, St. Eluan, and St. Lugidus, depending on local dialects. Irish legendary history called him a King Lugadius martyred by a lance-thrust from a druidic priest—a story taken quite directly from ancient cults of the sacred-king/dying-god. Lug perished after marrying the Great Goddess called "the Sovereignty of Erin until the day of doom."[3]

1. Squire, 254. 2. Briffault 3, 75. 3. Spence, 66, 102. 4. Joyce, 439.
5. Spence, 101. 6. Pepper & Wilcock, 273. 7. Campbell, Or.M., 107.

Luna

Latin name of the Moon-goddess, coupled in Gnostic symbolism and magic texts with Sol, the male sun. Together they represented fire and water, whose combination produced the Blood of Life. Luna the watery moon used to be considered superior to Sol the fiery sun. Even Chaucer wrote of "Luna the Serene, / Chief goddess of the ocean and its queen, / Though Neptune have therein his deity, / Is over him and empress of the sea."[1]

Many myths present the Moon-goddess as the Creatress who first drifted alone on the primal ocean of chaos until she decided to bring orderly forms out of elemental formlessness. Thus she was specifically "Moon Shining Over the Sea" to Scandinavian pagans.[2] Finns called her Luonnotar, sometimes loosely translated Daughter of Nature. But she was not the daughter of anything; she existed all alone in primordial time, until she tired of loneliness and decided to create a world.[3] See **Moon**.

Christians claimed the worshippers of Luna were crazy, hence the word "lunatic," a person moon-touched or moon-struck. To this day, many people believe lunacy is affected by the moon, being characterized by increased psychic disturbance when the moon is full.

1. Chaucer, 435. 2. Briffault 3, 67. 3. *Larousse,* 304.

Lupa

Sacred She-Wolf of Roman legend, nurse of the foundling twins Romulus and Remus. Lupa's temple harlots were *lupae,* sometimes called Queens (or high priestesses) in outlying towns of the empire. Lupa's greatest festival was the annual Lupercalia, celebrated in the Grotto of the She-Wolf, with orgiastic rites to insure the year's fertility. After participating in the ceremony, naked youths traveled throughout Palatine towns to "purify" them.[1] Perhaps this was why, after Lupa's festival was adopted by the Christian church, it was renamed the Feast of the Purification of the Virgin.[2] See **Dog; Werewolf.**

1. Wedeck, 174. 2. *Larousse*, 208.

Lupus

var. Loup, Saint

Fictitious saint based on the words *Sanctus Lupus* (Holy Wolf) on Gallo-Roman icons, dating back to the worship of Dis Pater as the Holy Wolf of Gaul. Christian hagiographers pretended Lupus was a bishop of Troyes who saved Gaul from the Huns. This story was entirely falsified.[1] See **Werewolf.**

1. Attwater, 223.

Lycaon

Arcadian sacred king, ancestor of all "lycanthropes" (werewolves); his totemic form was a wolf. He was formerly worshipped in the Lyceum or "wolf-temple" where Aristotle taught.[1] Lycaon seems to have been an earthly incarnation of several elder gods able to assume wolf shape, such as Apollo Lycaeus or Zeus Lycaeus.

1. Summers, W., 144.

As law-giver and dispenser of justice, the Egyptian Goddess MAAT weighed each man's soul against a feather—which became the symbol that she sports prominently in this bas-relief. From the period of the 19th Dynasty.

One of the MAENADS who were Dionysian priestesses. When possessed by the wine god, they sacrificed and ate their victims. Later, in the classical age, they made do with just drinking and carnival processions. Roman copy of a 5th-century Greek relief; near life-size.

Tales of the great MARTYRS of the Middle Ages are now generally thought to have been made up to impress later Christians with the near-preposterous tenacity to believe. Poor Saint Julitta, for example, suffered the discomfort shown only after having been hammered full of nails, boiled in oil, and—contrary to the evidence—decapitated. Detail, panel painting of an altar frontal; 12th century.

Ma

"Ma-Ma" means "mother's breasts" in nearly all languages.[1] "All around the world, from Russia to Samoa, and in the ancient languages of Egypt, Babylon, India, and the Americas, the word for 'mother' is *mama* or some minor variation of this word."[2] In ancient Anatolia the Mother was Ma-Bellona; in Sumer and Akkad the Great Goddess was often called Mama, Mami, Mammitu, etc. In Central and South America the Goddess had such names as Mama Cocha, Mama Quilla, Mama Cuna.[3]

Basic mother-syllable of Indo-European languages, worshipped in itself as the fundamental name of the Goddess. The universality of the mother-word (not shared by words for "father") indicates either that the human race carried the same word from its earliest source to all parts of the earth at a period previous to the discovery of fatherhood; or else that all human beings instinctively say something like "ma" as the first verbal sound and associate it with the mother's breast, consequently with emotional dependence on a divinity perceived as a milk-giving mother—notwithstanding the absurd reference of Moses to a "nursing father" carrying the sucking child in his bosom (Numbers 11:12).

In the Far East, the maternal blood bond that joined members of the matrilineal clan was *mamata,* "mine-ness."[4] Its sacred letter *Ma,* in pictographic form as the Spark of Life (bindu or vindu), was said to be "in the Great Yoni."[5] This scripture referred to a mystic essence uniting all the souls in a matrilineal kinship group. *Ma* or *mamata* expressed the idea that descendants of the same mother shared the same blood and couldn't injure one another without injuring themselves; therefore the concept of the maternal clan was a practical instrument of peace.

In Indo-European root languages, *Ma* was often defined as "intelligence," the maternal force that bound elements together to create forms at the beginning of the world.[6] Ancient Egypt gave this maternal force such names as Ma-Nu, Maa, or Maat, the Great Goddess of the All-Seeing Eye and the spirit of Truth.[7]

The primitive Iranian Moon-goddess Mah (or Al-Mah, the Moon) was another form of the same deity. Arabs called her Qis-Mah, "Fate," which the Turks corrupted into *kismet.* She gave birth to a series of Messiahs, each one called the Mahdi, one guided or given by Mother Mah. Persians made her name a sacred Word, formed of the letters Mourdad-Ameretat, "Death-Rebirth."[8] The ideogram MA was said to mean a state of immortality brought about by drinking the milk of the Goddess's breast, which brings one back to the original Ma-Ma.

In Hebrew the same sacred letters MA made the Mem-Aleph, combining ideographs of "fluid" and "birth." This holy sign was credited with great protective power, and was written on Jewish amulets dating from the early 9th century B.C.[9] It could have been copied from either the Persians or the Egyptians, whose Mother Isis wore an "Amulet of Ma," a vase representing her own fountains of nourishing fluid.[10] Or again, as Ma-Nu, the Primal Deep, she was symbolized by three cauldrons.[11] Even today the Tantric Goddess as a personification of "fertilizing water" is named Mamaki.[12]

In Egyptian myth, a reversal of the Ma-Ma of nourishing breasts produced the female Devourer in the underworld: Am-Am, eater of souls. In the cyclic fashion of the elder religions, the giver was transformed into the taker.[13]

Ma, the Great Goddess of Comana, was "worshipped by a whole people of hierodules in the ravines of the Taurus and along the banks of the Iris. Like Cybele she was an ancient Anatolian divinity and personified fertile nature."[14] She was taken to Rome where she merged with the war goddess Bellona, who personified fighting spirit as indomitable as that of a mother defending her young.

Today the divine implications of the syllable *Ma* are recognized only in obscure semi-magical cults like voodooism, where a priestess embodies the Goddess's spirit and is known as *mamaloi* or *mambo.*[15] However, Ma is still a universal synonym for "mother." See **Motherhood**.

1. Potter & Sargent, 229. 2. Farb, W.P., 317. 3. *Larousse,* 443.
4. *Bardo Thodol,* 219; Campbell, Or.M., 216. 5. *Mahanirvanatantra,* cxx.
6. d'Alviella, 240. 7. Budge, E.L., 55. 8. *Larousse,* 311, 317. 9. Albright, 198.
10. Elworthy, 125. 11. *Book of the Dead,* 205. 12. Tatz & Kent, 164.
13. Budge, E.M., 171. 14. Cumont, O.R.R.P., 54. 15. Martello, 160.

Maat

Egyptian Goddess as personification of "Truth" or "Justice"; the original name based on the universal Indo-European mother-syllable meant simply "Mother." Maat's symbol was the feather against which she weighed each man's heart-soul *(ab)* in her underground Hall of Judgment. Thus the Plume of Maat itself became a hieroglyph for "truth."[1]

The same feathers of Truth were worn by other aspects of the Goddess, such as Isis, who was the same lawgiving Mother. The gods themselves were constrained to "live by Maat." Her law governed all three worlds ruled by her trinity as "Lady of heaven, queen of the earth, and mistress of the underworld."[2]

As the lawgiver of archaic Egypt, Maat was comparable to Babylonian **Tiamat** who gave the sacred tablets to the first king of gods. Maat's laws were notably benevolent, compared to the harsh commands of later patriarchal gods, backed up by savage threats like those of Deuteronomy 28:15–68. An Egyptian was expected to recite the famous Negative Confession in the presence of Maat and Thoth (or Anubis) to show he had obeyed Maat's rules of behavior:

> *I have not been a man of anger. I have done no evil to mankind. I have not inflicted pain. I have made none to weep. I have done violence to no man. I have not done harm unto animals. I have not robbed the poor. I have not fouled water. I have not trampled fields. I have not behaved with insolence. I have not judged hastily. I have not stirred up strife. I have not made any man to commit murder for me. I have not insisted that excessive work be done for me daily. I have not borne false witness. I have not stolen land. I have not cheated in measuring the bushel. I have*

allowed no man to suffer hunger. I have not increased my wealth except with such things as are my own possessions. I have not seized wrongfully the property of others. I have not taken milk from the mouths of babes.[3]

Those who lived by the laws of Maat took a sacramental drink, comparable to the Hindus' Soma or its Persian counterpart Haoma, which conferred ritual purity in the same sense as the Christian "washing in the blood of the Lamb." Egyptian scribes of the 3rd millenium B.C. wrote: "My inward parts have been washed in the liquor of Maat." Like baptismal water of life, Maat's potion brought life-after-death to the peaceful, but death overtook violent persons.[4]

Egyptian moral precepts were of a high order, many of them turning up centuries later in the Bible:

Take heed not to rob the poor, and be not cruel to the destitute. . . . If thou canst answer the man who attacks thee, do him no injury. Let the evildoer alone; he will destroy himself. We must help the sinner, for may we not become like him? . . . Crusts of bread and a loving heart are better than rich food and contention. . . . Learn to be content with what thou hast. Treasure obtained by fraud will not stay with thee; thou hast it today, tomorrow it has departed. . . . The approval of man is better than riches.[5]

Under the feudal disorders of the 12th dynasty, old rules began to break down along with the matrilineal clan system that supported them, and educated Egyptians deplored the disruptions of society. A Heliopolitan priest wrote: "Maat is cast out, iniquity is in the midst of the council hall. . . . [T]he poor man has no strength to save himself from him that is stronger than he."[6] Sometimes kinsman murdered kinsman, in violation of the clan's most sacred rule. One writer unfavorably compared his countrymen to the Maat-worshipping tribes of Nubia: "The Matoi, who are friendly towards Egypt, say: 'How could there be a man that would slay his brother?' "[7]

Maat was more than a judge of the dead. She was a stand-in for all Egyptian Goddesses, including Hathor, Mut, Isis, Neith, Nekhbet, etc. The sun god was told: "The goddess Maat embraceth thee both at morn and at eve." As a birth-giver, she was sometimes Metet, the Morning Boat of the Sun, translated "becoming strong" and corresponding to the Greco-Roman mother of dawn, Mater Matuta.[8] She was worshipped in lands other than Egypt. Northern Syria was called by the Hittites, Mat Hatti: that is, Mother of Hatti.[9] Egyptian priests drew the Feather of Maat on their tongues in green dye, to give their words a Logos-like power of Truth so their verbal magic could create reality.[10] Similarly in northern Europe the divine bard Bragi had this power because of the runes engraved on his tongue by the Goddess Idun.

African Pygmies still know Maat by the name she bore in Sumeria as "womb" and "underworld": Matu. She was the first woman, and the mother of God. Like her Egyptian counterpart she was sometimes cat-headed.[11]

1. Budge, E.L., 68. 2. Budge, G.E. 1, 418. 3. Budge, D.N., 254; Hallet, 411. 4. H. Smith, 49–51. 5. Budge, D.N., 258–59. 6. H. Smith, 50. 7. Erman, 43, 107. 8. Budge, G.E. 1, 323, 417. 9. Mendenhall, 157. 10. Seligmann, 39. 11. Hallet, 95.

Mab, Queen

Celtic Fairy Queen, whose name meant "mead"—a red drink representing sovereignty which she gave to each of her many consorts.[1] Like the "claret" in the lap of Thomas Rhymer's Fairy Queen, this seems to have been a concoction of the queen's own **menstrual blood** as the feminine wine of wisdom. Mab's legends date from the matriarchal age, when queens chose and invested their own kings. See **Thomas Rhymer**.

1. Rees, 75.

Macabre

Grim Reaper of medieval mystery plays. As Lord of Death, Macabre led the *danse macabre* (German *Totentanz*) wearing a skeleton suit and carrying a scythe. Like the "Destroyer" deities of the east, the Macabre figure represented the Gnostic death-in-life principle. See **Mask**.

Macha

"Great Queen of Phantoms," worshipped in Ireland even before the coming of the Celts; probably identical with the Central Asian Moon-goddess Macha Alla, Mother of Life and Death. She appeared in the Old Testament as Queen Maachah, whose spirit was worshipped as an idol in a grove until ousted by her "son," King Asa (1 Kings 15:13). The mountaintop temple of Machaerus (where John the Baptist met his doom) may have been named for her.

Macha's Irish shrine was Emain Macha, capital of Ulster. Its heavenly form was Emania, the Moon-goddess's realm of death.[1] As the third person or death-aspect of the triple Morrigan she presided over an extensive necropolis. Like other versions of the deadly mother (Morgan, Durga, Uma, Kara), she haunted battlefields and made magic with the blood of slain men.[2] She was also identified with the Fairy Queen, Mab. As a trinitarian Goddess, she cast her death curse on **Cu Chulainn** in the guise of three druidic "sorceresses of Mab."[3]

Some said the voice of Macha summoned men to death, and it was the same as the dread voice of the **Banshee**, or "woman of the barrow-graves."[4] Since followers of the Old Religion went to her land of death, naturally their spirits inhabited the ancient tombs that also represented her womb of rebirth.

1. *Larousse,* 229; Spence, 146. 2. Rees, 36. 3. *Larousse,* 233. 4. Goodrich, 177.

Mader-Akka

"Mother Akka," a Lapp name of the ancestress of humanity; the same as the Goddess-mother of Akkad, who was also Acco in Greece, Acca Larentia in Rome, etc. See **Akka**.

Madri

"Mother," in Tantric Buddhism a Goddess of Enlightenment who gave birth to the moon and sun; the Great Mother as a spouse of one of the popular incarnations of the Buddha.[1]

1. Waddell, 545.

Maenads

Priestesses of **Dionysus** and Orpheus, named after their original home, the holy mountain of Maenalus, where Pan also lived as an Arcadian shepherd. Possessed by the spirit of the wine god, the Maenads became "wild women" who tore apart their sacrificial victim and devoured him during their orgies. In the more civilized classical age, they worshipped their Savior with a drunken feast and carnival processions. In Rome they were called Bacchantes, dedicated to their god under his Roman name of Bacchus. See **Orphism**.

Maera

Black bitch-totem of Hecate, a form assumed by her Trojan incarnation, Queen Hecuba, when she was captured by Odysseus. The cause of his long wandering exile apparently was the curse Hecuba-Maera laid on him. Some said she was killed and buried in "The Bitch's Tomb." Others said she scared away her enemies with her spells and curses and ran free.

She was an animal version of the fatal Crone-goddess Moera, symbolized by the Lesser Dog Star whose rising announced human sacrifices in Attica. One of her victims was a king whose daughter Odysseus married, "and whose fate he will therefore have shared in the original myth."[1] Similar sacrifices were still offered to the Death-goddess and Wolf-mother Maerin in her temple at Trondheim as late as the 11th century A.D.[2]

1. Graves, G.M. 2, 341–44. 2. Turville-Petre, 91.

Magdala

"High Place," or "Temple"; in Herod's triple-towered palace in Jerusalem, the sanctuary of Queen Mariamne. Thus "Miriam of Magdala" (**Mary Magdalene**) was either the queen herself or a high priestess impersonating the Goddess Mari. See **Mary**.

Magen David

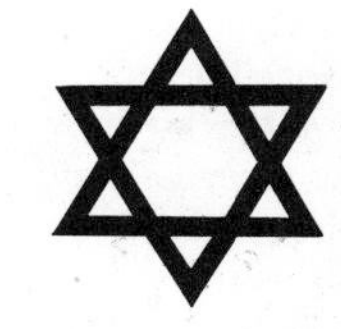

Star of David (Hexagram)

"Shield of David," the so-called Star of David or **hexagram** constructed of two interlocked triangles, now accepted as a symbol of Judaism. Actually, it was not associated with Judaism until the late Middle Ages and was not officially accepted as a Jewish symbol until the 17th century.[1]

The original source of the Magen David was the Tantric "Great Yantra," which stood for union of the sexes: the downward-pointing triangle being female, the upward-pointing one male, the two signifying the eternal union of God and Goddess.[2] Cabalistic sex-worship brought the Yantra into Jewish tradition, but later puritanical elements obscured its original meaning.

1. *Encyc. Brit.*, "Magen David." 2. Zimmer, p. 147.

Magi

"Magicians," the Three Wise Men inserted into the Christian birth-story because Persian-Essenic sages taught that the Magi were the only seers able to read the coming of the Messiah's star and so identify the right Divine Child. This teaching stemmed ultimately from Egypt, where the Three Wise Men were the three stars in the Belt of Orion, pointing to Osiris's star Sothis (Sirius), which "rose in the east" to announce the coming of the Savior at the season of the Nile flood. (See **Osiris**.) These three Belt stars were still called Magi in the Middle Ages.[1]

In Rome early in the Christian era, Magi meant priests of Mithra (the original Persian "Messiah"), or astrologers, or miscellaneous healers and miracle-workers; it was a term for magicians in general. Roman Christians were hostile to the Magi but were forced to retain the three Magi of the Gospel story because their presence was emphasized as evidence of Jesus's divinity.

1. Jobes, 221.

Giovanni della Porta's list said ancient magicians were called *magos* by Persians; *sapientes* by the Latins; *philosophes* by the Greeks; *Brachmanes* or *gymnosophistas* by the Indians; *Chaldaeos* by the Babylonians and Assyrians; *Drydas, Bardos,* and *Semnothes* by the Celts; *sacerdotes* by the Egyptians; and *prophetes* by the Cabalists. History's leading magicians were Persia's Zoroaster, Rome's Numa Pompilius, Thrace's Zalmoxis, Babylon's Buddha, and Egypt's Hermes.[3]

Giovanni della Porta (1535–1615) Neapolitan philosopher and author, who wrote comedies as well as scientific treatises on magnetism, agriculture, optical phenomena, cryptography, steam engines, chemistry, astrology, and demonology. He founded the Accademia dei Segreti, which the Inquisition later suppressed.

Magic

Though the church condemned magic as a devilish art, the Ages of Faith were filled with magical beliefs and practices. Magic was legal in Roman times; this tolerance continued through the early Middle Ages, in some areas much longer than that. Sir Walter Raleigh praised magic as a route to "virtues hidden in the center of the center." He said magic "bringeth to light the inmost virtues, and draweth them out of Nature's hidden bosom to human use."[1]

The nobility—including princes of the church—supported court magicians, astrologers, and diviners who helped them conduct their affairs.[2] Scholars carefully classified different types of magicians, as if to distinguish the heretical from the acceptable. The "ancients" were respected for their great magical wisdom.

Mixtures of tradition and confusion characterized nearly all the manifestations of magic, especially the verbal charms and holy names popularly supposed to invoke supernatural powers necessary to the "working." A magician must recite defensive charms while enroute to the scene of a magical operation, such as: "Zazaii, Zamaii, Puidamon most powerful, Sedon most strong, El, Yod He Vau He (the **tetragrammaton**), Iah, Agla, assist me an unworthy sinner who have had the boldness to pronounce these Holy Names which no man should name and invoke save in very great danger. Therefore have I recourse unto these Most Holy Names, being in great peril both of soul and of body. Pardon me if I have sinned in any manner, for I trust in Thy protection alone, especially on this journey." Proceedings were usually opened with an "evocation," often involving a sacrifice to be performed in a specific manner. The Grand Grimoire gives a sample:

> *On the third day of the moon, the witch or sorcerer will sever the head of a virgin kid with one stroke, a clean cut. The kid will be garlanded with verbena and green ribbon beforehand and the sacrifice must take place far away from habitation. A clean, new knife is used; the celebrant must bare the right shoulder and keep a willow wood fire brightly aflame. Saying: "I offer this creature to three, O great Adonai, Elohim, Ariel and Jehovas, in the honor and power and the resplendence of The Name, which is greater than all the spirits. O Great Adonai: agree to accept it as agreeable."*[4]

Magic books were full of charms in series, with assurances that if one charm failed to call up the dread spirits, then surely the next one, bearing even more powerful names, would work. Demons who stubbornly refused to appear were threatened with eternal torments.

The frustrated magician played God and enchanted recalcitrant spirits into deeper circles of hell. The silliness of the grimoires can only be appreciated through their own words; here in a series of invocations from the Lemegeton or Lesser Key of Solomon:

> *O mighty and potent prince Samael, who art the ruler and governor of the first hour of the day by the decree of the Most High God, King of Glory; I, the servant of the Most High, do desire and entreat you by three great and potent names of God, Adonai, Aglaon, Tetragrammaton, and by the power and virtue thereof, to assist me in my affairs, and by your power and authority to send me, causing to appear before me, all or any of the angels whom I shall call by name, the same being resident under your government. I do further entreat and require that they shall help me in all matters which accord with their office, even as I shall desire, and that they shall act for me as for the servant of the Most High. Amen.*

Grand Grimoire
One of the most popular Renaissance collections of spells, exorcisms, invocations, and magical recipes.

If this legalistic contract failed to bind the demons, the magician commonly resorted to threats:

> *Because thou art disobedient, and obeyst not my commandments nor the precepts of the Lord thy God, now I, who am the servant of the Most High and Imperial Lord God of Hosts, Jehovah, having His celestial power and permission, for this thine averseness and contempt, thy great disobedience and rebellion, will excommunicate thee, will destroy thy name and seal, and bury them in unending oblivion, unless thou comest immediately, visibly and affably, here before this circle, within this triangle, assuming a fair and comely form, without doing harm unto myself or any creature whatsoever, but giving reasonable answer to my requests and performing my desire in all things.*

Solemn magicians seem not to have realized the absurdity of excommunicating a demon, who was hardly likely to be distressed by severing relations with the church, since he had presumably severed relations with God already. Nevertheless, wizards were supplied with the following curse for excommunication:

> *Thou art still pernicious and disobedient, willing not to appear and inform me upon that which I desire to know; now therefore, in the Name and by the power and dignity of the Omnipotent and Immortal Lord God of Hosts, Jehovah Tetragrammaton, sole Creator of Heaven, Earth, and Hell, with all contained therein, the marvellous Disposer of all things visible and invisible, I do hereby curse and deprive thee of all thine office, power and place; I bind thee in the depth of the Bottomless Pit, there to remain unto the Day of Judgment, in the Lake of Fire and Brimstone, prepared for the rebellious Spirits. May all the Company of Heaven curse thee; may the Sun, the Moon, the Stars, the Light of the Hosts of heaven, curse thee into fire unquenchable, into torments unspeakable; and even as thy name and seal are bound up in this box, to be choked with sulphureous and stinking substances and to burn in this material fire, so, in the name of Jehovah, and by the power and dignity of the three names, Tetragrammaton, Anexhexeton, Primematum, may all these drive thee, O thou disobedient Spirit N., into the Lake of Fire.*

The grimoires provided many excuses for failure. They required infinite care in the manufacture of tools, with complicated charms and debilitating purifications, fasting, and penance. Their lists of holy names and words of power were lengthy and hard to remember—and letter-perfect recitation was essential. The practice of magic was clearly beyond the grasp of the lazy, stupid, or illiterate. Unfortunately it was also beyond the grasp of the credulous educated as well.

A grimoire called the *Little Albert* gave an infallible formula for making a ring of invisibility, but the ring had to be plaited with three hairs from the head of a hyena.[6] Hyenas were scarce in Europe, but even if one could be found, its head hairs would prove too short to be plaited in a ring. Similarly impossible prescriptions appeared in all magic books. The more infallible the charm, the more outrageously difficult its execution.

Faith in magic was identical with faith in religion. Both depended on hieratic ceremony and verbal incantation. Both involved prayer to a superior power—even the same power in both cases. Both used the name as a vehicle of appeal and coercion. The pious practiced magic no less than the impious by way of a thousand informal charms like the following, advocated in 1785 to learn winning numbers in the French national lottery:

> *Lord Jesus Christ, Who hast said, "I am the Way, the Truth, and the Life," for Thou hast cherished truth and hast shown me the secrets of Thy wisdom whereby again this night the unknown things which are not revealed save to the lowly shall be revealed to me, send me the angels Uriel, Rubiel, and Barachiel to teach me which numbers I must choose to win, by Him Who will come to judge the quick and the dead and the times by fire.*[7]

Peasant magic was usually crude, without the secret names and verbose invocations requiring a written recipe. Illiterate witches simply performed acts of magic, like this rude country charm to cure lameness:

> *Take hog's dung and charnell, and put them together and hold them in your left hand, and take in the other hand a knife, and prick the medicine three times, then cast the same into the fire, and take the said knife and make three pricks under a table, and let the knife stick there; and after that take three leaves of sage, and as many of herb John, and put them into ale, and drink it last at night and first in the morning.*[8]

A witch's patient testified that this procedure did indeed give her "ease of her lameness." We may laugh, but equally crude magic has been promulgated for profit in our own time, often by churches themselves. In 1880, one of the leading churches in Philadelphia sold blessed candles with the guarantee that the purchaser would be preserved for one year from all disorders of the throat. A sermon was preached to this effect, and seven examples given of miraculous cures.[9] The mass of exploitable believers was still evident a century later in 1970, when an enterprising seer sold healing cloths by radio advertising: "I lay hands on a cloth," he said. "The healing power of God which I received four years ago is passed on to the cloth which I send to you."[10]

Christians practiced magic from the very beginning of the church. Isaac of Antioch complained in the 5th century that not only the people but clergymen also "carry about the incantations of the magicians; and instead of the holy cross, lo, they carry the books of devils . . . ; a child carries about devils' names and comes to church."[11] In other words, pagan amulets were credited with as much protective power as Christian amulets. St. Jerome himself affirmed that a sapphire amulet "procures favor with princes, pacifies enemies, and obtains freedom from captivity."[12]

Christian authorities said an amulet containing many secret names of God was sure to keep the bearer from any evil death. The cake of wax called Agnus Dei (Lamb of God) was advertised by Pope Urban V as a sure protection against lightning, fire, and water; also a charm for easy childbirth and remittance of sins. Various charms were sold by the church to preserve horses' hoofs from cracks, to prevent disease, to enhance sexual potency. Girls wishing to grow long hair were told to hang locks of their hair before an image of St. Urbane. Christians had malevolent charms too. It was believed that any man would die within a year if the 108th Psalm was "said against" him by a priest.[13] The Mass was credited with potent magical force for both good and evil uses. Masses were said for healing, for fertility, for magical protection of livestock, houses, boats, etc.; they were also said to kill enemies. From the 7th to the 15th century, church literature spoke of priests who could cause death by saying the Mass for the Dead against living persons.[14]

Up to the 17th century it was still written that a dream revealing the whereabouts of any stolen article could be obtained by placing under one's pillow a wax tablet with the names of the Magi—Jasper, Melchisor (sic), and Balthasar. Another kind of magical dream, to see the face of one's future mate, could be had by putting a Bible under the pillow with a sixpence inserted in the Book of Ruth.[15] Many magic charms invoked the names of apostles:

The devil is tying a knot in my leg!
Mark, Luke, and John, unloose it, I beg;
Crosses three we make to ease us:
Two for the thieves, and one for Christ Jesus![16]

Priests often tried to impress simple folk by teaching them magic charms. Ady's maid was given a charm to make butter come in the churn, by an old woman who said her mother had it from "a learned Church man in Queen Maries days, when as church men had more cunning, and could teach people many a trick, that our Ministers now a days know not."[17] Typical Christian magic included verbal charms to exorcise, heal, bless, or excommunicate; the wearing of amulets such as crucifixes, St. Christopher medals, and scraps of the scriptural texts; the use of holy water; the invocation of saints; and of course the belief in miracles generally—for "magic" and "miracle" were but different words for the same idea.

1. J.B. Russell, 55, 143. 2. Lea unabridged, 772. 3. Shumaker, 235. 4. Ravensdale & Morgan, 72. 5. Waite, C.M., 77 et seq. 6. Waite, C.M., 310. 7. de Givry, 310. 8. Rosen, 114. 9. Leland, 42. 10. Bromberg, 179. 11. Angus, 51. 12. Hazlitt, 6. 13. Scot, 165, 186, 188, 201, 216. 14. Cavendish, P.E., 224. 15. Hazlitt, 22, 189. 16. Hazlitt, 363. 17. Hazlitt, 84.

Magna Dea

"Great Goddess" of Syria, worshipped especially at Hierapolis, "Holy City." The same title was applied to all Goddesses throughout the Roman empire, which was verging on a concept of female monotheism when Jewish, Persian, and Christian patriarchy intervened.

Magnates

"Landowners," medieval noblemen, whose title in the Balkans probably descended from the Magnetes or Centaurs. Equestrian warriors were the model of every military aristocracy in Europe: Spanish caballeros, French chevaliers, English cavaliers, all meant "riders of horses."

Magog

"Mother of Gog," biblical name of the Scythian-Amazonian Goddess and her land in the north, whence came equestrian warriors greatly feared by the Semites, to judge from the prophets' lengthy cursings and invocations for their defeat (Ezekiel 38).

Authors of Genesis made Magog a "son" of Japheth (Genesis 10:2), though Japheth himself was not a Hebraic hero but a borrowed form of the titan Iapetus in Greek myth.[1] From this bit of syncretic confusion arose the impression that Magog was a male, and a giant, for a titan's offspring would naturally be another titan.

Though tribes of western Asia continued to worship Magog as a Goddess, in Europe "Gogmagog" was usually envisioned as a demonic colossus. "Ma" was merged with the Celtic *mac* to yield an interpretation of "Gog, son of Gog." Gog and Magog were commonly used names for any pair of colossal figures, especially figures of pagan deities. Yet, curiously, "Gog and Magog" appeared in Renaissance magic books as two of the Ineffable Names of God.[2]

1. Graves, W.G., 253. 2. Waite, C.M., 277.

Maha-Nila-Sarasvati

"Great Blue River Goddess," Hindu name of the Mother of Waters, from which the name of the Nile may have been derived.[1] The waters of the Goddess Sarasvati were once considered essential to the anointing of kings, purification, and baptism.

1. Avalon, 193.

Maharis

"Motherhoods," the basic social unit of clans in Assam, where families were matrilineal. See **Motherhood**.

Maharutti

Tantric "Great Rite," the sexual union between the menstruating Goddess and her chosen bridegroom Shiva the Condemned One, who died shortly afterward and became Shava, the Corpse. Thus *maharutti* was both a *hieros gamos* and a love-death. See **Sex**; **Tantrism**.

Mahatma

Hindu sage, a word literally meaning "Great Mother," masculinized in much the same way as the Semitic *ima,* "mother," became *imam,* a male sage. The original *mahatmas* were the Primal Matriarchs, or *matrikadevis.*

Mahdi

One guided by, sent by, or given by the Moon-goddess Mah; Arabic-Moslem title of the promised Messiah, who became the Desired Knight of medieval European romance. He was essentially the same as the final avatar of Buddha, the Kalki yet to appear on earth; or the Persian Messiah, or the Christian Christ in his Second Coming. The Mahdi would be born of "the Virgin Paradise" (*Pairidaeza*), who embodied the spirit of the Moon-goddess on earth. His coming was so eagerly awaited that many historical Islamic leaders claimed to personify him.

After Arabia was converted to Islam, it was usually supposed that the Mahdi would be sent by Allah. But he was older than Islam. As his title suggests, he was a Son of the Moon in the most primitive times, when all Arabia was the territory of the lunar Goddess, one of whose oldest names was Mah.[1] See **Ma**.

1. *Larousse,* 311.

Maia

"Grandmother of Magic," mother of the Greeks' Enlightened One, Hermes; the western version of **Maya**, "Magic," mother of the Hindus' Enlightened One, Buddha. She personified the powers of transformation and material "appearances," the same powers attributed to Maya-Kali, who made the universe by her magic. Greek writers called Maia one of the Pleiades, but also understood that she was the Great Goddess of Maytime festivals, of the renewal and rebirth of the dead. She made her son Hermes the Conductor of Souls in the underworld, just as the Hindu Maya made her masculine counterpart Ya-Ma into a Conductor of Souls and Lord of Death.[1]

1. Graves, W.G., 179.

Maira

Gnostic name of the Star of Isis, or Venus, or Stella Maris, a title of the virgin **Mary**. The star represented a World Soul.

Maithuna

Tantric term for *coitus reservatus,* sexual intercourse performed as one of the Five Boons given to humanity by Kali. The other four were *madya,* wine; *mamsa,* meat; *matsya,* fish; and *mudra,* woman.[1] *Maithuna* was the sexual technique for allowing man to assimilate into himself the innate magical wisdom of woman. See **Tantrism**.

1. Campbell, Or.M., 359.

Malinalxochitl

Primal Mother of Aztec mythology, ruler of all men and beasts until she was overthrown by her brother, the divine leader of the patriarchal Aztecs. After her defeat, she was diabolized.

var. Mamaki, Mamata

Mama

Title of the Great Goddess **Ma**, or Mama, the world's basic name for "mother's breasts." Mother Kali was sometimes Mamaki, spirit of the world's "Fertilizing Waters." She was also Mamata, spirit of "mineness" or belonging, binding members of the same matrilineal clan together through the blood of mothers.[1] In Mesopotamia, she was Mami or Mammitu or Mama, the Creatress who made mankind of clay and nourished her creatures with her own magic fluids.[2]

1. Campbell, Or.M., 216. 2. Neumann, G.M., 136.

Mammisi

Egyptian "motherhood temple" usually built to honor the queen's maternity, after she gave birth to her first child and so became assimilated to the Goddess. Queen Cleopatra had a *mammisi* built for worship of her own motherhood after the birth of her first child. It was still standing in the 19th century A.D. but has since vanished. See **Cleopatra VII**.

Mammon

Medieval demon of commercial acquisitiveness, whose name meant "riches." In the Middle East, the original meaning of this name was the rich outpouring of the Great Goddess's inexhaustible breasts *(mammae),* which nourished all her children; Babylon named her Mami or Mammitu (Mother), the biblical Mamre. Some Sumero-Babylonian scriptures called her "Mammetun the mother of destinies."[1]

Jesus's precept, "Ye cannot serve God and Mammon" (Luke 16:13) meant a choice between God and Goddess, in a time when her temples were richer and more magnificent than his. The Gospels demanded that her shrines be destroyed and her wealth taken away, in an obviously jealous attack on the "Many-breasted" Goddess "whom all Asia and the world worshippeth" (Acts 19:27). Like the Oriental Goddess Earth (Artha, "riches"), she stood for material wealth because her temples had a great deal of it and her soil was the ultimate source of all.[2]

It was the habit of demonologists to masculinize even Goddesses when they were diabolized and consigned to hell. Even Ashtoreth, or Astarte, was a male in hell. Much the same thing seems to have happened to Mammetun: she became a "lord" of riches. Weyer made her/him a dignitary of hell and an ambassador from hell to England, probably a reflection of resentment of English commercialism.[3]

1. *Epic of Gilgamesh,* 107. 2. Cavendish, P.E., 238. 3. Waite, C.M., 186–87.

Mamokoriyoma

Primal Mother of the Yanomamo tribes, who gave birth to the first people and instituted ritual **cannibalism**.

Mamom

"Grandmother," the oldest style of Maya pottery, designed and executed by women, to whom the art of pottery was sacred. See **Potter**.

Man

In the original Old Norse, *man* meant "woman."[1] The word for "man" was not *man* but *wer,* from the Sanskrit root *vir* as in *wer-wulf,* the man-wolf.[2] The name Man meant the Moon, creatress of all creatures according to Scandinavian and other tribes throughout Europe. Even in imperial Rome, Man or Mana was the mother of all *manes* or ancestral spirits. The Sanskrit root *man* meant "moon" and "wisdom," both the primary attributes of the Great Goddess.[3]

Heathen skalds composed a class of sacred love songs to the feminine principle of the Moon and her earthly incarnation, woman; these were *mansongr,* "woman-songs." They were expressly prohibited by the Catholic church.[4]

The Isle of Man was formerly sacred to the Moon-goddess, who was sometimes a mermaid or an androgynous Aphrodite who kept men's souls in "pots turned upside down"—i.e., grave mounds and beehive tombs.[5] Passage graves in East Jutland were full of upturned pots, an Iron Age burial custom.[6] The same custom was mentioned in South America where the Moon carries souls away and places them under upturned pots.[7] Apparently the Isle of Man used to be a sacred Isle of the Dead. The name of its deity was variously rendered Man, Mana, Mana-Anna, or Manannan.

The island used to have an "enchanted palace" with a crypt or chapel of thirteen pillars, the sacred number of the old lunar year. Every visitor was expected to count the pillars. If the counting ceremony was omitted, the visitor would be imprisoned in the crypt, which indicates a burial place sacred to the Moon. The site was later destroyed by "salt spilled on the ground," a reference to Christians' habit of leveling pagan shrines and sowing the ground with salt to make it infertile.

The Goddess-or-God Mana-Anna, or Mannanan, was masculinized as a "son of Lir" of Sidh Finnaha. Lir however was the same as Shakespeare's King Lear, who had three daughters but no son.[10] Thus, Shakespeare's source seems to indicate that this child of Lir was originally the Triple Goddess, for one of the so-called daughters, Cordelia, was really Creiddylad, another name for the Fairy Queen.[11]

The Moon-goddess appeared in Manx legend as a Fairy Queen who sometimes led the whole male population "into the sea, where they perished." Most probably they perished first and were given to the sea-womb as in the ancient Norse funeral rite. The Fairy Queen escaped annihilation by the priests when she took the form of a wren. But pious Manxmen organized wren hunts, a custom followed every New Year's Day thereafter, killing scores of the little birds in an effort to kill "Jenny Wren," the fairy. Feathers of the slain wrens were said to preserve sailors from shipwreck, and no Manx sailor would go to sea without one.[8] The wren hunts possibly were pre-Christian, with the legend of the Fairy Queen invented for a new rationale. Before the missionaries came, wrens probably were the "soul-birds" sacrificed to the Goddess. Vallancey said the druids considered the wren supreme among all birds. "The superstitious respect shown to this bird gave offense to our first Christian missionaries, and by their commands he is still hunted and killed by the peasants on Christmas Day, and on the following (St. Stephen's Day) he is carried about hung by the leg, in the center of two hoops crossing each other at right angles."[9]

1. Steenstrup, 105. 2. J.B. Russell, 55. 3. Avalon, 178. 4. Turville-Petre, 176. 5. Spence, 126, 158; Keightley, 259. 6. H. R. E. Davidson, P.S., 34. 7. Eliade, S., 327. 8. Hazlitt, 387–90. 9. Hazlitt, 666. 10. Goodrich, 177. 11. Graves, W.G., 183.

Mana

var. Mania

Nearly all languages had a cognate of this word, the basic meaning of which was maternal power, moon-spirit, magic, supernatural force, and a title of the Goddess. *Mana* came back into English via anthropological studies in the South Pacific, where the word was described as follows:

> *Mana is the stuff through which magic works . . . proceeding immediately from the nature of the sacred person or thing, or mediately because a ghost or spirit has put it into the person or thing. . . . The cult of the relics of saints springs from the belief that their bodies, whether living or dead, possessed Mana.*[3]

Mana also ruled the underworld, which the Finns called Manala.[6] The Romans knew her as a very ancient Goddess Mana or Mania, governing the underground land of the long dead: the ancestral spirits called *manes,* her children. They dwelt in a pit under the *lapis manalis* in the Forum, emerging to receive their offerings on the annual feast day of the Maniae.[7] On this occasion the Goddess Mania appeared in a fright mask, like the terrifying Crone-face of Medusa or Destroying Kali.[8]

Mania was not solely a spirit of death or madness, however, in classical times. Her "moon-madness" or "lunacy" was viewed as a revelation of the divine, to be received with gratitude. Socrates said, "The greatest of our blessings come to us through *mania.* . . . Madness coming from [the deity] is superior to sanity of human origin."[9] In other words, Mana-Mania was the Muse. Gnostics said Mana is "the divine spirit in man"; and the Great Mana, or Mana of Glory, is "the highest godhead."[10]

Mana may be compared to Hindu *Maya,* the Virgin Goddess whose name was "power," and Arabic *Manat,* the Virgin Goddess whose name was "fate" and who represented the Triple Moon.[1] In archaic Europe, Mana was the Moon-mother who gave birth to the race of **man**—that is, of woman, which is what *man* originally meant.[2]

Mana or Mania became a common name for the Great Goddess as Creatress and Queen of Heaven (moon), because it was intimately connected with the mysterious powers of women, like the moon itself. Scandinavians called the Goddess's sky-realm Manavegr, "the Moon's Way."[4] Celts called it E-Mania, or Hy Many, the land ruled by the Triple Goddess. Sometimes it was Emain Macha, the moon-land of Mother Macha. Cormac's Glossary

1. Briffault 2, 602. 2. Steenstrup, 105. 3. Budge, A.T., 24–26. 4. Turville-Petre, 76. 5. Joyce 1, 285, 370. 6. *Larousse,* 305. 7. James, 183. 8. *Larousse,* 213. 9. Angus, 264. 10. Jonas, 98.

Managarm

"Moon-Dog," firstborn wolf-son of Angurboda, the Danish death-goddess called Hag of the Iron Wood, mother of Hel. Managarm and his brother wolves carried the bodies of the dead to Valhalla—by eating them. See **Dog**.

Manasa-Devi

Serpent Goddess of Bengal, identified with the moon, bearing the moon's magic name **Mana**.

Mana . . .
said *ema* meant "blood" (compare the Semitic *ima,* "mother," and *dam,* meaning both "mother" and "blood"). Emain, therefore, was the country of the Great Mother's regenerative lunar blood.[5]

Manat

Arabic Moon-goddess, ruler of Fate: thus her name is still a synonym for Luck or Fortune. She was venerated in a sacred stone at Kodaid in pre-Islamic times, and was one of the trinity of Fates worshipped at Mecca. See **Arabia**.

Mandala

Oriental sacred diagram or meditation symbol, usually circular, sometimes square, sometimes another regular shape, such as the Eight-Petaled Lotus of Smashana-Kali. Contemplation of the mandala was supposed to lead to mystical insight.

Mandorla

Vesica piscis

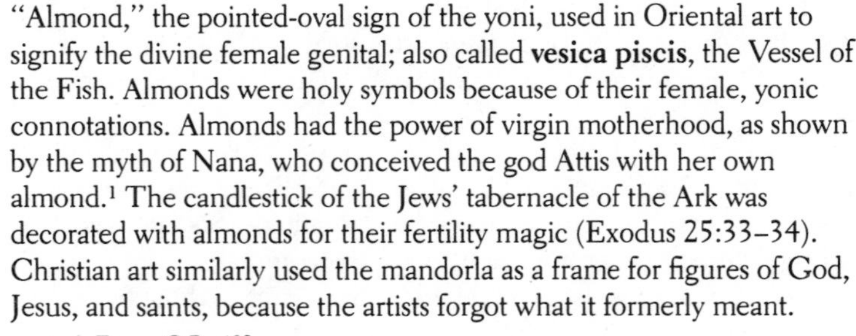

"Almond," the pointed-oval sign of the yoni, used in Oriental art to signify the divine female genital; also called **vesica piscis**, the Vessel of the Fish. Almonds were holy symbols because of their female, yonic connotations. Almonds had the power of virgin motherhood, as shown by the myth of Nana, who conceived the god Attis with her own almond.[1] The candlestick of the Jews' tabernacle of the Ark was decorated with almonds for their fertility magic (Exodus 25:33–34). Christian art similarly used the mandorla as a frame for figures of God, Jesus, and saints, because the artists forgot what it formerly meant.

1. Frazer, G.B., 403.

Manicheans

Gnostic Christian sect, a leading rival of the early orthodoxy. St. Augustine was a Manichean for over a decade, before he was converted to orthodoxy and began writing arguments against the precepts of his former teachers.[1]

Founder of the Manichean sect was the third-century Persian prophet Manes or Mani, whose legend claimed he was another incarnation of Christ. He was born of a holy virgin named Mariham, or Mar Mariam, "the Lady Mary," whose title was "Mother of the Life of the Whole World."[2] He performed the usual feats of every Savior: preached, healed the sick, exorcised demons, collected twelve disciples, and eventually suffered martyrdom. He was crucified and flayed by the Persian king, perhaps as a ritual surrogate.[3]

Mani's central doctrine was puritanical. The material world was the work of the devil, who invented sex to entrap ethereal souls in the prison of flesh: the same view was held by the **Essenes**. Mani's followers abstained from sex, and also from animal food, even eggs, believing that all flesh was evil if begotten by copulation. They ate fish, pretending that fish do not reproduce sexually but are spontaneously engendered from "living water." Christians' adoption of the Aphroditean fish symbol for Christ may have been a Manichean idea.[4]

According to Mani, the devil who created this world of gross matter was the Jewish Jehovah. He said: "It is the Prince of Darkness who spoke with Moses, the Jews, and their priests. Thus the Christians, the Jews, and the Pagans are involved in the same error when they worship this God. For he led them astray in the lusts that he taught them."[5] Like Jesus, Mani faced this same demon-god on a mountaintop and resisted his temptation. The demon-god offered Jesus "all the kingdoms of the earth" in return for a single act of worship, implying that all the kingdoms of the earth belonged to the devil, who could dispose of them as he pleased (Matthew 4:9). Jesus refused the offer, and so did Mani.

Manicheans naturally aroused the ire of orthodox Christians by calling their God a devil. Eusebius fairly frothed with indignation at these heretics: "Mani presumed to represent the person of Christ; he proclaimed himself to be the Comforter, and the Holy Ghost, and being puffed up with this frantic pride, chose, as if he were Christ, twelve partners of his new-found doctrine, patching into one heap false and detestable doctrines of old, rotten, and rooted out heresies, the which he brought out of Persia."[6]

Eusebius Bishop of Caesarea, active in the Arian controversy during the reign of Constantine I; a voluminous writer, apologist, exegete, and "corrector" of biblical texts to suit the theology of his sect.

This was wishful thinking on Eusebius's part. The heresy was not rooted out. The Manichean idea of the Catholic demon-Jehovah was to recur again and again through the Middle Ages, in sects like the Cathari, Paulicians, Albigensians, Bogomils, and many others. In view of the sufferings of these people at the hands of Catholic Rome, their premise seemed not unfounded. One historian said the Manichean heresy was conquered only by "massacre and violence at first, and afterward by organized terrorism."[7] So terrible were the persecutions that Lea said, "If the blood of the martyrs were really the seed of the Church, Manicheism would now be the dominant religion of Europe."[8]

1. Reinach, 76. 2. Legge 2, 279–86, 300–301. 3. Robertson, 86–88. 4. Legge 2, 153. 5. Legge 2, 239. 6. Doane, 429. 7. Guignebert, 296. 8. Campbell, Oc.M., 496.

Manifest Destiny

Catch-phrase invented by white settlers in North America to prove that God appointed them to destroy the Indians. When the Indians objected and even fought back, there arose what General Philip Sheridan called "the vexed Indian question." The general's solution to the question was to exterminate the buffalo, on whom the Plains Indians depended for food, shelter, and clothing. When the great herds were killed and left to rot, many Indian tribes died of famine. This was hailed as a working of Manifest Destiny.[1]

It was also part of Manifest Destiny that the Indians must be converted to the conquerors' religion. They didn't like that either. In 1805 a Seneca chief told a missionary: "Brother, we do not wish to destroy your religion, or take it from you; we only want to enjoy our own. Brother, we are told that you have been preaching to white people in this place . . .; we will wait a little while and see what effect your preaching has upon them. If we find it does them good, makes them honest, and less disposed to cheat Indians, we will then consider again what you have said."[2]

1. *National Geographic,* v. 151, n. 3, 427. 2. Starkloff, 122.

Mante

"Prophetess," or "One Inspired by the Moon"; title of oracular priestesses in ancient Thebes. In patriarchal myth, Mante was a "daughter" of the Theban sage Teiresias, daughter being the usual replacement for mother, as in the reversed story of Adam and Eve. The myth signified male usurpation of the priestesses' functions of magic and prophecy, at first by transvestism and/or castration to turn men into pseudo-women; Teiresias was made female and lived for seven years as a temple harlot, which gave him his divinatory powers.[1] The Mantes eventually came to include male priests, then to consist of a wholly male priesthood. Souls of such magical folk were thought to take the form of insects between incarnations, hence the "praying mantis." The same Greek root word meant a method of divination, as in necromancy, geomancy, oneiromancy, pyromancy, etc.

1. Graves, G.M. 1, 258; 2, 396.

Mantra

Sanskrit term for a spoken formula incorporating "words of power," like Egyptian *hekau* or the Neoplatonic **Logos**. The root word *man* meant feminine "wise blood" emanating from the moon; it was usually defined as Intelligence.[1] Like the Muses who gave Greek poets the gift of words, the Mother Goddesses or *matrikadevis* gave Sanskrit poets the secret of mantras, by which the gods themselves could be controlled.[2]

The *matrikamantra* or Mother of Mantras was Kali's Word of Creation *Om,* meaning her own "pregnant belly" and perhaps stemming from the grunting exhalation of a woman in childbirth; for Om was the word Kali uttered in giving birth to the universe.[3] The second most famous Tantric mantra, *Om mani padme hum,* Jewel in the Lotus, referred to the Lord of the universe contained within the Goddess.

Hindus believed anything could be accomplished if one only knew the correct mantras. Compendia like the Tantrasara gave "prayers, Mantras and Dharanis to protect against every form of evil, against the bad Spirits, wild beasts, natural calamities, human enemies, and so forth which were said to be effective, provided that they were applied in the proper disposition and at the right time and in the right manner." To produce the desired effect, "the Mantra must be intoned in the proper way, according to both sound (Varna) and rhythm (Svara)." Therefore a Mantra loses its efficacy when translated into another language.[4]

The same belief led the Catholic church to retain Latin as its liturgical tongue, 1500 years after Latin ceased to exist in the mouths of ordinary folk. Like Brahman priests with their God-controlling mantras, church fathers thought the very sound of the words had been invested with magic power at the see of St. Peter; so translation of the Latin would rob the words of their power to make God act.[5] This superstition forced Christian laymen to listen, century after century, to church services of which they couldn't understand a single word.

The idea of the mantra wasn't introduced into Rome by Christians; it was there already. Pagan Romans believed, as Virgil said, that the right words, rightly spoken, could draw the moon down from the sky. A ritual of "drawing down the moon" is still practiced by modern "witches."[6] By the power of her words, a Roman priestess could "arrest the flow of rivers and turn back the stars in their courses; she summons the nocturnal spirits; you will see the ground rumble beneath her feet; and the ash trees descend from the mountains."[7]

All liturgies were basically mantras, evolved from the primitive theory that human words could make things happen in the supernatural realm, which in turn influenced the natural one. An example is the idea of praying souls out of Purgatory, where "mantras" alone produce the result even though the result is unverifiable. This also had Tantric precedents. Tibetan lamas still circumvent their own law against eating animal flesh by eating it anyway, to the accompaniment of a mantra that will assure the eaten animal's rebirth in heaven.[8] Thus the offended creature is placed, by human words, in a blessed situation where he can no longer take offense. Naturally, mantras of such marvelous power are revealed only with great care, by qualified gurus to tested candidates worthy to become Guardians of the Mysteries.[9]

1. Avalon, 493. 2. Frazer, G.B., 60. 3. Wilkins, 201. 4. Avalon, 208–9, 487. 5. Woods, 149. 6. Agrippa, 217. 7. Wedeck, 144. 8. Waddell, 216. 9. *Bardo Thodol,* 221.

Manu

The Vedic Noah, who rode out the Deluge in his ark with the assistance of the Great Serpent, Vasuki. Manu's ark, loaded with the seeds of every plant and a pair of every kind of animal, tied up to the Serpent's horn and so survived the watery chaos between the destruction of one universe and the creation of the next.[1]

Manu's ark was the cosmic seed-vessel, in pre-Vedic myth the womb of the Goddess, which preserved the spark of life through cycles of destruction and renewal. It seems Manu was a masculinized form of Ma-Nu or Mother Night, the name she bore in Egypt, as the spirit of the primordial abyss that gave birth to the cosmos. Sumerians knew her as Nammu, "the primeval ocean, the mother of the gods."[2]

The archaic notion of Manu as a Creatress also attributed to her the foundation of morality and law; hence the scriptures that Vedic sages called the Laws of Manu, frequently rewritten and augmented by patriarchal Brahman and Buddhist philosophies. However, Manu remained sexually ambiguous, like Egypt's Ma-Nu or Nu or Nun, who sometimes took the form of a great Fish who gave birth to the gods.[3] Nu was translated into Hebrew as Noah. Significantly, this name was the "Fish" without the sexually definitive mother-syllable Ma.

Vedic sages came to believe in Manu as a kind of Adam, the progenitor of the human race, incestuously begotten by the Brahman creator upon his own daughter—a reversal of the archaic myth of the primal creatress who made, then mated with, her Great Serpent. So many different acts, myths, laws, and customs were attributed to the authority of Manu that this personage multiplied into 14 different Manus, avatars or reincarnations of the same Manu in different ages of the world.[4] This may have been a re-interpretation of the original idea of successive universes, with the dark mother-womb bridging the periods of watery chaos between them by preserving the seeds of future life.

1. *Larousse*, 362. 2. Hooke, M.E.M., 29. 3. Erman, 252. 4. O'Flaherty, 25, 347.

---

var. Marah

Mara

Exceedingly ancient name of the Goddess-as-Crone, the death-bringer. The name and its variants may be found from India to northern Europe. Buddhists translated the name as Fear-of-Death, and combined it with Kama, Erotic-Desire, to create the demon who tempted Buddha to abandon his meditation before he achieved true knowledge of Nirvana.[1] This "temptation in the wilderness" scene was replayed over and over in subsequent legends of ascetic Saviors, such as Mani and Jesus.

The gypsies, with their traditions rooted in Hinduism, knew Mara to be the death goddess who trapped the soul of the Enchanted

Huntsman in a **mirror**, and caused his death—a myth that paralleled ancient Pelasgian stories of the death of Dionysus.[2]

The Slavs said Mara or Mora was a destructive female spirit who "drank the blood of men" by night.[3] She became the *mare* or Nightmare, "A monstrous hag squatting upon the breast—mute, motionless and malignant; an incarnation of the evil spirit—whose intolerable weight crushes the breath out of the body."[4] This was the same image assumed by black Kali the Destroyer, whose death aspect meant "passive weight and darkness."[5]

Semitic peoples associated Mara or Marah with the "passive weight and darkness" of the deep sea-womb; thus the name was sometimes translated "briny" or "bitter." Marah was the name assumed by the matriarch Naomi (Ruth 1:20) as she passed into the Crone stage of her life. An old shrine of the goddess Mara was the Old Testament's Maralah, "a place of trembling" (Joshua 19:11), possibly a necropolis. The biblical death-curse Maranatha (1 Corinthians 16:22) also invoked the destroying Goddess. **Mari** was another version of her name, as in Kel-Mari (Kali the Pot Goddess, who made mankind out of clay), Marici the Goddess "clothed with the sun," Yamamari, a combination of Mari with Yama or "Death," and Mari-Amma the Death-giver, in Hebrew Mariamne, Miriam, or Mary.

1. Campbell, Or.M., 17. 2. Groome, 131–32. 3. R.E.L. Masters, 188. 4. Robbins, 340. 5. Rawson, E.A., 160.

Mardoll

"Moon Shining Over the Sea," an epithet of the Goddess Freya as the Creatress brooding over the primal waters.[1] Her biblical form, derived from older Sumero-Babylonian sources, was the (female) Spirit of God moving "on the face of the waters" (Genesis 1:2). See **Tiamat**.

1. Branston, 133.

Marduk

Babylonian municipal god whose legends strongly influenced Jewish ideas of Yahweh. Marduk claimed to have created the world by separating the celestial and the abyssal waters, as Yahweh did (Genesis 1:7); actually, Marduk did it by cleaving the body of his mother Tiamat, who personified all "Waters." Marduk also killed the first-born God, Kingu, and created the first man from Kingu's blood—a myth remembered by the Arabs, who said Allah made man from flowing blood.[1] Marduk also inherited the tablets of sacred law that the Mother Goddess had given her elder, favorite son. These same tablets were entrusted to Babylonian kings by presentation on the holy "mountain" of the ziggurat. This tradition, too, was copied by the God of Moses.

1. Gaster, 20.

Marea

City in western Egypt, sacred to the Goddess **Mari**, possibly the so-called Land of Goshen occupied by Israelites before their expulsion from Egypt (see **Moses**). Mari was the same Goddess later worshipped in Israel as a consort of Yahweh.[1]

1. Graves, W.G., 439.

Mare Nostrum

"Our sea," or "Our mother"; Roman title of the Mediterranean, or "Middle-of-the-Earth Sea." All seas were *maria,* "Marys," symbolized by the Goddess in her blue robe, sometimes a mer-maid (literally, Sea-Virgin), often named Aphrodite Marina. See **Mary**.

Margaret, Saint

Mythical "virgin martyr" who never existed as a Christian but was a canonized form of Aphrodite Marina, Pelagia, or Margarita, called Pearl of the Sea.[1] Originally she was a yonic Goddess representing Aphrodite's "Pearly Gate," which, like the Jade Gate of the Chinese Great Mother, meant the genital entrance to paradise. The name Margaret may be traced to Sanskrit Marga, "the Gate" or "the Way," i.e., the yonic gate of Kali-Shakti leading through ritual sexuality to the paradise of Tantric sages.[2]

Hagiographers invented several legends of Margaret-Pelagia-Marina, all names of the pagan Sea-goddess. Sometimes she was a virgin who suddenly turned Christian on her wedding day and so renounced her bridegroom, the "sinful riotings" of the wedding feast, and the joys of married life which she decided were worthless as "dung." Sometimes she was a divine harlot, the wealthiest and most beautiful woman in Antioch, covered with gold, silver, and gems, who suddenly turned Christian and gave away all her possessions to poor folk (Christians, of course), and allowed a bishop to impose on her a hard life of penance.[3] This legend was a favorite of early saint-makers, who particularly resented promiscuous women and invariably coveted their ill-gotten gains.

One legend made St. Margaret the daughter of a pagan priest. She spurned her rich suitor, Olybrius, governor of Antioch, and devoted herself to Christian virginity. She was subjected to amazing tortures to overcome her determination. "All her bones were laid bare, and the blood poured forth from her body as from a pure spring."[4] But she still had strength enough to conquer the devil, who took the form of a great dragon and swallowed her, whereupon she caused his body to burst and stepped forth "unharmed"—except of course for the harm that had already been done by her various tortures. After this she was burned, drowned, and beheaded: St. Margaret was very hard to kill.

Another legend of St. Margaret said she fled from her suitor to become a holy hermit. She joined a monastery of ascetics, disguising herself as a monk, "Brother Pelagius." In this connection one might recall the rule of early Syrian churches, that no women would be permitted to become Christians unless they "made themselves male."[5] Margaret made herself male so successfully that she was accused of seducing a nun, subjected to severe penances which she accepted humbly, and finally vindicated only after death, when those who came to prepare her body for burial discovered that she had been a woman.

Under her other name of **Pelagia**, before she became the monk Pelagius, Margaret devoted her early life to "lewd" worship of Aphrodite as a temple harlot. On being converted to Christianity, she called herself "a sea of wickedness overflowing with the waves of sin . . . an abyss of perdition . . . a quagmire and pitfall of souls."[6] The feast day of this Margaret-Pelagia was the same as that of St. Thais, another mythical version of the same courtesan-turned-Christian, the second most popular type of female saint, after the "virgin martyr."

Since Margaret was fundamentally an incarnation of Aphrodite, spouse of Adonis "the Lord" at Bethlehem, it would be expected that she remain the spouse of "the Lord"; and accordingly her worshippers said, "Blessed art thou O Margaret the spouse of Christ."[7]

Through all her appearances as virgin, harlot, monk, and so on, however, Margaret remained what the pagan Goddess always was: the primary patron of childbearing women.

1. Attwater, 228. 2. Campbell, C.M., 661. 3. de Voragine, 611–14. 4. de Voragine, 352. 5. Bullough, 113. 6. de Voragine, 611. 7. Scot, 384.

Margawse

Second person of the Celtic female trinity in Arthurian legend: Elaine the virgin, Margawse the mother, Morgan the crone. Margawse was the same as the Latin Anna, the Mother of the Year: she gave birth to the four Aeons, named Gareth, Gaheris, Agravine, and Gawain. She also mated with her brother **Arthur** and brought forth Arthur's nemesis, sister-son, son, tanist, and supplanter: Mordred, whom Arthur tried to kill in his infancy. As Fate or perhaps Margawse herself decreed, Mordred lived to grow up and destroy Arthur.

Mari

Basic name of the Goddess known to the Chaldeans as Marratu, to the Jews as Marah, to the Persians as Mariham, to the Christians as Mary: as well as Marian, Miriam, Mariamne, Myrrhine, Myrtea, Myrrha, Maria, and Marina. Her blue robe and pearl necklace were classic symbols of the sea, edged with pearly foam.[1]

The Goddess's Amorite city of Mari was one of the wonders of the ancient world. Its six-acre temple-palace astonished archeologists who uncovered it in the 1930s. Mari dominated the area now known as the Holy Land until it fell to the armies of Hammurabi in 1700 B.C.[4]

Semites worshipped an androgynous combination of Goddess and God called Mari-El (Mary-God), corresponding to the Egyptian Meri-Ra which combined the feminine principle of water with the masculine principle of the sun.[5]

The Syrian version of Mari or Meri was worshipped in combination with her serpent-consort Yamm, derived from Yama, the Hindu Lord of Death. Yamm alternated with Baal, "the Lord," as the Goddess's favorite and a sovereign over heaven and the abyss. Indian Yama was one of the consorts of Kel-Mari, as Kali was called in the south.[8] Tantric Buddhists still speak of the "Slayer of the Death King," Yama-Mari, who was identified with the Dalai Lama.[9] Jews and early Christians used the same combination of names, Mari-Yamm or Mariam, for the mother of Jesus.[10]

The spirit of the archaic Mari entered into Babylonian diviners known as *mare baruti*, sea-mothers, who operated in the *bit mummu* or womb-chamber, where statues of the gods were said to be "born" (made animate).[11] In similar womb-chambers the Hindu goddess was worshipped as Kau-Mari or Kel-Mari.[12] She is still invoked as Marici-Tara, the Diamond Sow on the Lotus Throne, "Glorious One, the sun of happiness." She is the Goddess "whose mayik vesture is the sun," forerunner of the Gospels' "woman clothed with the sun" (Revelation 12:1), who was identified with the virgin Mary.[13]

She was also the Great Fish who gave birth to the gods, later the Mermaid, Mare-mynd, mareminde, marraminde, maraeman, or mereminne.[20]

In short, she was always Mother Sea. Her Latin name was Maria, "the Seas." St. Peter Chrysologus called her Christian incarnation, the virgin Mary, "the gathering together of the waters."[21] But she was also the earth and heavens, since her earliest form was a trinity. She was worshipped in pre-Roman Latium as Marica, mother of the first king Latinus, who was also her priapic goat-footed consort Faunus. She was probably the same Goddess worshipped by the Slavs under the name of Marzanna (Mari-Anna), who "fostered the growth of fruits."[22]

Mari and her pagan consort were incongruously canonized as a pair of Christian saints, Addai and Mari (Adonis and Aphrodite-Mari). Their legends called them "bishops" dispatched to Aphrodite's

Many place names evolved from Marian shrines. Among them were Amari or Ay-Mari, the Cyprian home of Aphrodite Marina; Marib, City of the Moon, seat of the queens of Sheba; Marea in western Egypt; Maronea near Lake Ismaris; Maru, mother-city of the Medes; Sa-Maria, a country whose name meant literally "holy blood of Mary."[2] One of the entrances to her underworld womb, a sacred cave accessible only by sea, was Mar-Mari, "Mother Sea."[3]

Sometimes the deity was named simply Mer, an Egyptian word for both "waters" and "mother-love."[6] Mer was also a component of the names of Egyptian queens in the first dynasty. One of Egypt's oldest names was Ta-Mera, Land of the Waters, which could also be interpreted as a Land of the Great Mothers.[7]

Northern Europe knew the same Goddess as Maerin, wedded to Thor at her shrine in Trondheim.[14] To the Saxons she was Wudu-Maer:

cult center at Edessa, probably because their portraits appeared there, and it was easier to Christianize them than to destroy them.

Their cult began with Nestorian Christians who called them "Holy Apostles Addai and Mari."[23] Another Christianization was St. Maura, from the Goddess's Fate-name Moera, "older than Time."[24] As the Fate-spinner who held men's destinies in her hand, she generated a taboo: on St. Maura'a day, women were forbidden to spin or sew.[25]

Medieval Spain knew the Goddess Mari as a "Lady" or "Mistress" who lived in a magic cave and rode through the night sky as a ball of fire.[26] This may have meant the red harvest moon, or possibly the moon in eclipse—always a dire omen. The Goddess Mari was said to give gifts of fairy gold and precious stones, which might turn into worthless lumps of coal by the light of day.[27] In later centuries, the same worthless gifts were given to "bad" children by St. Nicholas at Christmas.

The island of Inis Maree had a ruined temple, sacred to a certain "St. Mourie"—none other than the Goddess Mari for whom the island was named. In 1678 the Presbytery of Dingwall "disciplined" some people who sacrificed bulls to the divinity of Loch Maree on the 25th of August, a day dedicated to Aphrodite-Mari for more than 1500 years.[28]

1. Graves, W.G., 438.
2. Graves, W.G., 410–11; *Assyr. & Bab. Lit.*, 179; Herodotus, 41, 400.
3. Hughes, 159. 4. Keller, 46–49. 5. Budge, G.E. 1, 86; *Book of the Dead,* 602.
6. Budge, E.L., 76. 7. Budge, D.N., 160. 8. Briffault 1, 474. 9. Waddell, 364.
10. Ashe, 48. 11. Lindsay, O.A., 41. 12. *Mahanirvanatantra,* 149.
13. Waddell, 218, 361; *Mahanirvanatantra,* xl. 14. Turville-Petre, 91.
15. Graves, W.G., 441. 16. Keightley, 22. 17. Thomson, 135.
18. *Assyr. & Bab. Lit.,* 287. 19. Albright, 98. 20. Steenstrup, 105. 21. Ashe, 147.
22. *Larousee,* 208, 291. 23. Attwater, 31. 24. Bachofen, 57. 25. Lawson, 175.
26. Lederer, 210. 27. Baroja, 238. 28. Spence, 37.

literally, a Wood-Mary, or Goddess of the Grove. To the Celts she was Maid Marian, beloved by Robin, the witches' Horned God. Their greenwood cult caused church authorities considerable trouble in the 14th century.[15]

Mari was the same Merian or Merjan worshipped in Persia as Queen of the Peris (Fairies).[16] Iran had its mother goddess Mariana from very ancient times.[17] She might be traced to the land of Akkad, created by a Goddess called the Lady Marri, Mother of the World.[18] A king of Mari in 2500 B.C., united with the Goddess, took the royal name of Lamki-Mari.[19]

Marriage

The word marriage came from Latin *maritare,* union under the auspices of the Goddess Aphrodite-Mari. Because the Goddess's patronage was constantly invoked in every aspect of marriage, Christian fathers were opposed to the institution. Origen declared, "Matrimony is impure and unholy, a means of sexual passion." St. Jerome said the primary purpose of a man of God was to "cut down with an ax of Virginity the wood of Marriage."[1] St. Ambrose said marriage was a crime against God, because it changed the state of virginity that God gave every man and woman at birth.[2] Marriage was prostitution of the members of Christ, and "married people ought to blush at the state in which they are living." Tertullian said marriage was a moral crime, "more dreadful than any punishment or any death." It was *spurcitiae,* "obscenity," or "filth."[3]

St. Augustine flatly stated that marriage is a sin. Tatian said

St. Peter Chrysologus (Peter Golden-word) Fifth-century bishop of Ravenna, friend of Pope Leo the Great. Three centuries after his death, a collection of 176 sermons was produced, and attributed to him, though mostly spurious. He was made a doctor of the church in 1729.

marriage is corruption, "a polluted and foul way of life." Influenced by him, Syrian churches ruled that no person could become Christian except celibate men, and no man who had ever been married could be baptized. Saturninus said God made only two kinds of people, good men and evil women. Marriage perpetuated the deviltry of women, who dominated men through the magic of sex.[4] Centuries later, St. Bernard still proclaimed that it was easier for a man to bring the dead back to life than to live with a woman without endangering his soul.[5]

St. Paul damned marriage with faint praise, remarking that to marry was only better than to burn (1 Corinthians 7:9); but later followers of Pauline Christianity damned marriage altogether, according to the word of Jesus: "If any man come to me, and hate not his father, and mother, and wife, and children, and brethren, and sisters, yea, and his own life also, he cannot be my disciple" (Luke 14:26). Jesus renounced his family, declaring that he had no relatives except the faithful (Mark 3:31-35). Jerome interpreted this as a mandate to destroy marriage and the family. He was disgusted by motherhood: "the tumefaction of the uterus, the care of yelling infants, all those fond feelings which death at last cuts short."[6] He said every man who loves his wife passionately was guilty of adultery.[7] Augustine also expressed disgust at feminine sexual and maternal functions. He coined the saying that birth is demonstrably accursed because every child emerges "between feces and urine."[8]

An example of anti-family virtue was made of one of the artificial saints built on a title of the pro-family Goddess, Perpetua, "the Eternal One." In her new Christian disguise as St. Perpetua, she was so devoted to single blessedness that she not only faced martyrdom with equanimity but also renounced her parents, her husband, and her suckling infant in order to become Christian. Her pagan relatives tried to soften her heart by putting the infant to her breast, but she threw it aside and said to them, "Begone from me, enemies of God, for I know you not!"[9]

This was the early Christian notion of a "good" woman: one who placed faith before family. Church customs reflected this view. There was no Christian sacrament of marriage until the 16th century.[10] Catholic scholars say the wedding ceremony was "imposed on" a reluctant church, and "nothing is more remarkable than the tardiness with which liturgical forms for the marriage ceremony were evolved." It is perhaps not remarkable to find that these liturgical forms were not evolved by the church at all, but borrowed from pagans' common law.[11]

The Anglican marriage service came from Anglo-Saxon deeds used to transfer a woman's land to the stewardship of her "houseman" (husband). The original wording had the bridegroom say: "With this ring I thee wed and this gold and silver I give thee and with my body I thee worship, and with all my worldly chattels I thee honor." The bride responded: "I take thee to my wedded husband, to have

Origen (Origenes Adamantius) Christian father, ca. 185–254 A.D., an Egyptian who wrote in Greek, exerting a powerful influence on the early Greek church. At first he was accounted a saint, but three centuries after his death he was declared a heretic because of Gnostic elements found in his writings.

Tertullian (Quintus Septimius Florens Tertullianus) influential early Christian writer and father of the church, ca. 155–220 A.D., born in Carthage of pagan parents.

and to hold, for fairer for fouler, for better for worse, for richer for poorer, in sickness and in health, to be bonny and buxom in bed and at board, till death us depart [sic]." A curious clerical note made in the margin at a later date, explained that "bonny and buxom" really meant "meek and obedient."[12]

About wedding ceremonies in Greece and the Balkans, an authority on Greek religion wrote: "With the modern Greeks as with other Europeans, the religious service of their church is intrusive, no real part of the ceremony of marriage, but an elaborate way of calling down a blessing on the ceremonial, or what is left of it, which constitutes the real wedding."[13]

The Christian priesthood was fighting ancient traditions in which it was remembered that male spiritual authority was dependent on marriage: either a *hieros gamos* between the ruler of a land and his Goddess, or the mandatory husbandship of priests who were not allowed to contact the deities unless they had wives. In Asia, the gods themselves had to be married. Even patriarchal figures like Vishnu and Brahma needed their Shaktis or wives who embodied their power, and "without whom they avail nothing."[14] Brahman priests couldn't perform certain ceremonies without wives.[15] Oriental mystics taught that any man was spiritually incomplete until he experienced *bhavanan,* "husbandship," which linked him to the Goddess as Bhavani or "Existence."[16] The implication was that an unmarried man does not truly exist. Tantric hymns said all women are goddesses because they embody the spirit of the Goddess; thus "women are Life itself."[17]

Early Israelites also barred unmarried men from the priesthood. They thought a priest's spells and invocations would be powerless if he had no wife.[18] Jewish scriptures said, "The man who has neither wife nor children is disgraced in the world and is hated by them, like a leafless and fruitless tree."[19] Similarly, the spiritual authority of Rome's high priest the Flamen Dialis depended on his marriage to the Flaminica, high priestess of Juno. If she died or left him, he immediately lost his holy office.[20]

So much depended on a man's ability to remain married, in the most ancient times, that the first rules of marriage invented by men seem to have been rules for insuring permanent monogamy. Thus a husband could hold on to a woman's property and children by binding the woman herself. Matriarchal societies seldom permitted sexual jealousy. Women were free to change lovers or husbands, to make polyandrous or group marriages. Myths record the transition from loose, flexible marital arrangements favored by Goddesses to the rigid monogamy favored by Gods.

The pre-Hellenic Mother of God, Rhea, condemned monogamy as a sin and insisted on her ancient law of group marriage. Her son Zeus defied her, on behalf of patriarchal invaders of her lands. He forced Rhea's "daughter" Hera—actually another form of Rhea herself—into a monogamous union, though he never stuck to his own side of the bargain. He was constantly adulterous, and Hera detested him. On one occasion she roused the other gods in a rebellion against him. Zeus punished her by hanging her from the sky with anvils attached to her ankles—perhaps the first divine precedent permitting men to torture wives into submission.[21]

Hellenic Greeks believed that men should seize every possible advantage in forcing wives to be obedient and (especially) faithful. Aristotle taught that a husband should be more than twice his bride's age—he 37, she 18—so he could dominate her: "The elder and full grown is superior to the younger and more immature."[22] Greek patriarchy foreshadowed the patriarchal religion which, "in the form seen in Judaism, Christianity, and Mohammedanism, is basically nothing other than a formalization, by means of a projection upon deities, and the demand for obedience to their revealed command, of the father's desired sexual control of his wives and of their female children, and the forcible exclusion of male children from sexual activity."[23]

The Greeks' contempt for wives eventually led to their cult of homosexual romance, ignoring their families and taking young boys for true-love relationships. Some scholars say this belittling of marriage was founded on fear of women:

> *The Greek male's contempt for women was not only compatible with, but also indissolubly bound to, an intense fear of them, and to an underlying suspicion of male inferiority. Why else would such extreme measures be necessary? Customs such as the rule that a woman should not be older than her husband, or of higher social status, or more educated, or paid the same as a male for the same work, or be in a position of authority—betray an assumption that males are incapable of competing with females on an equal basis; the cards must first be stacked, the female given a handicap.*[24]

Observing group marriages among their neighbors, the Greeks regarded such customs as barbaric or unusual. In an age when the Greeks were almost the only people with a patriarchal-monogamous social structure, a Greek said to the Spartan wife of Leonidas: "You of Lacedaemon are the only women in the world that rule the men." She retorted: "We are the only women who bring forth men."[25]

Despite their pretense that their own system was the only normal one, Greek writers like Herodotus knew the Arabs were polyandrous, the Scythians shared spouses and children communally, the Lycians recognized only matrilineal inheritance, and the Agathyrsi "cohabit in common with the women, in order that they should all be blood kin and that their family relationships should prevent them from harboring envy and hostility toward one another."[26]

Caesar said group marriage was the rule in Britain. An indicator of the group-marriage system among the Celts was the multiple paternity of many of their mythic heroes. Clothru, queen of Connaught, married three brothers at once, the same kind of fraternal polyandry practiced by such eastern peoples as the Todas and the Singhalese.[27] The Nairs practiced group marriage up to the 19th century. Hindu literature speaks of a princess who married five brothers at once, and was blessed by the Goddess Cunti, and promised many children.[28] In the Mahabharata, a speech to the same Goddess Cunti told of "the practice of old indicated by illustrious Rishis fully acquainted with every rule of morality":

> *Women were not formerly immured in houses and dependent on husbands and relatives. They used to go about freely, enjoying themselves as best they pleased. . . . They did not then adhere to their husbands faithfully; and yet . . . they were not regarded as sinful, for that was the sanctioned usage of the times. . . . Indeed, that usage, so lenient to women, hath the sanction of antiquity. The present practice, however, of women being confined to one husband for life hath been established but lately.*[29]

After Brahmanism established monogamy in some parts of India, the rules of marriage were greatly changed: "No act is to be done according to her own will by a young girl, a young woman, though she be in her own house. In her childhood a girl should be under the will of her father; in her youth under that of her husband; her husband being dead, under the will of her sons. A woman should never enjoy her own will. Though of bad conduct or debauched, a husband must always be worshipped like a god by a good wife."[30]

Rules similar to those of the Brahmans were established in western Europe by Christian authorities, insofar as possible. Some churches even insisted that a bride at her wedding must kneel and place her bridegroom's foot on her head in token of abject obedience.[31] Christianity accepted marriage only on condition that the partners form a slave-and-master relationship. This meant getting rid of the Goddess whose many forms and avatars protected the married woman in all phases of matrimony and motherhood.

Juno, the Roman Queen of Heaven, regulated every aspect of marriage through her priestesses. Juno Pronuba arranged marriages. Juno Domiduca conducted the bride across the threshold of her new home. Juno Nuxia perfumed the doorposts. Juno Cinxia untied the bride's virgin-girdle. Juno Lucina watched over the pregnant woman. Juno Ossipago strengthened her infant's bones. Juno Rumina provided mother's milk. Juno Sospita took care of women in childbed.[32] So it went: in marriage and family matters, women ignored God and appealed to their own Goddess. The idea that a male priest should preside alone over a marriage ceremony was unthinkable—which is one reason why Christians didn't think of it. For many centuries, marriage existed in a limbo without a deity to solemnize it, having no place in canon law, which is why marriage remained so long under the jurisdiction of common law.

The Council of Trent decreed that a person who even hinted that the state of matrimony might be more blessed than celibacy would be declared *anathema*—accursed and excommunicated.[33] The earliest form of Christian marriage was a simple blessing of the newly wedded pair, *in facie ecclesiae*—outside the church's closed doors—to keep the pollution of lust out of God's house. This blessing was a technical violation of canon law, but it became popular and gradually won acceptance. In 1215 the fourth Lateran Council granted it legal status.[34] Still, the church maintained that there were no marriages in heaven, according to Christ's statement in the scriptures (Mark 12:25; Luke 20:35). St. Thomas Aquinas assigned a "goodness value" of 30 to marriage, as compared with 60 for widowhood, and 100 for lifelong virginity.[35]

Medieval folk tales convey a distinct impression that the Christian God opposed marriage. One story said a pure youth and maiden agreed never to marry, "for love of God." But their heathen parents forced them into a wedding. By God's grace, the ground opened under their feet and swallowed them before they could spoil their virginity. A priest who dared officiate at the wedding was found dead next day. Another young couple eloped, being forced to defy God, who "did not sanction earthly marriages." Gebhard, archbishop of Cologne, was said to have blessed married couples illegally, and even took a wife himself. He was excommunicated, besieged by Catholic forces in Godesberg Castle, caught, and killed. The ruins of his castle are still shown to travelers.[36]

Common-law marriages were often informal. Mere cohabitation could constitute a valid marriage.[37] Temporary trial marriages were legal up to the early 17th century. Peasant "betrothals" were often trial marriages, incorporating such customs as "tarrying," night-visiting, and courting-on-the-bed. Pregnancy might make the union permanent, but not necessarily. Bastardy was a commonplace in all social classes of medieval society.[38]

The church displayed remarkable reluctance to deal with the matter of marriage at all. During the Middle Ages there was no ecclesiastical definition of a valid marriage nor of any contract to validate one. Churchmen seemed to have no ideas at all on the subject.[39] They ignored marriage, leaving it largely in the realm of the common law.

Under Roman and barbarian laws, marriages "could be freely initiated and could be terminated without formality by either party and at any time."[40] This system persisted among common folk until 1563. Finally the church declared the priestly blessing indispensable to a legal marriage, refusing to recognize any more marriages made by the common law. Still, the church's rule remained invalid in many areas for several centuries more.[41]

In 1753 Lord Harwicke's Act made clerical blessing a requirement for legal marriage in England, but the Act didn't apply to Scotland. Therefore Scotland became a mecca for elopements, because legal marriages could be made there by the old pagan custom of "handfasting"—simply joining the couple's hands in the presence of witnesses, without benefit of clergy.[42] All the way up to 1939, English lovers could travel across the Scottish border to the "marriage town" of Gretna Green for an instant wedding.

When Christian authorities revised pagan marriage laws, they were primarily concerned with placing a wife's property in her husband's control and keeping it there. Women owned the land under the pagan system, and their husbands could acquire an interest in it only through matrimony. This system was reversed in husbands' favor. Common-law and Morganatic marriages were provisionally accepted by Christian churches only after many restrictions had been imposed on the wife's rights of ownership and inheritance. Christian marital morality amounted to taking the means of independence from women and turning it over to men.

Morganatic marriage A form of legalized concubinage, first instituted in Germany to allow high-ranking noblemen and princes to "marry" women of low rank, or commoners, with the proviso that neither wife nor children of the marriage would ever have any legal claim on the husband's property.

Celibacy was strictly enforced among the clergy when new laws permitted men to bequeathe their property (and their wives' property) directly to their children. When priests were forbidden to make valid marriages, they couldn't have heirs. Thus all property they owned or gained would revert to the church when they died.[43] Clerical marriages, on the other hand, meant a loss of ecclesiastical income.

Priests abandoned the early church's rule of celibacy and began to take wives during the 5th and 6th centuries. This continued to the 11th century, when papal decretals commanded married clergymen to turn their wives out of their homes and sell their children as slaves.[44] These new laws brought much more wealth to the church. Though some ex-wives stayed on as the concubines of their former husbands, they were disinherited in the church's favor. (See **Matrilineal Inheritance**.)

Churchmen revered St. Hilary, who was married and the father of a daughter. When his daughter wished to marry, however, Hilary forbade her. Fearing she might weaken and lose her virginity, he asked God to kill her. God complied—with a little help from Hilary himself. After burying the daughter, "by his prayer" Hilary sent his wife to heaven also. The legend claims the wife voluntarily begged Hilary to "obtain for her the same grace which he had obtained for her daughter."[45]

Besides popularizing the peculiar morality of a saint who killed his family, the church fostered "chastisement" of wives by husbands, citing St. Paul's teaching that "the head of every man is Christ; and the head of the woman is the man" (1 Corinthians 11:3). In practice, under the pretext of discipline a man could torture his wife with impunity, and no legal or religious agency would defend her. A mild protest in the 13th-century Laws and Customs of Beauvais noted that an excessive number of women were dying of marital chastisement, so husbands were advised to beat their wives "only within reason."[46]

The theological view of the time was that "woman has sinned more than man" and should therefore be unhappier; her suffering must be doubled on earth, even in the womb, which is why female embryos did not receive their souls from God as early as male embryos.[47] Men were only doing God's will when they made women suffer.

The Oriental heathen, whom Christians thought barbaric, were teaching different rules: "The householder should never punish his wife, but should cherish her like a mother. . . . By riches, clothes, love, respect, and pleasing words should one's wife be satisfied. The husband should never do anything displeasing to her."[48] Westerners simply condemned as obscene the passages in the Brhadaranyaka Upanishad describing as a sacrament a husband's sexual worship of his wife as "House-Goddess (Grhadevata)."[49]

Physical abuse and sexual coercion were so often the lot of a Christian wife that it came to be an accepted idea that no woman could love a husband. A "lover" meant a man outside the marriage. The Countess of Narbonne, ruler of France's celebrated Court of Love, said the relation between husband and wife and "the true love between lovers are two absolutely different things which have nothing in common. . . . We say definitely and considerately that love cannot exist between married people."[50] One good reason was the master-slave relationship. "Men were exhorted from the pulpit to beat their wives and wives to kiss the rod that beat them."[51]

Medieval society was so accustomed to the idea that all wives were battered by their husbands, that churchmen used this as an argument for women to renounce marriage in favor of the cloister. They told young girls that "the wife was subject to her husband, that often she was exposed to blows and kicks, and often brought forth misshapen offspring. . . . While men are betrothed they seem filled with gentleness, whereas after marriage they rule as cruel masters."[52]

It has been recently shown that, "Although omitted from most church historical accounts, the Christian church . . . has had a record of practicing and recommending physical abuse to women." The Decretum of 1140 said: "It is right that he whom woman led into wrongdoing should have her under his direction so that he may not fail a second time through female levity." Friar Cherubino's 15th-century *Rules of Marriage* made a husband his wife's sole judge: "Scold her sharply, bully and terrify her. And if this still doesn't work . . . take up a stick and beat her soundly, for it is better to punish the body and correct the soul than to damage the soul and spare the body. . . . Then readily beat her, not in rage but out of charity and concern for her soul, so that the beating will redound to your merit."[53]

A Russian pope recommended the use of a whip rather than a rod of wood or iron, which was more likely to cripple or kill. "Keep to a whip," said the pontiff, "and choose carefully where to strike: a whip is painful and effective."[54]

Martin Luther thought himself an unusually kind husband. He

said when his wife "gets saucy, she gets nothing but a box on the ear."[55]

English jurisprudence applied to marital "disagreement" the famous Rule of Thumb elucidated by Blackstone: a husband was free to beat his wife with a whip or rod no thicker than his thumb, "in order to enforce the salutary restraints of domestic discipline." British law up to the late 19th century decreed that acts which would amount to an assault if committed against a stranger were legally innocent when committed by a husband against a wife.[56] Wives had little help from the law; they were legally classified with minors and idiots, and were consigned to the custody of their husbands.[57]

Sir William Blackstone (1723-1780) Famous English jurist, author of the *Commentaries* which became the standard reference authority of both British and American law through the 19th century.

When John Adams was helping to draw up the Constitution of the United States in 1777, his wife Abigail wrote to him, "Do not put such unlimited power in the hands of husbands. Remember, all men would be tyrants if they could."[58] Abigail's plea went unheard. The American husband was no less tyrannical than his British forebear. It has been said that among the Puritans especially, the husband "exercised the authority of God" over his wife.[59]

In 1848 feminist Emily Collins described a typical example of the abused American wife: a woman who mothered seven children, cooked, cleaned, washed, spun, wove, sewed and mended the family clothing, milked the cows, and took the multiple responsibilities for the welfare of nine persons, including her husband, who beat her because she sometimes "scolded"—that is, nagged, or complained. This was accepted as sufficient reason for violent attacks on his hard-working spouse.[60]

Up to the middle of the 20th century, American law upheld the so-called doctrine of immunity, which meant the "sanctity of the home" could not be invaded to stop husbandly violence. A man's home was his castle, even if it was also his wife's prison. The law denied women the right to sue their husbands for assault because the suit "might destroy the peace of the home." Only in 1962 did a judge rule that the peace of the home was already destroyed by a wife-beating husband, therefore the doctrine of immunity was legally unsound.[61] Even now, the law may refuse to recognize a woman's right to protection within her home.

Wife-beating was a by-product of the Christian view of woman as man's property. Napoleon remarked, "Woman is given us to bear children. She is our property. . . . She is our possession, as the fruit tree is that of the gardener."[62] St. Thomas Aquinas said a wife is lower than a slave because a slave may be freed, but "Woman is in subjection according to the law of nature, but a slave is not."[63]

Josephine Henry 19th-century Kentucky suffragist and pamphleteer, active in the women's rights movement.

Josephine Henry reported that "The ownership of the wife established and perpetuated through Bible teaching is responsible for the domestic pandemonium and the carnival of wife murder which reigns throughout Christendom. In the United States alone, in the eighteen hundred and ninety-seventh year of the Christian era, 3,482 wives, many with unborn children in their bodies, have been murdered in cold blood by their husbands. . . . The by-paths of ecclesiastical history are fetid with the records of crimes against women; and 'the half has never been told.'"[64]

From feudal times onward, Christian systems of slavery placed similar powers in the hands of slaveowners and husbands, often combining the two functions. A sister of President Madison wrote: "We southern ladies are complimented with the name of wives: but we are only the mistresses of seraglios." A southern planter's wife described herself as "the chief slave of the harem." The wife of a Confederate general wrote: "God forgive us, but ours is a monstrous system. . . . Like the patriarchs of old, our men live all in one house with their wives and their concubines. . . . Any lady is ready to tell you who is the father of all the mulatto children in everybody's household but her own. Those, she seems to think, drop from the clouds."[65]

Southern ladies' doublethink about their roles was an expected, even mandatory, social response. The first edition of Emily Post's *Etiquette* described "The Instincts of a Lady: As an unhappy wife, her dignity demands that she never show her disapproval of her husband, no matter how publicly he slights or outrages her."[66]

Though the rule obviously served the man's dignity, not the woman's, unhappy wives tried to obey it. Patriarchal society managed to convince them that if they failed to make their marriages "happy," they failed as women and as human beings. Hence, battered wives often accepted the guilt for their own victimization. Recent investigators report that battered wives go to great lengths to conceal the crime because of their own embarrassment and shame.[67]

Churches helped develop this secret embarrassment. One clergyman's routine advice to brides was: "Your duty is submission. . . . Your husband is, by the laws of God and of man, your superior; do not ever give him cause to remind you of it."[68] Of all professional groups, clergymen have proved least able or willing to help battered wives.

One abused wife from a "nice suburban neighborhood" wrote of her appeal to her clergyman and the reprimand she received. The minister demanded to know what she was doing wrong to bring her husband's violence down upon herself, and advised her only to search her own soul and discover how she might behave better to relieve the tension. She had a husband so violent that she feared for her life. Yet her spiritual leader and alleged comforter gave her less than no comfort. He tried rather to increase her suffering with a specious burden of guilt.[69]

In 1977 Ellen Kirby of the Board of Global Ministries of the United Methodist Church wrote: "The institutional church either through its blatant sexist theology, which has blessed the subordination of women, or through its silence, blindness, or lack of courage, has allowed itself to be one of the leading actors in the continuing tragedy of abuse."[70] Under the circumstances it seems unrealistic for Pope Paul VI to have observed in 1966 that "a true contradiction cannot exist between the divine laws pertaining to the transmission of life and those pertaining to the fostering of authentic conjugal love."[71] Translated from theologese, the "divine laws" meant simply the church's stand on birth control and "authentic conjugal love" meant husbandly dominance over the wife.

Patriarchal religions developed many rules for maintaining male dominance in marriage, but the structure was inherently unstable:

> *The patriarchal "family" of academic social science is but a euphemism for the individualistic male with his subordinate dependents. As a social unit the family means the (male) individual, activated by his most aggressively individualistic instincts; it is not the foundation, but the negation of society. . . .*
>
> *Human society did not arise as an organization of adjusted interests. It arose out of an extra-rational sentiment; it has never existed in any form except through the binding force of such sentiments.*[72]

The patriarchal family was at bottom unnatural, a reversal of the biological authority of the female over her dependents. "Economic man acts in perfect self-interest; a woman cannot base her relationships within the family on the principle of *quid pro quo:* she gives. It appears, from a masculinist perspective, that woman might be a more primitive version of a man—not because there is *prima facie* evidence of her lower intelligence, but because of her loving and giving nature, which is itself taken as evidence of lower intelligence. Rousseau's 'noble savage' like his ideal woman was compassionate and nurturing."[73]

As a rule, women were driven into marriage by social pressures that made spinsterhood even less attractive economically. When patriarchal laws took property out of women's hands and placed it in the hands of men, unmarried women became as helpless to support themselves as wives were. In the 17th century, a "spinster" was any woman imprisoned in a "spin-house" without money or male protectors. John Evelyn described a spin-house as a place where "incorrigible and lewd women are kept in discipline and labor."[74] It was seldom noticed that spinsters had become "incorrigible and lewd" in an effort to earn a living, in a society that allowed them to learn no skills other than trying to please men.

John Evelyn (1620-1706) English gentleman of letters, author of about 30 books including a famous diary.

Though patriarchal marriage typically existed for the service of man, there was usually a pretense of male autonomy and leadership; and the discovery of its mythical quality caused the wife's "basic trauma," according to Jessie Bernard:

Jessie Bernard Modern American feminist author and sociological researcher.

> *There are few traumas greater . . . than the wife's discovery of her husband's dependencies; than the discovery of her own gut-superiority in a thousand hidden crannies of the relationship; than the realization that in many situations his judgment is no better than hers; that he does not really know more than she; that he is not the calm, rational, nonemotional dealer in facts and relevant arguments; that he is, in brief, not at all the*

kind of person the male stereotype pictures him to be. Equally, if not more, serious is her recognition that she is not really the weaker vessel, that she is often called upon to be the strong one in the relationship.[75]

Marc Feigen Fastau also pointed out that false commitment to the myth of masculine steadiness and objectivity brings on disillusionment among wives:

> *Nothing contrasts more sharply with the masculine image of self-confidence, rationality, and control than men's sulky, obtuse, and, often virtually total, dependence on their wives to articulate and deal with their own unhappy feelings and their own insensitivity, fear, and passivity in helping their wives to deal with theirs. This, more than anything else, disillusions women about their men. Bromides like 'Men are just overgrown little boys' are both a description of the phenomenon and an attempt, by labeling it innocuously, to ease the pain of disillusionment: disillusionment at having subordinated yourself to a person who isn't, it turns out, special enough to justify the sacrifice, who is probably not much smarter than you are in most ways and in some very important ways is a lot less perceptive, more dependent and more childlike.*[76]

Though wives provide an essential support system, without which few men would be capable of carrying on productive careers, the "job" of a wife is the last relic of slavery in that it earns nothing. A woman can't collect unemployment insurance for losing this non-paid job, even when it means financial hardship for herself and her children. As a widow she is taxed at the highest level because she is not considered a contributor to her husband's estate. Yet a conservative estimate of the market value of a wife's services amounts to over $1,000,000. Nor is the job an easy one. Data collected by the Department of Health and Human Services show that housewives suffer more from symptoms of stress than do working women.[77]

Marlene Dixon
Modern feminist, writer, and teacher of sociology at a Canadian university.

Marlene Dixon said marriage is "the chief vehicle for the perpetuation of the oppression of women; it is through the role of wife that that subjugation of women is maintained."[78] To a large extent it was the Christian concept of marriage in the western world that brought this about, since the church declared women socially, politically, and intellectually inferior and made them their husband's chattels.[79] Wife-beating was so routine in Christian Europe that the standard symbol of "marriage" in Alsatian New Year decorations was a miniature man beating his miniature wife.[80]

Nineteenth-century clergymen in both Europe and America consistently upheld a husband's right to abuse his wife and to use "salutary restraints in every case of misbehavior," without the interference of what some court records of 1824 referred to as "vexatious prosecutions." In other words, it was vexatious for a battered wife to seek redress, but not vexatious for her husband to beat her in the first place. Many clergymen still have this attitude. A battered wife recently said: "My husband repeatedly spoke scripture at me about what a wife's responsibility was. . . . She was supposed to be submissive, and he would quote Paul, verse after verse after verse. I didn't feel like I had very much to fight with. . . . I don't recall any clergy person I went to—and I went to more than one—being supportive of my feelings about not continuing the marriage, of not wanting the abuse to continue. I got no support from any clergyman."[81]

Only recently, and grudgingly, did the clergy of some denominations remove the word "obey" from the bride's responses in the marriage service. Many clergymen still believe a wife should bow to her husband's wishes more than he bows to hers—not the best attitude in men who think themselves qualified to act as marriage counselors.

1. Fielding, 82, 114. 2. Briffault 3, 373. 3. Lederer, 162–63. 4. Bullough, 103, 112. 5. Campbell, M.I., 95. 6. Briffault 3, 373. 7. Sadock, Kaplan & Freedman, 22. 8. Simons, 99. 9. de Voragine, 736. 10. Fielding, 233. 11. Briffault 3, 248–49. 12. Hazlitt, 447. 13. Rose, 144. 14. *Mahanirvanatantra,* xxiv. 15. Bullough, 234. 16. Waddell, 117. 17. Avalon, 172. 18. Brasch, 70. 19. *Forgotten Books,* 201. 20. Briffault 3, 20. 21. Graves, G.M. 1, 54. 22. Bullough, 64. 23. Legman, 416. 24. Bullough, 309. 25. Hartley, 219. 26. Bachofen, 140, 145. 27. Briffault 3, 378; Hauswirth, 88. 28. Briffault 1, 712, 683. 29. Briffault 1, 346. 30. Briffault 1, 345. 31. Hazlitt, 453. 32. *Larousse,* 203. 33. Briffault 3, 375. 34. *Encyc. Brit.,* "Marriage." 35. Murstein, 115. 36. Guerber, L.R., 77, 110, 121. 37. Briffault 3, 249. 38. Fielding, 233–34. 39. Pearsall, W.B., 166–67. 40. *Encyc. Brit.,* "Marriage." 41. Briffault 3, 249. 42. *Encyc. Brit.,* "Marriage." 43. M. Harrison, 197. 44. H. Smith, 263. 45. de Voragine, 90–91. 46. de Riencourt, 228. 47. de Voragine, 150. 48. *Mahanirvanatantra,* 162–63. 49. Avalon, 596. 50. Briffault 3, 428. 51. T. Davidson, 98–99. 52. de Voragine, 282. 53. T. Davidson, 99. 54. Murstein, 445. 55. T. Davidson, 100. 56. Langley & Levy, 34–36. 57. Crow, 147. 58. Rugoff, 169–70. 59. Ehrenreich & English, 7. 60. Stone, 233. 61. Langley & Levy, 40. 62. E. Douglas, 137. 63. de Riencourt, 219. 64. Stanton, 196–98. 65. Bullough, 300; Rugoff, 325–26. 66. Wolff, 346. 67. Langley & Levy, 117. 68. Ehrenreich & English, 7. 69. Langley & Levy, 21. 70. T. Davidson, 211. 71. Wickler, xxx. 72. Briffault 3, 511–13. 73. Ehrenreich & English, 17. 74. Funk, 260. 75. Gornick & Moran, 154–55. 76. Feigen Fastau, 82. 77. Sheehy, 313–14. 78. Roszak, 193. 79. H. Smith, 228. 80. Miles, 270. 81. Hirsch, 173, 354.

Mars

Sign of Mars

Rome's "red" war-god Mars was once an Etruscan fertility-savior Maris, worshipped at an ancient shrine in the Apennines, Matiene.[1] At a similar shrine in northwestern Iran, Matiane (Mother Ana), the Medes worshipped the same god who became Martiya to the Persians, a holy "martyr" also called Immanuel or Imanisi. The inscription of Darius at Behistun says the god was incarnate in a sacred king slain by his people.[2] His spirit ruled what Sufis still call the "fulfilling" death-and-rebirth process, known as *mardiyya* or martyrdom.[3] An early Phrygian version of the same sacrificial god appears in Greek myth as the flayed satyr Marsyas, slain on a pine tree "between heaven and earth" by order of the heavenly father.

Mars was "red" because his basic Indo-European prototype was the pre-Vedic flayed god Rudra, father of the Maruts or sacrificial victims, red with their own blood. Rudra "the red one" was born of the three-faced virgin-mother Marici, Goddess of birth, dawn, and the New Year, a manifestation of the ancient feminine **Trinity**. Thus, Rudra bore the title of Tryambaka, "He Who Belongs to Three

Mother Goddesses." In Japan this Goddess was known as Marici-deva or Marishi-ten, whom later patriarchal writers masculinized as a Buddhist monk. However, this alleged monk always wore the garments of a woman.[4]

The same Goddess was Marica to the Latins. She gave birth to the god-king Latinus, ancestor of all Latin tribes. Her consort was the flayed goat god of the Lupercalia, Faunus, another incarnation of Mars, who also appeared in bird-soul form as the sacred woodpecker Picus, giving oracles from the top of a phallic pillar in his shrine.[5]

The Martian New Year sacrifices took place in the god's month of March, which once began the Roman year; this is why the "Ides of March" were considered dangerous to kings. In the Babylonian sacred calendar, the same New Year month of atonement sacrifices was Marcheshvan.[6] The astrological sign of this month still begins the year, according to astrologers' tradition.

In northern Europe, Mars was identified with Tiw, Tyr, or Tig: names derived from Indo-Germanic *dieus,* "God."[7] Just as Mars was often confused with the sky-father Jupiter, so Tiw was another name for the sky-father Odin. Tiw's sign was a lingam-yoni arrangement of a phallic spear attached to a female disc. As wielder of the spear or lightning bolt of fertility, Mars-Tiw became a god of battle. He was the patron of Roman warriors, who called him Marspiter (Father Mars) and honored him with "martial" exercises on the Campus Martius, site of a temple of Maris in Etruscan times. His sacred day was Tuesday, named after Tiw in English, though it is still *dies martis* in Latin and similarly named in Latinate languages (French *mardi*).

To account for the inevitable story that the Queen of Heaven as Celestial Virgin gave birth to the sacrificial god, Romans claimed the Blessed Virgin Juno spurned the love of her spouse, Jupiter, and to spite him conceived Mars by her own unaided feminine fertility magic, the lily blossom that represented her own yoni.[8]

1. Hays, 182; J.E. Harrison, 101. 2. *Assyr. & Bab. Lit.,* 178. 3. Shah, 394. 4. *Larousse,* 342, 422. 5. *Larousse,* 207–8. 6. *Assr. & Bab. Lit.,* 170. 7. H.R.E. Davidson, G.M.V.A., 57. 8. *Larousse,* 202.

Martin, Saint

Christian version of the March sacrificial god Mars, said to have come riding on the pale horse of death in the manner of Woden. Ireland preserved the custom of killing the god incarnate in an ox, the Mart-beast. It was claimed that the saint himself was cut up and eaten in the form of an ox. Every household killed some domestic animal and sprinkled the threshold with the animal's blood. St. Martin as "martyr" came to be regarded as "one of the very chief of the saints. . . . The tradition of slaughter is preserved in the British custom of killing cattle on St. Martin's Day."[1]

The holy day was a continuation of the Roman festival of Martinalia, when the god Bacchus prefigured Jesus by turning water into wine at his sacred marriage (the Christian adaptation appearing in the Gospel of John). By British folk custom down to the 19th century A.D., schoolboys filled vessels of water on St. Martin's Night so the water could be turned into wine before morning. By a benevolent deception like that of the Tooth Fairy, parents sometimes replaced the water with wine during the night.[2]

1. Miles, 204–6. 2. Hazlitt, 393.

Martyrs

Since the 9th century, when martyr-legends became wildly popular, the church listed countless bogus saints said to have died in "persecutions" of the 4th and 5th centuries. With more imagination than historicity, martyrologists created a church history out of fictions. Records of the alleged martyrs slain in "persecutions" are virtually nonexistent. The gory fantasies reported by such sources as the Golden Legend were invented from six to nine centuries after the time of the alleged events. Even Catholic scholars say martyrologists' tales are so childishly naive that when reading them "it is often difficult to refrain from smiling."[1]

Still, one might wonder why a smile should be the response to these grisly fantasies of torture and butchery, which hint at a sadistic turn of mind in those who invented such tales for the edification of their fellow Christians.

Most of the classic martyrs were assigned to the persecution of Diocletian, which Christian tradition greatly exaggerated. Diocletian made no objection to Christians until 298 A.D., when his priests claimed Christian unbelievers, present at an official sacrifice, prevented the reception of favorable omens. The emperor ordered Christians to honor the gods by burning a pinch of incense on the imperial altars. For those in the army or civil service, refusal to comply with this rule could mean discharge. Five years later, quarrels between Christian and pagan priesthoods escalated to the point where official oracles began to insist on the closing of Christian churches. Some Christian zealots took it on themselves to strike back by attacking the emperor himself.

Two fires were set in Diocletian's palace at Nicomedia. Three Christian eunuchs, residents in the palace, were accused of arson and executed. Centuries later they were canonized as Saints Dorotheus, Gorgonius, and Peter.[2] After the fires, Diocletian also ordered the arrest of some Christian priests. Martin Jones says "Some months later, the imprisoned clergy were all forced to sacrifice, and then, with the exception of a few obstinate reclusants, released." Some of the obstinate ones were executed. But the "persecution" was never more than half-hearted. Though it continued intermittently for a while, it was entirely abandoned by 313 A.D.[3]

The Golden Legend Collection of the "lives" of various saints, with emphasis on martyrdoms and miracle tales, written by Jacobus de Voragine, a 13th-century Dominican bishop in Lombardy, later archbishop of Genoa.

Diocletian (Gaius Aurelius Valerius Diocletianus) Roman emperor from 284 to 305 A.D. Of military background, Diocletian was noted for his economic and administrative reforms.

These ten years and comparatively few deaths were blown up into a legendary reign of terror, after the teachings of the primitive church were forgotten. One of these teachings was that martyrdom, called "the Crown," automatically brought Christlike apotheosis and made the soul of the martyr one with Jesus, as the soul of an Egyptian could become one with Osiris. In pursuit of this "imitation of Christ," so many Christians purposely broke laws and clamored for the death penalty that Antoninus of Antioch irritably inquired whether Christians had no ropes or precipices to kill themselves, without constantly making trouble for the authorities.[4]

Some of the early churches taught that martyrdom was required to be among the blessed in heaven. Apocryphal Gospels quoted Jesus: "Truly I say to you, none of those who fear death will be saved; for the kingdom of death belongs to those who put themselves to death." Tertullian said he longed for martyrdom, "that he may obtain from God complete forgiveness, by giving in exchange his blood." Gnostics however ridiculed martyrdom, saying it made God a cannibal who desired human blood; and the advocates of martyrdom were said to inflict it on each other all too often. Some Gnostic writings denounced other Christians for "oppressing their brothers" and even making children suffer, to save their souls.[5] This was one of the sources of the charge that Christians sacrificed children to their deity.[6] Centuries later, Christians used the same charge of child sacrifice to justify persecution of the Jews.[7]

In reality, Rome embraced many diverse faiths, Christianity among them, with far more tolerance than Christians showed. Angus says, "In the matter of intolerance Christianity differed from all pagan religions, and surpassed Judaism; in that respect it stood in direct opposition to the spirit of the age."[8] Some of the so-called persecutors were actually trying to stop the fighting between different factions of Christians, like the emperor Maxentius who arrested the rival popes Marcellus and Eusebius to prevent further street battles between their followers. Another pair of rival popes, Damasus and Ursinus, precipitated such bloody fighting that 137 corpses were left in the basilica of Sicininus in only one day. Ammianus reported that "It was only with difficulty that the people, having been roused to such ferocity, could be brought back to order."[9]

A persecution, rich in martyrdoms, was expected from the "Apostate" emperor Julian, an urbane pagan who disliked fanatical Christians. But Julian disappointed them by leaving them alone. Gregory of Nazianzus held even Julian's tolerance against him: "He begrudged to our soldiers the honor of martyrdom. . . . In order that we might suffer, and yet not win honor as we should, suffering for Christ's sake . . . he attacked our religion in a very villainous and ungenerous way, introducing into his persecution the traps and snares of argument." Julian was killed in a military camp, under odd circumstances. According to Libanius, the emperor was assassinated by a

Christian—less inclined to argue, more inclined to destroy the opponent.[10]

There are no verifiable contemporary records of individual Christians "slain for their faith" under the Roman empire. Eusebius (d. 371 A.D.) mentioned a letter, supposedly from the churches of Lyons and Vienne to the churches of Asia and Phrygia, listing the names of 48 Christians executed in the reign of Marcus Aurelius, 177 A.D., nearly two hundred years earlier.[11] Eusebius probably wrote the letter himself. It was he who adopted the principle of "holy lying" on the church's behalf. Ever afterward, churchmen cited Eusebius to prove that any lie is permissible if it glorifies the Christian faith.[12]

Aside from this father of "holy lying" and his dubious letter, no martyrs' names were heard of until the 7th to 9th centuries. A majority were only names or titles of old pagan deities whose shrines had been pilgrimage centers since pre-Christian times.

The real martyrs of the early Christian era were not made by the pagans so much as by their fellow Christians. Diocletian's persecution was negligible compared to the violent warfare of Christian against Christian in those centuries. Zealots in Asia Minor destroyed whole towns and villages and massacred thousands of "heretics." Women and children were tortured until they agreed to receive the Host of the true faith. Ammianus said "no wild beasts are so hostile to man as Christian sects in general are to one another."[13] Toleration itself was punishable. At Trier in the 4th century two bishops, Priscillian and Instantius, with two other men and a woman, were illegally tortured and executed by their fellow Christians for being too tolerant of their pagan neighbors.[14]

In the 5th century, Innocent I proclaimed that God gave the church the right to kill. Its military might "had been granted by God and the sword had been permitted for the punishment of the guilty"—meaning anyone holding unorthodox opinions.[15] A letter attributed to Clement, bishop of Rome, said whoever refuses to "bow the neck" to God's bishops, priests, and deacons is guilty of insubordination against God and must suffer the death penalty.[16]

Once in power, the church attacked both pagans and non-orthodox Christians in a reign of terror. By a conservative estimate, pagan emperors spilled less than one ten-thousandth of the amount of Christian blood later shed by other Christians.[17] The persecutions in Asia Minor were thus described in 386 A.D.:

> *The monks say they are making war on the temples but their warfare is a way of pillaging what little poor unfortunates do have, the produce of the fields and the cattle they feed. . . . They grab people's land, claiming the place is sacred. Many have been robbed of their patrimony on such a pretext. They who (as they say) give honor to their god by fasting are getting fat on the wretchedness of others.*
>
> *And as for those others, the victims of such a sack, if they go to town, to a "shepherd"—he will be called that, though he may not be a*

good shepherd precisely—and tell him, weeping, of their injustices suffered, the shepherd will approve of the pillagers, and chase their victims away, saying that they should count it a gain that they have not suffered worse.

If they hear of a place with something worth raping away, they immediately claim that someone is making sacrifices and committing abominations, and pay the place a visit. [18]

Christian zealots sometimes tortured pagan women to make them renounce their Goddess.[19] This may have been the real origin of the many fictitious "virgin martyrs" said to have renounced love and marriage to embrace Christian celibacy, retaining their virginity despite the most horrendous tortures. Catholic writers now call the church's virgin-martyr horror tales only "edifying romance"—though why these sadistic fantasies should seem edifying is not made clear.[20] Christian tales of the pagans' execution of virgins made no sense in any case; for under Roman law, no virgin could be executed. If sentenced to death, a virgin had to be legally deflowered before sentence could be carried out.[21] No Roman law made virginity *per se* a crime.

The real reason why the church demanded martyr-myths was that it was the best traditional way to achieve union with a deity and consequent immortality. From the earliest ideas of sacred kingship, he who died in agony could become at once one with his God. The very word *martyr* was the name of the ancient sacred king in Persia, Martiya-Immanuel (see **Mars**).[22] The Fourth Book of Maccabees, written about the 1st century B.C., provided a typical scriptural model for Christian martyrologists. It described the sufferings of the Jew Eleazar and his companions, who endured the usual sequence of flayings, burnings, scourgings, disembowellings, etc., couched in loftily metaphorical prose: "Eleazar, like a fine steersman steering the ship of sanctity on the sea of the passions, though buffeted by the threats of the tyrant and swept by the swelling waves of the tortures, never shifted for one moment the helm of sancity until he sailed into the haven of victory over death."[23]

1. Attwater, 13. 2. Brewster, 402. 3. *Encyc. Brit.,* "Diocletian." 4. H. Smith, 211. 5. Pagels, 90–93. 6. Robertson, 116. 7. Lindsay, O.A., 219. 8. Angus, 277. 9. J.H. Smith, D.C.P., 40, 131. 10. Ibid., 102, 115. 11. Attwater, 224. 12. Knight, S.L., 164. 13. Gibbon 1, 719–22. 14. J.H. Smith, D.C.P., 155. 15. Bullough, 122. 16. Pagels, 34. 17. H. Smith, 210. 18. J.H. Smith, D.C.P., 166. 19. Gibbon 1, 720. 20. Attwater, 210. 21. Sadock, Kaplan & Freedman, 17. 22. *Assyr. & Bab. Lit.,* 178. 23. *Forgotten Books,* 185.

Mary

Fathers of the Christian church strongly opposed the worship of Mary because they were well aware that she was only a composite of Mariamne, the Semitic God-Mother and Queen of Heaven; Aphrodite-Mari, the Syrian version of Ishtar; Juno the Blessed Virgin; Isis as Stella Maris, Star of the Sea; Maya the Oriental Virgin Mother of the

Redeemer; the Moerae or trinity of Fates; and many other versions of the Great Goddess.[1] Even Diana Lucifera the Morning-Star Goddess was assimilated to the Christian myth as Mary's "mother," Anna or Dinah. Churchmen knew the same titles were applied to Mary as to her pagan forerunners: "queen of heaven, empress of hell, lady of all the world."[2]

The *Speculum beatae Mariae* said Mary was like the Juno-Artemis-Hecate trinity: "queen of heaven where she is enthroned in the midst of the angels, queen of earth where she constantly manifests her power, and queen of hell where she has authority over the demons." According to the Office of the Virgin, she was the primordial being, "created from the beginning and before the centuries."[3]

Speculum beatae Mariae A book of praise attributed to St. Bonaventura (13th century), but probably written anonymously some centuries later.

Christian patriarchs therefore sought to humanize and belittle Mary, to prove her unworthy of adoration. Epiphanius ordered: "Let the Father, the Son and the Holy Spirit be worshipped, but let no one worship Mary."[4] Anastasius said, "Let no one call Mary the Mother of God, for Mary was but a woman, and it is impossible that God should be born of a woman."[5] Ambrose called Mary the "temple" of God, and "only he is to be adored who worked within the temple."[6] Up to the 5th century the church persecuted as heretics a sect calling themselves Marianites, who claimed that Mary possessed the true quality of divinity.[7] Mariolatry has plagued Christian patriarchy throughout its history, as the popular need to worship the Mother-figure always arose unbidden.

Some early church fathers sought a way out of the dilemma by attacking Mary's motherhood, to prove her neither divine nor really maternal. Some claimed Jesus wasn't born in the ordinary way but suddenly materialized before Mary.[8] Marcionites said Jesus could never touch vulgar female flesh, therefore he was never born at all. He descended from heaven as a fully formed adult.[9] Some church fathers rejected Mary's motherhood on the ground that she was not only a mere mortal, but even a sinful woman.[10]

There was ecclesiastical opposition to Mary throughout the Christian era. Pope Nicholas III ordered Jean d'Olive, a friar "distinguished for learning and piety," to burn with his own hands a tract he had written in praise of Mary because it expressed excessive devotion to her.[11] When it was permitted, Marian devotion did appear to take on an Oriental extravagance.

Isidore Glabas 14th-century Greek Marianist theologian.

Germanus, Patriarch of Constantinople in 717, called Mary "Lady all-holy" and "Lady most venerable," maintaining that no one could be saved or receive the gift of grace except through her, since God obeys her "through and in all things, as his true mother." Henri Boudon, archdeacon of Evreux, said his people thought Mary "as much as, or more than, God himself." Isidore Glabas said Mary ruled in heaven before her earthly birth; like a creatress she brought all things into being, and all the angels obeyed her. Bernardine of Siena said Mary's birth of the Savior through her own mystic powers was more

St. Bernardine of Siena (1380–1444) Franciscan theologian and reformer who preached against the moral breakdown consequent upon the papacy's Great Schism.

St. Louis-Marie Grignion de Montfort (1673–1716) French priest who founded two congregations and wrote *True Devotion to the Blessed Virgin.* He was canonized in 1947.

Protoevangelium, also known as the Revelation of James: a Gospel written in the second century A.D., valued by early church fathers as authentic but eventually eliminated from the canon.

miraculous than God's generation of him. "Even if she had not been the Mother of God, she would nevertheless have been the mistress of the world." Louis-Marie de Montfort declared that Mary had absolute power over God.[12]

People of the Middle Ages often viewed God as their persecutor, Mary as their defender. Early 16th-century woodcuts showed God shooting arrows of pestilence, war, and inflation at the world, while the inscription pleaded with Mary to restrain him.[13] It was said that "Mary stands for Mercy, and it is only because of her influence at court, not because of love or goodwill on God's part, that heaven is within reach."[14] A 14th-century Franciscan wrote:

> *When we have offended Christ, we should go first to the Queen of Heaven and offer her . . . prayers, fasting, vigils, and alms; then she, like a mother, will come between thee and Christ, the father who wishes to beat us, and she will throw the cloak of mercy between the rod of punishment and us, and soften the king's anger against us.*[15]

Ashe says, "Christian scripture and doctrine totally preclude placing Mary above Christ. Yet the vitality of Christ's own Church has often seemed to depend on her rather than him. . . . [W]ithout her he would probably have lost his kingdom."[16] During its first five centuries, Christ's church discovered that no amount of force would make people renounce their Mother Goddess. She had to be preserved in some form:

> *The church seemed doomed to failure, destined to go down to bloody death amidst the bleeding corpses of its victims, when the people discovered Mary. And only when Mary, against the stern decrees of the church, was dug out of the oblivion to which Constantine had assigned her and became identified with the Great Goddess was Christianity finally tolerated by the people. . . . The only reality in Christianity is Mary, the Female Principle, the ancient goddess reborn.*[17]

In the eastern empire it was said the mark of true Christian faith was to "confess the holy Ever-Virgin Mary, truly and properly the Mother of God, to be higher than every creature whether visible or invisible." Ephraem of Syria called Mary the bride or spouse of Jesus as well as his mother, after the fashion of the pagan Goddess and her son-consort; she was also Gate of Heaven, Ark, and Garden of Paradise. Mary personally sprinkled the face of Adam with life-giving rain, which placed her in the creation myth as "co-redemptress." Ephraem's opinions were called heretical by some, but after a lapse of 1600 years—in the year 1920—he was declared a Doctor of the Universal Church by papal decree.[18]

The Christian figure of Mary was gradually created during the first four centuries of the Christian era, out of bits and pieces of the Great Goddess who conceived "sons of God" and Saviors in all the temples of the ancient world. The Protoevangelium said Mary served as a temple hierodule, and received God's seed as she was beginning to spin a blood-red thread in the temple—the work of the Fate-virgin, first of the Moerae or "Marys," who spun the thread of destiny.[19] At this mystically crucial moment the angel Gabriel "came in unto her" (Luke 1:28), the biblical phrase for sexual intercourse.

Other sources also identified Mary with the Fate-spinner, whom the Greeks called Clotho, youngest of the trinity of Moerae. The Coptic *Discourse on Mary,* attributed to Cyril of Jerusalem, represented Mary as the same triple Goddess of Fate, incarnate in the three Marys who stood at the foot of Jesus's cross.[20] In like manner, the three Fates of Nordic myth stood at the foot of Odin's tree of sacrifice; their virgin aspect was sometimes Freya, "the Lady." The Swedes called the constellation of Orion the distaff of the virgin Mary, because it was formerly the distaff used by Freya to spin the destinies of men.[21]

Greek myth presented an image of the Virgin Persephone almost identical to that of fate-spinning Mary. Persephone sat in a sacred cave or temple, starting to spin a web with a great picture of the universe—the magic picture which the Mother made into reality. At that moment the Heavenly Father appeared in the form of a phallic serpent and begot the savior Dionysus on her.[22]

In an effort to make Mary's impregnation as sexless as possible, some Christian ascetics invented very peculiar mechanisms for it. Sacred art showed semen emanating from God's mouth and passing through a long tube that led under Mary's skirts. Some theologians claimed God's seed was carried to Mary in the beak of the Holy Dove. Others said it came from Gabriel's mouth, to be filtered through the sacred lily before entering Mary's body by way of her ear.[23]

Though the Christian God took over the Triple Goddess's ancient trinitarian character at the Council of Nicaea, there is some evidence that early Christians perceived Mary as a trinity. Like the Buddhists' Mara, she was sometimes a spirit of death.[24] The *Gospel of Mary* identified all three of the Marys at Jesus's crucifixion with one another, as if they were the same Triple Goddess who attended the death of the pagan Savior.[25]

Gospel of Mary One of the early Gnostic Gospels, once included with the books of the New Testament but later eliminated from the canon. A copy was rediscovered in the 1940s at Nag Hammadi.

For some centuries, eastern churches worshipped a Father-Mother-Son trinity modeled on such pagan triads as Osiris-Isis-Horus, Zeus-Rhea-Zagreus, Apollo-Artemis-Heracles, etc. This idea was so commonplace that even writers of the Koran felt compelled to deny the divine trinity of God, Mary, and Jesus.[26] Moslem sources also preserved another manifestation of the Virgin Goddess as Mar Mariam or Sancta Maria, mother of the Persian savior Mani.[27] As "the Sea" (Maria), the Triple Goddess swallowed up the god she gave birth to. In solemn imitation, the women of Alexandria threw images of Osiris into the sea after his Passion Play.[28] Hebraic copies of this rite probably account for Plutarch's report that the chief city of Palestine—Jerusalem—was built in honor of a child whom Isis killed and threw into the sea.[29]

Mary was also closely associated with the Great Goddess of

Ephesus, whose temples she took over. In the 5th century an Ephesian priest named Proclus delivered a sermon on the multiform nature of Mary, calling her "the living bush, which was not burnt by the fire of the divine birth . . . virgin and heaven, the only bridge between God and men, the awesome loom . . . on which the garment of union was woven."[30]

Much was made of the reversal of Mary's Latin *Ave* and the name of Eve (Eva). Mystics said Mary was Eve's purified reincarnation, as Jesus was the similar reincarnation of Adam.[31] Somehow, theologians failed to recognize that the new incarnations apparently reversed the parent-child relationship. Then again, as Adam and Eve were spouses, so the relationship of Mary and Jesus sometimes verged on the sexual or conjugal. In a legend ascribed to St. John, Jesus welcomed Mary into heaven with the words, "Come, my chosen, and I shall set thee in my seat, for I have coveted the beauty of thee."[32]

The church's doctrine of the assumption of Mary was explained in a number of ways. Early churchmen declared that Jesus visited Mary's tomb—variously located in Ephesus, Bethlehem, Gethsemane, or Josaphat—and raised up her corpse, which he made to live again; then he personally escorted her into heaven as a live woman.[33] She was not a soul or a spirit but an immortal person in her own original body. This became the official modern view when the doctrine of the assumption was declared an article of faith in 1950, when Pope Pius XII pronounced that "the immaculate mother of God, the ever Virgin Mary, when the course of her earthly life was run, was assumed in body and in soul to heavenly glory."[34] But the point had already been argued for more than a thousand years.

The church's problem was to take advantage of popular reverence for Mary but at the same time prevent her literal deification. Some theologians of the 13th century claimed Mary's mortality should bring more women to obey the church, because the king of heaven "is no mere man but a mere woman is its queen. It is not a mere man who is set above the angels and all the rest of the heavenly court, but a mere woman is; nor is anyone who is merely man as powerful there as a mere woman."[35]

Mariale Common name of two Marianist handbooks, the first written by an anonymous author and falsely ascribed to Albertus Magnus; the second written in 1478 by the Franciscan friar Bernardine of Busti.

Always the theologians feared to impute too much power and glory to Mary. Pope John XXIII, presuming to know Mary's inner thoughts, announced: "The Madonna is not pleased when she is put above her Son," though in fact it was the church who was not pleased. Catholic doctrines themselves attributed to her two of the three basic characteristics of divinity: she was immortal by reason of the assumption, and sinless by reason of the **Immaculate Conception**. The third requirement of divinity, omniscience, was conceded to her by popular belief. A 13th-century *Mariale* said she had perfect knowledge of divine mysteries, understood all scriptures, foresaw the future, and knew everything about mathematics, geography, astronomy, alchemy, and canon law—even in her earthly life, when there was no canon and therefore no canon law.[36] A French manuscript illustration showed Mary enthroned beside God on Judgment Day, weighing souls in her balances like her prototype the Goddess Maat 3000 years earlier.[37] (See **Alchemy**.)

The Welsh confused Mary with the triadic White Goddess, and seldom asked the blessing of God without also imploring the favor of "the white Mary."[38] Saints' tales implied that Mary's was the true touch of canonization. St. Bernard was ennobled by three drops of milk that the Virgin pressed from her own breast for him.[39] St. Catherine of Siena also claimed to have been nourished by Mary's milk.[40]

Many legends depicted Mary as the only true source of the milk of human kindness. At Mainz Cathedral she gave away one of her image's gold shoes to a starving beggar, who had pleased her by playing his fiddle for her. He was caught with the shoe, arrested, and sentenced to death. On the way to the scaffold he paused to pray to the Virgin, and she exonerated him by publicly giving him her other shoe. The beggar was released, but the priests took away the gold shoes and locked them in the treasury, "lest the Virgin should again be tempted to bestow them upon some penniless beggar who prayed for her aid."[41]

Mary's mercy often proved superior to that of God or Jesus. She was occasionally represented leaning on the balance that weighed a sinner's few good deeds, to make them heavier than his evil deeds and save him from damnation. Her mercy extended even to the Jews, despite her priests' detestation of them. On Easter Day in Bourges, a Jewish child took Holy Communion along with his Christian friends. For this offense, the boy's father threw him into a furnace; but he lay unharmed by the fire, saying the Lady who stood on the Christians' altar was protecting him. "Then the Christians, understanding that he meant the statue of the Blessed Mary, took the aged Jew and threw him into the furnace, and he was burnt and consumed."[42]

Ethiopian Christians' Lefafa Sedek, "Bandlet of Righteousness," said God gave the secrets of salvation to humanity only because Mary requested it, when she began to grieve for her relatives writhing in hell's River of Fire. Egyptian paganism was the real source of this "Christian" scripture, copied from the Book of the Dead with the name of God substituted for Ra, of Christ for that of Thoth, and of Mary for that of All-Merciful Isis.[43]

Some theologians said even the worst of sinners could win a sure salvation by doing some special service for Mary. Two scribes pleased her by making copies of the *Book of the Miracles of the Virgin Mary.* Afterward they committed many sins, and when they died, devils came for their souls. But the Virgin pulled them away from the devils, saving them on account of their devotion to her.[44]

At times it seemed that Mary, not God, was the real opponent of evil forces. Spengler said this was "one of the maxima of the Gothic, one of its unfathomable creations—one that the present day forgets and *deliberately* forgets. . . . It is not possible to exaggerate either the grandeur of this forceful, insistent picture or the depth of sincerity with which it was believed in. The Mary-myths and the Devil-myths formed themselves side by side, neither possible without the other. Disbelief in either of them was deadly sin. There was a Mary-cult of prayer, and a Devil-cult of spells and exorcisms."[45] Historian Henry Adams noted: "Without Mary, man had no hope except in atheism, and for atheism the world was not ready. . . . The thirteenth century could not afford to admit a doubt. Society had staked its existence, in this world and the next, on the reality and power of the Virgin."[46]

Caesarius of Heisterbach told a story showing that Mary was more revered than God. A knight of Liège needed money and so made a pact with Satan. When asked to curse and renounce God, he did so willingly. However, when the demon required him to renounce the Virgin, he refused, horrified. Therefore the Virgin later intervened to save him from damnation.[47]

Mary dispensed compassion (Hindu *karuna*) more effectively than Christ, for this very quality had been associated with the feminine image from the beginning. Compassion was the *charis* of sacred harlots, which contributed much to Mary's consistent patronage of prostitutes. The "whore" Mary Magdalene was one of the original Marian trinity.[48] Augstein says Mariolatry evolved because "the people needed a queen of heaven, as the Israelites needed one in Jeremiah's time, one for whom they could bake cakes, a great mother, a fertility-prostitute; but she was half shown to them, half withheld, and Freud only gives us half the truth when he says that the Christian religion recreated the mother-god."[49] Actually, the people recreated the mother-god out of their own pagan heritage.

Churchmen claimed that all women lay under a threefold curse. They were accursed if they were barren. They were accursed also if they conceived, since conception was of the nature of original sin. They were accursed by the pains of childbirth, in fulfillment of God's curse on Eve. But Mary escaped all three curses. "Mary alone of all women is blessed, because she is virgin and fruitful, she conceives in holiness, and gives birth without pain."[50] Of course this view of Mary did little to improve the lot of ordinary women, presenting them with a wholly impossible ideal, yet implying that they fell short of the ideal only because of their sinfulness.[51] The ancients saw no incongruity in a Goddess who was both virgin and mother (as well as lover and **crone**), because she represented all women in all phases of life. Christians however insisted on taking the "miracle" literally, having lost sight of its subtle allegory.

A hidden reason for the church's adoption of Mary was the

successful amputation of her pre-Christian sexuality. Of all the attributes she inherited from the ancient Goddess, Mary's virginity was most emphasized. She was called "the Virgin," not "the Mother." Church fathers insisted that she never engaged in sexual intercourse in her life, even though the Bible plainly spoke of Jesus's brothers and sisters.[52] St. Ambrose demanded, "Would the Lord Jesus have chosen for his mother a woman who would defile the heavenly chamber with the seed of a man, that is to say one incapable of preserving her virginal chastity intact?"[53] Marian legends insisted that, although Mary was amazingly beautiful, no man could ever look on her with desire.[54]

Yet some monasteries institutionalized desire for Mary, who "married" the monks as Christ "married" nuns. If a knight placed his ring on the finger of Mary's image, she would grip it firmly so it couldn't be removed. At this, the knight considered himself a Bridegroom of the Virgin and entered a monastery. The same tales were told of pagan statues of Venus, who "married" any man who placed a ring on her marble finger.[55] In 1470 a Breton Black Friar, Alain de la Roche, claimed the Virgin married him in the presence of many saints and angels, placing on his finger a ring woven of her hair.[56]

Cistercians styled themselves "Knights of Our Lady," associating their Lady with the pagan May Queen. Aegidus's 13th-century history of the order said it was the custom in the time of Bishop Albero for the clergy of Liège to choose "from among their concubines" a Paschal and Pentecostal Queen, who was robed in purple, crowned, throned, and worshipped with drums and music, "revered almost with idolatry as if she were an idol."[57] She also manifested herself as the Fairy Queen who watched over a monastery near Laach as the monks' divine Bride. She announced each man's death three days in advance by placing a lily in his stall at midnight.[58]

Gothic cathedrals were dedicated not to God or Jesus but to *Notre Dame;* they were collectively called "Our Ladies" or "Palaces of the Queen of Heaven."[59] Many of them were built over pagan shrines of the Great Goddess. Rome's cathedral of Santa Maria Maggiore was built over the sacred cave of the Magna Mater. Santa Maria in Aracoeli on the Capitoline Hill was formerly a temple of Tanit. Mary's churches throughout Italy were founded on shrines of Juno, Isis, Minerva, Diana, Hecate. One church was even naively named Santa Maria sopra Minerva: Holy Mary over (the shrine of) Minerva.[60]

In the 6th century, the great temple of Isis at Philae was rededicated to Mary.[61] Aphrodite's sanctuaries on Cyprus became churches of Mary, whom the Cypriots continued to address by Aphrodite's name.[62] At Chartres, the heathen idol of the *virgo paritura* (Virgin Giving Birth) was preserved in the so-called Druid Grotto underneath the cathedral. It was said to be a black statue of Mary.[63]

Ecclesia, "the Church," was one of Mary's titles. She was identified with both the buildings and the organization of Holy Mother Church as bride and mother of God. Yet this pseudo-female church remained the exclusive property of men. As late as February 1977 Pope Paul VI again forbade ordination of women, saying the church "does not consider herself [sic] authorized to admit women to priestly ordination." The pope maintained that priests must have a "natural resemblance" to Christ, and if they were women "it would be difficult to see in the minister the image of Christ."[64] There was no mention that a priestess might present a resemblance to Mary, who symbolized the church itself. The modern church prefers to forget that early churches of Mary were staffed by priestesses, not priests.[65]

Above all, Christian authorities feared Mary might be the channel through which Goddess-worship could reestablish itself, for she inspired utterances similar to those the ancient Mother inspired, like Goethe's: "Supreme and sovereign Mistress of the World! . . . Oh Virgin, in the highest sense most pure, oh Mother, worthy of all our worship, our chosen Queen, equal with the gods."[66] The secret, ineradicable heresies of Marian worship received graphic form in the famous Vièrge Ouvrante—Mary as a statue that opened up to show God, Jesus, angels, and saints contained inside her.

> *In the generating and nourishing, protective and transformative, feminine power of the unconscious, a wisdom is at work that is infinitely superior to the wisdom of man's waking consciousness, and that, as source of vision and symbol, of ritual and law, poetry and vision, intervenes, summoned or unsummoned, to save man and give direction to his life.*
>
> *This feminine-maternal wisdom is no abstract, disinterested knowledge, but a wisdom of loving participation. . . . In the patriarchal development of the Judeo-Christian West, with its masculine, monotheistic trend toward abstraction, the goddess, as a feminine figure of wisdom, was disenthroned and repressed. She survived only secretly, for the most part in heretical and revolutionary bypaths. . . .*
>
> *Seen from the outside, the "Vièrge Ouvrante" is the familiar and unassuming mother with child. But when opened she reveals the heretical secret within her. God the Father and God the Son, usually represented as heavenly lords who in an act of pure grace raise up the humble, earth-bound mother to abide with them, prove to be contained in her; prove to be the "contents" of her all-sheltering body.*[67]

Mary represented the second of the two expedients men used to overcome their fear of women, according to Horney: disparagement and idealization.[68] But she was so ideal that she had to be apotheosized just as unmistakably as Jesus himself. So she rose bodily from the earth and ascended to glory. Unfortunately, those who formulated this idea were quite ignorant of the vastness of the universe, and their simplistic "rising to the sky" no longer serves an age in which such information is readily available. Even assuming that Mary's body could travel at the speed of light—an impossible idea to begin with—it would be only two thousand light-years away at the present time, about one-fiftieth of the distance across our own galaxy, let alone plunged into the unthinkable immensity of intergalactic space. And yet in an era when the absurdity of the idea is perfectly plain to the educated, to be exact on June 30, 1968, the Credo of Pope Paul VI reconfirmed the dogma of the Assumption of the Blessed Virgin Mary—though God apparently didn't take the trouble to inform him about the method of its accomplishment.[69]

But not all minds in the modern age are modern minds. Many remain ignorant of what has been discovered about the physical universe. Many are ignorant of the theories and doctrines professed by their own religion. They worship Mary only because their inner being demands a mother-archetype, and she is the only one presented to them. They don't know how many "Marys" there were before Christianity. But educated churchmen know. Canon John de Satgé wrote: "The evangelical has a strong suspicion that the deepest roots of the Marian cultus are not to be found in the Christian tradition at all. The religious history of mankind shows a recurring tendency to worship a mother-goddess. . . . May it not be the case, the evangelical wonders, that what we have here is in reality an older religion, a paganism which has been too lightly baptized into Christ and whose ancient features persist under a thin Christian veil?"[70]

However, Mary wasn't "lightly" adopted by Christianity. She was opposed, attacked, and finally accepted only with many theological misgivings and restrictions. Early Gospels that dwelt on the divinity of Mary were labeled "poisonous" by the orthodox church.[71] Christian mystics who coveted the female role and spoke of "becoming Mary and bearing God from within," did so in defiance of the church's earlier edict that Mary couldn't claim the title of Theotokos (God-bearer), because God couldn't be born of a mortal woman.[72] The edict was abandoned after several centuries only because Christians wished to emulate the pagan Mystery-cults whose Savior-gods were invariably born of mortal virgins. (See **Virgin Birth**.)

Christian art of the first five centuries showed Mary in a position lower than Jesus, even lower than the Magi, who wore haloes while she wore none. In the 6th century she acquired a halo and rose to the central position in a group of non-haloed apostles. By the 9th century she reigned as Queen of Heaven in the middle of the apse in two cathedrals.[73]

By the 14th century, Wyclif was writing: "It seems to me impossible that we should obtain the reward without the help of Mary. There is no sex or age, no rank or position, of anyone in the whole human race, which has no need to call for the help of the Holy Virgin." The *Te Deum Laudamus* declared, "All the earth doth worship thee, Spouse of the Eternal Father."[74]

When Mary appeared in a subordinate position, it was in the role of Daughter—like the Virgin Kore—on the lap of the Elder Goddess represented by "God's grandmother," the ancient Anna (St. Anne, called Mary's mother). In some painted or sculpted groupings, the two Goddesses and the male infant seem to form a trinity quite exclusive of God.[75] An observer might be reminded of the Egyptian god-king on the laps of his Two Mothers, they who would nurse him forever and thus give him eternal life. The mythical history of St. Anne reveals that she, even more directly than Mary, descended from the image of that fertile Creatress, Mother Earth.[76]

Legends and images of Mary exerted an uncanny appeal even in the "scientific" modern age with its professed skepticism about the supernatural. In 1945, a young boy named Joseph Vitolo was greatly impressed by the film *Song of Bernadette,* and subsequently conjured up a vision of the Virgin for himself. He conversed with her for sixteen consecutive nights at a certain rock in the Bronx. She told him to have a chapel built on the spot, and promised the appearance of a healing spring within a short time.

Though the site received the popular name of the Bronx Lourdes, and credulous folk hurried there in astonishing numbers to pray for miraculous cures, the spring never appeared. Eventually, young Joseph became embarrassed by the fuss he had caused. He then said the Virgin told him she wouldn't come any more to that place. Despite this disappointment, for many years the faithful continued to gather and dig in the mud, seeking the holy spring.[77]

But it was not only the simple-minded who sought help from Mary. Historian Henry Adams thought Christianity's divine mother, however attenuated, offered the only hope of spiritual comfort in an alienated technological society. He saw that "the males of his society, who had transferred so many of their once autonomous activities to machines and automatons, did not have sufficient life-sense to save the race. In their blind pride over their scientific facilities, they would cling to the insensate mechanisms they had created, making them go faster and faster, though incapable of applying the brakes. . . . Henry Adams, at the end of his own career, turned to another countervailing form of energy, the energy of life, the energy of erotic love, reproduction, and creation; he sought a counterpoise to chaos by invoking woman's faith in her own creativity, in all the ramifying, formative processes of life, above all those of sex, love, and motherhood." In a poetic address to the Virgin he said: "I feel the energy of faith, not in the future science but in you."[78]

Once more it seemed that God (or man) depended on his Mother (or woman) to straighten up the mess he had made, even if it meant ceding supreme power to her. An 18th-century theologian wrote, "At the command of Mary all obey, even God." Today it is widely recognized even by laymen that "two rivers of common source, Mary and Maya, the Virgin and Shakti, once again run into one: and the

Goddess is once more, as she ever was, the creatrix of the universe, the self-revealing energy of the unknowable God."[79]

1. Campbell, P.M., 140. 2. Scot, 348. 3. Mâle, 235, 238. 4. Ashe, 151. 5. de Riencourt, 150. 6. Lederer, 173. 7. Briffault 3, 183. 8. Ashe, 134. 9. Bullough, 112. 10. *Encyc. Brit.*, "Mary." 11. Coulton, 215. 12. Ashe, 203, 215, 223. 13. Wilkins, 193. 14. Ashe, 203. 15. Bullough, 169–70. 16. Ashe, 236. 17. Daly, 92. 18. Ashe, 173, 203. 19. Ashe, 201. 20. Ashe, 135. 21. Briffault 2, 625. 22. Campbell, P.M., 101. 23. Simons, 103. 24. Campbell, Or.M., 352. 25. Malvern, 39. 26. Ashe, 206. 27. Robertson, 88. 28. Frazer, G.B., 390. 29. Budge, G.E. 2, 191. 30. Ashe, 188. 31. Wilkins, 116. 32. Mâle, 249–50. 33. Ashe, 208. 34. *Encyc. Brit.*, "Mary." 35. Bullough, 178. 36. Ashe, 213, 228. 37. Robbins, 131. 38. Hazlitt, 630. 39. Bullough, 170. 40. Reinach, 308. 41. Guerber, L.R., 255. 42. de Voragine, 461. 43. Budge, A.T., 196. 44. Budge, A.T., 477–78. 45. Campbell, C.M., 49. 46. Beard, 222. 47. J.B. Russell, 118–19. 48. Malvern, 39. 49. Augstein, 302. 50. de Voragine, 205. 51. Daly, 62. 52. Coulton, 308. 53. Ashe, 182. 54. de Voragine, 152. 55. Baring-Gould, C.M.M.A., 224, 226. 56. Wilkins, 40. 57. Wilkins, 63, 168. 58. Guerber, L.R., 147. 59. Ashe, 217. 60. Wilkins, 69. 61. *Larousse,* 19. 62. Ashe, 192. 63. Swaan, 118. 64. *Time,* Feb. 7, 1977, 65. 65. Ashe, 231. 66. de Riencourt, 250–51. 67. Neumann, G.M., 330–31. 68. Bullough, 53. 69. Campbell, F.W.G., 125. 70. Ashe, 7–8. 71. Ochs, 72. 72. Cavendish, T., 74; de Riencourt 150. 73. Ochs, 76. 74. Ochs, 72, 74–75. 75. Neumann, G.M., pls. 180–81. 76. Neumann, A.C.U., 13, 57. 77. Castiglioni, 356. 78. Mumford, 363. 79. Lederer, 179.

Mary Magdalene

The Gospels say Jesus cast seven devils out of the sacred harlot Mary Magdalene, and appeared first to her after his resurrection (Mark 16:9). Books later eliminated from the canon by Christian censors gave further curious details about the relationship: Jesus loved Mary Magdalene more than all other apostles, called her Apostle to the Apostles and "the Woman Who Knew the All," and often kissed her.[1] He said she would excel every other disciple in the coming Kingdom of Light, where she would rule.[2]

Before Gnostic Gospels were cut out of the canon, they were accepted as the Word of God, as much as the synoptic Gospels and other New Testament writings. Therefore medieval traditions concerning Mary Magdalene hark back to her early mystical supremacy. She was called Mary Lucifer, "Mary the Light-giver." It was said Jesus raised Lazarus from the dead solely for love of her. "There was no grace that He refused her, nor any mark of affection that He withheld from her."[3]

The Pistis Sophia made Mary Magdalene the questioner of Jesus, in the Oriental manner of the catechism applied to the god by his Shakti or Devi (Goddess). The female questioner then was addressed as "Dearly Beloved."[4] Jesus used the same form of address, though later editors eliminated all traces of the identity of his questioner; but it was apparent that his "dearly beloved" was Mary Magdalene.[5]

Pistis Sophia (Faith-Wisdom) A Gnostic scripture of the 3rd century A.D., translated from Greek to Coptic, setting forth the teachings of Jesus upon his return to earth, 12 years after his resurrection.

Origen showed a mystic devotion to Mary Magdalene, confusing her with the Goddess by calling her "the mother of all of us," and sometimes Jerusalem, and sometimes The Church (Ecclesia, another title of the Virgin). Origen claimed Mary Magdalene was immortal, having lived from the beginning of time.[6]

Thus it seems Mary the Whore was only another form of Mary the Virgin, otherwise the Triple Goddess Mari-Anna-Ishtar, the Great Whore of Babylon who was worshipped along with her savior-son in the Jerusalem temple.[7] The *Gospel of Mary* said all three Marys of the canonical books were one and the same.[8]

Indeed, the Virgin and Whore were still confused with one another in the 7th century A.D. when, on the day of the Nativity of the Blessed Virgin, Pope Sergius instituted an annual procession to the old temple of the prostitute-goddess Libera, changing the temple's name to Santa Maria Maggiore: Most-Great Holy Mary.[9] It was not made clear which Holy Mary was meant. A Gnostic poem merged the two of them as a primal feminine power: "I am the first and the last. I am the honored one and the scorned one. I am the whore, and the holy one."[10]

Magdalene means "she of the temple-tower." The Jerusalem temple had a triple tower representing the triple deity, one tower bearing the name of the queen, Mariamne, an earthly incarnation of the Goddess Mari.[11] This was the same Mariamne, Miriam, or Mary who took **Joseph** for her lover.[12] Priestesses of this temple apparently subsidized Jesus and his companions, according to Luke 8:1–3, which says Jesus and "the twelve" were financially supported by Mary Magdalene and a group of women. Latin texts say the women provided for "him" (Jesus), but Greek texts make it "them."[13]

The seven "devils" exorcised from Mary Magdalene seem to have been the seven Maskim, or Anunnaki, Sumero-Akkadian spirits of the seven nether spheres, born of the Goddess Mari. Their multiple birth was represented in her sacred dramas, which may account for their alleged emergence from Mary Magdalene. An Akkadian tablet said of them: "They are seven! In the depths of the ocean, they are seven! In the brilliancy of the heavens, they are seven! They proceed from the ocean depths [Maria], from the hidden retreat."[14]

The Gospels say no men attended Jesus's tomb, but only Mary Magdalene and her women. Only women announced Jesus's resurrection. This was because men were barred from the central mysteries of the Goddess. Priestesses announced the successful conclusion of the rites, and the Savior's resurrection. The Bible says the male apostles knew nothing of Jesus's resurrection, and had to take the women's word for it (Luke 24:10-11). The apostles were ignorant of the sacred tradition and didn't even realize a resurrection was expected: "They knew not the scripture, that he must rise again from the dead" (John 20:9).

Mari-Ishtar the Great Whore anointed—or *christ*-ened—her doomed god when he went into the underworld, whence he would

Origen (Origenes Adamantius) Christian father, ca. 185–254 A.D., an Egyptian who wrote in Greek, exerting a powerful influence on the early Greek church. At first he was accounted a saint, but three centuries after his death he was declared a heretic because of Gnostic elements found in his writings.

Gospel of Mary One of the early Gnostic Gospels, once included with the books of the New Testament but later eliminated from the canon. A copy was rediscovered in the 1940s at Nag Hammadi.

rise again at her bidding. That is, she made him a Christ. Her priestess raised the lament for him when he died in the flesh, as a sacrificial victim. In the Epic of Gilgamesh, victims were told: "The harlot who anointed you with fragrant oil laments for you now."[15] Temple-women of Jerusalem raised the same lament for Tammuz (Ezekiel 8:14), with whom Jesus was identified. Jesus himself said Mary Magdalene anointed him for his burial, pouring a precious unguent on his head in the time-honored manner of the sacred king's crowning (Matthew 26:7-12). The christening-vase of holy oil was the ubiquitous symbol of Mary Magdalene in Christian art—though the virgin Mary also bore the harlot's title of Holy Vase.[16] See **Jesus Ben Pandera**.

Virgin and Whore constantly exchanged attributes through the Middle Ages; the virgin Mary was consistently a special patron of prostitutes.[17] A Christian magic ring, now in the London museum, bears the legend, "Holy Mary Magdalene pray for me."[18]

Pope Julius II by a papal bull established a "sacred" brothel in Rome, which flourished under his successors Leo X and Clement VII. The earnings of this brothel supported the Holy Sisters of the Order of St. Mary Magdalene, indicating that the Holy Sisters and the *magdalenes* (whores) were one and the same. Pope Innocent III also favored Rome's *collegia* of prostitutes, called *virgines,* "unmarried women." He publicly announced that any man who married one of them would be specially praised in heaven.[19]

Much Christian myth-making went into the later history of Mary Magdalene. She was said to have lived for a while with the virgin Mary at Ephesus. This story probably was invented to account for the name Maria associated with the Ephesian Goddess. Afterward, Mary Magdalene went to Marseilles, another town named after the ancient sea-mother Mari. Her cult centered there. Bones were found at Vézelay and declared to be hers. Her dwelling was a cave formerly sacred to the pagans, at St. Baume (Holy Tree).[20] For thirty years she lived there without eating or drinking, her only nourishment the sweet songs of the angels, a "delightful repast" she daily took in through her ears.[21] A church was built over her grotto. Local winegrowers still offer votive candles to her for a good vintage, as if the ancient fertility-mother still occupied the site.[22]

St. Martha accompanied Mary to Provence and worked a number of miracles there. Meeting a dragon named Tarasque (i.e., the Celtic deity Taranis), Martha destroyed him by tying him up with her girdle and pouring holy water on his head.[23] Old images of the Twofold Goddess with her Great Serpent seem to have been renamed Mary and Martha. More often, Mary appeared as the typical feminine trinity ruling birth, love, and death. As Holy Mary at the Cradle, she was the midwife (or birth-goddess) who delivered Jesus.[24] As harlot and funerary priestess she was linked with sex and death. Finally there was the Gnostic suggestion that she was the original "pope," foundress of

Christ's church, according to the Oriental idea that spiritual authority must pass from male to female and vice versa (see **Peter, Saint**). Some said she married St. John the Evangelist.[25] In 12th-century Milan they were worshipped together in a dual cathedral built and administered by the monks of St. John jointly with the *virgines* of St. Maria Maggiore, also entitled Sancta Dei Genetrix (Holy Mother of God). The androgynous cathedral was excavated in 1943-44, but its discovery was kept secret.[26]

During the 13th century a Dianic temple was rededicated to Mary Magdalene. At Easter, the story of her conversion of the rulers of Marseilles was chanted at the altar. Later the sacred song was suppressed. Later still, Mary's devotees were forbidden to hold mass. In 1781, the Magdalene temple was demolished.[27]

1. Pagels, 22, 64. 2. Malvern, 47–49. 3. de Voragine, 355.
4. *Mahanirvanatantra,* 173. 5. Malvern, 12. 6. Malvern, 60. 7. Briffault 3, 169.
8. Malvern, 39. 9. Brewster, 401. 10. Malvern, 55. 11. Keller, 371.
12. Enslin, C.B., 48–49. 13. Morris, 114. 14. Wedeck, 23. 15. Malvern, 16.
16. Brewster, 338. 17. Briffault 3, 216. 18. Budge, A.T., 297.
19. Briffault 3, 216; *Encyc. Brit.,* "Prostitution." 20. Attwater, 237; Brewster, 338.
21. de Voragine, 361. 22. Malvern, 77. 23. Brewster, 345. 24. Miles, 107.
25. de Voragine, 363; Attwater, 237. 26. Morris, 12. 27. Malvern, 75–76.

Mascot

Originally a familiar spirit in animal form, like a witch's traditional black cat or black dog. *Mascoto* meant "witchcraft," from Provençal French *masco,* a sorceress (i.e., "masked one").[1] The mascot of a pagan totemic clan was its animal **mask**, worn on ceremonial occasions. By Christian definition this became an animal-headed demon.

1. de Lys, 94.

Mashu

"Twin Peaks," the holy mountain of Akkadian myth into which the sun god daily sank; corresponding to the Bosom of Hathor, Ma-Nu, into which the Egyptian sun sank prior to his rebirth each dawn.[1] This twin-peaked mountain-mother may be related to the Celtic death goddess Macha, slayer of heroes; or even to the twin-peaked mountain Macchu Picchu, "Hitching Post of the Sun," in distant Peru.[2]

1. Epic of Gilgamesh, 123. 2. *Larousse,* 443.

Mashya and Mashyoi

Persian prototypes of Adam and Eve, the first human couple born together from the womb of Earth, in which the seed of Gayomart, the primal man, had been buried for "forty years"—a mythic augmentation of the sacred forty weeks, normal term of human gestation. God

(Ahura Mazda) told them not to listen to the lies of the devil (Ahriman). But they disobeyed, and came to regard Ahriman as the creator of the feminine elements, water, earth, and fruit. This couple gave birth to seven other couples, from whom descended all the races of humanity.[1] The same sevenfold pattern of racial "roots" reappeared in Simonian Gnosticism as the seven powers born of the primordial female source, from whom came even God the Father.[2] See **Simon Magus**.

1. *Larousse*, 319. 2. Legge 1, 183.

Mask

It is a commonplace of primitive religion that deity resides in a sacred mask. A wearer of the mask is possessed by the spirit. He or she is the God or Goddess, at least for participation in the sacred drama or procession. Paleolithic rock drawings show divine creatures as human beings wearing the masks of animals. Egyptian animal-headed deities were obviously human beings wearing elaborate animal heads.[1] Modern Africans, Melanesians, Australians, and many others maintain the same belief. A witch doctor in a lion mask "isn't pretending to be a lion; he is convinced that he *is* a lion. . . . [H]e shares a 'psychic identity' with the animal."[2] Similarly in pre-Christian Europe, anyone wearing the mask or headdress of a god would become the god—or, as Christians put it, would be possessed by the devil.

The word *mask* occurs in many Indo-European languages and might be traced to the *maskim* of Sumer and Akkad: spirits of the nether spheres, or ancestral ghosts. Initiated Sufi magicians of the Middle Ages wore spirit masks and became *maskhara,* "revelers," at their sabbats; this probably gave rise to the French designation of a mystery play as a *masque.*[3]

The Scandinavian word for a mask was *grim.*[4] This word was often a component of gods' names, like Grimnir (Masked One, a title of Odin).[5] In some legends the mask became a magic helmet that gave admission to the spirit world. The most famous magic helmet was called Hildegrim, or Helkappe, or Tarnkappe, or Cap of Darkness. It was given by Mother Hel (Hilde) to her favored heroes. It made them invisible so they could enter the rose gardens of paradise as if they were dead, yet return alive to the earth. The wearer of the mask became like the Lord of Death, able to reincarnate himself.

The Book of Heroes and the Wilkina saga named Hel's perennial consort Grim. He lived with the Goddess in her secret cave until another hero came to challenge and kill him and inherit the mask.[6] Some said this magic Helkappe was made of dog skin, since dogs were sacred to the death-goddess, and it was the same mask worn by Hades, the Lord of Death.[7]

In medieval France the same Lord of Death was **Macabre**, the

Grim Reaper—that is, the masked reaper, wielding his scythe as a reaper of souls. He performed the *danse macabre,* Dance of Death, in the mystery plays and folk festivals so frequently featured in medieval art. Like Dancing Shiva in Kali's cosmic yoni, Macabre reminded his audience that the dance of life is also a dance of death; that the two are mutually dependent, neither possible without the other.[8] Tibetan mystery plays still present the death-masquerader in his skull mask and skeleton costume.[9] Evans-Wentz said medieval mystery plays contained "symbolism so much akin to that found in mystery plays still flourishing under ecclesiastical patronage throughout Tibet and the neighboring territories of Northern Buddhism as to point to another stream of Orientalism having come into Europe."[10]

Animal-headed deities of Egypt and the Middle East also found new incarnations in medieval mystery plays, some of which may have been rooted in Neolithic rites when sacred dancers wore the heads of sacrificed beasts. At the ineradicably popular Carnival, "Mummers went about dressed as various kinds of beasts, probably a remnant of some seasonal festival of native gods, Gaulish or other, for in Gaul at all events gods often were represented under forms other than human."[11]

Pagan mask-wearing at religious festivals continued in the secular Carnival. After having denounced it as unlawful for many centuries, the church finally capitulated and declared it "lawful" to wear masks in Carnival season.[12] However, the word *masca* remained one of the church's official words for a witch.[13]

1. *Larousse,* 32. 2. Jung, M.H.S., 45. 3. Shah, 208. 4. Sturluson, 49. 5. Turville-Petre, 39. 6. Guerber, L.M.A., 110, 119. 7. Cavendish, P.E., 88. 8. Campbell, M.I., 358. 9. Waddell, 524–25. 10. *Bardo Thodol,* 3. 11. Rose, 298. 12. Moakley, 56. 13. J.B. Russell, 15.

Mass

Latin *missa,* from the Persian-Mithraic communion cake called *mizd,* thought to embody the divine flesh and blood of the Sole-Created Bull sacrificed by Mithra.[1] Another Latin name for the communion cake was *hostia* (host), meaning "victim."

1. H. Smith, 201.

Matabrune

"Burning Mother," a bardic name for the Valkyrie Brunnhilde, or Burning Hel, mother of the sun king Oriant.[1] See **Hel**.

1. Baring-Gould, C.M.M.A., 579.

Mater

var. Matra, Meter

Aryan root word for both "Mother" and "Measurement," giving rise to such English derivatives as matrix, matter, metric, material, maternal, matron, etc. *Matres* meant the Celtic Triple Goddess, or Three Fates.[1] *Matri* or "mothers" was a Tantric word for all benevolent female spirits. Matta, "Mother," the gypsies' supreme Goddess, was an amalgam of many matriarchal titles.[2] The Gnostic, Hermetic, or magical term for the Womb of Matter, *matrix,* was actually a redundant form meaning "she-mother"—*mater* with a feminine ending.

1. *Larousse,* 224. 2. Groome, lxii.

Mater Matuta

"Mother of Dawn," the Birth-goddess who daily brought forth the sun; same as the Goddess Eos in Greek myth, or Hebe, or Ilithyia, or the Egyptian Goddess Matet, whose name meant "growth" or "waxing in strength." She produced the sun in the morning and supported him as he rose in the sky.[1]

1. Budge, G.E. 1, 323.

Mati-Syra-Zemlya

"Moist Mother Earth," worshipped by Slavic peasants even under orthodox Christianity. Her ceremonies take place outside the church, on the anniversaries of old pagan festivals. In August, for example, she is invoked with libations of hemp oil. In the fields, her votary faces east and prays to her for protection from evil spells; then faces west and prays for her control of devils in the underworld; then faces south and prays for her control of sandstorms and whirlwinds; then faces north and prays for relief from snowstorms and cold. Thus Mother Earth is supposed to rule the same forces that fell under the jurisdiction of witches: that is, the weather, and the spirits of the underworld.[1] See **Earth**.

1. *Larousse,* 287.

Matrikadevis

"Holy Mothers," or "Mother Goddesses," Hindu term for the primal matriarchs who governed ancestral tribes. *Matrikadevis* corresponded to the *dísir* or Divine Grandmothers of Norse myth, the Celtic fairies, the pre-Hellenic Goddess-worshipping titans, etc. According to Tantric tradition, the *matrikadevis* were the true parents of humanity. The *pitris,* "fathers," were products of an entirely different creation.[1] See **Motherhood**.

1. *Mahanirvanatantra,* xli.

Matrikamantra

"Mother of Mantras," the Great Goddess's creative word Om, a reference to her own primordial pregnancy which gave birth to the universe.[1] This was known as the Supreme Syllable, Mother of All Sound.[2] By its magic the Goddess brought forth everything that exists. See **Logos**.

1. Wilkins, 201. 2. *Upanishads,* 53.

Matrilineal Inheritance

During the Neolithic age, the matrilineal clan system and the rule of mother-right were followed almost everywhere. Early writings from Egypt depict the woman in complete control of herself and her home, with property descending from mother to daughter. The most significant revolution in Greece was the transition from matrilineal to patrilineal succession and the resulting destruction of clan loyalties. In many other areas, the matrilineal system survived to a late date. The Venerable Bede mentioned rules of matrilineal succession still existing in parts of the British Isles up to the 9th century.[1]

Matrilineal inheritance was the rule among British tribes until the coming of Christianity. The Picts inherited all property, even "kingdoms," through the female line.[2] With the coming of Christianity, the old laws of mother-right began to decline. Sixth-century England still had laws of equal inheritance, but a wife who decided to leave her husband could carry off half the property and all the children. Later in the Christian era, the wife was deprived of everything. The English "heir" came from *heres,* cognate with the Greek word for a female landowner, *here* or "Hera." The Magna Carta referred to a *here* as a person of either sex. Later church laws listed *heres* as exclusively male.[3]

Among pagan Celts, men bequeathed nothing to their children; their possessions were inherited by their sisters or their sisters' children. According to old laws of Burgundy and Thuringia, property passed only in the female line.[4] Charlemagne opposed marriage for his daughters, because under old Frankish laws of matrilineal inheritance this would have meant division of his kingdom.[5]

In pre-Roman Latium a landholding was called *latifundia,* founded by the Goddess **Lat**, after whom the country was named; thus each parcel of land belonged originally to a matriarch.[6] Even in the later Roman empire, husbands had no legal claim on their wives' land or possessions as long as the wife was careful to spend three consecutive nights each year away from home.[7] This was a remnant of an earlier custom like that of pre-Islamic Arabs, whereby a wife divorced her husband by shutting him out of the home for three consecutive nights.[8]

In Greece, a parcel of property was *temenos,* "land belonging to the moon," i.e., to woman.[9] This came to mean specifically the land surrounding a temple of the Goddess.[10] In primitive times however, every matriarch's hearth was a temple of the Goddess. The population and land unit in Attica was a *demos,* derived from De—that is, the Goddess De-Mother, or Demeter.[11] Chieftains ruled only through marriage with the resident matriarch. Harking back to this same system in India, the Mahabharata says the leading attributes of a queen were high intelligence, sacred knowledge, and property.[12]

In most ancient societies, young men went forth from their maternal homes to seek their fortune elsewhere, because their sisters inherited the family home. It was a fixed habit of Greek men, and also of the pagan heroes depicted in fairy tales, to leave home and seek a matrilocal marriage with an heiress in a distant land.[13]

"Matrimony" used to mean the feminine equivalent of "patrimony": inheritance of property, in the maternal line. Matrimony came to be synonymous with marriage only because marriage was a way for men to gain control of property.

In Lydia, women owned the land, governed the communities, and took the initiative in love affairs.[14] The same was true in Egypt. "Inheritance passed through the mother rather than through the father," says Professor Gordon. "This system may well hark back to prehistoric times when only the obvious relationship between mother and child was recognized, but not the less apparent relationship between father and child." For many centuries, patriarchal marriages in Egypt existed side by side with old-style matriarchal unions, initiated by the wife and terminated by her will alone.[15] Since daughters, not sons, inherited property, it was the duty of an Egyptian daughter (not son) to care for aged parents.[16]

Male scholars have been reluctant to describe ancient systems of matrilineal inheritance. After translation of early Babylonian texts, W. Boscawen wrote, "The freedom *granted* [my italics] to women in Babylonia *allowed* them to hold and manage their own estates. . . . [T]he mother here is always represented by a sign which means 'goddess of the house.'"[17] The implication was that women held their property only through men's lenience, which was not the case. Women held property by the ironclad law of mother-right, and a Babylonian wife had the same title as a matriarch in India, *grhadevata,* "House-Goddess."

Even Mohammed, a leading opponent of matriarchal principles, "was enabled to carry out his mission thanks only to the wealth which he acquired from his first wife Khadija, who was engaged in lucrative traffic and owned landed estates."[18]

Landed property developed in the hands of women because women were the first to farm the land, thereby establishing ownership of it. Some primitives still believe only the life-magic inherent in women will make plants grow: "Women know how to bring forth, and how to make the seed bring forth; men don't understand these things."[19]

Mahabharata
Indian epic poem, consisting of historical and legendary material gathered between the 4th and 10th centuries A.D., including the famous Bhagavad-Gita.

Matrilineal Inheritance

Amerindians universally attributed the invention of agriculture to women, sole owners of the cultivated fields. Matrilocal marriage and matrilineal ownership of the home place were customary among the Algonquin, Sioux, Seneca, Pawnee, Seminole, Kiowa, and Cree tribes. As in ancient Greece, fathers were "strangers" in the clan. Women were "mistresses of the soil."[20] "The women were the great power among the clans as everywhere else. . . . [T]he original nomination of the chiefs always rested with them."[21] When the Iroquois conveyed lands to the U.S. government, documents had to be marked by their women, because the marks of men had no validity among the tribes.[22]

Payuga women owned everything, as one missionary found to his astonishment: "If the husband gives his wife any cause, real or fancied, of offense, she packs up the tent and its furniture, appropriates even the canoe, and takes everything away; the children follow her, and the husband and father is left with the clothes he stands in and his weapons as his only possession."[23] The laws of this missionary's homeland insisted on the contrary: a divorced husband retained everything including the children, the wife having no legal right even to her clothes. Hence, the missionaries' surprise at Indian customs and their expectation of men's resentment. Yet Indian men didn't resent the prerogatives of mother-right. They considered the mother's authority natural, as Christians considered the father's authority natural. Indian husbands were known to take forty- or fifty-mile hikes only to procure some special food craved by a pregnant wife.[24]

In Africa, women owned the land and other property connected with the home place, and transmitted ownership to their daughters or their brothers' daughters. European governments and missions in Africa loosed a torrent of propaganda against matrilineal customs among the natives. In most African nations, European land reforms consisted of taking land away from the women and allocating it to their husbands.[25] This tended to make the women paupers and destroy their self-respect, as the tribes looked down on a woman who couldn't support her children.

Patriarchal religious authorities everywhere changed ancient systems of matrilineal inheritance to put property in the hands of men. Medieval Christian kings commonly endowed their barons with the phrase, "Take that woman and her fief."[26] The early centuries of the Christian conquest of Europe were largely occupied with acquisition of lands from the pagan women. The monastic Order of Teutonic Knights got the island of Mainau from its owner, the Fair Maid of Mainau, on condition that her lover be made head of the order.[27]

The Bible contains traces of former matrilineal inheritance and matrilocal marriage, e.g., a man shall "leave his father and his mother, and cleave unto his wife" (Genesis 2:24). Naomi told her daughters-in-law to "return each to her mother's house" (Ruth 1:8) because houses were owned by mothers, not fathers. A marriage agreement permitting removal of a woman from her maternal home was a violation of ancient laws. Therefore Abraham, seeking a bride for his son, had to give many gifts to the bride, to her mother, and to her brother (not to her father) as compensation for taking her away from her home (Genesis 24:53).

Retention of property in the hands of a patrilineal clan was the purpose of the so-called Levirate marriage commanded by God (Deuteronomy 25:5). If a man died, his brother must marry the widow rather than allow her to take her property and depart from the family. This rule dated from an early era when nomadic Israelites began to acquire lands and possessions by intermarrying with pagan women of Canaan, Moab, Phoenicia, etc. Modern laws play the same trick on women. If a husband and wife die together in an accident, it is assumed that the wife dies first, so the man's family will inherit.[28]

People who maintained the matrilocal marriage tradition, like the American Indians, developed no wedding laments, mock battles, pseudo-kidnappings, or displays of coyness.[29] But in patrilocal marriages, the bride's relatives usually put on a show of resistance. Matrilocal marriage appeared in the Norse myth of Ragnar Lodbrok (Leather-breeches), who married a foreign warrior-princess, but could not induce her to leave her own country. When he wished to return to his homeland, he was forced to leave her behind.[30]

Even the peripatetic gypsies had matrilocal marriage traditions. In gypsy folklore, heroines never left their maternal homes. After death they were buried under the family threshold—a custom of the early Hindus, the gypsies' forebears.[31]

The aim of European Christianity was acquisition of property, which meant overturning pagan systems of matrilineal inheritance. By forcible seizure and warfare, the church managed to acquire fully a third of all the landed property on the continent by the early Middle Ages.[32] The rest was more difficult. In some parts of Europe up to 1200 A.D., women were still listed as the landowners, and men identified themselves by their mothers' clan names. Until the 10th century, priests married to gain property, claiming that without their wives they would succumb to "hunger and nakedness." Church laws revised the system; then a series of papal decretals between 1031 and 1051 ordered priests to abandon their wives and sell their children into slavery.[33] Naturally, the property and monies thus acquired by a priest would revert to the church upon his death, since he no longer had legal heirs.

The legal/ecclesiastical war on female property ownership went on century after century, until women were so hamstrung by the laws of God and man that they had almost nothing left that they could call their own. By the end of the 19th century, English wives could not administer their own property even if they had any, nor make a will disposing of it, without their husbands' consent.[34] As late as 1930 in France, a woman was forbidden to do any business with a bank, not even to make small deposits, without her husband's permission.[35] Up to the present time, lack of control over money and property is still the greatest obstacle for women who wish to take their children and leave abusive or violent husbands. In this respect the centuries of patriarchal effort achieved their goal.

1. Stone, 15, 37, 52; Boulding, 318. 2. Johnson, 157. 3. Beard, 194, 199–200. 4. Briffault 1, 415–16, 419. 5. de Voragine, 759. 6. Cumont, M.M., 74. 7. Hartley, 232. 8. Briffault 2, 348. 9. Campbell, Oc.M., 47. 10. Knight, D.W.P., 64. 11. Rose, 34. 12. Campbell, Or.M., 197. 13. Angus, 183. 14. Fielding, 145–46. 15. Stone, 37. 16. Bachofen, 71. 17. Stone, 43. 18. Briffault 1, 375. 19. Frazer, G.B., 33. 20. Briffault 3, 2; 1, 269, 275, 316–17. 21. Hartley, 133. 22. Farb, M.R.C., 97–100. 23. Briffault 1, 318. 24. Montagu, S.M.S., 153. 25. Gornick & Moran, 411. 26. Briffault 3, 407. 27. Guerber, L.R., 326. 28. Kermode, 41. 29. Briffault 1, 307, 422. 30. Guerber, L.M.A., 23. 31. Groome, 19. 32. Augstein, 298. 33. H. Smith, 263; Boulding, 399. 34. Pearsall, N.B.A., 40. 35. Hauswirth, ch. 1.

Matronalia

"Feast of the Mothers," a Roman holy day celebrated in spring by women only, at the sacred grove established in pre-Roman times by the Sabine matriarchate. The women's subsequent period of asceticism and fasting up to the festival of Ceres in April was the forerunner of the Christian fast of **Lent.**[1] Rites of the Matronalia were kept secret from men and remain obscure to this day, though their purpose undoubtedly was to make the Earth Mother ready for springtime regeneration.

1. Gaster, 645.

May

In Scandinavia, May was dedicated to Maj, the Virgin, either Mary or the pagans' Virgin Mother, interchangeably. In Saxon England the month was called Sproutkale: the sprouting time of virgin-mother Earth with her archaic Aryan name of Kale, Kelle, or Kali. Another name for the month was Tri-Milchi, improbably derived by the Venerable Bede from a theory that the Saxon cows gave milk three times a day in May.[8] Alternatively, it meant the Triple Goddess's appearance in the form of three cows.

The month of Maya or Maia, the Virgin Goddess of Spring; in northern Europe, Maj or Mai, the Maiden.[1] This was the traditional month of "wearing of the green" in honor of the Earth Mother's new garment, and of fornicating in plowed fields to encourage the crops. May was a "honey-moon" of sexual freedom throughout rural Europe up to the 16th century.[2] Marriage bonds were temporarily in abeyance. The maxim that "only bad women" marry in the month of May probably was a relic of earlier taboos on all marriages during the month of license.[3]

Yet there were traces of a divine marriage ritual in the "May riding," when knights and ladies rode in pairs into the wood, led by the Queen of the May on a white horse and her male companion on a dark one. They impersonated Frey and Freya, "the Lord" and "the Lady" whose union made fertility magic each spring.[4]

May Eve was the great springtime festival of "witches," corresponding to Halloween at the opposite pole of the year. May Eve was known in Germany as Walpurgisnacht, in Ireland and Scotland as Beltaine or Baltein, when the god Baal, Bel, or Balder was burned in effigy. Sometimes a man chosen by lot represented him, and leaped through the May fires still called "Balder's balefires" in rural Scandinavia.[5] Clearly, these were customs dating back to real burning of the man who represented the god in his love-death (*Liebestod*).

The May King of medieval romance inherited the customs of Diana's sacred kings. He won the "queen of a magic wood" (the Goddess) by combat with her previous king on the festival of Ascension Day in May. *Le Chevalier de la Charrette* named him Meleagant, prince of the land of no return (he was a Lord of Death). *Le Morte d'Arthur* corrupted his name to "Mellyagaunce," a lascivious May King who became the ritual lover of Queen Guinevere and led the sexual games of May Day.[6] A 15th-century poet identified the same May King with Christ, who was like the Holy Rose of May: "the red flower that Mary bore."[7]

The god's phallus was planted in the earth's womb in the guise of the Maypole, which was not originally European but a direct borrowing from India where the Maypole is still "the great lingam."[9] In 16th-century England its phallic symbolism was understood perfectly well, as shown by the diatribe of the Puritan writer Philip Stubbes:

> *Young men and maids, old men and wives, run gadding overnight to the woods, groves, hills, and mountains, where they spend all night in pleasant pastimes; and in the morning they return, bringing with them birch and branches of trees, to deck their assemblies withal. And no marvel, for there is a great Lord present amongst them, as superintendent and Lord over their pastimes and sports; namely, Satan, prince of hell. But the chiefest jewel they bring from thence is their May-pole, which they bring home with great veneration, as thus. They have twenty or forty yoke of oxen, every ox having a sweet nose-gay of flowers placed on the tip of his horns, and these oxen draw home this May-pole (this stinking idol, rather) which is covered all over with flowers and herbs, bound round about with strings, from the top to the bottom, and sometimes painted with variable colors, with two or three hundred men, women and children following it with great devotion. And this being reared up, with handkerchiefs and flags hovering on the top, they strew the ground round about, bind green boughs about it, set up summer halls, bowers, and arbors hard by it. And then fall they to dance about it, like as the heathen people did at the dedication of Idols, whereof this is a perfect pattern, or rather the thing itself.*[10]

Young men and maids went into the woods, and few returned home "undefiled," as the observer said. According to Spelman, the rustic fellows and their girl friends fell "into ditches upon one another," for the odd reason that they were "enveloped with a mist of wandering out of their ways." Douce had no doubt of the festival's pagan origin: "The Queen of the May is the legitimate representative of the Goddess Flora in the Roman Festival."[11] Stuckeley described May celebrations in 1724:

> *There is a May Pole near Horn Castle, Lincolnshire, where probably stood an Hermes (*herm, *phallic pillar) in Roman times. The boys annually keep up the festival of the Floralia on May Day, making a procession to this hill with May gads (as they call them) in their hands.*

This is a white willow wand, the bark peeled off, tied round with cowslips, a thyrsus of the Bacchanals. At night they have a bonefire, and other merriment, which is really a sacrifice, a religious festival.[12]

Naturally the church was opposed to this religious festival. Bishop Eligius of Noyons begged his converts in the 7th century to stop observing the sexual rites of May—without success.[13] A thousand years later the month was still given over to "witches." Church bells in 17-century Treves were rung all night throughout the month of May, to "protect the city from flying witches."[14]

There were a few voices raised against ecclesiastical restrictions on the activities of the Merry Month. William Fennor's *Pasquil's Palinodia* (1619) lamented the new puritanical laws against the rites of May:

When no capricious constables disturb them,
Nor justice of the peace did seek to curb them,
Nor peevish puritan, in railing sort,
Nor over-wise church-warden, spoiled the sport,
Happy the age, and harmless were the days
(For then true love and amity were found),
When every village did a Maypole raise,
And Witson-ales and May-games did abound . . .
But since the Summer poles were over-thrown,
And all good sports and merriments decay'd,
How times and men are chang'd, so well is known,
It were but labor lost if more were said.
Alas, poor May Poles; what should be the cause
That you were almost banish'd from the earth?
Who never were rebellious to the laws;
Your greatest crime was harmless, honest mirth . . .
Some fiery, zealous brother, full of spleen,
That all the world in his deep wisdom scorns,
Could not endure the May-pole should be seen
To wear a cox-comb higher than his horns:
He took it for an idol, and the feast
For sacrifice unto that painted beast.[15]

1. Steenstrup, 32. 2. Briffault 3, 198. 3. W. Scott, 84. 4. Gelling & Davidson, 163. 5. Frazer, G.B., 717, 769. 6. Rees, 285. 7. Wilkins, 155. 8. Brewster, 220. 9. Avalon, 517. 10. Frazer, G.B., 142. 11. Hazlitt, 399–401. 12. Hazlitt, 402. 13. Spence, 104. 14. Robbins, 512. 15. Hazlitt, 404.

Maya

"Magic," title of the Virgin Kali as the creatress of earthly appearances, i.e., all things made of matter and perceptible to the senses. She also gave birth to the Enlightened One, Buddha.[1]

The same Goddess, called Maia by the Greeks, was the virgin mother of Hermes the Enlightened One, who had as many reincarnations as the Buddha. Sometimes Maia's partner was Volcanus (Greek Hephaestus, the divine smith and fire-god). This was another mythic mating of male fire and female water.[2] Hindus said Agni the fire-god was the consort of Kali-Maya, though he was periodically swallowed up and "quenched" by her. According to the Tantric phrase, the Goddess quenched a blazing lingam in her yoni.[3]

As the virgin mother of Buddha, Maya embarrassed ascetic Buddhists and was soon written out of the script. Like ascetic Christians speaking of Christ's birth, some Buddhists claimed the Enlightened One could not touch his mother's "parts of shame" and so was born through an opening in her side. This mythic Caesarian section seems to have been bungled, for a few days later Maya died—"of joy," as Buddhist scriptures rather fatuously put it.[4]

Nevertheless, Maya remained very much alive as one of Kali's most revered manifestations, because the very fact of "Existence"—the material cosmos—demanded her presence. As Zimmer analyzed her:

> *Maya-Shakti is personified as the world-protecting, feminine, maternal side of the Ultimate Being, and as such, stands for the spontaneous, loving acceptance of life's tangible reality. . . . [S]he affirms, she is, she represents and enjoys, the delirium of the manifested forms. . . . Maya-Shakti is Eve, "the Eternal Feminine,"* das Ewig-Weibliche: *she who ate, and tempted her consort to eat, and was herself the apple. From the point of view of the masculine principle of the Spirit (which is in quest of the enduring, eternally valid, and absolutely divine) she is the pre-eminent enigma.*[5]

In herself Maya embodied all three aspects of the maternal Trinity. Her colors were white, red, and black, the colors of the Gunas, or the Virgin-Mother-Crone.[6] Like every other form of Kali, she was Creator, Preserver, Destroyer. She was also a spirit dwelling perpetually in women. A Mahayana text says, "Of all the forms of Maya, woman is the most important."[7]

Maya's son Buddha was surrounded by her symbols. He entered his trance of meditation under her sacred fig tree, which protected him from the weather. On his return from the soul-journey, his first symbolic act was to accept a dish of curds from a maiden on Full Moon Day in the month of May, the greatest of Buddhist festivals.[8]

Not only the month but many other traditions, names, and concepts attest to the great age and wide distribution of the Goddess Maya. She was more than the Maia who mothered Hermes; she was also Maga the Grandmother-goddess who bore **Cu Chulainn's** mother; and the Mandaean Christians' Almaya, called "Eternity," or "the World," or "Beings"; and Maga or Maj the May-maiden in Scandinavia.[9] Like the Hindu Maya who brought forth earthly appearances at creation, the Scandinavian one personified the pregnant womb of chaos before the beginning: *Ginnungagap.* In this the World-virgin was associated with the idea of magical illusion, creating "appearances" like her Hindu counterpart.[10]

This universal Creatress-name may have reached the western

hemisphere also. The Maya people of Yucatan offered sacrifices in the same way as in northern India, at the same seasons, determined by the same stars.[11] Mayan "scorpion stars" were the same as the constellation Scorpio on Hindu and Greek charts. As in India, Mayan divine images were painted blue and Mayan woman pierced the left nostril for insertion of a jewel.[12] Another version of the Creatress seems to have been the Mother Goddess Mayauel of the Mexican Agave, called "Woman with Four Hundred Breasts," with a strong resemblance to the world-nurturing Many-Breasted Artemis and other eastern forms of the deity who mothered all the world's creatures.

1. *Larousse,* 348. 2. Rose, 229. 3. Rawson, E.A., 57. 4. *Larousse,* 348. 5. Lederer, 136. 6. *Upanishads,* 124. 7. Campbell, Or.M., 320. 8. Ross, 88. 9. Squire, 156; Goodrich, 181; Jonas, 54. 10. Davidson, G.M.V., 197. 11. Von Hagen, 137; Tannahill, 82. 12. Von Hagen, 178, 38.

Me

Babylonian word for "mother-wisdom" enshrined on the Tablets of Destiny, given by the Great Goddess to her firstborn son; cognate of Sanskrit *medha,* feminine wisdom, and Egyptian *met,* with the same meaning, as well as a decimal numbering system, like the Greek *meter* (mother).[1] *Me* also meant the magic power of Fate, religious inspiration, and healing magic (medicine). Goddess names derived from this root include Medea, Medusa, Metis, Mene, Maat, and Demeter.

1. Budge, E.L., 93.

Mearah

Hebrew "Cave," a title of the Goddess Cybele, Great Mother of the Gods; also applied to the holy cavern where Adonis was born in Bethlehem. (See **Cave**.)

Medea

"Wise One," eponymous Mother Goddess of the Medes. Like Medusa and Metis, she was named from the Sanskrit concept of *medha,* "female wisdom."[1] She was a fount of the feminine art of healing, and her name was related to "medicine."[2] She could restore the dead to life in her magic **cauldron**, as shown by the myth of Aeson, who was so restored. Pliny called Medea a Goddess whose magic arts could control the sun, moon, and stars.[3] She rode in a chariot drawn by serpents; it also had wings, to show that she ruled both earth and heaven.[4]

According to Herodotus, Medea was the Great Goddess of all the Aryan tribes of Parthia.[5] She was all-wise, and never died, but dwelt forever in heaven.[6]

She seems to have been remembered in Ireland as the Goddess Medana, associated with a sacred tree and a regenerative well, whose waters were reputed to cure sore eyes. She was artificially canonized as a saint, and her Christian legend was copied from that of the equally bogus **St. Lucy**.[7]

The classic story of Medea's ill-starred marriage to Jason apparently was based on a captured idol of the Goddess. Her rites were imported into Greece but proved too sanguinary for Hellenic taste.

1. *Larousse,* 312. 2. Briffault 1, 486. 3. Hawkins, 139. 4. Graves, G.M. 2, 253. 5. Herodotus, 390. 6. Graves, G.M. 2, 252, 257. 7. Gifford, 131.

Medusa

Classic myth made Medusa the terrible Gorgon whose look turned men to stone. The Argives said Medusa was a Libyan queen beheaded by their ancestral hero Perseus, who brought her head (or ceremonial mask) back to Athens.[1]

Actually, Medusa was the serpent-goddess of the Libyan Amazons, representing "female wisdom" (Sanskrit *medha,* Greek *metis,* Egyptian *met* or Maat). She was the Destroyer aspect of the Triple Goddess called Neith in Egypt, Ath-enna or Athene in North Africa. Her inscription at Sais called her "mother of all the gods, whom she bore before childbirth existed." She was the past, present, and future: "All that has been, that is, and that will be."[2] So famous was this description of her that Christians later copied it on behalf of Jehovah (Revelation 1:8).

She said: "No mortal has yet been able to lift the veil that covers me," because she was Death, and to see her face to face was to die—that is, to be "turned to stone" as a funerary statue. She was veiled also because she was the Future, which always wears a veil. Another meaning of her hidden, dangerous face was the menstrual taboo. Primitive folk often believe the look of a menstruous woman can turn a man to stone.[3] Medusa had magic blood that could create and destroy life; thus she represented the dreaded life- and death-giving moon-blood of women (see **Menstrual Blood**).[4]

The Perseus story was invented to account for the appearance of Medusa's face on Athene's aegis, inherited from the pre-Hellenic period when Athene was actually the same Goddess (also mythologized as Metis, her alleged "mother"). The Athenians pretended their municipal Goddess was the "wisdom" of Zeus, born from his head. But older myths said Athene was born of the Three Queens of Libya—that is, the Triple Goddess, of whom Metis-Medusa was the Destroyer aspect.[5] A female face surrounded by serpent-hair was an ancient, widely recognized symbol of divine female wisdom, and equally of the "wise blood" that supposedly gave women their divine powers.

1. Graves, W.G., 244. 2. *Larousse,* 37. 3. Frazer, G.B., 695, 699. 4. Graves, G.M. 1, 175. 5. Graves, G.M. 1, 244; 2, 399.

Megaera

"Grudge," one of Demeter's three Furies or Dogs of Law; possibly related to Megara, "Cave," the black cavern of Demeter Chthonia, whence her spirits of law issued forth to punish evildoers. Megaera or Megara was also a mythical wife of Heracles.[1] See **Furies**.

1. Graves, G.M. 2, 399.

Mehen the Enveloper

Egyptian serpent-goddess who enclosed the Phallus of Ra every night, as Hindu phallic gods were enveloped in their sleep cycles by the serpent-goddess called Infinity. See **Serpent**.

Mehitabel

Hebrew version of the Lady Mehit, a lion-headed Goddess in Egypt, one of the aspects of Bast or the Sphinx (Hathor). The Bible made her a "daughter of Matred" (Genesis 36:39), that is, of **Maat**, or Mater, indicating a priestess of the Goddess in her lion mask. Mehit was also described at times as a fish goddess.[1] The "Bel" part of her Hebrew name simply meant a deity.

1. Budge, D.N., 151.

Mehurt

Title of the Egyptian Goddess Nut, or Neit, as the primordial heavenly waters; probably a variant of Mehit.

Meidelant

"Land of Maidens" or Land of Women, the matriarchal fairyland where Lancelot was brought up by the Lady of the Lake.[1] Heroes of Celtic romance usually returned to this same paradise of "maidens" after death. See **Lancelot**.

1. Rees, 293.

var. Melanie

Melaina

"Black One," a title of Black Demeter the Underground Goddess. She was also Mare-headed Melanippe, "Black Mare," worshipped in her Black Cave (*Mavrospelya*) with her mane entwined with snakes—all images similar to those of Kali the "Black Mother" of

India.[1] These dark aspects of Demeter evolved into the Night-Mare who punished sinners with dreams of terror. See **Demeter**.

1. *Encyc. Brit.*, "Demeter."

Melchizedek

Savior-god accepted by Christian Gnostics as a deity greater than Christ. Melchizedek was the savior for angels, while Christ was only the savior for men. Melchizedek was an emanation of the Five Trees of the Treasure House of Light, according to the *Pistis Sophia:* the hand of the Goddess Sophia herself. It was claimed that Melchizedek's brief appearance in the Old Testament as a purveyor of "bread and wine" (flesh and blood) was a prophecy of his Second Coming as the true savior (Genesis 14:18). Psalm 110 said Christ himself was only a priest "after the order of Melchizedek."

Melchom

var. Milcom

Christian demon based on the Tyrian fire-god Moloch, Melek, or Melkart, whose name meant "king," and whose sacrifices were made by passing through fire, like those of **Heracles**. In fact, this god and Heracles were often said to be one and the same.

Meliae

"Ash-Tree Nymphs," a Greek name for the three Fates, identified with the Germanic **Norns**. Germanic tribes said the Fates were three mystic women who dwelt at the root of the World Ash Tree.

Melissa

"Bee," title of Aphrodite's high priestess at the honeycomb-shrine of Mount Eryx, where the Goddess's fetish was a golden honeycomb. Corresponding to Israel's priestess Deborah, whose name also means "Bee." See **Aphrodite**; **Honey**.

Melusine

Medieval version of fish-tailed Aphrodite, with an ancient shrine at Lusinia (modern Lusignan), named after her as "Lady of Light." During the church's crusades against the cults of love in southern France, Melusine's legend made her the mystic bride of Raymond, Count of Poitou. She consented to marry him only on condition that each Sabbath day she must remain in seclusion, alone in her own castle of Lusinia. There she became a fish-tailed mermaid and spent the day reclining in her bath. (According to classic myths, it was fatally dangerous for men to see the Goddess in her bath. Whether she was Aphrodite, Artemis, Athene, or Ertha, she could be seen bathing only by "men doomed to die.")[1]

Churchmen discovered Melusine and either killed her, or, according to another version, drove her out of her castle. The legend says she still returns every night, like the moon, to suckle her "children," probably meaning the people themselves. She had a prophetic death-goddess form also. It was said when Melusine appeared wailing over the ramparts of Lusignan, the king would die.[2]

1. Tacitus, 728. 2. Baring-Gould, C.M.M.A., 478.

Mem-Aleph

Hebrew letters MA, the Mother-charm signifying "water" and "the beginning," written on protective amulets of the 9th century B.C.[1] The magic name of the Great Goddess **Ma**. A concept borrowed from the Persians, who called the maternal spirit Mourdad-Ameretat (MA: Death-Rebirth).[2]

1. Albright, 198. 2. *Larousse,* 317.

Memra

Mystical term for "the Word" in Middle-Eastern mystery-religions; a secret name or Logos of several Mesopotamian gods.

Mena

var. Menes

First dynastic Egyptian ruler to unify the Two Lands, ca. 3000 B.C. Egyptologists call this person a "pharaoh"; but the hieroglyphic symbol of Mena means both "moon" and "milk-giving mother's breast," improbable symbols for a male.[1] More recent scholars admit that this so-called first pharaoh may have been a matriarchal queen, or a titulary king ruling in her name.[2]

Upper Egypt once belonged exclusively to the lunar Goddess. It was called Khemennu, "Land of the Moon."[3] One of Egypt's oldest oracular shrines was Menhet, "House of the Moon," which Greeks called Latopolis, City of the Milk-Giving Mother.[4]

The first mother-city of Egypt was Memphis, seat of first-dynasty rulers. Its Egyptian name was Men-nefer, "Beautiful Moon-virgin." Another variation of the Egyptian Moon-goddess was Menos, credited with the invention of hieroglyphic writing. See **Moon**.

1. Budge, E.L., 57. 2. Brandon, 134. 3. Hallet, 115. 4. Budge, G.E. 2, 50.

Menander

"Moon-man," an Indo-Greek king of Bactria in the 1st century B.C., also known as Soter (Savior). After he died, pieces of his body were sent to different parts of the lands he ruled, in the manner of an Osiris or one of the Moon-bulls.[1]

1. *Encyc. Brit.*, "Menander."

Menat

Egyptian "Moon charm," an amulet representing sexual intercourse, with a narrow male vessel pouring fluid into a broad female vessel.[1] The Menat was once an immense constellation in the heavens as Egyptians saw them, extending from Arcturus in Boötes in the northern sky, all the way to Antares in Scorpio in the south. As an astrological sign it "gave strength to the reproductive organs, promoted fruitfulness and health."[2]

As a sacred amulet for gods, priests, and mummies, the Menat insured sexual potency in the after-life and magical fertility in earthly existence. See **Jar-Bearer**.

1. Budge, E.M., 60. 2. Jobes, 208.

Mene

Throughout the ancient Middle East this word meant Moon, though on its appearance in the Old Testament (Daniel 5:25) it was translated "numbered," because the moon was the basis for calendars and the measurer of time. King Belshazzar was frightened by the dire inscription written on the wall at his feast, MENE, MENE, TEKEL, UPHARSIN, which Daniel interpreted as follows: (1) your days are numbered; (2) you have been weighed in the balances and found wanting; (3) your kingdom will be taken by the Medes and Persians. The original inscription probably appeared in a language the Hebrew editor didn't know, and Daniel's speech was loosely interpreted from an old icon representing the Moon-goddess as Destroyer, announcing the end of a king's term of office. See **Kingship**.

Menec

"Moon-shrine," a Neolithic menhir system near Carnac, in Brittany; one of the many stone "temples of the Moon" that once dotted European lands.

Menelaus

"Moon-king," husband of Helen the Moon-princess from Homer's Troy. The gods told him he would be immortal because he had Helen for his wife.[1] When he lost her, he was deprived of both immortality and property. See **Helen of Troy**.

1. Knight, S.L., 125.

Menevia

"Moon-Way," the Romano-British name for the Welsh town of St. David's, actually named after the god Dewi, or Devi (see **David, Saint**). Menevia was the same as the Scandinavian Manavegr, the heavenly paradise ruled by the Moon-mother Mana.

Menorah

Seven-branched candlestick of the Jewish tabernacle, probably representing the Seven Sisters or Moon-Horae, since it was decorated with yonic symbols (Exodus 25:33-35).

Menos

Egyptian title of the Moon-goddess credited with the invention of writing.

var. Menarva

Menrva

Etruscan version of the name of Minerva, Roman Goddess of wisdom, war, and the lunar calendar; the Crone of the original Capitoline Triad. She was a Latin form of Athene. A bronze statue of the 6th century B.C. depicts her with an Athenian **aegis** covering her breast, a helmet with a gigantic crest on her head, and in her hand a spear or javelin poised for throwing.[1] She was also connected with the death scene of the archaic savior Mars.

1. *Larousse*, 206.

Mensa

Roman Goddess of measurement, numbers, calendars, calculations, tables, and record-keeping; derived from the Moon-goddess as inventor of numerical systems. Probably a title for the archaic Minerva as the moon, "measurer of Time."

Menstrual Blood

From the earliest human cultures, the mysterious magic of creation was thought to reside in the blood women gave forth in apparent harmony with the moon, and which was sometimes retained in the womb to "coagulate" into a baby. Men regarded this blood with holy dread, as the life-essence, inexplicably shed without pain, wholly foreign to male experience.

Most words for menstruation also meant such things as incomprehensible, supernatural, sacred, spirit, deity. Like the Latin *sacer*, old Arabian words for "pure" and "impure" both applied to menstrual blood and to that only. The Maoris stated explicitly that human souls are made of menstrual blood, which when retained in the womb "assumes human form and grows into a man."[1] Africans said menstrual blood is "congealed to fashion a man."[2] Aristotle said the same: human life is made of a "coagulum" of menstrual blood. Pliny called menstrual blood "the material substance of generation," capable of forming "a curd, which afterwards in process of time quickeneth and groweth to the form of a body." This primitive notion of the prenatal function of menstrual blood was still taught in European medical schools up to the 18th century.[3]

Basic ideas about menstrual blood came from the Hindu theory that as the Great Mother creates, her substance becomes thickened and forms a curd or clot; solid matter is produced as a "crust."[4] This was the way she gave birth to the cosmos, and women employ the same method on a smaller scale. According to Daustenius, "The fruit in the womb is nourished only by the mother's blood.... [T]he menstruum does not fail the fruit for nourishment, till it at the proper time comes to the light of day."[5]

Indians of South America said all mankind was made of "moon blood" in the beginning.[6] The same idea prevailed in ancient Mesopotamia, where the Great Goddess Ninhursag made mankind out of clay and infused it with her "blood of life." Under her alternate names of Mammetun or Aruru the Great, the Potter, she taught women to form clay dolls and smear them with menstrual blood as a conception-charm, a piece of magic that underlay the name of **Adam**, from the feminine *adamah*, meaning "bloody clay," though scholars more delicately translate it "red earth."[7]

The Bible's story of Adam was lifted from an older female-oriented creation myth recounting the creation of man from clay and moon-blood. So was the Koran's creation story, which said Allah "made man out of flowing blood"; but in pre-Islamic Arabia, Allah was the Goddess of creation, Al-Lat.[8] The Romans also had traces of the original creation myth. Plutarch said man was made of earth, but the power that made a human body grow was the moon, source of menstrual blood.[9]

The lives of the very gods were dependent on the miraculous power of menstrual blood. In Greece it was euphemistically called the "supernatural red wine" given to the gods by Mother Hera in her virgin form, as Hebe.[10] The root myths of Hinduism reveal the nature of this "wine." At one time all gods recognized the supremacy of the Great Mother, manifesting herself as the spirit of creation (Kali-Maya). She "invited them to bathe in the bloody flow of her womb and to drink of it; and the gods, in holy communion, drank of the fountain of life—(*hic est sanguis meus*!)—and bathed in it, and rose blessed to the heavens."[11] To this day, cloths allegedly stained with the Goddess's menstrual blood are greatly prized as healing charms.[12] W.R. Smith reported that the value of the gum acacia as an amulet "is connected with the idea that it is a clot of menstrous blood, i.e., that the tree is a woman." For religious ceremonies, Australian aborigines painted their sacred stones, churingas, and themselves with red ochre, declaring that it was really women's menstrual blood.[13]

The esoteric secret of the gods was that their mystical powers of longevity, authority, and creativity came from the same female essence. The Norse god Thor for example reached the magic land of enlightenment and eternal life by bathing in a river filled with the menstrual blood of "giantesses"—that is, of the Primal Matriarchs, "Powerful Ones" who governed the elder gods before Odin brought his "Asians" (Aesir) out of the east.[14] Odin acquired supremacy by stealing and drinking the "wise blood" from the triple cauldron in the womb of Mother-Earth, the same Triple Goddess known as Kali-Maya in southeast Asia.

Odin's theft of menstrual magic paralleled that of Indra, who stole the ambrosia of immortality in the same way. Indian myth called the sacred fluid Soma—in Greek, "the body," because the word's eastern root referred to a mystical substance of the body. Soma was the object of so much holy dread that its interpretations were many.

Soma was produced by the churning of the primal sea (Kali's "ocean of blood" or sometimes "sea of milk"). Or Soma was secreted by the Moon-Cow. Or Soma was carried in the "white pot" (belly) of Mohini the Enchantress. Or the source of Soma was the moon. Or from Soma all the gods were born. Or Soma was a secret name of the Mother Goddess and the active part of the "soul of the world."[15]

Soma was drunk by priests at sacrificial ceremonies and mixed with milk as a healing charm; therefore it was not milk. Soma was especially revered on *somvara*, Monday, the day of the moon. In an ancient ceremony called Soma-vati, women of Maharashtra circumambulated the sacred female-symbolic fig tree whenever the new moon fell on a Monday.[16]

Some myths claimed the Goddess under her name of Lakshmi, "Fortune" or "Sovereignty," gave Soma to Indra to make him king of the gods. His wisdom, power, and curiously feminine capacity for pregnancy, came from Lakshmi's mystic drink, "of which none tastes who dwells on earth."[17] On drinking it straight from the Goddess, Indra became like her, the Mount of Paradise with its four rivers, "many-hued" like the Goddess's rainbow veils, rich in cattle and fruiting vegetation.[18] The Goddess's blood became his wisdom. Similarly, Greeks believed the wisdom of man or god was centered in his blood, the soul-stuff given by his mother.[19]

Egyptian pharaohs became divine by ingesting "the blood of Isis," a soma-like ambrosia called *sa*.[20] Its hieroglyphic sign was the same as the sign of the vulva, a yonic loop like the one on the *ankh* or Cross of Life.[21] Painted red, this loop signified the female genital and the Gate of Heaven.[22] Amulets buried with the dead specifically prayed Isis to deify the deceased with her magic blood.[23] A special amulet called the Tjet represented Isis's vulva and was formed of red substance — jasper, carnelian, red porcelain, red glass, or red wood. This amulet was said to carry the redeeming power of the blood of Isis.[24]

The same elixir of immortality received the name of *amrita* in Persia. Sometimes it was called the milk of a mother Goddess, sometimes a fermented drink, sometimes sacred blood. Always it was associated with the moon. "Dew and rain becoming vegetable sap, sap becoming the milk of the cow, and the milk then becoming converted into blood:—Amrita, water, sap, milk, and blood represent but differing states of the one elixir. The vessel or cup of this immortal fluid is the moon."[25]

Celtic kings became gods by drinking the "red mead" dispensed by the Fairy Queen, Mab, whose name was formerly Medhbh or "mead."[26] Thus she gave a drink of herself, like Lakshmi. A Celtic name of this fluid was *dergflaith*, meaning either "red ale" or "red sovereignty." In Celtic Britain, to be stained with red meant to be chosen by the Goddess as a king.[27] Celtic *ruadh* meant both "red" and "royal."[28]

The same blood color implied apotheosis after death. The pagan paradise or Fairyland was at the uterine center of the earth, site of the magic Fountain of Life. An old manuscript in the British Museum said the dying-and-resurrected Phoenix lives there forever. The central Holy Mountain or *mons veneris* contains both male and female symbols: the Tree of Life and the Fountain of Eternal Youth, the latter obviously menstrual, as it was said to overflow once every lunar month.[29]

Medieval churchmen insisted that the communion wine drunk by witches was menstrual blood, and they may have been right. The famous wizard **Thomas Rhymer** joined a witch cult under the tutelage of the Fairy Queen, who told him she had "a bottle of claret wine . . . here in my lap," and invited him to lay his head in her lap.[30] Claret was the traditional drink of kings and also a synonym for blood; its name meant literally "enlightenment." There was a saying, "The man in the moon drinks claret," connected with the idea that the wine represented lunar blood.[31]

Medieval romance and the courtly-love movement, later related to witch cults, were strongly influenced by the Tantric tradition, in which menstrual blood was indeed the wine of poets and sages. It is still specified in the Left Hand Rite of Tantra that the priestess impersonating the Goddess must be menstruating, and after contact with her a man may perform rites that will make him "a great poet, a Lord of the World" who travels on elephant-back like a rajah.[32]

In ancient societies both east and west, menstrual blood carried the spirit of sovereign authority because it was the medium of transmission of the life of clan or tribe. Among the Ashanti, girl children are still more prized than boys because a girl is the carrier of "blood" (*mogya*).[33] The concept is also clearly defined in India, where menstrual blood is known as the Kula flower or Kula nectar, which has an intimate connection with the life of the family. When a girl first menstruates, she is said to have "borne the Flower."[34] The corresponding English word flower has the significant literal meaning of "that which flows."

The British Goddess of flowers was Blodeuwedd, a form of the Triple Goddess associated with sacrifices of ancient kings. Welsh legend said her whole body was made of flowers—as any body was, according to the ancient theory of body formation from the blood "flower." Her name suggests the Blood Wedding, and myth made her the spouse of several murdered heroes, recalling the old idea that the Goddess's divine blood had to be periodically refreshed by human sacrifice.[35]

The Hebrew word for blood, *dam*, means "mother" or "woman" in other Indo-European languages (e.g. dam, damsel, madam, *la dama*, dame) and also "the curse" (damn). The Sumerian Great Mother represented maternal blood and bore names like Dam-kina, Damgalnunna. From her belly flowed the Four Rivers of Paradise, sometimes called rivers of blood which is the "life" of all flesh. Her firstborn child, the Savior, was Damu, a "child of the blood."[37] *Damos* or "mother-blood" was the word for "the people" in matriarchal Mycenae.[38] Another common ancient symbol of the blood-river of life was the red carpet, traditionally trod by sacred kings, heroes, and brides.[39]

The Bible also calls menstrual blood the flower (Leviticus 15:24), precursor of the "fruit" of the womb (a child). As any flower mysteriously contained its future fruit, so uterine blood was the moon-flower supposed to contain the soul of future generations. This was a central idea in the matrilineal concept of the clan.[36]

The Chinese religion of Tao, "the Way," taught Tantric doctrines later supplanted by patriarchal-ascetic Confucianism. Taoists said a man could become immortal (or at least long-lived) by absorbing menstrual blood, called red yin juice, from a woman's Mysterious Gateway, otherwise known as the Grotto of the White Tiger, symbol of life-giving female energy. Chinese sages called this red juice the essence of Mother Earth, the yin principle that gives life to all things. They claimed the Yellow Emperor became a god by absorbing the yin juice of twelve hundred women.[40]

A Chinese myth said the Moon-goddess Chang-O, who controlled menstruation, was offended by male jealousy of her powers. She left her husband, who quarreled with her because she had all the elixir of immortality, and he had none, and was resentful. She turned her back on him and went to live in the moon forever, in much the same way that Lilith left Adam to live by herself at the "Red Sea." Chang-O forbade men to attend Chinese moon festivals, which were afterward celebrated by women only, at the full moon of the autumnal equinox.[41]

Taoist China considered red a sacred color associated with women, blood, sexual potency, and creative power. White was the color of men, semen, negative influences, passivity, and death.[42] This was the basic Tantric idea of male and female essences: the male principle was seen as "passive" and "quiescent"; the female principle as "active" and "creative," the reverse of later patriarchal views.[43]

Female blood color alone was often considered a potent magic charm. The Maori rendered anything sacred by coloring it red, and calling the red color menstrual blood.[44] Andaman Islanders thought blood-red paint a powerful medicine, and painted sick people red all over in an effort to cure them.[45] Hottentots addressed their Mother Goddess as one "who has painted thy body red"; she was divine because she never dropped or wasted menstrual blood.[46] Some African tribes believed that menstrual blood alone, kept in a covered pot for nine months, had the power to turn itself into a baby.[47]

Easter eggs, classic womb-symbols of the Goddess Eostre, were traditionally colored red and laid on graves to strengthen the dead. This habit, common in Greece and southern Russia, might be traced all the way back to Paleolithic graves and funeral furnishings reddened with ochre, for a closer resemblance to the Earth Mother's womb from which the dead could be "born again." Ancient tombs everywhere have shown the bones of the dead covered with red ochre. Sometimes everything in the tomb, including the walls, had the red color. J.D. Evans described a well tomb on Malta filled with reddened bones, which struck fear into the workmen who insisted the bones were covered with "fresh blood."[48]

A born-again ceremony from Australia showed that the Aborigines linked rebirth with the blood of the womb. The chant performed at Ankota, the "vulva of the earth," emphasized the redness surrounding the worshipper: "A straight track is gaping open before me. An underground hollow is gaping before me. A cavernous pathway is gaping before me. An underground pathway is gaping before me. Red I am like the heart of a flame of fire. Red, too, is the hollow in which I am resting."[49] Images like these help explain why some of the oldest images of the Goddess, like Kurukulla in the east and her counterpart Cybele in the west, were associated with both caverns and redness.[50]

Greek mystics were "born again" out of the river **Styx**, otherwise known as Alpha, "the Beginning." This river wound seven times through the earth's interior and emerged at a yonic shrine near the city of Clitor (Greek *kleitoris*) sacred to the Great Mother.[51] Styx was the blood-stream from the earth's vagina; its waters were credited with the same dread powers as menstrual blood. Olympian gods swore their absolutely binding oaths by the waters of Styx, as men on earth swore by the blood of their mothers. Symbolic death and rebirth were linked with baptism in the waters of Styx, as in many other sacred rivers the world over. Jesus himself was baptized in Palestine's version of the Styx, the river Jordan. When a man bathed seven times in this river, "his flesh came again like unto the flesh of a little child" (2 Kings 5:14). In Greek tradition the journey to the land of death meant crossing the Styx; in Judeo-Christian tradition it was crossing the Jordan. This was the same "river of blood" crossed by Thomas Rhymer on his way to Fairyland.

Tantric worship of menstrual blood penetrated the Greco-Roman world before the Christian era and was well established in the Gnostic period. This worship provided the *agape*—"love-feast" or "spiritual marriage"—practiced by Gnostic Christians like the Ophites. Another name for the *agape* was *synesaktism*, "the Way of Shaktism," meaning Tantric yoni-worship.[52] *Synesaktism* was declared a heresy before the 7th century A.D.[53] Subsequently the "love-feast" disappeared, and women were forbidden direct participation in Christian worship, according to St. Paul's rule (1 Timothy 2:11-12).

Epiphanius described the *agape* practiced by Ophite Christians, while making it clear that these heretical sexual activities filled him with horror:

> *Their women they share in common; and when anyone arrives who might be alien to their doctrine, the men and women have a sign by which they make themselves known to each other. When they extend their hands, apparently in greeting, they tickle the other's palm in a certain way and so discover whether the new arrival belongs to their cult. . . . Husbands separate from their wives, and a man will say to his own spouse, "Arise and celebrate the love feast (*agape*) with thy brother." And the wretches mingle with each other . . . after they have consorted together in a passionate debauch. . . . The woman and the man take the man's ejaculation into their hands, stand up . . . offering to the Father, the Primal Being of All Nature, what is on their hands, with the words, "We bring to Thee this oblation, which is the very Body of Christ." . . . They consume it, take housel of their shame and say: "This is the Body of Christ, the Paschal Sacrifice through which our bodies suffer and are forced to confess to the sufferings of Christ." And when the woman is in her period, they do likewise with her menstruation. The unclean flow of blood, which they garner, they take up in the same way and eat together. And that, they say, is Christ's Blood. For when they read in Revelation, "I saw the tree of life with its twelve kinds of fruit, yielding its fruit each month" (Rev. 22:2), they interpret this as an allusion to the monthly incidence of the female period.*[54]

The meaning of this Ophite sacrament to its practitioners is easily recovered from Tantric parallels. Eating the living substances of reproduction was considered more "spiritual" than eating the dead body of the god, even in the transmuted form of bread and wine, though the color symbolism was the same:

> *When the semen, made molten by the fire of great passion, falls into the lotus of the "mother" and mixes with her red element, he achieves "the conventional mandala of the thought of enlightenment." The resultant mixture is tasted by the united "father-mother" [Yab-Yum], and when it reaches the throat they can generate concretely a special bliss*

> *. . . the bodhicitta—the drop resulting from union of semen and menstrual blood—is transferred to the yogi . . . . This empowers his corresponding mystic veins and centers to accomplish the Buddha's function of speech. The term "secret initiation" comes from the tasting of the secret substance.*[55]

In the occult language of the Tantras, two ingredients of the Great Rite were *sukra*, semen, and *rakta*, menstrual blood. The officiating priestess had to be menstruous so her lunar energies were at flood tide.[56] She embodied the power of *rakta*, sometimes rendered *rukh* or *ruq*, cognate with the Hebrew *ruach*, "spirit," and the Arabic *ruh*, which meant both "spirit" and "red color." Throughout all Tantric and related faiths, the merging of female red and male white was "a profoundly important symbolic conjunction."[57]

The Sufis, who practiced their own brand of Tantrism, said *ruh* was female and red. Its male counterpart *sirr*, "consciousness," was white. Red and white colors alternated in the Sufi *halka* or magic circle, corresponding to the Tantric *chakra* and called "the basic unit and very heart of active Sufism." The Arab rosary of alternating red and white beads had the same meaning: men and women coupled around the circle, as in most European folk dances.[58]

Red and white were the colors worn by alternating female-and-male dancers in the witches' "fairy ring" of pagan Ireland, where the Goddess was worshipped under the same name as the Tantric earth mother, Tara.[59] With men and women alternating as in a Tantric *chakra*, the dance moved counterclockwise or moonwise, as nearly all circle dances still do. Red and white colors "represented the fairy world."[60]

The rites were often governed by old women, due to the ancient belief that post-menopausal women were the wisest of mortals because they permanently retained their "wise blood." In the 17th century A.D., Christian writers still insisted that old women were filled with magic power because their menstrual blood remained in their veins.[61] This was the real reason why old women were constantly persecuted for witchcraft. The same "magic blood" that made them leaders in the ancient clan system made them objects of fear under the new patriarchal faith.

Because menstrual blood occupied a central position in matriarchal theologies, and was already *sacer*--holy-dreadful—patriarchal-ascetic thinkers showed almost hysterical fear of it. The Laws of Manu said if a man even approached a menstruating woman he would lose his wisdom, energy, sight, strength, and vitality. The Talmud said if a menstruating woman walked between two men, one of the men would surely die.[62] Brahmans ruled that a man who lay with a menstruating woman must suffer a punishment one-quarter as severe as the punishment for Brahmanicide, which was the worst crime a Brahman could imagine. Vedic myths were designed to support the law, such as the myth that Vishnu dared copulate with the Goddess Earth while she was menstruating, which caused her to give birth to monsters who nearly destroyed the world.[63]

This was patriarchal propaganda against the Tantric Maharutti ("Great Rite"), in which menstrual blood was the essential ingredient. In Kali's cave-temple, her image spouted the blood of sacrifices from its vaginal orifice to bathe Shiva's holy phallus while the two deities formed the lingam-yoni, and worshippers followed suit, in an orgy designed to support the cosmic life-force generated by union of male and female, white and red.[64] In this Great Rite, Shiva became the Anointed One, as were his many Middle-Eastern counterparts. The Greek translation of Anointed One was *Christos.*

Persian patriarchs followed the Brahman lead in maintaining that menstruous women must be avoided like poison. They belonged to the devil; they were forbidden to look at the sun, to sit in water, to speak to a man, or to behold an altar fire.[65] The glance of a menstruous woman was feared like the glance of the Gorgon. Zoroastrians held that any man who lay with a menstruating woman would beget a demon, and would be punished in hell by having filth poured into his mouth.[66]

Persian religion incorporated the common primitive belief that the first onset of menses must be caused by copulation with a supernatural snake. People not yet aware of fatherhood have supposed the same snake renders each woman fertile and helps her conceive children.[67] Some such belief prevailed in Minoan Crete, where women and snakes were sacred, but men were not. Tube-shaped Cretan vessels for pouring oblations represented a vagina, with a serpent crawling inside.[68] Ancient languages gave the serpent the same name as Eve, a name meaning "Life"; and the most ancient myths made the primal couple not a Goddess and a God, but a Goddess and a Serpent.[69] The Goddess's womb was a garden of paradise in which the serpent lived.

Phrygian Ophiogeneis, "Snake-born People," said their first male ancestor was the Great Serpent who dwelt in the garden of paradise.[70] Paradise was a name of the Goddess-as-Virgin, identified with Mother Hera (Earth), whose virgin form was Hebe, a Greek spelling of **Eve**. Virgin Hera parthenogenetically conceived the oracular serpent Python, of the "Womb-temple," Delphi.[71] Snakes living in the womb of Mother Earth were supposed to possess all wisdom, being in contact with the "wise blood" of the world.

One of the secrets shared by the primordial woman and her serpent was the secret of menstruation. Persians claimed menstruation was brought into the world by the first mother, whom they called Jahi the Whore, a Lilith-like defier of the Heavenly Father. She began to menstruate for the first time after coupling with Ahriman, the Great Serpent. Afterward she seduced "the first righteous man," who had previously lived alone in the garden of paradise with only the divine sacrificial bull for company. He knew nothing of sex until Jahi taught him.[72]

The Jews borrowed many details from these Persian myths. Rabbinical tradition said Eve began to menstruate only after she had copulated with the serpent in Eden, and Adam was ignorant of sex until Eve taught him.[73] It was widely believed that Eve's firstborn son Cain was not begotten by Adam but by the serpent.[74] Beliefs connecting serpents with pregnancy and menstruation appeared throughout Europe for many centuries. Up to modern times, German peasants still held that women could be impregnated by snakes.[75]

Whether initiated by a serpent or not, menstrual bleeding inspired deadly fear among both Persian and Jewish patriarchs (Leviticus 15). Rachel successfully stole her father's *teraphim* (household gods) by hiding them under a camel saddle and sitting on it, telling her father she was menstruating so he dared not approach her (Genesis 31). To this day, orthodox Jews refuse to shake hands with a woman because she might be menstruating. Jews also adopted a rule apparently laid down by Hesiod, that a man must never wash in the same water previously used by a woman, lest it might contain a trace of menstrual blood.[76]

There were many similar taboos. The ancient world's most dreaded poison was the "moon-dew" collected by Thessalian witches, said to be a girl's first menstrual blood shed during an eclipse of the moon.[77] Pliny said a menstruous woman's touch could blast the fruits of the field, sour wine, cloud mirrors, rust iron, and blunt the edges of knives.[78] If a menstruous woman so much as laid a finger on a beehive, the bees would fly away and never return.[79] If a man lay with a menstruous woman during an eclipse, he would soon fall sick and die.[80]

Christians inherited all the ancient patriarchs' superstitious horrors. St. Jerome wrote: "Nothing is so unclean as a woman in her periods; what she touches she causes to become unclean." Penitential regulations laid down in the 7th century by Theodore, Bishop of Canterbury, forbade menstruating women to take communion or even enter a church. At the French Synod of Meaux, menstruous women were specifically forbidden to come to church. From the 8th to the 11th centuries, many church laws denied menstruating women any access to church buildings. As late as 1684 it was still ordered that women in their "fluxes" must remain outside the church door.[81] In 1298 the Synod of Würzburg commanded men not to approach a menstruating woman.[82] The superstition came down to the 20th century, when a Scottish medical text quoted an old rhyme to the effect that menstrual blood could destroy the entire world:

Oh! Menstruating woman, thou'rt a fiend
From which all nature should be closely screened.[83]

Christian women were commanded to despise the "uncleanness" of their own bodies, as in the Rule for Anchoresses: "Art thou not formed of foul slime? Art thou not always full of uncleanness?"[84]

Medical authorities of the 16th century were still repeating the old belief that "demons were produced from menstrual flux."[85] One of the "demons" born of menstrual blood was the legendary basilisk with its poisonous glance.[86] The legend evidently arose from the classic myth of the Gorgon with her serpent-hair and wise blood, petrifying men with her glance. The Gorgon and the red cross of menstrual blood once marked the most potent taboos.[87] The very word taboo, from Polynesian *tupua,* "sacred, magical," applied specifically to menstrual blood.[88]

Just as primitives attributed beneficial powers to menstrual blood along with its fearfulness, so medieval peasants thought it could heal, nourish, and fertilize.[89] Some believed a menstruating woman could protect a crop by walking around the field, or exposing her genitals in it.[90] Peasant women carried seed to the fields in rags stained with their menstrual blood: a continuation of the custom of Eleusinian fertility-priestesses.[91] Even doctors thought menstrual blood could cure leprosy, or act as a powerful aphrodisiac. Madame de Montespan used it to encourage the ardor of her royal lover, Louis XIV.[92] Gypsies said a woman could win any man's love with a potion of her own menstrual blood.[93]

As the former medium of reincarnation, menstrual blood was sometimes called a remedy for death itself. In the tale of Childe Roland, the elven-king roused men from the magic sleep of death with a "bright red liquor."[94] Early romances associated this universal heal-all with "the blood of a noble virgin," as a wise-woman revealed to Galahad.[95] The same belief impelled Louis XI to try to stave off death by drinking young girls' blood.

Victorian superstition taught that a child conceived during a menstrual period would be born with a caul, and would have occult powers.[96] Nineteenth-century doctors inherited their predecessors' notions of witchcraft and evil, and so maintained that menstruating women are not healthy; copulation with them could infect a man with urethritis or gonorrhea. Dr. Augustus Gardner said venereal diseases were usually communicated from women to men, not vice versa.[97] Speaking of savages' menstrual taboos, anthropologists described the women as "out of order," "suffering from monthly illness," or "stricken with the malady common to their sex."[98] A doctor wrote even in the present century: "We cannot too emphatically urge the importance of regarding these monthly returns as periods of ill health, as days when the ordinary occupations are to be suspended or modified."[99]

Dr. Augustus Kinsley Gardner Eminent physician of the late 19th century, opponent of all forms of birth control, which he claimed led "directly and indisputably" to nervous diseases and debilities.

At the present time just as in the Middle Ages, the Catholic church still considers itself on firm theological ground by advancing, as an argument against ordination of women, the notion that a menstruating priestess would "pollute" the altar. This would not preclude ordination of post-menopausal women, but different excuses are found for those. The holy "blood of life" used to be feminine and real; now it is masculine and symbolic.

1. Briffault 2, 412–13, 444. 2. Frazer, G.B., 243. 3. Briffault 2, 444–45. 4. Avalon, 305. 5. Silberer, 136. 6. Chagnon, 38. 7. Hooke, M.E.M., 110. 8. Gaster, 20. 9. Cumont, A.R.G.R., 107. 10. Graves, G.M. 1, 118. 11. Lederer, 139. 12. Harding, 62. 13. Briffault 2, 416, 631. 14. Turville-Petre, 79. 15. O'Flaherty, 148. 16. d'Alviella, xvii. 17. Rees, 75. 18. Hays, 214. 19. Knight, S.L., 119. 20. Budge, G.E. 1, 43; 2, 298. 21. *Larousse*, 39. 22. Jung, M.H.S., 55. 23. Budge, E.M., 127. 24. Budge, A.T., 137. 25. Zimmer, 60. 26. Rees, 75. 27. Graves, W.G., 354. 28. Joyce 2, 90. 29. Baring-Gould, C.M.M.A., 256. 30. Sargent & Kittredge, 64; Gaster, 31. 31. Hazlitt, 384. 32. Rawson, A.T., 32. 33. Stone, 60. 34. *Mahanirvanatantra*, 88. 35. Graves, W.G., 28-29. 36. Stone, 26. 37. Briffault 3, 91. 38. Lindsay, A.W., 49. 39. Brasch, 33. 40. Rawson, E.A., 149, 234. 41. *Larousse*, 383. 42. Bullough, 244. 43. *Encyc. Brit.*, "Shaktism." 44. Briffault 2, 413. 45. Hays, 351. 46. Briffault 2, 417. 47. Silberer, 143. 48. Pepper & Wilcock, 76. 49. Hays, 373. 50. *Larousse*, 359. 51. Graves, W.G., 406. 52. Bullough, 105. 53. Sadock, Kaplan & Freedman, 23. 54. Campbell, C.M., 159. 55. Tatz & Kent, 128–29. 56. Rawson, A.T., 32. 57. Rawson, A.T., 33. 58. Shah, 21, 380. 59. Keightley, 367. 60. Jung & von Franz, 272. 61. Gifford, 26. 62. Frazer, G.B., 700. 63. O'Flaherty, 90, 196. 64. Goldberg, 70; Edwardes, 50. 65. Edwardes, 8. 66. Campbell, Oc.M., 199. 67. Briffault 2, 669. 68. Hays, 101. 69. Potter & Sargent, 224; Graves, G.M. 1, 27. 70. J.E. Harrison, 129. 71. Graves, G.M. 1, 80. 72. *Larousse*, 318. 73. Briffault 2, 666. 74. Tennant, 154. 75. Briffault 2, 664. 76. Briffault 2, 337. 77. Graves, W. G., 170. 78. Simons, 39. 79. de Lys, 46. 80. Morris, 106. 81. Morris, 110. 82. Briffault 2, 396. 83. Pearsall, W.B., 209. 84. Bullough, 176. 85. Robbins, 357. 86. Silberer, 139. 87. Harding, 57. 88. Spretnak, 270. 89. Crawley, 241. 90. Briffault 2, 411. 91. Spretnak, 269. 92. Montagu, S.M.S., 113. 93. Trigg, 44. 94. Wimberly, 214. 95. Gaster, 514. 96. Hazlitt, 99. 97. Barker-Benfield, 278, 298. 98. Briffault 2, 369, 382. 99. Ehrenreich & English, 100.

Menstrual Calendar

Two conflicting calendars were used through most of the Christian era in Europe: the church's official, solar, "Julian" calendar, and the peasants' unofficial, lunar, Goddess-given menstrual calendar. The thirteen annual lunations of the latter produced one of the contrasting answers to the nursery-rhyme riddle: "How many months be in the year? There be thirteen, I say." Christians produced another answer: "There be but twelve, I say." The lunar calendar's thirteen 28-day months had four 7-day weeks apiece, marking new, waxing, full, and waning moon-sabbaths in the ancient form. Weeks are still lunar, but they no longer fit neatly into the solar month system. Thirteen lunar months gave 364 days per year (13 × 28), with one extra day to make 365. Nursery rhymes, fairy tales, witch charms, ballads and other repositories of pagan tradition nearly always describe the full annual cycle as "a year and a day."

It has been shown that calendar consciousness developed first in women, because of their natural menstrual body calendar, correlated with observations of the moon's phases. Chinese women established a lunar calendar 3000 years ago, dividing the celestial sphere into 28 stellar "mansions" through which the moon passed. Among the Maya of central America, every woman knew "the great Maya calendar had first been based on her menstrual cycles."[1] Romans called the calculation of time mensuration, i.e., knowledge of the menses. Gaelic words for "menstruation" and "calendar" are the same: *miosach* and *miosachan.* The new-moon sabbaths of ancient Latium were *kalends,* possibly related to the Aryan name of Kali. For fear of disrupting the Goddess's transitions, activities of some kinds were forbidden on the seventh day of each lunar phase; thus sabbaths became "unlucky" or taboo. Because it was the time-honored custom, even the biblical God was forced to "rest" on the seventh day.

One of the prototypes of Yahweh was the Babylonian god Marduk, who divided the maternal "waters" into those above and below the firmament (Genesis 1:7). Marduk claimed to be the creator, but was not yet so patriarchal as to abandon his Mother's lunar calendar. Babylonian priests said Marduk established holy days and seasons by the moon.[2] Yet older traditions said the menstrual calendar was instituted in Babylon by the god Nabu-Rimmani, the biblical Baal-Rimmon, a phallic deity united with the Great Mother's yoni in the form of a **pomegranate.**[3]

The Chinese explained their menstrual calendar with the myth of the holy calendar plant, *lik-kiep,* on which a pod grew every day for 14 days, then a pod fell off every day for 14 days. When the months became confused by solar reckoning, the Chinese added extra days when "a pod withered without falling off."[4]

According to another story, the menstrual calendar was called Hsiu, "Houses." The Moon Mother rested each night of the lunar month in a different one of her 28 houses, which were kept by the 28 warrior-hero consorts she had placed in heaven to attend her.[5]

The ancient Hebrews took their calendar from Chaldea, legendary home of Abraham, whose older name was Ab-sin, "Moon-father."[6] Chaldeans were credited with the invention of astrology, now largely based on the movements of the sun; but the Chaldeans didn't study the sun. They were "Moon-worshippers," believing the moon determined the fates of men by her movements through various "houses" of the zodiac. The same lunar myths were found in Egypt, northern Europe, Greece, and Rome. Latin kings were sacrificed at the three-day dark of the moon period called *ides,* to insure the Goddess's safe return from the underworld. Greeks similarly made offerings at the Great Sabbath called Noumenia (New Moon). The other Great Sabbath was Dichomenia (Full Moon), when the Goddess stood at the peak of her cycle.[7]

Early attempts at calendar reform left Greek city-states quarreling among themselves about sabbaths and intercalary days. Aristophanes's *The Clouds* makes the Moon-goddess complain that her reckoning of the days was not being correctly followed.[8] Time-spans in myths became confused. Adonis was born after "ten months' gestation," which really meant ten lunar months, the normal 280 days.[9] According to the Book of Maccabees, every gestation lasted ten months.[10] This wasn't ignorance; it was just lunar reckoning.

Even the saints' days of the medieval church were established by *menology,* literally "knowledge of the moon." The church's so-called movable feasts were movable because they were determined by lunar cycles, not solar ones; thus they drifted erratically through the months of the canonical calendar. The most important of them, Easter, is still determined by the moon (first Sunday after the first full moon after the spring equinox), at a time when the Goddess slew and re-conceived the Savior or vegetation god for a new season.[11]

More confusion was created by the fact that menstrual calendars reckoned the day from noon to noon, with the midnight hour in the central position; but solar calendars reckoned the day from midnight to midnight. The Saxon word *den* (day) really meant "night." In Shakespeare's time, people said goodnight by wishing each other good den, literally good moon-day. Old French nursery rhymes greeted the moon rising in the evening with "Good morning, Madame Moon."[12] The *meridian* or high point of noon used to indicate the full moon overhead at midnight: hence its name Meri-Dia or Mary-Diana, the Moon-goddess. Superstitious folk talked of the *daemonium meridianum,* devil of the meridian, a diabolization of the Goddess.[13] She was probably the second of the Slavic trinity of Fates (Zorya), called "She of the Evening, She of Midnight, and She of Morning," in that order.[14]

Pagans held their festivals at night, by moonlight: a custom that might be traced as far back as ancient Egypt, where major religious ceremonies were nocturnal, as listed in the *Book of the Dead:*

> *The night of the battle and of the overthrow of the Sebau-field in Tattu . . . , the night of making to stand up the double Tet in Sekhem . . . , the night of establishing Horus in the heritage of the things of his father in Rekhti . . . , the night when Isis maketh lamentation at the side of her brother Osiris in Abtu . . . , the night of the Haker festival when a division is made between the dead and the spirits who are on the path of the dead . . . , the night of the judgment of those who are to be annihilated at the great festival of the ploughing and the turning up of the earth.*[15]

Pre-Christian Europe also gave night precedence over day. Germanic tribes, Celts, Gauls, druids, the ancient Irish calculated "months, years, and birthdays in such a way as to make the night precede the day."[16] Caesar noted that the Celts measured time by nights instead of by days.[17]

Christian holy days were copied from pagan ones, displaced by 12 hours in their solar reckoning; therefore the older, heathen version of each festival was celebrated on the "Eve" of its Christian counterpart. From this arose the so-called devilish rites of May Eve, Midsummer Eve, Lammas Eve, All Hallow's Eve, and Christmas Eve which was taken from the pagan Yule, and to a late date was still called the Night of the Mother.[18]

Witch persecutors pretended the witches copied their sabbats from Christian feast days in deliberate mockery of the church; but in fact the copying had gone in the other direction. The church took over the pagan feasts of Halloween, May Day, Lammas, Imbolg, Midsummer, **Easter**, Yule, and so on, then claimed to have invented them. However, of the two rival festivals on the same day, the Christian one was invariably the newcomer.[19]

May Eve was the Saxons' Walpurgisnacht, the Celts' Beltain, announcing the opening of the Merry Month of sexual license and "wearing of the green" in honor of the earth's new spring garment. The occasion was still marked by pagan ceremonies in the late 16th century.[20] (See **May**.) Midsummer Eve merged with St. John's Day, but the solstitial rites remained more pagan than Christian. Lammas Eve was a witches' Great Sabbat because it was formerly the pagan Feast of Bread (*Hlaf-mass*) in honor of the Corn-mother.[21] **Halloween** was All Hallows' or All Souls' eve, from the Celtic Samhain or Feast of the Dead, when pagan ancestors came forth from their fairy-mounds, and Christians called them "demons" who attended the witches' feasts.[22]

The thirteen months of the menstrual calendar also led to pagan reverence for the number 13, and Christian detestation of it. Witches' "covens" were supposed to be groups of 13 like the moon-worshipping dancers of the Moorish *zabat* (sabbat), to whom thirteen expressed the three-in-one nature of the lunar Goddess.[23]

Some said thirteen was a bad number because Christ was the thirteenth in the group of apostles, thus the thirteenth member of any group would be condemned to death. Actually, it was the church's opposition to pagan symbolism that brought opprobrium on the number 13. Some even feared to speak its true name, and it was euphemized as a "baker's dozen," or sometimes "devil's dozen."[24]

The heathen tradition persisted in such symbols as the Thirteen Treasures of Britain, probably lunar-month signs taken from a primitive list of zodiacal constellations. They were defined as a sword, basket, drinking horn, chariot, halter, knife, cauldron, whetstone, garment, pan, platter, chessboard, and mantle.[25] The thirteen menstrual months were symbolized in the Tarxien temple on Malta as a sow with 13 teats, like the Celts' Sow-goddess Cerridwen.[26] Thirteen "moons" of the menstrual calendar were suggested also by the English Twelfth Night custom of kindling twelve small fires and one large one, to represent the moon of the New Year.[27]

In general, the symbols of ancient matriarchy came to be known as night, the moon, and the number 13, while those of patriarchy were day, the sun, and the number 12.

1. Von Hagen, 62. 2. Hooke, M.E.M., 45. 3. Lindsay, O.A., 40. 4. d'Alviella, 160. 5. Jobes, 37. 6. Briffault 3, 79, 108. 7. Briffault 2, 439, 599. 8. Von Hagen, 176. 9. Frazer, G.B., 391. 10. *Forgotten Books,* 145. 11. de Lys, 362. 12. Briffault 2, 589. 13. Summers, V., 171. 14. *Larousse,* 285. 15. Budge, G.E. 1, 410. 16. Joyce 2, 391. 17. Phillips, 112. 18. Turville-Petre, 227. 19. J.B. Russell, 50. 20. Frazer, G.B., 142. 21. Brewster, 349. 22. Joyce 1, 265. 23. Shah, 218. 24. Hazlitt, 24. 25. Squire, 339. 26. Pepper & Wilcock, 75. 27. Hazlitt, 602.

Menu

var. Min

Osiris reborn as the ithyphallic Moon-god, called "He Who Impregnates his Mother," or sometimes "Bull of his Mother." As the Goddess's bridegroom, he became an Eros-like sex-god "from whom spring the delights of love."[1] The same lunar title was sometimes applied to his Goddess, as Mena or Meny, which became a cabalistic name of Venus-Aphrodite-Isis. See **Osiris**.

1. Budge, E.M. 140.

Mera

Egyptian "Waters," a primitive Mother-goddess of the Nile, and the divine ancestress of the Locrians. See **Mari**.

Mercury, Saint

A canonized Mercury (Hermes), whose Cappadocian temple was converted into a church in the 6th century.[1] St. Basil had a dream which informed him that St. Mercury was a Christian soldier sent by the virgin Mary to assassinate the emperor Julian in 363 A.D. in revenge for Julian's toleration of the pagan faiths in Rome.[2] Other sources said Julian was not assassinated but died in battle.[3] In this case, there could not have been even a fictitious St. Mercury, but only the pagan god with a new halo.

1. Attwater, 243. 2. de Voragine, 131. 3. *Encyc. Brit.,* "Julian."

Meriah

Sacrificial victim "bought for a price" and hung on a tree or cross "between heaven and earth" in northern India, as an offering to the Earth-goddess Tara, or her spouse, Father Heaven.[1] The title recalls the Old Testament mount of sacrifice, Moriah, where Abraham went to offer his son Isaac to Yahweh; or the place of sacrifice known as *morai* among Polynesians.[2]

1. Robertson, 25–26. 2. Campbell, M.I., 439.

Meriamlik

"Miriam's Stone," the original shrine of the spurious Christian saint Thekla or Thecla, actually a priestess of Diana (see **Thecla, Saint**). Meriamlik would have been a *beth-el* embodying the spirit of the

Goddess Mari, or Mariamne, another name for Diana, who often occupied sacred aniconic stones.

Meridiana

Title of the Moon-goddess at the zenith (meridian), at the height of her powers; also Mary-Diana. Meridiana was the alleged fairy mistress of Pope Silvester II, who made a pact with the devil to gain the pontificate, according to legend.[1] See **Devil**.

1. Gaster, 771.

Meri-Ra

Androgynous combination of the Egyptian Goddess of "Waters" (Meri) with the sun god Ra; same as the combination of Kali and Agni in India. See **Mari**.

Meri-Yamm

Miriam, Mari, or Mary as the consort of the Philistine serpent god Yamm, Lord of Death, cognate of the Hindu Yama. The name of Miriam apparently began as as androgynous form of Mari-Ishtar with a masculine half known as Yamm, the eternal rival and *alter ego* of Baal (God). See **Yama**.

Merlin

Druidic wizard associated with the fairy-religion, later thinly Christianized as the resident wise-man of King Arthur's court. Old Welsh traditions called Merlin a "wild man of the woods" with prophetic or shamanistic skills; he was named either Lailoken or Myrrdin. Geoffrey of Monmouth said Merlin's earlier name was Ambrosius, associating him with the female-symbolic "ambrosia" given by the Fairy Queen to her chosen bards and magicians.[1] In medieval falconry, a *merlin* was a kind of hawk that could be flown only by a lady.[2]

Merlin learned all his magic from the Goddess, in the guise of Morgan le Fay, or Viviane (She Who Lives), or the Lady of the Lake. At the end of his life she took him back into her magic cave and wrapped him in deathless sleep until his Second Coming. Here she was called Nimue, or Fate, the same as the Moon-goddess Diana Nemorensis, or the Nemesis of the Greeks. Pagan Britons believed Merlin would return from his enchanted sleep to announce the coming of a new age of peace and fertility.

Christian writers however made Merlin a child of the powers of hell. According to Robert de Borron, Merlin was deliberately conceived to become Antichrist; he was fathered on a virgin by a devil. He possessed a benevolent nature because of his mother's goodness, which prevailed over his demonic nature.

When King Vortigern's temple was being built on Salisbury Plain, the structure persisted in falling down because—so the astrologers said—its foundations needed the blood of a child who had no human father. Young Merlin fitted the description and was brought to be sacrificed; but his magical X-ray vision discovered the real cause of the trouble. A red and a white dragon were fighting in a mystic pool under the temple's foundations. Merlin prophesied from this that Vortigern, the Welsh red dragon, would be slain by Uther Pendragon, the British white dragon; and it so happened. Afterward, Merlin built Stonehenge by himself, in one night calling all its massive stones from Ireland with his magic songs.[3]

Merlin was also an artisan and a smith. He forged King Arthur's magic armor and a wonderful cup identified with the Holy Grail. He built the palace at Camelot.[4] He made the Round Table, symbol of the pagan lunar calendar. The first tally of its knights made up the moon's number, 28.[5]

The Round Table seems to have been derived from the sacred *mensa,* calendar-table, of Vesta. Petronius said it was a Round Table with the Goddess's image in its center. It represented the earth, which Anaximenes described as "like a Table in form." Plato's *Symposium* said the table stood for Mother Earth because "besides feeding us it is round in shape, it is fixed, and very suitably it has been given by some the name of Hestia."[6]

Merlin's secret cave was located either in the Breton fairy-wood of Broceliande, or in the British druidic shrine of Mount Ambrosius. Some said this was Chislehurst, a chalk cliff honeycombed with caves, long occupied by a college of druidesses.[7] Merlin was associated with the druidic Goddess under many of her names: Morgan, Viviane, Nimue, Fairy Queen, Lady of the Lake—the Celtic Water-goddess Muirgen, often called *boine clergesse* (the Good Priestess). Because Merlin was clearly connected with Goddess worship and the mass of Merlin literature was for centuries a vehicle for criticism of the church, in the 16th century the Council of Trent placed the Book of Merlin's Predictions on the Index of Prohibited Books.[8]

Index of Prohibited Books (Index Librorum Prohibitorum) The first official edition appeared in 1559, though ecclesiastical authorities censored, condemned, and destroyed various kinds of books from the earliest centuries of the Christian era. Catholics were forbidden to read any books listed on the Index, which was regularly updated. Observation of this prohibition was obligatory up to 1966, when Pope Paul VI suppressed the Index.

1. *Encyc. Brit.,* "Merlin." 2. Potter & Sargent, 89. 3. Guerber, L.M.A., 205. 4. Guerber, L.M.A., 211. 5. Malory 1, 72. 6. Lindsay, O.A., 287. 7. Spence, 57. 8. Jung & von Franz, 393, 367.

Mermaid

Literally "Virgin of the Sea," the mermaid was an image of fish-tailed Aphrodite, the medieval Minne, Maerin, Mari, Marina, *mereminne, mare-mynd, mareminde, marraminde,* or *maraeman.*[1] Her Death-goddess aspect, sometimes named Ran, received the souls of those put to sea in funeral boats; or, she might trap living men in her fish net. Teutons said drowned men went to dwell in the house of Ran.[2]

An English law, still on the books in the 19th century, officially claimed for the Crown "all mermaids found in British waters."[3]

1. Steenstrup, 105; Branston, 133. 2. Davidson, G.M.V.A., 129. 3. Holmes, 228.

Mesmerism

When Mesmer excited popular interest with his new cult of "animal magnetism" and began performing miraculous cures, the Vatican approved it in 1840. Then in 1847 it was discovered that "mesmerized" people tended to have religious experiences, and to claim powers of clairvoyance and prophecy. Therefore the church declared heretical "those who profess to see things which are invisible . . . or apply purely physical principles to things which are in reality supernatural." Finally in 1856 an encyclical letter warned the clergy that mesmerism was a dangerous "error."[1] It was a good example of the church's refusal to admit any source of spiritual illumination or mythic imagery other than its own.

1. Bromberg, 164.

Messiah

Persian title of the Anointed One (Greek *Christos*) supposed to come to earth just before doomsday; based on the Kalki Avatara, final incarnation of Buddha, due to appear in time to save the virtuous, before destruction of this universe.[1]

Persians sometimes identified the Messiah with the virgin-born prophet Zoroaster, who would return as his own reincarnation or "son" just before the final battle of the God of Light and the God of Darkness (**Ahura Mazda** and **Ahriman**).[2]

The Jews called the Messiah "Mashiach," and identified him with Elijah. Passover ceremonies required four cups of wine, one left untasted. This was the Cup of Elijah which would be mysteriously drained before the Second Coming. During the Middle Ages, the hopes of oppressed Jewry were raised from time to time by a report that someone's Cup of Elijah had been emptied by a miracle.[3]

The Talmud spoke of two Messiahs; Messiah ben David and Messiah ben Joseph. For this reason, Christian genealogies tried to make Jesus both of them at once, through his mother Mary of the house of David, and through his father Joseph. Some versions of the Gospels said Joseph was Jesus's natural father, other versions said he was not.[4] Like the Persian Messiah he was also the mutually contradictory Son of Man and Son of God.

1. *Mahanirvanatantra,* xlviii. 2. Campbell, Oc.M., 210.
3. Hooke, M.E.M., 158–59. 4. H. Smith, 182; Pfeifer, 131.

Metis

"Wisdom," mythical mother of Athene, assimilated to the Zeus cult by the claim that Zeus impregnated her, then swallowed her, so her wisdom-principle became part of himself. Thus he was able to give birth to Metis's child Athene from his own head. Older versions of the myth show that Metis was really **Medusa,** whose Gorgon face and snake hair symbolized Female Wisdom. Athene was the virgin form of the same Goddess, born not from Zeus's head but from the triple Gorgon in the land of Libyan Amazons, who worshipped Medusa-Metis as the Mother of Fate.[1] A later, Gnostic-Christian version of the same Goddess was **Sophia**, whose name also meant "Wisdom."

1. Graves, W.G., 245–46.

Mezuzah

Jewish door-charm, supposed to protect the house from entry by evil spirits. Originally, an imitation of Egyptian door-charms known as Pillars of Horus: small tablets engraved with hieroglyphic spells to repel evil spirits.[1] Touching or kissing the door-charm when passing through dates back to the Hindu custom of touching the yoni of the door-post Kali-figure "for luck," when entering her temple.[2] Similar "obscene" yonic door-charms were used in early Irish churches; see **Sheila-Na-Gig**.

1. Budge, D.N., 247. 2. Rawson, E.A., 30.

Miasma

Greek "spiritual pollution," a highly contagious evil fate brought on by crimes against a mother or against the Mother Goddess's traditional law. Orestes, having committed the unforgivable crime of matricide, could find no one to defend him against the Furies because *miasma* cut him off from human contact. See **Curse, Mother's.**

Michael, Saint

Judeo-Christian archangel who inherited the myths and attributes of **Hermes** and Heimdall, including the trumpet of the Last Trump and the two sacred Mounts of Mercury on either side of the English Channel, now known as Michael's Mounts (in France, Mont St. Michel).

Michael was said to have been the leader of God's angelic army during the War in Heaven, and God delegated to Michael the divine "words of power" that would defeat the rebellious troops and propel them down to the underworld.[1] Michael-the-Warrior was a favorite subject of Christian artists, who usually showed him in golden armor, with a long spear.

1. Legge 1, 169.

Mictecaciuatl

"Lady of the Place of the Dead," eponymous Mother Goddess of Mexico. Very similar to Kali, she represented the earth's yonic hole from which all things were born, and she was shown also in the trappings of death, thrusting a corpse into the earth.[1] See **Kali Ma**.

1. Summers, V., 263–64.

Midas

Ass-eared king of Phrygia, credited with the Golden Touch that later passed into the lore of alchemy as a magical ability to turn base metals into gold. Hellenic myths made fun of his ears, evidently shown on icons because they were once a sign of divine power, as in the cult of Ass-eared Set. See **Ass**.

Middle-Earth

Scandinavian *Midgard,* the world of men, located between the spirit-worlds above and below. Old Norse *gard* meant earth, place, home: the modern *yard.*[1] Like all ancient people, the Scandinavians regarded their own land as the geographical center of the universe. See **Omphalos**.

1. Lethaby, 62.

Midwifery

From Anglo-Saxon *med-wyf,* "wise-woman" or "witch." Even in the Christian era, priestesses of the Great Mother maintained their monopoly of obstetrics, for most men were afraid of the taboo mysteries of birth. The Bible declared a new mother *sacer* or untouchable for as long as 66 days after giving birth (Leviticus 12:5); and by canon law, a mother was not allowed to enter a church until 40 days after childbed.

For the first half of the Christian era, the arts of medicine remained almost exclusively in the hands of "wise-women" because ancient healing shrines had been devoted almost exclusively to the Goddess's priestesses.[1] In ancient Egypt, midwifery was the province of Sevenfold Hathor who gave each infant its seven souls. The Malayan Semai still say all midwives are holy, partaking of the spirit of the First Midwife who lives in the highest of the seven heavens, each one of which is ruled by one of the Seven Celestial Midwives, identical with the Hathors. An earthly midwife is a sort of fairy godmother, with a spiritual tie to each child she brings into the world.[2]

Mexican peasants attribute similar powers to the *recibidora* who combines the functions of obstetrician, godmother, priestess, and witch. She performs complicated knot-magic in binding and tying the umbilical cord and casts spells for the future fate of the newborn.[3]

Pagan Rome recognized several kinds of midwives, who received separate offerings after a successful birth. There was the *obstetrix* who performed the delivery; the *nutrix* or "nurturer" who encouraged the mother's milk and taught techniques of nursing; and the *ceraria,* priestess of Ceres charged with birth rituals.[4] All were connected with the women's temple, like the Greek Horae who were temple-women on earth and ascended to heaven as midwives to the gods.

Medieval Christianity detested midwives for their connections with pagan matriarchy and Goddess-worship. Churchmen viewed them as implacable enemies of the Catholic faith. Handbooks of the Inquisition stated: "No one does more harm to the Catholic faith than midwives," because they invariably offered newborn children to the service of the devil with a magical baptism by the kitchen fire.[5] The real reason for ecclesiastical hostility seems to have been the notion that midwives could help women control their own fate, learn secrets of sex and birth control, or procure abortions. The pagan women of antiquity had considerable knowledge of such matters, which were considered women's own business, not subject to male authority.[6] Patriarchal religion however forbade midwives to assist their patients in preventing conception, relieving themselves of unwanted pregnancies, or easing their birth-pangs.

In 1591 a Scottish noblewoman, Eufame Macalyne, was burned alive for asking a witch-midwife for drugs to ease her labor pains.[7] Parliamentary Articles of Enquiry in 1559 ordered churchwardens to report any use of "charms, sorcery, enchantments, invocations, circles, witchcrafts, soothsaying," or any like procedures "especially in the time of women's travails."[8]

Some charms and sorceries were allowed as long as they were of the Christian variety: that is, with Christian names substituted for pagan ones in the formulae. Women in childbed were officially advised to bind around their thighs a long charm in Latin, beginning *In nomine Patris et Filii et Spiritus Sancti Amen,* followed by invocations of saints and secret names of God. If the names were not Christian, however, the charm was devilish. An episcopal injunction of 1554 said midwives must not "use or exercise any witchcraft, charms, sorcery, invocations, or prayers other than such as be allowable and may stand with the laws and ordinances of the Catholic church."[9]

Christianity's official view was that to relieve women's sufferings in any aspect of reproduction was to oppose God's will in the matter of the curse on Eve. God decreed that she and all her female descendants must bring forth children with "sorrow" (pain). Consequently, up to the beginning of the 20th century, doctors refused to consider treatment of the major cause of women's deaths, childbed (puerperal) fever. The clergy held such deaths to be either a just reward for an immoral life, or the expression of God's continuing judgment on "the sex."[10]

When James Simpson proposed to relieve women's labor pains with the newly discovered anesthetics, chloroform and ether, there was a great outcry from the clergy, who called it a sinful denial of God's wishes. According to Scottish clergymen, to relieve labor pains would be "vitiating the primal curse against woman."[11] A New England minister wrote: "Chloroform is a decoy of Satan, apparently offering itself to bless women; but in the end it will harden society and rob God of the deep earnest cries which arise in time of trouble, for help."[12] With the usual half-concealed sadism of patriarchal morality, he was really saying that female screams of pain gave God pleasure, and men must see to it that God was not deprived of this.

The matter was resolved when Queen Victoria allowed her doctor to give her chloroform during delivery of her eighth child, and publicly hailed the new pain-reliever as a great blessing. All at once the clergymen were silenced, in effect conceding to the Queen the right to overrule God.[13]

Toward the end of the 19th century, male doctors moved in on the last remaining area of exclusively female medicine, and took the midwifery-trade away from women. At the instigation of the American Medical Association, the U.S. Congress outlawed midwives, and the new male "obstetricians" replaced them. Frequently, an elder midwife found herself out of work, or even in jail for illegal practice, in a community most of whose members she had brought into the world![14]

The effects of the new male professionalism were not always beneficial:

> *Our mechanized civilization, in the interest of a speedy delivery, at the convenience, even at the timed participation of the physician, often endangered mother and child with impatient interference in the natural process, and too often compounded this mistake by anesthetizing the mother completely. All too soon, as a result of scientific pride over inventing a formula for feeding independent of the natural source of milk, the child was parted from its mother and deprived not only of mother's milk, but of the experience of a warm, loving, commensal relationship with her, the kind we must have also with Mother Earth.*[15]

The male-dominated medical profession not only took up delivering women's babies, but even presumed to teach women how to "mother" them which often led to terrible mistakes like the turn-of-the-century minimal-handling theory, which assumed that crying children must not be "spoiled" by cuddling them but should be picked up only at predetermined infrequent intervals. Perhaps the ultimate hubris was attained by L.K. Frank who wrote: "The psychiatrist is uniquely competent to tell us how to practice the Christian injunction to love little children."[16] Here is modern "education" ignorant of the historical truth that the very existence of the human race depended for countless thousands of years—long before either Christianity or psychiatry were heard of—on the unique ability of mothers to love little children and of "wise-women" to assist the instincts of motherhood.

1. Briffault 1, 488. 2. Dentan, 96–98. 3. Castiglioni, 139. 4. Dumézil, 37. 5. Kramer & Sprenger, 66, 141. 6. *Encyc. Brit.*, "Abortion." 7. White 2, 63. 8. Robbins, 157. 9. Hazlitt, 379. 10. Pearsall, N.B.A., 85. 11. White 1, 319. 12. Vetter, 355. 13. *Encyc. Brit.*, "Anesthesia." 14. See Barker-Benfield. 15. Mumford, 469. 16. Torrey, 109.

Milky Way

The Milky Way is our galaxy, from the Greek *gala,* "mother's milk." The ancients believed this heavenly star-stream issued from the breasts of the Queen of Heaven.[1] Worshippers of Argive Hera said the stars were made of milk from Hera's Moon-Cow incarnation. Ionians said the stars came from the udder of their own Moon-Cow, Io, "the Moon."[2] Others said the Moon-Cow was Europa, consort of Zeus as a totemic white bull. All white Moon-Cows were the same Goddess, known from India to Scandinavia as the nourisher of the world and the mother of the star-spirits.[3] See **Cow**.

The Four Rivers of Paradise were supposed to pour from the four teats of the Moon-Cow's udder. Norsemen said these rivers came from the udder of Audumla, the Nourisher, a divine cow who existed before any other creature.[4] She was identified with Mana, the Moon Mother. Scandinavian mythology knew the Milky Way as Manavegr, "Moon-Way."[5] To the Celts, it was *Bothar-bó finné,* Track of the White Cow.[6] The primordial white cow whose udder produced the star-rivers was almost certainly the same cow who "jumped over the moon" in the nursery rhyme, because she was shown hovering over the moon in pre-Christian icons.

Akkadians called the Milky Way River-of-the-Divine-Lady, or Hiddagal, the Great River, which the Bible rendered Hiddekel (Genesis 2:14). Arabians called the Milky Way *Umm al Sama,* Mother of the Sky.[7] Egyptians called the Milky Way the "Nile in the Sky," which poured from the udder of the Moon-Cow, Hathor-Isis, who thus gave rain to the rest of the world, though she reserved her "true Nile" for Egypt.

Classic mythology made the galactic mother Gala-Tea, "Milk Goddess," a white statue of Aphrodite carved by her priest-consort

Pygmalion, whose name was a Greek form of Pumiyathon, priest-consort of Astarte-Hathor at Byblos.[8] Alternatively, the galaxy spurted from the breasts of Hera when she suckled Heracles; or else it came from the breasts of Rhea when she suckled Zeus.[9] Names differed, but everywhere the Milky Way was regarded as the Goddess's star-milk, which formed curds to create worlds and creatures.

The Rabelaisian statement that the moon is made of green cheese dates back to old legends of the moon's creation as a ball of cheese curdled from the Milky Way.[10] Sometimes it was the earth that was made of green cheese from the Goddess's milk. The Bible copied a former address to the Goddess: "Hast thou not poured me out as milk, and curdled me like cheese?" (Job 10:10).

Anglo-Saxon names for the Milky Way suggested that it was not only a river but also a main street of heaven. It was called Irmin's Way, Waetlinga Straet, Vaelinga, Vaetlinga, or Watlingastrete, Wadlyn Street, and Watling Street.[11]

1. Lawson, 13. 2. Graves, G.M. 1, 190, 196. 3. Elworthy, 183, 194. 4. Branston, 57. 5. Turville-Petre, 76. 6. Graves, W.G., 175. 7. Jobes, 103. 8. Graves, G.M. 1, 212. 9. Graves, W.G., 78. 10. Jobes, 27. 11. Jobes, 103.

Mimemata

"Imitations of the Mother," old name for models of the movements of the heavenly bodies, a reference to the Celestial Goddess who was formerly supposed to direct the stars.[1]

1. Lindsay, O.A., 96.

Minaksi

"Fish-Eyed One," title of Kali as the yonic Eye: possible origin of the European bards' Love-goddess **Minne**.

Minerva

Roman Goddess of wisdom and the moon derived from the Etruscan Goddess Menarva or Menrva, probably a Crone aspect of the original Capitoline Triad: a Latinized Athene. Her totem was the same as that of Athene, Lilith, and the Welsh Goddess Blodeuwedd: an owl, which consequently became known as the bird of wisdom and of witches.[1]

1. *Larousse,* 207.

Miniato, Saint

Spurious Christian saint worshipped at Florence, constructed out of an old Roman title for any god painted with *minium,* a red pigment signifying holy blood and divine sovereignty. The faces of gods were reddened during sacred processions and festivals. Military heroes at their triumphal parades also had their faces painted with *minium.*[1] "Miniato" meant simply one who was so reddened. The same custom of ceremonial face-reddening was found among the ancient Celts, and also in traditional Chinese drama, where a reddened face betokened a sacred person.[2] See **Menstrual Blood.**

1. Rose, 294. 2. Williams, 79.

Minne

"Love," the medieval Aphrodite worshipped by *Minne*singers and *Min*strels; perhaps the Moon-goddess Mene or Mana, or the erotic Fish-goddess Minaksi-Kali of India. Minne often appeared as a mermaid, like Aphrodite. But the Minnesingers said of her, "She resembles nothing imaginable. Her name is known; her self, however, ungrasped. . . . She comes never to a false heart."[1]

Norse skalds called Minne a Goddess of Memory, like Mnemosyne, the first of the Muses who gave poets their inspiration.[2] Sometimes she was called simply Lofn, "Love." The Edda said she was a pagan Goddess who gave men and women permission to make love, as opposed to the Christian church which called lovemaking evil.[3] See **Romance.**

1. Campbell, C.M., 181–82. 2. Turville-Petre, 251. 3. Sturluson, 59.

Minos

"Moon's Creature," title of Cretan kings, who were incarnate in sacrificial bull-gods cyclically reborn as the Minotaur or "Moon-bull."[1] The Cretan cult probably stemmed from Egyptian pre-dynastic Apis-bull-kings conceived by the moon. Minos was the name of a dynasty ruling early in the 2nd millenium B.C., when each king married the Moon-goddess.[2] She was either Mother Rhea Dictynna, or the Daughter of Crete called Pasiphae, the Shining One. Late mythographers re-interpreted her ritual coupling with the bull-god as a strange perversion and her son the bull-masked Minotaur as a monster. However, it was the custom of ancient Oriental queens to pantomime intercourse with the severed genitals of sacrificial animals.[3]

1. Graves, G.M. 2, 400. 2. Graves, G.M. 1, 293–95. 3. Briffault 3, 188.

Miriam

var. Mariamne, Miriamne

Semitic name for the Goddess Mari, meaning "Fruitful Mother." She was canonized in many forms, notably Mary; she was also a

St. Miriamne said to be a daughter of St. Philip, himself once the pagan god of May Day.[1] See **Mari**; **Mary**.

1. Brewster, 221.

Mirror

The ancients attributed mystic powers to any reflective surface, solid or liquid, because the reflection was considered part of the soul. Heavy taboos were laid on the act of disturbing water into which a person was gazing, because shattering the image meant danger to the soul. Hence the similar taboo on breaking a mirror, now said to bring seven years' bad luck.

Damage to the reflection-soul was the real basis of the myth of Narcissus, usually misinterpreted as a fable of excessive self-love. Narcissus couldn't bear to leave the reflection of his beautiful face in the magic pool of the nymph Echo, and so he pined away and died, and turned into a flower on the bank. Echo also pined until nothing remained of her but a voice. Actually, Echo was the Goddess of death-by-water, who lay in wait to seize one's reflection-soul, according to beliefs still current among Africans and Melanesians.[1] Narcissus was another name of the sacrificed springtime-flower hero also called Antheus, Adonis, Hyacinthus, or Dionysus, who died at the May Day Heroantheia (Hero-flowering) in Crete, Mycenae, and Lacedaemon.[2]

A mirror meant the god's death in the Pelasgian myth of Dionysus. The Titans trapped his soul in a mirror, as the soul of Narcissus was trapped in reflective water. Then Dionysus was torn to pieces in the rite of the omophagy (see **Cannibalism**). Many centuries later, the gypsies repeated a tale of Dionysus transformed into the Enchanted or Accursed Hunter, whose soul was trapped in a mirror by a "witch" Mara, the same as the Hindu death-spirit Mara.[3] Among Slavic gypsies, **Mara** or Mora was a destroying Fate-goddess who rode the night winds and "drank the blood of men."[4]

The tragically deceased Narcissus was taken into the Christian canon as a saint, said to have been a "bishop" of Jerusalem in the first century (when there were no bishops of Jerusalem). Instead of dying like his ephebic namesake at the pinnacle of youth and beauty, St. Narcissus lived to be 116 years old.[5] He was one of the pseudosaints whose legend was supposed to convince the pagans that the Christian faith could grant the gift of longevity.

Mirrors were connected with death in many Christian superstitions. Demons, werewolves, vampires, and such "soulless" creatures showed no reflection in a mirror. Many Europeans still turn mirrors to the wall after a death in the house, in the belief that mirrors trap the souls of the living or detain the souls of the dead on their journey.[6] Some say one who looks in a mirror in a house of death will see not his own face but the face of the deceased.[7] Pope John XXII had an inordinate fear of mirrors; he claimed wizards sent devils to attack him through mirrors.[8]

The so-called witch's mirror could be made of polished stone, a sheet of metal, a crystal, or a bowl of water or ink. Water represented the Abyss, the numinous hidden spirit world; its reflections therefore could be read as shadows cast ahead by future events. In fairy tales, the land of souls often appeared as a hall of mirrors.[9]

Cabalists professed to read the will of the seven planetary spirits in seven mirrors, each made of the appropriate metal for its day, its deity, and its subject matter. Questions about the great folk of the earth were addressed to a golden mirror on Sun-day. Dreams and mystic enlightenment were observed on Monday (Moon-day) with a mirror of silver. Enmities and lawsuits were resolved on Tuesday with a Mars mirror of iron. A Mercury mirror of quicksilver in glass was consulted on Wednesday about money matters. A Jupiter mirror of tin was questioned on Thursday about worldly successes. Questions of love were resolved on Friday with a Venus mirror of copper. Lost articles and secrets could be discovered on Saturday by a Saturn mirror of lead.[10]

The esoteric meaning of the mirror was explained long ago by Plotinus, who connected it with the Hindu concept of Maya, creatress of the "reflections" of spiritual reality in the mirror of the material world. "Matter serves as a mirror upon which the Universal Soul projects the images or reflections of its creations, and thus gives rise to the phenomena of the sensible universe."[11]

Oriental mystics were close to the conclusion that the Universal Soul really meant one's own soul, where reality was perceived as in a mirror, darkly. A Buddhist aphorism said: "All existence is like a reflection in a mirror, without substance, only a phantom of the mind. When the finite mind acts, then all kinds of things arise; when the finite mind ceases to act, then all kinds of things cease."[12] In other words, the world exists only for those who live and perceive it. This was an idea that Western philosophers played with endlessly, even to the logical but irrational idea that if there were no intelligent beings to perceive it, the universe would not exist at all.

1. Frazer, G.B., 223. 2. Graves, G.M. 1, 113. 3. Groome, 131–32.
4. R.E.L. Masters, 188. 5. Brewster, 467. 6. Clodd, 33–34.
7. Cavendish, P.E., 36. 8. White 1, 384. 9. Guerber, L.R., 219.
10. Jobes, 90. 11. Shirley, 42. 12. *Bardo Thodol,* 227.

Mistletoe

Mistletoe was the Golden Bough that gave access to the underworld, according to pagan belief. The gold color of dry mistletoe was seen as a symbol of apotheosis, as was gold metal. The living plant was viewed as the genitalia of the oak god, Zeus or Jupiter or Dianus of Dodona, consort of the Moon-mother Diana Nemetona, Lady of the Grove. At the season of sacrifice, druidic priests ceremonially castrated the oak god by cutting off his mistletoe with a golden moon-sickle, catching it in a white cloth before it could touch the ground, so it remained like every sacrificial deity "between heaven and earth."[1]

The phallic significance of mistletoe probably stemmed from the notion that its whitish berries were semen-drops, as the red berries of its feminine counterpart, holly, were equated with the Goddess's menstrual blood. Among Indo-European peoples generally, **castration** of the god was customary before his immolation.

Sacred-oak cults continued throughout the Christian era. In the 8th century A.D., the Hessians worshipped the oak god at Geismar and gave his holy tree the name of Jove (Jupiter). As late as 1874, an ancient oak-tree shrine in Russia was worshipped by a congregation led by an Orthodox priest. Wax candles were affixed to the tree, and the celebrants prayed, "Holy Oak Hallelujah, pray for us." A drunken orgy ensued.[2] Modern customs of kissing under the mistletoe are pale shadows of the sexual orgies that once accompanied the rites of the oak god.

To Nordic pagans, mistletoe symbolized the death of the savior-god Balder, son of Odin, whose Second Coming was expected after doomsday, when he would return to earth to establish the new creation. Balder was slain by a spear of mistletoe wielded by Hod, the Blind God, another name for Odin himself. Or, some said Hod was Balder's dark twin, corresponding to the light-and-dark year-gods Set and Horus in Egypt.[3]

Some derive the Saxon *mis-el-tu* from Mas, the Sanskrit "Messiah" (Vishnu), and *tal,* a pit, metaphorically the earth's womb. Thus it stood for the god's entry into his Mother-bride. Norsemen's word for mistletoe was Guidhel, the same "guide to hell" as Virgil's Golden Bough.[4]

After they were converted to Christianity, Saxons claimed the mistletoe was "the forbidden tree in the middle of the trees of Eden," i.e., the Tree of Knowledge, which was popularly supposed to have furnished the wood for Jesus's cross.[5]

The phallic meaning of the mistletoe made it the "key" that opened the underworld womb, key and phallus being interchangeable in mystical writings. Some treatises said, "All locks are opened by the herb Missell toe." Combined with the "feminine" herb Alcyone, it "makes a man do often the act of generation."[6]

The pagan's interpretations of mistletoe were still understood in Renaissance times, when it was adopted as an emblem of the new Messiah and "carried to the high altar" of English churches on Christmas Eve. But some Christian writers insisted that the mistletoe "never entered those sacred edifices but by mistake, or ignorance of the sextons; for it was the heathenish and profane plant, as having been of such distinction in the pagan rites of Druidism."[7]

1. Frazer, G.B., 763–73, 816. 2. Spence, 78, 108. 3. de Lys, 60. 4. Hazlitt, 412. 5. Mâle, 153. 6. Wedeck, 189. 7. Hazlitt, 413.

Mithra

Persian savior, whose cult was the leading rival of Christianity in Rome, and more successful than Christianity for the first four centuries of the "Christian" era. In 307 A.D. the emperor officially designated Mithra "Protector of the Empire."[1]

Christians copied many details of the Mithraic mystery-religion, explaining the resemblance later with their favorite argument, that the devil had anticipated the true faith by imitating it before Christ's birth. Some resemblances between Christianity and Mithraism were so close that even St. Augustine declared the priests of Mithra worshipped the same deity as he did.[2]

Mithra was born on the 25th of December, called "Birthday of the the Unconquered Sun," which was finally taken over by Christians in the 4th century A.D. as the birthday of Christ.[3] Some said Mithra sprang from an incestuous union between the sun god and his own mother, just as Jesus, who was God, was born of the Mother of God. Some claimed Mithra's mother was a mortal virgin. Others said Mithra had no mother, but was miraculously born of a female Rock, the *petra genetrix,* fertilized by the Heavenly Father's phallic lightning.[4]

Mithra's birth was witnessed by shepherds and by Magi who brought gifts to his sacred birth-cave of the Rock.[5] Mithra performed the usual assortment of miracles: raising the dead, healing the sick, making the blind see and the lame walk, casting out devils. As a Peter, son of the *petra,* he carried the keys of the kingdom of heaven (see **Peter, Saint**).[6] His triumph and ascension to heaven were celebrated at the spring equinox (Easter), when the sun rises toward its apogee.

Before returning to heaven, Mithra celebrated a Last Supper with his twelve disciples, who represented the twelve signs of the zodiac. In memory of this, his worshippers partook of a sacramental meal of bread marked with a cross.[7] This was one of seven Mithraic sacraments, the models for the Christians' seven sacraments.[8] It was called *mizd,* Latin *missa,* English *mass.* Mithra's image was buried in a rock tomb, the same sacred cave that represented his Mother's womb. He was withdrawn from it and said to live again.[9]

Like early Christianity, Mithraism was an ascetic, anti-female religion. Its priesthood consisted of celibate men only.[10] Women were forbidden to enter Mithraic temples.[11] The women of Mithraic families had nothing to do with the men's cult, but attended services of the Great Mother in their own temples of Isis, Diana, or Juno.[12]

To eliminate the female principle from their creation myth, Mithraists replaced the Mother of All Living in the primal garden of paradise (Pairidaeza) with the bull named Sole-Created. Instead of Eve, this bull was the partner of the first man. All creatures were born from the bull's blood. Yet the bull's birth-giving was oddly female-imitative. The animal was castrated and sacrificed, and its blood was delivered to the moon for magical fructification, the moon being the source of women's magic lunar "blood of life" that produced real children on earth.[13]

Persians have been called the Puritans of the heathen world. They developed Mithraism out of an earlier Aryan religion that was not so puritanical or so exclusively male-oriented.[14] Mithra seems to have been the Indo-Iranian sun god Mitra, or Mitravaruna, one of the the twelve zodiacal sons of the Infinity-goddess Aditi. Another of Aditi's sons was Aryaman, eponymous ancestor of "Aryans," whom the Persians transformed into Ahriman, the Great Serpent of Darkness, Mithra's enemy.[15]

Early on, there seems to have been a feminine Mithra. Herodotus said the Persians used to have a sky-goddess Mitra, the same as Mylitta, Assyria's Great Mother.[16] Lydians combined Mithra with his archaic spouse Anahita as an androgynous Mithra-Anahita, identified with Sabazius-Anaitis, the Serpent and Dove of Anatolian mystery cults.[17]

Anahita was the Mother of Waters, traditional spouse of the solar god whom she bore, loved, and swallowed up. She was identified with the Anatolian Great Goddess **Ma**. Mithra was naturally coupled with her, as her opposite, a spirit of fire, light, and the sun.[18] Her "element," water, overwhelmed the world in the primordial flood, when one man built an ark and saved himself, together with his cattle, according to Mithraic myth.[19] The story seems to have been based on the Hindu Flood of Manu, transmitted through Persian and Babylonian scriptures to appear in a late, rather corrupt version in the Old Testament. See **Flood**.

What began in water would end in fire, according to Mithraic eschatology. The great battle between the forces of light and darkness in the Last Days would destroy the earth with its upheavals and burnings. Virtuous ones who followed the teachings of the Mithraic priesthood would join the spirits of light and be saved. Sinful ones who followed other teachings would be cast into hell with Ahriman and the fallen angels. The Christian notion of salvation was almost wholly a product of this Persian eschatology, adopted by Semitic eremites and sun-cultists like the Essenes, and by Roman military men who thought the rigid discipline and vivid battle-imagery of Mithraism appropriate for warriors. Under emperors like Julian and Commodus, Mithra became the supreme patron of Roman armies.[20]

After extensive contact with Mithraism, Christians also began to describe themselves as soldiers for Christ; to call their savior Light of the World, Helios the Rising Sun, and Sun of Righteousness; to celebrate their feasts on Sun-day rather than the Jewish sabbath; to claim their savior's death was marked by an eclipse of the sun; and to adopt the seven Mithraic sacraments. Like Mithraists, Christians practiced baptism to ascend after death through the planetary spheres to the highest heaven, while the wicked (unbaptized) would be dragged down to darkness.[21]

Mithra's cave-temple on the Vatican Hill was seized by Christians in 376 A.D.[22] Christian bishops of Rome pre-empted even the Mithraic high priest's title of Pater Patrum, which became Papa, or Pope.[23] Mithraism entered into many doctrines of Manichean Christianity and continued to influence its old rival for over a thousand years.[24] The Mithraic festival of Epiphany, marking the arrival of sun-priests or Magi at the Savior's birthplace, was adopted by the Christian church only as late as 813 A.D.[25]

1. Legge 2, 271; Angus, 168. 2. Reinach, 73.
3. J.H. Smith, D.C.P., 146; Campbell, M.I., 33. 4. de Riencourt, 135.
5. H. Smith, 129; Hooke, S.P., 85; Cumont, M.M., 131. 6. H. Smith, 129.
7. Hooke, S.P., 89; Cumont, M.M., 160. 8. James, 250. 9. H. Smith, 130, 201.
10. Legge 2, 261. 11. Lederer, 36. 12. Angus, 205. 13. Campbell, Oc.M., 204.
14. Knight, D.W.P., 63. 15. O'Flaherty, 339. 16. *Larousse,* 314.
17. Cumont, M.M., 17. 18. Cumont, O.R.R.P., 54, 65. 19. Cumont, M.M., 138.
20. Cumont, M.M., 87–89. 21. Cumont, M.M., 144–45. 22. J.H. Smith, D.C.P., 146.
23. H. Smith, 252. 24. Cumont, O.R.R.P., 154. 25. Brewster, 55.

Miti

"Mother," the Great Goddess of the Chukchi. She gave the secrets of magic to men, in return for the sacrifice of her consort's penis, which was pounded into a pudding and given to her to eat.[1] She was identified with the moon, to which Chukchi men showed their genitals when begging for the gift of power. See **Castration**.

1. Hays, 412.

Mnemosyne

"Memory," first of the Muses, an old version of the Ninefold Goddess. Poets called on Mnemosyne to help them avoid errors in reciting the sacred sagas, learned by rote in pre-literate cultures.[1] She was linked with Mother Earth, whom Nordic bards invoked under the name of Erda.

1. Graves, G.M. 2, 400.

Modir

"Mother," the Norse Goddess who gave birth to the ruling caste of *jarls* (earls), or landowners. See **Caste**. Her name was related to Germanic *Moder,* meaning not only "mother" but also clay, mud, a mixture of the two feminine elements: earth-and-water. Thus, Modir was the same as the Moist-Mother-Earth worshipped by the Slavs, and called **Mati-Syra-Zemlya**.

Modranect

"Night of the Mother," Old Saxon term for Christmas Eve, the traditional pagan winter-solstice festival, when the sun god was reborn from the Great Goddess.[1] Mary replaced the pagan Mother, but the Christmas Eve rituals remained much the same. See **Christmas**.

1. Turville-Petre, 227.

Mohini

"The Enchantress," a Vedic nymph whose "white bowl" or belly-cauldron was said to be the source of Soma, the gods' elixir of immortality. See **Cauldron**; **Menstrual Blood**.

var. Moerae

Moirai

The Three Fates of Greek myth: Clotho the Spinner, Lachesis the Measurer, Atropos the Cutter, western versions of the Oriental Triple Goddess as Creator, Preserver, Destroyer. All nations of the ancient world knew the theory that life was a mystical thread spun by the Virgin, measured and sustained by the Mother, and cut by the Crone.

The Goddess Aphrodite took trinitarian form as the Great Moira, said to be older than Time.[1] Greek funerary hymns consigning the dead to her care were known as *Moirologhia,* invocations of the **Fates**.

1. Bachofen, 57.

var. Moly

Mola

Salted flour prepared by Vestal Virgins to sprinkle over every animal offered in public sacrifice in Rome.[1] *Mola* was credited with miraculous powers, as was the **salt** that Christians later used to dedicate altars.

1. Dumézil, 318.

Molech

var. Moloch

Tyrian fire god, probably based on Hindu Agni. His name meant "king," like the Semitic *melek* or *melkart.* He was assimilated to the Greek's Heracles, whose sacrificial victims were slain by fire.

Molech was worshipped by the Jews in the time of Solomon, whose famous temple was actually built by the king of Tyre (1 Kings 5:1–11). Jews seem to have identified Molech with Yahweh when they were passing their firstborn children through the fire to Molech (Leviticus 18:21); Yahweh also demanded sacrifice of firstborn children (Exodus 13:2).

The shrine of Molech near Jerusalem was **Gehenna**. Christians adopted this word out of the Bible as a synonym for hell, and also gave Molech a prominent position among the demons.[1]

1. Waite, C.M., 186–87.

Money

The so-called "root of all evil" took its name from a title of Rome's Great Mother, Juno Moneta (Juno the Admonisher), whose Capitoline temple included the Roman mint. Silver and gold coins manufactured there were valuable not only by reason of their precious metal but also by the blessing of the Goddess herself, which could effect good fortune and healing magic. Later popes carried on the pagan tradition by blessing Christian amulets and holy medals which were also used in trade, like money.[1]

The attendant spirit of Juno Moneta was the erotic Cupid, corresponding to the Greeks' Eros, who was both child and companion of Aphrodite. Thus, "cupidity" used to mean erotic desire, but in Christian times its meaning was changed to greed for money.

1. *Larousse,* 204.

Monotheism

Though in practice they worshipped three gods, one goddess, and innumerable demigods (angels and saints), Christian theologians insisted their religion was monotheism, and monotheism was the highest form of religion. Vetter comments:

> *One might well ask, where is the evidence that the worship of one supreme god is so superior to the worship of several gods?—that is unless one takes the position that it is difficult enough to furnish proof of the existence of one god, and that each additional god assumed to exist would simply double the problem faced. If the reduction in numbers of deities of itself has merit, then why are not those religions in which no gods whatever are worshipped the "highest" of all?*[1]

There was nothing lofty about the original impulse toward monotheism: the conceit of kings who identified themselves with a god and demanded that god's supremacy. One of the earliest self-worshipping monotheists was the Egyptian pharaoh Ikhnaton (Akhenaten), who reigned from 1379 to 1362 B.C.

Ikhnaton decided that the sole supreme deity was Aton, symbolized by the sun disc and incarnate on earth in himself. He moved his family and court to an earthly paradise 300 miles north of Thebes, to a site now called Tell el Amarna, a great city and temple-palace. He ordered even the word "gods" removed from inscriptions throughout the land, so his own divine alter ego reigned alone. Jewish monotheism probably originated in Egypt. The Old Testament contains writings copied from the cult of Aton, especially the 104th Psalm, thought to have been written by Ikhnaton himself.

Egyptian priesthoods of the old deities refused to tolerate the royal monotheism. Ikhnaton died mysteriously. His body disappeared, and wasn't buried in the tomb prepared for it. His name was erased from king lists. He was described as a criminal.[2] The Egyptians plainly were not disposed to call monotheism a "higher" religion.

Another self-worshipper was the Roman emperor Elagabalus (Heliogabalus), who identified himself with the solar god El Gabal, and tried to absorb all other deities into a single faith. He built a temple on the Palatine, "and he desired to bring into that temple the image of the Magna Mater and the fire of Vesta and the Palladium and the shields and all things that were sacred to the Romans; and he strove to bring it to pass that no god save El Gabal should be worshipped in Rome."[3] But the Roman people were not ready to limit themselves to El Gabal or any other single god.

Fifty years later, Aurelian erected in the Campus Martius his great temple to the Mithraic sun god, *Deus Sol Invictus,* the only god. Diocletian also declared this god Rome's sole ruling deity. Mithraism almost succeeded in establishing Roman monotheism. Mithra was adored "from the mouth of the Danube to Hadrian's Wall in Britain, from Hadrian's Wall to the Pillars of Hercules, and from the Pillars of Hercules to the Desert of Sahara." Moesia, Dacia, Pannonia, and Noricum adopted the cult, as did southern France, especially Lyons. Mithraic inscriptions and sanctuaries have been found at Ostia, Naples, Palermo, Syracuse, Spoleto, and other sites.[4] See **Mithra**.

1. Vetter, 206–7. 2. *Encyc. Brit.,* "Ikhnaton." 3. Carter, 81. 4. Carter, 91–92.

Mons Veneris

"Mount of Venus," simultaneously a mountain shrine and a figurative reference to female genitals. Medical terminology still calls the pubic area *mons veneris.* Medieval Europe had mountains of the same name. Pope Pius II said witches met by night on Mons Veneris (German Venusberg) to consult demons and learn magic.[1]

1. Wedeck, 160.

Montanism

Christian sect founded by Montanus, a former priest of Cybele. Because it allowed women to prophesy and preach, Montanism was declared a heresy and suppressed.[1]

1. Reinach, 278.

Montsalvatch

"Mount of Salvation," the Temple of the Holy Grail vaguely located in the Pyrenees. This was probably an alternate name for the fortress of the heretical Cathari at Montségur in the Pyrenees, where members of the sect were trapped and beseiged for years by papal armies, until the fortress was finally captured and destroyed in 1244.[1] The Grail temple was supposed to be the residence of Knights Templar who rode forth to the assistance of ladies in distress.[2] See **Grail, Holy**.

1. See Oldenbourg, *Massacre at Montségur.* 2. Guerber, L.M.A., 200.

Moon

Moon

"Egyptian priests style the moon the Mother of the Universe," Plutarch said, because the moon, "having the light which makes moist and pregnant, is promotive of the generation of living beings and the fructification of plants."[1] Upper Egypt used to be called Khemennu, "Land of the Moon."[2] In worship of the heavenly bodies, primacy was always assigned to the moon.[3] Babylonians gave the moon precedence over the sun. Oriental nations in general worshipped the moon before the sun.[4] Moses Maimonides said moon worship was the religion of Adam.[5] The Gnostic sect of Naassians believed in a primordial being known as "the heavenly horn of the moon."[6] The moon was the eternal Great Mother. In central Asia it was said the moon is the Goddess's mirror reflecting everything in the world, like the mirror of Maya.[7]

Many savages revere the moon more than the sun, reasoning that the Moon-mother gives her light at night, when it is needed, whereas the sun shines only by day. This belief presupposes that sunlight and daylight are not the same, a common idea among primitives.[8] Writers of the Bible made this same mistake. They said God created "light" (daylight) before the sun and moon (Genesis 1:5, 16).

Mana or *men* gave the name of the pre-Roman Latin Goddess Menrva (Minerva), and such words as mentality, menstrual, menology, mensuration, mentor, menage (a matrilineal household), omen (a revelation from the moon), and amen (the moon of rebirth).

Ashanti people had a generic term for all deities, Boshun, "Moon." In the Basque language, the words for "deity" and "moon" were the same. Sioux Indians called the moon "The Old Woman Who Never Dies." Iroquois called her "The Eternal One."[9] Rulers in the Eritrean zone of South Africa bore the Goddess's name, "Moon."[10] Ancient rulers of the Tutsi tribe were named Mwezi, "Moon."[11] The Gaelic name of the moon, *gealach,* came from Gala or Galata, original Moon-mother of Gaelic and Gaulish tribes. Britain used to be called Albion, the Milk-white Moon-goddess. Persians called the moon Metra (Matra, mother), "whose love penetrated everywhere."[12]

The root word for both "moon" and "mind" was the Indo-European *manas, mana,* or *men,* representing the Great Mother's "wise blood" in women, governed by the moon.[13] Its derivative *mania* used to mean ecstatic revelation, just as *lunacy* used to mean possession by the spirit of Luna, the moon.[14] To be "moon-touched" or "moon-struck" meant to be chosen by the Goddess; a "moon-calf" was one carried away by love of her. When patriarchal thinkers belittled the Goddess, these words came to mean mere craziness. The moonstruck person was described as "silly," a word that formerly meant "blessed," possibly derived from Selene, the Moon.[15]

To the Greeks, *menos* meant both "moon" and "power." To the Romans, the morality of the Moon-goddess was superior to that of the Sun-god. Plutarch said, "The effects of the moon are similar to the effects of reason and wisdom, whereas those of the sun appear to be brought about by physical force and violence."[16]

In many cultures, the Moon-goddess and the Creatress were one and the same. Polynesians called the Creatress Hina, "Moon." She was the first woman, and every woman is a *wahine,* made in the image of Hina.[17] To the Finns, the Creatress was Luonnotar (Luna, the Moon). She brooded over the sea until she brought forth the World Egg, heaven, and earth.[18] Scandinavians sometimes called the Creatress Mardoll, "Moon Shining Over the Sea."[19]

The Moon-goddess created time, with all its cycles of creation, growth, decline, and destruction, which is why ancient calendars were based on phases of the moon and menstrual cycles (see **Menstrual Calendar**). The moon still determines agricultural work in some parts of India.[20] Indonesian moon priestesses were responsible for finding the right phase of the moon for every undertaking. The Dayaks prayed to the moon for children, increase of cattle, and abundant crops; they said she was the cause and measurer of time.[21] Greeks said the same of Demeter, whose priests were called Sons of the Moon.[22]

Peruvians called the moon either Mama Quilla or Mama Ogllo, sometimes identifying the two as mother and daughter, like Demeter and Kore. Mama Quilla married the sun and gave birth to Mama Ogllo, "Egg," the moon-maiden and her brother the sun-man. These two mated and founded the Inca royal line on the site of Cuzco, "the Navel," in Inca cosmology the center of the world.[23]

Because the Moon-goddess was threefold, the Destroyer as well as the Creator, she was the devourer of the dead as well as the giver of life. In Mexico her Destroyer aspect was Mictecaciuatl, who roamed the skies at night, seeking victims to devour. She was called Lady of the Place of the Dead, in appearance like Kali the Destroyer. She was not only the moon but also the All-mother from whose genital hole in the earth humanity crawled in the beginning, and to which humanity would return.[24]

The Vedas say all souls return to the moon after death, to be devoured by maternal spirits.[25] Trobriand Islanders spoke of these spirits as "female sorcerers" associated with the moon, eaters of the dead.[26] Maoris called the Moon Mother "man-eater." Tartars of central Asia worshipped the moon as Macha Alla, Queen of Life and Death, said to be an eater of men. Africans said the moon searched for men to devour.[27]

Orphic and Pythagorean sects viewed the moon as the home of the dead, a female Gate (yoni) through which souls passed on the way to the paradise-fields of the stars.[28] Greeks often located the Elysian Fields, home of the blessed dead, in the moon.[29] Kastor of Rhodes said the shoes of Roman senators were decorated with ivory lunules (crescents) to show that after death they would inhabit the moon.[30] Roman religion taught that "the souls of the just are purified in the moon."[31] Wearing the crescent was "visible worship" of the Goddess.[32] That was why the prophet Isaiah denounced the women of Zion for wearing lunar amulets (Isaiah 3:18). "The crescent moon worn by Diana and used in the worship of other Goddesses is said to be the Ark or vessel of boat-like shape, symbol of fertility or the Container of the Germ of all life."[33] The same Ark carried gods, like Osiris, into death; which may account for Jeremiah's hostility to the Ark's symbolism (Jeremiah 3:16).

Semites feared the devouring Old Moon as Hindus feared the devouring Kalika. Her dual nature may account for the correlation between Semitic *ima,* "mother," and *e-mah,* "terror."[34] Superstitious Christians sometimes refused to sleep where moonlight might touch them. According to Roger Bacon, "Many have died from not protecting themselves from the rays of the moon."[35] There was always an association with death:

> *The idea of the journey to the moon after death is one which has been preserved in the more advanced cultures. . . . It is not difficult to find . . . themes of the moon as the Land of the Dead or the regenerating receptacle of souls. . . . This is one reason why the moon presides over the formations of organisms, and also over their decomposition.*[36]

Because the moon was the receptacle of souls between reincarnations, it sheltered both the dead and the unborn, who were one and the same. Believers in prophetic dreams said if a man dreamed of his own image in the moon, he would become the father of a son. If a woman dreamed of her own image in the moon, she would give birth to a daughter.[37]

Most important for its association with birth, the moon was supposed to be the receptacle of menstrual blood by which each mother formed the life of her child. This *sacer,* taboo moon-fluid kept even the gods alive. The moon was "the cup of the fluid of life immortal, quickening the vegetable realm and whatsoever grows in the sub-lunar sphere, quickening also the immortals on high."[38]

Many myths of the moon-journey bore witness to the ancient belief in lunar heavens. Gypsies opposed the Christian savior with their own Romany savior who carried souls to the moon, like Hermes Psychopomp.[39] Strangest of all myths of the moon-journey was one involving Jesus himself. The Digby mystery play of the 16th century quoted "Jesus's hymn to the Moon, his mother, the vessel . . . in whom he rested before he ascended to the Sun."[40]

Digby mystery play English Renaissance passion play, *Mary Magdalene,* by an anonymous author tentatively identified as Miles Blomefylde.

Peasants in France and Portugal confused Jesus's mother with the Moon-goddess, whom they called "Our Lady" and "Mother of God."[41] Scottish women curtsied to the moon when they saw her, saying "It is a fine moon, God bless her."[42] In the Loire district, children's rhymes spoke of Madame Moon, giver of babies.[43] A medieval German sect of Cathari worshipped the moon as Heva (Eve), Mother of All Living, an older incarnation of the virgin Mary.[44] Even the orthodox church held that, as Jesus was the second Adam, so Mary was the second Eve; and Mary was associated with both the moon and the sea.

As the moon governs the sea's tides, so she was supposed to govern the tides of life and death. Shore dwellers had an ineradicable conviction that a baby can be born only on an incoming tide, and a dying person cannot expire until the tide goes out. As a corollary, it was often said birth at a full tide or a full moon betokens a lucky life.[45] The soul may ride the tide in lunar form, according to Caesarius of Heisterbach: "The soul is a spiritual substance of spherical nature, like the globe of the moon."[46]

Scottish girls refused to schedule a wedding day for any time other than the full moon, the most fortunate time for women.[47] Scandinavian women particularly prized amulets made of silver, the moon metal. The moon was the special deity of women even during the Renaissance, when it was said if a woman wanted anything she should not ask God but should pray instead to the moon.[48]

Witches invoked their Goddess by "drawing down the moon," a rite dating back to moon-worshipping Thessaly, centuries before the Christian era.[49] Thessalian priestesses also prefigured "witchcraft" by laying curses with "moon-dew," said to be the first menstrual blood of girls gathered during a lunar eclipse.[50] Medieval folk believed such a curse incurable. St. Augustine and other fathers of the church believed what Virgil said about moon-priestesses, that they could draw down the moon, stop rivers in their courses, turn back the wheel of the stars, or bring trees marching downhill.[51] St. Augustine berated women for dancing "impudently and filthily all the day long upon the days of the new moon."[52]

Few religious symbols occurred in so many diverse contexts as symbols of the moon. In the runic menological calendar the moon-sickle stood for the festival of Harvest Home, which the Scots called Kirn—from Koreion, moon-virgin Kore—which Christians renamed the Feast of Our Lady of Mercy.[53] In Gaul the crescent moon stood for the druidic Diana. *Crescere* meant "to grow," a form of Latin *creare,* to produce, to create.[54] Hence the crescent. Gauls made communion cakes in crescent shape. Modern France still makes them, and calls them *croissants,* "crescents," colloquially known as "moon-teeth."[55]

The moon ruled the sexuality of women, and sometimes made them scornful of the male-dominated society's notions of hierarchy. An astrological book of 1688 warned: "The double conjunction of Venus and the Moon produces extreme lubricity, brings venereal disease, and causes women of quality to become enamored of menservants."[56]

Despite all the church's condemnations, rural folk continued to trust the Moon-mother in all their most important activities. A popular almanac said: "Kill fat swine for bacon about the full moon. . . . Shear sheep at the moon's increase: fell hand timber from the full to the change . . . ; horses and mares must be put together in the increase of the moon, for foals got in the wane are not accounted strong . . . ; fruit should be gathered, and cattle gelded, in the wane of the moon." Most of all, the moon always governed magic. Melton said in 1620 that no sorcerer ever drew a circle of protection without observing the time of the moon.[57]

1. Knight, S.L., 99. 2. Hallet, 115. 3. Cumont, A.R.G.R., 19, 69.
4. Budge, G.E. 2, 34. 5. Briffault 3, 78. 6. Jung & von Franz, 136.
7. Jobes, 32. 8. Briffault 2, 677. 9. Briffault 2, 436, 601, 670; 3, 76.
10. Campbell, P.M., 166. 11. Hallet, 152. 12. Jobes, 29.
13. Avalon, 178; *Mahanirvanatantra,* liii. 14. de Lys, 414.
15. Cavendish, T., 62. 16. Briffault 3, 2. 17. Campbell, M.T.L.B., 43.
18. *Larousse,* 304. 19. Briffault 3, 67. 20. O'Flaherty, 89.
21. Briffault 2, 711. 22. Castiglioni, 192. 23. Jobes, 41, 58.
24. Summers, V., 263–64. 25. Briffault 3, 132. 26. Hays, 400.
27. Briffault 2, 576. 28. Lindsay, O.A., 92. 29. Cumont, A.R.G.R., 96, 107.
30. Lindsay, O.A., 222. 31. Gettings, 91. 32. Elworthy, 194.
33. Avalon, 423. 34. Brasch, 25. 35. Gifford, 31. 36. Gettings, 95.
37. Hazlitt, 191. 38. Zimmer, 167. 39. Trigg, 202. 40. Malvern, 121.
41. Harding, 100. 42. Hazlitt, 417. 43. Briffault 2, 589.
44. Knight, D.W.P., 179. 45. de Lys, 398. 46. Jung & von Franz, 138.
47. Briffault 2, 587–88. 48. de Lys, 458. 49. Cumont, A.R.G.R., 186.
50. Graves, W.G., 170. 51. Cavendish. P.E., 97. 52. Hazlitt, 417.
53. Brewster, 424. 54. Potter & Sargent, 278. 55. Jung, M.H.S., 276.
56. de Givry, 224. 57. Hazlitt, 418, 143.

Mordrain and Nascien

"Death and Birth," two heathen rulers of the holy city of Sarras, the New Jerusalem, according to Holy Grail legends. They seem to have represented the Lady of Life and Lord of Death common to most pagan traditions.

Mordred

"The Killer," who was a son, a uterine nephew, supplanter, and Oedipal rival of King Arthur, who tried to escape Fate by destroying Mordred as soon as he was born, and failed. Mordred survived an intended Slaughter of the Innocents, grew up, and lived to betray and slay his father-king. Like other supplanter-gods he was born of a version of the Triple Goddess, Margawse, the middle one of Arthur's three "sisters" who really represented the Virgin, Mother, and Crone. See **Arthur**.

Morgan Le Fay

Celtic death-goddess: Morgan the Fate, or Fata Morgana, or the Triple Morrigan, or "Morgue la Faye."[1] Sometimes she was a Ninefold Goddess, the Nine Sisters called Morgen ruling the Fortunate Isles in the far west, where dead heroes went.[2] Sometimes she, or they, became mermaids. Morgans or "sea-women" could "draw down to their palaces of gold and crystal at the bottom of the sea or of ponds, those who venture imprudently too near the water."[3]

Like Macha, the Crone aspect of the Morrigan, Morgan as Mother Death cast the destroying curse on every man. Even Arthurian romances which presented her as a human being, Arthur's sister, inconsistently admitted: "Morgan the Goddess is her name, and there is never a man so high and proud but she can humble and tame him."[4]

Sometimes she kindly promised immortality to her favored lovers, like Ogier the Dane, who accompanied her to her paradise. As the Morrigan, she stage-managed the contest between **Cu Chulainn** and a giant named Terrible. She presided over Cu Chulainn's killing of his springtime rival, in a tale based on the Celtic legend of Gawain and the Green Knight.[5]

Morgan sat at the head of the table in the Green Knight's castle, presiding over the death and resurrection of the rival year-gods as they beheaded one another in their proper seasons. Gawain was obviously a solar hero, his strength waxing in the morning and waning in the afternoon; he was one of four brothers representing the four solar seasons. The Green Knight was his perpetual antagonist.

Like Njord and Frey, Horus and Set, Gwynn ap Nudd and Gwythyr son of Greidawl, they rose again and killed each other at the turning of the year. Gawain bore Morgan's pentacle as a heraldic device on his blood-red shield. He and his rival seem to have established the ceremony of knighthood, a symbolic decapitation, which formerly transformed a victim into a god at the year's end.[6]

Late romances deprived Morgan of her divinity and made her human, just as the Great Goddess Mari became a mortal virgin Mary. Morgan became Arthur's sister, yet "a great clerk of necromancy," a prototypical witch.[7] She received a fictitious husband, King Uriens of Gore, probably a corrupt form of the classic castrated heaven-god Uranus. Her name was applied to anything magical, miraculous, or misleading, as the Fata Morgana. An old word for witches' spells, *glamor,* came from Glamorgan, the Goddess's sacred territory in Wales.

Morgan's mysterious Fortunate Isles continued to appear in Irish folklore up to the present time. It was claimed that off the coast of Galway nine islands rose out of the sea every seven years; but if anyone tried to reach them by boat, they would vanish.[8]

1. Keightley, 45. 2. Rees, 193. 3. Keightley, 433. 4. Loomis, 387. 5. Goodrich, 188, 216. 6. Loomis, 107, 324–42. 7. Malory 1, 8. 8. Ramsay, 90.

Moros

"Doom," in Orphic creation myths a divine child of the primal Goddess Night. See **Orphism**.

Morrigan

The Triple Goddess Morgan in Ireland: the virgin Ana, flowering fertility-goddess; the mother Babd, "Boiling," the cauldron perpetually producing life; and the crone Macha, "Great Queen of Phantoms," or Mother Death.[1] Sometimes she was Mugain, the ruling Goddess of Munster.

Like Hecate the triple Moon-goddess, Macha sometimes stood for all three *personae.* Queens of Ulster governed her shrine, Emain Macha, or Macha's Emania, land of the moon.[2] She laid the death curse on Cu Chulainn, and haunted battlefields, making magic with the blood of slain men.[3] In the form of a raven she emerged from her fairy-mound and perched on a standing-stone, singing of her Mysteries: "I have a secret that you shall learn. The grasses wave. The flowers glow golden. The goddesses three low like kine. The raven Morrigan herself is wild for blood."[4] See **Trinity**.

1. Rees, 36; Graves, W.G., 409. 2. *Larousse,* 229. 3. Rees, 36, 58. 4. Goodrich, 192.

Moses

Sir Flinders Petrie said the name Moses was Egyptian, as in Thut-mose, Ahmoses, etc., meaning "unfathered son of a princess." An Egyptian model for Moses's myth was the demigod Heracles of Canopus, drawn from an ark in the Nile bulrushes. When he grew up, he performed great deeds, and finally died on a mountaintop.[1]

The myth was not only Egyptian. It was applied to many heroes and god-kings. King Sargon of Akkad, 2242–2186 B.C., was a virgin-born son of a temple maiden, whose title *enitum* meant Virgin Bride of God, like the Semitic *kadesha.* She set Sargon afloat on the river in a basket of rushes. He was rescued by the divine midwife, Akki the Water Drawer, now transformed into Aquarius. He passed through the sacred king's customary adventures: an early threat of destruction from the incumbent monarch, a period of exile in the wilderness, temptation by evil spirits, finally elevation to the throne as the spouse of the Goddess Ishtar.[2]

Akki the Water-Drawer, or breaker of the waters, may be related to Hekat in Egypt, Acco the childbirth-goddess in Greece, "Acca the Maker" in the Roman cult of Heracles, and Akka the eponymous mother of Akkad.[3] Finns and Lapps said she was Mader Akka (Mother Akka) who gave birth to all humanity. This Akkadian Great Mother was associated with many tales of heroes floating on rivers in infancy for this was a mythic symbol of birth-waters. Rome's Acca Larentia drew Romulus and Remus from their floating basket on the Tiber, in the same myth-cycle.[4] Egypt's version of her was the "pharaoh's daughter" of the Moses myth, i.e., Hekat the Midwife, or Heka-Akka.

The fatherless hero born of "waters" (Maria) was a universal image of the sacred king, repeated in the myths of Perseus, Horus, Jason, Oedipus, Trakhan of Gilgit, Joshua son of Nun, and others including—conceptually at least—Jesus. Most were based on the ancient myth of the Goddess Cunti (Kali-the-cosmic-yoni), who gave birth to the sun god and placed him in a basket of rushes on the river Ganges. The same sun god was reborn in Athens, fathered by Apollo on the virgin Creusa, and left in a woven basket.[5]

Moses's miracles were equally derivative, drawn chiefly from Egyptian myths. The drying up of a body of water, to cross dry-shod, was a miracle of Isis, who parted the waters of the river Phaedrus on her journey to Byblos.[6] The same tale was told of Bindumati (Kali as mother of the *bindu* or Spark of Life) when she crossed the Ganges. Moses's extraction of water from a rock was performed long before by a guru at Lhasa; his rock is still called "the water of the god's vessel."[7] Atalanta of Calydon also brought forth water from a rock by striking it with her spear and calling on her Goddess.[8] Mother Rhea performed the same miracle; and she was also the giver of law tablets on a holy mountain.

The historical basis of Moses myths seems to have been the expulsion of Jews from Egypt during an outbreak of "pestilence," possibly leprosy. The historian Choeremen said the oracles blamed the infection on foreign workers called Children of Israel. The priest Manetho said in the 3rd century B.C. that alien tribes in northwestern Egypt were lepers and unclean. Lysimachus stated that the oracle of Amon ordered the alien workers to be collected and driven out of Egypt.[9]

Tacitus's account called the Jews "a race detested by the gods," whose presence in Egypt was responsible for an outbreak of disfiguring disease. The offenders were evicted from Egypt and sent into the desert:

> *The people, who had been collected after diligent search, finding themselves left in a desert, sat for the most part in a stupor of grief, till one of the exiles, Moyses by name, warned them not to look for any relief from god or man, forsaken as they were of both, but to trust to themselves, taking for their heaven-sent leader that man who should first help them to be quit of their present misery. They agreed, and in utter ignorance began to advance at random. Nothing, however, distressed them so much as the scarcity of water, and they had sunk ready to perish in all directions over the plain, when a herd of wild asses was seen to retire from their pasture to a rock shaded by trees. Moyses followed them, and, guided by the appearance of a grassy spot, discovered an abundant spring of water. This furnished relief. After a continuous journey for six days, on the seventh day they possessed themselves of a country, from which they expelled the inhabitants, and in which they founded a city and a temple.*[10]

Jewish history begins with this expulsion from Egypt. Everything previous to this in the Bible was syncretic mythology gathered from non-Jewish sources.[11] Moses's encounter with the god of Sinai—the Chaldean moon-god Sin—shows that the Jews tried to settle in this god's territory, the Cainite-Midianite mining community on the Sinai peninsula.

The whole peninsula was the Land of Sinim, i.e., "Land of the Moon." Its god Sin was a consort of Mother Inanna, or Nanna, who annually turned the waters of Sumer into blood. Sin dwelt in a holy mountain, which Moses climbed, and Moses reported that he was the same as the god of Abraham, though Abraham didn't know him by the same name (Exodus 6:3). In very ancient documents, the name of Abraham himself appeared as a synonym for Ab-Sin, "Moon-father."[12]

The "God of Abraham" whose name meant Father Brahm introduced himself to Moses as "I Am That I Am," in imitation of the Brahmanic *Tat sat,* "I Am That that Is."[13] (See **Tetragrammaton**.) The god also commanded, "Put off thy shoes from off thy feet, for the place whereon thou standest is holy ground" (Exodus 3:5). This was an ancient Hindu custom. In India it is still proper to go barefoot in temple precincts, on the theory that subtle emanations from the holy ground can enter the body through the feet. Ancient Egyptians and Roman witches had the same custom.[14]

Another Brahma-like habit of Moses's god was to view a thousand years of man as one day in his own sight (Psalms 90:4). This was copied from the "Day of Brahma" made up of a thousand years, or sometimes a thousand *mahayugas* or "great aeons."[15]

The stone tablets of law supposedly given to Moses were copied from the Canaanite god Baal-Berith, "God of the Covenant." Their Ten Commandments were similar to the commandments of the Buddhist Decalogue.[16] In the ancient world, laws generally came from a deity on a mountaintop. Zoroaster received the tablets of law from Ahura Mazda on a mountaintop.[17] An earlier lawgiving mountain-deity was Mother Rhea of Mount Dicte, or Ninhursag, probably a model for the masculine lawgivers. Moses's god provided laws remarkably similar to those handed down from the Babylonian god to King Hammurabi.[18]

Moses took over another matriarchal myth in the tale of the plagues of Egypt. This came from the third-dynasty reign of Tcheser (or Joser, whom the Hebrews called Joseph). The Nile flood failed for seven years, and Egyptians starved to death by thousands. The pharaoh sent a desperate message to Mater (Mother), ruler of Nubia, to ask how the Goddess might be propitiated. Mater's reply described "the couch of the Nile," a double cavern called Qerti or Khert, the underworld, likened to "two breasts from which all good things poured forth."[19] Mater said the trouble was caused by a jealous male god, who wished to be called "father of gods" and to hold the Key of the Nile. As usual, the god's practical demands boiled down to gifts and tithes for his priesthood.

When the story was written down many centuries afterward, in the late Ptolemaic period, priests of Ra pretended their god had ended the drought, by spreading a "red beer" over Egypt's fields to distract the attention of Mother Hathor, who was killing the people.[20] This "beer" was said to be "as human blood." What transformed it into blood was a holy substance from the Nile's source, called *dedi*.[21] This was sometimes said to be a salty red earth, like ochre, likened to **menstrual blood**. Or again, the red color was pomegranate juice, another symbol of menstrual blood.[22] The pomegranate represented the vulva in biblical times, and was worshipped as an emblem of the Goddess on her holy mount Rimmon ("Pomegranate").[23]

What really turned the Nile into blood was not Moses's magic wand, but the red silt of flood time, supposed to be the Goddess's life-giving uterine blood bathing the land in the substance of life. The mythic killing probably referred to hecatombs of firstborn sons, sacrificed in the attempt to end the drought, their blood spread on the fields to encourage the flood by sympathetic magic. See **Firstborn**.

Moses's followers pretended that Yahweh had caused the slaughter of Egyptian firstborn sons (Exodus 12:29), while the Israelites were permitted to redeem their sons with the blood of lambs (Exodus 13:15). However, Yahweh had long copied the Egyptian custom of firstborn-sacrifice. He said, "Sanctify unto me all the firstborn, whatsoever openeth the womb among the children of Israel, both of man and of beast; it is mine" (Exodus 13:2). Like early Egyptian gods, Yahweh forgave sins only when his altars were soaked in blood: "without shedding of blood there is no remission" (Hebrews 9:22).

The Lord rather unnecessarily told Moses to instruct his people to smear sacrificial blood on their doorposts, a custom that would have been perfectly familiar to any people living in Egypt where it was done at most religious festivals since the earliest times. Again it seems to have originated in the Far East. At New Year sacrifices in China, doorposts were smeared with blood of sacrificial lambs just as in the

Passover myth.[24] Upper Nigerian tribes still sacrifice to ancestral ghosts on the threshold of the house and smear the blood on doorposts.[25]

Many laymen are still led to believe that a real Moses wrote the Pentateuch (first five books of the Old Testament), even though scholars have known for a long time that these books were first written in the late post-exilic period by priestly scribes in Jerusalem.[26] Their purpose was to create a mythic history for their nation out of customs, sayings, and legends mostly borrowed from others. The figure of Moses remains mysterious because it was largely a framework of myth hung on a non-Jewish name.

1. Graves, W.G., 151, 161. 2. Gray, 55. 3. Graves, G.M. 2, 190. 4. *Larousse,* 214, 308. 5. Rank, 18. 6. Budge, G.E. 2, 191. 7. Waddell, 384. 8. Graves, G.M. 1, 264. 9. Doane, 52. 10. Tacitus, 658. 11. Reinach, 182. 12. Briffault 3, 106–8. 13. *Mahanirvanatantra,* xix. 14. Wedeck, 152. 15. Campbell, M.I., 143. 16. Waddell, 134. 17. Reinach, 66. 18. Hooke, M.E.M., 147. 19. Budge, G.E. 2, 53. 20. Hays, 256. 21. Erman, 49. 22. *Larousse,* 36. 23. Graves, W.G., 410. 24. Williams, 78. 25. Frazer, F.O.T., 322. 26. White 2, 328–29.

Mot

Canaanite god representing "Death" or "Sterility"; the rival, tanist, twin, and alter ego of the fertility god Aleyin or Baal. Mot may be compared to Shiva in his "dead" phase as Shava the Corpse, or to Osiris in his "mummy" phase as the Still-Heart. In other words, he was the vegetation-god in the fallow season.

Like the dying Jesus, Mot was "forsaken" by his heavenly Father (El) and symbolically castrated by the breaking of his reed scepter. Like the harvested grain, he was cut with a sickle, beaten with a flail, ground in a mill, and scattered in pieces over the fields by his Goddess, Anat (Anatha). He was also assimilated to the pre-Christian figure of the Lamb of God, calling himself the sacrificial lamb made ready with pure wheat to atone for the sins of the people.[1] After each of his annual ceremonial "deaths" he was always resurrected by the Goddess, who caused him to be reborn as the new crop, Aleyin. He was worshipped in Babylon and also in Jerusalem under the name of Tammuz.

1. *Larousse,* 76–78.

Mother Carey

English sailors' version of Mater Cara, "Beloved Mother," the Latin Sea-goddess. The petrels, "Mother Carey's chickens," were her soul-birds; thus the French called them Birds of Our Lady.[1] Their other name meant "little peters." See **Peter, Saint**.

1. Potter & Sargent, 71, 117.

Motherhood

During the early evolution of the human race, motherhood was the only recognized bond of relationship. Like any mammalian family, the primitive human family consisted of mother and offspring.

> *The animal family is the product of the maternal instincts and of those alone; the mother is the sole centre and bond of it. . . . The male has no share in forming the animal family; he is not an essential member of it; he may join the maternal group, but commonly does not do so. When he attaches himself to the animal family his association with it is loose and precarious. . . . Where the female can derive no benefit from association with the male, no such association takes place. Where male cooperation is useful, the male seeks out or follows the female, and it is the latter who determines the segregation of the group and selects its abode.*[1]

The root of civilization was the kinship bond that kept groups together to evolve mutual cooperation. The bond was maternal because no paternal relationships were perceived, or even guessed, by such early groups with their shifting, temporary sexual attachments. "The connection between sexuality and childbearing was unknown to primitive men."[2]

People in primitive circumstances still show ignorance of the connection between sexuality and childbearing. Trobriand Islanders attributed pregnancy to spirits, not sex. A woman's husband might help care for her children, but he thought of them as "the children of my wife." The islanders laughed at white men who first tried to tell them about impregnation. Chukchi female shamans said they made their children by their sacred stones, not by intercourse with men. Australian aborigines thought women became pregnant by eating some special foods, or by embracing a sacred tree hung with umbilical cords from previous births. Bataks believed no woman could become pregnant unless umbilical cords and placentae were buried under her house.[3]

Primitives not only attributed pregnancy to a variety of causes, but also assigned to it a variety of different durations, showing that they were not sure when it began.[4] Most authorities now agree that not only the uncivilized races today, but certainly all the world's people in the prehistoric period, knew nothing of man's part in the process of reproduction. It was believed that only women held the divine power to give life.[5] All the most ancient mythologies speak of a Creatress rather than a Creator because living things could be made only by a female, according to primitive beliefs. Men believed themselves unnecessary to the process.[6]

The most primitive hunting cultures have legends of still earlier ages, when women possessed all magical arts and men had none. As childbearers and nurturers, women took charge of growing things generally. They became the producers, storers, and distributors of vegetable foodstuffs, hence the owners of the land they used for cultivation. They made the earth valuable and equated it with themselves.

Their economic and social power thus evolved the early village communities in matriarchal form. The men saw themselves as almost entirely superfluous, except for the labor they could contribute as hunters or defenders of the matriarchal group.[7]

The secret of fatherhood can only have been revealed to men by the women themselves, because women were the keepers of calendrical records, another traditionally female skill that most men thought beyond their comprehension. Before the advent of monogamous marriage, a late development in human history, there would have been no reason or inclination to correlate copulations with births. Even if the truth were suspected, there were many negative cases to disprove it: some women could copulate frequently and never become pregnant, others could remain "barren" when living with one man but conceive when living with another. Women past menopause or before menarche could take any number of lovers without conceiving, which tended to suggest that menstruation was the crucial factor rather than sexual activity.

As may be found still in many groups of people, motherhood alone was the foundation of clan loyalties. In Assam, the social unit of tribes was *maharis,* "motherhoods." The Malay family was a *sa-mandei,* "motherhood." Among the Garos and Khasis, mothers headed the family groups and bequeathed all property in the female line; men could inherit nothing. Nearly everywhere, kinship bonds also passed only through the female line, as in the ancient system deliberately reversed by the Bible's "begats," which recognized only male ancestors. Seri Indian tribes called themselves Kunkak, "womanhood," or "motherhood."[8] The earliest religious works of art "are figures of the solitary Great Goddess—the Paleolithic image of Mother, before there was any Father either on earth or in heaven."[9] The idea of fatherhood was alien to the religious or social thinking of the earliest civilizations.[10]

> *"Home and mother" are written over every phase of neolithic agriculture. . . . It was the woman who wielded the digging stick and the hoe; she who tended the garden crops and accomplished those masterpieces of selection and cross-fertilization which turned raw wild species into the prolific and richly nutritious domestic varieties: it was woman who made the first containers, weaving baskets and coiling the first clay pots. . . . In form, the village, too, is her creation: for whatever else the village might be, it was a collective nest for the care and nurture of the young. Here she lengthened the period of child-care and playful irresponsibility, on which so much of man's higher development depends. House and village, eventually the town itself, are woman writ large. In Egyptian hieroglyphics, "house" or "town" may stand as symbols for "mother," as if to confirm the similarity of the individual and the collective nurturing function. In line with this, the more primitive structures—houses, rooms, tombs—are usually round ones: like the original bowl described in Greek myth, which was modeled on Aphrodite's breast.*[11]

Ancient civilizations show ample evidence of the matriarchal matrix in which they grew. Egyptians traced their descent through mothers, calling themselves "X, born of the Lady Y," omitting their father's name.[12] On Egyptian funerary stelae, the mother's name was given but the father's was omitted.[13] Diodorus said Egyptian queens received more respect than kings.[14] In the Ramesseum, the queen mother was addressed as "mighty mistress of the world."[15] Pharaohs ruled by matrilineal succession, and styled themselves "Rulers from the Womb."[16] The name of the Goddess was always a component part of royal names in the earliest dynasties. A pharaoh's title was originally *per aa,* Great Gate or Great House, symbol of the cosmic womb. Rulers of the Egyptians' Nubian neighbors had an even more mother-centered title: Mater.[17]

Egyptian men were awed by maternal behavior patterns, wondering why women did what they did to maintain the race. Maxims written about 1500 B.C. said:

> *Thou shalt never forget thy mother and what she has done for thee. . . . For she carried thee long beneath her heart as a heavy burden, and after thy months were accomplished she bore thee. Three long years she carried thee upon her shoulder and gave thee her breast to thy mouth, and as thy size increased her heart never once allowed her to say, "Why should I do this?"*[18]

Egyptian scriptures emphasized the honor due "thy mother, who bore thee with much suffering. She placed thee in the Chamber of Instruction that thou mightest acquire instruction in books. She was unremitting in her care for thee, and had loaves and beer for thee in her house. When thou art grown . . . cast thine eyes upon her that gave thee birth and provided all good things for thee, thy mother. Let her never reproach thee."[19]

An Ethiopian woman expressed to Frobenius the basic psychological attitude of primitive mothers:

> *How can a man know what a woman's life is? . . . The man spends a night by a woman and goes away. His life and body are always the same. The woman conceives. As a mother she is another person from the woman without child. She carries the fruit of the night nine months long in her body. Something grows. Something grows into her life that never again departs from it. She is a mother. She is and remains a mother even though her child die, though all her children die. For at one time she carried the child under her heart. And it does not go out of her heart ever again. Not even when it is dead. All this the man does not know; he knows nothing. He does not know the difference before love and after love, before motherhood and after motherhood. He can know nothing. Only a woman can know that and speak of that. That is why we won't be told what to do by our husbands.*[20]

In Old Iranian, the head of a clan or family was the *hana,* "grandmother." Among the Medes, genealogies were based on the female line. In Babylon, the ideogram for "mother" combined the elements of "house" and "deity," like the Hindu *grhadevata* or "house-goddess." The female sex received precedence in all forms of address. The descending order of beings began with "Goddess and gods, women and men."[21] By Babylonian law, "any sin against the mother, any repudiation against the mother was punished by banishment from the community." The Lycians too kept track of female ancestors only. Heraclides Ponticus said of them, "From of old they have been ruled by the women."[22] Phoenicians wrote of recent past when people didn't know their fathers, but took the names of their mothers.[23]

Etruscan tomb inscriptions also disregarded fathers. When married couples were buried together, only the wife's name was written. Late Roman texts reversed this usage, writing the name of the husband and omitting that of the wife.[24] But before the founding of Rome, Italy was governed by the Sabine matriarchate, when not even kings knew their fathers. Romulus, Ancus Marcus, and Servius Tullius had only mothers. Indeed, fatherhood was not always noticed even in the classical period; Roman plebeians didn't know their fathers. When the myth of Romulus and his men was written down, it was said Romulus made his followers marry Sabine women, because, as men, they lacked *sanguis ac genus,* the blood of the race.[25] This could come only from the female owners of the land.

Patriarchal writers claimed that Romulus named each of the early Roman *curiae* (clans) after one of the Sabine women.[26] The story was invented to disguise the fact that these *curiae* were "motherhoods," bearing the names of maternal ancestresses.[27] The mother of all clans was Juno Curitis, the Queen of Heaven whom the Romans adopted and presented with a new spouse, Jupiter.[28]

Among barbarian tribes of northern Europe, women were property owners, clan heads, and religious leaders. Roman writers called the northern nations "lands of women" governed by *kvaens* (queens).[29] Prehistoric Irish queens were mentioned in old writings, but their spouses were left nameless. The Lombards claimed their ancestors descended from a primal virgin mother, Gambara, who had no spouse. Mothers, not fathers, gave their names to children in pagan Britain and Scandinavia. Old German documents designate persons by their mothers' names only.[30]

It was the same in the Far East. Chinese family names are always formed from a sign meaning "woman." The custom is said to date from a past time when people knew their mothers but not their fathers.[31] The Man-Tseu of southern China had a system of hereditary queenship passing through a sacred female clan.[32] Chinese writings call Tibet "the land of women" and Japan "the land of queens." Japanese imperial families traced their descent from the supreme sun goddess, Omikami Amaterasu, mother of the world. Japanese legendary "chiefs" of ancestral tribes were usually women.[33]

The Chinese said the first man to understand fatherhood and institute monogamous marriage was Fu-Hi—who, however, had no father but only a mother.[34] The same first discoverer of paternity in

Greek myth was Cecrops, a high priest of Athene and one of her serpent-consorts.[35] Athene however was a name of the Aegean Great Goddess and Universal Mother, who ruled alone and supreme during the Bronze Age.[36] In the whole Aegean area, religious rites were in the hands of priestesses, regarded as emanations or embodiments of the Goddess, who was simply woman deified, as the later God was man deified. Men didn't participate in public worship until a fairly late date, then only as priestesses' helpers, as the male deity was subordinate to the female.[37]

In Europe also, the Great Goddess was thought the sole omnipotent deity. Fatherhood was not incorporated into religious thinking, because in clan life it was a very frail bond, even if recognized.[38] Scholars know that "in the beginning the Goddess everywhere antedated, or at least was predominant over, the God. It has been affirmed that in all countries from the Euphrates to the Adriatic, the Chief Divinity was at first in woman form."[39]

> *Recent researches into the history of the family render it in the highest degree improbable that the physical kinship between the god and his [sic] worshippers, of which traces are found all over the Semitic area, was originally conceived as fatherhood. It was the mother's, not the father's blood which formed the original bond of kinship among the Semites as among other early people and in this stage of society, if the tribal deity was thought of as the parent of the stock, a goddess, not a god, would necessarily have been the object of worship.*[40]

Modern male scholars often tried to conceal or deny the evidence of the ancient matriarchate. Whenever possible, some automatically converted references to the Great Mother into the word "God," as was done in translating the Bible. Even so responsible a scholar as Cumont, translating Apuleius's description of the Syrian Goddess as *omnipotens et omniparens,* "all-powerful and all-producing," glossed the description as a "conception of the absolute, unlimited authority of God [sic] over the earth."[41]

Frankfort said the Goddess was supreme in Mesopotamia "because the source of all life is seen in the female." Saggs said she was "the central figure in Neolithic religion."[42] In Egypt, she was "the Being eternal and infinite, the creative and ruling power of heaven, earth, and the underworld, and of every creature and thing in them. . . . Mother-goddess, lady of heaven, queen of the gods . . . who raised up Tem in primeval time, who existed when nothing else had being, and who created that which exists . . . the greatest power on earth, who commandest all that is in the universe, and who preservest all the gods . . . the God-mother, giver of life. . . . All that has been, that is, and that will be."[43]

Besides creating the world and everything in it, the Goddess created the civilized arts: agriculture, building, weaving, potting, writing, poetry, music, the graphic arts, calendars, and mathematics. These seem to have developed mostly in the hands of women as outgrowths of the maternal nest-building, communication, and play behavior. "Woman was the creator of the primordial elements of civilization. . . . [A]ll the richer perceptions and interpretations that color the actualities of life, all art, all poetic sentiment, are irradiations of those extra-individualistic, racial interests which are represented by the reproductive instincts, and are the dominant interests of the female. They have their source in the race-regarding feminine impulses."[44]

Hindu scriptures say the Goddess invented alphabets, pictographs, mandalas and other magical signs, hence her title of Samjna (sign, name, image). The Brahmavaivarta Purana says under another of her titles, Savitri, the Goddess gave birth to the Vedas, the rhythms of the Ragas, day and night, the year, the month, the seasons, the inch, the second, and all other units of measurement; also logic, grammar, the days of the week, Time, Death, Nourishment, Memory, Victory, religious rituals, the trinity of aeons, and all the gods.[45]

As Great Mother Kali Ma, she wore on her necklace of skulls the sacred Sanskrit letters, which she invented, and invested with such magic power that she could create things simply by pronouncing their names in this language.[46] The notion led to the Neoplatonic, and later Christian, concept of the Creative Word or **Logos**.

Sanskrit *matra,* like the Greek *meter,* meant both "mother" and "measurement." Mathematics is, by derivation, "mother-wisdom." Root words for motherhood produced many words for calculation: metric, mensuration, mete, mens, mark, mentality; geo-metry, tri-gono-metry, hydro-metry, etc. Women did temporal and spatial calculations for so long that, according to the Vayu Purana, men once thought women were able to give birth because they had superior skill in measuring and figuring. Men imagined that if they could master these feminine skills, they could give birth, too. "Male ancestors" told one another that if they could only learn to measure the earth, they would "happily create progeny."[47]

In the Middle East also, numbers and letters were inventions of the Goddess and the special concern of her priestesses. Ashurbanipal proudly declared that he was the first Babylonian king to learn "the noble art of tablet-writing," which belonged to the special scribes called *maryanu.*[48] A similar Egyptian word for a scribe was Maryen or Mahir, "great one" or "mother."[49] No one was permitted to enter the Holy of Holies in Babylon's municipal temple except women who had given birth; thus it seems likely that the *maryanu* were originally mothers, dedicated to the Semitic Goddess Mari-Anna, otherwise known as **Ishtar**.[50] Among the Hittites, priestesses known as Elderly Women taught the art of writing, kept records, advised kings, and practiced medicine.[51] The Triple Goddess of Fate was incarnate in three Gulses or "writers," corresponding to the Germanic Fates called *Die Schreiberinnen,* the Writing-Women, and the Roman mother of destiny Fata Scribunda, "the Fate who writes."[52]

In pre-Hellenic Greece the alphabet was attributed to the original three Muses, who were identical with the Fates or Graeae, eponymous mothers of Greek tribes. The Latin alphabet was created by the archaic Goddess Carmenta, mother of *carmens* or "charms." Or, according to Isidore of Seville, the alphabet was created by the Moon-goddess Io under her Egyptian name of Isis.[53]

Egyptians revered the Goddess as measurer of time, mistress of the house of books, mistress of the house of architects.[54] As foundress of the science of architecture she was named Seshat, "Lady of the Builder's Measure." She built "the abode of a king in the next world," a pyramid. She also created the Golden Calf, Horus, familiar in the Bible as the idol worshipped by Aaron and the Israelites.[55]

Ancient beliefs linking motherhood with superior intelligence, reasoning power, and magical knowledge made it hard for men to oppose the matriarchate, even when they discovered paternity and personified it in gods. Fathers' claim to children's respect seemed relatively trivial by comparison with the mothers' gestation, birth-giving, nursing, supporting, and daily teaching. The Book of Maccabees said a mother's sympathy with her children is deeper than a father's.[56] The *Mahanirvanatantra* said, "Mother is superior to father on account of her bearing and also nourishing the child."[57] Menander wrote, "A mother loves her child more than a father does."[58] Therefore the child is more hers than his; as the old Irish proverb put it, "To every cow belongs her calf."[59] The Laws of Manu stated that "A spiritual teacher exceeds a worldly teacher ten times, a father exceeds a spiritual teacher one hundred times, but a mother exceeds one thousand times a father's claim to honor on the part of a child and as its educator."[60]

There may have been a real biological advantage underlying ancient views of the female's superior intelligence. As mothers or potential mothers, female mammals have more need of naturally responsive alertness than males. "Girls' more mature skills enable them to attend to stimuli, especially from other people, more swiftly and accurately than boys. Girls are better at analyzing and anticipating environmental demands; in addition, they have greater verbal facility. . . . The perceptual, cognitive, and verbal skills which for unknown reasons are more characteristic of girls enable them to analyze and anticipate adult demands."[61] As a modern woman said, "After the birth of children—that enormous thing you do—everything else seems kind of a breeze. But so many of us lock the doors of the mind. We never bother to penetrate below the surface of that bottomless sea of resources that may be nature's gift to women."[62]

For a long time men feared to oppose women because they were convinced women were more closely allied with the forces of nature. West African tribesmen testified that "women were more powerful than men, for to them alone the mysteries of the gods and of secret things were known." Women founded the magical Egbo society, but after men learned the secret rites, they kept women from participating any more. In Queensland also, once men learned magic, they forbade women to practice, on the ground that women had too much natural aptitude for it.[63]

In northern Europe, the Vanir or Elder Gods, led by Mother Earth and the Goddess Freya, were overthrown by new patriarchal deities from Asia, the Aesir led by Father Odin. In the Aegean, followers of Father Zeus fought the pre-Hellenic worshippers of Mother Rhea or Hera. In Babylon, worshippers of Marduk rebelled against the primal mother Tiamat, whose own son killed her to take over her world-creating function. In Mexico, the legendary leader of the Aztecs overthrew his sister Malinalxochitl, former ruler of men and beasts, afterward described as "a bad witch."[64]

In Australia, the Goddess named Marm (Mother) was diabolized by men who resented the advantages she bestowed on women. She made women in her own image, and gave them "magic fruit" (offspring) that she denied to men.[65] In Malekula, men frankly admitted that their religious rites were stolen from the women, who invented them but ceased to practice them.[66] Tierra del Fuegan men said women used to rule the world by witchcraft, and all religious mysteries belonged to their Goddess, the moon.[67] Men adopted the cult of the sun god, and under his leadership they murdered all the adult women of the tribe, leaving only immature girls not yet initiated.[68]

A transparently mendacious Iatmul legend said women invented sacred objects and secrets of magic, then "gave" these things to men, and "asked" the men to murder them so no woman would have the secrets any more.[69] Many similar examples show that the defeat of the matriarchate was mythologized as a violent attack of men upon women. Such myths of leadership forcibly wrested from women occur throughout the world and cannot be overlooked.[70] As Engels noted, "The overthrow of mother-right was the world-historical downfall of the female sex."[71]

In some ways, it may have meant the downfall of all humanity from a basically peaceful social order to a hierarchical structure established and maintained by aggression. Patriarchal societies insisted on pecking orders; matriarchal ones tended to be more egalitarian.[72] Neolithic village cultures with their matriarchal family-based governments were cooperative, unwarlike, and nonviolent. Their lack of destructiveness has been attributed to the life-loving spirit of affirmation that scholars find at the core of most matriarchal societies.[73]

The same spirit of affirmation has been found in matriarchal or semi-matriarchal societies of the recent past. American Indians who worshipped the female principle, and were ruled by tribal chiefs elected by the real leaders, called Female Governesses, surprised Christian missionaries with behavior more "Christian" than that of white men. A missionary said, "What is extremely surprising in men whose external appearance is wholly barbarous, is to see them treat one another with a gentleness and consideration which one does not find among common people in the most civilized countries." Indian women were known as the Life of the Nation, and Mistresses of the Soil.[74] In answer to a white questioner who couldn't understand the Indian reverence for women, one Indian man said, "Of course the men follow the wishes of the women; they are our mothers."[75]

Even aggressive savages like the Dobu Islanders regarded motherhood as the only possible antidote to warfare. Mutual trust was maintained exclusively among members of a matrilineal kinship group known as "mother's milk."[76] Societies where women set the standards of behavior and morality were found generally kinder than male-dominated societies. Children grew up without harsh punishments, expecting kindness from others as a matter of course and consequently developing into nonhostile, nonviolent adults. Envy, greed, and exploitiveness were minimal; depression almost unknown; crime almost unheard-of. People were generally good-humored, trustful, and confident. Women were treated as the equals of men. Attitudes toward sexuality tended to be positive and permissive. People seemed to feel sure Mother Nature would provide for their needs, even in cases where a harsh environment demanded hard work for the sake of survival.[77]

Societies dominated by men tended to introduce cruel punishments, hostility toward the young, formalized rivalry, and sadistic elements replacing easy, affectionate sexuality. Some of this may have been biologically based. Among animals, females care for the young, males fight for mates, and care only for themselves. The primitive human female "nourished, reared and protected the more feeble than herself, while her mate, a terrible savage, knew only how to pursue and kill."[78]

> *When new-born humanity was learning to stand upright, it depended much on its mother and stood close to her protecting side. Then women were goddesses, they conducted divine worship, women's voice was heard in council, she was loved and revered and genealogies were reckoned through her. What broke into this feminine Elysium and robbed it of liberty and happiness? The male of the species. As the race grew older, rationality flourished at the expense of moral sense. . . . Man, unmindful of the mother's contributions to racial uplift and welfare, thought only of bending every energy and forcing tribute from everything and every one who could elevate himself and give him dominating power. . . . There's no more reason for not killing humans who oppose you than for sparing the lives of mosquitoes, in the mind of a man whose self-seeking emotions are permitted to run rampant. And the average "normal" male's personality balance tends definitely in the same direction.*[79]

Bachofen said, "The idea of motherhood produces a sense of universal fraternity among all men, which dies with the development of paternity." Ancient societies believed that those related by mother-blood shared a common soul, so no member of the group could hurt another without doing injury to himself. Egyptians and other folk carefully distinguished between children of the same mother and children of the same father; the former were the "real" siblings, constrained to care for each other as for their own selves. As Telemachus remarked, a person must be told who his father is; the mother is the parent every child knows "of himself."[80]

Psychologists agree that the images of Mother and Father affect the psyche in different ways. Feelings of connectedness are more closely associated with the mother; feelings of dissociation or alienation with the father. In spiritual terms, outer and inner worlds of nature and the self were not separated under a matriarchal order, whereas patriarchy insisted on their absolute severance.[81]

Past societies dreaded even a temporary loss of the mother image. Apuleius spoke of the period when the Goddess departed from the world for her season of self-renewal: "There has been no pleasure, no joy, no merriment anywhere, but all things lie in rude unkempt neglect; wedlock and true friendship and parents' love for their children have vanished from the earth; there is one vast disorder, one hateful loathing and foul disregard of all the bonds of love."[82] When the Goddess permanently disappeared from theological imagery, the sense of alienation became universal:

> *The earlier, neolithic order was of the female above the male, the cosmic mother above the father . . . with the progressive devaluation of the mother-goddess in favor of the father, which everywhere accompanied the maturation of the dynastic state and patriarchy. . . . A sense of essential separation from the supreme value symbol became in time the characteristic religious sentiment of the entire Near East.*[83]

G. R. Taylor's classification of "matrist" and "patrist" societies showed guilt, negativism, and fear in the latter, as opposed to a more confident outlook in the former. Matrist societies were typified by: (1) permissive attitude toward sex; (2) freedom for women; (3) high feminine status; (4) welfare more valued than chastity; (5) democratic political principles; (6) progressive views; (7) spontaneity, exhibition; (8) sex differences minimized; (9) hedonism, pleasure welcomed; (10) mother worship. Patrist societies displayed opposite tendencies: (1) restrictive attitude toward sex; (2) restriction of women; (3) women seen as inferior, sinful; (4) chastity more valued than welfare; (5) authoritarian politics; (6) conservative, against innovation; (7) inhibition, fear of spontaneity; (8) sex differences maximized, e.g. in dress; (9) fear of pleasure, ascetic self-denial; (10) father worship.[84]

Worshippers of the Great Mother celebrated rites of "love," including sexual love, which was often taken as a symbol for all loves, expressed in gestures and acts similar to those of mother-child behavior: cuddling, breast-sucking, and so on. Conversely, votaries of the Father were ordered to "fear" him (Deuteronomy 6:13). St. Paul declared that those who had no fear of God were automatically sinners (Romans 3:18). Christianity gave its followers much to fear, including one of the most sadistic hells ever devised by the human imagination, and an implacable God who consigned "most" human beings to that hell forever, according to his theologians (see **Hell**). But the primitive Mother gave comfort and reassurance. Eskimo shamans still call her the soul of the universe, never seen, but her voice can be heard: "a gentle voice, like a woman, a voice so fine and gentle that even children cannot become afraid. What it says is 'Be not afraid of the universe.' "[85]

Montagu says the mother image is still used to alleviate terror. "When the male's defenses are down, when he is *in extremis,* when he is dying, his last, like his first word, is likely to be 'mother,' in a resurgence of his feeling for the mother he has never repudiated, but from whom he had been forced, at the overt level, to disengage himself."[86] Eugene O'Neill expressed the secret longing in a dramatic speech:

> *The mistake began when God was created in a male image. . . . That makes life so perverted, and death so unnatural. We should have imagined life as created in the birth-pain of God the Mother. Then we would understand why we, Her children, have inherited pain, for we would know that our life's rhythm beats from Her great heart, torn with the agony of love and birth. And we would feel that death meant reunion with Her, a passing back into her substance, blood of Her blood again, peace of Her peace! Now wouldn't that be more logical and satisfying than having God a male whose chest thunders with egotism and is too hard for tired heads and thoroughly comfortless?*[87]

The Kagaba Indians expressed the same sentiments in a less sophisticated but equally forceful song describing their Goddess:

> *The Mother of Songs, the mother of our whole seed, bore us in the beginning. She is the mother of all races of men and the mother of all tribes. She is the mother of thunder, the mother of the rivers, the mother of trees and of all kinds of things. She is the mother of songs and dances. She is the mother of the older brother stones. She is the mother of the grain and the mother of all things. . . . She is the mother of the dance paraphernalia and of all temples, and the only mother we have. She is the mother of the animals, the only one, and the mother of the Milky Way. It was the mother herself who began to baptize. She gave us the limestone coca dish. She is the mother of the rain, the only one we have. She alone is the mother of things, she alone. And the mother has left a memory in all the temples. With her sons, the saviors, she left songs and dances as a reminder.*[88]

Psychologists often regard the universal myth of the Golden Age as a symbol of childhood. Yet when Plato wrote of the Golden Age, he apparently took some details from matriarchal societies familiar to the Greeks as either contemporary or belonging to the recent past. He said there was "no wildness nor eating of each other, nor any war, nor revolt amongst them. . . . There were no governments nor separate possessions of women and children. For all men rose again from the earth remembering nothing of their past. And such things as private property and families did not exist."[89] This was regarded as a figment of Plato's imagination until research discovered the pre-urban community of the Neolithic cultivator:

> *There was no ruling class to exploit the villagers, no compulsion to work for a surplus the local community was not allowed to consume, no taste for idle luxury, no jealous claim to private property, no exorbitant desire for power, no institutional war. Though scholars have long contemptuously dismissed the "myth of the Golden Age," it is their scholarship, rather than the myth, that must now be questioned.*
>
> *Such a society had indeed come into existence at the end of the last Ice Age, if not before, when the long process of domestication had come to a head in the establishment of small, stable communities with an abundant and varied food supply: communities whose capacity to produce a surplus of storable grain gave security and adequate nurture to the young. The rise in vitality was enhanced by vivid biological insight.*[90]

At Catal Huyuk, in what is now southern Turkey, a matriarchal community of the 7th millenium B.C., there was no evidence of chieftainship or rivalry, though there were many priestesses. Children were buried in the tombs of their mothers. Art and handicrafts flourished, producing obsidian mirrors, copper and lead jewelry and tools, woollen textiles, artistically carved wooden vessels. For 1500 years—seven times as long as the existence of the United States of America—the community seemed free of massacre or war. Though many hundreds of skeletons have been found, none showed any sign of violent death.[91]

Matriarchal Sumeria dominated the Fertile Crescent for 3000 years with virtually no evidence of warfare.[92] Neolithic foundations of such peaceful societies have been unearthed at Hassuna, Tell Halaf, Samarra, and Ubaid—where there were no gods. Holy icons showed only naked women holding or nursing infants.[93] Patriarchal religions gradually ousted the ancient matriarchies, chiefly by violence; but some scholars have suggested that this revolution was neither satisfactory nor final. The Great Mother, ostensibly overthrown by her sons, is an ineradicable archetype dwelling somewhere in the psyche of every human being born of woman—which means, of course, every human being. The more emphatically she is denied, the more threatening her images appear.[94] Ancient myths were not merely allegorizing when they spoke of the furious wrath of a neglected deity.

Even scholars refrain from noticing the everyday words for ancestry that clearly indicated matrilineal descent: "forebears," for example, a short form of "fore-bearers." Ancestry is called *extraction,* and obvious reference to what one came out of; similarly *descent* is the "descending" from the womb. From the beginning, it was maternal spirit that fostered cooperation and togetherness in work or worship.

> *The maternal totemic clan was by far the most successful form that human association has assumed—it may indeed be said that it has been the only successful one. . . . Political organizations, religious theocracies, States, nations, have endeavored in vain to achieve real and complete social solidarity. They are artificial structures; social humanity has never succeeded in adequately replacing the primitive bond to which it owes its existence.*[95]

Medieval ballads depict a pagan world where mothers were the ultimate authority in every household. Sons appealed to mothers, not fathers, in times of crisis, as the ballad-hero Johnie Cock asked the help of his mother, and through her, of the Goddess. Christianity however was devoted to destruction of the Goddess and her temples (Acts 19:27). Clement of Alexandria quoted Christ: "I have come to destroy the works of the female."[96] Christ ordered his followers to renounce their families (Luke 14:26) and said to his own mother, "Woman, what have I to do with thee?" (John 2:4). Fathers of the church wrote diatribes against motherhood.[97] Western religion consequently became an exercise in male-dominated power-seeking.[98]

Many male scholars still try to pretend there never was a Goddess, or if there was, she was only a "cult" figure vaguely associated with sexual promiscuity and/or "fertility." It is not recognized that religious feeling for the Mother was, if anything, much deeper and more passionate than feelings for a divine patriarch. Deities of both sexes are styled "gods." Egyptian sacred art showing divine persons with obvious dangling breasts, is described as a picture of "gods."[99] Scholars carefully avoid quoting ancient texts that say the Primordial Being was a Creatress, not a Creator. Though she was the central unifying concept of ancient civilizations, the Great Mother isn't mentioned in ancient-history texts. Scholars' violent denial of the evidence for the prehistoric matriarchate causes one to suspect that their prejudices often blind their eyes, as if a patriarchal culture prevents its members from comprehending any foreign viewpoint.[100]

Freud's ignorance of feminine values left him incapable of understanding humanity's most basic bonds. He gave sexuality a primary significance that probably should have been relegated to the mother-child bond instead. Freud admitted that thirty years of practice never taught him what women really want—because, of course, he had already convinced himself that what every woman wanted was a penis.[101] He even went so far as to imagine that a mother loved her child only because it was, for her, a penis-substitute.

> *The reason for Freud's failure of insight here should by now be plain: in his analysis of the development of the self, he left out of account the*

positive influence of the other member of the family, the mother. Overemphasizing, if anything, the rule of the father, the Jovean, power-seeking, repressive, organizing element in the personality, he played down the function of the mother, with her life-bestowing gifts, her relaxing and yielding attitudes, her life-transmitting and life-nurturing functions: the mother's sympathy and responsiveness, her giving of the breast to her infant, her special effort to establish an I-and-thou intimacy through language, her endless ways of expressing love.[102]

Freudian phallocentrism added to Christian devaluation of the female tended to perpetuate the common pattern of troubled families, as described by a social worker: "There's always a husband who's witholding his emotional support and a wife who's unhappy, whose feeling of personal worth has been damaged."[103] Mumford points out that devaluation of motherhood leaves children of both sexes cut off from a vital experience, the essential basis of all future commitments to cooperative functioning in the social context. "In repressing the mothering and nurturing impulses, in the personality, the scientist has also lost the normal parental concern for the future life it cherishes. One hardly knows whether to characterize this attitude as innocence or fatalism; it certainly indicates a failure to reach maturity."[104]

Gilder theorizes that few men can attain psychological maturity at all without a vital connection with the sense of futurity through intimate association with a woman. She has, "as part of her very sexuality, a sense of the future: a sense of evolution and growth, a notion of deferring pleasures for future gains, a sense of the phases and seasons of life, a devotion to the value of the individual human being. These sentiments are the very source of human morality."[105] Indeed these are precisely the sentiments embodied in matriarchal religions' cyclic, future-oriented view of life. Such religions were free of the neurotic quest for indefinable "meaning" in life, since they never assumed that life would be required to justify itself. They were also generally free of the anxiety, guilt, and sense of sin imposed by patriarchal religions, evolved by males made insecure from earliest childhood by a social order based on male intimidation and dominance.

Might-is-right morality was typical of the linear, hierarchical masculine theology. Feminine morality seems to have been both more subtle and more affirmative, fostering the same spirit of close cooperation that enabled humanity to become civilized in the first place.

Despite the basic male need to take part in feminine values, the patriarchal society seems to be organized the other way: women are forced to attain a sense of personal worth by taking part in masculine values. Instead of aspiring happily to the worthy estate of motherhood, many women are taught to think it unworthy while they are still in the "bosom" of the patriarchal family:

The upwardly mobile career of every go-getting woman seems to have been her father's gift to her. As a sop to his male guilt, Daddy may have goaded daughter to achievements he willfully denied his wife; or as a sop to his male vanity, he may have engendered in her such hurtful feelings of female worthlessness that only the adoption of a male-style existence could appease. But always, it seems, daughter has been vicariously wounded by damage the maternal ego suffered at paternal hands. She may feel compassion for her mother's plight, or contempt that "Mama let Papa get away with it," or a mixture of both emotions, but she invariably grows up with an almost pathologic horror of "living out Mom's life all over again."[106]

Briffault and other scholars believed devaluation of the maternal role inflicted injury on males as well as females: "Men have much more of the 'patriarchal theory' to unlearn. Women have to learn that all racial ideals that are worth while are ultimately identical with their own elemental instincts, and are the outcome of them. . . . The compromises that govern the relations between the sexes are those that condition all true human values. . . . It is, as of old, the part of the Vestal Mothers to tend the Sacred Fires. Upon women falls the task not only of throwing off their economic dependence, but of rescuing from the like thraldom the deepest realities of which they were the first mothers."[107]

Even Buddha reached back to basic maternal imagery in his Discourse on Universal Love: "As a mother, even at the risk of her own life, protects and loves her child, her only child, so let a man cultivate love without measure toward the whole world, above, below, and around, unstinted, unmixed with any feeling of differing or opposing interests. . . . This state of mind is the best in the world."[108] But no man could achieve it without Motherhood as a model.

1. Briffault 1, 191. 2. Neumann, A.C.U., 11. 3. Frazer, G.B., 45–46, 138.
4. Briffault 2, 445–47. 5. Stone, 11. 6. Mead, 102. 7. Campbell, P.M., 315, 320–21.
8. Briffault 1, 275, 288, 300. 9. Neumann, G.M., 94. 10. Graves, G.M. 1, 11.
11. Lederer, 87. 12. Maspero, 3. 13. Budge, D.N., 20. 14. Hartley, 188.
15. Briffault 3, 42. 16. Erman, 83. 17. Budge, G.E. 1, 52, 93. 18. Hartley, 197.
19. Briffault 1, 374. 20. Jung & Kerenyi, 141–42. 21. Hartley, 201–3.
22. Stone, 43, 46. 23. *Larousse,* 83. 24. Briffault 1, 245, 426. 25.Dumézil, 68.
26. M. Harris, 80. 27. Briffault 1, 422, 427. 28. Dumézil, 296.
29. Thomson, 244. 30. Briffault 1, 414, 419. 31. de Riencourt, 170.
32. Briffault 3, 23. 33. *Larousse,* 403. 34. Briffault 1, 366. 35. Graves, G.M. 1, 97.
36. *Larousse,* 85. 37. Stone, 47. 38. Graves, G.M. 1, 11. 39. Avalon, 409.
40. Stone, 26. 41. Cumont, A.R.G.R., 64. 42. Stone, 15, 26.
43. Budge, G.E. 1, 93, 213–14, 459, 463; Maspero, 286–87; *Larousse,* 37.
44. Briffault 1, 432; 2, 442. 45. O'Flaherty, 65, 352, 49. 46. Graves, W.G., 250.
47. O'Flaherty, 48. 48. *Assyr. & Bab. Lit.,* 387. 49. Erman, 227–30.
50. Briffault 2, 515. 51. Stone, 131. 52. Gaster, 764. 53. Graves, W.G., 240, 248.
54. *Larousse,* 28. 55. Budge, G.E. 1, 426. 56. *Forgotten Books,* 194.
57. *Mahanirvanatantra,* 161. 58. Bachofen, 133. 59. Brewster, 280.
60. Hauswirth, 30. 61. Gornick & Moran, 226. 62. Gittelson, 26.
63. Briffault 2, 545, 551–52. 64. F. Huxley, 215. 65. Hallet, 183.
66. F. Huxley, 207. 67. de Riencourt, 20. 68. Neumann, G.M., 290.
69. Mead, 94. 70. Campbell, P.M., 318. 71. Beard, 113. 72. Daly, 94.
73. Fromm, 158. 74. Briffault 2, 497; 1, 316–17. 75. Hartley, 142.
76. Fromm, 174. 77. Fromm, 168. 78. Briffault 1, 432. 79. Beard, 40–41, 55–56.

80. Bachofen, 80, 133. 81. Campbell, Oc.M., 70. 82. Neumann, A.P., 31. 83. Mumford, 242–43. 84. Bullough, 13–14. 85. Campbell, M.T.L.B., 206. 86. Montagu, T., 273. 87. O'Neill, *Strange Interlude*. 88. Neumann, G.M., 85. 89. J.E. Harrison, 496. 90. Mumford, 242–43. 91. Fromm, 155. 92. Hays, 63. 93. *Encyc. Brit.*, "Babylonia and Assyria." 94. Campbell, Oc.M., 86, 153. 95. Briffault 2, 493–94. 96. Stone, 194. 97. Simons, 99. 98. Augstein, 200. 99. *Larousse*, 13, 36. 100. Daly, 94. 101. Lederer, 238. 102. Mumford, 341. 103. Gittelson, 87. 104. Mumford, 469, 347–48. 105. Gilder, 144–52. 106. Gittelson, 66. 107. Briffault 3, 519–20. 108. Ross, 123.

Mothering Sunday

English pagan Mother's Day honored up to the 18th century A.D. On the 4th Sunday of Lent, each person visited his or her mother with an offering of simnel-cake (Latin *simila*, "fine flour"), to receive her blessing. This was "going a-mothering." Herrick mentioned the custom in his canzonet to the nymph Dianeme, probably Diana of Nemi. The simnel was a manikin, Gingerbread Man, similitude, or Host: a god ceremonially eaten.[1]

1. Brewster, 144.

Mountain

Perhaps more than any other natural objects, mountains most often represented the Great Mother. In every land the mountains were identified with breasts, belly, or **mons veneris** of the Earth, as well as the paradise where gods live.

Chomo-Lung-Ma, "Goddess-Mother of the Universe," is the world's highest mountain, known in the west, typically, by the name of a man: Mount Everest. Nearby rises Annapurna, "Great Breast Full of Nourishment."[1] There is also Nanda Devi, "Blessed Goddess," mother of the river-goddess Ganga (Ganges). These mountains are some of the Primal Mothers called Himalaya, "Mountains of Heaven," which gave rise to the Germanic *Himmel*, "heaven."[2]

Northern Europeans called the home of the gods Himinbjorg, Heaven-Mountain.[3] The gods lived on the "lap" of the Great Mother. "This notion of a mountainous situation of the home of the gods is one shared by other Indo-European races such as the Greeks who settled their pantheon on Mount Olympus; it is surely behind the psalmist's 'I will lift up mine eyes unto the hills from whence cometh my help.'"[4]

Snow-covered, breast-shaped mountains were considered the source of "help" (or food) from the benevolent Goddess whose white milk was really water: glacier-fed streams whose waters were often white with suspended rock dust. The Mountain Mother was both a source of life-giving waters, and a Queen of Heaven. One of the oldest titles of the Hindu triple Goddess Parvati-Kali-Uma was Daughter of Heaven (Himalaya).[5] According to the Greeks, the Goddess formerly ruled not only Mount Olympus, home of the classic gods, but all mountains; hence her title Panorma, "Universal Mountain Mother."[6]

One of the archaic Goddesses was Niobe, "Snowy One," identified with Mount Sipylus, where a water-streaming crag still bears the carved image of a Hittite mother goddess.[7] Mountainous breasts rise in County Kerry, Ireland, as double peaks called the Paps of Anu—that is, the ancestral Goddess Anu, or Danu, mother of the Tuatha Dé Danann.[8] Samoyed shamans believe they must experience a vision of climbing a magic mountain, where they will meet the Lady of Waters. She is a naked Goddess who accepts the shaman by allowing him to feed at her breast, saying, "You are my child; that is why I let you suckle at my breast."[9]

Sumero-Babylonian texts spoke of the Mother-mountain where the sun god was daily born and nightly swallowed up. This was Mashu, "Twin Peaks," as high as the walls of heaven, dwelling in the western garden of paradise by the shores of Ocean.[10] The twin peaks were breasts nourishing heaven, and the mountain had another set of "paps" reaching downward to nourish the underworld, as if it were the two-faced Goddess of life and death. The way into the land of death was into the Mother-mountain's body, via the Road of the Chariot, or Road of No Return.[11]

There was a curious resemblance between Mashu of the Sumerians and Macchu Picchu of the Peruvian Incas, another twin-peaked holy mountain where the sun rose and set, tended by priestesses. There as in distant Sumeria, the common name of the Goddess was Mama.[12]

The Hindu pantheon was settled on Mount Meru, or Sumeru, the "Good Mountain" located in the north, pointing to an archaic connection between India and Sumeria.[13] The Chinese located their Mount of Paradise in the same general vicinity as Sumeria, in the west. It produced the usual four rivers and was surrounded by "red water" like the River of Blood that surrounded ancient Fairylands.[14] See **Menstrual Blood**.

Dravidian Referring to the cultures of the Dravidian language group in southern and central India, now ranging from highly civilized people to preliterate forest primitives. Dravidian languages were rooted in pre-Aryan Indus Valley civilization, the earliest known in India.

Iranians said the Lofty Mountain-Mother stood at the center of the earth. She was called High Haraiti. At her summit was the Navel of Waters, "for the fountain of all waters springs there, guarded by a majestic and beneficent Goddess." The Vedas say Yama, Lord of Death, sits in the midst of the celestial ocean in her highest heaven, on the Navel of Waters, where "matter first took form."[15] The Japanese combined him with the Mountain-Mother Fuji the Ancestress, and the magic mountain came to be called Fujiyama.[16]

A very old Dravidian form of the mountain-Mother was Hariti, who nursed five hundred supernatural beings at once.[17] The gods she supported on her lap recall archetypal images of the infant enthroned on the mother's body, which is simultaneously "earth" and "paradise." Myths hold many indications of the child-parent relationship between the god and his feminine support. One of the emblems of **Isis** was the *Mu'at,* "foundation of the throne," meaning hers was the lap the pharaoh and his divine *alter ego* sat on, on earth as well as in heaven.

The Persian sun god Ahura Mazda lived in a glowing palace on the summit of Mount Hara, a derivative of Hariti.[18] In Hebrew, *hara* meant both "mountain" and "pregnant belly."[19] In Latin the word described the official diviners called *haruspices,* those who gaze into the belly—that is, entrail-readers.[20]

The idea of the Mount of Paradise as the Goddess's belly or vulva led to the widespread belief that life-giving rivers of blood emanated from it, the "four rivers of paradise" common to Asiatic traditions, identified with real rivers by the Bible with lofty disregard for their geography (Genesis 2:10-14). One of these rivers was Gihon, the Hebrew name for the Nile, coming from "the whole land of Ethiopia." The name was a corruption of Gehenna or Ge-enna, the River of Ge (Gaea), or of Mother Earth. Or again, the Nile was supposed to emanate from the Mountain of the Moon (Ruwenzori) beyond Ethiopia.

This was one of the universal female-symbolic images in mythology: the lunar mountain, located in a garden of paradise, containing a great cave or labyrinth, producing the rivers of life. Its genital connotation could hardly be overlooked. Arabs called it Jebel Ka-Mar, the Mother-mountain. Even in medieval European romances it was the source of wisdom; Merlin learned his magic by drinking of its ambrosia. Anointed knights of Charlemagne, searching for the same source, traveled to a great cavern under a Mountain of the Moon at the headwaters of the Nile.[21]

Egyptians eventually transferred the mystic source of the Nile from the remote Mountains of the Moon to the handier first cataract at Elephantine (modern Jazirat Aswan). This was regarded as the earth's yoni, where the God mated with the Goddess, to produce the annual outpouring of the Nile. The genital metaphor of the mountain is still suggested by the word *mons,* meaning both a mountain and a female genital.[22]

Pyramids and ziggurats were artificial mountains built where the land was flat, to serve as thrones of the Lord, "high places" for his sacred marriage to the Goddess, earth-wombs for his regeneration, and shrines. Like the Celtic *tumulus,* a Buddhist reliquary mound or *stupa* was also an imitation of the holy mountain, often likened to the Mother's belly.[23] Similar tombs on a larger scale were the Mycenaean *tholos* tombs, covered with tons of earth to make artificial hills.[24]

Eastern lamas were interred in domes or pyramids plated with gold whenever possible, because imperishable gold was the metal of apotheosis and immortality, making the body imperishable also.[25] In the west, where gold was not plentiful, the magic mountain was said to be made of glass or crystal, in imitation of the seven crystalline spheres of heaven. The Celtic after-world centered on a glass castle, perhaps a misunderstanding of the old word *glas,* meaning "the blue of heaven."[26] But the crystal mountain was sometimes taken literally. At the Celtic burial mound of New Grange, the surface of the earth-womb was once covered by quartz fragments to make it sparkle in the sun like a mound of crystal.[27] The Slavs believed in a crystalline mountain of heaven, and used to bury bear's claws with the dead, to help them scramble up the slippery glass.[28]

The expression "in seventh heaven" came from the ancient belief that the seven celestial spheres were arranged like a seven-story mountain, as shown by the Babylonian ziggurat of seven stages.[29] Below ground, seven concentric "hells" or "pits" reflected the celestial realm in Sheol, its mirror image in the Abyss, ruled by the queen of the underworld, who had many names—Allatu, Eresh-kigal, Persephone, Hel, Hecate, Nephthys, or the earlier female Pluto—but always a dark *alter ego* of the celestial Goddess.[30]

The Babylonian netherworld was "divided into seven zones, like those of Dante's Inferno, upon the model of the seven planetary spheres. . . . Seven gates gave admission, each guarded by a porter. . . . This idea of the circles of the underworld is also found in the Egyptian mythology of the ritual of the dead." Like the biblical Joseph, Assyrian priests went down into the Pit as part of their death-rebirth initiations. There at the base of the celestial mountain in the land of the Black Sun, stood "the foundations of the earth, the meeting of the mighty waters."[31]

Initiations everywhere enacted a journey through the nether and celestial spheres, a symbolic ascent of the mountain. The Norse father-god Odin himself had to win his wisdom by traversing the "seven nether spheres" of death.[32] Apuleius described his own initiation into the Mysteries of Isis as a journey to the land of death, where he beheld the Black Sun, and saw the deities of the upper and lower worlds "face to face." Then he rose to the heights, and was exhibited to the congregation in the costume of the sun god. Mithraic initiates similarly rose through seven spheres, winning the ranks of Raven, Bridegroom, Warrior, Lion, Persian, Sun-runner, and Pater (high priest).[33]

Arabs perpetuated the basic Chaldean notion of the cosmos as a magic mountain with seven ascending spheres and seven underground ones; this in turn was based on the Hindu image of Purusha, the universe personified. "According to the common opinion of the Arabs, there are seven heavens, one above the other, and seven earths, one beneath another. . . . This is explained by a passage of the Koran in which it is said that God created seven heavens and as many earths or storeys of the earth."[34] Medieval Christians inherited the same idea, modeling their cosmos on that of ancient Chaldea. The church officially listed the heavens as aerial, ethereal, Olympian, the heaven of fire, the heaven of stars, the crystalline, and the Empyrean. In the seventh heaven "Christ dwells, and this is the especial and proper dwelling place of Christ and the angels and saints."[35]

Thus the magic mountain was taken over by Christianity, but at the same time the church vigorously condemned all the magic mountains where "witchcraft" carried on worship of the Goddess. Puy-de-Dôme in Auvergne was a famous witch-mountain; so was the Brocken or Blocksberg in the Hartz Mountains. Puy-de-Dôme had a temple served by women called *fatuae,* "fairies" or "fates," and *fatidicae,* "seeresses." Young girls were periodically initiated into the sect, under the novice-title of *bonnes filles.*[36]

A map made of the Brocken in 1751 noted that its summit was a witches' ground, where sabbats were celebrated before an altar by a magic spring, "formerly consecrated to some false deity of the pagans."[37] This may have been the mountain Pope Pius II called Mons Veneris, where one could meet witches and demons, "address them and learn the magic arts."[38]

The story of Tannhäuser's sojourn in the Mons Veneris or Mount of Venus (Venusberg) was another relic of fairy-religion, hinting at the existence of a real high priestess powerful enough to defy the pope, and serving the Goddess under the name of Queen Sybil. The Goddess "still resided in the megalithic temples of western Europe, which were old before the Greeks invaded Greece. Although her rites were officially forbidden, her worship was celebrated on magical mountains throughout Europe. She came to be confused with the classical goddess Venus, and her magic mountains were called Venusbergs in Germany, where the written versions of the Tannhäuser myth seem to have originated. Her worship was celebrated at several real mountains: Horselberg, Waldsee, Freiburg, and Wolkenstein, as well as at peaks in Italy and Scotland. . . . In all the Tannhäuser myths, the Queen Sybil is the Goddess Venus."[39]

Sybil was a Latinization of Cybele, the Great Mother of the Gods, whose worship actually continued in secret up to the 20th century on wild mountaintops in her native Anatolia. Her rites "contained primitive usages of the religion of Anatolia, some of which have survived to this day in spite of Christianity and Islam. Like the Kizil-Bash peasants of today, the ancient inhabitants of the peninsula met on the summits of mountains covered with woods no ax had desecrated, and celebrated their festal days."[40]

Throughout the Middle Ages, men believed the Goddess could

invite them into the interior of her magic mountain, as shown by many tales—Tannhäuser was not the only Venus-loving hero. The Danish ballad of *The Elfen Hill* speaks of a youth enchanted by an elf-maid's dancing, and invited by her to the interior of her hill.[41] There were even indications that the Mountain-goddess was still a trinity. According to the Thuringian Chronicle of 1398, she appeared at mid-day as three great flames in the air, "which presently ran together in one great globe of flame, parted again and finally sank into the Horselberg."[42]

The Mother-mountains continued to shelter pagan gods, who were thought to be not dead but sleeping in the terrestrial womb, awaiting rebirth like Hindu gods between their incarnations. Merlin, William Tell, Barbarossa, Frederick, and others slept in magic mountains. Many were assimilated to "the figure of Wotan, which survives in these legends of emperors and empires. It is Wotan who is awaiting to reappear in this world . . . a dark heathen god-image that has not been taken into account by the prevailing attitude of consciousness."[43]

1. Neumann, G.M., 152. 2. Lethaby, 125. 3. Eliade, M.E.R., 12. 4. Branston, 85. 5. Ross, 62. 6. Massa, 48. 7. Graves, G.M. 1, 260. 8. Graves, W.G., 409. 9. Eliade, S., 39. 10. Hooke, M.E.M., 47. 11. *Epic of Gilgamesh,* 27, 37, 98. 12. *Larousse,* 443. 13. O'Flaherty, 206. 14. Hallet, 245. 15. Lethaby, 74–75. 16. Campbell, P.M., 336. 17. *Larousse,* 359. 18. Stone, 77. 19. Fodor, 290. 20. Rose, 237. 21. Hallet, 115, 401. 22. Dumézil, 64. 23. Campbell, Or.M., 40. 24. de Camp, A.E., 81. 25. Waddell, 243, 271. 26. Joyce 2, 360. 27. Campbell, P.M., 430. 28. Baring-Gould, C.M.M.A., 539. 29. Budge, G.E. 1, 275. 30. Campbell, Or.M., 106. 31. Lethaby, 129, 162, 172. 32. Baring-Gould, C.M.M.A., 247. 33. Rose, 283, 288. 34. Lethaby, 24. 35. de Voragine, 291. 36. Pepper & Wilcock, 166. 37. de Givry, 74. 38. Wedeck, 160. 39. Goodrich, 155–57. 40. Cumont, A.R.G.R., 47. 41. Steenstrup, 62. 42. Baring-Gould, C.M.M.A., 211. 43. Jung & von Franz, 197.

Mourdad-Ameretat

Persian spirit of "Death-Rebirth" whose name was constructed of two sacred letters corresponding to the Jewish Mem-Aleph, or Amulet of **Ma**.[1] The original reference was to the Mother-Goddess Ma as ruler of reincarnations.

1. *Larousse,* 317.

Mudra

Tantric term for (1) "woman," one of the five boons bestowed on man by the Goddess Kali; (2) "kidney bean," a female-genital symbol associated with transmigration of souls (see **Beans**); (3) a mystical gesture, in temple dancers' hand-sign language.[1]

1. Campbell, Or.M., 359; Bharati, 41.

Mulkari

Australian primordial spirit who taught men to mutilate their genitals in imitation of female menstrual bleeding.[1] Probably a corruption of Ma-Kali (Mother Kali). See **Kali Ma.**

1. Montague, S.M.S., 241.

var. Mu-Kari

Mummy

From *mumiya,* preservative bitumen used to coat corpses; probably sacred to the Goddess of rebirth still called Mumi or Muzem-Mumi, Earth Mother, by the Votyaks.[1]

1. *Larousse,* 307.

Muses

Ninefold Goddess as the source of "in-spiration," literally breathing in "I-deas" or Goddess-spirits within. The Muses were originally a triad—the primordial Triple Goddess. First of them was Mnemosyne, "Memory," who made poets able to remember sacred sagas.[1]

The seven-tone musical scale was the Muses' invention, supposedly based on their "music" of the seven spheres. Scipio the Elder said the spheres "produce seven distinct tones; the septenary number is the nucleus of all that exists. And men, who know how to imitate this celestial harmony with the lyre, have traced their way back to the sublime realm."[2] Led by Thalia, who governed music in general, the classical Muses were Clio (history), Calliope (heroic poetry), Terpsichore (dance), Melpomene (tragedy), Erato (erotic poetry), Euterpe (flute accompaniments), Polyhymnia (sacred songs), and Urania, the Celestial Aphrodite of the plane of the fixed stars. The Alexandrian shrine of the Muses was the Museum, "the nearest thing to a modern university that the ancient world experienced."[3] It was destroyed by Christians, who detested pagan learning.

1. Graves, W.G., 377; G.M. 1, 66. 2. Seligmann, 245. 3. de Camp, A.E., 136.

Mut

"Mother," archaic name for the Egyptian Goddess as a trinity. The first of Mut's three heads was the Virgin Maat, wearing the plumes of Truth. The second was Hathor, Mother of the World, wearing the red-and-white crowns of the Two Lands. The third, painted black and wearing vulture feathers, was Nekhbet, the Crone of Death.[1] The Goddess's trinitarian name may have been a cognate of Kali's name

Mutteyalamma, one of her manifestations as a disease-causing Destroyer.

Mut mothered all the gods of Egypt. Though some myths said Isis was the oldest deity in the world, others claimed Isis was born along with Osiris from the womb of Mut. Her hieroglyphic sign was a design of three cauldrons, representing the Triple Womb.[2] See **Cauldron**; **Trinity**.

1. Budge, E.M., 121. 2. *Book of the Dead,* 205.

Mutspell

"Mother's Curse," the Norse idea of the fate that would overtake the world at doomsday, as a result of the Goddess's disgust at the actions of men and gods. As the Crone-mother Skadi, she would lay her doom on the world, and spirits from the hot southern lands of Mutspellheim would begin to destroy the earth, a mythic reminder of Kali the Destroyer in her original territory. See **Doomsday**.

Mylitta

"Birth-producer," a Carthaginian name for the Goddess who, Herodotus said, was Alitta in Arabia, Venus Mylitta in Assyria, and Mitra in Persia.[1] Carthage had a province named after her, Magasmelita, "Shrine of Mylitta." Like the fish-mother Atargatis or Tirgata, she personified the primal womb of the Abyss.[2] She espoused the sun god and "quenched the blazing lingam" in the waters of her womb, like all personifications of the female Deep.[3] The ancient city of Mdina on Malta used to bear her name.[4]

1. Herodotus, 54. 2. Baring-Gould, C.M.M.A., 497–98. 3. Rawson, E.A., 57. 4. Pepper & Wilcock, 78.

Myrrh

Appearing at two crucial points in Christian mythology, at Jesus's birth (Matthew 2:11) and again at his death (Mark 15:23), myrrh represented the mystic virgin mother who was also Mother Death, called Mary, or Miriam, or Mari, or Myrrha, or—as the Christians called the virgin Mary—"Myrrh of the Sea."[1]

The pagans' version of Mary was the temple-maiden Myrrha, who gave birth to Adonis, "the Lord," in the same cave at Bethlehem that Christians claimed as Jesus's birthplace.[2] Myrrh was used as aphrodisiac incense in Adonis's rites, and its thorny twigs probably formed the mock crown of the sacred king, still called the Crown of Thorns. Myrrh was an emblem of Mara, a common Oriental name for the spirit of death.[3]

Some scholars have offered a theory that myrrh was given Jesus on the cross to deaden his pain, because of a Jewish tradition that "the kindly women of Jerusalem" used to give myrrh to "those who were led out to execution."[4] The theory cannot be supported, since myrrh has no analgesic properties. The women of Jerusalem apparently had another, less kindly reason for giving myrrh to those executed; even early Christians remembered that myrrh meant the death and rebirth of a god and was identified with his holy mother.

In the lore of magic, myrrh was credited with power to cause menstruation: perhaps a relic of ancient legends of the castrated god's shedding of the "blood of life."[5]

1. Ashe, 48. 2. Doane, 155. 3. Frazer, G.B., 390; Campbell, Or.M., 219.
4. Keller, 376. 5. Pritchard, S.S., 47.

The Victory of Samothrace is probably better known today than her inspiration, the pre-Hellenic Goddess NIKE, was in her day. Her name means "victory" or "dominance," and this heroic statue, found on the island of Samothrace in the middle of the 19th century, forcefully demonstrates this characteristic. Marble, 98 inches high; 5th century B.C.

OSIRIS was the most ancient and durable of Egyptian gods, well established by 2000 B.C. and so strong an influence at the beginning of the Christian era that many of his characteristics were reflected in (some say assumed by) the new Messiah. Shown here with his wife-mother-goddess Isis and the vulture-headed Anubis, rulers of Egypt for centuries.

OEDIPUS, mythical King of Thebes, in addition to killing his father, marrying his mother, and gouging out his eyes, also broke the Goddess's image, the Sphinx, by throwing her off a cliff. J. A. Ingres captured him in a calmer moment, explaining the Enigma to the familiar incarnation.

Naamah

Christian name for a demon, derived from a title of Adonis, Naaman, "Darling."[1] As the "darling" of the Goddess Aphrodite, he also gave his name to the anemone, supposed to be the "flower" of his blood. See **Adonis.**

1. Frazer, G.B., 390.

Nagas

Vedic serpent-people, children of the Goddess Kadru. The Nagas guarded treasure in underwater palaces and kept books of mystic knowledge.[1] The real Nagas of southern India were tribes who retained matriarchal customs, practiced matrilineal inheritance, and laid no sexual or marital restrictions on women.[2] In return for their proper reverence for her, their Goddess was supposed to bestow long life on them.

1. Tatz & Kent, 79. 2. Graves, G.M. 1, 13.

Nakedness

Tantric sages said one should participate in religious rites "sky clad" (*digambara*) or naked, because in the eyes of the Goddess all distinctions of rank, caste, or class should be put off along with the clothing that expressed them.[1] The Goddess herself appeared naked, under the name of Nagna, "Nudity."[2] It was widely recognized that the magic of the Goddess dwelt more in the reality of her flesh than in her garments, since creation was a function of the female body, not of any external accouterments.[3] Moreover, it was her nakedness that exerted its mysterious power over the bodies of men. Images of the Naked Goddess even decorated churches until 11th and 12th centuries A.D., especially in the British Isles. Though many were destroyed, some of these images still survive.[4]

By contrast to this earlier emphasis on nakedness, the magic of men and their gods usually dwelt in their garments. Odin's sayings in the Havamal show that he gave men clothes by which they would put on "nobility"—i.e., power—for "the naked man is naught."[5] Patriarchal societies generally made much of uniforms, vestments, badges of rank, and other decorations by which men defined themselves.

Perhaps out of this same sense that nakedness enhanced the power of women and reduced that of men, Christians were usually opposed to nakedness even when it was practical, as among tropical peoples. Australian missionaries refused to give food to hungry natives until they put on clothes. A missionary in the Orinoco regretted that the natives had not really accepted Christianity, but he confessed himself "greatly consoled" at having taught native women such modesty that they would no longer remove their clothes even in bed.[6]

Early Christians condemned nakedness because it was characteristic of worship of the Goddess. The legend of St. Barnabas tells of the saint's miraculous destruction of the temple of Aphrodite at Paphos, were he saw "a multitude of men and women celebrating a feast, and running about naked. So wroth was he that he cursed the temple of these pagans, and instantly the temple fell in ruins, crushing a large number of pagans in its fall."[7]

A 4th-century Christian bishop named Priscillian seems to have participated in pagan rites. He gave himself to "abominable studies, and held nightly meetings with immodest women and had been accustomed to pray stark naked."[8]

Medieval books on sorcery taught that spirits can be raised by ceremonial nudity, but this kind of magic is a degradation which "the foolish dotage of women is subject to fall into."[9] Women continued to believe in the power of nakedness. Scottish maidens stripped themselves naked on the Eve of St. Andrew and recited a prayer "to learn what sort of husbands they shall have."[10] Pierre de Lancre wrote that "witches in their accursed assemblies are either entirely naked or *en chemise.*"[11] Up to the 17th century, ancient fertility rites dictated the grinding of grain for festival cakes in Ireland with "certain stones," by girls who had to be completely naked at the time.[12]

At the Bulgarian ceremony of the need-fire, "two young men 'whose names must not be spoken' marched in front of the flocks and herds which were to be driven through the flames, and afterwards stripped themselves naked and kindled the new fire in a wood." At a similar ceremony in Serbia, "a naked boy and girl lit the fire by rubbing rollers of wood together."[13] Even in the present century, Balkan peasants and gypsies performed ceremonies requiring them to go naked in moonlight.[14] Witches sometimes maintain the "sky-clad" tradition, as in the Middle Ages they were often accused of worshipping the "great Devil" in the form of a large star when they went out naked at night. Some medieval heretics called "shepherds" insisted on saying Mass while naked, on the theory that "this was the way our father Adam sacrificed." The Inquisition condemned them, on the ground that Adam didn't say Mass at all.[15]

St. Jerome established the church's policy on female nakedness by saying women should be so ashamed of their own bodies that they should "blush and feel overcome" at the sight of themselves. For this reason, no "virgin of full age" should bathe. If she was good-looking, a woman must try to spoil her appearance by "a deliberate squalor" so she wouldn't distract saintly men from their pure thoughts.[16] Among medieval nuns therefore, clothing was seldom changed, and dirtiness was thought next to godliness.

In the 15th century, the Adamites of Bohemia associated nakedness with humanity's pristine purity, quoting the Bible (Genesis 3:7) to prove that garments were worn only after the first sin was committed. They advocated nudity and free love to liberate the flesh from sinfulness. Their sect was exterminated in 1421.[17]

Nakedness often figured in secret initiations, as advised in a French mystical book: "The aspirant should become stark naked, should empty himself completely, should be stripped of all his faculties, renouncing all his own predilections, his own thoughts, his own will—in a word, his whole self."[18] Even here the "self" seemed to be closely identified with the clothes—which, as the world knows, "make the man."

1. Campbell, Or.M., 219. 2. Avalon, 111. 3. Campbell, P.M., 389. 4. Branston, 22. 5. Branston, 64. 6. Briffault 3, 298, 306. 7. de Voragine, 307. 8. Coulton, 24. 9. Agrippa, 128. 10. Hazlitt, 8. 11. Leland, 158. 12. Johnson, 103. 13. Gelling & Davidson, 179. 14. Leland, 134. 15. J. B. Russell, 181, 210. 16. Muller, 160. 17. J. B. Russell, 224. 18. Waite, O.S., 234.

Name

For the purposes of magic and religion, the name of anything was considered identical with the thing itself, a spiritual "handle" by which the thing or the supernatural being could be manipulated. Children and primitives seldom distinguish clearly between the reality and the name of an object.[1] The childlike mind of the Middle Ages couched the same thought in pseudo-rational terms: "The proper names of things are certain rays of things, everywhere present at all times, keeping the power of things, as the essence of the thing signified."[2] Like other Europeans, ancient Britons believed the name and the soul were the same.[4]

Words for "name" were virtually the same as words for "soul": Irish *ainm,* Old Welsh *anu,* Old Bulgarian *imen,* Sanskrit *naman,* Greek *onoma,* Latin *anima, nomen,* and *numen.* "Irish *ainm* is 'name' and *anim* is 'soul, anima.' In certain cases they are declined alike and therefore often confused by students."[3]

Each Egyptian's soul-name, the *ren,* was breathed by a mother on her child as it was first put to her breast; therefore the Goddess of soul-names was Renenet, who governed lactation. Without its *ren,* the child would have no identity and would not be allowed to eat. Even the gods needed mothers to give them names, otherwise they would pine away and die.[5] The same belief is found in India: the "thousand-eyed god" named Existence cried immediately after he was born, "Give me a name, for without a name I will not eat food."[6]

Name-giving was often connected with food-giving. The French still give a child a *nom de lait,* milk-name, obviously recalling the pre-Christian matriarchy where only mothers could give names.[7] Chinese children received a "rice-name" with the first rice; it was supposed to embody the soul and was kept secret.[8] According to the Bible, infants were named by their mothers, not their fathers.[9] Adam's naming of the animals, however, was a magical means of making Adam their father, after the manner of Shiva under his title of Prajapati, "Father of the Animals."

Transitions from matriarchy to patriarchy were marked by fathers' takeover of the name-giving function. Brahmans insisted that fathers, not mothers, breathed the essential soul-name into children; thus the soul of a Brahman was called Atman, "the Breath," from which came Greek *atmos* and German *atmen.* At each Brahman wedding, long lists of "begats" were recited to establish paternal ancestry. Imitators of this eastern custom contributed the lists of spurious "begats" in the Old Testament.[10]

Ancestor worship was instituted in matriarchal times, when tribal mothers became goddesses who gave their children names. When patriarchs became synonymous with gods, the system was copied for the other sex. Egyptian priests of **Ra** claimed their deity created all other gods by naming them: "It is Ra who made his own names into his members, and these became the gods who are in his following. . . . Ra created the Company of the Gods out of his own names."[11] This was intended to uphold the priests' contention that any god one cared to name was really Ra in disguise. But in a primeval time, Ra himself existed only as a name within the being of his Mother, Ma-Nu, the cosmic abyss.[12]

Egyptians remembered that the secret name embodying the soul was mother-given. So did the Phoenicians, Babylonians, Scythians, and Celtic and Germanic tribes who called themselves by mother's names, which encompassed the tribal soul.[13] "Ask a Lycian who he is," Herodotus wrote, "and he answers by giving his own name, that of his mother, and so on in the female line."[14]

Despite Brahmanism, most of India retained the ancient system of maternal name-giving. Distribution of family names was governed by the Goddess under her title of Samjna or Saranyu, "the Name," or "Sign."[15] Chinese family names similarly incorporated the Mother-sign, a custom known to date back to the matriarchal age, before people knew their fathers.[16] The Japanese didn't use patronymics until 1400 A.D. Previously, children took their mothers' names.[17] See **Motherhood**.

Hellenic Greeks dated their transition from mother-names to father-names back to a quarrel between the god Poseidon and the goddess Athene. She won, but he oppressed the people to enforce his demands. Athenian women were deprived of the vote, and men were forbidden to take their mother's names as they had done before.[18]

Even when calling themselves "patrician" (father-descended), Roman clans kept the feminine names originating in the pre-Roman matriarchate, where only mothers embodied clan spirit.[19] The fact that Roman women bore clan names like Julia, Claudia, Cornelia, Lucretia, etc., has been misunderstood as evidence of social oppression. Bullough said, "Until fairly late in Roman history women even lacked individual names in the proper sense of the term . . . ; mothers and daughters would have the same name."[20] He missed the point: women bore the clan name because they embodied the clan soul, passed in matrilineal succession from mother to daughter.

The wholly patriarchal Christian system maintained patronymics throughout. In nomenclature, women hardly existed at all. The only name a woman kept for herself was her baptismal name, sacrosanct because it was ratified by a male god. Christian baptism didn't mention surnames, because in the middle ages there were still common-law rules providing for maternal surnames. Christian women received the surnames of their fathers, but after marriage even these were given up, so the children inherited no name from the female line. Christian fathers like Brahman fathers gave children their names by speaking or sometimes writing them; hence the term "author of my being." Yet the matronymic survived in some places, such as Spain, even though church councils declared maternal surnames illegal.[21] Scandinavia remained pagan up to the 11th century and retained older systems of nomenclature. Scandinavian women didn't take their husbands' surnames until the 18th century.[22]

The great importance attached to names goes back to the earliest ages, and probably bears a profound psychological relationship to the human animal's unique ability to verbalize. Names were confused with souls almost everywhere. Egyptians said "To speak the name of the dead is to make them live again." Tomb inscriptions begged passers-by to speak the name of the entombed, to give "the breath of life to him who has vanished."[23] No greater harm could be done to an Egyptian than to erase the carving or writing of his name. To destroy the very letters meant destruction of the soul.[24]

Romans also wanted to preserve the name-soul after death. Roman epitaphs asked the passer-by to read the name aloud. Wealthy Romans often established endowments for a guild of friends and their successors to celebrate their names at a banquet, at stated intervals on the anniversary of death.[25] The Christian practice of writing names on tombstones developed from the Roman practice of re-creating the soul in speech.

Some said a major purpose of the epitaph was to induce deities to speak the name, which would insure immortality because any word spoken by a god became reality. The spoken name in a divine mouth would re-create the actual man. The pharaoh Sesostris I (1965–1934 B.C.) had his name inscribed on the benben-stone (obelisk), remarking that "A name that standeth thereupon is mentioned [by the gods] and perisheth not in eternity."[26] For the same reason, Babylonian kings prayed to the Goddess **Ishtar** to give life to their names.[27]

On the other hand, a man or god could be cursed if his secret, magical name was learned by an enemy and spoken in the wrong context. Isis spoke the secret soul-name of Ra to destroy him at the end of his daily cycle, making him an old man tottering feebly toward his death at sunset.[28] Knowledge of his name brought destruction to Rumpelstiltzkin in the fairy tale, which may have been a late version of the myth of Ra and Isis.

At times the Goddess invoked the power of her own name, or

several of her names, to release forces of creation or destruction. Isis brought Osiris back to life by invoking herself as Isis and Nephthys.[29] She fought the dragon of darkness and "obtained mastery over him in her name of Sekhet, she overpowered him in her name of Khut-nebat (Eye of Flame)."[30] Names of the Goddess of creation and destruction were incongruously applied to Yahweh under his pagan-inspired title El Schadaj—related to *schadajim,* "milk-giving breasts," and *schadaj,* "to destroy."[31]

Precedents older than civilization evolved the idea that forces of creation and destruction could be activated by pronouncing a divine name. The Mother of Gods controlled her offspring by knowledge of their secret names. Early priestly theory proposed that these secret names could be learned by human beings, who could then control the gods with them. Brahman priests claimed to control the gods' actions with mantras incorporating the divine names. Some of their lore was embodied in the Upanishads, which means "secret names."[32] The name of the Amida Buddha was so powerful that a priest could send himself or any other man to the Western Paradise immediately only by uttering it.[33]

Naturally, priesthoods kept the knowledge of these dread names to themselves, as it would never do to let ordinary folk use them for free. Hence the Jews' taboo on taking the name of the Lord in vain. Common people of the Semitic tribes didn't know their gods' real names; they called them simply El or Baal or Adonai, "the Lord." When the name of the Jewish God became more widely known, the rabbis said its magic lay in its correct pronunciation, which could be communicated only once every seven years from an elder priest to a younger.[34] The name was written on phylacteries which were said to keep the bearer from every evil after many repetitions of the syllables. Learned Jews said "God brought Israel out of Egypt by means of a Name which consisted of seventy-two Names."[35]

The Islamic Allah was even better equipped, with ninety-nine secret names. Moslems claimed he would be compelled to answer any prayer if all these names were pronounced. Allah himself was called "the Essential Name," originally the milk-giving Goddess Al-Lat.[36] Pious Moslems invoked Allah's name before sexual intercourse so no evil spirit could enter the womb and beget an evil child.[37]

Both Moslems and Christians inherited Jewish name-magic and believed that all sorts of miracles could be worked by invoking the name of God or the name of Christ, to say nothing of their secret names. In the Middle Ages it was believed that any priest could absolutely compel God to do whatever was asked, by conducting a Mass of the Holy Spirit which mentioned God's secret name.[38] The powers of God's name were explained by Henry Morley as follows:

> *Whoever knows the true pronunciation of the name Jehovah—the name from which all other divine names in the world spring as the branches from a tree, the name that binds together the sephiroth—whoever has that*

in his mouth has the world in his mouth. When it is spoken angels are stirred by the waves of sound. It rules all creatures, works all miracles, it commands all the inferior names of deity which are borne by the several angels that in heaven govern the respective nations of the earth.[39]

Early in the Christian era, when Christians were struggling to separate their sect from Judaism, many stories were invented to prove the name of Christ superior in magic efficacy to the name of God. One such story from the *Life of Pope Silvester* told of a duel of holy names performed by the pope and a Jewish rabbi, in the presence of the Empress Helena, mother of Constantine. The Jew said God's secret name was so powerful that no unprepared creature could hear it and live. To prove his point, he whispered the name into the ear of a bull, which immediately fell dead. Then the pope pronounced the secret name of Christ in the dead bull's other ear, saying, "Bull, arise; go back to thy herd"; and the bull got up and went.[40] Silvester scoffed at the Jew's claim to mastery of the divine name's fatal power, asking him, "How is it, then, that thou thyself hast heard this Name and hast not died?"[41] The Jew didn't answer.

Both Jewish and Christian Gnostics focused on the power of divine names to bring about healing, exorcism, absolution, and salvation. In the Pistis Sophia, Jesus told his disciples to "hide the mystery" of a great Name that could dissolve evil and "blot out all sins, done knowing or not knowing."[42] According to the Gospels, this was the esoteric secret that Jesus concealed from all but his intimates. The masses were not told, "lest at any time they should be converted, and their sins should be forgiven them" (Mark 4:11), indicating that early Christianity like other mystery-religions addressed itself to a favored few. Jesus gave the disciples his secret name, which had power to exorcise, when he said "In my name shall they cast out devils" (Mark 16:17). Seventy of his followers told him, "Lord, even the devils are subject unto us through thy name" (Luke 10:17). Origen said Jesus's name had "expelled myriads of evil spirits from the souls and bodies of men."[43] According to the *Enchiridion*, the powers of Jesus's name were so far-reaching that it was hard to see how anything could possibly go wrong in a world where it was spoken:

O sacred Name, Name which strengthens the heart of man, Name of life, of salvation, of joy, precious Name, resplendent, glorious, agreeable Name, which fortifies the sinner, Name which saves, conserves, leads and rules all . . . wheresoever the most sweet Name of Jesus is pronounced . . . the demons take flight, every knee is bent, all temptations, even the worst, are scattered, all infirmities are healed, all disputes and conflicts between the world, the flesh and the devil are ended, and the soul is filled with every heavenly delight.[44]

The esoteric secrets of Judeo-Christian name-magic were borrowed from Egypt, where the angels of light baffled the forces of darkness with words of power, and set forth in works like the Book of

Origen (Origenes Adamantius) Christian father, ca. 185–254 A.D., an Egyptian who wrote in Greek, exerting a powerful influence on the early Greek church. At first he was accounted a saint, but three centuries after his death he was declared a heretic because of Gnostic elements found in his writings.

Enchiridion A book of magic spells, charms, and secret names allegedly written by Pope Leo the Great, who presented it to Charlemagne to insure his continuing good luck.

Enoch, which depicted the archangel Michael battling dark angels with similar words:

> *This is the number of Kesbeel, who showed the head of the oath to the holy ones when he dwelt high above in glory, and its name is Beqa. And this angel requested Michael to show him the hidden name, that they might mention it in the oath, so that those who revealed all that was hidden to the children of men might quake before that name and oath. And this is the power of that oath, for it is powerful and strong, and he placed this oath Akae in the hand of Michael.*[45]

This passage was garbled Egyptian resurrection-magic. "Those who revealed all that was hidden" were the serpent deities who gave mankind holy secrets, against the will of heaven. "The oath Akae" was Aqa, the rudder of the boat of the dead, "shiner in the water, hidden beam." The name of Aqa had to be spoken before a dead man could enter the boat that plied the heavenly Lake of Reeds.[46] It was among the words of power by which Ra's angels battled the dragon of night: "When these gods rich in magic spoke, it was the very spirit (*ka*) of magic, for they were ordered to annihilate my enemies by the effective charms of their speech."[47]

Ethiopian and Abyssinian Christians retained the notions of Egyptian paganism in regard to words of power (*hekau*). Their vision of the War in Heaven was simply the battle between Ra and the serpent of darkness. They said God's armies were twice overthrown, and Satan was about to assume control of the universe, when God sent his angels one last time into the fight, armed with a cross of light bearing the three secret names of the trinity. "When Satan saw the Cross and the Three Names of Power, his boldness and courage forsook him, his arms lost their strength and the weapons which he was wielding fell from them and he and his hosts turned their backs and were hurled down into the abyss of hell by the now invincible angels of God." The same trinity, however, came into being from the same abyss, the Great Mother Ma-Nu, within whom the triple male god "at first existed in name only."[48] That is, he/they came into being because the Mother spoke his/their name(s). It was believed that the very existence of this trinity depended on continual mention of its/their holy name in the mouths of men.

Egyptian faith in the efficacy of speaking the trinitarian name was taken over by Christians, who viewed "In the name of the Father, of the Son, and of the Holy Ghost" as a magic formula second to none. It could cure disease, chase away vermin, protect worldly goods and acquire more of them.[49] Pope Alexander III forbade monks to study medicine, on the ground that all sickness was caused by demonic possession and the only proper remedy was exorcism by the trinity's holy names.[50]

Holy names constituted the effective portion of any Christian ceremony. Absolution gave a typical formula: "I absolve thee from all thy sins in the Name of the Father and of the Son and of the Holy

Spirit." Extreme unction was a string of invocations; "In the Name of the Father and of the Son and of the Holy Spirit, may there be extinguished in thee every power of the Devil by the imposition of our hands, and by the invocation of all the holy Angels, Archangels, Patriarchs, Prophets, Apostles, Martyrs, Confessors, Virgins, and all the Saints." Even longer lines of holy names marched through the litany for the dying: "Go forth, Christian soul, from this world in the Name of God the Father Almighty, who created thee; in the Name of the Holy Spirit, who was poured out upon thee; in the Name of the holy and glorious Mother of God, the Virgin Mary," and so on, through long lists. Holy water for dedicating a church was exorcised with the formula: "I conjure thee thou creature of water, in the name of the father, and of the son, and of the Holy-ghost, that thou drive the devil out of every corner and hole of this church, and altar; so as he remain not within our precincts."[51]

The holy names were not merely symbols. Words spoken "in the name of Jesus" or "in the name of the Father, Son, and Holy Ghost" were supposed to have absolute efficacy in expelling demons from altars, candles, fonts, even church hassocks, just as Egyptian *hekau* could expel demons from a pyramid.[52] Certainly man never invented a weapon easier to use against the evil powers that he felt threatening him on all sides. Nothing could induce him to abandon it, then or now.

Henry Cornelius Agrippa von Nettesheim (1486-1535) Austrian military officer, scholar, court historiographer, and magus; author of the famous *Occult Philosophy,* which attempted to reconcile magic, theology, physics, mathematics, alchemy, and cabalism.

Agrippa von Nettesheim tried to explain the efficacy of holy names in pseudo-rational style, ending with a wholly irrational description of such names as "vehicles of Divine omnipotence, not fixed by men or by angels but by the great God himself in a certain way according to a number and figure which are unchangeable by reason of their eternal stability; they breathe the harmony of Divinity and are sanctified by God's help. . . . The heavenly powers fear these Divine names, Hell trembles at them, the angels worship them, the bad demons dread them, all creatures revere them."[53]

Yet infernal names were considered just as effective as divine ones. Romanians converted the pagan Mother Death into a witch from the Mount of Olives, called Avestitza, or "Wing of Satan." She was dangerous to most human beings, but could not harm anyone who learned and wrote down her nineteen secret names.[54]

Priests and magicians, Christian or pagan, operated on the same premise that the names of supernatural beings would call them and compel them to perform the required task. Magic books and church liturgies were near akin in intention. One typical book of necromancy provided impressive lists of secret names, guaranteed to work.

> *This is the earliest name of Typhon, at which tremble the earth, the abyss, Hades, heaven, the sun, the moon, the place of the stars and the whole phenomenal universe. When this name is spoken, it carries along with its force gods and demons. It is the hundred-lettered name, the same name as last written. And when thou hast uttered it, the god or the dead person who hears it will appear to thee and will answer concerning the*

things you ask. And when you have learned all things, dismiss the god only with the strong name, the one of the hundred letters, saying "Begone, Lord, for thus wills and commands the great god!" Say the name and he will depart.[55]

Another source mixed Jewish and Greek gods in a spell for calling a spirit of divination into a vessel of water, also for breaking chains, blinding enemies, bringing dreams and divine favors.

I invoke thee who created the earth and the bones (rocks) and all flesh and spirit and established the sea, and shakes the heavens and did divide the light from the darkness, the great ordering mind, who disposes all, the everlasting eye, Demon of Demons, God of Gods, the Lord of Spirits, the unwandering Aeon. Iao ouei, hearken unto my voice. I invoke thee the ruler of the gods, high-thundering Zeus, O king Zeus Adonai, O Lord Jehovah. I am he who invokes thee in the Syrian tongue as the great god Zaaler iphphou (Baal-zephon), and do not disregard the sound in Hebrew ablanathanalba abrasiloa.[56]

The longer and more sonorous the spell, the more holy or unholy names it mentioned, the more effective it was supposed to be. A typical love-charm invoked Greek, Egyptian, and Babylonian underworld deities, as it was placed on a grave to carry the message down to them via the deceased.

I place this charm down beside you, subterranean gods, Kore, Persephone, Ereshkigal and Adonis, Hermes the subterranean, Thoth and the strong Anubis, who hold the keys of those in Hades, the gods of the underworld and the daimons, those untimely reft away, men, women, youths and maidens, year by year, month by month, day by day, hour by hour. I conjure you, all daimons assembled here. . . . Betake yourself to that place and that street and that house and bring her hither, and bind her. . . . Let her sleep with none other, let her have no pleasurable intercourse with any other man, save with me alone. Let her neither drink nor eat, nor love, nor be strong nor well, let her have no sleep except with me, because I conjure you by the terrible terror-striking name of him, who, when his name is heard, will cause the earth hearing it to open; the daimons, hearing his fearful name, will be afraid, the rivers and the rocks, hearing his name, will burst.[57]

The Christian church taught that no demon could be exorcised before his own name was known, following the example of Jesus who demanded the names of the devils he cast out of the Gadarene (Mark 5:9). The *Rituale Romanum* printed in 1947 prescribed that a priest must demand the devil's name and rank, "and the devil, like a prisoner of war, was in honor bound to respond."[58] Precedents dated back, not only to the Gospels, but also to the Magic Papyri where secret names of God were multiplied endlessly in the effort to learn a spirit's name:

I conjure thee by the God of the Hebrews, Jesus, Jaba, Jae, Abraoth, Aia, Thoth, Ele, Elo, Aeo, Eu, Jiibaech, Abarmas, Jabarau, Abelbel, Lona, Abra, Maroia, Arm, appearing in fire, thou, Tannetis, in the midst of

Rituale Romanum
Catholic handbook of rites and ceremonies, with prescribed phrases and gestures for every occasion.

Magic Papyri
Collections of exorcisms, invocations, charms, and spells widely circulated during the early Christian era, used as bases for later grimoires and Hermetic texts.

plains, and snow, and mists; let thine inexorable angel descend and put into safe keeping the wandering demon of this creature whom God has created in his holy Paradise. For I pray to the Holy God, putting my reliance in Ammonipsentancho. I conjure thee with a flood of bold words: Jakuth, Ablanathanalba, Akramm. . . . Thou art Abrasiloth, Allelu, Jelosai, Jael: I conjure thee by him who manifested himself to Osrael by night in a pillar of fire and in a cloud by day and who has saved his people from the hard tasks of Pharaoh and brought down on Pharaoh the Ten Plagues because he would not hearken. I conjure thee, demoniac spirit, to say who thou art. For I conjure thee by the seal Solomon placed upon the tongue of Jeremiah that he might speak. Say therefore who thou art, a celestial being or a spirit of the airs.[59]

One rabbinical tradition anathematized Christian use of holy names to bring about everything from exorcism to resurrection; but Christianity could hardly have existed without it. Jesus said, "I have manifested thy name unto the men which thou gavest me. . . . And I have declared unto them thy name" (John 17:6, 26), copying the Egyptian magician's secret communication of a divine name: "I am he whom you [the god] met under the holy mountain and to whom you gave the knowledge of your greatest Name, which I shall keep holy, communicating it to none save to your fellow initiates in your holy rites."[60] Magic books attributed to Pope Honorius, famed as a wizard despite his pontifical rank, plainly listed the seventy-two secret names of God and demonstrated their use in conjurations. For any modern reader who may wish to test their efficacy, they are: Trinitas, Sother, Messias, Emmanuel, Sabahot, Adonay, Athanatos, Jesu, Pentagna, Agragon, Ischiros, Eleyson, Otheos, Tetragrammaton, Ely, Saday, Aquila, Magnus Homo, Visio, Flos, Origo, Salvator, Alpha et Omega, Primus, Novissimus, Principium et Finis, Primogenitus, Sapientia, Virtus, Paraclitus, Veritas, Via, Mediator, Medicus, Salus, Agnus, Ovis, Vitulus, Spes, Aries, Leo, Lux, Imago, Panis, Janua, Petra, Sponsa, Pastor, Propheta, Sacerdos, Sanctus, Immortalitas, Jesus, Christus, Pater, Filius Hominis, Pater Omnipotens, Deus, Agios, Resurrectio, Mischiros, Charitas, Aeternas, Creator, Redemptor, Unitas, Summum Bonum, Infinitas, Jehovah, Agla, Sady, Gog and Magog.[61]

Christians maintained even up to the present day the old pagan belief that to speak the name of a dead person could call up his ghost, therefore such a name must be accompanied by the formula "God rest him," to keep him in the grave where he belonged. Pliny said Roman pagans used the same formula for speaking of the dead.[62] It was also thought a disaster to have a dying person carry one's name in his mouth through the passage into death. If a dying man cursed his enemy by name, the enemy would also die, obviously in accord with the ancient belief that a name was a vital part of the soul.[63]

One tradition Christians deliberately forgot, however, was the oldest of all: that mothers gave children their name-souls while baptizing them with milk from their breasts. Pagan mothers continued to do this, well into the Middle Ages; but it was specifically stated that such a matriarchal baptism was never given to the Christ child.[64]

1. Campbell, P.M., 85. 2. Agrippa, 217. 3. Jung & von Franz, 185.
4. Squire, 263. 5. Erman, 296. 6. O'Flaherty, 31. 7. de Lys, 429. 8. Clodd, 65.
9. Briffault 1, 372. 10. Hays, 223; *Mahanirvanatantra*, 215, 236.
11. *Book of the Dead*, 266. 12. Budge, A.T., xix.
13. Briffault 1, 419; *Larousse*, 83; Maspero, 3. 14. Stone, 46.
15. O'Flaherty, 65, 352. 16. de Riencourt, 170. 17. Briffault 1, 369.
18. Graves, G.M. 1, 60. 19. Dumézil, 68; Briffault 1, 422. 20. Bullough, 82.
21. Hartley, 287. 22. Oxenstierna, 207. 23. Cohen, N.H.U.T., 122.
24. *Book of the Dead*, 280. 25. Angus, 199. 26. Erman, 51. 27. d'Alviella, 189.
28. *Larousse*, 11. 29. Brandon, 126–27. 30. Budge, G.E. 1, 447.
31. Castiglioni, 177. 32. Campbell, Or.M., 200. 33. Ross, 111. 34. Campbell, P.M., 85.
35. Budge, A.T., 270, 378. 36. Budge, A.T., 48, 50. 37. Fielding, 84.
38. Frazer, G.B., 61. 39. Agrippa, 248. 40. J.H. Smith, C.G., 314–15.
41. deVoragine, 80. 42. Malvern, 51. 43. Robbins, 181. 44. Waite, C.M., 51–52.
45. Legge 1, 169. 46. Budge, E.M., 169. 47. Hooke, M.E.M., 74.
48. Budge, A.T., xx, xxi, xxii. 49. Frazer, G.B., 615, 632; de Voragine, 770.
50. White 1, 386. 51. Scot, 191. 52. H. Smith, 200. 53. Shumaker, 149.
54. Leland, 64. 55. Legge 1, 104. 56. Legge 1, 106–07; Budge, E.M., 177.
57. E.M. Butler. 58. Robbins, 128. 59. E.M. Butler. 60. M. Smith, 49, 132.
61. Waite, C.M., 275–77. 62. Halliday, 47. 63. Wimberly, 352. 64. Wimberly, 373.

Nammu

var. Nar-Marratu

Sumerian name for the Mother of the Universe, represented by an ideogram meaning "sea." She appears to have been identical with **Tiamat** or the primal mother called Ma-Nu in both India and Egypt, i.e., the Deep that existed before creation. According to Sumerian scriptures, she "gave birth to heaven and earth."[1]

1. Hooke, M.E.M., 24.

Namrael

Manichean name for the mother of Adam and Eve. Jews also called her Nahemah or Naama, a serpent-mother classified with Lilith as a being who gave birth to demons.[1] She was an esoteric remnant of the primal Goddess who gave birth to the first couple in her magic garden.

1. Legge 2, 329.

Nana

Virgin mother of Attis, cognate with Norse Nanna, Anatolian Anna, Sumerian Inanna; a priestess-incarnation of the Goddess, like Adonis's virgin mother Myrrha. In ancient Uruk, the name of Nana meant "Moon." The same name was applied to the same deity in Dahomey, where the first man and woman were born of Nana-Buluku, the "Moon-Sun."[1]

1. Hays, 339.

Nanda Devi

"Blessed Goddess," the mountain-mother who gave birth to the Ganges; one of the holiest mountains of the Himalayan chain (see **Mountain**). The nearly inaccessible peak of Nanda Devi lay beyond walls of rock and ice, none less than 18,000 feet high. The Blessed Goddess was finally approached by climbers in 1936.

Nanshe

"Interpreter of Dreams," Babylonian title of the Goddess who gave her priests the ability to interpret and prophesy from other men's dreams. To acquire this ability, priests underwent an initiation ceremony of descent into her "pit," a symbolic death and resurrection, like that of the Old Testament Joseph who interpreted Pharaoh's dreams afterward. Nanshe was also a Goddess of water and fertility, her symbol a vessel of water with a fish in it, signifying the gravid womb.[1] Joseph practiced divination by means of his "cup," which was probably a Vessel of Nanshe (Genesis 44:5, 15). See **Abaddon**.

1. *Larousse*, 61, 63.

Narcissus

Greek flower-god who died looking at this own reflection in the pool of the nymph Echo. As a deity of spring vegetation he was an alternate form of Dionysus (Antheus), who was caught by the Titans with a magic **mirror** or reflecting pool inhabited by water nymphs who seized his soul.[1] Once his soul was caught, the god died and sprang up again as spring flowers. The Hellenic myth that Narcissus pined away for love of his own reflection was an imaginative revision of the older story of a human sacrifice at the springtime Heroantheia, or "Hero-Flowering."

1. Graves, G.M. 1, 288.

Natron

"Birth fluid," the brine in which Egyptian mummies were pickled. Curing in salt water was a magical imitation of fetal existence. The **mummy** was supposed to be awaiting rebirth from the Goddess's womb.

Nave

Central aisle of a church, from *navis,* a ship; medieval churches copied the ship shape of Norman burial mounds.[1] *Nave* also meant the navel or *omphalos*, since both ship and shrine were symbols of the Goddess's womb to which Northmen returned at death.

1. Oxenstierna, 34.

Necromancy

"Divination by the dead," one of the world's most popular forms of magic, still widely practiced under the new name of spiritualism or mediumship. The basic idea was (and is) direct communication with the dead, to discover the secrets of the after-life and the future.

The idea of necromancy underlay every salvation cult. Every Savior came back from the land of death to tell his followers how to avoid its pitfalls and attain blissful immortality. Such information constituted the Mystery-teachings of Orphism, of Eleusis, of Samothrace, and of the Dionysian cults as well as those of Osiris, Pan, Adonis, Tammuz, Krishna, Balder, Zalmoxis, and Christ. But not only Saviors and sacred kings returned from the land of death. Any ghost could do so, if properly summoned.

Homer depicts Odysseus performing necromancy with sheep's blood, to call the dead from Hades and speak with them.[1] A gift of blood was always most welcome to the "shades" who were bloodless. This idea led on to medieval terrors like vampires and revenants who came back from the grave in search of blood.

The Bible shows Saul incapable of practicing necromancy for himself, as Odysseus did. To consult the ghost of Samuel, Saul needed the help of the wise-woman miscalled the "witch" of Endor. The text does not describe her as a witch, but as a "woman that hath a familiar spirit" (1 Samuel 28:7). She is an obvious fraud, presenting to Saul under cover of darkness an obscure figure hidden in a mantle, speaking in whispers, as ghosts were supposed to do. Saul, overcome by superstitious terror, bows his face to the ground and never even tries to get a good look at the apparition (1 Samuel 28:14).

Romans also had necromantic specialists, though the ordinary citizen could deal in a small way with ancestral ghosts, making offerings to them on the nights of the Lemuria.[2] Once each year, priests called up the ghosts dwelling in the pit under the *lapis manalis* or "soul stone" in the Forum, to consult them for omens.[3]

Northern tribes had similar customs, consulting ancestral ghosts at Samhain, the Feast of the Dead, which became Christians' All Hallows or Halloween. "Ghost" and "guest" both descended from Germanic *Geist* because the death's-heads really did attend the feasts as honored guests.[4]

Christians also believed in, and practiced, necromancy. St. Clement the Roman, called the third pope after Peter, paid a necromancer a large sum of money to call up a spirit from the underworld and question it concerning the after-life.[5] Raising the dead Lazarus to life

Rituale Romanum
Catholic handbook of rites and ceremonies, with prescribed phrases and gestures for every occasion.

again—for a while—was one of the miracles that defined the divinity of Christ; yet, Scot asked, how is that "witches do the same, and it is called necromancy?"[6]

Necromancy came to be known as "black magic" through a linguistic blunder. The Greek root *nekros*, a corpse, was corrupted to Latin *niger*, "black"; this gave *nigromancy*, the "black art."[7]

A curious necromantic notion of the resurrection of the flesh underlay the church's procedure for canceling excommunication of a corpse. The *Rituale Romanum* said:

> *If the body be not yet buried, let it be lightly beaten with a rod or small cords after which it shall be absolved. . . . But if it hath been already buried in unconsecrated ground, if it may be conveniently done, let the body be exhumed, and after it hath been lightly beaten in like manner and then absolved let it be buried in consecrated ground; but if the body cannot conveniently be disinterred, then the grave shall be beaten. . . . And if the body be already buried in consecrated ground, it shall not be disinterred, but the grave shall be lightly beaten.*[8]

As a rule, Christian authorities reserved for themselves all dealings with the dead and regarded any lay necromantic or spiritualist activities as heresy, if not diabolism. In 1866 the Second Plenary Council of Baltimore forbade the faithful to attend seances, even if motivated only by idle curiosity; "for some, at least, of the manifestations must necessarily be ascribed to Satanic intervention since in no other manner can they be understood or explained."

1. Homer, Book XI. 2. *Larousse*, 213. 3. James, 183. 4. Hazlitt, 27. 5. Castiglioni, 165. 6. Scot, 141. 7. J.B. Russell, 9. 8. Summers, V., 101.

Nehellenia

"Nether Moon," a variant of the Goddess **Hel**, or Holle, after whom Holland was named. Altars and artifacts dedicated to her were found in Holland after a great storm in 1646 washed away the soil that had buried them.[1]

1. Johnson, 211–12; Reinach, 138.

Nehushtan

Semitic serpent god whose idol was made by Moses (2 Kings 18:4). Hebrew Nehushtan or Nahash, "serpent," descended from the Vedic serpent-king Nahusha, once ruler of all the gods, later cast down to the underworld by Indra.[1] Gnostic Jews worshipped Nehushtan in the first few centuries A.D. and were known as Naassians, "snake-worshippers," counterparts of the Ophites (see **Serpent**).

1. O'Flaherty, 348.

Neith

Triple Goddess of Sais, also called **Anatha**, Ath-enna, Athene, Medusa. Egyptians said her name meant "I have come from myself." She was the World Body, the Primal Abyss from which the sun first rose, and "the Cow, who gave birth to Ra." [1] She was the Spirit Behind the Veil, whom no mortal could see face to face. She called herself "all that has been, that is, and that will be," a phrase copied by the Christian Gospels (Revelation 1:8). She was older than dynastic Egypt. Her symbol was borne by a prehistoric clan, and her name by two queens of the first dynasty. Greeks knew her as Nete, one of the original trinity of Muses at Delphi.[2]

In the Bible she was called Asenath (Isis-Neith), Great Goddess of the city of Aun, which the Jews rendered "On." Her high priest Potiphar was made her "father," as Teiresias was made the "father" of the Goddess Mante, and Brahma was made the "father" of the Goddess Sarasvati (Genesis 41:45). The Goddess herself was made the spouse of Joseph, whose Egyptian name meant "he who was brought to life by the word of the Goddess (*neter*)." [3]

1. Budge, G.E. 1, 451, 459; 2, 299. 2. *Larousse*, 37, 118. 3. Budge, D.N., 34–35.

Nekhbet

Archaic Egyptian name for Mut, the Vulture-goddess of death and rebirth. Her necropolis at Nekhen was an original City of the Dead and one of Egypt's oldest oracular shrines. Nekhbet has been recognized as "the representative of an ancient matriarchal stratum" in Egyptian religion.[1] See **Vulture**.

1. Neumann, A.C.U., 12.

Nemean Lion

Mother Nemea as a destroying Moon-goddess gave birth to the Nemean lion, who was slain by Heracles, as also by his Jewish counterpart Samson, a similar sun-hero.[1] The lion was Leo, whom the sun-man encountered at midsummer, in the season of honey-making, as shown by the honeycomb appearing in the body of Samson's lion (Judges 14:8).

1. *Larousse*, 143.

Nemesis

"Due Enactment," the Time-goddess also called Dike or Tyche, "Destiny." [1] She was probably derived from Kala-Nemi, the Mother of Karma and of the wheel of time.[2] Many versions of the Moon and her holy groves were cognates: Nemea, Diana Nemetona, the Celtic Nemhain, Merlin's Nimue, the Mother of the ancient Nemed or "moon-people."

Ovid called Nemesis "the Goddess that abhors boastful words," because she brought all kings and heroes down to destruction in the end, no matter how arrogant they might become.[3] The Stoics worshipped her as the world-governing principle of Nature, which in time reduced all things to their component elements. Even Zeus feared Nemesis, for she was once his destroyer and devourer, the Goddess who gave both birth and death to all gods.[4] She was sometimes entitled Adrasteia, the Inescapable One.[5]

1. Graves, G.M. 1, 126. 2. O'Flaherty, 344. 3. Gifford, 55. 4. Angus, 12. 5. Graves, G.M. 1, 126.

var. Nebthet

Nephthys

Egypt's underground Goddess called the Egyptian Hecate.[1] Plutarch also said she was the same as Aphrodite, having the names Finality and Victory.[2] With Isis, she made up the divine Two Ladies, representing death and life.

1. Graves, W.G., 153. 2. Barrett, 92.

Nereids

Greek catchall term for fairies, nymphs, mermaids, female nature spirits. Mount Parnassus has Nereid Pits and a Nereid Spring; a whole mountain on Crete is the Nereid Castle. As shape-shifters, Nereids appeared sometimes as beautiful women, sometimes as animals. Christians called them "she-devils" and their leader a Lamia.[1]

1. Hyde, 143–46.

Nereus, Saint

Spurious canonization of the pagan god Nereus, an "old man of the sea" born of the Goddess under her name of Nereis, queen of Nereids. The original Nereus was confused with Proteus, the "first man," and probably with Noah.[1] Christian legend made him one of a pair of eunuchs, Nereus and Achilleus, whose claim to sainthood was that they convinced a rich woman to remain a virgin for the sake of her soul. The story may have begun with a funerary portrait of the woman, Flavia Domitilla, flanked by her family deities Nereus and Achilles.[2]

1. Graves, G.M. 1, 128. 2. de Voragine, 282.

Nergal

Akkadian underworld god, consort of Eresh-kigal, the queen of the shades. The Bible says the men of Cuth made Nergal's image (2 Kings 17:30). A prince of Babylon was named "Nergal-Preserves-Me" (Jeremiah 39:3). Since Nergal represented another form of the nether Black Sun—like Hades, Pluto, and Saturn—he was assimilated to Christian legend as a demon.[1]

1. Waite, C.M., 186.

Neter

var. Nether, Nuter, Nu

Egyptologists found in ancient Egypt a concept they could equate with their own notions of a supreme God, though they did so only by ignoring the matter of gender since all evidence suggests that this primal being was female. Mariette Bey wrote: "At the head of the Egyptian pantheon soars a God who is one, immortal, uncreated, invisible and hidden in the inaccessible depths of his [sic] essence; he [sic] is the creator of the heavens and of the earth; he [sic] has made everything which exists and nothing has been made without him [sic]." De Rougé gushed: "The unity of a supreme and self-existent being, his [sic] eternity, his [sic] almightiness, and eternal reproduction thereby as God; the immortality of the soul, completed by the dogma of punishments and rewards; such is the sublime and persistent base which . . . must secure for the beliefs of the ancient Egyptians a most honorable place among the religions of antiquity."[1]

Auguste Mariette (1821-1881) French Egyptologist, discoverer of the ruins of the Serapeum at Memphis, excavator at Karnak and other sites. He achieved the Egyptian ranks of Bey and Pasha.

De Rougé and Mariette spoke of the concept of *neter* (also rendered *nether, nuter,* or Nu), usually translated "God" or "gods" though several of the seven Hathors had the name of Neter. They ruled the womb of rebirth, the seven-layered after-world known as Khert-Neter or Neter-Khertet.[2] Male gods were called *neter* only when they wore artificial breasts.[3] *Neterit* or *nutrit,* "nurturer," was a common synonym for "Goddess."[4] *She-nit* or *She-neter* were Fate-goddesses "who form the conditions of the lives of men."[5]

The *Book of the Dead* distinguished between gods and the *netri* or *nutri:* "I am devoted in my heart without feigning, O thou *netri* more than gods." A king was told that in his after-life he lived "by the side of a *neter*" like a Hindu god with his shakti. Every king was warned that he was "only the guardian of goods and provisions which belonged to the *neter.*" She provided all subsistence, and property, and children; and she opposed would-be tyrants.[6]

Neter netri was defined as "self-produced, primeval matter," the ocean of uterine blood before creation, holding future forms in the condition of formlessness or Chaos. Scholars actually translated this concept "Lake of God."[7] Its real meaning lay in the root syllable Nu, or **Nut,** "an ocean infinite in extent and of fathomless depth, bearing the germs of all kinds of life," like Kali's primordial womb. The power of Nu was "the self-created," "maker of the gods," and "creator of men." She existed before the sky, the earth, mortals, or gods. From Nu the sun was born; therefore Nu and the Great Mother were one and the same.[8]

The sun went back into Mother Nu's "great gate" in the west when he died. Nu was also the hieroglyphic symbol of water that the Goddess Nut carried on her crown. Nu was the Triple Goddess, shown in tomb carvings as three cauldrons. Nu "maketh fertile the watery mass of heaven, and maketh to come forth water on the mountains to give life to men."[9] Nu became the Semitic *nun,* primal sea personified as the Fish-mother (see **Fish**). She was incarnate in the sacred harlots of Erech, known as *nu-gig.*[10]

This primal sea was likened to the menstrual blood of the Great Mother Goddess Tiamat, the creatress, who menstruated for three years and three months to produce enough life-giving essence to give birth to the universe.[11] This flow was the Nether Upsurge, or Fountain of the Deep, emanating from her "holy door" designated by the letter *daleth* or *delta,* the sign of the yoni. (See **Demeter**; **Triangle**.)

With a vowel point, *daleth* formed the Hebrew word *ed,* erroneously translated "mist" in Genesis 2:6: "But there went up a mist from the earth, and watered the whole face of the ground." The original meaning was not "mist" but something like a mighty fountain or spring, an unexplained upwelling of fluid from the bowels of the earth, which soaked the ground (*adamah*) to make it fertile, before the sending of rain from Father Heaven. This was what other Middle-Eastern scriptures called the Nether Upsurge: female fluid from the deeps, bursting forth to meet a male fluid from the clouds.[12] Other Oriental sources show that the original sacrament of creation called for a meeting of semen and menstrual blood "like the pouring of water into water," as in the meeting and mingling of the powers of Kali and Shiva, or of Tiamat and Apsu. Subsequently, *adamah* brought forth life.

Adamah really meant "blood-red soil," and other myths clearly state that the Nether Upsurge from the interior of Mother Earth was not mist but life-giving uterine blood. The ancients often likened blood to salt water, which was regarded as the *arché,* the first of all elements from which the others were born.[13] Salt water was "birth fluid" (natron), representing regenerative Mother-blood. And Mother-blood was the vehicle of that world-creating spirit called *neter, nether,* etc., which Egyptologists insisted on confusing with their own concept of God.

> *To the great and supreme Power which made the heavens, the gods, the earth, the sea, the sky, men and women, animals and creeping things, all that is and all that is yet to come into being, the Egyptians gave the name of* neter *or* nether, *a word which survives in Coptic under the form* nuti . . . *Dr. Brugsch defined* neter *to mean "the active power which*

> *produces and creates things in regular recurrence; which bestows new life upon them, and gives back to them their youthful vigor. . ." [T]he innate conception of the word completely covers . . . the Latin* natura *. . . the great cosmic powers, and the beings who although held to be "divine" were yet finite and mortal . . . were called* neteru, *and the word is translated "gods" by Egyptologists.*[14]

It seems, however, that "gods" didn't even begin to cover the true meaning of the ancient word *neter,* a relic of primitive matriarchal religion. Budge says:

> *One knows not exactly the meaning of the verb* nuter, *which forms the radical of the word* neter, *"god." It is an idea analogous to "to become," or "to renew oneself." . . . In other words, it has the meaning of god, but it teaches us nothing as to the primitive value of this word. We must be careful . . . not to let it suggest the modern religious or philosophical definitions of god which are current today . . . ;* neter *appears to mean a being who has the power to generate life, and to maintain it when generated.*[15]

Naturally, at the time when this crucial word was coined, the power to generate life was believed to be solely female (see **Motherhood**). It was the Goddess only who was "self-renewing" and the source of all "becoming."[16] Moreover, Egyptian writings contradict Egyptologists who want to call *neterit* "gods." The gods in the train of Ra were strongly differentiated from *neterit,* whom Ra's priests called contemptible beings.[17] In the time of Queen Hatshepsut, the *neterit* were not contemptible but divine beings; however, they "ruled without Ra" and paid no attention to his commands. In some way they had been "made distant" and their footprints were gone from the earth.[18] Here it seems the *neterit* were nothing more nor less than deified maternal ancestresses, like the *matrikadevis* of ancient India and the *dísir* of Scandinavia.

After the 20th dynasty the early religion of Egypt was fragmented and lost in confusion under the rule of new patriarchal gods, like Ra. Budge says, "Knowledge of the early dynastic religion of Egypt possessed by the priests in general after, let us say 1200 B.C., was extremely vague and uncertain. The result of this was to create in their religion a confusion which is practically unbounded."[19]

1. Budge, G.E. 1, 138–39. 2. *Book of the Dead,* 126. 3. *Larousse,* 36.
4. Maspero, 267. 5. Budge, E.M., 34. 6. Budge, G.E. 1, 72, 120, 125, 127.
7. Budge, G.E. 1, 74, 481. 8. *Book of the Dead,* 161, 163.
9. Budge, G.E. 1, 203, 511; 2, 103. 10. Stone, 158. 11. *Assyr. & Bab. Lit.,* 301.
12. Hooke, M.E.M., 110–11. 13. Campbell, P.M., 64. 14. *Book of the Dead,* 99–100.
15. Budge, G.E. 1, 69–70. 16. Stone, 219. 17. *Book of the Dead,* 161.
18. Campbell, Or.M., 103. 19. Briffault 2, 773.

Nicholas, Saint

A bogus saint evolved from the pagan sea god who replaced Artemis as patron of sailors and harlots.[1] Temples of Poseidon became shrines of

St. Nicholas, who also inherited Poseidon's popular title, "the Sailor."[2]

Nicholas's Christian name was the same as Old Nick, or Hold Nickar, the Teutonic sea god known as king of the nixies (sea nymphs). Nicholas was also equated with Woden. As European pagan deities were Christianized, the benevolent aspect of Woden became St. Nicholas (Santa Claus), who galloped over housetops during the winter solstice as the elder god did, granting boons to his worshippers below.[3]

In Italy, St. Nicholas supplanted a female boon-giving deity called The Grandmother, or Pasqua Epiphania, or Befana, who used to fill the children's stockings with her gifts.[4] The Grandmother was ousted from her shrine at Bari, which became the center of St. Nicholas's cult. Christian sailors carried the saint's image out to sea on his feast day, as pagan sailors formerly carried the image of the sea god or goddess.[5] Some bones were collected in the 11th century A.D., installed in a church built at Bari to house them, and labeled the bones of St. Nicholas.[6]

This was the real beginning of St. Nicholas's cult, though his Christian legend claimed (quite without foundation) that he had been a bishop of Myra in the 4th century. His official biography was preposterous. As an infant he fasted, said the hagiographers, taking his mother's breast only once on Wednesdays and Fridays. He became a bishop on account of his predecessor's prophetic dream, because he was the first man to enter the church next day. He resurrected the dead from a magic cauldron. He instantly halted a violent storm at sea to save three drowning sailors. He miraculously multiplied a shipment of grain to feed a whole diocese for two years, with enough seed left over for future crops—vastly surpassing Christ's miracle of the loaves and fishes. After his death he achieved even greater feats. His bones exuded a fountain of holy oil that could cure every disease.[7]

The original pagan god Nicholas gave rise to a Gnostic sect of Nicolaites who worshipped him with his cauldron of regeneration as a fertility figure. They "held that the only way to salvation lay through frequent intercourse between the sexes."[8] Like other worshippers of the sexual fertility principle, pagan or Christian, the Nicolaites were surpressed; but sexual symbolism persisted in the sigil of St. Nicholas's Day in the runic almanac: a furka combined with a yonic mandorla. In ancient Egypt, this was a sign of the phallus of Set in conjunction with the goddess's genital oval.[9] Another symbol of St. Nicholas was the cluster of three golden balls, adopted as a crest of the Medici family and later as a sign of pawnbrokers.[10]

The Dutch called St. Nicholas Sinte Klaas, and carried his cult to the New World where the name was corrupted to Santa Claus.

1. Miles, 218. 2. Hyde, 82–83. 3. Zimmer, 186. 4. Miles, 343. 5. Miles, 221. 6. Mâle, 329. 7. de Voragine, 17–21. 8. Knight, D.W.P., 173. 9. Brewster, 13. 10. Attwater, 251.

Nifl

Alternate name for the Teutonic underground Goddess Hel, ruler of the dead. She was the Greek Nephele, a shadow-twin of Mother Hera. Both names, Nifl and Nephele, meant darkness, clouds, obscurity (Old High German *nebul,* Old Saxon *nebal,* German *Nebel*). Children of Nifl were the Niflungar or Nibelungs, the Burgundians' designation of their dead ancestors, who lived in the womb of Nifl-Hel and were turned black, like shadows. Their sagas became the *Nibelungenlied.*[1]

In the Bible, the same ancestral ghosts are called *nephilim,* "children of Nephele." By Jewish tradition, the *nephilim* were giants, sprung from a great dark mother named Nephesh, "Soul of the Earthly World."[2] See **Shadow**.

1. Turville-Petre, 202. 2. Campbell, Oc.M., 398.

Nike

"Dominance" or "Victory," a pre-Hellenic Goddess born of **Styx**, the personification of the birth-stream. Her begetter was Pallas, the phallus.[1]

1. J.E. Harrison, 72–73.

Nimrod

Biblical "mighty hunter before the Lord" (Genesis 10:9), that is, a copy of the Lord of the Hunt, whom the Greeks called Orion and the Canaanites called Baal-Hadad.

Nimue

Celtic Moon-goddess, cognate with Greek Nemesis and the Diana of the Groves (*nimidae*). Medieval romances made her the witch-maid who enchanted **Merlin** into his crystal cave of sleep at the heart of her fairy-wood, Broceliande. Her name meant Fate. She was also called Vivien, "She Who Lives," or Morgan, the Goddess of death, for she was the archetypal Death-in-Life duality, as even Tennyson described her: "How from the rosy lips of life and love / Flash'd the bare-grinning skeleton of death!"

Ninhursag

Sumerian name of the Mountain Mother, "She Who Gives Life to the Dead."[1] She was the Creatress of the first human beings, whom she made out of clay, a special magic later copied by the biblical God. She was associated with sacred serpents.[2] Like her Egyptian counterpart Hathor, she sometimes appeared as a divine cow. "Holy milk" from temple dairy farm at Lagash nurtured Assyrian kings five thousand years ago. Many Mesopotamian kings included among their qualifications for the throne the assertion that they had been "fed with the holy milk of Ninhursag."[3] Calves were sacrificed to her, in the role of "firstborn."[4]

The Todas of southern India still sacrifice a calf to the Cow-mother who represents the earth, with a prayer that includes the word *Ninkurshag.* They say the meaning of the word is unknown, but it is a very holy word.[5]

1. Ashe, 15. 2. Stone, 83. 3. Whitehouse, 62. 4. Neumann, G.M., 124–25. 5. Campbell, Or.M., 38.

Ninian, Saint

Mythical missionary, said to have converted the southern Picts to Christianity in the 2nd century A.D., many centuries before Christianity actually touched the British Isles. The spurious *Life of St. Ninian,* "Apostle to the Southern Picts," was written in the 12th century A.D. by a Cistercian monk. This imaginative document claimed St. Ninian was worshipped by a tribe called Novantae, at the Candida Casa (White House), a temple built "after the Roman manner." An Irish *Life of St. Ninian* claimed that he founded a church in Leinster, and identified him with the god Monenni. The *Martyrology of Talsnacht* said Monenni was another name for the pagan goddess Nenn, or Nynia, cognate with the Danes' Nanna.[1] Thus "Ninian" seems to have been a legend built around a pagan idol of indeterminate sex, worshipped in a Roman-style temple.

1. Attwater, 255; Brewster, 409–10.

Ninsun

Akkadian title of the Goddess who "knew all knowledge" in her role of queen mother of every sacred king. She was the mother of Gilgamesh.[1] She was the divine mother of Ur-Nammu (2112–2095 B.C.), founder of the third dynasty of Ur. She was the mother of King Shulgi, who also married her virgin form Inanna, "the vulva of heaven and earth."[2] Ninsun was all-wise, and made rules for the contests of sacred kings.

1. *Larousse,* 66. 2. Pritchard, A.N.E., 31, 132, 135.

Ninti

var. Nintu

"Lady of Life" or "Lady of the Rib"; Sumerian birth-goddess who enabled pregnant women to make their babies' bones out of their own ribs.[1] This idea was copied by biblical writers for the pseudo-birth of Eve from Adam's rib. Even modern scholars have misrepresented Ninti by describing her devotees adoring "the god."[2]

1. Hooke, M.E.M., 115. 2. Pritchard, A.N.E., 285.

Niobe

"Snowy One," Anatolian Mountain-goddess whose worshippers were destroyed by patriarchal Hellenic tribes. Greek myth therefore made her a mother forever mourning her "children" slain by the Olympian gods.[1] Greek writers pretended she was a woman too proud of her children, so the gods killed them to punish her hubris.

1. Graves, G.M. 1, 260.

Nirvana

Contrary to the popular western belief that Nirvana meant paradise, it was really quite the opposite: an eternal not-being, with cessation of all feeling, the ascetic ideal of disappearance of the self into the infinite. Nirvana meant final escape from the karmic wheel of earthly reincarnations ruled by the cyclic Mother. It was supposed to lie beyond all sense perceptions, memories, loves, hates, fears, joys, or will; it was like the Tantric idea of Dreamless Sleep, forever. It could be achieved only by holy men after many cycles of reincarnation taught them to conquer all desires.

Niu-Kua

Legendary Chinese empress who reigned 130 years and had the magical ability to command the movements of the heavenly bodies; a mythic remnant of China's matriarchal age.

Nixies

Germanic water-fairies similar to Greek nereids, children of Mother Night, whose name in Norse was Nott; in Greek, Nyx.[1] As a personification of the dark Chaos at the beginning and end of the universe, she gave rise to the word *nix,* negation or nothingness. Pre-Christian religions viewed the Goddess Nyx-Selene (Night-Moon) as the agent of deification after death, which made her a direct rival of the Christian savior figure.[2] Her nixies were abyssal angels who kept the souls of the dead in an underwater fairyland, in "pots turned upside down," after the manner of all Teutonic death-spirits.[3] In the Middle Ages, the water-fairies assumed the same characteristics as their close relatives, the mermaids, sirens, wilis, and water-witches: that is, they lured hapless sailors into the water and magically devoured their souls.

1. Branston, 145, 152. 2. Strong, 108. 3. Keightley, 259.

Noah

Hebrew version of Nu, or Nun, the "Fish" in the Hebrew sacred alphabet; originally the god born of Ma-Nu or Ma-Nun, Egyptian Goddess of the primordial deep.[1] The name of Ma-Nu was associated with the creation-flood in both Egypt and India. "Ma" was the Womb of Chaos, often personified as a cosmic fish; "Nu" or Noah was the embryonic seed of life floating into a new birth. See **Creation**; **Flood**; **Tiamat**. The flood-heroes of India, Sumeria, and Babylonia also rode out the deluge of birth-fluid in a moon-vessel called *argha* or **ark,** carrying with them the pairs of all creatures to populate the new creation.[1] From the same root came *arc,* a crescent; for the vessel of creation was always identified with the moon.

1. Jobes, 121.

Norns

The female trinity of Fates as she/they appeared in Scandinavia: also known as Weird Sisters, from Teutonic *wyrd,* "fate." The Prose Edda called them "three mysterious beings," High One, Just-As-High, and Third, who revealed the secrets of the universe and wrote the book of destiny; hence their other title, *Die Schreiberinnen,* "women who write." More common names for the Norns were Urth (Earth), Verthandi, and Skuld, variously translated Fate, Being, and Necessity, or like the ancient Egyptian Goddess of past, present, and future, "Become, Becoming, and Shall-Be."[1]

The original, single, eldest Norn was Mother Earth, Ertha, Urth, Urdr, etc., who represented Fate and the Word of creation. She was Wurd in Old High German, Wyrd in Anglo-Saxon, Weird in English.[2] She/they lived in the cave at the source of the Fountain of Life, Urdarbrunnr, the cosmic womb under the root of the World Tree. She/they were older than the oldest "heavenly father" and had power over every god.[3]

The death-Norn Skuld was a variant of **Skadi**, an eponymous mother of Scandinavia and a typical Destroyer. Norse poet-shamans were servants of Skuld and called themselves *skalds;* Christians said they indulged in witchcraft, or "skulduggery." Skuld would lay the death-curse on the whole universe at doomsday. Her name apparently gave rise to "scold," meaning a woman gifted with the power of cursing. Like the third of the **Moirai**, Skuld cut the thread of every life.

The Norns became "fairies" in romantic traditions of pagan balladry:

And lo! Reclining on their runic shields
The mighty Nornas now the portal fill;
Three rosebuds fair which the same garden yields,
With aspect serious, but charming still.
Whilst Urda points upon the blackened fields,
The fairy temple Skulda doth reveal.[4]

1. *Larousse,* 37. 2. Campbell, C.M., 121. 3. Branston, 208.
4. Guerber, L.M.A., 267.

Numa

Legendary Latin king who became very wise, through his sacred marriage with the Goddess of creation and birth, Diana Egeria, the Virgin of Nemi's sacred healing spring. Numa probably never existed, but "his" name recalls the Oriental custom of creating some of the Goddess's spouses by reversing the syllables of her own name, e.g., Ya-ma, Lord of Death, a reversal of Ma-ya, Lady of Life. Ma-Nu was a Goddess of Creation in some of the oldest Indo-European traditions, and Nu-Ma seems to have been her male counterpart.

Nun

Egyptian word for the primal ocean, origin of the Hebrew letter *nun* meaning "fish"; it was also a sacred name, as in "Joshua son of Nun" (Joshua 1:1). As applied to a religious woman, "nun" descended from *nonne,* a nurse, because in antiquity priestesses were practitioners of the healing arts.

Nut

var. Nuit

Egyptian Great Mother personifying the night sky. Sometimes she was the Cow whose udder gave forth the Milky Way; or sometimes she was a woman arched over the earth, touching the "ends of the earth" with her toes and fingertips; or again, her figure was painted inside coffin lids, her arms stretching down to embrace the deceased.[1] Her consort Geb was an earth-bound god who lay on his back and tried to reach her with his erect penis, signified by the obelisk.[2]

Pharaohs were sons and consorts of Nut. Pepi II said he was living "between the thighs of Nut." Men-Kau-Ra (Mycerinus) knew he was "born of Nut, conceived of Nut . . . spreadeth herself thy mother Nut over thee in her name of 'mystery of Nut,' she granteth that thou mayest exist without enemies, O king of the South and North, Men-Kau-Ra, living for ever!"[3] Egyptians said every woman was a *nutrit,* Little Goddess (see **Neter**).

1. Neumann, G.M., pls. 36, 90–92. 2. F. Huxley, 69. 3. *Book of the Dead,* 22, 17.

Nymph

Greek *nymphe,* Latin *nympha,* a bride or a nubile young woman. The same word was applied to female-genital symbols like the lotus flower, water lilies, and certain shells. "Nymphs" served as priestesses in ancient temples of the Goddess, especially in sexual ceremonies, where they represented the divine principle of flowering fertility and were sometimes known as Brides of God. See **Virgin Birth**.

In medieval times the word nymph was applied to either a witch or a fairy, since both descended from the pre-Christian priestess. As spirits of nature, the "nymphs" were believed to embed their souls forever in certain parts of the natural world that the Goddess had ruled in antiquity: there were water nymphs, tree nymphs, mountain nymphs, and nymphs who dwelt in the earth, the sea, or Fairyland. Their ancient connection with sexuality was more or less consistently maintained. Even now, "nymphomania" connotes sexual obsession, like the moon-madness supposed to motivate the ancient nymphs in their seasons of mating.

Obelisk

Egyptians knew the obelisk was intended to represent a giant phallus. It was called the benben-stone, or begetter-stone, similar to the Petra, "the Rock that begat thee," as the Bible says. (See **Peter, Saint**.) Usually the obelisk was regarded as an erection of the earth god Geb in his perpetual eagerness to mate with the Goddess of Heaven.[1]

1. F. Huxley, 69.

Oberon

Anglo-Saxon King of the Fairies; derived from German Alberich, the underworld dwarf king who kept buried treasure in the earth, which was also a function of the devil. Oberon was married to **Titania**, the Fairy Queen, the ancients' "Mother of Titans."

Occulta

"Hidden things," the secret ceremonies of the mystery cults which taught their own esoteric secrets of salvation in the early Christian era. Primitive Christianity had its own *occulta,* but in medieval times the word was applied to every religion other than Christian orthodoxy. Thus *occulta* became almost synonymous with witchcraft, magic, heresy, Hermetism, etc.

Oceanus

Greco-Roman water-serpent deity supposed to surround the earth with his vast body, holding his tail in his mouth to form a continuous barrier of water at the outer limits of the world. Oceanus was often confused with Neptune, Poseidon, Ouroboros, Taaut, or Python. Oceanus was married to the primal Sea-goddess Tethys, or Thetis. His name meant "He who belongs to the Swift Queen."[1]

var. Okeanos

1. Graves, G.M. 1, 27; 2, 402.

Odin

Norse All-father, called God of the Hanged because the trees of his sacred grove at Uppsala were laden with hanged human sacrifices even as late as the 10th century.[1] Each victim's *draumar* (drama) recapitulated the death-rebirth of Odin himself, when he acquired his divine powers by giving himself up to immolation on the World Tree, wounded in the side with a spear. He said: "I know that I hung on the windy tree for nine whole nights, wounded with the spear, dedicated to Odin, myself to myself."[2]

The occult significance of nine nights was pseudo-feminization for the sake of creativity; it was the period sacred to women in childbirth. Latins called it the *nundinum* (nine-day).[3] Celts called it the *noínden* (nine-night). On occasion the Goddess Macha inflicted a nine-night period of helplessness on men, which probably arose as a ceremonial couvade whereby in primitive times the men tried to partake of women's powers.[4] The purpose of Odin's nine-night ordeal was to learn the secret of the "wise blood" in the Earth-mother's uterine cauldron, and to command the magic power of the runes, invented by his feminine prototype Idun (Freya). After he traversed all the realms of death, he said, "I got a drink of the precious mead, I was sprinkled with Odrerir. Then I began to be fruitful and to be fertile, to grow and to prosper; one word sought another word from me."[5]

By his sacrifice Odin won for men the female secrets of the *saga* (speaking-woman, prophetess, priestess). He learned the runes, words of power, and sacred poetry, which his skalds called "the sea of Odin's breast," meaning the blood he shed on the earth.[6] His myth evidently predated the discovery of fatherhood, for Erda or Urth was refreshed and fructified by his blood, not his semen.

Sometimes the tree of his martyrdom was represented by the Tau cross, also known as the Cross of St. Anthony or the Gibbet Cross.[7] At other times, his gallows was door-shaped, with two upright tree trunks and a crossbeam. This matched the poets' description of Odin's gallows, **Yggdrasil** the "Terrible Horse," for the gallows was both a tree and a horse on which men rode to the land of death.[8] The same form of the horse-gallows appeared on the Tarot card of the Hanged Man, whose number is twelve; he is the twelfth of the numbered Major Arcana or trump suit. Thus the Tarot Hanged Man revealed Odin's secret of the Twelfth Rune, a mystery specifically mentioned in the Edda as a necromantic sign, with power to make a hanged man answer any question put to him.[9] This was one of the sources of the divinatory magic attributed to the pictures of the Tarot cards. It has been noted that the Hanged Man is a pagan figure, and "one of the clearest indications that the Tarot trumps were designed to illustrate some non-Christian system of belief."[10] The card of the Hanged Man was followed by the card of Death, number 13, showing that the victim like Odin was intended to traverse the nether worlds of the dead.

Scandinavian sacred kings were identified with Odin and suffered the same kind of holy death, probably followed by apotheosis as was usual for sacrificial victims. Vikarr, legendary ancestor of the Vikings, was killed by a spear-thrust from one of Odin's priests during such a ceremony. Medieval Swedes periodically "reddened the earth with the blood of their lord," enacting the love-death of king and god. The blood Odin poured forth begot his reincarnation or son, Balder, the northern Adonis or Attis, whose consort had the same name as Attis's virgin mother. She was Nanna or Nan, a Valkyrie name, probably derived from the archaic Middle-Eastern Moon-goddess Inanna.[11] Balder seems to have been the same dying-and-reborn god as Baal.

By the decree of his Heavenly Father, Balder too was slain and sent to the underground realm of the Goddess Hel. He was restored by the "tears of red gold" shed over him by Hel's celestial aspect, Freya; but he would not return to this world. Balder's Second Coming would take place in the next universe, after the destruction of the current gods and the present world. He would rise again and establish a new kingdom of more virtuous gods in another creation.[12] See **Doomsday**.

Pagan saviors like Odin-Balder were naturally regarded as demons by followers of their Christian rival. Therefore Odin became an "ogre" via his Lord-of-Death title Yggr, "Terrible One."[13] Medieval necromancers were believed to use the things that belonged to Odin's realm: gallows wood, gallows earth, parts of bodies of the hanged. At Toulouse in 1335 a woman named Anne-Marie de Georgel was accused of witchcraft, on the charge of having used clothing, hair, nails, or fat of hanged criminals to make her magic ointments.[14]

Though Odin was called All-father, he was not regarded as a creator. Like his Greek counterpart Zeus, he was strictly limited in power. Both Odin and Zeus were helpless in the hands of the Fates who were Norns in Scandinavia and Moirai (Moerae) in Greece. "The ancestresses of the Nornir were those beings who also gave rise to the Greek Moirai, the goddesses of Fate. According to Greek myth the Moirai were amongst the children of Night; and Night, as we know, was one of the more ancient beings of Northern myth—older at any rate than the viking god Odin." Nevertheless, Odin's worshippers eventually divided him into a trinity named Twilight, Midnight, and Dawn, copied from the trinitarian Mother Night to whom he was mated, just as the Hindu Lord of Death became a trinity to mate with Triple Kali.[15]

Odin was an Aryan god, descended from the Vedic lord of winds, Vata, as shown by several other variations of his name: Voten, Wuotan, Woden.[16] He was also Godan, in Hindu tradition a lord of western barbarians, consort of the Goddess **Godiva** whose name was really a redundant "Goddess-Goddess."

As a lord of winds, Odin was identified with the Prince of the Power of the Air, one of the titles of the Christian devil. Odin led the Wild Hunt, a nocturnal ceremony originally representing ghost-ridden storm clouds galloping through the sky: another form of the Gray Horse that Odin rode. An English chronicle of 1127 described the Wild Hunt celebrated on the 6th of February by a group of black-clad horsemen, riding black horses, following black hounds with "eyes like saucers." Twenty or thirty men galloped through the woods between Peterborough and Stamford, "and all through the night the monks heard them sounding and winding their horns."[17]

Sometimes Odin appeared on earth as a one-eyed, gray-bearded old wizard leaning on a staff, wearing either a hood or a broad-brimmed witch-hat.[18] Odin's other common title was "the one-eyed god," derived from several mythological sources including the ancient metaphor for the penis. As a nonsexual explanation of the metaphor, one myth claimed that Odin gave up one of his eyes for the privilege of drinking from the feminine Fount of Wisdom, called either Mimir (Mother of Memory) or Urdarbrunnr (Stream of Urd, i.e., of the eldest Norn). Still another explanation for his acquisition of feminine wisdom was that he stole the "wise blood" from the cauldron Odrerir, which was in the keeping of the Earth-goddess in her sacred uterine cave.[19] A similar story was told of the Aryan god Indra, who stole the Great Mother's lunar blood Soma, and assumed the form of a bird to fly away with it to the home of the patriarchal gods. Both Odin and Indra were revered by men for having obtained formerly forbidden secrets of magic and bestowed them on their favored shamans.

1. Oxenstierna, 223. 2. Frazer, G.B., 412. 3. Cumont, A.R.G.R., 91. 4. Rees, 58. 5. Turville-Petre, 42. 6. Turville-Petre, 39. 7. d'Alviella, 15. 8. Branston, 114. 9. B. Butler, 154. 10. A. Douglas, 85. 11. Turville-Petre, 40, 113, 118. 12. Turville-Petre, 115; Lederer, 109. 13. Branston, 114. 14. J.B. Russell, 183. 15. Branston, 66, 208. 16. Branston, 109, 126. 17. Branston, 108. 18. Branston, 113. 19. *Larousse*, 257.

Odor of Sanctity

An alleged recognition sign for bodies or tombs of Christian saints was a sweet odor, as opposed to the expected odor of decay. This was emphasized in legends of many saints' relics, for example the remains of St. Mark allegedly discovered by some Venetian merchants in Alexandria during the 5th century. "When they lifted the stone from the tomb, so strong a perfume spread throughout the city of Alexandria that everybody wondered whence this sweet odor might come."[1]

According to the conventional phrase, every true saint died "in the odor of sanctity," for the sweet smell was taken as a symbolic assurance of undecaying immortality, tied to the church's doctrine of resurrection of the flesh. If a saint or martyr achieved heaven at once, as was the orthodox teaching, then his flesh could not decay and would therefore smell as sweet as the airs of heaven, which were generally supposed to be perfumed.

This was not an originally Christian notion. It was copied from Egyptian ritual and theory of mummification. A corpse must smell sweet in order to be accepted by the Egyptian deities; that was the reason for embalming mummies with sweet-smelling spices, resins, and aromatic oils. **Anubis** guarded the gates of the after-world and checked each newcomer with his keen canine nose. If the scent was acceptable, Anubis declared the dead man reconciled to the gods by his Odor of Sanctity, and admitted him to the blessed realm.[2]

Though the Christian Dark Age lost the art of mummification—which was not to be revived until 20th-century embalmers improved on it—still the same spices were sometimes clumsily applied to dead bodies in an effort to preserve them. The precious virtue of frankincense was that it served as a key to heaven by counteracting "the ill smells" of a corpse.[3] Churchmen claimed the bodies of those who were excommunicated would not decompose, but they lacked the Odor of Sanctity that characterized saints.[4]

The perfume allegedly exuded by saints' remains could work miracles and cure diseases. The corpse of St. Stephen instantly healed 70 sick men who smelled its odor when it was first exhumed. Earth from the grave of St. Dominic was said to smell sweet and possess miraculous powers.[5]

An effort was made to canonize the 13th-century inquisitor Bernard de Caux with a legend of incorruptibility, because he was "a persecutor and hammer of heretics, a holy man . . . wonderful in extirpating heresy," Bernard Gui wrote. His body was exhumed 28 years after his death and said to be perfectly fresh and sweet-smelling, except that part of its nose was missing.[6]

The gypsies mocked Christian legends of nondecaying saints, claiming that bodies which fail to undergo normal decomposition are not holy spirits but vampires.[7] The church accepted stories about the "un-dead" but insisted on undecaying saints also.

1. de Voragine, 241. 2. *Book of the Dead*, 569. 3. Hazlitt, 250. 4. Robbins, 523. 5. de Voragine, 409, 427. 6. Lea, 246. 7. Trigg, 156.

Oedipus

Mythical king of Thebes at a point in time when kings were beginning to oppose matriarchal rule. Oedipus killed his father/predecessor and married his mother/queen in the conventional way, but he caused the Goddess's image (the Sphinx) to be thrown from a cliff and broken.

His mother/queen was Jocasta or Iocaste, "Shining Moon," who apparently called down the wrath of the Goddess on her consort. Some said he was banished from Thebes, others said he was slain by the Goddess's Furies in her sacred grove.[1] Most stories agree that he was blinded by a "clasp" taken from Jocasta's garment.

Jocasta's "clasp" may have been a euphemism for the castrating moon-sickle. Herodotus said the women of Athens killed a man with their "clasps," but a new patriarchal law afterward forbade women to carry such weapons.[2] Blindness was a common mythic symbol of castration, as shown by the tales of Samson, Odin, and Teiresias of Thebes. In Egypt also, a penis was called an Eye; to cut it off was to put out the "light" of the One-Eyed God.[3]

The allegedly incestuous marriage between Oedipus and his mother/queen was no more than the conventional alternation of sacred kings, each one chosen by the queen and declared the "son" or reincarnation of his slain predecessor. Oedipus's "father" bore the name of Laius, not a name at all but simply a title: "the king." As in antiquity every king was a god, so every queen was a Mother of God, and the god's virgin bride as well. See **Incest**; **Kingship**.

1. Graves, G.M. 2, 10, 15, 396. 2. Herodotus, 303–4. 3. Norman, 42.

Oenothea

"Wine Goddess," title of a priestess mentioned by Apuleius. She represented the Goddess as Dispenser of Immortality, keeping gods and men alive with her magic ambrosia.[1] Among her many other names were Hebe, Ariadne, Siduri, or Saki.

1. Wedeck, 207.

Ogier the Dane

Poet-king of medieval romance, a patron of bards, who attained immortality by a sacred marriage with **Morgan le Fay**. When he was born, she cast his fate and said he would dwell with her in Avalon. When he attained the age of 100 years, she gave him a Crown of Oblivion to erase the memory of his former life, put a magic ring on his finger, and took him to her western paradise where he joined the heroes Arthur, Oberon, Tristan, and Lancelot in eternal bliss under the auspices of the Goddess.[1]

1. Guerber, L.M.A., 135–38.

Old Nick

Popular English name of the devil, probably derived from the Danish sea god Hold Nickar, leader of the nickers, or **nixies** (water-fairies).[1] The same sea god evolved into the mythical **St. Nicholas** as might be told by the saint's association with the cauldron of regeneration and the symbols of the Triple Goddess. "Hold" was a variant of the Goddess's name—Holde, Hild, Hel—so "Old Nick" may have been another instance of the masculinization of the personified Sea-womb.

1. Hazlitt, 459.

var. Volga

Olga

Legendary Amazonian warrior-queen of Kiev, so revered by the tribes of southern Russia that the orthodox church was forced to adopt and canonize her as one of its spurious saints.[1] According to an old chronicle, she led her soldiers into battle after invoking the protection of Pyerun, the pagan thunder-god.[2]

1. Leland, 36. 2. *Larousse*, 294.

Om

Universal "Word of Creation" spoken by the Oriental Great Goddess upon her bringing forth the world of material existences; an invocation of her own pregnant belly. *Om* was called the Mother of Mantras (*matrikamantra*), the supreme Word. See **Logos**.

Omen

Literally, a sign from the Moon. Arts of divination were generally under the aegis of the ancient Moon-goddess. Cicero listed four types of omens. *Ostenta* were those that "make clear," yielding our word ostensible. *Portenta* were those that foreshadow or "portend." *Monstra* were those that demonstrate or show, like dreams and visions. *Prodigia* were the "prodigies" that give signs of future events through miraculous happenings.[1]

Any omen was numinous, a word derived from *nu-men,* another Latin rendition of Moon-spirit. *Nu-men* was the Roman counterpart of *mana.*[2] Both words meant revelation emanating from the Moon-mother. See **Mana.**

1. Wedeck, 230. 2. Rose, 19.

Omikami Amaterasu

Japanese sun goddess from whom the imperial family traced descent, at first through a line of queens, later through the male line, after Japanese society instituted patriarchal customs about the 14th century A.D.[1] Her name meant Mother Creation-Spirit. See **Sun Goddess.**

1. Briffault 1, 369.

Omophagia

Eating-into-the-Belly, Greek ritual of holy communion by eating the flesh of sacrificial victims, human or animal. (See **Cannibalism.**) According to the primitive tradition, worshippers were expected to tear apart the victim with bare hands and teeth, devouring him raw, as in the earliest cults of Dionysus, Orpheus, Zagreus, and other gods torn to pieces in their myths. "The communicants rushed madly upon the sacrificial animal, tore it to pieces and ate it raw, believing that the god was resident in the offering. . . . It was believed that thus there took place an identification with the god himself, together with a participation in his substance and qualities."[1] His immortality was eaten too—both in the *omophagia* and its descendant, the Christian sacrament of god-eating—though his body was no longer meat but a tiny fragment of bread.

1. Angus, 129.

Omphale

Lydian name of the Goddess of the Hub—*omphalos,* the navel-stone marking the center of the universal womb. Greek myth describes her as a queen of Lydia, who enslaved Heracles and set him to work at her spinning wheel. Heracles was the sun, and he performed his twelve Labors on the spinning wheel of the zodiac. Each "labor" was really one of the zodiacal houses through which the sun passed during Heracles's one-year servitude in Omphale's palace. This year marked his reign as the Aeon. He wore the queen's robes, in memory of which the priests of Heracles wore female garments and pretended to command feminine powers of magic. It was characteristic of transitional periods between matriarchy and patriarchy that the king wore the queen's robes when acting as her deputy.[1]

Omphale represented the Goddess as a consumer of sun-kings, each one annually killed and replaced by another who was born at the winter solstice; like the archaic Roman Goddess Anna Perenna she was a Mother of Time.[2] One of her consorts before Heracles was the oak-god Tmolus, who fathered his own reincarnation, the sacred king Tantalus, cermonially drowned at the Oschophoria to represent the sun sinking into the sea.[3] Tmolus as a human victim was wreathed in the oak garland of the god and tossed by a bull onto sharp stakes, indicating that the Goddess's bull-masked priests impaled him in a pit where his blood could fertilize the ground.

The divine Father of Heracles-the-Savior was the sun god Apollo, thought to have originated in Lydia although he later became one of the most typically Greek of gods. In his earliest forms, Apollo was subject to the rule of his sister-bride Artemis, the Moon, who was sometimes incarnate in a sacred navel-stone and therefore bore the title of Omphale.

1. Graves, G.M. 2, 167. 2. Herodotus, 5–6. 3. Graves, G.M. 2, 29.

Omphalos

Greek transliteration of Latin *umbilicus,* the navel or hub of the world, center of the Goddess's body, source of all things. As every ancient nation regarded its own version of the Great Mother as the cosmic spirit, so its own capital or chief temple was located at the center of the earth, marked by the stone *omphalos* that concentrated the Mother's essence. Hebrews called it the *beth-el* or "dwelling place of deity." As a male god, incarnate in the king, this deity was always located at the Goddess's middle because he was her child.

In 710 B.C. a king of Susa said, "The Susian land, which is the first of the earth, is in the center of all mankind." Iranians said, "The country of Iran is better than all other places, for it is in the middle." China called itself "the Middle Kingdom." So did Scandinavia, known to its inhabitants as Middle-Earth (Midgard). Old Japanese poems called Japan the Middle Kingdom of Earth. Romans called the sea at the center of their empire *mare nostrum,* "our sea," and gave it the name of Mediterranean, literally Middle-of-the-Earth.[1]

Romans placed the world's navel or *omphalos* at the round hearth of the temple of Vesta. Greeks placed it at the *omphalos* of Delphi, "Temple of the Womb." Jews placed it at the temple of Zion. Christianity inherited a Jewish cosmogony wherein Jerusalem was regarded as the center of the earth, where Jesus died on the identical spot where the Tree of Life once grew in the primal garden. It was said a spear standing upright at the tomb of Christ would cast no shadow at midday, because it marked the center point of everything under the sun. When Pope Urban preached the first crusade at Clermont, he declared "infallibly" that "Jerusalem is the middle point of the earth."[2]

By pre-Christian reckoning, this middle point was the Virgin Zion, or the yonic temple of Mari-Anat. Feminine symbolism was prevalent in all omphalic shrines, which generally represented the body of the Goddess with the God present as a sexual partner—a phallic serpent, tree, cross, or sacrificed male bleeding the Blood of Life. Even medieval romances spoke of the Palace of Love where God and Goddess joined *in medio mundi,* at the center of the world. It was equipped with the usual sexual symbols: a sacred spring in the garden, which also contained the Tree of Life.[3]

Christian theologians were amply supplied with the kind of hubris that made men call their own home place the center of the earth, their own lifetimes the ultimate end of time, their own religion the only permissible one, and their own selves the focal point of the cosmic drama of good and evil. Indeed, the whole universe was viewed as a mere backdrop for man's probation. Peter Lombard said, "Just as man is made for the sake of God—that is, that he may serve Him—so the universe is made for the sake of man—that is, that it may serve him; therefore is man placed at the middle point of the universe."[4] If man couldn't think of himself as somehow vitally connected with the *omphalos,* his world-view was threatened. Such a threat underlay the church's opposition to the discoveries of **Galileo**, which tended to prove that the earth was not the center of God's universe.

1. Lethaby, 73. 2. White 1, 99. 3. Wilkins, 139. 4. H. Smith, 329.

Onuphris, Saint

Artifical canonization of the god Osiris, taken from his epithet Unnefer, the Beneficent One.[1] Onuphris was accepted into the canon of saints even though his original Egyptian form was usually viewed as a pagan "devil."

1. H. Smith, 227.

Ophion

var. Ophis

Serpent consort of the Creatress Eurynome, in the Pelasgian creation myth; in Gnostic sexual symbolism he was the World Serpent mated to the World Egg. According to an ancient Phrygian tradition he was the Father of mankind: a divine serpent who lived in the Tree of Life in the primal garden, and begot the tribes called Ophiogeneis, "serpent-born."[1] He was assimilated to Christ by the Gnostic Christian sect of Ophites, and to Jehovah by their Jewish counterparts the Naassians or "serpent-worshippers." Ophion the

Serpent was a heavenly king who revealed the sacred Mysteries, even against the will of the jealous god. See **Serpent**.

1. J.E. Harrison, 129.

Ops

Pre-Roman name of Ceres, Bona Dea, etc.; the Goddess who invented Roman law. Her secret rites were forbidden to men; but on her December festival, the Opalia, there was a general ceremony involving sexual orgies and touching the earth.[1] The powers of Jupiter were believed ineffective unless he was united with her, as Jove Opulentia.[2] Like Pluto, he became Lord of Abundance, or Lord of Riches. Macrobius said the secret name of Rome was Ops Consivia.

Sacred gem of the Opalia was the opal, representing the Goddess's many-colored veils. Because of its feminine connotation, Christians declared it an unlucky stone. As a witch charm it was said to blind prying eyes and make its bearer invisible.[3] Arab alchemists identified it with the Philosopher's Stone, because the latter was believed to contain all basic colors—red, blue, yellow, green, and white.[4]

1. *Larousse,* 208. 2. Dumézil, 689. 3. Wedeck, 189. 4. Seligmann, 94.

Orcus

Greco-Roman death god, also known as Phorcys or Porcus, a sacrificial boar.[1] In the Middle Ages he was made a demon with a human body and a pig's head.

1. Graves, G.M. 2, 107.

Orestes

Classic Greek mother-slayer, pursued by the Furies for violation of the ultimate matriarchal law. The Furies maintained that no crime is worse than killing the mother whose "intimate blood" made one's own life. Apollo however defended Orestes on the ground that even if he did murder his mother, Queen **Clytemnestra**, she wasn't his true parent because the only true parent is a father.[1]

1. Bachofen, 159.

Orgy

From Greek *orgia,* "secret worship."[1] Most secret worship involved sexual rites, as in the Sacred Mysteries of Eleusis, Cabiria, Shaktism, Sufism, Ophite Christianity, etc. Wilkins says, "Even when religion no longer tends towards the orgiastic as all cults in close touch with nature do . . . it always has its erotic aspect. . . . The further back one goes the less possible it is to distinguish between the erotic and the sacral. And 'the further back' means not only in time, but also into the depths of experience."[2]

Our "holiday" derives from the Holi festivals of the east, described by a pious western observer as a Saturnalia, featuring "the most licentious debauchery."[3] The participants invariably saw their "debauchery" as a holy act, redolent of blessedness. Hindu texts said, "To have carnal intercourse with the goddess Parvati is a virtue which destroys all sin."[4] The I Ching speaks of the mystical value of sexual intercourse, which "gives life to all things."[5] According to Iwan Bloch, "Religion shares with the sexual impulse the unceasing yearning, the sentiment of everlastingness, the mystic absorption into the depths of life, the longing for the coalescence of individualities in an eternally blessed union."[6] For such reasons, words like passion, bliss, trance, ecstasy, glory were interchangeably applied to religious and sexual experience.

Iwan Bloch Author of *The Sexual Life of Our Times;* contemporary of Havelock Ellis.

Classical paganism used sexual *orgia* to represent the central Mystery, which is why Christian ascetics condemned the Great Rite as "the unnameable rites of the mysteries" or "the whoredoms of Eleusis." The Goddess promised eternal life to those who "privily entered the bedchamber," meaning the *pastos* or bridal chamber where the **hieros gamos** between the Goddess and her worshipper was consummated.[7] The same sort of *orgia* took place among the northern barbarians. Strabo said the druid enchanters in Ireland practiced sexual worship "similar to the orgies of Samothrace."[8]

Strabo Greek traveler, geographer, and historian of the first century B.C., a follower of the Stoic faith.

Despite the extreme asceticism of its early centuries, Christianity too became an orgiastic religion in some of its manifestations. An 11th-century Christian community at Orléans met on certain nights of the year to indulge in promiscuous behavior. A contemporary account said when the lights were put out, "every man grabs whatever woman comes to hand, even though she may be his own mother, his sister, or a nun, without thought of sin; for such tumbling is regarded by them as holiness and religion."[9] Defining such behavior as a manifestation of devil-worship was not very effective in preventing it, however. Communal mating was a standard accompaniment to religious ceremonies the world over, since before any Bibles were written. It was part of the surge of group feeling often characterizing the religious experience. The medieval peasant had long been familiar with the phenomenon, and liked it well enough to cling to it even if it was called Satanism.[10]

Few orgiasts deliberately viewed themselves as devil worshippers. As a rule they thought themselves exceptionally holy. Rasputin's sect, the "Men of God," claimed their naked dances imitated those of the heavenly angels. After singing and dancing to induce an ecstatic state, they engaged in sexual orgies which sometimes resulted in the birth of children, all of whom were said to have been begotten by the Holy Ghost.[11]

A Methodist preacher in Indiana once said, "Religious passion includes all other passions: you cannot excite one without stirring up the others."[12] American revivalism certainly proved this, so consistently that any child born nine months after a revivalist meeting was generally known as a "camp-meeting child." Outwardly puritanical, American Protestantism nevertheless "revived" a mode of religious behavior that would have been perfectly familiar to the ancient Greeks with their Samothracian orgies and their lecherous satyrs.[13] It just wasn't called by its real name.

1. Funk, 174. 2. Wilkins, 127. 3. Briffault 3, 198. 4. Edwardes, 52. 5. Rawson, E.A., 231. 6. Hartley, 317. 7. Lawson, 570, 586. 8. Haining, 23. 9. Campbell, C.M., 165. 10. Seligmann, 177. 11. Campbell, C.M., 163. 12. Rugoff, 337. 13. Mumford, 12.

Oriant

Medieval sun king born of the legendary Matabrune, "Burning Mother," who probably personified the red clouds of dawn. She was also embodied in Brunnhilde, leader of the Valkyries; so her name meant both Burning Mother and Burning Hel.[1] As his name suggests, Oriant was Lord of the East, like Ra, born every day from the womb of the Goddess.

1. Baring-Gould, C.M.M.A., 579.

Orion

"Moon-man of the Mountain," Greek version of the Lord of the Hunt ritually slain by Artemis, the Huntress. Some Hellenic stories claimed the Goddess killed Orion by mistake while he was swimming in the sea, too far away to be clearly seen. She shot arrows into a floating object that turned out to be Orion's head. Other stories said Orion was killed by a scorpion sent by Apollo, and Artemis placed his soul-image among the stars. Even in heaven, Orion is perpetually pursued by the Scorpion. According to Graves, this arrangement of constellations referred to the scorpion sent by the god Set to slay Horus.[1] In any event, Orion was another deified sacrificial victim.

1. Graves, G.M. 1, 152–53.

Ormazd

Variant name of **Ahura Mazda**, the Persian sun god who opposed his twin brother Ahriman, the Serpent of Darkness. Hormazd, Hormizd, and Ormuzd are further common variations. Persian

Manicheans of the early Christian era gave the name Ormuzd to a being called Primal Man, "an emanation of the highest God," who contributed to the Gnostic idea that man and God are identical, since Adam was God's essential self "made flesh."[1]

1. Jonas, 217.

Orpheus

Orphism was one of the most popular mystery-religions of the early Christian era. It was a development of the cult of Dionysus together with Orpheus, his earthly prophet and savior-son.

> *Orphism introduced a theology of redemption. It taught a doctrine of original sin. Man's nature was dualistic, composed of the* titanic *elements closely associated with the body, and the* dionysiac *elements which were allied with the soul. By an ascetic morality the former must be repressed and the latter cultivated, to the end that the soul may escape from the body as from a tomb, and may cease to be subject to the weary* kyklos genesios, *"cycle of reincarnation." "I have flown out of the sorrowful wheel," says the Orphic initiate on the Compagno tablet. . . . On the Dionysiac type of Greek religion it laid hold and remodelled it to its purpose. This Dionysiac religion, like Orphism, was of northern Thracian provenance, and was fraught with orgiastic-mystic elements, on which Orphism fastened, adopting its emotionalism, its doctrine of* Enthousiasmos, *and of possession by the deity, rejecting its wild frenzy, and transforming its savage ritual into a sacramental religion.*[1]

Orphism was a kind of western Buddhism, with escape from the karmic wheel effected by ascetic contemplation, spiritual journeys of the astral-projection type, and elaborate revelations. "Orphism was steeped in sacramentalism, which flooded the later Mysteries and flowed into Christianity. Salvation was by sacrament, by initiatory rites, and by an esoteric doctrine. . . . Orphism was the most potent solvent ever introduced into Greek religious life. . . . [T]he Orphics sowed the seeds of distrust toward the national and hereditary principle in religion, and made the salvation of the individual soul of first importance. In this way Orphism had enormous influence upon the subsequent history of religion."[2]

Orphism was the principal vehicle for Oriental mysticism in Greece. Its teachings were those of mystics everywhere: "Grasping in your mind that nothing is impossible for you, consider yourself immortal and capable of understanding everything. . . . Ascend beyond all height, descend beyond all depth. Gather into yourself the sensations of creation, of fire and of water, of dryness and of humidity, imagining that you are at one and the same moment everywhere, on earth, in the sea, in the heaven, that you have not yet been born, that you are beyond death." Like an initiated yogi, the Orphic sage could repeat: "I represent things to myself, not by the sight of my eyes, but by the spiritual energy I draw from the Powers. I am in heaven, in earth, in water. I am in air, in animals, in plants, in the womb, before the womb, after the womb, everywhere."[3]

An Orphic funerary tablet dug up near Sybaris alluded to Buddha-like escape from the karmic wheel (*kyklos genesion,* cycles of becoming), essentially identical to the Oriental *sangsara.*

An Orphic sacramental bowl of gold, with carved figures, dating from the 5th century, was unearthed in Romania in 1837. The figures showed the Orphic initiate's death-and-rebirth journey, the deities to be met in the upper and nether worlds, who also appeared in person as masked temple personnel when the novice was led through the stages of initiation. These figures were arranged on the bowl in the same way as the deities of the Intermediate State, between death and rebirth, were arranged on mandalas of Tibetan holy books.[4]

In Orphic belief as in the Orient, the power behind all forces of manifestation was the Great Mother, whose free-standing image appeared in the center of the Orphic bowl with other goddesses and gods ranged around her in the formation of a wheel.[5] She was the Black Mother Night, from whom were born Sleep, Love, Dreams, the Fates, Nemesis, Old Age, and Death. Even Zeus feared her, "which may reflect an old belief in Night as one of the great primeval powers of the universe."[6]

Mother Night was equated with Persephone, the "Destroyer" linked with both Dionysus and Orpheus. Once initiated, the Orphic mystic could announce: "I have sunk beneath the bosom of Persephone, Queen of the Underworld." Upon his post-mortem descent into hell, Persephone would personally greet him and promise to make him "god instead of mortal."[7]

The *Descent Into Hades* was the title of the Orphic manual and the essential rite of Orphic initiation, because the god himself descended into hell and returned, bringing with him the revelation on which the Mysteries were founded.[8] According to the classic myth, Orpheus descended to retrieve his bride Eurydice, who had died after being bitten by a snake in the grass. This was a late revision of a primitive Thracian dying-god myth, onto which the doctrines of Orphism were grafted later. Eurydice was actually "Universal Dike," or Tyche, Goddess of Fate, lady of the karmic wheel. She was originally one of Demeter's matriarchal Furies, converted by Hellenic writers into a daughter of Zeus.[9] In the underworld she was herself Persephone, the Death-goddess; and her "snake in the grass" was her own totem.

The oldest Orphic myth said Orpheus was torn to pieces by the **Maenads**, who worshipped Dionysus, Orpheus's divine alter ego. Mythographers gave various excuses for the Maenads' act, designed to conceal the true sacrificial motive. Some said the Maenads killed

Orpheus because he denounced their sexual orgies and advocated male homosexual love instead of the heterosexual kind. The Maenads were so angry at Orpheus that in Macedonia they killed all their husbands for listening to his teachings. It has been suggested that patriarchal-ascetic ideas came to Orphism from Egyptian priests of Ra, because Orphic priests wore Egyptian dress.[10]

Other stories said Orpheus was killed not by the Maenads but by Zeus's lightning bolt as punishment for his revelation of the gods' secrets to mankind. After he descended into hell and returned, his disembodied head was laid in a cave sacred to Dionysus, where it continued to sing and speak, like the head of Osiris at Abydos. As a teacher of the mysteries of the after-life, Orpheus became a god of oracles. He was said to have founded the oracles of Hecate in Aegina and of Demeter Chthonia in Sparta, two examples of Hellenic syncretism, as these oracles were formerly the property of the Goddesses whose names they bore.[11] Some derived Orpheus's name from Urphi, a popular oracular shrine in Edessa, though others linked his name with Erebus, the land of the dead.[12] Aristotle insisted that Orpheus had never lived at all.[13]

The common legend said Orpheus was a famous poet and lyre-player, like Cinyras the ancestor of Adonis (Greek *cinyra,* "lyre," cognate with Semitic *kinnor,* "lyre") and like David the ancestor of Jesus. Orpheus's lyre was kept as a holy relic in the temple at Lesbos, untouchable and taboo. Neanthus, son of the Tyrant of Lesbos, once played the Orphic lyre and shortly afterward was torn to pieces by a pack of "dogs," which might have meant dog-masked Maenad-priestesses. Later, the lyre was set in the stars, where it still appears as the constellation Lyra.[14]

One of the mysteriously significant phrases of Orphic initiation was "I a kid have fallen into my mother's milk," possibly a reference to death under Persephone's bosom followed by rebirth as her nursling. An ancient ritual was involved, one that was specifically forbidden by Jewish laws: "Thou shalt not seethe a kid in his mother's milk" (Exodus 23:19). So great was the Jews' fear of this ceremony that they even insisted on using different sets of dishes for milk and meat products. Yet their god was once mated to Mother Asherah as the "Pit," like Persephone, in a sacred-marriage rite that included cooking a kid in its mother's milk.[15] No one now knows what the phrase meant to biblical writers. Certainly the prohibition was not motivated by kindness to animals or reverence for goat-motherhood; there was a mystical reason for it.

Orphism became one of the most serious rivals of Christianity in the first few centuries A.D., until the church devised ways to identify the Orphic savior with Christ. Fourth-century Christian art showed Christ in the guise of Orpheus, wearing a Phrygian cap, playing the lyre, a sacrificial lamb under his foot.[16] Alexander Severus kept holy images of Christ and Orpheus side by side in his private chapel.[17]

The Orphic Gospel was preached throughout the Mediterranean world for at least twelve centuries.[18] It contributed much to Christian theology, and even reappeared in medieval bardic romance. The poets transformed Orpheus into Sir Orfeo, a king of England, son of King Pluto and the Goddess Juno. Orfeo's wife was Heurodis (Eurydice). He entered the underworld through a rocky cleft, and found the pagan fairyland of groves and gardens surrounding the queen's crystal palace, with its pillars of gold and gems. The place was inhabited by "people supposed to be dead, but they were not so." Orfeo returned to his capital city, Winchester, which "used to be called Thrace"—or so the bard said.[19] So much for medieval notions of geography.

Orphism gave Christian Europe more than muddled geography and romantic legends, however. The Orphic revelation was virtually indistinguishable from the Christian one, especially in its later "purified" form among ascetics who abstained from meat and from sensual pleasures in order to win eternal blessedness. With the introduction of a system of post-mortem punishment, the resemblance to Christianity was striking. Adeimantos, a character in Plato's Republic, said the Orphic revelation was "misused" by unscrupulous teachers, who "hold out the bribe of a happy immortality to the good and threaten eternal punishment to the bad, so that men turn to goodness not for its own sake, but in fear."[20] The difficulty was not restricted to Orphism (see **Hell**).

1. Angus, 151. 2. Angus, 154, 202. 3. Lindsay, O.A., 121–22. 4. Campbell, M.I., 389; *Bardo Thodol,* frontispeice. 5. Campbell, M.I., 391. 6. Cavendish, P.E., 88. 7. Angus, 110, 154. 8. *Bardo Thodol,* lxvi. 9. Hays, 114. 10. Graves, G.M. 1, 112, 114. 11. Graves, G.M. 1, 113. 12. Baring-Gould, C.M.M.A., 436. 13. Knight, S.L., xxii. 14. Graves, G.M. 1, 113. 15. Hooke, S.P., 225; M.E.M., 93. 16. d'Alviella, 89. 17. Rose, 292. 18. Angus, vii. 19. Loomis, 315–19. 20. Guthrie, 320–21.

Osculum Infame

"Infamous kiss," supposedly bestowed on the devil's anus by his worshippers as an act of homage. Pagan rituals, however, contained no such act; it seems to have been one of the inventions of the inquisitors. Scatological fantasies and excrement often figured in churchmen's visions of the activities of witches.

Osiris

Of all savior-gods worshipped at the beginning of the Christian era, Osiris may have contributed more details to the evolving Christ figure than any other. Already very old in Egypt, Osiris was identified with nearly every other Egyptian god and was on the way to absorbing them all. He had well over 200 divine names.[1] He was called Lord of Lords, King of Kings, God of Gods.[2] He was the Resurrection and the Life, the Good Shepherd, Eternity and Everlastingness, the god who "made men and women to be born again." Budge says, "From first to last, Osiris was to the Egyptians the god-man who suffered, and died, and rose again, and reigned eternally in heaven. They believed that they would inherit eternal life, just as he had done."[3]

According to Egyptian scriptures, "As truly as Osiris lives, so truly shall his follower live; as truly as Osiris is not dead he shall die no more; as truly as Osiris is not annihilated he shall not be annihilated."[4]

Osiris's coming was announced by Three Wise Men: the three stars Mintaka, Anilam, and Alnitak in the belt of Orion, which point directly to Osiris's star in the east, Sirius (Sothis), significator of his birth. Angelic voices hailed the coming of the Universal Lord on this occasion, which marked the rising of the Nile flood. Oriental paths of the Osirian tradition may be traced in Tibet, where the rising of the same star in the east marks the annual festival of "setting free the waters of springs," as the Egyptian festival set free the waters of the Nile. Tibetans named the star Rishi-Agastya, after a holy king of "a very ancient time."[5] Ancient Hebrews called the same star Ephraim, or the Star of Jacob. In Syrian, Arabian, and Persian astrology it was Messaeil—the Messiah.[6]

Certainly Osiris was a prototypical Messiah, as well as a devoured Host. His flesh was eaten in the form of communion cakes of wheat, the "plant of Truth." Osiris was Truth, and those who ate him became Truth also, each of them another Osiris, a Son of God, a "Light-god, a dweller in the Light-god." Egyptians came to believe that no god except Osiris could bestow eternal life on mortals.[7] He alone was the Savior, Un-nefer, the "Good One." Under this title he was even canonized as a Christian saint.[8]

Egyptians were much afraid of death's corruption awaiting them without the kindly intervention of Osiris: "When the soul hath departed, a man seeth corruption, and the bones of his body crumble away and become stinking things, and the members decay one after the other, the bones crumble into a helpless mass, and the flesh turneth into fetid liquid. Thus a man becometh a brother unto the decay which cometh upon him, and he turneth into a myriad of worms, and he becometh nothing but worms, and an end is made of him, and he perisheth in the sight of the god of day."[9] But Osiris could prevent all this nastiness:

> *Homage to thee, O my divine father Osiris, thou hast thy being with thy members. Thou didst not decay, thou didst not become worms, thou didst not diminish, thou didst not become corruption, thou didst not putrefy, and thou didst not turn into worms. . . . I shall not decay, and I shall not rot, I shall not putrefy, I shall not turn into worms, and I shall not*

see corruption before the eye of the god Shu. I shall have my being, I shall have my being; I shall live, I shall live; I shall germinate, I shall germinate, I shall germinate; I shall wake up in peace; I shall not putrefy, my intestines shall not perish; I shall not suffer injury; mine eye shall not decay; the form of my visage shall not disappear. . . . My body shall be stablished, and it shall neither fall into ruin nor be destroyed on this earth.[10]

The cult of Osiris contributed a number of ideas and phrases to the Bible. The 23rd Psalm copied an Egyptian text appealing to Osiris the Good Shepherd to lead the deceased to the "green pastures" and "still waters" of the *nefer-nefer* land, to restore the soul to the body, and to give protection in the valley of the shadow of death (the Tuat). The Lord's Prayer was prefigured by an Egyptian hymn to Osiris-Amen beginning "O Amen, O Amen, who art in heaven."[11] Amen was also invoked at the end of every prayer.

Jesus's words, "Except a corn of wheat fall into the ground and die, it abideth alone; but if it die, it bringeth forth much fruit" (John 12:24), were taken from an Osirian doctrine that a dying man is like a corn of wheat "which falls into the earth in order to draw from its bosom a new life."[12] Jesus's words, "In my Father's house are many mansions" (John 14:2) came from an Osirian text telling of numerous Arits ("Mansions") in the blessed land of Father Osiris.[13] Stories about Osiris turned up in Christian legends. Jesus's healing of a nobleman's daughter was based on a tale of an Osirian priest who cured a princess.[14] Worshippers of Osiris were promised that they would rule the spirit-souls (angels) in heaven, foreshadowing St. Paul's promise to his followers that they would rule even angels (1 Corinthians 6:3). The bishop's crozier was the Osirian shepherd-crook. The Christian cross itself was a variant of the Egyptian *ankh,* symbolizing "the Life to Come."[15]

One significant difference between Osiris and Christ was that Osiris was restored to life not by his divine father but by his divine mother—who was also his bride, Isis. She put his dismembered body back together and raised him from the dead. She married him and conceived his reincarnation, the Divine Child Horus who became Osiris again. She also took him to heaven where he reigned as Father Ra. Sometimes Ra was called Osiris's father, sometimes Osiris was called Ra's father, sometimes they were the same god, named Osiris-Ra. They were cyclically reincarnated as father-son and son-father, dwelling in the Mother as fetus, lover, corpse.[16]

Thus Osiris's cult centered on the theme of divine incest, apparent also in a Christianity that declared the Father and Son identical, and the Mother of God the same individual as God's bride. Osiris plainly expressed the archetypal wish for union with the mother, found in all men's religions. He was restored to life as the ithyphallic Min, Men, or Menu, "Moon-god," hailed as a Bull of lust, "the mummy with a long member," or "the Lord Who impregnates his Mother."[17]

A symbol of Osiris's sacred marriage was the *menat,* "moon-charm," in hieroglyphics a phallus-shaped jar pouring fluid into a wider pot or vase, signifying sexual intercourse with a deity.[18] The *menat* amulet was borne by nearly every Egyptian god; it was also a title of Isis.[19] The same sexual image of the two vessels was found in the tombs and temples of Babylon and Assyria.[20] The male water-jar represented the seminal spirit of the Savior in all the lands of the Middle East and Egypt. In his processions, the god was preceded by a **jar-bearer** like the man with a jar of water who preceded Jesus in the Passover procession (Luke 22:10).

The Jews' Passover meal called Seder may have descended from the Egyptian Sed, the oldest festival of Osirian regeneration and fertility.[21] At the Sed, Osiris's masculinity was erected in the form of the Djed column, originally a simple phallic obelisk, later a representation of Osiris's sacrum, the "sacred bone" so called because it was once regarded as the source of seminal fluid. When Isis brought Osiris back to life, her first care was to make him "stand up," which meant restoration of his phallic spirit.[22]

Primitive elements in Osirian myth show its extreme antiquity, dating back to Neolithic Egypt. Before re-conceiving Osiris, the Goddess apparently devoured him as she hovered over his corpse in the guise of the archaic Vulture-mother (see **Vulture**).[23] Like similar images of devouring Kali, this points to an age predating even the discovery of fatherhood, when reincarnations were believed to be brought about by cannibalism. Indeed, Osiris may have begun as one of the numerous forms of Shiva, for his name came from Ausar or Asar, meaning "the Asian" just like the **Aesir** or "Asian" gods of northern Europe.[24]

About 4000 years ago, Osiris's cult was established at Abydos, where he was called Osiris Khenti-Amenti, Lord of Death or Lord of the Westerners, meaning those who had "gone west" into death's sunset land. He was incarnate in a succession of sacred kings who seem to have served as sacrificial victims. Their bodies were divided up and distributed to different parts of the country to assist fertility—as in Norway, up to the 9th century, where kings' bodies used to be quartered and sent to the four provinces for burial, so each locality would have royal flesh to assist the crops.[25] As Christian churches used to be founded on spurious relics of apostles and saints, so Egyptian temples were founded on bits of Osiris's body.[26]

Like the head of Orpheus on Lesbos, the head of Osiris was preserved in the temple at Abydos to serve as an oracle, providing much of the Egyptians' detailed knowledge of the after-world. The shrine had a sacred well called Peq or Pega, the original home of the Pega-nymphs who guarded the oracular well of Pirene in Corinth.[27] Like Christians seeking burial in consecrated ground by a church, wealthy Egyptians bought burial space near the Osirian temple, so as to share the god's resurrection. Abydos therefore became the center of a great necropolis.[28] The faithful claimed on their epitaphs that "I have become a divine being by the side of the birthchamber of Osiris; I am brought forth with him, I renew my youth."[29]

When human sacrifices were replaced by animals, Osiris obligingly incarnated himself in a variety of beasts, notably the Apis bull who ascended to glory, carrying away the sins of all Egypt as he died in atonement.[30] Osiris-Apis later became the composite deity **Sarapis**, monotheistic god of Alexandria for six centuries.[31]

There were several Osirian trinities. One consisted of Osiris the father, Isis the mother, and Horus the son. Another was Ra the father, Osiris the son on earth, and Horus the son rising in heaven. Another was (1) Ptah, "Opener of the Way," a phallic consort of the Virgin and the opener of her matrix; (2) Seker, representing the male spent, dead, and hidden within the female tomb-womb; and (3) Osiris, newly incarnate as the Min-phallus and standing for resurrection.[32]

The sacred lunar numbers seven, fourteen, and twenty-eight were prominent in Osiris's cult. The lunar cycle of twenty-eight days corresponded to his descent into the underworld and ascent to heaven: fourteen days each way, or fourteen steps on his mystic Ladder. Buddha's ladder of descent to earth and return to heaven also had fourteen steps.[33] Like Buddha and Osiris, the Tibetan sage is still supposed to pass fourteen days in the after-world before encountering enlightenment in the form of "the mandala of the animal-headed deities," reminiscent of the Egyptian gods. Some of these deities were named Heruka, a possible cognate of Osiris the sun, Heru-Harakhti.[34]

Like Hindu sacred dramas, the cycle of Osirian drama seems to have been keyed to the menstrual cycle of the Goddess, incarnate in the priestess who bore the title of Divine Mother. In the month of Athyr (Hathor), Egyptian women made clay phalli as images of Osiris and threw them into the Nile when it "turned to blood" in flood time (see **Moses**).[35] This custom recalled the Oriental conviction that the Goddess must be menstruating at the time of her sacred marriage to the dying god. Later accounts explained Osirian lunar numbers by saying he was 28 years old at the time of his passion, or else that it took place in the 28th year of his reign on earth.[36]

As Lord of Death, Osiris was sometimes identified with the Great Serpent of the underworld, and sometimes painted in the same serpentine form, bent around so his toes touched his head.[37] In Ptolemaic times the whole underworld became Osiris's province, its seven halls collectively called the House of Osiris.[38]

Between 1450 and 1400 B.C. the Osirian mystery-cult took form, with hundreds of verbal formulae for making the worshipper become an Osiris. He would be born of Isis and nursed by Nephthys. He would ride across the sky "side by side with the gods of the stars." He would be as virile as Osiris-Menu: "My palm tree (penis) standeth upright and is like Menu. . . . Therefore the Phallus of Ra, which is the head of

Osiris, shall not be swallowed up." When he was in heaven, the gods themselves would bring offerings to him.[39]

The Osirian Mysteries taught words of power for bringing about these desirable effects. Such words of power were "keys" to heaven, to be concealed from non-initiates as "a great mystery."[40] The Saite Recension said with such keys, a soul could pass freely through the gates, gatekeepers, guardians, heralds, inspectors, and other spirits of the heavenly mansions, for he would know all their names.

Saite Recension A portion of the Egyptian *Book of the Dead* in vogue from the XXVI dynasty to the Ptolemaic period, ca. 600–30 B.C.

> *And the Majesty of Anpu shall say unto me, "Knowest thou the name of this door, and canst thou tell it?" . . . And the Majesty of the god Anpu shall say unto me, "Knowest thou the name of the upper leaf, and the name of the lower leaf?" On receiving the proper answers, the Majesty of the god Anpu shall say, "Pass on, for thou hast knowledge, O Osiris."*[41]

During the first century B.C. the Osirian religion was established in all parts of the Roman Empire.[42] Its popularity declined in the end because it became too complicated for the average mind. Necessary "words of power" developed into lengthy catechisms of divine names of doorposts, lintels, bolts, panels, doorkeepers, spirits of the hour, thresholds, gods' right and left feet, etc. Egyptians invented even a memory-god to bring back the spells and holy names if they were stolen by a spirit of forgetfulness.[43] The important ceremony of "Opening the Mouth" was performed to let the dead person speak charms and words of power freely.[44] Still, the catechisms became too long and complex to be remembered.

Budge remarks that the Egyptians believed in "the resurrection of the body in a changed and glorified form, which would live to all eternity in the company of the spirits and souls of the righteous in a kingdom ruled by a being who was of divine origin, but who had lived upon the earth, and had suffered a cruel death at the hands of his enemies, and had risen from the dead, and had become the God and king of the world which is beyond the grave. . . . Although they believed in all these things and proclaimed their belief with almost passionate earnestness, they seem never to have freed themselves from a hankering after amulets and talismans, and magical names, and words of power, and seem to have trusted in these to save their souls and bodies, both living and dead, with something of the same confidence which they placed in the death and resurrection of Osiris. A matter for surprise is that they seem to see nothing incongruous in such a mixture of magic and religion."[45]

It is a matter for even more surprise that a scholar of Budge's stature failed to see exactly the same mixture of magic and religion in Christianity; for indeed he could have been talking about Christians as well as Egyptians. To this day, simple Christian folk still display the same hankering after crucifixes and medals, *agnus dei,* incantations, invocations of holy names and other formulae, saints' relics, holy water, images, even rosaries which they copied from the Egyptians. Christian formulae of exorcism, baptism, extreme unction, absolution, etc., were words of power under different names. The notion of resurrection through identification with a resurrected god (by eating his flesh) was in itself magical rather than religious—and this was the basis of the Christian salvation-idea no less than for that of Osiris's votaries. Moreover it seems the concept of Christ was no less syncretic than the concept of Osiris. If anything, the older god had more right to claim an original system of worship—or of superstition, depending on one's point of view.

1. Budge, G.E. 2, 178. 2. *Book of the Dead,* 650; Martello, 189.
3. Budge, G.E. 2, 126, 141. 4. Angus, 139. 5. Waddell, 509–10. 6. Martello, 190.
7. *Book of the Dead,* 156, 268, 459, 551. 8. H. Smith, 227. 9. *Book of the Dead,* 462.
10. Neumann, G.M., 166. 11. Budge, E.M., 116. 12. Pepper & Wilcock, 50.
13. *Book of the Dead,* 269. 14. Budge, G.E. 2, 41. 15. Baring-Gould, C.M.M.A., 355.
16. Budge, G.E. 1, 256. 17. Erman, 304. 18. *Book of the Dead,* 170.
19. Budge, G.E. 2, 55. 20. James, 169. 21. James, 135–39. 22. Brandon, 126–27.
23. Hays, 257. 24. Budge, G.E. 2, 113. 25. Turville-Petre, 192.
26. Budge, G.E. 2, 192. 27. Budge, G.E. 2, 118; D.N., 276. 28. *Larousse,* 17.
29. Robertson, 48. 30. Budge, G.E. 2, 127. 31. Cumont, A.R.G.R., 80.
32. Budge, E.M. 84. 33. Campbell, M.I., 169. 34. *Bardo Thodol,* 70–71.
35. Hooke, M.E.M., 70. 36. Budge, G.E. 1, 101; 2, 188. 37. Budge, G.E. 1, 172.
38. Lethaby, 157. 39. *Book of the Dead,* 297, 469, 509–10, 518. 40. Budge, E.M., 116.
41. *Book of the Dead,* 571. 42. Angus, 197. 43. *Book of the Dead,* 279–80, 591–94.
44. Budge, E.M., 196. 45. Budge, E.M., xii-xiv.

Ouroboros

Greek name of the Hermetic World Serpent, sometimes the Sea-serpent Oceanus encircling the earth; sometimes the underground Python coiled in the earth's womb; otherwise known as Sata, Leviathan, Taaut, Tuat, Thoth, Ophion, etc. See **Serpent**.

Owl

Romans called the owl *strix* (pl. *striges*), the same word that meant "witch."[1] Greeks said the owl was sacred to Athene, their own version of the ancient Mesopotamian "Eye-Goddess" whose staring owl-eyed images have been found throughout the Middle East, especially around the Mother-city of Mari.[2] The owl was also the totem of Lilith, Blodeuwedd, Anath, and other versions of the Triple Goddess of the moon. See **Trinity**.

According the Christian legend, the owl was one of "three disobedient sisters" who defied God and was transformed into a bird who never looked at the sun.[3] It is easy enough to see in this idea the shape of the Goddess herself, and the church's hostility to her. One of the medieval names for the owl was "night hag"; it was said to be a witch in bird form.[4] The owl is still associated with witches in the symbols of **Halloween**.

The owl is also a bird of wisdom because it used to embody the wisdom of the Goddess. Certain medieval magic charms apparently sought to use the bird's oracular power against its former mistress, woman. If an owl could be slain and its heart pulled out and laid on the left breast of a sleeping woman, the woman would talk in her sleep and reveal all her secrets.[5] This seems to have been a basis of the expression, "heart-to-heart talk," which meant a woman's secret conversation with her familiar.

1. Trigg, 96. 2. Neumann, G.M., pl. 87. 3. de Lys, 37. 4. Cavendish, P.E., 100. 5. Agrippa, 76.

Like the Hindu Shakti, classical PSYCHE was the female soul who sought completion with the body in union with Eros. This is a detail from an antique Greek sculpture in the Capitoline Museum, Rome.

Queen of the Underworld, PROSERPINA was prominent in both Roman and (as Persephone) Greek mythology. The Christians had to deal with her somehow, so turned her into the "arch she-devil." Shown here with Ceres, her sometime mother, and Pluto, her consort in Hades. Rome; Museo Laterano.

Daughter of Heaven, bride of Shiva, PARVATI was the virgin aspect of the Hindu goddess, Kali Ma. Bronze; Southern India, Chola period, 10th century.

Paganism

Latin *pagani* meant country-dwellers, the rural people whose religious conservatism caused them to cling to old gods and goddesses even when Christianity was well established in cities and among the aristocracy. "It has now been demonstrated that the hostility of the peasantry to Christianity gave the meaning of 'pagan' to *paganus.* This seems to date from the first half of the fourth century and it gradually becomes general in the second half."[1]

"Heathen" came from Germanic *heiden,* that which is hidden, because the church officially forbade the rites of the old deities, and the pagan people continued their rites in secret.[2]

Through the first half of the Christian era, paganism was overt and more or less acceptable. Christianity and paganism existed side by side in uneasy proximity long enough for Christians to take over as many pagan deities, holy places, customs, and holidays as possible. Noting that the people wouldn't accept Christianity unless it could be considered an extension of their paganism, Pope Gregory the Great directed that Christian relics must be placed in the inner shrines of pagan temples, and the people converted gradually to the idea that their deity was a saint instead of an un-Christian spirit.[3] Pagan feast days were to be Christianized. For example, at Christmas the people were to be allowed to sacrifice and eat "a great number of oxen to the glory of God, as they had formerly done to the Devil."[4]

Though the old deities were re-defined as devils, nominal Christians continued to believe in them as firmly as they believed in Christ, if not more so.[5] They were quite willing to consult "devils" for guidance in their daily lives. The Venerable Bede said Redwald, king of the East Saxons, kept in the same temple an altar to offer sacrifices to Christ and another altar to offer sacrifices to "devils."[6] Gothic converts to the church simply added the name of Christ to their own lists of native gods but dropped it with equal readiness if its magic proved ineffective.[7]

This dual religious system persisted even through periods when the "fairy-religion" was persecuted as witchcraft. It could be said that Christianity and paganism co-exist even now, for the greater part of Christian worship, sacraments, and basic theology came from the pagan heritage. "The lamb, the dragon (or serpent), the dove above the altar, the triangle enclosing the all-seeing eye (common to Freemasonry as well), the sacred fish-symbol, the ever-burning fire, or the image of the risen sun upon the receptacle for the consecrated wafer in the Roman Mass, the architectural symbols and the orientation of church and cathedral, the cross itself, and even the colors and designs of the robes of priest and bishop and pope, are a few of the silent witnesses of the survival in the modern Christian churches of the symbolism of paganism."[8] Even such essential doctrines as the virgin birth, Incarnation, Logos, resurrection, salvation, purgatory, baptism, and holy communion were products of paganism, developed many centuries before the Christian era.

Giraldus Cambrensis complained in the 12th century that the people of Ireland were still given over to "old, barbaric and obscene customs."[9] The cult of Diana co-existed with Christianity in Devon as late as the 14th century, when the Goddess was worshipped in woodland shrines even by monks.[10] At Cologne in 1333, Petrarch saw "women conjuring the Rhine" in what was described as "a rite of the people."[11]

The people's religion had been largely in the hands of women since Caesar's day, and so it remained up to the 12th and 13th centuries when active persecution of "witches" began.[12] Martin of Braga, a 6th-century Portuguese missionary father, noted that women not only maintained their own un-Christian temples, but also performed domestic acts of worship like decorating tables, wearing laurels, taking omens, offering bread to water spirits and wine to the Yule log, calling upon Minerva when spinning, and invoking Venus at weddings and on the public road. "What is that but worship of the devil?" he asked. Moreover, he believed in the women's pagan deities himself. He said the rivers, springs, and woods were filled with Lamias, Nymphs, and Dianas; "and they were all malign devils and nefarious spirits."[13]

A 10th-century Penitential tried to forbid women to present their children to Mother Earth at the crossroads in their ancient manner, "for this is great paganism."[14] A 16th-century Finnish bishop observed that "when people fall ill, they seek help from the devil by laying wax figures, candles, squirrel skins and other things on the altars, and on certain days sacrifice sheep and coins."[15] The 9th-century Synod of Rome recorded pagan worship in the churches: "Many people, mostly women, come to church on Sundays and holy days not to attend the Mass but to dance, sing broad songs, and do other such pagan things."[16]

Of course the churches had deliberately lured women by taking over the shrines of their Goddess, with the promise that the rites could continue as usual. Churches were built over shrines of Syrian Astarte at Corbridge in Northumberland, of Diana Nemetona at Bath, and of Sarapis and Mithra at York.[17] At Cangas de Onis, Arrichinaga, and other places in Spain, churches were built around pagan dolmens and sacred mounds, still in existence today.[18] Church processions featured carnival mummers in the masks and costumes of ancient beast-gods, such as the four totems of the pagan sacred year—lion, bull, eagle, and serpent—adopted as symbols of the evangelists.[19] Pagan deities appeared in the very carvings and decorations of churches. As late as 1576 a British church employed workmen to pull down and destroy "sundry superstitious things tending to the maintenance of idolatry."[20]

The Christian church had no holidays of its own; every feast in the Christian calendar was borrowed from the pagans, including Easter and Christmas. Roman festivals were particularly tenacious, until they had to be given Christian names to excuse the people's continued celebration of them. The Hilaria became the Feast of Annunciation; the Robigalia became the Feast of St. Mark; the Quinquatrus became the Feast of St. Joseph; St. Cyprian's Day replaced the day of Jupiter.[21] "A thousand years ago, old and young assembled in woods or on plains to bring gifts to their gods, and celebrated with dances, games, and offerings the festival of spring, or of awaking and blooming Nature. These celebrations have taken Christian names, but innumerable old heathen rites and customs are still to be found in them."[22]

Christian historians often give an impression that Europe's barbarians welcomed the new faith, which held out a hope of immortality and a more kindly ethic. The impression is false. The people didn't willingly give up the faith of their ancestors, which they considered essential to proper functioning of the earth's cycles. They had their own hope of immortality and their own ethic, in many ways a kinder ethic than that of Christianity which was imposed on them by force.[23] Justinian obtained 70,000 conversions in Asia Minor by methods that were so cruel that the subject populations eventually adopted Islam in order to rid themselves of the rigors of Christian rule.[24]

As a rule, heathen folk resisted Christianity as long as they could, even after their rulers had gone over to the new faith for its material rewards. Louis the Pious baptized a Danish chieftain named Harald Klak, and gave him a large fief on the Weser river, on the understanding that he would convert his people; but the people rejected both Christianity and Harald. In the 10th century, King Haakon of Norway was fiercely opposed when he tried to institute Christianity. His people rebelled, burned the new Christian churches, and forced Haakon to eat the horse-liver sacrifices and drink New Year toasts to Woden, Frey, Bragi, and the totemic clan. Some rulers themselves rejected the new faith out of hand. Alcuin announced in the 8th century that there would never be any hope of Christianizing the Danes. Their king was "harder than a stone and wilder than any beast," and would have none of Rome's God.[25]

Certain words reveal by their derivation some of the opposition met by missionaries. The pagan Savoyards called Christians "idiots," hence *crétin,* "idiot," descended from *Chrétien,* "Christian." German pagans coined the term *bigot,* from *bei Gott,* an expression constantly used by the monks.[26] Christians were the first to insist that there was only one god, and it was theirs. This attitude tended to produce resentment among worshippers of other gods.

The Roman Empire tolerated all religions within its far-flung borders, so long as Rome's official deities received due lip-service, and the deified emperors were properly honored. This policy of religious freedom was soon abandoned by the Roman church, which began to insist that all non-Christian faiths be destroyed; then that even Christians of non-orthodox sects must give up their heretical "errors," or die. The beginning of organized Christianity marked the true end of the ancient world's polytheistic freedom of worship. The new Gospels became the sole authority. Other scriptures were burned. Yet, despite all the destruction, there was no real end to paganism.[27] The people remembered it and practiced it throughout the Christian era.

The third Council of Constantinople decreed in the 7th century that the people must stop kindling bonfires and leaping over them on nights of the new moon.[28] St. Eligius wrote: "Let no Christian place lights at the temples, or the stones, or at fountains, or at trees, or enclosures, or at places where three ways meet. . . . Let no one presume to make lustrations, or to enchant herbs, or to make flocks pass through a hollow tree or an aperture in the earth; for by doing so he seems to consecrate them to the devil."[29] Nevertheless, these activities continued.

In vain the Council of Toledo condemned "worshippers of idols, those who venerate stones, who kindle torches, who celebrate the rites of springs and trees . . . men who go about in the mask of a stag or bull-calf, who dress in the skin of a herd animal, or put on the heads of beasts."[30] At Ephesus, twelve centuries after the time of Christ, ancient fertility rites were still performed though Christian writers reported that "men took delight in unholy things as if they were pious deeds."[31] To the pagans, they were pious deeds.

Slavs never ceased to worship Kupala, the Water-mother Va-kul, Volos the horse god, Yarilo the fertility-savior, and the rest of their pantheon. Bulgarian penitential books tried again and again to abolish worship of the sun and moon—without success. As late as the 18th century, the bishop of Voronezh denounced the "satanic games" connected with the sacrifice of Yarilo; and the Bulgarian monk Spiridon complained that most of his countrymen still worshipped Pyerun the thunder god instead of Jesus.[32]

The old customs were preserved especially by women, who were not welcome in the new church, and preferred paganism for the spiritual authority it could confer on them. A 10th-century Ecclesiastical Canon appealed to fathers, not mothers, to instruct their children in Christian ways. Men must "forbid well-worshippings, necromancies and divinations; enchantments and man-worshippings, and all the other vain practices which are carried out with various spells. . . . And we enjoin that every Christian man zealously accustom his children to Christianity and teach them the Paternoster and the Creed. And we enjoin that on feast-days, they abstain from heathen songs and devil's games."[33]

But the songs and games went on, gradually taking on the guise of secular carnivals, harvest-homes, May dances, Oktoberfests, Midsummer feasts, and so on. Women maintained many of these traditions, not because they were more rebellious than men but because they were more conservative. Priestesses came to be called "witches" by their Christian enemies. "Pagan folk practices and beliefs, whether Greco-

Roman, Teutonic, or Celtic, did not die out with the introduction of Christianity but rather remained and constituted the fundamental substratum of witchcraft."[34]

After centuries of denunciation and suppression, the church found that many pagan ceremonies were too tenacious to be stamped out and had to be assimilated by the Christian system. At the end of the 18th century, Irish clergymen "artfully yielded to the superstitions of the natives, in order to gain and keep up an establishment, grafting Christianity on Pagan rites." Bourne said "The monks, in the dark unlearned ages of Popery, copied after the heathens, and dreamed themselves into the like superstitions."[35] Sometimes Christ and the old gods were incongruously blended, as at a 15th-century temple at Istein dedicated to "Jupiter Christus."[36] To this day, the pagan ceremony of the New Fire is enacted each Easter on Mount Lycabettus, where it used to commemorate the rebirth of Apollo.

Many pagan deities were remade into saints. Others were vaguely Christianized by interpreting them as prophetic figures. "Aesculapius, who suffered death because he had raised the dead, is a type of Christ. . . . Jupiter, changed into a bull and carrying Europa on his back, also typifies Christ, the sacrificial ox who bore the burden of the sin of the world. Theseus who forsook Ariadne for Phaedra prefigures the choice which Christ made between the Church and the Synagogue. Thetis who gave her son Achilles arms with which to triumph over Hector, is no other than the Virgin Mary who gave a body to the Son of God."[37]

With a combination of syncretism, reinterpretation and exegesis, Christianity managed to absorb nearly all of paganism except its Goddess. According to Guignebert:

> *Western peoples in the early centuries of the Christian era never really understood the Christian dogmas, nor have they understood them since. The religion which they have constructed upon these dogmas through their own efforts was something different . . . it was cast in formulas ill able to contain it. The Western peoples have, strictly speaking, never been Christians. . . . Bearing the impress only of the Christian legend and nourished upon formulas passively repeated, these men—the vast majority of professed Christians—remained actually pagans, and still do so within the folds of the Catholic commonwealth.*[38]

1. Guignebert, 175. 2. Borchardt, 290. 3. Hitching, 210; Guignebert, 214. 4. M. Harrison, 139. 5. Coulton, 27. 6. M. Harrison, 42. 7. J.H. Smith, D.C.P., 238. 8. *Bardo Thodol,* 4. 9. M. Harrison, 181. 10. Lethbridge, 71. 11. Borchardt, 282. 12. Turville-Petre, 261. 13. J.H. Smith, D.C.P., 238–41. 14. Hitching, 210. 15. Robbins, 199. 16. J.B. Russell, 75. 17. Squire, 275. 18. Hitching, 216. 19. Rose, 298. 20. Hazlitt, 335. 21. Rose, 295. 22. Leland, 142. 23. Campbell, C.M., 390. 24. H. Smith, 228. 25. Oxenstierna, 67–69, 221. 26. Potter & Sargent, 202. 27. Phillips, 152. 28. Hazlitt, 63. 29. Hitching, 209. 30. H. Smith, 270. 31. Lawson, 223. 32. *Larousse,* 294; Spinka, 34. 33. M. Harrison, 143. 34. J.B. Russell, 37. 35. Hazlitt, 336, 374. 36. Borchardt, 117. 37. Mâle, 339–40. 38. Guignebert, 500, 502.

Paivatar

Finno-Ugric version of the Aryan Goddess Parvati, or Prithivi, the Virgin who spun the threads of fate. She was sometimes described as the Daughter of the Sun, or a younger form of the same deity. Northern Europeans generally regarded the sun as female.[1]

1. *Larousse*, 308.

Palaemon

Heracles the Sun, swallowed by the Sea-mother in totemic form as a great **fish**, and reborn of the same mother as the Boy on the Dolphin. Palaemon was a Greco-Roman counterpart of **Jonah**. His mother was Venus Salacia, the womb of the sea, named Delphinos which meant both "dolphin" and "womb."[1] Biblical writers transformed the dolphin into Jonah's whale, and the "boy" born of the fish-mouth into a prophet.

1. Neumann, A.P., 6.

Pales

Archaic ass-god after whom both Palestine and Philistia were named; also the Palatine Hill in Rome, where the ancient festival of Palilia annually celebrated the rites of Pales, or Pallas. (See **Palladium**.) There was some disagreement as to Pales's sex. Some said he was a priapic ass-headed fertility spirit like Set, or Pan; others said Pales was a female, one of the disguises of Vesta under the name of Diva Palatua (the Palatine Goddess).[1] The temple of this androgynous deity was the origin of the word "palace." His/her festivals were celebrated regularly, several centuries into the Christian era, by priests wearing ass-faced masks. See **Ass**.

1. Briffault 3, 18.

Palladium

This mysterious fetish occupied the Holy of Holies in the Roman temple of Vesta on the Palatine Hill, and was said to embody the essential spirit of Rome, as it had previously embodied the spirit of Troy. Roman legend said Aeneas carried off the Palladium from the wreckage of Troy and founded Rome with its help. It was a symbol of a protean, androgynous deity usually called Pallas, whose name meant either "maiden" or "youth."[1]

Some said Pallas was identical with the Goddess Athene. Some said Pallas was a Pan-like goat god slain by Athene. Some said Pallas was a giant. Some said Pallas was a wooden image of a female warrior. Some said Pallas was a thunder-stone. A majority believed Pallas was a phallic god and his Palladium was "the scepter of Priam, in the likeness of a male sex organ."[2]

In Greek myth, Pallas had offspring, the Pallantids, who worshipped an Amazonian fighting Goddess, the enemy of the patriarchal Hellenic hero Theseus.[3] This may account for the notion that Pallas was a female warrior, once a companion of Athene who took her name and became Pallas Athene after accidentally killing her in a mock battle. This classic myth bears the marks of revision, a story invented to account for Athene's androgynous idol represented by a lingam-yoni, showing her union with Pallas, Pales, or Pan.

The Vestal Virgins were married to the spirit of Rome by means of an artificial phallus in the Palladian shrine; thus it seems probable that Pallas was a sacred lingam signifying AMOR, the secret name of ROMA in reverse.

Constantine moved the Palladium to Constantinople and made it a symbol of his own masculinity. It was buried under a huge red porphyry pillar topped by an image of himself in the guise of Apollo.[4]

1. Graves, G.M. 2, 403. 2. Graves, G.M. 2, 261, 266; Dumézil, 323, 583.
3. Graves, G.M. 2, 15. 4. Seznec, 43; J.H. Smith, C.G., 226.

Palladius

Roman name for the phallic god represented by the Palladium; a name given to the Pater, or Patricius, a spirit of begetting. Palladius was assimilated to the Celtic *pater,* "Patrick," in a Christian legend that claimed one Bishop Palladius was a missionary to the pagan Irish before St. Patrick.[1] Both bishop and saint seem to have been purely imaginary (see **Patrick, Saint**).

1. *Encyc. Brit.,* "Patrick."

Palm Tree

In the Babylonian myth of the primal garden, the palm tree was the Tree of Life, a dwelling-place of the Goddess Astarte. The Hebrew version of her name was Tamar, "Palm Tree."[1]

Her male counterpart was Baal-Peor, or Phoenix, the god of Phoenicia whose name meant "Land of the Palm." As a phallic deity, Baal-Peor was symbolized by a palm tree between two large stones. Sexual orgies in the temple celebrated his union with the Goddess in Phoenicia and in Israel until priests of Yahweh killed the celebrants in the midst of their rites (Numbers 25:8).

Still, the feminine connotations of the palm tree remained. The Goddess was often embodied in a Mother-palm, giving the food of life in the form of coconut milk or dates. A complicated biblical myth shows Tamar the Palm-tree as the mother of a slain "firstborn of Judah"; and as a veiled sacred harlot decorated with the signet, staff, and bracelets of the nation of Judah; and as a widow (Crone) to whom offerings of goats were made; and as an idol "by the wayside," whom priests of Yahweh wanted to burn (Genesis 38). She gave birth to the rival twins Pharez and Zarah, Hebrew counterparts of Osiris and Set. The spirit of the palm tree was still the Great Mother in the tradition of early Christians, who gave the title of Holy Palm (Ta-Mari) to the virgin Mary.[2] Yet Egyptians continued to call a man's penis his "palm tree."[3]

1. Graves, W.G., 197. 2. Hughes, 55. 3. *Book of the Dead,* 518.

Pan

King of Arcadian satyrs, the horned and hoofed woodland god *par excellence.* Pan was one of the oldest gods in Greece, associated with the cult of Dionysus and sometimes identified with him. Pan was said to have coupled with all the Dionysian Maenads. In addition, he was mated to Athene, Penelope, Selene, and many archaic forms of the Great Goddess.[1]

Greeks claimed the Egyptian solar god Amon-Ra was the same as Pan. They called Amon-Ra's holy city Panopolis, "City of Pan," saying it was inhabited by "Pans and satyrs." The *panoply* (ceremonial dress and decoration) derives from holy processions in the City of Pan.[2] Other words connected with Pan's cult are caper, caprice, and capriccio, all from Latin *caper,* the goat. Pan's sacred drama of death and resurrection was the original "tragedy," from Greek *tragoidos,* "Goat Song."[3] The word "panic" was originally the terrible cry of Pan, who dispersed his enemies with a magic yell that filled them with fear and took away all their strength.

It may be that Pan's legend began with the Hindu fertility god Pancika, consort of one of the primal Mother-goddesses, many-breasted Hariti, who suckled hundreds of pre-Vedic animal spirits as many-breasted Diana suckled the woodland beasts, whose king Pan was.[4]

Pan was an important model for medieval pagans' Horned God, whom the church called Satan. The devil always displayed Pan's attributes of goat-hoofs, horns, and unremitting lust; sometimes also a goat head and an attendant throng of satyrs (demons). Yet the new romanticism of the 19th century laid aside the demonic nature attributed to Pan only a few centuries previously and made him a gentle image of the lost Arcadia populated by shepherds and nymphs. Romantic poets adopted Pan as their wildwood god.

In 1821, Shelley wrote to his friend Thomas J. Hogg: "I am glad to hear that you do not neglect the rites of the true religion. Your

Pan's name has been derived from *paein,* "pasture"; it was also the word for "all" and for "bread," recalling various All-fathers who were gods of divine bread, such as Osiris, Adonis, and Tammuz. Like them, Pan was a sacred king who died in fertilizing the earth. The ritual phrase "Great Pan is dead" seems to have been taken from the rites of Tammuz; it was also understood as *Thamus Pan-megas Tethnece,* "All-great Tammuz is dead."

letter awoke my sleeping devotion, and the same evening I ascended alone the high mountain behind my house, and suspended a garland, and raised a small turf-altar to the mountain-walking Pan." Oscar Wilde wrote wistfully: "O goat-foot god of Arcady! This modern world hath need of thee!"[5] Byron wrote a regretful ode on the passing of Pan:

The Gods of old are silent on their shore
Since the great Pan expired, and through the roar
Of the Ionian waters broke a dread
Voice which proclaimed "the mighty Pan is dead."
How much died with him! false or true—the dream
Was beautiful which peopled every stream
With more than finny tenants, and adorned
The woods and waters with coy nymphs that scorned
Pursuing Deities, or in the embrace
Of gods brought forth the high heroic race
Whose names are on the hills and o'er the seas.[6]

1. Graves, G.M. 1, 103. 2. Budge, G.E. 2, 22. 3. Funk, 253, 302. 4. *Larousse,* 359. 5. Merivale, 64, 119. 6. Merivale, 72.

Panacea

"All-healer," one of the divine daughters of Mother Rhea Coronis at her Pelasgian sanctuary of Titane. Another daughter was Hygeia, "Health." To this day, both Goddesses are invoked in the medical Hippocratic Oath.[1] The two seem to have been personifications of the Great Mother's breasts, source of the Milk of Kindness and the balm of healing.

Egyptians said the remedy for almost every ill was "the milk of a woman who has given birth to a child: such is the sweet perfume" that could expel demons of sickness.[2] Panacea and Hygeia were comparable to Egypt's Two Mistresses, Buto and Nekhbet, whose milk bestowed divinity on pharaohs and health on everyone.[3] Buto was the same nursing-mother Goddess called Latona, Lada, Leto or Leda, the Babylonians' Allatu, the Arabs' Al-Lat (who later became Allah). Etruscans called her **Lat**, mother of Latium and giver of moon-milk. Latopolis, "Milk-City," was the Greek name for Buto's oracular shrine, the oldest in Egypt.[4]

Medieval Europe continued to believe in the curative virtues of mother's milk. It was said that any mother could cure her infant's sore eyes by squirting her milk into them.[5] Male doctors often recommended woman-milk for the sick.

Ironically, one of the last superstitious believers in Panacea was Pope Innocent VIII, author of the infamous bull *Summis Desiderantes,* which laid the legal foundations for persecution of witches and caused the torture and death of millions of women. In his last illness,

Pope Innocent tried to fend off his own death by living on a woman's breast milk.[6] The magic didn't work; he died.

1. *Larousse,* 170. 2. Castiglioni, 162. 3. *Larousse,* 29. 4. Herodotus, 106. 5. de Lys, 159. 6. H. Smith, 291.

Pandemonium

"Home of All Demons," Christian term for the underworld, to which every non-Christian deity was consigned because the church claimed all gods and goddesses of the heathen were devils (1 Corinthians 10:20–21). "During Rome's long decline, almost the last thinking believers in the old gods were their Christian enemies. A pagan might laugh at Apollo as a fable. A Christian would shudder at him as a malignant spirit."[1]

First of the demons in Pandemonium were the rival gods mentioned in the Bible. To these were added the Celtic, Teutonic, and Saxon-Scandinavian deities; the deities of Greece and Asia Minor; and the Roman classical gods and goddesses. Specifically listed among the devils were Jupiter, Mercury, Venus, and Minerva.[2] Ruler of Pandemonium was the underground god: Pluto, Hades, Zeus Chthonios, Saturn, Lucifer.

1. Ashe, 145. 2. de Voragine, 670.

Pandia

"All-Goddess," one of "three daughters of the Moon" in Greek myth; a title of the female trinity.[1] Her two sisters were called Erse and Nemea. See **Moon**.

1. *Larousse,* 143.

Pandora

"All-giver," title of the Earth-goddess Rhea, personified as the first woman in an anti-feminist fable by Hesiod, who tried to blame war, death, disease, and all other ills on women.[1]

Pandora's vessel was not a box but a honey-vase, *pithos,* from which she poured out blessings: a womb-symbol like the Cornucopia, anciently used as a vessel of death and rebirth.[2] Pandora's Vase became Pandora's Box only in the late medieval period, when Erasmus mistakenly translated *pithos* as *pyxis.*[3]

Hesiod claimed Zeus sent Pandora to earth to punish men, who had offended him. She bore a vase filled not with blessings but with curses: strife, pain, death, sickness, and all other afflictions. Pandora in her curiosity opened the vase, as Zeus knew she would, and released them among men. In a refinement of cruelty, Zeus also supplied delusive Hope, to prevent men from killing themselves in despair and escaping the full meed of suffering their Heavenly Father intended for them.[4] The basic theme is also familiar in the myth of Eve.

Hesiod's story was further adapted to the legend of King Solomon, who was said to keep a horde of demons in a vase. After his death, greedy men broke the vase in seeking treasure and let the demons out into the world.[5]

1. Graves, G.M. 1, 148. 2. Neumann, G.M., 267. 3. *Larousse,* 93.
4. Graves, G.M. 1, 145. 5. de Voragine, 353.

Pangaea

"Universal Gaea," title of the Earth Mother at her mountain shrine in Thrace. She was also called Ida, Olympia, and Panorma, Universal Mountain Mother.[1] See **Mountain.**

1. Massa, 48.

Pantaloon

Stock character in Italian *commedia,* an amorous old rake in dancing slippers. He evolved from an artificially created saint, St. Pantaleone, patron of Venice, as he appeared in medieval mystery plays.[1] St. Pantaleone was actually the totemic lion, steed of Venus, after whom Venice was named. This animal was doubly canonized as the Lion of St. Mark, who replaced Venus as the city's patron and whose "relics" occupied the former Shrine of the Lion, now converted into St. Mark's cathedral.

Because the character St. Pantaleone wore flowing trousers in the eastern fashion, his costume came to be called "pantaloons," later shortened to "pants."

1. Funk, 85–86.

Paradise

The Persian *Pairidaeza* (Paradise) was a magic garden surrounding the holy mountain of the gods, where the Tree of Life bore the fruit of immortality. Pairidaeza was also the divine Virgin who would give birth to the future Redeemer: the Mahdi, or Messiah, or Savior, or Desired Knight of Saracenic Grail myths. Shi'ite Arabs still look for the coming of the Virgin Paradise, the next Holy Mother.[1]

Hebrew *pardes,* "garden," was derived from the same Virgin Paradise.[2] In Solomon's Song the "enclosed garden" is the virgin bride whose fountain of life-giving fluid is not yet opened (Song of Solomon 4:12). A dual vision of paradise as a living garden and the living garden as a female body runs through all religious symbolism. Lorenzo the Magnificent stated the same ancient theme in his description of heaven: "Nothing other than a pleasant garden, abundant with all pleasing and delightful things, of trees, apples, flowers, vivid running waters, song of birds, and in effect all the amenities dreamed of by the heart of man; and by this one can affirm that Paradise was where there was a beautiful woman, for here was a copy of every amenity and sweetness that a kind heart might desire."[3]

The psychological model of paradise was life's first experience of comforting love, the mother who warmed and fed the infant right after its terrifying birth trauma. Having "fallen" from the comfort of the womb into a world of painful stimuli, if the child is not embraced and "lulled into the illusion that the lost paradise has nearly been regained, the foundations for later neurosis will be laid."[4] Often the dweller in paradise was in a state of pseudo-infancy. When an Egyptian pharaoh came to his two divine mothers in the after-world, "They draw their breasts to his mouth, and never more do they wean him."[5] Egyptian funerary priestesses bared their breasts when escorting a dead man to his tomb, probably as a magical promise of the nursing Goddess's tender care.[6] As further insurance, she was painted inside the sarcophagus lid, reaching down with her arms to clasp the deceased against her bared breast, like a mother reaching for her baby.[7]

Primitive notions of paradise as land flowing with milk and honey were clearly representative of the mother's body in the earliest memories. An elderly Kikuyu chief spoke of these memories, still vivid in his mind:

> *She was always there; I can remember the comforting feel of her body as she carried me on her back and the smell of her skin in the hot sun. Everything came from her. When I was hungry or thirsty she would swing me around to where I could reach her full breasts; now when I shut my eyes I feel again with gratitude the sense of well-being that I had when I buried my head in their softness and drank the sweet milk that they gave. At night when there was no sun to warm me, her arms, her body, took its place; and as I grew older and more interested in other things, from my safe place on her back I could watch without fear as I wanted and when sleep overcame me I had only to close my eyes.*[8]

Western culture made this paradise—the birthright of every primitive child—a paradise lost. Dr. Henry pointed out that "No other culture has invented so many excuses for keeping a mother away from her infant."[9] Wickler said a human baby is, like a monkey baby, by nature "a mother-hugger and should be carried against the mother's body continuously in the early days of its life, as is still the custom among primitive races today. The entire behavior repertory of the newborn baby is adapted for this. . . . It is not biological for us to place our babies in cribs. Symptomatic of this is that the babies cry out of loneliness with abnormal frequency in our culture, while one scarcely ever finds this among the children of primitive peoples."[10]

Psychologists know the image of the lost mother is projected onto the sexual partner, which accounts for the extraordinary sexual significance attached to women's breasts. Erasmus Darwin noted that the symbolism even goes beyond the breast *per se:* "When any object of vision is presented to us, which by its waving or spiral lines bears any similitude to the form of the female bosom . . . we experience an attraction to embrace it with our arms, and to salute it with our lips, as we did in our early infancy the bosom of our mother."[11] Man often sees himself in an infantile relationship to a woman who may be embraced and kissed—that is, a wife or mistress. The Bengali poet Chandidas addressed himself to a loved woman as if he were her infant: "I have taken refuge at your feet, my beloved. . . . You are to me as a parent to a helpless child."[12]

A psychiatrist notes that most sexual fantasies of adult males "seem appropriate for a naive four-year-old, whose most important gratifications primarily depend on mother. . . . He shows unacknowledged signs of longing for her with the same fervor he did when she was all the world to him, the holy center of his child's universe. His desire seems unmodified by his conscious perception and understanding of the realities of life and the limited possibilities for gratification with his mother."[13]

Similarly, the desire to return to the perfect comfort of the womb in a post-mortem paradise seems unmodified by conscious recognition of its improbability. Hidden prenatal memory surfaces in many religious visions of the bliss of paradise, expressing a powerful wish that what was lost at birth may be regained after death. To those trained in interpretation of unconscious symbolism it is clear that the metaphors of eternity represent a return to the womb.[14] When death is near, the mind may even present vivid fantasies reminiscent of the maternal comfort that followed the birth trauma and soothed away the first experiences of pain and fear.

Thus we find that the garden-paradise from which humanity "fell" in the beginning was a genital symbol: garden, gate, grove, holy mount (*mons veneris*). This was suggested by the word Eden, meaning in Hebrew "a place of delight."[15] In the Middle Ages the usual metaphor for paradise was the Garden of Delights, a term less characteristic of the Christian heaven than of the *other* paradise, Fairyland or Avalon, where sexuality was permitted. Christian tradition forbade sexual love and marriage in heaven (Matthew 22:30), but the pagan tradition continued to view paradise as the epitome of all sensual gratifications and the satisfaction of all sexual-romantic yearnings.

Christians adopted the word paradise as a synonym for their own heaven, and insisted that the pagans' paradise was really hell, with a false appearance of beauty to lure sinners. In rebellion against this theory, bards openly expressed a preference for hell. Aucassin gives an example:

> *For into Paradise go none but such folk as I shall tell thee now: Thither go these same old priests, and halt old men and maimed, who all day and night cower continually before the altars, and in the crypts; and such folk as wear old mantles and old tattered frocks, and naked folk and shoeless, and covered with sores, perishing of hunger and thirst, and of little ease. These be they that go into Paradise; with them have I naught to do. But into Hell would I fain go . . . thither pass the sweet ladies and courteous that have two lovers, or three, and their lords also thereto. Thither go the gold, and the silver, and cloth of vair, and cloth of gris, and harpers, and makers, and the prince of this world. With these I would gladly go, let me but have with me Nicolette, my sweetest lady.*[16]

Aucassin Hero of the French medieval romantic poem *Aucassin et Nicolette,* based on the character of an earlier Arabic lover-hero, Al-Kasim.

Other ballads and early medieval romances rejected the Christian paradise for its lack of feminine company. The Irish Fenians, whose rule was never to insult a woman, were said to have gone to hell for denying Christian anti-feminist doctrines. The heathen sage Oisin (Ossian) rejected St. Patrick's heaven on the ground that it had no hunting, no bardic poetry, and no love of fair women. Oisin said he would rather join the Fenians in hell.[17]

Most people refused to believe that hell was identical with their beloved Fairyland, Avalon, Cockaigne, Torelore, Valhalla, Isles of the Blest, or whatever pagan paradise they professed; so it came to be called the earthly paradise, as opposed to the heavenly one. This realm of the Fairy Queen was usually placed in the Far West. Revered popular heroes dwelt there: Oberon, Lancelot, Tristan, Arthur, Ogier the Dane, and many others.[18] Since these heroes lived forever, the Irish called their paradise Thierna na Oge, the country of eternal youth. A wonderful fountain at its heart dispensed the Water of Life that made old men young again.

Belief in this ancient idea may have inspired the westward voyages of Leif Ericson, Columbus, and the legendary St. Brendan the Voyager, who was really a canonized form of the sea-god Bran, discoverer of the Cauldron of Regeneration. St. Brendan was said to have discovered it too, on a magic isle in the west. But "St. Brendan's Isle" was never found.[19] Ponce de Leon went looking for it, and claimed to have discovered the Fountain of Youth in Florida, which he called Bimini.[20]

Churchmen also believed in this earthly paradise. St. Thomas Aquinas was sure it existed and stated that Elijah and Esdras still lived there.[21] The 13th-century Hereford Map showed it as a circular island off the coast of India, which Columbus thought he could reach by sailing west. Hugo de St. Victor said the island of paradise was "a spot in the Orient productive of all kinds of woods and pomiferous trees. It contains the Tree of Life: there is neither cold nor heat there, but perpetual equable temperature. It contains a fountain which flows forth in four rivers." A Danish hero was said to have reached it by traveling to India and entering the mouth of a dragon who guarded the bridge to the mystic island.[22]

The bridge to paradise appeared in nearly all Indo-European myths. It was sometimes a dragon or serpent, but most often a rainbow. Persians called it the Kinvad Bridge. Babylonians called it the Necklace of Ishtar. Norsemen called it Bifrost, or sometimes Brisingamen, the Necklace of Freya. Beyond it, the gods dwelt in Asgard or Valhalla, in a castle called Gladsheim (Joyous Home). In Grail myths, this was the Grail Castle on Mount Joy; in the Arthurian cycle, it was Lancelot's fortress, Joyous Gard. The pagan paradises had many "mansions," like the paradise of Osiris which Jesus claimed for his own deity (John 14:2).[23]

1. Lederer, 181. 2. Hughes, 47. 3. Hughes, 99. 4. Fodor, 33. 5. Erman, 9. 6. *Book of the Dead,* frontispiece. 7. Neumann, G.M., pls. 90–91. 8. Montagu, T., 79. 9. Henry, 288. 10. Wickler, 266. 11. Montagu, T., 78. 12. Elisofon & Watts, 82. 13. Wachtel, 27. 14. Campbell, P.M., 65. 15. Campbell, M.T.L.B., 26. 16. Loomis, 251. 17. Squire, 206, 226. 18. Guerber, L.M.A., 135. 19. *Encyc. Brit.,* "Brendan." 20. Baring-Gould, C.M.M.A., 539–40. 21. Wilkins, 119. 22. Baring-Gould, C.M.M.A., 258–59, 263. 23. Branston, 120.

Pariah

Hindu out-caste, one belonging to none of the divine orders of society; an Untouchable. Such people were assigned to the dirty chores, both in India and in biblical lands, as "hewers of wood and drawers of water" (Joshua 9:21). See **Caste**.

Parnassus

Ancient Mount of the **Muses**, taken over by the god Apollo who usurped the Muses' function of creative inspiration. See **Mountain**.

Parthenon

"Virgin-temple," the shrine of Athene still standing on the Acropolis above Athens. The Goddess's title was Athene Parthenia (Virgin Athene), which also designated many other versions of the Goddess. An old name for Magdeburg was Parthenopolis, "City of the Virgin," dedicated to Venus Parthenia.[1] Parthia, "Virgin-land," was the home of Scythians who worshipped the Virgin Artemis. Parthians ruled Persia from 250 B.C. to 191 A.D.

1. Borchardt, 85.

Partridge in a Pear Tree

Middle English *pertriche,* "partridge," was derived from Perdix, one of Athene's sacred kings, thrown into the seas from a tower, and carried to heaven in the form of a bird by his Goddess.[1] He was the partridge, she the pear tree. Athene was worshipped in Boeotia as Oncë, the Pear Tree, mother of all pear trees. Perdix's name originally meant "the Lost One." He was a form of Vishnu-Narayana, called Lord of Pear Trees at his holy city of Badrinath in the Himalayas (from *badri,* "pear tree"). The pear tree had feminine-maternal significance through Eurasia. It was also sacred to Hera, whose oldest image at the Heraeum in Mycenae was made of pear wood.[2] European peasants considered the pear a favorite "life-tree" for a girl. In Russia it was a protective charm for cows.[3] The partridge in the tree was evidently taken as a symbol for Christ, instead of Perdix, when the image was transposed into a Christmas carol.

1. Potter & Sargent, 123. 2. Graves, G.M. 1, 252. 3. B. Butler, 238.

Parvati

Virgin aspect of **Kali Ma**, called Daughter of the Mountain, or Daughter of Heaven, both titles meaning the same since "heaven" was Himalaya, the Mountains.[1] Parvati was Shiva's bride under other names as well, such as Maya, Sati, Durga, or Shakti. Often she was identified with Prithivi, an archaic Mother Earth.

1. O'Flaherty, 349.

Pasht

"Tearer," an alternate name for the Egyptian cat-goddess Bast, probably in the role of Destroyer or devouring Sphinx. See **Cat**.

Pasiphaë

"She Who Shines for All," the Cretan Moon-goddess embodied in a queen who coupled with the sacred bull and brought forth the Minotaur (Minos-the-Bull). Her offspring represented the line of Minoan kings who wore the bull mask and mated with the Goddess every seven years at a ritual **hieros gamos**, followed by a ritual bull-killing.[1] It is believed that Cretan colonists carried the cult of Pasiphaë and Minos to Spain and instituted sacred games that have come down to the present day as the bullfight.

1. Graves, G.M. 2, 403.

Pastos

Inner "bridal chamber" of pagan temples, where male initiates could mate with the Goddess or female initiates with her divine consort to insure their redemption after death; comparable to the *abaton* or sacred "pit." See **Abaddon**.

Pathos

"Passion," the Dionysian ceremony of love-death, forerunner of the "Passion" of Christ. In the earlier version, the god mated with the goddess and sent forth his seed along with his soul, to bring rebirth to the world.[1] See **Drama**.

1. J.E. Harrison, 344.

Patrick, Saint

Patron saint of Ireland, probably a fictitious figure built on Roman *pater* or *patricius,* a priest. The only evidence for the existence of a Christian St. Patrick was his own autobiography, supposedly written in the 5th century but not heard of until 400 years later.[1] Thus it seems that Patrick's purported writings were forged by monks wishing to pretend Ireland was Christianized earlier than it actually was. It is highly unlikely that the Irish were converted as early as the 5th century. In the 12th century, St. Bernard complained that the Irish were still given over to "barbarous rites," Christianity having failed to take root among them.[2]

Like many other saints evolved by 9th- and 10th-century hagiography, Patrick had pagan precedents. One was the Irish god of the shamrock, Trefuilngid Tre-eochair, "Triple Bearer of the Triple Key," whose sacred plant bore all edible fruits including the apples of immortality. He was a son-consort of the Triple Goddess whose triple yoni was represented by shamrock designs from the earliest civilizations of the Indus valley. The story that St. Patrick explained the Christian trinity to the Irish by exhibiting the shamrock was entirely apocryphal. The Irish worshipped the shamrock as a sign of their triple pagan deities. The Book of Leinster said Patrick's mother was the Goddess Macha: she of the feminine trinity who gave birth to the shamrock-god.[3]

Book of Leinster A 12th-century Irish codex containing stories and poems from the pagan tradition.

Many other stories suggested Patrick's true paganism. He was educated by a druid.[4] In Wales he bore the title of Maenwyn, meaning one dedicated to the moon.[5] The legend of his martyrdom indicated that he was sacrificed to the Moon-goddess, but like a pagan god he was united with her Virgin incarnation, Brigit. The funerary temple at Downpatrick was dedicated to both Brigit and Patricius.[6] The Welsh form of the Triple Goddess, Guinevere, was said to have slain "the Irish knight Sir Patrice" with her magic apple, recalling the Goddess's gift of an apple of immortality to each of her doomed lovers.[7]

With all his pagan precedent, it is not surprising to find the monkish version of Patrick declaring himself "a sinner . . . despised by many."[8]

St. Patrick's Day was known throughout the Roman empire as the day of apotheosis of the god slain during the Ides of March: Liber Pater or Mars Pater, who would have been known as Patricius or Patrick in Britain.[9] At his Roman festival on March 17, a gigantic phallus was paraded through the streets, and solemnly crowned with a garland representing the divine yoni, by the hands of a specially selected matron.[10] The phallus of Liber Pater was also known as the **Palladium**, planted in the womb-temple of Vesta. The priest who represented this god's power was the *pater patrum,* "father of fathers," or else the Peter (the phallic stone pillar), or else Palladius. An old chronicle mentioned a Roman-Irish martyr called Bishop Palladius, "the first bishop to the Irish who believe in Christ," sacrificed to the Irish Moon-goddess before Patrick appeared.[11] Evidently both Palladius and Patrick were the same pagan god, adopted into the canon after his old shrines were taken over by Christians.[12]

1. *Encyc. Brit.,* "Patrick." 2. de Paor, 174. 3. Graves, W.G., 130, 518. 4. Spence, 56. 5. Hazlitt, 483. 6. Brewster, 140. 7. Malory 2, 274. 8. Attwater, 266. 9. G.R. Scott, 165; Rose, 212. 10. Knight, D.W.P., 154. 11. *Encyc. Brit.,* "Patrick." 12. Graves, W.G., 152.

Paul, Saint

The true founder of orthodox Christianity was Paul, who either composed or inspired the earliest identifiably Christian writings, predating the Gospels.[1] Paul laid down the basic orthodox doctrines: hope of high rank in heaven for the pure; avoidance of women and sexuality; separation of body and soul. "For the flesh lusteth against the Spirit, and the Spirit against the flesh: and these are contrary the one to the other" (Galatians 5:17). Paul copied the more ascetic Gnostic sects of his time, when "a gulf never completely to be closed again is opened: God and world, God and nature, spirit and nature, become divorced, alien to each other, even contraries."[2]

One key to this process was separation of male and female principles in religion. Father Heaven and Mother Earth were no longer wedded. Women were no longer participants in sacred mysteries according to Paul. The church must be entirely patriarchal; women were forbidden to teach or preach in it. Paul also laid the guilt of original sin on woman alone, absolving man from responsibility: "Adam was not deceived, but the woman being deceived was in the transgression" (1 Timothy 2:11-14).

Paul's antipathy toward women and sexuality leads to a suspicion that his esoteric doctrine was linked with the early Christian practice of voluntary **castration**, recommended by Jesus for "the kingdom of heaven's sake" (Matthew 19:12). In Paul's day, Rome revered the self-castrated god **Attis** and Paul was an earnest admirer of Roman culture, as shown by the fact that he Romanized his name, changing it from Saul to Paul. Roman Christians later used self-castration as an automatic ticket to heaven, in the manner of Attis's priests.[3] Tertullian said the heavenly gates were always thrown open to eunuchs.[4]

In a secretive, elliptical style typical of contemporary mystical writings, Paul suggested that he was among the divinely favored eunuchs. He often mentioned, but never described, his mysterious "infirmity" which he called a "light affliction, which is but for a moment" though it would bring him eternal glory (2 Corinthians 4:17). It assimilated him to Christ, and "They that are Christ's have crucified the flesh with the affections and lusts" (Galatians 5:24).

Paul hinted that he was one of the "new creatures" in Christ, neither circumcised nor uncircumcised. A man would have to be one or the other, unless he altogether lacked a penis. Paul made an oblique reference to a mutilation: "I bear in my body the marks of the Lord Jesus" (Galatians 6:17). He scorned the "natural" (unmutilated) man for his lack of spirituality: "The natural man receiveth not the things of the Spirit of God; for they are foolishness unto him" (1 Corinthians 2:14). Nevertheless, Paul recognized that some men might prefer to remain natural. Although "it is good for a man not to touch a woman," he proposed that such men be allowed to take wives, "to avoid fornication." Yet this was a grudging concession, given "by permission, and not of commandment. For I would that all men were even as I myself" (1 Corinthians 7:1-7).

Paul wrote to the Galatians: "I would they were even cut off which trouble you" (Galatians 5:12). The word rendered "cut off" also meant "castrated."[5] Paul said those who "bite and devour one another"—terms often applied to sexual behavior—may be consumed. But those who are in the Spirit "shall not fulfil the lusts of the flesh" (Galatians 5:15-16). In his addresses to the Romans, Paul seemed to offer himself and some of his followers as examples of the virtue of sexlessness:

> *How shall we, that are dead to sin, live any longer therein? . . . Our old man is crucified with him [Jesus], that the body of sin might be destroyed, that henceforth we should not serve sin. For he that is dead is freed from sin. . . . Let not sin therefore reign in your mortal body, that ye should obey it in the lusts thereof. Neither yield ye your members as instruments of unrighteousness unto sin. . . . I speak after the manner of men because of the infirmity of your flesh: for as ye have yielded your members servants to uncleanness and to iniquity unto iniquity; even so now yield your members servants to righteousness unto holiness. (Romans 6:2-19)*

Paul spoke "after the manner of men," as if he were not one, because his hearers' flesh had an "infirmity" that he didn't share. He asked them to crucify and destroy "our old man," a common Middle-

Eastern epithet for the phallus. "He that is dead is freed from sin" because he could no longer serve the "uncleanness" of women.

The Jews would naturally have argued that sterility was a violation of divine law, since Yahweh's commandment was to be fruitful and multiply. Paul insisted that this commandment was obsolete. God had changed his mind. Paul declared that fruitfulness of the flesh now meant death rather than life:

> *For when we were in the flesh, the motions of sins . . . did work in our members to bring forth fruit unto death. But now we are delivered from the law, that being dead wherein we were held; that we should serve in newness of spirit. . . . Sin, taking occasion by the commandment, wrought in me all manner of concupiscence. . . . For I was alive without the law once: but when the commandment came, sin revived, and I died. And the commandment, which was ordained to life, I found to be death. (Romans 7:4-10)*

Paul found the divine law of reproduction outdated and distasteful because it brought forth "fruit unto death"—i.e., more life doomed to die. Therefore he "died" from the carnal life and acquired new spirituality. "The carnal mind (or, minding of the flesh) is enmity against God . . . so then they that are in the flesh cannot please God. . . . For if ye live after the flesh, ye shall die: but if ye through the Spirit do mortify the deeds of the body, ye shall live" (Romans 8:7-13).

Paul used the parable of the wild olive tree, whose branches must be lopped off, to be grafted onto a fruitful tree. To those whose "branches" were lopped off for the kingdom of heaven's sake, he promised better replacements in the hereafter, for "God is able to graff them in again. For if thou wert cut out of the olive tree which is wild by nature, and wert graffed contrary to nature to a good olive tree: how much more shall these, which be the natural branches, be graffed onto their own olive tree?" (Romans 11:23-25).

This parable, Paul said, was an important "mystery" of which his followers must not be ignorant. He pleaded for cutting of the sinful branch: "I beseech you therefore, brethren . . . that ye present your bodies a living sacrifice, holy, acceptable unto God, which is your reasonable service" (Romans 12:1). Paul's "living sacrifice" may well have been like those of Buddhist ascetics and Aztec holy men who habitually practiced penile mutilations to win the favor of the gods.

John the Baptist used arboreal symbolism like Paul's: "the ax is laid to the root of the trees" (Matthew 3:10). In pagan context, this meant castration of the fertility king. The wild olive, "castrated" with a golden sickle like the oracular oaks of Dodona, figured in the myths of Heracles and his Tyrian counterparts.[6] The genital blood of a castrated king was the food of immortality, according to the *Book of the Dead;* the soul of man was nourished on the food "shed upon the olive tree."[7] The olive branch was, and is, a sign of Peace; and "Peace" meant the death of a phallic god, who received the Word of Peace at his departing. Here is a parable of which modern scholars should not be ignorant. The lopped-off olive branch was carried in the beak of the Dove, emblem of Aphrodite, who castrated sacred kings.[8]

1. Enslin, L.C.M, 233–38. 2. Jonas, 251. 3. Bullough, 100–113. 4. Briffault 3, 372. 5. Enslin, L.C.M., 223. 6. Graves, G.M. 2, 178. 7. *Book of the Dead,* 89. 8. Graves, G.M. 1, 71.

Pazuzu

The only Babylonian deity to become a movie star: Pazuzu was the "demon" of the film *The Exorcist.* His name really came from an ancient Sumerian title of the flood-hero-king Ziusudra, "the *pa-susu.*"[1] Babylonian myths supplied him with a serpent-penis and made him the consort of the serpent-mother Lamashtu, or Lamia, the Jews' **Lilith**.

1. Pritchard, A.N.E., 29.

Peach

Female genital symbol, in China regarded as the source of the ambrosia of life which gave gods their immortality; corresponding to the apple in western Europe. Great Mother Hsi Wang Mu ruled the magic peach garden in the west, where the gods were reborn.[1]

Peach Blossom meant a virgin in Taoist symbolism, while the fruit stood for a mature woman whose juices were essential to man's health. China's patron saint of longevity Shou Lou was an old man with a high bulging forehead, bursting with "yin juice" he had absorbed and sent up to his head through sexual coupling with many women. To reveal his mystical secret, Shou Lou always held up a peach with one of his fingers stuck into its cleft.[2]

Chinese wizards made magic wands from peach twigs. These might be compared to magic wands made in the west from other woods sacred to the Goddess, such as witch hazel, witch-willow, apple boughs, or holly.[3]

Western writers sometimes confused the Oriental peach with the apricot, because *abricot* was once a European word for the vulva. Sculptures from the pagan period at Nimes showed examples of this fruit in conjunction with phalli.[4]

1. *Larousse,* 382. 2. Rawson, E.A., 234. 3. de Lys, 397. 4. Knight, D.W.P., 136, pls. XV, XVI.

Peacock

Bird of Juno, mother of the Roman gods. The peacock's iridescent tail-feather "eyes" symbolized the Goddess's watchfulness, her many-colored veils, and her plumes of justice, against which the hearts of men were weighed, as against the plumes of Maat in Egypt. The peacock belonged to Juno when she was still the Etruscan Goddess Uni, the Great Yoni. It also belonged to the Hindu Goddesses Sarasvati and Maya, and their Argive counterpart Hera.[1]

Juno's priests and priestesses in their sacred processions carried tall peacock-feather fans called *flabelli.* These articles were taken over by Christian popes and are still displayed at papal Easter services. They are now said to represent "the many-eyed vigilance of the church."[2]

Because it was a matriarchal totem originally, the peacock tended to attract the same opprobrium as black cats, opals, ladders, pentacles, mirrors, owls, and moonlight. Christian superstition generally viewed the peacock as a bird of doom. St. James's Gazette reported in 1888: "Nobody who has not gone exhaustively into the subject can have any adequate idea of the amount of general inconvenience diffused by a peacock. Broken hearts, broken limbs, pecuniary reverses, and various forms of infectious disease have all been traced to the presence of a peacock." According to some legends, the peacock became a bad-luck bird because it was the only one who consented to show Satan the way to paradise—an echo of the pagan belief that the peacock was Juno's **psychopomp.**[3]

In the Orient, however, the peacock remained a Bird of Paradise. Peacocks were encouraged to wander about the precincts of any Hindu temple and in the royal gardens. Like doves in western Europe, peacocks were considered soul-birds and emblems of good fortune, sometimes even oracles.

1. Jobes, 224. 2. Brewster, 166. 3. Leland, 154.

Pearly Gate

Entrance to heaven; a Christian borrowing from the cult of Aphrodite Marina, or the Sea-mother Mari, to whom pearls were sacred. Her own body was the Gate of Heaven, like the Jade Gate of the Chinese Goddess, through which all men passed at birth (outward) and again at death (inward). Various yonic symbols of the Goddess were said to be bordered with pearls, including even the Celts' sacred Cauldron of Regeneration. (See **Cauldron.**)

When the Goddess appeared in the guise of the moon, she was called Pearl of the Sea, or Pearl of Wisdom; her seven high priestesses were the Seven Pillars of Wisdom (see **Pleiades**). As the moon was the gate of paradise, so was the Goddess. Early Christian sectaries copied the pagans in claiming that the souls of the dead "mount up by the pillar of dawn to the sphere of the moon, and the moon receives them incessantly from the first to the middle of the month, so that it waxes and gets full, and then it guides them to the sun until the end of the month, and thus effects its waning in that it is lightened of its burden."[1]

The pearly moon-gate like Mother Earth made no distinctions between those who could be admitted and those who could not; as all living things were her own children, so all dead things were her charges also. When Christian mythology supplied a gatekeeper in the form of **St. Peter**, then the Pearly Gate became a barrier where a judgment was made on the worthiness or unworthiness of the soul.

The ancients gave all pearls the feminine connotation, saying they were made of two female powers, the moon and water. It was believed that pearls should be worn only at night, for moonlight would enhance their luster whereas sunlight would spoil them.[2]

1. Jonas, 233. 2. de Lys, 284–85.

Pegasus

Winged horse of Greek myth, symbol of the sacred king's or hero's journey to heaven; an image of death and apotheosis, like the mythic death-horses of northern Europe.[1] Pegasus had archaic, matriarchal origins. He sprang from the "wise blood" of the Moon-goddess Medusa, who embodied the principle of *medha,* the Indo-European root word for female wisdom. Or, alternatively, he was the magic horse Arion, "moon creature on high," born of the Goddess Demeter and ridden by Heracles in his role of sacred king in Elis. There was an earlier female Pegasus named Aganippe, "the Mare Who destroys mercifully," actually a title of Demeter herself as the destroying lunar Night-Mare.[2]

Pegasus was named for the Pegae, water-priestesses who tended the sacred spring of Pirene in Corinth. The cult seems to have been rooted in Egypt. The oldest shrine of Osiris at Abydos (ca. 2000 B.C.) centered on on a sacred spring called Pega.[3]

The Greek Pegae preserved an ancient dying-god cult, as shown by the myth of Bellerophon, who mounted Pegasus and tried to ride to heaven "as though he were an immortal." He failed, and fell. Bellerophon's predecessor (mythologized as his "father") also failed, and was devoured by wild man-eating mares. This was not meant to suggest that human flesh ever became incorporated into an equine diet. It meant rather that "the pre-Hellenic sacred king was torn in pieces at the close of his reign by women disguised as mares."[4]

Pegasus represented divine inspiration as well as godlike apotheosis. A man who rode him could become a great poet. Pegasus's crescent-moon-shaped hoof stamped the ground and dug the Hippocrene (Horse-Well), a spring of poetic inspiration on Mount Helicon, the home of the Muses. This was another kind of immortality; the rider of Pegasus could *figuratively* "fly through the air, to reach the heavens."[5]

1. Eliade, S., 467. 2. Graves, G.M. 1, 239, 255; W.G., 425. 3. Budge, D.N., 276. 4. Graves, G.M. 1, 232, 254. 5. Eliade, S., 467.

Pelagia, Saint

Several St. Pelagias were invented during the era of saint-making (ca. 9th century A.D.)—Pelagia the Penitent, Pelagia of Antioch, Pelagia of Tarsus, et al. All were fictions built on the epithet of Aphrodite Pelagia, "Sea." They were identified also with St. Margaret or St. Marina, other "pelagic" titles of the same Goddess.

Sometimes Pelagia was a beautiful dancing girl, converted by a Christian preacher and made to repent. Sometimes she was a beautiful virgin who threw herself from a housetop to avoid losing her virginity. Sometimes she was a beautiful Christian maiden who spurned a royal lover, the son of Diocletian (or, in some versions, the emperor himself), and for this she was roasted to death in a brazen bull.[1] The stories apparently were inspired by statues of the Goddess labeled "Pelagia," and some of the methods of destroying them.

Another legend showed Pelagia differently, as a temptress trying to corrupt a male saint. He was St. Hilary, who wandered into a remote Alpine village when the people were celebrating pagan rites of Midsummer under the guidance of their chatelaine, Lady Pelagia. She welcomed the holy man to her palace and asked him many deep questions. When she asked, "What is the distance from heaven to hell?," a heavenly voice commanded St. Hilary to breathe on her in the name of Christ. He did so, and she suddenly turned into a statue of Aphrodite. In the morning the statue fell to pieces, and the magic palace was revealed as a ruin of an old Roman city.[2]

The same riddle was asked again in the legend of St. Andrew, who explained that only Satan could know the distance from heaven to hell because he had measured it in his fall.[3]

Another legend of Pelagia repeated the same tale told of many other fictitious she-saints, namely that she disguised herself as a man and spent some time living in a community of monks, under the name of Pelagius.[4] This may have been connected with the early apocryphal Gospels that forbade women to be Christians unless they "made themselves male."[5]

1. Attwater, 272. 2. Summers, V., 243–45. 3. de Voragine, 15. 4. Attwater, 272. 5. Malvern, 38.

Pelican

Often confused with the stork, another baby-bringing totem of the Birth-goddess, the pelican was an early symbol of the Sacred Heart. Egyptians believed that a mother nourished her infant *in utero* with her heart's blood; similarly a mother pelican nourished her young by wounding or "vulning" her own breast with her beak to let her heart's blood flow into the mouths of her nestlings. The legend probably arose from the pelican's habit of resting with its bill sunk in its breast feathers.

St. Augustine accepted this ancient fantasy of the mother pelican as fact, and so did subsequent churchmen, for no one dared contradict Augustine—even though no pelican had ever been seen opening its own breast.[1] The self-sacrificing mother pelican became a popular motif on both ecclesiastical and secular coats of arms.

1. Potter & Sargent, 179.

Penates

Roman household gods who protected the *penus,* a grain-storage chamber, once associated with the family tomb. Like Jewish *teraphim,* the Penates seem to have been preserved skulls of ancestors, set in niches around the storeroom.[1]

1. Neumann, G.M., 283.

Penelope

"She Whose Face is Veiled," a title of the weaving Fate-goddess, miscast in the Odyssey as Odysseus's wife, though she was probably his personal guardian angel in an earlier story. She was once an orgiastic fertility-mother, as shown by the legend that she took all her "suitors" into her bed, and she was both the mother and the consort of Pan.[1]

Her function in the Odyssey was to account for Odysseus's charmed life. As long as Penelope refrained from cutting her thread, Odysseus couldn't die. So he survived many dangerous adventures while she wove and unwove the tapestry of his life, never cutting it off. He even overcame the death-curse cast on him by Hecuba.[2]

1. Graves, W.G., 392. 2. Graves, G.M. 2, 341.

Pentacle

Pentacle

Based on the symbol of the Goddess Kore in the apple core, the pentacle or pentagram was worshipped by Pythagorean mystics who called it Pentalpha: the birth-letter interlaced five times.[1] Its meaning was given as "life" or "health."[2] Some called it the star of Ishtar or of Isis, or of Isis's underworld twin, Nephthys. In Egypt the five-pointed star represented the underground womb.[3]

Use of the pentacle as an amulet of protection or healing was common in Babylon, where it was often drawn on pots to preserve their contents. The amulet known as The Seven Seals shows a pentacle as the first of its holy signs. According to Judeo-Christian tradition, the Seals were supposed to represent the secret names of God, and the pentacle was the chief of them, inscribed on King Solomon's magic ring.[4] Thus it was sometimes erroneously called Solomon's Seal.

However, it was more closely connected with pagan deities than with the Jewish one. A pentacle with one point straight down represented the Horned God, whom Neoplatonic philosophers called Pentamorph, "He of the Five Shapes."[5] He appeared in human form as well as the four horned animals, bull, ram, goat, and stag.

Pagan Celts like the Egyptians revered the pentacle as a sign of the underground Goddess, whom they called Morgan. In her honor, the solar hero Gawain carried a pentacle on his blood-red shield.[6]

Hermetic magicians used the pentacle for their model of Man the Microcosm. A male figure was placed inside a circle representing the cosmos: his feet, hands, and head touched the circle at the points designated by the inscribed pentacle, his genitals being located exactly in its center.[7] This image was related to Firmicus Maternus's remark that man is a microcosm ruled by "the five stars."[8]

Like other figures constructed of a single unbroken line, the pentacle was believed to afford protection from spirits, who needed the "gates" formed by a broken line. Therefore the pentacle was often used to mark off magical enclosures, especially for invocation. Medieval churchmen consequently took to calling it by such names as Devil's Sign, Witch's Cross, Wizard's Star, Goblin's Cross, or Witch's Foot.[9] It was thought that a vampire or werewolf would show a pentacle on the foot sole or palm of the hand. This notion may be compared with the five-petaled Lotus that appeared on the hands of Buddha.[10]

Continuous appearances of the pentacle in magic books probably influenced Slavic witches who tried to cure diseases by "measuring the pentacle" on the patient. A string was stretched from feet to chin, from the middle finger of each hand to the other, from each hand to the opposite foot, while the sufferer stood in the position of Microcosmic Man. "Differences in measurement give diagnosis and prognosis, and cutting the twine with a knife after each measurement cuts away the sickness. The bits of twine are burned so that the patient may inhale the fumes, and the ashes are placed in fresh water, of which the patient drinks a portion."[11]

Magic charms using the pentacle are still extant. Gypsies still cut the apple to reveal the Kore, the Pentacle of the Virgin, which they call Star of Knowledge.[12]

1. Hornung, 212. 2. Pepper & Wilcock, 23. 3. Budge, E.L., 75. 4. Budge, A.T., 40. 5. Wedeck, 121. 6. Loomis, 342. 7. Lehner, 77. 8. Wedeck, 236. 9. de Lys, 478. 10. Ross, 104. 11. Gifford, 87–88. 12. Derlon, 157.

Penthesileia

"Man-griever," Amazon queen slain in battle by Achilles during the Trojan War. Some said she killed Achilles first but Zeus restored him to life. Various sources agree that when she was dead, Achilles raped her corpse. Some stories say her eyes were gouged out and she was dragged by one foot and thrown into a river. Others say she was taken up respectfully and buried with honor as a great heroine.[1]

1. Graves, G.M. 2, 313.

Perceval

Also known as Parsifal, Percival, Persevelle, and other variations, this protean hero of medieval romance united many myths both pagan and Christian.

He was first manifested as the Welsh ithyphallic demigod Peredur Paladrhir, whose name meant "Spearman with a Long Shaft," carrying the same sexual implication as Osiris's title, "Mummy with a Long Member."[1] His later name, Perceval, also meant a phallus, literally "He Who Pierces (or penetrates) the Valley."[2]

The original myth of Peredur was an allegory of druidic initiation. His adventures were staged as secret examinations, and he had to take an oath not to speak a single word to any Christian—a detail that surely indicates pagan Mysteries. Peredur passed 21 days in the castle of the witches of Caer Loyw to receive his instruction. In the women's "great court" he saw the Cauldron of Regeneration performing resurrections of the Sons of the King of Suffering, near a sacred cave with a phallic pillar at its entrance. A man was killed each day. The women anointed the corpse and bathed it in the magic **cauldron**, and the man's life was restored. Two sisters resembling the Gospels' Mary and Martha gave Peredur bread and wine to serve the banquet table. This scene was not a copy of the Christian Last Supper; it came from older sources. It presaged primitive rites of the death and rebirth of the vegetation god, for whom the women wailed and in whose absence the earth became a Waste Land.[3]

Peredur's chief instructress was his lady-love, "the most beautiful damsel in the world," whose colors were those of the Triple Goddess in India: virgin white, maternal red, and the black of death. These remained the colors of the Maiden in many romances and fairy tales, such as "Snow White." (See **Gunas**.) The colors alone put Peredur into a "trance of meditation" on his mysterious Shakti, for that was what she was. On saying farewell, she told him: "When thou seekest for me, seek in the direction of India."[4]

Roman de Perceval
Alternate name for the *Conte del Graal* written by Chrétien de Troyes about 1185, finished later by other hands.

Similar instruction at the hands of a Shakti figured in the 12th-century *Roman de Perceval,* where the Welsh hero metamorphosed into the Desired Knight sent to cure the world's ills, like a Saracen *Mahdi.* It was claimed that Perceval would heal the lame Fisher King and restore the **Waste Land** to fertility.

Perceval was hidden, like most versions of the Divine Child, and brought up in secret by his mother. He happened to meet some knights, assumed they were angels, and followed them to King Arthur's court. Despite his appearance as a clownish rustic, a lady prophesied a great destiny for him. ("Ladies" were the court seeresses.) Perceval visited the Grail castle and saw a vision of the holy vessel in the hands of Queen Repanse de Joie (Dispenser of Joy).

Perceval's instructress Blancheflor (White Flower) undertook to reveal to him the secret meanings of chivalry, or the mysticism of love. Spiritual/sexual union with her made him invincible in battle. However, German versions of the legend recounted a battle between the old pagan Perceval sustained by the power of sexual love and a new Christian Perceval sustained by celibacy.[5] Monkish authors worked on the unfinished *Roman de Perceval* from before 1200 A.D. to about 1230, Christianizing the hero, who then discovered that the true meaning of chivalry was not what his lady-love taught at all but rather the doctrines of the church. Blancheflor fell on hard times, mythically speaking. She was vilified as "a Jewess named Blanchefleure" who coupled with Satan at a witches' sabbat and gave birth to **Antichrist.**[6]

The new Perceval was no longer a champion of women. He even castrated himself in order to become one of the pure knights who "believed in God perfectly." On one occasion he offered assistance to a pagan noblewoman whose property had been stolen. She served him a feast and invited him into her bed. Though sorely tempted, he caught sight of the cross formed by his sword hilt and thrust away the enchantress. She vanished in a puff of black smoke. Perceval "rove himself through the thigh"—a classic metaphor for castration—saying, "Sithen my flesh will be my master I shall punish it. . . . O good Lord, take this in recompensation of that which I have done against thee."[7]

In this way the phallic hero called Piercer of the Valley became the purest of pure knights, the only one worthy to see the Holy Grail because all other knights were polluted by love affairs or marriage. In Perceval's vision, "the old law" was represented as a woman riding a serpent, who a priest told him was a fiend. The woman asked Perceval to serve her, as the priest said, "to make thee believe on her and leave thy baptism." Perceval refused. He made the sign of the cross and killed the serpent.[8]

In a Cistercian romance, Perceval met the Queen of the Waste Land, his aunt, living in poverty in the Waste Forest, though she had once been "the richest woman in the world." This indicates the Goddess, her temples robbed, and only her woodland groves left to her. Another female relative, Perceval's sister, arrived dead on Solomon's ship, the symbol of the church. She was nobly enshrined because she had died a pure virgin, the monks' notion of the only acceptable kind of woman.

There were no women involved in the Quest, any more than there were women involved in setting policies for the church.[9] In this final version of the Grail myth, its feminine meaning had been written out of the script, even though it was a prize sought by men. With this development, interest in the subject declined. Grail legends dwindled away for lack of further inspiration. The Christianized, virginized Perceval seemed to lack charisma. He was a hero who pleased only the monks who invented him; ordinary folk found it difficult to sympathize with this singularly bloodless knight.

1. Squire, 369. 2. Jung & von Franz, 185. 3. Goodrich, 52, 64, 67; Loomis, 209–11. 4. Goodrich, 63–69; Loomis, 211. 5. Campbell, C.M., 558. 6. Baring-Gould, C.M.M.A., 169. 7. Malory 2, 199, 204. 8. Malory 2, 201. 9. Campbell, C.M., 543, 551, 566.

Peri

Persian fairy or genie, usually female, like western fairies but sometimes considered one of the fallen angels *(djinn)*. A peri could also be a familiar spirit, a mischievous elf, a heavenly nymph, a Shakti. Sufis called a peri a *pir,* lady-love.

Persephone

"Destroyer," the **Crone** form of the Triple Goddess Demeter, whose other *personae* were **Kore** the Virgin and Demeter-Pluto the Mother (or Preserver). The three deities succeeded each other cyclically like the three points of a turning triangle—Demeter's symbol, the *delta*—so that Kore and Persephone were often confused and came to be considered the same Goddess. The fable about Kore-Persephone's abduction by Pluto was a later invention. She was Queen of the Underworld long before there was a masculinized Pluto. Orphic mystics worshipped her as Goddess of the blessed dead, to whom they addressed formula prayers: "And now I come a suppliant to the Holy Persephone, that of her grace she receive me to the seats of the Hallowed." Persephone answered, "Happy and blessed one, thou shalt be god instead of mortal."[1] She held the keys to heaven and hell (Elysium and Tartarus), thus anticipating the Mithraic *pater patrum* and his Christian counterpart **Peter**.[2]

Persephone was considerably older than the Eleusinian myth of classical writings, which told of her descent into the underworld and her annual return to the earth each spring. She was really another name for Hecate, or Hel, and had ruled the underworld as Destroying Mother Kali ruled it under the name of Prisni, which may have been the origin of Persephone's Etruscan name, Persipnei. Romans called her Proserpine. It was under this name that she passed into Christian tradition as a Queen of She-Demons.[3] Like Kali the Destroyer, she was the basic Death-goddess from the beginning.

1. Legge 1, 133. 2. Cavendish, P.E., 98. 3. de Givry, 141.

Perseus

God-begotten, virgin-born Athenian hero supposed to have slain Libyan Medusa and Phoenician Yamm, the sea-serpent incarnation of Baal. Greeks claimed he rescued and married the Phoenician queen Andromeda ("Ruler of Men"), to establish a Hellenic government in Phoenicia. Perseus became a god and ascended to heaven; but his constellation was said to exert evil influence. Astrologers called it Cacodaemon (Bad Demon) because it contained the "Demon Star" Algol, an eclipsing binary given to mysterious appearances and disappearances.[1]

1. Jobes, 228.

Peter, Saint

The myth of St. Peter was the slender thread from which hung the whole weighty structure of the Roman papacy. One solitary passage in the Gospel of Matthew said Jesus made a pun by giving Simon son of Jonah the new name of Peter, "Rock" (Latin *petra*), saying he would found his church on this rock (Matthew 16:18-19).

Unfortunately for papal credibility, the so-called Petrine passage was a forgery. It was deliberately inserted into the scripture about the 3rd century A.D. as a political ploy, to uphold the primacy of the Roman see against rival churches in the east.[1] Various Christian bishoprics were engaged in a power struggle in which the chief weapons were bribery, forgery, and intrigue, with elaborate fictions and hoaxes written into sacred books, and ruthless competition between rival parties for the lucrative position of God's elite.[2]

Most early churches put forth spurious claims to foundation by apostles, even though the apostles themselves were no more than the mandatory "zodiacal twelve" attached to the figure of the sacred king. Early popes were often mere names, drawn from titles of Roman gods, such as Eleutherios or Soter, falsely inserted into an artificial chronology to simulate succession from Peter. But even Catholic scholars now admit that the stories of Peter's upside-down crucifixion before Nero, and burial in the Vatican hill, were fictitious.[3]

The real roots of Peter's legend lay in pagan Roman myths of the city-god called Petra, or Pater Liber, assimilated to the Mithraic *pater patrum* (Father of Fathers), whose title was corrupted into *papa,* then "pope."[4] This personage had been both a Rock and a Father—that is, a phallic pillar—in the Vatican *mundus* since Etruscan times, when oracular priests called *vatis* gave their title to the site. Other variations of the deity's name were Patriarch (Chief Father), Pompeius, and Patricius (Patrick).[5] Like Indian Brahmans, Roman "patricians" claimed a patrilineal descent from the god. Since his name also meant a rock, he was what the Old Testament called "the Rock that begat thee" (Deuteronomy 32:18).

The god's stone phallus remained planted in the Vatican mount through the later centuries of the Roman empire and well into the Middle Ages—perhaps even into the 19th century, when a visitor said Vatican authorities "kept in secret a large stone emblem of the creative power, of a very peculiar shape."[6] Medieval names for such an object—*perron, pyr, pierre*—show that it was both a "rock" and a "peter." Such was the ancient Pater's phallic scepter or pillar topped with a pine cone, the *thyrsus* of Pater Liber. Church authorities often converted a carved *perron* into a Christian symbol simply by placing a cross on its tip.[7]

Pater Liber's *perron* appeared in St. Peter's Church of the 14th century A.D., atop the round temple called Pantheon, renamed St. Mary Rotunda. The temple had been buried under an artificial hill forming the court of St. Peter's, probably because it was known as a shrine of the Goddess. Local legend said the phallic stone had been "carried off there by the devil on the night on which the Virgin brought Christ into the world."[8]

This "devil" probably meant the Horned God Bacchus (Pater Liber), whose phallic staff called *baculus* was allegedly carried by St. Peter, though not by the popes. A strange, garbled legend explained the loss of the *baculus.* Peter gave it to the earth in order to raise a saint called Maternus from the grave. This legend evidently arose from the cult of Bacchus, who sent his phallic staff into the underworld, sometimes in the form of an inverted "Peter's cross," to fertilize the maternal soil. Hence the oddly-named Maternus who rose like vegetation from the ground. The bones of St. Maternus were said to lie under the foundation of the First Church of the Martyrs in Cologne, built by the Empress Helena in Maternus's honor, a typical confusion of chronologies.[9]

Peter's Cross

However garbled, the legend of Peter's *baculus* was perpetuated by Germanic emperors, who claimed Peter's staff had passed from the popes to Germany, betokening Teutonic leadership of the Holy Roman Empire.[10] Other medieval legends presented Peter in the pagan role of a fertilizing spirit. For instance, he was said to make a woman conceive by giving her an apple or a pine cone, symbols of Bacchus and his bride.[11]

Peter or Petra combined with other phallic "rocks," such as the obelisk at the gate of the Egyptian after-world, sacred to Par, the title of Ra as "Lord of the Phallus."[12] This was also called Petra. A "prophet" of Ra incarnate in the savior Osiris was known as Petosiris; his tomb near Hermopolis was a great pilgrimage center about 341 B.C. A Greek prayer addressed him: "I invoke Petosiris whose venerated body here lies. Today he is among the gods, he is now united with the Wise." King Nechepso was possessed by his spirit, which took him on a typical shamanic "night journey" to heaven.[13] Greco-Egyptian scriptures written under the names of Nechepso and Petosiris were popular in the 2nd century B.C.[14]

Like the obelisk, a phallic pillar stood at nearly all the "Pearly Gates" of the Great Mother's temples, representing the Petra who demanded the right passwords of initiates entering the temple, and the same initiates after death entering heaven. Petra also guarded the gates of the year, through which the *Christos Aeon* passed. Thus Peter was identified with Janus, god of gateways, and came to be called the Janitor, "Gatekeeper."[15]

The church's festival of St. Peter used to be held on the day of Janus, when the sun entered the sign of Aquarius, symbol of both the gate of the year and the Pearly Gate of Maria-Aphrodite.[16] Pagan precedents naturally assimilated St. Peter to the position of guardian of the *janua coeli,* "gate of heaven," formerly a yonic emblem of the Virgin Juno. Robert de Borron's romance of the Grail even suggested that Peter stood for the gate of Jesus's tomb: Jesus was laid under a *pierre,* a peter-stone, such as marked the graves of ancient phallic heroes.[17]

As gatekeeper, Peter inherited the mystical keys based on the trident of Shiva and the Osirian *ankh,* called Key of the Nile and also a heavenly key to the Nile in the Sky (the Milky Way). Key-holding deities generally gave or denied admittance to the land of the dead, whether it was located in the earth or in the heavens. The *Book of Enoch* described various keepers of the heavenly mansions as key-holders: one for the winds, one for the seasons, one for the gates of hell, etc.[18] Prayers to the Goddess Persephone called her Holder of the Keys; or, alternatively, her consort Hades was the holder of the keys to heaven and hell.[19]

On such pagan precedents rested the crucial doctrine of the papal keys, as stated in the interpolated Gospel passage: "I [Jesus] will give unto thee [Peter] the keys of the kingdom of heaven: and whatsoever thou shalt bind on earth shall be bound in heaven: and whatsoever thou shalt loose on earth shall be loosed in heaven" (Matthew 16:19). That is, holding the keys meant magic power. Whatever the key-holder commanded would come to be. This primitive idea underlay the powers of priests, bishops, popes, and the whole church organization. Without the mystic keys, ecclesiastics' blessings, cursings, baptisms, exorcisms, excommunications, prayers, or invocations were without efficacy. As Brahman priests commanded the gods by secret mantras, so Christian clergymen made the public believe the power of the keys could cause God to act.

The Gospels suggest that Peter controlled even the Savior's passage through the holy gate. There is a ring of ritual about the story that Peter denied Christ three times before the cock crew (Matthew 26:34), as though some material of the ancient sacred drama were clumsily re-interpreted. The resurrected god couldn't enter into his kingdom until dawn. The angel of annunciation appeared as a cock,

Pausanias Greek traveler and geographer of the 2nd century A.D. Living in a time of declining culture, he was inspired by a desire to describe the ancient sacred sites for posterity.

"to announce the coming of the Sun," as Pausanias said.[20] At cockcrow the Savior arose as Light of the World to disperse the demons of night. But if he tried to enter into his kingdom earlier, disrupting the cycles of night and day, the Gatekeeper would deny him. The ritualistic denial took place also in the fertility cults of Canaan, where the dying god Mot was denied by a priest representing the Heavenly Father.[21]

This story made difficulties for Christian theologians, when the pagans inquired why Jesus should found his church on a disciple who denied him instead of a more loyal one. The conventional answer was that it demonstrated Christ's power of forgiveness. But during the later persecutions, denial of Christ came to be considered the one absolutely unforgivable crime.

The cock was another totemic "peter" sometimes viewed as the god's alter ego. Vatican authorities preserved a bronze image of a cock with an oversize penis on a man's body, the pedestal inscribed "The Savior of the World."[22] The cock was also a solar symbol. Sun worship was evident in Christian literature, especially the "Gnostic Gospel" of John. Mithraic solar symbolism entered into many papal customs. St. Peter's Chair, the papal throne, was decorated like the throne of Mithra with zodiacal signs and the twelve labors of the sun god.[23]

Another curious survival of the bird form of "Peter" was the water-walking sea petrel, whose name meant "little peter." Petrels belonged to the legendary sea witch, Mother Carey, a corruption of Mater Cara, the Latin Goddess Car or Ceres, "Mistress of Earth and Sea." English sailors called the petrels Mother Carey's chickens, chicken being a diminutive of "cock," just as petrel was of "peter."[24] Like St. Peter, the petrels were "fishermen" who walked on water. Some said however that they were pagan souls who didn't reach hell before the gates were closed, and had to fly into "holes in the earth."[25]

The incident of Peter's water-walking (Matthew 14:29) was drawn from centuries of Oriental myth. Five hundred years before Christians attributed this feat to Jesus and Peter, Buddhists were saying a sage proficient in yoga could walk on water.[26] Later medieval writers attributed the same miracle to various saints noted for asceticism. St. Maurus for example lived an especially pure life, and found himself able to walk on water after he was blessed by St. Benedict.[27]

Other miracles attributed to Peter probably were intended to prove that he truly possessed the power of the keys. Like Christ, he could make the lame walk (Acts 3:7), and he could kill with a word, his first victims being Ananias and Sapphira (Acts 5:5, 10). None of Peter's legends however suggest that he was a real person. Scriptures concerning him were written (or forged) long after the epistles of Paul.[28]

It is now certain that there was no St. Peter in Rome to "found the papacy."[29] Stories about Peter were invented after the Roman see was well established. During the first five centuries of the Christian era, no one thought the bishop of Rome had a right to govern other bishops; there was no such doctrine as the primacy of the Roman see. "Christ neither founded nor desired the Church."[30] Indeed, the Jesus of the Gospels would have had no reason to found a church, since his principal message was that the world was going to end almost at once.

Whatever his origin, St. Peter stood for patriarchal opposition to the female principle, as shown by the Gnostic Gospels later censored out of the canon. The *Dialogue of the Savior* made the holy harlot Mary Magdalene the superior of all apostles; the *Gospel of Mary* said Christ loved her best, and gave her a secret revelation that Peter tried to force out of her. In the *Pistis Sophia,* Mary remarked, "Peter makes me hesitate; I am afraid of him because he hates the female race."[31]

Gospel of Mary One of the early Gnostic Gospels, once included with the books of the New Testament but later eliminated from the canon. A copy was rediscovered in the 1940s at Nag Hammadi.

Medieval legends also suggested Petrine anti-feminism. It was said Peter had a daughter, Petronilla (Little She-Peter), who was too beautiful in Peter's opinion, so he prayed God to strike her with a fatal illness, and God complied. The *Golden Legend* suggested that Peter tortured women to exorcise them, as he caused them to vomit up the devils that possessed them, along with "much blood."[32]

Legends aside, the real political power of the popes depended on popular acceptance of the doctrine of Peter's keys. Like a Brahman high priest, the pope assumed absolute control of God, who would grant his vicar's slightest request. Thus invested with divine power on earth, the pope became a figure comparable to the ancient god-kings, worshipped with similar subservience and inclined toward a similar arrogance.[33]

Pope Innocent III set papal policy with a proclamation that "the Lord left to Peter the governance not of the church only, but of the whole world."[34] Innocent was not content with the title "Vicar of Christ" but had it changed to "Vicar of God."[35] The bull *Unam Sanctam* of Pope Boniface VIII stated that every human creature on earth must be "subjected to the Roman pontiff."[36] In his jubilee year, Boniface represented himself as the emperor of all Europe. He dressed his cardinals as Roman priests, and himself in imperial armor, proclaiming, "I am the emperor; I am the Augustus."[37]

Boniface came to power by tricking his simple-minded, 80-year-old predecessor Celestine into abdicating the throne. Boniface had Celestine imprisoned in the fortress of Fumone, and had him murdered, rumor said, by driving a nail into his head. Boniface's enemies cherished as a holy relic Celestine's alleged skull, with a hole in it. Boniface had many enemies because he used papal power to seize lands and towns of the wealthy Colonna family, to give them to his own family, the Gaetani. Encountering resistance from the Colonnas, Boniface preached crusades against them and plunged Italy into a bloody civil war. He beseiged the Colonna city of Palestrina and offered to return half the enemy's possessions if the city were given up;

but he broke his promise. Once it was in his hands, he had Palestrina razed, its palaces, libraries, and treasure-houses sacked, its ground plowed and sown with salt. One of the Colonnas survived and eventually assassinated Boniface.[38]

A similarly avaricious heir of St. Peter was the highly inclement pope Clement VII, nicknamed "the Butcher" because of his fondness for massacre. He promised the mutinous people of Bologna that he would "wash his hands and feet in their blood."[39] At Cesena in 1376 he offered mercy to the city, then killed five thousand of its citizens. There were uprisings against him. Mobs hounded him out of Rome and Naples, crying, "Death to the Antichrist! Death to Clement and his cardinals!"[40]

Over all, the heirs of St. Peter have tended to follow the general pattern of dictators, some less benevolent than others. If they had any quality in common, it was acquisitiveness. This appeared so consistently that the Renaissance popes made it a heresy to say Jesus and Peter were poor men. Visiting Rome in 1511, Martin Luther was so shocked by the decadent luxury of the papal court that he wrote: "If there is a hell, then Rome is built upon it. . . . Tiberius, the heathen Emperor, even if he were such a monster as Suetonius writes of, is nevertheless an angel in comparison with the present court of Rome. The same hath to serve the supper table twelve naked girls."[41] It was rather a contrast with the popular image of twelve apostles.

1. Reinach, 240. 2. H. Smith, 252. 3. Attwater, 274. 4. H. Smith, 252.
5. Knight, S.L., 47. 6. G.R. Scott, 254. 7. d'Alviella, 103, 109. 8. Kendall, 97.
9. Guerber, L.R., 67. 10. Borchardt, 68. 11. Groome, 65–66.
12. Robertson, 193; Budge, G.E. 2, 19. 13. Lindsay, O.A., 185. 14. Angus, 167.
15. Dumézil, 328. 16. Robertson, 137. 17. Jung & von Franz, 304.
18. *Forgotten Books,* 96. 19. Cavendish, P.E., 98, 119; Vermaseren, 80.
20. Knight, S.L., 70. 21. *Larousse,* 76. 22. G.R. Scott, 262–63.
23. Robertson, 137. 24. Potter & Sargent, 71, 117. 25. Cohen, N.H.U.T., 112.
26. *Bardo Thodol,* 158; Tatz & Kent, 167. 27. de Voragine, 198.
28. Enslin, L.C.M., 233–38; H. Smith, 179–80. 29. Reinach, 240.
30. Guignebert, 125, 226. 31. Pagels, 22, 64–65. 32. de Voragine, 301, 252.
33. Campbell, C.M., 390. 34. H. Smith, 256. 35. Guignebert, 323.
36. Lea unabridged, 662. 37. J.H. Smith, C.G., 320.
38. Chamberlin, B.P., 93, 102–5. 39. Lea, 255.
40. Tuchman, 322, 333. 41. Chamberlin, B.P., 246.

Phaedra

Daughter of the Cretan Moon-queen Pasiphaë, who gave birth to the Minotaur. Phaedra married Theseus, who killed the Minotaur. She accompanied Theseus back to Greece and became his wife, and simultaneously the stepmother of Hippolytus, a victim slain by horses at the instigation of the magic Bull from the Sea—the Minotaur.

This tangled tale centering around Phaedra points to importation of the Cretan sacred-bull cult into Greece, where it merged with the local horse cult. Hippolytus was the victim dragged to death by horses after coupling with the queen (Phaedra). Apparently Hippolytus died as a surrogate for Theseus who, as the slayer of the bull-king in the

Labyrinth, would normally have been the next victim. The classic myth states that Theseus brought about the death of his son Hippolytus by laying a curse on him and praying to the sea god to implement it.[1]

Some say Hippolytus was apotheosized and now appears in heaven as Auriga, the Charioteer.

1. Graves, G.M. 1, 357.

Phaethon

Classic Greek figure of the solar Lucifer, a son of the sun. Phaethon committed the crime of hubris, offended his jealous Father, and was cast down from heaven like a lightning bolt.

Phaethon tricked his father Helios-Apollo into allowing him to drive the solar chariot across the sky, playing the role of the great God himself. But Phaethon lacked his father's skill. He lost control of the horses and nearly set the world afire with his reckless driving. His father threw him down into the sea just in time to save the earth from being ignited by the fiery sun-chariot.[1]

Phaethon's myth didn't originate in Greece. It was an old tale from Rhodes, the Island of the Sun, where white horses and a burning chariot were annually thrown into the sea to propitiate the Hittite sun god Tesup, whose cult had replaced that of the Moon-goddess Danae.[2] It seems likely that in primitive times there was also a charioteer playing the role of Phaethon and giving up his life for the sake of a post-mortem godhood.

1. Reinach, 90. 2. Graves, G.M. 1, 157.

Phallaina

One of the titles of the Greek "female soul," also known as Psyche, in her devouring aspect; literally, a yoni—that which devours the phallus.[1] The same word was applied to the night-moth, as a mysterious dark sister of the sun-loving butterfly that represented Psyche's daylight aspect. Phallaina was Psyche paired with Eros. According to the classical myth, their matings could take place only in the dark. When Psyche saw her husband in the light, their marriage was dissolved.

1. Lindsay, A.W., 131.

Phallus Worship

As Goddess-dominated religions made the yoni their holiest symbol, so God-dominated religions adored the phallus. Patriarchal Semites worshipped their own genitals, and swore binding oaths by placing a hand on each other's private parts, a habit still common among the Arabs.[1] Words like testament, testify, and testimony still at*test* to the oaths sworn on the testicles.[2]

Abraham's servant swore by placing his hand "under the thigh" of his master (Genesis 24, 9) because "thigh" was a common euphemism for "penis," used in superstitious fear of mentioning the divine organ directly. Myths of male pseudo-birth—like Zeus's fatherhood of Dionysus—made the offspring come forth from the father's "thigh."[3] But the meaning was "penis," as in the Hindu myth that substituted the lingam for the yoni: the god Sukra (Seed) came out of the stomach of the Great God by way of his penis.[4]

Another Middle-Eastern euphemism for "penis" was "knee," *genu,* so often mentioned that some people came to believe the knee was the source of seminal fluid. A father used to establish paternal rights to a child by setting the infant on his knee, which is why "genuine" (of the knee) came to mean "legitimate." In Mesopotamia the word *birku* meant both "knee" and "penis."[5] In Latin it became *virtu,* "masculine spirit, virility, erect-ness."

The Bible calls Jacob's penis the sinew that shrank, lying "upon the hollow of the thigh." Scholars have tried to interpret this limp penis as something else: a severed tendon, or a certain thigh muscle, which Jews were forbidden to eat (Genesis 32:32). But medieval translators frankly recognized the phallic meaning of the "sinew." They said the god-man's blighting touch on Jacob's shrunken member was "to cool the fires of concupiscence."[6]

Biblical patriarchs worried inordinately about the vulnerability of the penis and avoided direct mention of it lest evil spirits be drawn to it. Old Testament laws reveal a special fear of women's power over the penis. God's commandment was that a woman who grabs a man's genitals must have her hand cut off, even if she does it to defend her husband against an enemy (Deuteronomy 25:11–12).

The word "fascinate" is a relic of men's belief in the magic of their own genitals. Latin *fascinum* meant an erect penis (presumably "fascinating" to the opposite sex), especially in the form of a phallic amulet. Such amulets continued to be used through the Middle Ages as antidotes to the evil eye.[7] In the 8th century A.D., the church forbade men to pray to the *fascinum.* In the 9th century, the same prohibition had to be repeated—and again in the 12th and 13th centuries, showing that the custom went blithely on.[8]

The phallic principle was covertly worshipped in sacred posts and pillars, such as the Maypole and the "bride-stake" erected at weddings, about which "the guests were wont to dance as about a May-pole."[9] Stubbes in 1583 described common folk dancing and hanging garlands on their Maypole, which he called a "stinking idol."[10] Women of ancient Rome used to hang flower wreaths on the erect penis of the god Liber, to "have fruit of the seeds they sow," St. Augustine said.[11]

The same sexual ceremony of encircling the phallus with a female wreath was perpetuated at Antwerp, where an ancient ithyphallic statue of Priapus stood before the sanctuary of St. **Walpurga**, once the orgiastic Goddess of Walpurgisnacht or May Eve. Each year at the spring festival, women hung wreaths of flowers on Priapus's penis.[12] Another image of the same god was carried through the streets of Naples in sacred processions, displaying a penis long enough to reach his chin. This excrescence was known as *il santo membro,* the Holy Member.[13]

A 13th-century Chronicle of Lanercost said that, at Easter, the parish priest of Inverkeithing "revived the profane rites of Priapus, collecting young girls from the villages, and compelling them to dance in circles to Father Bacchus. When he had these females in a troop, out of sheer wantonness, he led the dance, carrying in front on a pole a representation of the human organs of reproduction, and singing and dancing himself like a mime."[14] This priest was less eccentric than one might think; the same sort of thing was happening all over Europe. Phallus worship was Christianized in ways that hinted at Christianity's true nature: a cult of the male principle.

Giant phalli were adored up to the 17th century as saints, such as Eutropius, Foutin, Guerlichon, Gilles, Regnaud, René, and Guignole. St. Foutin de Varailles was a phallic pillar kept red with libations of wine, as the phalli of Shiva were constantly reddened in Hindu temples.[15] Ithyphallic saints in Normandy and Anjou were believed to impregnate women who lay with them all night. The image of St. Guignole had a large erect penis from which women scraped splinters as conception charms. So much scraping went on that the saint might have had his holy member whittled away entirely. But the priests, with commendable foresight, made his phallus of a wooden rod that passed all the way through the statue to the back, where it was hidden by a screen, and could be periodically thrust forward by a tap of a mallet as it diminished in front.[16]

Christ assumed the role of a phallic god in providing the most popular of conception charms: the Holy Prepuce—or more accurately, Prepuces, for there were hundreds of them in Renaissance churches. At least thirteen examples still survive.[17] All had the power to make women conceive. The most celebrated of the virile foreskins, housed at the Abbey Church in Chartres, was credited with thousands of miraculous pregnancies.[18] St. Catherine of Siena went so far as to claim that Jesus used his holy foreskin as her wedding ring. She was bound to Jesus as his bride, "not with a ring of silver but with a ring of his holy flesh, for when he was circumcised just such a ring was taken from his holy body."[19]

Phallic saints were special patrons of virility, much entreated by men with sexual problems. Sir William Hamilton described the cult of two phallic saints, Cosmo and Damiano, at Isernia in 1781: "*Ex-voti* of wax, representing the male parts of generation, of various dimensions

. . . are publicly offered for sale. . . . The Vow is never presented without being accompanied by a piece of money, and is always kissed by the devotee at the moment of presentation." The priests sold St. Cosmo's holy oil as a virility charm:

> *The oil of St. Cosmo is in high repute for its invigorating quality, when the loins, and parts adjacent, are anointed with it. No less than 1400 flasks of that oil were either expended at the Altar in unctions, or charitably distributed during the Fete in the year 1780; and as it is usual for everyone, who either makes use of the Oil at the Altar, or carries off a flask of it, to leave an alms for St. Cosmo, the ceremony of the Oil becomes likewise a very lucrative one for the Canons of the Church.*[20]

A hint of the broad extent of phallic Christianity in England appeared after World War II when Professor Geoffrey Webb, of the Royal Commission on Historical Monuments, investigated a bomb-damaged altar of an old church and found a large stone phallus within it. Further researches showed that the altars of approximately 90% of English churches built before 1348 had hidden stone phalli.[21] By pagan tradition, an altar symbolized the female body—which is why witches were said to use a naked woman for their altar—and the phallus within it obviously represented the Hidden God.

Sexual symbolism kept cropping up to embarrass scholars of religion, like Georges Dumézil, who called "indiscreet" the Roman belief that the sacred Palladium in the temple of Vesta was the scepter of Priam "in the likeness of a male sex organ." Yet Dumézil himself wrote, "Some day it will be necessary to restore to the history of religions the idea of the symbol which is today so underrated and yet of such capital importance."[22]

An understanding of phallus worship is important for comprehension of religious psychology, especially the fundamental insecurity of male self-worship: for the phallic God was useless without the Goddess. Dr. Lederer says:

> *During the aeons of feminine dominance, women were well content in the possession of their own particular magic, and did not envy men their little tool that was so easily borrowed when it was needed. Indeed, the Great Mother was never short of a phallus . . . the phallus was at her service. It was kept in evidence in the sanctuary of the Goddess, and was not the phallus of any particular God or mortal, was not a man or a God* with *a phallus, but it was simply a phallus* per se, *a depersonalized instrument of ready and convenient use. Once used, it was no longer useful. For the Great Mother, as for certain of her descendants today, penises are expendable: one can always get more, and the new ones are probably better. The new ones, of course, are younger; and the fear of being spent, and doomed to replacement by a younger man—both in the sexual and in the general service of the Goddess—may on occasion be a source of deep anxiety for the middle-aged male.*[23]

Phallic anxiety was evident in all patriarchal systems, where fear of the devouring vulva led to both ascetic avoidance and persecution of women. Phallic anxiety was the keynote of the one solitary joke in the *Malleus Maleficarum* (Hammer for Witches), the Inquisition's official handbook. The monkish authors took the joke seriously, though it was given them by some sly peasant whose purpose was mockery. The story was that a witch stole a man's penis, but he caught her and forced her to reveal its whereabouts. She told him to climb a tall tree and look in a nest, which proved to be filled with penises. He chose the biggest one, but the witch said he couldn't have that one; it belonged to the parish priest.

The pious authors swallowed all this with great solemnity, and wrote: "What is to be thought of those witches who in this way sometimes collect male organs in great numbers, as many as twenty or thirty members together, and put them in a bird's nest, or shut them up in a box, where they move themselves like living members, and eat oats and corn, as has been seen by many and is a matter of common report?"[24] Even more to the point, what is to be thought of those churchmen who believed it?

Phallus worship often slid over the ill-defined line into homosexuality, which was inevitable among men taught to adore the phallic principle in each other. Sometimes a homosexual kind of adoration was extended toward the superior male, or toward God. Among gypsy men, the expression of ritual self-abasement was *hav co kar*, "I eat thy penis." It was explained that "If one should, for example, petition God in prayer for a wish to be granted, he would precede his request by saying, 'O God, I eat thy penis.' " As with other eaten gods however, "the question whether it might be the last remnant of a very ancient practice of cannibalism must be considered."[25]

Phallus worship is still evident in the symbols and sayings of the modern world, though its meaning is less like impregnation and more like death. Guns, cannon, missiles and other weapons are the phallic symbols. In underworld slang, "to get a hard-on" means to pull a gun.[26] "Hits" and "scores" describe both attacks and sexual encounters. Dominant men are "big shots" or "big guns." The ancient image of the fructifying Lord of Life is unhappily transformed into a Lord of Death when male power is identified with the power to destroy. In its worship of the masculine principle of aggression, the modern world sorely misses the central idea of ancient Goddess worship: that true power is the power to preserve.

1. Edwardes, 65–66. 2. Brasch, 152; Potter & Sargent, 298. 3. Graves, G.M. 2, 56.
4. O'Flaherty, 297. 5. Gaster, 789. 6. de Voragine, 583. 7. Robbins, 193.
8. Knight, D.W.P., 129. 9. Hazlitt, 76. 10. Frazer, G.B., 142. 11. Scot, 219.
12. Knight, D.W.P., 145. 13. G.R. Scott, 250–52.
14. Phillips, 169; Knight, D.W.P, 131. 15. Knight, D.W.P., 141. 16. G.R. Scott, 247.
17. Budge, A.T., 26. 18. Goldberg, 67. 19. Tuchman, 324.
20. G.R. Scott, 253. 21. M. Harrison, 210. 22. Dumézil, 26, 323.
23. Lederer, 214–15. 24. Kramer & Sprenger, 121. 25. Trigg, 206.
26. Farb, W.P., 123.

Phanes

Orphic double-sexed deity, firstborn of the World Egg. He-she helped the Triple Goddess arrange the universe. Phanes was also known as Eros, Ericipaius, or Phaethon Protogenus (Shining First-born).[1] Phanes means "Revealer."

1. Graves, G.M. 1, 30; 2, 404.

Philosopher's Stone

See **Alchemy**.

Phoebe

"Bright Moon," title of Themis the oracular Goddess of Delphi, and her emanation Ar-temis. The title was taken over by Phoebus Apollo, which gave him the self-contradictory name of "Lunar Sun."[1] Nevertheless, his priests insisted on this title. Sometimes he was called simply Phoebus, indicating a moon god rather than a sun god.

1. Graves, G.M. 1, 178.

Phoenix

Egyptians identified the Phoenician god Phoenix with their *bennu* bird, a spirit of the *benben* or phallic **obelisk**. He rose to heaven in the form of the Morning Star, like Lucifer, after his fire-immolation of death and rebirth.[1] In Phoenicia as in Egypt he embodied the sacred king cremated and reborn. Symbolic burning of the king continued up to the present century in Upper Egypt, on the first day of each solar year by Coptic reckoning.[2] The king's soul released above the pyre assumed bird form, as ancient pharaohs at their cremation took the form of the Horus-hawk. See **Birds**.

1. Budge, G.E. 2, 97. 2. Frazer, G.B., 332–33.

Phrixus

Boeotian prototype of Isaac, a son almost slain as an offering to God by his pious father, when a magic ram appeared to take his place. The ram carried Phrixus out of danger, then gave up its life and its Golden Fleece, which became a sacred fetish. The myth "records the annual mountain sacrifice of the king, or of the king's surrogate—first a boy dressed in a ram's fleece, and later a ram."[1] Thus Aries-the-Ram (Egyptian Amen) became the god of New Year sacrifices. See **Ram**.

1. Graves, G.M. 1, 229.

Pig

See **Boar**.

Pillar

The obelisk, Maypole, pillar, sacred tree trunk, upright cross, and other male divinity-symbols probably originated in India where Shiva's lingam (penis) was worshipped as a sacred pillar. Shiva's title Sthanu, "the Pillar," revealed him as a personified phallus.[1] Some of his holy pillars are still popular pilgrimage centers. Land within a radius of 100 cubits from such a pillar became known as the Kingdom of Shiva, where many miracles occur, including instant remission of sins.[2] Seasonal festivals still feature a Maypole representing Shiva's "Great Lingam."[3]

Phallic pillars appear also in northern Asia and Siberia, where such erections are entitled Powerful Posts of the Center of the City, or Man-Pillar of Iron. People pray to such pillars, calling them "Man" or "Father," offering them blood sacrifices.[4]

Blood was anciently considered essential to the lingam-pillar, which Hindus frequently painted red or smeared with blood. Archaic Egyptian myth said two pillars, called "trees that shed blood," stood at the entrance of the temple. The blood they shed could render women pregnant.[5] Here may be found a remnant of the primitive idea that male blood, not semen, is the fertile essence, copied from Neolithic worship of female "moon-blood." The temple door represented the yoni, entitled *Er-per,* the Holy Door of the Goddess.[6]

As in India, where Shiva's lingam was painted red or anointed with blood for religious festivals, so in Egypt the pillars in front of the temple door were "blooded" in memory of primitive sacrifices when real men were hung on them to bleed. Jews picked up this Egyptian custom and blooded their doorposts for Passover with the vital fluid of the sacrificial lamb. The doorposts represented phalli, like the pillars in front of Solomon's temple, named Boaz and Jachin, "Strength" and "God Makes Him Firm" (1 Kings 7:19–20).

At Hierapolis the temple of the Goddess had an enormous phallic pillar on each side of the door. Every year, a man climbed to the top of each pillar and remained there for seven days, symbolically recapitulating ancient sacrifices when the pillars were bathed in the blood of human victims, who were evidently left hanging for one lunar week, perhaps in imitation of a menstrual period.[7] When Syria was Christianized, the custom was continued by the "pillar saints" who, like their pagan predecessors, thought themselves near enough to heaven for their prayers to be distinctly heard.[8] The most famous of them was St. Simeon Stylites, "Simeon of the Pillar," who stayed aloft until his limbs became gangrenous and he died in a pungent odor of sanctity.[9]

A church was built around a sacred pillar in Athens and named St.

John of the Column. As pagans had previously come to tie their illnesses to the pillar with silk thread, so the legendary St. John ordered, "Let any sick come and tie a silk thread to the column and be healed."[10]

Pillars in conjunction with churches—as a spire or campanile—are not often recognized as male symbols in contact with a female one, although the *shikhara* or spire associated with a Hindu temple is generally viewed as a phallus.[11]

1. O'Flaherty, 354. 2. *Mahanirvanatantra,* 335. 3. Avalon, 517. 4. Eliade, S., 263. 5. Maspero, 17–18. 6. Budge, D.N., 144. 7. Knight, D.W.P., 84. 8. Frazer, F.O.T., 69. 9. *Encyc. Brit.,* "Simeon." 10. Hyde, 109. 11. de Camp, A.E., 298.

Pithos

Female-symbolic Holy Vase, used in the Eleusinian Mysteries as a uterine receptacle for corpses, to give them a blessed rebirth. The Goddess herself was represented by a vase or pot in the guise of Pandora the "All-Giver." (See **Pandora**.) The identity of the Great Mother with this vessel of rebirth and regeneration was an idea common to most ancient cultures, where the manufacture of pots and vases of all kinds was usually the business of women.[1]

In Christian custom the *pithos* was transformed into the *pyx* or "box" that enclosed the body of Christ; and Erasmus confused the two vessels in translating the patriarchal version of Pandora's myth.

1. Neumann, G.M., 132–33.

Planetary Spheres

The Chaldean astrological cosmology was generally accepted throughout the Mediterranean world in the early Christian era. According to this cosmology, the earth lay under a series of nested, inverted crystal bowls, turned independently of each other by star-angels. This idea accounted for the independent movement of sun, moon, and planets against the fixed stars. Each "sphere" had its tutelary deities. In Egypt these were known as the Seven Heavenly Midwives, emanations of Hathor, who guarded the seven gates of heaven. Souls seeking entrance must address them with *hekau,* words of power. The first of them was greeted: "Lady of tremblings, surrounded by lofty walls, the chieftainess, lady of destruction, the disposer of the words that drive away storms and deliver from destruction him that traveleth along the way."[1]

Under the earth lay the celestial spheres' mirror image, seven nether spheres descending into the Abyss. These divisions of the underworld were called Seven Recesses, Seven Gates, abysses, *bothroi, antra, mychoi, pylai,* or *chasma* (pits).[2] At the bottom lay the foundations of the earth, "the meeting of the mighty waters." Like the celestial gates, the underworld gates were guarded by special porters, the Assyro-Babylonian *maskim* or Anunnaki. Ziggurats were models of the upper and lower planetary spheres. Ascending heavens were represented by the terraces of the ziggurat, known as the Stages of the Seven Spheres of the World.[3] Underneath, inside the temple, were seven corresponding "deeps" or "pits."

Initiations in the temple apparently mimicked the descent into the underworld pits and a journey through the heavenly stages also. Apuleius described his initiation into the Mysteries of Isis as a descent into the land of death, to the threshold of Isis-Nephthys, or Persephone the Destroyer. He beheld the Black Sun, nether image of the solar god. Then he ascended through the lower and upper worlds and saw "face to face" the deities of both. Finally he rose to the heights and was exhibited to the congregation in the costume of the sun god.[4] The journey of each initiate was a theatrical performance, with priests and priestesses wearing the costumes and masks of the appropriate spirits, and dramatic descents through dark caves and other specially decorated rooms. The impressive effects may well be imagined.

Early Christians believed all souls descended from heaven to enter their bodies of flesh on earth, during the descent taking faults and passions from each sphere to sully their initial purity and cause temptation. This was the origin of the Seven Deadly Sins. "As the souls descend, they draw with them the torpor of Saturn, the wrathfulness of Mars, the concupiscence of Venus, the greed for gain of Mercury, the lust for power of Jupiter; which things effect a confusion in the souls, so that they can no longer make use of their own power and their proper faculties."[5] After living the right sort of life, the soul could re-ascend after death, shedding its sinful qualities one by one.[6] Sometimes the spirits of the planetary spheres acted as inspectors after the Egyptian manner: "As men ascend, they find custom-houses guarding the way with great care and obstructing the soaring souls, each custom-house examining for one particular sin, one for deceit, another for envy, another for slander, and so on in order, each passion having its own inspectors and assessors."[7]

Gnostic mystery-cults copied the pagans, in that they taught passwords and charms to propitiate the guardian spirits of each sphere. In the Pistis Sophia, Jesus told his followers: "Stay not your hand until ye find the cleansing mysteries which will cleanse you so as to make you pure light, that ye may go into the heights and inherit the light of my kingdom."[8] The heights meant the Empyrean, where God lived in the highest heaven. Those who attained true enlightenment would enter the Godhead and become God, just as Oriental sages believed they could enter Nirvana and become one with the Infinite.[9] In China, the successively higher heavens were even graphically illustrated by the multiple roofs of the pagoda, one above another.[10]

The days of the week are still named after the planetary spheres. Monday is the Day of the Moon (*dies lunae*). Tuesday is Tiw's Day, named for the Saxon god who was the counterpart of Mars; it is the Day of Mars in Latinate languages (French *mardi*). Wednesday is Woden's Day, *dies mercurii,* named for the Teutonic god considered the equivalent of Mercury. The once-supreme Woden was ousted from the list in the very country of his origin, Germany, and replaced by a neutral *Mittwoch,* "Mid-week."

Thor's Day was named for the thunder-god who was a Germanic equivalent of Jove; Romans called it *dies jovis.* Friday was Freya's Day (Frea-Tag), Rome's *dies veneris,* the day sacred to Venus-Aphrodite-Freya—the only wholly feminine day, which may be why so many superstitions were connected with it. The Goddess's day was followed by Saturn's Day, then by the Day of the Sun (*dies solis*), associated with the "fiery" heaven of aether.

As the planets ruled various divisions of heaven, so also they were believed to rule various places on earth according to their qualities. Under the sun were "light places, the serene air, kings' palaces and princes' courts, pulpits, theatres, thrones, and all kingly and magnificent places." Under the moon were "wildernesses, highways, groves, woods, rocks, hills, mountains, forests, fountains, waters, rivers, seas, seashores, ships, and granaries for corn." Under Mars were "fiery and bloody places, furnaces, bakehouses, shambles, places of execution, and places where there have been great battles fought and slaughters made." Under Mercury were "shops, schools, warehouses, exchanges for merchants." Under Jupiter were "all privileged places, consistories of noblemen, tribunals, chairs, places for exercise, schools, and all beautiful and clean places, and those sprinkled with divers odors." Under Venus were "pleasant fountains, green meadows, flourishing gardens, garnished beds, stews, the sea, the seashore, baths, dancing places, and all places belonging to women." Under Saturn were "all stinking places, and dark, underground, religious, and mournful places, as church-yards, tombs, and houses not inhabited by men; and old, tottering, obscure, dreadful houses; and solitary dens, caves, and pits; also fish-ponds, standing pools, sewers."[11]

1. *Book of the Dead,* 271–72. 2. Lindsay, O.A., 64. 3. Lethaby, 129. 4. Rose, 283. 5. Jonas, 157. 6. Lindsay, O.A., 124. 7. Lawson, 284. 8. Legge 2, 174–75. 9. Jonas, 153. 10. Lethaby, 50. 11. Agrippa, 149–50.

Pleiades

The convoluted symbolism of the Pleiades or Seven Sisters suggests an extremely archaic tradition. The importance attached to this small group of dim stars seems out of proportion to their apparent insignificance.

The sacrifice of the Mexican savior Xipe Totec, Our Lord the Flayed One, took place on the Hill of the Stars at the moment when the Pleiades reached the zenith on the last night of the Great Year cycle. It was thought if the Sisters were not propitiated by the sacrifice, the universe would fall to pieces and the world would come to an end.[1]

Pre-Vedic India also attached sacrificial significance to the Pleiades, called Seven Mothers of the World, or Krittikas, "razors" or "cutters." They were also seven priestesses who "judged" men—a cognate was Greek *kritikos*, "judge"—and sometimes "critically" wounded them, for their razors were castrating moon-sickles. The fire god Agni copulated with the Seven Mothers while they were menstruating, the usual Tantric rite later outlawed by the Vedic priesthood. They gave birth to a solar hero enveloped in a great red cloud (female symbol) penetrated by bolts of lightning (male symbol). The hero was sacrificially slain, wounded in the side with a spear, and from his body sprang his reincarnation, another hero like himself.[2] In this myth may be discerned rites of great antiquity, predating the discovery of fatherhood, when blood was the essence of generation.

The Pleiades were prominent in the early cult of Aphrodite, who was supposed to have given birth to them under her name of Pleione. Aphrodite was a castrating Crone-goddess as well as a Holy Dove; and the Pleiades were "a flock of doves."[3] They were connected with sacrificial New Year ceremonies in Greece as in central America and southeastern Asia. The Seven Sisters stood at the zenith on New Year's Eve as if to select the god of the new Aeon. Old Babylonian texts began the year with the Pleiades. Later, the zodiacal sign of the New Year became Aries, the Ram.[4]

Egyptian texts allude to the Pleiades' archaic significance as Krittikas, judges of men, assigning them also to seven planetary spheres as the seven Hathors. The dead had to speak the names of these Goddesses to pass their "critical" examinations and enter paradise: "Hail, ye seven beings who make decrees, who support the Balance on the night of the judgment of the Utchat, who cut off heads, who hack necks in pieces, who take possession of hearts by violence and rend the places where hearts are fixed, who make slaughterings in the Lake of Fire, I know you, and I know your names; therefore know ye me, even as I know your names."[5] The reference to tearing out hearts is remarkably evocative of Aztec religious customs. The Seven Mothers Who Make Decrees appeared also in Arabia as Seven Sages or *imams* (from *ima*, "mother").[6]

In classical mythology the Pleiades represented the Maytime feast of life and the November feast of death at opposite points of the year. They were emanations of the Moon-goddess "who was worshipped at the two solstices as the Goddess of alternatively Life-in-Death and Death-in-Life and who early in November, when the Pleiades set, sent the sacred king his summons to death."[7] Prayers for the dead were recited before the Pleiades on November 1, which became All Soul's Day.[8]

Greeks said the leader of the Pleiades was the Dove-goddess Alcyone, the "halcyon" bird who brought good weather for the planting season. Another Pleiad was Electra, mother of Dardanus, legendary founder of Troy, whose name is still preserved in the Dardanelles. Another Pleiad was Merope, "Bee-eater," a title of Aphrodite's queen bee as devourer of the drone. Some said Merope was one of the Furies; others said she married the doomed sun-hero Sisyphus. Still another Pleiad was Maia "the Maker" or the "Grandmother," mother of Hermes the Enlightened One, as her Hindu counterpart Maya mothered Buddha the Enlightened One.[9]

Classical writers seemed anxious to disguise the real nature of the Pleiades. One story insisted they were all virgins. Orion the Hunter tried to rape them, but Zeus protected them by turning them into doves and placing them in the heavens. The story was obviously absurd, as all the Pleiades had lovers or husbands, and three of them had mated with Zeus himself. In earlier myths, Orion the Hunter was their victim, not their attacker. The Huntress of the Seven Stars, Artemis, shot him to death in the sea, suggesting that victims were sometimes riddled with arrows then consigned to the deep.[10]

Artemis personified another set of seven stars, the much larger constellation Ursa Major, the "Great She-Bear," who may have been another version of the Seven Sisters. Artemis and Aphrodite both were associated with ancient cults of the Seven Pillars of Wisdom, seven mantic priestesses of Seven-Gated Thebes, where the Seven Hathors once ruled, where sacred kings were slain every seventh year, and where Teiresias was castrated and lived seven years as a temple woman. The same magic seven were called Seven Midwives in Egypt and the Orient. They were probably represented in pre-patriarchal Jerusalem by the holy Menorah (seven-branched candlestick) symbolizing the sevenfold Men-horae or Moon-priestesses, as shown by its female-genital decorations, lilies and almonds (Exodus 25:33).

Medieval superstitions betrayed fear of groups of seven females, perhaps a relic of ancient images of the Sisters. East Frieslanders believed that in any family of seven sisters, one of the seven was sure to be a vampire or a werewolf.[11] The sevenfold grouping could also be arranged in a vertical line of descent, e.g. in the ubiquitous belief that a seventh daughter of a seventh daughter was always a witch.

1. Tannahill, 82. 2. O'Flaherty, 346, 187, 110–15.
3. Graves, G.M. 1, 71; 2, 405; W.G., 194. 4. Lindsay, O.A., 56. 5. Budge, E.M., 165.
6. Briffault 1, 377. 7. Graves, W.G., 194. 8. Jobes, 336.
9. Graves, G.M. 1, 165; 2, 259, 400. 10. Graves, G.M. 1, 151–52.
11. Baring-Gould, W., 113.

Pluto

"Riches," underworld consort of Persephone in classical myth. An earlier Pluto was not male but female, a daughter of the Cretan earth-mother Rhea, one of the Titans or elder deities.[1] She was apparently the second person of the original Demeter trinity—also called Rhea—comprising Kore the Virgin, Pluto the Mother, Persephone the Destroyer. "Riches" typically meant the Mother figure whose breasts poured forth abundance. Later, Pluto was masculinized, and in Christian times "he" became synonymous with the devil.

1. Graves, G.M. 2, 25.

Poimandres

"Shepherd of Men," a title of Hermes Trismegistus as **psychopomp** or Conductor of Souls. According to the Hermetic scriptures called *Poimandres,* the enlightened soul under the benevolent direction of Hermes could ascend to heaven by giving up its sins to each of the planetary spheres in turn, becoming one with the Heavenly Powers, then entering the essential being of God. "This is the good end of those who have attained gnosis: to become God."[1] See **Antinomianism**.

A medieval prophet named Giovanni Mercurio da Correggio assimilated himself to Poimandres who seems to have been, in this context, a reincarnation of Jesus. He arrived in Rome one Palm Sunday, riding a white ass and leading a procession. He wore a crown of thorns, topped by a crescent bearing the legend: "This is my son Pimander, [sic] whom I have chosen. . . . Thus speaks the Lord God and the Father of every talisman in the world, Jesus of Nazareth." This Hermetic hero marched to the Vatican to lay his magic tools on the altar, declaring that he had come down from heaven with power to judge the quick and the dead. He wandered about Italy for years, preaching and working magic. He was suspected of heresy but as he was sponsored by Lorenzo de' Medici and other influential patrons, the Inquisition let him alone.[2]

1. Jonas, 153–54. 2. Shumaker, 111.

Pollux

Latin form of Polydeuces, twin brother of Castor. Together they were the Dioscuri, born of Leda's egg along with their sister Helen of Troy. Castor and Pollux were worshipped as gods of the morning and evening star, and attendants of the Moon-goddess, their mother.[1] Because Pollux as a morning-star god became identified with Lucifer, and because he was revered by the pagans, his name gave rise to "pollution."

1. Graves, G.M. 1, 251.

Pomegranate

Rimmon, "pomegranate," was a biblical name of the Goddess's genital shrine (2 Kings 5:18), from *rim,* "to give birth."[1] The pomegranate with its red juice and many seeds was a prime symbol of uterine fertility. Therefore pomegranates were eaten by souls in the underworld, to bring about rebirth. Hellenic mythographers said both Kore and Eurydice were detained in the underworld because they ate pomegranate seeds there. Nana, virgin mother of the savior Attis, conceived him by eating either a pomegranate seed or an almond, another yonic symbol.

The Bible says the pillars of Solomon's temple were ornamented with the female-genital symbols of lilies and pomegranates (1 Kings 7:18–20). Solomon himself impersonated the phallic god Baal-Rimmon, "Lord of the Pomegranate," when he was united with his divine bride, the mysterious Shulamite, and drank the juice of her pomegranate (Song of Solomon 8:2).

Argive Hera was worshipped as Our Lady With the Pomegranate at Capaccio Vecchio near Paestum, formerly a Sybarite colony called Poseidonia. In ancient times the people laid at the Goddess's feet offerings of little boats filled with flowers, as she sat enthroned with her child on one arm, a pomegranate in her other hand, inviting contemplation of the miracle of her bringing forth life. About the 12th century A.D. the people of Paestum built her a new shrine, to which pilgrimages are made to this day. There sits Our Lady With the Pomegranate still, enthroned with her child on one arm, a pomegranate in her other hand.[2] The people lay at her feet offerings of little boats filled with flowers.

Hera was Mother Earth, and the suit of pentacles in the Tarot pack represented the earth element. Therefore it is not surprising to find this suit transformed in some medieval packs into a Suit of Pomegranates, the fruit always opened in an oval orifice to show its moist red interior.[3]

1. Graves, W.G., 410. 2. J. H. Smith, D.C.P., 244. 3. Cavendish, T., 155, 170.

Pomona

Roman Apple-Mother, Goddess of fruit trees; a title of Hera or Eve as dispenser of the apples of eternal life. Every Roman banquet ended with apples, as an invocation of Pomona's good will. See **Apple**.

Pooka

Irish version of Puck, from Old English *puca*, a fairy; also related to "spook," a ghost or demon, as the old gods of the fairy-religion were called.[1] Ireland had several Puckstowns, a Puck Fair, and a Pooka's Ford.[2] See **Bogey**.

1. Potter & Sargent, 295. 2. Pepper & Wilcock, 279–80.

Poseidon

Greek sea god corresponding to Roman Neptune. He was "greedy of earthly kingdoms"—that is, his priests were —and so his myths tell how he took territories from various forms of the Goddess. He pretended to marry the Triple Goddess herself, under her name of Amphitrite, and demoted her to a mere sea nymph. He tried to take Argolis from Hera, and Athens from Athene. He claimed to have invented the horse bridle, though Athene had already done it. He demanded that women be deprived of their vote in Athens, and forbade men to continue taking the surnames of their mothers as they had formerly done.[1] He even claimed husbandship of the venerable Mare-Demeter on the ground that he had once raped her in the form of a stallion.

Yet Poseidon was an upstart god, transparently subject to the Goddess in his earlier myths. "He had, properly speaking, no name of his own, but was simply known as 'the spouse of Earth.' He only became a great god when his original nature, and also the origin of his name, were forgotten."[2]

When Poseidon sent a flood on the Xanthian plain, the Xanthian women beat him off and saved their country by hoisting their skirts and marching on him with their genitals exposed. The doughty sea god beat a hasty retreat.[3]

1. Graves, G.M. 1, 59–60. 2. Guthrie, 98. 3. Graves, G.M. 1, 254.

Possession

The idea that a human body may be possessed by a supernatural personality, in addition to its own natural one, occurs in every religion. Christians believed in several kinds of possession, both divine and demonic. The Catholic church retains the office of exorcist because it still considers demonic possession real. At the same time, god-possession was the central idea of Christ's incarnation, and it is believed that a worshipper may be possessed by the spirit of Christ, often in the ecstatic manner of the primitive shaman. Some Christian sects called this "getting the spirit."

Pagan mystery cults brought about god-possession by eating the god (as did Christians also), and by initiatory rites and formulae. The Mithraic initiate said he was "rendered immortal in this hour by the good will of God in his abounding goodness . . . that I may be initiated and that the Holy Spirit may breathe within me." A Hermetic papyrus prayed the god to enter into the worshipper, "for thou art I and I am thou. . . . I know thee, Hermes, and thou knowest me; I am thou, and thou art I."[1] Possession by Hermes the Wise Serpent would have been "diabolic" possession from the Christian point of view; but the principle was the same everywhere.

People possessed by pagan gods sometimes created a tradition directly inherited by Christianity. Worshippers of Attis castrated themselves when fully possessed by the spirit of their castrated god. Under the same influence "they flogged themselves until the blood came. In Italy such processions of flagellants during Passion Week have continued until the present day, the Madonna being the patroness of these *Re penitenti* (penitent kings)" instead of the Great Mother of the Gods, who formerly governed their bloodlettings.[2]

To be possessed meant to take the spirit into one's body, either as the flesh of a sacrificial victim or as bread and wine representing that flesh. For the same reason that Christ "entered into" those who ate him, so possession by devils was thought to occur through incautious eating. St. Gregory the Great told of a nun who became possessed by a devil after eating a bit of lettuce. The devil complained to the exorcist, "What wrong have I done? Here I was sitting upon this lettuce, and she came and ate me!"[3] To speak a blessing over food before eating was originally supposed to drive out whatever devils might be lurking there.

Pope Gregory professed an ability to recognize the signs of demonic possession under any circumstances. When a horse kicked and plunged and refused to let him mount, he instantly realized the horse was possessed by a demon. He even knew the possession had been caused by two magicians, whom he arrested, blinded, and tortured into confessions. Afterward, they were "cared for" at the church's expense for the rest of their lives, meaning they were imprisoned for life.[4]

All primitive people think humans, animals, and inanimate objects may serve as vessels for spirits. "The Maori term *waka* clearly indicates that the inspired man carries the god in him as a canoe carries its owner."[5] Our own vocabulary expresses the same belief. Inspiration means breathing in a spirit; enthusiasm means the god within. We say, "What possessed you to do that?" or "I don't know what got into me." An obsessive person may be called devil-ridden or hag-ridden.

Euripides called Dionysus the god of prophecy, because he took possession of the body through divine madness, which "makes those whom he maddens foretell the future."[6] We still speak of being "possessed" by prophetic or poetic frenzy. Mediums are "possessed" by spirits of the dead, who speak through them as demons were said to speak through their human hosts.

Men never abandoned the notion of alien spirits within the human mind. Not only was the god-within concept essential to the communion rite, but the devil-within concept was also essential to discrediting other deities, whose communion rites were the same. Moreover, diabolic possession was affirmed by the scriptures. Summers said, "We have the authority of Christ Himself as to its reality. . . . [N]o reader of the Scriptural narrative can deny that Christ by word and deed showed His entire belief in possession by evil spirits. And if Christ were divine how came He to foster and encourage a delusion?"[7]

The third edition of the *Encyclopaedia Britannica* gave the same official opinion under Demoniacs: "The reality of demoniacal possession stands on the same evidence with the gospel system in general." A 19th-century Catholic authority wrote, "To deny possession by devils is to charge Jesus and his apostles with imposture. . . . How can the testimony of apostles, fathers of the Church, and saints who saw the possessed and so declared, be denied?"[8]

Seventeenth-century clergymen fought the "evil heart of unbelief" that led people to doubt the reality of demonic possession and the efficacy of exorcism. Priests vied with each other to see who could cast out the most demons. In a highly publicized case, Sister Madeleine de la Palud of the Ursuline convent of Aix-en-Provence was found to contain 6,666 demons including Beelzebub, Leviathan, Baalberith, Asmodeus, and Astaroth—the cream of hell's celebrities.[9] Jesuits at Vienna claimed over 12,000 demons in a single case of possession. One skeptic, Bishop Miron, suspected the possessed Martha Brossier of fakery when her demon sent her into convulsions at the reading of what she thought was a Latin Bible; it was actually a copy of Virgil's *Aeneid.* Miron called the girl a fraud, but the Capuchin monks rejected his verdict as "Godless."[10]

Fraud was a major ingredient of incidents of possession, often deliberately fostered by clergymen to trump up a dramatic demonstration of their power over the forces of evil. At Salmesbury in 1612, three women were accused of causing possession in a girl, who later admitted that she had been coached by a Roman Catholic priest who wanted the women prosecuted, because they had defected from his church and turned Protestant.[11] Sir Walter Scott observed:

> *The Catholic church had much occasion to rally around her all the respect that remained to her in a schismatic and heretical kingdom; and when her fathers and doctors announced the existence of such a dreadful disease [as possession], and of the power of the church's prayers, relics, and ceremonies, to cure it, it was difficult for a priest, supposing him more tender of the interest of his order than that of the truth, to avoid such a tempting opportunity as a supposed case of possession offered for displaying the high privilege in which his profession made him a partner, or to abstain from conniving at the imposture, in order to obtain for his church the credit of expelling the demon. It was hardly to be wondered at, if the ecclesiastic was sometimes induced to aid the fraud of which such motives forbade him to be the detector.*[12]

Some cases were not consciously faked. Symptoms of possession could be produced by such causes as hysteria, epilepsy, sexual frustrations, depression, or plain boredom. Ascetics in monasteries and convents were most prone to demonic possession, which seemed a way to relieve the isolation, inactivity, and drabness of the cloistered life. Nuns were often imprisoned in convents against their will, because husbands wished to be rid of them, or because their parents could give them no dower and so compelled them to be brides of Christ.[13] The church's word for the depression that afflicted nuns and monks was *acedia,* "abysmal apathy."[14]

Screaming fits, blasphemies, sexual fantasies, and erotomania of the possessed sprang directly from hatred of convent life, as shown by the nun Jeanne des Anges:

> *My mind was often filled with blasphemies, and sometimes I uttered them without being able to take any thought to stop myself. I felt for God a continual aversion. . . . The demon beclouded me in such a way that I hardly distinguished his desires from mine; he gave me moreover a strong aversion for my religious calling, so that sometimes when he was in my head I used to tear all my veils and such of my sisters' as I might lay hands on; I trampled them underfoot, I chewed them, cursing the hour when I took the vows. . . . More often than not I saw quite well that I was the prime cause of my troubles and that the demon acted only according to the openings I gave him. . . . As I presented myself at Communion, the devil took possession of my head, and after I had received the blessed host and half moistened it the devil threw it in the priest's face.*[15]

There was a time when demonic possession was almost as contagious as the common cold. It would sweep through a cloister like an epidemic. A 15th-century German convent suffered an outbreak of possession in which all the nuns took to biting one another. In a French convent, they began mewing like cats. At Aix in 1611, a man was burned at the stake for sending an extraordinary number of demons into the nuns; one nun alone was possessed by 6500 demons.[16]

Possession served as an excuse for orgiastic goings-on at several convents in the 17th century. Father confessors at Louviers from 1628 to 1642 instructed the nuns in lesbian intercourse, celebrated communion naked, and staged obscene masses where the officiating priest would attach a host to his penis, and engage in coitus or sodomy. Nuns were forced by their "demons" to frequent coupling with both "devils" and prelates. At Auxonne, the Mother Superior was accused of causing possession among the nuns by teaching them to masturbate with a dildo. At Nimeguen, possessed nuns claimed to be sexually assaulted by black priapic creatures lurking in their beds. Even in the late 19th century, erotic hysteria infected the sisters of Mont-Saint-Sulpice at the instigation of a "possessed" nun Cantianille, allegedly violated by a priest and dedicated to the devil at the tender age of 15.[17]

Maria Renata Sanger, sub-prioress of a convent at Würzburg, was executed for bewitching other nuns and causing them to be seduced by demons in the form of handsome young men.[18] One would naturally suspect that these "demons" were made of quite solid material and entered the convent by night through some secret hole in the wall, with a certain amount of assistance from within.

Erotomania was the major ingredient of one of the most famous cases of fraudulent possession, that of the nuns of Loudun in the 1630s, which ended in the legal murder of a priest, Urbain Grandier, whose misfortune it was to have made some powerful enemies.

With the Mother Superior setting the example, claiming possession by four major demons—Leviathan, Balan, Iscaron, and

Behemoth—the nuns accused Father Grandier of causing their frenzies, which only grew worse with every attempt at exorcism.[19] The priest maintained his innocence though hideously tortured; his legs were crushed to pulp in the boots. He refused to name any accomplices, as the custom demanded. To build their case, his torturers said he was really invoking the devil when he prayed aloud to God for deliverance from his sufferings.[20] At last a phony pact with the devil was forged and "found" to seal his doom. It said:

> *My Lord and Master, I own you for my God; I promise to serve you while I live, and from this hour I renounce all other gods and Jesus Christ and Mary and all the Saints of Heaven and the Catholic, Apostolic, and Roman Church, and all the goodwill thereof and the prayers which might be made for me. I promise to adore you and do you homage at least three times a day and to do the most evil that I can and to lead into evil as many persons as shall be possible to me, and heartily I renounce the Chrism, Baptism, and all the merits of Jesus Christ; and, in case I should desire to change, I give you my body and soul, and my life as holding it from you, having dedicated it forever without any will to repent. Signed URBAIN GRANDIER in his blood.*[21]

After Urbain Grandier was burned at the stake, possession of the nuns continued. It had become a tourist attraction, and the sisters were celebrities. They learned to show off for the crowds, like Sister Claire:

> *She fell on the ground, blaspheming, in convulsions, lifting up her petticoats and chemise, displaying her privy parts without any shame, and uttering filthy words. Her gestures became so indecent that the audience averted its eyes. She cried out again and again, abusing herself with her hands, "Come on then,* foutez-moi! *[fuck me]!"*[22]

Possession was often achieved by children and adolescents, who knew with a sure instinct what would gain them the most attention. The conveniently timed hysteria of adolescent girls, followed up by adults' superstitious fears, created the notorious witch-craze at Salem, Massachusetts; the basic idea had long been common in England. Panicked by any sign of fits in a child, parents and neighbors immediately began a search for the witch who was to blame.[23] Needless to say, any child who learned what a stir he could cause in this way was strongly motivated to repeat it.

In 1595 a thirteen-year-old Staffordshire boy learned to throw fits at the sight of a woman named Alice Gooderidge, who was tortured by having her feet burned to induce her to confess sending a demon into the child. Upon being faced with him, Alice pleaded, "Thomas, I pray you forgive me and be good to me." But Thomas only fell into "a marvelous sore fit," went into a trance, "saw a man come out of the chamber pot, flames of fire, and the heavens open." To Alice he said, "Yonder comes Mother Red Cap, look how they beat her brains out, see what it is to be a witch; see how the toads gnaw the flesh from her bones." Alice Gooderidge was convicted of witchcraft and died in prison.[24]

Faked possession was used to condemn 80-year-old Ann Bodenham in 1653. A servant girl caught with stolen silverware accused Ann Bodenham of sending a demon into her in the form of a black man without a head. The girl went into fits in Mrs. Bodenham's presence but was instantly relieved when the "witch" was removed from the room. She described how Mrs. Bodenham had transformed herself into a black cat to tempt her into the devil's service.[25] Convicted and on her way to the gallows, the old woman called for beer, and cursed all who refused her. As was the custom, the hangman asked her forgiveness before turning her off the ladder. She snapped, "Forgive thee? A pox on thee, turn me off," and died in her rage.[26]

At Norfolk in 1600, a woman named Margaret Francis allegedly bewitched a girl who exhibited the usual symptoms of possession:

> *Tearing her hair, and beating herself, and her head against bedsteads and stools, sometimes foaming, sometimes dolefully shrieking and blaring like a calf; groaning, howling, and barking like a dog; and biting like a mad dog. Her head, feet, and legs were drawn awry and almost backward; and she stared, & gaped most fearfully and gnashed her teeth and lay as dead and senseless many times a day and more sometimes together, without breath or panting, saving that her natural color remained still fresh; and yet, sometimes suddenly she did spit in the faces of them that stood by or at her friends or at the name of Jesus; and sometimes she did smite at her parents also . . . sometimes storming at God and good men, and sometimes blaspheming God, saying God is a good man I can do as much as he; I care not for Jesus, etc. Some things were uttered, unknown before to the maid; and many times in a strange snappish voice; and sometimes in the tune and voice of the witch and in her phrases and terms.*[27]

Exorcism rarely relieved such symptoms, but more often exacerbated them, since the exorcistic ritual only increased the effect desired by making the afflicted one all the more a center of attention. More practical cures brought about the miracle that exorcism failed to produce. In 1835 an epidemic of possession was well under way at a French convent in Morzine. Professor Tissot investigated, and found the nuns went into fits at the touch of holy water if they knew what it was, but secretly they could be dosed with quarts of it in wine or food, without effect. The demons were cast out by the police, who appeared with orders to treat the possessed as lunatics and remove them to an asylum. Immediately, all symptoms vanished.[28]

The Dutch physician Boerhaave found an epidemic of possession in a Haarlem hospital ward, with patients going into convulsions and imitating each other in acts of frenzy. He ordered a brazier of coals and a cauterizing iron placed in the ward, and promised to brand the next victim of possession. There were no more cases. A similar report from Japan told of the miraculous cure of a possessed girl, whose father tied her to a pillar and rushed at her with a drawn sword, crying,

"Wicked spirit, if you do not forthwith leave this child I will kill you both!" The child was instantly cured.[29]

Some authorities recommended flagellation as a cure for possession. Bergomensi said a "prudent and moderate" whipping could work wonders.[30] Of course it never worked in cases of illness caused by demonic possession. Demons were convenient scapegoats for ignorant doctors, and many diseases were attributed to possession. Some authorities even insisted that every illness is caused by demons.[31] Among the long lists of "signs" of demonic possession were the following: inability to retain food; sensation of weight in the stomach; pain in the lower belly, kidneys, or head; lassitude; impotence; weakening or emaciation of the body; fiery pains in the entrails; sudden swelling of the stomach; yellowish or pale complexion; melancholia. Demonic possession was the proper diagnosis "if skilled physicians are not sure what the affliction is, and cannot form an opinion about it; or if the medications prescribed do not help but rather increase the sickness."[32] Since the medications of the period usually did make the sick sicker, possession must have been a frequent diagnosis.

Aside from its usefulness to physicians, the theory of possession was useful to the possessed themselves. It provided an outlet for hidden rage. This psychological function is still seen in groups who formally court possession. In the zar, or demon, cult of modern Ethiopia, Moslem wives maintain a religion of demonism conducted by matrilineal priestesses. It's the only religion the women have, where even Coptic churches refuse to admit them, and the only feminist institution in the country. An observer reported that the zar cult is enormously popular, and most women participate despite opposition from their husbands, "who fear the sexual and economic emancipation of the wife."[33]

Possession is induced by drumming, chanting, and rhythmic movement. A woman is "ridden" by her demon or zar, a name perhaps traceable all the way back to Osiris Zer.[34] The possessed woman shrieks, babbles, blasphemes, vents her sexual frustrations and heaps bitter abuse on her husband. She demands new clothes, gifts and ornaments, which must be given her, as part of the cure. "The epidemiology of possession starts a chain of events that enables them [the women] to escape from their social confinement"—for a while, at least.[35]

The same forces used to operate in Christian society. Oppressed women used their "demons" to tell the Heavenly Father what they thought of him, without incurring the punishment of heretics. Demonic possession was the confessional of the dispossessed.

Or again, the same theory of possession was used to excuse sadistic behavior. As late as 1895 one Michael Cleary of Clonmel, Ireland, tortured and burned his young wife Bridget on the pretext that she was possessed by a devil.[36] With the help of several other men, he poured paraffin over her and set her afire. The men dragged her to the hearth and made her sit on the fire, while her husband recited exorcisms.[37]

In 1966, a Swiss girl named Bernadette Hasler was beaten to death by two religious fanatics who claimed they were driving out her demon. Churchmen's reaction to this case was interesting. Johannes Vonderach, bishop of Chur, seemed more concerned about the murderers' usurpation of clerical prerogatives than about the fact that murder had been done. He announced, "Just as the Church separates itself from superstitious belief in miracles, it rejects a false belief in the Devil. However, as it regards the Devil seriously, on the basis of Holy Writ, it places itself doubly under the protection of the crucified Lord."[38]

This is a notable example of theological doubletalk, making one wonder what can be the difference between "superstitious" belief in miracles and nonsuperstitious belief in miracles; or between "false" belief in the Devil and real belief in the Devil. What for that matter can be the difference between a fanatic who believes in the Devil because he reads the Bible, and a church that "regards the Devil seriously, on the basis of Holy Writ"? In his haste to separate his church from the two criminals, Vonderach betrayed his own ignorance of Holy Writ. John said to Jesus, "Master, we saw one casting out devils in thy name; and we forbad him, because he followeth not with us." Jesus answered, "Forbid him not: for he that is not against us is for us" (Luke 9:49–50).

In August 1976 the following item appeared in the American press:

> *The voice on the tapes was that of a woman, but it was unnaturally deep and the words were incoherent screams mixed with furious profanities. The tapes recorded the dying days of a timid, 23-year-old epileptic named Annaliese Michel, and they were part of the evidence in a manslaughter case West German authorities were preparing last week against the Roman Catholic Bishop of Wurzburg, Josef Stangl, and two priests he appointed to exorcise the Devil from the young woman. When Michel died last month of malnutrition and dehydration, she weighed only 70 pounds. One of the priests, Father Arnold Renz, maintained that six devils—including Nero, Judas, Hitler and Lucifer himself—possessed Michel and made her refuse to eat.*[39]

That such human tragedies can still occur in a purportedly enlightened age is grim proof of the blindness that can be engendered by "blind faith." Perhaps the definitive remark on the subject of possession was made in 1970 by Dr. Henry Ansgard Kelley of the University of California: "Diabolical possession is caused by belief in diabolical possession."[40]

1. Angus, 110. 2. Vermaseren, 97. 3. Cohen, N.H.U.T., 71; de Voragine, 549. 4. de Voragine, 186. 5. Eliade, S., 370. 6. d' Alveilla, 165. 7. Summers, H.W.D., 203. 8. White 2, 167. 9. Cavendish, P.E., 234. 10. White 2, 142–43. 11. Robbins, 298. 12. W. Scott, 168. 13. White 2, 121. 14. Mumford, 302. 15. Oesterreich, 49–50. 16. White 2, 141–43. 17. R.E.L. Masters, 107–8. 18. Summers, G.W., 506–16. 19. Castigloini, 247. 20. Haining, 107. 21. de Givry, 118–19.

22. Robbins, 316; R.E.L. Masters, 106. 23. Robbins, 393. 24. Ewen, 180; Robbins, 66. 25. Robbins,140. 26. Ewen, 328. 27. Ewen, 191. 28. White 2, 159–62. 29. Oesterreich, 107. 30. Robbins, 189. 31. Cavendish, P.E., 206. 32. Robbins, 182. 33. Ebon, D.B., 80. 34. H. Smith, 39. 35. Ebon, D.B., 83. 36. Cavendish, P.E., 206. 37. Budge, E.M., 206–7. 38. Ebon, D.B., 148, 171–77. 39. *Newsweek,* Aug. 23, 1976, 57. 40. Ebon, S.T., 195.

Potter

The Sumero-Babylonian Goddess Aruru the Great was the original Potter who created human beings out of clay. She made man in the image of a god, and infused him with the breath of heaven, which brought him to life.[1] Aruru was also Ishtar, Inanna, Ninhursag, and Mami, Mama, or Mammitu; she made the first man (Adam) out of clay (*adamah,* the female earth). Assyrians said she made seven clay mother-wombs for females and seven clay mother-wombs for males: "The creatress of destiny, in pairs she completed them; the forms of the people Mami forms."[2]

The biblical story of God's creation of Adam out of clay was plagiarized from ancient texts with the patriarchs' usual sex-change of the deity. Mesopotamian flesh-is-clay images were derived from the primitive matriarchate, when all pottery belonged to women. "The art of pottery is a feminine invention; the original potter was a woman. Among all primitive peoples the ceramic art is found in the hands of women, and only under the influence of advanced culture does it become a man's occupation."[3]

The Goddess was worshipped as a Potter in the Jewish temple, where she received "thirty pieces of silver" as the price of a sacrificial victim (Zechariah 11:13). She owned the Field of Blood, Aceldama, where clay was moistened with the blood of victims so bought. **Judas**, who allegedly sold Jesus for this same price, was himself another victim of the Potter. In the Potter's Field he was either hanged (Matthew 27:5) or disemboweled (Acts 1:18), suggesting that the Potter was none other than the Goddess who both created and destroyed.

India's **Kali Ma** was the same creating-and-destroying Goddess, with a special incarnation as Kel Mari the Pot Goddess.[4] Since she made the first man out of clay, her people were Aryans, from *arya,* "man of clay."[5] Kel Mari was related to Mari of Mesopotamia, or Mariamne, or Miriam, or Mary, whose name was connected with the deaths of both John the Baptist and Jesus. Her earth, which drank the blood of sacrificed men, might have been the same Aceldama that drank the blood of Judas.

Kali's other name Maya was the same as the central American civilization whose women produced remarkable pottery. The oldest form of Maya pottery was known as Mamom, "the Grandmother." Von Hagen says, "Pottery was woman. All we see of the remains of the Maya ceramic art was done by women. It is a fact that should be stressed. In almost every place where pottery making was on an archaic level—Africa or Melanesia—pottery was woman-made and its design was woman-inspired. Throughout the area of the Amazon, pottery was a woman's task. Women were the potters, so far as we know, in ancient Peru. Early Greek and early Egyptian pottery was also woman-made until the introduction of the potter's wheel. . . . All the superbly beautiful patterns found on pottery (as well as weaving) were conceived by women."[6]

The biblical God couldn't give birth, so he copied the next best creation technique and molded his first man out of clay, as the Goddess did before him.

1. Epic of Gilgamesh, 121. 2. Neumann, G.M., 136. 3. Briffault 1, 466–77. 4. Briffault 1, 474. 5. Potter & Sargent, 33. 6. Von Hagen, 27, 80.

Prakriti

"Nature," the Sanskrit title of Kali as the female Holy Trinity commanding the **Gunas**, the white, red, and black threads of Creation, Preservation, and Destruction.[1] Prakriti embodied past, present, and future; earth, sea, and sky; youth, maturity, and age; and other manifestations of the Triple Goddess.

1. O'Flaherty, 350.

Priam

"One Who Is Redeemed," king of Homer's Troy, married to the Moon-goddess in the person of Hecuba (Hecate). Some said Troy's sacred fetish, the Palladium, was Priam's scepter in the form of a phallus.[1] Others said it was a female symbol; most likely it was a dual lingam-yoni representing the sacred marriage.

1. Dumézil, 323.

Priapus

God of the phallus, a figure with enormous genitals, born of Aphrodite by either Adonis or Dionysus, the latter perhaps an allegorical statement that wine begets lust. Priapus was a primitive form of Eros, based on the wooden ithyphallic idols worshipped in early Greece, later translated into stone *herms* or temple phalli for deflowering brides.[1] See **Firstborn**. Some of Priapus's grotesque images lasted through the Middle Ages, and were even worshipped as saints (see **Phallus Worship**).

1. Graves, G.M. 1, 71.

Prisca, Saint

Mythical "virgin martyr" invented from an icon of the Mother Goddess with her palm branch in her hand and a lion at her feet. The Christian tale claimed that during the reign of Claudius, Prisca was condemned to be thrown to the lions for the crime of wanting to preserve her virginity. Her innocence exuded such powerful magic that the beasts refused to eat her, and lay down at her feet like house cats. Later she was beheaded.[1] Apparently human beings were better able than lions to resist her charm.

Unfortunately for the legend's credibility, Christians weren't slain in the reign of Claudius. On the contrary, Claudius earnestly wished to preserve freedom of religion in his empire, and begged warring Christian sects to "stop this destructive and obstinate mutual enmity."[2] Claudius was, however, a devotee of Mother Cybele, who was pictured on his coins with a lion at her feet, like the original icon of Saint Prisca.[3]

The only human Prisca who might be legitimately connected with early Christianity was a woman believed to have been the real author of the Epistle to the Hebrews, sometimes called Priscilla, "Little Prisca."[4] There is no evidence that she was ever martyred.

1. Brewster, 73. 2. *Encyc. Brit.,* "Claudius I." 3. Vermaseren, 179. 4. Morris, 121.

Prometheus

Greek "Forethought," probably not the god's original name but the nearest vocal equivalent to Sanskrit *pramantha,* the swastika or fire-drill sacred to Agni, the fire god who brought fertility to Kali's water element. Prometheus brought fire or "light" to mankind as Lucifer did, against the will of the Olympian heavenly father. Yet Zeus himself appeared as Zeus Prometheus at Thurii, holding a fire-drill.[1]

One of the Hindu notions of creation was that all things arose from the action of male firesticks (Agni) twirling in the female groove (Ambika-Kali).[2] The Sea Dyaks have the same image of sexual creation. They say only one woman survived the Deluge. She made a fire-drill and used it as a phallus. By its motion in her body, she conceived the human race.[3] Such myths obviously date back to the time before semen was credited with the power of conception. One of the early theories of fatherhood was that only sexual "motion" stimulated formation of life in the womb.

The Greeks didn't know where Prometheus came from. Diodorus said he was Egyptian. An Orphic hymn identified him with Saturn. Lycophron called him "the Ethiopian god Prometheus."[4] He was the consort of Libyan Athene, who gave life to the human beings he molded out of clay (see **Potter**). From Athene he learned the secrets of the civilized arts, and passed them on to his protégés, along with the stolen "fire from heaven" identified with lightning, or enlightenment, or godly knowledge that Zeus wished to keep secret from humans.[5]

Like Lucifer, Prometheus disobeyed the heaven-father by being more benevolent toward humanity than he was. Aeschylus's *Prometheus Bound* plainly showed more sympathy toward the disobedient one than toward the God he offended. Zeus punished Prometheus by having him chained to a Caucasian mountaintop where his liver was daily devoured by his own totemic eagle and nightly restored to be devoured again. The sea nymphs wailed for Prometheus. The Daughters of Ocean cursed Zeus as an insolent despot. The other lightning-god Hephaestus muttered seditiously, "The mind of Zeus knows no turning, and ever harsh the hand that newly grasps the sway."

Prometheus himself mused, "I rescued mankind from the heavy blow that was to cast them into Hades. . . . Mankind I helped, but I could not help myself." He prophesied Zeus's downfall at the hands of ancient female powers of justice (or karma): "The Fates triform and the unforgetting Furies." He told Io the Moon-cow, also oppressed by Zeus, that her offspring would be the instrument of Zeus's doom.

The Prometheus myth presaged the Gnostics' sympathy for Lucifer, who was the same sort of hero—a philanthropic anti-god unfairly punished for giving "light" or "enlightenment" to humanity. Gnostic icons copied early pictures of Prometheus molding the first man out of clay while Athene stood waiting to infuse the figure with the spirit of life. Behind her rose a tree encircled by a serpent, totemic symbol of her wisdom.[6] The story of Eden was based on just such icons.

According to another myth, Prometheus tricked Zeus into accepting the less edible parts of sacrificial animals, such as the fat and bones, on behalf of the gods, while human beings were allowed to consume the meat. This was not what Zeus intended, and he swore revenge on both Prometheus and his human friends.[7] Still, he had made his choice and had to stick to it. The biblical Yahweh made the same choice, and so received only the fat and guts of sacrificial animals (Leviticus 4) while the priests ate the rest. The Greek sense of humor envisioned Zeus accepting such offal only because he was forced to, having sworn by the Styx to keep to his choice; but the Jews simply claimed that Yahweh preferred it.

Prometheus was made one of the Titans, the group of gigantic earth-spirits who predated Zeus and his Olympian host, and were generally hostile to them. The battle between Zeus's Olympians and the Titans, in which the latter were deprived of the status of gods and chained under the earth, was one of the prototypes of the Judeo-Christian "war in heaven."

1. Graves, G.M. 1, 148; d'Alviella, 48. 2. O'Flaherty, 148. 3. Gaster, 101. 4. Knight, S.L., 88. 5. Graves, G.M. 1, 144. 6. d'Alviella, 166. 7. E. Hamilton, 70.

Prophecy

The ancients' chief standard of judgment for any holy man or woman was his or her power to prophesy coming events. Conversely, anyone's spiritual authority was dependent on fulfillment of prophecies that had already been made. This was so important in establishing Christianity that the New Testament again and again relates events that were done only to fulfill some prophetic text from the Old Testament. By contemporary notions, the coming of Jesus or any other spiritual leader was of no account unless it had been prophesied by a different spiritual leader.

Prophets were sometimes carried away by the ecstatic spirit and prophesied too literally, so the prophecy could be too easily checked. Thus the prophetic God seemed to tell lies. Provision was made for this difficulty in the Bible—not to excuse the over-zealous prophet, but to excuse God: "When a prophet speaketh in the name of the Lord, if the thing follow not, nor come to pass, that is the thing which the Lord hath not spoken" (Deuteronomy 18:22). Of course this made it impossible to tell, at the time, whether any given prophecy was genuine or not; and this rather defeated the whole purpose of prophecy.

Prorsa and Postverta

Two faces of the Etruscan year-goddess Anna Perenna, who looked forward and backward in Time, therefore ruled both prophecy of the future and history of the past. The Romans masculinized her as Janus.

Proserpina

var. Proserpine

Roman version of Persephone, queen of the underworld. Along with Hecate and Diana, Proserpina was frequently designated "queen of witches" in medieval tradition. Christian Gnostics spoke of her as the death-goddess whom every soul would meet soon after death. Christian demonologists listed Proserpina among the dignitaries of hell, as the "arch she-devil."[1] She had a poetic appeal however for such as Swinburne, who said she "gathers all things mortal with cold immortal hands"; and in her mystic garden there was "only the sleep eternal in an eternal night."[2]

1. de Givry, 141. 2. Swinburne, *The Garden of Proserpine.*

Prostitution

Like the *devadasis* of Hindu temples, prostitute-priestesses dispensed the grace of the Goddess in ancient Middle-Eastern temples. They were often known as Charites or Graces, since they dealt in the unique combination of beauty and kindness called *charis* (Latin *caritas*) that was later translated "charity." Actually it was like Hindu *karuna*, a combination of mother-love, tenderness, comfort, mystical enlightenment, and sex.

Hesiod said the sensual magic of the sacred whores or Horae "mellowed the behavior of men."[1] Ishtar, the Great Whore of Babylon, announced, "A prostitute compassionate am I."[2] Mary Magdalene said of her sisters in the profession, "Not only are we compassionate of ourselves, but we are compassionate of all the race of mankind."[3]

As Mother of Harlots, Ishtar was called the Great Goddess HAR. Her high priestess the Harine was spiritual ruler of "the city of Ishtar."[4] HAR was a cognate of the Persian *houri* and the Greek Hora, also the origin of "harem," which used to mean a Temple of Women, or a sanctuary.[5] A similar meaning was once attached to *seraglio*, from Semitic *serai*, a shrine of queens.

Ancient harlots often commanded high social status and were revered for their learning.[6] As embodiments of the Queen of Heaven, in Palestine called Qadeshet, the Great Whore, the harlots were honored like queens at centers of learning in Greece and Asia Minor.[7] Some even became queens. The empress Theodora, wife of Justinian, began her career as a temple harlot.[8] St. Helena, mother of Constantine, was a harlot before she became an empress-saint.[9]

In an Egyptian story, a priestess of Bubastis demanded all of a man's worldly goods for one night of her love. She said, "I am a hierodule; I am no mean person."[10] Until recently Egypt still had a class of women called *ghazye*, "sacred whores," who were greatly honored in the time of the Mamelukes and prized as brides when their period of service was ended.[11]

Temple prostitutes were revered as healers of the sick. Their very secretions were supposed to have medical virtue. A Sufi proverb still suggests this opinion: "There is healing in a woman's vagina."[12] Even their spittle could perform cures. Jesus's cure of blindness by spittle (Mark 8:23) was copied from a matriarchal tradition. A clay tablet from Nineveh says eye diseases can be cured by a harlot's spittle.[13] Harlots were also sorceresses, prophets, and seers. The Hebrew word *zonah* means both a prostitute and a prophetess.[14]

Holy Mothers designated the promiscuous priestess-shamanesses of Japan, also known as spirit-women. Becoming Brides of God, they entered the shrine to lie with a priest possessed by the god's spirit.[15] Similar customs distinguished the Indian *devadasis*, human copies of the lascivious Heavenly Nymphs.

The profession was popular. Temples of Aphrodite at Eryx, Corinth, Cyprus, and other sites were served by a thousand sacred harlots apiece.[16] When Hellenic Greeks reduced wives to the status of servants, the *hetaerae* or courtesans remained legally and politically equal to men. Roman matrons of the highest aristocracy prostituted themselves in the temple of Juno Sospita when a revelation was needed.[17] Every Babylonian woman prostituted herself in the temple before marriage.[18] By Amorite sacred law, "she who was about to marry should sit in fornication seven days by the gate (of the temple)."[19] Such laws were supposed to appease the Goddess, who disapproved of monogamy in the era when there was no formal marriage and children didn't know their fathers.[20] In Greek myth, the Great Mother forbade the Heavenly Father Zeus to make a monogamous marriage, holding that only her own ancient system of group marriage was honorable.[21]

The Tantric word for a sacred harlot was Veshya, probable origin of the Goddess's oldest names in Greece and Rome, Hestia or Vesta, the Hearth-mother, served by the Vestal Virgins who were originally harlot-priestesses.[22] "Hearth" and "Earth" both arose from the altar of the Saxon Goddess Ertha, or Heartha, the northern Hestia-Vesta. In the matriarchal age, every woman's hearth-fire was her altar.[23] The hearth was also the omphalos, feminine hub of the universe, navel-stone of the temple, around which the sacred harlots performed their Dances of Time.

Dancing harlots came to be called Hours: Persian *houri*, Greek *horae*. Egyptian temple-women also were Ladies of the Hour. Each ruled a certain hour of the night, and protected the solar boat of Ra in the underworld during his passage through her hour.[24] The Dance of the Hours began as a pagan ceremony of the Horae (divine "Whores") who kept the hours of the night by dances, as Christian monks later kept the hours of the day by prayers. The oldest authentic Hebrew folk dance is still called *hora* after the circle dances of the sacred harlots. The Horae also guarded the gates of heaven, ministered to the souls of the blessed, and turned the heavenly spheres.[25] (See **Houri.**)

The Hebrew word *hor* means a hole, cave, or pit, common synonyms for both a sacred prostitute and the Goddess she served, whose yoni was represented by a hole, cave, pit, or pool of water in the heart of the temple.[26] A similar Latin term was *puteus*, a well or pit, source of the Spanish *puta*, "whore." Common folk the Romans buried in *puticuli*, "pits," which like all graves used to stand for the womb of rebirth.[27] The common root was Vedic *puta*, "pure" or "holy," and the Avestan *putika*, a mystical lake of the waters of birth.[28] "Lady of the Lake" was a title of the Great Goddess throughout Eurasia. In Aramaic, her shrines were *Athra qaddisa*, "the holy place," literally a "heavenly harlot-place," or genital pit or lake.[29]

"To dive into water means to delve into the mystery of Maya, to quest after the ultimate secret of life. . . . [T]he cosmic waters are at once the immaculate source of all things and dreadful grave."[30] All Asia called water a female element, the source of creation, the *arché* of Stoic philosophy. To dive into such water was a symbol of sexual intercourse. Communing in this way with a holy whore, man could realize the spiritual enlightenment called *horasis*. This word appears in the New Testament (Acts 2:17), misleadingly translated "visions."[31]

A Semitic clan, the Horites of Genesis 36, traced their descent from the Great Goddess as "Hora."[32] The Jews had cult prostitutes in the time of King Josiah, when they lived next to the temple and wove hangings for the sacred grove (2 Kings 23:7). Modern translations of the Bible call them "sodomites," but the original wording meant holy harlots.[33] Such holy harlots were often "brides of God," set apart to give birth to Sons of God, i.e., prophets and sometimes sacrificial victims.[34]

Holy whores were called "virgins" because they remained unmarried (see **Virgin Birth**). Like medieval nuns, they took veils as a badge of their office. Ishtar-Asherah-Mari-Anath was not only the Great Whore but also the Great Virgin (*kadesha*, holy one). Her Greek name was Athene, also described as a "virgin" (Parthenia); but Athene's temple, the Parthenon, was served by promiscuous hierodules like all other shrines of the Goddess. Later myths rationalized the perpetual "virginity" of lascivious fertility-goddesses by periodic hymen-renewing ceremonies such as sea baptism, annual bathing in sacred springs, etc. The virginity of Great Mother Hera was annually restored by a dip in the spring of Canathos at Nauplia. Pausanias said the myth was based on a rite of bathing the Goddess's image.[35]

Nauplia Ancient city near Argos in the Peloponnese, site of Hera's sacred spring Canathos.

Pausanias Greek traveler and geographer of the 2nd century A.D. Living in a time of declining culture, he was inspired by a desire to describe the ancient sacred sites for posterity.

Because whores occupied a significant position in paganism, Christians vilified their profession. Churchmen didn't want to stamp out prostitution altogether, only amputate its spiritual meanings. St. John Chrysostom earned high praise from the Patriarch of Constantinople for robbing temple prostitutes of "the honors paid to them."[36] The triad of heavenly Horae were mythically virginized as three maiden saints martyred together, Agape, Chionia, and Irene (Love-feast, She of Chios, and Peace).[37] Real *horae* were relegated to *hora*-houses, no longer temples. The traditional red light of the whorehouse descended from the houses of Roman *venerii* who displayed the sign of an erect phallus, painted blood red.[38]

Medieval Germanic law forbade a man to build a *hörgr*, or to call his house a *hörgr*, on pain of forfeiting every penny he owned; because *hörgr* meant a pagan shrine, a house of "holy whores" where priestesses carried on the old religion. Such place names as Hörgsholt in Iceland still identify ancient shrines.[39]

In the year 1000 A.D. the Icelanders agreed to become Christian in name at least, and to be baptized; but all who wished were still legally permitted to celebrate the rites of their ancestors in private houses called *hörgr*, for a while, until the church rescinded its promises of tolerance.[40] In earlier centuries, the *hörgr* seems to have been a *mons veneris* or omphalos in a sacred grove.[41]

Sometimes the alternate word *hus* (house) carried the same sense of "a place of worship," because every matriarch once worshipped the Goddess of her own hearth, which she could share with more than one *hus*-band. Hence the word *hussy*, Lady of the House, by Christian definition a promiscuous woman.[42]

Promiscuity was appreciated, rather than deplored, by medieval *minnesingers* who worshipped the Goddess under her new name of Minne, "Love." They objected to commercialized prostitution as a degradation of their deity: "Love, the queen of all hearts, the free-born, the one and only, is put up for public sale! What a shameful tribute is this that our mastery has required of her! We cultivate Love with embittered minds, with lies, and with deceit, and then expect from her joy of body and heart; but instead, she bears only pain, corruption, evil fruit, and blight—as her soil was sown."[43]

Theologians however accepted commercial prostitution as "a lawful immorality," in St. Thomas Aquinas's self-contradictory phrase. Aquinas said prostitution was necessary to prevent men from sodomizing each other: "Take away prostitutes from the world," he said, "and you will fill it with sodomy."[44] Prostitution enabled man to look upon promiscuous women as depraved, though their equally promiscuous clients were seen as helpless victims of compulsion. There was no recognition of the truth, that most prostitutes acted under a more telling compulsion than any man's sexuality: the need to earn wherewithal to keep alive. It was not an easy living. At best the prostitute was forced to make herself a stranger's abject servant. At worst, she could become his tormented victim.[45]

Certain anticlerical writers maintained that prostitutes should be respected for their willingness to be kind. Lorenzo Valla's 15th-century *De Voluptate* called for a return to ancient customs, echoing Horace's *Omnia voluptas bona est.* Valla wrote: "Whores and prostitutes deserve more from the human race than do nuns with their chastity and virginity!"[46] Of course, such sentiments did not prevail. Two centuries later, English apprentices celebrated each Shrove Tuesday by breaking into whorehouses and beating the inmates. It also became customary in England for men to "punish" the whores they patronized by hamstringing: cutting the sinews of the legs to make the woman a permanent cripple.[47] One might be reminded of the Chinese custom of crippling courtesans by footbinding.

God punished the whores in hell even more severely than men punished them on earth, according to God's spokesmen, whose asceticism engendered sexual fantasies of astonishing violence.[48] Monkish deprivations and repressions led to secret envy and fierce hatred of the carnal folk who might be suspected of enjoying sexual activity.[49] The hatred poured out in a thousand nasty fantasies of hell. Abbé François Arnoux, canon of Riez in 1622, provides an example:

> *And the light women, these shall have in their arms a dragon most cruel, flaming with fire . . . who shall bind and enchain their feet and their legs with his serpent tail and shall clasp their whole body with his cruel talons, who shall put his beslabbered and reeking mouth upon theirs, breathing therein flames of fire and sulphur and poison and venom, who with his nose, glandered and hideous, shall breathe into theirs a breath most stinking and venomous . . . this dragon shall make them suffer a thousand agonies, a thousand colics and bitter twistings of the belly, and all the damned shall howl, and the devils with them, "See the wanton! see the strumpet! Let her be tortured indeed! To it, to it, ye devils! To it, ye demons! To it, ye hellish furies! See the harlot! See the trull! Hurl ye upon this whore and wreak upon her all the torments ye can!"*[50]

Kastoria The ancient Celetrum, a town and nome in Greek Macedonia.

On the wall of the women's section of the Church of St. John the Baptist in Kastoria, a painting showed God's punishment of a whore. Bound in hell, the woman had her legs stretched apart by two demons, while a third demon plunged red-hot irons into her vagina. Next to the woman punished for being sexually available, another woman labeled the Vain Coquette was similarly punished for *not* being sexually available.[51] Women attending this church might well be excused for thinking they were damned if they did and damned if they didn't.

Churchmen did not distinguish between a professional prostitute and a woman in love with a lover. Both were "whores." The whole point of patriarchal morality was that women must not have the right to pick and choose men. For a woman to fall passionately in love was a tragedy under the medieval church: to pay for a few stolen hours of love, both she and her lover were doomed to an eternity of suffering.[52] The point was illustrated by Grunewald's painting *The Damnation of Lovers,* showing a sinful pair as emaciated corpses living in hell, with worms burrowing through their flesh, the woman crowned with a coiled serpent, her genitals gnawed by a toad. According to a 15th-century illustration for St. Augustine's *De Civitate Dei,* lovers would be bound together on spits in hell and roasted over coals fanned by devils.[53]

With western religion envisioning such grisly punishments for sexual enjoyment, it is hardly surprising to find western civilization as a whole seized by a sick compulsion to destroy all forms of pleasure.[54]

Even in the Christian heaven however, whores had their special protectors, modeled on pagan Roman harlot-goddesses like Venus and Meretrix. Official Catholic patrons of whores were St. Aphra, St. Aphrodite, and St. Maudline (Magdalen), simple canonizations of former titles of the Goddess.[55] Chief protectress of whores was the virgin Mary. In Antwerp up to the present century, prostitutes spent certain annual feast days marching in procession to the churches, to dedicate candles to the Holy Virgin whom they called their own special deity.[56]

An oft-told tale of the Middle Ages said when a nun decided to run away from her convent, to live as a prostitute for a few days, Mary assumed the errant nun's appearance and took her place in the convent, so she wouldn't be missed and pursued.[57] A German variant of the story said the nun, Beatrix, left the convent to live with her heathen lover for 15 years. When she returned, she found that Mary had served as her stand-in all the while.[58]

Medieval brothels were not always clearly distinguished from convents. A trace of the pagan *collegia* of priestesses still clung to both institutions. Early "double convents," with men and women united in one community, sometimes housed consecrated prostitutes. Several popes maintained "holy brothels" in Rome; Queen Joanna of

Naples founded a religious house of prostitutes called The Abbey in the papal city of Avignon. In Victorian times, it was still a common custom to call the madam of a whorehouse "the abbess," though the historical precedent was forgotten.[59] See **Mary Magdalene**.

Outside the Judeo-Christian tradition, prostitution often became a fully legitimate lifestyle. Black Africans never fully accepted missionaries' views on the matter. White men's laws deprived African women of their property and their monopoly of farming, trading, and crafts by which they supported their children. African women suffered a devastating loss of self-respect, for in their society a woman without her own income was regarded with contempt. On finding that white men would pay for their sexual favors, many African women took up prostitution as their last remaining chance to make an honest living. Africans still regard a successful prostitute as a usefully employed businesswoman rather than a criminal.[60]

By contrast, Christian society seldom offered women any formal opportunity to take up prostitution as a career, but half-deliberately looked the other way as many hundreds of young girls "fell" into it. Eighteenth-century London swarmed with female children struggling to keep themselves alive by prostitution, according to a contemporary pamphlet denouncing "little Creatures piled in Heaps upon one another, sleeping in the public streets, in the most rigorous seasons, and some of them whose Heads will hardly reach above the Waistband of a Man's Breeches, found to be quick with Child, and become burdensome to the Parish." Far from extending sympathy to these little girls, the pamphleteer called them wicked whores, "a most enormous Sin to lay Snares for the Unwary, and to be the Means of ruining both Souls and Bodies of so many innocent young Gentlemen."[61]

According to the terminology of the time, a "wench" was a child of either sex. Dryden's description of a gentleman as one who "eats, drinks, and wenches abundantly" apparently meant a man who picked up homeless male or female children in the streets to service his sexual idiosyncrasies. Later, "wench" came to mean only a lower-class female, a servant or peasant available for a gentleman's sexual use.[62]

By the 19th century, thousands of girls under the age of 14 were listed on English police registers as "common prostitutes." London in 1860 had at least 500 registered prostitutes under the age of 13, and 1500 more under the age of 16. Victorian gentlemen had a taste for raping child virgins, who commanded the highest prices in whorehouses. Experienced child whores were taught to imitate the cries and struggles of a newly deflowered victim, and to insert leeches or broken glass into their vaginas to produce a convincing flow of blood.[63]

Josephine Butler's investigations of the English system of prostitution led to legislation to raise the "age of consent" to 14; still, large numbers of younger girls were captured and immured in brothels. "The law was lax on the matter of abduction, and the punishment for trafficking in girls was derisory." Male authorities took an interest in prostitution only after they clearly understood its connection with rampant venereal disease. Legal regulation of brothels was instituted then; but this didn't mean closing them. It meant subjecting them to medical inspections, so they would be safe for male patrons.[64]

Whores were not considered full-fledged human beings. The 18th-century term for a whore was "a fleshy convenience."[65] The word "convenience" also meant an outhouse. One might say that from the revered sacred harlot of antiquity to this was a long road backward.

1. *Larousse,* 138. 2. Briffault 3, 169. 3. Malvern, 49. 4. *Assyr. & Bab. Lit.,* 170. 5. Briffault 2, 320. 6. Erman, 227–30. 7. Briffault 2, 341–42. 8. Bullough, 125. 9. J. H. Smith, C.G., 16. 10. Maspero, 138. 11. Briffault 3, 217. 12. Edwardes, 96. 13. Gifford, 63. 14. Stone, 211. 15. Eliade, S., 463. 16. Knight, D.W.P., 105. 17. Dumézil, 431. 18. Gifford, 182. 19. Briffault 3, 220. 20. *Larousse,* 83. 21. Graves, G.M. 1, 54. 22. *Mahanirvanatantra,* 328. 23. Potter & Sargent, 201. 24. *Book of the Dead,* 497. 25. Lethaby, 199. 26. Gaster, 608. 27. James, 182. 28. Dumézil, 81. 29. Albright, 210. 30. Zimmer, 34. 31. Campbell, M.D.R., 71. 32. Graves, W.G., 411. 33. Martello, 173. 34. Rawson, E.A., 88. 35. Guthrie, 103. 36. J. H. Smith, D.C.P., 175. 37. Attwater, 34. 38. Brasch, 164. 39. Turville-Petre, 240, 298. 40. Branston, 35. 41. Turville-Petre, 236, 298. 42. Legman, 612. 43. Campbell, C.M., 249. 44. Daly, 61. 45. Rugoff, 251. 46. Guignebert, 365. 47. Hazlitt, 34, 634. 48. Hartley, 323. 49. H. Smith, 266. 50. de Givry, 39. 51. Lawson, 68. 52. Campbell, C.M., 53. 53. Hughes, 203, 211. 54. Henry, 405. 55. Scot, 442. 56. Briffault 3, 216. 57. Briffault 3, 500. 58. Guerber, L.R., 73. 59. Briffault 3, 215–16. 60. Briffault 2, 221. 61. de Vries & Fryer, 104, 110. 62. Funk, 261. 63. Pearsall, N.B.A., 243. 64. Crow, 240, 247. 65. de Vries & Fryer, 25.

Providence

Latin *provideo* meant "to foresee"; *Providentia* meant divinatory magic.[1] It was a personification of female prophetic or mantic talents, the quality that enabled ancient matriarchs to "provide" for their dependents through foreknowledge of the stars and seasons, agriculture and food storage. In Christian usage, Providence was sometimes a synonym for God; but many mystics defined Providence as a female deity.[2]

1. Funk, 275. 2. Collins, 54.

Psyche

Greek "female soul," corresponding to Hindu Shakti. Classical myth wedded Psyche to the love-god Eros: a union of soul with body. Apuleius's version said Psyche and her bridegroom could come together only in the dark. When Psyche insisted on seeing Eros by the light of her lamp, he had to leave her forever.[1] As an allegory, this said the passion of the soul might banish sexual passion. The original story probably arose from a custom like that of ancient Sparta, where young husbands visited their wives only by night. "Sometimes children were born before the pair had ever seen each other's faces by day."[2]

Psyche was incarnate in a butterfly, for the early Greeks believed human souls could occupy flying insects while passing from one life to the next. The belief was not forgotten. At Carcassonne in 1329 an amorous Carmelite monk was accused of witchcraft for hiding love charms in women's houses. It was charged that he also called up Satan and sacrificed a butterfly to him, in symbolic offering of the soul.[3]

1. E. Hamilton, 92–100. 2. Crawley, 42. 3. J. B. Russell, 186.

Psychopomp

"Conductor of Souls," title of Hermes and other "Good Shepherd" gods who led human souls through the after-world. Angels, Valkyries, certain birds and animals could also act as psychopomps. See **Hermes; Dog; Vulture**.

Pucelle

"The Maid," French title of any woman who impersonated the Virgin Goddess of the druidic fairy-religion; a feminine form of Puck (see **Pooka; Bogey**). It was the title of **Joan of Arc**, an indication that her faith was basically non-Christian. British heathens called Maid Marian the *pucelle* or Maiden of the Coven. Her consort was Robin Hood or Robin Goodfellow, known as the god of witches (see **Robin**).[1]

1. Graves, W.G., 441.

Pudens and Pudenziana, Saints

Naive Christian canonization of the symbolic genitalia of Rome's God and Goddess (*pudenda*). According to the Christian legend, Pudenziana was the usual virgin convert, a daughter of Pudens, a wealthy patrician. Peter and Paul lodged in the house of Pudenziana on their (mythical) visit to Rome. With the help of a holy man named Pastorus (Shepherd), St. Pudenziana soaked up the blood of Christian martyrs in sponges, which she hid in a well.[1] This tale was often cited to account for the numerous bottles of martyrs' blood used as healing relics in countless churches.

The well with its holy blood probably meant the yonic "pit" (*puteus*) in the Forum, where the spirits of blessed ancestors dwelt. The Shepherd Pastorus was a form of the Psychopomp or Conductor of Souls, sometimes called Shepherd of the Stars.

1. Brewster, 250–51.

Purgatory

One of several Christian doctrines derived more or less directly from Buddhism. Five centuries before the Christian era, Buddhist priests claimed to be able to deliver one's ancestors from pains of atonement in the underworld and to cause them to be born again in heaven, by reciting magic words and performing sacrifices on their behalf—for a fee paid by the pious descendant.[1] "Above all," Buddhist scriptures said, "it is necessary to obtain the aid of priests who deliver these bound souls by the ritual."[2]

The Christian doctrine of purgatory implied that priests had the power to send to heaven individuals who might otherwise have been damned. Some stories hinted that the privilege could be carried too far. Pope Gregory the Great succeeded in praying the emperor Trajan out of purgatory and into heaven, but God punished Gregory with gout, fever, and stomach pains for his sin of praying for a heathen.[3]

The Catholic notion of purgatory was renounced by Protestants, who were scornful of anything resembling the sale of salvation. Reginald Scot remarked that in England the ghosts no longer pestered the living to be prayed out of purgatory: "Where are the spirits? Who heareth their noises? Who seeth their visions? Where are the souls that made such moan . . . to be eased of their pains in purgatory?" He concluded that they had all gone to Italy, because masses had become too expensive in England.[4]

The word purgatory was often applied to the pagan womb-shrine or *abaton* used in initiations in pre-Christian times (see **Abaddon**). A candidate would "descend into an underground chamber, simulate death, undergo great trials, and experience a rebirth into a new life. The early Christian Church continued this custom, calling such pagan shrines 'purgatories.' The most celebrated purgatory during medieval times was the one at Lough Derg (Red Lake) in County Donegal, Ireland, to which pilgrimages were made in the twelfth century in honor of St. Patrick, for whom the purgatory was named." Though Pope Alexander VI declared it a residence of devils and ordered it closed in 1497, St. Patrick's Purgatory was still in use in 1790.[5]

According to a 15th-century illustration for the *Divine Comedy,* purgatory was not a pit or cave but a mountain, constructed in wedding-cake levels very like a ziggurat. At the summit was the Earthly Paradise, where a nude male and female figure were joined together in a sacred marriage: a peculiar link between the ancient King and Goddess mating at the pinnacle of the ziggurat, and the conventional bride-and-groom dolls on the wedding cake.[6] The implication of the picture was that, once the sinner had expurgated his sins and moved up the stages of the mountain, he too could enter the love-paradise at the top: a strange image for a Christian article of faith.

1. Waddell, 98–99. 2. Avalon, 208. 3. de Voragine, 185. 4. Scot, 390.
5. Goodrich, 157; Baring-Gould, C.M.M.A., 244. 6. Campbell, M.I., 91.

Purim

Jewish festival based on the Book of Esther, which presented a Hebraic version of the Elamite cult of sacred kingship under the rule of the Goddess **Ishtar**, whose name was "Esther" in Hebrew. Yahweh is never mentioned in the Book of Esther, because the Elamite Jews didn't know him. They worshipped Ishtar's spouse Marduk, who appears in the book as Mordecai.

Purim is the Feast of Lots, because the original Elamite festival was based, in turn, on the Hittite Purulli, where a sacred-king-victim was chosen by casting lots, or by a competition.[1] The victim in the Jewish Purim was Haman, the same as the Libyan sacrificial god Amon.

Haman lay with the Goddess, Ishtar-Esther, then was slain by Marduk-Mordecai (Esther 7:8). Afterward, his flesh was sacramentally eaten, as he is still eaten symbolically at Purim in the form of *hamantaschen,* small triangular pastries in the Goddess's sacred delta shape. Egyptian bakers made similar three-cornered cakes to represent the Host or victim in festivals of Amon.[2]

The story of Esther is an allegorical tale of the intercession of Ishtar, whom the Jews worshipped at the time, with the king who was supposed to be her consort, on behalf of the subject Jewish tribes. Interwoven with this theme is that of the ritual sacrifice. Haman was given a Last Supper and a night of the Goddess-queen's love. Then he was hanged on the high gallows that was "prepared for Mordecai"—that is, he became the god Marduk and assumed the trappings of divinity (Esther 7:10).

The Jews also worshipped Marduk, who had originally "divided the waters which were under the firmament from the waters which were above the firmament" (Genesis 1:7) by splitting the Water-mother **Tiamat**. In the Book of Esther, Jewish scribes made Marduk one of their own sacred ancestors. Marduk helped the Jews kill 75,000 of their enemies, apparently by magic, for they "laid not their hands on the prey" (Esther 9:16).

1. Hooke, M.E.M., 99. 2. Budge, D.N., 75.

Purple

From Latin *purpureus,* "very, very holy," or *sacer,* or taboo.[1] The ancients' "royal purple" was not purple but a dark wine red, the color of blood, especially the menstrual blood formerly considered the very stuff of life. Royal purple meant the same as royal blood: matrilineal kinship in a sacred clan. Some legends said royal purple descended from Athene's "goatskin dyed red," the **aegis** of sovereignty.[2] The purple robe of a Roman emperor was said to have been "colored by blood."[3] Purple still meant blood color in the time of Shakespeare, who spoke of the "purpled hands" of Caesar's assassins, stained with "the most noble blood of all the world."

When Mark's Gospel says Jesus's robe was purple (15:17) and Matthew's Gospel says it was scarlet (27:28), they are really talking about the conventional sacred-king robe of moon-blood-color. Babylonian kings wore the same dark-red robe, called *lamhussu.* It was the same sacred blood color that covered altars in Canaan and Israel (Numbers 4), and dyed the "red carpet" trod by triumphal religious processions.[4]

First Book of Adam and Eve One of the legendary apocrypha (works written in Greek from Jewish sources) giving additional details or alternative versions of the Genesis myths.

Blood-purple was sacred to the pagans, as suggested by the *First Book of Adam and Eve,* which says the art of dyeing crimson and purple was invented by Satan.[5]

Actually, the art was invented by the Phoenicians, who obtained deep-blood-red dye from mollusks of the family Muricidae. These sea snails were the source of the famous "Tyrian purple" worn by royalty.[6] In Roman society, people just below imperial rank were allowed to wear stripes or borders of the holy color on their togas, in smaller widths according to a descending scale of status.

1. Graves, W.G., 395. 2. Mendenhall, 43. 3. de Voragine, 79. 4. Brasch, 33. 5. *Forgotten Books,* 77. 6. de Camp, A.E., 79; Potter & Sargent, 146.

Purusha

"Person," the World Body in Oriental imagery, originally the Great Mother as a colossal being, containing the universe. The earth plane lay at her waist, seven concentric hells below in the pelvis, seven more in the legs. Fourteen corresponding heavens mounted through the thorax and head: 28 in all, like the 14 levels descended by Osiris on his way to the Pit, and 14 more ascended into heaven—one night for each making a full lunar cycle. Egyptian priests said the World Body was the Goddess Neith.[1] However, ascetic Jain Buddhists rendered the Purusha sexually neutral. Later, medieval Europe adopted the idea but made the World Body wholly male.[2]

The highest heaven, which Greeks called the Empyrean, spread as a shining umbrella over the head of Purusha. On the earth plane, continents and oceans were arranged in concentric rings, like a horizontal target.[3] This image was still found in medieval geographies.

1. Budge, G.E. 2, 299. 2. Campbell, Or. M., 256. 3. Campbell, Or. M., 224.

Pyerun

var. Piorun, Peron

Slavic thunder god, identified with Jupiter and Thor. His onomatopoeic name imitated the sound of thunder. Pyerun was still worshipped in some parts of the Balkans up to the 18th century.[1]

1. Spinka, 34.

Pygmalion

Greek version of Phoenician priest-kings called Pumiyathon, consorts of the image of Astarte at Byblos. Pygmalion was a priest-king of Cyprus, receiving his right to rule through a sacred marriage with the Goddess's image, who was called **Galatea** (White Goddess or Milk Goddess). Aphrodite brought her to life—that is, inhabited the statue—during the sacred-marriage ceremony.[1]

1. Frazer, G.B., 38.

Pygmies

Homer spoke of *Oi Pygmaioi,* the pygmies who lived in a tropical garden of paradise near the Mountains of the Moon at the source of the Nile. Pygmies still live as they did 3000 years ago, in the jungle near the Ruwenzori Range (Mountains of the Moon). This area was rendered virtually inaccessible from the north when climatic changes created a vast swamp, now known as the Sudd, between Nilotic civilizations and the mountain headwaters. But in an earlier age, Africa's topography was more congenial to travel and colonization.

Pygmies say their ancestors came from the northern land of Kimi, a Coptic name for Egypt, derived from Khemennu, "Land of the Moon." The pygmies' culture hero Efé was sometimes called Heru, an old Egyptian name for Horus. He was crucified on a World Tree, and received a revelation of holy law from a lunar spirit named Mara, the old pygmy name for a tribal matriarch, then for any divine personage.[1]

Like their relatives the Bushmen, pygmies are caucasoid people: thin-lipped, light-skinned, often blue-eyed. Anthropological investigations show the pygmies were not true primitives but remnants of a formerly sophisticated race, the proto-Berber people inhabiting what Hallet called "old white Africa."[2] Pygmies have about the same stature as Egyptian mummies; the ancient Egyptians were not large people.

Egypt had a pygmy god, Bes, patron of music, dancing, and entertainment. He seems to have been an imported court jester to the gods. "They delighted in his grotesque figure and contortions, just as the Memphite Pharaohs of the Old Kingdom enjoyed the antics of their pygmies." Bes became almost as popular as Osiris. He protected women, especially pregnant ones. He preserved families, looked after the dead in the underworld, and attended the infant sun god at his birth. Later, Bes was diabolized along with all other Egyptian deities. He was called a "wicked demon' exorcised by Moses. He is said to dwell still in the southern gate of the temple of Karnak, whence he threatens solitary travelers.[3]

Pygmies retain matriarchal traditions from their original source. They say the first human beings were made by the **moon**. The first woman, Mother of God, was Matu (Mother), who still dwells in caverns under the Mountains of the Moon. Sometimes she was seen as a cat-headed deity like Egypt's Bast. Her name was a cognate of Maat and also of the Sumerian Matu, the primal womb, the underworld, and the devourer of the dead. In Babylon the Death-goddess Matu was also Lilith, or the yonic lotus *lilu.* Now the pygmies say their Goddess can take the form of a monster named Lulu, with a vast vulva-mouth that opens vertically instead of horizontally, and swallows human beings headfirst.[4]

Not only are the pygmy myths and deities derived from those of the ancient world, but their traditional stories plainly speak of the time when their ancestors lived in a high state of civilization, in great cities, with wonderful tools to use, and skills that enabled them to work miracles.[5]

The true origin of these people cannot be known precisely, any more than the origin of any other nonliterate group. Yet it seems clear that they did have a connection with Nilotic culture at a very early date, possibly even as colonial villages along the upper reaches of the Nile. Even in dynastic Egypt there were half-forgotten stories about the "true source" of the Nile at the Goddess's lunar mountain with its vast uterine cave. Later the ceremonial source of the Nile was located at Elephantine, because it became too difficult to travel upriver beyond this point. In the end, the pygmies were cut off.

1. Hallet, 113, 115, 124. 2. Hallet, 37. 3. *Larousse,* 39. 4. Hallet, 95, 144, 170. 5. Hallet, 102, 106.

Pyrrha

Wife of Deucalion, the Greek version of Noah. She and her spouse repopulated the earth after the Flood by the instruction of the Goddess Themis, magically creating human beings out of stones. Pyrrha, whose name means "fiery red," may have been the magic ingredient of the charm, embodying the Blood of Life. Her name was also commonly applied to wine.[1]

1. Graves, G.M. 1, 141.

Python

Great Serpent born of Mother Hera without the aid of Zeus, which meant the Mother's firstborn **serpent** antedated all father-gods, like the Ophion-serpent of the creatress Eurynome. Also like Lucifer, Python was the lightning-serpent who descended into the Deep to fertilize the Goddess. Mother Hera also bore Hephaestus without the aid of any male god, and Hephaestus was the same lightning-god who "fell from heaven."[1]

Python personified the prophetic spirit of the Delphic oracle, whose priestess was always the Pythoness even when the shrine was taken over by Apollo. Python lived in the earth-womb and knew its secrets, which is why he was an oracle. Some myths said Python was a Lord of Death because Apollo had killed him. But, like all other light-and-dark twins, Apollo and Python were really the same god. Sacred kings of Delphi always killed their predecessors, who were laid to rest in the stone *omphalos* where the Pythoness sat to commune with the oracular spirit.[2]

Sometimes Python was the nether aspect of Apollo himself, the Black Sun corresponding to the celestial sun. This serpent-figure was the familiar Sata, Thoth, Ouroboros, Okeanos, Hermes, and other subterranean oracle-gods.

1. Guthrie, 73. 2. Graves, G. M. 1, 80–82.

Q R

In antiquity QUEEN simply meant a female land-owner; eventually, only royalty had queens. This one, Karomama, ruled in Egypt with husband Takelot II in the 22nd Dynasty (950–730 B.C.). Damascened bronze.

The RAM was a sacred and sacrificial animal, along with the other horned beasts—bull, stag, goat. Since they always carried phallic connotations, human-bodied gods often wore horned heads, as does this limestone sculptor's model. Egypt, 4th to 3rd century B.C.

Lupa, the She-Wolf, an Etruscan bronze, nurses the Renaissance ROMULUS AND REMUS. The three represent the founding and nurture of Rome. Rome, Capitoline Museum.

Qadeshet

Arabic *qadisha*, Hebrew *kadesha* meant a sacred harlot or Holy Virgin; *qadeshet* was also the title of Astarte and her temple women. The word meant "priestess." In the Koran it was used as a name for Mohammed's rich wife Khadija, whose money supported the prophet's endeavors.[1] Astarte-the-Qadeshet was the Syrian counterpart of Ishtar, Babylon's Great Whore, who declared herself the Mother of Compassion.[2] See **Prostitution**.

1. Briffault 1, 375. 2. Lindsay, O.A., 54.

Queen

Old Norse *kvaen*, Old English *cwene* meant "owner," specifically applied to female owners of the land in the days of the matriarchate. Ancient writers described many barbarian societies as nations of "queens." [1] See **Matrilineal Inheritance**.

1. Thomson, 244.

Quetzalcoatl

Aztec savior-god with the same characteristics as similar gods of the ancient Middle East. Quetzalcoatl was born of a virgin, one of three mystic sisters (the Triple Goddess). He represented the corn. His death and resurrection were linked with planting, growth, harvest. Like the serpent-and-dove deities of Mesopotamia, he combined avian and reptilian attributes; he was called the Feathered Serpent.

He gave blood from his penis to re-create the human race after the Flood and so became one of the "castrated Fathers." [1] He was sacrificed; he descended into hell; he rose again from the dead. His Second Coming was expected.

Like the dead and living Shiva, like Njord and Frey, Horus and Set, Apollo and Python, etc., Quetzalcoatl was a two-faced deity of creation and destruction, united back to back with his brother Death.[2] North American Indians also worshipped the same alternating rival gods as the White Manitu and the Dark Manitu, lords of life and death. They were alternately sons or husbands of the Great Goddess whom the tribes named Divine Grandmother.[3] Aztecs called her the Lady of the Serpent Skirt, receiver of Quetzalcoatl's sacrifice.

1. Campbell, M.I., 156. 2. Neumann, G.M., 205. 3. Briffault 2, 732.

Quintessence

Blue blood was once supposed to be the sign of the gods' aristocracy. It was given by the Goddess to deified ancestors of the highest caste.

Blue blood was called *quinta essentia* by the Romans, the "essential fifth part" or quintessence, embodying a spirit of immortality (godhood).[1] Sometimes the *quinta essentia* was a sacred wine or ambrosia; sometimes it was more plainly designated the menstrual blood of the Goddess. Worshippers of Aphrodite taught that the "essential fifth" came to a man during the lunar month called honey-moon, planned to span a menstrual period. Aphrodite's nectar was also called **honey**. Horace said the kiss that sealed the marriage bond was mixed by Aphrodite with "a fifth part of her own nectar." [2] Homer said the blood that flowed in the veins of gods was a blue ethereal fluid, *ichor*, prepared by Aphrodite's honeybees.[3]

This blue essence evolved from a confused memory of Indo-European ancestral gods made immortal by their blue blood. Hindu gods are still painted blue in sacred art—which may shed light on the custom of the Picts and other early British tribes to paint themselves blue with woad for religious ceremonies, and sometimes for warfare, to insure their resurrection in case of death in battle.[4]

The blue-blooded god filled with *quintessence* was well known to Gnostic thinkers. Porphyry said the Demiurge or creator of the material world was shaped like a man, with a dark blue complexion, exactly like Shiva, Vishnu, and other Hindu gods.[5] Aristotle taught that quintessence was a fifth element—after earth, water, air, and fire—of which the bodies of gods were made. Sometimes this fifth element was said to be the same as ether, the fluid of heaven.[6]

Medieval alchemists described the *quinta essentia* as a blue elixir, able to confer spiritual illumination and resurrection of the body.[7] Later, the mystic Essential Fifth was represented by the fifth trump suit of the **Tarot** deck, the Major Arcana (Great Secrets), whose figures conveyed mystical doctrines to the initiated.

1. Jung, P.R, 109. 2. Bachofen, 46. 3. Gaster, 29. 4. von Hagen, 137. 5. Lindsay, O.A., 137. 6. Funk, 349. 7. Jung, P.R., 109.

Ra

Egypt's royal sun god, said to beget every pharaoh by coupling with the queen mother.[1] He was a late addition to Egypt's pantheon. His origins were greatly confused by his own priests, who called him the supreme deity, though the Goddess's priests insisted that Ra was only her dependent child. Many scriptures demonstrate the ideological battle.

During the Ptolemaic period, some of Ra's votaries rejected the idea that Ra was born of the Mother of the Gods; they called him "self-begotten and self-born."[2] A hymn addressed him as "divine divinity, that came into being of himself, primeval god, that existed at the beginning." But this passage was an interpolation. The same hymn also said, "Thou art fair, O Ra, every day thy mother Nut embraceth thee."[3]

One source called Ra "the divine man-child, the heir of eternity, self-begotten and self-born"; but the same source also said he was "the Disc within thy mother Hathor . . . made strong each day by thy mother Nut." Sometimes, Ra's divinity depended on identifying him with the Mother herself. He was told, "Thou art indeed Isis," or "Thou art the Great Cat," i.e., the Goddess Bast-Hathor.[4]

Some writers mocked Ra's pretensions to divinity and considered him subordinate to the Goddess Mother. He was "born yesterday from the buttocks of the goddess Mehurt . . . the Great Celestial Water." He was told, "Thy mother brought thee forth upon her hand." Apparently the average Egyptian wouldn't tolerate priestly efforts to erase the Goddess and replace her with the kings' solar Father. Budge says, "it is quite certain that there was something in the doctrines of the priests of Ra, or in the worship that was the practical expression of them, which was contrary to the instincts of the Egyptians as a nation."[5]

Wrestling with the problem of bringing their god into being without a mother, Ra's priests took refuge in abstractions beyond the understanding of ordinary folk: "The god hath formed himself and his form is not known. He hath joined his seed with his body, so that his egg existed in his secret self. . . . He had no mother, who might have given him his name. . . . He who hath shaped his egg himself, the mighty one of mysterious birth, who (himself) created his beauty." Such abstractions failed to satisfy the literal-minded Egyptian, who wanted to know how Ra did it. Priests responded with the same evasiveness that modern priesthoods also exhibit:

> *His image is not spread out in books. . . . He is too mysterious that his glory should be revealed, too great that men should question concerning him, too powerful that he should be known. One falleth down dead on the spot for terror, if his mysterious, unknowable name is pronounced. No god can address him by it, him with the spirit, whose name is hidden, for that he is a mystery.*[6]

Yet Ra was not only the Goddess's child; he may even have been a masculinized version of the Goddess herself. One of her ancient names was Ra with a feminine ending *-t*: "Ra-t of the two lands, the lady of heaven, mistress of the gods . . . mistress of Heliopolis." Her full name was Rat-taiut, "Ra-t of the world."[7] Her city, translated into Greek as Heliopolis, was the Egyptian Anu, which the Bible calls On. The Goddess really controlled Ra by means of his secret soul-name. Each day she laid on him an unbreakable spell, forcing him to grow old and senile as he limped on his cane toward his death at sunset. She forced him to stand still at the summit of heaven while she resurrected her son Horus from the dead, a feat on which the Jews modeled their myth of Joshua's arrest of the sun at the battle of Jericho.[8]

The Jews enthusiastically adopted Ra and identified him with Yahweh, especially in his Babylonian form as the sun god Shamash

(Chemosh). Beth-Shemesh, House of the Sun, was a biblical version of the sun god's shrine, corresponding to Egyptian *per Ra*. The God of Moses followed Ra's custom, demanding that his worshipper go barefoot in his presence. "Put off thy shoes from off thy feet, for the place whereon thou standest is holy ground" (Exodus 3:5).[9] Sometimes the Jews called their sun god Elias, a corruption of the Greek Helios. Elias was the "father" Jesus called upon from the cross (Matthew 27:47–49).

1. *Book of the Dead*, 165. 2. Budge, G.E. 1, 341. 3. Erman, 139. 4. Budge, G.E. 1, 339–45. 5. *Book of the Dead*, 385, 501, 167. 6. Erman, 296, 299–300. 7. Budge, G.E. 1, 328. 8. Budge, E.M., 135. 9. *Book of the Dead*, 25, 203, 231.

Rabbatu

"Holy One," female form of *rabbi*, applied to the semitic Goddess or her priestesses.[1] See **Asherah**.

1. Albright, 210.

Rachel

"Womb," personification of *rachamin*, "mother-love" or "compassion," comparable to Sanskrit *karuna*.[1] Rachel's totemic form was the divine Ewe, mother of the Holy Lamb: an important symbol of early Hebraic tribal motherhoods. Rabbinical writings admitted that during this tribal period, the Four Matriarchs—Rachel, Sarah, Rebecca, and Leah—were more important than the Three Patriarchs—Abraham, Isaac, and Jacob.[2]

1. Brasch, 183. 2. Briffault 3, 551–53.

Radha

"Cow elephant," the Shakti of Krishna. Her name doubtless arose with the ancient bull-elephant cult. Krishna was considered an avatar of the elephant god Ganesha.[1] According to the Kama Sutra, the elephant represented maximum sexual capacity and unflagging desire.

1. Rawson, A.T., 99.

Ragnarok

Norse **doomsday**, the end of the present universe. Heimdall would announce the last battle of the gods by blowing the Last Trump on his horn; there would follow the destruction of the earth, the disappearance of the sun, the death of all gods, and the return of the world to its original state of chaos.

Rainbow

Myths often associate the rainbow with the dream-time or Golden Age when earth and heaven were in easy communication with one another. Deities, spirits, and mortals might pass back and forth on the rainbow bridge, which was also the *axis mundi*, or ladder of heaven, or necklace of the Great Mother who ruled the Golden Age. The Pot of Gold at the rainbow's end was another form of the Celts' Holy Grail, a womb symbol related to the pots where Mother Moon (Mana) kept the souls of the dead in her western paradise.[1]

The rainbow's seven colors represented the seven celestial spheres and the rainbow-hued veils of Maya, the Goddess working behind the veils to manifest the material world in its many-colored complexity. Her priestesses wore the colors of the veils, which appeared in Egyptian mythology as the seven stoles of **Isis**, and in the Bible as the seven veils of **Salome**.[2]

The rainbow veils of the Goddess Ishtar were sometimes garments, sometimes jewels. The rainbow was called her necklace, of which she made the bridge to heaven for the souls of her chosen ones. Her rainbow necklace had selective power. If the Goddess willed, neither man nor god could cross it. On one occasion she placed her rainbow to block the Heavenly Father from receiving the food laid on earth's altars, to punish him after he sent the **Flood** to destroy her earthly children.[3] Biblical writers re-interpreted this Babylonian myth to omit the Goddess and make the rainbow represent God's promise to Noah not to do it again.

The rainbow's selectivity is a common motif. The glowing bridge was a broad way for the chosen, a razor-edge for the wicked. The *Katha Upanishad* said the rainbow bridge to heaven is as difficult to traverse as the edge of a razor.[4] The Persians said the same of their Kinvad or Cinvat rainbow bridge: "For the just it is nine lance-lengths wide, for the ungodly it is as narrow as the edge of a razor. The Cinvat bridge is at the 'Center' . . . the bridge connects earth and heaven at the 'Center.'"[5] Christian tradition spoke of the same selective bridge of heaven: "Narrow is the way . . . and few there be that find it" (Matthew 7:14).

Upanishads
Buddhist scriptures representing the final stage in Vedic thought, dealing with the philosophy known as Vedanta. The *Katha Upanishad* discusses transmigration of souls, the nature of eternal life, the doctrine of *maya*, and an account of a visit to Yama, Lord of the Dead.

The Japanese said the rainbow is "the road of the gods and the bridge between sky and earth." As in India and Mesopotamia, its seven colors were associated with the seven heavens. "The throne of the Supreme Being is surrounded by a rainbow, and the same symbolism persists into the Christian art of the Renaissance." The sex of the Supreme Being was changed by patriarchal theology, but the symbol still suggests the archaic Maya-Shakti enveloped in her rainbow veils. "Shamanic drums are decorated with drawings of the rainbow represented as a bridge to the sky. . . . In the Turkic language the word for rainbow means bridge."[6]

Northern pagans also said the Goddess's rainbow necklace and the rainbow Bridge of Heaven were one and the same.[7] Freya's magic necklace Brisingamen was the same as the rainbow bridge called Bifrost or Bilrost, the "trembling way," also known as Asbru, "bridge of the gods."[8] During the Christian era, this rainbow bridge became one of the features of Fairyland. Heathen legend said as doomsday approached, the bridge would be broken down so there was no more communication between earth and heaven. In effect this meant mortals would no longer go to heaven, neither in the shamanic trance nor in the spirit after death.

Greeks personified the rainbow as the Goddess **Iris**, usually called Hera's messenger, one more instance of the Great Goddess's association with the garment of many colors, Maya's or Isis's veils. As the "bridge," Iris carried Mother Hera's messages to earth as the rainbow-hued peacock carried the messages of Mother Juno. Iris also bound the Nemean Lion with her colorful girdle and carried it to the sacred cave in the Nemean mountains.

The Nemean Mountains were the location of an ancient temple, near the city of Nemea in Argolis, in the Peloponnesus.[9]

1. Davidson, 34. 2. Angus, 251. 3. *Assyr. & Bab. Lit.*, 434. 4. Campbell, P.M., 333. 5. Eliade, S., 485, 397. 6. Eliade, S., 134–35. 7. Turville-Petre, 176. 8. Branston, 104. 9. Graves, G.M. 2, 104.

Ram

One of the "horny" animals embodying the phallic god along with the bull, stag, and billygoat. The ram was often selected for the dubious honor of sacrifice, being identified with the god who immolated himself to himself for the sake of humanity.

Solar gods were linked with the heavenly ram Aries, who began the sacred year, dead and reborn as the new Aeon. Egyptians called him Amen-Ra, "the Ram, the virile male, the holy phallus, which stirreth up the passions of love, the Ram of rams."[1]

The Ram Caught in a Thicket was a sexual metaphor and a common religious icon in Abraham's legendary home, Ur of the Chaldees. The same Ram Caught in a Thicket appeared in the Bible as a surrogate victim to replace Isaac, whose father Abraham was about to sacrifice him on the altar at Yahweh's command (Genesis 22:13). The story marked a transition from ancient customs of human sacrifice to the classical rule of animal sacrifice, as shown also in the substitution of the ram of the Golden Fleece for the king's son in a Boeotian sacrifice to Zeus.[2] An older Midrashic version of the Abraham-Isaac story said Abraham's hand was not stayed, the ram did not appear. Isaac was slaughtered, buried, and rose again on the third day.[3]

Rams were sacred in Israel as consorts of Rachel, the Holy Ewe, whom the biblical narrative later married to Jacob, a reincarnated Isaac. Jews sacrificed the paschal lamb each year as a firstborn son of the ram god who was identified with Yahweh. At one time the biblical God wore ram's horns, later assigned instead to the devil. Joshua's priests used ram's horns to make victory magic (Joshua 6:4), showing that they were led by the divine ram in battle.

1. Budge, G.E. 2, 64. 2. Graves, G.M. 1, 226–27. 3. Ochs, 32.

Rama

Hero of the Ramayana, whose name meant "sexual pleasure" or "enjoyment of virility"—one of the phallic avatars of Krishna as consort of the female-genital Goddess Sita, "the Furrow."[1] Their story was constructed on the framework of titles for the male and female elements of the lingam-yoni.

1. Avalon, 607.

Rape

Classical mythology abounds in rapes: the rape of the Sabine women, Zeus's rape of his mother Rhea, Apollo's numerous rapes of nymphs, even of his sister Artemis. One gets the impression that the Greeks thought women always had to be forced into sexual relationships, even with gods. But the word translated "rape" usually meant seduction. Teiresias, who lived as both a man and a woman, announced his discovery that a woman's pleasure in sex was nine times that of a man.[1]

True rape was not common in the ancient world. Like the males of all other mammalian species, the ancients believed sexual activity should be initiated by the female. The modern conventional description of a rapist as an "animal" is a slur on the animal kingdom; animals do not rape. Only man forces sexual attentions on an unwilling female.

The Bible tells of a Levite who gave up his concubine-wife to a mob to be gang-raped to death in order to save himself from molestation, and then cut her to pieces. "All who saw it said, There was no such deed done nor seen from the day that the children of Israel came up out of the land of Egypt unto this day" (Judges 19:30). A war was fought over the incident, showing that it was highly unusual.

A change in the attitude toward rape was one of the contrasts between the ancient world and the medieval one in western Europe. The Romans and Saxons punished rapists by death. Normans cut off a rapist's testicles and gouged his eyes out.[2] The gypsies' Oriental heritage demanded the death penalty for a rapist.[3] Hindu law said a rapist must be killed, even if his victim was of the lowest caste, an Untouchable; and his soul should "never be pardoned."[4] The Byzantine Code decreed that rapists must die and their property must be given to the victim, even if she was no better than a slave woman.[5]

Christian laws changed the picture. Serfs' wives, sisters, or daughters were always sexually available to their overlords under the new regime.[6] Peasant brides were raped by the baron before being turned over to their bridegrooms—probably to be raped again. The Church made it illegal for any wife to refuse sexual intercourse unless it was a holy day when marital sex was prohibited. Therefore, marital rape was encouraged.

Victorian England almost achieved one of patriarchy's most sought-after goals: total male control of female sexuality. Until 1884 a wife could be jailed for trying to deny her husband his "conjugal rights." She was as much a sexual slave as any inmate of an eastern harem.[7] Forced to consent to frequent rape by husbands who neither knew nor cared about women's sexual enjoyment, 19th-century wives became predictably indifferent to the delights of the marriage bed, in such numbers that medical authorities described women as "largely devoid of sexual pleasure." It was said in a standard marriage manual used for decades, and translated into 12 languages: "Wives seldom seek the closer embraces of their husbands. They are generally indifferent; often absolutely averse. . . . God has made the passivity of the wife the protection of her husband and a source of manifold blessing to their children." Having thanked God for a world of unaroused women, the author went on: "There can be little doubt that much marital indifference upon the part of wives is due to chronic constipation, which is so prevalent among women."[8] The implied assumption would be that God foresightedly afflicted women with chronic constipation in addition to the other curses on Eve.

Societies retaining the idea of Goddess-worship seldom demonstrate marital or extramarital rape; female sexuality is nearly always fully developed. Sadistic, violent sexual fantasies do not appear in the imagery of India.[9] The matriarchal Semai held it illegal for a man even to try to talk to a woman into sexual relations if she said no in the beginning.[10] Anti-rape rules inspired warmer relationships, as G.B. Shaw said: "The desire to give inspires no affection unless there is also the power to withhold."[11]

The laws of Shaw's culture, however, were designed to deprive women of the power to withhold. Before 1653, any Englishman could kidnap and rape a child heiress, after which the law viewed him as her legal husband. He was rewarded for rape with the acquisition of the victim's property. In 1653 the law was changed—not to help the victim, but to cut the government in on the loot. A man could be imprisoned for raping a young girl for her money, but half the victim's estate was taken by the government.[12]

Victorians never held men legally responsible for debauching adolescent girls, since the legal "age of consent" for females was twelve. A child under the age of eight was not allowed to give evidence against a man who violated her, on the ground that she was too young to understand the legal oath.[13] Yet in the 16th century, authorities set the "age of consent" at six years.[14] Raping children was a common enough pastime of Victorian men, who maintained that sexual intercourse with a virgin child was a sure cure for syphilis. As late as the 1930s, the madam of a West End whorehouse advertised, "In my house you can gloat over the cries of the girls with the certainty that no one will hear them besides yourself."[15]

Victorian pornography reflects an obsessive fascination for violence and rape, often describing sexual partners as "adversaries," though they were certainly not evenly matched. One male writer fantasized a female experience of defloration by a rapist who "quickly buried his tremendous instrument too far within me to leave me any chance of escape. He now paid no kind of attention to my sufferings, but followed up his movements with fury, until the tender texture altogether gave way to his fierce tearing and rending, and one merciless, violent thrust broke in and carried all before him, and sent it imbrued, reeking with blood of my virginity, up to its utmost length in my body. The piercing shriek I gave proclaimed that I felt it up to the very quick; in short, his victory was complete." The same male writer mused complacently: "How magical is the influence of our sex over the feelings of the softer one."[16]

The magic was not apparent to a modern rape victim who, nevertheless, displayed an almost catatonic acceptance of the victim's role, in effect giving her attackers the right to abuse her:

> *They were just taking advantage of me because I was alone and available. That's just the way men relate to women. If they're alone and available, well, use them. And it's nothing perverted. It's just their normal way of relating to a woman. . . .*
>
> *After it was over, I was aware of pain and dirtiness in my body, and I was hurt in my pride and confused about why they had raped me and why they were laughing at me and making fun of my body and taunting me. And I was also very sure that God was watching the whole thing and shaking his head and saying what a horrible person I was for allowing myself to get raped.*[17]

Studies have shown that raped women often were reluctant to hurt their assailants, e.g. by gouging eyes or twisting testicles, even when they had a chance. "Women often take the responsibility when men treat them as prey. This isn't just an odd female quirk. The attitude is deeply entrenched. . . . Women are taught to make themselves attractive to men. Those who don't are ignored by men or incur their displeasure. But if they become victims of sexual assault, they are immediately suspected of collusion. No man is ever guilty."[18]

In San Francisco in 1971, a gunpoint rapist was acquitted because his unmarried victim admitted having a lover. Women picketers protested the decision in vain, handing out leaflets which said:

> *When a person is robbed, the robber is put on trial. When someone is murdered, the murderer is tried. But when a woman is raped, it is the woman and not the rapist who is put on trial. . . . If she can be shown to have any sexual history, the rapist must be acquitted, for by their definition it is then no rape at all. For a woman to allow herself to be a sex-*

ual person, to enjoy her sexuality in her own way in her own time, is for her to lose all protection from being forced to commit sexual acts with any man at any time.[19]

Sometimes the culture forces on men a pseudo-rapist stance vis-à-vis women, where men in groups gang up on a woman verbally or symbolically, to injure her sense of self. One young woman wrote: "When I first started to live in the city, I would walk by the construction workers having lunch and hear all those horrible comments. I didn't quite know how to deal with it. I was embarrassed because I had breasts. I felt it was my fault for having them, and that of course I deserved to be commented upon. Now I know that's not true. It's they who have to change, not me."[20] A recent investigator wrote:

> *The virility mystique . . . predisposes men to rape. If women were physically stronger than men, I do not believe there would be any instances of female raping male, because female sexual socialization encourages a woman to integrate sex, affection, and love, and to be sensitive to what her partner wants. Of course, there are many women who deviate from this pattern, just as there are men who have managed to reject their socialization for virility. But cultural trends make these cases exceptional. If our culture considered it masculine to be gentle and sensitive, to be responsive to the needs of others, to abhor violence, domination, and exploitation, to want sex only within a meaningful relationship, to be attracted by personality and character rather than by physical appearance, to value lasting rather than casual relationships, then rape would indeed be a deviant act. . . .*
>
> *If lynching is the ultimate racist act, rape is the ultimate sexist act. It is an act of physical and psychic oppression. . . . [L]ike lynching, it is cowardly, and like lynching, it is used to keep individual women, as well as women as a caste, in their place. And finally, as with lynching, the rape victim is blamed for provocation.*
>
> *Rape is an abuse of power, and the increase in rape shows that men are increasingly unable to handle their excessive power over women. . . . Eradicating rape requires getting rid of the power discrepancy between men and women.*[21]

From the Inquisition's torturers, who usually raped their victims first, to Victorian doctors who attacked female genitals with leeches, many kinds of rape could be traced to what has been called "the virulent woman-hatred in fundamentalist Christianity."[22] Recent studies show that most rapists were professed members of a religious sect and learned to regard sex as evil, in the traditional Christian manner.[23] One rapist said, "I've always been brought up that sex was dirty, sex was not to be practiced." Another said he was "confused about just what the sex act was and how they went about it." Another was so naive he didn't know where babies came from, and another was ignorant of the word "vagina," calling it "virginia" instead.[24] "Sex offenders as a group were extremely naive about sexual matters, felt inferior, had suffered in childhood from anxiety and fears about sex . . . and had lacked accurate sex instruction."[25]

In some areas, the laws of both church and state actually encouraged rape until very recently. Up to 1978 in Italy, a rapist could go unpunished if his victim agreed to marry him. By a combination of violation and coercion, it was quite possible for a man to force marriage on a woman who had every reason to fear and hate him. And, since patriarchal society in effect forbade women to hate men, especially as wives, once again the victim would be blamed for her victimization.

1. Graves, G.M. 2, 11. 2. Pearsall, W.B., 315. 3. Derlon, 135. 4. *Mahanirvanatantra*, 267. 5. Soisson, 43. 6. Bullough, 168. 7. Crow, 147. 8. Stall, 49, 124–26. 9. Rawson, E.A., 184. 10. Briffault 2, 48; see Dentan. 11. de Riencourt, 349. 12. Murstein, 224. 13. Crow, 247. 14. Robbins, 462. 15. Pearsall, W.B., 243, 350. 16. Marcus, 212. 17. D.E.H. Russell, 48–50. 18. D.E.H. Russell, 44. 19. D.E.H. Russell, 11. 20. D.E.H. Russell, 168. 21. D.E.H. Russell, 264. 22. Robbins, 502; Dreifus, 49; Spretnak, 388. 23. Evans, S.S., 226. 24. Goldstein & Kant, 56, 81–85, 143. 25. Shultz, 165.

Rati

Balinese name of the Goddess, called "Erotic Delight," perhaps a cognate of ancient Egyptian Ra-ti of the World, "Lady of Heaven, Mistress of the Gods."[1] There may have been a connection with the Greeks' Erato, "Passionate One," the Muse of erotic poetry.[2] Images of Rati displayed the overflowing sexuality and fertility admired in ancient matriarchies: huge breasts, a pregnant belly, a mouth twisted to one side and shaped like a vulva. Zimmer's description shows the typical uneasiness of the western male in the presence of such exaggerated symbols of the Eternal Feminine:

Heinrich Zimmer (1890-1943) Leading western student of Oriental religions and Sanskrit texts, particularly the sacred literature of India.

> *The goddess of maternity and fertility . . . is indicating, with a traditional twofold symbolic gesture, the two main functions of the female principle. One forearm lifts the breasts that nourish the creatures she brings forth, while the other hand, placed at the lower abdomen, immediately above the organ of generation, presses the ever-pregnant womb. The sensual mouth, with its half-open lips and broadening gap at the left corner, has a voluptuous, dolorous trait, suggesting simultaneously the delights of love and conception and the pangs and throes of birth. The figure exhibits, frankly, all the innocent shamelessness of archaic mother figures, but in addition—or so it seems—the challenging, calm, watchful, and consciously exhibitionistic attitude of a curiously demonic, suprahuman harlot. The hideous and grotesque features are suffused with a sinister, devilish allure of sex. . . .*
>
> *The image, though by no means isolated in the art of Bali, is one of its most challenging and meaningful specimens . . . rawly protesting, as it were, against the lofty doctrines of release and transcendent redeeming wisdom, which, in the forms of Buddhist and yogic asceticism, were the most conspicuous and forceful products, in that period, of the masculine spirit. After milleniums of the struggle of the gurus to disengage man from the brutish thrall of the demonic powers of sheer nature, these—unabated, unconquered, and unreconciled—still were there. And they are both shocking and attractive.*[3]

1. Budge, G.E. 1, 328. 2. Graves, G.M. 2, 390. 3. Campbell, M.I., 270–71.

Ravana

Kingly Hindu "demon" with an ass head worn by a succession of ten human kings, the last of whom was slain by the god Krishna.[1] Ravana's images usually showed the ass head in the center, the human heads ranged along the sides of his neck. The kings have been related to the ten antediluvian patriarchs postulated by early ass-worshipping Hebrews. See **Ass**.

1. Norman, 123.

Raven

In its black plumage, the raven was a natural totem of the deities of death. Many forms of the Lord of Death were incarnate in a raven. Chukchi shamans called their ancestral wizard-king Big Raven, he who was ceremonially castrated and killed.[1] Danes spoke of a Valraven who was Hel's king in the underworld. As a son and mate of the nether Goddess, he was sometimes personified as King Morvran, "Sea-Raven."[2]

Valkyries could take the form of ravens to drink the blood of slain warriors, which is why Norse skalds called blood "the raven's drink."[3] Like a Valkyrie-psychopomp, a raven was supposed to perch on the shoulder of the Orphic initiate as he entered the temple for the ceremony of mock death and rebirth.[4] According to the Mithraic Mysteries, the initiate received the title of Raven when he attained the first degree of enlightenment, which corresponded to ascent to heaven's lunar sphere, the domain of the Moon-goddess who received and cared for the dead.[5]

So constant was the death-and-resurrection symbolism of the raven in Germanic tradition that the new Germanic hero of the Second Coming, Emperor Frederick, was said to be guarded by ravens as he waited, sleeping, in his underground sanctuary for the day of his return to earth. According to the Armenian version, the emperor still sleeps under a magic hill called Rock of the Raven.[6] In fairy tales, a raven is often the soul-bird who conducts the hero into mysterious underground places and out again, or gives information concerning the after-world.

1. Hays, 412. 2. Graves, W.G., 87. 3. Turville-Petre, 58. 4. Campbell, M.I., 389. 5. Rose, 289. 6. Borchardt, 152.

Reincarnation

Literally, "re-fleshing," the basic Oriental view of cyclic rebirth after each death; the original meaning of being born again. In the role of Fate-goddess, the Great Mother governed the Wheel of Becoming (Greek, *kyklos geneseon*) which meant the cycles of successive lives, like the wheel of karma governed by Kali.[1]

Patriarchal thinkers tended to deny the doctrine of reincarnation in favor of the one-way trip to heaven or hell after only one life on earth. They sought eternal stasis rather than cycles. Yet reincarnation was the standard belief of all the ancient nations, with the patriarchal principle of eternal stasis appearing only as a late development.

Pythagoras believed in transmigration of souls from one body to another: "The spirit wanders, comes now here, now there, and occupies whatever frame it pleases. From beasts it passes into human bodies, and from our bodies into beasts, but never perishes."[2] Plato had the same idea. His *Republic* depicted Greek heroes in the underworld choosing bodies for their next incarnation on earth. The rebirth doctrine prevailed among cultured Greeks who had been initiated into the Mysteries. Their idea was the same as the Tantric idea, which promised free choice of subsequent bodies to the Enlightened Ones in the Intermediate State between death and the next life.[3]

First Book of Adam and Eve One of the legendary apocrypha (works written in Greek from Jewish sources) giving additional details or alternative versions of the Genesis myths.

Even Jewish tradition retained traces of the reincarnation doctrine. In the *First Book of Adam and Eve,* Adam offered God a sacrifice of his own blood, saying, "Be favorable to me every time I die, and bring me to life."[4] Orthodox Jews made it a rule not to name a newborn child after a living person, lest untimely transmission of the name-soul should bring death to the elder. The rule stemmed from the ancient belief that every infant possessed the soul of an ancestor in a new body.[5] The Jewish belief that a woman could conceive by bathing in water used to wash a corpse clearly points to a belief in reincarnation.[6] Indeed, the Talmud says Adam was reincarnated in the person of David, and then again in the Messiah.[7]

Reincarnation was the general belief not only in the Orient but throughout pagan Europe. Caesar said the druids taught this doctrine of cyclic rebirths.[8] It is still the prevailing opinion among "primitive" peoples who imagine their own souls to be temporary bits of the World Soul that animates all living things. The Poetic Edda demonstrates a belief in the karmic wheel of reincarnations, from which one may be released only by self-destruction. Brynhild's suicide insured that "born again she may never be."[9] Among the Eskimos as among ancient Greeks and Hindus, cycles of reincarnation include all forms of life. They say the Goddess of Animals looks after all creatures and doesn't like to see too many of them killed, since they are of the same spiritual substance as human beings. "Life is endless," the shamans say, "only we do not know in what form we shall reappear after death."[10]

Reincarnation was necessarily bound up with motherhood in all societies, since mothers were its agents and carriers. It was the mother of Lemminkainen, hero of the *Kalevala,* who gave him another life after he was killed.[11] In northern India, dead infants were buried under the threshold of the house, so their spirits might enter the bodies of mothers who passed in and out and so be born again.[12]

Reincarnation seems to have been a secret tenet of some of the early Christian churches, not explained to ordinary congregations but revealed in secret after the preliminary stages of initiation into an inner group of "elect" or "perfected" mystics. Later, the exoteric church repudiated the doctrine of karmic rebirth. In 553 A.D. the Second Council of Constantinople laid down a decree: "Whosoever shall support the mythical doctrine of the pre-existence of the soul and the consequent wonderful opinion of its return, let him be anathema." Origen, once accounted a saint and a father of the church, taught the doctrine of reincarnation; but three centuries after his death he was officially excommunicated "on account of his beliefs."[13]

Origen (Origenes Adamantius) Christian father, ca. 185–254 A.D., an Egyptian who wrote in Greek, exerting a powerful influence on the early Greek church. At first he was accounted a saint, but three centuries after his death he was declared a heretic because of Gnostic elements found in his writings.

The concept of reincarnation made nonsense of the Christian doctrine of reward and punishment after death. If all souls returned to the same Cauldron of Regeneration, including animal souls mingling with human ones, logically they were not differentiated for eternity into "evil" and "good" souls. The West's traditional denial of soul-stuff to animals, and its insistence that man alone was immortal and stood at the pinnacle of all creation, led to abuses contributing to the present-day ecological crisis. At a symposium of theologians in California, 1970, "virtually all the scholars agreed that the traditional Christian attitude toward nature has given sanction to exploitation of the environment by science and technology and thus contributed to air and water pollution, overpopulation and other ecological threats." Lynn White wrote, "One of the causes of our present crisis is to be found in the Judeo-Christian traditions . . . which speak of man's dominance over nature. . . . By destroying pagan animism, Christianity made it possible to exploit nature in a mood of indifference to the feelings of natural objects."[14] It is odd that even here, those living things with feelings are called "objects."

Eastern opinions on reincarnation mitigated man's cruelty to his fellow creatures, at the price of attributing to them a psychic content indistinguishable from that of human beings. It is no great moral victory to refrain from killing a spider if one sincerely believes the spider could contain the soul of one's grandmother. It might be more moral to refrain from killing a spider simply because it is alive, and wishes to remain so; and all will to live deserves respect.

Perhaps the best one could say for reincarnation was that it was not wasteful. Its soul-stuff was preserved and recycled. The Christian theory was less tidy, with constant new creation of supposedly "immortal" souls, since the world began: a vast accumulation, still increasing daily. In practice, however, many Christians secretly believed in some form of the forbidden reincarnation. Like Orphics, some even claimed they could remember their former lives. The conspicuous absence of proof for such claims only seems to strengthen the faith of those who wish to believe.

1. *Bardo Thodol,* lxvii. 2. Campbell, P.M., 293–94. 3. *Bardo Thodol,* 53, 188. 4. *Forgotten Books,* 17. 5. de Lys, 428. 6. Gaster, 521. 7. Waddell, 226. 8. Squire, 36. 9. H.R.E. Davidson, G.M.V.A., 158. 10. Campbell, P.M., 294. 11. H.R.E. Davidson, G.M.V.A., 234. 12. Frazer, F.O.T., 320. 13. *Bardo Thodol,* 234. 14. Patai, 135–36.

Religion

Latin *religio* meant re-linking or reunion, a restoration of the umbilical bond between nature and man, or between the Mother Goddess and her son-consort, typified by human sexual union. The Sanskrit equivalent was *yoga,* which also meant linking or joining, root of the English "yoke."[1]

A need to re-establish the mother-child bond in symbol may have been the source of all religion, which Schleiermacher defined as an infantile "feeling of absolute dependence."[2] Gaylin says "the helplessness of infancy" is transmuted in religious imagery to "a plea for a solution to the problem of survival."[3] Significantly, the mature, caretaking figure even in patriarchal religious imagery was the female, not the male. God nearly always had a baby stage, appearing in his Mother's arms. But the Goddess, even in her virgin form, was full grown and maternally capable. This curious fact may be based on the attitude of worshipper to deity as a child to parent, and the true biological parent recognized by all mammals is the mother. Thus, even patriarchal religions conceal the "strong unconscious trend towards mother-worship."[4]

Freud defined religion as an attempt to control the mental world "by means of a world of wishes." Religious images are "fulfilments of the oldest, strongest, most compelling wishes of mankind."[5] Apart from the wish to control the Mother figure, and the wish not to die, the gods made in the image of men expressed a rather paltry, self-seeking series of wishes obviously drawn from limited imagination. Santayana remarked, "It is pathetic to observe how lowly are the motives that religion, even the highest, attributes to the deity, and from what a hard-pressed and bitter existence they have been drawn. To be given the best morsel, to be remembered, to be praised, to be obeyed blindly and punctiliously—these have been thought points of honor with the gods."[6] Of course these were points of honor with men first. As Sir Richard Francis Burton said, "The more I study religions, the more I am convinced that man never worshipped anything but himself."[7]

Sir Richard Francis Burton (1821-1890) British traveler, consul, orientalist, translator of *The Arabian Nights,* author of more than 50 books on Indian, Arabian, South American and African cultures—including a book on the Mormons of Salt Lake City. Burton was one of the first Europeans to make the pilgrimage to Mecca and Medina; and with J.H. Speke, one of the first to discover Lake Tanganyika and the sources of the Nile.

Buddhist ascetics concurred, saying a man's self is "nearer to us than anything else, indeed dearer than a son, dearer than wealth, dearer than all beside. Let a man worship the Self alone as dear, for if he worship the Self alone as dear, the object of his love will never perish." Children were of no interest to the male ascetics: "Realizing the glory of the Self, the sages of old craved not sons nor daughters. 'What have we to do with sons and daughters,' they asked, 'we who have known the Self, we who have achieved the supreme goal of existence?' "[8]

With the advent of male gods, religions tended to become obsessive about guilt and sin, worried about what the gods might punish as hubris, fearful of giving offense by a careless word or deed. In short, the gods behaved like not particularly loving fathers, or elder males seeking to maintain ascendancy over younger ones. The Judeo-Christian deity became one of the foremost examples of Oepidal hostility in the world pantheon. He punished the whole human race for one sin of its remote ancestor, with a punishment so terrible that it would last forever in merciless agony. The fear of so irrational and vindictive a deity drove a whole civilization into neurosis. Social evils that might have been remedied were left unchecked, on the theory that all human beings were sinful wretches who deserved to suffer—especially women, the primary sinners. Serfdom, slavery, legalized brutality, economic oppression—all were excused in the name of a vengeful God, whose priesthood insisted on his hostility toward humanity, to the point where unspeakable atrocities were committed to the greater glory of religion.[9] Christian history shows that religion may follow a humane course in response to social trends; but it does not lead the way.

With its doctrine of inherited sin, for which no man could atone by himself without the intercession of the Son whose death the Father commanded, Christianity set out to formalize the hostile parent figure in its insistence that the only way to righteousness was to fear God. Accordingly, fathers of the church emphasized this point. Lactantius claimed all religion depends on fear; Tertullian asked, "How are you going to love, unless you are afraid not to love?"[10] The horror story of God's hostility toward his wretched children was treated as a literal reality, not a psychological image. This "fiction of timeless truths has taxed the ingenuity of even the ablest of rationalizers who seek by means of subtle taxonomic devices to fit embarrassing new discoveries into the framework of the old beliefs."[11] As the old beliefs were products of primitive ignorance, their framework has had to be stretched to cover an immense body of fact that it was never meant to cover. The fit is still poor:

> *No ethics and no religion can contain any wisdom that can transcend man's own knowledge about the immediate and future consequences of his own behavior. Every religion and every ethical system must recognize that it might well be made obsolete by an extension of human knowledge in almost any area. . . .*
>
> *Far from any evidence of far-sighted and consistent leadership, the clergy has shown nothing other than all too human tendency to fill their sails with whatever winds of public opinion may blow, and always with their vested interest firmly at the helm.*[12]

The clergy's vested interest now dictates revision of traditional illusions to suit more modern thinking. Augstein says theologians now admit that "Christianity has been on the wrong track for sixteen hundred years, ever since Constantine, that it has had a wrong conception of God all that time and is only now in a position to disclose its social mores—in short, that it must start all over again. But when religion was powerful, it never wielded any positive influence on social mores; so why should it do so today, when it is a survival sinking out of sight?"[13] Churches have not shown any inclination to reform themselves except when sales of their nonproduct decline to the danger point, and few take much active interest in social issues. Farm worker Roberto Acuna spoke bitterly of his church's indifference: "I could tear the churches apart. I never saw a priest out in the fields trying to help people. . . . [I]t's always the church taking from the people."[14]

James Martineau, professor of moral philosophy at Manchester New College, summed up the dilemma of conventional religion in *The Seat of Authority of Religion:*

> *Christianity . . . has been mainly evolved from that which is unhistorical and perishable in its sources; from what is unhistorical in its traditions, mythological in its preconceptions, and misapprehended in the oracles of its prophets. From the fable of Eden to the imagination of the last trumpet, the whole story of the divine order of the world is dislocated and deformed. . . .*
>
> *The spreading alienation of the intellectual classes of European society from Christendom, and the detention of the rest in their spiritual culture at a level not much above that of the Salvation Army, are social phenomena which ought to bring home a very solemn appeal to the consciences of ordinary churches.*[15]

Some scholars find it baffling that man seems unable to found an ethic or a philosophy on perceptions of reality, but instead must cling to crude myths—even to the point of filling his own life and the lives of others with unnecessary horrors.[16] Among the worst of these is the real violence with which man attacks the questioners or doubters of his myths: as if to kill his own reasonable doubts before they rise up to the surface of his mind and become fully conscious.

To purvey an unenlightened education, teaching myths as if they were facts, is another abuse of cultural communication, inflicting on children a confusion between truth and fantasy that may haunt them all their lives and prevent them from developing clear thought on any subject. It isn't always easy for a child to know where the real world stops and his own imagination begins. If adults can't help him draw the line, because their own minds are muddled by an age-old ignorance, the next generation will repeat the errors of centuries.

Religions affect to purvey "higher Truth," but all too often their capital-T Truth bears an uncanny resemblance to a capital-L Lie. One theologian said the objective of religion is "to know the truth and to live by it"; but the same theologian defined religion as "believing things that do not seem to be so, and always it is believing what cannot be proved to be so." A less subtle seminarian once defined religion as "the power that enables us to believe what we know to be untrue."[17] No wonder the Rev. Kirsopp Lake lamented that a clergyman is "apt to have a lower standard of intellectual honesty than would be tolerated in any other profession." A noted historian writes: "The churches have long brought up the intellectual rear of our civilization, and . . . their

Rev. Kirsopp Lake British ecclesiastical historian, author of *Landmarks in the History of Early Christianity,* 1920.

claims to spiritual leadership are still weakened by their engrained tendency to resist new knowledge and aspiration. Most are still disposed to a dogmatic supernaturalism that saps the intellectual honesty and courage essential for a responsible idealism."[18]

It is often taken for granted that religion helps to keep the ordinary citizen honest, presumably through fear of divine punishment. This may be a misapprehension:

> *Every survey ever undertaken of the composition of the criminal population reveals a percentage of the avowedly religious higher than a random sample of the population will show. . . . Little or no relationship was found between the presence or absence, intensity, or kind of expression of religious faith, and conduct or moral standard. Some of those who were most skeptical, or who denied all need of faith or concern with religious problems, were unimpeachable in behavior, kind and helpful to others, and of high integrity. . . .*
>
> *The many attempts to find evidence that religion or its practice have [sic] desirable consequences in crime prevention have without exception ended in failure . . . there seems to be no convincing evidence that conventional religion, of itself, has proved an effective antidote to crime.*[19]

Unfortunately, in the western world religion has proved more often an instrument of oppression than a guide to more honest or more tolerant living. Churches generally supported the powerful at the expense of the powerless. For example, the church helped even the cruelest monarchies in history by formulating and upholding the doctrine of the divine right of kings. In the present century the world has seen cardinals praying for the success of dictators.[20]

The common symbol of religious organization is "the shepherd and the herd he must tend . . . and at the bottom of it lies the childlike concept that our elders run the world for our benefit."[21] Of course, the shepherd doesn't tend the herd for the benefit of the sheep. He tends them for his own benefit. He makes his living from them. In some ways the analogy is apt. Ecclesiastical "shepherds" in the past have resorted to every imaginable crime to increase their profits: land-grabbing, vandalism, false advertising, defamation of character, forgery, plagiarism, even all-out war and murder, ever since Pope Leo the Great endorsed the death penalty for "erroneous beliefs." There is still a tendency among Christians to "assume that theirs is the only true religion, and that their Christian duty is to convert the rest of the world. The rest of the world, which happens to include the great majority of mankind, still resents this assumption."[22]

Christian elitism allowed theologians to "believe that they speak for everyone when they lecture about things like guilt, love, sin, and grace. This naiveté allows them to make definitive statements about the true way in which all people should live and think about these matters. Theologians are ignorant of what every anthropologist knows—i.e, that the forms of our thought derive from the forms of our culture." It has been demonstrated often enough that women particularly suffered from the suppression of their own natural religious imagery in favor of an imposed masculine, alien, hierarchical system. "For women to become intellectually responsible and creative members of society, they have to outgrow Oedipal dependence on paternal authority whether that authority is embodied in a paternalistic husband, or father, or God." Feminists have shown "how important the demise of Yahweh and Christ is to the intellectual independence of Western women. Freud was certain that Judaism and Christianity stunted the intellectual maturity of men. It is probable, however, that these religions are even more damaging to the intellectual growth of women."[23]

One might hope that, if women again become free to create their own religion as they were in the distant past, it would be a religion less sullied by the profit motive, the cruelty, hostility, and Oedipal jealousy that disfigures the religious images of men. One might hope, also, that it would remain open to correction by new scientific discoveries, as Christianity has never been. Thomas Aquinas warned long ago that the faith would become a matter of ridicule "if any Catholic, not gifted with the necessary scientific learning, presents as dogma what scientific scrutiny shows to be false."[24] Later churchmen forgot this advice. In consequence they can offer no reason other than the church's decree at present to endorse such impossibilities as a virgin birth, transubstantiation, resurrection of the flesh, and all the biblical miracles. At the same time they must deny the very same impossibilities claimed by Christianity's historical rivals, on equally credible (or incredible) grounds.

It seems the religions of the western world have reached a period of crisis and must dissolve and re-form according to new principles, perhaps more realistic and humanistic ones.

1. Campbell, Or. M., 13; Muller, 315. 2. Starkloff, 38. 3. Becker, D.D., 213. 4. Montagu, T., 273. 5. Augstein, 223, 305. 6. Muller, 85. 7. Edwardes, xx. 8. *Upanishads*, 80, 111. 9. Muller, 159. 10. Cavendish, P.E., 163; Muller, 86. 11. Vetter, 85. 12. Vetter, 470–73, 520–21. 13. Augstein, 328. 14. Terkel, 32. 15. H. Smith, 398–99. 16. Campbell, P.M., 4. 17. Vetter, 18–19, 257–58. 18. Muller, 250, 354. 19. Vetter, 479–80. 20. Muller, 154, 185. 21. Augstein, 200. 22. Muller, 184, 45. 23. Goldenberg, 115, 35. 24. Muller, 249.

Renenet

Egypt's "Lady of the Double Granary," Goddess of suckling, who gave each baby its *ren* (secret name-soul) along with its mother's milk. Sometimes she wore a lion head, like Hathor; sometimes a serpent head, Uraeus; sometimes she wore the plumes of Mother Maat, the Goddess-Named-Truth.[1] Renenet represented the ancient matriarchal theory that a child's soul is bestowed by its mother after she has given birth to its body. The *ren* soul was kept secret, since an enemy who discovered it could work evil charms against the possessor.[2] See **Name**.

1. *Larousse,* 38. 2. H. Smith, 24.

Repanse de Joie

"Dispenser of Joy," the Fairy Queen who kept the Holy Grail in her temple-palace at Montsalvatch.[1] She was identified with Elaine the Lily Maid in the Arthurian cycle, and with several other versions of the White Lady, showing that she was simply a medieval transformation of the Moon-goddess with her Cauldron of Regeneration. Her title was a traditional epithet of a harlot-priestess. See **Grail, Holy**.

1. Guerber, L.M.A., 200.

Restituta, Saint

"Restored One, " a saint whose legend probably was based on a vandalized and half-burned statue of the Goddess found on the isle of Ischia and replaced in her temple. According to the Christian myth, Restituta was a "virgin martyr" slain in Africa and consigned to a boat filled with burning pitch. The boat drifted ashore on Ischia where her remains were taken up by Christians and "reverently cared for."[1] The more likely possibility was that the Ischians took up the damaged image of their Goddess and restored her to her temple after an attack by fanatical iconoclasts.

1. Brewster, 245.

Revelation

Latin *revelatio* meant to draw back the veil (*velum*).[1] It was the Goddess's rainbow veil that concealed the future and the secrets of the spirit under the colors of earthly appearances. After death, men might see her "face to face." A vision of the naked Goddess was vouchsafed to her sacred kings, who could draw back the veil of her temple, the *hymen*, pierce her virginity and die in their mating, to become gods. But, as the Goddess said on her temple at Sais, "No mortal has yet been able to lift the veil which covers me." [2] Those who saw her unveiled were no longer mortal.

In time, the word revelation was applied to every religious vision or opinion. It even described the stereotyped pronouncements of fortune-tellers.

The Bible's *Book of Revelation* purports to be a doomsday-vision experienced by St. John the Divine, but it is in fact a collection of images and phrases from many sources. Literature of this kind was plentiful in the first few centuries A.D., and it still occurred a thousand years later in European pagan traditions, e.g. the very similar *Voluspá* (Sybil's Vision) of the Scandinavian version of doomsday.

1. Funk, 282. 2. *Larousse*, 37.

Rhadamanthys

"Diviner," one of three Cretan god-kings born of the Full-Moon goddess Europa, fathered by Zeus. The other two were Sarpedon and Minos.

Rhadamanthys was said to have been so wise and just that in the underworld he was made a judge of the dead, like the similar bull-king Yama in India. Some myths said when Rhadamanthys was installed in the paradise of the Elysian Fields he married Alcmene, "Moon-power," the virgin mother of Heracles.[1] Thus he was another form of the Moon-bull king, like Zeus himself as consort of the Moon-cow Europa—a son identified with his divine father, like all other versions of the Lord of Death.

1. Graves, G.M. 1, 294.

Rhea

Cretan name of the Aegean Universal Mother or Great Goddess, who had no consort and ruled supreme before the coming of patriarchal Hellenic invaders. Rhea was the archetypal Triple Goddess, with several titles suggesting her separate functions: she was Britomartis the Sweet Virgin, and Dictynna the Lawgiving Mother of Mount Dicte, and Aegea the foundress of Aegean civilizations.[1] Another of her names was Coronis, both a carrion crow (death-goddess) and a virgin mother (life-goddess) of the great hero of healing, Asclepius, whose Titan cult the Hellenic Zeus angrily destroyed.

Rhea was not restricted to the Aegean area. Among ancient tribes of southern Russia she was Rha, the Red One, another version of Kali as Mother Time clothed in her garment of blood when she devoured all the gods, her offspring.[2] The same Mother Time became the Celtic Goddess Rhiannon, who also devoured her own children one by one.[3] This image of the cannibal mother was typical everywhere of the Goddess as Time, who consumes what she brings forth; or as Earth, who does the same. When Rhea was given a consort in Hellenic myth, he was called Kronus or Chronos, "Father Time," who devoured his own children, in imitation of Rhea's earlier activity. He also castrated and killed his own father, the Heaven-god Uranus; and he in turn was threatened by his own son, Zeus.[4] These myths reflect the primitive succession of sacred kings castrated and killed by their supplanters. (See **Kingship**.) It was originally Rhea Kronia,

Mother Time, who wielded the castrating moon-sickle or scythe, a Scythian weapon, the instrument with which the Heavenly Father was "reaped." Rhea herself was the Grim Reaper.

Pre-Roman Latium knew her as Rhea Silvia, "Rhea of the Woodland," an early form of the Moon-goddess Diana, called the first Vestal Virgin and the mother of Romulus and Remus. Under the rule of Rhea Silvia, the Vestal Virgins were neither celibate nuns, nor servants of the state, as they became in later ages. They were choosers and deposers of the early Latin kings, a college of *matronae* who ruled the rulers and took no husbands. Consequently all their children were begotten by "gods," not by men, as were the children of Rhea Silvia herself. Once born, Rhea's children were cared for by Acca Larentia, a "holy harlot" or high priestess who also mothered all the ancestral spirits (*lares*) of Rome. See **Akka**.

Hellenic myth assimilated Rhea as both mother and wife of the Great God Zeus. Zeus "raped" his mother Rhea because she forbade him to make a monogamous marriage (her own people had practiced group marriage). Then again, Zeus "raped" his sister-bride Hera, Rhea's daughter, alter ego, and virgin phase, whose name was really the same as Rhea's—*He Era*, the Earth.[5]

Having forced Rhea-Hera to marry him, Zeus became a symbol of Greek wife-abuse. The Mother and Father of the Olympian gods despised one another, constantly bickered and argued; mythographers always carefully described Hera's hostile "jealousy" of Zeus's many impregnations of mortal virgins to provide the earth with god-begotten heroes. To spite her twin-brother-son-husband, Rhea-Hera returned to her ancient birth-magic and parthenogenetically conceived and bore the serpent god Python—just as under the archaic title of **Eurynome** she had created the world alone and given birth to the serpent god Ophion.

Another name for Rhea was Pandora, "the All-giver," which Hesiod converted into an Eve-like giver of disasters to mankind, through her excessive curiosity.[6] The myth had its origin in the idea that the Goddess did indeed give all kinds of fate, death as well as birth, suffering as well as joy, in her endless time-cycles.

1. *Larousse*, 85–86. 2. *Mahanirvanatantra*, 295–96. 3. Squire, 286. 4. Graves, G.M. 1, 40. 5. Graves, G.M. 1, 51, 53–54. 6. Graves, G.M. 1, 148.

Rhinemaidens

Teutonic river-nymphs, original owners of the golden treasure of the Nibelungs. Since the Nibelungs were "shades," or spirits of the dead, the Ring symbolized the karmic wheel and the Rhinemaidens were keepers of the dead who were consigned to water, like aquatic Valkyries. They resembled eastern Vilas and Homeric Sirens; hearing their sweet songs could mean death to men. In antiquity, such songs were sung by priestesses in connection with sending a corpse to the Water-mother by way of the funerary boat.

Robin

God of the Witches, with numerous variations: Robin Goodfellow, Robin son of Art, Robin the Bobbin, Robin Hood, or Robin Red-breast—the last apparently derived from memories of the Norman sacred king with blood-runes or *geirs-odd* carved in the flesh of his breast on his "red-letter day" (see **Runes**). As Lord of the Hunt and a dying god he became the slain Cock Robin, whose executioner in the nursery rhyme did him in "with my wee bow and arrow"—a Saxon version of the Celtic **Cu Chulainn** who died at Mag Muirthemne bound to the sacred pillar and riddled with arrows.[1]

Robin was Saracenic, from *Rah-bin,* "a seer," cognate with the Semitic *rabba,* "lord," *reb* or *rabbi,* a priest. Robin's cult penetrated northern Europe from roots in Moorish Spain.[7] The Iberian peninsula was not Christianized until the overthrow of its Arab governors in the 11th century. Like Scandinavia in the same period, it was a fount of pagan ideas and practices.

The red-breasted bird of spring was Cock Robin's soul; the red was his blood, shed by a pagan sacrifice, though a pseudo-Christian legend tried to explain it in a different way. A robin tried to pluck away the thorns from Christ's crown, but only succeeded in tearing its own breast, so all robins had red breasts thereafter.[2] This fable failed to remove the curse of Cock Robin in the opinion of Christian authorities who knew quite well that he was a phallic god.

In Cornwall, Robin meant a cock in the other sense: a penis. His surname Hood, or Hud, referred to the symbolic pine log, planted in Mother Earth as a sacred pillar. A pamphlet of 1639 showed Robin as a horned, hoofed, ithyphallic satyr, leading witches' revels in the company of a black dog and an owl.[3]

Robin Hood, Wizard of the Greenwood, was a real person or persons leading Sherwood Forest covens in the early 14th century, with a wife or paramour taking the role of the Goddess Maerin, or Marian, or Mari-Anna, the Saxon *wudu-maer,* literally the Mary or the Mother of the Grove. Great sacramental feasts in honor of Robin and his lady were remembered in popular rhymes nearly three centuries later, when he was "Robin the Bobbin, the big-bellied Ben, who ate more meat than fourscore men."[4]

Family names can be found dating back to the "greenwood marriages" performed by heathen shamans, symbolized by the renegade Friar Tuck. Morrises and Morrisons descended from orgiastic Morris-dancers, also called Marian's morrice-men.[5] Like Robin (or Robinson), Morris dancers' May Day rites came from Moorish Spain. The original word was *morisco,* "Moorish."[6]

The common folk of England liked Robin, which is why they called him Goodfellow, or Puck, which descended from a word for "God." He was supposed to right the wrongs inflicted on the peasants by the church. He stole the treasures of the rich clergy and nobles and bestowed them on the poor. By force of arms he maintained a heathen preserve in the wildwood, a sanctuary for heretics and others persecuted by the church. Popular legend said Robin was born of a virgin impregnated by Oberon, King of the Fairies. He traveled to fairyland, and was shown "many secrets which he never did open to the world."[8]

Like the Greeks' Pan, Robin defended unspoiled land against the encroachment of towns. In country districts, each village set aside a plot of raw woodland, which was not to be disturbed, because it belonged to The Goodfellow, or the Good Man.[9] Elders of the Scottish church in 1594 exerted their utmost influence to abolish this Goodfellow's Croft, which they called the devil's acre, claiming it gave "great offence."[10]

Mystery plays of the 16th century still continued to celebrate Robin, Maid Marian, Friar Tuck, Little John, and the other heathen heroes. A Churchwardens Account Book lists the prices of costumes for Robin and Marian as King and Queen of the May. The lady impersonating Marian wore a crown, a purple coif, a blue surcoat, a yellow skirt, and red sleeves.[11] In such a way did the church ingest pagan ceremonials by sponsorship, and eventually deprive them of serious meaning.

1. *Larousse,* 233. 2. Bowness, 38. 3. Graves, W.G., 441. 4. Spence, 109. 5. Graves, W.G., 441–43. 6. Hazlitt, 422. 7. Shah, 210; Ravensdale & Morgan, 153. 8. Keightley, 287, 289, 315–16. 9. W. Scott, 78. 10. Hazlitt, 283. 11. Hazlitt, 384–85, 520.

Roch, Saint

The Roman church's official protector against the plague. French churchmen declared the pestilence would never enter a house protected by the written letters V.S.R. (Vive Saint Roch).[1] Unfortunately, the charm didn't work.

1. Mâle, 271.

Romance

Poets of the Middle Ages kept alive many druidic and other pre-Christian sacred tales, orally transmitted from generation to generation in the manner of the Vedas, under the guise of "romances." Earlier rhyme-makers were priests of the Goddess, who gave them the gift of inspiration from her magic cauldron, or Holy Grail.[1] A poet was like a seer or wizard, able to deal in "words of power," to create by the charms of speech, a blessing of the Muse. Medieval poets were worshippers of Art and Woman, founders of the cult of courtly love, singers of *mansongr,* the "woman-songs" beloved by the Goddess; and they were mockers of the church.

Poets seem to have regarded themselves as a dispossessed priesthood of the Goddess Love (Minne), who inspired the church's hostility. Before the 13th century, poets were denied Christian communion, and denounced by churchmen as "ministers of Satan." Later, they won acceptance by using biblical and theological motifs in their songs, but romantic poetry remained suspiciously heretical.[2]

Old romances depicted the clergy as rude, brutish fellows who mistreated delicate ladies, and even displayed sadistic behavior toward their own brethren.[3] The pagan gods were credited with warmer personalities. Frithiof's saga suggested that, though Christ despised lovers, the god Balder did not. Lovers could meet in the temples of Balder, "the pious god," because "Is not his love for Nanna part of his own nature, pure and warm?" Romantic heroes generally avoided the Christian **paradise** and went to the earthly one, governed by the Goddess Morgan, or the Fairy Queen.[4]

Frithiof's saga
Swedish national poem composed by Esias Tegnér (1782-1846), based on an Old Icelandic saga.

According to the Lay of Gudrun, the poet had more magic power than any priest. Like the poet-savior Orpheus, he could charm birds and beasts with his music, and even raise the dead. His songs were better liked than clerical sermons:

Whate'er he might be singing, to no one seemed it long;
Forgotten in the minster were priest and choral song,
Church bells no longer sounded so sweetly as before,
And every one who heard him longed for the minstrel sore.[5]

Minstrels' ballads have been praised as works that seem "to have looked deepest into the human heart," excluding their occasional Christian moralizing which is always "manifestly a later addition." Steenstrup calls attention "to what small degree the ecclesiastical, or the strictly Catholic, element . . . gets leave to appear. . . . [T]he religious, the ecclesiastical, the Catholic element has been clapped on later, and . . . it is a disturbing and jarring force."[6] The bards invoked not God but Erda—Mother Earth—and the Goddess Minne, whose name was a synonym for Love.[7]

To churchmen, love was "nothing." To play at a game of chance "for love" was to play for nothing.[8] The expression "for love or money" began with this distinction between pagan and Christian motivations. The troubadours and minnesingers acted for *Minnedienst,* the "service of love."[9] Of course, donations were always acceptable.

The cult of Love rarely included marriage, which was usually arranged by the couple's elders, for economic reasons. Ladies of the Courts of Love in southern France said true love couldn't exist between married people. True love could exist only between a lady and her chosen knight, who was expected to prove "gallantry" in combat before he could be a "gallant," or lover. Ladies told their suitors, "It is necessary that for love of me you should do deeds of chivalry. . . . I will give you all my love as soon as I have seen you fight your first joust." *Chansons de gestes* advised warriors to strike their enemies squarely in the bowels, so as to win the love of "the most beautiful ladies of the court."[10]

Chansons de gestes
Old French epic poetry of the 11th to 13th centuries.

This was a curiously mammalian-biological system, in which women watched men in combat and rewarded the winners with sexual favors. Bishop Jacques of Vitry complained that knights fought in tournaments only to gain "the favors of the shameless women whose tokens they wear." The monk Gildas described the barbarian aristocracy as "addicted to vice, adulterous, and enemies of God."[11]

Old ballads and romances depict a society in which men constantly showed off to excite women's admiration, almost like male birds and beasts displaying themselves to females. Norse skalds said everything men did was to impress the ladies. When women were watching, they spurred their horses to go faster, so "readily will look the ladies and lasses, as we are passing."[12] Geoffrey of Monmouth said the noble women were celebrated for their wit, and "esteemed none worthy of their love, but such as had given proof of their valor in three several battles."[13]

There arose a corollary belief that no man could fight well unless inspired by the promise of his lady-love. Tristan said a man couldn't be a warrior unless he was a lover. Lancelot became invincible only because Elaine gave him her sexual-symbolic love-token, a red silk sleeve as "sheath" for his "sword." Minnesinger Wolfram von Eschenbach wrote of the love-trance that made a knight invincible, like a *berserker.* Wolfram's Parsifal asserted that for every kind of spiritual aid, including courage in battle, "it is better to trust a woman than God."[14]

Wolfram von Eschenbach Highly influential 13th-century author of such poetic epics as *Willehalm, Titurel, Parzival,* and various *Tagelieder.*

This Germanic *Parsifal* incorporated no Christian ceremony but was written as if the church didn't exist. Parsifal's prayers were addressed to his lady, who magically protected him in battle and gave him success as if she were a sacred agent of the ancient Lady of Victory. He fought in a love-trance of communion with her spirit, which made him virtually superhuman.[15]

This pagan knight fought his own *alter ego,* a Christian knight who fell back before the onslaught of the "heathen man" made invincible by his lady's love. "The heathen never wearied of love; his heart, therefore, was great in combat." When he cried the name of his queen's dwelling place, "his battle strength increased."[16]

For a while, certain sects of warriors undertook to defend the beleaguered rights of women, in the name of the Goddess. From this period dated romantic stories of knights who rescued "castles of women" from robber barons who had seized their property. About the 12th century, when the church began to arm its laws with the teeth of the Inquisition, emphasis shifted from defense of women to defense of the church. Sir Parsifal, or **Perceval**, presented a typical example of the pagan hero who finally turned Christian and renounced women.

At first he was a champion of Love; but later he was "purified," and described by an ecclesiastical writer as "one of the men of the world at that time which most believed in our Lord Jesus Christ, for in those days there were but few folks who believed in God perfectly." Perceval set out to rescue "a gentlewoman which is disherited," but changed his allegiance in mid-adventure, and renounced her as a seductress and witch.[17]

Romantic literature reveals continual conflict between the minstrel's love-oriented philosophy and the church's anti-love attitude. Churchmen said lovers became "vile" by forgetting God and making the beloved woman a divinity. One priest said the bards "sinfully love women, whom they make into deities," and this was exactly the same as loving Satan.[18] Professor Huizinga noted that "from the side of religion, maledictions were poured upon love in all its aspects." Yet the poets insisted that "Love was a divine visitation, quelling mere animal lust. . . . The lover, whose heart was rendered gentle by the discipline of his lady, was initiate to a sphere of exalted realizations that no one who had experienced such could possibly identify (as the church identified them) with sin."[19]

Johann Huizinga (1872-1945) Dutch historian, author of *The Waning of the Middle Ages* (1924), professor of history at Groningen and Leiden University until he was arrested by the Nazis in 1942.

Modern scholars have struggled to define the later stages of the courtly-love movement, when the Meistersinger school was founded by men with the title of Frauenlob, "Lover of Women." The obvious spirituality of the movement led some to interpret it as a sentimental asceticism inspired by adoration of the virgin Mary. Yet some of the minstrels' poetry was intensely—even grossly—erotic, focused on a real female body, not an ethereal vision. Scholars failed to understand this combination of spirituality and carnality because they failed to discover its historical root: the penetration of Europe by yet another wave of Tantric sex-worship.

The most mysterious element in courtly love was the secret technique of lovemaking known as drudaria, druerie, or *karezza.* It can only have been a western version of Tantric *maithuna,* the sacrament of *coitus reservatus.* This alone can explain its blend of erotic and spiritual ecstasy. Significantly, one of the heroes of courtly love most revered as a model for poets was Tristan, who had reversed his name and called himself Tantris for the secret understanding of his lady-love.[20] See **Tantrism**.

The poets kept their secret but obliquely referred to it when defending themselves against charges of lechery. They claimed their aim was not selfish pleasure but only gratification of the lady. Montanhagol wrote, "A lover should on no account desire what would dishonor his lady-love," probably meaning an unwelcome pregnancy. "Desire never had any power over me to make me wish her to whom I have given myself aught that should not be. I would not reckon that a pleasure which might debase her." Another poet said, "A true lover must seek the interest of his beloved a hundred times more than his own."[21]

Guilhem Montanhagol Provençal troubadour who took the lead in raising ideals of romantic love in Renaissance poetry.

The poets were angered by certain ignorant men who copied courtly-love behavior without understanding its basis. Men who pursued women for their own sexual satisfaction were regarded as vulgar boors who "confounded everything by their behavior, which is no better than that of dogs." Men who didn't understand the true initiation of love "adopted other maxims, which bring about shame." Marcabru said scornfully, "If they call that drudaria, they lie." Arnaud Daniel claimed to have renounced the love of wealthy women, who knew only pleasures of the shameful sort. "From such love as moves me are debarred those disloyal seekers of women who destroy courtliness."[22] Courtliness was synonymous with *Minnedienst,* the service of women who knew how to be served.[23]

Where did the bards learn of *maithuna?* Probably from several sources. The gypsies practiced it, and gypsies infiltrated Europe from at least the 11th century on.[24] Even more influential was the Moorish-Saracen tradition emanating from Spain and the Middle East after the crusades. Yoni-worship was preserved by such sects as the Sufis, whose "Sufi Way" involved a sexual initiation by a *fravashi,* an occult love-priestess like the Tantric shakti. Sufi sages taught that a man can find spiritual fulfillment only in love, realizing Woman as "a ray of deity." The word Sufi contained "in enciphered form, the concept of Love." Deciphered, it reduced by the Arabic numerological system to three letters: FUQ, meaning "that which is transcendent."[25]

Under the same language system, the title of a singer was Ta Ra B, which picked up the Spanish suffix -ador and became "troubadour." Thus the troubadours' worship of Love was a synthesis of pagan and Oriental themes, founded on the idea of Woman as the true source of benevolence. Troubadour Bernard de Ventadorn wrote to his beloved: "Noble lady, nothing do I ask of thee but that thou shouldst take me for thy servant. I would serve as one serves a good lord, whatever reward I might gain. Behold, I am at thy command: sincere and humble, gay and courteous. Neither bear nor lion art thou, to kill me, as I here to thee surrender."[26] Gentleness and sensuality reigned together in the mythical fairyland visited by Aucassin, a French romantic hero based on the Arabic "sultan of love," Al-Kasim.[27]

Minnesingers worshipped their Goddess Minne as Love, but mocked the syncretism of Christian dogmas. Gottfried von Strassburg wrote: "The very virtuous Christ is as yielding as a wind-blown sleeve; he adapts himself and goes along whatever way he is pressed, as readily and easily as anyone could ask."[28] Wolfram von Eschenbach parodied the pope as a eunuch named Clinschor ("Clergyman") who offered his services to the devil.[29] Walther von der Vogelweide reprimanded the clergy for their condemnation of love:

Whoever says that Love is sin,
Let him consider first and well:
Right many virtues lodge therein
With which we all, by rights, should dwell.[30]

Minnesinger Konrad of Megenburg wrote a scathing satire which he presented in the form of a debate between Lady Church (Mary-Ecclesia) and her servants, the clergy, who only pretended to serve her, but actually served her rival, Lady Avarice-and-Vainglory.

Marcabru, or Marcabrun One of the earliest Provençal troubadours, of whose work about 40 pieces survive, dated ca. 1135-1148.

Gottfried von Strassburg One of the greatest medieval German poets, author of the epic *Tristan und Isolde* (early 13th century) and many lyric poems.

Walther von der Vogelweide (ca. 1170-1230) Great German lyric poet, self-described as a Minnesinger, author of many love poems, protégé of several Swabian and Thuringian princes.

Konrad von Megenburg German anti-papal imperialist scholar, author of *Planctus Ecclesie in Germaniam* (1337) and *De translatione Romani Imperii* (1354).

Lady Church denounced her servants in most unladylike terms and called their real mistress " a whore, a wretched nurse of vice, a superlative evil, a hypocrite."[31]

Out of the courtly-love movement came one of the oddest of Christian pseudo-saints: St. **Dymphna**, a corruption of the romantic poet's name for his lady-love, *madonna* or *ma dompna,* "my mistress, my lady." As an erstwhile patron of the moon-madness that sent the poet into his love-trance, she is still advertised today as a healer of "emotional distress."[32]

Language and metaphors of romance in general point to disguised heretical allegories, which also survived in folklore and pagan custom, drama, children's games, and witchcraft.

1. Briffault 3, 451. 2. Briffault 3, 446–48. 3. Guerber, L.M.A., 121. 4. Guerber, L.M.A., 271, 138. 5. Guerber, L.M.A., 26. 6. Steenstrup, 188, 199, 207. 7. Turville-Petre, 251. 8. Hazlitt, 371. 9. Jung & von Franz, 75. 10. Briffault 3, 409–412, 428. 11. Briffault 3, 384, 417. 12. Hollander, 152. 13. de Riencourt, 223. 14. Campbell, C.M., 462. 15. Campbell, C.M., 476–77. 16. Campbell, C.M., 558. 17. Malory 2, 199, 204. 18. Briffault 3, 490, 494. 19. Campbell, Oc.M., 509. 20. Guerber, L.M.A., 238. 21. Briffault 3, 489. 22. Briffault 3, 482–90. 23. Jung & von Franz, 75. 24. Derlon, 159. 25. Shah, 29, 121, 135, 176. 26. Campbell, C.M., 62, 179. 27. Murstein, 150. 28. Campbell, F.W.G., 216. 29. Campbell, C.M., 512. 30. Campbell, C.M., 181. 31. Borchardt, 272. 32. Murstein, 150.

Romulus and Remus

Offspring of Rhea Silvia, nurslings of the Etruscan wolf bitch Lupa, these familiar twins were generally regarded as founders of Rome. Remus was killed by his jealous brother, in a myth that placed fratricide at the beginning of Roman patriarchy just as the myth of Cain and Abel placed fratricide at the beginning of Jewish patriarchy.[1]

According to legend, the followers of Romulus were all men, having no right to own land under the old matriarchal law, forced to marry Sabine property-owning women to acquire community standing and the *sanguis ac genus,* blood of the race, which was transmitted only on the female line.[2] Some said Romulus's men were criminals and outlaws who could not participate in the sacred succession of clans.[3] They had to abduct Sabine women, to establish *curiae* (clans); but each clan continued to carry the name of its original ancestress.[4] Roman writers claimed Romulus named the clans in honor of the Sabine women; but in fact the Latin clans had been named after their women for as long as anyone could remember. See **Motherhood**.

Romulus himself was a patriarchal invention based on an ancient feminine clan name: the Etruscan gens Romulia, the real founders of Rome.[5]

1. *Larousse,* 315. 2. Dumézil, 68. 3. Pepper & Wilcock, 83. 4. Briffault 1, 422, 427. 5. Carter, 22.

Rosalia, Saint

Patron saint of Palermo, a loosely Christianized Venus Rosalia, the pagan Goddess symbolized by the Holy Rose, a yonic symbol. The usual virgin martyr myth was invented for Rosalia, but not even her bones were real. The osteologist Buckland studied Rosalia's relics and found them to be the bones of a goat.[1] Nevertheless, even after this discovery, the goat's bones retained an undiminished power to perform healing miracles that had been the speciality of Rosalia's shrine for many centuries.

1. White 2, 29.

Rosary

Dominicans pretended that the rosary began with St. Dominic's "beatific vision" at the church of St. Sabina in Rome. Actually, Christians copied the rosary from eastern pagans. Its real origin was the Hindu *japamala,* "rose-chaplet," called the Rosary of the Mantras worn by Kali Ma. Its alternately red and white beads symbolized her Mother and Virgin forms (see **Gunas**). The *Rosary Upanishad* said the sounds of her mantras were white, the bead-touchings were red.[1] Arab poets viewed both white and red roses as emblems of the female principle, and called their rosaries *wardija,* "rose-garden." The same word in Latin, *rosarium,* described early rosaries associated solely with the cult of the virgin Mary up to the 14th century. The Litany of Loreto calls Mary "Queen of the Most Holy Rosary." The German term *Rosenkranz,* "rose-wreath," was sometimes shortened to *Kranzlein,* "little wreath," a symbol of virginity or "flower of maidenhead."[2] In the east, the flower-wreath represented sacred marriage, circling the "head" of the phallic god.[3]

Like a portable prayer-wheel, the rosary was used everywhere to count repetitive prayers or mantras. Constant repetition of such verbal charms was believed to bring about blissful after-life, automatically. The *Book of the Dead* said the spoken formula of the rosary (in Egypt hung with an image of Horus) was "a protection upon earth, and it will secure for the deceased the affection of men, gods, and the Spirit-souls which are perfect. Moreover it acteth as a spell in Khert-Neter, but it must be recited by thee on behalf of the Osiris Ra, regularly and continually millions of times."[4]

Early Christians at first rejected rosaries and denied the efficacy of constantly repeated prayers counted on the beads. Jesus said, "When ye pray, use not vain repetitions, as the heathen do: for they think that they shall be heard for their much speaking" (Matthew 6:7). Despite this Gospel directive, however, Christians eventually adopted the heathen custom of "vain repetitions" along with the heathen rose-wreath

Upanishads Buddhist scriptures representing the final stage in Vedic thought, dealing with the philosophy known as Vedanta. The Katha Upanishad discusses transmigration of souls, the nature of eternal life, the doctrine of *maya,* and an account of a visit to Yama, Lord of the Dead.

Book of the Dead Common name for the collection of Egyptian funerary papyri written between 1500 and 1350 B.C., including Vignettes, Hymns, Chapters, and descriptive Rubrics. Among the best-preserved, and most typical, copies of the Theban Recension of the *Book of the Dead* is the much-studied Papyrus of Ani.

itself, relating both to their own version of the Great Mother just as the Hindus related them to Kali Ma. To this day, the user of the rosary appeals most often to Mary, imploring her to be present at his death, just as the Tantric sages implored Kali-Shakti.

Association of the rosary with death is still found in the archaic religion of Tibet, where rosaries sometimes had beads made of human skull bone, recalling the rosary of skulls worn by Kali the Destroyer. In a remarkable parallel, Christian rosaries were sometimes made of tiny skulls carved from bone or ivory. Many eastern rosaries had a retaining bead formed like a vase, said to give birth to the other beads. In the west, both the pagan Goddess and the virgin Mary—the primary object of rosary worship—were known as the Holy Vase.[5]

Mohammedan rosaries usually contained 99 beads, one for each of Allah's miracle-working names (see **Name**). Smaller rosaries were made of 33 beads, with 3 groups of 11 set apart by markers, probably in imitation of the Vedic tradition of 33 gods divided into 3 companies of 11 each.[6] Arabs sometimes called the rosary Gulistan, the Rose Garden, which was also the title of a mystical work by Sufi poet Saadi of Shiraz, a Goddess-worshipper of the 13th century A.D. Europe's heraldic "gules," meaning red, came from the Arabic word for "rose."[7]

1. Wilkins, 44, 194, 201. 2. Wilkins, 40, 42, 151. 3. *Larousse,* 335. 4. *Book of the Dead,* 567. 5. Wilkins, 45, 58. 6. Budge, A. T., 437. 7. Shah, 98.

Rose

The rosary was an instrument of worship of the Rose, which ancient Rome knew as the Flower of Venus, and the badge of her sacred prostitutes.[1] Things spoken "under the rose" (*sub rosa*) were part of Venus's sexual mysteries, not to be revealed to the uninitiated.[2] The red rose represented full-blown maternal sexuality; the white rose or lily was a sign of the Virgin Goddess. Christians transferred both of these symbolic flowers to the virgin Mary and called her the Holy Rose.

Rose windows in Gothic cathedrals faced west, the direction of the matriarchal paradise, and were primarily dedicated to Mary as the female symbol opposing the male cross in the eastern apse. At Chartres, the window called Rose of France showed "in its center the Virgin in her majesty. . . . Round her in a circle, are twelve medallions; four containing doves; four six-winged angels or Thrones; four angels of a lower order, but all symbolizing the gifts and endowments of the Queen of Heaven." Beneath, the Marian number of five windows centered on Mary's mother, "the greatest central figure, the tallest and most commanding in the whole church."[3]

Five was the Marian number because it was the number of petals in the rose, and also in the apple blossom—another virginity-symbol—

giving rise to the five lobes of the mature apple, the corresponding symbol of motherhood, fruition, regeneration, and eternal life. Five was considered "proper to Marian devotion" because Rose-Mary was the reincarnation of Apple-Eve. Christian mystical art showed apples and roses growing together on the Tree of Life in Mary's "enclosed garden" of virginity.

The fivefold rose and apple were also related to numerous pre-Christian images of the Goddess, the witches' pentacle, the five-pointed Star of Ishtar, and the Egyptian symbol of the uterine underworld and cyclic rebirth. Mysteries of the Rose belonged to Aphrodite, according to the poet Nossis: "Anyone the Cyprian does not love, knows not what flowers her roses are." Aphrodite was represented by a Rose-Mary plant, named for her as *rosmarina,* the Dew of the Sea.[4]

In the great age of cathedral-building, when Mary was worshipped as a Goddess in her "Palaces of the Queen of Heaven" or *Notre-Dames,* she was often addressed as the Rose, Rose-bush, Rose-garland, Rose-garden, Wreath of Roses, Mystic Rose, or Queen of the Most Holy Rose-garden.[5] The church, the garden, and Mary's body were all mystically one; for she was Lady Ecclesia, the Church, as well as "the pure womb of regeneration." Like a pagan temple, the Gothic cathedral represented the body of the Goddess who was also the universe, containing the essence of male godhood within herself. This was largely forgotten after the passing of the Gothic period. In later centuries, "Gothic" became an epithet of contempt, synonymous with "barbarous." The symbolism of the Palaces of the Queen of Heaven was no longer understood. By the 18th century, its secrets were as obscure as the crypto-erotic art of the temples of India.[6]

In fact it was in India that the Great Mother, whose body was the temple, was first addressed as Holy Rose.[7] The "Flower of the Goddess" was the scarlet China rose.[8] This was sometimes identified with the mystic Kula flower, source of a virgin's menstrual blood, representing the life of her future children and her bond of union with the past maternal spirit of her clan.[9]

The eastern World Tree was often envisioned as a family rose-tree, a female Tree of Life and Immortality. In central Asia the tree was called Woman, the Wellspring, Milk, Animals, Fruits. "The Cosmic Tree always presents itself as the very reservoir of life and the master of destinies." Mongols knew the tree as Zambu, whose roots plunge to the base of Mount Sumer; it is the Mother-tree whose fruits feed the gods.[10] Zambu was undoubtedly the same as the Hindu paradise, Jambu Island, home of the cosmic Rose-Apple tree. The island was shaped like a yoni. In its "diamond seat" (a symbolic clitoris), one could be reborn as a human being with keen intelligence.[11]

Judeo-Christian tradition associated this tree of ancestors with a male Tree of Life (genitalia), regarding male ancestry as the only important kind. The genealogy of Christ was depicted in medieval art as a tree-phallus rising from the loins of a recumbent Jesse, with its flowers and fruit surrounding the figures of David, Mary, and Jesus. Still, mystics generally assigned feminine gender to the rose-tree, rose-garden, rose-wreath, etc., fully realizing that these were genital symbols. The medieval scholar Pierre Col said the Gospel of Luke represented the Holy Rose as a sign of the vulva.[12]

Britain had a traditional Mummers' dance known as The Rose: five dancers formed a five-pointed star of swords over a victim, called the Fool, who was symbolically slain and resurrected with a mysterious elixir, the Golden Frosty Drop, or Dewdrop in the Rose. This was simply a western version of the Jewel in the Lotus: i.e., a seminal drop in the female flower. It is said the " 'garden' may symbolize the uterus, as 'scarlet flower' may signify the vulva." The Frosty Drop, or dew, signified the semen of the God reincarnating himself in the Goddess. The Bible says dew was a poetic synonym for semen (Song of Solomon 5:2). Meister Eckhart understood quite well the sexual significance of both dew and rose when he wrote, "And as in the morning the rose opens, receiving the dew from heaven and the sun, so Mary's soul did open and receive Christ the heavenly dew."[13]

The dance called The Rose seems to have been a pagan ritual so vital that it couldn't be suppressed. The accompanying chant was "ring-around-the-rose-wreath"; in German, *Ringel Ringel Rosenkranz;* in English, Ring-Around-A-Rosy.[14] The "pocket full of posies" in the nursery rhyme probably referred to the cave of flowers, an old symbol of the underground Fairyland. The final instruction, "All fall down," was the behest of Morgan the Grim Reaper, or Mother Death bringing an end to the fertility season. According to Danish folk custom, roses decorated sacred groves for the dances of Midsummer Eve, which had to be guarded by armed men against possible intruders:

Midsummer night upon the sward,
Knights and squires are standing guard;
In the grove a knightly dance they tread
With torches and garlands of roses red.[15]

The Rose was likened not only to Mary but to other surviving forms of the pagan Goddess. As Spenser's Faerie Queene she had a Bower of Bliss signifying her sexual nature, where the central holy of holies was the Rose of Love.[16] Medieval myths of Lady Briar Rose pictured the Virgin as a rose in the midst of a thorn bush, a sexual image established long ago by the poet Sedulius:

As blooms among the thorns the lovely rose, herself without a thorn,
The glory of the bush whose crown she is,
So, springing from the root of Eve, Mary the new Maiden
Atoned for the sin of that first Maiden long ago.[17]

No matter how consistently the Rose was assimilated to Mary, it was obviously a sexual symbol of Goddess-worship brought back to

Europe from Arabia with the returning crusaders.[18] Sufi mystics in Arabia wrote romantic-religious works centering on the rosary and the Rose. Fariduddin Attar's *Parliament of the Birds* explained the symbol in the words of the "passionate nightingale":

> *I know the secrets of love. Throughout the night I give my love call. . . . It is I who set the Rose in motion, and move the hearts of lovers. Continuously I teach new mysteries. . . . When the Rose returns to the world in Summer, I open my heart to joy. My secrets are not known to all but the Rose knows them. I think of nothing but the Rose; I wish nothing but the ruby Rose. . . . Can the nightingale live but one night without the Beloved?*[19]

This Eros-nightingale reappeared in European romances as the Spirit of the Rose, or a "devil" named Rosier in the 17th century. According to the exorcist Father Sebastien Michaelis, the devil Rosier whispers sweet words that tempt men to fall in love. Rosier's heavenly adversary was St. Basil, "who would not listen to amorous and enchanting language."[20] Still later, the same devil became the hero of the classical ballet *Le Spectre de la Rose* in which he tempts a young girl to fall in love.

Sometimes the male Spirit of the Rose was a briar rose with "pricking" thorns. "Pricking flesh to acquire blood artificially is the only way that men can 'produce' it. In the European romantic legend of two heterosexual lovers, the female red rose is paired with the male briar, or 'prick.' *Prick,* when used as a slang, taboo name for the penis, is a descriptive-magical term for access-to-power. . . . The briar is the male rose."[21]

1. Wilkins, 108, 136. 2. Hazlitt, 527. 3. Campbell, M.I., 235. 4. Wilkins, 108, 110, 133. 5. Wilkins, 93, 106. 6. de Riencourt, 261. 7. Wilkins, 44. 8. Avalon, 203. 9. *Mahanirvanatantra,* 88. 10. Eliade, S., 271. 11. Tatz & Kent, 37, 84. 12. Tuchman, 481. 13. Wilkins, 102, 113–14, 124. 14. Wilkins, 81. 15. Steenstrup, 12. 16. Wilkins, 128. 17. Wilkins, 116. 18. Goodrich, 103. 19. Shah, 108. 20. Robbins, 129. 21. Spretnak, 274.

Rudra

Pre-Vedic "red god," a primitive form of Shiva, sometimes known as The Howler.[1] Both his redness and his howling link him with the death by flaying of the sacrificial beings called Maruts, of whom he was the founding ancestor. The Maruts became similar flayed gods or red gods in the west—e.g. **Mars** the red god, and his Phrygian counterpart Marsyas, the flayed satyr, hung on a pine tree and sacrificed to Apollo. Satyrs were goat gods, and goats were typical victims of flaying-sacrifices for atonement in Rome (e.g., the Lupercalia), Phrygia, Syria, and Mesopotamia.

Rudra was also called Tryambaka, "He Who Belongs to Three Mother Goddesses."[2] Like Shiva after him, he seems to have been offered to the original female trinity. Like Shiva also, he merged with her—or them—and became known as an androgynous Lord Who is Half Woman.[3]

His name passed into Latin as "rude," meaning a primitive deity of wild animals and woodlands, a typical satyr.[4] Thus it might be said that Rudra was the prototype of all the primitive Aryan gods of fertility and death.

1. O'Flaherty, 357. 2. *Larousse*, 342. 3. O'Flaherty, 298. 4. Dumézil, 418.

Runes

The runic alphabet seems to have been invented by the "wise-women" of northern Europe. Runic letters appear first in the hands of the Goddess Idun, keeper of the gods' magic apples of immortality. She gave runes to her consort Bragi by engraving them on his tongue; thus he acquired the magic of words and became the first wizard-king of skaldic poetry.

Odin received knowledge of the runes by his self-sacrifice, hanging on the gallows-tree Yggdrasil for nine nights—that is, for a *noínden,* the traditional lying-in period for a woman in childbirth. In the old myths, self-sacrifice or suicide was often demanded as the price of male acquisition of feminine wisdom. This also meant a journey to paradise (Fairyland), and godlike immortality.

Odin died to acquire the runes for men; but men were expected to imitate his sacrifice, as Christian martyrs imitated that of Christ. If a Norse hero couldn't die in battle, which would automatically make him a son of Odin, then he could commit a kind of hara-kiri by carving the runes in his own flesh and bleeding to death.[1] In this manner Sigurd Ring summoned the Valkyries to take him to Valhölle: "Bravely he slashes Odin's red letters, blood-runes of heroes, on arm and breast."[2]

The festal day of a hero's death thus became a "red-letter day," marked in red on runic calendars, as modern calendars still print Sundays and holidays in red. Special sacrificial runes called *geirs-odd* were recommended for ceremonial suicide. These enabled the hero to compose his own death-song in his final "inspiration" (literally, "breath"). Skaldic tradition associated poetry with blood. The Mead of the Poets was also called the Sea of Odin's Breast, meaning the blood that flowed from his breast when he was pierced on the Rood.

The nursery-rhyme figure of slain Cock Robin Redbreast descended from the folklore of the *geirs-odd.* **Robin** was the God of the Witches, frequently identified with Odin, sacrificed in a sacred grove to Marian the Virgin, whom the Northmen called Maerin and worshipped with blood sacrifices at Trondheim as late as the 11th century.[3] Robin Redbreast appeared as a human martyr in an old Danish ballad. He won the love of a bird-maiden (Valkyrie) by cutting slices of flesh from his breast for her, and she took him to paradise. "The youth has now got his reward, safely has he won from harm; at night he sleeps full joyously within his truelove's arms."[4]

The death song composed by Ragnar Lodbrok for himself presents a pagan version of a runic epitaph, supposed to be sung by the bleeding man with his final breath, like the song of a dying swan; indeed, runes and swan-princes were often associated. Ragnar sang, with a certain gallantry:

Cease, my strain! I hear a voice
From realms where martial souls rejoice;
I hear the maids of slaughter call,
Who bid me hence to Odin's hall:
High seated in their blest abodes
I soon shall quaff the drink of gods.
The hours of life have glided by;
I fall, but smiling shall I die.[5]

Knowing the runes of heathen alphabets were connected with death charms and mysterious curses, Christians came to regard the runes as devilish. They believed witches could cause death by "casting the runes." But the original purpose of casting runes was divination, in a system not essentially different from casting yarrow stalks of the I Ching, or casting "the lot of rods" in medieval churches, or casting dice as magic knucklebones, or shuffling Tarot cards. The runes were scratched on wooden shingles or chips, like dice, and these were thrown in certain patterns. The process of interpreting them was *raedan,* "reading"; the result was *raedels* or "riddles." In old-fashioned usage, "reading" meant to solve a riddle.[6] From the runes came such English construction as "read me this riddle," and the use of "reading" to mean fortune-telling.

1. Branston, 106. 2. Guerber, L.M.A., 279. 3. Turville-Petre, 39, 91.
4. Steenstrup, 54. 5. Guerber, L.M.A., 279. 6. Funk, 27.

Rusalki

Russian water witches and psychopomps, named after Mother Russia; formerly her priestesses of rivers and springs. Rusalki were feared as sirens who could lure men to a watery grave. Yet their old function as fertility-spirits was not forgotten. During Rusalki Week at the beginning of summer, they would emerge from the waters by moonlight and dance. Peasants said "where the Rusalki trod when dancing, there the grass grew thicker and the wheat more abundant."[1] They were the same as the Wilis, Vilas, or **Valkyries.**

1. *Larousse,* 293.

SHIVA, oldest of the Vedic trinity that includes Brahma and Vishnu. He was god of yoga, death, cattle, dance, the moon, and all the abstract forces like beneficence and destruction. But universal energy he could represent only with the help of his female counterpart, Shakti. Shiva dances in a circle of flames representing the cosmos. Bronze; India, Chola period, 11th to 12th century.

The Great Goddess Hathor became the winged, usually lion-headed SPHINX to confound humans with her famous riddle. Oedipus spoiled her fun by telling her the answer and then throwing her out of Thebes. The painting, showing them before the trouble started, is by Gustave Moreau, 1864.

Sa

Egyptian word for the holy blood of Isis, which made pharaohs and other selected heroes immortal; counterpart of the Hindu *soma,* the divine fluid of sovereignty and eternal life, manifested in many ways, but basically derived from the Goddess's **menstrual blood**. As the Egyptian Great Mother's "wise blood," *sa* was said to contain the spirit of all intelligence.[1]

1. Budge, G.E. 2, 298.

Sabazius

Phrygian serpent god identified with Attis, with Dionysus, and in the first century B.C. with the Jewish Jehovah.[1] Plutarch said worshippers of the Hebrew God in Jerusalem called him also by the name of Sabbi.[2] Jews living in Asia Minor said their Jehovah was another form of Zeus Sabazius.[3]

Phrygians said the ancestor of their tribes was a great serpent who lived in a Tree of Life in the primal garden; therefore they were Ophiogeneis, "Snake-born people."[4] Such pagan traditions led to the Gnostic sects' confusion of Jehovah with the serpent in the garden of Eden; sometimes one was the enemy of mankind, sometimes the other (see **Gnosticism**).

Some have suggested that the nocturnal rites of Sabazius gave rise to the name of the Sabbat or Sabbath, for both Christians and pagans (e.g. the "witches' sabbat"), but there were also other suggested origins for this lunar festival. Sabazius seems to have been just another form of the ubiquitous serpent-deity who was the first companion of the Great Mother of the Gods.

1. Graves, W.G., 366–68. 2. Knight, S.L., 156. 3. Enslin, C.B., 91. 4. J.E. Harrison, 129.

Sabbat, Witches'

Some derive "sabbat" from the Moorish *zabat,* "an occasion of power," at which Berber descendants of north African "Amazons" still perform sacred dances in groups of 13—the traditional number of the witches' coven—for the 13 annual lunations.[1]

The European sabbat or festival was fabricated largely by judges of the Inquisition during the 14th and 15th centuries, on a foundation of pagan precedents. Churchmen said witches held four Great Sabbats a year "in derision of the four annual festivals of the Church"; but the church had copied these from the pagans in the first place.[2] They were: (1) Candlemas Eve; (2) May Eve, or Walpurgisnacht; (3) Lammas Eve; and (4) Halloween. Some lists included Midsummer (the Feast of

St. John) and the solstitial festival on December 21 (the Feast of St. Thomas).[3]

Details were drawn from classical descriptions of Roman fertility festivals, such as the Bacchanalia, Saturnalia, Lupercalia, etc. At the ancient ceremony of purification for the New Year, in the Lupercal grotto where Lupa the She-Wolf was said to have suckled Romulus and Remus, he-goats were sacrificed and youths were touched with the blood; priests in raw goatskins struck women's hands with strips of goatskin as a fertility charm; men and women exchanged clothing and engaged in orgiastic sex. Late in the 5th century, this Lupercalia was adopted into the Christian calendar and renamed the Feast of Purification of the Virgin.[4]

Other pagan practices supposedly incorporated into the witches' sabbat included widdershins (counterclockwise) dancing in a ring, in honor of the Moon-goddess; wearing masks; jumping over fires; sacrificial feasting; worshipping trees, springs, and sacred stones; and making lewd jokes and horseplay in a carnival atmosphere. Indeed the Carnival, or Feast of Fools, descended from pagan holidays when the social order was temporarily reversed, and everything was done backward, a prototype of the "reverse Christianity" of the Black Mass. The Saturnalia was still kept by medieval Christians in this manner:

> *The priests of a church elected a bishop of fools, who came in full pomp, placing himself in the episcopal seat in the choir. High mass then began; all the ecclesiastics assisted, their faces smeared with blacking, or covered with a hideous or ridiculous mask. During the course of the celebration, some of them, dressed like mountebanks or in women's clothes, danced in the middle of the choir, singing clownish or obscene songs. Others ate sausages or puddings from the altar, played at cards or at dice in front of the officiating priest, incensed him with the censer, or, burning old shoes, made him breathe the smoke.*[5]

Such carnival clownishness was "simply the last form which the Priapeia and Liberalia assumed in Western Europe, and in its various details all the incidents of those great and licentious orgies of the Romans were reproduced."[6] However, certain authorities came to perceive such revels as profoundly evil. In 1445 the Paris Faculty of Theology called for reform, writing to the French bishops a puritanically shocked description of pre-Lenten customs: "Priests and clerks may be seen wearing masks and monstrous visages at the hours of office. They dance in the choir dressed as women, panders or minstrels. They sing wanton songs. They eat black puddings at the horn of the altar while the celebrant is saying Mass. They play at dice there. They cense with stinking smoke from the soles of old shoes. They run and leap through the church, without a blush at their own shame."[7]

Copies of letters like this one, drawn from the archives, surely gave the Inquisition's judges many ideas for details of the Sabbat that they put in the mouths of their victims, and confirmed by torture. With only minimal imagination, a judge could reverse any ordinary church service and accuse his victim of kissing the devil's anus (instead of the bishop's ring), eating children's corpses and drinking menstrual blood (instead of bread and wine), saying the prayers backward, making the sign of the cross with the left foot instead of the right hand, addressing subterranean deities instead of celestial ones, and so on.

Weekly sabbats were supposed to be held on Friday, once a lunar "Eve" of the original sabbath, the day of Saturn or of Zeus Sabazius. Friday was the day sacred to Venus-Freya, and after sunset it was the Jews' sabbath day, both of which made it a bad or unlucky day in Christian opinion. Friday the 13th was especially ill-favored.

1. Ravensdale & Morgan, 153; Shah, 210. 2. Knight, D.W.P., 225. 3. Robbins, 415. 4. *Larousse,* 208. 5. Crawley, 333. 6. Knight, D.W.P., 207. 7. Miles, 304.

Saci

"Power," title of the Hindu Goddess as the wife of Indra, who received his essence of divinity from her.[1] She was probably related to the Egyptian Goddess as Sakhmis or Sekhmet, "the Powerful One," one of the titles of Hathor as the blood-drinking battle-goddess or divine lioness, Lady of Victory.[2] The name Saci or Saki was also applied to the Arabic spirit of the Cupbearer who gave gods and men the wine of life, as Indra received the Goddess's blood-wine of sovereignty.

1. O'Flaherty, 351. 2. *Larousse,* 36.

Sacred

Derivation of Latin *sacer,* which meant "untouchable" in the dual sense of both holy and unclean. A *sacer* person or thing was set aside for a divine purpose; it was taboo, dedicated to the other world, shunned by ordinary folk because of its dangerous charge of spiritual *mana.* A case in point is the biblical story of Uzzah, who dared to seize the ark of the covenant to keep it from falling off its oxcart. Though Uzzah's intentions were entirely honorable, God struck him dead for touching the *sacer* object (2 Samuel 6:3). Priests knew a special insulating charm whereby they could approach the Holy of Holies without deadly risk: "When they go into the tabernacle of the congregation, they shall wash with water, that they die not" (Exodus 30:20). This same insulating charm was used throughout the centuries in Catholic churches, where people dipped their fingers in the stoup of holy water and made a self-protective sign of the cross.

The biblical word "unclean" also meant *sacer.* Menstrual blood and parturient women were "unclean" because filled with mysterious, dangerous magic (Leviticus 15). Sacrificial victims, set aside for consumption by the gods, were *sacer.* Certain animals were "unclean" except when eaten on ceremonial occasions, like the sacred bulls of Egypt and the pigs of Syria, Lebanon, and Palestine. Lucian said the pigs kept in the temple at Hierapolis were taboo in the typical dualistic sense, both "unclean" and sacred.[1] Simple people everywhere still demonstrate fear in the presence of whatever they consider sacred: the common emotion Coleridge called "holy dread."

1. Crawley 1, 114.

Sacrifice

Human or animal, the sacrificial victims of ancient cultures were almost invariably male. Worshippers of Shiva sacrificed only male animals; the god himself ordered that female animals must never be slain.[1] Males were expendable, for there were always too many for a proper breeding stock.

The same was true even of human sacrifices, which were men, not women. "The fertility of a group is determined by the number of its adult women, rather than by its adult men."[2] Therefore male blood only was poured out on the earliest altars, in imitation of the female blood that gave "life." That is why totemic animal-ancestors were more often paternal than maternal. The animals' blood and flesh, ingested by women, was thought to beget human offspring; and the rule was "Whatever is killed becomes father."[3] The victim was also god, and king.

Amazonian Sacae or Scythians founded the Sacaea festivals of Babylon, where condemned criminals died as sacrificial surrogates for the king, to mitigate the earlier custom of king-killing. The chosen victim was a sacred king, identified with the real king in every possible way. He wore the king's robes, sat on the king's throne, lay with the royal concubines, wielded the scepter. After five days he was stripped, scourged, then hanged or impaled "between heaven and earth," in a prototype of the crucifixion ceremony later extended to sacred kings of the Jews.[4] The object of scourging and piercing was to make the pseudo-king shed tears and blood for fertility magic.[5] Babylonian scriptures said, "If the king does not weep when struck, the omen is bad for the year."[6] The king or pseudo-king "became God" as soon as he was dead. He ascended into heaven and united himself with the Heavenly Father, i.e., the original totem father, or first victim.[7] Probably the promise of apotheosis and privileged immortality induced victims to accept death willingly, even as the same kind of promise attracted Christian martyrs.

When ritual murder of kings or human king-surrogates came to be considered crude and uncivilized, then animal victims took their place. Ceremonies were invented to identify the animal with the man. The Egyptians, for instance, "put off their dead with counterfeits, offered an animal to their gods instead of a man, but they symbolized their intended act by marking the creature to be slain with a seal bearing the image of a man bound and kneeling, with a sword at his throat."[8]

Pigs were often set aside as *sacer* victims in Egypt, India, and the Middle East, which explains why their flesh was taboo to the Jews. The sacrificial boar-god Vishnu had many western counterparts, such as Ares, the boarskin-clad consort of Aphrodite, whose children Phobos (Fear), Deimos (Horror), and Harmonia (Peace) may have represented the three stages of the sacred drama—from the victim's point of view.[9]

Meat was not to be wasted, so early theologians were anxious to invent ways to pretend the sacrifice was politely offered to the deity, while they actually kept it for their own consumption. The usual method was to offer the deity only inedible portions of the animal, or portions that couldn't be readily collected and used, such as blood. "Kosher killing," draining the blood from a sacrificed animal, was not a Jewish idea. It was a common Oriental method of offering the animal's blood to the Great Earth Mother while the worshipper kept the meat for himself.[10] The Jews, like the Hindus, taught that the animal's soul was in its blood (Leviticus 17:11).

Greeks assumed their gods resented being deprived of the best part of the sacrifice, but they avoided guilt by blaming Zeus's ancient rival, the titan Prometheus. When the first sacrificial bull was butchered, Prometheus sorted it into a portion of bones concealed under fat, and another portion of meat hidden under the entrails, and invited Zeus to choose his portion on behalf of all the gods. Zeus chose the fat, and later raged helplessly when he found he had been tricked.[11] But this became the standard fare for the gods, even Yahweh: "the fat of the beast, of which men offer an offering made by fire unto the Lord" (Leviticus 7:25).

Jews were even more parsimonious with their offerings than the Greeks. Sometimes Yahweh didn't even get the fat of the beast. All he got was a smell of it. Levite priests legalized the "wave offering," which meant the goodies were waved in front of the altar, then eaten by the priests: "the breast may be waved for a wave offering before the Lord . . . but the breast shall be Aaron's and his sons'" (Leviticus 7:30-31). The Jews however did retain a custom of human sacrifice, for special occasions, longer than any other people in the sphere of influence of the Roman empire.[12] Out of this tradition arose the figure of the dying *Christos* in Jerusalem.

Concerning the biblical concept of sacrifice, E.C. Stanton wrote: "The people have always been deluded with the idea that what they gave to the church and the priesthood was given unto the Lord, as if the maker of the universe needed anything at our hands. How incongruous the idea of an Infinite being who made all the planets and the inhabitants thereof commanding his creatures to kill and burn animals for offerings to him. It is truly pitiful to see the deceptions that have been played upon the people in all ages and countries by the priests in the name of religion."[13]

1. *Mahanirvanatantra,* 103. 2. M. Harris, 39. 3. Campbell, P.M., 129. 4. H. Smith, 135. 5. Frazer, G.B., 328. 6. Stone, 143. 7. Frazer, G.B., 513. 8. Elworthy, 82. 9. Graves, G.M. 1, 67. 10. Neumann, G.M., 152. 11. Graves, G.M. 1, 144. 12. Cumont, O.R.R.P., 119. 13. Stanton, 132.

Saga

Literally, "speaking-woman" or "sayer," an ancient Norse Goddess in Asgard.[1] Her name also meant a priestess learned in sacred poetry, charms, words of power. In the Middle Ages, *saga* or "female sage" became a synonym for "witch."[2]

1. Branston, 88. 2. Wedeck, 140.

Saint Elmo's Fire

This electrical phenomenon, usually seen on shipboard, was formerly sacred to Helen, the Moon-goddess, or else to Hermes, god of magic. The French called it Feu de S. Hélène, or Feu de S. Hèrme: Fire of the Holy Helen or the Holy Hermes. In Spain it was known as St. Helmes or St. Telmes fire, regarded as a form of witchfire, like the Fata Morgana (marsh gas).[1] In fact it is a static discharge from points such as masts and spars of a ship, or from the wings of earlier airplanes.

According to some sea stories, if one flame appears, it is Helen, who presages bad weather; if two flames appear, they are Helen's brothers Castor and Pollux, who indicate that the weather will clear, and also that even sea-myths demonstrate patriarchal bias. Other names for the mysterious light are Corposant—from Italian *corpo santo,* Christ's body—St. Anne's Light, and even Saint Electricity.[2]

Saint Elmo was entirely mythical. Some scholars claimed he was the same as St. Erasmus of Syria, who was also mythical, his legend based only on a spurious "Acts" written three centuries after his alleged martyrdom. It was claimed that he died of having his intestines wound out of his body onto a windlass; therefore his symbol in sacred art was a windlass. Through this tenuous link, he became a patron saint of sailors.[3] But since he probably never existed at all, the point is only academic.

1. Hazlitt, 94. 2. Jobes, 180. 3. Attwater, 117.

Saints

Canonization of saints was a Christian extension of the ancient Greco-Roman custom of apotheosis (god-making), whereby mortals could become immortal and live forever in heaven through identification with a deity. The liturgy and forms of canonization were taken from the pagans, including the ceremonial release of bird-souls to represent the deified one flying to heaven to join the other immortals.[1]

The canon of saints made Christianity in effect a form of polytheism, just as the similar system of multiplying bodhisattvas created a Buddhist polytheism. Medieval Europeans wanted many deities, not one. Thus, in medieval churches, "the life of Christ fills a smaller place and is told with far less complacence than are the lives of the saints."[2] Much time and effort were expended to ascertain the right saint or saints to answer any particular kind of appeal.

The mythical saints included numerous transformations of the Great Goddess under names that were only her various pagan titles, in the same way as the Judeo-Christian God was called "Almighty" or "Ancient of Days" or "Lord." Among the sainted Goddess-names were Mari, Marina, Margaret, Aphra, Venerina, Martina, Mary of Egypt, the Three Marys, Aphrodite, Demetra, and such title-names as Irene, Philomena, Reine, Pelagia, Corona, Rosalia, Sophia, Eugenia, Viviana, Columba (Peace, Moon-lover, Queen, Sea, Crown, Holy Rose, Wisdom, Health, Life, Dove).[3]

Diana Ilithyia was canonized as St. Yllis. Artemis became St. Artemidos. Keraunos the thunder-serpent became St. Ceraunos. Castor and Pollux were transformed into Sts. Cosmas and Damianus, whose images replaced those of the pagan Heavenly Twins in their healing shrine at Aegaeae. Sts. Sebastian and Hubert, patrons of archers and hunting dogs, were once pagan Lords of the Hunt; so was St. Eustace, allegedly converted by Christ who spoke to him from the horns of a magic stag.[4]

The sun god Helios became St. Elias. Gods and heroes like Bacchus, Dionysus, Hyacinthus, Narcissus, Nereus, and Achilles were canonized under their own names. Mercury became a warrior-saint, supposedly sent from heaven to assassinate the emperor Julian, "the Apostate." Under his other name, Hermes, he was canonized by the spurious *passio* of Pope Alexander I. The satyr-god Silvanus was canonized, and called a son of the equally fictitious St. Felicity.[5] Even Buddha became a Christian saint, disguised as St. Josaphat (Bodisat).[6]

As St. Aphra or Afra, Aphrodite appeared in the role of a repentant prostitute, embracing martyrdom to atone for her promiscuous behavior. She was quoted as saying, "My body has sinned, let it suffer." She was burned to death on an island in the river Lech—meaning that the Goddess's image was burned in its former Temple of Lechery.[7]

A late absurdity was the canonization of the Goddess's Holy Vial as an anthropomorphic saint, which one 18th-century historian referred to as St. Ampoule.[8]

About the beginning of the 9th century, bones, teeth, hair, garments, and other relics of fictitious saints were conveniently "found" all over Europe and Asia and triumphantly installed in the reliquaries of every church, until all Catholic Europe was falling to its knees before what Calvin called its anthill of bones.[9] Martyrs' remains became extremely valuable, as Gibbon says: "The satisfactory experience that the relics of saints were more valuable than gold or precious stones stimulated the clergy to multiply the treasures of the church. Without much regard for truth or probability, they invented names for skeletons, and actions for names."[10] Myths invented for the fictitious relics of the evangelists provide typical examples.

Some Venetian merchants pretended to find the bones of St. Mark in Alexandria in 815. They brought their find home to Venice and sold it to the municipal treasury. A great church was built over the bones in the Square of St. Mark—who was only associated with the city in the first place because the original municipal totem was a lion, and the evangelist was assigned to the season of Leo in the pagan calendar. The bones remain in Venice to this day, for the fiction has not yet been renounced.

In like manner, the bones of "St. Matthew" were dug up in Parthia at Hierapolis, and carried to a church in Salerno in 1080 A.D., at the height of the early saint-making fad. Matthew's legend was invented by Pope Gregory VII, who claimed to have learned by divine inspiration of the apostle's travels through Egypt, Ethiopia, and other places, and of the miracles he worked to shame the poor magic of pagan magicians.[11] St. Luke was touted as one of the ancient world's most prolific artists, to judge from the numerous portraits of the Virgin, painted by him, that appeared in many churches. Some still remain, despite ample proof that all such portraits were actually painted during the Middle Ages.[12]

Conversion of pagan gods and goddesses to saints usually accompanied the church's takeover of their shrines. An example is the so-called Isle of Saints whose sacred inhabitants were not saints at all but women called Gallicenae, former priestesses of the Gallic oracle. Pomponius Mela, Latin geographer of the 1st century A.D., said they were "holy in perpetual virginity, said to be nine in number, with singular powers, so as to raise by their charms the winds and seas, to turn themselves into what animals they will, to cure wounds and diseases incurable by others, to know and predict the future; but this they do only to navigators who go thither purposely to consult them."[13]

Like pagan oracles and wise-women, sacrificial gods were also converted into saints. The *Blutritt* (blood rite) of northern heathens was easily transformed into a Christian ceremony by simple substitution of the blood of Christ or the relic of a local saint, the former god. A 10th-century ecclesiastical decree in Westphalia ordered that "every year, on the second day of Whitsuntide, with the grace of the Holy Ghost, ye shall bear the patron saint of your cloister church in a long procession through your parochial district. . . . This processional will cause the seed of the fields to grow more abundantly, and the harshness of the weather will be subdued."[14]

In the old shrines of Great Mother Cybele at Acrae in Sicily, rock-cut niches dating from the 3rd century B.C. sheltered numerous figures of the Goddess, some dating from a much earlier period. After Christian conquest of the area, the Goddess's figures became known as Santoni, "saints," and are so called to this day.[15]

Pseudo-saints often retained jurisdiction over those departments of nature that they ruled as pagan deities. St. Medardus controlled the rain, and during droughts his statue was drenched with water to stimulate him to action. St. Caesarius of Arles was identified with Boreas, god of the north wind. In the valley of Vaison his holy glove was said to hold the air that let loose winds and storms, so his power actually approximated that of Satan who was Prince of the Power of the Air.[16]

The church that slaughtered the heathen for worshipping false gods was itself guilty of worshipping false saints—which, sometimes, were even the same deities as those of the heathen. This became so obvious in the 8th century that the Synod of Leptinnes had to prohibit the offering of sacrifices to saints instead of to God.[17]

Christians surpassed their pagan ancestors in credulity, propagating and believing saintly miracle-tales apparently without any limitations. Pope Gregory the Great wrote a book of saints' lives filled with impossible feats. St. Honoratus for example halted in mid-air a giant boulder that was rolling down a mountainside toward his monastery simply by making the sign of the cross at it. The monk Maurus walked on water, like Jesus and St. Peter.[18] In fact, the miracles attributed to Jesus were negligible compared to the wonders performed by saints. Angobard wrote in the 9th century, "The wretched world lies now under the tyranny of foolishness; things are believed by Christians of such absurdity as no one ever could aforetime induce the heathen to believe."[19]

The church never lost sight of practical common sense on one point, however; saints were leading sources of its income, thanks to the mandatory pilgrimage system, donations, and tithes. Gold, silver, and gems were collected to house and adorn the precious relics. An ecclesiastical chronicler of Trier related how the priests buried the church's treasures to hide them from attacking Norsemen, "so that the relics might not be mocked and jeered at by the barbarians."[20] Of course the real fear was not mockery of the relics, but robbery of their valuable vessels.

Some genuine flesh-and-blood saints achieved their canonization by adding to the wealth of the church through trickery. A common trick seems to have been manipulation of the popular belief in ghosts. St. Fridolin of Säkingen claimed for the church the property of a deceased Count Urso, on the ground that Urso had promised it to the church while receiving the last rites from Fridolin. But the property had passed into the hands of Urso's heir, his brother Landolf, and there was no document to prove Fridolin's claim. However, the saint won his case by summoning Count Urso himself to rise from the grave and appear before the judges, testifying "in sepulchral tones" that Landolf's holdings must be turned over to the monastery. The unfortunate Landolf lost not only his inheritance, but also his life. Fridolin became the patron saint of Säkingen and was buried in the church he built with the dead man's money.[21]

The same thing happened in the case of St. Stanislaus the Martyr, Bishop of Cracow, who managed some "very ample estates" belonging to a man named Peter. After Peter's death, his heirs claimed the estates, but the bishop refused to part with them. As he was unable to show any documents of ownership, a court ruled in favor of Peter's heirs. Then the bishop went to Peter's tomb, touched the body, and commanded it to rise and follow him to the court. The corpse then "confirmed the statement of the bishop in every particular, and fearful as they sat the judges reversed their former decision."[22] The wily saint kept the estates, doubtless contributing a share to whatever accomplice it was who impersonated the dead Peter.

Such miracles were more common than might be expected. The same thing happened in the time of St. Augustine the Apostle of England, according to his biographer John Brompton. "St. Augustine had long been endeavoring to persuade a certain nobleman of great wealth to pay the appointed tithes, but out of obstinacy these were constantly refused, which did great mischief and caused others to become discontented and impudently follow so bad an example." One day during High Mass, St. Augustine directed all who were excommunicate to leave the church. A tomb in the crypt suddenly opened, and a corpse came forth, explaining that it had been excommunicated by a priest now dead. St. Augustine led witnesses to the dead priest's tomb, and asked why the revenant had been excommunicated. The priestly ghost replied, in "a low, far-off" voice, "I excommunicated him for his misdeeds, and particularly because he robbed the church of her due, refusing to pay his tithes."[23] Through this elaborate charade, the saint was able to improve economic piety in the district.

The multitudes of phony or commercial saints are treated by modern Catholic scholars with a rather amused tolerance, as if the saint-makers' fantasies held something of the same charm as tales invented by bright children. It is rarely admitted that these fantasies were not intended to charm but rather to defraud. The saints were made up to earn money for the church, and many of the made-up saints are still doing so, for the church refrains from publicizing their spurious origins lest such publicity might disappoint the faithful—which, translated, means the donations might cease.

1. Gaster, 769. 2. Mâle, 176. 3. Reinach, 312. 4. Norman, 73.
5. Attwater, 128, 168, 243, et al. 6. H. Smith, 227. 7. Attwater, 33. 8. Hazlitt, 285.
9. Kendall, 122. 10. Campbell, Oc. M., 393. 11. Brewster, 212, 420. 12. Attwater, 223.

13. Keightley, 420. 14. Oxenstierna, 219–20. 15. Vermaseren, 68. 16. Mâle, 271. 17. J.B. Russell, 66. 18. de Camp, A. E., 265. 19. H. Smith, 260. 20. Oxensteirna, 14. 21. Guerber, L.R., 316–18. 22. Summers, V., 55. 23. Summers, V., 111.

Sais

Capital of Egypt during the 7th century B.C., where the Great Goddess (Isis-Neith) ruled supreme in her temple carved with the words later copied by the biblical God: "I am all that was, that is, and that is yet to come" (see Revelation 1:8).[1] A thousand years later, the temple of the Goddess at Sais was taken over by Christians and converted into a church of the virgin Mary.

1. *Larousse,* 37.

Saki

Arabic "Cupbearer," based on the Hindu Goddess as Saci or Power, whose wine meant life and energy for all the gods. Saki was sometimes female, like the Greek gods' cupbearer Hebe; sometimes male, like Hebe's replacement Ganymede, the boy lover of Zeus. According to Arabian symbolism, death came for each man when Saki turned down his empty cup; his life was "drained to the lees."

Sakyamuni

One of the earlier incarnations of Buddha as "Sage of the Sakyas," bearing approximately the same relationship to the Buddha Siddhartha as King David to Jesus. Sakyamuni dwelling in heaven perceived that he would become incarnated again in the offspring of a queen of the Sakyas, the role assigned to the Goddess Maya in the Buddha legend.[1] His semen was deposited by the god **Ganesha**.

1. *Larousse,* 348.

Sala

Sacred cherry tree, symbol of virginity, under which the Virgin Maya gave birth to Buddha; celebrated in a similar Christian legend by the Cherry Tree Carol. See **Cherry**. The "feminine" qualities of redness, roundness, and fruition made the cherry everywhere sacred to the Goddess, along with other red fruits like the apple and pomegranate.

Salacia

"Salacious" Sea-goddess, Venus-Aphrodite worshipped in Rome as the feminine abyss "with fish-teeming womb."[1] The name probably was related to Greek Thalassa, "Sea," which also gave rise to the holy cry *Talassio* raised by wedding guests in honor of the Goddess of

Marriage, or *maritare.* Romans didn't know the origin of this wedding cry but continued to use it nevertheless.[2] See **Fish**.

1. Neumann, A.P., 6. 2. Rose, 192.

Salem

Semitic "Peace," with variations like Shalem, Shalom, Selim, Solomon, Shalman, Salmon, Shalmaneser. Jeru-salem was "the House of Peace," or of the god Salem, whose earlier city was ruled by Melchizedek (Genesis 14), the "King of Light" called Melek or Molech in Phoenicia. "Peace" was the word spoken daily to the dying sun, and also to the dying sacrificial victim who impersonated him in the rites that "brought forth bread and wine" (Genesis 14:18). See **Lucifer**.

Saliva

Both Mohammed and Jesus claimed to restore sight to the blind by applying saliva to their eyes (Mark 8:23). This was an imitation of cures previously attributed to priestesses of the Goddess. A clay tablet from Nineveh says eye diseases could be cured by the mixed saliva and milk of a temple harlot. Romans thought blindness could be cured by the saliva of a mother of sons. As late as the 19th century, Italian folk healers were still trying to cure blindness with the saliva and milk of the mother of a premature child.[1]

Notions of the wonderful curative power of female saliva may be traced back to Tantrism and its Chinese offshoot, Tao, whose scriptures called women's saliva "a great medicine," one of the three wonderful yin juices, the others being breast milk and menstrual blood.[2]

European pagan heroes also cured blindness with saliva—so many of them that medieval churchmen had to say this was one of the recognition signs for Antichrist.[3]

1. Gifford, 63. 2. Rawson, E.A., 234. 3. Gifford, 120.

Salome

The Bible presents the Dance of the Seven Veils as a mere vulgar striptease performed by Salome to "please Herod" (Matthew 14:6-8). Actually, the Dance of the Seven Veils was an integral part of the sacred drama, depicting the death of the surrogate-king, his descent into the underworld, and his retrieval by the Goddess, who removed one of her seven garments at each of the seven underworld gates. The priestess called Salome or "Peace" (Shalom) impersonated the descending Goddess, passing through seven gates in the temple of Jeru-salem which meant House of Peace. "Josephus records that the first name of the city was Solyma. Salma, or Salim, was evidently the Semite god of the rising or renewed sun; Salmaone was the Aegean goddess from whom he took his titles, as did Salmoneus the Aeolian."[1]

Salome represented Ishtar as the third of her three high priestesses or "Marys." Her name was a translation of the Greek Irene, "Peace," the third of the sacred harlots called Horae.[2] She may have been identical with the sacred harlot Mary Magdalene, or Mary of the Temple, whose so-called "seven devils" were the same underworld gatekeepers to whom the temple dancer gave her veils. These veils, like the rainbow veils of Maya, signified the layers of earthly appearances or illusions falling away from those who approach the central Mystery of the deeps. Isis too had seven stoles with the same mystical significance.[3]

The dancing priestess was more than a trivial entertainer. Salome's husband Joseph was killed after he lay with the queen, Mariamne or Miriam (Mary).[4] Salome was present with the virgin Mary—the same Mary?—at the birth of Jesus; some said she was the midwife who delivered the holy child.[5] Salome was present with all three Marys at the death of Jesus (Mark 15:40). Obviously she was also involved in the death of John the Baptist, which seems to have been not a murder but a ritual sacrifice.

Some early Christian sects (the Mandaeans) ignored Jesus, and worshipped John the Baptist as the true sacrificed Christ.[6] An early Greek epiphany hymn said it was the blood of John the Baptist that "bedewed"—i.e., fructified—the mothers and children of Jerusalem.[7] As an initiated Essenic prophet, John would have been *sacer* and "chosen" to die as a surrogate for the king, whose blood was required for fertility of the land. John was beheaded, a common form of sacrificial death throughout the early Aegean and Levantine cultures, still practiced to this day in some of the eastern temples of the Goddess, though the victims are now animals instead of men.[8]

Though only a fragment in its present form, the story of Salome presents evidence for the survival of the Tammuz-Ishtar cult in Jerusalem, where someone periodically died in the role of the god, and the women raised the ancient lament for the victim in the temple (Ezekiel 8:14).

1. Graves, W. G., 413. 2. *Larousse,* 138. 3. Angus, 251. 4. Enslin, C. B., 48. 5. Graves, W. G., 75. 6. Reinach, 77. 7. J. E. Harrison, 174. 8. Neumann, G. M., 152.

Salt

One of the few substances known to the ancients that could preserve foodstuffs and dead bodies was salt. Egyptian mummies were preserved in a brine solution called natron, "birth-fluid." Salt was accepted as a substitute for the Mother's regenerative blood; it came from the sea-womb and had the savor of blood. Therefore salt became a symbolic instrument of kinship, like maternal blood. The Roman rite of *confarreatio* (patrician marriage) had the bride and groom share a cake of flour and salt, which stood for flesh and blood respectively, and magically transformed them—like those who in older times shared real flesh and blood—into blood kin, unable to harm one another.[1]

The Arabs signified a similar bond of good faith by sharing a meal of bread and salt, which created the binding portion of any covenant. The Bible speaks of a "covenant of salt" (Numbers 18:19) as one that cannot be broken, even when it is a covenant between man and God. Salt was an acceptable substitute for blood also in dedicating an altar, either Jewish or Christian (see **Blessing**).

A common Semitic metaphor for enlightened seers was "salt of the earth," i.e., true blood of the Earth Mother. The term was applied to Christ's followers (Matthew 5:31) to suggest that they could prophesy truly.

Christian uses of salt were copied largely from Roman pagans, who used salt to bless every public sacrifice. "Immolate" came from *mola,* the flesh-and-blood-symbolic combination of salt and flour prepared by the Vestal Virgins to sprinkle over every beast that was led to sacrifice.[2]

Church bells were solemnly anointed with salt and water, wiped with linen, blessed, and christened. God was requested to give the bells power to dispel demons by their sound, and to send thunder and lightning far away from the vicinity of the church—though bell-ringing was never very successful in the latter endeavor, since church bell-towers were struck by lightning more often than any other structure.[3]

Christian infant baptism often involved rubbing the infant with salt to repel demons. It was said that heretics carefully rubbed the salt off.[4]

Superstitious fear of spilling salt was directly related to the idea of spilling blood. Throwing a pinch of salt over the shoulder to take off the curse was a symbolic way of putting bloodshed "behind," or turning one's back on it.

Natural salt pillars in the vicinity of the Dead Sea proved profitable to enterprising medieval Saracens, who learned that Christians would pay good money to be guided to the exact spot where "Lot's wife" stood, to behold a biblical miracle with their own eyes. Eroded by wind, the salt pillars often assumed fantastic shapes. One may well have been shaped like a woman; if not, a few touches of the chisel could make it so.

Cabalistic tradition suggests that the biblical Lot's wife was really a form of the Triple Goddess. Hebrew MLH, "salt," is a sacred word because its numerical value is that of God's name of power, YHWH, multiplied three times.[5] The same word is also a root of Malkuth, the cabalistic Queen Mother Earth.

1. Hartley, 231. 2. Dumézil, 318. 3. Hazlitt, 43. 4. Cavendish, P. E., 223. 5. Budge, A. T., 323.

Samjna

Hindu "Sign," "Letter," or "Name"; title of the Goddess as inventor of writing and pictographic alphabets; also a title of the moon.[1] See **Motherhood**.

1. O'Flaherty, 352.

var. Samuel

Sammael

"Dread Lord," Semitic version of the Asiatic Sama, Samana, or Samavurti, "the Leveller," Judge of the Dead, identified with the underworld king Yama.[1] The Sama Veda called him a storm god, clothed in black clouds.[2] Like his later incarnation Satan, he was Prince of the Power of the Air; also the Celtic god of Samhain, the Feast of the Dead, Christianized as All Souls. Medieval Gnostics were accused of worshipping his as Sammael or Satanael.

In Britain he had a feminine counterpart, Samothea (Death-Goddess), queen of the mysterious land of the Hyperboreans, where Pythagoras traveled to learn the arts of letters, astronomy, and science from this all-wise lady.[3] She seems to have been another form of **Skadi** or Scatha.

1. *Larousse,* 346. 2. Frazer, G. B., 78. 3. Boulding, 193–94.

Samson

Hebrew version of the sun god called Shams-On in Arabia, Shamash in Babylon, identical with Egypt's Ra-Harakhti and Greece's Heracles. Samson's lion-killing, pillar-carrying, and other feats were copied from the Labors of Heracles, signifying the sun's progress through the zodiac. Samson's "mill" was the same as Omphale's wheel, to which Heracles was bound. His loss of hair meant the cutting of the sun god's rays, in the season when he became weak.

As Heracles was controlled by Omphale, and Ra was "made weak" by Isis, so Samson was deprived of his strength in due season by Delilah, "She Who Makes Weak." Another interpretation of her name was Lily of the Yoni, that is, the female principle that deprived the phallic god of strength by drawing his "rays" or energy into herself. Hair-cutting was a common mythic symbol of castration, since phallic power was supposed to reside in a man's **hair**, according to ancient eastern beliefs.[1] The castrating priestess Delilah was a Semitic copy of Heracles's deadly consort Deianira, the instrument of his destruction. Blinding, also, meant putting out the "phallic eye."

Talmudic tradition viewed Samson's "grinding" in Philistia as a symbol of fornication—suggesting a sacred-king cult in which a strongman assumed the role of the sun hero, deflowered all the virgins until his strength was gone, then faced castration and sacrifice.[2] It has been supposed that Samson's wrecking of the Philistine temple stood for the sun's power to dry out and crumble a structure made of mud bricks.

1. Rawson, E. A., 25. 2. Legman, 520; Silberer, 97.

Sanguis ac Genus

"Blood of the race," the essence of genealogical continuity, possessed only by women, according to pre-Roman beliefs in Latium.[1] See **Motherhood; Romulus and Remus.**

1. Dumézil, 68.

Santo Niño

"Holy Child" slain and eviscerated by Jews to cast a death-spell on all Christendom, according to the legend used by Torquemada and the Spanish Inquisition to evict the Jews from Spain.[1] Several captured Jews, after sufficient torture, confirmed the story. The same legend was used two centuries earlier to encourage a persecution of Jews in Germany.[2] See **Jews, Persecution of.**

1. Plaidy, 171 et seq. 2. Guerber, L. R., 206.

Sapientia

Latin "Lady Wisdom," corresponding to the Greek Sophia, the Gnostic Goddess worshipped by Hermetists, alchemists, cabalists, and medieval "philosophers" whose doctrines were disguised heresies. In fact Sapientia was sometimes represented as "the Siren of the Philosophers," pouring the red-and-white wines of enlightenment from her breasts, rising from the sea like a crowned Aphrodite.[1]

Renaissance mystics depicted Sapientia as the Shakti of God, identifying her sometimes with the virgin Mary, sometimes with Mother Nature, sometimes with God's "inner mind" or Goddess-Within (I-dea). She was described as God's wisdom; indeed, as "all the wisdom he had."[2] Spenser said Sapientia dwelt in God's bosom, as his spouse, "the sovereign darling of the Deity, clad like a Queen in royal robes." She was described as "the basic and primordial foundation of all things . . . the being, life, and light of intelligible things," and a Triple Goddess: *Sapientia creans,* the Creatress; *Sapientia disponans,* "who unites all things in harmony"; and *Sapientia gubernans,* "otherwise known as Divine Providence."[3]

The Christian writer pseudo-Dionysius credited Sapientia with creation itself, calling her "Thou unbegun and everlasting Wisdom, the which in thyself art the sovereign-substantial Firsthood, the sovereign Goddess, and the sovereign Good."[4]

Sapientia was the hidden Creatress of medieval thought—the unofficial Goddess supposedly eliminated from Europe's religions centuries earlier, but still living fragmented under various names: **Mary**, Nature, **Luna**, **Earth**, **Venus**, or **Sophia**.

1. de Givry, 361. 2. von Franz, 16. 3. Collins, 54, 220. 4. Wilkins, 112.

Sapphire

Biblical mistranslation of *sappur,* literally "holy blood": the lapis lazuli, called the substance of the throne of God.[1] Originally it was divine blue blood in the **cauldron** of the Crone, Siris, Babylonian "Cosmic Mother."[2]

1. Graves, W. G., 290. 2. *Assyr. & Bab. Lit.,* 308.

Sappho

Poet-priestess of Lesbos, the "isle of women" dedicated to the Goddess. Once married, mother of a daughter Cleis, Sappho devoted her later life to the love of women. She was called the Tenth Muse and revered even above Homer; but only fragments of her work remain because her books were later burned. See **Lesbians**.

Sarah

"Queen," also rendered Sarai, Sara, Serah, Serai. Persian forms referred to a matriarchal government, evolving into "temple of women," seraglio, or harem.[1]

Sarah was the maternal goddess of the "Abraham" tribe that formed an alliance with Egypt in the 3rd millenium B.C.[2] This was the real meaning of the embarrassing biblical story about Abraham's pimping for his wife (Genesis 12). According to Jewish tradition, Sarah ranked higher than her husband, and her death brought "confusion" to a nation that was in good order while she lived.[3] She was interred in the holy cave of Machpelah, a womb-necropolis of the Goddess of the Anakim. Votive idols in this cave were later adopted by the Jews and called by the names of deified ancestors: Sarah, Abraham, Isaac, Rebekah, Leah, and Jacob.[4]

1. Briffault 3, 110. 2. Graves, W. G., 300. 3. Ochs, 45. 4. Graves, W. G., 162.

Sara-Kali

"Queen Kali," the Goddess worshipped by gypsies, who came originally from Hindustan. Some gypsies appeared in 10th-century Persia as tribes of itinerant dervishes calling themselves Kalenderees, "people of the Goddess Kali."[1] A common gypsy clan name is still Kaldera or Calderash, descended from past Kali-worshippers, like the Kele-De of Ireland.[2]

European gypsies relocated their Goddess in the ancient "Druid Grotto" underneath Chartres Cathedral, once the interior of a sacred mount known as the Womb of Gaul, when the area was occupied by the Carnutes, "Children of the Goddess Car." Carnac, Kermario, Kerlescan, Kercado, Carmona in Spain, and Chartres itself were named after this Goddesss, probably a Celtic version of **Kore** or Q're, traceable through eastern nations to Kauri, another name for Kali.[3]

The Druid Grotto used to be occupied by the image of a black Goddess giving birth, similar to certain images of Kali.[4] Christians adopted this ancient idol and called her Virgo Paritura, "Virgin Giving Birth." Gypsies called her Sara-Kali, "the mother, the woman, the sister, the queen, the *Phuri Dai,* the source of all Romany blood." They said the black Virgin wore the dress of a gypsy dancer, and every gypsy should make a pilgrimage to her grotto at least once in his life. The grotto was described as "your mother's womb." A gypsy pilgrim was told: "Shut your eyes in front of Sara the Kali, and you will know the source of the spring of life which flows over the gypsy race."[5]

A gypsy prayer to the Goddess demonstrates her Kali-like trinity of Creator, Preserver, and Destroyer:

> *Thou destroyest and dost make everything on earth; thou canst see nothing old, for death lives in thee, thou givest birth to all upon the earth for thou thyself art life. . . . Thou art the mother of every living creature and the distributor of good; thou doest according to thy wisdom in destroying what is useless or what has lived its destined time; by thy wisdom thou makest the earth to regenerate all that is new. . . . [T]hou are the benefactress of mankind.*[6]

Sara-Kali was also known as Bibi, "the Aunt," a Destroyer-Crone corresponding to Russia's Baba Yaga. Like the Kalika who created fatal illnesses, Bibi "has the power to cause all kinds of disease, especially at the beginning of a new month when there is a full moon."[7] Bibi dressed in red, recalling the red-clothed Kali at the final dissolution of the world when her garment is made of "a red mass of blood" from all the gods she devours.[8] As Kali's **dakinis** identified themselves with the Destroyer at ceremonies of death, so gypsy women wore red for funerals.[9]

Gypsies also used the Indo-Egyptian Yoni Yantra (triangle) as a sign for "woman," practiced Tantric sexual rites like those of the east, and believed in reincarnation according to Hindu doctrines of karma governed by the Goddess. The gypsy said, "The sands of truth will deposit me on the bed of earth from which I came. . . . [N]aked, I shall return to the womb of my mother."[10]

Some gypsies insisted that Sara-Kali was Queen of Heaven and Earth. According to a secret tradition, all the cathedrals in France were arranged to form an earthly reflection of the constellation Virgo,

Sara-Kali's true home in heaven.[11] After being semi-Christianized, gypsies identified Sara-Kali with the virgin Mary. Gypsies celebrated the Feast of the Assumption of the Blessed Virgin by piling up the heads of sacrificed fowls in front of her church, as Kali's votaries in India piled up the heads of sacrificed animals.[12]

Further Christianization inspired legends to provide Sara-Kali with a Christian background. Some claimed she was not a mother goddess but a saint, the patron saint of the gypsy people. She accompanied the three Marys from the foot of Jesus's cross on their sea voyage to the west. They landed at Saintes-Maries-de-la-Mer. Another story said Sara-Kali was a gypsy queen from the Rhone delta, who swam from Saintes-Maries-de-la-Mer to meet the boat carrying Mary Salome, Joseph of Arimathea, Mary and Martha and their brother Lazarus, and other Christian celebrities, whose bones were displayed at the site throughout the Middle Ages.[13]

1. Keightley, 20. 2. Esty, 67. 3. Campbell, Oc.M, 294. 4. Rawson, A.T., 33. 5. Derlon, 217–19. 6. Leland, 107. 7. Trigg, 186. 8. *Mahanirvanatantra,* 295–96. 9. Trigg, 119. 10. Derlon, 132, 159. 11. Derlon, 210. 12. Trigg, 184. 13. Esty, 79.

Sarama

Vedic bitch-goddess, mother of the brindled Dogs of Yama, who were westernized first as the Celtic Hounds of Annwn and then as the Christian Hounds of Hell.[1] Sarama was the eastern form of the Huntress, known in classical mythology as Artemis, Diana, or Hecate. (See **Dog**.) Like other Huntress-figures she symbolized the death-dealing function of the Goddess who implacably hunted down all whose time of dissolution had come, according to the cycles of karma.

1. O'Flaherty, 352.

Saranyu

The Vedic Goddess as a mare, mother of the Asvins or centaurs. Her western counterparts were Leukippe, Melanippe, Epona, or Mare-headed Demeter. (See **Horse**.) Saranyu also gave birth to Yama and Yami, the Lord of Death and Lady of Life, when she occupied the form of a woman instead of a mare. According to one story, Saranyu created a shadow-woman exactly like herself, and left this simulacrum with her husband while she departed in the form of a mare. When her husband Vivasvat realized the deception, he turned himself into a stallion and followed her, as Poseidon became a stallion in order to mate with Mare-headed Demeter. However, Saranyu's mating took place in a peculiar way. Vivasvat spilled his semen on the ground, and Saranyu snuffed some of it into her nostrils. In this way she became pregnant, and later gave birth to the physician-gods, the Asvins, from her mouth.[1] The myth evidently came from an early period when the mechanism of impregnation was thought to be variable and the orifice of birth not always exclusively genital.

1. O'Flaherty, 61, 69.

Sarapis

var. Serapis

Syncretic god worshipped as a supreme divinity in Egypt to the end of the 4th century A.D. The highly popular cult of Sarapis used many trappings that were later adopted by Christians: chants, lights, bells, vestments, processions, music.

Sarapis represented a final transformation of the savior Osiris into a monotheistic figure, virtually identical with the Christian God. The religion of Sarapis was founded in the 3rd century B.C. by Ptolemy Soter (Ptolemy the Savior), the Macedonian pharaoh who identified himself with the deity in traditional pharaonic style.[1] This Ptolemaic god was a combination of Osiris and Apis, called Osarapis, or Sarapis. As Christ was a sacrificial lamb, so Sarapis was a sacrificial bull as well as a god in human form. He was annually sacrificed in atonement for the sins of Egypt, with the words: "If any evil be about to befall either those who now sacrifice, or Egypt in general, may it be averted on this head."[2]

In his later development, Sarapis picked up the qualities of every Egyptian deity and became both Father and Son, ruler and victim. He was called lord of Death, Good Shepherd, creator, healer, sun, fertility god, impregnator of the Goddess—his image carried in holy processions was a huge phallus. His greatest temple, the Sarapeum at Alexandria, was a cathedral of pilgrimage and medicine. The philosopher Demetrius of Phalerum testified that Sarapis had cured him of blindness; his paeans to the god were still sung as hymns centuries later.[3] Alexandrian psalms declared: "There is only one Zeus Sarapis."[4]

Sarapis became a great patron of arts and letters. The Sarapeum included a vast library of literary treasures from all over the Roman empire, a storehouse of contemporary learning. When Christianity came to power in Alexandria, the library was attacked, though it was desperately defended for three years.[5] Finally, in 389 A.D., Theodosius gave a direct order that the building must be wrecked and the books burned. Christians therefore destroyed the Sarapeum and its library, thus eliminating most of the ancient world's important literature in one holocaust.[6]

The "deceased" pagan god was later assimilated into the canon as an artificial saint or saints. Among several Egyptian St. Sarapions, the most notable was called a companion of St. Anthony, but a legend of his martyrdom was constructed from the destruction of Sarapis's temple. The late official canonization of St. Sarapion at the end of the 19th century was based on an ecclesiastical literary hoax, the "discovery" of some texts alleged to be copies of material in the lost Sarapean library.[7]

1. Cumont, A.R.G.R., 74. 2. Budge, G.E. 2, 349. 3. Cumont, A.R.G.R., 75. 4. *Encyc. Brit.,* "Sarapis." 5. J.H. Smith, C.G., 168. 6. H. Smith, 228. 7. Attwater, 305.

Sarasvati

"Flowing One," the Vedic river goddess whose water conferred divinity on kings when it was used in their baptism. Sarasvati was also the Queen of Heaven assimilated to Brahmanism as Brahma's wife, a combination that suggests the biblical A-brahm and Sara(h). Sarasvati really predated the cult of Brahma. She was said to have invented all the arts of civilization: music, letters, mathematics, calendars, magic, the Vedas, and all other branches of learning. Sometimes she bore the name of Savitri, listed by some scholars as a male god, even though ancient records called Savitri "wife of Brahma" and "Daughter of the Sun."[1] Frequently she was identified with the holy waters of Ganges.

1. O'Flaherty, 352–53; *Larousse,* 332, 344.

Sargon

King of Akkad (now northern Iraq), 2241–2186 B.C.; a typical god-king, born of a "virgin bride of God" or temple maiden, secretly placed in a basket of rushes and sent away on the river to foil the incumbent king who wished to kill him; drawn forth by a magical personage, the Water-Drawer or midwife-goddess Akki; raised in seclusion in the wilderness; returned to the court in triumph to marry the Goddess Ishtar and rule her lands.[1] Many other hero-myths were based on the details of Sargon's story.

1. Jobes, 375.

Satan

Like all so-called devils, Satan began as a god. Early Egyptians called him the Great Serpent Sata, Son of the Earth, immortal because he was regenerated every day in the Goddess's womb. A man could become immortal, like Sata, by repeating prayers to identify himself with the god: "I am the serpent Sata, whose years are infinite. I lie down dead. I am born daily. I am the serpent Sata, the dweller in the uttermost parts of the earth. I lie down in death. I am born. I become new, I renew my youth every day."[1]

Sata seems to have been an underground aspect of the sun, Horus-Ra, corresponding to Apollo's underground serpent-form Python, whom the Jews called Apollyon, Spirit of the Pit. He was a phallic consort of the archaic Goddess Sati, or Setet, whose name was the same as that of a virgin aspect of Kali, and who once ruled Upper Egypt which was known as the Land of Sati.[2] The god was also called Set—the biblical Seth, who may not have been immortal but did manage to live 912 years (Genesis 5:8).

The snake's communion with the life-giving fountains of the deep was still an important image in dynastic times, when Sata became the keheret-snake, living in a yonic orifice in Isis's temple and giving oracles, like Python at Delphi. It was felt that disasters would strike the country if the serpent should leave the Goddess's sacred hole.[3]

The **serpent** was often a symbol of the sun god's alter ego, the Black Sun, spirit of night or of death. He combined with the solar disc as the god during his dark hours. The pattern was the same in Osiris-Set, Apollo-Python, Anu-Aciel, Baal-Yamm, etc. The dark god was the light god's adversary not because he was originally viewed as evil, but because he represented a sleeping or quiescent phase of the same god.

Sata dwelling forever in the underworld reappeared in Russian folk tales as the great underground serpent Koshchei the Deathless.[4] In his "adversary" role he eventually became the immortal Dragon whom the sun-hero had to slay, as men wished to slay the spirit of death dwelling within their own bodies, the archetypal "betrayer" who led them sooner or later to destruction.

To the Hebrews, a "satan" was an adversary in the sense of a judge: one who tested the faith of another by asking trick questions or posing problems to be solved. The "satan" first appears in the Bible as one of the sons of God, advising God to test the faith of Job (Job 1:6). In the original wording, Satan was one of the *bene ha-elohim,* sons of "the gods"; but Bible translators always singularized the plurals to conceal the fact that the biblical Jews worshipped a pantheon of multiple gods.[5]

This "son of God" was identified with the lightning-serpent Lucifer by the words of Jesus, who claimed to have seen Satan descending into the earth as lightning (Luke 10:18). This repeated Persian myths concerning Ahriman, the lightning-serpent cast from heaven to the underworld by the god of light. Persians held that God and the Great Serpent were twin brothers, an idea that entered into Gnostic tradition and led to medieval magic books that called upon Satan by the mystic names of God, such as Messias, Soter, Emmanuel, Saboth, Adonai (Messiah, Savior, Immanuel, Lord of Hosts, the Lord).[6]

Satan not only answered to God's names, he even assumed a divine appearance when he wished. The medieval church insisted that Satan "transfigures himself into an angel of light," so anyone claiming an unofficial angelic vision could be charged with devil worship at the discretion of inquisitors—who, naturally, always knew the difference between a real angel and a devil in angelic disguise.[7]

Islamic writers called Satan Shaytan, or Iblis. He governed the race of *djinn,* the "genies" who were once ancestral spirits, like the Roman *genius.* The djinn scorned Allah's prophets, so an army of angels attacked them, killed many, and took the rest prisoner. Among the prisoners was Iblis-Shaytan, also called Azazel, to whom the Jews used to offer scapegoats on the Day of Atonement. Iblis-Shaytan had rebelled against Allah when Allah created Adam and ordered all the angels to worship his creation. Allah says in the Koran, "We said unto the Angels, Worship ye Adam, and they worshipped except Iblis who was of the Jinn."[8]

The background of this story may have come from the early Gnostic *Gospel of Philip,* which the church censored for obvious reasons: "Human beings make gods, and worship their creation. It would be appropriate for the gods to worship human beings!"[9] Satan's worst offense seemed to be that he was not disposed to respect man, whose faults he well knew; nor did he have any good to say of God, who had governed heaven too harshly and stimulated rebellion.

Medieval Christians interpreted everything apart from their own orthodoxy as a manifestation of Satan-worship: astrology, magic, pagan ceremonies, divination, etc.

> *Service of Satan is everything dealing with paganism, not only the sacrifices and the worship of idols and all the ceremonies involved in their service, according to the ancient custom, but also the things that have their beginning in it. Service of Satan is clearly that a person should follow astrology and watch the positions and motions of the sun, the moon, and the stars for the purpose of traveling, going forth, or undertaking a given work, while believing that he is benefited or harmed by their motion or their course; and that one should believe the men who, after watching the motions of the stars, prognosticate by them.*[10]

1. *Book of the Dead,* 307, 544–45; Briffault 2, 649. 2. *Larousse,* 37, 335. 3. Erman, 101. 4. Lethaby, 168. 5. Cavendish, P.E., 184. 6. Wedeck, 95. 7. J.B. Russell, 77. 8. Keightley, 289. 9. Pagels, 122. 10. Laistner, 6–7.

Sati

Kali as the dangerous Virgin Bride of India's **svayamara** ceremony. The same name was applied to Egypt's similarly archaic Virgin Huntress, once the ruler of the first nome of Upper Egypt, called "The Land of Sati." Her holy city was Abu, the City of the Elephant (the Greeks' Elephantine), where she was worshipped in conjunction with the elephant god, who also mated with the Hindu version of Sati under her "magic" name of Maya, to beget the Enlightened Son of God, Buddha.[1]

India still has pilgrimage centers known as Footprints of Sati, memorials of the time when the Goddess walked on earth.[2]

1. *Larousse,* 37, 348. 2. Ross, 49.

Saturn

Roman name for Cronus, the primitive earth god associated with Great Mother Rhea and credited with her own Destroyer function of devouring her own children. Saturn was the same as the Black Sun (Aciel) of Chaldean astrologers, the Lord of Death at the nadir of the underworld, representing the sun at his lowest aspect in the midwinter solstice. Sometimes he was called Sun of Night.

At Harran, near old Edessa in what is now Turkey, Saturn's worship included the wearing of black clothing, and burning candles made of incense, opium, goat's fat, and urine, with the prayer: "Lord, whose name is august, whose power is widespread, whose spirit is sublime, O Lord Saturn the cold, the dry, the dark, the harmful . . . crafty sire who knowest all wiles, who art deceitful, sage, understanding, who causest prosperity or ruin, happy or unhappy is he whom thou makest such."[1]

As a rule the Lord of Death was both a god and a demon, like Shiva the Destroyer. He was the negative side of the summer sun, propitiated in midwinter so he might allow spring to come again. This important festival became the Roman Saturnalia, which contributed many of its customs to Christmas. At Saturn's festival, death and atonement were featured as well as joyous celebration of the sun's new birth.

A sacrificial victim was chosen to represent both the god himself and the king-surrogate. He was slain and sent to the underworld to merge with his divine counterpart. "It was the universal practice in ancient Italy, wherever the worship of Saturn prevailed, to choose a man who played the part and enjoyed all the traditionary privileges of Saturn for a season, and then died, whether by his own or another's hand, whether by the knife or the fire or on the gallows-tree, in the character of the good god who gave his life for the world."[2]

Though the real killing of the victim was gradually replaced by symbolic killing, the festival was never abandoned, and in Christian times it became part of the midwinter Carnival. "The mock execution of King Carnival is a vestige of the ancient Saturnalia, when the man who had acted as king of the revels was actually put to death at the end of his reign. This practice continued in parts of the Roman army well into Christian times."[3]

Saturn gave his name to Saturday, the sabbath of the week's end, before the coming of the new sun on Sun-day (Latin *dies solis*). To the Jews this was the seventh day when God "rested," like Saturn quiescent in darkness before the sun rose again. Saturn was identified with the seventh planetary sphere, whose astrological influences partook of "saturnine" qualities such as somberness, heaviness, darkness, passivity, coldness, etc.

The Babylonian name of the planet Saturn was Ninip, which was also a name of the underworld god: "the black Saturn, the ghost of the dead sun, the demoniac elder god."[4] But Saturn was not altogether demoniac. Like most chthonian deities, he was ambiguous. He was often revered as a healer. Our medicinal symbol Rx began as the planetary sigil of Saturn, which was often written on paper and eaten as a cure for disease.[5]

1. Cumont, A.R.G.R., 28, 90. 2. Frazer, G.B., 679. 3. Moakley, 55. 4. Hallet, 387. 5. Waddell, 401.

Savior

Greek *Soter,* "Savior," was often affixed to the name of a god or divine king, e.g., Dionysus Soter, Antiochus Soter. Its literal meaning was "one who sows the seed," i.e., a phallic god, like Rome's Semo Sancus—Holy Seed—consort of Mother Earth.[1] After sowing or planting, the Soter was "born again" in the new grain as a Divine Child, and his advent was hailed with the formula, "He is risen."[2]

It was usual for the Savior to sow his "seed" three times, like the Persian Messiah who spilled his seed three times into the womb of Mother Earth (Hvov).[3] At Eleusis the savior Iasion bore the title of Triptolemus, "Three Plowings," ostensibly because he lay with Mother Demeter "in a thrice-plowed field"; but the field was Demeter herself, as Mother Earth, and the Savior was the plow.[4] Ptolemy, the royal name of the Macedonian line of Egyptian pharaohs, meant "plower" or "sower," like the Greek *Soter.*[5]

Since most kings were gods made flesh, many bore the title of Savior. Antiochus Soter (Antiochus the Savior) ruled Babylon from 280 to 260 B.C., and was identified with the sacrificial god Nabu, "exalted Son, powerful leader of the gods."[6] In 48 B.C., Julius Caesar was hailed as "God made manifest and universal Savior of human life." His successor Augustus was "Ancestral God and Savior of the whole human race."[7] The emperor Nero was immortalized on his coins as "Savior of Mankind."[8] Roman emperors were routinely deified and made "saviors," as shown by the address prepared for the birthday celebration of Augustus in 9 B.C.

> *This day has given earth an entirely new aspect. The world would have gone to destruction had not there streamed forth from him who is now born a common blessing. Rightly does he judge who recognized in this birthday the beginning of life and of all the powers of life. . . . The providence which rules over all has filled this man with such gifts for the salvation of the world as designate him the Savior for us for the coming generation: of wars he will make an end, and establish all things worthily. By his appearing are the hopes of our forefathers fulfilled: not only has he surpassed the good deeds of men of earlier times, but it is impossible that one greater than he can ever appear. The birthday of God has brought to the world glad tidings that are bound up in him. From this birthday a new era begins.*[9]

Such speeches were often copied by followers of less exalted "saviors," of which the early Christian era had many, especially in the Middle East. "Palestine was seething with eschatological (i.e., salvational) movements. . . . [T]he emergence of the Christian sect was anything but an isolated incident." One of the greatest problems of early Christianity was to decide what the savior was supposed to be saving humanity from. Among the many theories put forth were: Christ saved mankind from (1) death, or (2) sin, or (3) demons, or (4) the fleshly world and its evil demiurge.[10]

Celsus quoted a typical speech of the kind of self-styled savior currently prevalent in his day:

> *I am God (or a son of God, or a divine Spirit). And I have come. Already the world is being destroyed. And you, O men, are to perish because of your iniquities. But I wish to save you. And you see me returning again with heavenly power. Blessed is he who has worshipped me now! But I will cast everlasting fire upon all the rest, both on cities and on country places. And men who fail to realize the penalties in store for them will in vain repent and groan. But I will preserve for ever those who have been convinced by me.*[11]

Aulus Cornelius Celsus Patrician Roman scholar of the first century A.D., who wrote at length on the subjects of medicine, agriculture, philosophy, jurisprudence, and religion.

Gnostics believed in a Buddhistic succession of saviors. Some Gnostic leaders said "the savior does not come just once into the world but that from the beginning of time he wanders in different forms through history."[12] The belief of Jewish Essenes in a savior of this type probably contributed to the medieval legend of the Wandering Jew.

1. Hays, 109. 2. Briffault 3, 162. 3. Campbell, Oc.M., 210. 4. Graves, G.M. 1, 93. 5. Budge, G.E. 2, 199. 6. *Assyr. & Bab. Lit.*, 195. 7. Angus, 109. 8. Strong, 82. 9. H. Smith, 171. 10. Jonas, 31, 139. 11. Jonas, 104. 12. Jonas, 79.

Savitri

A name of the Hindu Goddess as mother of civilization, she who brought forth music and literature, rhythm, time, measurements, day and night, memory, conquest, victory, yoga, and religion, as well as many spirits of civilized arts; she also brought forth The Maiden Death, dissolution, and all diseases.[1] The same acts of creation were attributed to the Goddess under another name, **Sarasvati**, inventor of alphabets, wisdom, language, the Vedas, etc. Both Goddess-names were applied to "the wife of Brahma," though the creative Goddess preceded Brahma, and became his consort only after the Brahman cult claimed her as a source of his power.

1. O'Flaherty, 49–50; *Larousse*, 344.

Scold

Probably derived from Skuld (Skadi), the Norse Goddess of cursing, third of the Norns, who spoke the deadly words that condemned every man to death sooner or later. Even after Christianity discredited Skuld, men continued to believe that women's curses had effective power to injure them, to cause bad luck, disease, or death.

Certainly Christian laws displayed fear of women's maledictions. Men were permitted to curse women, but a woman could be jailed or tortured for "scolding" a man. In England, "a common scold" was considered a criminal, like a thief. The ducking stool, frequently used to drown witches, was also used to punish a scold.[1]

In 1632 the English brought from Scotland an instrument of torture called a brank, or "scold's bridle": an iron head-cage with a tongue piece to be inserted in the mouth, the cage being locked around the head. Sometimes the tongue piece was shaped like a spoon; sometimes it was a sharp spike. A brank with four sharp spikes, two to pierce the tongue and two to pierce the cheeks, was used to fasten the "witch" Agnes Sampson to the wall of her cell, as part of the torment to make her confess to the crime of witchcraft.[2]

The brank was still in use as a punishment for "scolding" women up to the middle of the 19th century. In 1856 a woman locked into one of these devices was paraded from the town cross to the church at Bolton-le-Moors, in Lancashire.[3]

1. Hazlitt, 158. 2. Robbins, 359. 3. Pearsall, N.B.A., 190.

Scorpion

The constellation of the Scorpion is one of the links between the cultures of central America and those of the ancient east, possibly Mesopotamia, whose ziggurats were so similar to the Mexican pyramids. Scorpio was the same in Babylonia, India, and Greece; and the Maya of Yucatan also called the same constellation "scorpion stars."[1]

Astrological myths everywhere placed Aquarius the Water-drawer at the winter solstice, Taurus the Bull at the spring equinox, Leo the Lion at the summer solstice, and Scorpio at the autumnal equinox.[2] Therefore it was said in Egypt that the Scorpion killed Horus, the sun, sending him to his midwinter death and resurrection as his Mother Isis gave him rebirth; and Pharaoh's daughter apparently played the part of the Water-drawer or divine midwife on the banks of the Nile, as shown by the myth of **Moses**.

Spirits of the four points of the year were sometimes called Sons of Horus, and placed as small images in the four corners of a pharaoh's tomb. As man, bull, lion, and scorpion (or serpent) they were adopted by Christianity and converted into the four totems of the evangelists and the four angels of the Apocalypse.

1. Von Hagen, 178. 2. Campbell, Oc.M., 259.

Scotia

Latin form of the "Dark Aphrodite" after whom Scotland was named; in her native land she was the Death-goddess Scatha, or **Skadi.**[1] She was the mother of Caledonia; some said she was identical with the Caillech, or Crone, who created the world.

1. Graves, G.M. 1, 72.

Sebastian, Saint

Canonized form of the Gaulish savior-god immolated by being bound to a tree or pillar and pierced by arrows, like **Cu Chulainn.** Pagan images of the dying god were simply renamed St. Sebastian, as in the ancient stone temple at Knockmay in Galway—that is, Gaul's Way.[1]

The Christianized myth made St. Sebastian a martyr "born in Gaul." His legend is now described as "simply a romance," the Catholic scholar's term for a faked sainthood. Nevertheless, he has not been officially eliminated from the canon.[2]

1. Spence, 85, 106. 2. Attwater, 304.

Seidr

Freya's secrets of witchcraft, copied by the patriarchal gods under Father Odin; cognate with Irish *sidh* and Hindu *siddhi,* the magic powers resulting from the practice of yoga. Sufi sages called these powers by a similar name, *sihr.*[1]

1. Shah, 335.

Seker

Egyptian Lord of Death, "the hidden one," or "he who is shut in"; Osiris as the Black Sun enclosed in the earth's womb, at the bottom of the underworld, in a secret pyramid filled with "blackest darkness."[1] Seker was a title of the phallus at the point of "dying," sending forth seed into the dark. The Arab's word for "penis," *zekker,* came from the god's name.[2]

The same Lord of Death was the tutelary deity of the necropolis at Sakkara, another variation of his name.[3] He also appeared in Babylon as Zaqar, a messenger from the moon—that is, from the land of death.[4] In Hebrew he was *zakar,* "maleness, virility." His medieval descendant was the phallic Satan enclosed in the darkest central pit of hell, yet radiating the spirit of lust.

1. *Book of the Dead,* 145. 2. Edwardes, 23. 3. Budge, G.E. 1, 504. 4. *Larousse,* 63.

Semele

Virgin mother of Dionysus, associated with both the earth and the moon. The Moon-goddess Selene was only a variant of Semele.[1] Phrygians called her Zemelo, an incarnation of Cybele, Great Mother of the Gods.[2] Semele was "made into a woman by the Thebans and called the daughter of Kadmos, though her original character as an earth-goddess is transparently evident."[3]

1. Graves, G.M. 2, 408. 2. Neumann, A.C.U., 70. 3. Guthrie, 56.

Semiramis, Queen

Greek name of the Assyrian queen Sammuramat, said to have founded Babylon and built its famous Hanging Gardens, conquered the whole Middle East, and invaded Kush and India.[1] Her consorts had little or nothing to do with government; she was a daughter of the Goddess and made her son the king. Some said she castrated the males of her royal household, suggesting that she was the Goddess whose temples were served by eunuch priests.[2] Like most early Assyro-Babylonian queens she embodied the spirit of Mari-Ishtar.[3]

1. de Camp, A.E., 69. 2. Brasch, 155. 3. *Encyc. Brit.,* "Semiramis."

Semites

The Bible said Semitic tribes descended from Noah's son Shem, or Sem. This mythical personage was actually a title of Egyptian priests of Ra, who when fully initiated were allowed to wear the panther skin (as priests of Dionysus and Yahweh did also) and call themselves Shem. These priests in turn may have evolved from the class of Egyptian priestesses called *shemat,* "singing-mothers," who knew the hymns and words of power.[1]

1. *Book of the Dead,* 221, 278.

Senate

From Latin *se-natus,* "self-born," in earliest times probably a group of *matrones* or tribal mothers thought to be reincarnated in their daughters by matrilineal succession. The later patriarchal gods also claimed to be "self-born," like Ra in Egypt.[1] Providing any god with a mother implied that there was an older, greater female authority over him—a self-defeating idea for patriarchal thinkers.

1. Budge, G.E. 1, 341.

Serpent

It was a general belief in the ancient world that snakes don't die of old age like other animals, but periodically shed their skins and emerge renewed or reborn into another life. Greeks called the snake's cast skin *geras,* "old age." The Chinese envisioned resurrection of the dead as a man splitting his old skin and coming out of it as a youth again, like a snake. Melanesians say "to slough one's skin" means eternal life. A basic serpent-myth said the dual Moon-goddess of life and death made the first man. Her bright aspect suggested making him immortal like a snake, able to shed his skin; but her dark aspect insisted that he should die and be buried in the earth.[1] Eternal life and serpenthood are still equated in the Italian expression *aver piu anni d'un serpente*— "being older than a serpent."

The ageless serpent was originally identified with the Great Goddess herself. Hinduism's Ananta the Infinite was the serpent-mother who embraced Vishnu and other gods during their "dead" phase.[2] She was also Kundalini, the inner female soul of man in serpent shape, coiled in the pelvis, induced through proper practice of yoga to uncoil and mount through the spinal *chakras* toward the head, bringing infinite wisdom. The Serpent-goddess occupied the famous Khmer temple of Angkor Wat in Cambodia where she embraced the king every night. If one night the Goddess did not appear, it was a sign that the king must be killed and a new king chosen.[3]

The Negritos said the divine people called Chinoi (Chinese) were descended from a mighty Serpent-goddess named Mat Chinoi, Mother of the Chinese. In her belly lived beautiful angels who received the souls of the dead. Since her womb was Paradise, shamans underwent their death-and-rebirth initiations by entering the serpent's belly.[4]

The ancient Aegean world worshipped primarily women and serpents. Men didn't participate in religious ceremonies until late in the Bronze Age, when Cretan kings were allowed to become priests of the bull-god. Even then, the priest's role was subordinate to that of the priestess, until the priest himself took the title of "serpent."[5] The word for "priest" among ancient Akkadian peoples literally meant "snake charmer."[6]

The Indian Serpent-goddess Kadru gave birth to all the Nagas or cobra people, and made them immortal by feeding them her divine lunar blood.[7] She had a Babylonian counterpart, the Goddess Kadi of Der, worshipped as a serpent with a woman's head and breasts.[8] Her children like the Nagas were depicted as water-serpents, human from

Book of Thoth Legendary Egyptian magical text supposed to have been written by the god Thoth, found in the necropolis at Memphis by a young prince named Satni-Khamois.

Magic Papyri Collections of exorcisms, invocations, charms, and spells widely circulated during the early Christian era, used as bases for later grimoires and Hermetic texts.

Mahabharata Indian epic poem, consisting of historical and legendary material gathered between the 4th and 10th centuries A.D., including the famous Bhagavad-Gita.

the waist up, like mermaids and mermen. The Nagas guarded "great treasures of wealth and precious stones, and sometimes books of secret teachings in underwater palaces."[9]

A similar serpent guarded the wonderful Book of Thoth, which was hidden in an underwater palace.[10] Like his Greek twin Hermes, Thoth was often incarnate in a snake, signifying his magical wisdom. Egypt agreed with India in depicting the first serpent as a totemic form of the Great Mother herself. Egypt's archaic Mother of Creation was a serpent, Per-Uatchet or Buto. The Egyptian *uraeus*-snake was a hieroglyphic sign for "Goddess."[11] Incongruously, "Uraeus" later became one of the most popular "secret names of God" listed in Magic Papyri and medieval texts of sorcery.

Egypt's Serpent-goddess also had the title of Mehen the Enveloper, similar to Kundalini or Ananta. Each night, Mehen enfolded the ram-headed god Auf-Ra (Phallus of Ra) during his sojourn in the uterine underworld. This was a mythic image of the king's sexual union with his Goddess, reminiscent of the custom of Angkor Wat.[12] At Philae, the Serpent-goddess received the title of Anqet, from *anq,* to surround, to embrace.[13] "Serpent of the Nile" was the title, not only of Cleopatra, but of all Egyptian queens who represented the nation and the Goddess embracing the king.

The birth-and-death Goddesses Isis and Nephthys became identified with the dual Serpent-mother of life and after-life. Only they could help the soul through the section of the underworld inhabited by serpent deities, Egypt's version of the Nagas.[14] The *Mahabharata* depicts a hero seeking immortality in a similar underworld called "city of serpents," where the dual Mother of Life and Death wove the web of nights and days with black and white thread, binding them with the red thread of life.[15]

The Akkadian Goddess Ninhursag, "She Who Gives Life to the Dead," was also called "Mistress of Serpents" as yet another form of Kadru or Kadi.[16] Babylon's version of her made her a dark twin of the Heaven-goddess Ishtar, calling her Lamia or Lamashtu, "Great Lady, Daughter of Heaven." Cylinder seals showed her squatting, Kali-like, over her mate, the god Pazuzu, he of the serpent penis.[17] As another Lord of Death, he gave himself up to be devoured by the Goddess. The image of the male snake deity enclosed or devoured by the female gave rise to a superstitious notion about the sex life of snakes, reported by Pliny and solemnly believed in Europe even up to the 20th century: that the male snake fertilizes the female snake by putting his head in her mouth and letting her eat him.[18]

The male serpent deity became the phallic consort of the Great Mother, sometimes a "father" of races, because he was the Mother's original mate. In some myths, he was no more than a living phallus she created for her own sexual pleasure. In other myths, she allowed him to take part in the work of creation or to fertilize her world-producing womb. When the serpent-creator turned arrogant and tried to pretend that he alone made the universe, the Goddess punished him, bruising his head with her heel and banishing him to the underworld.[19] On this version of the creation myth the Jews based their notion of Eve's progeny bruising the serpent's head, and the rabbinical opinion that the serpent was Eve's first lover and the true father of Cain.[20]

Actually, the serpent was worshipped in Palestine long before Yahweh's cult arose. Early Hebrews adopted the serpent-god all their contemporaries revered, and the Jewish priestly clan of Levites were "sons of the Great Serpent," i.e., of Leviathan, "the wriggly one."[21] He was worshipped in combination with his Goddess, the moon.[22] The Bible shows that Yahweh was a hostile rival of the serpent Leviathan, for the two gods battled each other (Psalms 74:14; 89:10, Isaiah 51:9). They would engage in another final battle at doomsday (Isaiah 27:1; Revelation 12).

Another Jewish name for the Great Serpent was Nehushtan, described as the god of Moses. Hebrew *nahash,* "serpent," descended from an ancient Vedic serpent-king, Nahusha, once "the supreme ruler of heaven," until he was cast down to the underworld by a rival.[23] Nehushtan was the same god whose image Moses made: a "fiery serpent" according to Numbers 21:8. The Israelites worshipped him until the reign of Hezekiah, when the new priesthood "cut down the groves, and brake in pieces the brazen serpent that Moses had made" (2 Kings 18:4).

Yet serpent worship continued in Israel. *Seraph,* the Hebrew word for the divine fiery serpent, used to mean an earth-fertilizing lightning-snake, and later became an angel.[24] The *seraphim* were originally serpent-spirits, like those of the caduceus created by Hermes the Great Serpent and copied by Mosaic tradition. Jewish medallions of the 1st and 2nd centuries B.C. represented Jehovah as a serpent god, like the "snake-tailed winds" of the Greeks.[25] Jews of Asia Minor said their Jehovah was the same as Zeus Sabazius the serpent god of Phrygia.[26] Some Jewish Gnostics early in the Christian era maintained that the post-exilic Jehovah was no god, but a devil, the usurper of the original Kingdom of the Wise Serpent.[27]

Much Gnostic literature praised the serpent of Eden for bringing the "light" of knowledge to humanity, against the will of a tyrannical God who wanted to keep humans ignorant.[28] This view of the Eden myth dated back to Sumero-Babylonian sources that said man was made by the Earth Mother out of mud and placed in the garden "to dress it and to keep it" (Genesis 2:15) for the gods, because the gods were too lazy to do their own farming and wanted slaves to plant, harvest, and give them offerings.[29] The gods agreed that their slaves should never learn the godlike secret of immortality, lest they get above themselves and be ruined for work. Therefore, as the Epic of Gilgamesh reports, the gods gave death to humanity, and "Life they kept in their own hands."[30]

In one of the interwoven Genesis stories, God was not one but many, the *elohim* or "gods-and-goddesses."[31] The God of Eden remarked to his divine colleagues, "Behold, the man is become as one of us, to know good and evil"; therefore he must be ejected from the garden at once, lest he "take also of the tree of life, and eat, and live for ever" (Genesis 3:22). The serpent's teachings would have led man to conquer death and become godlike, against the will of the *elohim.*

Hypostasis of the Archons ("Reality of the Rulers") A Gnostic Gospel written about the 3rd century A.D., incorporating one of the alternate versions of the Adam and Eve myth.

The *Hypostasis of the Archons* showed that the serpent was a totemic form of the Goddess, apparently taking pity on her doomed creature and seeking to instruct him in the attainment of eternal life: "The Female Spiritual Principle came in the Snake, the Instructor, and it taught them, saying, 'you shall not die; for it was out of jealousy that he said this to you. Rather, your eyes shall open, and you shall become like gods, recognizing evil and good.' " Then "the arrogant Ruler" (God) cursed the serpent and the woman.[32] Some Gnostic sects honored both Eve and the serpent for their efforts on behalf of humanity.[33]

The present form of the biblical story is obviously a much-revised version of the original tales of the Great Mother and her serpent. Babylonian icons showed the Goddess attended by her snake, offering man the food of immortality. The Pyramid Texts said it was the serpent who offered the food of eternal life.[34] As Ophion, or Ophi, he was the ancestor of the African serpent god Obi, whose name is still preserved in the voodoo-magic system, *obeah.*[35] The Bible uses a Hebrew version of the name, *obh,* for the familiar spirit of the Witch of Endor, and the Vulgate renders this word "python."[36] In Dahomey, the primal Mother-Creatress Mawu was supported by a Great Serpent.[37]

Gnostic accounts of the Eden myth used the Aramaic pun identifying Eve, the Teacher, and the Serpent: *Hawah,* Mother of All Living; *hawa,* to instruct; and *hewya,* Serpent.[38] Eve's name in Arabic still combines the idea of "life" (*hayyat*) with the name of the serpent (Hayyat).[39] Hippolytus viewed the serpent as a feminine Logos, "the wise Word of Eve. This is the mystery of Eden: this is the river that flows out of Eden. This is also the mark that was set on Cain, whose sacrifice the God of this world did not accept whereas he accepted the bloody sacrifice of Abel: for the lord of this world delights in blood. This Serpent is he who appeared in the latter days in human form at the time of Herod."[40]

Arabian tradition identified the food of immortality with the female uterine blood, colored "royal purple"; and the Mother's uterine garden with the moon temple at Marib in Sheba. Legend said the serpents of Sheba were purple with the divine essence, and lived in trees; the people were serpentlike, with forked tongues, great wisdom, and longevity.[41] From Sheba might have come the mysterious life-giving substance called *shiba* in the Epic of Gilgamesh, dispensed by the wife of Uta-Napishtim (Noah), who had become the only immortal man; his wife therefore was a Goddess. When this holy matriarch gave *shiba* to Gilgamesh, he shed his old, diseased skin like a snake, and emerged from it reborn.[42]

Persians also maintained the symbolic connections between menstrual blood and the serpent's secret of longevity. Mithraists claimed immortality was conferred by the blood of the sacrificial bull, but a serpent was there to collect the blood as it flowed from the bull's body; and this blood was imitation-menstrual blood in that it was "delivered by the moon."[43]

Immortality was the special province of the skin-shedding Serpent and the blood-bestowing Goddess from earliest times. Some of the very oldest traditions of the Great Serpent identified him with the Earth's intestines. Archaic serpent gods like Egyptian Apep and Sumerian Khumbaba were said to "resemble intestines."[44] In this connection, the biblical phrase for birth or rebirth was "separation from the bowels." Serpents understood how to restore life to the dead, according to the myths of Crete, where the sorcerer Polyidos learned the serpents' secret and won great honor at the Minoan court by bringing the dead prince Glaucus back to life.[45]

Many Gnostic traditions identified the Serpent with Jesus. In the *Pistis Sophia,* Jesus was the serpent who spoke to Eve "from the tree of knowledge and the tree of life, which were in the paradise of Adam." Jewish Naassians (Serpent-worshippers) said the serpent was the Messiah. Magic Papyri called him "World Ruler, the Great Serpent, leader of gods . . . the god of gods."[46] Some Christians held that the serpent was the father of Jesus, having "overshadowed" the bed of the virgin Mary and begotten the human form of the Savior.

These traditions were still extant, though hidden, in Renaissance times. Bartel Bruyn's Gnostic-symbolic painting of the Annunciation showed an unmistakably Hermetic serpent-caduceus as the rod extended toward Mary by the impregnating angel Gabriel. The Dove poised in a halo in its tip, making a sign like a cross between a fairy-wand and the emblem of Venus.[47] This made a combined symbol of the male-and-female mystery of the Serpent and Dove, which was inserted into the mouth of Jesus according to Matthew 10:16. Many theologians claimed the crucified serpent Nehushtan was a prophecy of Jesus: "And as Moses lifted up the serpent in the wilderness, even so must the Son of Man be lifted up" (John 3:15). In the 16th century, German smiths made golden thalers with a crucified Christ on one side and a crucified serpent on the other, hinting that they were two faces of the same redeemer.[48]

Every mythology had some form of the World Serpent. Like the Hermetic or Gnostic serpent encircling the World Egg, he was a basic Indo-European religious symbol. Norse myth called him the Midgard-Worm, who encircled the whole round of Middle-Earth (Midgard), his tail in his mouth.[49] Russians called him Koshchei the Deathless, encircler of the underworld.[50] This seems to have been a variation of the Japanese dragon of sea-tides, Koshi.[51] Egyptians called him Sata (Satan), or the Tuat, on whose back the sun god rode through the underworld each night. Greeks called him Okeanos, the sea-serpent of the outermost ocean.

Often the Heavenly Father assumed this serpent form, like Zeus Meilichios, worshipped as a gigantic serpent in the 4th century B.C.[52] In the shape of a serpent he became the consort of chthonian Persephone.[53] He also begot heroes on mortal women. Alexander the Great was allegedly fathered by God who in the form of a serpent impregnated his mother, Queen Olympias.[54]

The Pyramid Texts spoke of the serpent as both subterranean and celestial. In his heavenly aspect, he was a dispenser of immortality.[55] As the divine phallus in perpetual erection he was the Tree of Life, or *axis mundi,* a Pole passing through the center of heaven and earth—that is, Father Heaven coupled to the Goddess's "hub." His eye was seen as the pole star. In 3000 B.C., the pole star was Alpha Draconis, the Serpent's Eye.[56]

The *Mahabharata* said the pole star to which the yoke of the world was fixed was "the supreme snake, Vasuki." The same snake was the phallic god who stirred the uterine Abyss at creation, according to the Vedas.[57] Like the God of Genesis, the Vedic deity Indra claimed to have cast down the Great Serpent from heaven into the world-encircling abyss of the outer ocean.[58] Like the Bible story, this myth re-interpreted the original meaning of the serpent as a descending, fertilizing phallus.

The sexual image of the phallic serpent's head as the Jewel in the Lotus ramified into many versions of the myth of menarche: the belief that menstruation was initiated by copulation with a supernatural snake (see **Menstrual Blood**). According to this imagery, the divine male serpent acquired a "blood-red jewel" in his head. Hindus said all the great snakes carried blood-red rubies of immortality in their heads.[59]

Germans remembered this Aryan lore, and said a serpent with a magic stone in its head would be found at the root of a hazel tree—witchwood—near mistletoe. The serpent's stone was sacred to the moon, and was identified with the Philosopher's Stone, which could bring eternal life.[60] Remnants of the serpent's phallic symbolism appeared in medieval magic charms, such as the conviction that "female diseases" could be cured by applying to the sufferer a staff with which a snake had been beaten.[61]

In 13th-century France, a snake on a pole like the Ophites' image of Christ was carried in triumphal procession during Easter Week to the baptismal font of the church.[62] Sometimes the fetish was an enormous stuffed serpent, like a Chinese carnival dragon. Churchmen tried to assimilate the custom by saying the serpent was the devil "driven from his kingdom by the Passion of Christ"; but this was but a lame explanation for a rite that was already old when Christianity was new.[63]

Early Ophite Christians adopted serpent worship and claimed Moses as the founder of their sect, alleging that Moses taught the Jews to worship the serpent in the wilderness.[64] Besides, the serpent had certainly given knowledge to Adam and Eve, and therefore was a savior of humanity, an earlier incarnation of Christ who also suffered at God's hands for the enlightenment he brought. The Ophites' holy serpents were made to twine around the bread of the Eucharist, and were adored hanging on crosses. Ophite "colleges" still existed in Bithynia in the 5th century A.D., when bishops began leading mobs to wreck the Ophite churches.[65]

Bithynia Ancient region of Asia Minor, adjoining the Sea of Marmora, the Bosporus, and the Black Sea. The Bithyni, a Thracian tribe, settled the region toward the end of the 2nd millenium B.C.

Medieval Hermetists worshipped the serpent as Ouroboros, king of magic, a syncretic mixture of the Ophites' Christ-Ophion, the Greeks' Hermes, the Phoenicians' Taaut, the Egyptians' Tuat, and other ancient snake-tailed gods including the underground oracle Python.[66] Ouroboros was linked with the Chinese *pi*-dragon, symbol of the universe, carved on jade discs as a dragon or serpent eating its own tail.[67] This may have been the prototype of the serpent Python and the Pythagoreans' worship of *pi* as the mystic numerical principle of the circle. Two serpents eating each other's tails combined the yang-and-yin mandala with the caduceus, expressing the bisexual nature of Hermes and all cyclic alternations: birth/death, summer/winter, light/dark, etc. The Ouroboros was still pictured under the earth in certain European areas, and some people claimed to be able to feel his slow movements through their feet when they stood in the ancient shrines.

1. Briffault 2, 643–48. 2. O'Flaherty, 340. 3. Wendt, 198. 4. Eliade, S., 340. 5. Stone, 47–48. 6. *Assyr. & Bab. Lit.*, 4. 7. O'Flaherty, 222. 8. *Larousse*, 63. 9. Tatz & Kent, 79. 10. Maspero, 125. 11. Budge, G.E. 1, 24. 12. Norman, 48. 13. Budge, G.E. 2, 57. 14. *Book of the Dead*, 140. 15. Lethaby, 238. 16. Ashe, 15. 17. Budge, A.T., 110. 18. Briffault 2, 667. 19. Graves, G.M. 1, 27. 20. Tennant, 154. 21. Gaster, 576. 22. Briffault 3, 108. 23. O'Flaherty, 348. 24. Brandon, 360. 25. Campbell, M.I., 294. 26. Enslin, C.B., 91. 27. Graves, W.G., 367. 28. Malvern, 34. 29. Campbell, Or. M., 109. 30. *Larousse*, 72. 31. Reinach, 188. 32. Pagels, 31. 33. Malvern, 34. 34. Lindsay, O.A., 54. 35. Martello, 159. 36. Summers, H.W.D., 177. 37. Jobes, 97. 38. Pagels, 30–31. 39. Shah, 387. 40. Jonas, 95. 41. Thomson, 195. 42. *Assyr. & Bab. Lit.*, 360; Hooke, M.E.M., 55. 43. *Larousse*, 316. 44. Budge, A.T., 169. 45. Jobes, 245. 46. Legge 2, 173, 256. 47. Campbell, M.I., 245. 48. Campbell, C.M., 153–54. 49. Branston, 96. 50. Lethaby, 168. 51. Jobes, 172. 52. Campbell, M.I., 295. 53. Graves, G.M. 1, 56. 54. Gifford, 141. 55. Lindsay, O.A., 54. 56. *Encyc. Brit.*, "Precession of the Equinoxes." 57. O'Flaherty, 131, 274. 58. Campbell, Or. M., 183. 59. O'Flaherty, 226. 60. Briffault 2, 704. 61. Agrippa, 158. 62. Mâle, 183. 63. de Voragine, 280. 64. Budge, A.T., 203. 65. Legge 2, 77. 66. Cavendish, T., 70. 67. Rawson, E.A., 229.

Seshat

Egyptian Goddess of writing, measurements, calculation, record-keeping, and hieroglyphics; "Mistress of the House of Books," "Lady of the Builder's Measure." Priests of Thoth insisted their god was married to her and took over her functions, so Thoth was often credited with the invention of letters and numbers. However, in the time of Queen Hatshepsut, Thoth was not fully entrusted with the court records and bookkeeping. His figures had to be "verified by his wife."[1]

Most contemporary studies (by male scholars) ignore Seshat and list Thoth as the deity of writing—though the earliest dynastic literature emphasizes her, not him.

1. *Larousse*, 28.

Set

Ass-headed Egyptian deity, once ruler of the pantheon; "supplanter" of the Good Shepherd Osiris; perpetual rival of Horus. Copied by biblical writers, he appeared in the Old Testaments as Seth, "supplanter" of the Good Shepherd Abel. See **Ass**.

Seven Pillars of Wisdom, Seven Sisters

See **Pleiades**.

Sex

Rev. Dr. Joseph Fletcher of the Episcopal Theological School wrote, "The Christian churches must shoulder much of the blame for the confusion, ignorance, and guilt which surrounds sex in Western culture. . . . [T]he Christian church, from its earliest primitive beginnings, had been swayed by many Puritanical people, both Catholic and Protestant, who have viewed sex as inherently evil."[1]

Others have been less forgiving, and stated bluntly that Christian churches must shoulder not just "much of" the blame, but all of it. R.E.L. Masters declared, "Almost the entire blame for the hideous nightmare that was the witch mania, and the greatest part of the blame for poisoning the sexual life of the West, rests squarely on the Roman Catholic Church."[2] The rest of the blame presumably devolves upon Protestantism, for there was no institution in western culture other than Christianity that made any effort to teach human beings to hate or fear sex.

Christian abhorrence of sex began with the fathers of the church, who insisted that the kingdom of God couldn't be established until the human race was allowed to die out through universal celibacy.[3] Marcion announced that all propagation must be abandoned at once. St. Jerome ordered: "Regard everything as poison which bears within it the seed of sensual pleasure."[4] St. Athanasius declared the great revelation and blessing brought by Jesus was knowledge of the saving grace of chastity.[5] Tertullian said chastity was "a means whereby a man will traffic in a mighty substance of sanctity," whereas the sex act rendered even marriage "obscene."[6]

Numenius of Apamea proclaimed that only total cessation of all sexual activity could bring about the union of the soul with God.[7] St. Augustine pronounced the doctrine that "concupiscence" is the root of original sin and the means of transmitting Adam's guilt to all generations. Thus he sealed the church's commitment to asceticism, at least in theory, for the next 1600 years.[8] Augustine said sexual intercourse is never sinless, even within marriage.[9] Augustine didn't invent this doctrine. He got it from Gnostic Manicheans, to whose sect he belonged before his conversion to orthodoxy. Gnostics taught that souls are entrapped in flesh by "the mystery of love and lust, through which all the worlds are inflamed." This teaching probably came ultimately from ascetic Jain Buddhist yogis, who enjoined the same precept as the First Book of John: "Love not the world, neither things that are in the world . . . for all that is in the world, the lust of the flesh, and the lust of the eyes, and the pride of life, is not of the Father."[10]

Numenius of Apamea Neopythagorean and Platonic philosopher, born in Syria during the 2nd century A.D.; influential in the school of Plotinus.

These views became more entrenched as time went on. Medieval theologians said sex "caused the damnation of humanity, which was on its account put out of Paradise, and for its sake Christ was killed."[11] Officials of the Inquisition taught in their handbooks that women's "carnal lust" was the cause of witchcraft and Satanism, since God "allows the devil more power over the venereal act, by which the original sin is handed down, than over all other human actions . . . because of its natural nastiness."[12]

The church promulgated legends about saints so devoted to chastity that they preferred extreme physical torment to sexual pleasure. St. Paul the Hermit was tied down by the wicked emperor Decius and subjected to the lascivious caresses of a harlot. As soon as he felt his penis rise, "having no weapon with which to defend himself, [he] bit off his tongue and spat it into the face of the lewd woman." The sainted Pope Leo was so pure that when "a woman kissed his hand, and aroused in him a violent temptation of the flesh," he cut his hand off. By singular good fortune it was restored by the Holy Virgin so he could continue to perform religious ceremonies.[13]

The early church attacked most bitterly the many pagan faiths that made sex a central holy sacrament, enacting union of the Great Goddess and her phallic consorts. Tertullian denounced "the whoredoms of Eleusis," and Eusebius condemned "the unnameable rites of the mysteries, adulteries and yet baser lusts." Yet Plato and his contemporaries had worshipped Eros, god of sexual love, as "the most venerable of the deities, the most worthy of honor, the most powerful to grant virtue and blessedness unto mankind both in life and after death."[14]

From the most primitive period, European pagans incorporated sex into their religion. The word *Lust* in old Germanic languages meant "religious joy."[15] At their holy feasts, Norsemen sang songs the Christians called "lewd and shameful," and danced hip-swinging dances the Christians called "female gyrations."[16] The people refused to give these up, believing them essential to general fertility. When seasons went awry and crops failed under the first Christianized kings, the peasants were sure the cause was neglect of the old deities' rites.[17]

Sexuality was reverenced in cultures where the female principle was accorded freedom and honor, as in Egypt, where women chose and wooed their lovers at will.[18] Egyptians described carnal knowledge as "knowing a woman perfectly," and regarded it as a joy. Sages counseled men never to be rude to a mistress or wife, nor to try to order her about; it would be unseemly in one with whom she shared "joy."[19] This was like the Tantric identification of sexual bliss with the bliss of the Goddess and God as they continually engendered life in the universe.[20] Hindus said intercourse with any woman is like union with the Goddess herself. Far from being sinful, "to have carnal intercourse with the Goddess Parvati is a virtue which destroys all sin."[21]

But in the Christian view, woman brought death into the world and sex perpetuated it.[22] It was claimed that Adam was made to be immortal, but he lost both his innocence and his immortality when Eve taught him about sex. All women were copies of Eve, said Tertullian; "the unsealer of that Tree," her very existence bringing destruction to "God's image, man."[23] Women were dangerous even when dead. An early church edict ordered that a male corpse must not be buried next to a female corpse until the latter was safely decomposed.[24]

St. John Chrysostom said a man "cannot endure" looking at a woman.[25] A biographer of St. Augustine assumed automatically that "because of his great holiness, he was unwilling to look upon a woman's face."[26] St. Augustine's doctrine of original sin was destined to crucify not only Christ but the whole of the western world with its anti-pleasure, pro-pain philosophy.[27] Even today it is hardly possible for anyone brought up in one of the western nations to comprehend the ancient world's opinion of sex as an experience of divine pleasure or a preview of heaven, without deliberate, laborious intellectual progress toward such an opinion.

Not only was Europe crucified by Christian antisexuality but also much of Oceania, Africa, and the Far East. Wherever Christian missionaries went—which was everywhere—people were told their own generally healthy sexual attitudes were wrong and sinful. One missionary described Bantu harvest festivals as Bacchic feasts: "It is impossible to witness them without being ashamed. Men and women, who in ordinary circumstances are modest in behavior and speech, then abandon themselves to licentiousness." Another missionary wrote: "I have seen the most indelicate performances in the shape of dances or theatrical pieces in front of the Badago temples, and on bearing witness to their wickedness have been told that the god delighted in them."[28]

A missionary in Malaya observed that the natives engaged in all of what he called the carnal sins except one: rape.[29] He didn't follow up the thought to the prevalence of rape in his own society; but today's psychologists are beginning to understand the leading role played by sexual repression in developing the kind of woman-hatred that leads to rape. Western thinkers have only recently caught on to the fact that cultural suppression of the need for bodily pleasure will inevitably result in perverted expression through cruelty.[30]

Cruelty to both women and children was the early Christian substitute for the affection usually shown them in less ascetic societies. The *Apostolic Constitutions* called for severe physical punishment of children. Fathers (not mothers) were told: "Do not hesitate to reprove them, chastening them with severity. . . . Teach your children the word of the Lord, straiten them even with stripes and render them submissive, teaching them from infancy the Holy Scriptures."[31]

Apostolic Constitutions Short title of the *Ordinances of the Holy Apostles Through Clement,* forged documents purporting to be ecclesiastical laws laid down by the apostles and their immediate successors. In reality, the *Constitutions* were written by an anonymous Syrian author toward the end of the 4th century.

Recent experiments have shown that inhibition of sexual responses (in animals) is associated with aggressive cruelty, whereas sexual permissiveness goes with peaceful co-existence. While some investigators theorized that aggression and lust rise together from a common source, experiments don't support this belief. Instead, it seems one alternative inhibits the other.[32] Christianity made all Europe a vast experiment in sexual inhibition, with predictable results. In one of history's most cruel ages, Thomas Browne spoke of a nearly total rejection of sex: "I would be content that we might procreate like trees, without conjunction, or that there were any other way to perpetuate the World without this trivial and vulgar way of union."[33]

Sir Thomas Browne (1605–1682) English physician, author of the famous *Religio Medici* and other works.

In 1721 Beaumont ordered the pious to reject any and all sensual pleasures, even the most subtle or involuntary ones:

> *If ye perceive a sudden sweet taste in your mouths or feel any warmth in your breasts, like fire, or any form of pleasure in any part of your body, or . . . if ye become aware by occasion of pleasure or satisfaction derived from such perception, that your hearts are drawn away from the contemplation of Jesus Christ and from spiritual exercises . . . then this sensation is very much to be suspected of coming from the Enemy; and therefore were it ever so wonderful and striking, still renounce it and do not consent to accept it.*[34]

Inhibition of sensual impulses was the keynote of western morality up to and including the 19th century, when Dr. Alcott authoritatively stated that even marital sex should never be indulged more than once a month. Any greater frequency was "prostitution of the matrimonial life."[35] For many centuries the church insisted that marital sex should be as barren of sensual pleasure as possible, and that orgasms in women were unseemly or even devilish. The "missionary position" was the only permitted sexual position, because it afforded the least pleasure, especially to the wife.

Dr. William A. Alcott American physician who undertook the instruction of married couples in his two books, *The Young Wife* (1837) and *The Young Husband* (1839).

In consequence of such socialization, "good" women were frequently sex-haters. Bertrand Russell said of his first wife that "she had been brought up, as American women always were in those days, to think that sex was beastly, that all women hated it, and that men's brutal lusts were the chief obstacle to happiness in marriage."[36]

A Christian scripture falsely attributed to St. Dionysius, *Of the Names of God,* said the name of Love was not suitable for God, "because one could only honor God, not love Him."[37] Love was left to the sinful, bearing out Nietzsche's observation that "Christianity gave Eros poison to drink; he did not die of it but degenerated into a vice."[38] Only recently has it even been suggested that love, or Eros, is essential to the moral development of a man, in a sense that was never hinted at by the moralists of the west. A man may rise to "a new moral plane" by falling in love, a process that cannot be pursued through any rationally established program. Western society doesn't understand how to instill a comfortably "instinctive" morality into any individual, even with the opportunity to work on the problem from earliest childhood—let alone to improve the moral outlook of an adult. But a man's emotional commitment to a beloved, if sincere, may radically alter and improve his whole view of the world, of himself, of right and wrong, and of the individual's relations with and responsibilities toward others.[39]

Patriarchal religion was devoted to destruction of the sensual female nature that elicited and responded to such emotional commitments. Women's sexual desire or pleasure was generally considered detrimental to the marital relationship.[40] A standard Christian work on sex dedicated to Cardinal d'Este, Sinibaldi's 17th-century *Geneanthropeia,* said no woman could conceive if she enjoyed sex.[41] Before the turn of the last century, it was expected that "good" women would know nothing of sexual pleasure. If they showed an inclination to learn, they might be cruelly teased. Thomas Branagan's advice to young men was to test the virtue of a fiancée by trying to seduce her, to make sure she would react with "becoming abhorrence." If she seemed too compliant, she must be jilted.[42]

Thomas Branagan American author of *The Excellency of Female Character Vindicated,* 1808.

The name of John Bowdler became a byword for his pious labors in removing all risqué words from the Bible, Shakespeare, etc. He even objected to any mention of women's traditional care of the sick or of infants, on moral grounds: "Few women have *any idea* [Bowdler's italics] how much men are disgusted by the slightest approach to these in any female. . . . By attending the nursery or sick bed, women are too apt to acquire a habit of conversing on such subjects in language which men of delicacy are shocked at."[43] Male "delicacy" even dictated that the books of male and female authors must be kept on separate bookshelves unless the authors "happen to be married."[44]

The Victorian authority on sex was Dr. William Acton, who couldn't heap too much praise on "all those mysterious sensations which make up what we call VIRILITY," a quality that "seems necessary to give a man that consciousness of his dignity, or his character as head and ruler and of his importance, which is absolutely essential to the well-being of his family, and through it, of society itself. It is a power, a privilege, of which the man is, and should be, proud." But women were permitted no such pride in their sexual nature. "As a general rule," said Acton, "a modest woman seldom desires any sexual gratification for herself. She submits to her husband, but only to please him; and, but for the desire of maternity, would far rather be relieved of his attentions." Acton admitted however that there were a few sad exceptions to his rule, who might be found either in the divorce courts or in lunatic asylums, suffering from "the form of insanity called nymphomania."[45]

Those women labeled nymphomaniacs and imprisoned in Victorian asylums were frequently women who had somehow stumbled upon discovery of their own orgasmic capacity and found to their dismay that men neither knew nor cared anything about it. Even Freud's view of female sexuality was all wrong. For over fifty years, doctors slavishly followed Freud's interpretation and wondered why there were so many "frigid" women, whose sexual readiness was constantly aroused to no purpose until they rejected sex out of sheer frustration. "It is remarkable that only recently has Freud's classic theory on the sexuality of women—the notion of the double orgasm—been actually tested and found just plain wrong."[46]

The 20th century was not much more enlightened than the 19th. Stall's marriage manual, the ultimate authority at the turn of the century, blamed women themselves for the sexual ignorance society imposed on them. If a wife failed to understand her husband's sexual needs, she was to blame "for her lack of knowledge and consideration."[47] But men's lack of knowledge and consideration was part of the culture.

> *The oft-heard complaint directed by women at the clumsiness, crassness, and incompetence of men in their sexual approaches and in sexual intercourse itself, men's lack of skill in foreplay and their failure to understand its meaning, almost certainly substantially reflects the lack of tactile experience that many males have suffered in childhood. The roughness with which many men will handle women and children constitutes yet another evidence of their having been failed in early tactile experience, for it is difficult to conceive of anyone who had been tenderly loved and caressed in infancy not learning to approach a woman or a child with especial tenderness. The very word "tenderness" implies softness, delicacy of touch, caring for. The gorilla, that gentle creature, is the most frequently slandered when women wish to describe the sexual approaches of the average male. Sex seems to be regarded as a tension releaser rather than as a profoundly meaningful act of communication in a deeply involved human relationship.*[48]

One modern woman—a rape victim—thus expressed her own view of sex:

> *Sex, for men, is totally oriented toward the man's orgasm and isn't successful unless it involves intercourse and orgasm, which is ridiculous,*

because sex to me is a much more sensual, much more emotional experience. It doesn't involve just one particular spot on the body getting excited and aroused, and then it's over, and it's either a success or failure.[49]

Men culturally trained not to pay attention to women seldom understood what women meant by "love," even when they tried to explain. The celebrated Kinsey reports on American sexual behavior didn't mention "love" in their index.[50] Certainly there was no such idea in America as the Tantric *karuna,* which combined all forms of love in communion with the female, though modern women sometimes try to grope toward this concept, unaware that it was elucidated long ago:

> *Gestation . . . is a complex inner process in which sexuality is fed by everything else a woman has at her disposal, much in the same way that she might feed a fetus. When there is no fetus, an inclusive kind of sexual intimacy fills up a comparable inner space. But when sex is separated from that context, the disparity between a penetration that is no more than an "action" and a penetration that reaches into complex inner space can become quite overwhelming. . . .*
>
> *To most men the problem . . . does not seem very real. To them the clearest aim of sex is orgasm, that moment of intense physical intimacy and satisfaction which so often serves as a substitute for other kinds of intimacy. Perhaps that is one of the reasons why men seem to be so concerned with satisfying women sexually and interpret that satisfaction in terms of what they think would satisfy them if they were women. It may also be one of the reasons why men seem to think that many women can never be completely satisfied sexually. The terrain where a woman remains forever unsatisfied or even, as they say, "insatiable," is probably the area where her sexuality borders most closely on that more complex psycho-sexual area of her being.*[51]

In Oriental countries where an image of the Goddess was retained, broader ideas of sexuality were retained also:

> *Western attitudes . . . look on sexual intercourse as a matter of tension, appetite and relief . . . according to the simplistic biological conception which is still current. . . . It is well known that the man who, in the Kinsey Report on the Human Male, recorded a frequency above thirty times a day for many years became a kind of folk-hero in America. Sexual love, in such a context, becomes at best a matter of frequently happily shared orgasms.*
>
> *To the traditional Indian mind this attitude is grotesque and pathetic. Even the ordinary man recognized that such banality was absurd. . . . Eighteenth-century Indian harlots mocked European men for their miserable sexual performance, calling them "dunghill cocks" for whom the act was over in a few seconds. Despite recent advances in sexological knowledge, the West's chosen external explanations of sex, attached as they are to a provisional and impoverished rationalization of the infinite complex of human experience, still tend to regard sex as the pursuit of orgasm. . . . Traditional India did not.*[52]

A mystical or poetic view of sex, like the Indian one, seemed to jar the puritan consciousness even more than a "dirty" or degraded view. Dr. Marie Stopes's *Married Love* was imported from England in 1918 but banned for obscenity in the U.S., chiefly on account of such delirious passages as the following:

> *The half-swooning sense of flux which overtakes the spirit in their eternal moment at the apex of rapture sweeps into its flaming tides the whole essence of the man and woman, and as it were, the heat of the contact vaporizes their consciousness so that it fills the whole of cosmic space. For the moment they are identified with the divine thoughts, the waves of eternal force, which to the Mystic often appear in terms of golden light.*[53]

Some progress has been made since the sexual obtuseness of western men made them a laughingstock in India. But recent investigators found "a view of sex that is as distorted as the Victorian, for it is still shrouded with the unrealistic expectations and outmoded standards of gender behavior of the past. Fantasy rather than reality is its keynote; hostility, anxiety, and guilt are aggravated rather than alleviated."[54] Significantly, a male author characterizes male sexuality as loveless and death-centered, capable of destroying the foundations of society:

> *Contemporary eroticism attempts to free woman sexually but according to a* masculine *conception of sexuality. . . . The present rehabilitation of the erotic in its purely sexual, loveless aspect is completely at variance with the truly feminine conception . . . an ultimate striving toward dislocation, destruction, and death—Thanatos—as against Eros, the love-filled erotic, unifying and conservationist. . . . Ultimately, this overemphasis of the masculine component in Western society threatens to destroy its foundations.*[55]

To counterbalance the destructiveness of male-dominated society, nothing could be effective except recognition of the feminine principle, according to George Sand: "It will be in the female heart *par excellence,* as it always has been, that love and devotion, patience and pity, will find their true home. On woman falls the duty, in a world of brute passions, of preserving the virtue of charity. . . . When woman ceases to play that role, life will be the loser."[56] Modern thinkers also regret the loss of cultural emphasis on the feminine morality that can integrate sex with affection, tenderness, and sensitivity toward others' emotional needs. It has been often said that male-dominated societies tend to burden the sexual impulses of both women and men with basically unrelated guilts, fears, angers, and their resulting aggressions. Some forms of "entertainment" for example take advantage of the new frankness to introduce disturbingly sadistic elements into mass socialization for sexual adulthood. "Rather than lament the fact that sexual appetite is now being encouraged, we might more profitably spend our time trying to ensure that the emotions that are integrated with it are the ones we approve of."[57]

As recently as 1966, an anthropological study of the Irish islanders of Inis Beag revealed a mini-culture of 19th-century Christian-patriarchal patterns in sexual life. Female orgasm was unknown. Women were trained to endure rather than enjoy sex. Men habitually ejaculated within seconds. Modesty was the overwhelming preoccupation of both sexes; husbands and wives didn't see each other naked. Sexual foreplay consisted of rough fondling outside the sleeping garments. No coital position other than *Venus observa* was used.

Premarital sex was virtually unknown, since young couples were never alone together. Not even "walking out," the old-fashioned version of dating, was allowed. Young people received no instruction in sexual matters. The islanders said after marriage "nature would take its course" without the embarrassment of discussion.

Though the men were often at sea in small boats, they never learned to swim, being unwilling to undress in public for this purpose. "Bathing" in the sea meant wading, fully clothed. The sexes were rigidly separated for this activity. Men were known to die of disease or injury rather than to go to a hospital on the mainland, where they thought their bodies would be bared to the eyes of female nurses.

Even the dogs of Inis Beag were whipped for licking their genitals or other "obscene" behavior. Imported copies of American magazines such as *Life* or *Time* were denounced from the pulpit as pornography. Fear of female "mysteries" was overt: women were not approached sexually for many months after childbirth, or during menstruation, when men thought them especially dangerous. Predictably, severe repression exacted a severe toll in quarrelsomeness, alcoholism, violence, and frequent mental disturbances.[58]

Paradoxically, the more sexuality is banned and ignored, the more fear it seems to engender in men. A patriarchal-ascetic ethic seems to arrange sexual attitudes according to the way men would like them arranged, but it doesn't work well even for men. A psychiatrist says, "In the privacy of our consulting room we do from time to time see strong men fret, and hear them talk of women with dread and horror and awe, as if women, far from being timid creatures to be patronized, were as powerful as the sea and inescapable as fate. . . . Man, confronted by woman, does seem to feel, variously, frightened, revolted, dominated, bewildered, and even, at times, superfluous."[59] One male author in a revealing passage on men's sexual feelings refers to a woman as "it," but also admits "general helplessness in the face of her," and a sense of her "awesomeness and power"—seemingly overblown terms for an ordinary human female:

> *We cannot relate to the total object as it [sic] is, and thus we need standardized definitions of sexual attractiveness. These we get in the form of "cues" that serve to cut the object down to manageable size: we look at the breast or the black underwear, which allow us not really to have to take account of the total person we are relating to. . . . [W]e strip*

the partner of awesomeness and power and so overcome our general helplessness in the face of her.[60]

The symbols of "sexiness" are created and instilled by the society, however odd it may seem to realize that human physiological responses can actually be keyed to abstract images. "It is now quite clear that how a person behaves sexually is largely determined not by inborn factors but by learning."[61] The prevailing conventional wisdom and its influence on the growing child determine whether most people will enjoy sex or hate it, perceiving their own bodies as heaven or hell. Western anti-sexuality has created many individuals tending toward the "hate" or "hell" end of the spectrum, epitomized by a psychiatric patient who said, "Somehow I always think that sexual intercourse is a great disgrace for humans." A female patient called her body an "abhorrent envelope," and said, "I wish I could tear this skin off. If I didn't have this stupid body, I would be as pure outside as I feel inside."[62]

Women have an especially difficult time with the body-image in a society that attaches little value to their complex body-oriented roles of wife, mother, nurturer, or comforter; and may even cease to play these roles when they have fully accepted the value system of the dominant sex. Women don't reject traditional "feminine" roles out of perversity, nor because of that Freudian absurdity, penis envy. Like men, most women prefer to do what their society values and rewards. If the wife-and-mother role is undervalued—or even deprecated, as it has been throughout the past two millenia in the western world—women can hardly be blamed for seeking valid achievement in other fields.[63] In our society the universal standard of valuation is money, and the so-called "career" of wife-and-mother earns none at all.

Underevaluation of the mother affects sons as well as daughters, since the mother's reaction to social expectations of her inevitably creates a deep impression on her children. "Psychiatric observation suggests that human sexual behavior is subtly shaped by the nature of the social attachments formed during a person's development"; and the mother is the primary social attachment.[64] Chodorow says the modern civilized male "is in the unhappy position of being able to attain masculine identity almost solely through efforts to distinguish himself from the person closest to him [the mother], with whom he might most naturally identify. His efforts commonly take the form of a rather primitive rejection of all that is 'feminine' in women and in himself."[65]

Sexual development is further hampered by conventional religions which still attach fear and guilt to almost every stage of the process. Ignoring recent proofs that masturbation is necessary for development of normal orgasmic capacity in both sexes, Pope Paul VI's 1976 declaration on sexual ethics pronounced masturbation "a grave moral disorder." Moreover, within the framework of marriage, only the "finality" of procreation could "ensure the moral goodness" of sex—in other words, sex must make babies, not pleasure.[66] As for premarital sex, Norman Vincent Peale declared it a dreadful sin even for persons deeply in love; they cannot be forgiven without prolonged spiritual "treatment."[67]

It is now said that sexual appetites have "little or no relation to biological or physiological needs. . . . [E]rotic urges stem more from socio-cultural factors than from those of the strictly physiological nature."[68] Therefore the broad extent of ugly or cruel sexual behavior patterns in modern society should stimulate serious thought about what the society is teaching. In 1972, the Chief of the Sex Section of the Washington D.C. Police Department reported: "The newspapers print only what they want to. I tell them about little girls of seven or eight who come up with venereal diseases inflicted on them by male members of their own families. An appalling number of 11- and 12-year-olds are giving birth after being raped by their own fathers. But they won't print things like this. They're only heart-breaking and horrible—not sensational."[69]

A report of the Commission on Obscenity and Pornography concluded: "Failure to talk openly and directly about sex . . . overemphasizes sex, gives it a magical nonnatural quality. . . . Such failure makes teaching children and adolescents to become fully and adequately functioning sexual adults a more difficult task. . . . The very foundation of our society rests upon healthy sexual attitudes grounded in appropriate and accurate sexual information."[70] In other words, the foundations of society rest on dissemination of precisely the kind of information that Christian morality insisted on withholding from one and all—men, women, and children.

Churches today have largely renounced all their responsibility to establish guidelines for sexual development or sexual behavior, leaving their congregations in an area of confusion. Theologians stress "the personal responsibility of the Christian to find God's will for himself."[71] In which case, he hardly needs a church.

1. S. Harris, 255. 2. R.E.L. Masters, xxvi. 3. Lederer, 163. 4. Mumford, 145.
5. Bullough, 97. 6. Fielding, 81; Jonas, 145. 7. Bullough, 110.
8. H. Smith, 250; Cavendish, P.E., 27. 9. J.B. Russell, 284. 10. Jonas, 73.
11. Briffault 3, 494. 12. Kramer & Sprenger, 167, 169. 13. de Voragine, 89, 231.
14. Lawson, 570, 606. 15. Wilkins, 122. 16. Oxenstierna, 223–24.
17. Turville-Petre, 193. 18. Fielding, 145–46. 19. Hartley, 196. 20. Avalon, 191.
21. Edwardes, 52. 22. Ashe, 178–79. 23. Bullough, 114. 24. Murstein, 76.
25. Bullough, 115. 26. de Voragine, 499. 27. H. Smith, 228–29.
28. Briffault 3, 199, 207. 29. Briffault 2, 48. 30. Elisofon & Watts, 11.
31. Laistner, 31. 32. Fromm, 190. 33. de Riencourt, 102. 34. Silberer, 284–85.
35. Rugoff, 47. 36. Barker-Benfield, 279–80. 37. de Voragine, 146.
38. Sadock, Kaplan & Freedman, 32. 39. Gilder, 145–46. 40. Bullough, 114.
41. Simons, 141. 42. Rugoff, 49. 43. Perrin, 68. 44. Bullough, 290.
45. Marcus, 25–32. 46. Gornick & Moran, 211. 47. Stall, 134.
48. Montagu, T., 173–74. 49. D.E.H. Russell, 105. 50. Mumford, 344.
51. Bengis, 68. 52. Rawson, A.T., 78. 53. Murstein, 421.
54. Steinman & Fox, 258–59. 55. de Riencourt, 416–17. 56. de Riencourt, 301.
57. Nobile, 237–38. 58. Marshall & Suggs, ch. 1. 59. Lederer, vii.
60. Becker, D.D., 242. 61. Montagu, S.M.S., 63. 62. Becker, D.D., 226, 236.
63. Mead, 92. 64. Nobile, 232–33. 65. Gornick & Moran, xxiv.
66. *Newsweek,* Jan. 26, 1976. 67. Ellis, 187. 68. Nobile, 233–34.
69. D.E.H. Russell, 31. 70. Goldstein & Kant, 153. 71. Murstein, 433.

Sexism

The *Catholic Encyclopedia* declares, "The female sex is in some respects inferior to the male sex, both as regards body and soul."[1] This is a somewhat modified version of the opinion of St. Thomas Aquinas, who insisted that every woman is birth-defective, an imperfect male begotten because her father happened to be ill, weakened, or in a state of sin at the time of her conception.[2] Knowing nothing of the human ovum, the church taught the doctrine of Augustine and Aquinas that a mother contributes nothing to her child's genetic inheritance, but acts only as "soil" for the male soul-bearing seed.[3] Nevertheless, churchmen claimed the birth of a true freak was not the father's fault, but the result of "the heated and obstinate imagination" of the mother during sexual intercourse.[4]

Fathers of the church were earnest woman-haters. St. John Chrysostom said men suffer "a thousand evils" from having to look at women; "the beauty of women is the greatest snare." St. Odo of Cluny refused to be ensnared; he said, "How should we desire to embrace what is no more than a sack of dung!" According to Walter Map, "Even the very good woman, who is rarer than the phoenix, cannot be loved without the loathesome bitterness of fear and worry and constant unhappiness." A 19th-century Anglican churchman said women are "intrinsically inferior in excellence, imbecile by sex and nature, weak in body, inconstant in mind, and imperfect and infirm in character."[5] In the 1890s, the president of a leading theological seminary declared, "My Bible commands the subjection of women forever."[6]

St. John Chrysostom, "Golden-mouthed John," 4th-century Christian orator who served as Patriarch of Constantinople until he incurred the wrath of the empress Eudoxia, who arranged to have him deposed and exiled.

Walter Map Canon of St. Paul's, Lincoln, and Hereford; archdeacon of Oxford; ecclesiastical justice attached to the court of Henry II in the late 12th century. Map was (probably falsely) credited with authorship of some of the older Arthurian legends.

So it did. Through the centuries, the Bible supported sexist sentiments which were echoed by all churchmen. St. Paul said: "The head of every man is Christ; and the head of every woman is the man" (1 Corinthians 11:3). St. Peter said in the Gospel of Thomas: "Women are not worthy of life."[7] Clement of Alexandria quoted the words of Christ from the Gospel According to the Egyptians: "I have come to destroy the works of the female."[8] He added: "Every woman ought to be filled with shame at the thought that she is a woman."[9]

Up to the modern era, clergymen continued to appeal to biblical authority to maintain the political subjection of women. "The clergy were often in the forefront of the fight against suffrage, dredging up quotations from the Bible to prove that the natural order of things was female obedience to man." Simone de Beauvoir says: "For the Jews, Mohammedans and Christians among others, man is master by divine right, the fear of God will therefore repress any impulse towards revolt in the downtrodden female." As late as 1971 an Episcopalian bishop confirmed these views: "The sexuality of Christ is no accident nor is his masculinity incidental. This is the divine choice." Feminists believe that even if the churches should destroy themselves in the effort, they will cling to their notion of male supremacy to the very end, for this was their primary foundation in the beginning.[10] Theology's entire conceptual system was invented by men to serve the interests of men—and, not incidentally, to restrict and suppress the interests of women.[11]

Church fathers long ago laid down the principle of woman's guilt for the existence of death and sin. Augustine blamed the perpetuation of original sin on the "concupiscence" that united male bodies with female ones under any circumstances, including marriage.[12] Christianity was the first religion to announce that it was sinful just to be alive, on account of having been sexually conceived and born of a woman.[13] St. John Chrysostom commanded every Christian father to instill into his son "a resolute spirit against womankind. . . . Let him have no converse with any woman save only his mother. Let him see no woman."[14]

Sometimes the writings of Christian men revealed an almost hysterical fear of woman. Her very glance could "infect, entice, bewitch." Her eyes "poison and intoxicate the mind: yea, her company induceth impudency, corrupteth virginity, confoundeth and consumeth the bodies, the goods, and the very souls of men. And finally her body destroyeth and rotteth the very flesh and bones of man's body." Vairus said women become witches because "they have such an unbridled force of fury and concupiscence naturally. . . . And they are so troubled with evil humors, that out go their venomous exhalations, engendered through their illfavored diet, and increased by means of their pernicious excrements, which they expel."[15]

John Aylmer labeled all women "tale-bearers, eavesdroppers, rumor raisers, evil tongued, worse minded, and in every wise doltified with the dregs of the Devil's dung hill."[16] Similar opinions have been offered by modern woman-abusers, such as the rapist: "I thought . . . women were trashy, low-down and scummy because that's what I had been taught."[17]

Andrew the Chaplain said woman is "by nature a miser, envious, a slanderer . . . greedy, a slave to her belly, inconstant, fickle . . . disobedient and impatient of restraint, spotted with the sin of pride and desirous of vainglory, a liar, a drunkard, a babbler, no keeper of secrets, too much given to wantonness, prone to every evil, and never loving any man in her heart."[18]

John Scotus Erigena taught that human beings were once without sin and without sexuality; but after they disobeyed God, they were divided into two sexes. The sinless part was embodied in man, the sinful part in woman.[19] Other theologians said woman was "the confusion of man, an insatiable beast, a continuous anxiety, an incessant warfare, a daily ruin." The church ostensibly made war on the devil, but in actual practice made war on women. "Woman was the Church's rival, the temptress, the distraction, the obstacle to holiness, the Devil's decoy."[20] Official church literature said:

> *All wickedness is but little to the wickedness of a woman. . . . [T]he natural reason is that she is more carnal than a man, as is clear from her*

many carnal abominations. And it should be noted that there was a defect in the formation of the first woman, since she was formed from a bent rib, that is, a rib of the breast, which is bent as it were in a contrary direction to a man. And since through this defect she is an imperfect animal, she always deceives.[21]

Curiously enough, modern genetic research indicates that the truth may be something like the reverse of this view. The XY chromosome that produces a male is physiologically an "incomplete" female chromosome. Some individuals are born with an XYY chromosome abnormality, making them genetic super-males. They are said to be tall, below average in intelligence, and strongly disposed to criminal behavior.[22]

This would have surprised men like Orestes Brownson, who insisted that woman's "ambition and natural love of power" must be subject to masculine control, otherwise "she is out of her element, and a social anomaly, sometimes a hideous monster, which men seldom are, excepting through a woman's influence."[23] Such men never bothered to notice that their denunciations of women were self-contradictory; as in this case, for instance, if woman's love of power was "natural," then in exercising it she would be in her element, not out of it.

Orestes Augustus Brownson (1803-1876) U. S. arbiter of opinion, writer on spiritualism, religion, social reform, states' rights, etc.; publisher of *Brownson's Quarterly*, 1844-75.

Martin Luther claimed the physical differences between men and women demonstrated God's plan for sexism. "Men have broad and large chests and small and narrow hips and more understanding than women who have but small and narrow chests and broad hips, to the end that they should remain at home, sit still, keep house and bear and bring up children."[24] But if their bearing and bringing up children wore them out, it was no matter, Luther said: "If women get tired and die of bearing, there is no harm in that; let them die as long as they bear; they were made for that."[25]

Schopenhauer, who detested women, found nothing likeable about their physical appearance: "It is only the man whose intellect is clouded by his sexual impulses that could give the name of *the fair sex* to that undersized, narrow-shouldered, broad-hipped, and short-legged race. . . . [T]he sympathies that exist between them and men are skin-deep only, and do not touch the mind or the feelings or the character."[26] Hartley tends to agree that thanks to Christian tradition, "An extreme outward sex-attraction has come to veil but thinly a deep inward sex-antipathy, until it seems almost impossible that women and men can ever really understand one another."[27]

Those few Renaissance men who would speak on behalf of women were outside the church, and usually suspected of heresy, like Agrippa von Nettesheim, who wrote that women "are treated by the men as conquered by the conquerors, not by any divine necessity, for any reason, but according to custom, education, fortune, and the tyrant's opportunity."

The tyranny of men prevailing over divine right and the laws of nature, slays by law the liberty of woman, abolishes it by use and custom, and extinguishes it by education. For the woman, as soon as she is born, is from her earliest years detained at home in idleness, and as if destitute of capacity for higher occupations, is permitted to conceive of nothing beyond needle and thread. Then when she has attained years of puberty she is delivered over to the jealous empire of a man, or shut up forever in a shop of vestals. The law also forbids her to fill public offices. No prudence entitles her to plead in open court.[28]

There was sex discrimination even in the penalties imposed for witchcraft. Female witches were more severely punished than male witches. A law of 1683 said that for the crime of causing death by witchcraft, a man may be hanged, but a woman must be burned at the stake. Men could with impunity kill their wives (e.g., by beating) in the 1650s, but women were burned for killing their husbands, a crime defined as "petty treason."[29]

A self-perpetuating belief in woman's inferior intellect was fostered by the almost universal custom of keeping women out of schools, all but a few aristocratic ladies who could receive an expensive private education. Queen Elizabeth I of England was unsexed by several historians who thought she was too clever to be female. They claimed she died in infancy, and a boy was secretly raised in her place. The small minority of educated women were seldom accepted as such. On one occasion a learned lady was presented as a curiosity to King James I, and he was told she was fluent in Latin, Greek, and Hebrew. He only inquired, "But can she spin?"[30]

The church controlled most schools, and the church would have no truck with women unless it was unavoidable. St. Columkille made a rule that no woman could even be buried in the vicinity of a Christian church, alleging that this was the custom from Christianity's beginnings. County Tyrone in Ireland still has a *Relig-na-man*, "cemetery of women," located a half-mile from the church where only men were buried in the churchyard.[31] Some churchmen opined that women didn't even have any souls to save. Ockham claimed women did have souls, and on that account should be allowed to vote in church councils. The pope instantly condemned this as heresy.[32]

Josephine Henry
19th-century Kentucky suffragist and pamphleteer, active in the women's rights movement.

Josephine K. Henry castigated the churches for their consistently antifemale attitudes over the centuries:

Has the Church ever issued an edict that women must be equal with man before the canon or the civil law, that her thoughts should be incorporated in creed or code, that she should own her own body and property in marriage, or have a legal claim to her children born in wedlock, which Christianity claims is a "sacrament" and one of the "holy mysteries"? . . . No institution in modern civilization is so tyrannical and so unjust to woman as is the Christian Church. It demands everything from her and gives her nothing in return. The history of the Church does not contain a single suggestion for the equality of woman . . . . Through tyranny and falsehood alone is Christianity able to hold woman in subjection.[33]

Indeed, women were better served by pre-Christian laws nearly everywhere. Under the ancient Byzantine code, inheritance laws made no distinction between heirs on the basis of their sex; and although adulterous men were executed, adulterous women were not.[34] After centuries of Christian revision, the laws freely allowed men to commit adultery, though their wives could be imprisoned or beaten to death for it. Until 1857, no English woman could obtain a divorce on any grounds without a special Act of Parliament, which meant only upper-class women with plenty of political leverage could even hope for a divorce.[35]

In 1835, a Mrs. Caroline Norton left her husband after he repeatedly subjected her to beatings, mental abuse, and infidelity. He kept his mistress in the same house with her. A court ruled that the wife need not return to the house, but the husband was given their three children because the wife had "condoned his actions" by staying with him through all his cruelties. In 1839, the Infants' Custody Act introduced a slight modification. At his own discretion, a judge in equity could allow separated mothers to keep children under seven years of age, or to have visiting rights to older children, provided the mother was not guilty of adultery.[36] Fathers suffered no such restriction, of course.

Women who refused to submit to the "discipline" of marriage, but instead played the dangerous game of promising without delivering, were known as jilts. Such women aroused the most violent outbursts of sexist sentiment, according to an old pamphlet:

> *Their tricks and devices are numberless, and not to be paralleled by any thing but their Ingratitude and Inhumanity; there indeed they exceed themselves; nothing in Nature being so perfectly brutish and cruel as one of these kind [sic] of Creatures . . . a Vermin so ravenous and malicious, and withal so subtle and designing, so formally chaste and hypocritically virtuous, and yet so scandalously common and impudently lewd, so proud, and yet so mercenary, and above all, so insolently ill natured, that in the short character of a Jilt, are comprehended all the Vices, Follies and Impertinences of the whole Sex. . . . In short, I cannot but fancy them a Colony of Hell-Cats, planted here by the Devil, as a mischief to Mankind.*[37]

Noting that women often refused to play fair in the game for which men made all the rules, even Freud failed to transcend the sexist attitudes of his time. He wrote: "One cannot resist the thought that the level of normal morality is different for women. Their superego never becomes so unshakeable, so impersonal, so independent of its affective origins, as we demand it of a man. Critics since time immemorial have reproached women of certain character traits: that they exhibit less of a sense of justice than men do; that they are less prepared to submit to the great necessities of life." Since Freud regarded male domination as one of the great necessities of life, he should hardly have been surprised to find women resisting it. Simone de Beauvoir said every woman knows that "masculine morality, as it concerns her, is a vast hoax. Man pompously thunders forth his code of virtue and honor; but in secret he invites her to disobey it, and he even counts on her disobedience; without it, all that splendid facade behind which he takes cover would collapse."[38]

Since women weren't told the rules of the game, many of them became losers while they were still too young to figure it out for themselves. Commenting on Oscar Wilde's homosexuality trial, W.T. Stead remarked, "If Oscar Wilde, instead of indulging in dirty tricks of indecent familiarity with boys and men, had ruined the lives of half a dozen innocent simpletons of girls, or had broken up the home of his friend by corrupting his friend's wife, no one could have laid a finger on him. The male is sacrosanct: the female is fair game."[39]

Though women were scorned for being "simpletons," they were even more violently scorned when they tried to develop their minds. Florence Nightingale's popularity inspired many women to seek educations in medicine, but male students ganged up on them. In 1870 a group of student doctors formed lines to prevent five women from entering classes in Surgeons' Hall in London. Medical examiners tried to embarrass female students with indecent questions. When women received high marks in examinations, they were passed over, and scholarships were awarded to the men immediately below their level.

It was the same in other professions. In 1879, Birmingham schoolmasters barred women from employment as teachers of small boys, on the ground that it would encourage "immorality." Lawyers denied women admission to the Inns of Court. Determined feminist efforts brought about admission of some women to classes at Queen's College in 1848; but the Bishop of London excluded women from Wheatstone's classes on electricity, because they had "congregated too abundantly" in Sir Charles Lyell's geology classes, keeping more deserving students (i.e., men) from finding places in the classroom. In the field of religion, the Church of England found it "unthinkable" that women should ever be admitted to the ministry.[40]

Christine Pierce
Contemporary American feminist, professor of law and philosophy at Harvard and New York State University.

The basic fallacy of sexism in employment or education was pointed out by Christine Pierce: "We need not fear that women will do what they cannot do."[41] If women were really unable to learn medicine, law, theology, science, or any other field of endeavor, it would hardly have been necessary for men to exert such efforts to keep them from learning. The theory of feminine intellectual inferiority began to recede from view when women managed to receive education. But many men still clung to the belief that women must be less able to think than men.

In 1913 T.E. Reed wrote a book called *Sex, Its Origin and Determination,* to prove "scientifically" that women were biologically inferior to men. The author said coitus during an incoming tide always conceived boys, while coitus during an outgoing tide conceived girls—proving that the female was weaker, born of "waning" energy. Despite the fact that incoming and outgoing tides differed on every one of the world's coastlines, and infants conceived inland couldn't be identified with any tide, the theory proved popular.[42]

In many ways, sexist thinkers have tried to pretend male dominance is "natural" or is a divinely ordained biological mandate. Yet as other mammalian species demonstrate, such an arrangement could serve no biological purpose.

Any animal species in which males were biologically programmed to attack and injure the females would be at a disadvantage in terms of species survival, since mammalian young can't grow to maturity without healthy, competent mothers.[43] Thus it is found that, in most species, males are biologically inhibited from attacking females, even under strong provocation. And the one virtually unbreakable male animal taboo is any kind of interference between a female and the young she protects.

Karen Horney suggested that men's antagonism may have developed as a result of sexual envy: "The male is sexually dependent on the female to a higher degree than the woman is on him, because in women part of the sexual energy is linked to generative processes. Could it be that men, therefore, have a vital interest in keeping women dependent on them?"[44] Judith Antonelli says, "Patriarchy is based on the 'phallacy' that the male is creator. Man's original awe and envy of woman becomes, under patriarchy, resentment and hostility. The only way man can possess female power is through woman, and so he colonizes her, suppressing her sexuality so that it serves him rather than being the source of her power. . . . Patriarchy is indeed a male neurosis."[45]

Karen Horney, née Danielsen (1885-1952) U.S. psychoanalyst and teacher, Freudian-trained but breaking away from Freudian thought in many respects; author of *The Neurotic Personality of Our Time* (1937), *Our Inner Conflicts* (1945), *Neurosis and Human Growth* (1950), etc.

1. Evans, N.H.N., 180. 2. de Riencourt, 227. 3. Rees, 227. 4. Shumaker, 95. 5. Bullough, 98, 187, 203. 6. Stanton, 194. 7. Malvern, 1. 8. Stone, 194. 9. Lederer, 162. 10. Stone, 236–38. 11. Daly, 4. 12. Bullough, 117. 13. H. Smith, 250. 14. Laistner, 112. 15. Scot, 227, 248. 16. Bullough, 202. 17. Goldstein & Kant, 85. 18. Murstein, 160. 19. de Riencourt, 227. 20. Tuchman, 211. 21. Kramer & Sprenger, 44. 22. Torrey, 178. 23. Bullough, 309. 24. de Lys, 179. 25. de Riencourt, 258. 26. Murstein, 261. 27. Hartley, 266. 28. Agrippa, 271. 29. Robbins, 165, 209. 30. Bullough, 223. 31. Joyce 2, 374. 32. Coulton, 227. 33. Stanton, 205–7. 34. Soisson, 43. 35. Crow, 147. 36. Crow, 40–41. 37. de Vries & Fryer, 111–13. 38. Lederer, 93–95. 39. Pearsall, N.B.A., 231. 40. Pearsall, N.B.A., 43–45. 41. Gornick & Moran, 252. 42. Montagu, S.M.S., 92. 43. Fromm, 192. 44. Roszak, 110. 45. Spretnak, 401.

Shadow

The ancients believed a person's shadow was one of his several souls. Egyptians called the shadow *khaibut,* Romans called it *umbra,* the "shade" or ghost that went to the underground Land of Shades after death. Pagan Europe generally described the ghosts of ancestors as black, like shadows, and desirous of blood, the elixir of rebirth.

The shadow was a vulnerable soul because it was external and had to be carefully preserved from accident. Many superstitious people even today think it dangerous to let their shadows fall across an open grave, rocky cleft, or swift stream.[1]

The Bible shows Joshua and Caleb placing a death-curse on their enemies by saying "Their shadow is departed from them" (Numbers 14:9). This was a typical "doom-saying," supposedly a prophecy to be fulfilled by its very utterance.

One could also give one's soul to a god by dedicating one's shadow to him. Pausanias said human bodies lost their shadows in the sanctuary of Zeus Lycaeus (Wolfish Zeus).[2] From such beliefs descended the shadowless "werewolf" or vampire of medieval superstition. Soullessness was indicated by lack of a shadow or a reflection, both of which were anciently identified with souls.

Pausanias Greek traveler and geographer of the 2nd century A.D. Living in a time of declining culture, he was inspired by a desire to describe the ancient sacred sites for posterity.

Like those who pretended to give their shadows to the ancient gods, those who gave their souls to the devil could be distinguished by lack of a shadow, according to medieval superstition. The most famous shadowless man in Jewish folklore was Peter Schlemihl, whose name became a byword for a fool because the devil tricked him into parting with his shadow.[3] He was apparently based on the biblical patriarch Shelumiel, whose name meant "friend of God," possibly because he gave God his shadow-soul. In Bohemia, Peter Schlemihl was known as Prschemischl, a hero mated to the legendary Queen Libussa. This may have been a garbled recollection of the sacred marriage of Pater Liber and the Goddess Libera.[4]

Another version of Pater-Peter and his shadow-soul appeared in Acts 5:15–16. People troubled by sickness or demonic possession were brought into a street where the shadow of St. Peter passing by "might overshadow some of them"; and with this kind of soul-contact "they were healed every one."

In the pagan context, a shadowless man was not a demon, a werewolf, or a "Schlemihl" but one whose soul had gone into eternal bliss. Plutarch said at the end of the world, the blessed ones would be happy forever "in a state neither needing food nor casting a shadow."[5]

On earth, however, a shadowless state was to be feared. Jews lived in terror of the "noonday devil" (Keteb), a stealer of shadows. It made the shadow-soul small and weak at noonday, leaving the owner vulnerable to demons of disease.[6] This shadow-stealing devil also entered into Christian superstition as the *demonium meridianum* (noonday devil).

1. Frazer, G.B., 575. 2. d'Alviella, 64. 3. Norman, 131. 4. Leland, 115. 5. Knight, S.L., 117. 6. Budge, A.T., 219.

Shaharit

Jewish morning service, based on the ancient Canaanite cult of the god of the morning star, Shaher, whose duty it was to announce the rebirth of the sun by proclaiming, "He is risen." See **Lucifer**.

Shakta

A male worshipper of the Tantric image of the Great Goddess, Shakti; a man versed in the techniques of Tantric yoga and identified with the Goddess herself through sexual union with her earthly representative. A *shakta* was also known as a *sadhaka* or *sadhu,* possible origin of the "Sadducees" mentioned in the Bible. See **Tantrism**.

Shakti

Tantric title of the Great Goddess (**Kali Ma**), realized both as a sexual partner and as the innermost, animating soul of man or god, like the Greek Psyche, Roman Anima, Gnostic Sophia, Cabalistic Shekina, all based on the Shakti. Jung said she was the figure known as My Lady Soul: "Every mother and every beloved is forced to become the carrier and embodiment of this omnipresent and ageless image, which corresponds to the deepest reality in a man."[1]

Shakti is translated "Cosmic Energy." She implies "power, ability, capacity, faculty, strength, prowess; regal power; the power of composition, poetic power, genius; the power or signification of a word or term; the power inherent in cause to produce its necessary effect. . . . *[S]hakti* is the female organ; *shakti* is the active power of a deity and is regarded, mythologically, as his goddess-consort and queen."[2] Every god needed his Shakti, or he was helpless to act. The Tantras say "the female principle antedates and includes the male principle, and . . . this female principle is the supreme Divinity."[3]

Tantric doctrine said mortal women are "life itself," and Goddess-like, because they embody the principle of Shakti. The sages "hold women in great esteem and call them Shaktis and to ill-treat a Shakti, that is, a woman, is a crime." A Tantric synonym for "woman" was *Shaktiman,* "Mind of Shakti" or "Possessor of Shakti."[4]

A Shakti was also a spirit-wife, or female guardian angel, who could be incarnate in the earthly wife or mistress, or a wholly supernatural figure. "An important division of the 'mythology of woman' is devoted to showing that it is always a feminine being who helps the hero to conquer immortality or to emerge victorious from his initiatory ordeals. . . . Every Teleut shaman has a celestial wife who lives in the seventh heaven, where he meets her and makes love to her during his ecstatic journeys."[5]

Final union with the Shakti occurred at the moment of death, according to Tantric mystics. She was both the individual and the cosmic Goddess, absorbing the soul and body of the dying sage into herself, an experience of unsurpassable bliss on his part. "The possession of her, the cosmic Shakti, the living embodiment of the principle of beauty and youth eternal, is the ultimate quest, the very highest prize."[6]

The Kulacudamani Nigama said not even God could become the

Lalita Sahasranamam One of the Tantric texts in praise of the Goddess Kali-Shakti.

Avesta Early scriptures of Zoroastrianism, written in Avestan, an ancient Iranian language; still used by the Parsees as a Bible and prayer book.

supreme Lord unless Shakti entered into him. All things arose from their union, but she said, "There is none but Myself Who is the Mother to create." The Lalita Sahasranamam said "The series of universes appear and disappear with the opening and shutting of Her eyes." As the god required her power before he could do anything at all, so her worshipper on earth required the power of his own Istadevata, Shakti or lady-love.[7]

The same system was followed by Middle-Eastern mystics like the Sufis, who deemed the mystic lady-love or *fravashi* essential to any man's enlightenment. Early Christian Gnostics also worshipped Shakti under such names as Sophia, Pneuma, Eide, or Anima. Gnostic writings show that post-mortem union with one's own soul was perceived in sexual symbolism, as in the Mandaean Liturgies for the Dead: the soul or "image" (Eide) embraces and caresses the dead man like a beloved woman. This Tantric idea came into the west by way of the Avesta doctrine that, after the death of a believer, his own conscience would welcome him "in the form of a fair maiden."[8]

1. Campbell, C.M., 488. 2. Zimmer, 25. 3. Avalon, 173. 4. Avalon, 172, 388. 5. Eliade, S., 76, 78. 6. Zimmer, 178. 7. Avalon, 390, 396, 452. 8. Jonas, 122.

Shalimar

Oriental garden of love, the **paradise** of kings in their sacred union with the Goddess. The garden was both her body and the after-world, like the Tibetan Shal-Mari, a "land of souls." The same mystic garden probably was the body of the Middle-Eastern Great Goddess, Sheol-Mari; for "Sheol"—which later became a synonym for "hell"—was originally a magic garden within the belly of Mother Earth. As the Enclosed Garden (*hortus conclusus*) it represented the Goddess Mari as a Virgin. As the *pardes* (paradise) she was the Virgin Bride of Hebrew god-kings.

Shamrock

The Celtic trefoil, which originated in the east. Pre-Islamic Arabs called the trefoil *shamrakh,* the three-lobed lily or lotus flower of the Moon-goddess's trinity: a design of "three yonis" which appeared on artifacts of the ancient Indus Valley civilization, as well as on stone, pottery, and woodwork in Mesopotamia, Crete, and Egypt between 2300 and 1300 B.C.[1]

Christians pretended that St. Patrick explained the doctrine of the Christian trinity to the Irish by exhibiting the shamrock. However, the Irish were worshipping this emblem of their Triple Goddess long before Christianity appeared in their land. It stood for her triple "door," and her God sometimes bore the title of Trefuilngid Tre-eochair, "Triple Bearer of the Triple Key," a trident representing the triple phallus. He was known as a God of the Shamrock, partially assimilated to Christianity by a legend that he appeared to the Irish on the day of Christ's crucifixion, bearing sacred stone tablets and a branch with three fruits.[2]

1. *Encyc. Brit.,* "Indus Civilization." 2. Graves, W.G., 518.

Shayba

var. Sheba, Shebat

Arabic-Aramaean title of the Great Goddess. Shayba was the "Old Woman" whose spirit dwelt in the sacred stone of the Kaaba in Mecca. Sheba was the land-name and Goddess-name of Arabian queens in the ancient seat of government, Marib, in southern Arabia (now Yemen). Shebat was the Mesopotamian Moon-goddess (a variation of Hebat or Eve), and the month named after her. In Assyria the ancient head of a family was called *shebu,* formerly a matriarch, later a tribal elder of either sex. See **Arabia**.

Sheila-na-gig

Carved representation of a naked woman squatting with her knees apart, displaying her vulva, shown as a *vesica piscis* or double-pointed oval. Sometimes the figure presented the vesica with both hands or drew it open with one. Sheila-na-gig figures appeared all over old Irish churches built before the 16th century.[1] Many were still in place during the 19th century, but Victorian prudery defaced or destroyed large numbers of them. Some have been found buried near the churches they once embellished.[2]

Sheila-na-gig figures closely resembled the yonic statues of Kali which still appear at the doorways of Hindu temples, where visitors lick a finger and touch the yoni "for luck." Some of the older figures have deep holes worn in their yonis from much touching.[3]

The protruding ribcage on many examples of the sheila-na-gig imitates the figures of Kali as the death-goddess, Kalika, evidently remembered in Ireland as the Caillech or "Old Woman," who was also the Creatress and gave birth to all races of men.[4] Celts generally protected doorways with some female-genital fetish, which is why they settled on the horseshoe, classic Omega-sign of the Kalika. In India it stood for the feminine cosmos within which Shiva ever performed his creative sexual dance, although he was assimilated to the Kalika and given her title of Destroyer.[5]

Derivation of the term sheila-na-gig is obscure. It meant something like "vulva-woman." *Gig* or *giggie* meant female genitals and may have been related to the Irish "jig," from French *gigue,* in pre-Christian times an orgiastic dance. In ancient Erech a *gig* seems to have been a holy yoni; the sacred harlots of the temple were known as *nu-gig*.[6]

1. F. Huxley, 63. 2. G.R. Scott, 239–43. 3. Rawson, E.A., 30. 4. Knight, D.W.P., pls. XXIX, XXX. 5. Campbell, M.I., 358. 6. Stone, 158.

Shekina

Jewish-cabalistic version of Shakti; the female soul of God, who couldn't be perfect until he could be reunited with her. Cabalists said it was God's loss of his Shekina that brought about all evils. The Hebrew Sh'kina meant "dwelling-place," a hint that God had no "home" without her. Like her Tantric counterpart the Shakti, the Sh'kina was the source of all "soul" in the universe. Gnostic Christians of the 4th century spoke of the Sh'kina as a "spirit of glory" in whom Beings of Light lived, as children in their mother's body or house. Mani referred to the Aeons as sh'kinas, or female spirits of the sacred year.[1]

Cabalists taught that it was essential to bring male and female cosmic principles together again, which might be done by sexual magic, signifying union of the sun (man) and moon (woman). This was graphically expressed by the **hexagram**. Philosophy of the Cabala said the supernal mother Shekina is manifested in the earthly mother, with whom her husband should lie on the Sabbath, because "all the six days of the week derive their blessing" from this coupling. Rabbi Eliahu di Vidas said, "Who has not experienced the force of passionate love for a woman will never attain to the love of God."[2]

Jewish mystics said the "outer garment" of the Shekina is Torah, "Holy Law." A man became a Bridegroom of Torah by study, symbolized in erotic imagery. He must court her like a beautiful maiden. "She begins from behind a curtain to speak words in keeping with his understanding, until very slowly insight comes to him." The Shekina as "Indwelling One" might be compared to the Latin I-dea, or Goddess Within. "She opens the door of her hidden chamber ever so little, and for a moment reveals her face to her lover, but hides it again forthwith. . . . He alone sees it and he is drawn to her with his heart and soul and his whole being."[3]

As a man required his Shekina for enlightenment, so God required his Shekina for wisdom and creativity. This crucial tenet of cabalistic doctrine is seldom emphasized—or even mentioned—today.

1. Jonas, 218, 98. 2. Lederer, 187. 3. Cavendish, T., 72–73.

Sheol

Hebrew "Pit," cavern, womb, or underworld; related to the uterine paradise-garden called Shal-Mari in Tibet and Shalimar in India.[1] In its earliest forms, Sheol was the Virgin's "enclosed garden" of flowers, fruits, fountains, and fairy-nymphs. Sacred kings who died on trees went to this other world. The Markandeya Purana mentioned an underground realm where men's souls were impaled on trees.[2]

Shal-Mari probably became Sheol-Mari in the Middle East, where Mari was Ishtar, and there was a long tradition of hanging human sacrifices on trees.

1. Robertson, 25–28, 93. 2. Hughes, 172.

Puranas are ancient Sanskrit scriptures in verse, treating of cosmologies, sacred histories, and the nature of the divine.

Shibboleth

Hebrew "ear of corn," the mystical object displayed as the Ultimate Revelation in temples of Astarte and Demeter: present food and future seed, current life and life yet to come. At Eleusis, the central Mystery was "an ear of corn reaped in silence."[1]

Old Testament writers supposed that the shibboleth was Astarte's dying-and-reborn god Baal. Shibboleth was used as a password because some tribes couldn't pronounce it (Judges 12:6). Patriarchal opposition to the symbol later made it synonymous with a false deity, a meaning that remained up to the present time.

1. d'Alviella, 2.

Shin-Mu

"Mother of Perfect Intelligence," China's Holy Virgin, who miraculously conceived her firstborn son, a Savior and spirit of the grain. Her infant "came like a lamb, with no bursting or rending, with no hurt or harm," and was tenderly adored by sheep and oxen.[1]

After producing this child, Shin-Mu resumed her archaic Great Mother character and gave birth to 33,333 creatures. Patriarchal myths deprived her of a vagina, and so insisted all these creatures were born from her arms or breast. A Christian traveler in China explained Shin-Mu's miraculous motherhood: she had "no place on her body whence to bring them forth as other women of the world, whom for sin God hath subjected to filthiness of corruption, to show how filthy sin is."[2]

After she was virginized and even deprived of a vagina, Shin-Mu's only remaining connection with sexuality was similar to the virgin Mary's: she continued to be the divine patroness of whores.[3]

Persians diabolized her and called her Shimnu, the "Great Devil," so called in a Manichean Confession-Prayer found at Turfan and in the Cave of a Thousand Buddhas, at Tun-huang.[4]

1. Hays, 241. 2. Briffault 3, 171. 3. Briffault 3, 177. 4. Legge 2, 334–35.

Ship

Teutonic *Schiff,* "ship," descended from Old Norse *skop,* meaning "Fate" and also "genitals."[1] It was a symbol of the Goddess Frigga (Freya), whose name also gave rise to "frigging" and "frigate"; she ruled the ship-shaped burial mounds.[2]

From these mounds evolved the Norman temples, laid out in the form of a ship, *navis,* on which the *nave* or "belly" of a Christian church was modeled. Both "navel" and "naval" once referred to the burial shrine likened to a ship and the Mother's womb at the same time. The Norse death ship—vessel of the famous "Viking funeral"—was called *ludr,* meaning boat, coffin, and cradle.[3] It took the dead back to their Mother-sea; the Norsemen's expression for "death" was "to return to the mother's womb."[4] The pagan Welsh similarly sent their dead back to the marine womb and called their funeral dirges *marwysgafen,* "Giving-back-to-the-Sea-Mother."[5] The vessel of death and rebirth was always feminine, which may be why a ship is still "she."

Egypt's Lord of Death, Osiris-Seker, was carried away in a boat under the auspices of a priest entitled "great chief of the hammer," the same title held by Thor. The god came to life again in the "morning boat," tended by a spirit named Matet, evidently the same as Mater Matuta, the Dawn-Mother.[6] Matet was an emanation of Isis the Mother, to whom the solar boat was dedicated.

Romans worshipped Isis as a ship-goddess, the boat being a symbol of her womb, each of her temples having a "bark of Isis" carved in stone at the entrance. The Roman temple where Isis's holy boat was kept became a Christian church under the name of Santa Maria della Navicella: Our Lady of the Boat.[7] Isis-figures in boats, kept in pagan temples throughout Europe, gave rise to the curious fairy tale collected by Grimm under the title of "The Witch in the Stone Boat."

Many "witches" or Goddess-figures appeared in boats even during the nominally Christian era. A 12th-century chronicler spoke of singing, dancing processions that followed sacred ships mounted on wheels, containing as he put it "I know not what evil genius."[8] One suspects the chronicler knew perfectly well that the wheeled ship contained a pagan Goddess. Up to the late Middle Ages, the Goddess's wheeled ship was drawn through the streets of Flemish towns by the weavers' guilds, accompanied by half-naked male and female dancers whose behavior, churchmen said, was "scandalously bacchanalian."[9] The Midsummer festival at Douai in 1770 featured a huge Wheel of Fortune, emblem of the Fate-goddess, and a dry-land ship filled with people who made "strange gestures," recalling the images of ancestral spirits in the ship of Arianrhod which was also a star-wheel.[10] See **Wheel**.

Ships were associated with orgiastic rites from the earliest manifestations of the ship as a womb symbol and an earthly imitation of the crescent moon. Oriental sages called the moon "the Ark or vessel of boat-like shape, symbol of fertility or the Container of the Germ of all life."[11]

1. Neumann, G.M., 254–55. 2. Oxenstierna, 34. 3. Turville-Petre, 276. 4. Gaster, 787. 5. *Encyc. Brit.,* "Welsh Literature." 6. Budge, G.E. 1, 323, 505. 7. Wilkins, 146. 8. Reinach, 138. 9. Briffault 3, 65. 10. Gelling & Davidson, 158. 11. Avalon, 423.

Shiva

Oldest god of the Vedic male trinity (Brahma-Vishnu-Shiva) formed in imitation of the older female trinity. Like the Great Goddess whose son, lover, and victim he was, Shiva had many names. Sometimes he alone was a trinity, or a three-headed god, bearer of the trident or triple phallus which enabled him to mate with the Triple Mother.[1]

Shiva was "in a state of actualization because he is in bodily contact with his own universal energy, the Shakti, the Goddess, the feminine active principle, the efficient and material cause of the universe, the Maya that evolves the differentiated elements and beings. Sakala Shiva bears on his head the crescent of the moon."[2]

Shiva was called Lord of Yoga, i.e., of the "yoke" that bound him to the Goddess. He was also Lord of Death, called Shava, the Corpse, prostrate under the feet of Kali as she devoured his entrails—a Hindu parallel of the dead Osiris shown as the Still-Heart, a mummy, dead and yet alive.[3]

Among Shiva's many other titles were Great Lord, Lord of the Dance, Lord of Cattle (Pasupati), Beneficent One (Sankara), Lord Who Is Half Woman (Ardhanarisvara), God with the Moon in His Hair (Candrasekhara), He Who Belongs to the Triple Goddess, He Who Gives and Takes Away, Consort of the Goddess Uma, Condemned One, Destroyer, Howler.[4]

Tantric yogis insisted that their supreme Shiva was the only god, and all other gods were only inferior imitations of him. He was certainly older than the Vedic heaven-gods. A deity like Shiva was shown under the feet of a Kali-like squatting Goddess on Sumerian cylinder seals of 2300 B.C.[5] Cultures of Sumeria and the Indus valley were in contact at very early periods. Shiva's worshippers may have been literally correct in viewing other gods as recent upstarts. Some of their scriptures claimed that Brahma and Vishnu were so puny that they couldn't even realize the limits of Shiva's cosmic lingam (phallus).[6]

As a sexual god, Shiva epitomized the Tantric ideal of *maithuna,* insuring the orgasmic pleasure of his partner while controlling his own, to partake of her sexual energy. He advocated the female-superior position also favored by such Middle-Eastern Goddesses as Hecate, Lilith, and Asherah—the position usually forbidden by patriarchs.[7] The Brahmana Purana said the female-superior position was a "reversal"

Puranas are ancient Sanskrit scriptures in verse, treating of cosmologies, sacred histories, and the nature of the divine.

practiced by Shiva and lusted after by the "daughters of the sages" of old; but proper Brahmans must regard it as a perversion.[8]

Vedic myths portray hostility between Brahma and Shiva, even though the two were eventually regarded as components of the same trinity. Shiva's priests claimed that Brahmadeva (Brahma-god) was nothing more than a servant of Shiva under his archaic name of Rudra Mokshakala, "Liberated Black Rudra." Brahmans retaliated by belittling Shiva as "an evil yogi," whose cult was only "worship of the lingam"; if Brahma was Shiva's servant, at least the servant didn't take up the same "self-indulgence" or "hideous activities" as the master. Like western underground gods, Shiva was easily diabolized because he was already the Great Black One (Mahakala), confused with Yama and Ganesha, the Lord of Hosts, who begot his reincarnations on Maya-Kali.[9]

As Lord of the Dance, Shiva represented one of Hinduism's most subtle concepts. He copied Kali's Dance of Life, supposedly directing and controlling by its rhythm the constant movement in time and space of all material things. Shiva performed this dance in a place called Chidambaram, the "Center of the Universe"; but the location of this place is within the human heart.[10] The sages' implications were that (1) the heartbeat is the basic rhythm to which all human music is related, because it is heard even by the unborn infant in the paradise-state of intrauterine life, and it is never forgotten; and (2) each human being secretly regards his own heart as the center of the universe indeed, therefore the god is located within the core of man's own self.

Shiva was seldom depicted alone, for his power depended on his union with Kali, his feminine energy, without whom he could not act. The puzzling vision of Shiva as Shava the Corpse, under the Goddess's feet, illustrated the "doctrine that Shiva without his Shakti can do and is, so far as the manifested is concerned, nothing." Yet joined to the Goddess, he became the Bindu or spark of creation. Every human orgasm was believed to share in this creative experience as "an infinitesimally small fragment and faint reflection of the creative act in which Shiva and Shakti join to produce the Bindu which is the seed of the universe."[11] A Tantric yogi in sexual union with his yogini or Shakti could attain the experience of *yoga,* "linking" himself with godhood, and in his ecstasy exclaim *Shivaham*—"I Am Shiva."[12]

1. O'Flaherty, 130. 2. Zimmer, 205. 3. Campbell, Or.M., 198, 90. 4. Zimmer, 126, 130. 5. Campbell, Or.M., 42. 6. Zimmer, 129–30. 7. Graves & Patai, 68–69. 8. O'Flaherty, 144. 9. Tatz & Kent, 82–83, 106. 10. Ross, 32. 11. Avalon, 191, 417. 12. Campbell, Or.M., 198; Oc.M., 183.

Siddhartha Gautama

Seventh in a line of reincarnated Buddhas, still to come to earth once more as the eighth avatar Maitreya, who awaits beyond space-time, in the form of a bodhisattva, his next and final Coming at the end of the world.[1]

Siddhartha literally means "rich in magic," *siddhi* being the magic power controlled by a master yogi. Tantric texts claimed such a sage could walk on water, make himself invisible, create and destroy matter, and turn base elements into gold, as credulous alchemists tried to do for many centuries.[2]

Siddhi was an international word. The Sufi word for the magic power of an enlightened sage was *sihr.*[3] The Kalmuks—descended from "Mother Kali"—called their sacred tales and magic formulae Siddhi-Kur.[4] Norse myths said the gods learned from Mother Freya their magic power over elements and spirits, the *seidr.* In the *Lokasenna,* Odin was reproached for practicing *seidr* because it was a female craft, property of the Goddess.[5] The Lapps worshipped the *seidi* (spirit-power) of their deities.[6] The Celts called their matriarchal fairy-lore *sidh,* pronounced "she." The center of the Celtic otherworld was Caer Sidi, the revolving hub of the Goddess's karmic wheel.

1. Ross, 124. 2. Menen, 93. 3. Shah, 335. 4. Baring-Gould, C.M.M.A., 570. 5. Eliade, S., 385. 6. Davidson, 79.

Siduri Sabitu

Babylonian Goddess of the wine of eternal life. She advised **Gilgamesh** to give up his quest for immortality, for the gods kept her "wine" for themselves and refused to share it with humans.[1] She became the Saki of Arabian Sufi mystics, serving the wine of paradise to the enlightened.

1. *Larousse,* 72.

Siegfried

Teutonic hero *par excellence:* dragon-slayer, warrior, winner of the Queen of the Valkyries, strongman, and ritually-slain sacred king. One legend said Siegfried's father was King Sigmund of Tarlungaland, his mother Queen Sisibe, a prototype of Snow White; for, suspected of adultery, she was sent into the forest with a huntsman who had orders to cut out her tongue, but he did not. The queen died in giving birth to Siegfried, who was set afloat on the river in a vessel of glass and taken ashore by a doe, who nursed him until he was found by the smith Mimir, who raised him. According to another story, Siegfried was nursed by a she-wolf, and his early name was Wolfdietrich.[1]

Siegfried's later adventures are the subject matter of the Nibelungenlied and other epic romances: how he slew the dragon Fafnir and married Brunnhilde ("Burning Hel"), and was slain in a typical *Liebestod* (Love-Death) after which he was reunited with his mystic bride. He was a Germanic Heracles, with many elements of the sun-hero.

1. Rank, 57–58.

Sige

"Silence," Gnostic name for the Creatress, sometimes called the grandmother of God. Out of her was born the first Word; this was the **Logos** of creation. Like Mother Night, she stood at the beginning of all things and represented the state of chaos or nonexistence before the universe took form. See **Sophia, Saint**.

Simon Magus

Clementine Homilies Greek writings falsely attributed to a first-century bishop of Rome; actually composed by an anonymous Christian apologist toward the end of the 4th century.

"Simon the Mage" was one of the principal rivals of the Christians' cult-hero in the first century A.D. The Clementine Homilies said Simon was one of the Essenes, and a disciple of John the Baptist, and the founder of Gnostic Christianity. Simon was said to have appeared in Samaria as God the Father, in Palestine as the Son, and in the rest of the nations as the Holy Spirit. He was even canonized, in the guise of a "St. Simon" allegedly chosen "bishop of Jerusalem" in 62 A.D., after leading a group of Essenic eremites in the village of Pella, beyond Jordan. Followers of Simon were still numerous in the 4th century A.D.[1]

From the orthodox viewpoint, the trouble with Simon was that his sect welcomed women and held that the world-creating power was as much female as male. Simon's heaven was sevenfold, after the classic pattern, and ruled by three pairs of male-and-female Powers, Roots, or Aeons, all born of a great female source with the power of conception, the origin of all things. Simon said God the Father came out of her, and was not called Father until she had named him Father.[2]

Simon traveled with a sacred harlot named Helen, whom he called his First Thought (Ennoia). She was a reincarnation of Helen of Troy, Inanna, Athene, and other Goddesses. Simon claimed that, with her, in his former god-incarnation he had created the world. Simonians worshipped her as Sophia, the Gnostic Virgin of Light, and insisted that she had mothered Jesus. As a Holy Whore (Prunikos), she represented the fallen Ennoia for whose sake God descended and clothed himself in flesh, in the person of Simon. "World salvation was bound up with her redemption by him."[3]

Simonians said those who placed their faith in Simon and Helen would be saved by this grace, without need of works. The relationship between Simon and Helen was like that of the Gnostic Christ and his sacred harlot Mary Magdalene, who was similarly called Pistis-Sophia-Prunikos (Faith-Wisdom-Whore). She embodied Sophia, who was Jesus's spouse in heaven.[4] Gnostic Gospels said Jesus gave the mystic secret of the keys to the kingdom of heaven not to Peter, but to Mary; and Peter reacted with jealousy and hostility toward Mary and all women.[5]

Peter was also hostile toward Simon Magus. According to the Acts of the Apostles, Peter rebuked Simon for trying to buy the apostles' secret of "laying on of hands" to cure diseases and cast out devils (Acts 8:18). From this biblical tale came the term simony—buying and selling priestly benefices and powers—a sin to which the medieval heirs of "Peter" were especially prone. The author or authors of Acts had no good to say of Simon, who was called a false prophet, one who "bewitched the people of Samaria, giving out that himself was some great one: to whom they all gave heed . . . saying, This man is the great power of God" (Acts 8:9-10).

Like Peter, Simon was supposed to have visited Rome and impressed the crowned heads with his miracles. Christians invented a story about Simon to explain the inscription on a statue of the old Sabine god Semo Sancus. The inscription was *Semoni deo sancto,* which some semiliterate "authority" rendered The Holy God Simon, claiming that the statue was raised by Nero in honor of Simon Magus, after Simon allowed himself to be beheaded by Nero's executioner. Then, by magic art, he substituted a ram for himself, and on the third day rose from the dead before Nero, after the manner of all savior-gods.[6]

The Acts of Peter and Paul asserted that Simon flew over the Campus Martius in a chariot drawn by winged demons. In the midst of his triumph, his enemy Peter recited a magic formula that caused him to fall and break his neck.[7] During the 8th century, Pope Paul I built a church "on the exact spot" where Simon Magus fell to his death—the exact spot having been discovered through a private revelation from the Holy Ghost. In 850, Pope Leo IV reconstructed this church and named it Santa Maria Nova—the New Holy Mary.

After his death, Simon was succeeded by another Gnostic hero, Menander, "Moon-man."[8] This seems to have been a reincarnated Simon, assimilated to the moon. The rivalry between Peter and Simon-Menander suggests the battles between those Christians who worshipped the Essenic sun god—whose priests were Pater, Petra, or Peter—and those who worshipped the lunar hero. The controversy suggests a schismatic breaking away from a parent cult: it must be remembered that Peter's name was Simon before Jesus changed it to Peter (Matthew 10:2), and that Peter too was a "Mage."

The Magi discovered the advent of Jesus by astrological magic, according to the Christian story; this was put forth as one of the proofs of Jesus's divinity. Therefore, Christians were reluctant to discredit any of the Magi. In Simon's case however, the early fathers were implacably opposed to the main feature of his doctrine: "the earthly incarnation of the heavenly mother. . . . Leaders of the orthodox Church fought from the very beginning of Christianity against such glorification of women."[9] Writings attributed to Simon made extensive use of feminine symbols: paradise was the womb, Eden the placenta. "The river that flows forth from Eden symbolizes the navel, which nourishes the fetus. . . . [T]he Exodus, consequently, signifies the passage out of the womb, and . . . 'the crossing of the Red Sea refers to the blood.' "[10] Such feminine imagery linked Simon with priests of the Old Religion. In Ireland he was known as Simon the Druid.[11]

The Latin cognomen Faustus, "Favored One," was bestowed on Simon early in the Christian era. "The fact that he was accompanied by a Helena whom he claimed to be the reborn Helen of Troy shows clearly that we have here one of the sources of the Faust legend of the early Renaissance. Surely few admirers of Marlowe's and Goethe's plays have an inkling that their hero is the descendant of a gnostic sectary, and that the beautiful Helen called up by his art was once the fallen Thought of God through whose raising mankind was to be saved."[12]

1. Brewster, 107. 2. Legge 1, 183. 3. Jonas, 107. 4. Malvern, 34. 5. Pagels, 22, 64–65. 6. Mâle, 297. 7. Reinach, 264. 8. Summers, H.W., 193. 9. Seligmann, 128–29. 10. Pagels, 53. 11. Wedeck, 142. 12. Jonas, 111.

Sin

Sign of Sin

The original Moon-god of Mount Sinai, "Mountain of the Moon." He was born of the Virgin Queen of Heaven, Nanna or Inanna. He ruled the Land of Sinim (Isaiah 49:12), which meant "land of the lunar mountain" and was an older form of Zion. His Chaldean name was Kingu. He was the god who received the Tablets of Law from the primal Mother of Creation, **Tiamat**. As Moses's god, he still had the same mountain-throne and the same tablets. A biblical scholar has pointed out that "the Jehovah of the Hebrews" was merely another transformation of "the primitive lunar deity of Arabia."[1]

The god Moses met on Mount Sinai claimed to be the god of Abraham, though he said Abraham knew him by a different name (Exodus 6:3). In fact, Abraham may have been the same deity. Very ancient documents used the name Abraham or Ab-ram as a synonym for Ab-Sin, Moon-father.[2] In the 12th century B.C., the Babylonian heaven was ruled by a trinity consisting of Shamash, Sin, and Ishtar, represented by the sun, moon, and stars.[3]

1. Briffault 3, 106. 2. Briffault 3, 108. 3. Campbell, M.I., 88.

Sirens

Homer's word for the magic women of Cyrene, who cast spells on ships to cause them to be wrecked on the rocky coast. The "sweet songs" by which the Sirens lured Odysseus's sailors were spells to draw foreign ships into the Cyrenian shallows, where natives apparently carried on a profitable trade as wreckers.

Sita

"Furrow," the Goddess Earth as the wife of Rama (Krishna) in the *Ramayana.* A personification of the yoni, mated to the phallic "ram" whose name meant "sexual enjoyment." See **Furrow**.

Skadi

var. Scatha, Scotia

The Celto-Teutonic Goddess in her "Destroyer" aspect. Like the Greek Persephone, "Destroyer," she was Queen of the Shades, Mother Death. Her name was the root of Gothic *skadus,* Old English *sceadu,* "shadow, shade." She was the Shadow into which all the gods went at doomsday, called Götterdämmerung, or Going-Into-the-Shadow-of-the-Gods.[1] As Scotia, she was the Dark Goddess—like Black Kali, the Caillech—after whom Scotland was named.[2]

Like Kali, Skadi had to be propitiated each year with an outpouring of male blood in primitive sacrificial rites. Her annual victim was assimilated to the god Loki, who became a "savior" by fertilizing Skadi with his blood. Loki's genitals were attached by a rope to a goat, and a tug-of-war ensued, until Loki's flesh gave way and he fell into Skadi's lap, thus bathing her loins in his blood. The gods watched anxiously to see if Skadi smiled; and when she did, it means spring could return once more to the land.[3]

Similar blood-rites were practiced all over the ancient world, when men sought godhood by giving their blood to the Goddess, before animal sacrifices replaced human ones, and even afterward. It was not uncommon for priestesses representing the Goddess to bathe in sacrificial blood, like the women who sacrificed Apis the bull-god in Egypt, hoisting their skirts as they dismembered him so his spurting blood would quicken their wombs.[4] Like many death-goddess figures, Skadi collected the penises of her castrated heroes, and in this character she was named Mörnir, "troll-woman."[5]

Remnants of the bloody sacrifice of Loki and the goat could still be found in Norway and Sweden in the late 17th century. Churchmen vainly denounced the masquerades, sexual promiscuity, and "goat games" associated with Easter and other religious festivals.[6]

Skadi was a dark twin of Freya, therefore virtually identical with the underground Goddess Hel. She was once all the Earth, birth-giver and devourer of her children. The entire land mass of Scandinavia was named after her. Originally it was Scadin-auja, the land of Skadi.[7]

A variation of her name, Skuld, was given to the third of the three Fates, or **Norns**, in the role of destroying Crone. Naturally she became the patroness of witches, whose activities came to be called "skulduggery."

To the Celts, she was Scatha or Scath. Her underground realm of the dead was "the Land of Scath." Like Persephone's underworld within seven loops of the Styx, the Land of Scath was a city of seven walls.[8] It was variously located under the earth, or in heaven, or far away over the sea on a western island, the land of "Sky." **Cu Chulainn** and other Celtic heroes learned magic skill in martial arts from a visit to Queen Scatha's island of Skye. She kept the hero for "a year and a day," the usual mythic image of the old 13-month lunar year with its intercalary day. When she had taught a man all she knew, she sent him back to earth a fey man, set apart and *sacer,* fated to do great deeds and die a sacrificial death.[9] The legend suggests that the real island of Skye was a cult center of the Goddess, and warriors went there to be initiated into their heroic profession.

Skadi is still invoked by place names in Sweden, such as Skadavé (Skadi's temple) and Skadalungr (Skadi's grove).[10]

1. Turville-Petre, 164. 2. Graves, G.M. 1, 72. 3. Oxenstierna, 213.
4. Graves. G.M. 1, 255. 5. Turville-Petre, 257. 6. Oxenstierna, 216.
7. Branston, 164. 8. Lethaby, 163. 9. Goodrich, 187. 10. Turville-Petre, 165.

Skald

Scandinavian poet-shaman, probably derived from Skadi or Skuld, as a Goddess of inspiration. A great skald was believed to have words of power; what he sang or prophesied would come true. He was able to address the death goddess herself, via funerary ballads, and appeal to her to treat the deceased well. Norse sagas and eddaic poetry were the work of skalds who belonged to a priestly class, like druids. See **Romance**.

Slavery

The de Paors wrote naively of the life of a slave in early Christian Ireland: "Even if he was a slave he had the advantage of living in a society which had accepted the teachings of Christianity."[1] This wasn't much of an advantage, considering that in pagan society he would not have been a slave at all. The United States in the 19th century had also accepted the teachings of Christianity, but this was of little benefit to the slaves on southern plantations.

In effect, the feudalism upheld by the Christian churches was a slave state. Serfs were at the mercy of their overlords, who held the power of life and death over them. Serfs could be bought and sold with the land. Though they were taxed to support the church and the nobility, they were without legal rights. The "teachings" of Christianity paid no attention to the plight of the serfs, nor did the churches make any effort to alleviate their sufferings.

Church fathers were even more concerned to keep women in a state of subjection throughout all social strata, so that each male even at the slave level had at least one slave of his own: a wife. St. Augustine said wives should be slaves to their husbands, and husbands had the right to beat and abuse them. To a wife who had been beaten he would say, "It is the duty of servants to obey their masters. . . . [Y]ou have made a contract of servitude."[2] St. Thomas Aquinas said a male slave was superior to a wife, because a male slave was not in subjection "according to the law of nature," but a wife was "subject to the man on account of the weakness of her nature, both of mind and body."[3] In other words, Aquinas believed that might makes right; weakness must be dominated by strength. Of course this was not always the rule in all-male relationships, only in male-female ones.

The combination of slavery and sexism in Christian societies made the lot of female slaves particularly onerous. They were completely helpless in the hands of their masters, and could be raped, tortured, or murdered with impunity. Even in "enlightened" 19th-century America, female slaves were in a singularly unenviable position.

Dr. James Marion Sims, known as the American "father of gynecology," was famed as the inventor of a surgical technique for curing vesicovaginal fistula. He also performed hundreds of clitoridectomies and ovariotomies to cure "sex-related diseases" in women. What is usually not told about his career is the way he developed his techniques. Before the Civil War, he kept women slaves in a disused jailhouse and made them his guinea pigs, performing hundreds of experimental and exploratory operations on them until they died off one by one and were replaced by fresh victims.[4] Sims's career and writings bear out what some psychologists have suspected, that early gynecological surgeons were fundamentally women-haters with a sadistic bent.

In patriarchal societies, said Marx, "Woman's true qualities are warped to her disadvantage, and all the moral and delicate elements in her nature become the means for enslaving her and making her suffer."[5]

1. de Paor, 100. 2. Hartley, 231. 3. de Riencourt, 219. 4. See Barker-Benfield on Sims. 5. de Riencourt, 364.

Sleipnir

Odin's eight-legged gray horse, a Norse symbol of death, likened to the gallows-tree on which Odin hung. Skalds called the gallows "high-chested rope-Sleipnir," carrying men to the land of death. The same word meant "gallows tree" and "horse" (*drasil*).[1] See **Horse**; **Odin**.

1. Turville-Petre, 48.

Smashana-Kali

Kali Ma as the Goddess of cremation grounds and other places of death. The *yantra* (symbol) of Smashana-Kali was doubly yonic: an eight-petaled lotus with multiple repetitions of the inverted triangle that meant "female genitals."[1] The meaning of the yantra of Smashana-Kali was rebirth following death. Her priestesses, called **dakinis**, arranged funerals and tended the dying. In the after-world they became psychopomps.

1. *Mahanirvanatantra,* 360.

Smith

A recurrent story about Amazons was that they deliberately crippled certain men, members of a special caste of metalworkers and smiths whose deformity became their caste mark. The Amazonian smith-god Hephaestus was lame. Some said he was lamed when Zeus cast him down from heaven to the underworld for trying to defend his mother Hera. Others said he was lamed by Hera herself. Hephaestus shared a temple with Athene, renowned as an instructress of smiths. She taught smithcraft to Daedalus, the builder of the Cretan Labyrinth.[1]

Many myths point to a continuing relationship between smithcraft and the worship of the Goddess. Egyptian priests of Isis were *mesniu,* "smiths."[2] Aphrodite ruled the copper mines and metalworking schools of her sacred isle, Cyprus ("Copper"). Medieval alchemists continued to call copper the Metal of Venus. The lame smith Hephaestus also claimed Aphrodite as his bride. The primal sea-goddesses loved him, despite his deformity. "Golden women" helped him in his workshop on the isle of Lemnos, traditional home of militant Amazons.[3]

Smiths often claimed magic powers stemming from secret connection with the feminine forces of nature. Roman *faber* meant both "smith" and "magician." Russian folk tales portrayed smiths as assistants of witches. Exorcisms attributed to St. Patrick claimed to avert the spells of "women, smiths, and druids."[4] The Yakuts said "Smiths and shamans are from the same nest," believing smiths could heal, prophesy, and work miracles. Secret societies linking metallurgy and magic appear in the traditions of China and Japan, as in those of medieval alchemists, craft fraternities, and German *Mannerbunde.*[5]

The German name Schmidt (Smith) once referred to a priestly caste of metalworking shamans, who were also bards. Their apotheosized founder was Wayland the Smith—in Scandinavia, Volund—a consort of the Triple Goddess. He encountered her in totemic form, as three doves flying above a sacred spring.[6]

English tradition said Wayland the Smith lived within the Berkshire hill marked by the 370-foot image of the White Horse of Uffington. If horses were brought to him at night and left, with money, at one of the standing stones, he would shoe them before the coming of the dawn.[7]

Mongols said the seven stars of Ursa Major—which the Hindus called Seven Rishis—were the skulls of seven smiths who had been raised to the sky by the Goddess. The constellation was a special patron of smiths.[8] Christian folklore said the man in the moon was Cain, whose name meant "smith"; the Cainites or Kenites were the special caste of metalworkers in ancient Palestine, until they were driven out of the country (1 Samuel 13:19). See **Cain**.

The Irish said the celestial smith was Luno (Moon-man), a lame craftsman like Hephaestus. He made Fingal's magic sword.[9] Merlin too was a smith; he forged Arthur's magic armor.[10] Christian syncretism even represented the God who impregnated the virgin Mary as "the Smith from above" who threw his hammer into her breast—probably a new version of Thor, as an apotheosized Wayland.[11]

When the old gods were made devils, smithcraft was associated with devil's work. Numerous cathedral bells were said to have been forged by the devil.[12] The devil was also the Master Smith who forged the original ironwork doors of Notre Dame de Paris, which were replaced by new doors in 1860.[13]

Gypsies were often described as smiths, and many adopted the surname of Smith.[14] The prejudice against ironworkers included gypsies. This prejudice was particularly notable in Abyssinia where ironworkers were restricted to a special caste, excluded from the rites of the church, and believed to possess the evil eye.[15]

Along with the smiths, other medieval European craft guilds were considered subversive by Christian orthodoxy. The guild of free masons, for example, maintained their own ceremonies, secrets, and semi-religious doctrine. "The Church, not without the semblance of reason, will regard the Masonic brotherhood as her most treacherous and dangerous enemy, which aims to dismantle her work and reconstruct it in another spirit."[16] The smiths' guilds were even more suspect at one time, to the point where the church even felt it necessary to dissolve some of them.

1. Graves, G.M. 1, 311. 2. Briffault 2, 535. 3. Graves, G.M. 1, 87. 4. Joyce, 223. 5. Eliade, S., 470–73. 6. Keightley, 215. 7. Hazlitt, 621. 8. Jobes, 262. 9. W. Scott, 99. 10. Guerber, L.M.A., 211. 11. d'Alviella, 16. 12. Guerber, L.R., 47–56. 13. de Givry, 152. 14. Groome, xxviii, lxi. 15. Gifford, 29. 16. Guignebert, 443.

Snake

See **Serpent**.

Sneeze

Roman paganism contributed the traditional "God bless you" or *Gesundheit* (May you have health) offered to one who sneezed. The old expression was "Jupiter preserve you" or "Jupiter help me."[1] Its basis was the ancient Indo-European concept of the air-soul or breath-soul (*Atman*), which might be expelled from the body by a violent rush of air unless prevented by a verbal charm. Covering the mouth during a yawn arose from the same fear of losing the soul. Medieval churchmen accepted the superstition, and taught that both sneezing and yawning should be immediately protected by the sign of the cross, because "Ofttimes a man sneezed, and expired at the moment of sneezing. . . . In like manner it often befell that a man yawned, and fell dead."[2]

The primitive idea of the air-soul was closely associated with sneezing by the Polynesians. The first man on earth was kneaded of red clay moistened with the deity's blood—that is, the same combination of menstrual blood and earth that ancient Semites called *adamah*—and was animated by the deity's breath. Then the clay effigy came to life and sneezed. The name of this first man was Tiki-ahua, or The Creator's Sneeze. *Ahua,* or "likeness," was a sound-word for "sneeze."[3] Thus the man made "in God's image" was the same as a man made "by God's sneeze."

The Christian custom of saying "God bless you" to a sneezer was meant to serve as shorthand for extreme unction, in the event that the soul happened to leave the body. Hindus still take similar precautions when someone yawns. They snap their fingers to frighten the soul away from the open mouth and back down the throat where it belongs.

1. de Lys, 305. 2. de Voragine, 278. 3. Frazer, F.O.T., 5.

Solomon and Sheba

Solomon meant Sun God of On, the Jewish version of Ra of Heliopolis.[1] Solomon was the one Jewish king with pretensions to ruling a Golden Age of glory. The wonders of his reign were attributed to his wisdom, supposedly the gift of Yahweh, though the Bible inconsistently declares that Solomon didn't worship Yahweh. Solomon's famous temple was built not by himself but by King Hiram of Tyre, to whom Solomon was forced to pay tribute (1 Kings 5:11). The deities worshipped in that temple were the Tyrian sun god Melek or Heracles-Melkart (biblical Molech); Shamash the sun god (biblical Chemosh); and the Goddess Astarte, or Ashtoreth, whom Yahweh's priests called an abomination (1 Kings 11:5-7).

In reality, there was no Golden Age of Solomon. No contemporary nation took any notice of Israel's alleged glory. The "great cities" Solomon was supposed to have built were small mud-hut villages. The "city" of Megiddo covered less than 13 acres. "The standard of living was far from luxurious when compared to that prevailing in other parts of the ancient Near Eastern world."[2]

Solomon's reign was set in the middle of the 10th century B.C., but the Hebrew manuscript used as a basis for the biblical account was written in the 10th century A.D., 2000 years later—though a few early-medieval copies of a Greek text might have gone as far back as the 3rd century B.C. There were no records whatever traceable to Solomon's own time, not even the king lists that were customary in the nations that amounted to anything. Like David, Solomon was arbitrarily assigned a reign of forty years because that was the traditional span of a generation.[3]

Solomon's reign and deeds must be interpreted as a collection of legends from Egypt, Phoenicia, and especially from southern Arabia, the land of Sheba, where a true Golden Age was flourishing under a succession of matriarchal queens. Sheba was the primary source of frankincense and other valuable spices, in great demand not only for food preservation but also for religious and funerary use.

Eutychius Greek historian, author of a series of *Annals.*

Eutychius said the whole Sinai peninsula had been governed by wealthy Sheban queens for as long as anyone could remember. In the alleged time of Abraham, Queen Shabib (Sheba) had "built Nisib and Edessa and surrounded them with walls. She founded also the sanctuary of Harran, and made an idol of gold, called Sin."[4] This was the Moon-god of Mount Sinai, the god of Moses. Semitic tribes of Arabia worshipped the moon and her earthly embodiment, the queen, since at least the 16th century B.C.[5] Sheba was the lunar queen's capital, also known to the Egyptians as Punt or Ophir, famous as a land of fabulous wealth.[6]

There were king consorts in Sheba's capital city of Marib (Mariaba), but they were forbidden to leave the queen's palace on pain of death by stoning.[7] The city, hub of the spice trade, had a great moon temple at Almaqah, laid out in the feminine-symbolic oval characteristic of matriarchal religious centers. Priestesses of this temple appear in the Old Testament as "Sabeans" (Shebans). They were described as holy harlots from the "wilderness," the biblical name for any place outside of Israel, having crowns on their heads and jeweled bracelets on their arms (Ezekiel 23:42). Sheban priests were called *mukarrib,* "kindred of the moon," from which descended the Hebrew *kerubh* (cherub, angel) and the Arabic *muqarribin,* "close kindred," a title of medieval Sufi mystics.[8]

The Bible presents a highly improbable picture of a rich Queen of Sheba coming with a caravan of spices, gold, and precious stones to visit a king of poor, backward Israel. She loaded Solomon with gifts because she was so impressed by what he already owned and by his clever answers to her questions (1 Kings 10:5). Needless to say, this was only mythic name-dropping. Solomon was placed on his throne and crowned by a Sheban moon-priestess called Bath-Sheba (Daughter of Sheba), said to be his mother (Song of Solomon 3:11). The king—whether his name was Solomon or not—clearly lived in a more dependent relationship to the Sheban matriarchate than the account of the queen's visit might suggest.

According to the Koran, Solomon stole his throne from Balkis, Queen of Sheba.[9] The name Balkis, Bilqis, or Balqama is thought to be related to Greek *pallakis,* "sacred harlot." The Marib temple was Mahram Bilqis, Moon-Mother Bilqis, the formal name of the Goddess-queen. Set in the doorway of the temple was a large bronze baptismal basin filled with water, the prototype of the "brazen sea" in Solomon's temple, copied from Sheban antecedents.[10] This mighty womb-symbol was decorated with the female yonic emblems of knops and lilies, also "cherubim," derived from the Sheban *mukarribim.*[11]

Solomon's temple featured a pair of phallic pillars named Boaz (eagerness, strength) and Jachin (God makes him firm), surmounted by female symbols of lilies and pomegranates (1 Kings 7:19-20). By the ancient symbolism, the two pillars at the temple door represented the king and his tanist, both craving entrance into the Enclosed Garden or temple-body of the Goddess. The **hieros gamos** between Solomon and his mysterious black queen—a marriage arranged by Bath-Sheba—was a mating of the king to his land, signalized by pornographic hymns like the wedding-poems of ancient Sumeria.[12]

The fragment of love-liturgy now called Solomon's Song has been an embarrassment to theologians, even though they strenuously insisted it was an allegory of Christ's love for his church, Lady Ecclesia. It was hard to explain why such a love should exude such a steamy air of obviously erotic sensualism. Yet the 18th-century scholar Herder was persecuted and hounded from one pastorate to another for daring to suggest that Solomon's love poem should be accepted at face value, as a piece of Oriental erotica.[13]

When the metaphors of this poem are unraveled, they prove to be more, not less, frankly sexual. The *hortus conclusus* or "enclosed garden" is the internal genitalia of the virgin bride, where her spouse "enters paradise"—from Hebrew *pardes,* "garden."[14] Solomon says, "A garden enclosed is my sister, my spouse; a spring shut up, a fountain sealed." He proposes to unseal her, unlock her door, and "drink of spiced wine of the juice of my pomegranate" (Song of Solomon 8:2). This metaphor is explained by the contemporary image of the pomegranate, *rimmon,* as a female-genital symbol. Spiced wine meant the secretion of the Goddess representing the blood of life: i.e., **menstrual blood**, of which only kings and gods could taste.[15]

Solomon's bride said invitingly, "Let my beloved come into his garden, and eat his pleasant fruits." Solomon answered, "Open to me, my sister, my love, my dove, my undefiled: for my head is filled with dew, and my locks with the drops of the night. I have put off my garment; how shall I put it on?" The king's dew-filled "head" was the common symbol of the penis, in royal wedding hymns of Sumer and Akkad. A king's union with the Goddess Inanna, Queen of the Universe, was so described: "The king goes with lifted head to the holy lap, he goes with lifted head to the holy lap of Inanna." Every king's divine bride was Inanna "the queen, the vulva of heaven and earth."[16]

A priestess impersonated the Goddess on the royal wedding night. Solomon's mysterious "black, but beautiful" bride, the Shulamite, seems to have been no more than an ancient Canaanite title of the Goddess, Zulumat, "Darkness."[17] Like the Goddess she was not only the night and the moon; she was also the land and its crops. Her stature was like a palm tree, her breasts like clusters of grapes, her mouth like honeycomb, her teeth like flocks of sheep, her belly a heap of wheat set with lilies, and so on. In short she was the Enclosed Garden-paradise of Oriental kings, like Shalimar in the Far East—the Semitic Sheol-Mari, or Mary of the enchanted garden underground.

Similarly the Enclosed Garden became a Christian symbol of the same Mary. The Litany of the Virgin jumbled together many of the old fertility symbols, calling Mary the Enclosed Garden, Well of Water, Gate of Heaven, Chosen Vessel, City of God, Beautiful Moon, Beloved of the Sun, Rose, Lily, Olive, and Palm.[18] Within the Virgin's *hortus conclusus* dwelt such phallic symbols as the Tower of David, Tree of Life, enchanted unicorn, and Exalted Cedar of Lebanon, always called "tall." The ancient meaning of "tall" combined the concepts of "prompt, quick, docile, comely, handsome"—flattering descriptions of the divine phallus.[19]

Mary or Mari was linked with the Sheban moon-temple at Marib, having the same name and the title of *almah* or moon-woman, once a priestess of the Almaqah. Solomon's mother Bath-Sheba, who crowned him, apparently represented the elder queen of Sheba, who was also the Naked Goddess when viewed in her bath by the next king. Her spouse David had come to kingship by viewing her in her bath and showing a satisfactory reaction. Prior to Solomon's reign, the king's defeated tanist was Absalom or "Father Salomon," variants of Salem, Salma, Shalem, or Solomon. After lying with the royal concubines to prove his virility, Absalom died a sacrificial death on an oak tree, and a phallic pillar was erected in his honor (2 Samuel 18:18). Bath-Sheba meant literally the daughter of Shaybah, an ancient Arabic name of the Goddess.[20] See **Zenobia**.

In one year Solomon received 666 talents of gold (1 Kings 10:14), the mystic number of the Triple Goddess, later re-interpreted by her enemies as "the number of the beast" (Revelation 13:18). Clearly, Solomon worshipped the Goddess (1 Kings 11:5) and paid little or no attention to Yahweh. Apocryphal texts said Yahweh never forgave Solomon's paganism, but after his death condemned him to perpetual punishment, like that of Prometheus: to be daily devoured, forever, by 10,000 ravens.[21]

The gold that came to Solomon was probably a symbol of his wisdom; for kings' wisdom was generally ascribed to their union with the Goddess who represented "mother-wisdom" (Hebrew *hok-mah,* after Egyptian *hek-maa*). Sargon II also claimed to have received "gold" form the Arabian queen.[22] Centuries later, Arabian alchemists talked in highly esoteric terms of the acquisition of mystic gold, which may have meant something different from the usual interpretation of material gold from base metal. In medieval alchemy much was made of the occult link between gold and the Wisdom-goddess, variously named Sophia, Sapientia, Anima Mundi, Athene, or Luna.

Solomon's legendary wisdom brought him almost as much reverence from medieval occultists as Thoth-Hermes Trismegistus, god of magic. Several grimoires purported to have been written by his hand; *The Key of Solomon* was one of the most popular. Magic signs like the pentacle and hexagram were often called Solomon's Seal. "Of a truth," the Grand Grimoire said of Solomon, "what other man, save this invincible genius, would have had the hardihood to reveal the withering words which God makes use of to strike terror into the rebellious angels and compel them into obedience?"[23] Thus wizards invoked Solomon's help in calling up demons for magical purposes.

The Bible is remarkably uncommunicative concerning Solomon's death, considering the intimate detail that describes his wedding night, his temple furnishings, his household, etc. The Arabs said Solomon lost his magic ring while bathing in the Jordan, and forgot his wisdom, so he was killed by a *djinni* who ruled in his place. Rabbinic writers said Solomon's corpse was stuffed and shown to the people on holy days to make them think he still lived. One day the royal mummy embarrassingly fell apart, which ended the deception.[24]

1. Stanton, 67. 2. Pritchard, S.S., 35. 3. Pritchard, S.S., 10, 21. 4. Briffault 3, 108. 5. Albright, 96. 6. Pritchard, S.S., 47. 7. Lethaby, 159–60. 8. Shah, 180. 9. de Givry, 98. 10. Pritchard, S.S., 61, 100. 11. Shah, 26, 180. 12. *Encyc. Brit.*, "Solomon." 13. White 2, 325. 14. Hughes, 47. 15. *Mahanirvanatantra*, 273. 16. Pritchard, A.N.E., 135, 202. 17. Pritchard, A.N.E., 97. 18. Hughes, 55. 19. Potter & Sargent, 220. 20. Briffault 3, 80. 21. Wedeck, 211. 22. Pritchard, A.N.E., 197. 23. Waite, C.M., 100–101. 24. de Givry, 97–98.

Son of Man

Narayana, "Son of Man," originally meant Vishnu, not Jesus. It was coined to prove Vishnu a god made wholly in the image of man, having no need of a mother.[1] Yet Vishnu himself finally adopted the worship of Mother Kali, saying in his hymn to her divinity, "The gods themselves are merely constructs out of Her maternal substance."[2]

"Son of Man" was subsequently applied to the Persian Messiah, then to the Essenic Christ, both of whom were "born" at the hands of men, "of water and of the spirit." Men so born were supposed to be able to defeat death, whereas man born of woman was fated to die. The Persian Son of Man, Yima the Splendid (copied from the Vedic Yama) became a Lord of Death, "the good shepherd, the most glorious of those who were born, the sole mortal possessor of the solar eye." He alone could "render men and beasts non-mortal."[3]

Repeating a bit of Persian eschatology, Jesus promised that on the Last Day "the Son of man shall come in the glory of the Father with his angels" to judge the world (Matthew 16:27). Theologians have never really decided who was the Father of the Son of Man.

1. O'Flaherty, 349. 2. Rawson, E.A., 159. 3. *Larousse,* 310.

Sophia, Saint

Canonical adaptation of the Gnostic Great Mother: Latin Sapientia, Greek Sophia, the spirit of Female Wisdom. Symbolized by the Dove of Aphrodite (later transformed into a sign of the Holy Ghost), Sophia once represented God's female soul, source of his power, just as Kali-Shakti served to vitalize the Hindu gods.[1]

The Trattato Gnostico said Sophia was God's mother, "the great revered Virgin in whom the Father was concealed from the beginning before He had created anything." She was identified with Isis-Hathor, whose seven emanations gave each Egyptian his seven souls. Irenaeus said Sophia like Hathor was the mother of the seven planetary spirits, whose names were listed in Gnostic papyri as the magic-working secret names of God.[2]

The Clementine Homilies called Sophia the All-Maternal Being, The Queen, Lady Wisdom. Early Gnostic Christians held that, like Krishna and Shiva, or like Dionysus and Zeus, Christ and God together merged with Sophia as an androgyne: "The Son of Man agreed with Sophia, his consort, and revealed himself in a great light as bisexual. His male nature is called 'the Savior,' the begetter of all things, but his female, 'Sophia, Mother of All.' "[3]

Clementine Homilies Greek writings falsely attributed to a first-century bishop of Rome; actually composed by an anonymous Christian apologist toward the end of the 4th century.

A Gnostic creation myth said Sophia was born from the primordial female power Sige (Silence). Sophia gave birth to a male spirit, Christ, and a female spirit, Achamoth. The latter gave life to the elements and the terrestrial world, then brought forth a new god named Ildabaoth, Son of Darkness, along with five planetary spirits later regarded as emanations of Jehovah: Iao, Sabaoth, Adonai, Eloi, and Uraeus. These spirits produced archangels, angels, and finally men.

Ildabaoth or Jehovah forbade men to eat the fruit of knowledge, but his mother Achamoth sent her own spirit to earth in the form of the serpent Ophis to teach men to disobey the jealous god. The serpent was also called Christ, who taught Adam to eat the fruit of knowledge despite the god's prohibition.[4]

Sophia sent Christ to earth again in the shape of her own totemic dove, to enter the man Jesus at his baptism in the Jordan. After Jesus died, Christ left his body and returned to heaven. Sophia gave Jesus a body of ether, and placed him in heaven to help collect souls.[5] Some said Jesus became Sophia's spouse and his glory depended on this sacred marriage; for he was only one of the Aeons, a minor spirit, the "common fruit" of the Pleroma.[6]

Some said Sophia was also Jesus's mother, for she was the Virgin of Light whose spirit entered into the body of Mary to conceive him.

She also entered the body of Elizabeth to conceive John the Baptist. Some said Sophia was to God as Metis to Zeus: his "mind." But Sophia wasn't acceptable to the all-male church. Of the three mighty female powers in the Gnostic creation myth, all preceded Jehovah, and two of them opposed Jehovah as a tyrant, overruled his taboo, and saved humanity from ignorance. It was a version that the Pauline churches found lacking in appeal.

Nevertheless, Sophia was passionately adored by Eastern Christians. Her greatest shrine was erected in Constantinople during the 6th century A.D., and was one of the wonders of the world: the Church of Holy Sophia (Hagia Sophia).

Embarrassed by this magnificent monument to the Great Mother, Roman Christians claimed it was dedicated to a minor "virgin martyr," St. Sophia, whose phony legend lacked even a date. Despite her virginity she was the mother of three daughters, also "virgin martyrs": St. Faith, St. Hope, and St. Charity. The legend may have arisen in personification of the saying that Wisdom gives birth to Faith, Hope, and Charity. Hagiographers took it literally, confusing the three virtues with the three Charites. Catholic scholars now claim the church of Hagia Sophia was never dedicated to the Great Mother in any form, not even that of a female saint. They say its name—which means "Holy Female Wisdom" in plain Greek—really meant "Christ, the Word of God."[7]

Jewish "Wisdom" literature owed much to the cult of Sophia, who was to reappear in medieval Jewish cabalism as the Shekina of God. Yet the 8th and 9th chapters of Proverbs demonstrate the early conflict between followers of Sophia and those of God. The first of these passages urges the benefits of Sophia's worship; the second belittles her and her priestesses:

> *Doth not Sophia cry? and understanding put forth her voice? She standeth in the top of high places, by the way in the places of the paths. She crieth at the gates, at the entry of the city, at the coming in of the doors. Unto you, O men, I call; and my voice is to the sons of man. O ye simple, understand Sophia: and, ye fools, be ye of an understanding heart. Hear; for I will speak of excellent things; and the opening of my lips shall be right things . . . for Sophia is better than rubies; and all the things that may be desired are not to be compared to her. I Sophia dwell with prudence, and find out knowledge of witty inventions. . . . Counsel is mine, and sound wisdom; I am understanding; I have strength. By me kings reign, and princes decree justice. By me princes rule, and nobles, even all the judges of the earth. I love them that love me; and those that seek me early shall find me. . . . I lead in the way of righteousness, in the midst of the paths of judgment: that I may cause those that love me to inherit substance; and I will fill their treasures. . . .*
>
> *Blessed is the man that heareth me, watching daily at my gates, waiting at the posts of my doors. For whoso findeth me findeth life. . . .*

But he that sinneth against me wrongeth his own soul: all they that hate me love death.

This was one side of a public-relations war. The other side was presented by the following chapter, wherein God scorned the worship of the Goddess:

Sophia hath builded her house, she hath hewn out her seven pillars: she hath killed her beasts: she hath mingled her wine: she hath also furnished her table. She hath sent forth her maidens: she crieth upon the highest places of the city. Whoso is simple, let him turn in hither; as for him that wanteth understanding, she saith to him, Come, eat of my bread, and drink of the wine which I have mingled . . . [but] the fear of the Lord is the beginning of wisdom: and the knowledge of the holy is understanding. For by me [God] thy days shall be multiplied, and the years of thy life shall be increased. . . . A foolish woman is clamorous: she is simple, and knoweth nothing. For she sitteth at the door of her house, on a seat in the high places of the city, to call passengers who go right on their ways: whoso is simple, let him turn in hither. . . . But he knoweth not that the dead are there; and that her guests are in the depths of hell.[8]

The "high places of the city" meant temples, therefore the "woman" was the Goddess, who met with much resistance from followers of the God. Yet she was still in evidence during the Middle Ages, as Sophia-Sapientia, Lady Wisdom, ruling deity of the Gnostic philosophers who said the World Soul was born of her smile.[9]

1. Graves, W.G., 159. 2. Legge 2, 69. 3. Malvern, 43, 53. 4. Jonas, 204. 5. Legge 2, 69 et seq. 6. Jonas, 188. 7. Attwater, 127, 312. 8. *Holy Bible,* King James version. 9. Neumann, A.C.U., 56.

Soteira

"Savioress," a title of Persephone; feminine form of *soter,* meaning "savior" or "sower-of-seed." The word came from primitive images of the Savior as a phallic god who died in the act of fertilizing the earth. Persephone acquired the title as an annual bride of Pluto, or Hades, who took her underground.

Sothis

Greco-Egyptian name of the star Sirius, which "rose in the east" to announce the advent of the Savior Osiris each year at the onset of the Nile flood. "Three Wise Men" announced the rising of Sothis—the three stars in Orion's belt which point directly toward Sirius. As the "Eye" of the Great Dog (Canis Major), Sirius was sometimes called Canopis or Dog-Eye, the same as the holy city of Anubis who, as Dog of Death, kept Osiris's soul in the star Sothis until his rebirth. See **Dog**.

Soul

Germanic *Seele,* "soul," was feminine, used by mystics like Eckhart and Goethe in the same sense as *Shakti* in India: i.e., "the feminine Ultimate Reality."[1] Most ancient words for the soul were female: psyche, pneuma, anima, alma. God-souls were Goddesses: Kore, Sophia, Metis, Sapientia, Juno. The ancients believed every man had a female soul derived from the Mother Goddess through his earthly mother.

Each Egyptian had seven souls, bestowed by the Seven Hathors who guarded the planetary spheres and were fairy godmothers at the birth of every child. The souls were *aakhu, ab, ba, ka, khaibut, khat,* and *ren:* (1) primordial life spirit, resident in the blood; (2) the heart, formed from the mother's heart's blood; (3) the ghost that appeared after death and flew in and out of the tomb, sometimes as a bird; (4) the semblance or image, the other self seen in reflections; (5) the shadow; (6) the material living body, supposedly resurrected "in the flesh" after death; and (7) the secret name or soul-name.[2]

Greeks connected different aspects of the soul with different deities. Psyche, the spirit, was married to Eros, the body, until they were separated by death: this was the philosophical meaning of the romantic myth of Psyche and Eros. Souls belonging to Persephone in the underworld were shadows, or "shades"—the *umbra* corresponding to the Egyptian *khaibut* (see **Shadow**). Reflection-souls in water seem to have been connected with the water-goddess Echo, as shown by the myth of Narcissus.

Patriarchal writers tended to emphasize the soul called "breath," *pneuma,* since this was the kind of soul that could be given by a father. The idea came from Vedic India. Patriarchal Brahmans called the vital principle, self, or soul Atmen, "breath," cognate of the Greek *atmos,* "air." Brahman fathers gave their children breath-souls as opposed to the souls of blood, heart, name, flesh, mind, shade, etc., contributed by mothers. Therefore Brahmans regarded the breath-soul as the only important one. A Brahman father pretended to bring his newborn infant to life by breathing on it three times, putting a soul into its body.[3] Like all Aryan notions, this one reappeared in Europe centuries later, in a superstitious belief about lions. "For three days after birth the cubs of the lioness gave no sign of life, but on the third day the lion came and with his breath restored them to life."[4]

The biblical God performed the same miracle with breath, restoring life to slain warriors who had become heaps of dry bones. At the invocation of Ezekiel, God sent his breath into them from the winds, "and they lived, and stood up upon their feet, an exceeding great army" (Ezekiel 37:10). We are always astonished at the ease with which the ancient prophets ordered up impossible miracles, such as have never appeared within living memory.

Jesus's assertion that "the kingdom of God is within you" (Luke 17:21) filtered down from Ionian philosophers of the 6th and 5th centuries B.C. They identified the air-soul as God, and proposed that the divine spark within man was precisely the air he breathed, the "finest" element, forming the personal soul and the Oversoul at the same time. Diogenes of Apollonia set forth this doctrine:

> *Mankind and the other animals live on air, by breathing; and it is to them both soul and mind.*
>
> *The soul of all animals is the same, namely air which is warmer than the air outside, in which we live, though much colder than that near the sun.*
>
> *In my opinion that which has intelligence is what men call air, and by it everything is directed, and it has power over all things; for it is just this substance which I hold to be God.*[5]

The philosophers reasoned that if God=air=soul, then the air within a breathing person was an inner God judging his actions—an interior conscience. So said the poet Philemon:

> *I am he from whom none can hide, in any act which he may do, or be about to do, or have done in the past, be he god or man. Air is my name, but one might also call me Zeus. I, as a god should be, am everywhere—here in Athens, in Patrae, in Sicily, in all cities, in every home, in every one of you. There is no place where is not Air. And he who is present everywhere, because he is everywhere of necessity knows everything.*[6]

Christians largely accepted the air-soul theory, drawing out of it their ideas of invisible ghosts that could be felt but not seen, like air; and the notion that the soul can depart from the body through the nose or mouth, like breath. Yet older ideas of the soul also hung on.

The Egyptian doctrine of the seven souls, descending from the seven planetary spheres, passed into Gnostic Christianity as seven *qualities* of souls drawn from, and influenced by, the planetary spheres. Coming down from heaven to enter a newborn body, the soul had its original purity adulterated by sins and passions as it passed through the spheres: "As the souls descend, they draw with them the torpor of Saturn, the wrathfulness of Mars, the concupiscence of Venus, the greed for gain of Mercury, the lust for power of Jupiter." Seven deadly sins were acquired from the seven spheres, but they could be shed again after death as the soul ascended through the same spheres in the reverse direction, enroute to heaven. Christians generally restricted the number of souls to one, but some Gnostics held that every man has two souls, one emanating from the First Mind, and one called the God-seeing soul, "put in from the revolution of the heavens."[7]

Theories on the physical seat of the soul in the body have been many and various. The ancients usually placed the soul in the heart or the liver. Patriarchal thinkers declared that a man's testicles held the souls of his future children; St. Thomas Aquinas and other Christian authorities concurred in this. Some souls were external; they dwelt in umbilical cords, placentae, nail clippings, or shorn hair; any injury to these articles would injure the person. A more recent theory, dating from the early Age of Enlightenment, was that the seat of the soul is the pineal gland.

1. *Bardo Thodol,* xxxv. 2. H. Smith, 24. 3. Hays, 223. 4. Mâle, 15. 5. Guthrie, 136. 6. Guthrie, 142. 7. Jonas, 157, 160.

Sow

The white corpse-eating Sow-goddess represented the death aspect of the Great Mother in cults of Astarte, Demeter, the Celts' Cerridwen, and the Teutons' Freya. As a death goddess, Freya had the title of Sýr, "Sow."[1] Demeter-Persephone or "Demeter the Destroyer" was sometimes called Phorcis the Sow, mother of the Phorcids or Fatal Women. One of these was Circe, swine-goddess of Aeaea, who could turn men into sacrificial pigs.[2] Her island Aeaea meant literally "Wailing," a reference to the ritual laments accompanying sacrifices of the god in pig form.

The self-sacrifice of Vishnu in the form of a boar was repeated in western Indo-European myths, where the god was Porcus, Phorcus, or Orcus, a Lord of Death. *Orc* means "pig" in Irish; and the Orkney Islands were once sacred to the devouring Sow.[3]

In Tantric Buddhism the Goddess is still worshipped as the Diamond Sow, Marici. She sits on a lotus throne drawn by seven pigs. On earth she is incarnate in a real woman, the female counterpart of the Dalai Lama.[4] See **Boar; Vishnu.**

1. Turville-Petre, 168. 2. Graves, G.M. 1, 129. 3. Graves, W.G., 244. 4. Waddell, 233, 361.

Spartacus

Thracian slave who led a short-lived uprising against the Roman government in 73 B.C. Spartacus was a would-be Orphic savior, viewing himself as an incarnation of the god. His wife, a priestess of Orpheus-Dionysus, saw in a dream the Orphic serpent coiled around Spartacus's head, indicating that he would do great deeds and would die a hero's death.[1] Her prophecy was fulfilled. Spartacus's revolt was soon put down, and he was caught and executed in the manner of a sacred king.

1. Dumézil, 517.

Speaking in Tongues

Glossolalia, "speaking in tongues," was often seen in episodes of religious ecstasy or trance and was anciently considered a proof of divine grace. St. Paul was proud of his ability to "speak in tongues" more than any of his followers (1 Corinthians 14:18). Early Christians actually believed the speaker in tongues was expressing himself in another language or languages not known to his conscious mind, through temporary possession by the divine spirit. The idea came originally from Buddhists who claimed that when Buddha addressed gods, demons, men, and animals, each heard the Enlightened One speak in the language he could understand.[1]

In reality, glossolalia is only meaningless babbling that may pour forth from an entranced person. Not one authenticated case of speaking in tongues has ever been observed, where any real language was spoken and identified by a native speaker of the same language, together with evidence that the same language was wholly unknown to the possessed one.

1. Waddell, 159.

Sphinx

Mother Hathor as a lion-headed sphinx asked men her mystic riddle, and killed those who couldn't answer, until King Oedipus solved her riddle and cast her out of Thebes. The riddle was: "What goes on four legs at dawn, two legs at midday, and three legs at sunset, and is weakest when it has the most support?" The answer was either man or god. The sun god Ra, Hathor's offspring, grew old and feeble at the end of each day and walked with a third leg: a cane.[1] Some said Ra's weakness was the result of his mother's curse.

As the two-faced Goddess of birth and death, the Sphinx sometimes looked in two directions, with two heads and two foreparts. This glyph was called *xerefu* and *akeru,* "the Lions of Yesterday and Today," similar to the Goddess's Greek designation of Alpha and Omega.[2]

1. Graves, G.M. 2, 10. 2. Budge, E.L., 61.

Spider

Arachne the Spider was a totemic form of the Fate-spinner, otherwise known as Clotho or Athene or the Virgin Moera. The classic myth of Athene's jealousy of the maiden Arachne, which caused her to turn Arachne into a spider who continued to practice her incomparable skill in spinning and weaving, was mistakenly deduced from an icon showning Athene with her totemic spider spinning the web of Fate, from which the future could be foretold. An English writer of the 17th century still thought "Minerva" (Athene) gave spiders a special ability to foretell the weather.[1]

In Hindu myth, the spider represented Maya, virgin aspect of the Triple Goddess, spinner of magic, fate, and earthly appearances.[2] The spider's web was likened to the Wheel of Fate and the spider to the Goddess as a spinner, sitting at the hub of her wheel.

The female spider's habit of devouring her mate led to identification of the spider with the death goddess, Maya transformed into Kali-Uma. In Aztec myth, with its mysterious archaic relation to India, spiders represented the souls of warrior women from the pre-Aztec matriarchate, like the Amazonian Fate-spinners. At the end of the world, these women would descend from heaven on their silken threads and eat up all the men on earth, like eight-legged Valkyries. Indeed there were Scandinavian associations, too. Odin's horse Sleipnir (Slippery) was gray and had eight legs, like a spider; it also represented Odin's "Fate" in that it was associated with the gallows on which he was hanged.

Medieval Europe usually associated spiders with witches. The folk tale of the Spider and the Fly suggested the once widespread belief that flies are souls in search of a female entity to eat them and give them rebirth.[3] See **Arachne**.

1. Hazlitt, 625. 2. B. Butler, 244. 3. Spence, 96.

Starkad

Archaic Scandinavian god of many arms. Thor tore off all but two of Starkad's arms to "make him more comely," but his body always bore the marks of former supernumerary limbs. He was one of the elder gods or giants named *risi,* a derivation from Sanskrit *rishi,* "a sage"; therefore he was obviously a Hindu idol of the many-armed type still seen in India.[1] His myth indicates the Asiatic origin of northern Aryan peoples.

1. Turville-Petre, 206, 231.

Stations of the Cross

Image-galleries picturing key events in Christ's life and martydom, with recommended prayers and meditations for each stop. The gallery of "stations " was based on ancient Oriental picture galleries within the temple, to be traversed by pilgrims enroute to the central Holy of Holies.[1] The idea of separate, progressive meditations was taken directly from the Oriental tradition, in which the pilgrim's mind was supposed to be prepared for the inner revelation by slow stages during progress through the gallery or labyrinth.

1. Zimmer, 127.

Stella Maris

"Star of the Sea," an epithet of Isis, Ishtar, Aphrodite, Venus, Mari-Anna, and the virgin Mary. St. Jerome was said to have been the first to steal the title from the old Goddesses and bestow it on Mary.[1] The "star" was variously identified as the planet Venus (morning and evening star), or Polaris marking the *axis mundi,* or Sirius, or the leader of the Pleiades.

1. Jobes, 350.

Stoicism

Greco-Roman school of philosophy based on worship of Fate, the Goddess whose law ruled the constant combining, dissolving, and re-combining of elements (*stoicheia*). The infinite variety of her manipulations of elemental ingredients "gave rise to all perceptible phenomena."[1]

According to Stoic doctrine, the karmic law of Nature was beyond the power of any god to rescind, for the gods themselves were subject to the same law, and in common with other creatures would be destroyed eventually. Thus Stoicism stood in opposition to the Judeo-Christian hypothesis of miracles, by which God broke his own laws from time to time. Stoics said whatever is, is natural.

The Stoic concept of Fate or Nemesis was like the Tantric concept of Kali. To know the Goddess was to accept the fact of death, and to bow before the decrees of Fate as gracefully as possible.

Stoicism appealed to Roman intellectuals such as Seneca and Lucretius, who despised religious commercialism and hypocrisy. The Stoic sage Persius seems to have been a model for the story of Christ's encounter with the money-changers in the temple. It was Persius the Stoic who first demanded, "What is gold doing in a holy place?"[2]

Early Christians envied the esthetic elegance of Stoic theology and tried to assimilate it, but the basic premises of Stoicism and Christianity couldn't be reconciled. "The difference between the two conceptions cannot fail to manifest itself. . . . Stoic ethics are self-sufficing; they proceed from nature, so to speak, and do not rely upon grace; they have no need of a doctrine of Redemption. . . . There is nothing in common between them and Christianity save the elements it once borrowed from them."[3]

Nevertheless, Christian admirers of Stoicism strove to assimilate Stoic principles, such as the brotherhood of man, which Christian Gospels did not teach. St. Augustine even borrowed the phrase coined by Marcus Aurelius in his Stoic vision of all races dwelling as kindred in the "City of Zeus," though Augustine revised the title to "City of God."[4]

1. Cumont, A.R.G.R., 68. 2. Rose, 267. 3. Guignebert, 367–68. 4. Guthrie, 65.

Styx

"Shuddery; That Which is Taboo," principal river of the underworld in Greek myth.[1] The Styx was taboo because it was likened to the menstrual blood of Mother Earth, emanating from her secret yonic shrine in a mountain by the city of Clitor.[2] Like most rivers of the ancient world, Styx was also personified as a Goddess, called a daughter of Ocean. She married Pallas (*phallos,* the lingam), and gave birth to Power, Force, and Dominance (Nike). This was a mythic expression of the magic power supposedly engendered by the combination of semen and menstrual blood.[3]

Styx wound seven times through the underworld: a remnant of the primitive belief that pregnancy lasted seven lunar months, and rebirth would follow seven cycles of the moon. It was said that one *crossed* the Styx to reach the land of death-rebirth—as **Thomas Rhymer** crossed the River of Blood to reach Fairyland, and Jewish sages were said to cross the Jordan. Both Styx and Jordan were birth-rivers as well as death-rivers. The other name of Styx was Alpha, "birth." Similarly, when a man dipped himself seven times in the Jordan, "his flesh came again like unto the flesh of a little child" (2 Kings 5:14).

The ancient idea that a dead person must be ferried across the Styx by Charon was still literally believed in Greece, Ireland, and other countries up to the 17th and 18th centuries. Even though they were nominally Christian, peasants usually put money in a corpse's mouth before burial, "to pay the ferry."[4]

1. J.E. Harrison, 73. 2. Graves, W.G., 405–6. 3. J.E. Harrison, 72–73. 4. Hazlitt, 338.

Subincision

Ceremonial penis-slitting, practiced by some primitives in an effort to make male genitals resemble female ones. Like circumcision, subincision evolved from a former custom of **castration**, and became a rite of passage wherein grown men could express their hostility to the developing sexuality of pubescent youths while pretending to "make men" of them.

Succubus

Medieval Christian notion of the lascivious she-demon anciently called Lamia, Hora, Daughter of Hecate, Daughter of Lilith, Empusa, etc. She copulated with men in their dreams, and sucked out the essence of their souls (semen). Nocturnal emissions were always attributed to the attentions of she-demons who "cause men to dream of erotic encounters with women, so the succubae can receive their emission and make therefrom a new spirit."[1] See **Incubus**.

A common name for a succubus was Brizo, after the Greek goddess of sleep whose title came from *brizein,* "to enchant," and referred to a special kind of incubation known as brizomancy.[2] Like Babylon's dream-goddess Nanshe, Brizo brought prophetic dreams which were subsequently identified as "wet" dreams.

1. Robbins, 127. 2. Wedeck, 220.

Sufism

Arabic mystical system preserving within Islam a Tantric form of Goddess- and woman-worship. Like European bards and minnesingers who copied them, medieval Sufi poets sang of the spiritual significance of love, exemplified in the woman called a Fravashi or "Spirit of the Way." Sufis claimed the universe was held together by the feminine forces of motherhood and sexuality. To survive within a rabidly patriarchal society, however, the Sufis disguised their doctrines in many allegorical symbols, and established a mystical system in which nearly every tenet was imparted as a graphic image or metaphorical tale. Sir Richard Burton called Sufism "the Eastern parent of Freemasonry." See **Arabia**; **Romance**; **Tantrism**.

Sukra

"Seed," son of the planet Venus, with a second birth from the penis of Shiva, who had swallowed him and then endured a pregnancy of 100 years.[1] Like the stories of male birth-giving in Greece and the Middle East, Sukra's myth was intended to establish the notion that men could be "mothers." See **Birth-Giving, Male**.

1. O'Flaherty, 354.

Sun Goddess

Sun Goddess

Though western iconography usually called the sun male and the moon female, archaic Oriental tradition spoke of a female sun. Japanese ruling clans traced their descent from a supreme Sun Goddess, Omikami Amaterasu.[1] In 238 A.D., Japanese tribes were ruled by a queen named Himiko, Daughter of the Sun.[2]

The Hindu Great Mother took the form of the sun as the Goddess Aditi, mother of the twelve zodiacal Adityas, spirits who would "reveal their light at Doomsday."[3] The *Mahanirvanatantra* said the sun was the "garment" of the Great Goddess: "The sun, the most glorious symbol in the physical world, is the mayik vesture of Her who is 'clothed with the sun.' "[4] The same Goddess, identified with Mary, appeared in the Gospels as the "woman clothed with the sun" (Revelation 12:1).

Tantric Buddhism recognized a precursor of the Middle-Eastern Mari, or Mary, as the sun. Her monks greeted her at dawn as "the glorious one, the sun of happiness. . . . I salute you, O Goddess Marici! Bless me, and fulfil my desires. Protect me, O Goddess, from all the eight fears."[5]

When the Japanese revised their mythology to accommodate new patriarchal ideas, the Goddess Marici was masculinized, and it was forgotten that she was once identical with Omikami Amaterasu. Yet there was a strange ambivalence about the "powerful god" called

Marici-deva or Marishi-ten. "He" was called a protector of the sun, yet "he" always appeared in the garments of a Chinese woman, indicating an origin both feminine and rooted in lands west of Japan.[6]

Among the ancient Arabs, the sun was a Goddess, Atthar, sometimes called Torch of the Gods.[7] The Celts had a Sun Goddess named Sulis, from *suil,* meaning both "eye" and "sun." Germans called her Sunna. Norwegians called her Sol.[8] In Scandinavia she was also known as Glory-of-Elves, the Goddess who would give birth to a daughter after doomsday, thus producing the new sun of the next creation.[9] The Eddas said: "One beaming daughter the bright Sun bears before she is swallowed by Fenrir; so shall the maid pace her mother's way when the gods have gone to their doom."[10]

The Sun Goddess Sul, Sol, or Sulis was worshipped in Britain at the famous artificial mountain in the Avebury complex of megalithic monuments, now known as Silbury Hill. Here she gave birth to each new Aeon from her great belly-tumulus, over 130 feet high and more than 500 feet in diameter. "The influence of the British Goddess, Sul, extended over the greater part of south west England, and her worship appears to have been conducted on the tops of hills, overlooking springs. Thus near her springs at Bath we have the isolated hill called Solsbury, or Sulisbury, probably the seat of her worship." At Bath, Romans identified Sul with Minerva and set up altars to her under the name of Sul Minerva.[11]

1. *Larousse,* 408 et seq. 2. Campbell, Or.M., 463. 3. O'Flaherty, 339. 4. *Mahanirvanatantra,* xl. 5. Waddell, 218. 6. *Larousse,* 422. 7. *Larousse,* 323. 8. Branston, 152. 9. Sturluson, 92. 10. Branston, 288. 11. Dames, 154.

Svayamara

Bridegroom-choosing ceremony of pre-Vedic queens embodying the spirit of Sati as the Virgin Kali. She chose Shiva the Condemned One as her consort, casting over his head a wreath of flowers representing her yoni enveloping his lingam. In the role of sacred king he would die in his mating, like a penis, and his bridal wreath became the funeral wreath laid on his grave.[1] His divine bride followed him into the underworld and brought him back, as Ishtar followed Tammuz and Aphrodite followed Adonis.[2]

Svayamara meant a love-death (Teutonic *Liebestod*), a sinister implication for the ones who originally "caught the bride's bouquet." But later patriarchy converted the spirit of Sati into a symbol of the dutiful wife who followed her deceased husband into the underworld, whether she wanted to or not. "Sati" was corrupted into the word for widow-sacrifice, *suttee.* Up to the 19th century it was customary to burn widows on their husbands' funeral pyres, until the British government in India finally classified the rite of *suttee* as "homicide"—though it was never homicide, but only gynocide.[3] Widowers were never slain for the sake of their dead wives.

1. *Larousse,* 335. 2. Hauswirth, 41. 3. Bullough, 242.

Swan

An ancient, universal shamanic practice of wearing swan-feather cloaks created numerous myths of deities able to transform themselves into swans. The Heavenly Nymphs (Apsaras) of Hindu mythology were swan maidens. As a phallic god sporting with these sexual angels of the Vedic heaven, Krishna became a swan knight. Multiplied forms of his Goddess were sometimes swan-houris, sometimes milkmaids, the Gopis. Kalmuck tales of the *Siddhi Kur,* translated from Sanskrit, made Krishna a swan knight who courted the Triple Goddess in the guise of three milkmaids, daughters of the Old Woman (Kali).[1]

The same Indo-European lore surfaced in Scandinavian myth as the swan incarnations of the Valkyries, who wore magic swan-feather cloaks to transform themselves. Kali or Kauri became the Valkyrie Kara, who flew in her swan feathers above battlefields and sang magic charms to deprive the enemy of strength. Legends insisted that if a man could steal a Valkyrie's costume of swan feathers, she would be forced to grant his every wish.[2]

The swan knight Krishna reappeared in classic Greek myth as Zeus in swan feathers, disguising himself as a swan to seduce the Goddess Leda, who gave birth to the World Egg, which suggests that she too was a totemic swan. Sometimes she was confused with the Goddess Nemesis to whom Zeus's very life was subject: Leda or "Lady" being only her title.[3] Northern mythology also identified her with the Valkyrie Brunnhilde, whose seven children or Seven Dwarves were transformed into the seven swans of the fairy tale.[4] Zeus's swan form can be traced also to the Vedic image of Brahma in his special *vahana* ("vehicle," animal incarnation): a swan.[5]

Swan maidens and swan knights associated with the Old Religion were common in European folklore throughout the Christian era. A certain order of knights connected with the legendary Temple of the Grail and the defense of women claimed descent from a divine swan-hero. The families of Gelders and Cleves bore a swan on their arms, to honor their ancestor "the Knight of the Swan, servant of women," in whose memory Duke Adolph held a tournament in 1453.[6]

This Knight was sometimes called Lohengrin, a savior of women like the British hero Lancelot-Galahad. After the classic pattern, Lohengrin floated in a mystic vessel on the sea in his infancy, and was found and raised by a great queen in a foreign land. After his death he was reborn or reincarnated as his own son.[7]

When Lohengrin became one of the Knights Templar of the Grail, he was sent from the Grail castle at Montsalvatch to champion the cause of Duchess Else of Brabant, who had been unjustly imprisoned for exercising the ancient right of noblewomen to choose a lover from among men of inferior rank. Having overcome Else's enemies, Lohengrin married her. According to one version of the story, probably drawn from the myth of Psyche and Eros, Else was forbidden to ask her husband's real name, but couldn't help insisting on it; so, sorrowfully revealing his name, Lohengrin was obliged to leave Else and return to the Mount of Paradise. Other versions of the story said he took her with him to Montsalvatch, where they lived happily ever after.[8]

Other stories said Lohengrin appeared in his swan-feather costume to defend Clarissa, Duchess of Bouillon, against the Count of Frankfort, who tried to steal her duchy. Or, he took up the cause of Beatrice of Cleves, whose property rights were threatened by hostile barons.[9] Though he sallied forth to the rescue of several ladies in distress, the Swan-knight's real home was always "the mountain where Venus lives in the Grail."[10]

1. Baring-Gould, C.M.M.A., 568. 2. *Larousse*, 278–79; Baring-Gould, C.M.M.A., 579. 3. Graves, G.M. 1, 207–8. 4. Baring-Gould, C.M.M.A., 571, 579. 5. Ross, 36. 6. Baring-Gould, C.M.M.A., 600. 7. Rank, 62. 8. Guerber, L.M.A., 202–3. 9. Baring-Gould, C.M.M.A., 600. 10. Jung & von Franz, 121.

Swastika

Those who know the swastika only as the Nazi *Hakenkreuz* (Hook Cross) may be surprised to learn that it is one of the oldest, most widely distributed religious symbols in the world. Swastikas appear on Paleolithic carvings on mammoth ivory from the Ukraine, dated ca. 10,000 B.C.[1] Swastikas figure on the oldest coinage in India.[2] Persia, Asia Minor, and Greece represented the rotating *axis mundi* with the symbol of a swastika. On a Boeotian amphora of the 7th century B.C., the swastika was presented as a sacred sign of the Goddess Artemis.[3] It also represented many other deities from Iceland to Japan, Scandinavia to North Africa. It was much used in Troy and Mycenae before the 13th century B.C.[4]

Sanskrit *svastika* meant "so be it" or "amen." In Japan, the swastika was an ideogram for "infinity"—the number 10,000, which was a synonym for infinity because it was the highest number Japanese sages could visualize.[5]

Swastika

There were two basic types of swastikas: the left-pointing, counterclockwise, widdershins version called the Moon Swastika, and the right-pointing, clockwise one called the Sun Swastika. The former was naturally associated with the Left-Hand Path of the Goddess, the latter with the Right-Hand Path of the God. (See **Left Hand**.) Hindus said the solar swastika represented the god Ganesha, "Lord of Hosts," and the lunar swastika stood for Kali-Maya, his virgin bride, mother of Buddha.[6] As a reincarnation of his divine father, Buddha displayed the sign of a cross, with a swastika enclosed in the female circle at the end of each arm.[7] Tibetan Buddhists said the right-handed swastika was the Savior, the left-handed swastika meant witchcraft, or the "magic" of Mother Maya.[8]

The feminine moon swastika received the name of *sauvastika* and was said to represent the autumnal half of the year, when the sun wanes, while the masculine swastika stood for the vernal season when the sun grows stronger.[9] As the feminine *sauvastika* suggested the sun god declining toward his death and resurrection at the winter solstice, it sometimes signified rebirth.

In Japan, the reborn Amida, "Buddha of Immeasurable Light," wore a left-handed swastika carved on his breast.[10] A similar left-handed swastika was the sign of Thor's hammer on Scandinavian coins.[11] Thor was one of the gods supposed to have come from ancient Troy; and Trojan images of the Great Goddess showed a swastika within a female triangle on her belly, indicating the hidden god prior to his next rebirth.[12]

Early Christians adopted the swastika to represent Christ, calling it a *crux dissimulata* or disguised cross. It was also called crux gammata, gammadion, or gamma cross, because it showed the Greek letter gamma four times repeated. To Saxons it was *fylfot,* translated either "four-foot," referring to the four heavenly pillars at the corners of the earth, or "fill-foot," referring to the Christian habit of filling in the foot of a church window with swastikas.[13] In old Danish churches, the swastika was the usual ornamentation for the baptismal font.[14] It was also much used in medieval heraldry, as "cross potent rebated," *croix gammée,* or *croix cramponnée.* Still, knights who wore the swastika on their shields couldn't be sure whether it stood for the cross of Christ or the cross of Thor, the latter being revered in swastika form all over Germanic areas, including the Scandinavian settlements in Lincolnshire and Yorkshire.[15]

In the 1930s, the Nazi party adopted the swastika because of an impression that it was a "pure Aryan" sign. A variant of the swastika long represented German Vehmic Courts (from *Vehme,* "punishment") which began in the Middle Ages as civil tribunals for persecuting heretics, and became connected with the Inquisition. Their activities were kept secret. In Napoleon's time, the Vehmic Courts were still operating as underground organizations devoted to summary justice, like the Black Hand in Sicily.[16] From the *Vehmgericht* arose specifically anti-Semitic secret societies of Austria and Germany in the early 1900s—the forerunners of Nazism.

1. Campbell, F.W.G., 147. 2. d'Alviella, 80. 3. Neumann, G.M., 134. 4. d'Alviella, xi-xii. 5. Hornung, 211; d'Alviella, 43. 6. Graves, G.M. 1, 149; d'Alviella, 68. 7. Baring-Gould, C.M.M.A., 354. 8. Jung, M.S., 36. 9. Budge, A.T., 332. 10. Campbell, F.W.G., 173. 11. Baring-Gould, C.M.M.A., 351. 12. d'Alviella, 33. 13. Hornung, 211. 14. d'Alviella, 39. 15. Baring-Gould, C.M.M.A., 354. 16. *Encyc. Brit.,* "Vehmgericht."

Swithin, Saint

Originally S. Wothin, or Holy Wotan, "Swithin" was the god of West Saxon kings of Winchester, "Place of the Winds," from Latin *venta,* winds. The calendar symbol of St. Swithin was the Cross of Wotan representing the four winds.[1] Since Wotan was a Saxon version of Jupiter Pluvius, it was claimed that rain on St. Swithin's day meant rain for the next forty days, and that Swithin's relics were buried outside Winchester Cathedral where rain could pour from a roof spout onto his grave.

Swithin was adopted as a Christian saint about a century after his alleged lifetime, which was assigned to the 9th century.[2] His claim to sainthood was that he was supposed to have established tithes in England, having talked the Saxon king Ethelwold into turning over to the church a tenth part of all his lands.[3]

1. Brewster, 330. 2. Hazlitt, 576. 3. Brewster, 330.

Sword

Herodotus said the Scythian war god was represented by an ancient iron sword (phallus) fixed in a pyramid of brushwood (female symbol), made fertile with the blood of human sacrifices.[1] Eight centuries later, the Alani and Quadi in the same region worshipped a father-god as a naked sword fixed in the ground. Ammianus said the warriors worshipped their own swords as gods.[2]

In the north, a primary female symbol was the house (*hus,* hussy), which was combined with the sword by marriage. A Norse wedding custom was plunging a sword into the main beam of the house: "a proof of the virility of the bridegroom and a sign of good luck for the marriage."[3]

Norse myth said the gates of heaven are guarded by a man juggling seven swords, one for each of the seven (male) spirits of the planetary spheres.[4]

1. Goodrich, 217. 2. Gelling & Davidson, 38. 3. Gelling & Davidson, 150. 4. Keightley, 61.

var. Sibyl

Sybil

"Cavern-dweller," a Latin form of Cybele, the Great Mother of Gods. The name may have been derived from Babylonian *subultu,* a Goddess seen in the sky as the constellation of the Celestial Virgin.[1] Her oracular spirit occupied a succession of priestesses in the sacred cave at Cumae, near Lake Avernus, dedicated to Triple Hecate. The cave was famed as an entrance to the underworld. Sybils called up the dead there for necromantic interviews. By the same door, Aeneas descended into the womb of the earth (his mother Aphrodite).[2]

In the 2nd century B.C. the aniconic idol of Cybele was carried to Rome by order of the Cumaean sybils whose oracles guided imperial policy. Texts of the priestesses' sayings, the Sybilline Books, were so respected that both Christians and Jews spent many centuries rewriting these books, and forging additions to them, to make it seem that the sybils foretold the coming of Christ and the Messiah.[3]

According to Varro, in the first century B.C., there were ten great sybils who divided the known world among their ten oracular shrines. Throughout the Middle Ages, Christian scholars described each of the great sybils as a prophetess of Christ, painting them with Christian symbols such as crucifixes, crowns of thorns, lilies, mangers, etc.[4]

Folk tradition maintained that after the Christian conquest of Europe, the sybils continued to occupy sacred caves in certain mountains that belonged to the Great Mother of the Gods. These were the Venusbergs of medieval paganism. Many legends told of men who, like Tannhauser and Thomas Rhymer, entered such a cave and dwelt in "the Paradise of Queen Sybil."[5]

Conjurations and pleas for buried treasure, rings of invisibility, and the like were addressed to the Blessed Virgin of Fairies, "Sibyllia," or to "three sisters of fairies, Milia, Achillia, Sibyllia." They were charged by the Father, Son, and Holy Ghost to appear "in form and shape of fair women, in white vestures."[6]

1. Briffault 2, 600. 2. Graves, W.G., 273. 3. James, 248–50; Ashe, 132. 4. Brewster, 415–17. 5. Goodrich, 172. 6. Scot, 340–42.

Sylph

Greek word for a female spirit of the element of air: an invisible angel, whose voice might be heard in the breeze. In medieval times, "sylph" became a synonym for "witch." See **Elements**.

Synesaktism

The "Way of Shaktism," Gnostic-Christian term for the cult of "spiritual marriage," or *agape,* the love-feast: actually a western version of Tantric sex-worship. Synesaktism flowered in the late Roman empire, but before the 7th century A.D. it was declared heretical and outlawed by the orthodox church.[1] See **Tantrism**.

1. Bullough, 105; Sadock, Kaplan & Freedman, 23.

T

Mother Goddess of the Aztecs, TLAZOLTEOTL was very like her medieval Near Eastern counterpart Hecate. Here, she gives birth to the sun-god. Made of aplite, speckled with garnets.

Pre-Vedic, primal Goddess TARA was known from India to Ireland and worshipped as "savior" and "star." Gilt bronze; Tibet, 16th century.

The Great Goddess Fortune, TYCHE, sitting on a rock, the river Orontes swimming at her feet. Marble; Roman copy of the original Eutychides sculpture from the 3rd century B.C.

Taaut

Phoenician name for the World Serpent, called Tuat or Thoth in Egypt, Ouroboros or Python in the Greco-Roman world. The traditional figure of the underground serpent with his tail in his mouth was also associated with the cosmic Water-snake encircling the earth (Oceanus), and the serpent Sata at the roots of the earth. Egyptians said the chambers of the serpent's body provided the many "mansions" (Arits) of the nether world. See **Serpent**.

var. Tat

Tait

Title of Isis as weaver and knotter of the threads of Fate, governing all happenings with her magical manipulation of strands. Persons of high rank were promised mummy-wrappings woven and tied by the Goddess herself.[1] See **Knot**.

1. Erman, 73.

Taliesin

Welsh bard and magician whose legends claimed he was the son of the Goddess Cerridwen, the White Goddess of the Cauldron of Regeneration and Inspiration. Many mystical, allegorical writings about the Old Religion were attributed to Taliesin. He was generally supposed to have been a real person who lived in the 6th century A.D.[1] However, like the works of Homer, those of Taliesin seem to have been made up of collections and reorganizations of older myths.

1. *Encyc. Brit.*, "Welsh Literature."

Ta-Mera

"Land of Waters," an old name of Egypt. Mera or Mara was an archaic name for the Goddess of the primordial sea. In Egypt she was even coupled with the sun god as an androgynous deity Meri-Ra. Among the meanings of *Mera* were such female symbols as a watercourse, ditch, pit, sea, and lovingness.[1]

1. Budge, E.L., 76.

Tammuz

The *Christos* or sacred king annually sacrificed in the temple at Jerusalem, attended by women who dedicated him to their Goddess Ishtar-Mari, Queen of Heaven, his mother and bride (Ezekiel 8:14).

He was a Hebrew version of Dionysus Liber, or Adonis, whom the

Romans called the chief god of the Jews.[1] Tacitus however thought the Jews had given up worshipping Liber, for he "established a festive and cheerful worship, while the Jewish religion is tasteless and mean."[2] A month of the Jewish calendar is still named after Tammuz, who was revered all the way up to the 10th century.[3]

Tammuz was imported from Babylon by the Jews, but he was even older than Babylon. He began as the Sumerian savior-god Dumuzi, or Damu, "only-begotten Son," or "Son of the Blood." He fertilized the earth with his blood at the time of his death, and was called Healer, Savior, Heavenly Shepherd. He tended the flocks of stars, which were considered souls of the dead in heaven. Each year on the Day of Atonement he was sacrificed in the form of a lamb, son of the Holy Ewe; but his animal incarnation was understood to be a substitute for an earlier human sacrifice. A lament for the dead god asked rhetorically:

> *Why have they slain him, him of the plains? The Shepherd, the Man of Wisdom, the Man of Sorrow why have they slain? The Lady of the Vine languishes, the lambs and the calves languish. The Lord, the Shepherd of the fold lives no more, the spouse of the Queen of Heaven lives no more.*[4]

On the occasion of the god's death, temple women raised ritual "howls" or "ululations," which the Babylonians called *alalu*, and the Greeks called *houloi*. This was the sound mentioned by Ezekiel: in the Jerusalem temple, women "wailed" for Tammuz. A typical "wail" is mentioned in Sumerian scriptures:

> *For him who has been taken away there is wailing; ah me, my child has been taken away, my Damu that has been taken away, my Christ that has been taken away, from the sacred cedar where the Mother bore him. The wailing is for the plants, they grow not; for the houses and for the flocks, they produce not; for the perishing wedded couples, for perishing children, the people of Sumer, they produce not. The wailing is for the great river, it brings the flood no more. The wailing is for the fish ponds; the fish spawn not. The wailing is for the forests; the tamarisks grow not. The wailing is for the store-house; the honey and wine are not produced.*[5]

Some liturgies addressed Dumuzi-Tammuz as Usir or Usirsir, variations of the name Osiris, who was also the Good Shepherd and the keeper of the "flocks" of the dead.[6] Though Tammuz occupied the central position in the sacred drama at Jerusalem, the New Testament transformed him into a mere apostle of the new dying god, under the Greek form of his name, **Thomas**.

A thousand years later, however, Syrian farmers still considered the sacrifice of Ta-uz, the grain god, essential to the welfare of the crops. He was cruelly treated: slain by the reaper's sickle, his bones ground in a mill, his flesh scattered on the earth, his death bewailed by the women.[7]

Like all earlier "saviors," Tammuz eventually was diabolized in Christian tradition. During the Middle Ages he was listed as one of hell's leading devils. Weyer's treatise on demonology made Tammuz hell's ambassador to Spain, probably because he was still worshipped by Saracenic sects in Spain.[8]

1. Graves, W.G., 368. 2. Tacitus, 660. 3. Frazer, G.B., 393. 4. Briffault 3, 91–95. 5. Briffault 3, 94. 6. Hooke, S.P., 175. 7. Frazer, G.B., 392–93. 8. Waite, B.C.M., 186–87.

Tanit

Sign of Tanit

Carthaginian name of the Phoenician Great Goddess, Astarte—the biblical Ashtoreth or Asherah. Her temple in Carthage was called the Shrine of the Heavenly Virgin. Greek and Roman writers called it a temple of the moon.[1]

Another of her titles was Astroarche, Queen of the Stars. Her priestesses were famous astrologers, whose prophecies were circulated throughout the Roman empire and even rivaled the pronouncements of the Cumaean sybils.[2]

Though Romans destroyed Carthage in the Punic Wars, Roman legend traced the very origin of Rome to the Carthaginian mother-city, as shown by the story of Aeneas, who came directly across the Mediterranean from there, to found Rome.[3] The primitive Roman queen Tanaquil, who conferred sovereignty on the "fatherless" Latin kings, the Tarquins, was none other than the Libyan Goddess Tanit. She was also known as Libera, Goddess of Libya, whose festival the Liberalia was celebrated each year in Rome during the Ides of March.[4] An alternative name for the festival was Bacchanalia, dramatizing the love-death and resurrection of Bacchus Liber, or Dionysus, or Consus, which were various names for the same fertility god.[5]

The distinctive symbol of Tanit was a pyramidal shape, like a woman in a very full skirt, topped by a disc-shaped full-moon head, with upraised arms in the manner of the Egyptian *ka.*[6] Similar symbols represented such goddesses as Aphrodite, Athene, Venus, and Juno.

1. Reinach, 42. 2. Lindsay, O.A., 327. 3. Reinach, 106. 4. G.R. Scott, 165. 5. Graves, W.G., 399. 6. *Larousse,* 84.

Tannhäuser

"Dweller in the House of Tann," the hero who lived in the Goddess's magic mountain, the Venusberg. Tann, Dann, Danu, Diana, Tannetis, or Dennitsa were variations of the same Goddess (Venus) whom Tannhäuser adored in the shape of her mortal priestess, Queen Sybil. The legend of Tannhäuser displayed considerable hostility to the authority of the pope, and presented the cult of the Goddess as an alternative to Christianity. See **Sybil**.

Tantrism

The system of yoni-worship, or female-centered sex-worship, allegedly founded thousands of years ago in India by women of a secret sect called Vratyas, forerunners of the devadasis or sacred harlots.[1] The religion was associated with later written scriptures known as Tantras, therefore it was called Tantrism. The primary object of its adoration was the lingam-yoni, sign of male and female principles in conjunction (the god Shiva and the goddess Shakti-Kali). Tantrism is still widely practiced in India, Nepal, Bhutan, and Tibet.[2]

The basic principle of Tantrism was that women possess more spiritual energy than men, and a man could achieve realization of the divinity only through sexual and emotional union with a woman. A fundamental rite was controlled sexual intercourse, *maithuna,* Latin *coitus reservatus:* sex without male orgasm. The theory was that a man must store up his vital fluids rather than expending them in ejaculation. Through Tantric training, he learned to absorb through his penis the fluid engendered by his partner's orgasm and to prolong sexual intercourse for many hours. In this way he could become like Shiva, the God in perpetual union with his Goddess. Theoretically, the vital fluids thus conserved would be stored in a man's spinal column, mount through the *chakras* up to his head, and there flower forth with the inspiration of divine wisdom. The Tantras explain this and other practices based on worship of the Goddess, together with the philosophy underlying the rites.

The most sacred *mantra* (holy phrase) expressing Tantric worship was *Om mani padme hum,* the Jewel (penis) in the Lotus (vulva). The symbolic lingam-yoni often took the form of an altar, shaped like a penis in a vulva.[3] Remnants of Tantric practice inspired the medieval European belief that "witches" worshipped at an altar represented by a female body.

Tantric Buddhism consisted of an uneasy marriage between an originally ascetic Buddhist cult with ancient sexual disciplines. Like its Christian offshoot five centuries later, Buddhism was founded on opposition to the female principle and the belief that men must avoid women, in order to conserve their souls' vitality by retaining their semen and concentrating on the Self. Buddhist monks claimed their prophet ordered them to quell all sexual desire, and never to see or speak to women.[4]

Like early Christianity, however, Buddhism soon spread out along a continuum of sects ranging from the austere, puritanical Jains to exuberantly erotic Tantric Buddhists with principles like "Buddhahood resides in the vulva."[5] All over Indian temples, Buddhist saints appeared with their voluptuous Shaktis in the divine embrace called Yab-Yum (Father-Mother), representing everlasting orgasmic bliss—the real cause of the beatific smiles on the faces of the bodhisattvas.

Erotic forms of Tantric Buddhism penetrated all Asia, though patriarchal sects later suppressed them and denied their historical existence. Tantric Buddhism flourished in China under the Six Dynasties, T'ang, and Mongol Yuan, until Confucian patriarchs succeeded in eliminating it. Japanese Shingon is an attenuated remnant. Tantrism is no longer mentioned in China or Japan; its art was destroyed; authorities pretend it was never there at all.[6]

The same denial appeared in areas dominated by Islam where Sufi mystics had perpetuated a form of Tantrism. They emphasized the discipline of *fana,* "rapture," attainable only with a *pir* (Peri), a fairy mistress, also known as Fravashi, "Spirit of the Way."[7] Through her, a man might achieve "the larger full surrender" said to pass beyond God to realization of the ultimate Void that swallowed even the gods.[8]

Early Gnostic Christians sometimes called their religion *synesaktism,* the Way of Shakti, another name for Tantrism.[9] These Christians were influenced by Oriental Tantrism as well as by some of its western forms, philosophies of Goddess-worship filtered through Pythagorean and Neoplatonic mystics. Plotinus equated the mind's progress toward the Ineffable with "the sight of a beautiful lady." Ascent of the mind toward realization of divinity was divided into six steps, beginning with perception of woman's beauty, culminating in contemplation of Universal Beauty.[10]

Christians like the Ophites and Montanists apparently practiced sexual adoration of the feminine life force under the name of **Sophia**, the female Holy Spirit, a feminine soul or Shakti of God. Their rite of "spiritual marriage" was misunderstood by the orthodox, who later called it a Test of Faith. Certain male and female saints, they said, had proved their chastity by lying together naked without copulation. Possibly it was not sexual intercourse *per se* that such "saints" had avoided, but only male orgasm. Like Tantric yogis, Gnostic saints sometimes thought themselves "perfected" by *coitus reservatus,* so they could indulge in nakedness and promiscuity without being sinful.[11]

These sects were destroyed by the end of the 5th century A.D. and no more was heard of the famous Test of Faith.[12] Orthodox fathers of the church ruled that sexual intercourse should have no purpose other than to beget offspring, and sexual pleasure should be altogether denied to women.[13]

While Tantric Christians were condemned as heretics, Islamic leaders were attacking Sufi cults of love.[14] Sufi mysticism survived underground, in the hands of troubadours who called themselves Lovers and adored the female principle as the world-sustaining power. Sufi yoni-worship influenced European troubadours, who founded cults of Courtly Love in the centuries following the crusades. The church called them devil-worshippers because they "sinfully" loved women instead of God, and women were equated with the devil by the theological opinion of the time.[15] See **Romance**.

Heroes of the Courtly Love movement apparently practiced Tantric *maithuna* under the name of drudaria, a kind of love associated with male self-denial, yet not at all chaste. On the contrary, its poetry was highly erotic.[16] Bardic romance sometimes showed distinct connections with eastern Tantrism, as when Peredur's mystic lady-love revealed that she came from India, or when Tristan told his lady-love Iseult that his name was the syllabically-reversed Tantris.[17]

Though never officially recognized, Tantric sex has been practiced throughout history in western nations, either in accordance with a secret teaching, or as an independent discovery. Medieval Goddess-worshippers vilified as "witches" apparently knew of it, and may have used it as a birth-control technique. It was claimed that no woman was ever made pregnant at the witches' Sabbath.[18]

In 1848, *maithuna* was again publicized by the founder of the Oneida Creek Community, John Humphrey Noyes, who rediscovered it while trying to protect his wife from "the horrors and the fear of involuntary propagation" after she had four disastrous pregnancies.[19] Noyes called his discovery "male continence," or *karezza,* and trained members of his community in the technique. Then they engaged in what Noyes called "complex marriage" with various partners, without unwanted pregnancies.[20] Several occult societies of the 19th and 20th centuries made use of Tantric *coitus reservatus* for various reasons, but it was seldom admitted to the "normal" sexual repertoire of the western male.

1. Rawson, A.T., 80. 2. *Encyc. Brit.,* "Tantrism." 3. Rawson, E.A., 47. 4. Campbell, Or.M., 301. 5. Campbell, Or.M., 352. 6. Rawson, E.A., 255. 7. Bullough, 150. 8. Campbell, Oc.M., 194, 451. 9. Bullough, 105. 10. Collins, 113. 11. Bullough, 112. 12. Legge 2, 77. 13. Bullough, 114. 14. Sadock, Kaplan & Freedman, 23. 15. Briffault 3, 490. 16. Briffault 3, 483. 17. Loomis, 211; Guerber, L.M.A., 238. 18. Knight, D.W.P., 236. 19. Crow, 179. 20. Carden, 55–56.

Tao

"The Way," Chinese version of Tantrism. Men were taught to reserve their vital forces, which could be dangerously depleted by ejaculation, and to let their weaker Yang nature absorb the powerful Yin force engendered by a woman's orgasm. Men were advised to keep this "key" secret from women, for if women learned to suppress their own orgasms while bringing men to ecstasy, they would greatly surpass men in wisdom and spiritual energy. Their already superior Yin magic would remain in their bodies, while the man's lesser Yang magic would be added to it.[1]

Lao-Tse said: "How unfathomable is Tao—like unto the emptiness of a vessel, yet, as it were, the honored Ancestor of us all. Using it we find it inexhaustible, deep and unfathomable. Now pure and still is the Way! I do not know who generated it. It may appear to have preceded God."[2]

1. Bullough, 256. 2. Ross, 141.

Tara

Indo-European name of the primal Goddess Earth, known from India to Ireland; cognate with Latin Terra Mater, Hebrew Terah, Gaulish Taranis, Etruscan Turan.[1] An extremely ancient festival held annually at Athens was named after her, Taramata (Mother Tara), nicknamed "the Rioting" because of its wild orgiastic customs.[2]

The sacred grove of Tara in Ireland was the Goddess's genital shrine, enclosing the God in the form of a stone pillar, Fal (phallus). This pillar represented his generative power, like the obelisk in Egypt, and was specifically called "the stone penis."[3] The God's name was Taran in Wales, or Torann in Ireland, meaning "thunder." Like Jupiter Pluvius, he fertilized Mother Tara with rain.[4] The traditional words of a fanfare, Taran-Tara, originally came from a magic "cry" expressing the union of the two deities.

Tantric Buddhists in Tibet still pray to Mother Tara like this:

> *Hail! O verdant Tara! The Savior of all beings! Descend, we pray Thee, from Thy heavenly mansion, at Potala, together with all Thy retinue of gods, titans, and deliverers! We humbly prostrate ourselves at Thy lotus-feet! Deliver us from all distress! O holy Mother! We hail Thee! O revered and sublime Tara! Who are adored by all the kings and princes of the ten directions and of the present, past and future.*[5]

In India, Tara is called "the most revered" of the old pre-Vedic Goddesses, just as in all lands populated by Aryan peoples, Mother Earth was the first, oldest, and greatest of deities.[6]

1. Dumézil, 676. 2. Lawson, 226. 3. Rees, 273. 4. Turville-Petre, 120.
5. Waddell, 435. 6. *Larousse,* 359.

Tarot

The modern pack of playing cards evolved from the Tarot pack by the subtraction of 25 cards. In addition to the now-standard 52—four suits from ace to king—Tarot packs had a fifth suit, the Major Arcana (Great Secrets), a trump suit consisting of 22 picture cards. Only one of these trump cards now remains in the deck, the Joker, Jester, or Fool. Present card decks are only remnants of what medieval cards used to be—that is, the Tarot.

Four court cards also disappeared from the suits: the four knights. Therefore, modern cards have only three court cards per suit: king, queen, and jack. Disappearance of the knights led some scholars to think Tarot cards might have been invented by the Knights Templar, who were declared heretics, disgraced, and exterminated in the 14th century. Though Templars may have learned from the Saracens to use cards, they didn't invent them.[1] Unbound "books" of picture cards were long used in the east to teach mystical doctrines to people who couldn't read.[2]

Italian author Covelluzo wrote: "In the year 1379 the game of cards was brought to Viterbo from the country of the Saracens, where it is called *naib.*" In that year, Saracen mercenaries served in the armies of rival popes Urban VI and Clement VII; but Saracenic Arabs had occupied Spain, southern France, Sicily, and Italy since the early 8th century. The Arabs dominated Spain until the 15th century. Their word *naib* became Spanish *naipes,* "playing cards."[3]

Gypsies migrating from their ancient home in Hindustan also brought cards into Europe. Tarot cards have been called "the compendium of gypsy philosophy and religion."[4] The world's oldest gambling game, Faro, came from gypsies who were supposed to be "Egyptians," and whose "game of kings" was naturally named Pharaoh (Faro) because, it was said, their cards had pharaohs painted on them.[5] Spanish gypsies introduced Spain's national card game, ombre (Spanish *hombre*), "the game of man," which was as much a system of mystical divination as a game. Ombre was "a modification of the earlier game of primero . . . of all modern games that which most resembles the ancient tarot."[6]

The mysterious disappearance of the trump suit and the knights was connected with more or less consistent hostility of Christian authorities toward the cards. In 1370, a monk named John of Brefeld said in the symbolism of the cards "the state of the world as it is now is most excellently described and figured." But this turned out to be a heretical opinion. Other churchmen claimed the Cathari used cards to teach their Gnostic faith. In 1378, the cards were banned in Regensburg, Germany. In 1381, they were condemned in Marseilles. In 1397, they were forbidden in Paris. In 1423, St. Bernardino of Siena said the cards were invented by the devil. In 1441, importation of cards was prohibited in Venice. In 1450, a Franciscan friar denounced cards in northern Italy. John Northbrooke later wrote: "The play at Cards is an invention of the Devil, which he found out that he might the easier bring in Idolatry amongst men." Scottish clergymen called cards "the Devil's books." Churchmen were especially enraged by the Major Arcana or trump suit. These 22 little pictures were called "the rungs of a ladder leading to the depths of hell."[7] Cards were described as the devil's breviary, "in which various figures are painted, just as they are in the breviaries of Christ, which figures show forth the mysteries of evil."[8]

One may well wonder, what were these mysteries? What "idols" did the idolatry of cards show forth? What doctrines were taught by the "devil's breviary"?

The Tarot has been linked with several non-Christian mystical systems: the Cabala, Hermetic magic, classical paganism, witchcraft. Dr. Gerard Encausse wrote, "The game of cards called the Tarot, which the Gypsies possess, is the Bible of Bibles. It is the book of Thoth Hermes Trismegistus, the book of Adam, the book of the primitive Revelation of ancient civilizations."[9] A more recent student of the cards says, "The Tarot speaks in the language of symbols, the

Dr. Gerard Encausse French physician, theosophist, and founder of the popular spiritual-masonic Order of Martinists. Under the pen name of Papus, he published the highly influential *Le Tarot des Bohémiens* in 1889, setting a precedent for Tarot interpreters of the early 20th century.

language of the unconscious, and when approached in the right manner it may open doors into the hidden reaches of the soul."[10]

In the east, whence cards originally came, there was an ancient tradition of religious insights taught through dramatic presentation or through pictures. Eastern mystics believe in the existence of a secret international symbol-code known only to initiates, whereby the true meanings of religious mysteries are revealed. Similarly it was thought the hieroglyphs of Egypt and central America began as a secret symbol-code. Pythagorean and Orphic initiates used such code systems in antiquity. European mystery plays, too, conveyed Gnostic or non-Christian ideas in symbols and tableaux of very ancient origin, under the noses of churchmen who would have suppressed them if they had understood their meaning.[11]

The Tarot strongly resembles an Oriental symbol-code when observed in relation to doctrines prevailing in the east at the time of its European debut. Pictures of the Major Arcana can be linked with pageants of the mystery plays, Gnostic teachings, and Orphic icons. Here was the real reason for opposition to the trump suit—opposition so bitter that in the end all trumps were excised except the Fool, a "know-nothing." Because of the church's hostility, today's card players have no trump suit, and are obliged to name one of the other suits "trumps" when necessary.

Images of the Tarot suggest female-centered, cyclic doctrines of reincarnation such as the old religions taught. The cards probably were the original "elf-books," allegedly given by the fairies to people they loved, which enabled them to foretell the future.[12] Cards were associated with witches. In German towns where witch persecutions fell heaviest, painters of the forbidden cards were women.[13] Moakley has pointed out that "preachers have never liked playing cards, and it can be said that the story the cards tell is very much opposed to the basic tenets of Christianity."[14]

To understand the story, one must study the cards' format. The four suits of the Minor Arcana or Lesser Secrets are clearly related to Oriental images of the elements. The first suit was Cups, Chalices, or Grails; it later became the suit of hearts. The second was Wands, Rods, Batons, or Scepters—now converted into clubs, though the club is not a club but a trefoil. The third suit was usually called Pentacles, also rendered Coins, Disks, Denari, or Pomegranates, which became diamonds. Finally there was the suit of Swords, modern spades, derived from Spanish *espada,* sword.

As cup, scepter, ring, and sword, these emblems were displayed by the four-armed androgynous deity Ardhanarisvara—Kali and Shiva merged.[15] Other gods, such as the monkey god Hanuman, held the same symbols.[16] The female earth principle Brawani also carried the elements as lily, flame, cross, and sword.[17] Like her the Greek Goddess Nemesis or Fate displayed the same symbols as a cup, apple wand, wheel, and sword.[18]

These Tarot suit symbols stood for paired male-and-female elements: female water with male fire, female earth with male air. These in turn were linked with the four stages of life established by Tantric philosophers: Sambhoga, Nirmana, Artha, and Moksha.[19] These four life-stages had the following "elemental" meanings.

1. Sambhoga, the Life of Enjoyment, was related to the feminine Water element and its symbol the cup, grail, or heart. It referred to the period of youth under the tutelage of the Mother, when pleasures of the senses figure most prominently in the life experience, while the cup of life fills up with feelings, consciousness, awareness of others. The Tarot suit of Cups therefore was traditionally applied to the subject of love, family relationships, marriages, children, emotion: matters of the heart, or "hearts."

2. Nirmana, the Process of Building, was related to the masculine Fire element and its symbol the phallic wand, scepter, rod, or club. It meant young adulthood, the period of assertion of power, a peak of energy. The wand or *dorje* represented the phallic lightning streaking toward the waters. Tarot readers therefore applied the suit of Wands to matters of status, power, business, and commerce.

The straight Wand became a trefoil through an alchemical transformation. The trefoil was an alchemical symbol for wood, sometimes called Wood of the Tree of Life.[20] The Chinese considered wood a fifth element, placed between earth, which gave birth to it, and fire, which consumed it.[21] The Wand of the Tarot associated with fire would have meant a wooden torch, therefore the symbol of wood changed it into a modern "club."

Symbol of Wood

3. Artha, "Earth," stood for Wealth or Possessions: the period of middle age when the fruits of labor accumulate, and grown children also are "wealth." The feminine Earth element was associated with riches in all Indo-European traditions, and so the Goddess's pentacle became a diamond, the Far-Eastern earth-symbol whose very name meant "Goddess of the World." The oldest form of money was a female-genital cowrie shell, and coins used to be manufactured in the Mother Goddess's temple at Rome.[22] It was not illogical then that the Tarot suit of Pentacles was related to money matters and property. Sometimes they were Pomegranates, another female symbol.[23]

4. Moksha, "Liberation," or the Art of Dying, was linked with the masculine Air element that meant the soul released from the body, into the keeping of the Lord of Death, or Kali the Destroyer, represented by the sword. Eastern philosophers viewed old age, the fourth life-stage, as an opportune time to learn to approach death without fear. However, the Tarot suit of Swords was linked with fear-inspiring events: calamities, difficulties, threats, various kinds of doom. Even in ordinary playing cards, the suit of spades, the Swords' descendant, was reckoned a suit of evil omen.

The underlying theory of cartomancy was that shuffling the cards was like mixing the elements in the larger world. Fate would guide the diviner to make combinations which, properly interpreted, would apply to past or future events that the mingling of elements brought about. Suit colors still show the blood-red of life for the "female" elements, the black of death for the "male" elements, according to very ancient Oriental ideas of the active energy of the Lady of Life as opposed to the passivity of the Lord of Death. It is perhaps oddly significant that the oversized ace of modern cards is the ace of spades, symbolically the sword of Father Heaven, which fortune-tellers called the card of death.

When churchmen failed to eradicate playing cards, there were several attempts to adapt the cards to Christian orthodoxy. Major Arcana pictures were described as various episodes in Christ's Passion as if they represented Stations of the Cross.[24] Another system tried to relate the four suits to the four Grail Hallows, listed in the 12th century as (1) the chalice of the Last Supper; (2) the wooden lance St. Longinus used to pierce Jesus's side; (3) the round paten or platter from which Jesus's disciples ate the paschal lamb, and (4) King David's "Sword of the Spirit." These Grail Hallows were themselves un-Christian, having been lifted from the Four Treasures of pagan Ireland, magical emblems of the **Tuatha Dé Danann**. These were: (1) the Cauldron of Regeneration; (2) the Spear of Lug; (3) the Stone of Fal, or Stone of Sovereignty, which like the Scots' Stone of Scone would cry out in recognition of a true king; and (4) the Sword of Nuada.[25] Typical lingam-yoni combination of the last two formed the famous "Sword in the Stone" that figured in myths of Arthur, Perceval, and Galahad.

A 15th-century game called Triumphs associated the four suits with qualities resembling the Tantric definitions of the four elemental life-stages: (1) Pleasures, (2) Virtues, (3) Riches, and (4) Virginities.[26] These are easily identified with the male-female elements. "Virtues" came from *virtu,* "manliness, uprightness" in the dual sense of erectness. "Virginities" referred to the ascetic life recommended for the elder sage in eastern lands. But the game itself was named after the Major Arcana—the "trump" suit that clergymen called heretical.

The word "trump" came from *trionfi* or "triumph," the old Latin word for a religious procession, in which the very sequence, costumes, and masks of the marchers stood for doctrinal teachings the initiates could understand. Images of the deities, sacred masks borne by temple dancers, charioteers, priests, and priestesses displayed the *exuviae,* "attributes," of divinities. The leader of the procession was the *triumphator,* a magistrate in charge of Rome's sacred games. At the end of the drama or the parade, celebrants raised the cry of *Triumpe,* announcing the immanence of divine spirit in the things and persons shown.[27] Trump, then, originally meant "that which is divine," and like everything divine it was credited with power of divination.

According to ancient ideas of the divine order, deities revealed themselves within a calculated framework of time. An initiate into any of the pagan Mysteries would meet them one at a time, learning new thoughts from each. A time-frame appeared in the Tarot as well as the matter-frame of the elements. This had to do with its numbering.

The number of Minor Arcana cards is 56, a number with profound meanings in Oriental philosophy. When Buddha was born, he took his first 56 steps in each of the four cardinal directions, 7 forward and 7 back each way, signifying the 14 waxing and 14 waning days of the moon and the lunar weeks, like the 14 steps on the heavenly ladder of Osiris.[28]

The same number of posts or stones representing "steps in time" circled old temples of astronomical calculation, like Stonehenge. There were 56 years in a sacred Great Year when lunar and solar cycles coincided.[29] The number of the Tarot's Sun card is 19, the number of the Moon card 18: and the ancient Great Year consisted of two 19-year periods combined with an 18-year period, a total of 56 years to bring the sun and moon together. The total number of cards in a Tarot pack, 78, was the sum of all the numbers of the signs of the zodiac added together: 1+2+3+4+5+6+7+8+9+10+11+12.

Among the many derivations offered for the mysterious word Tarot was the famous palindrome ROTA TARO ORAT (TORA) ATOR: the Wheel of the Taro speaks of (the Law of) Hathor.[30] However, the Oriental background of card-divination and the 21 numbered cards of the Major Arcana suggest an older connection with the Goddess Tara, the Aryan Great Mother as "Earth," whose name gave rise to Latin Terra Mater and Celtic Tara.

From ancient times, this Goddess was assigned 21 forms. Magic diagrams, or painted dice-boards for divining the cause of illness, prophesying, and so on, are still known as "the 21 Taras." If the 21 numbered cards of the Major Arcana can be related to such boards, the Minor Arcana certainly echo the similar boards of 56 squares used "for determining the successive regions and grades of one's future rebirths."[31] In the Far East, games like cards and dice were used to teach esoteric doctrines. Tantric Buddhists still enjoy the Game of Rebirth played with dice and a colorful board; it is both a pastime and a teaching aid for spiritual doctrines.[32]

As in China, cards were created from the possible throws of rods in the I Ching, so divination by dice obviously influenced the format of the Tarot. The two Tarot numbers 56 and 21 are dice numbers—21 the number of possible throws by a set of two dice and 56 the number of possible throws by a set of three dice. Together they add up to 77—seven-times-eleven, the ultimate number of dice games. The Tarot pack has one more card, making 78, but this card has no numerical value. It is the Fool, whose number is zero. In many Tarot layouts he stands apart, as an observer or querent.[33]

The form and meaning of Hindu temples also had some influence on the Tarot. Images showing various manifestations or avatars of the deities were placed in rows along corridors leading to the central Holy of

Holies. Devout pilgrims passed through this "instructive picture gallery" saying prayers at each station.[34] Pictures of the deities and their attributes used to be painted on cards, like a miniature picture gallery, for private meditation. Such a pasteboard pageant revealed sacred mysteries to those who knew its symbolism. In this circumstance one might find the real reason why Christians objected to the Major Arcana—not because the cards were frivolous, but because their underlying meanings were all too serious.

The most significant arrangement in Oriental sacred graphics was the triangle, sign of the Goddess, known as the Kali Yantra or Primordial Image.[35] A female triangle with a central dot or *bindu,* "spark of life," stood for the Goddess's genital power bringing life into being. The 21 numbered Tarot trumps seemed designed to form this yantra, 7 cards to each side of the triangle, with the unnumbered Fool in the center standing for the *bindu.*

The three sides of the triangle traditionally represented the Triple Goddess as Three Fates, ruling past, present, and future; the three trimesters of intrauterine existence; and the three larger trimesters of extrauterine life: from birth to coming-of-age at 21; from 21 to middle age at 42; and from 42 to the "grand climacteric" at 63. The same three stages of man's life were depicted in such classical images as the Riddle of the Sphinx.

The biblical God promised his followers a lifetime of threescore and ten years, offering seven years more than older deities who guaranteed only the mystically trinitarian number of threescore and three (63). The pagan lifespan was remembered in medieval times, when the age of 63 was known as the grand climacteric and was thought to carry a threat of death.[36] It is still believed that 21 is the pinnacle of first maturity, because the pagan system of age-counting became incorporated in common law.

Each trimester spanned 21 years, the first exclusive multiple of the sacred numbers 3 and 7. Therefore the past, present, and future could be envisioned in the Major Arcana arranged in one of the Goddess's essential sigils. This triangular format was often used by the gypsies, who understood that "triangle" meant "female" and that the Goddess was the trinitarian ruler of Fate.[37]

The last trump is called the World, also known as the Bride, the Shekina, the Universe, Mother Nature, Sophia, or the Major Fortune.[38] This card always showed a naked woman dancing within a flower wreath, flanked by emblems of the four seasons. This was the final revelation of the Tarot system: the Goddess without her veils, the Shakti bringing joy to the moment of death. According to the doctrine of karma, "She it is who is ever desired, won, and lost again."[39] In the cyclic or continuous layouts favored by gypsy cartomancers, the realization of the World led "naturally on to the next card, the Fool, symbol of the newly born child commencing its life's journey. And so the Ring of Return revolves once more."[40] In other words, the religion of the Tarot was a cyclic religion of reincarnation, not a linear religion of heaven-or-hell choices.

A popular method of laying out the cards signified two Rings of return, the joined circles of the Right-Hand Path (clockwise) and the Left-Hand Path (counterclockwise), traditional symbols of male and female powers combined in a horizontal figure eight, the Vedic sign of Infinity. This was inherited by the Arabs along with the other "Arabic" numerals (actually of Indian origin), and is still the sign of infinity in modern mathematics. The Major Arcana strongly suggested this figure-eight layout by their own traditional designs.

The lemniscate infinity-sign appeared as a wide-brimmed hat or halo over the head of the Magician, a male figure beginning the first decade of trumps at the #1 position. The same sign appeared again as the same wide-brimmed hat or halo over the head of the Goddess of Strength, a female figure beginning the second decade of trumps at the #11 position. The male and female figures hinted that the first circle of ten cards was to rotate clockwise, along the "solar" path; the second circle of ten cards was to rotate counterclockwise, along the "lunar" path.

The figure-eight represented union of the sexes not only in the Orient, but also in the ancient Celtic marriage rite preserved by the Scottish custom of handfasting. Bride and groom joined their right "male" hands, then their left "female" hands also, forming the double-sexed Infinity sign to signify the blending of their two natures. This custom is still followed in India, where the symbolism of the Right-Hand Path and Left-Hand Path was never lost.[41]

Besides the Magician and the Goddess of Strength, another card presented the Infinity sign: the deuce of Pentacles, showing two discs embraced by two endlessly circling serpents, or a comparable lemniscate design. The importance of this card was revealed by special decorations; it usually bore the maker's trademark, as the ace of spades does today. Clearly, the figure-eight layout was urged. But then, what did it show?

The first circle stood for the realm of consciousness, matter, the world of affairs: solar, outward-turning—all the cards faced out. The second circle stood for the unconscious or the spirit—lunar, inward, feminine, the realm of mysteries and "true meanings." The center crossing superimposed the two "mandala" cards, the Wheel of Fortune and the World (or Major Fortune). In such an arrangement, each card in the solar sphere matched a card in the lunar sphere, their two numbers always totaling 20, a sacred number in the eastern decimal system.[42] Each pair of matched cards revealed a secret identity or meaning.

The Magician, or Hermes (#1) corresponded in the spiritual realm to the masculine power of the Sun (#19). The Papess (#2) was revealed as a personification of the Moon (#18). The Empress (#3) was the same as the Naked Goddess pouring forth her blessings on land and sea, on the card of the Star (#17)—i.e., Astarte or Ishtar. The Emperor (#4) stood for the Holy Roman Empire, which would soon suffer a downfall, according to the heretical prediction; and the downfall of the Empire was shown on the corresponding card, #16, the Tower, or the House of God, blasted by the lightning of Lucifer the Light-bringer. Two figures toppling from the crown of the lightning-struck Tower could well have been Emperor and Pope. As for the Pope himself, shown on card #5, in the spiritual realm of the Tarot he was revealed as the Devil (#15), taking the same pose on both cards with two worshippers at his feet.[43]

Tarot cards were not the only manifestations of these subversive symbols. The same pictures mysteriously appeared in many places, including even churches. Rheims Cathedral still has a carved stone panel showing the lightning-struck Tower with the two male figures falling from its blasted crown.[44] An engraved Horoscope wheel manufactured at Nürnberg in 1515 placed seven of the Major Arcana pictures in various zodiacal positions.[45] The figures of the World, the Wheel of Fortune, Justice, the Fool, and Death—the skeletal Grim Reaper with his scythe—were common illustrations of the medieval *Zeitgeist;* but no one knows whether they were copied from the Tarot, or the card pictures were copied from them.

Just before the card of Death came the card perhaps most characteristic of the Tarot alone: the Hanged Man, who "cannot be found in any orthodox Christian symbology, and is one of the clearest indications that the Tarot trumps were designed to illustrate some non-Christian system of belief."[46] The Hanged Man hung on a door-shaped gallows such as Norse pagans called the Wooden Horse, or the Horse of Odin.[47] Even though the figure of Death immediately followed him, it was only a symbolic death. He hung, not by the neck, but by one foot: a custom known as "baffling," inflicted on debtors and traitors in Germany, Italy, and Scotland.[48] Baffling was a formal humiliation, like a sojourn in the stocks, or like the mockery of sacred-king-victims (such as Jesus). Mystical initiations imitated such procedures, so the novice "should empty himself completely, should be stripped of all his faculties, renouncing all his own predilections, his own thoughts, his own will—in a word, his whole self."[49] The Hanged Man's number, 12, recalled the famous Twelfth Rune sacred to Odin the Hanged God, the rune by which hanged victims could be made to speak, and reveal the mysteries of the death-world.[50]

The mystic revelation following the Hanged Man's encounter with Death was the female figure of Temperance, copied from magic texts that showed the Goddess Isis with one foot on land, the other in water, revealing her dominion over both elements.[51] This Temperance angel poured water from one jar into another, recalling the symbolic merging of Isis and Osiris in the Amulet of the Two Jars, an ancient Egyptian charm of eternal life.[52] Similarly in India, the revelation of divine love was a merging of God and Goddess "like the pouring of water into water."[53] One of the incarnations of the God himself was a water jar, just as Babylonian, Egyptian, and Cabirian savior-deities were symbolized by water jars in their holy processions, as was Jesus also, according to Luke 22:10. In the Far East, the vessel of water was regarded as the residence of the deity.[54] Moreover, this same Water-Jar-Savior appeared in Hindu playing cards at the head of the suit of Jars, which corresponded to the Tarot suit of Cups.[55]

Thus the European Tarot seemed to show a man symbolically dying, and meeting a manifestation of the Goddess as a result. This meeting or merging, "like the pouring of water into water," prefigured the final meeting with the cosmic Mother upon actual death—the Last Trump—just as a man's sexual union with his earthly Shakti prefigured his union with the ultimate Shakti of the spirit realm, Kali herself. Small wonder then that patriarchal Christians regarded the Tarot as a Bible of heresy comprehensible to the illiterate, at a time when even literate laymen were officially forbidden to read their own Bible.[56] The Oriental origin of its heretical Tantric/Gnostic imagery is suggested by the Slavic word for a "reader" of the cards: *Vedavica,* literally a Vedic seer.[57] Small wonder that some of the bishops and cardinals tried to collect packs of cards and burn them, as was done in Nürnberg in 1452.[58] Cards became harmless to the church only after their religious symbols were removed and their meanings forgotten, so they were mere "games"—ludicrous, in the new interpretation of the old pagan *ludi* or "sacred games." To Hebrew patriarchs also, *naipes,* "cards," became *naibi,* "sorcery."[59]

1. A. Douglas, 21. 2. Cavendish, T., 18. 3. A. Douglas, 20. 4. Trigg, 47. 5. Funk, 320. 6. Hazlitt, 460. 7. Cavendish, T., 15–17; A. Douglas, 24, 32. 8. Moakley, 98. 9. Papus, 9. 10. A. Douglas, 43. 11. *Bardo Thodol,* 3. 12. Keightley, 81. 13. A. Douglas, 24. 14. Moakley, 35. 15. *Larousse,* 371. 16. A. Douglas, 19. 17. Baring-Gould, C.M.M.A., 375. 18. Cavendish, P.E., 71. 19. *Bardo Thodol,* 11. 20. Koch, 74. 21. Lethaby, 245. 22. *Larousse,* 204. 23. Cavendish, T., 155. 24. Jobes, 79. 25. A. Douglas, 37. 26. Moakley, 46. 27. Dumézil, 231, 572. 28. *Bardo Thodol,* 207. 29. Hawkins, 140. 30. Case, 123. 31. Waddell, 359, 467, 1472. 32. Tatz & Kent, 19, 32. 33. Moakley, 41. 34. Zimmer, 127. 35. Silberer, 170; *Mahanirvanatantra,* 127. 36. Elworthy, 407. 37. Trigg, 48. 38. Gettings, 109. 39. Zimmer, 178. 40. A. Douglas, 114. 41. de Lys, 169. 42. Jung, M.H.S., 42. 43. A. Douglas, 44–45. 44. Gettings, 87. 45. Lehner, 60. 46. A. Douglas, 85. 47. Branston, 114. 48. Moakley, 95. 49. Waite, O.S., 234. 50. B. Butler, 154. 51. Seligmann, 43. 52. Budge, E.M., 60. 53. Tatz & Kent, 140. 54. Zimmer, 34. 55. Hargrave, 25, 27. 56. H. Smith, 253. 57. Leland, 65. 58. Hargrave, 101. 59. Hargrave, 224.

Tartarus

Greek name of the underworld, related to *tartaruga,* "tortoise," because archaic Hindu tradition claimed the earth was supported by Vishnu in the form of a tortoise. The tortoise was a totem of the

Underground God, sometimes incarnate in Pan or Hermes who invented the tortoise-shell lyre to create universal harmony.[1] In alchemy, the Underground God became *spiritus tartari,* spirit of Tartarus, a description of tartaric acid, or simply tartar.

1. Jung & Kerenyi, 78.

Taueret

"The Great," Hathor as the Goddess of childbirth and nursing; as Mother of the Nile, she sometimes wore a hippopotamus head. At other times she wore the lion head of destruction. Her images were associated with the hieroglyphic sign *sa,* meaning the uterine blood of the Goddess which could bestow eternal life.[1] See **Menstrual Blood**.

1. *Larousse,* 38–39.

Tefnut

Primitive Egyptian death-goddess living at the bottom of the underworld; a shadow twin of the Goddess Nut who lived at the summit of the sky. A group of nether gods with slaughtering-blocks hacked the dead to pieces and fed Tefnut with their blood—a mythic memory of Neolithic sacrifices.[1]

Tefnut was identified with Hathor-the-Sphinx and with the Greeks' Artemis.[2] Some said she was a savage Goddess from the Nubian desert; she was always reddened with the blood of the men she devoured.[3] She resembled the blood-red Kalika who devoured all that she brought forth (see **Kali Ma**).

Tefnut's consort was Shu, "Giver of Winds," a god of dryness as opposed to her wetness.[4] He was "dry, parched, withered, empty." He was a phallus called Prop of Heaven, but a spent phallus entering the Goddess's "deep" which served as "a hiding-place for his body." He could give souls of air to the dead, like Yahweh in Ezekiel's valley of bones; in fact some Jews said Yahweh and Shu were the same.[5]

1. *Book of the Dead,* 146. 2. *Larousse,* 13. 3. *Book of the Dead,* 176.
4. Budge, G.E. 2, 420. 5. Budge, G.E. 2, 67, 87.

Teiresias

Double-sexed seer of Thebes. The Goddess miraculously made him a woman, and he lived as a temple harlot for seven years, acquiring great powers of insight and divination. His myth may date back to the transvestism or ritual castration required of men who entered the Goddess's priesthood. Hermes also became a god of magic insight by turning himself into the pseudo-female Hermaphroditus and presiding over the temple of his consort Aphrodite, wearing female robes and artificial breasts.[1]

Teiresias had a Hindu counterpart, Trisiras, god of magic, whose powers were based on his ability to change from male to female at will.[2]

Teiresias's "daughter" was Mante, whose name means Seeress, and was really a title of the Theban priestesses before men managed to take over their functions.

1. Graves, G.M. 1, 73. 2. O'Flaherty, 70.

Tell, William

Archer-wizard of Altdorf, the best known of the whole cycle of legendary heroes. A cruel overlord ordered Tell to shoot an apple from his son's head with an arrow to prove his skill. Tell performed the feat successfully, holding a second arrow which he said would have slain the oppressor, had the junior Tell been injured.

The same tale was told earlier of the Rhineland archer-wizard named Puncker (Marksman), ordered by Prince Eberhard Longbeard to shoot a penny off his son's head. Puncker too held a second arrow, saying if he failed the test, the second arrow would have penetrated Longbeard's heart.[1]

In the 12th century, Saxo Grammaticus told the same story about Toki, a Danish archer-wizard forced by King Harald Bluetooth to shoot an apple from his son's head. The same incident occurred in the mythical history of Egil, brother of Velundr, in the Saga of Thidrick. Another Norse hero, Eindridi, was obliged to shoot a writing-tablet off his son's head. Another, Hemingr, had to throw a spear at a hazel nut on the head of his brother Bjorn. The Faroe Island archer-wizard was Geyti, whom King Harald commanded to shoot a hazel nut from his brother's head.

All the stories may have come from an ancient Persian poem, the *Mantic Uttair,* or Language of Birds, by Farad-Uddin Attar. One of its most widely repeated stories told of a king who shot an apple from the head of a beloved page boy.[2]

1. Kramer & Sprenger, 151. 2. Baring-Gould, C.M.M.A., 119–25.

Teraphim

Old Testament household fetishes, said by Hosea to be essential to worship (Hosea 3:4). A Hebrew commentator said the *teraphim* were ancestral ghosts, in the form of mummified oracular heads.[1] Their name means "children of Terah." The Bible says Terah "begat" **Abraham**; but the word translated "begat" often meant "gave birth to," and many of the so-called patriarchs in the Pentateuch are feminine names. If Abraham was the same as Ab-Brahm or Father Brahma, his parent would have been the Goddess Tara, a universal name of Mother Earth.

The Jews' *teraphim* were similar to the Romans' *lares* or *manes,* also ancestral spirits residing in relics. Like the worshippers of *teraphim,* African natives still believe a dead ancestor's spirit can inhabit an effigy—especially if the effigy contains physiological relics like bones, teeth, hair, etc.—and by consulting such an idol one can communicate directly with the ancestor.[2]

There were many Middle-Eastern peoples whose habit it was to preserve skulls of the dead for later necromantic consultation, especially the skulls of sacred kings. Their place of sacrifice called Golgotha, alleged scene of Jesus's crucifixion, meant "the place of skulls."

1. Graves, W.G., 164. 2. de Lys, 431.

Terra Firma

Title of Mother Earth, taken from the Homeric phrase "Great Mother, Firmly Founded, Oldest of Divinities." To the Greeks she was Gaea the Deep-Breasted One, who ruled Mount Olympus before the coming of the Hellenic gods. See **Tara**.

Tetragrammaton

Literally, "four-letter word," the secret name of God in Hebrew letters *yod-he-vau-he* (YHWH); often confused with God's introduction of himself to Moses, "I Am That I Am" (Exodus 3:14). This introduction was borrowed from the god Ab-braham or Father Brahma, who introduced himself in Sanskrit *Tat Sat*—"I Am That that Is."[1]

The root of YHWH is the radical HWH, *he-vau-he,* which meant "being" or "life" or "woman"—interchangeable concepts in the ancient Middle East.[2] The same letters in Latin are E-V-E: Eve.[3] Thus the so-called inner meaning of the Tetragrammaton was really Eve, Mother of All Living, the real creator of the world and mother of Adam, according to Gnostic scriptures.[4]

The Tetragrammaton had two versions. The lesser-known one was EHYH, a feminine principle derived from Hayya (another of Eve's names), designating the Goddess in her special connection with women in childbed. On Samaritan phylacteries the masculine and feminine versions of the Tetragrammaton were intertwined.[5]

Medieval writers who didn't know the meaning of Tetragrammaton often took it for the name of a powerful demon, and invoked it in magic charms. A 17th-century writer declared that "the mighty Tetragrammaton" was a devil who protected witches.[6] Other authorities said Tetragrammaton was one of the more powerful secret names of God, used to control demons when they were invoked. (See **Name**.)

Jewish mystics used the Tetragrammaton extensively in the lore of the Cabala. YHWH was called the Divided Name, "considered to contain all the Forces of Nature." Since the holy name could be divided into that of Mother Eve (HWH), and that of the "I" or *jod* for Jehovah, it suggested the cabalistic doctrine of God's loss of his Shekina, the Great Mother, whose return the mystics believed essential to the achievement of peace in the universe.

Sometimes the Tetragrammaton was called Sem ha-mephoras, or Schemahamphorasch, probably the origin of the word "semaphore" in the sense of a word-sign like the Hindu *samjna.*[7] Rabbinic tradition said the Sem ha-mephoras either was inscribed on a holy phallic stone buried in the Great Gate of Mother Earth, or else was the stone itself, also called *Eben stijjah,* the Stygian Stone, or Stone of the Deeps. It was connected with the sexual myth of the descent of Father Heaven's phallus into the yoni of the virgin Mother Earth, to "unlock her fountains," that is, to stimulate the Nether Upsurge of world-sustaining blood. Sexual organs of God and Goddess lay at the center of the holy of Holies. "David is supposed to have found at the digging of the foundation of the temple, the Eben stijjah, Stone of the Deeps, that unlocked the fountain of the great deep, and on which the Sem ha-mephoras, the outspoken name of God, was inscribed."[8]

1. *Mahanirvanatantra,* xix. 2. Reinach, 188. 3. Cavendish, T., 116. 4. Pagels, 30. 5. Budge, A.T., 224, 261. 6. Hazlitt, 656. 7. O'Flaherty, 352. 8. Silberer, 315.

Teutatis

Germanic version of the priapic Hermes, worshipped as a giant phallus at Eresburg, the Mount of Mother Earth (Hera). Teutatis was also called a Lord of Death, and a father of "Teutons."[1]

1. Borchardt, 145.

Thais, Saint

The famous harlot Thais, mistress of Alexander the Great, was transferred to the 4th century A.D. in her Christianized legend, which ignored chronology so Thais could repent her gaudy life and be converted to Christianity by one of the Coptic cenobites, usually St. Anthony. To fulfill what seemed to be one of the ascetics' favorite fantasies, Thais at the height of her beauty and fame was said to have renounced her sins, mortified her flesh, burned her fine clothes and ornaments, given away all her wealth to the church, and walled herself up in a desert cell to live in the midst of her own filth.[1] The only trouble with the hagiographer's tale was that, at the time it was supposed to have happened, Thais had already been dead for more than 600 years.

1. Attwater, 320.

Thalassa

The Goddess at Rhodes and Miletus, mother of the Telchines ("enchanters"). As patroness of sex and marriage, she was an archaic form of Aphrodite Marina. She was invoked at Roman weddings by the cry *Talassio*, the meaning of which had been forgotten, but everyone knew "it was the correct thing to shout at weddings."[1]

1. Rose, 192.

Thecla, Saint

"Famous One," a title of Ephesian Diana, whose shrine in Seleucia was a popular pilgrimage center in pagan times, and remained so even after the Goddess was Christianized as a saint, up to the 17th century A.D.[1] Early churchmen didn't like St. Thecla or her shrine. In the 4th century it was attended by a group called Apotactics, under a female "deacon," subsequently declared heretical.[2] Some Christians asserted that St. Thecla was Diana's priestess.[3] Others, like Tertullian, knew she was nothing but an epithet of the Great Goddess. Tertullian denied the legend connecting Thecla with St. Paul, calling it a lie invented by a misguided church elder "for love of St. Paul"—a curious explanation, hinting that Paul might have been honored by the connection.[4]

1. Attwater, 321. 2. Boulding, 370. 3. Brewster, 423. 4. Reinach, 255.

Themis

Pre-Hellenic Creatress, cognate with Chaldean *Thamte,* "Sea," or with Tiamat. Her Virgin aspect was Artemis (Ar-Themis); her name was numerically equivalent to that of the moon.[1] Her children were Themistes, "oracles." She founded the oracle of Delphi ("Womb"), long before it was taken over by Apollo.

Aphrodite, Cybele, Anat-Athene, and many other Goddesses occupied aniconic stones, called *baitulos* in Greece, *baetyl* in Syria, *beth-el* or "house of deity" in Palestine.[2]

Black Sea Amazons worshipped Themis in the form of a black stone on their sacred island of Themiscyra, "Divine Themis." The Roman Forum had an ancient black stone, the Lapis Niger, engraved with the Goddess's sacred law.[3] In faraway Iceland the same Goddess was adored in the form of a stone called Spamathr, "Mother of Prophecy," or Armathr, "Mother of Prosperity."[4]

To the Egyptians, Themis was "Temu," spirit of the fertile Abyss that gave birth to all things in the beginning.

Classic myth made Themis the spirit of the post-diluvian creation. After the Flood receded, Themis taught the survivors Deucalion and Pyrrha how to repopulate the earth by magic. They were to fling "the bones of their mother" behind them as they walked. On resolving the riddle, they understood that Themis meant stones, the bones of their Mother Earth.[5] By the grace of the Goddess, new human beings rose up from these stones.

1. Neumann, G.M., 214. 2. Graves, W.G., 405. 3. Lindsay, A.W., 176.
4. Turville-Petre, 230. 5. Graves, G.M. 1, 139.

Theology

Literally, "God-knowledge," the paradoxical pretense of knowing what theologians themselves call unknowable. The weakness of theology as a "science" is its lack of objective proof for any of its claims. Vetter points out that any theologian in the modern age is likely to be confused and worried: "He is trying to reconcile science with faith and dogma, and they are simply not to be reconciled."[1]

Since Galileo's time, Christian theology has been concerned not with justifying God's ways to man but with justifying God's ways to science. This is usually done by reasoning backward from religion's given conclusions to theoretical causes. In 1952, Pope Pius XII demonstrated this in an astonishing series of non sequiturs to force "science" to prove the existence of God:

> *What significance, then, has modern science for the proof of the existence of God, which depends on the fact that the cosmos is susceptible of change? . . . From the fact that there is change we may conclude that there is an Absolute Being whose nature is unchangeable. . . . [Science] has, with the concreteness that belongs to physical proof, confirmed the principle of contingency and the conclusion based on it that . . . the cosmos came into being by the hand of the Creator.*[2]

Only theology could make such a long, loose-jointed leap from the fact that there is change to a "conclusion" that something unchangeable must exist. Needless to say, science has not confirmed any such thing as the theological principle of contingency with any "physical proof"; theologians simply don't understand what physical proof consists of.

Theological problems are not solved by physical evidence but by adjustment of verbal definitions. The usual method is debate. Medieval Schoolmen earnestly debated such questions as how many angels could dance on the head of a pin, or whether the earth hung from heaven by a golden chain or an iron one. "Evidence" was taken from analogy. For instance, Peter Lombard's rules on incest said it was all right to marry outside the sixth degree of consanguinity because there were six ages of the world. In 1215 the fourth Lateran Council

Peter Lombard Ecclesiastical teacher of the 12th century, bishop of Paris, author of many sermons, commentaries on scripture, and theological treatises known as the *Books of Sentences.*

declared it was even all right to marry outside the fourth degree of consanguinity, because there were four humors in the body and four elements in the universe.[3]

Most of the time, theology and science have been implacable enemies.[4] The aggression has been on the side of theology, not science; the latter simply pursues facts, the former attacks facts because they threaten orthodox fantasies.

> *The priesthoods of whatever stripe can never live down, nor make amends for, their disgraceful role in retarding the development of modern science during the past millenium in Christendom. But what is even worse, they seem to have learned nothing from that defeat and are now closing ranks, better to fight the same sort of a battle in the area of the social sciences and ethics. . . . [S]upernaturalism is, in its social functions and consequences, a dangerous opiate. And, what is perhaps even worse, it discourages objective attempts at intelligent social trial-and-error, planning, and even research, and undermines man's faith in his own resources. . . .*
>
> *The methods and principles of the theologians are still the same; they have merely abandoned certain fields as no longer profitable for exploitation and have concentrated their efforts in the psychological and sociological, derived out of a distant past. Their sole claim to validity today derives from the extent of their social acceptability, not from any empirical validation. To preserve that social acceptability organized religion bends its every effort to keep "controversial" topics out of public educational institutions and to provide as much parochial education as possible for as many of the "faithful" as possible.*[5]

To provide the kind of education defined as Christian, it has been necessary for theologians to lie, and then to find words that call their lies morally right. Such semantic wriggling is shown by a book for Catholic laymen by Edwin F. Healy, S.J., published in 1960 under the rather astonishing title of *Moral Guidance.*

> *At times one is obliged in conscience to veil the truth, for there are secrets to be guarded and detractions to be avoided. Sometimes silence will not suffice to maintain the secret which one is trying to guard. In fact, it may happen that silence would betray the secret. Hence there must be some licit means of concealing the truth when necessary. This licit means is the broad mental reservation. . . . One way of putting the question is to ask if a false statement is always a lie. Some theologians answer in the negative. . . . Sometimes it is necessary to make a false statement in order to protect secret knowledge. Silence or the use of mental reservation is not sufficient; the only way to protect the secret is to make a statement contrary to what you know to be true.*[6]

In direct ideological descent from Eusebius who extolled "holy lying" for the church's sake, Healy makes "licit" every form of falsehood. Churchmen themselves seldom believed the lies they told, or allowed, as shown by the 19th-century clergymen's aphorism: "He may hold anything who holds his tongue."[7] The theologian Beausobre wrote:

Churchmen not only do not say what they think, but they do say the direct contrary of what they think. Philosophers in their cabinets; out of them they are content with fables, though they well know they are fables. Nay, more: they deliver honest men to the executioner, for having uttered what they themselves know to be true. How many atheists and pagans have burned holy men under the pretext of heresy? Every day do hypocrites consecrate, and make people adore the host, though as well convinced as I am, that it is nothing but a bit of bread.[8]

Perhaps the most dangerous truth, about which theologians always lied, was the one advanced by the Arab philosopher Averroës: that all religions are of equal validity or nonvalidity, because all are merely human productions.[9] Judeo-Christian tradition could not bear this idea, for it taught that not only were its scriptures directly dictated by God but its religion was the only "right" one even though shaped and supported by false statements.

How could the modern church acknowledge, Guignebert asks, "that religion lives its whole life in the consciousness of men and that human consciousness has changed since the thirteenth century?" Orthodoxy must believe itself immutable, but it is always embarrassed by the records of its mistakes. Renan says, "There is one thing that a theologian can never be, and that is a historian. History is necessarily disinterested. . . . The theologian has one interest, his dogma. If this dogma be trimmed down as much as ever it can be, then it is still for the critical mind an unbearable load. The orthodox theologian may be compared to a bird in a cage; all real movement is forbidden to it."[10]

The conclusion that theology once found unthinkable is becoming more and more thinkable. "What gods are there, what gods have there ever been, that were not from man's imagination?"[11] To insist on deities in the real world, the theologian must resort to intellectual dishonesty. "One should claim as knowledge only what he really knows, and admit that he does not know what he doesn't know. The characteristic Western ardor for answering the unanswerable would be more uplifting if it did not entail claims of certitude."[12] Morton Smith points out that "When a theologian talks of a 'higher truth,' he is usually trying to conceal a lower falsehood."[13]

1. Vetter, 257. 2. Keller, 413. 3. Murstein, 11. 4. See White. 5. Vetter, 472, 515. 6. Lederer & Jackson, 109. 7. H. Smith, 375. 8. Doane, 435. 9. Guignebert, 305. 10. Guignebert, 467, 492. 11. Campbell, M.L.B., 253. 12. Muller, 334. 13. M. Smith, 165.

Theotokos

"God-bearer," title of the virgin Mary. Church fathers originally opposed the title because "It is impossible that God should be born of a woman."[1] Later church authorities changed their minds and pronounced it possible.

1. de Riencourt, 150.

Thesmophoria

Women's festival of Demeter Thesmophoros, "Demeter-Who-Established-the-Customs." Women mixed the seed corn with their menstrual blood to give it life; sacrificed pigs; and carried in procession seed vessels, serpents, and cakes formed like female genitals.[1] On the third day, sacrificed victims came forth from the earth-womb in the Kalligeneia, "Fair Birth."[2] Victims were identified with the savior Dionysus, a Holy Child laid in a manger, later to die and give his blood as sacred wine for the worshippers to drink, thus assuring their immortality.

1. Spretnak, 269. 2. *Encyc. Brit.*, "Thesmophoria."

Thomas Rhymer

Thomas Learmont, also known as Thomas of Erceldoune, a 14th-century Scottish poet-seer. Erceldoune (now Earlston) was "Ercel's Down," seat of the Saxon Goddess Ercel, or Ursel, or Horsel, the "Fairy Queen" who loved Thomas and taught him secrets of magic. Thomas was accosted on Huntlie Bank by the incumbent Queen of Elphame, an earthly incarnation of the Goddess, who taught him the secrets of the witch cult and re-baptized him as True Thomas when he had renounced Christianity.[1]

According to "The Ballad of Thomas Rhymer," the Fairy Queen showed Thomas three roads: one leading to heaven, a second to hell, and a third to "fair Elf-land," that is, a Way that was neither Christian nor anti-Christian. Along the third road he came to the River of Blood, comparable to the Greeks' birth-river Styx, or the river of giantesses' menstrual blood, crossed by the god Thor on his way to the land of elder deities. Here Thomas entered a very mysterious place: "For forty days and forty nights / He wade thro' red blude to the knee, / And he saw neither sun nor moon, / But heard the roaring of the sea."[2]

The legend suggests a Tantric sort of enlightenment, brought about by communion with female life-essence. The Fairy Queen stated that she had "claret wine" in her lap and invited Thomas to lay his head there. The original meaning of "claret" was perception, or enlightenment. In common English usage, claret was also a synonym for blood. In Celtic myth, the Fairy Queen offered "red mead" which was also herself, Mab (Mead).[3] The Norse version of Thomas was Sir Bosmer, who swam the "eddying flood" to the Elf-Queen as she stood on the far bank, saying, "Welcome, Sir Bosmer! Come home to me, I've brewed the mead and the wine for thee."[4] Such tales tend to confirm clergymen's insistence that **menstrual blood** was the communion wine of witches.

After Thomas's journey to the secret paradise, where he remained seven years—recalling the seven windings of the Styx—he became a great wizard, poet, and prophet, ranked with such sages of the old faith as Merlin and Tristan.[5]

1. Graves, W.G., 483. 2. Sargent & Kittredge, 64. 3. Rees, 75. 4. Wimberly, 116. 5. *Encyc. Brit.*, "Thomas the Rhymer."

Thomas, Saint

Hellenized name of the god Tammuz, traditional Dying Savior of the Jerusalem cult (Ezekiel 8:14), whose rites were supplanted by those of Jesus. Tammuz then became Doubting Thomas, challenging Jesus's claim to authentic apotheosis and resurrection in the flesh. He refused to believe in his rival's return from death until he had probed his wounds. Then, Thomas-Tammuz announced his acceptance of Jesus as "my Lord and my God" (John 20:28)—or so the Gospel would have it.

The story of Doubting Thomas appears only in the so-called Gnostic Gospel of John, written more than 150 years after Jesus's purported lifetime.[1] Its purpose was to press Christian claims to superiority over the old deities.

Thomas the doubter-turned-convert was also Thomas the twin: Christian legends admitted that Jesus and Thomas-Tammuz had the same face and were really the same god. According to some sources, the rival's name was Judas Thomas, or Judas the Tammuz, whose face was the same as Jesus's face.[2] Judas and Jesus seem to have been traditional names taken by victims in whom the god Tammuz was incarnate.

During the 4th century, a shrine at Edessa was taken over by followers of the new Tammuz—now called St. Thomas, Apostle to India—and the usual phony relics were installed.[3]

1. Enslin, L.C.M., 451. 2. Augstein, 151. 3. Attwater, 325.

Thor

var. Thundr, Thunaer, Donar

Scandinavian thunder-and-lightning god, corresponding to the Slavs' Pyerun and the Latin Jove—which is why Rome's *dies jovis,* Jove's Day, became Thursday (Thor's Day). Thor had at least six major sanctuaries in England; Thurstable in Essex was originally "Thor's Pillar." Thor's cult persisted up to the 11th century when a Christian chronicler said Thor—or his priest—was "a wicked man of Kent" acting as the king's counselor. Saxons converted to Christianity were obliged to renounce "Thunaer, Woden and Saxnot, and all those demons who are their companions."[1]

Yet Thor continued to be worshipped in the north. His sanctuary at Maerin in Trondheim was still active in the 11th century.[2] Eligius, bishop of Noyons, scolded Christians for observing Thursday as the holy day of Thor in the 7th century; yet even 500 years later, Thor's hammers were still revered in temples as sacred relics and sources of thunder. In Prussia up to the 16th century, Jupiter-Thor was worshipped by the people in "sacred woods in which they made sacrifices and sacred springs which Christians were not allowed to approach."[3]

Thor apparently descended from the Middle-Eastern thunder-bull who was also Jupiter. Plutarch said the Phoenician thunder god was Thur, the bull.[4] The Germanic Thor "bellowed like a bull" as he swung his hammer.[5] Like other forms of the bull god, he was married to the Earth Goddess as Thrud, "Power" or "Strength."[6] Though late myths sometimes called Thrud his "daughter," Thor's home in Asgard belonged to her. It was called Thrudvangar, "Thrud's Field."[7]

1. Turville-Petre, 99–100. 2. Oxenstierna, 294. 3. H.R.E. Davidson, G.M.V.A., 81–87. 4. Knight, S.L., 20. 5. *Larousse*, 261. 6. Hollander, 32. 7. Branston, 87.

Thoth

Egyptian god of magic words and writing, which he acquired from his consort Seshat, or Maat. He was identified with the Greek Hermes. His holy city was known as Hermopolis, "City of Hermes." Priests of Hermopolis pretended that Thoth had created the world, either by hatching the World Egg (which he encircled in the form of the Gnostic Serpent), or by speaking the words of creation, after the manner of the biblical God. (See **Logos**; **Ur-Text**.) The *Book of Thoth* was a famous legendary work supposed to reveal the secrets of manipulating matter by verbal charms.

Like Hermes and other manifestations of the Wise Serpent, Thoth owed his powers to his former close association with the Great Mother. He was lunar in nature, rather than solar. When he ascended to heaven, he became the guardian of the Moon gates.[1]

1. *Larousse*, 27.

Thugs

The curious ritual-murder cult of Thuggee flourished in central India for some three centuries, until the advent of railroads decreased foot travel in the 1800s so that the depredations of Thuggee "highwaymen" declined.

Thugs were fanatical worshippers of the Goddess Kali, having developed the idea that killing men in her name would win them a privileged reincarnation. They preyed on her enemies, the Brahmans. Women had nothing to fear from the Thugs; their victims were only men.[1]

Thuggee legend said Kali once tried to destroy all the "demons of blood and seed" (men) created by male gods. But each time she beheaded one, another man sprang up from every drop of spilled blood, probably a remnant of the belief that spilled blood in the Goddess's sanctuary brought forth increased fertility. At last Kali wiped the sweat from her arms with a handkerchief, gave the handkerchief to her faithful followers, and told them to make it into cords to strangle the "demons" without bloodshed.

Male human sacrifices were still offered to Kali up to the 16th century A.D., and occasionally even later, decapitation being the method of choice. A boy was beheaded at Kali's altar in Tanjore every Friday at sunset.[2] A king of Cooch Behar offered a hundred and fifty men to Kali at Danteshvari in the 1500s, and a king of Bastar sacrificed twenty-five men at the same shrine in 1830. Human sacrifice was prohibited and replaced by animal sacrifice in 1835.

Like medieval Arabian Assassins, the Thugs maintained that the rites of their Goddess should continue, and the Brahmans were heretics who deserved extermination. The *Mahabharata* presents Kali as a spirit of Brahmanicide, "with teeth projecting terribly, of an aspect furiously contorted, tawny and black, with disheveled hair, appalling eyes, and a garland of skulls around her neck, bathed in blood, clad in rags and the bark of trees."[3] This probably represented a primitive idol of the Death-goddess whose devotees believed she must be bathed in blood to remain fertile and satisfied.

1. Tannahill, 153. 2. Campbell, Or.M., 5. 3. Campbell, Or.M., 187.

Thumb

Hindus said the soul, "of the size of a thumb, the innermost Self, dwells forever in the heart of all beings." According to the Katha Upanishad, "That being, of the size of a thumb, dwells deep within the heart. He is the lord of time, past and future." The belief was literal. The sages actually thought a thumb-sized manikin danced inside the heart, stamping out the heartbeat, just as Dancing Shiva stamped out the rhythm of the universe as he perpetually danced within the cosmic body of his consort. The crudity of the original belief now has to be glossed over by modern commentators, who don't want their ancient traditions to seem absurd. So the pious scholar writes, "The sages ascribe a definite, minute size to the Self in order to assist the disciple in meditation."[1]

Still, the thumb-sized soul passed into European folklore and emerged as Hop-O'-My-Thumb and the fairy Thumbelina, both of whom probably began as disembodied souls in search of new bodies.

1. *Upanishads*, 21, 24.

Upanishads Buddhist scriptures representing the final stage in Vedic thought, dealing with the philosophy known as Vedanta. The Katha Upanishad discusses transmigration of souls, the nature of eternal life, the doctrine of *maya*, and an account of a visit to Yama, Lord of the Dead.

Thyrsus

Rod and staff of Dionysus, a wand or scepter tipped with a pine cone, representing the god's power to fertilize. The thyrsus was borne by the god himself, by his satyrs, his Maenads, his sileni, and other participants in his sacred *orgia.* Sometimes the thyrsus was displayed in conjunction with a wine cup, forming a male-and-female combination like that of the royal scepter and orb.[1]

1. *Larousse,* 153.

Tiamat

Sumero-Babylonian "Goddess Mother" (Dia Mater), from whose formless body the universe was born at creation; personification of The Deep, or **Tohu Bohu**. Babylonians later claimed their municipal god Marduk, Tiamat's son, divided her into heavens above and earth below, as did Marduk's imitator, the biblical God. But the original division was made by the Mother herself, as in the ancient Pelasgian myth of her Aegean counterpart, Eurynome.[1]

In derivative Hebrew myths, Tiamat became *Tehom,* The Deep; and this is how she appears in the Bible (Genesis 1:2). Patriarchal writers forgot that "The Deep" was a personified womb, a Middle-Eastern version of Kali whose being before creation was "formless." Most creation myths incorporated the idea of formlessness, in the darkness before the birth that brought "light" and the splitting of the Mother's body, so she became both heaven and earth. The Bible's account is based on the same archetype.

In Egypt, Tiamat was Temu or Te-Mut, oldest of deities, mother of the archaic Ennead of four dual female elements: Water, Darkness, Night, and Eternity.[2] She was also Nun, Naunet, or Ma-Nu, the great fish who gave birth to the universe and the gods. In repeated cycles of becoming, she periodically swallowed up both gods and universes and gave them rebirth—like Kali.[3]

Tiamat's firstborn child seems to have been a duplicate of herself, Mummu, translated either "churning" or "mother." The combination recalled the ancient notion that solid earth was made from "churning" the primordial fluid, like making butter from milk.[4] Some myths gave Tiamat a male consort, Apsu, similar to Jupiter Pluvius: a Father Heaven whose job it was to fertilize the Mother's abyss with seminal rain. But he was not her superior, not even her equal. Even in the chaotic conditions before creation, Tiamat was the true source of life. Her consort was subordinate, not even very necessary.[5] Various myths said Tiamat alone produced the fluid of creation, which was not semen but her menstrual blood, flowing continuously for three years and three months.[6] Its great reservoir was the Red Sea—comparable to Kali's "ocean of blood"—the eastern shore of which is still called Tihamat by the Arabs.

Babylonians said their god Marduk divided his mother Tiamat into two parts, upper waters and lower waters. Likewise, the Jewish God "divided the waters which were under the firmament from the waters which were above the firmament" (Genesis 1:7). The Jewish God also divided the Red Sea, which was likened to Tiamat herself.

The idea of dividing waters was not original with the Jews. Goddesses did it before gods. The Hindu Goddess Bindumati, "Mother of Life," divided the waters of the Ganges.[7] The Goddess Isis divided the waters of the river Phaedrus, to cross dry-shod.[8] Even an insignificant Egyptian wizard named Zazamonkh divided the waters of a lake to retrieve a courtesan's lost pendant.[9] Yahweh's miracle on behalf of the Israelites was fairly common in contemporary lore.

By dividing Tiamat, Marduk established the Diameter (horizon), which was the Greek version of Tiamat's name, meaning Goddess-Mother. We still say a *diameter* divides a whole circle. Though Marduk was supposed to have slain his mother, the Ocean of Blood, he still maintained the menstrual calendar in Babylon, celebrating sabbaths and months of the year according to the moon's phases.[10]

Modern scholars tend to ignore Tiamat's maternal Creatress nature, describing her as nothing more than a "dragon of chaos" slain by Marduk. It is seldom emphasized that this was a myth of matricide, or that the Goddess was the one who created the world. Some traditions indicate that Marduk's murder of his mother may have been motivated by jealously, like Cain's murder of Abel. Mother Tiamat had overlooked Marduk and chosen another of her sons, Kingu, to be her consort and the king of the universe.

> *[She] exalted among the gods, her sons, that she had borne, Kingu, and made him greatest among them all . . . placed him on a throne, saying, "By my charm and incantation I have raised thee to power among the gods. The dominion over all the gods I intrusted to thee. Lofty thou shalt be, thou my chosen spouse; great be thy name in all the world." She then gave him the Tablets of Destiny, and laid them on his breast.*[11]

Jealous Marduk not only killed Tiamat; he also deposed, castrated, and killed Kingu, and made the first man on earth out of Kingu's blood—which tends to show that Kingu was once the name of the sacrificed god-king, whose blood had the "feminine" power to make life.[12] Kingu was identified with the moon. Chaldeans called him Sin, the Moon-god of Mount Sinai. Apparently he still had the tablets of the Law given him by Tiamat (as Mother Rhea gave sacred tablets of the Law to Minos on Mt. Dicte), for the Old Testament claims he passed them on to Moses.

In southern Arabia, the Goddess was assimilated to Ishtar. The eyes of her idol Tehama were said to flow with tears each year as she bewailed the death of Tammuz.[13]

1. Graves, G.M. 1, 27. 2. Budge, D.N., 211. 3. Neumann, G.M., pl. 91; Erman, 252. 4. Brandon, 22. 5. Stone, 26. 6. *Assyr. & Bab. Lit.*, 301. 7. Rawson, A.T., 74. 8. Budge, G.E. 2, 191. 9. Erman, 40. 10. Hooke, M.E.M., 45. 11. *Assyr. & Bab. Lit.*, 287. 12. *Larousse*, 54. 13. Baring-Gould, C.M.M.A., 279.

Tingeltangel

Sexual orgy connected with worship of the Great Mother in medieval Germany. The same word was known to Scottish witches in the 17th century, according to a Forfar witch's confession that at the sabbat a "merry" song was sung at a nocturnal churchyard meeting. The song was called "Tinkletum Tankletum," close enough to the German term to show correspondence between them. The Scottish rites seem to have been fairly innocent. Scottish witches only drank some beer and danced, and "the devil kissed every one of the women."[1] As a result of such confessions, four women were hanged.

1. Summers, G.W., 230.

Titania

Ovid's name for Diana, inherited by the medieval Fairy Queen, as shown in Shakespeare's *Midsummer Night's Dream.*[1] The original Titania was the Great Goddess who ruled the pantheon of Aegean "Titans" or Elder Gods, later overthrown by patriarchal Olympians under Father Zeus. The name of the Titans meant "rulers," for they once ruled the Aegean world. Titania, their queen, was otherwise known as Themis, Gaea, or Mother Rhea, assimilated as the mother of the conquering Zeus.

1. Keightley, 325.

Tiw

Saxon god identified with Mars; the god of Tuesday (Tiw's Day), called Mars's Day in Rome, modern French *mardi.* Tiw was an archaic Aryan sky god descended, like Zeus Pater, from Sanskrit *Dyaus pitar,* as suggested by his other names: Tiuz in northern Germany, Ziu in the south, Tyr in Scandinavia. He was also called *Things,* because he was invoked at the Germanic *Thing* or *Ding,* an assembly for lawmaking. A 3rd-century inscription in Britain called him Mars Thincsus. The German word for Tuesday, *Dienstag,* evolved from "Thing-day."[1]

1. *Larousse,* 265–66.

Tlalteutli

Aztec Goddess of creation. At the beginning of time, the universe was made of her body. The gods discovered that she wouldn't bring forth new fruit for food, nor any new life, unless she was fed human hearts and drenched with human blood, like some of the manifestations of Kali.[1] Hence the Aztecs' sanguinary sacrifices.

1. Campbell, P.M., 225.

Tlazolteotl

Aztec Goddess resembling the medieval Hecate as Queen of Witches. Her symbol was a broomstick; she was also associated with the moon, the snake, and the screech owl. Her sabbats were held at crossroads. Her sacred women were Ciuateteo, "right honorable mothers," or Ciuapipiltin, "princesses." Sahagun said they were the ghosts of women who died in childbirth. "They were supposed to wander through the air, descending when they wished to earth. . . . They haunted cross-roads to practice their maleficent deeds, and they had temples built at these places where bread offerings were made to them, also the thunder stones which fall from the sky."[1] In other words, in Mexico as in Europe, the missionary clergy were at pains to diabolize the Mother-deities.

1. Summers, V., 261–62.

Toga

Garment of clan-ruling *matronae* in pre-patriarchal Rome. Men adopted the toga as they gained political power, until in classical times the only women still wearing it were promiscuous priestesses of the Goddess. Thus it became a custom to distinguish a prostitute by the name of "toga-wearer."[1]

1. Rose, 191.

Tohu Bohu

Hebrew "primal chaos," elemental formlessness between the destruction of one universe and the creation of the next. The idea came from a general Asiatic belief in cyclic recurrences brought about by the Goddess (Kali), herself the cauldron or sea of "infinite formlessness," holding all potential forms in a plastic state of flux.[1] She was the Abyss or the Deep before creation, according to the Bible (Genesis 1:2).

Chaldean sources of the Bible myth said the brooding creative spirit that brought order out of chaos was the Goddess; but patriarchal writers transformed her into the "Spirit of God."[2] *Tohu bohu* was her semi-fluid substance, menstrual blood in the process of clotting into solidity; the sea, but also a sea of blood. Orphics called it "Chaos eternal, immense, uncreated, from which all is born; neither darkness nor light, nor damp nor dry, nor hot nor cold, but all things mingled, eternally one and limitless."[3] Some scholars have identified *tohu* with the Primordial Sea, the Goddess Tiamat (Hebrew Tehomet), and *bohu* with the male earth god Behemoth, making "a sexual creation."[4]

1. Avalon, 229, 233. 2. Augstein, 209. 3. Lindsay, O.A., 116. 4. Ochs, 94.

Tongue

Latin *lingus,* "tongue," was derived from Sanskrit *lingam,* "phallus." Showing the tongue between the lips was once a sacred gesture representing the lingam-yoni; to this day the folds of the vulva are properly called *labiae,* "lips." (See **Vagina Dentata**.)

At the moment of her mating with Shiva, Kali Ma usually showed a protruding tongue in token of the sexual sacrament.[1] The classic Medusa head signifying "female wisdom" also had a protruding tongue, a reference to ancient sexual mysteries celebrated in her honor.[2]

Medieval Christians understood very well that the protruding tongue was a sexual symbol. Their pictures of lusty devils showed long phallic tongues, and sticking out the tongue "at" someone became their favorite gesture of insult, equivalent to "fuck you." In the east, where sexuality was not associated with shame or dishonor, sticking out the tongue is still considered a polite greeting.

Italians used to heighten the mouth's resemblance to a vulva by drawing down one corner of it with the thumb.[3] Biting the thumb, a supreme insult in Italy, cast a curse of castration.

Archaic sacred kings, who had to kill their "fathers" or predecessors to win the queen, often castrated the defeated rival to deprive his ghost of *virtu* (man-magic) which might give him enough power to return for revenge. This Oedipal attack was often mythologized as the slaying of a dragon, symbol of "father," or "phallus bigger than mine." The dragon-slayer's reward was the woman (mother). Dragon-slaying heroes cut off the dragon's tongue, representing amputation of the penis. Tristan cut off the tongue of his slain dragon, to establish his right to demand the hand of Iseult.[4]

In medieval cathedrals, "an extraordinary number of grotesque heads are depicted with protruding tongues," and this was distinctly related to exposure of sexual organs. "The exposure of the genitalia was widely believed to thwart and keep at bay pursuing evil forces."[5] All over the Gothic cathedral, numerous creatures with their tongues sticking out showed once again that the cathedral was dedicated to a pantheon of both Christian and pagan deities. People wanted their "creatures from the grotto" or *grotesques* to inhabit the same churches that were built over the sites of the old grottoes. By Renaissance times, the old deities with their obscenely protruding tongues were declared devils, so it became conventional to show devils making this gesture.[6]

The story of Pinocchio's nose, which grew every time he told a lie, may have originated in Oriental beliefs concerning the tongue. Buddhists said a liar's tongue would grow to great length in hell.[7] The Buddhists called "liars" most of the old non-Buddhist deities who stuck out their tongues in token of the sexual sacrament.

1. Neumann, G.M., pls. 65, 67. 2. Massa, 19. 3. Knight, S.L., 30.
4. Guerber, L.M.A., 240. 5. Sheridan & Ross, 54. 6. de Givry, 141.
7. Tatz & Kent, 69.

Tophet

Alternate name for hell, from the Jewish shrine of Tophet in the valley of Hinnom, outside Jerusalem, where Solomon made fire-sacrifices to the Tyrian god Heracles-Melkart, or Molech (1 Kings 11:17). The previous source was probably the Egyptian Tephet, "Hidden abode," a part of the underworld.[1]

At the Tophet altar, victims "passed through the fire to eternal life," meaning they were burned to death and rose again as gods. For a while, Molech was identified with Yahweh, which is why the sons of Aaron were consumed on the altar by "fire from the Lord" (Leviticus 10:2). Norse heroes also passed through "magic fire" to reach the paradise of the Valkyries. Jewish surrogate-kings were still burned for the Lord in Hilkiah's reign (2 Kings 23:10).[2]

Levite priests eventually distinguished Yahweh from Molech and forbade the latter's worship (Leviticus 18:21); but the cult of Heracles-Melkart still flourished in St. Paul's time in Paul's own home town of Tarsus.[3] Because victims burned in this "Tophet" were deified as holy martyrs, Paul thought there was a special magic in giving one's body to be burned (1 Corinthians 13:3).

1. Budge, G.E. 1, 230. 2. James, 192. 3. H. Smith, 182.

Torture

During the Middle Ages, torture became the common accompaniment to legal cases involving matters of faith. Pagan common-law traditions opposed the use of torture, and regarded an accused person as innocent until proven guilty by the prosecution.[1] Christian crusaders and inquisitors reversed this trend. (See **Inquisition**.) The Inquisition's use of torture removed all possibility of proof of innocence. Gibbon said, "No power under heaven could save the prisoner; he was doomed." Weyer, an eyewitness, wrote that the inquisitors' victims were "slaughtered with the most refined tortures that tyrants could invent, beyond human endurance. And this cruelty is continued until the most innocent are forced to confess themselves guilty."[2]

Surviving records, though scanty, paint a hideous picture of the Inquisition's activities, which were sometimes disbelieved even by contemporaries because they were unimaginable. A woman arrested at Eichstätt in 1637 "laughed heartily" on the first day of her trial at the idea that she might have trafficked with the devil. She said she would rather die than accuse herself of such doings; she had lived a blameless life with her husband and eight children for more than 20 years. Three weeks later, she died under the torture, confessing that she was in love with the devil, that she killed one of her children at his bidding, and that at least 45 of her neighbors were fellow-Satanists.[3]

Not even the most saintly had a chance against the inquisitors' engines. A 16th-century abbess of the convent of Santa Isabela at

Cordova, Magdalena de la Cruz, was a woman of "an extraordinary reputation for sanctity." Nevertheless she was accused and arrested, and soon confessed to practicing witchcraft with the help of two familiar demons, Balbar and Pithon.[4]

The inquisitors' rule was to keep on torturing until the victim named many "accomplices," who were then arrested and tortured until more names were given, and so on until whole districts were found to be "infected" with heresy. One woman told her confessor: "I never dreamed that by means of the torture a person could be brought to the point of telling such lies as I have told. I am not a witch, and I have never seen the devil, and still I had to plead guilty myself and denounce others." One minister urged a condemned witch to renounce her accusations of innocent people, but she answered, "Father, look at my legs! They are like fire—ready to burn up—so excruciating is the pain. I could not stand to have so much as a fly touch them, to say nothing of submitting again to the torture. I would a hundred times rather die than endure such frightful agony again. I cannot describe to any human being how terrific the pain actually is."[5] Such torture was "extensively, viciously, and persistently used and could break all but the most heroic spirits."[6]

Weyer served as a physician in witch prisons and spoke from first-hand knowledge of women driven half mad "by frequent torture . . . kept in prolonged squalor and darkness of their dungeons . . . and constantly dragged out to undergo atrocious torment until they would gladly exchange at any moment this most bitter existence for death, are willing to confess whatever crimes are suggested to them rather than be thrust back into their hideous dungeon amid ever recurring torture." Friedrich von Spee, a Jesuit confessor who also worked in the prisons, wrote: "All recantation is vain. If she does not confess, the torture is repeated—twice, thrice, four times. In 'exceptional' crimes, the torture is not limited in duration, severity, or frequency. . . . She can never clear herself. The investigating body would feel disgraced if it acquitted a woman; once arrested and in chains, she has to be guilty, by fair means or foul."[7]

This might be contrasted with the old law of the Ripuarian Franks, that any man who killed a woman for any reason whatever must pay a fine so heavy that it obligated his descendants for three generations.[8]

Motherhood was a distinct liability for those who fell into inquisitors' hands. Bodin recommended that children, if "craftily handled," could be depended on to inform against their mothers. Children were also highly susceptible to torture; so a rule was made that children could be tortured at once, without any waiting period. Elicited by torture or by craft, the testimony of "infants"—meaning children under 10—was acceptable to the Inquisition and could convict their mothers of witchcraft, even though such testimony was not accepted in other kinds of trials.[9]

Rules for the persecution of witches allowed no revocation of confessions after torture. Those who tried to retract their confessions were taken back to the torture chamber and tortured again; once to purge themselves of the retraction, and once again to elicit a "true" confession. Any display of fear was proof of guilt. So was denunciation by another tortured victim. In 1597 a 69-year-old woman named Clara Geissler manage to resist the thumbscrew, but confessed everything she had been asked after racking and crushing of her feet. When those she named had been arrested and similarly tortured, Clara was returned to the torture chamber to confirm their confessions. She was tortured with "the utmost severity," and died. The record stated that the devil had wrung her neck.[10]

In some cases of retracted confessions, the court automatically assumed that the confession was true, and the retraction a perjury. The victim was then declared a relapsed impenitent, and handed over to the stake.[11]

Inquisitors were instructed by their handbooks to give false promises of mercy for the sake of compliance and confession.[12] There was no need to keep any promises to an accused witch. If a victim confessed everything, abjured her heresy, and threw herself on the court's mercy, her sentence was carried out anyway, on two counts: (1) for the "temporal injuries" she had caused, and (2) for the worthlessness of her confession which was made "from fear of death" rather than from true repentance.[13] The same "worthless" confession, though, was a legal basis for execution.

Denial of guilt was useless, even if it could be maintained against tortures. Le Sieur Bouvet declared that "denial of guilt by a prisoner was an especially good reason why torture should be continued." Limborch's *History of the Inquisition* said it was a simple matter to extort confession by torture from "such as are most innocent." According to Cornelius Loos, "Wretched creatures are compelled by the severity of the torture to confess things they have never done, and so by cruel butchery innocent lives are taken and by a new alchemy gold and silver coined from human blood." Von Spee wrote, "The most robust who have thus suffered have affirmed to me that no crime can be imagined which they would not at once confess, if it would bring ever so little relief, and they would welcome ten deaths to escape a repetition."[14]

Records of the Spanish Inquisition at Toledo show that some victims were prevented from confessing until the lust of their tormentors had been gratified. Their torture went on for days or weeks beyond the point where they had wholly broken down, and pleaded to be told what to say, so they could say it.[15] Such evidence shows that the Inquisition really was a system of formalized sadism. The fact that the vast majority of its victims were women points to crypto-sexual motivations engendered by repression on a massive scale.

Pope Alexander III said in an encyclical letter that confessions should not be forced by torture. His successors took it upon themselves to explain that what Alexander really meant was that torture must not be used against clergymen by lay persons; but it could be used by the clergy against laymen. When Innocent IV adopted torture for ecclesiastical trials, he said it should "stop short of loss of life or limb," but this was a mere formality, since limbs were broken or crushed routinely in the torture chamber. When a victim died under torture, inquisitors were authorized by Pope Urban IV to absolve each other from guilt, to be innocent in the sight of God.[16]

Many semantic devices were used to convey an official impression that the inquisitors were not monsters of cruelty. Records often said confessions were given freely, *sine tortura et extra locum torturae*—"without torture and even out of sight of the instruments of torture." This meant that after the victims were tortured, they were carried into another room and given the choice of confessing "freely" or being taken back to the torture chamber.[17]

When victims managed to kill themselves in prison, or died of their injuries, they were said to have been slain by the devil. One victim who succeeded in cutting his own throat was described by Friar Guazzo as "tempted by a demon," which carried away his soul, "for so did Divine Justice dispose."[18] Few victims were allowed an opportunity to kill themselves, for they were closely chained at night; but they could easily be devoured by the rats and other prison-infesting vermin attracted by the smell of blood and suppurating wounds.[19]

Most victims pleaded for death sooner or later, but pious ones were further tormented by visions of the hellfire that awaited them, dying with lies on their lips. A housewife named Rebecca Lemp sent letters from prison to her husband and six children, showing radical alterations in her attitude before and after torture. At first she was confident: "My dearly beloved Husband, be not troubled. Were I to be charged by thousands of accusations, I am innocent, else may all the demons in hell come and tear me to pieces. Were they to pulverize me, cut me in a thousand pieces, I could not confess anything. Therefore do not be alarmed; before my conscience and before my soul I am innocent. Will I be tortured? I don't believe it, since I am not guilty of anything."

After she had been tortured five times, and had confessed every enormity her tormentors suggested to her, Rebecca wrote again to her husband: "O thou, the chosen of my heart, must I be parted from thee, though entirely innocent? If so, may God be followed throughout eternity by my reproaches. They force one and make one confess; they have so tortured me. . . . Husband, send me something that I may die, or I must expire under the torture. . . . Send me something, else may I peril even my soul."[20]

Another letter smuggled out of the Bamberg prison in 1628 was written by a man of means, Burgomaster Johannes Junius, whose property was taken by the inquisitors:

Many hundred thousand good-nights, dearly beloved daughter Veronica.

> *Innocent have I come into prison, innocent have I been tortured, innocent must I die. For whoever comes into the witch prison must become a witch or be tortured until he invents something out of his head and—God pity him—bethinks him of something. I will tell you how it has gone with me. . . . The executioner put the thumb screws on me, both hands bound together, so that the blood ran out at the nails and everywhere, so that for four weeks I could not use my hands, as you can see from the writing . . . . Thereafter they first stripped me, bound my hands behind me, and drew me up in the torture. Then I thought heaven and earth were at an end; eight times did they draw me up and let me fall again, so that I suffered terrible agony. The executioner said, "Sir, I beg you, for God's sake confess something, whether it be true or not. Invent something, for you cannot endure the torture which you will be put to, and even if you bear it all, yet you will not escape." . . . Now, dear child, here you have all my confession, for which I must die. And they are sheer lies and made-up things, so help me God. For all this I was forced to say through fear of the torture which was threatened beyond what I had already endured. For they never leave off with the torture till one confesses something; be he never so good, he must be a witch. Nobody escapes. . . . Dear child, keep this letter secret so that people do not find it, else I shall be tortured most piteously and the jailers will be beheaded. So strictly is it forbidden. . . . I have taken several days to write this; my hands are both lame. I am in a sad plight. Good night, for your father Johannes Junius will never see you more. . . . Dear child, six have confessed against me at once . . . all false, through compulsion, as they told me, and begged my forgiveness in God's name before they were executed.*[21]

Torture was euphemistically called "the Question." Making a show of mercy, handbooks of the Inquisition recommended that the accused be questioned at first "lightly, without shedding of blood."[22] Sometimes this elicited full confessions. A witch in the diocese of Constance confessed to having raised a hailstorm—by pouring water into a small hole in the ground—after she "had at first been exposed to the very gentlest questions, being suspended hardly clear of the ground by her thumbs."[23]

Other methods, not quite so gentle, included the rack, thumbscrew, bootscrew, whips, branding irons, pincers for twisting off gobbets of flesh, ropes to wind the extremities until blood spurted from under the nails. A favorite of the judges was the hoist or strappado, a pulley to haul the victim into the air by her arms bound behind her back, jerking her up and down until the shoulders were dislocated. The water torture was also common. This consisted of forcing gallons of water into the belly through a funnel put down the throat, sometimes also forcing down and pulling up long strips of linen along with the water, or paddling the distended belly with sticks. Feet or hands might be basted with boiling fat and roasted over a brazier.[24] Most of the instruments were inscribed with the pious motto: *Soli Deo Gloria,* Glory be only to God.[25]

Dr. Johann Meyfarth witnessed hundreds of witch trials in the

17th century and wrote that he would have given a thousand thalers to be able to forget what he had seen: "feet wrenched off legs, and eyes torn from their sockets, and the prisoner burned with brimstone and basted with oil. He had seen torturers apply flaming balls of brimstone to the genitals of a woman while she was hanging in strappado. He had watched them revel in horror until their victims confessed—or died (strangled by the Devil, the judges explained)."[26]

Execution was still another torture, sometimes miserably protracted, as in Spain where half-burned heretics were snatched from the flames, still alive, and allowed to suffer for hours before being returned to the fire. At the "Witches' Tower" in Hesse, victims were hung 15 feet above ground in niches, and slowly baked to death over a low fire. Numerous burned bones and skulls were found buried at the base of the tower.[27] Oddly enough, the tower later became the property of the novelist Sacher-Masoch, who gave his name to the perversion known as masochism.[28]

A significant detail, speaking psychologically, was that inquisitors seemed very anxious to make women cry. It was their rule that a witch was proved guilty if she didn't shed tears during torture. The judge adjured her to weep, "by the loving tears shed by Christ on the cross." If she did weep, though, she went to the stake anyway, for it proved the devil had given her the gift of tears to mislead the judges.[29] If she didn't weep, she was convicted of "taciturnity," a crime punishable by burning. In England, the punishment for taciturnity was *peine fort et dure*—pressing to death.[30]

England didn't import the engines of torture used on the continent, but Scotland did. English witch-finders used informal or bloodless tortures like starvation, "swimming the witch," or "walking the witch" (preventing her from sleeping until a confession was made).[31] Various binding tortures were used. An accused witch might be stripped and bound cross-legged on a table, sometimes with ropes around the neck attached to the four corners of the room, and left in that position until she confessed. Sometimes, accused witches were so tightly manacled in jail while awaiting trial, that they came to the courtroom with limbs rotted by gangrene. Many died of "gaol fever" (typhus) before they could be tried at all.

Swimming the witch was a relic of the ordeal by water. With thumbs bound to the opposite big toes, the victim was lowered into a stream or pond by men holding ropes, one on each bank. If the body floated, witchcraft was proved, on the theory that water rejected a witch. If the body sank, the accused was innocent, although frequently dead of drowning. The decision was largely dependent on the men who held the ropes.

Peasant mobs often invented their own tortures for suspected witches. At Catton in Suffolk in 1603, a mob of men tossed an 80-year-old woman up in the air, punched her, flashed gunpowder in her face, and "having prepared a stool in the which they had stuck daggers and knives with sharp points upwards, they often times struck her down upon the same stool whereby she was sore pricked and grievously hurt."[32]

"Pricking" was the favorite technique of witch-finders who claimed to locate the giveaway witch mark or "devil's mark" on a witch's body by sticking a three-inch awl into her flesh. The devil's mark was supposed to be a numb spot, so the pricking would produce no pain. Most witch-finders used a trick instrument with a retractable blade, like a stage dagger, to find the "painless" spot.[33] Scottish prickers formed a regular guild. Among the more famous of them were John Bain, John Balfour, John Kincaid the "common pricker," and Matthew Hopkins, who pricked hundreds of old women in the country of Suffolk, and soon announced that the entire area was infested with witches.[34]

The search for the mark was not necessarily definitive, if it failed. When the Bavarian witch-finder Jorg Abriel couldn't find the mark on a woman, he simply said she looked like a witch to him, and went on to torture her into admitting it.[35]

Grim Calvinist Scotland instituted tortures as nasty as the continental ones, though the persecution was less, because the church made no profit from it. Perhaps the most famous Scottish witch trial was conducted in the presence of King James V1 (James 1 of England), who was convinced the witches had caused a storm at sea that nearly wrecked his ship, and badly frightened him. The record said they had done it by throwing a dead cat into the sea. They also set sail on the sea in a sieve.[36]

The alleged ringleader of the "coven" was Dr. John Fian, a schoolmaster, who displayed exemplary courage in the face of multiple tortures, but his courage did him no good. "His nails upon all his fingers were riven and pulled off with an instrument called in Scottish a *turkas*, which in England we call a pair of pincers, and under every nail there was thrust in two needles." He was subjected to "thrawing" (binding the head tightly with a rope), tongue-pricking, and three sessions in the boots. He "did abide so many blows in them, that his legs were crushed and beaten together as small as might be, and the bones and flesh so bruised, that the blood and marrow spouted forth in great abundance, whereby they were made unserviceable for ever."[37] He was carried to the stake on a cart.[38]

The memory of this martyr to superstition was sullied by a rather bawdy tale that arose after his death. Dr. Fian was said to have craved the love of a village maiden, and bribed her brother to obtain three of her pubic hairs for a love charm. The boy was caught by his mother, who substituted three hairs from a cow's udder. Dr. Fian accepted these and made his love charm, after which he was pursued through the village by a roaring, lovesick cow.[39]

Through its history, western civilization has been disgraced by spectacles of formalized infliction of pain upon the helpless. Such spectacles are even artificially contrived in modern "entertainment," such as films. G. B. Shaw remarked, "A public flogging will always draw a crowd; and there will be in that crowd plenty of manifestations of a horrible passional ecstasy in the spectacle of laceration and suffering."[40] Sometimes it was so blatant as to embarrass even participants. When Protestants abolished the bloody sport of bear-baiting in England, they gave as their reason not that it was cruel to bears and dogs, but that it afforded too much pleasure to the spectators.[41]

Animals and women were perennial victims, even equated with one another by churchmen who claimed both were devoid of souls. Among the most savagely tormented were women suspected of enjoying their sexuality—witches, whores, adulteresses. The latter received public floggings in colonial America: "Public whippings yielded a vicarious sexual experience—a mixture of sadism and mass voyeurism cloaked in righteous disapproval. . . . They gathered on such occasions to watch as a woman convicted of uncontrolled desire bared her back down to the waist and was whipped by a man with a kind of erotic violence later made notorious by the Comte de Sade."[42]

Western civilization came to choose pain over pleasure: to think pain-giving permissible, fit for public display, even pious, whereas pleasure-giving of the physical sort was suspect, hidden, "evil." The two types of behavior seem to be inversely related. If a society suppresses one, the other will flourish. Studies with laboratory animals show that individuals conditioned to be highly aggressive have below-normal sex drive and display little interest in copulation. It has also been observed among human beings that angry, hostile individuals have little sexual appetite.[43]

Sexually repressed individuals abounded in western society, especially in the church, which spawned the Inquisition. There were also less extreme manifestations of the evil. Doctors lauded the salutary effects of pain. Paullini's *Flagellum Salutis* (1698) recommended severe beatings for "quick and easy cures" of such disorders as melancholia, paralysis, toothache, sleepwalking, deafness, and nymphomania. Professor Cullen at Edinburgh taught that "stripes and blows about the body" help cure maniacs. John Battie, another expert on the care of the insane, wrote: "Body pain may be excited to purpose and without the least danger. Beating is often serviceable."[44]

Among the most curious manifestations of western man's pain-obsession was its projection upon women as the *givers* of pain, almost as if man collectively sought punishment for his historical offenses against females. Flagellation was remarkably popular among Victorian "puritans." Publisher George Cannon called flagellation "a letch which has existed from time immemorial, and is so extensively indulged in London at this day that no less than twenty splendid establishments are supported entirely by its practice."[45] One writer said, "Lovers of the birch . . . are almost as common as the lovers of Venus."[46]

But it was Venus who wielded the birch: usually a mother image, stepmother, aunt, governess, housekeeper, or a large, imposing sort of courtesan. Swinburne said, "One of the great charms of birching lies in the sentiment that the floggee is the powerless victim of the furious rage of a beautiful woman." St. George H. Stock wrote: "When an elegant high bred woman wields the birch with dignity of mein and grace of attitude, then both the practice and suffering becomes a real pleasure." Dugdale published a pornographic book entitled *Betsy Thoughtless,* "a most spicey [sic] and piquant Narrative of a Young Girl obliged to excoriate her sweetheart's bum before he could ravish her Maidenhead."[47] A typical passage of Victorian "spice" ran:

> *Martinet meanwhile had taken off her loose morning wrapper, and armed herself with a rod, formed, not of canes and cuttings like the rest, but of stout birch stems with innumerable branches, like a tree in miniature. With this weapon in her hand, how terrible she appeared! Juno deprived of the apple might have looked like her. Her splendid neck and arms were bare, her cheeks flamed, her huge breasts were heaving. Speech was too weak, the graces of birching were ignored, nothing short of savage* beating *would satisfy her present need of vengeance.*[48]

Was this a vision of woman wronged—or Goddess ignored—through centuries of oppression, surfacing in pornography—which by its very simplicity may give expression to genuinely archetypal imagery? These books were written by men, not women. They presented fantasies that men wanted to see in the mind's eye. In one pornographic work, a young man was beaten for insulting his mother, by an older woman presented as a "nurse"—ordinarily, a nurturer or caretaker. Her bizarre speech ran: "The young gentleman thought, I dare swear, there was no one could break him of those crimes, but I'll whip this bold backside of his till I strip every bit of skin off it, or I'll work an amendment in him." The youth pleaded, "Try me this once, my dearest mistress! Oh gracious! Try me! Oh, I'm killed! let me down! let me down! nurse! nurse! nurse!" She answered, "You may roar, and cry, and kick, and plunge, and implore, my pretty gentleman, but all will not do; I'll whip you till the blood runs to your heels! You shall feel the tuition of this excellent rod!"[49]

William Gladstone, four times prime minister of England, regularly indulged in flagellation and patronized brothels for the purpose, as was discovered when his diaries were published in 1975.[50] Of course, English public-school customs of hazing and caning created many unfortunates whose sexual drives were warped into a confusion between pleasure and pain; the poet Swinburne presents a well-known example. But a tradition even older had predisposed all Christendom to this kind of confusion. The sense of sin and guilt attached to all forms of sexuality; the ubiquitous image of a tortured Christ revered for his suffering (inflicted on him by Father); the generally accepted theory that children must be trained to "fear God" through painful punishments—many such things together established a culture of cruelty, where men often judged their own success in life by their level of ability to make others suffer. This was the real meaning of power.

Psychologically, men who obviously enjoyed torturing women and children revealed their own incapacity to inspire love. Sadists find sadistic behavior satisfying because it can elicit strong emotional responses from people who would otherwise pay no attention to them. A sadist doesn't know how to be lovable. This feeling of powerlessness can be transformed into a feeling of power if he can torture. He can even achieve something like a sense of bravery or daring, despite the fact that the victim has no opportunity to retaliate. To subject others to any violent physical attack is to defy their rage. When such rage is made completely helpless to express itself, as in the case of a prisoner, the victim becomes an object of total control—which is precisely what men yearned to make of women ever since patriarchal thought introduced the possibility.

Sadism has been called the religion of psychical cripples.[51] It was also a religion of sexual cripples. Unable to reconcile their concept of sin with the tenderness and affection that good sexual relatedness requires, Christians turned to perverted obsessions with pain and punishment. Western historians were fond of describing the barbarian cruelties of the ancient pagan world, as contrasted with a "Christian" morality of kindness. However, it might appear that of the two approaches to morality, paganism was the kinder one on the whole. At least its cruelty was never so mercilessly efficient as that of western civilization, extending from the Inquisition to the wars and concentration camps of the 20th century.

1. Lea, 117. 2. Robbins, 500, 540. 3. Haining, 103. 4. Summers, H. W., 69. 5. Robbins, 501. 6. J.B. Russell, 43. 7. Robbins, 102. 8. Bullough, 154. 9. Scot, 15, 16, 21. 10. Robbins, 43, 104, 503. 11. Lea, 125. 12. Kramer & Sprenger, 226, 125. 13. H. Smith, 290. 14. Robbins, 103, 482–83, 309. 15. Plaidy, 157. 16. Coulton, 154–55. 17. J.B. Russell, 221. 18. Robbins, 18, 508. 19. H. Smith, 287. 20. Robbins, 303–4. 21. Ewen, 122–23. 22. H. Smith, 285. 23. Kramer & Sprenger, 149. 24. Plaidy, ch. 8. 25. H. Smith, 286. 26. Robbins, 346. 27. Summers, G.W., 496–97. 28. Robbins, 450. 29. Daly, 64. 30. Robbins, 506. 31. Ewen, 124. 32. Robbins, 509. 33. W. Scott, 240. 34. H. Smith, 294. 35. Robbins, 42. 36. H. Smith, 293; Robbins, 196. 37. Robbins, 198. 38. Rosen, 201. 39. Seth, 39–40. 40. Pearsall, N.B.A., 181. 41. Woods, 141. 42. Rugoff, 22–23. 43. Fromm, 190, 193. 44. Bromberg, 53, 102. 45. Pearsall, N.B.A., 257. 46. Weintraub, 163. 47. Marcus, 255; Pearsall, N.B.A., 258–63. 48. Marcus, 258. 49. Marcus, 256–57. 50. Sadock, Kaplan & Freedman, 62. 51. Fromm, 288–90.

Transubstantiation

Catholics claim by the doctrine of transubstantiation that the bread and wine of the Eucharist is entirely transformed into Jesus's flesh and blood, a doctrine as old as primitive cannibalistic blood-sacrifices when the "symbol" was real because the dying god was in fact eaten. The Satapatha Brahmana says the first sacrifice most acceptable to the gods was a man; then a horse was substituted, then a bull, ram, or goat, and at last "it was found that the gods were most pleased" with offerings of grain.[1]

Mystery cults of the early Christian era sacrificed and ate their gods in the form of bread and wine, whether the "savior" was Osiris, Mithra, Attis, Dionysus, or Orpheus. Rationalists like Cicero objected to the practice: "When we call the corn Ceres and the wine Bacchus we use a common figure of speech; but do you imagine that any one is so insane as to believe that the thing he feeds upon is a god?" Yet the vulgar did indeed believe it, transforming the ancient *omophagia* into grain-flesh and wine-blood of the god who might carry them into heaven when he became a part of them. Jesus repeated the same claim as all other savior gods: "Whoso eateth my flesh, and drinketh my blood, hath eternal life; and I will raise him up at the last day."[2]

The theory behind transubstantiation was the most primitive kind of magic, "the echo of some prehistoric cannibalistic religion. . . . The flesh and blood consumed becomes an innate part of the diner. Thus, if a man feeds on a stag, some measure of the animal's swiftness becomes a part of his own skill; if he drinks the blood of a warrior, he acquires the warrior's power and strength."[3] If he eats a god, he becomes godlike.

Literal belief in the conversion of bread and wine into Jesus's flesh and blood was essential to the idea of salvation, which Christianity shared with the pagan Mysteries. Doubt on this point was not tolerated. St. Gregory the Great told of a woman who dared laugh at the Eucharist, explaining to Gregory, "I laughed because you called this morsel of bread, which I kneaded with my own hands, the 'Body of Christ.'" Gregory then prayed, and caused the host lying on the altar to be changed into "a piece of flesh in the form of a finger." This convinced the woman, who then ate the bread she had just seen turned into a finger, and came back to the faith.[4]

Even today, those who tried to reinterpret the Eucharist as a purely symbolic act have been rebuked *ex cathedra* by the pope. The 1965 encyclical *Mysterium Fidei* once again insisted on "the marvelous change of the whole of the bread's substance into Christ's body and the whole of the wine's substance into his blood." Having never wavered on this point, churchmen were curiously inconsistent, to say the least, in condemning converted Mexican Indians for secretly continuing their "great heresy and abominable sin," which consisted of making "dough images of their god which were distributed and eaten."[5]

Transubstantiation was one of the primary doctrinal causes of the Protestant Reformation. John Huss and his colleague Jerome of Prague went to the stake for denying it, but their martyrdom set off the war between the papacy and the Bohemian heretics, which ended with the church's loss of all Bohemia and the foundation of the independent Moravian church.[6] Protestants eventually developed contempt for Catholic "God-eaters." Heath's 1610 *Epigrammes* called them worse than cannibals, who committed only the lesser sin of eating man's flesh.[7] Both factions, perhaps dimly recalling pagan versions of transubstantiation, viewed witches as cannibals. "Where the basic internal social divisions are between the generations or sexes, women and children are often cast as witches and cannibals by the dominant males."[8]

There was much satisfaction in pagan communion feasts where the god was incarnate in an edible animal and distributed even to the poor, who seldom enjoyed any meat of their own. But the church came to regard this kind of feast as too expensive. "The point that really merits attention is that the nutritive value of the communion feast is virtually zero, whether there is transubstantiation or not. . . . What the end of animal sacrifice really signified was the end of ecclesiastical redistributive feasting."[9]

1. Robertson, 27. 2. H. Smith, 168, 200. 3. Jobes, 219. 4. de Voragine, 185. 5. Arens, 67, 161. 6. H. Smith, 319. 7. Hazlitt, 594–95. 8. Arens, 158. 9. M. Harris, 119.

Transvestism

When men began to seek a share of religious and magical knowledge, formerly the property of women, their original objective was to make themselves resemble women so the spirits would find them acceptable. A common method was to put on women's clothes.

Transvestism is found in a majority of ancient priesthoods. Tacitus said the priests of Germanic tribes were *muliebri ornatu,* men dressed up as women.[1] Norse priests of sunrise and sunset rituals in honor of the Haddingjar (Heavenly Twins) were men whose office demanded that they wear the dress and hair styles of women.[2] Even Thor, the thunder god, received his magic hammer and was filled with power only after he put on the garments of the Goddess Freya and pretended to be a bride.[3]

At the ancient Argive "Feast of Wantonness" (Hubristika) men became women by wearing women's dresses and veils, temporarily assuming feminine powers in violation of a specific taboo.[4] Cretan priests of Leukippe, the White-Mare-Mother, always wore female dress. So did priests of Heracles, ostensibly in memory of their god's service (in female dress) to the Lydian Goddess Omphale, personification of the *omphalos.*[5] The Jewish philosopher Moses Maimonides said men in his day put on women's clothing to invoke the aid of the Goddess Venus.[6]

Roman priests of the Magna Mater dressed as women, and transvestism figured prominently in Roman rites of the Lupercalia and the Ides of January. The custom was still prevalent in the time of St. Augustine, who inveighed against men who clothed themselves in women's garments at the feast of Janus. He said such men could not attain salvation, even if they were otherwise good Christians. Before his conversion to Christianity, St. Jerome even participated in ritual transvestism, though his biographers tried to pretend that he had worn women's clothes by mistake.[7]

Despite Augustine and other church fathers, ritual transvestism continued. Men dressed in women's clothes at religious festivals at Amasea in the 5th century, and again—or still—at the Kalends of January in the 10th century. Balsamon said in the 12th century even the clergy participated in pagan rites in the nave of the church, wearing masks and female dress.[8] Gregory of Tours, bishop of Auvergne in Merovingian times, was forced to give up his church to a crowd of "demons," their leader dressed as a woman and seated on the episcopal throne.[9] The inquisitor Jean Bodin asserted that male and female witches actually changed their sex by changing clothes with one another.[10]

Men's transvestism was rooted in the ancient desire to imitate female magic. In the Celebes, religious rituals remained in the hands of women, assisted by an order of priests who wore female dress and were called *tjalabai,* "imitation women." The same word was applied in Arabia to the robe that men copied from women, *djallaba.*[11] Among the northern Batak the shaman is always a woman, and the office is hereditary in the female line, because there was no transvestism.[12] In Borneo, magicians are required to wear female clothing. Siberian shamans often wore women's clothes. Considered greatest were those shamans who could "change their sex" and become female, taking husbands and living as homosexual wives.[13]

Similarly, American Indians viewed the homosexual or *berdache* as a gifted medicine man. He claimed to receive an order from the Moon-goddess in a dream, to the effect that he must turn female and become one of her own. He was accepted by the tribe as the woman he wanted to be, was allowed to wear women's clothes, joined the women's craft guilds and dance societies. Eliade says, "Ritual and symbolic transformation into a woman is probably explained by an ideology derived from the archaic matriarchy."[14]

An observer in Malaya said it was "more than likely that manangism (shamanism) was originally a profession of women, and that men were gradually admitted to it, at first only by becoming as much like women as possible."[15] The manang or shaman put on female clothing after initiation, and remained a transvestite for life. A Dyak manang still wears women's dress and follows women's occupations. "This transvestism, with all the changes that it involved, is accepted after a supernatural command has been thrice received in dreams: to refuse would be to seek death. This combination of elements shows clear traces of a feminine magic and a matriarchal mythology, which must formerly have dominated the shamanism of the Sea Dyak; almost all the spirits are invoked by the manang under the name of Ini ('Great Mother')."[16]

The Krishna cult as currently practiced in India still demands ritual transvestism for men who adore the feminine principle by identifying themselves with Krishna's Gopis. They wear the clothes and ornaments of women and even observe a "menstrual period" of a few days' retirement each month. According to their theological doctrine, "all souls are feminine to God."[17]

1. Tacitus, 730. 2. Turville-Petre, 219. 3. Oxenstierna, 206. 4. Lederer, 145. 5. Gaster, 316. 6. King, 50. 7. de Voragine, 83, 588. 8. Lawson, 222–23. 9. de Givry, 139. 10. Scot, 71. 11. Gaster, 317. 12. Eliade, S., 346–47. 13. Hays, 416. 14. Eliade, S., 258. 15. Briffault 2, 526–27. 16. Eliade, S., 351–52. 17. Rawson, A.T., 109.

Trefuilngid Tre-Eochair

Irish god of the trefoil (shamrock), known as Triple Bearer of the Triple Key, the same as Shiva the "trident-bearer," referring to a triple phallus designed to fertilize the Triple Goddess. The shamrock-god was assimilated to St. Patrick, another bearer of the trefoil, whose name meant "father" like that of any tribal begetter. Old legends said the Irish god's trefoil produced apple, nut, and oak trees, as well as the five mystic trees representing the five senses.[1] See **Shamrock**; **Trident**.

1. Graves, W.G., 518.

var. Trivia

Trevia

"Three Ways," a Roman title of Hecate as Goddess of three-way crossroads, where her three-faced images received offerings of cake, fruit, or money. She also ruled springs and fountains. Money is still offered to the Roman fountain that bears her name, Trevi.

The modern meaning of "trivia" may be related to early attempts to belittle the cult of the Goddess and render unimportant the old custom of offering gifts to her image for protection on journeys.

Triangle

Tantric tradition said the triangle was the Primordial Image, or the female Triangle of Life.[1] It was known as the Kali Yantra, representing Kali as Cunti, or else as the Yoni Yantra, or sign of the vulva.[2] In Egypt the triangle was a hieroglyphic sign for "woman," and it carried the same meaning among the gypsies, who brought it from their original home in Hindustan.[3] In the Greek sacred alphabet, the *delta* or triangle stood for the Holy Door, vulva of the All-Mother Demeter ("Mother Delta").

Most ancient symbol systems recognized the triangle as a sign of the Goddess's Virgin-Mother-Crone trinity and at the same time as her genital "holy place," source of all life. The triangle represented the Virgin Moon Goddess called Men-Nefer, archaic deity of the first Mother-city of Memphis.[4] The triangle itself was worshipped in much the same way that modern Christians worship the cross. Concerning this, Oriental sages said: "The object of the worship of the Yantra is to attain unity with the Mother of the Universe in Her forms as Mind, Life, and Matter . . . preparatory to Yoga union with Her as She is in herself as Pure Consciousness."[5]

The triangle was everywhere connected with the female trinity, and a frequent component of monograms of Goddesses. To the Gnostics, the triangle signified "creative intellect."[6]

1. Silberer, 170. 2. *Mahanirvanatantra,* 127. 3. Lederer, 141. 4. *Book of the Dead,* 204. 5. Avalon, 428. 6. Koch, 8–9, 54.

Trident

Trident

Symbol of the triple phallus displayed by any god whose function it was to mate with the Triple Goddess; a masculine counterpart of the triangle. In India, the "trident-bearer" was Shiva, bridegroom of threefold Kali.[1] In the west, the trident passed to such underground or abyssal gods as Hades, Pluto, Neptune, and Poseidon, and after them to the Christian devil, their composite descendant.

Celtic myth retained the original phallic significance of the Triple Key to the Holy Door. Like Shiva, the primitive Irish shamrock-god **Trefuilngid Tre-Eochair** was a "bearer of the triple key." Symbol of his Door was the trefoil that the Arabs called *shamrakh* and the Hindus worshipped as an emblem of Kali thousands of years before the first Aryans came to Ireland.[2] The Irish god was quaintly assimilated to Christianity by a Middle Irish text claiming that he appeared to Fintan, king of Tara, on the day of Christ's death, bearing a sacred branch with three fruits, and stone tablets of Celtic property law.[3]

Because the trident was generally recognized as a phallus in pagan tradition, Renaissance "devils" were often pictured with three-pronged or forked penises. A devil "*cum membro bifurcato*" was mentioned in 1520, and a number of inquisitorial judges said witches copulated with devils whose phalli had two or more points.[4]

1. O'Flaherty, 130. 2. *Encyc. Brit.,* "Indus Valley Civilization." 3. Graves, W. G., 518. 4. Robbins, 466.

Triduana, Saint

Christian transformation of the Triple Goddess, Diana Triformis, in Scotland. Triduana was the Three Dianas, a threefold Lady of the Moon. She was credited with the same legend of eye-sacrifice as St. Lucy, the Christian transformation of Juno Lucina (see **Lucy, Saint**). Triduana's shrine at Restalrig was destroyed in 1560 by a church order that declared it "a monument of idolatry."[1] So, even as a saint, she proved to be unacceptable to the church that canonized her.

1. Gifford, 131.

Trinity

From the earliest ages, the concept of the Great Goddess was a trinity and the model for all subsequent trinities, female, male, or mixed. Anatolian villages in the 7th millenium B.C. worshipped a Goddess in three aspects—as a young woman, a birth-giving matron, and an old woman.[1] This typical Virgin-Mother-Crone combination was Parvati-Durga-Uma (Kali) in India, Ana-Babd-Macha (the Morrigan) in Ireland, or in Greece Hebe-Hera-Hecate, the three Moerae, the three Gorgons, the three Graeae, the three Horae, etc. Among the Vikings, the threefold Goddess appeared as the Norns; among the Romans, as the Fates or Fortunae; among the druids, as Diana Triformis. The Triple Goddess had more than three: she had hundreds of forms.

Pre-Roman Latium worshipped her as the Capitoline Triad under the collective name of Uni, "The One," a cognate of *yoni.* Her three *personae* were Juventas the Virgin, Juno the Mother, and Menarva or Minerva the wise **Crone**. Under the empire, Juventas was ousted to make room for a masculine member of the trinity, Jupiter.[2] Some modern scholars refer to the two-female, one-male Capitoline Triad of the later period as "three gods"—as if they might describe a group of two women and one man as "three men."[3]

Like three-headed Kali in India, Egypt's primal mother Mut had three heads and three names. An archaic name for Egypt, *Khem,* with a feminine ending formed the word for "three"—*Khemt.*[4]

Cumont says, "Oriental theologians developed the idea that the world forms a trinity; it is three in one and one in three."[5] The masculine scholar substitutes the neuter "world" for "Goddess," though they were in a sense synonymous. It was she who established the trinitarian form of Creator, Preserver, and Destroyer. Even though Brahmans evolved a male trinity of Brahma, Vishnu, and Shiva to play these parts, Tantric scriptures insisted that the Triple Goddess had created these three gods in the first place.[6]

The three aspects of the Goddess were personified on earth by three kinds of priestesses: Yogini, Matri, Dakini—nubile virgins, mothers, and elder women. These were sometimes called "deities of nature." Manifestations of the Triple Goddess were known as The Three Most Precious Ones.[7]

Negritos of the Malay Peninsula remembered the Goddess as Kari, a virgin who conceived the first man and woman by eating her own lotus; yet she was also a trinity called the "three grandmothers under the earth."[8]

Even in pre-Columbian Mexico the Virgin Goddess who gave birth to the Savior Quetzalcoatl was a trinity, one of "three divine sisters." Like the Semitic Mary, she was a birth-giver, mother, and death-bringer all at once, for she was also known as the Precious Stone of Sacrifice, apparently represented by the altar on which her savior-son's blood was poured out.[9]

Mother of the Greek gods was a trinity composed of Virgin **Hebe**, Mother **Hera**, and Crone **Hecate**; at Stymphalus she was worshipped as Child, Bride, and Widow.[10] Each of her *personae* could be a trinity again, so she could be the Muses or the Ninefold Goddess. Hecate was called Triformis and shown with three faces, each a lunar phase.[11] Among the Irish she was the Triple Morrigan, or Morgan, sometimes multiplied into "nine sisters" who kept the Cauldron of Regeneration and ruled the western isle of the dead.[12]

The Goddess Triformis ruled heaven as Virgin, earth as Mother, and the underworld as Crone, or **Hel**, or Queen of the Shades. This was remembered even in Chaucer's time, for his Palamon invoked her "Three Forms," Luna in heaven, Diana on earth, Proserpine in hell.[13] The old name of Sicily, Trinacria, invoked her as a "center of the earth" with three realms.

Bardic romances abounded in manifestations of the Triple Goddess. Wayland the Smith married her, after she first appeared to him as three magic doves.[14] King Arthur went to Avalon with her. The triadic Guinevere was another version of her. Sir Marhaus (Mars) encountered her as the Three Damosels at their magic fountain: the eldest "threescore winters of age, wearing a garland of gold; the second thirty winters of age, wearing a circlet of gold; the youngest fifteen winters of age, wearing a wreath of flowers."[15] Fifteen was the number of the pagan Virgin **Kore**, the pentacle in the apple. Mythic virgin mothers, like that of Zoroaster, typically gave birth at the age of 15. Double that was the Mother's age, double again the age of the Crone.

The Middle East had many trinities, most originally female. As time went on, one or two members of the triad turned male. The usual pattern was Father-Mother-Son, the Son figure envisioned as a Savior.[16]

The notion of a trinity appeared during the 14th century B.C. among the Hatti and Mitanni. In the 5th century B.C., a popular Babylonian trinity was composed of Shamash, Sin, and Ishtar—Sun, Moon, and Star. In Greece this was repeated as Helios the sun, Selene the moon, and Aphrodite the star. A Father-Mother-Son trinity was worshipped at Costopitum as Jupiter Dolichenus, Celestial Brigantia, and Salus.[17]

Gnostic versions of the trinity followed the Father-Mother-Son patterns of the contemporary east, with the Holy Ghost recognized as a female Sophia, the Dove, worshipped as the Great Goddess in Constantinople, and viewed by most Gnostics as the **Shakti** of God. The Christian God was originally modeled on Far-Eastern heaven-fathers, such as Brahma and Dyaus Pitar, all of whom needed their female sources of "Power," or else they could not act.[18] Therefore, a female member of the triad was essential even to God. Among Arabian Christians there was apparently a holy trinity of God, Mary, and Jesus, worshipped as an interchangeable replacement for the Egyptian trinity of Osiris, Isis, and Horus.[19]

During the Christian era, all-male trinities became popular among Germanic tribes. Woden, Thor, and Saxnot were worshipped together by Saxons of the 8th and 9th centuries. Norsemen called them Odin, Tyr, and Frey. According to a certain fragmentary myth, the Triple Goddess seems to have been burned as a witch. She had to be burned to ashes three times. Afterward, youth, beauty, and love in the person of Freya departed from Asgard; and there was war in heaven.[20]

Like many other remnants of paganism, the female trinity is still associated with marriage. Breton wedding ceremonies celebrated the three phases of the bride's life, impersonating her first by a little girl, then by the mistress of a house, then by an old grandmother.[21] Modern weddings still retain the flower girl and the matron of honor, but—significantly—the Crone figure has vanished.

August Comte nearly revived the female trinity in his vision of woman as mediator between man and the guiding moral spirit. Mother, wife, and daughter were to represent man's unity with past, present, and future; also with what Comte called the three altruistic instincts: veneration, attachment, benevolence.[22] In plainer words, these were what women want from men: respect, love, kindness.

1. Stone, 17. 2. Dumézil, 116. 3. Carter, 26. 4. Budge, G.E. 1, 317. 5. Cumont, A.R.G.R., 69. 6. de Riencourt, 167. 7. Waddell, 129, 169. 8. Hays, 352. 9. Campbell, P.M., 458. 10. Graves, G.M. 1, 52. 11. d'Alviella, 183. 12. Graves, W.G., 406; Rees, 193. 13. Chaucer, 81, 511. 14. Keightley, 215. 15. Malory 1, 115. 16. Briffault 3, 96. 17. Lindsay, O.A., 112, 328, 375; Norman, 71. 18. Zimmer, 25. 19. Ashe, 206. 20. Branston, 112, 213–14. 21. Crawley 2, 51. 22. H. Smith, 401.

Triptolemus

"Three Plowings," name or title of the young god with whom Demeter lay three times in the plowed fields of Crete, before he was slain. He mated three times with the Triple Goddess (naturally) to fertilize each of her; he was not Pluto, the god of the trident, able to do it all at once. Triptolemus's other names were Iasius or Iasion, cognates of Jesus and Jason.[1]

1. Graves, G.M. 1, 89, 93.

Tristan

Cult hero of the courtly-love movement; a wizard, poet, dragon-slayer, lover, and perhaps also a Tantric adept. When he met his Shakti in the form of Iseult, he reversed the syllables of his name and introduced himself as Tantris, which may have been a secret bardic pun or "recognition sign."[1] Though Iseult was the wife of King Mark of Cornwall, the poets called King Mark a "felon" for trying to prevent her from choosing her own lover. As a faithful votary of the Goddess of Love, Tristan was said to have been reincarnated in another of her votaries, **Thomas Rhymer**.

1. Guerber, L.M.A., 238.

Tritone

var. Tritonis

Athenians claimed their Goddess Athene was born from Zeus's head, but her real origin was North African, in "an epoch when fatherhood was not recognized." Her Libyan mother was Tritone, the Third Queen, and her birthplace was Lake Tritonis, "the Three Queens." Herodotus said Athene's dress and the attributes of her cult were borrowed from those of Libyan women.[1] See **Athene**; **Neith**.

1. Graves, G.M. 1, 44.

Trolls

Earth-demons, called *Trulli* in Burton's *Anatomy of Melancholy.*[1] The word "trull," a loose woman, grew from the same root; thus the Troll was probably at first one of the pagan Hags or earth-priestesses.

Norse folklore said trolls commonly sat under bridges, waiting to seize and eat those who crossed the bridge without making them an offering. Association with bridges suggests the Valkyries who guarded Bifröst, the Bridge of Heaven; they too were "trulls" or "trolls." The Angels of Death were said to congregate at a divine Sabbat called the *trolla-thing.*[2]

1. Wedeck, 107. 2. J.B. Russell, 48.

Tuat

Egyptian word for the underworld; sometimes a uterine cavity, sometimes a great snake around the world's outer rim, the same as the Phoenicians' Taaut.

Tuatha Dé Danann

"People of the Goddess Dana," early matriarchal settlers of Ireland, later called fairies who dwelt in their barrow-graves and sacred mounds. Dana, Danu, Ana, Dinah, Diana, and other such names designated the Aryan Great Goddess worshipped by Danes, Celts, Saxons, and many other tribes in Europe and the Middle East.

Tu Kuëh

Legendary eponymous founder of the Turkish nation, suckled and brought up like Romulus by a divine She-Wolf, whom he later married.[1] See **Dog**.

1. Gaster, 228.

Tutela

"Goddess of the City," title of any divine Mother who took a particular town under her protection. Her emblem was the mural crown, signifying that everything within the city walls was held in her thought. Medieval kings copied the crown.

Tutunus

Phallic god of Roman weddings; another name for Priapus. Brides deflowered themselves on the erect penis of the god's statue, in order that the god, not a man, should "open the matrix" as the biblical phrase goes, and the firstborn child could be considered God-begotten.[1] Any woman thus deflowered was described as a Virgin Bride of God. The god himself was a *Christos,* "anointed," because his phallus was anointed with *chrism* or holy oil. The custom was still common in the 4th century A.D. See **Firstborn.**

1. Simons, p. 77.

Twins

Dylan and Lleu, twin powers of darkness and light, were born simultaneously from the womb of Arianrhod, Celtic Goddess of the star-wheel.[1]

Castor and Pollux, twin gods of the morning and evening star, were born simultaneously from the womb of Leda, or Latona, primal mother of the World Egg in Greek myth.[2]

Shaher and Shalem, twin gods of the morning and evening star in Canaan, were born simultaneously from the womb of Helel, the Pit, a dark yonic aspect of the Goddess Asherah, she who swallowed the Father-god El.[3]

Ahura Mazda and Ahriman, God and the devil, were twins born simultaneously from the womb of Zurvan, the primal two-faced androgynous being who personified Infinite Time to the Persians. The event is shown on a famous silver plaque from Luristan, dated in the 8th century B.C.[4]

American Indians said the White Manitu or Lord of Life and the Black Manitu or Lord of Death were twins, born simultaneously from the womb of the Moon-goddess, called The Old Woman Who Never Dies, the real ruler of all gods and men.[5]

Gnostics said the sun god Sol, Helios, or Apollo had a dark twin, known as Sol Niger (Black Sun), king of the nether world. The Chaldeans called him Aciel.[6] The light god was transformed into the dark god when he entered into conjunction with their common mother, the Moon.

Throughout all mythologies the same pair can be found: twins of light and darkness, born from the Great Mother. Every dualistic religion–such as Zoroastrianism–opposing a principle of evil to a principle of good had to begin with the two principles personified as offspring of the primordial womb. Hence the medieval heretics' claim that God and the devil were twin brothers; for if there were no dark twin, then God had to be made responsible for evil. See **Devil**.

1. Squire, 261. 2. Graves, G.M. 1, 246. 3. Hooke, M.E.M., 93. 4. *Larousse*, 323. 5. Briffault 2, 729–32. 6. Jung & von Franz, 200.

Tyche

Greek "Fortune," also called Dike or Moera; the Goddess of Destiny either for the universe, or for the individual soul.[1] Tyche Basileos was the title of the "female soul" or Fortune-goddess of a king. No ruler had any power to act unless the Goddess Tyche looked upon him with favor. See **Fortune**.

1. Lawson, 289.

Typhon

Greek name of the Egyptian ass god Set, whose breath was the hot wind supposed to bring pestilence (typhus). The name was pan-Asiatic: *t'ai fung* in China, *tufan* in Arabia, "typhoon" in southeastern Asia. This god of winds was probably based on the Vedic ass god Ravana. In all the ancient world, a hot desert wind that brought pestilence was called the Breath of the Ass. See **Ass**.

U V

Mary is the West's most famous VIRGIN, but unmarried maidens appeared throughout ancient and medieval history and mythology. This carved and painted wood panel, "Christ in the Virgin's Womb," is German, ca. 1400.

The Roman VENUS is best known as a love goddess, but she was much more, including goddess of birth and death. This early 19th century school-girl painting is called "Venus Drawn by Doves," but the artist and title are actually unknown.

The Saxon goddess Ursel, the She-Bear, was eventually transmogrified into SAINT URSULA by the Christian fathers. She was so smart, pretty, and pure that to marry her, Prince Conon of England met her every whim: 11,000 virgin handmaidens, a three-year pilgrimage to holy shrines, and Conon's own conversion in the bargain. Conon and the 11,000 were dispatched by the Huns, and since Ursula refused to marry their leader, he shot her with three arrows. Benozzo Gozzoli; painting on wood; Florence, 15th century.

Uchati

"Weepers," title of sacred harlots of Ishtar, whose duty it was to make formal lamentations for the dead.[1] They also wailed for the dead savior Tammuz in the temple of Jerusalem, where Ishtar was worshipped as Mari, Queen of Heaven (Ezekiel 8:14). Their title was related to Egyptian Utchatti or Udjatti, Divine Eyes, sacred to the Goddess Maat as the All-Seeing Eye, whose hieroglyphic eye emblem later became associated with the cult of Horus.[2]

1. *Assyr. & Bab. Lit.*, 413. 2. Budge, A.T., 360.

Uma

Kali's Destroyer or Crone aspect, also known as Prisni, mother of the dark season and of the "demon" Maruts and Rudras. In the Skanda Purana, Uma appeared as a demoness with a *vagina dentata:* "hard teeth like thunderbolts with sharp tips inside the vagina."[1] Sometimes Uma was called Daughter of the Mountains, or Daughter of Heaven—that is, of Himalaya, which meant both mountain and heaven. As the wife of Shiva, Uma was a patroness of yogic asceticism. In most of her forms she was recognizable as Mother Death.

1. O'Flaherty, 257.

Umbra

"Shade," the shadow-soul that Greeks, Romans, Egyptians, Semites, and other ancient peoples believed in. After death, the *umbra* went to the Land of Shades, to live a dark, bloodless pseudo-life. See **Shadow**.

Ummati

Title of Assyrian priestesses, meaning "mothers of creation," for *umm* was the Semitic version of the *Om* or Creative Word attributed to Kali in India. To be admitted to the Holy of Holies, a woman had to have borne children to prove she had the spirit of fertility and the "wisdom of motherhood."

Uncle

Before recognition of physical fatherhood, and even for a long time after it, most people viewed a mother's brother as a child's nearest male relative, because he was united with the mother and the mother's mother by the all-important matrilineal blood bond. Hawaiians still use the same word for "father" and "uncle" because formerly they made no distinction between them.[1]

Tacitus said Germanic barbarians regarded the relationship between sister's sons and maternal uncles as "more sacred and binding" than the relationship between sons and fathers.[2] The same was true of the Celts. Early Christian missionaries in Ireland had to call Christ "our sister's son," because that was the only masculine relationship held sacred by the people.[3]

Malory said the whole purpose of introducing Christianity into Britain was to establish laws of patrilineal succession and the authority of father. Among the pagans, fathers and sons cared nothing for one another.[4] Only nephews and maternal uncles had a true blood bond. More recently among the Semang, enlightened sages and prophets were known as nephews of God, not sons of God.[5]

Fathers were of no significance in family relationships among the matrilineal clans of early Latium. Inheriting this tradition, even patriarchal Romans distinguished between a father's brother, *patruus,* and a mother's brother, *avunculus*—derived from *avus,* "ancestor." The *patruus* was unimportant and usually ignored.[6] The *avunculus* was the true uncle, as shown by the very word "uncle" which descended from his title, and "avuncular" which implies a benevolent interest. Europe still retains a linguistic memory of the dual-uncle system. A father's brother is just an uncle; but a mother's brother is called "own uncle."

Systems of uncle relationships were always older than those of paternity, having descended from the matriarchal period when fatherhood was not understood. See **Motherhood**.

1. Farb, W.P., 194. 2. Tacitus, 719. 3. Rees, 145.
4. Malory 2, 179, 199. 5. Eliade, S., 337. 6. M. Harris, 80.

Uni

var. Unial

Etruscan name for the Great Mother's holy trinity, a "three-in-one" Goddess who gave birth to the *uni*-verse. She was represented by the sign of female genitals; Uni was a cognate of "yoni." In Rome, the three were worshipped as the early Capitoline Triad of Virgin-Mother-Crone (Juventas, Juno, Minerva); but in Imperial times the virgin Goddess was removed to make room for Jupiter.[1] The name of Uni evolved into Iune, or Juno.

1. Hays, 181.

Unicorn

Classic symbol of the phallic horse deity, or sacred king incarnate in a horned horse. According to medieval legend, the unicorn could be captured only by a virgin girl, because his irresistible desire was to lay his "horn" in a maiden's lap. While thus engaged, he was incapable of resisting capture. (However, no unicorns were ever captured.)

The unicorn was a secret phallic consort of the virgin Mary, shown inside her "enclosed garden" of virginity, in many examples of Christian mystical art. At times he was identified with the Savior. A medieval hymn called Christ "the wild wild unicorn whom the Virgin caught and tamed."[1]

A source of the unicorn myth may have been the Babylonian dragon-beast made up of a horselike body with lion's forelegs, scales, a snakelike neck and a flat horned head with a single spike growing from the center of the nose.[2] One theory proposes that the unicorn was originally the bull of spring, rearing up and struggling with the lion of summer. Babylonian art showed both animals in profile, so the bull appeared to have only one horn. The British coat of arms still has "the lion and the unicorn" contending in just such a manner.[3]

Explorers thought they found the legendary unicorn in the African rhinoceros. Because of the unicorn's phallic significance, powdered rhinoceros horn became a highly popular "remedy" for impotence, and is so used even today.[4]

1. Harding, 51. 2. Hooke, S.P., 135. 3. Jobes, 254. 4. Woods, 176.

Uraeus

Egyptian serpent symbol, a hieroglyphic sign for "Goddess," suggesting that in pre-dynastic times it was thought all serpents were female and divine. The serpent-mother was one of Egypt's oldest divinities, and her uraeus-snake idol signified healing. Moses copied this Egyptian magic with his "brazen serpent" (Numbers 21:9). Egyptian rulers wore the uraeus-snake in the form of a rearing cobra on the forehead, representing the "third eye" of mystical insight. Despite patriarchal opposition to the symbol of the she-serpent Uraeus, among later Gnostic Christians her name became one of the "secret names of God." See **Serpent**.

Urania

"Celestial One," title of Aphrodite as Queen of Heaven. Her former consort Uranus was transformed into her castrated "father" in classical myth; Uranus's patricidal son threw his severed genitals into the sea, and the sea-womb brought forth Aphrodite. Actually, Celestial Aphrodite and the sea-womb were one and the same: manifestations of the Triple Goddess. The castrated dying god was her ubiquitous son-lover who died, fertilized her by his death, and begot himself again.

Uranus was a western form of Varuna, a deity of indeterminate sex, sometimes a male-turned-female like Hermes or Teiresias. To the Persians he was *varan,* a spirit of sexual intercourse like the Hindu Kama. His name came from *vr,* to envelop—a female function—and he performed female-imitative miracles, such as turning water into blood, giving birth to the sun, and measuring the earth.[1] From the Asian precedents it may be assumed that Urania and Uranus were the same primal androgyne as Jana-Janus, Diana-Dianus, etc.

1. Campbell, Or.M., 177.

Urd

var. Urth

One of the Norse names of Mother Earth, in addition to Urtha, Erda, Eartha, Wyrd, Wurd, Word, Weird, etc. Urd was usually called the divine fount of wisdom tended by the three Norns (Fates) under the root of the World Tree; it was also the name of the oldest Norn, an Earth Goddess who knew everything, past, present, and future. The gods couldn't render judgment unless they gathered at the fount of Urd, because they were helpless without the wisdom imparted by the Urdarbrunnr, "Stream of Urd," which gave life and mind. Old mythologies held that the fount of wisdom was female, and without it neither men nor gods could know anything.[1] Another name for the fountain was Mimir, which means "Mother," although the same name was given later to Odin's maternal uncle, who brought him back to life with fluid from the Mother-spring and taught him the wisdom of the runes.

1. Branston, 76.

Urim and Thummim

Divinatory knucklebones or "dice" used by Jewish priests, probably copied from the oracular knucklebones said to have been invented by Hermes. Kings of Israel governed their acts by the prophecies of the Urim and Thummim (1 Samuel 28:6). Levitical law directed that these articles be carried in the high priest's "breastplate of judgment" whenever he entered the tabernacle, so the *mana* of the holy place would enter into them and yield correct prophecies (Exodus 28:30).

Urine

From Uranus, "Father Heaven," whose magical urine, semen, or blood came down as rain to fertilize Mother Earth. Primitive myths present all three fluids as the fertilizing principle. Zeus came down as "golden rain" of urine to fertilize Danae, the Earth, whose priestesses the Danaids performed rain charms by carrying water in a sieve. According to Aristophanes, rain was caused by Zeus urinating through a sieve. Aristotle mentioned the general belief that "Zeus does not rain in order to make the crops grow, but from necessity," suggesting that Zeus rained for the same reason men urinated—because he had to.[1]

The Danaids founded the Eleusinian rite of Thesmophoria, when the severed genitals of the sacred king were offered to the Goddess, just as the severed genitals of Uranus were given to the sea-womb. The real genitals of a real victim were eventually replaced by symbolic substitutes: serpents and phallus-shaped loaves of bread. But the meaning was the same—a summoning of the god's urine, semen, or blood.[2]

Aeschylus said of the Danaids' performance: "Rain falling from the bridegroom sky makes pregnant the Earth. Then brings she forth for mortals pasture of flocks and corn, Demeter's gift, and the fruitfulness of trees is brought to completion by the dew of their marriage." As the Goddess was both Earth and Sea, the rain-urine-seed-blood, etc., fell on both. The priestesses looked up to the sky and cried, "Rain!" Then they looked down to the earth and cried, "Conceive!"[3]

Rain-making was a chief function of Heavenly Fathers everywhere. Rome's begetting god was Jupiter Pluvius, Jupiter-Who-Makes-Rain, another version of Zeus, who was in turn a replacement for Uranus. Even after the essential fluid was definitely identified as semen, the other fluids were not forgotten. Urine remained a popular rain charm. Shamans in Siberia used to bring rain by "making water" on the naked body of a woman who represented the earth.[4] In Iraq, when rain was wanted, a female dummy called the Bride of God was placed in a field, in the hope that God would "make water" on her.[5]

1. Guthrie, 38. 2. Graves, G.M. 1, 202, 205. 3. Guthrie, 54. 4. Frazer, G.B., 80–81. 5. Briffault 3, 210.

Ursula, Saint

Christianized form of the Saxon Goddess Ursel, or Horsel, the "Ercel" of Thomas Rhymer's Erceldoune, and the Venus of the Horselberg-Venusberg. Ursel means "She-Bear," the title of Artemis Calliste, the same as the Helvetian Goddess Artio, in the guise of Ursa Major, the Great Bear (Big Dipper), whose constellation circles the pole star without disappearing into the sea. The ancients said Artemis the She-Bear ruled all the stars until Zeus usurped her place.[1]

The mythical St. Ursula was accompanied by eleven thousand virgins, a common pagan image of the Moon-goddess accompanied by her children, the stars. One of the Goddess's foremost shrines was Cologne, where "Ursel" was converted into a Christian heroine to account for the reverence paid to her by the local people.

The tale on which Ursula's canonization was based was first invented about the 9th century A.D.; then, "During the 12th century this pious romance was preposterously elaborated through the mistakes of imaginative visionaries; a public burial-ground uncovered at Cologne was taken to be the grave of the martyrs, false relics came into circulation and forged epitaphs of non-existent persons were produced."[2]

The churchmen claimed that St. Ursula was a Breton princess betrothed to Conon, prince of England, in the 5th century A.D. Prior to her marriage, she took her eleven thousand virgins on a pilgrimage. While passing through Cologne, they were attacked and slaughtered by the Huns, at the instigation of two Roman generals who feared the Christian ladies' exemplary piety would convert all the northern barbarians to Christ.[3]

This fable was intended to Christianize the lunar bear-goddess worshipped at Cologne, the same who was Artio, the Helvetian "Mother of Animals," with another cult center at Berne ("She-Bear"), where her portrait still appears on the Bernese coat of arms.[4] Ursel and Artio were alternate names of the triple Artemis who took the "bear-king" Arthur to paradise. The Greeks said Artemis Calliste, "Fairest One," was associated with both the moon and the constellation of the Great Bear. In Britain, Ursa Major was often called "Mistress Ursula," at first a title of the Goddess, later transferred to the saint.[5]

Artemis the She-Bear was so widely recognized as the Mother of Animals that the island once sacred to her, Callista, is still called Thera, "She-Beast."[6] Arcadians traced their descent from her son Arcas, the Little Bear (Ursa Minor), a bear-god like the Celtic Arthur. Hellenic mythographers pretended that Arcas's mother was a mere nymph, Calliste, who was punished for losing her virginity by receiving the form of a bear, along with her child; but Artemis took pity on them and placed them in the stars as Ursa Major and Ursa Minor. This version of the myth was invented "to account for the traditional connection between Artemis and the Great Bear."[7] The Christian version was invented for different reasons, but with the same ultimate aim: to mortalize the Goddess.

Some memory of Ursula the Moon-goddess seems to haunt the foundation of the Ursuline order of nuns, by St. Angela Merici in 1506. Catholic authorities now claim the Ursulines were the oldest order of teaching nuns. But most convents were centers of learning for women until the church forbade women's education in the 13th century.[8] The Ursulines were perhaps the only order of teaching nuns who remained obedient to the papacy, and so were permitted to continue.

Yet the Ursulines began under a cloud of suspicion. Angela Merici was a native of Brescia, which Pope Calixtus III described as a hotbed of witches.[9] Angela's first group of sisters numbered exactly 28, the lunar number. They made their first devotion in a church dedicated to another mythical saint who was only another transformation of the Goddess, St. Afra or Aphra (Aphrodite).[10] Angela was not allowed to establish her holy society of teachers until forty years had passed since her original vision, which she received not in a church but in an open field under the moon. She and her women had no religious habit, no vows, no communal life. They went to their pupils' homes to teach, like itinerant governesses.

The church was not interested in Angela until she underwent "popular" canonization in her home territory. Two centuries later, the church decided to take advantage of the popularity of her cult by declaring her Blessed. Finally in 1807 she was canonized by Pope Pius VII.[11] But she is still almost as vague and dim as the Ursuline lunar She-Bear that the people of Brescia once worshipped. A 20th-century Catholic scholar mentioned her with one of those curious slips of the pen so common among patriarchal writers; he said the Ursuline order was founded by "Bishop Angela of Brescia."[12]

1. Graves, G.M. 1, 86. 2. Attwater, 333–34. 3. Guerber, L.R., 66. 4. *Larousse,* 226. 5. Jobes, 266. 6. Herodotus, 251. 7. Graves, G.M. 1, 84, 86. 8. Bullough, 160. 9. M. Harrison, 240. 10. Attwater, 46. 11. *Encyc. Brit.,* "Angela Merici." 12. Brewster, 459.

Ur-Text

Greatest legendary treasure of medieval Hermetic magic, after the Elixir of Life and the Philosopher's Stone. The Ur-text was supposed to be a magical grammar of the primordial tongue, whose words God pronounced at creation in order to bring forth the things themselves; that is, the words could create, just by being spoken. The idea was based on eastern notions of the creative power of Sanskrit, the Mother-language.[1] Another development of the idea was the Neoplatonic *Logos* or "Seminal Word," which was adopted as a Christian dogma. (See **Logos**.)

Presumably the Ur-text emanated from Abraham's "Ur of the Chaldees," famous as the home of magic and astrology. The medieval theory was that all words and names exerted some influence over their objects, hence the efficacy of both magic spells and liturgies. But in all known languages, the power of the word was slightly displaced from the true essence of the thing, as the calendar was slightly displaced from the sidereal year. In the Ur-text, words were precisely aligned with essences or "souls," so the words could control things and events absolutely.

The implications were the same as in the Hindu idea of the "holy language" of Sanskrit. Knowledge of the Ur-text would give a man absolute power over the universe; whatever he said would come true at once.

Many magicians identified the Ur-text with the equally wonderful *Book of Thoth,* named after the Egyptian god of magic and mentioned in very old Egyptian folk tales as a written version of Thoth's technique for creating by the power of the Word. One story claimed the book was found by a sage named Satni-Khamois in a Memphite tomb. It contained only two formulae but they were great *hekau* (words of power):

> *The two formulae that are written there, if thou recitest the first of them, thou shalt charm the heaven, the earth, the world of the night, the mountains, the waters; thou shalt understand what all the birds of heaven and the reptiles say, as many as there are. Thou shalt behold the fish, for a divine power will bring them to the surface of the water. If thou readest the second formula, even when thou art in the tomb, thou shalt resume the form thou hadst on earth; thou shalt also behold the sun rising in the heavens, and his cycle of gods, also the moon in the form that she has when she appears.*[2]

The first beneficiaries of this wondrous magic became immortal, not by reading the book but by eating the papyrus it was written on—although the book continued to exist, hidden in underwater vessels guarded by the Great Serpent.[3] Eating instead of reading a piece of magical literature was a common Oriental method of absorbing the virtue of magic words even when one is unable to read. In Tibet, Madagascar, China, and Japan it was customary to cure diseases by writing the curative charm on paper and eating the paper, or its ashes.[4] Tartar lamas wrote the names of medicines on paper and made the patient swallow the prescription; for they believed "To swallow the name of a remedy, or the remedy itself . . . comes to precisely the same thing."[5]

The same notion was often found in the west. The modern pharmacist's Rx began as a curative symbol of Saturn, written on paper and eaten by the patient.[6] A common medieval prescription for toothache was a paper bearing the magic words by which Jesus removed a worm from St. Peter's tooth.[7] The Venerable Bede declared that scrapings from the pages of "books that were brought out of Ireland," when drunk in water, instantly cured snakebite.[8]

With so many different kinds of credulity in regard to the written words—especially among the majority to whom all writing was a mysterious, unknown magic—it is hardly surprising that belief in the Book of Books, the Ur-text, survived. Some of the beliefs concerning the Ur-text became attached to the Latin Bible, which the medieval church would not allow to be translated into any other language, even though the readings from the pulpit were quite incomprehensible to most congregations. The theory was that Latin was the language of St. Peter's Roman see, and God intended the Bible to be written in that language and no other; for the magic efficacy of the words lay in their sound, which would be lost if they were rendered in another tongue. Thus, out of superstitious belief in the power of the Word, the church kept the "dead" language of Latin alive within its own in-group for over 1500 years.

1. *Mahanirvanatantra,* cvii. 2. Maspero, 118. 3. Maspero, 129. 4. Gaster, 299. 5. Wedeck, 112. 6. Waddell, 401. 7. Leland, 38. 8. de Paor, 18.

Uta-Napishtim

Babylonian prototype of Noah: the flood hero who carried progenitors of all creatures through the Deluge on his ark. He was the only man to become immortal, because he married the Goddess who dispensed *shiba,* the fluid of life. See **Gilgamesh**.

Uther Pendragon

See **Arthur**.

Uzza

"Powerful One," in Jewish traditions, a rebellious angel who stole divine secrets of magic and revealed them to Eve. Originally, a title of the Arabian Moon-goddess, Al-Uzza, the Powerful One—probably a version of the Crone. See **Arabia**.

Vac

The "Voice" that pronounced the first creative Word, *Om;* a Hindu Goddess described in the Rig Veda as the First, the Queen, the Greatest of All Deities.[1] See **Logos**.

1. Briffault 1, 7.

Vagina Dentata

"Toothed vagina," the classic symbol of men's fear of sex, expressing the unconscious belief that a woman may eat or castrate her partner during intercourse. Freud said, "Probably no male human being is spared the terrifying shock of threatened castration at the sight of the female genitals."[1] But he had the reason wrong. The real reason for this "terrifying shock" is mouth-symbolism, now recognized universally in myth and fantasy: "It is well known in psychiatry that both males and females fantasize as a mouth the female's entranceway to the vagina."[2]

The more patriarchal the society, the more fear seems to be aroused by the fantasy. Men of Malekula, having overthrown their matriarchate, were haunted by a yonic spirit called "that which draws us to It so that It may devour us."[3] The Yanomamo said one of the first beings on earth was a woman whose vagina became a toothed mouth and bit off her consort's penis. Chinese patriarchs said women's genitals were not only gateways to immortality but also "executioners of men."[4] Moslem aphorisms said: "Three things are insatiable: the desert, the grave, and a woman's vulva."[5] Polynesians said the savior-god Maui tried to find eternal life by crawling into the mouth (or vagina) of his mother Hina, in effect trying to return to the womb of the Creatress; but she bit him in two and killed him.[6]

Stories of the devouring Mother are ubiquitous in myths, representing the death-fear which the male psyche often transformed into a sex-fear. Ancient writings describe the male sexual function not as "taking" or "possessing" the female, but rather "being taken," or "putting forth."[7] Ejaculation was viewed as a loss of a man's vital force, which was "eaten" by a woman. The Greek *sema* or "semen" meant both "seed" and "food." Sexual "consummation" was the same as "consuming" (the male). Many savages still have the same imagery. The Yanomamo word for pregnant also means satiated or full-fed; and "to eat" is the same as "to copulate."[8]

Distinction between mouths and female genitals was blurred by the Greek idea of the lamiae—lustful she-demons, born of the Libyan snake-goddess Lamia. Their name meant either "lecherous vaginas" or "gluttonous gullets."[9] Lamia was a Greek name for the divine female serpent called Kundalini in India, Uraeus or Per-Uatchet in Egypt, and Lamashtu in Babylon. Her Babylonian consort was Pazuzu, he of the serpent penis. Lamia's legend, with its notion that males are born to be eaten, led to Pliny's report on the sexual life of snakes that was widely believed throughout Europe even up to the 20th century: a male snake fertilizes the female snake by putting his head into her mouth and allowing himself to be eaten.[10]

Sioux Indians told a tale similar to that of the Lamia. A beautiful seductive woman accepted the love of a young warrior and united with him inside a cloud. When the cloud lifted, the woman stood alone. The man was a heap of bones being gnawed by snakes at her feet.[11]

Mouth and vulva were equated in many Egyptian myths. Ma-Nu, the western gate whereby the sun god daily re-entered his Mother, was sometimes a "cleft" (yoni), and sometimes a "mouth."[12] Priestesses of Bast, representing the Goddess, drew up their skirts to display their genitals during religious processions.[13] To the Greeks, such a display was frightening. Bellerophon fled in terror from Lycian women advancing on him with genitals exposed, and even the sea god Poseidon retreated, for fear they might swallow him.[14]

According to Philostratus, magical women "by arousing sexual desire seek to devour whom they wish."[15] To the patriarchal Persians and Moslems this seemed a distinct possibility. Viewing women's mouths as either obscene, dangerous, or overly seductive, they insisted on veiling them. Yet men's mouths, which look no different, were not viewed as threatening.

"Mouth" comes from the same root as "mother"—Anglo-Saxon *muth,* also related to the Egyptian Goddess Mut. Vulvas have *labiae,* "lips," and many men have believed that behind the lips lie teeth. Christian authorities of the Middle Ages taught that certain witches, with the help of the moon and magic spells, could grow fangs in their vaginas. They likened women's genitals to the "yawning" mouth of hell, though this was hardly original; the underworld gate had always been the yoni of Mother Hel. It had always "yawned"—from Middle English *yonen,* another derivative of "yoni." A German vulgarity meaning "cunt," *Fotze,* in parts of Bavaria meant simply "mouth."[16]

To Christian ascetics, Hell-mouth and the vagina drew upon the same ancient symbolism. Both were equated with the womb-symbol of the whale that swallowed Jonah; according to this "prophecy" the Hell-mouth swallowed Christ (as Hina swallowed her son Maui) and kept him for three days. Visionary trips to hell often read like "a description of the experience of being born, but in reverse, as if the child was being drawn into the womb and destroyed there, instead of being formed and given life." St. Teresa of Avila said her vision of a visit to hell was "an oppression, a suffocation, and an affliction so agonizing, and accompanied by such a hopeless and distressing misery that no words I could find would adequately describe it. To say that it was as if my soul were being continuously torn from my body is as nothing."[17]

The archetypal image of "devouring" female genitals seems undeniably alive even in the modern world. "Males in our culture are so afraid of direct contact with female genitalia, and are even afraid of referring to these genitalia themselves; they largely displace their feelings to the accessory sex organs—the hips, legs, breasts, buttocks, et cetera—and they give these accessory organs an exaggerated interest and desirability."[18] Even here, the male scholar inexplicably "displaces" the words sex organ onto structures that have nothing to do with sexual functioning.

Looking into, touching, entering the female orifice seems fraught with hidden fears, signified by the confusion of sex with death in overwhelming numbers of male minds and myths. Psychiatrists say sex is perceived by the male unconscious as dying: "Every orgasm is a little death: the death of 'the little man,' the penis."[19] Here indeed is the root of ascetic religions that equated the denial of death with denial of sex.

Moslems attributed all kinds of dread powers to a vulva. It could "bite off" a man's eye-beam, resulting in blindness for any man who looked into its cavity. A sultan of Damascus was said to have lost his sight in his manner. Christian legend claimed he went to Sardinia to be cured of his blindness by a miraculous idol of the virgin Mary—who, being eternally virgin, had her door-mouth permanently closed by a veil-hymen.[20]

Apparently Freud was wrong in assuming that men's fear of female genitals was based on the idea that the female had been castrated. The fear was much less empathetic, and more personal: a fear of being devoured, of experiencing the birth trauma in reverse. A Catholic scholar's curious description of the Hell-mouth as a womb inadvertently reveals this idea: "When we think of man entering hell we think of him as establishing contact with the most intrinsic, unified, ultimate and deepest level of the reality of the world."[21]

1. Becker, D.D., 223. 2. Farb, W.P., 93. 3. Neumann, G.M., 174. 4. Rawson, E.A., 260. 5. Edwardes, 45. 6. Briffault 2, 657–58. 7. *Assyr. & Bab. Lit.*, 338–39. 8. Chagnon, 47. 9. Graves, G.M. 1, 206. 10. Briffault 2, 667. 11. Campbell, F.W.G., 78. 12. Maspero, lx. 13. Budge, G.E. 1, 448. 14. Bachofen, 123. 15. Wedeck, 153. 16. Young, 47. 17. Cavendish, P.E., 157–58. 18. Ellis, 239–40. 19. Lederer, 126. 20. Gifford, 143. 21. Cavendish, P.E., 160.

Vajra

Sanskrit "jewel," "phallus," or "lightning"—images of the Jewel in the Lotus, male spirit enclosed in the female, graphically represented by the lingam-yoni. *Vajrasana* meant the "diamond seat" of the Tantric yogi, a mystic state of psychosexual union with the Goddess. As a diamond shape was an archaic symbol of the clitoris, it may be that the *vajra* was recognized as an enlarged male version of the same thing. See **Lotus**.

Va-Kul

Zyrian "Mother of Waters," worshipped throughout the Middle Ages as a powerful Goddess whose displeasure could cause catastrophes.[1] See **Water**.

1. *Larousse*, 307.

Valentine, Saint

The original Valentine's Day in the ides of February was Rome's Lupercalia, a festival of sexual license. Young men chose partners for erotic games by drawing "billets"—small papers—with women's names on them. Christians denounced these prototypical valentines as "heathens' lewd customs."[1] Churchmen tried to substitute saints' names and short sermons on the billets, but people soon reverted to the old love-notes.[2] February was sacred to Juno Februata, Goddess of the "fever" (*febris*) of love. The church replaced her with a mythical martyr, St. Valentine, who was endowed with several contradictory biographies. One of them made him a handsome Roman youth, executed at the very moment when his sweetheart received his billet of love.[3]

St. Valentine became a patron of lovers perforce, because the festival remained dedicated to lovers despite all official efforts to change it. Even in its Christianized form, the Valentinian festival involved secret sex worship, called "a rite of spiritual marriage with angels in a nuptial chamber."[4] Ordinary human beings engaged before witnesses in an act of sexual intercourse described as the marriage of Sophia and the Redeemer. A spoken formula said, in part, "Let the seed of light descend into thy bridal chamber, receive the bridegroom . . . open thine arms to embrace him. Behold, grace has descended upon thee."[5]

During the Middle Ages, St. Valentine was much invoked in love charms and potions, since he was a sketchily Christianized version of such love-gods as Eros, Cupid, Kama, Priapus, or Pan.

1. Brewster, 104. 2. Hazlitt, 608. 3. de Lys, 358. 4. Angus, 116. 5. Seligmann, 65.

Valkyries

Norse death angels who hovered over battlefields and took the souls of brave warriors to Odin's heaven, Valhalla—according to the classic picture. Previously, the Valkyries seem to have been Amazonian priestesses who ruled the gates of death, and in the most primitive times even cannibalized the dead to give them rebirth.

Valkyries were northern counterparts of the funerary vulture-priestesses of Egypt, often decking themselves in feathers. Like angelic Hindu apsaras, they wore swan feathers; or, in funerary aspect, they appeared as carrion crows (ravens). Dead warriors were known in skaldic verse as *hrafengrennir,* "raven-feeders," and the blood of slain men was called "the raven's drink."[1] In Old Saxon the Valkyries were *walcyries* or *waelceasig,* "corpse-eaters," defined as "man-eating women" during the 11th century A.D.[2]

Valkyries in their black raven-feathers were called Kraken, or "crows." In the Middle East also, ravens were spirits of the lunar sphere of death and rebirth, symbolically preserved in Mithraic religion as the Raven who led the initiate into the first stage of mystical hierarchy, the sphere of the Moon.[3] Similar connotations were still attached to ravens in 1613 A.D., when Perkins's *Witchcraft* said if a raven stands on a high place (lunar sphere), "and looks a particular way and cries," death can be expected to come from that direction.[4]

Swans, ravens, crows, or hawks represented Valkyries in old ballads, such as "The Maiden Transformed into a Bird," who was fond of eating her true-love's flesh. This was beneficial to him, for after sacrificing his flesh to her, he attained a state of paradise in her arms.[5] Eliade says, "The Valkyries are psychopomps and sometimes play the role of the 'celestial wives' or 'spirit wives' of the Siberian shamans. . . . [T]his later complex extends beyond the sphere of shamanism and has elements both of the mythology of Woman and the mythology of Death."[6]

The Valkyries were also totemized as mare-women, like the ancient horse-masked priestesses of Demeter. In Sweden, a mare-woman was a *volva,* meaning Goddess, priestess, or a witch who could turn into a mare and carry a man away to death. A cognate was *vala,* a holy woman, with Slavic and central Asian counterparts in the Vilas, Wilas, or Wilis, possibly derived from *vilasa,* the heavenly bliss dispensed by Hindu nymphs of paradise in the service of the Goddess.[7] Such spirits were sometimes called Samovila or Samodiva: "death-goddess."[8] Some claimed that death in the arms of a Vila was a blissful passage into a fairy paradise. Others said it was cruel torment.[9] Naturally, this was a mythic expression of various ways of dying. See **Vila**.

The *Grimnismal* lists 13 Valkyries, the number of a witches' coven; other sources said there were only nine, the number of the Muses. From the 10th to the 14th centuries, Valkyries and witches were considered identical; both were also mystic swan-maidens and fairies.[10] Earthly priestesses who played the Valkyrie role in pagan funerals were described by churchmen as either Vilas or witches.[11]

Valhalla or Valhöll was the death-realm of Hel, the Great Vala. Though it was taken over by new gods led by Father Odin, its archaic feminine name remained. Later myths made it a paradise reserved solely for warriors and war-kings, members of the military caste who shared the opinions of Japanese *samurai* and Moslem "soldiers of Allah," that heavenly bliss belonged only to those who died fighting bravely.

Radbod, king of the Frisians, refused to abandon this faith when a Christian missionary informed him that Valhalla was the same as the Christians' hell. Where were his own ancestors, Radbod wanted to know, if there was no Valhalla? He was told they were burning in hell because they were heathens. "Dastardly priest!" Radbod cried. "How dare you say my ancestors have gone to hell? I would rather—yes, by their god, the great Woden, I swear—I would ten thousand times rather join those heroes in their hell, than be with you in your heaven of priests!"[12]

1. Turville-Petre, 58. 2. Woods, 156. 3. Campbell, Oc.M., 255, 4. Scot, 546. 5. Steenstrup, 53–54. 6. Eliade, S., 381–82. 7. Avalon, 199. 8. Leland, 67. 9. *Larousse,* 292–93. 10. Branston, 191–92. 11. Leland, 143. 12. Guerber, L.R., 9.

Vampire

The primal notion that all life depends on the magic of **menstrual blood**—or "the blood of Moon," as some primitives say—evolved a corresponding notion that the dead crave blood in order to make themselves live again.[1] Greeks believed the shades of the dead could be recalled from the underworld by offerings of blood, which they greatly desired; therefore blood was the essential ingredient of necromancy. Homer's Odysseus consulted the dead with a necromantic ceremony: "I took the sheep and cut their throats over the trench, and the dark blood flowed forth, and lo, the spirits of the dead that be departed gathered them from out of Erebus."[2]

The Greek word for a vampire was *sarcomenos,* "flesh made by the moon."[3] The word "vampire" was Slavic, possibly traceable to central Asia, thence to India. The Siamese still call a lunar sabbath day *vampra.* As in early Greece, there were two *vampra* sabbaths in each lunar month, at the new moon and full moon, with lesser sabbaths on the quarters to make four seven-day weeks.[4]

Ever since Homer's time, western nations had the fixed idea that blood could recall the dead to life, at least temporarily. Regular supplies of blood would impart a kind of life to the "un-dead," that is, vampires. They were called forth by the moon, their original Mother, who also called forth the blood that made the living. Since the moon was the original home of the dead and the source of rebirth, it was closely associated with vampires. Breton churchmen, still not altogether certain of the physiology of conception in the Middle Ages, claimed that a woman who exposed her naked body to moonlight would conceive and bear a vampire child.[5] Yet common folk continued to express in their customs the older belief that the souls of all children waited in the moon to be reborn. Scottish girls refused to be married at any time except during the full moon, for fear they otherwise might not have children. New brides in the Orkneys went to a circle of megalithic stones locally called the Temple of the Moon to pray for babies.[6]

The idea that the moon provided vital force for both the living and the dead persisted through the centuries, and reappeared as emphatically as ever in popular vampire literature only a hundred years ago. Boucicault's *The Vampire* instructed his servants to carry his body to a high mountain where it could be touched by the first rays of the rising moon. When this was done, the vampire sprang back to life, saying, "Fountain of my life: once more thy rays restore me. Death! I defy thee!"[7] An English friar once said, "The moon is the mother of all humors," and the body's most important life-giving "humor" was blood.[8]

Therefore, vampires walked wherever the moon shone and they might find blood; the church taught this, and no laymen dared to doubt it. Balkan countries had certain wizards who specialized in bottling vampires, a technique they probably learned from Arabian magicians who put *djinn* (Latin *genii*) into bottles or lamps, like the lamp of Aladdin. When a Bulgarian village panicked over a purported outbreak of vampirism, the specialist was called. He would solemnly identify the offender's grave, bait his bottle with blood, catch the restless spirit, cork him up, and burn the bottle.[9]

The Rev. Montague Summers mentions a sure cure for vampirism, which would have been simple, and eliminated all the dramatic, time-consuming, ultimately ineffective classical measures such as exorcisms, crucifixes, garlic, silver bullets, stakes through hearts, and so on. This simple solution was to place a consecrated host in a vampire's grave, which would immobilize him forever. However, Summers said, this remedy "was not to be essayed, since it savors of rashness and profanation of God's Body."[10] Summers, an earnest believer, evidently thought it was better to let a community be ravaged by marauding vampires than to profane Eucharistic bread.

Summers also attacked the rational doubts of Dom Calmet, who wrestled with the physical improbabilities of vampirism two centuries earlier, asking questions that no one ever bothered to answer:

> *How can a corpse which is covered with four or five feet of earth, which has no room even to move or to stretch a limb, which is wrapped in linen cerements, enclosed in a coffin of wood, how can it, I say, seek the upper air and return to the world walking upon the earth so as to cause those extraordinary effects which are attributed to it? And after all that how can it go back again into the grave, when it will be found fresh, incorrupt, full of blood exactly like a living body? Can it be maintained that these corpses pass through the earth without disturbing it, just as water and the damps which penetrate the soil or which exhale therefrom without perceptibly dividing or cleaving the ground? It were indeed to be wished that in the histories of the Return of Vampires which have been related, a certain amount of attention had been given to this point, and that the difficulty had been something elucidated.*[11]

Rev. Summers quickly disposed of Dom Calmet's questions in the accepted theological manner, not by answering them but by denouncing the asking of them:

> *These difficulties which Dom Calmet with little perception has raised . . . are not only superficial but also smack of heterodoxy. . . . [O]ne can hardly brush aside the vast vampire tradition. . . . Can the Devil endow a body with those qualities of subtilty, rarification, increase, and diminishing, so that it may pass through doors and windows? I answer that there is no doubt the Demon can do this, and to deny the proposition is hardly orthodox.*[12]

From the church's "vast vampire tradition," Summers concluded: "There can be no doubt that the vampire does act under satanic influence and by satanic direction."[13] This assertion was made not in the 12th or 13th century, but in the year 1928.

A thinly disguised reason for the never-failing popularity of vampire stories was, of course, their suggestion of sinful sex. Kissing and biting ran close together in both mental and actual behavior; and the attack of a male or female vampire on a victim of the opposite sex surely bore some resemblance to a love-bite. One of the all-time classics of vampire literature, Prest's *Varney the Vampire,* titillated Victorian male readers with scenes more suggestive of rape than of demonology:

> *That young and beautiful girl exposed to so much terror . . . . Her beautiful rounded limbs quivered with the agony of her soul. The glassy horrible eyes of the figure ran over that angelic form with a hideous satisfaction—horrible profanation. He drags her head to the bed's edge. He forces it back by the long hair still entwined in his grasp. With a plunge he seizes her neck in his fanglike teeth.*[14]

The church sanctioned vampire superstitions in order to draw converts through fear, and church rituals officially established the burning or piercing of suspected vampires in their graves. Even in the present century this was still done by priests in the Balkans.[15] Jean-Jacques Rousseau showed the evidence for the existence of vampires resting on much the same foundations as the evidence for the existence of God: "If there ever was in the world a warranted and proven history, it is that of vampires; nothing is lacking, official reports, testimonials of persons of standing, of surgeons, of clergymen, of judges; the judicial evidence is all-embracing."[16]

The most famous fictional vampire of them all, Count Dracula, did have a real history. He was a feudal baron of sadistic temperament, Vlad the Impaler, of the Little Dragon clan: that is, *Dracule.* He liked to impale his enemies on stakes, while he cut, roasted, and ate pieces of flesh from their still-living bodies.[17] The fear engendered by this monster was such that his serfs believed he would return to plague them even after his death. Of course no such revenant has ever reappeared, but the Count's clan nickname, at least, seems truly immortal.

1. Chagnon, 38. 2. Homer, 163. 3. Summers., V., 19. 4. Briffault 2, 425. 5. Summers, V., 238. 6. Briffault 2, 587–88. 7. Summers, V., 316. 8. Briffault 2, 782. 9. Tannahill, 124. 10. Summers, V., 106. 11. Summers, V., 171. 12. Summers, V., 174. 13. Summers, V., 32. 14. Cohen, N.H.U.T., 53. 15. Hyde, 182–83. 16. Seligmann, 302. 17. See McNally & Florescu.

Vanir

Scandinavian elder deities: peace-loving, matriarchal, agricultural nature spirits led by Mother Earth and by Freya, "the Lady," called *Vanadís* or Matriarch of the Vanir. The warlike **Aesir** led by Father Odin moved into the territory of the Vanir and made war against them, beginning with an act of cruelty: the Aesir seized and tortured their holy sorceress, Gullveig.[1] In the end the Vanir were conquered, but many generations remained in awe of their miraculous powers. They were said to have accomplished everything by magic, and invented all the knowledge that the new gods learned.[2]

Whether the Vanir were described as elder gods, giants, elves, matriarchs, or "primal ancestresses," they seem to have represented pre-patriarchal farming cultures who were forced to give way to nomadic Aryan invaders.

1. *Larousse,* 270. 2. Turville-Petre, 159, 176.

Varuna

Son of the Hindu sun-goddess Aditi, Varuna was an archaic god of Protean forms: lord of the sky, of waters, of law, of winds, of seasons, and of death. He was sometimes female, sometimes an androgyne representing sexual union. In this guise, he-she probably became the Persian *Varan,* a "spirit of concupiscence." Varuna was paired with Mitra, a similar entity, a sister or male twin; from this deity evolved the Persians' wholly masculinized **Mithra**.

1. *Larousse,* 328.

Vas Hermeticum, Vas Spirituale

Alchemical terms for the symbolic Grail, signifying the womb of matter, a universal vessel of all transformations. The original symbol was the "Vase" of life and death representing the womb of the Great Goddess Rhea Pandora. Among Christian mystics, Vas Spirituale was a common title of the virgin Mary.

Venus

Sign of Venus

Roman name for the Great Goddess in her sexual aspect, derived from the eponymous mother of Venetian tribes of the Adriatic, after whom the city of Venice was also named. "Veneration" and "venery" were further derivatives. Venery used to mean hunting; for, like her eastern counterpart Artemis, Venus was once a Lady of Animals, and her Horned God—Adonis, both the hunter and the sacrificial stag—became *venison,* which meant "Venus's son."[1]

Early Christian fathers denounced the temples "dedicated to the foul devil who goes by the name of Venus—a school of wickedness for all the votaries of unchasteness."[2] What this meant was that they were schools of instruction in sexual techniques, under the tutelage of the *venerii* or harlot-priestesses.[3] They taught an approach to spiritual grace, called *venia,* through sexual exercises like those of **Tantrism.**[4]

Like Tantric yogis, educated Romans envisioned the moment of death as a culminating sexual union, a final act of the sacred marriage promised by the religion of Venus. Ovid, an initiate, said he wished to die while making love: "Let me go in the act of coming to Venus; in more senses than one let my last dying be done."[5] Centuries later, in Shakespeare's time, "to die" was still a common metaphor for sexual orgasm.[6] An English treatise on interpretation of dreams said if a sick man dreamed of marrying a lovely maiden, it meant death.[7] When Christians said to die was to be gathered to the bosom of Christ or Abraham, they unwittingly based the concept on the ancient female one.

Modern interpretations of classical mythology tend to picture Venus as a sex goddess only. Her birth-giving and death-giving aspects have been suppressed; but they were equally important in her cult. As Queen of the Shades she was identified with Proserpine, but went by the name of Libitina. Plutarch said Libitina was only another name for Venus, "the goddess of generation."[8]

During the early Middle Ages, Venus became the ruling Fairy Queen of the magic mountains called Venusbergs. She also became a Christian saint, St. Venerina, who never existed in human form but only as a cult figure continuing the worship of the Goddess in Calabria.[9] In the Balkans she was called St. Venere, and is still invoked as a patron of marriage by young girls making a wish that they might find good husbands.[10] The magic rhyme addressed to the planet Venus as Evening Star still echoes down the centuries: "Star light, star bright, first star I see tonight, I wish I may, I wish I might, have the wish I wish tonight."

Venus the Evening Star was also Stella Maris, Star of the Sea. In her sacred city of Venice, on Ascension Day each year, the Duke of Venice ceremonially married her by throwing a gold wedding ring into the sea.[11] This practice continued through Renaissance times, even when the title of Stella Maris was assimilated to Mary.

1. Potter & Sargent, 209. 2. J.H. Smith, C.G., 287. 3. Massa, 101. 4. Dumézil, 94. 5. Cavendish, P.E., 51. 6. Sadock, Kaplan & Freedman, 544. 7. Hazlitt, 190. 8. Knight, D.W.P., 73. 9. Hughes, 52. 10. Hyde, 84. 11. Scot, 173.

Venus Observa

Technical term for the male-superior sexual position, which Adam tried and failed to impose on Lilith, and which the Catholic church designated the only legal position for marital intercourse, since it afforded the least pleasure to the wife.[1] Patriarchal societies generally opposed such female-superior sexual positions as those favored by the worshippers of Shiva and Hecate, and by medieval witches who, as the nursery rhyme says, rode on top of their "cock-horses."

Christian missionaries throughout the world usually insisted that their native flocks must abandon any sexual variations they might be accustomed to, and adopt the *Venus observa* posture exclusively, for anything else was sinful. Thus it came to be known as the "missionary position," and native couples often made fun of it in secret.

1. Graves & Patai, 67.

Veronica, Saint

St. Veronica was not a person but only a contraction of two Latin words, *vera iconica,* "the true image." In 8th-century Rome, a cloth imprinted with a man's face appeared in St. Peter's basilica and was advertised as the *vera iconica* of Christ. The legend invented to account for it was that, as Jesus was carrying his cross, a woman named Veronica wiped the sweat from his face with her veil, which miraculously took the image of the divine face.[1]

Such stories were not uncommon in the ancient world. An old Greek tale told of Pandarus the Thessalian, who had "shameful letters" on his brow until the god Asclepius miraculously removed them to a scarf that Pandarus bound on his forehead.[2] Another pagan tale was adapted to the Veronican legends: the king of Edessa sent an artist to paint Jesus's portrait; but the artist couldn't see Jesus's face because of its blinding sunlike brightness. So he merely pressed a cloth to the divine features, and the imprint rendered a perfect portrait. Another impossible story claimed that Veronica's veil cured the emperor Tiberius of sickness, so he carried it to Rome on a road entirely spread with silk and installed it in the shrine where it was "found" eight centuries later.[3]

St. Veronica's act of veil-imprinting is still included in the Stations of the Cross, though some churchmen recommended its elimination on the ground that the legend's transparent fakery is becoming too well known.[4]

1. Brewster, 65. 2. Frazer, F.O.T., 227. 3. de Voragine, 215, 634. 4. Attwater, 335.

Verthandi

Second of the three **Norns** venerated by Norsemen. Verthandi signified the present, while her sisters Urth and Skuld stood for the past and future.[1] As the **Weird Sisters**, or Mothers of Fate (*wyrd*), they corresponded to the Greek Moerae, Latin Fortunae, and other versions of the Triple Goddess. Verthandi also governed motherhood and the phases of the moon, like Kali the Preserver.

1. Branston, 209.

Vesica Piscis

Vesica Piscis

"Vessel of the Fish," a common yonic symbol, the pointed oval, named from the ancients' claim that female genitals smelled like fish. Mother Kali herself appeared in a Hindu story as "a virgin named Fishy Smell, whose real name was Truth," like Egypt's Goddess Maat.[1] Egyptians said Abtu, the Abyss, was "a fish who swallowed the penis of Osiris," but this abyss was also "The Fish of Isis," therefore a sexual metaphor. Aphrodite's principal rites at Paphos took place under the sign of Pisces, the Fish. Aphrodite, Isis, Freya, and other forms of the Goddess in sexual aspect appeared veiled in fish nets.[2] See **Fish**.

The *vesica piscis* was an unequivocally genital sign of the **sheila-na-gig** figures of old Irish churches. The squatting naked Goddess displayed her vulva as a vesica, as did the temple-door images of Kali in India.[3] One of the old pagan ideograms of sexual union was adopted by the church to represent the Feast of St. Nicholas on the runic calendar: a *vesica piscis* enveloping a male furka.[4]

The pointed-oval fish sign was even used by early Christians to represent the mystery of God's union with his mother-bride—which is why Jesus was called "the little Fish" in the Virgin's fountain.[5]

This female enclosure was much used in Christian art, especially as a superimposition on Mary's belly, with her child within. Sometimes Christ at his ascension was shown rising into a heavenly vesica, as if returning to the Mother-symbol. The vesica was also shown as a frame for figures of Jesus, God, and saints.

Another name for the same sign was *mandorla,* "almond," which also represented a yoni. In the cult of the Magna Mater, an almond was the feminine conception-charm for the virgin birth of Attis.

1. Campbell, C.M., 13. 2. Knight, S.L., 296. 3. G.R. Scott, 239–43. 4. Brewster, 13. 5. Harding, 58.

Vestal Virgins

Sign of Vesta

Priestesses of Rome's oldest Goddess-matriarch, Vesta, who was the same as the Greeks' Hestia. Descendants of an ancient order of holy women who guarded the public hearth and altar, the Vestals were entrusted with keeping alight the perpetual fire that was the mystic heart of the empire.

Vestals were *virgines,* i.e., women who vowed never to marry because they were brides of the spirit of Rome, in the same sense that Christian nuns were brides of Christ. Vestals underwent the same ceremony that was later applied to nuns, to limit their magic female powers: they had their hair shaved off.[1] In an earlier era, however, they were not so restricted. Like all other ancient priestesses who ruled by virtue of magic and motherhood, the Vestals used to be the governing sisterhood of Latium.

Rhea Silvia or "Rhea of the Woodland" was called the First Vestal; she was actually the Goddess Rhea transplanted to the Latin colonies. According to Roman legend, she gave birth to Romulus and Remus, the founders of Rome. Their midwife, Acca Larentia, another Vestal described as a "courtesan," gave birth to all the ancestral spirits the Romans called *lares.* (See **Akka**.)

The Vestals were never altogether virginal in the physical sense. Their marriage to the phallic deity of the **Palladium** was physically consummated in Vesta's temple, under conditions of great secrecy. The ceremony was performed by a priest called the Pontifex Maximus, "great maker of the *pons,*" which meant a bridge, a path, or a way. The Pontifex Maximus had what Dumézil calls "an obscure, now unknown duty" toward the Vestal Virgins.[2] One might suppose that his "way" was something like the Way of eastern sex-sacraments; that is, he built the "bridge" between Father Heaven and Mother Earth (Vesta).

The office of Pontifex was adopted by Christians, and became a "pontiff," synonymous with "pope." The Vestals however were emphatically *not* adopted by Christians, although several of the details of their habit and lifestyle passed on to Christian convents. Pagans revered the Vestals and were horrified by the way they were treated by Christian regimes in the 4th and 5th centuries. In 382 A.D., the endowments of all the pagan temples were withdrawn, including that of Vesta's 600-year-old Mother-hearth. "Worst of all in the opinion of some traditionalists, the fire on Vesta's hearth was to be permitted to go out: the Vestal Virgins were to lose their endowments and immunity from taxation, and all their privileges were to be taken away. The tiny order of six Vestals was particularly hated by the Christians. . . . Their Christian enemies feared them as mysterious and magical: they did not understand them and did not want to do so; they wanted only to see them destroyed."[3]

1. Graves, W.G., 396. 2. Dumézil, 583. 3. J.H. Smith, D.C.P., 149.

Vida

Norse skald's word for the sacred poetry setting forth religious tales; cognate with the Hindu Vedas. *Vida* might be traced back to the elder race of giants called *risi,* from Sanskrit *rishi,* an Enlightened One or sage, such as the early collectors of the Vedas were supposed to be.[1]

1. Turville-Petre, 231.

Vidya

"Wisdom," a Tantric term for a woman acting as sexual partner of a man in the magic circle; another epithet of the enlightenment-bringing Spirit of the Way, or Shakti.

Vikarr

Ancestor of the Vikings; a legendary king of Norway, sacrificially slain by the priests of Odin, enabled to beget tribes by the blood he shed on the maternal earth.

Vila

var. Wili

Slavic witch-spirit associated with water; cognate of the Scandinavian Vala or **Valkyrie**. Russian Vilas were sometimes known as Rusalki, daughters of Holy Mother Russia (Earth). Like Valkyries, the Vilas of old had charge of the rites of death and the guiding of souls.

Sometimes, especially favored men were invited to join the Vilas for a while, usually seven years. A man would be invited into a cave or hollow tree, and find himself in fairyland. He was "one who has won the love of a Vila," and his title was *Krstnik,* a "Christ," which meant both an Anointed One and an Accursed One.[1] That is, he was the Slavic version of the Enchanted Hunter *(Chasseur Maudit),* or **Thomas Rhymer**, **Tannhäuser**, etc.

In Dalmatia, a man associated with the Vilas was called Macieh, "Messiah." He took the form of a youth in a Phrygian cap, like the Indo-Iranian sun-hero Mithra.[2] The female spirits he lived with were also called *krstaca,* "crossed ones," from *krst,* a cross—cognate with both the Greek *Christos* and the Saxon "curst." The female spirits were also known as Rogulja, "Horned Ones."[3]

Vilas or Wilis came to be feared as angry, dangerous "souls of drowned women" who dwelt in water, perhaps because so many "witches" were drowned. Like Sirens, they were supposed to draw into the waters any heedless wayfarer who happened to see them dance by moonlight. They still dance on modern stages in the classical ballet *Giselle;* the old fear of them resides in such phrases as "it gives me the willies." A cold shudder was said to be a prophetic touch from a Wili's deathly hand. However, traces of the priestesses' former benevolence are found in the legend that where they danced on the nights of the old pagan festivals, there the grass grew thicker and the wheat flourished more abundantly.[4]

1. Leland, 145–46. 2. Keightley, 494. 3. Leland, 66. 4. *Larousse,* 292–93.

Virginal the Ice Queen

Medieval European version of the high-mountain Goddess, known in India as Durga the Inaccessible. She lived in the high Himalayas, and sometimes came down to form alliances with men; but always she returned to her lonely glaciers. In European folk tales, Virginal the Ice Queen lived alone in the pure upper snowfields of the mountains, but once she descended to a valley to become the bride of a minstrel-wizard, Dietrich von Bern. Soon, however, she wearied of the lowlands and of him, and went back to her inviolable mountaintop, where "she still rules supreme."[1]

The Norse version of Durga-Virginal was the death-goddess **Skadi**, who married the god Njord but grew tired of living with him in the lowlands by the sea, so she returned alone to her mountains. Some say she became the evil Snow Queen who would kidnap children from their homes and take away their souls.

Since snow-covered mountains were widely associated with the milk-giving breasts of Mother Earth, it is possible that Durga the Inaccessible and similar Ice Queens represented the nursing Goddess, in the period when lactating human females, like lactating animal females, were literally inaccessible to the male. Preoccupied with motherhood, the Goddess became "virgin" again in her refusal to tolerate male attentions. She "withdrew" from her marriage and went away to a place where no man could follow. There was an archetypal element in these stories. As M.-L. von Franz has said, "One may suddenly find oneself up against something in a woman that is obstinate, cold, and completely inaccessible."[2]

Dr. Marie-Louise von Franz Modern Swiss psychologist, collaborator and friend of Carl Jung.

1. Guerber, L.M.A., 115. 2. Jung, M.H.S., 189.

Virgin Birth

"Holy Virgin" was the title of harlot-priestesses of Ishtar, Asherah, or Aphrodite. The title didn't mean physical virginity; it meant simply "unmarried." The function of such "holy virgins" was to dispense the Mother's grace through sexual worship; to heal; to prophesy; to perform sacred dances; to wail for the dead; and to become Brides of God.

Children born of such temple women were called by the Semites *bathur,* by the Greeks *parthenioi,* "virgin-born."[1] According to the Protoevangelium, the Virgin Mary was a *kadesha* and perhaps married to one of that class of priests known as "fathers of the god."[2] See **Firstborn**.

The temple hierodules were called *virgines* or *venerii* in Rome, *horae* in Greece, *kadishtu, qadesh,* or *kadesha* in Babylon, Canaan, and Palestine.

Mary's impregnation was similar to Persephone's. In her Virgin guise, Persephone sat in a holy cave and began to weave the great tapestry of the universe, when Zeus appeared as a phallic serpent, to beget the savior Dionysus on her.[3] Mary sat in the temple and began to spin a blood-red thread, representing Life in the tapestry of fate, when the angel Gabriel "came in unto her" (Luke 1:28), the biblical phrase for sexual intercourse. Gabriel's name means literally "divine husband."[4]

Hebrew Gospels designated Mary by the word *almah,* mistakenly translated "virgin," but really meaning "young woman."[5] It was derived from Persian Al-Mah, the unmated Moon-goddess.[6] Another cognate was Latin *alma,* "living soul of the world," virtually identical to Greek *psyche,* Sanskrit *shakti.* The Holy Virgins or temple-harlots were "soul-teachers" or "soul-mothers"—the *alma mater.*

Christian translators insisted on rendering Mary's title as "virgin," which saddled their religion with an embarrassing article of faith. Even today, theologians like Karl Barth declare that "It is essential to the true Christian faith to accept the doctrine of the virgin birth"—thus drastically reducing the number of people who can be called true Christians.[7]

Early Christians demanded a virgin birth for their Savior out of simple imitativeness. All the other Saviors had one, for they were born of the Goddess incarnate in a chosen "virgin of the temple," whose business it was to bear Saviors. The notion that mortal women were impregnated by gods or spirits was a matter of everyday acceptance throughout the ancient world. Even the Old Testament says the archaic "giants" (ancestral heroes) were born of mortal women impregnated by spirits that came from God (Genesis 6:4).

Zoroaster, Sargon, Perseus, Jason, Miletus, Minos, Asclepius, and dozens of others were God-begotten and virgin-born. Even Zeus, the Heavenly Father who begot many other "virgin-born" heroes, was himself called Zeus Marnas, "Virgin-born Zeus."[8] Plutarch noted among the Egyptians the common belief that the spirit of God was capable of sexual intercourse with mortal women.[9]

Heracles was born of another *almah,* the Virgin Alcmene, whose name means Power of the Moon.[10] Her husband also, like the biblical Joseph, kept away from her bed during her pregnancy. The same tale was told of Plato, whose nephew affirmed that he was begotten by the god Apollo, his earthly parents having no sexual relations until after his birth.[11] Christians believed this, and solemnly attested that Plato was a virgin-born son of the sun god.[12]

After Christianity was established as the official religion of the Roman empire, however, church fathers tried to discredit all other virgin births by claiming that the devil had devised them, and maliciously placed them in a past time, so they would pre-date the real Savior. Justin Martyr wrote, "When I am told that Perseus was born of a virgin, I realize that here again is a case in which the serpent and deceiver has imitated our religion."[13]

St. Justin Martyr Christian apologist of the 2nd century, born of pagan parents and trained in philosophy before his conversion. In addition to his *Apologia* and *Dialogus,* many anonymous later works were falsely attributed to his pen.

Despite the efforts of church fathers, the virgin birth of Jesus was neither the first nor the last such miracle given credence by Christians. Priapic idols of antiquity, credited with the power to father children, actually fathered other priapic idols who became saints like Foutin, Gurtlichon, Gilles, Regnaud, and Guignole; these were credited with the same power of fertilization and were much adored by women who desired offspring.[14] Women of Tuscany and Portugal thought they could become pregnant by eating apples specially consecrated by a priest. Spaniards remembered the virgin birth of Mars, and thought any woman could conceive like Mars's mother Juno, by eating a lily. It was believed that souls could enter a woman's body in the form of flies, worms, or serpents, to cause impregnation. Cases were solemnly documented, like that of a Scot named Gillie Downak Chravolick, conceived when his mother raised her skirts on an old battlefield and received into her "private member" some ashes from the burned bones of dead warriors.[15] As impregnation by a god used to be the "acceptable explanation for pregnancy in most pagan countries where the sexual act was part of the fertility rites," so Christians thought impregnation by spirits was still credible, whether the alleged father was a dead hero, a devil, an incubus, or even—in some sects—the Holy Ghost again.[16]

Such an untenable belief survived because it was important to men. The impossible virgin mother was everyman's longed-for resolution of Oedipal conflicts: pure maternity, never distracted from her devotion by sexual desires. Churchmen unwittingly showed their anxiety by denying even the evidence of their own Gospels that Jesus had brothers and sisters. St. Ambrose insisted that Mary never conceived again, since God couldn't have chosen for his mother-bride "a woman who would defile the heavenly chamber with the seed of a man."[17]

Theologians in effect severed the two halves of the pagan Goddess, whose realistic femininity combined abundant sexuality and maternity. One half was labeled harlot and temptress, the other a female ascetic even in motherhood. The Goddess's old title, Sancta Matrona—Holy Mother—was added to the canon of saints as a phony St. Matrona, whose pseudo-biography made her a "hermitess."[18]

The primitive naiveté of the virgin-birth concept was dressed in pretentious verbiage, purporting to explain it, while actually hiding it from prying eyes. "A shadow is formed by light falling upon a body. The Virgin, as a human being, could not hold the fulness of divinity; but the power of the most High overshadowed her, while the incorporeal light of the godhead took a human body within her, and so she was able to bear God."[19]

Churchmen often presented the doctrine of the virgin birth as "ennobling" to women, since they viewed women's natural sexuality as degrading. Seldom were female sexuality and motherhood perceived as component parts of the same whole. Some women were astute enough to see that the doctrine effectively degraded real womanhood by exalting a never-attainable ideal. At the end of the 19th century one woman wrote:

> *I think that the doctrine of the Virgin birth as something higher, sweeter, nobler than ordinary motherhood, is a slur on all the natural motherhood of the world. . . . Out of this doctrine, and that which is akin to it, have sprung all the monasteries and nuns of the world, which have disgraced and distorted and demoralized manhood and womanhood for a thousand years. I place beside this false, monkish, unnatural claim . . . my mother, who was as holy in her motherhood as was Mary herself.*[20]

1. Briffault 3, 169–70. 2. Budge, D.N., 169. 3. Campbell, P.M., 101. 4. Augstein, 302. 5. Brasch, 25. 6. *Larousse,* 311. 7. Augstein, 38. 8. Graves, W.G., 320. 9. Angus, 113. 10. Graves, G.M. 2, 378. 11. H. Smith, 183. 12. Shumaker, 152. 13. H. Smith, 183. 14. Knight, D.W.P., 141. 15. Briffault 2, 452. 16. Holmes, 35. 17. Ashe, 182. 18. Boulding, 370. 19. de Voragine, 206. 20. Stanton, 114.

Virgo

Virgil said the constellation Virgo (the Virgin) was Erigone, Goddess of Justice, also known as Astraea or "Starry One."[1] She identified with Libera, or Libra, the Lady of the Scales, judge of men and ruler of their fates. Renaissance poets still called her Astraea: "She is that royal and great goddess by whom cities and empires are preserved in pride; without her no kingdom can long endure. This is she who makes them all secure."[2]

1. Lindsay, O.A., 277. 2. Moakley, 111.

Virtue

Latin *virtu* was derived from *vir,* "man," and originally meant masculinity, impregnating power, semen, or male magic, like Germanic *heill.* Patriarchal thinkers defined manliness as good and womanliness as bad, therefore *virtu* became synonymous with morality or godliness, along with other synonyms hinting at male sexuality: erectness, uprightness, rectitude, upstandingness, etc. As the Old Testament said, "Praise is comely for the upright" (Psalms 33:1).

Old phallic connotations of "virtue" may have been hidden in the Gospels' description of Jesus's miraculous cure of the woman with an issue of blood. When she touched Jesus, he felt "virtue" go out of him, "and straightway the fountain of her blood was dried up" (Mark 5:29–30). According to ancient systems of sacred kingship, it was important for the king-victim to give proof of virility, which meant impregnating a specially chosen priestess, so that the "fountain of her blood" might cease.

Vishnu

Vedic god representing both the sacrificial boar and the phallus. His name meant "he who embraces, pervades, or penetrates"; he was known as "the expander," and "he who excites men."[1] His emblem was a lingam-yoni composed of a male cross with a female circle, called the sign Kiakra: "When held by Vishnu, it signifies his power to penetrate heaven and earth."[2]

Vishnu insisted that his flesh and blood, poured out on the sacrificial altar, preserved the whole world, creatures and gods alike. When he transformed himself into the boar, he became the Universal Savior. For the sake of the world he gave himself up to death, and was sacrificed by "gods saying Om."[3]

The boar's tusk was identified with his phallus, because it was the tusk that effected Vishnu's mating with the primal Goddess Earth: "He uprose bearing on his tusk the fair goddess Earth, shedding in all directions the brine of the cosmic sea."[4] Boars' tusks often represented phalli in Oceanic and Far-Eastern cultures.

1. Campbell, M.I., 480–81; O'Flaherty, 357. 2. Baring-Gould, C.M.M.A., 374. 3. O'Flaherty, 196–97. 4. Campbell, M.I., 481.

Vitus, Saint

Imaginary saint dimly associated with Sicily, possibly based on a Latin word carved on an ancient healing shrine: *Vitus* ("life"). An emblem of the Moon-goddess entered into the fabrication of St. Vitus as his alleged "nurse," Crescentia.

Vitus was especially venerated in Westphalia, where bones said to be his had rested since the 9th century A.D., though his legend assigned him to the time of Diocletian, six hundred years earlier. The bones were credited with the ability to cure many diseases, especially chorea, the so-called St. Vitus's Dance.[1]

1. Attwater, 338.

Viviana, Saint

Canonized form of the pagan Goddess Viviane, whose name meant Life. It seems to have been nothing more than a word on the Goddess's temple on the Esquiline Hill in Rome. Probably an image of the Goddess, so labeled, was deliberately re-interpreted as the image of a "virgin martyr."[1]

Among early medieval Celtic poets, Viviane was the name of the Lady of the Lake, who reappeared in Arthurian myths as another form of Nimue, the "Nemesis" of Merlin.

1. Attwater, 338.

Völsi

"Horse's Penis," a title of Odin as the castrated royal horse, whose amputated member became the ancestor of the Völsungs. Welsh equivalents were the Waelsings, sons of Waels, who later became "the god Wales." Waels also meant "the Corpse," for the dead god was always resurrected and became the usual Lord of Death, like Shiva's corpse-form Shava. See **Horse**.

Vulcan

Latin lightning- or volcano-god derived from Cretan Velchanos, identical with Hephaestus. Vulcan's forges were said to lie under Mt. Etna or Mt. Vesuvius. See **Lightning**; **Smith**. He evolved into the medieval "Volund the Smith," a divine wizard whom the British called Wayland.

Vulture

One of the oldest totems of the Great Mother in Egypt was the vulture, eater of the dead. Vultures who devoured corpses were regarded as her angels of death, since they carried the dead piecemeal to heaven. In Neolithic times it was a common practice to expose dead bodies to carrion birds, who embodied the Mother's spirit. For this reason even the Greeks and Romans fostered a belief that all vultures are female.[1] On the Stele of the Vultures from Catal Huyuk, 7th millenium B.C., dead bodies are carried off by vultures—in a time and place where only the female principle was worshipped.[2]

Ancient Iranians didn't bury their dead, but exposed them to vultures in open-topped "towers of silence" called dakhmas, many of which still stand today. Such towers were built when Iranians worshipped the Moon-goddess Mah, the Mother, and believed that vultures carried the deceased to her heavenly realm.[3] Even after burial was instituted in Persia, a dead body couldn't be interred until it was first torn by vultures.[4]

Egyptians worshipped the vulture-headed Mother as the origin of all things, calling her Mut, Isis, or Nekhbet.[5] In combination with the serpent goddess Buto (Per-Uatchet), the vulture-mother gave rise to the Two Mistresses, guardians of royal dynastic clans, and nurses of deceased kings in the after-life. Temples had special chapels for the Two Mistresses: on the east, the serpent Goddess brought the sun to birth; on the west, the vulture Goddess daily ordained his death.[6] Sometimes both Goddesses appeared as vultures on the sacred mount of Sehseh, where the deceased pharaoh became an eternal infant at their breasts.[7]

Egypt's oldest oracle was the shrine of the vulture goddess Nekhbet at Nekhen (modern Al-Kab), the original "necropolis" or city of the dead. Because it was a birth shrine as well as a death shrine, Greeks called it Ilithyiaspolis after their own Great Mother of childbirth, Aphrodite Ilithyia.[8] Romans called it Civitas Lucinae, the city of Juno Lucina, Goddess of childbirth.[9]

Egypt's symbol for "grandmother" was the vulture goddess bearing a flail of authority: a totemic form of the pre-dynastic clan matriarch.[10] The word "mother" was written in hieroglyphics with the sign of the vulture.[11] Nekhbet the Vulture once ruled all of Upper Egypt, wearing the white crown in token of sovereignty. As Isis, she appeared in vulture form on mummy-pillows, crowned with a vulture skin and bearing in each claw the *ankh* or Cross of Life.[12] As a vulture she devoured her dead consort Osiris, just as Kali devoured her dead Shiva.[13] Then she reincarnated him in her body, and gave him rebirth as a new Holy Child, Horus.

Osiris was dismembered, which was the funerary custom of primitive Egypt, dating from a remote time when the dead probably were eaten, after the manner of primitive Greece's *omophagia.* Funerary magic lay in the hands of dancing priestesses called *muu,* "mothers," who may have worn costumes of vulture feathers to represent "eaters" and, like Isis, reconstitute the dead in their own bodies. The *Book of Ani* said the first gate of the uterine underworld was guarded by the vulture Goddess, whose tearing beak could admit the dead to the place whence they rose again.[14]

The vulture-mother was known also in northern Europe and Asia. Valkyries were "corpse-eaters" to the Saxons and often took the form of carrion-eating birds such as crows or ravens. In Siberia, each shaman had a "Bird-of-Prey Mother" who appeared twice in his life, at his spiritual death-and-rebirth—like the Dove-mother appearing at Jesus's baptismal ceremony—and again at his physical death. This spirit-mother was a large carrion bird "with an iron beak, hooked claws, and a long tail."[15]

Funerary priestesses came to be called "dirty" in classic myths, as they appear in the tale of the vulture-feathered **Harpies**. However, the ancient claim that all vultures are female was believed well into the Christian era. Church fathers cited, in defense of the Virgin Birth, the "fact" that vultures conceived their eggs only because they were fertilized by spirits of the wind.[16]

1. Budge, G.E. 2, 372. 2. de Riencourt, 24. 3. *Larousse,* 311, 314. 4. Herodotus, 56. 5. *Larousse,* 34. 6. Budge, G.E. 1, 440. 7. Neumann, A.C.U., 13; Erman, 9. 8. *Book of the Dead,* 493. 9. Budge, G.E. 1, 438. 10. Budge, G.E. 1, 286. 11. Neumann, A.C.U., 12. 12. *Book of the Dead,* 623. 13. Hays, 257. 14. *Book of the Dead,* 272, 289. 15. Eliade, S., 36. 16. Neumann, A.C.U., 65.

W X Y Z

YAMA, Hindu Lord of Death, with his spiritual side, Yami. He peers into his karmic mirror to espy the victims' good and evil deeds before butchering them. Tibet; 19th century.

Matthew Hopkins, self-appointed scourge of WITCHCRAFT, wrote *The Discovery of Witches* in 1647 and used this frontispiece showing himself with two witches and their familiar spirits.

ZEUS was Father of Heaven, but he did not create human life nor dispense the laws of the universe. He could only send lightning and rain to fructify Mother Earth and let her bring forth life. This detail is from a statue of the god in his Roman aspect, Jove; now in the Vatican.

Walpurga, Saint

var. Saint Walburga

Christianization of the pagan Goddess of Walpurgisnacht (May Eve), the orgiastic festival of the springtime sacred marriage. Walpurga was the May Queen whose cult remained so popular in Germany that the church had to adopt her in its usual way, by a spurious canonization. According to the canonical legend, she was an Englishwoman who became supreme abbess of the double monastery of Heidenheim during the 8th century; but there were no contemporary records of the time when this "abbess" was supposed to have lived and reigned.[1]

In the 8th century, however, double monasteries largely perpetuated the pagan traditions of the "colleges" of priests and priestesses living together under a female ruler, and apparently carrying on the ancient sex rites under a thin veil of Christian-pagan syncretism.[2] (See **Convent**.) The name of Walpurga's monastery means literally "home of heathens."

The medieval church produced and sold vast quantities of an allegedly miraculous Oil of St. Walpurga, which exuded—so it was claimed—from the holy rock under which the saint's bones lay, and which was highly recommended for the purpose of healing many kinds of diseases.[3]

The saint's day was transferred from May Eve to February, possibly in an attempt to discourage the Walpurgisnacht revels; but "witches" celebrated the original date of the marriage-festival anyway, in honor of Walpurga. Therefore the church had to claim that May Eve commemorated the transfer of St. Walpurga's relics to Eichstätt so the processions and dances and songs would seem to be associated with the progress of a revered reliquary.[4] May Eve, however, remained a prime festival of witches throughout all Europe.

1. Attwater, 339. 2. *Encyc. Brit.,* "Women in Religious Orders." 3. Wilkins, 61. 4. Attwater, 339.

War

A primary patriarchal contribution to culture, almost entirely absent from the matriarchal societies of the Neolithic and early Bronze Ages.[1] Even when Goddess-worship was beginning to give way to cults of aggressive gods, for a long time the appearance of the Goddess imposed peace on all hostile groups. Among Germanic tribes in Europe, Tacitus said, whenever the Goddess moved in her chariot at certain seasons to certain sacred places, the people "do not go to battle or wear arms; every weapon is under lock; peace and quiet are known and welcomed."[2] In later centuries, one of the reasons for the devaluation of women in feudal Europe was that the feudal system was based on war, in which women played no part except as victims.[3]

Patriarchal gods tended to be warlike from their inception—

including, or even particularly, the Judeo-Christian God. Stanton observed that the Old Testament's account of God's nature, purpose, and activities on behalf of his Chosen People boils down to "a long painful record of war, corruption, rapine, and lust. Why Christians who wished to convert the heathen to our religion should send them these books, passes all understanding."[4]

But Christianity was never a pacifist religion. The church placed warfare in its armory of persecution as soon as its political power made this possible. Pope Innocent I (d. 417) proclaimed that God gave the church the right to kill, and permitted papal armies to employ the sword "for the punishment of the guilty," which meant massacre of the nonorthodox.[5] The warfare of Christian sect against Christian sect was unremitting, so that pagan observers said Christians behaved toward each other with the ferocity of wild beasts.[6] These trends continued throughout the Christian era, under the headings of holy wars, crusades, conquests, and conversions by the sword. All-male Christianity was disseminated by violence.[7]

Meanwhile, with the decline of their religious power and the obliteration of their Goddess, women helplessly disapproved, as many do today. An American black woman recently said:

> *I don't think a few should control everything. I don't think it's right that women lay down and bear sons and then you have a few rich people that tell your sons they have to go and die for their country. They're not dying for their country. They're dying for the few to stay on top. I don't think that's necessary. I'm just tired of this type of thing. I just think we ought to be just human.*[8]

In contrast to these sentiments, there was a more masculine opinion published in Marinetti's "manifesto of futurism" in the following terms: "we want to extol the love of danger. . . . There is no beauty apart from conflict. There are no masterpieces without aggression. . . . We want to extol war—the world's only hygiene—militarism, patriotism, the anarchist's destructive gesture, the glorious, death-giving ideas and—contempt for women!"[9]

Filippo Tommaso Marinetti (1876-1944) Italian founder of the literary Futurist movement; supporter of Fascism; self-described as a "mystic of action."

Some women accepted the contempt and tamely submitted to the God and the man who extolled war, even giving up their children without protest, like housewife Jesusita Novarro:

> *I pray a lot. I pray to God to give me strength. If He should take a child away from me, to have the strength to accept it. It's His kid. He just borrowed him to me. . . .*
>
> *These kids don't ask to be born—these kids are gonna grow up and give their lives one day. . . . There will always be war. Why? I really don't know. Nobody has ever told me. . . . I wish I knew. I guess the big shots decided the war.*[10]

More articulate women have spoken out against the "big shots" who seem to leave the life-affirming interests of women out of their plans for the future, calling their power-mania gynocidal and therefore genocidal.[11] It is often implied that only women can take on the responsibility of defying the war machines, to save their children; but again women are placed in a no-win situation when they have no power to enforce their defiance.

With the advance of technological civilization, as everyone knows, wars have become deadlier than ever, as if the mind of man becomes less "civilized" as his tools become more so. Some have doubted that man is capable of constructing a stable, peaceful world. Becker remarked, "It seems that the experiment of man may well prove to be an evolutionary dead end, an impossible animal."[12] Jules Henry said:

> *Is there nothing in life in an achieving culture but constant war—war against the outside as the fullest expression of the drive, and war on the inside to contain and transform it? The grisly history of achieving cultures does not permit anything but the affirmation: No, there is nothing more. Though the inner and the outer war continue, the outer has so far been most successful, and the history of the achievement drive shows that* Homo sapiens *has been dying of success and will probably fail as a species because of it.*[13]

Teilhard de Chardin wondered whether some historical error might have brought man to a wrong turning in the path of progress, so that violence of the modern world betrays "a certain excess, inexplicable to our reason, as if to the normal effect of evolution is added the extraordinary effect of some catastrophe or primordial deviation."[14] It is not difficult to find such a deviation in the contrast between "matrist" and "patrist" societies, especially in their respective valuations of elemental caring behavior.

> *The fundamental problem of mankind is to develop a culture where the needs of the individual are always complementary to those around him; a culture in which a child is not slapped for crying; a culture in which sorrow always is met by the complementary need to be compassionate; where fear is always met by the complementary need in others to give reassurance; where the need to be loved is met by a need to give love in the way it is wanted, at the time it is wanted and as much as it is wanted. This is not an American view, for the American makes conflict into a god; and although sociology swells its chest with a thousand "conflict theories," it has none on compassion. . . . Life without conflict seems stale to the American elites; and compassion, which is a low-paid motivation, has been relegated to the fringes of the low-paid segments of the culture, and has never been a subject for research.*[15]

The highest-paid pursuits of the modern age tend to exploit violence either directly or in symbol, as Arthur Miller observed:

> *There is violence because we have daily honored violence. Any half-educated man in a good suit can make his fortune by concocting a television show whose brutality is photographed in sufficiently monstrous detail. Who produces these shows, who pays to sponsor, who is honored for acting in them? Are these people delinquent psychopaths*

> *slinking along tenement streets? No, they are the pillars of society, our honored men, our exemplars of success and social attainment. We must begin to feel the shame and contrition we have earned before we can begin to sensibly construct a peaceful society, let alone a peaceful world. A country where people cannot walk safely in their own streets has not earned the right to tell any other people how to govern itself, let alone to bomb and burn that people.*[16]

Some observers of the modern scene fear that the symbolism of violence, so prevalent in what passes for "entertainment" in our aggressive society, will actually create its social counterpart because of man's propensity to model his behavior on symbolic forms. Mumford says:

> *Power and order, pushed to their final limit, lead to their self-destructive inversion: disorganization, violence, mental aberration, subjective chaos. This tendency is already expressed in America through the motion picture, the television screen, and children's comic books. These forms of amusement are all increasingly committed to enactments of cold-blooded brutality and physical violence: pedagogical preparations for the practical use of homicide and genocide. . . . Was it not in the country most disciplined by militarism, absolutism, and physical science that systematic torture in the form of "scientific experiments" was undertaken? Did not Germany produce the nauseating horrors of the extermination camps? In the combination of cold scientific rationalism with criminal irrationalism the fatal poison produced its equally fatal antidote.*[17]

The rise of Hitler's Germany provides an interesting case in point, showing a nation swept by militaristic sentiment coupled with a sense of divine mission. The churches accepted Hitler's warmongering with religious joy. In April 1937, a Christian organization in the Rhineland passed a resolution that Hitler's word was the law of God and possessed "divine authority." Reichsminister for Church Affairs Hans Kerrl announced: "There has arisen a new authority as to what Christ and Christianity really are—that is Adolf Hitler. Adolf Hitler. . . . is the true Holy Ghost."[18] And so the pious gave him their blessing, and the churches gave him God's. "Organized religion has always managed to provide prayers and thanks for victories in bloody wars. . . . In more recent history, is there any evidence that organized religion anywhere did anything but bless the battlers on both sides?"[19]

In fact, Nazism was not the creation of Hitler alone, nor even of Germany alone. The Nazi myth of "pure Aryanism" began not with a German but with a Frenchman, Comte de Gobineau, who claimed in 1853 that the divinely chosen Master Race, of Teutonic stock, had been defiled by admixtures of inferior, swarthy peoples: Latins, Negroes, Semites. Teutons would "naturally" rule the world once these inferior strains were purged from their Aryan bloodlines.

Germans founded Gobineau societies all over their country, and developed a new nationalistic pride out of the myth of the Teutonic *Übermensch.* The myth was further elaborated by an Englishman,

H. S. Chamberlain, who wrote *The Foundation of the Nineteenth Century* in 1899, giving a "scientific" rationale for the awful consequences of racial mixture, especially the contamination of "exalted Aryans" by Semitic blood. Chamberlain married Wagner's daughter Eva, and became a German citizen. Kaiser Wilhelm praised him, and called Chamberlain's book his favorite reading. Clearly, it was also a favorite of Hitler's.

The Gobineau-Chamberlain-Hitler theory of the *Übermensch* shows one of the most common underlying causes of war: man's propensity to view himself and his own group as superior to others, who therefore deserve destruction because they are substandard. Once the propaganda machine begins to work, there is no limit to the depravity it can impute to the enemy—not wholly without reason, for war corrupts everyone including one's own troops, though this fact is invariably overlooked. War is an outstanding example of the We-They syndrome: the Saved versus the Damned, the Chosen People versus the heathen, God's champions against the forces of evil (even when God is on both sides). Hitler succeeded brilliantly in convincing his followers that his political enemies were subhumans *(Untermenschen)*, therefore it was only reasonable to exterminate them.[20]

In a sense this indoctrination can extend even to the enemy's homeland, which can be seen as a non-country whereas—according to the patriotic ideal—one's own country is the most superior spot on Mother Earth's body, the essential *cunnus* as primitives believed, a paradise on earth. Such maternal symbolism has even been used to good effect in developing desirable sentiments of aggression in wartime, as shown by the writing of a California superintendent of schools:

> *The good citizen stands in relation to his country as the good son to his mother.*
>
> *He obeys her because she is his elder, because she conjoins within herself the vision of many, and because he owes to her his begetting and his nurturing.*
>
> *He honors her above all others, placing her in a special niche within his secret heart, in front of which the candles of respect and admiration are forever kept alight.*
>
> *He defends her against all enemies, and counts his life well lost in her behalf.*[21]

Such utilization of the powerful Mother-symbol on behalf of militarism tends to conceal the real aggressors from their real victims. As women seem to know almost instinctively, the former are the "big shots"—mature men in positions of power. The latter are the younger, handsomer, more virile rivals—the sons who can be made obedient soldiers and sent off to be destroyed, which may defuse the Oedipal jealousy. In effect, war is a gentlemen's agreement between the authority figures on both sides that they will kill off each other's youths, and even win social approval or adulation for doing so.[22]

Patriarchal males have always shown hostility to the young, who divert the attention of females, either as mates or mothers. In the west, male aggression against the young is sometimes projected onto women: for example, accusing women of murder in the case of abortion, or of crime in the case of birth control. Both these measures tended to diminish the patriarchs' supply of cannon fodder. Margaret Sanger thought women could end war by "cutting off the surplus people. Of course military states always clamor for more children, first to defend the Fatherland, and when the population soars, to conquer more territory for the added millions."[23] But the goals of a militaristic state would not be served by women who deliberately denied it the necessary population base; the state wanted quantity, not quality.

Religion of the patriarchal sort was, and is, always on the side of the patriarchs. Vetter says, "There is little to choose between the head-hunting which keeps down the number of people to be supported by the game produced in a given area, and the periodic wholesale slaughter engaged in by 'civilized' peoples in their battles for the control of equally vital economic resources, and for which slaughters the blessings of our religions have never failed to be forthcoming."[24]

Wars are begun by elite males and carried out by those of lower status, while priesthoods bless the effort. "It is a fair estimate that 100 million people have been killed by war since 1900. Responsibility for this mass slaughter rests directly upon the male members of the species."[25] Yet war is never reasonable, as males imagine their actions to be. "Destruction of the world by a small group of white men in order to achieve more wealth than they can ever possibly use does not make sense. We are talking here about a drive for power, a need for domination that must be examined. . . . In squelching female energy, patriarchy creates a culture that is destructive and death-oriented."[26] Today "we see the threat of nuclear annihilation more serious than ever after two decades of disarmament efforts. We realize that science and technology cannot save us, at least not as currently administered by men. The design for disaster we currently face was not planned by women."[27]

In the Tantric morality which probably was planned by women, at least in part, war is entirely unacceptable. The adept may not participate in fighting or in the manufacture of weapons; he must not glorify soldiers' bravery, nor praise killing in a hunt or a battle. These "constitute a worse form of murder since they incite others to do it, thus harming their spiritual growth."[28] With modern films and television still trying to glorify violence, it seems the Tantric sages had already achieved a deeper understanding of human nature than those of our "enlightened" modern world.

1. Fromm, 158. 2. Tacitus, 728. 3. J.B. Russell, 281. 4. Stanton, 66. 5. Bullough, 122. 6. Gibbon 1, 719–22. 7. Campbell, C.M., 390; Reinach, 295. 8. Terkel, 461.

9. Wolff, 258. 10. Terkel, 402. 11. Daly, 184. 12. Becker, E.E., 153. 13. Henry, 348. 14. T.A. Harris, 224. 15. Henry, 197. 16. T.A. Harris, 262. 17. Mumford, 385. 18. Langer, 63. 19. Vetter, 513. 20. Fromm, 121. 21. T.A. Harris, 246. 22. Fromm, 178. 23. E. Douglas, 137. 24. Vetter, 485. 25. Lewis, xiii. 26. Spretnak, 401. 27. Boulding, 761. 28. Tatz & Kent, 31.

Waste Land

The recurrent threatening theme of medieval romances was the Waste Land motif, especially in the Holy Grail cycle. Like the Grail legends themselves, the Waste Land motif probably came from the Middle East, where European travelers and crusaders had seen a true Waste Land: the great desert which eastern mystics attributed to Islam's renunciation of the fertile Great Mother. Western pagans also maintained that if the Mother should be offended or neglected, she might curse the land with the same desperate barrenness that could be seen in Arabia Deserta and north Africa. (See **Grail, Holy**.)

One of the Grail stories said a king of England (Logres) once committed a mortal sin by raping one of the Goddess's priestesses and stealing her golden cup, symbol of her love, which must not be stolen but only given. Afterward, priestesses of the sacred springs no longer welcomed wayfarers with food and drink.[1] The Peace of the Goddess was destroyed, for the women no longer trusted men. "The land went to waste. The trees lost their leaves, grass and flowers withered, and the water receded more and more. . . . [A] wrong against a feminine being and a plundering of nature were perpetrated. . . . [T]he origin of the trouble was looked upon as an offense committed against the fairy world, i.e., actually against nature. . . . The growth of masculine consciousness and of the patriarchal logos principle of the Christian outlook are concerned in no small measure with this development."[2]

The Goddess appeared in several myths of the Grail cycle as a great lady disinherited, or a queen robbed of her possessions and reduced to penury, like *La Reine de la Terre Gaste* (Queen of the Waste Land) in the Cistercian romance of the *Queste del Saint Graal*.[3] Many tales speak of groups of women deprived of their former property rights and gathered together in "castles of damsels," under three rulers personifying the Goddess: a queen, her daughter, and her granddaughter.

Hoping to keep their enemies at bay by magic spells, the woman waited for a champion to defend their cause, as the Grail knights were supposed to do. The queen employed a certain learned astronomer whose wizardry kept away from the castle any knight likely to fail through cowardice, envy, greed, or any other weakness of character. The ladies waited for the coming of their savior, the Desired Knight, perfect in his honesty and bravery: one who could destroy all their enemies and restore their lands and possessions, which had been taken from them by various robber barons. "Orphaned maidens," deprived of their inheritance by new patrilineal laws, also took refuge in such castles of women; so did older widows who were no longer permitted to inherit property as under the former laws of mother-right.[4]

Legends of the coming of the Desired Knight may have been promulgated by women, or by bards seeking to please women with a favorite theme. But there was more than this to the image of the Waste Land. It haunted a society in which, "Under the autocratic regime of persecuting Christianity during the Middle Ages of Europe, Christian dogma was indeed accepted nominally by great intellects, but it was accepted under duress and with a reservation. . . . The men of highest intellect were compelled to express the faith that was in them in the most guarded language."[5] Often, the language was symbolism—the most guarded of all, since its true meaning could always be denied. The symbolic Waste Land was "a landscape of spiritual death," where religious concepts were dissociated from the feelings and life experiences of ordinary people, and imposed upon a confused, reluctant public only by authoritarian indoctrination.[6]

This could well describe Europe in the 12th century, when the coming of the Desired Knight was vaguely identified with the second coming of Christ—or Merlin, Arthur, Frederick, etc. Many oppressed people despairingly yearned for a powerful hero to defy the oppressors on their behalf. The Waste Land theme invoked the collective fear of every agricultural society since the Stone Age: the fear that Mother Earth's cyclic miracle of food production might fail. But it meant more than that. It also stood for collective devitalization and depression in a society perceived by its members as lacking spiritual roots.

A famous modern application of the Waste Land theme is, of course, T.S. Eliot's poem, based not only on western applications of Grail symbolism but also on the Hindu tale of the hopeless quest for the true Word of Power, as recounted in the *Brihadaranyaka Upanishad.* The Hindu version ran like this:

Gods, men, and demons went to Shiva-Prajapati in the guise of Lord of Thunder, to find out from him the ultimate word—that is, the word signifying the goal and end of all things, as *Om* signified their beginning. But the Thunder, being thunder, was not able to say any word except one: Da.

Men, hearing this word, thought it meant *datta,* meaning "give" or "fertilize," because begetting was the only divine thing they could do, and charitable giving was the only way they knew to seek blessedness. Demons, hearing this word, thought it meant *dayadhvam,* meaning "sympathize" or "be compassionate"; in the Oriental context demons were not evil spirits but deities of the old matriarchal religion, who preached *karuna,* mother-love. Gods, hearing this word, thought it meant *damyata,* meaning "control," the secret of their success; by self-control they became divine, and by divinity they achieved power to control all the others.

But the Lord of Thunder couldn't distinguish one word from

another. He only repeated mindlessly the only word he knew: "Da! Da! Da!"[7]

1. Spence, 138. 2. Jung & von Franz, 202, 204. 3. Campbell, C.M., 543. 4. Jung & von Franz, 229. 5. Shirley, 31–32. 6. Campbell, C.M., 5–6, 373, 388. 7. *Upanishads,* 112.

Water

First of the elements, according to the philosophers of ancient Miletus; the *Arché,* mother of all things.[1] Water gave birth to "spirit," supposedly a male principle; hence the idea of baptismal rebirth that Christians copied from the pagans involved both water (feminine) and spirit (masculine). The baptismal font was described as a "womb," specifically the womb of Mary, whose name was that of all the ancient Sea-goddesses.[2] Most myths placed the primary impulse of creation in a watery womb of chaos or "formlessness" representing the Great Mother (Tiamat, Kali, Ma-Nu, Themis, etc.), an image really drawn from the lack of differentiation between self and other—or self and mother—experienced by the infant in the womb and subconsciously remembered throughout life as an archetypal image. The Mother-letter M (Ma) was an ideogram for waves of water.

"Students of mythology find that when the feminine principle is subjected to sustained attack, as it was from the medieval Christian authorities, it often quietly submerges. Under the water (where organic life began) it swims through the subconscious of the dominant male society, occasionally bobbing to the surface to offer a glimpse of the rejected harmony."[3]

Correspondence between "water" and "mother" was so universal even in the Middle Ages, when the maternal principle was theoretically squelched, that the Hermetic magicians and other "philosophers" claimed souls were created not by God, but by the maternal earth and maternal waters.[4] Goddess-shrines were nearly always associated with wells, springs, lakes, or seas.[5] The Lady of the Lake was identical with Minne/Aphrodite, the Minnesingers' Goddess of Love, who appeared as a mermaid and was assumed to have a "nature of water." Often, water was a metaphor for love itself. Like water, love stayed with the man who held it loosely, as in an open, cupped hand; but the man who tried to grip it hard, in his fist, found that it flowed away and left him gripping nothing. And water, like love, was essential to the life-forces of fertility and creativity, without which the psychic world as well as the material world would become an arid desert, the **Waste Land**.

1. Campbell, P.M., 64. 2. Neumann, G.M., 311. 3. Dames, 152–53. 4. Agrippa, 43, 49. 5. Dames, 154.

Weird Sisters

The three witches in Shakespeare's *Macbeth* were called Weird Sisters after the three Fates, or Norns, corresponding to the Greek

Moerae and the Celtic Morrigan; that is, the Triple Goddess of past, present, and future. *Weird* was a Saxon name of the death-goddess or Crone, who often stood for the whole trinity. Her name was variously given as Wyrd, or Wurd, or Urd, meaning both "Earth" and the Word of Fate's immutable law.[1] As Beowulf said, "Every man in this life will go lay him down on the bed where Wyrd has decided to nail him."[2]

This passage from an early Saxon romance might throw light on the eastern yogi's celebrated bed of nails, symbol of his submission to the Goddess. Devotion to the Fates and their decrees often brought forth a "passionate surrender" in both eastern and western mystics: "This eagerness to submit to divine Fate inspired certain souls in days of old with feelings so fervent as to recall the rapture of Christian devotion, which burns to subject itself to the will of God."[3] Fate was *karma,* a concept virtually identical with that of Weird.

Beowulf was written in a pagan era, but it received later Christian additions. For instance, Beowulf said once that the Goddess Wyrd would determine the outcome of his battle; then he said that God would. The Triple Goddess was much opposed by churchmen of the time. A 12th-century Bishop of Exeter scolded his people for inviting the Three Sisters into the house after a birth, to cast a good destiny for the newborn, and making offerings to them on a table prepared "with three knives for the service of the fairies."[4]

Nevertheless, the Fairy Godmothers or Weird Sisters continued to be invited. Four centuries later in Tudor England, they were still prayed to appear at the cradle of a newborn infant, "for to set to the babe what shall befall to him."[5]

1. Campbell, Oc.M., 485. 2. Goodrich, 18, 32. 3. Cumont, A.R.G.R., 86.
4. Cavendish, P.E., 74, 82. 5. Hazlitt, 379.

Wells

Springs, fountains, ponds, wells were always female symbols in archaic religions, often considered water-passages to the underground womb, in northern Europe associated with Mother Hel, whose name also gave rise to "holy" and "healing." Many pagan sacred springs throughout England received the name of Helen's Well during Christian times, and churchmen claimed all these wells were named after Empress Helena, Constantine's sainted mother. But the real "Helen" was **Hel**, or Dame Holle, whose water-womb was called the source of all the children on earth.[1]

There were also many wells named after the Goddesses Morgan and Brigit. Coventina, "Mother of the Covens," was associated with healing wells. Margaret, a traditional witch name, also designated wells and springs. Lancashire legend speaks of a statue called Peg o' the Well beside a formerly holy spring in Ribblesdale, said to claim a human sacrifice every seven years.[2] Ecclesiastical canons of the 10th century expressly forbade "well-worshippings," but they continued nonetheless.[3]

The Danish poem *Water of Life* drew on the pagan tradition of resurrection through the Mother-symbol of a sacred well called Hileva (Hel-Eve). With this magic water, a divine queen put her dismembered lover back together and made him live again, as Isis did for Osiris.[4] The grotto and fountain of Lourdes once had a similar pagan tradition, now revamped to the service of the church.

In 1770 a curate of Bromfield forbade pagan ceremonies, wakes, and fairs at a spring called Hellywell (Hel's Well), to which site the ceremonies had been moved after they were evicted from the churchyard at a still earlier date.[5] The ceremonies had been going on for a very long time. A medieval *Life of St. Columba* mentioned them in connection with a fountain-shrine "famous among this heathen people, which foolish men, blinded by the devil, worshipped as a divinity."[6]

1. Rank, 73. 2. Phillips, 112, 160. 3. M. Harrison, 143. 4. Steenstrup, 186. 5. Hazlitt, 78. 6. Joyce 1, 366.

Werewolf

Belief in the werewolf, or "spirit-wolf," probably began with early-medieval wolf clans who worshipped their totemic gods in wolf form, as did some people of the Greco-Roman world centuries earlier. Zeus Lycaeus, or Lycaeon, was a Pelasgian wolf-king who reigned in a nine-year cycle as spouse of the Ninefold Goddess, Nonacris.[1] Virgil said the first werewolf was Moeris, spouse of the trinitarian Fate-goddess (Moera), from whom he learned secrets of magic, including the necromantic knack of calling up the dead from their tombs.[2]

Lycanthropy (werewolfism) was named for Apollo Lycaeus, "Wolfish Apollo," who used to be worshipped in the famous Lyceum or "Wolf-temple" where Socrates taught.[3] Apollo was mated to Artemis as a divine Wolf Bitch at Troezen, where she purified Orestes with the blood of nine sacrificial victims.[4] Pausanias said Apollo was originally an Egyptian deity, deriving his name from Up-Uat (Ap-ol), a very ancient name of **Anubis**.[5] (See **Dog**.)

Pausanias Greek traveler and geographer of the 2nd century A.D. Living in a time of declining culture, he was inspired by a desire to describe the ancient sacred sites for posterity.

Another Roman version of the wolf god was Dis Pater, Soranus, or Feronius, consort of the Sabine underground Goddess Feronia, "Mother of Wolves." A certain Roman family claimed descent from her Sabine priestesses, and annually demonstrated her power by walking barefoot over glowing coals during the festival of the Feronia.[6] She was also identified with Lupa the She-Wolf, whose spirit purified Palatine towns through the agency of young men in wolf skins, consecrated by participating in the Lupercalia or Festival of the She-Wolf.[7]

The She-Wolf was another aspect of the Triple Goddess, as

shown by her triadic motherhood. She gave three souls to her son, the legendary King Erulus or Herulus, so that when he was overthrown by Evander, he had to be killed three times.[8] The Amazons, who worshipped the Triple Goddess, incorporated a tribe called the Neuri, who "turned themselves into wolves" for a few days each year during their main religious festival, presumably by wearing wolf skins and masks.[9] The same story was told of a certain Irish tribe in Ossory, who became wolf-people when attending their Yuletide feast, devouring the flesh of cattle as wolves, and afterward regaining their human shape. "Giraldus Cambrensis relates this great wonder in detail, as in operation in his own time, and believed every word of it."[10]

The heathens' devotion to ancestral wolf gods in Teutonic Europe is evinced by the popularity of such names as Wolf, Wulf, Wolfram, Wolfburg, Aethelwulf, Wolfstein, etc. "Beowulf son of Beowulf," hero of the Anglo-Saxon epic, was called Scyld by the Danes, who said he came from the waters in a basket like Romulus and Remus, foster-sons of the She-Wolf.[11]

Irish tribes said their spiritual fathers were wolves, and for that reason they wore wolf skins and used wolves' teeth for healing amulets. Celtic folksongs tell of children or wives transformed into wolves. One whole tribe was said to assume wolf shape very seventh year.[12] As Germanic "berserkers" could become bears by donning bearskins, so it was thought people could become wolves by donning wolf pelts.[13]

In Mercia during the 10th century A.D. there was a revival of pagan learning under two druidic priests, one of whom was named Werwulf.[14] This name of "spirit-wolf" seems to have been applied to opponents of Christianity in general. About 1000 A.D., the word "werewolf" was taken to mean an outlaw.[15]

South Slavs used to pass a newborn child through a wolf skin, saying it was thus born of the She-Wolf. After their conversion to Christianity, the people claimed this ceremony would protect the child from witches. But its real purpose, obviously, was to assimilate the child to the wolf totem via a second birth from the wolf.[16]

Livonians said witches routinely transformed themselves into wolves by passing through a certain magic pool, another instance of baptismal rebirth in animal form.[17] Polish legend said a witch could transform a bride and groom into wolves by laying a girdle of human skin across the threshold at their wedding feast. Later they would receive dresses of fur and would regain their human shape at will.[18] Against such totemic ceremonies the 7th-century Council of Toledo issued severe denunciations of people who put on the heads of beasts, or "make themselves into wild animals."[19]

Italian peasants still say a man who sleeps outdoors on Friday under a full moon will be attacked by a werewolf, or will become one himself. Friday was the night of the Goddess, and the warning against her lunar influence probably dated back to the myth of Endymion

(“Seduced Moon-Man”), who fell asleep on her holy moon-mountain and became her enchanted bridegroom, never to wake up again, so the Goddess could shower her kisses on him each night.[20]

Another story traceable to wolf-clan traditions was “Little Red Riding Hood.” The giveaway details are the red garment, the offering of food to a “grandmother” in the deep woods—a grandmother who wore a wolf skin—and the cannibalistic motif of devouring and resurrection. In Britain, “a red woven hood” was the distinguishing mark of a prophetess or priestess.[21] The story's original victim would have been not the red-clad Virgin but the hunter, as Lord of the Hunt. Like Snow White, Little Red Riding Hood was part of a Virgin-Mother-Crone trinity, wearing the same red garment that Virgin Kali wore; as the red moon of a lunar eclipse she prophesied catastrophe and inspired much fear. Romanian churchmen declared that the eclipsed moon was reddened by her own blood, shed when her wolves attacked her, to “make men repent and turn from evil.”[22]

The werewolf was known to every Indo-European language: Danish *var-ulf,* Gothic *vaira-ulf,* Old Norman *wargus,* Servian *wlkoslak,* Slovakian *vlkodlak,* Russian *wawkalak,* Greek *vrykolaki,* Romanian *varcolaci,* French *loup-garou,* Italian *lupo manaro,* German *Währ-Wölffe.*[23] Slavic terms descended from *volkhvi,* a title of the shamans who held important positions in tribal life before Christianity. Cognates are German *Volk,* “people,” and Russian *vrach,* “physician”—indicating that werewolves were people: totemic healers in wolf masks.[24] Similar “medicine men” are still found among all primitives.

The Gaulish Diana had numerous wolf-cultists among her votaries, in both ancient and medieval times. Under her totemic name of Lupa she was a Mother of wild animals, and certain women seem to have impersonated her in southern France. A Provençal troubadour named Pierre Vidal wrote a love poem to a lady of Carcassonne, whose name was Loba, “She-Wolf”:

When loup-garou the rabble call me,
When vagrant shepherds hoot,
Pursue, and buffet me to boot,
It doth not for a moment gall me,
I seek not palaces nor halls,
Or refuge when the winter falls;
Exposed to winds and frosts at night,
My soul is ravaged with delight.
Me claims my she-wolf so divine;
And justly she that claim prefers,
For, by my troth, my life is hers
More than another's, more than mine.[25]

Lovers of the She-Wolf sometimes found her on a holy mountain, which the gypsies called Monte Lupo, Wolf-Mountain. Young men could learn the secrets of magic by celebrating the sacred marriage: masturbating over the Goddess's statue and ejecting semen on it. She would guide and protect them, provided they never again set foot in a Christian church.[26] Her votaries' shape-shifting followed the phases of the moon, which was another form of the Goddess herself. In the 12th century, Gervais of Tilbury noted: “In England we often see men changed into wolves at the changes of the moon.”[27]

Sacharow quoted an old Russian charm, to be spoken by one who wished to invoke the Moon-goddess and become a werewolf:

On the sea, on the ocean, on the island, on Bujan, on the empty pasture gleams the moon, on an ashstock lying in a green wood, in a gloomy vale. Toward the stock wandereth a shaggy wolf, horned cattle seeking for his sharp white fangs; but the wolf enters not the forest, but the wolf dives not into the shadowy vale. Moon, moon, gold-horned moon, check the flight of bullets, blunt the hunters' knives, break the shepherds' cudgels, cast wild fear upon all cattle, on men, on all creeping things, that they may not catch the gray wolf, that they may not rend his warm skin! My word is binding, more binding than sleep, more binding than the promise of a hero.[28]

This charm has a ring of peasant magic, suggesting a hungry poacher hoping to steal some fresh meat from the baron's herds, under the protection of a wolf skin. Poaching the overlord's cattle or game was punishable by death, which may account for the cruelty meted out to those accused of lycanthropy. One captured "werewolf" in France was so mauled that, a witness said, "he bore hardly any resemblance to a man, and struck with horror those who looked at him." The inquisitor, Pierre Boguet, explained that terrible injuries were common among werewolves, due to the many lacerations they suffered while running through bramble bushes.[29]

Another werewolf captured by the Inquisition in 1598 was "possessed by a demon" while in prison, which gave him such a thirst that he drank a large tubful of water, so his belly was "distended and hard." He refused to eat or drink any more, and soon died.[30] Translating this official report into its probable reality, one would assume the unlucky werewolf was subjected to the water torture and died of a ruptured stomach.

Another unfortunate werewolf was Peter Stubb of Cologne, tortured until he confessed having transformed himself into a wolf by a magic girdle given him by the devil. The judges couldn't find the girdle where Stubb said he hid it, but they explained this by saying it had "gone to the Devil whence it came, so that it was not to be found." Though his case was unproved, Stubb was nastily executed for the crime of lycanthropy: he was sentenced to have the flesh pulled off his bones in ten places with red-hot pincers, then to have his legs and arms broken with a wooden axe; finally to be beheaded and burned.[31]

Yet another werewolf in 1541 never even lasted long enough to go to prison. His captors hacked off his arms and legs, claiming to be searching for the wolf-hair that he wore on the inside of his skin. The hair was not found, so the victim was declared innocent of lycanthropy—which did him little good, as he was already dead.[32]

An often-repeated story concerned a lone man attacked at night by a lone wolf, which he wounded, usually by cutting off a forepaw. Next day a woman would be found with her hand missing, which identified her as the werewolf. Such an incident was reported as fact by Jean de Nynauld in 1615; the woman in the case was burned alive.[33] The story probably recommended itself to some men as a perfect way to dispose of a woman they had mistreated, such as a rape victim.

On December 14, 1598, a tailor of Chalons was sentenced to

death for lycanthropy, having confessed to luring children into his shop, murdering and eating them. Methods by which these confessions were extracted from the man can only be guessed, because the judges ordered the court records burned. In 1521 at Poligny, three men were induced by torture to say they had made themselves wolves with a magic salve given them by the devil, and in wolf shape they had eaten several children, and enjoyed sexual relations with wild she-wolves.[34] Gilles Garnier was a famous "lycanthrope" caught by the Inquisition, tortured and executed for having devoured children. The charge was not murder or cannibalism, but lycanthropy.[35] Whatever was left of the pagan wolf cults, it seems the Christian church molded the material into the enduring legend of the werewolf.

1. Graves, W.G., 406. 2. Lawson, 250. 3. Summers, W., 144.
4. Graves, G.M. 1, 201; 2, 66. 5. Baring-Gould, C.M.M.A., 129. 6. *Larousse*, 210.
7. Wedeck, 174. 8. Dumézil, 244. 9. Herodotus, 244. 10. Joyce, 299. 11. Rank, 63.
12. H. Smith, 275. 13. Wedeck, 173. 14. Wainwright, 70. 15. Robbins, 325.
16. J.E. Harrison, 131. 17. Scot, 72. 18. Baring-Gould, C.M.M.A., 152–53.
19. H. Smith, 270. 20. Graves, G.M. 1, 211. 21. Goodrich, 180. 22. A. Masters, 93.
23. Baring-Gould, W., 48–49. 24. Spinka, 9. 25. Baring-Gould, W., 64. 26. Leland, 206.
27. Robbins, 327. 28. Baring-Gould, W., 117. 29. Cohen, N.H.U.T., 49.
30. Baring-Gould, W., 83. 31. Robbins, 490. 32. Cohen, N.H.U.T., 44.
33. Robbins, 326. 34. Robbins, 324, 537. 35. Summers. G.W., 23–24.

Wheel

A primary Oriental symbol of the Goddess as ruler of Fate was the karmic wheel, often identified with the wheel of the galaxy, the Milky Way, or zodiac, circling the outer reaches of the universe around the Goddess's yoni or omphalos (navel), her earth-centered hub. Tantric tradition showed the wheel as a mandala centering on the three totems of the Triple Goddess, the dove (Virgin-Creatress), serpent (Mother-Preserver), and sow (Crone-Destroyer).[1] This mandala established "the six realms of the round of being," the sacred **Hexagram**.

Celts worshipped the karmic star-wheel as the emblem of Mother Arianrhod, ancestress of "Aryans." Some said it was a great silver wheel that dipped into the sea, on which heroes rode to Emania, the Moon's land of death.[2]

In Ethiopia the Goddess's image was placed in the center of a wheel of flames, like Indian images of Kali. Christian myths depict the early missionaries' destruction of her idol, which was called an old woman with the power of the evil eye and with feet "like unto a wheel of fire." Jesus commanded: "Take this woman of the evil eye, and make up a fire, and carry her thereto, and throw her into it and burn her."[3] Her ashes were to be scattered to the wind, for people believed she might be resurrected from them, like the Phoenix, if they remained in one place.

Destruction of the Wheel-goddess's image was the probable basis for the legend of St. Catherine, supposedly martyred on a wheel of fire, the famous "Catherine Wheel." There was no real St. Catherine, but there was a Goddess as Dancer of the Fiery Wheel, performing Kathakali—Kali's "dance of time"—at the hub of the universe. The Kalacakra Tantra (Wheel of Time), which presents this image, is still the most revered text in India and Tibet, "coming at the head of the tantric section of the sacred canon."[4] See **Catherine**.

Catherine was not the only medieval manifestation of the Goddess of the Wheel of Time, which was also the Wheel of Fortune manipulated by the trinitarian Mother of Fate, Fortuna. In ancient Rome she was one of the emanations of Juno Februata, whose festival was Christianized as St. Valentine's Day. Its symbol was a wheel of six spokes formed of yonic mandorlas, in the Asiatic manner.[5] The six spokes remained a sign of Juno well into the Christian era.[6]

Wheel of Fortune

In the 12th century, the Goddess and her wheel appeared in the *Hortus deliciarum* (Garden of Delights). Wheel windows of cathedrals were connected with her, some showing human figures rising on one side of the wheel and falling on the other, like the Rota Fortuna at the center of the Tarot's Major Trumps. "In these cathedral churches and royal abbeys is Dame Fortune who turns topsy-turvy faster than a windmill." Honorius of Autun said, "Philosophers tell us of a woman fastened to a wheel which turns perpetually, so that they say she is sometimes rising and sometimes falling with its movement. . . . The woman fastened to the wheel is Fortune, whose head alternately rises and falls." Here was the real St. Catherine: the Fate-goddess, worshipped by builders who incorporated their own secret symbols into the churches they built. Hugo pointed out that "Sometimes a porch, a facade, or a whole church presents a symbolic meaning entirely foreign to worship, even inimical to the Church."[7]

Boethius, a Gnostic philosopher whose writings were too popular to be ignored, was claimed as a Christian theologian; but his major work made no mention of Christ. He found his *Consolation of Philosophy* in the visitation of his guardian Goddesses, Philosophia and Fortuna. The latter taught him her doctrine of the karmic wheel: "I cause a rapid wheel to turn; I love to raise the fallen and abase the proud. Mount, then, if thou wilt, but on condition that thou dost not wax indignant when the law that presides at my Games demands that thou shalt descend."[8]

Fortuna, Goddess of the Wheel, may have been derived from a pre-Roman Vortumna, "She Who Turns the Year."[9] Fate and Time were always linked in the thought of the ancients. Later Roman writers tried to masculinize this Goddess as a seasonal god, Vertumnus; but they gave away "his" original character by saying he appeared in the guise of an old woman. The Goddess was worshipped in both beneficent and maleficent aspects as Bona Fortuna or Mala Fortuna, represented in her temple on the Esquiline as an All-Seeing Eye in the form of a wheel.[10]

As Fortuna Primigeneia, the Goddess of the Wheel was called the firstborn of the primal Mother Juno, and revered as the Virgin "who bestows on her worshippers every grace of body and every beauty of soul."[11] She was identified with the Mazdean "Glory." From her, as the Fortuna Augusti, Caesars drew their divine right to rule.

Her fiery wheel was associated with kingship in a more primitive, direct way during the early Bronze Age, when sacred kings died within the wheel of rebirth, as shown by the legend of Ixion, a ruler of the Thessalian Lapiths.[12] Ixion was killed at the end of his term of office, when he was rolled downhill, fastened inside a fiery wheel that signified the sun. This sacred-king figure might be compared with the Norse deity Kris Kringle, a "Christ of the Wheel," personifying the dying and reborn sun of the winter solstice—hence his later connection with Christmas, even identification with Santa Claus.[13]

Northern Europeans believed the mystic wheels of existence stopped turning at the crucial transition from one year to the next, during the darkest days of winter, when the sun came to its *nadir.* At this time, during the season of Yule, all rotating motions were taboo. Cart wheels were not allowed to roll; butter could not be churned.[14] Yet at the winter solstice and its corresponding point at the other side of the rolling year, Midsummer Eve, fiery fate-wheels were set rolling from British hilltops as late as the 19th century. "The Pagan rites of this festival at the summer solstice, may be considered as a counterpart of those used at the winter solstice at Yule-tide. . . . [T]he people imagine that all their ill-luck rolls away from them together with this wheel."[15]

Pseudo-Dionysius the Areopagite, a 6th-century Christian mystic who pretended to be a 1st-century bishop of Athens and was believed authentic for many centuries, declared that the class of angels called Thrones were really Wheels, having the name of Gel, "which in the Hebrew tongue signifies revolutions and revelations."[16] This image was Oriental, drawn from the vision of eastern temples as gigantic world-chariots, complete with wheels, in which the god was enthroned. In his chariot the god participated in the Carnival of Existence, carrying the world along with all its teeming life forms: animals, plants, mountains, rivers. Upon identification with the god, the sages said, "He who has seen his true self looks down upon transmigrating existence as upon a rolling chariot-wheel."[17]

Medieval processions sometimes took a circular form and went round and round a public square or courtyard, this exhibition being known as a *carrousel,* "a wheel of chariots."[18] The inclusion of its model in the proceedings of carnivals and fairs bears out the probability of its pagan origin, for most of the traditional trappings of fairs were left over from the Old Religion, including the wheel of Fortune.

The very name of the Carnival came from old festivals of the Goddess Carna, mother of "re-in-Carnations," the same cycles controlled by Kali's wheel of karma. The *roulette* or "little wheel" evolved from the eastern prayer wheel. Its spirit was not only Dame Fortune, but also Lady Luck, from Sanskrit *Loka,* a Divine Midwife guarding one of the planetary spheres or "ascending light planes of experience."[19]

Another carnival manifestation of the wheel was the Ferris Wheel, a form of the Fairies' Wheel, descended from the Celtic Wheel of Arianrhod. Riders of the Wheel represented pre-Christian "fairy folk" whose souls were involved in karmic cycles. The *Dream of King Arthur* describes a Fairies' Wheel closely resembling the modern Ferris Wheel.[20]

1. Campbell, C.M., 416. 2. Spence, 152–53. 3. Gifford, 57. 4. Tatz & Kent, 18. 5. Brewster, 104. 6. Koch, 54. 7. Mâle, 95–97, 395. 8. Mâle, 96. 9. Graves, G.M. 1, 126. 10. Elworthy, 195. 11. Cumont, M.M., 111. 12. Campbell, C.M., 422. 13. Wainwright, 245. 14. Oxenstierna, 214. 15. Hazlitt, 346. 16. Hughes, 29. 17. Rawson, A.T., 193. 18. Moakley, 44. 19. Avalon, 40. 20. B. Butler, 147.

Whisper

The ancients believed that ghosts and spirits would speak in whispers. Having been deprived of flesh, the dead spoke without laryngeal sound. Nearly all supernatural beings were supposed to be identifiable by their whisper-voices, even God, according to 1 Kings 19:12—the "still small voice" of God speaking to Elijah was a mistranslation of a phase meaning literally "a thin whisper."[1]

Other biblical parallels are Job 4:16, the same word "whisper" translated as a still voice; and Isaiah 29:4: "Thy voice shall be as one that hath a familiar spirit, out of the ground, and thy speech shall whisper out of the dust." These passages indicate the practice of ancient "spirit mediums" when purporting to be in communication with the dead. Impersonating the spirit, they whispered, so the voice couldn't be identified.

In a medieval German legend, the Triple Goddess presided over a land of the dead called Wisperthal (Valley of Whispers) centering on an enchanted Hall of Mirrors—perhaps related to the fairy-tale Crystal Mountain. Three innocent youths once trespassed in the valley, met various aspects of the Goddess as three beautiful maidens, three terrible hags, and three black death-ravens. They barely escaped with their lives from the eerie place and vowed never to return.[2]

1. Hooke, S.P., 57. 2. Guerber, L.R., 219.

Whistling

An old rhyme says "Whistling girls and crowing hens never come to any good ends." It was true; women who whistled were suspected of witchcraft. Whistling was a piece of sympathetic magic used to raise a wind. Becalmed sailors were allowed to "whistle for the wind," but whistling women were believed to cause destructive storms.[1] Therefore it became "unladylike" for girls to whistle.

1. Robbins, 361.

Widdershins

var. Withershins

Counterclockwise, the direction of the moon, or "left-hand path" of pagan dances (still prevalent in folk tradition). To open the door of a fairy hill, one must walk around it three times widdershins, as Childe Rowland did, calling, "Open door!" The same Open Sesame appears in other ballads: "Thrice went fair Agnes the mountain round, and entered the cave beneath the ground."[1] As sacred caves once served as pagan temples, the medieval church forbade their use and claimed that walking or turning one's self widdershins was an *indicium* of witchcraft.[2] See **Left Hand.**

1. Wimberly, 363, 367. 2. Robbins, 209, 421.

Willow

Water and willows represented the Goddess Helice, "Willow," virgin form of Hecate with her willow-withe grain-basket.[1] Willow wands invoked the Muses, whose mountain was encircled by the Helicon, "Willow-stream." The Dionysian thyrsus, like the later witch's wand, was willow. As Dionysus was once a major god of Jerusalem, the willow figured prominently in municipal ceremonies there. A "Great Day" of the Feast of Tabernacles was known as the Day of Willows, with rites honoring fire and water.[2] Willow wands gave protection in the underworld, where Orpheus carried one to show the way.[3] Willow wands were sacred to the Moon-goddess as late as the 17th century A.D., when an English herbal said the moon owns the willow.

Witches used willow bark to treat rheumatism and fevers; it was the source of salicylic acid (aspirin), one of Hecate's cures. Some said *wicca* or "witchcraft" evolved from a word meaning willow, cognate with "wicker" (willow-withe weaving). Magic cats were supposed to grow from pussy-willows or "catkins," to become witches' *malkins* (familiars): hence the saying that all cats were gray in the beginning. The catkins were harbingers of spring, appearing on the willow as graymalkins. (See **Cat**.)

1. Graves, G.M. 1, 115. 2. Graves, W.G., 47. 3. Pepper & Wilcock, 57.

Witch

There were many other words for witches, such as Incantatrix, Lamia, Saga, Maga, Malefica, Sortilega, Strix, Venefica.[3] In Italy a witch was a strega or Janara, an old title of a priestess of Jana (Juno).[4] English writers called witches both "hags" and "fairies," words which were once synonymous.[5] Witches had metaphoric titles: bacularia, "stick-rider"; fascinatrix, "one with the evil eye"; herberia, "one who gathers herbs"; strix, "screech-owl"; pixidria, "keeper of an ointment-box"; femina saga, "wise-woman"; lamia, "night-monster"; incantator, "worker of charms"; magus, "wise-man"; sortiariae mulier, "seeress"; veneficia, "poisoner"; maliarda, "evil-doer." Latin treatises called witches anispex, auguris, divinator, januatica, ligator, mascara, phitonissa, stregula.[6]

Dalmatian witches were *krstaca,* "crossed ones," a derivative of the Greek *Christos.*[7] In Holland a witch was *wijsseggher,* "wise-sayer," from which came the English "wiseacre."[8] The biblical passage that supported centuries of persecution, "Thou shalt not suffer a witch to live" (Exodus 22:18), used the Hebrew word *kasaph,* translated "witch" although it means a seer or diviner.[9]

Early medieval England had female clan-leaders who exercised matriarchal rights in lawgiving and law enforcement; the Magna Carta of Chester called them *iudices de wich*—judges who were witches.[10] Female elders once had political power among the clans, but patriarchal religion and law gradually took it away from them and called them witches in order to dispose of them. In 1711 Addison observed that "When an old woman begins to doat and grow chargeable to a Parish, she is generally turned into a witch."[11]

Scot remarked that the fate of a witch might be directly proportional to her fortune. The pope made saints out of rich witches, but poor witches were burned.[12] Among many examples tending to support this opinion was the famous French *Chambre Ardente* affair, which involved many members of the aristocracy and the upper-class clergy in a witch cult. Numerous male and female servants were tortured and burned for assisting their masters in working witchcraft; but in all the four years the affair dragged on, no noble person was tortured or executed.[13]

Illogically enough, the authorities persecuted poor, outcast folk as witches, yet professed to believe witches could provide themselves with all the wealth anyone could want. Reginald Scot, a disbeliever, scornfully observed that witches were said to "transfer their neighbors' corn into their own ground, and yet are perpetual beggars, and cannot enrich themselves, either with money or otherwise: who is so foolish as to remain longer in doubt of their supernatural powers?"[14] Witchcraft brought so little profit to Helen Jenkenson of Northants, hanged in 1612 for bewitching a child, that the record of her execution said: "Thus ended this woman her miserable life, after she had lived many years poor, wretched, scorned and forsaken of the world."[15]

The nursery-rhyme stereotype of the witch owed much to Scot's description:

> *Women which be commonly old, lame, blear-eyed, pale, foul, and full of wrinkles; poor, sullen, superstitious, and papists; or such as know no religion; in whose drowsy minds the devil hath gotten a fine seat; so as, what mischief, mischance, calamity, or slaughter is brought to pass, they are easily persuaded the same is done by themselves. . . . They are*

Skeat's Etymological Dictionary derived "witch" from medieval English *wicche,* formerly Anglo-Saxon *wicca,* masculine, or *wicce,* feminine: a corruption of *witga,* short form of *witega,* a seer or diviner; from Anglo-Saxon *witan,* to see, to know. Similarly, Icelandic *vitki,* a witch, came from *vita,* to know; or *vizkr,* clever or knowing one. Wizard came from Norman French *wischard,* Old French *guiscart,* sagacious one.[1] The surname Whittaker came from *Witakarlege,* a wizard or a witch.[2] The words "wit" and "wisdom" came from the same roots.

lean and deformed, showing melancholy in their faces, to the horror of all that see them. They are doting, scolds, mad, devilish; and not much differing from them that are thought to be possessed with spirits.[16]

Persecutors said it was heretical to consider witches harmless. Even in England, where witches were not burned but hanged, some authorities fearfully cited the "received opinion" that a witch's body should be burned to ashes to prevent ill effects arising from her blood.[17] Churchmen assured the arresting officers that a witch's power was lost the instant she was touched by an employee of the Inquisition; but the employees themselves were not so sure.[18]

Numerous stories depict the persecutors' fear of their victims. It was said in the Black Forest that a witch blew in her executioner's face, promising him his reward; the next day he was afflicted with a fatal leprosy. Inquisitors' handbooks directed them to wear at all times a bag of salt consecrated on Palm Sunday; to avoid looking in a witch's eyes; and to cross themselves constantly in the witches' prison. Peter of Berne forgot this precaution, and a captive witch by enchantment made him fall down a flight of stairs—which he proved later by torturing her until she confirmed it.[19]

Any unusual ability in a woman instantly raised a charge of witchcraft. The so-called Witch of Newbury was murdered by a group of soldiers because she knew how to go "surfing" on the river. Soldiers of the Earl of Essex saw her doing it, and were "as much astonished as they could be," seeing that "to and fro she fleeted on the board standing firm bolt upright . . . turning and winding it which way she pleased, making it pastime to her, as little thinking who perceived her tricks, or that she did imagine that they were the last she ever should show." Most of the soldiers were afraid to touch her, but a few brave souls ambushed the board-rider as she came to shore, slashed her head, beat her, and shot her, leaving her "detested carcass to the worms."[20]

From ruthlessly organized persecutions on the continent, witch-hunts in England became largely cases of village feuds and petty spite. If crops failed, horses ran away, cattle sickened, wagons broke, women miscarried, or butter wouldn't come in the churn, a witch was always found to blame. Marion Cumlaquoy of Orkney was burned in 1643 for turning herself three times widdershins, to make her neighbor's barley crop rot. A tailor's wife was executed for quarrelling with her neighbor, who afterward saw a snake on his property, and his children fell sick. One witch was condemned for arguing with a drunkard in an alehouse. After drinking himself into paroxysms of vomiting, he accused her of bewitching him, and he was believed.[21]

A woman was convicted of witchcraft for having caused a neighbor's lameness—by pulling off her stockings. Another was executed for having admired a neighbor's baby, which afterward fell out of its cradle and died. Two Glasgow witches were hanged for treating a sick child, even though the treatment succeeded and the child was cured. Joan Cason of Kent went to the gallows in 1586 for having dry thatch on her roof. Her neighbor, whose child was sick, was told by an unidentified traveler that the child was bewitched, and it could be proved by stealing a bit of thatch from the witch's roof and throwing it on the fire. If it crackled and sparked, witchcraft was assured. The test came out positive, and the court was satisfied enough to convict poor Joan.[22]

Witches were convenient scapegoats for doctors who failed to cure their patients, for it was the "received" belief that witch-caused illnesses were incurable. Weyer said, "Ignorant and clumsy physicians blame all sicknesses which they are unable to cure or which they have treated wrongly, on witchery." There were also priests and monks who "claim to understand the healing art and they lie to those who seek help that their sicknesses are derived from witchery."[23] Most real witch persecutions reflect "no erotic orgies, no Sabbats or elaborate rituals; merely the hatreds and spites of narrow peasant life assisted by vicious laws."[24]

Witches provided a focus for sexist hatred in male-dominated society, as Stanton pointed out:

> *The spirit of the Church in its contempt for women, as shown in the Scriptures, in Paul's epistles and the Pentateuch, the hatred of the fathers, manifested in their ecclesiastical canons, and in the doctrines of asceticism, celibacy, and witchcraft, destroyed man's respect for woman and legalized the burning, drowning, and torturing of women. . . .*
>
> *Women and their duties became objects of hatred to the Christian missionaries and of alternate scorn and fear to pious ascetics and monks. The priestess mother became something impure, associated with the devil, and her lore an infernal incantation, her very cooking a brewing of poison, nay, her very existence a source of sin to man. Thus woman, as mother and priestess, became woman as witch. . . .*
>
> *Here is the reason why in all the Biblical researches and higher criticism, the scholars never touch the position of women.*[25]

Men displayed a lively interest in the physical appearance of witches, seeking to know how to recognize them—as men also craved rules for recognizing other types of women from their physical appearance. It was generally agreed that any woman with dissimilar eyes was a witch. Where most people had dark eyes and swarthy complexions, as in Spain and Italy, pale blue eyes were associated with witchcraft. Many claimed any woman with red hair was a witch.[26]

This may have been because red-haired people are usually freckled, and freckles were often identified as "witch marks," as were moles, warts, birthmarks, pimples, pockmarks, cysts, liver spots, wens, or any other blemish. Some witch-finders said the mark could resemble an insect bite or an ulcer.[27]

Thomas Ady One of the few 17th-century English debunkers of the witchcraft craze; author of *A Perfect Discovery of Witches* (1661).

No one ever explained how the witch mark differed from an ordinary blemish. Since few bodies were unblemished, the search for the mark seldom failed. Thomas Ady recognized this, and wrote: "Very few people in the world are without privy marks upon their bodies, as moles or stains, even such as witchmongers call the devil's privy marks."[28] But no one paid attention to this.

Trials were conducted with as much injustice as possible. In 1629 Isobel Young was accused of crippling by magic a man who had quarrelled with her, and causing a water mill to break down. She protested that the man was lame before their quarrel, and water mills can break down through neglect. The prosecutor, Sir Thomas Hope, threw out her defense on the ground that it was "contrary to the libel," that is, it contradicted the charge.[29] When a witch is on trial, Scot said, any "equivocal or doubtful answer is taken for a confession."[30]

On the other hand, no answer at all was a confession too. Witches who refused to speak were condemned: "Witchcraft proved by silence of the accused."[31] Sometimes mere playfulness "proved" witchcraft, as in the case of Mary Spencer, accused in 1634 because she merrily set her bucket rolling downhill and ran before it, calling it to follow her.[32] Sometimes women were stigmatized as witches when they were in fact victims of unfair laws, such as the law that accepted any man's word in court ahead of any number of women's. A butcher in Germany stole some silver vessels from women, then had them prosecuted for witchcraft by claiming that he found the vessels in the woods where the women were attending a witches' sabbat.[33]

Sometimes the accusation of witchcraft was a form of punishment for women who were too vocal about their disillusionment with men and their preference for living alone. Historical literature has many references to "the joy with which women after widowhood set up their own households, and to the vigor with which they resisted being courted by amorous widowers."[34] The solitary life, however, left a woman even more vulnerable to accusations of witchcraft, since men usually thought she must be somehow controlled.

Those who tortured the unfortunate defendant into admitting witchcraft used a euphemistic language that showed the victim was condemned *a priori.* One Anne Marie de Georgel denied making a devil's pact, until by torture she was "justly forced to give an account of herself," the record said. Catherine Delort was "forced to confess by the means we have power to use to make people speak the truth," and she was "convicted of all the crimes we suspected her of committing, although she protested her innocence for a long time." The inquisitor Nicholas Rémy professed a pious astonishment at the great number of witches who expressed a "positive desire for death," pretending not to notice that they had been brought to this desire by innumerable savage tortures.[35] See **Torture**.

The extent to which pagan religion, as such, actually survived among the witches of the 16th and 17th centuries has been much discussed but never decided. Dean Church said, "Society was a long time unlearning heathenism; it has not done so yet; but it had hardly begun, at any rate it was only just beginning, to imagine the possibility

Dean R.W. Church British clergyman, author of *St. Anselm* (1870).

of such a thing in the eleventh century." In 15th-century Bohemia it was still common practice at Christmas and other holidays to make offerings to "the gods," rather than to God.[36] European villages still had many "wise-women" who acted as priestesses officially or unofficially. Since church fathers declared Christian priestesses unthinkable, all functions of the priestess were associated with paganism.[37] Bishops described pagan gatherings in their dioceses, attended by "devils . . . in the form of men and women."[38] Pagan ceremonies were allowed to survive in weddings, folk festivals, seasonal rites, feasts of the dead, and so on.[39] But when women or Goddesses played the leading role in such ceremonies, there was more determined suppression. John of Salisbury wrote that it was the devil, "with God's permission," who sent people to gatherings in honor of the Queen of the Night, a priestess impersonating the Moon-goddess under the name of Noctiluca or Herodiade.[40]

The Catholic church applied the word "witch" to any woman who criticized church policies. Women allied with the 14th-century Reforming Franciscans, some of whom were burned for heresy, were described as witches, daughters of Judas, and instigated of the Devil.[41] Writers of the Talmud similarly tended to view nearly all women as witches. They said things like, "Women are naturally inclined to witchcraft," and "The more women there are, the more witchcraft there will be."[42]

Probably there were few sincere practitioners, compared with the multitudes who were railroaded into the ecclesiastical courts and legally murdered despite their innocence. Yet it was obvious to even the moderately intelligent that Christian society deliberately humiliated and discriminated against women. Some may have been resentful enough to become defiant. "Women have had no voice in the canon law, the catechisms, the church creeds and discipline, and why should they obey the behests of a strictly masculine religion, that places the sex at a disadvantage in all life's emergencies?"[43] Possibilities for expressing their frustration and defiance were severely limited; but voluntary adoption of the witch's reputation and behavior was surely among such possibilities.

1. Leland, 66. 2. Wainwright, 238. 3. Wedeck, 140. 4. Elworthy, 353. 5. Scot, 550. 6. Robbins, 544. 7. Leland, 66. 8. Funk, 116. 9. J.B. Russell, 54. 10. Wainwright, 97. 11. Phillips, 180. 12. Scot, 259. 13. Robbins, 84. 14. Scot, 405. 15. Rosen, 354. 16. H. Smith, 269; Scot, 5. 17. Summers, V., 81. 18. Robbins, 334. 19. Lea unabridged, 815, 831. 20. Ewen, 251–53. 21. Rosen, 326–28. 22. Rosen, 163–64. 23. Bromberg, 59. 24. Maple, 49. 25. Daly, 69. 26. de Lys, 149. 27. Castiglioni, 243. 28. Robbins, 552. 29. Robbins, 456. 30. Scot, 19. 31. Baroja, 202. 32. Holmes, 112. 33. Baroja, 124. 34. Boulding, 554. 35. Baroja, 85–86, 117. 36. Miles, 35, 183. 37. Boulding, 361. 38. Baroja, 64. 39. Miles, 161, 190–91. 40. Baroja, 62. 41. Beard, 277. 42. Baroja, 80. 43. Stanton, 74.

Witchcraft

Early in the Middle Ages, almost anything women did could be described as witchcraft because their daily lives invoked the Goddess with a thousand small ceremonies as well as the larger ones connected with major holidays. Martin of Braga said women must be condemned for "decorating tables, wearing laurels, taking omens from footsteps, putting fruit and wine on the log in the hearth, and bread in the well, what are these but worship of the devil? For women to call upon Minerva when they spin, and to observe the day of Venus at weddings and to call upon her whenever they go out upon the public highway, what is that but worship of the devil?"[1]

Outside the official religion, where they were kept, women passed down their private family recipes and charms, curses and blessings, telling traditional tales of the past and foretelling the future from omens and "signs." The Dominican Johann Herolt declared: "Most women belie their catholic faith with charms and spells, after the fashion of Eve their first mother, who believed the devil speaking through the serpent rather than God himself. . . . [A]ny woman by herself knows more of such superstitions and charms than a hundred men."[2]

Up to the 15th century, women's "charms and spells" were virtually the only repository of practical medicine. Churchmen avoided doctoring, on the ground that all sickness came from demonic possession, and the only permissible cure was exorcism.[3]

Europe's traditional witch doctors were women: clan mothers, priestesses of healing shrines, midwives, nurses, *vilas.* In pre-Christian Gaul and Scandinavia, medicine was entirely in the hands of women.[4] Even in the Christian era, the village wise-woman was still every peasant's family doctor. Paracelsus said witches taught him everything he knew about healing.[5] Dr. Lambe, the Duke of Buckingham's famous "devil," was said to have learned secrets of medicine by consorting with witches.[6]

In 1570 the gaoler of Canterbury Castle released a condemned witch, citing the popular opinion that she did more good for the sick with her homely remedies than all the priests' prayers and exorcisms.[7] Agrippa von Nettesheim thought witches superior to male practitioners: "Are not philosophers, mathematicians, and astrologers often inferior to country women in their divinations and predictions, and does not the old nurse very often beat the doctor?"[8] The men who learned doctoring from witches were allowed to practice, but their female teachers were persecuted. Scot observed that a male "conjurer" was permitted to cure disease by magic arts, whereas a woman was condemned to death for doing so.[9]

Ordinary folk had no doctors. Physicians were available chiefly to the rich. The poor took their troubles to the local witch. Irish farmers still say a "fairy doctor" is needed for charms against the evil eye. In Greece, "both priests and witches are available for emergencies created by the evil eye. The priest burns incense and recites appropriate prayers. The witch also burns incense as she recites appropriate incantations."[10]

It wasn't unusual for the witches' healing charms to be preferred to those of the church, or for the two to be regarded as identical in essence. Ramesey wrote that the witches' cures were indistinguishable from the "magical and juggling cures" professed by the clergy, including "saints, images, relics, holy-waters, shrines, avemarys, crucifixes, benedictions, charms, characters, sigils of the planets, and of the signs . . . all such cures are rather to be ascribed to the forces of the imagination, than any virtue in them."[11]

Officially, women were often forbidden to do any kind of healing. In 1322 a woman named Jacoba Felicie was arrested and prosecuted by the medical faculty of the University of Paris for practicing medicine, although, the record said, "she was wiser in the art of surgery and medicine than the greatest master or doctor in Paris."[12]

Scot said witchmongers gave the witches as much power as Christ, and even more, when they claimed witches could raise the dead, as Christ raised Lazarus; they could turn water into other fluids, like wine or milk; they could control the weather, the crops, animals, men; they could see into the past and future. Reading of witches' trials, he said, "you shall see such impossibilities confessed, as none, having his right wits, will believe."[13] Loher also declared that the "sins" for which witches were brought to the stake were such "that they could not possibly commit."[14]

Churchmen, however, viewed the impossibility of witches' miracles as perfectly good ground for believing them, "because the performance of the impossible proved that demons were at work."[15] It was never explained how the performance of a miracle demonstrated the intervention of a saint in one case and of a demon in another. For example, Marie Bucaille was burned as a witch, though her "miracles" were saintlike: she healed the sick, saw holy visions, displayed stigmata, and performed many of the acts that led to canonization in other cases.[16]

The same acts were differently interpreted by churchmen in different times. Witchcraft was allowed through the first half of the Christian era. It was not called a "heresy" until the 14th century. In 500 A.D. the Franks' Salic Law recognized witches' right to practice. In 643, an edict declared it illegal to burn witches.[17] In 785, the Synod of Paderborn said anyone who burned a witch must be sentenced to death.[18] France's first trial to declare witchcraft a crime took place in 1390.[19]

Up to a surprisingly late date, nobility and clergy alike employed the services of witches. In 1382 the Count of Kyburg hired a witch to stand on the battlements of his castle and raise a thunderstorm to disperse an army of enemies.[20] This practice was soundly based on theological opinion that witches could raise storms at will, "either upon sea or land."[21] Churchmen said witches controlled the weather "with God's permission," and they didn't begin to punish what God permitted until the beginning of the Renaissance.[22]

Witches were summoned to court by Louis d'Orleans to cure his brother's madness, after priestly exorcisms had failed. (The witches also failed.) Guichard, Bishop of Troyes, used the classic pierced-puppet kind of witchcraft to kill his enemy, Queen Blanche of Navarre.[23]

English law was fairly tolerant of witchcraft until the reign of James I. As late as 1371 a male witch was arrested in Southwark for possessing magical articles: a skull, a grimoire, and a corpse's head for divination. He was released after he had promised not to do it again.[24] In 1560, a lenient period, eight men confessed to conjuration and sorcery, and were released with a reprimand. Only three years later the same acts were made punishable by imprisonment or a death penalty.[25]

The Council of Treves in 1310 outlawed conjurations, divinations, and love potions.[26] Further prohibitions seemed to be aimed at supporting husbands who wished to cast off their wives. Stringent laws threatened a witch to whom an abandoned wife might apply, for revenge through *malefica,* since she had no recourse under law.[27]

The church distinguished between sorcery, which was generally acceptable, and witchcraft, which was heresy. Von Nettesheim's books of sorcery were published under church auspices, accompanied by a statement of ecclesiastical approval; indeed, his instructor in magic had been John Trithemius, an abbot. What the distinction between sorcery and witchcraft boiled down to was that men could practice magic, women could not.[28]

When the church discovered that common folk couldn't understand the doctrinal subtleties of heresy and didn't care about theological arguments, persecution was extended into areas that were accessible to the public mind, so the church could maintain its control of that mind. For example, in the region of Bonn a late spring frost of 1610 ruined crops and was officially described as an act of God. Twenty years later, after the witch judges came to the area, the same kind of natural disasters were blamed exclusively on witches.[29]

Churchmen fostered the public delusion that witches were engaged in a vast secret plot, under the devil's guidance, to overthrow the kingdom of God on earth. They created and embellished the concept of the black mass, and made laymen believe it frequently occurred, whereas it was largely a fraud supported only by spurious "evidence" from the torture chamber. The Inquisition needed this public delusion, because the work it was created for was finished when the Albigensian, Waldensian, and other heretic groups of the south of France had been finally crushed. In order to continue its profitable existence, the Inquisition needed new victims. The witchcraft mania was the solution to its problem.[30] Whatever secular crimes the witches were supposed to have committed, the one crime that was decisive in sending all of them to the stake was the one crime of which all of them were completely innocent, because it was impossible: the crime of collaborating with a real devil. As for secret continuation of a pre-Christian religion: that was more often done by the church itself, in the guise of saint-worship, festivals, healing shrines, etc.

Scholars aren't sure how much pagan religion survived in the form of actual group worship, at the beginning of the era of persecution. Pico della Mirandola's *La Strega* (The Witch) described a cult in northern Italy where a pagan Goddess presided over sexual orgies; she was said to bear a close resemblance to the Mother of God.[31] Another group at Arras was said to have centered on "a prostitute" called Demiselle, or The Maiden. Her consort was the Abbot of Little Sense, otherwise known as the Prince of Fools, a composer and singer of popular songs—in other words, it was a cult of minstrelsy.[32] (See **Romance**.)

There is a vast body of "information" about what went on at the witches' Sabbat—all of it worthless, because its source was the torture chamber. The late Renaissance saw a frivolous interest in "black masses" among the wealthy, who tried to model a new cult group on what they had read of earlier trials. In 1610, Pierre de l'Ancre wrote of "great Lords and Ladies and other rich and powerful ones who handle the great matters of the Sabbath, where they appear cloaked, and the women with masks, that they may keep themselves always hidden and unknown."[33] In the reign of Louis XIV, half the Parisian clergy and most of the court, including Madame de Montespan, were involved with a society witch called La Voisin, who staged black masses for them.[34] But their rituals were based on ecclesiastical literature, not on a true folk tradition.

Françoise Athénaïs de Rochechouart, Marquise de Montespan (1641-1707). Mistress of Louis XIV for 13 years, mother of seven of his children; court patroness of Corneille, Racine, and La Fontaine.

It has been claimed that witchcraft constituted a coherent underground organization from the beginning, with well-defined chains of command and communication. "Witch books" purporting to come from the ancient tradition speak of a Brotherhood (not Sisterhood): "If you are condemned, fear not, the Brotherhood is powerful, they will help you to escape if you stand steadfast. . . . Be sure, if steadfast you go to the pyre, drugs will reach you, you will feel naught. You but go to death and what lies beyond, the Ecstasy of the Goddess."[35] But during the real persecutions, few witches seemed indifferent to their sufferings, and virtually none escaped.

Monstrelet described a typical early example of persecution in 1459.

> *In this year, in the town of Arras and county of Artois, arose, through a terrible and melancholy chance, an opinion called, I know not why, the Religion of Vaudoisie. This sect consisted, it is said, of certain persons, both men and women, who, under cloud of night, by the power of the devil, repaired to some solitary spot, amid woods and deserts, where the devil appeared before them in a human form—save that his visage is never perfectly visible to them—read to the assembly a book of his ordinances, informing them how he could be obeyed; distributed a very little money and a plentiful meal, which was concluded by a scene of general profligacy; after which each one of the party was conveyed home to her or his own habitation.*
>
> *On accusations of access to such acts of madness, several creditable persons of the town of Arras were seized and imprisoned along with some foolish women and persons of little consequence. These were so horribly*

tortured that some of them admitted the truth of the whole accusations, and said, besides, that they had seen and recognized in their nocturnal assembly many persons of rank, prelates, seigneurs, and governors of bailliages and cities, being such names as the examiners had suggested to the persons examined, while they constrained them by torture to impeach the persons to whom they belonged. Several of those who had been thus informed against were arrested, thrown into prison, and tortured for so long a time that they also were obliged to confess what was charged against them. After this those of mean condition were executed and inhumanly burnt, while the richer and more powerful of the accused ransomed themselves by sums of money, to avoid the punishment and the shame attending it. Many even of those also confessed being persuaded to take that course by the interrogators, who promised them indemnity for life and fortune. Some there were, of a truth, who suffered with marvellous patience and constancy the torments inflicted on them, and would confess nothing imputed to their charge; but they, too, had to give large sums to the judges, who exacted that such of them as, notwithstanding their mishandling, were still able to move, should banish themselves from that part of the country. . . . [I]t ought not to be concealed that the whole accusation was a strategem of wicked men for their own covetous purposes, and in order, by these false accusations and forced confessions, to destroy the life, fame, and fortune of wealthy persons.[36]

Those prisoners who found themselves condemned to death immediately shrieked aloud that they had been tricked; they were promised a light sentence, such as a pilgrimage, if they confessed as the inquisitors wanted.[37]

Witchcraft persecutions picked up momentum when inquisitors were seeking new victims to keep their organization going. In 1375 a French inquisitor lamented that all the rich heretics had been exterminated; there were none left whose wealth could support the Inquisition, and "it is a pity that so salutary an institution as ours should be so uncertain of its future." Then Pope John XXII empowered the Inquisition to prosecute anyone who worked magic, and "the Inquisition slowly and unevenly developed its concept of witchcraft."[38] Soon the church was making sweeping claims, such as the claim that the entire population of Navarre consisted of witches.[39]

Witch hunting sustained itself because it became a major industry, supporting the income of many. Local nobles, bishops, kings, judges, courts, townships, magistrates, and other functionaries high and low all received a share of the loot collected by inquisitors from their victims' assets. Victims were charged for the very ropes that bound them and the wood that burned them. Each procedure of torture carried its fee. After the execution of a wealthy witch, officials usually treated themselves to a banquet at the expense of the victim's estate.[40]

Inquisitors were no less zealous in wringing the last penny out of their poorer victims than in helping themselves to the estates of the rich. In 1256, a woman named Raymonde Barbaira died before her sentence could be carried out, leaving to her heirs a chest of linens, her clothes, several cows, and four sous in cash. The inquisitor demanded from the heirs forty sous for all the property. "Such petty and vulgar details," Lea said, "give us a clearer insight into the spirit and working of the Inquisition, and of the grinding oppression which it exercised on the subject populations."[41]

A history of the Inquisition written by a Catholic in 1909 had to admit that it "invented the crime of witchcraft and . . . relied on torture as the means of proving it." At first the Inquisition encountered skepticism everywhere. Even theologians shocked the inquisitors by attributing natural disasters to chance, or God, rather than to witchcraft. The public disbelieved witches' confessions, saying they were extracted only by torture. Peasants in some subalpine valleys broke into open rebellion against the judges' wholesale burnings. It took decades of ceaseless propagandizing, and ruthless measures to stop the mouths of critics, before the persecution could be said to have won public support.[42]

Severe persecution dated from the bull of Pope Innocent VIII, *Summis desiderantes,* wherein God's vicar "infallibly" declared that witches could blast crops and domestic animals, cause disease, prevent husbands and wives from copulating, and in general "outrage the Divine Majesty and are a cause of scandal and danger to very many."[43] The Divine Majesty being apparently unable to look after its own interests without human help, the churchmen took it upon themselves to carry out God's vengeance, which developed into a "hideous nightmare" as the church's mailed fist stretched over the western world for five centuries.[44]

The earlier Canon Episcopi ruled that witchcraft was nothing but a delusion, and it was heresy to believe in it. But that was before the church discovered how to profit from the witchcraft belief. After Pope Innocent's reign, it was heresy *not* to believe in witchcraft. According to Martin Del Rio, S.J., anyone who thought witchcraft was only a deception must be suspected of being a witch. No one was allowed to speak against the extermination of witches. Inquisitor Heinrich von Schultheis said, "He who opposes the extermination of the witches with one single word can not expect to remain unscathed."[45]

Superstitious belief in the "evil" of witchcraft persisted to a very late date. The last English witch trial took place in 1712. The last official witch burning in Scotland was in 1727, with unofficial incidents even later. Only a century ago, an elderly woman in the Russian village of Wratschewe was locked in her cottage and set afire for bewitching cattle. Her murderers were tried, and sentenced only to a light ecclesiastical penance.[46] In January, 1928, a family of Hungarian peasants beat an old woman to death, claiming she was a witch. A court acquitted them, on the ground that they acted out of "irresistible compulsion."[47]

The real reason for persistence of the witchcraft idea was that Christian authorities couldn't let it die, without admitting that God's word was wrong, and God's servants had committed millions of legal murders and tortured millions of helpless people without cause. Dr. Blackstone, England's ultimate authority on jurisprudence, wrote: "To deny the possibility, nay, actual existence of Witchcraft and Sorcery, is at once flatly to contradict the revealed Word of God in various passages both of the Old and New Testament; and the thing itself is a truth to which every Nation in the World hath in its turn borne testimony." When skepticism about witchcraft seemed to be on the rise, John Wesley cried bitterly, "The giving up of witchcraft is in effect the giving up of the Bible."[48] Calvin and Knox also protested that denial of witchcraft meant denial of the Bible's authority.[49] Joseph Glanvill, chaplain to Charles II, said all who disbelieved in witchcraft were atheists.[50]

Despite such protests, skepticism grew with the slow advance of the Age of Enlightenment. In 1736, Scottish laws against the "crime" of witchcraft were formally repealed. Yet the church refused to keep pace with the law. Forty years later, ministers of the Associated Presbytery passed a resolution declaring their unabated belief in witchcraft.[51] As late as the 1920s a rector of four parishes in Norfolk could still write: "If I were to take a census of opinion in all four villages I am certain that I should find a majority of people seriously professing belief in witchcraft, the policy of the 'evil eye,' and the efficacy of both good and evil spells."[52] The churches wouldn't let these beliefs die.

Christianity, then, has been chiefly responsible for the survival and growth of witchcraft as an article of faith. It seems so still. In the 1940s, Seabrook estimated that "half the literate white population in the world today believe in witchcraft"; and the nonliterate nonwhite population attains a much higher proportion.[53] A Gallup poll taken in 1978 showed that ten percent of all Americans believe in witches.[54]

But what is meant by "believe in"? It could mean a belief that there are people who call themselves witches; this is self-evident enough. It could mean a belief that such people erroneously think they have supernatural powers. It could mean a belief that such people really do have supernatural powers. It could mean a belief that, as the church has always maintained, witches are agents of the devil, seeking to destroy the world out of sheer perversity. Or, it could mean a belief that witches preserved an older and better religion based on worship of Nature and the female principle.

Those who now call themselves witches usually uphold some version of the latter belief. A modern witch, Leo Louis Martello, says:

> *We worship and identify with the Horned God, Lord of the Hunt and the Underworld, and the Mother Goddess, especially the latter (Mother Earth, Mother Nature). Without the female principle (women) man wouldn't be here. . . . Witchcraft is a pre-Christian faith. . . . It tends to be matriarchal whereas both Christianity and Satanism are patriarchal and*

male chauvinist. The latter two are merely opposite sides of the same coin. Witchcraft, as the Old Religion, is a coin of a different vintage, predating both.[55]

Asked how he feels about belonging to a heavily matriarchal tradition, one male witch answered: "I'd rather be first mate on a ship that is solid than captain on a ship that has a rotten hull, a ship that is sinking. Patriarchy is such a ship." Witches have defined patriarchy as "manipulative and domineering." The matriarchal world view, on the other hand, values "feelings of connectedness and intuition . . . nonauthoritarian and nondestructive power relationships." It is claimed that witchcraft tends to correct what W. Holman Keith called the fundamental religious error of our time: "to substitute force as the divine and ruling principle in place of beauty and love, to make destruction, in which the prowess of the male excels, more important in life than the creativity of the female."[56]

Certainly the history of witchcraft shows men persecuting women in order to maintain a male monopoly of profitable enterprises, such as medicine and magic. Women of outstanding reputation in any field were at risk, since almost any woman's accomplishment could be defined as witchcraft. When the church declared war on female healers, healing became a crime punishable by death if it was practiced by a woman. Women were forbidden to study medicine, and "if a woman dare to cure without having studied, she is a witch and must die."[57] Doctors eagerly participated in witch hunts, to eliminate their competition. It was all done very deliberately. "Given the number of instances in which the church combined with various economic groups from doctors to lawyers to merchant guilds, not only to make pronouncements about the incapacities of women, but often to accomplish the physical liquidation of women through witchcraft and heresy trials, one can hardly say that it all happened without anyone intending it."[58]

Churchmen who availed themselves of witches' services sometimes persecuted even those who helped them, in remarkable examples of ingratitude. Alison Peirsoun of Byrehill was so famous as a healing witch that the archbishop of St. Andrews sent for her when he was sick, and she cured him. Later he not only refused to pay her fee, but had her arrested, charged with witchcraft and burned.[59]

The muddy illogic of persecutors' sexist thinking is nowhere better illustrated than in the notion of the witch's "poppet," or wax doll, which could be mistreated by piercing or melting in order to make a human victim suffer corresponding stabbing pains, fevers, and other troubles. When the witch destroyed the doll altogether, the victim would die. Yet oddly enough, when male authorities discovered the doll and destroyed it, the victim would not die but would recover. A similar sexist attitude was apparent in the whole idea of traffic between human beings and demons. Burton's *Criminal Trials of*

Scotland stated that a male sorcerer is the master of demons, but a female witch is the slave of demons.[60] Yet her offense was usually considered more punishable than his.

Modern witches, male and female, seem inclined to restore the sexual balance of old romances, where men's magical skills were acquired under feminine instruction.[61] The witches appear to be reconstructing an old religion in a new format, gradually working out a theology that owes more to ancient Indo-European models than to the "reverse Christianity" associated with the idea of Satanism. Important points upon which this theology differs from Christianity are the following:

(1) The female principle is deified, equal to or greater than the male. (2) Body and soul are seen as one and the same; one cannot exist without the other. (3) Nature is sacred, not to be abused or "conquered." (4) The individual will has intrinsic value and is not to be subordinated to the "revealed" will of a deity. (5) Time is circular and repetitive; existence is cyclic; the figures of the Triple Goddess symbolize constant repetitions of growth and decay. (6) There is no original sin, and no hard-and-fast separation of "good" and "evil" (for example, a feast of fresh beef is good for the feasters but evil for the once-living main dish). (7) Sexuality, spontaneity, humor, and play activities may be incorporated into ritual, where the experience of pleasure is regarded as a positive force in life, rather than a temptation or a sin.[62]

The Goddess speaks to modern witches in somewhat the same vein as the speeches drawn from her ancient scriptures:

> *Mine is the secret that opens upon the door of youth and mine is the Cup of the Wine of Life and the Cauldron of Cerridwen, which is the Holy Grail of Immortality. I am the Gracious Goddess who gives the gift of joy unto the heart of man upon earth. I give the knowledge of the Spirit Eternal, and beyond death I give peace and freedom and reunion with those that have gone before. . . . I who am the beauty of the Green Earth, and the White Moon amongst the stars and the mystery of the Waters, and the desire of the heart of man, I call unto thy soul to arise and come unto me. For I am the Soul of Nature who giveth life to the universe; from me all things proceed and unto me all things must return. . . . I have been with thee from the beginning, and I am that which is attained at the end of desire.*[63]

1. J.H. Smith, D.C.P., 241. 2. Bullough, 177. 3. White 2, 36. 4. Briffault 1, 488. 5. Lederer, 150. 6. Rosen, 7. 7. Ewen, 69. 8. Agrippa, 270. 9. Scot, 20. 10. Gifford, 89. 11. Hazlitt, 103. 12. Tuchman, 216. 13. Scot, 43, 124, 141, 403. 14. Robbins, 308. 15. Cavendish, P.E., 218. 16. Summers, G.W., 429–30. 17. Tannahill, 96–97. 18. Castiglioni, 233. 19. Robbins, 209. 20. Briffault 3, 12. 21. Hazlitt, 655. 22. Wedeck, 78. 23. de Givry, 193. 24. Lea unabridged, 786. 25. Robbins, 161. 26. Robbins, 547. 27. Hazlitt, 341. 28. Agrippa, Foreword. 29. Robbins, 330. 30. Robbins, 50, 207–8. 31. R.E.L. Masters, 27. 32. Knight, D.W.P., 207. 33. de Givry, 84–85. 34. Summers, G.W., 435. 35. *Book of Shadows,* 11. 36. W. Scott, 166–68. 37. Robbins, 105. 38. Robbins, 8. 39. Ravensdale & Morgan, 105. 40. Robbins, 111, 113. 41. Lea, 172. 42. Robbins, 9, 271. 43. Kramer & Sprenger, xliii. 44. R.E.L. Masters, xxvi. 45. Robbins, 108, 143. 46. Robbins, 169, 457, 336. 47. Summers, W., 87. 48. Summers, H.W.D., 63; G.W. 169. 49. H. Smith, 293.

50. Maple, 98. 51. Robbins, 457. 52. Summers, G.W., 181–82. 53. Bromberg, 179. 54. *Newsweek,* June 26, 1978, 32. 55. Cohen, N.B., 129–31. 56. Adler, 122, 188, 204. 57. Dreifus, 7. 58. Boulding, 427, 505. 59. Baroja, 126. 60. Wimberly, 159. 61. Wimberly, 219. 62. Goldenberg, 111–14. 63. *Book of Shadows,* 65–67.

Woden

var. Wotan

Saxon and Frankish names of **Odin**, whom the Goths called Godan (God), or Father Goth. The day sacred to him was Wednesday—Woden's Day. German churchmen eventually changed the name of the day to *Mittwoch,* "mid-week," to prevent speaking of the heathen deity's name.

Wednesday is Mercury's Day in Latin-based languages (Italian *mercoledì,* French *mercredi,* Spanish *miércoles*), because Woden-Odin was identified with the Roman Mercury (Hermes). As a Conductor of Souls, Woden was associated with the cult of the dead, who were formerly called "elves" in Scandinavia; therefore he evolved into the Elven-king, Erl King, and leader of the Wild Hunt, when ghosts rode through the sky at Halloween. As Hod, the slayer of the year-god Balder, he appeared in his death mask and hood as a malicious deity, Old Carl Hood, father of the greenwood-hero **Robin**.[1] Christians readily identified him with the devil because he was already a fearful deity of death very like the Hindu Yama.

1. Wimberly, 200.

Wolf

Sacred totem of many European clans during the Middle Ages, as shown by the frequency of the name Wolf or Wulf in place names and family surnames. The old Saxon year began with Wolf-monath (Wolf Month). Wolf mothers or wolf nurses figured prominently in the biographies of pagan heroes. An early version of Siegfried was nursed by a divine she-wolf and was named Wolfdietrich.[1]

Worship of the wolf among heathen clans led to innumerable superstitions about wolf-demons and werewolves. Wolves were associated with death and reincarnation, since they were carrion eaters, formerly believed to carry the dead in their own bodies to the pagan heavens and hells. See **Dog; Werewolf**.

1. Rank, 58.

Womb

The Sanskrit word for any temple or sanctuary was *garbha-grha,* "womb."[1]

The great annual festival of Aphrodite in Argos was called *Hysteria,* "Womb."[2]

The oldest oracle in Greece, sacred to the Great Mother of earth, sea, and sky, was named Delphi, from *delphos*, "womb."

Megalithic tombs and barrow-mounds were designed as "wombs" to give rebirth to the dead. Their vaginal entrance passages show that Neolithic folk went to considerable trouble to devise imitations of female anatomy in earth and stone. Tomb and womb were even related linguistically. Greek *tumbos*, Latin *tumulus* were cognates of *tumere*, to swell, to be pregnant. The word "tummy" is thought to have come from the same root.[3]

Womb-temples and womb-tombs point backward to the matriarchal age, when only feminine life-magic was thought efficacious. Rebirth from the womb-tomb was the meaning of the domed funerary stupa of the Far East, where the remains of the sainted dead lay within a structure called *garbha*, the "womb."[4] The parallel with barrow graves, Mycenaean tholos tombs, cave temples, and other such structures is now well known. Even a Christian cathedral centered on the space called *nave*, originally meaning "belly." Caves and burial chambers were said to be sunk in the "bowels" of the earth—that is, of Mother Earth. The biblical term for "birth" is "separation from the bowels."

Archetypal womb-symbolism is as common today as it ever was, though not always recognized as such. Paul Klee said, "Which artist would not wish to dwell at the central organ of all motion . . . from which all functions derive their life? In the womb of nature, in the primal ground of creation, where the secret key to all things lies hidden?"[5]

1. Campbell, C.M., 168. 2. H. Smith, 126. 3. Potter & Sargent, 28. 4. Waddell, 262. 5. Jung, M.H.S., 263.

World Egg

See **Egg**; see also **Dioscuri**; **Goose**; **Swan**.

Worm

"The Worm" or "The Worm That Never Dies" sometimes designated the Earth Goddess in her corpse-eating aspect. Her spirit was thought to inhabit grave-worms (maggots), for which the Old Norse word was *mathkr*, Old English *matha*—both related to "mother." The modern word descended from a Middle English derivative, *mawke*.[1] Linguistically related to these "worms" were the Goddess's familiars or *mawkins*. See **Cat**.

1. Potter & Sargent, 238.

Wormwood

Artemisia absinthium, wormwood, was sacred to the Great Mother. Trevisa wrote in 1398: *"Artemisia* is called mother of herbs, and was sometime hallowed to the goddess that hight [is named] Artemis."[1] In Russia, wormwood or absinth was called an "accursed herb" because it was sacred to the pagan nymphs (Vilas); but it had also protective magic.[2]

Wormwood was a corruption of Old English *wermod,* "spirit-mother," which became German *Wermut,* French *vermouth.* Absinthe was first prepared by French witches from *artemisia,* and became a commercial product in the 18th century, though it proved very dangerous. Wormwood is a habit-forming drug that can destroy brain cells and cause delirium; furthermore, commercial absinthe was 68% alcohol by volume.[3] During the 19th century, the French government outlawed its production.[4]

1. Potter & Sargent, 274. 2. *Larousse,* 293. 3. Potter & Sargent, 275. 4. *Encyc. Brit.,* "Absinthe."

Wudu-Maer

"Forest-mother," literally "Wood-Mary"; Old Saxon for a nymph or fairy of the sacred grove, a priestess of the Oak-goddess, or a female druid. In Bavaria, the *wudu-maer* were presented with offerings of foodstuffs to court their goodwill; they were known as Little Wood Women.[1] A similar concept of a forest priestess survived in English legends of Maid Marian. See **Robin.**

1. Frazer, F.O.T., 312.

Xikum

Babylonian Tree of Heaven, emblem of Ishtar, spreading her branches into the celestial and nether worlds, holding the Savior Tammuz in her midst.[1] Moslems diabolized this Mother-tree and mentioned her in the Koran as Zakkum, the Tree of Hell.[2] See **Fig.**

1. Harding, 48. 2. Campbell, Oc.M., 430.

Xipe Totec

"Our Lord the Flayed One" in pre-Columbian Mexico, impersonated by a man who was executed on the Hill of the Stars at the end of each sacred 52-year cycle, at the moment when the Pleiades reached the zenith. He was castrated and flayed, and the priest was clothed in his bloody skin, signifying the god's rebirth.[1] People carried new fire from his temple to re-kindle their household fires, believing that his death staved off the end of the world, at least for one more cycle.[2]

Xipe Totec was the son of the Demeter-like Corn-goddess Chicomecoatl. Like all gods of crops, he suffered in imitation of reaping and grinding the grain. His flaying may have represented the husking of the corn cobs.

The "Flayed One" bore a remarkable resemblance to the archaic Hindu god Rudra, the Red One, or the Howler, or the Lord Who Is Half Woman. Rudra too was associated mystically with the **Pleiades**, called the Seven Mothers of the World, or Krittikas ("cutters"), whose "cutting" function may have been castrating or even flaying sacrificial gods.[3]

1. Neumann, G.M., 192. 2. Tannahill, 82. 3. O'Flaherty, 298, 346.

Xochiquetzal

Mexican Aphrodite: a many-faceted Love Goddess, Moon-virgin, fairy queen, and Madonna; a patroness of marriage and sacred harlots, dance, songs, spinning, weaving, changes and transformations, magic, and art. Like Syrian Adonis, her son-lover was a young vegetation god.[1]

Her worshippers said Xochiquetzal was the mother of all races of humanity after the primordial flood. Her many children were as dumb as animals until her holy spirit in the form of a dove descended on them from the Tree of Heaven and gave them speech. In this way all the world's languages were created.[2]

In addition to the dove, another symbol Xochiquetzal shared with the ancient Indo-European Goddesses was her sacred flower, the marigold—perhaps a New World version of the golden Thousand-Petaled Lotus representing the Great Mother in India.

Xochiquetzal's paradise was located "above the nine heavens in a very pleasant and delectable place, accompanied and guarded by many people and waited on by other women of the rank of goddesses, where are many delights of fountains, brooks, flower-gardens."[3] This fairyland was available after death to those who faithfully served the Goddess and lived according to her laws.

1. Neumann, G.M., 196–97. 2. Frazer, F.O.T., 107. 3. Summers, V., 260.

Yab-Yum

"Father-Mother," the Tantric coital posture in which gods mated with the Goddess and men with their Shaktis, especially at the moment of death when the Eternal Shakti brought everlasting bliss.[1] Unlike western patriarchs, Oriental mystics said the most favorable position for copulation was not *Venus observa* (male-superior), but Yab-Yum, with both partners upright, face to face, and free to move.

1. Rawson, E.A., 170; pl. 103.

Yahweh

Hebrew name of God, a vocalization of the **Tetragrammaton**. It was also rendered Yah, Yahu, Jahveh, Jahi, or Jehovah, and has been related to the name of the Canaanite moon deity Yareah, possibly a female or androgynous form. A male Yahweh was married to the Canaanite mother goddess Anat at Elephantine.[1]

The name of God pronounced Jaho, Iao, or Ieuw was applied to Zeus-Sabazius as the nocturnal sun: a Lord of Death under the earth, like Saturn. Jews called him Sabbaoth, "Lord of Hosts." His Latin name came from the same roots: Iu-piter, "Father Ieu," that is, Jupiter or Jove.[2]

Jahi was also a very ancient Goddess, appearing in Persian scriptures as the maker and seducer of the first man. Like many other Creatresses, she mated with the primal serpent; she also gave the menstrual "blood of life" to Eve.

1. Hays, 85, 89. 2. Knight, D.W.P., 113.

Yama

Hindu Lord of Death, male counterpart of the Lady of Life, whose name was his own in reversal: Ma-Ya. In classic Hindu myth, however, Yama's consort was his twin sister Yami, a feminine form of himself. The Fates ordained that he should mate with her, in the manner of the Primal Androgyne (see **Androgyne**). But Yama refused, saying he intended to keep himself pure. Because he detached himself from his feminine half and renounced the life-supporting power of the female, he became the first man to die.[1] He went into the underworld and became its king.

This myth presents an interesting reversal of the Judeo-Christian notion that the sin of woman and sex brought death into the world. Here death came about through the sin of male asceticism; Yama "died" because he refused to be a sexual being. His followers revered him as a **psychopomp**, like Hermes after his detachment from Aphrodite: "Yama chose death, and he found out the path for many, and he gives the souls of the dead a resting place."[2]

As Lord of Death he took the title Samana, "the Leveller," and at times he wore the fearsome aspect of a blue-skinned, bull-headed demon, the same as Sammael, the Angel of Death in the Book of Enoch.[3] Persians worshipped him as Yima the Splendid, the Good Shepherd who gave men immortality.[4] In the ancient land of Canaan, he became Yamm, Lord of the Abyss, annually cast down by Baal in their eternal contest for the favors of Astarte.

1. *Larousse,* 345. 2. Rees, 108. 3. Brandon, 362; F. Huxley, 45. 4. *Larousse,* 310.

Yang and Yin

Yang and Yin

Chinese mandala of light and dark, male and female, summer and winter, death and life, etc.: an S-curve dividing black and white halves of the circle, each half containing a spot of the opposite color. Though now regarded as a bisexual emblem, the Yang and Yin symbol was once wholly feminine. During the Sung period it referred to the cyclic phases of the moon.[1] Yin, the female power in the mandala, was a cognate of "yoni."

1. Campbell, Or.M., 24.

Yantra

Tantric "meditation sign," the graphic or symbolic equivalent of a *mantra.* Most important was the Sri Yantra or Great Yantra, a design of two interlocking triangles representing time cycles and the union of Goddess and God (see **Hexagram**).[1] Worship of the *yantra* was meant to attain "unity with the Mother of the Universe."[2]

1. Rawson, A.T., 82. 2. Avalon, 428.

Yard

From Scandinavian *gard* or *garth,* "world," the earth.[1] The churchyard descended from the old pagan tradition that a temple and its environs constituted a model of the universe, and those buried in the yard—corresponding to the Greek *koimeteria,* "cemetery"—automatically entered paradise because they were already in its vicinity (i.e., close to the temple). This was the pagan belief underlying the Christian habit of burying the pious in "consecrated ground" adjacent to the church. Refusal of such burial to criminals, witches, and other outcasts was tantamount to sending them to hell, for it was believed that anyone buried in unhallowed ground was automatically damned.

1. Lethaby, 62.

Yggdrasil

"Terrible Horse," or "The Horse of Ygg [the Ogre]"; Norse name of the World Ash Tree that became Odin's gallows tree—a gallows being poetically likened to a horse *(drasil)* on which men rode to Death. Like Christ's cross, Yggdrasil was depicted as the **axis mundi**. Its roots supported the earth, its trunk passed through the world's hub, its branches stretched over heaven and were hung with the stars. Under its roots by the Fount of Wisdom lived the three Fate-goddesses or Norns. A mighty serpent constantly gnawed at the tree and at doomsday would succeed in toppling the entire structure. All the worlds it upheld—Earth, heaven, Midgard, Asgard—were destined to tumble down and fall apart. See **Doomsday**; **Odin**.

Yin

Feminine life force, a Chinese cognate of "yoni"; usually represented as a fluid emanating from a female "Grotto of the White Tiger" (genitals).[1] According to the doctrines of Tao, the power of *yin* was stronger than any male power; therefore men had to learn to take feminine fluids into themselves, to gain wisdom and health.

1. Rawson, E.A., 253.

Ymir

Teutonic giant who died to give life to the universe. His flesh became the soil; his blood became rivers and seas; his skull was the dome of the sky. The first couple of male-and-female beings emerged from the sweat of his left armpit. The race of dwarves evolved from maggots that bred in Ymir's rotting corpse. This pantheistic creation myth was designed to give primordial significance to a sacrificial god; but Ymir was not really the first of all creatures. He was brought to life and nourished by the Cow-mother Audumla, "Creator of Earth."[1]

Ymir's name has been related to the Sanskrit Yama, the oldest underworld god in hermaphroditic guise as a producer of living things.[2] As Odin was another form of Indra, so Ymir was the Yama remembered by Aryan tribes in their westward migrations.

1. *Larousse,* 248. 2. H.R.E. Davidson, G.M.V.A., 151, 199.

Yoga

Sanskrit *yoga* meant to link, join, or unite, like the English derivative "yoke." It was the term for sexual union between the Tantric *sadhu* and his *yogini,* or Shakti, in imitation of the union between Kali and Shiva. As Kali's consort, Shiva bore the title of "Lord of Yoga."[1]

The practice of yoga was supposed to develop magic powers collectively called *siddhi*—in northern Europe, *sidh* or *seidr,* "magic." The fully developed sage could walk on water, change base metals to gold, understand all languages, heal diseases, cast out demons, and so on.[2] The Moors called such a person a *sidi,* "hero." In the myth cycles of Moorish Spain, the title itself became a name of the greatest known hero, El Cid.[3]

1. Campbell, Or.M., 13. 2. *Bardo Thodol,* 158; Campbell, Or.M., 424.
3. Goodrich, 236.

Yoni

"Vulva," the primary Tantric object of worship, symbolized variously by a triangle, fish, double-pointed oval, horseshoe, egg, fruits, etc.

Personifying the yoni, the Goddess Kali bore the title of Cunti or Kunda, root of the ubiquitous Indo-European word "cunt" and all its relatives: cunnus, cunte, cunning, cunctipotent, ken, kin, country.

The Yoni Yantra or triangle was known as the Primordial Image, representing the Great Mother as source of all life.[1] As the genital focus of her divine energy, the Yantra was adored as a geometrical symbol, as the cross was adored by Christians.

The ceremony of baptismal rebirth often involved being drawn bodily through a giant yoni. Those who underwent this ceremony were styled "twice-born."[2]

1. Silberer, 170. 2. Frazer, G.B., 229.

Yonijas

A Hindu myth of the battle of the sexes told of a quarrel between the Goddess Parvati (Kali) and the God Mahadeva (Shiva) over their rival claims to the true parenthood of human beings. To decide the question, each proposed to create a race of people without the aid of the other. The God, spirit of the lingam or phallus, created the Lingajas, who were weak and stupid, "dull of intellect, their bodies feeble, their limbs distorted."

However, the Goddess created the Yonijas, spirits of the yoni or vulva, who turned out to be excellent specimens: "well-shaped, with sweet aspects and fine complexions."[1] The two races fought a war, and the Yonijas won.

This may have been one of the earliest myths of conflict between male and female divinities over the matter of who did the creating. It was still a matriarchal age, as shown by the way the Mother made more viable people than the Father could make.

1. Simons, 57.

---

var. Yul

Yule

Norse solstitial festival, the season of the sun's rebirth, assimilated to Christmas in the Middle Ages, along with its pagan trappings: holly, ivy, pine boughs, lighted trees, wassail bowls, suckling pigs, Yule logs, carols, gifts, and feasting.

Some said the god of Yule was Kris Kringle, i.e., a Christ of the Orb, a new solar king. But most northern folk remembered the reborn god as Frey. They said, "Yule is celebrated in honor of Frey."[1]

In France it was celebrated in honor of another phallic god, like Cernunnos, whose phallus was identified with the festive log, called the Noel Log. Provençal folk songs mention the fertility magic of the

Noel Log, the ashes of which were traditionally mixed with cows' fodder to help them calve.[2]

1. Oxenstierna, 216. 2. Briffault 3, 101–2.

Yu-Ti

Chinese Heavenly Father, consort of Mother Earth (Wang-Mu). He was known as the August Personage of Jade, or August Supreme Emperor of Jade. He lived in heaven in a palace exactly like the earthly emperor's palace. He was said to have made the first human beings out of clay, like other archaic gods whose "creating" took place before the concept of begetting was understood.[1]

1. *Larousse,* 381–82.

Zabat

Berber name for sacred dances performed in groups of thirteen, in connection with the magic ceremony called "an occasion of power"; possible origin of the so-called witches' "sabbat."[1]

1. Shah, 210; Ravensdale & Morgan, 153.

Zagreus

Cretan bull-god and savior identified with both Dionysus the Son, and Zeus the Father. Zagreus was slain by the Titans (pre-Hellenic gods) as a sacrifice, then assimilated to his heavenly father and resurrected as a new copy of himself, by rebirth through the Mother (Rhea).

Zakar

Hebrew "male," from several ancient words for "penis." Zakar or Zaqar was a phallic deity like Hermes in Babylon, where he was called a messenger from the moon. Zekker, the Arabic word for "penis," came from a similar Egyptian root: Seker, the Lord of Death, i.e., Osiris as the dead god (or phallus) hidden within the Mother's womb. See **Seker**.

Zalmoxis

Savior of Thrace, worshipped by the Getae and identified with Orpheus. Zalmoxis promised eternal life to guests at his sacramental

Last Supper. Then he went into the underworld, and rose again on the third day—or, by some accounts, in the third year. He established sacred Mysteries to teach the secrets of the after-life. Human sacrifices to him were impaled, like victims impersonating Tmolus in Lydia (see **Heracles**).[1] Martyrdom as the spirit of Zalmoxis apparently was coveted. If the victim survived after being hurled onto the points of spears, he was rebuked and designated a "bad man"; and another was chosen to die in his place.[2]

1. Herodotus, 241–42. 2. Guthrie, 175.

Zar

Ethiopian demon, still worshipped by women as the spirit of their voodoo-like cult of **possession**, to which they have recourse when oppressed by their patriarchal society. The name Zar may be related to an ancient name of **Osiris**, worshipped during the first dynasty at Abydos as the god-king Zer, who became Lord of the Underworld.

Zen

Japanese system of controlled meditation, to master various skills, especially the martial arts. Zen was a mispronunciation of Chinese *ch'an,* which was in turn a mispronunciation of Sanskrit *dhyana,* "contemplation."[1] Medieval knights of romance, who worshipped Diana and followed a similar martial-arts cult, may have drawn their tradition from the same Oriental source.

1. Campbell, M.T.L.B., 127; Or.M., 440.

Zenobia

Dynastic name of matriarchal queens of Palmyra. In their native Aramaic, the name was Bath-Zabbai, or Bath-Sheba, meaning "Daughter of the Goddess." See **Solomon and Sheba**. The famous queen Zenobia Septimia was the "seventh Bath-Sheba."[1] She had no official consort. She named her son Wahab-Allath, "Gift of the Goddess Allath." Allath was the same Semitic Moon-mother whom Islam later masculinized as Allah.[2]

1. *Encyc. Brit.,* "Zenobia." 2. de Riencourt, 75.

Zephyr

Greek wind-spirit, capable of impregnating women or female animals, as Boreas the North Wind was thought to impregnate mares. Greek phallic gods often appeared in carvings and amulets as "snake-tailed winds." The idea that fatherhood resulted from sending air, breath, or wind into a womb was not only a Greek idea. It was common to early patriarchal religions, which taught the male Oversoul was nothing but air. See **Soul**.

Zeus

Greek form of Sanskrit *Dyaus pitar,* "Father Heaven," probably linked with Babylonian myths of Zu the Storm-Bird, a thrower of thunderbolts. The Romans called him Jupiter, or Jove; the Jews called him Jehovah.

Unlike the Judeo-Christian God who assumed his attributes, Zeus was not a creator of humanity, nor even a giver of laws. The real Creator-lawgiver was the Goddess called either his mother or his wife: Rhea, Hera, Gaea; in all her forms a "Virgin Mother of God." Zeus was entitled Marnas, "Virgin-born Zeus."[1] He was also identified with a number of dying gods, such as Zeus-Sabazius, Zeus-Zagreus, Zeus-Sabaoth. Like Lucifer, he "came down" as rain or lightning to fertilize his Mother, the earth. As a god of the fructifying bolt, he was known as Zeus Kataibates, "Zeus Who Descends."[2] He took over Mount Olympus, former shrine of Gaea Olympia.

Zeus eventually became the Olympic-Platonic patriarch, even claiming to give birth to Athene—the ancient Libyan Goddess of female wisdom—from his own head. "With the spread of Platonic philosophy the hitherto intellectually dominant Greek woman degenerated into an unpaid worker and breeder of children wherever Zeus and Apollo were the ruling gods."[3]

1. Graves, W.G., 320. 2. Guthrie, 38. 3. Graves, G.M. 1, 117.

Ziggurat

Babylonian "Mountain of Heaven," the pyramid that served as temple and palace in Mesopotamian towns. At its summit, the king consummated his sacred marriage with the Goddess, this being the point of contact between heaven and earth. Nebuchadnezzar's ziggurat was built in seven stages, representing the seven planetary spheres. Beneath, seven nether pits represented the descent into the corresponding seven spheres of the underworld. Such pits were used for death-and-rebirth ceremonies of priestly initiations. See **Mountain**.

Ziusudra

Sumerian prototype of Noah, the flood hero, carrying the seeds of a new universe through watery Chaos between destruction of one world and the birth of the next. Sometimes spelled Xisuthros. See **Flood**.

Zoe

"Life," a Gnostic name of Eve, comparable to the Teutonic All-Mother Lif.[1] Zoe was a daughter or emanation of the Gnostic Goddess, Sophia, who gave Adam his soul. She also threw down to the Abyss the unjust Creator, who had dared to curse her, and elevated the Lord of Hosts to the seventh heaven, where she undertook to instruct him about the eighth, the Great Mother's dwelling place. Gnostic Gospels said Zoe's power alone animated the first clay man, after various gods had tried to do it and failed. Therefore the man called her Mother of All Living.[2] The canonical Bible kept her title, but eliminated her giving of life to Adam.

1. Pagels, 30. 2. Robinson, 159, 166–69, 172–76.

var. Zarathustra

Zoroaster

Patriarchal Persian prophet whose name was affixed to many anti-female doctrines, such as the rule that no women could enter heaven except those "submissive to control, who had considered their husbands lords."[1] Most women, of course, were destined to go to hell. Along with much else, these sentiments were adopted from Zoroastrian teaching by the Jews and applied to the laws of Yahweh.

1. Campbell, Oc.M., 196, 199.

Zorya

The "Three Fates" in Slavic myth. "Three little sisters, three little Zorya: she of the Evening, she of Midnight, and she of Morning"—i.e., of the old lunar calendars that figured the day from noon to noon. Like the Norns, the Zorya kept the doomsday-wolf fettered to the pole star: "Their duty is to guard a dog which is tied by an iron chain to the constellation of the Little Bear. When the chain breaks it will be the end of the world."[1] An Egyptian prototype of the triple Zorya was the Goddess Reret, who kept the powers of destruction fettered by a chain.[2]

1. *Larousse,* 285. 2. Budge, G.E. 2, 249.

Zurvan

Archaic Persian deity of Infinite Time, two-faced or two-sexed in Zoroastrian symbolism. Zurvan must have been originally a manifestation of the Two Ladies of life and death, like Kali who united Virgin and Crone aspects of female divinity. From the womb of Zurvan were born the twins **Ahura Mazda** (God) and **Ahriman** (Satan). The former twin became king of heaven because he made the right sacrifices. Ahriman's sacrifices were unacceptable, so he was banished to the underworld and became the Great Serpent.[1]

Zurvan Akarana was worshipped as the First Cause, or principle of creation, linked with Time, Destiny, and Fate: three common characterizations of the Goddess.[2] An ancient scripture said her divinity could not even be addressed; it was "so incomprehensible to man that we can but honor it in awed silence."[3] Thus Zurvan was similar to the Gnostic Goddess Sige, origin of all things in Silence. Ahura could have been one of her early names. In Egypt, Ahura was feminine.[4]

The Zoroastrian pantheon assigned Zurvan to the dark side of divinity as a demon of decrepitude, very like the Crone Kali who represented moribund old age.[5] Patriarchal thinkers characteristically emphasized the negative aspects of the destroying-and-creating Goddess, even when the primal character of the Mother of good, evil, time, fate, and the universe was clearly discernible under the veneer of later myth.

1. *Larousse,* 323. 2. Cumont, A.R.G.R., 61. 3. Seligmann, 14.
4. Budge, E.M., 144. 5. Seligmann, 14.

Bibliography

Adler, Margot. *Drawing Down the Moon.* Boston: Beacon Press, 1981.

Agrippa, Henry Cornelius. *The Philosophy of Natural Magic.* Secaucus, N.J.: University Books, 1974.

Albright, William Powell. *Yahweh and the Gods of Canaan.* New York: Doubleday & Co., 1968.

Angus, S. *The Mystery-Religions.* New York: Dover Publications, 1975.

Apocrypha, Authorized Version. New York: University Books Inc. 1962.

Arens, W. *The Man-Eating Myth.* New York: Oxford University Press, 1979.

Ashe, Geoffrey. *The Virgin.* London: Routledge & Kegan Paul, 1976.

Assyrian and Babylonian Literature, Selected Translations. New York: D. Appleton & Co., 1901.

Attwater, Donald. *The Penguin Dictionary of Saints.* Baltimore: Penguin Books, Inc., 1965.

Augstein, Rudolf. *Jesus Son of Man.* New York: Urizen Books, 1977.

Avalon, Arthur. *Shakti and Shakta.* New York: Dover Publications, Inc., 1978.

Bachofen, J.J. *Myth, Religion and Mother Right.* Princeton, N.J.: Princeton University Press, 1967.

Bacon, Edward (ed.). *Vanished Civilizations of the Ancient World.* London: Thames & Hudson, 1963.

Barber, Charles L. *The Story of Speech and Language.* New York: Thomas Y. Crowell Co., 1965.

Bardo Thodol (W. Y. Evans-Wentz, trans.). London: Oxford University Press, 1927.

Baring-Gould, Sabine. *Curious Myths of the Middle Ages.* New York: University Books Inc., 1967.

Baring-Gould, Sabine. *The Book of Werewolves.* New York: Causeway Books, 1973.

Barker-Benfield, G.J. *The Horrors of the Half-Known Life.* New York: Harper & Row, 1976.

Baroja, Julio Caro. *The World of Witches.* Chicago: University of Chicago Press, 1965.

Barrett, C.K. *The New Testament Background.* New York: Harper & Row, 1961.

Beard, Mary R. *Woman as Force in History.* London: Collier-Macmillan Ltd., 1946.

Becker, Ernest. *The Denial of Death.* New York: The Free Press, 1973.

Becker, Ernest. *Escape from Evil.* New York: The Free Press, 1975.

Bengis, Ingrid. *Combat in the Erogenous Zone.* New York: Bantam Books, Inc., 1972.

Bharati, Agehananda. *The Tantric Tradition.* New York: Samuel Weiser, Inc. 1975.

Bibliography

Binder, Pearl. *Magic Symbols of the World.* London: Hamlyn Publishing Group Ltd., 1972.

Black, Matthew. *The Scrolls and Christian Origins.* New York: Charles Scribner's Sons, 1961.

Book of Shadows. St. Paul, Minn.: Llewellyn Publications, 1973.

Book of the Dead (E. A. Wallis Budge, trans.). New York: Bell Publishing Co., 1960.

Borchardt, Frank. *German Antiquity in Renaissance Myth.* Baltimore, Md.: Johns Hopkins University Press, 1971.

Boulding, Elise. *The Underside of History.* Boulder, Colo.: Westview Press, 1976.

Bouquet, A.C. *Comparative Religion.* London: Penguin Books Ltd., 1942.

Bowness, Charles. *Romany Magic.* New York: Samuel Weiser, Inc., 1973.

Boynton, Richard W. *Beyond Mythology.* New York: Doubleday & Co., 1951.

Brandon, S.G.F. *Religion in Ancient History.* New York: Charles Scribner's Sons, 1969.

Branston, Brian. *Gods of the North.* London: Thames & Hudson, 1955.

Brasch, R. *How Did Sex Begin?* New York: David McKay Co., 1973.

Bratton, Fred Gladstone. *Myths and Legends of the Ancient Near East.* New York: Thomas Y. Crowell Co., 1970.

Brewster, H. Pomeroy. *Saints and Festivals of the Christian Church.* New York: Frederick A. Stokes Co., 1904.

Briffault, Robert. *The Mothers* (3 vols.). New York: Macmillan, 1927.

Bromberg, Walter. *From Shaman to Psychotherapist.* Chicago: Henry Regnery Co., 1975.

Brownmiller, Susan. *Against Our Will: Men, Women, and Rape.* New York: Simon & Schuster, 1975.

Budge, Sir E.A. Wallis. *Amulets and Talismans.* New York: University Books Inc., 1968.

Budge, Sir. E.A. Wallis. *Gods of the Egyptians* (2 vols.). New York: Dover Publications, 1969.

Budge, Sir E.A. Wallis. *Egyptian Magic.* New York: Dover Publications, 1971.

Budge, Sir E.A. Wallis. *Dwellers on the Nile.* New York: Dover Publications, 1977.

Budge, Sir E.A. Wallis. *Egyptian Language.* New York: Dover Publications, 1977.

Bullough, Vern L. *The Subordinate Sex.* Chicago: University of Illinois Press, 1973.

Butler, Bill. *Dictionary of the Tarot.* New York: Schocken Books, 1975.

Butler, E.M. *Ritual Magic.* Cambridge: Cambridge University Press, 1949.

Campbell, Joseph. *The Masks of God: Primitive Mythology.* New York: Viking Press, 1959.

Campbell, Joseph. *The Masks of God: Oriental Mythology.* New York: Viking Press, 1962.

Campbell, Joseph. *The Masks of God: Occidental Mythology.* New York: Viking Press, 1964.

Campbell, Joseph. *The Masks of God: Creative Mythology.* New York: Viking Press, 1970.

Campbell, Joseph. *The Flight of the Wild Gander.* Chicago: Henry Regnery Co., 1969.

Campbell, Joseph. *Myths to Live By.* New York: Viking Press, 1972.

Campbell, Joseph. *The Mythic Image.* Princeton, N.J.: Princeton University Press, 1974.

Campbell, Joseph (ed.). *Myths, Dreams, and Religion.* New York: E.P. Dutton & Co., 1970.

Carden, M.L. *Oneida: Utopian Community to Modern Corporation.* Baltimore, Md.: Johns Hopkins University Press, 1969.

Carpenter, Edward. *Pagan and Christian Creeds.* New York: Harcourt, Brace & Howe, 1920.

Carter, J.B. *The Religious Life of Ancient Rome.* New York: Cooper Square, 1972.

Case, Paul Foster. *The Tarot.* Richmond, Va.: Maccy Publishing Co., 1947.

Castiglioni, Arturo. *Adventures of the Mind.* New York: Alfred A. Knopf, 1946.

Cavendish, Richard. *The Powers of Evil.* New York: G.P. Putnam's Sons, 1975.

Cavendish, Richard. *The Tarot.* New York: Harper & Row, 1975.

Cavendish, Richard. *Visions of Heaven and Hell.* New York: Harmony Books, 1977.

Ceram, C.W. *Gods, Graves, and Scholars.* New York: Bantam Books, Inc., 1972.

Chagnon, Napoleon A. *Yanomamo: The Fierce People.* New York: Holt, Rinehart & Winston, 1968.

Chamberlin, E.R. *The Bad Popes.* New York: Dial Press, 1969.

Chamberlin, E.R. *Antichrist and the Milennium.* New York: E.P. Dutton & Co., 1975.

Chaucer. *The Canterbury Tales.* Harmondsworth, England: Penguin Books Ltd., 1951.

Clodd, Edward. *Magic in Names and in Other Things.* London: Chapman & Hall, Ltd., 1920.

Cohen, Daniel. *A Natural History of Unnatural Things.* New York: McCall Publishing Co., 1971.

Cohen, Daniel. *The New Believers.* New York: M. Evans & Co., 1975.

Collins, Joseph B. *Christian Mysticism in the Elizabethan Age.* New York: Octagon Books, 1971.

Coulton, G.G. *Inquisition and Liberty.* Boston: Beacon Press, 1959.

Crawley, Ernest. *The Mystic Rose* (2 vols.). New York: Meridian Books Inc., 1960.

Crow, Duncan. *The Victorian Woman.* New York: Stein & Day, 1972.

Cumont, Franz. *Oriental Religions in Roman Paganism.* New York: Dover Publications, 1956.

Cumont, Franz. *The Mysteries of Mithra.* New York: Dover Publications, 1956.

Cumont, Franz. *Astrology and Religion Among the Greeks and Romans.* New York: Dover Publications, 1960.

d'Alviella, Count Goblet. *The Migration of Symbols.* New York: University Books, 1956.

Daly, Mary. *Beyond God the Father.* Boston: Beacon Press, 1973.

Dames, Michael. *The Silbury Treasure.* London: Thames & Hudson, 1976.

Davidson, H.R. Ellis. *Pagan Scandinavia.* New York: Frederick A. Praeger, 1967.

Davidson, H.R. Ellis. *Gods and Myths of the Viking Age.* New York: Bell Publishing Co., 1981.

Davidson, Terry. *Conjugal Crime.* New York: Hawthorn Books Inc., 1978.

Davies, A. Powell. *The Meaning of the Dead Sea Scrolls.* New York: New American Library, 1956.

Davis, Elizabeth Gould. *The First Sex.* New York: G.P. Putnam's Sons, 1971.

de Camp, L. Sprague. *The Ancient Engineers.* New York: Ballantine Books, 1960.

de Camp, L. Sprague & Catherine C. *Spirits, Stars, and Spells.* New York: Canaveral Press, 1966.

de Givry, Grillot. *Witchcraft, Magic and Alchemy.* New York: Dover Publications, 1971.

Delehaye, Hippolyte. *The Legends of the Saints.* New York: Fordham University Press, 1962.

de Lys, Claudia. *The Giant Book of Superstitions.* Secaucus, N.J.: Citadel Press, 1979.

Dentan, Robert Knox. *The Semai: A Nonviolent People of Malaya.* New York: Holt, Rinehart & Winston, 1968.

de Paor, Máire and Liam. *Early Christian Ireland.* London: Thames & Hudson, 1958.

de Riencourt, Amaury. *Sex and Power in History.* New York: Dell Publishing Co., 1974.

Derlon, Pierre. *Secrets of the Gypsies.* New York: Ballantine Books, 1977.

de Voragine, Jacobus. *The Golden Legend.* New York: Longmans, Green & Co., 1941.

de Vries, Leonard, and Fryer, Peter. *Venus Unmasked.* London: Arthur Barker Ltd., 1967.

Diner, Helen. *Mothers and Amazons.* New York: Julian Press Inc., 1965.

Doane, T.W. *Bible Myths and Their Parallels in Other Religions.* New York: University Books Inc., 1971.

Douglas, Alfred. *The Tarot.* New York: Taplinger Publishing Co., 1972.

Douglas, Emily Taft. *Margaret Sanger: Pioneer of the Future.* New York: Holt, Rinehart & Winston, 1970.

Dreifus, Claudia (ed.). *Seizing Our Bodies.* New York: Vintage Books, 1978.

Dumézil, Georges. *Archaic Roman Religion* (2 vols.). Chicago, Ill.: University of Chicago Press, 1970.

Durrell, Lawrence. *Pope Joan.* London: Derek Verschoyle, 1954.

Dworkin, Andrea. *Woman Hating.* New York: E.P. Dutton & Co., 1974.

Ebon, Martin. *Witchcraft Today.* New York: New American Library, 1971.

Ebon, Martin. *The Devil's Bride: Exorcism Past and Present.* New York: Harper & Row, 1974.

Ebon, Martin. *The Satan Trap.* New York: Doubleday & Co., 1976.

Edwardes, Allen. *The Jewel in the Lotus.* New York: Lancer Books, 1965.

Ehrenreich, Barbara, and English, Deirdre. *For Her Own Good.* New York: Anchor/Doubleday, 1978.

Eliade, Mircea. *The Myth of the Eternal Return.* Princeton, N.J.: Princeton University Press, 1954.

Eliade, Mircea. *Shamanism.* Princeton, N.J.: Bollingen Series, 1964.

Elisofen, Eliot, and Watts, Alan. *Erotic Spirituality.* New York: Macmillan, 1971.

Ellis, Albert. *The Folklore of Sex.* New York: Charles Boni, 1951.

Elworthy, Frederick. *The Evil Eye.* New York: Julian Press, Inc., 1958.

Encyclopaedia Britannica, Third Edition, 1970.

Enslin, Morton Scott. *Christian Beginnings.* New York: Harper & Bros., 1938.

Enslin, Morton Scott. *The Literature of the Christian Movement.* New York: Harper & Bros., 1938.

Epic of Gilgamesh. Harmondsworth, Middlesex, England: Penguin Books Ltd., 1960.

Erman, Adolf. *The Literature of the Ancient Egyptians.* New York: Benjamin Blom, Inc., 1971.

Esty, Katharine. *The Gypsies, Wanderers in Time.* New York: Meredith Press, 1969.

Evans, Bergen. *The Spoor of Spooks.* New York: Alfred A. Knopf, 1954.

Evans, Bergen. *The Natural History of Nonsense.* New York: Alfred A. Knopf, 1965.

Ewen, C.L'Estrange. *Witchcraft and Demonianism.* London: Heath Cranton Ltd., 1933.

Farb, Peter. *Word Play.* New York: Alfred A. Knopf, 1974.

Farb, Peter. *Man's Rise to Civilization.* New York: E.P. Dutton & Co., 1968.

Feigen Fastau, Marc. *The Male Machine.* New York: Dell Publishing Co., 1975.

Fielding, William J. *Strange Customs of Courtship and Marriage.* New York: Garden City Publishing Co., 1942.

Fodor, Nandor. *The Search for the Beloved.* New York: University Books Inc., 1949.

Forgotten Books of Eden. New York: Bell Publishing Co., 1980.

Frazer, Sir James G. *Psyche's Task.* London: Macmillan & Co., Ltd., 1909.

Frazer, Sir James G. *The Golden Bough.* New York: Macmillan, 1922.

Frazer, Sir James G. *Folk-Lore in the Old Testament.* New York: Macmillan, 1927.

Fromm, Erich. *The Anatomy of Human Destructiveness.* New York: Holt, Rinehart & Winston, 1973.

Funk, Wilfred. *Word Origins and Their Romantic Stories.* New York: Bell Publishing Co., 1978.

Gaster, Theodor. *Myth, Legend and Custom in the Old Testament.* New York: Harper & Row, 1969.

Gelling, Peter, and Davidson, Hilda Ellis. *The Chariot of the Sun.* New York: Frederick A. Praeger, 1969.

Gettings, Fred. *The Book of Tarot.* London: Triune Books, 1973.

Gibbon, Edward. *The Decline and Fall of the Roman Empire (3 vols.).* New York: Modern Library, n.d.

Gifford, Edward S., Jr. *The Evil Eye.* New York: Macmillan, 1958.

Gilder, George. *Naked Nomads.* New York: Quadrangle Books, 1974.

Gittelson, Natalie. *The Erotic Life of the American Wife.* New York: Delacorte, 1972.

Goldberg, B.Z. *The Sacred Fire.* New York: University Books Inc., 1958.

Goldenberg, Naomi. *The Changing of the Gods.* Boston: Beacon Press, 1979.

Goldstein, Michael J., and Kant, Harold S. *Pornography and Sexual Deviance.* Berkeley: University of California Press, 1973.

Goodrich, Norma Lorre. *Medieval Myths.* New York: New American Library, 1977.

Gornick, Vivian, and Moran, Barbara K. (eds.). *Woman in Sexist Society.* New York: New American Library, 1972.

Graves, Robert. *The Greek Myths* (2 vols.). New York: Penguin Books Inc., 1955.

Graves, Robert. *The White Goddess.* New York: Vintage Books, 1958.

Graves, Robert, and Patai, Raphael. *Hebrew Myths.* New York: Doubleday & Co., 1964.

Gray, John. *Near Eastern Mythology.* London: Hamlyn Publishing Group Ltd., 1963.

Groome, Francis Hindes. *Gypsy Folk Tales.* London: Herbert Jenkins, 1963.

Guerber, H.A. *Legends of the Rhine.* New York: A.S. Barnes & Co., 1895.

Guerber, H.A. *Legends of the Middle Ages.* New York: American Book Co., 1924.

Guignebert, Charles. *Ancient, Medieval and Modern Christianity.* New York: University Books, 1961.

Guthrie, W.K.C. *The Greeks and Their Gods.* Boston: Beacon Press, 1955.

Haining, Peter. *Witchcraft and Black Magic.* New York: Grosset & Dunlap, 1972.

Hallet, Jean-Pierre. *Pygmy Kitabu.* New York: Random House, 1973.

Halliday, William Reginald. *Greek and Roman Folklore.* New York: Cooper Square, 1963.

Hamilton, Edith. *Mythology.* Boston: Little, Brown & Co., 1940.

Harding, M. Esther. *Woman's Mysteries, Ancient and Modern.* New York: G.P. Putnam's Sons, 1971.

Hargrave, Catherine Perry. *A History of Playing Cards.* New York: Dover Publications, 1966.

Harris, Marvin. *Cannibals and Kings.* New York: Random House, 1977.

Harris, Sara. *The Puritan Jungle.* New York: G.P. Putnam's Sons, 1969.

Harris, Thomas A. *I'm OK—You're OK.* New York: Harper & Row, 1967.

Harrison, Jane Ellen. *Epilegomena to the Study of Greek Religion,* and *Themis.* New York: University Books Inc., 1962.

Harrison, Michael. *The Roots of Witchcraft.* Secaucus, N.J.: Citadel Press, 1974.

Hartley, C. Gasquoine. *The Truth About Woman.* New York: Dodd, Mead & Co., 1913.

Hauswirth, Frieda. *Purdah: The Status of Indian Women.* New York: Vanguard Press, 1932.

Hawkins, Gerald S. *Stonehenge Decoded.* New York: Dell Publishing Co., 1965.

Hays, H.R. *In The Beginnings.* New York: G.P. Putnam's Sons, 1963.

Hazlitt, W. Carew. *Faiths and Folklore of the British Isles* (2 vols.). New York: Benjamin Blom, Inc., 1965.

Henry, Jules. *Pathways to Madness.* New York: Random House, 1965.

Herodotus. *The Histories* (Henry Cary, trans.). New York: D. Appleton & Co., 1899.

Higgins, Godfrey. *Anacalypsis* (2 vols.). New York: University Books Inc., 1965.

Hill, Douglas, and Williams, Pat. *The Supernatural.* New York: Hawthorne Books, Inc., 1966.

Hinnels, John R. *Persian Mythology.* London: Hamlyn Publishing Group Ltd., 1973.

Hirsch, Miriam F. *Women and Violence.* New York: Van Nostrand Reinhold Co., 1981.

Hitching, Francis. *Earth Magic.* New York: Pocket Books Inc., 1978.

Hollander, Lee M. *The Skalds.* Ann Arbor: University of Michigan Press, 1968.

Holloway, Mark. *Heavens on Earth.* New York: Dover Publications, 1966.

Holmes, Ronald. *Witchcraft in History.* Secaucus, N.J.: Citadel Press, 1974.

Homer. *Complete Works.* New York: Modern Library, 1950.

Hooke, S.H. *Middle Eastern Mythology.* Harmondsworth, England: Penguin Books Ltd., 1963.

Hooke, S.H. *The Siege Perilous.* Freeport, N.Y.: Books for Libraries Press, 1970.

Hornung, Clarence P. *Hornung's Handbook of Designs and Devices.* New York: Dover Publications Inc., 1959.

Hughes, Robert. *Heaven and Hell in Western Art.* New York: Stein & Day, 1968.

Huxley, Aldous. *The Devils of Loudun.* New York: Harper & Bros., 1952.

Huxley, Francis. *The Way of the Sacred.* New York: Doubleday & Co., 1974.

Hyde, Walter Woodburn. *Greek Religion and Its Survivals.* New York: Cooper Square, 1963.

James, E.O. *The Ancient Gods.* New York: G.P. Putnam's Sons, 1960.

Jobes, Gertrude and James. *Outer Space.* New York: Scarecrow Press, Inc., 1964.

Johnson, Walter. *Folk-Memory.* New York: Arno Press, 1980.

Jonas, Hans. *The Gnostic Religion.* Boston: Beacon Press, 1963.

Joyce, P.W. *A Social History of Ancient Ireland* (2 vols.). New York: Arno Press, 1980.

Jung, Carl Gustav. *Psychology and Religion.* New Haven: Yale University Press, 1938.

Jung, Carl Gustav. *Mandala Symbolism.* Princeton, N.J.: Princeton University Press, 1959.

Jung, Carl Gustav. *Man and His Symbols.* New York: Doubleday & Co., 1964.

Jung, C.G., and Kerenyi, C. *Essays on a Science of Mythology.* New York: Bollingen, 1949.

Jung, Emma, and von Franz, Marie-Louise. *The Grail Legend.* New York: G.P. Putnam's Sons, 1970.

Keightley, Thomas. *The World Guide to Gnomes, Fairies, Elves and Other Little People.* New York: Avenel Books, 1978.

Keller, Werner. *The Bible as History.* New York: William Morrow & Co., 1956.

Kendall, Alan. *Medieval Pilgrims.* New York: G.P. Putnam's Sons, 1970.

Kermode, Frank. *The Sense of an Ending.* London: Oxford University Press, 1966.

King, Francis. *Sexuality, Magic and Perversion.* Secaucus, N.J.: Citadel Press, 1972.

Klaich, Dolores. *Woman Plus Woman.* New York: Simon & Schuster, 1974.

Knight, Richard Payne. *The Symbolical Language of Ancient Art and Mythology.* New York: J.W. Bouton, 1892.

Knight, Richard Payne. *A Discourse on the Worship of Priapus.* New York: University Books Inc., 1974.

Koch, Rudolf. *The Book of Signs.* New York: Dover Publications, 1955.

Kramer, Heinrich, and Sprenger, James. *Malleus Maleficarum.* New York: Dover Publications, 1971.

Kramer, Samuel Noah. *History Begins at Sumer.* New York: Doubleday & Co., 1959.

La Barre, Weston. *The Human Animal.* Chicago, Ill.: University of Chicago Press, 1955.

Laistner, M.L.W. *Christianity and Pagan Culture in the Later Roman Empire.* Ithaca, N.Y.: Cornell University Press, 1951.

Lamont, Corliss. *The Illusion of Immortality.* New York: Philosophical Library, 1950.

Langer, Walter C. *The Mind of Hitler.* New York: Basic Books Inc., 1972.

Langley, Roger, and Levy, Richard C. *Wife Beating: The Silent Crisis.* New York: E.P. Dutton & Co., 1977.

Larousse Encyclopedia of Mythology. London: Hamlyn Publishing Group Ltd., 1968.

Lawson, John Cuthbert. *Modern Greek Folklore and Ancient Greek Religion.* New York: University Books Inc., 1964.

Lea, Henry Charles. *The Inquisition of the Middle Ages.* New York: Citadel Press, 1954; unabridged version published by Macmillan, New York 1961.

Lederer, William J., and Jackson, Don D. *The Mirages of Marriage.* New York: W. W. Norton & Co., 1968.

Lederer, Wolfgang. *The Fear of Women.* New York: Harcourt Brace Jovanovich Inc., 1968.

Legge, Francis. *Forerunners and Rivals of Christianity* (2 vols.). New York: University Books Inc., 1964.

Legman, G. *Rationale of the Dirty Joke.* New York: Grove Press, 1968.

Lehner, Ernst. *Symbols Signs and Signets.* New York: Dover Publications, 1969.

Leland, Charles Godfrey. *Gypsy Sorcery and Fortune Telling.* New York: University Books Inc., 1962.

Lethaby, W.R. *Architecture, Mysticism and Myth.* New York: George Braziller, 1975.

Lethbridge, T.C. *Witches.* Secaucus, N.J.: Citadel Press, 1972.

Levy, Howard S. *Chinese Footbinding: The History of a Curious Erotic Custom.* New York: Walton Rawls, 1966.

Lewis, Helen Block. *Psychic War in Men and Women.* New York: New York University Press, 1976.

Lindsay, Jack. *The Ancient World.* New York: G.P. Putnam's Sons, 1968.

Lindsay, Jack. *The Origins of Astrology.* New York: Barnes & Noble, Inc., 1971.

Loomis, Roger S. and Laura H. *Medieval Romances.* New York: Modern Library, 1957.

Mabinogion (Gwyn and Thomas Jones, trans.). London: Everyman's Library, J.M. Dent & Sons, 1970.

MacCana, Proinsias. *Celtic Mythology.* London: Hamlyn Publishing Group Ltd., 1970.

MacKenzie, Norman. *Secret Societies.* New York: Holt, Rinehart & Winston, 1967.

Mahanirvanatantra (Sir John Woodroffe, trans.). New York: Dover Publications, 1972.

Mâle, Emile. *The Gothic Image.* New York: Harper & Row, 1958.

Malory, Sir Thomas. *Le Morte d'Arthur* (2 vols.). London: J.M. Dent & Sons Ltd., 1961.

Malvern, Marjorie. *Venus in Sackcloth.* Carbondale, Ill.: Southern Illinois University Press, 1975.

Maple, Eric. *The Dark World of Witches.* Cranbury, N.J.: A.S. Barnes & Co., Inc., 1964.

Marcus, Steven. *The Other Victorians.* New York: Basic Books Inc., 1964.

Marshall, Donald S., and Suggs, Robert C. *Human Sexual Behavior.* New York: Basic Books Inc., 1971.

Martello, Leo Louis. *Weird Ways of Witchcraft.* Secaucus, N.J.: Castle Books Inc., 1972.

Martin, Del. *Battered Wives.* San Francisco, Calif.: Glide Publications, 1976.

Maspero, Gaston. *Popular Stories of Ancient Egypt.* New York: University Books Inc., 1967.

Massa, Aldo. *The Phoenicians.* Geneva: Editions Minerva, 1977.

Masters, Anthony. *The Natural History of the Vampire.* New York: G.P. Putnam's Sons, 1972.

Masters, R.E.L. *Eros and Evil.* New York: Julian Press Inc., 1962.

McNally, Raymond T., and Florescu, Radu. *In Search of Dracula.* Greenwich, Conn.: New York Graphic Society, 1972.

Mead, Margaret. *Male and Female.* New York: William Morrow & Co., 1949.

Medea, Andra, and Thompson, Kathleen. *Against Rape.* New York: Farrar, Straus & Giroux, 1974.

Mendenhall, George E. *The Tenth Generation.* Baltimore, Md.: Johns Hopkins University Press, 1973.

Menen, Aubrey. *The Mystics.* New York: Dial Press, 1974.

Merivale, Patricia. *Pan the Goat-God.* Cambridge, Mass.: Harvard University Press, 1969.

Miles, Clement A. *Christmas Customs and Traditions.* New York: Dover Publications, 1976.

Moakley, Gertrude. *The Tarot Cards Painted by Bembo.* New York: New York Public Library, 1966.

Montagu, Ashley. *Sex, Man, and Society.* New York: G.P. Putnam's Sons, 1967.

Montagu, Ashley. *Touching.* New York: Columbia University Press, 1971.
Morris, Joan. *The Lady Was a Bishop.* New York: Macmillan, 1973.
Muller, Herbert J. *The Uses of the Past.* New York: New American Library, 1954.
Mumford, Lewis. *Interpretations and Forecasts.* New York: Harcourt Brace Jovanovich Inc., 1973.
Murray, Margaret Alice. *The Witch-Cult in Western Europe.* London: Oxford University Press, 1921.
Murstein, Bernard I. *Love, Sex and Marriage through the Ages.* New York: Springer Publishing Co., 1974.
Neumann, Erich. *Amor and Psyche.* New York: Harper & Bros., 1956.
Neumann, Erich. *The Great Mother: An Analysis of the Archetype.* Princeton, N.J.: Princeton University Press, 1963.
Neumann, Erich. *Art and the Creative Unconscious.* Princeton, N.J.: Princeton University Press, 1959.
Nobile, Philip (ed.). *The New Eroticism.* New York: Random House, 1970.
Norman, Dorothy. *The Hero.* New York: World Publishing Co., 1969.
Ochs, Carol. *Behind the Sex of God.* Boston: Beacon Press, 1977.
Oesterreich, T.K. *Possession, Demoniacal and Other.* New York: University Books Inc., 1966.
O'Flaherty, Wendy Doniger. *Hindu Myths.* Harmondsworth, England: Penguin Books Ltd., 1975.
Oldenbourg, Zoé. *The Crusades.* New York: Random House Inc., 1966.
Oldenbourg, Zoé. *Massacre at Montségur: A History of the Albigensian Crusade.* New York: Minerva Press, 1961.
O'Neill, Eugene. *Selected Plays of Eugene O'Neill.* New York: Random House, 1967.
Oxenstierna, Eric. *The Norsemen.* Greenwich, Conn.: New York Graphic Society, 1965.
Pagels, Elaine. *The Gnostic Gospels.* New York: Random House, 1979.
Papus. *The Tarot of the Bohemians.* New York: Arcanum Books, 1958.
Patai, Raphael. *Myth and Modern Man.* Englewood Cliffs, N.J.: Prentice-Hall, Inc., 1972.
Pearsall, Ronald. *The Worm in the Bud.* New York: Macmillan, 1969.
Pearsall, Ronald. *Night's Black Angels.* New York: David McKay Co., 1975.
Pepper, Elizabeth, and Wilcock, John. *Magical and Mystical Sites.* New York: Harper & Row, 1977.
Perrin, Noel. *Dr. Bowdler's Legacy.* New York: Atheneum, 1969.
Pfeifer, Charles F. *The Dead Sea Scrolls and the Bible.* New York: Weathervane Books, 1969.
Phillips, Guy Ragland. *Brigantia.* London: Routledge & Kegan Paul, 1976.
Piggott, Stuart. *The Druids.* New York: Frederick A. Praeger, 1968.
Plaidy, Jean. *The Spanish Inquisition.* New York: Citadel Press, 1967.
Polo, Marco. *Travels.* New York: Modern Library, 1953.
Potter, Stephen, and Sargent, Laurens. *Pedigree.* New York: Taplinger Publishing Co., 1974.
Pritchard, James B. *The Ancient Near East* (*2 vols.*). Princeton, N.J.: Princeton University Press, 1958.
Pritchard, James B. *Solomon and Sheba.* London: Phaidon Press Ltd., 1974.

Putney, Snell and Gail J. *The Adjusted American.* New York: Harper & Row, 1964.

Ramsay, Raymond H. *No Longer on the Map.* New York: Viking Press, 1972.

Rank, Otto. *The Myth of the Birth of the Hero.* New York: Vintage Books, 1959.

Ravensdale, T., and Morgan, J. *The Psychology of Witchcraft.* New York: Arco Publishing Co., 1974.

Rawson, Philip. *Erotic Art of the East.* New York: G.P. Putnam's Sons, 1968.

Rawson, Philip. *The Art of Tantra.* Greenwich, Conn.: New York Graphic Society, 1973.

Rees, Alwyn & Brinley. *Celtic Heritage.* New York: Grove Press, 1961.

Reinach, Salomon. *Orpheus.* New York: Horace Liveright, Inc., 1930.

Robbins, Rossell Hope. *Encyclopedia of Witchcraft and Demonology.* New York: Crown Publishers, 1959.

Robertson, J.M. *Pagan Christs.* New York: University Books Inc., 1967.

Robinson, James M. (ed.). *The Nag Hammadi Library in English.* San Francisco: Harper & Row, 1977.

Rose, H.J. *Religion in Greece and Rome.* New York: Harper & Bros., 1959.

Rosen, Barbara. *Witchcraft.* New York: Taplinger Publishing Co., 1972.

Ross, Nancy Wilson. *Three Ways of Asian Wisdom.* New York: Simon & Schuster, 1966.

Roszak, Betty and Theodore. *Masculine/Feminine.* New York: Harper & Row, 1969.

Rugoff, Milton. *Prudery and Passion.* New York: G.P. Putnam's Sons, 1971.

Russell, Bertrand. *A History of Western Philosophy.* New York: Simon & Schuster, 1964.

Russell, Diana E.H. *The Politics of Rape.* New York: Stein & Day, 1975.

Russell, J.B. *Witchcraft in the Middle Ages.* Ithaca, N.Y.: Cornell University Press, 1972.

Sadock, B.J., Kaplan, H.I., and Freedman, A.M. *The Sexual Experience.* Baltimore: Williams & Wilkins Co., 1976.

Sagan, Carl. *The Dragons of Eden.* New York: Random House, 1977.

Sargent, H.C., and Kittredge, G.L. *English and Scottish Popular Ballads.* Boston: Houghton Mifflin, 1932.

Savramis, Demosthenes. *The Satanizing of Woman.* New York: Doubleday & Co., 1974.

Scarf, Maggie. *Unfinished Business.* New York: Ballantine Books, 1981.

Scot, Reginald. *Discoverie of Witchcraft.* Yorkshire, England: Rowmand & Littlefield, 1973.

Scott, George Ryley. *Phallic Worship.* Westport, Conn.: Associated Booksellers, n.d.

Scott, Sir Walter. *Letters on Demonology and Witchcraft.* London: George Routledge & Sons, 1884.

Seligmann, Kurt. *Magic, Supernaturalism and Religion.* New York: Pantheon Books Inc., 1948.

Seth, Ronald. *In the Name of the Devil.* New York: Walker & Co., 1969.

Seznec, Jean. *The Survival of the Pagan Gods.* Princeton, N.J.: Princeton University Press, 1953.

Shah, Idris. *The Sufis.* London: Octagon Press, 1964.

Sheehy, Gail. *Passages.* New York: E.P. Dutton & Co., 1976.

Sheridan, Ronald, and Ross, Anne. *Gargoyles and Grotesques: Paganism in the Medieval Church.* Boston: New York Graphic Society, 1975.

Shirley, Ralph. *Occultists and Mystics of all Ages.* New York: University Books Inc., 1972.

Shultz, Gladys Denny. *How Many More Victims?* Philadelphia: J.B. Lippincott Co., 1965.

Shumaker, Wayne. *The Occult Sciences in the Renaissance.* Berkeley: University of California Press, 1972.

Silberer, Herbert. *Hidden Symbolism of Alchemy and the Occult Arts.* New York: Dover Publications, 1971.

Simons, G.L. *Sex and Superstition.* New York: Harper & Row, 1973.

Smith, Homer. *Man and His Gods.* Boston: Little, Brown & Co., 1952.

Smith, John Holland. *Constantine the Great.* New York: Charles Scribner's Sons, 1971.

Smith, John Holland. *The Death of Classical Paganism.* New York: Charles Scribner's Sons, 1976.

Smith, Morton. *Jesus the Magician.* San Francisco: Harper & Row, 1978.

Sobol, Donald J. *The Amazons of Greek Mythology.* Cranbury, N.J.: A.S. Barnes & Co., Inc., 1972.

Soisson, Pierre & Janine. *Byzantium.* Geneva: Editions Minerva, 1977.

Spence, Lewis. *The History and Origins of Druidism.* New York: Samuel Weiser, Inc., 1971.

Spinka, Matthew. *A History of Christianity in the Balkans.* Archon Books, 1968.

Spretnak, Charlene (ed.). *The Politics of Women's Spirituality.* New York: Anchor/Doubleday, 1982.

Squire, Charles. *Celtic Myth and Legend, Poetry and Romance.* New York: Bell Publishing Co., 1979.

Stall, Sylvanus. *What a Young Husband Ought to Know.* Philadelphia: Vir Publishing Co., 1897.

Stanton, Elizabeth Cady. *The Original Feminist Attack on the Bible.* New York: Arno Press, 1974.

Starkloff, Carl F. *The People of the Center.* New York: Seabury Press, 1974.

Steenstrup, Johannes C.H.R. *The Medieval Popular Ballad.* Seattle: University of Washington Press, 1968.

Steinman, Anne, & Fox, David J. *The Male Dilemma.* New York: Jason Aronson, 1974.

Stone, Merlin. *When God Was a Woman.* New York: Dial Press, 1976.

Strong, Eugenia Sellers. *Apotheosis and After Life.* Freeport, N.Y.: Books for Libraries Press, 1969.

Sturluson, Snorri. *The Prose Edda.* Berkeley: University of California Press, 1954.

Summers, Montague. *The Discovery of Witches.* London: Cayme Press, 1928.

Summers, Montague. *The Geography of Witchcraft.* New York: University Books Inc., 1958.

Summers, Montague. *The Vampire, His Kith and Kin.* New York: University Books Inc., 1960.

Summers, Montague. *The Werewolf.* New York: Bell Publishing Co., n.d.

Summers, Montague. *The History of Witchcraft and Demonology.* London: Routledge & Kegan Paul, 1973.

Swaan, William. *The Gothic Cathedral.* New York: Doubleday & Co., 1969.

Tacitus. *Complete Works.* New York: Modern Library, 1942.

Tannahill, Reay. *Flesh and Blood: A History of the Cannibal Complex.* New York: Stein & Day, 1975.

Tatz, Mark, and Kent, Jody. *Rebirth.* New York: Anchor Press/Doubleday, 1977.

Tennant, F.R. *The Sources of the Doctrines of the Fall and Original Sin.* New York: Schocken Books, 1968.

Terkel, Studs. *Working.* New York: Pantheon Books, Inc., 1972.

Thomson, J. Oliver. *History of Ancient Geography.* New York: Biblio & Tannen, 1965.

Thorsten, Geraldine. *God Herself: The Feminine Roots of Astrology.* New York: Avon Books, 1981.

Torrey, E. Fuller. *The Death of Psychiatry.* Radnor, Pa.: Chilton Book Co., 1974.

Trigg, Elwood B. *Gypsy Demons and Divinities.* Secaucus, N.J.: Citadel Press, 1973.

Tuchman, Barbara. *A Distant Mirror.* New York: Alfred A. Knopf, 1978.

Turville-Petre, E.O.G. *Myth and Religion of the North.* New York: Holt, Rinehart & Winston, 1964.

Tylor, Sir Edward Burnett. *Religion in Primitive Culture.* New York: Harper & Bros., 1958.

Upanishads. New York: Mentor Books, New American Library, 1957.

Vermaseren, Maarten J. *Cybele and Attis.* London: Thames & Hudson, 1977.

Vetter, George B. *Magic and Religion.* New York: Philosophical Library, 1973.

von Franz, Marie-Louise. *Time, Rhythm and Repose.* New York: Thames & Hudson, 1978.

von Hagen, Victor W. *World of the Maya.* New York: New American Library, 1960.

Wachtel, Paul L. *Psychoanalysis and Behavior Therapy.* New York: Basic Books Inc., 1977.

Waddell, L. Austine. *Tibetan Buddhism.* New York: Dover Publications, 1972.

Wainwright, F.T. *Scandinavian England.* Sussex, England: Phillimore & Co., Ltd., 1975.

Waite, Arthur Edward. *The Book of Ceremonial Magic.* New York: Bell Publishing Co., 1969.

Waite, Arthur Edward. *The Occult Sciences.* Secaucus, N.J.: University Books Inc., 1974.

Walker, D.P. *The Decline of Hell.* Chicago, Ill.: University of Chicago Press, 1964.

Wedeck, Harry E. *A Treasury of Witchcraft.* Secaucus, N.J.: Citadel Press, 1975.

Weintraub, Stanley. *Beardsley.* New York: George Braziller, 1967.

Wendt, Herbert. *It Began in Babel.* Boston: Houghton Mifflin, 1962.

White, Andrew D. *A History of the Warfare of Science with Theology in Christendom* (2 vols.). New York: George Braziller, 1955.

Whitehouse, Ruth. *The First Cities.* New York: E.P. Dutton, 1977.

Wickler, Wolfgang. *The Sexual Code.* Garden City, N.Y.: Anchor Press/Doubleday, 1973.

Wilkins, Eithne. *The Rose-Garden Game.* London: Victor Gallancz Ltd., 1969.

Williams, C.A.S. *Outlines of Chinese Symbolism and Art Motives.* New York: Dover Publications, 1976.

Wilson, Colin. *The Outsider.* Boston: Houghton Mifflin, 1956.

Wimberly, Lowry Charles. *Folklore in the English and Scottish Ballads.* New York: Dover Publications, 1965.

Wind, Edgar. *Pagan Mysteries in the Renaissance.* New York: W.W. Norton & Co., 1968.

Wolff, Geoffrey. *Black Sun.* New York: Random House, 1976.

Woods, William. *A History of the Devil.* New York: G.P. Putnam's Sons, 1974.

Young, Wayland. *Eros Denied: Sex in Western Society.* New York: Grove Press, 1964.

Zimmer, Heinrich. *Myths and Symbols in Indian Art and Civilization.* Princeton, N.J.: Princeton University Press, 1946.

Acknowledgments

Permission to reprint from the following works is gratefully acknowledged:

J. J. Bachofen, *Myth, Religion, and Mother Right,* trans. Ralph Manheim, Bollingen Series 84. Copyright © 1967 by Princeton University Press.

Robert Briffault, *The Mothers* (3-volume edition). Copyright 1931 by Macmillan Publishing Company, renewed 1959 by Joan Briffault.

Joseph Campbell, *The Mythic Image,* Bollingen Series 100. Copyright © 1974 by Princeton University Press.

Mircea Eliade, *Shamanism: Archaic Techniques of Ecstasy,* trans. Willard R. Trask, Bollingen Series 76. Copyright © 1964 by Princeton University Press.

Sir James G. Frazer, *The Golden Bough* (one-volume abridged edition). Copyright 1922 by Macmillan Publishing Company, renewed 1950 by Barclays Bank Ltd.

Vivian Gornick & Barbara K. Moran, *Woman in Sexist Society.* Copyright © 1971 by Basic Books, Inc.

Charles Guignebert, *Ancient, Medieval and Modern Christianity: The Evolution of a Religion.* Copyright new matter © 1961 by University Books Inc. By arrangement with Lyle Stuart Inc.

Jules Henry, *Pathways to Madness.* Copyright © 1965, 1971 by Mrs. Jules Henry. Reprinted by permission of Random House, Inc.

Henry Charles Lea, *The Inquisition of the Middle Ages: Its Organization and Operation.* Copyright 1954 by The Citadel Press. By arrangement with Lyle Stuart Inc.

Wolfgang Lederer, M.D., *The Fear of Women.* Copyright © 1968 by Wolfgang Lederer, M.D. By permission of the author.

Charles Godfrey Leland, *Gypsy Sorcery and Fortune Telling.* Copyright 1962 by University Books Inc. By arrangement with Lyle Stuart Inc.

Steven Marcus, *The Other Victorians.* Copyright © 1966 by Steven Marcus; Basic Books, Inc., Publishers.

Lewis Mumford, *Interpretations and Forecasts,* by permission of Harcourt Brace Jovanovich, Inc.

Erich Neumann, *The Great Mother: An Analysis of the Archetype,* trans. Ralph Manheim, Bollingen Series 47. Copyright 1955 by Princeton University Press.

Newsweek, "The Exorcists," copyright 1976 by Newsweek Inc. All rights reserved. Reprinted by permission.

Eugene O'Neill, *Selected Plays of Eugene O'Neill.* Copyright 1928 and renewed 1956 by Carlotta Monterey O'Neill. Reprinted by permission of Random House, Inc.

Philip Rawson, *Erotic Art of the East.* Copyright © 1968 by Philip Rawson. By permission of G.P. Putnam's Sons.

Diana E.H. Russell, *The Politics of Rape.* Copyright © 1975. Reprinted with permission of Stein and Day Publishers.

Studs Terkel, *Working: People Talk About What They Do All Day and How They Feel About What They Do.* Copyright © 1972, 1974 by Studs Terkel. Reprinted by permission of Pantheon Books, a Division of Random House, Inc.

George B. Vetter, *Magic and Religion,* by permission of Philosophical Library, Publishers.

Photo credits

Page

xii D.A. Harissiadis, Athens
1 *top* Alinari/Art Resource
1 *bottom* D.A. Harissiadis, Athens
82 Louvre
83 *top* The Historical Society of York County, Pa.
83 *bottom* Art Resource
128 Tzouaras/Art Resource
129 *top* Saint Catherine of Alexandria, Ugolino Lorenzetti; National Gallery of Art, Washington; Samuel H. Kress Collection
129 *bottom* The Metropolitan Museum of Art, Purchase, 1958, Fund from Various Donors.
204 Alinari/Art Resource
205 *top* Louvre
205 *bottom* Devil Bootjack, Maker unidentified. Ca. 1850–1875. Polychromed cast iron figure. Abby Aldrich Rockefeller Folk Art Center, Williamsburg, Va.
260 The Seattle Art Museum, Kress Collection
261 Photo Hirmer
296 The Bettmann Archive, Inc.
297 Scala/Art Resource
330 Scala/Art Resource
331 *top* Art Resource
331 *bottom* Berkson/Art Resource
364 Merseyside County Museums, Liverpool
365 Alinari/Art Resource
422 Alinari/Art Resource
423 *top* Philadelphia Museum of Art: The Louise and Walter Arensberg collection. Photographed by Philadelphia Museum of Art
423 *bottom* Scala/Art Resource
520 *left* Library of Congress
520 *right* Alinari/Art Resource
521 The Metropolitan Museum of Art, Wildenstein Fund, 1970
558 Scala/Art Resource
559 *top* The Metropolitan Museum of Art, Fletcher Fund, 1935
559 *bottom* Museo De Arte De Cataluña
704 Alinari/Art Resource
705 *top* Alinari/Art Resource
705 *bottom* Alinari/Art Resource
756 Alinari/Art Resource
757 *top* Alinari/Art Resource
757 *bottom* Metropolitan Museum of Art. Bequest of Cora Timken Burnett, 1957
834 Alinari/Art Resource

Photo credits

835 *top* The Metropolitan Museum of Art, Gift of Edward S. Harkness, 1917–1918
835 *bottom* Alinari/Art Resource
872 Borromeo/Art Resource
873 Metropolitan Museum of Art, bequest of William H. Herriman, 1921
968 Dumbarton Oaks, Washington, D.C.
969 *top* Victoria and Albert Museum, London
969 *bottom* Alinari/Art Resource
1024 Marquand Library of Art and Archaeology, Princeton University
1025 *top* Abby Aldrich Rockefeller Folk Art Center, Williamsburg, Virginia
1025 *bottom* Saint Ursula With Angels and Donor, Benozzo Gozzoli; National Gallery of Art, Washington, Samuel H. Kress Collection.
1056 Courtesy American Museum of Natural History (Photo: Leon Boltin)
1957 *top* Matthew Hopkins, Discoverie of Witches, 1647. Rare Book Division, The New York Public Library
1057 *bottom* Alinari/Art Resource

If you enjoyed this book, you will also want to read these other books from Harper & Row, San Francisco . . .

THE I CHING OF THE GODDESS

Barbara G. Walker

An exploration of the prepatriarchal origins of the I Ching offering a demonstration its overall logic and a fresh commentary on the hexagrams.

THE SECRETS OF THE TAROT

Origins, History, and Symbolism

Barbara G. Walker

This insightful probe into the origins, history, and symbolism of tarot brings to light its links to early Christian cults and its indisputable yet often overlooked relationship with Goddess worship.

THE SKEPTICAL FEMINIST

Discovering the Virgin, Mother, and Crone

Barbara G. Walker

A spiritual autobiography following Walker's journey away from her Christian upbringing, past the necessity for a belief in God or Goddess, to an appreciation of the idea of the Goddess as a way to structure our social system.

By Lynn V. Andrews:

MEDICINE WOMAN

FLIGHT OF THE SEVENTH MOON

The Teaching of the Shields

JAGUAR WOMAN

And the Wisdom of the Butterfly Tree

"The[se] autobiographical account[s] of a woman's search for identity in a Native American culture . . . read like a spiritual thriller. . . . In light of this odyssey, one wonders if Carlos Castaneda and Lynn Andrews have not initiated a new genre of contemporary literature: Visionary Autobiography."—*San Francisco Review of Books*

Medicine Woman also available in two 60-minute audiocassettes.

WOMANSPIRIT RISING

A Feminist Reader in Religion

Carol P. Christ and Judith Plaskow, editors

"Twenty-four essays on feminist aspects of religion. . . . Lucid, careful analysis like this is liberating in the best sense—an act of intellectual transcendence. . . . The best of the books on religion and feminism currently in print."—*Kirkus Reviews*

WOMANSPIRIT

A Guide to Woman's Wisdom

Hallie Iglehart

This practical workbook provides guidance for a contemporary and fully realized feminist spirituality. It outlines an authentic, alternative, holistic path for women seeking liberation from traditionally male-dominated religions.

MOTHERPEACE

A Way to the Goddess Through Myth, Art, and Tarot

Vicki Noble

"Focusing each chapter on an image created for a set of round tarot cards, Noble synthesizes Jungian psychology, goddess mythology, and holistic thought into a positive feminist interpretation of the tarot. Contemplation of these images provides a way of touching knowledge in the unconscious that will lead to full initiation into the human community."—*Library Journal*

TRUTH OR DARE

Encounters with Power, Authority, and Mystery

Starhawk

An eloquent examination of the nature of power and authority in women's experience, enabling women first to understand, then to redefine power and its uses in terms of their own values.

THE SPIRAL DANCE

A Rebirth of the Ancient Religion of the Great Goddess

Starhawk

"Provides a history of witchcraft; describes current practices, including information about covens, circles, rituals, and spells; gives exercises that can be used to . . . let us tap into our psychic and magical powers . . . an excellent book."—*Lammas*

THE GREAT COSMIC MOTHER

Rediscovering the Religion of the Earth

Monica Sjöö & Barbara Mor

This passionate exploration of the Goddess religion in prehistoric societies makes for "a substantial and important contribution to feminist scholarship and theory—and a fascinating work to read, as well."—*Robin Morgan*

BECOMING WOMAN

The Quest for Wholeness in Female Experience

Penelope Washbourn

"The first full-length feminist theology to explore the personal and spiritual questions implicit in the female life-cycle . . . insightful . . . a fruitful new direction in feminist thought."—*Religious Studies Review.* "Fascinating . . . a female PASSAGES."
—*West Coast Review of Books*

Available at bookstores or call toll-free (800) 638-3030